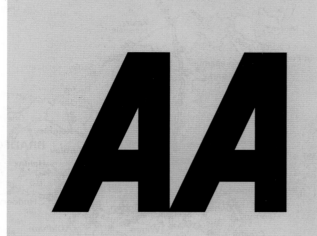

AA

BIG ROAD ATLAS
BRITAIN

2

CW00541132

**Scale 1:190,000
or 3 miles to 1 inch**

31st edition June 2022 © AA Media Limited 2022
Original edition printed 1991.

All cartography in this atlas edited, designed and produced by the Mapping Services Department of AA Media Limited (A05813).

This atlas contains Ordnance Survey data © Crown copyright and database right 2022. Contains public sector information licensed under the Open Government Licence v3.0. Ireland mapping and Distances and journey times contains data available from openstreetmap.org © under the Open Database License found at opendatacommons.org

Published by AA Media Limited, whose registered office is Grove House, Lutyens Close, Basingstoke, Hampshire RG24 8AG, UK.
Registered number 06112600.

All rights reserved. No part of this publication may be reproduced, stored in a retrieval system, or transmitted in any form or by any means – electronic, mechanical, photocopying, recording or otherwise – unless the permission of the publisher has been given beforehand.

ISBN: 978 0 7495 8295 1 (spiral bound)
ISBN: 978 0 7495 8294 4 (paperback)

A CIP catalogue record for this book is available from The British Library.

Disclaimer: The contents of this atlas are believed to be correct at the time of the latest revision, it will not contain any subsequent amended, new or temporary information including diversions and traffic control or enforcement systems. The publishers cannot be held responsible or liable for any loss or damage occasioned to any person acting or refraining from action as a result of any use or reliance on material in this atlas, nor for any errors, omissions or changes in such material. This does not affect your statutory rights.

The publishers would welcome information to correct any errors or omissions and to keep this atlas up to date. Please write to the Atlas Editor, AA Media Limited, Grove House, Lutyens Close, Basingstoke, Hampshire RG24 8AG, UK. **E-mail:** *roadatlasfeedback@aamediagroup.co.uk*

Acknowledgements: AA Media Limited would like to thank the following for information used in the creation of this atlas: Cadw, English Heritage, Forestry Commission, Historic Scotland, National Trust and National Trust for Scotland, RSPB, The Wildlife Trust, Scottish Natural Heritage, Natural England, The Countryside Council for Wales. Award winning beaches from 'Blue Flag' and 'Keep Scotland Beautiful' (summer 2021 data): for latest information visit *www.blueflag.org* and *www.keepscotlandbeautiful.org*. Road signs are © Crown Copyright 2022. Reproduced under the terms of the Open Government Licence. Ireland mapping: Republic of Ireland census 2016 © Central Statistics Office and Northern Ireland census 2016 © NISRA (population data); Irish Public Sector Data (CC BY 4.0) (Gaeltacht); Logainm.ie (placenames); Roads Service and Transport Infrastructure Ireland
Printed by 1010 Printing International Ltd, China

Contents

Map pages	inside front cover
Route planning	**II–XVI**
Route planner	II–V
London district	VI–VII
Restricted junctions	VIII
Smart motorways	IX
Caravan and camping sites in Britain	X–XI
Traffic signs and road markings	XII–XIII
Ferries and port plans	XIV–XVI
Atlas symbols	**1**
Road maps 1:190,000 scale	**2–112**
Channel Islands 1:135,000 scale	6–7
Isle of Man 1:190,000 scale	60
Orkney and Shetland Islands 1:709,000 scale	106
Skye & The Small Isles 1:340,000 scale	100
Western Isles 1:709,000 scale	106

Ferry ports

Aberdeen Harbour........XVI	Harwich International	Liverpool Docks............XVI	Port of Tyne..................XVI
Calais XIV	Port XVI	Newhaven Harbour XV	Portsmouth Harbour.....XIV
Channel Tunnel.............XV	Heysham Harbour XVI	Pembroke Dock XVI	Southampton, Port of...XIV
Dover, Port of XV	Holyhead Harbour XVI	Plymouth, Port of XIV	
Fishguard Harbour........XVI	Hull, Port of XVI	Poole, Port of XIV	

Tourist sites with satnav friendly postcodes	**113**
Ireland road maps 1:1 million scale	**114–115**

Town plans

Aberdeen......................99	Dundee 117	Liverpool......................54	Plymouth 121
Aberystwyth 32	Durham 118	Llandudno 53	Portsmouth 121
Bath 116	Edinburgh...................118	London........................119	Salisbury.....................121
Birmingham.................116	Exeter 118	Manchester 120	Sheffield 121
Blackpool 116	Glasgow 118	Middlesbrough 71	Southampton 121
Bradford......................116	Great Yarmouth 51	Milton Keynes.............120	Southend-on-Sea.........23
Bristol.........................116	Harrogate 118	Newcastle upon	Stratford-upon-Avon....122
Cambridge 116	Inverness....................118	Tyne..........................120	Sunderland...................71
Canterbury 117	Ipswich.......................119	Newquay 3	Swansea 122
Cardiff.........................117	Kingston upon Hull......119	Norwich.......................120	Swindon 122
Chester 117	Leeds 119	Nottingham..................120	Wolverhampton 122
Coventry......................117	Leicester.....................119	Oxford.........................120	Worcester....................122
Derby 117	Lincoln........................119	Peterborough 121	York.............................122

Index to place names	**123–144**
County, administrative area map	123
Place name index	124–144
Distances and journey times	**inside back cover**

Discover rated hotels, B&Bs and campsites at RatedTrips.com

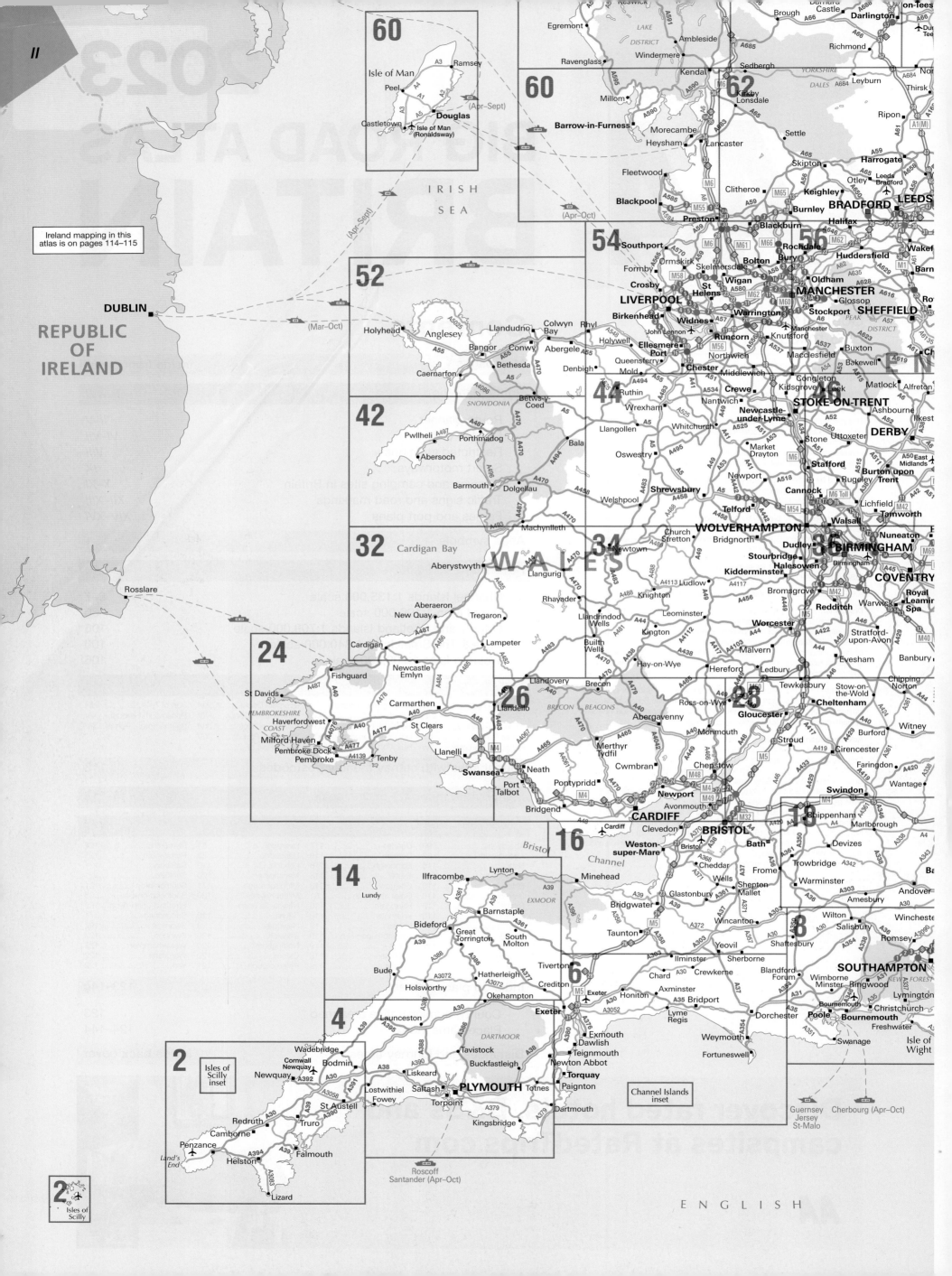

EMERGENCY DIVERSION ROUTES

In an emergency it may be necessary to close a section of motorway or other main road to traffic, so a temporary sign may advise drivers to follow a diversion route. To help drivers navigate the route, black symbols on yellow patches may be permanently displayed on existing direction signs, including motorway signs. Symbols may also be used on separate signs with yellow backgrounds.

FERRY INFORMATION

Information on ferry routes and operators can be found on pages *XIV–XVI*.

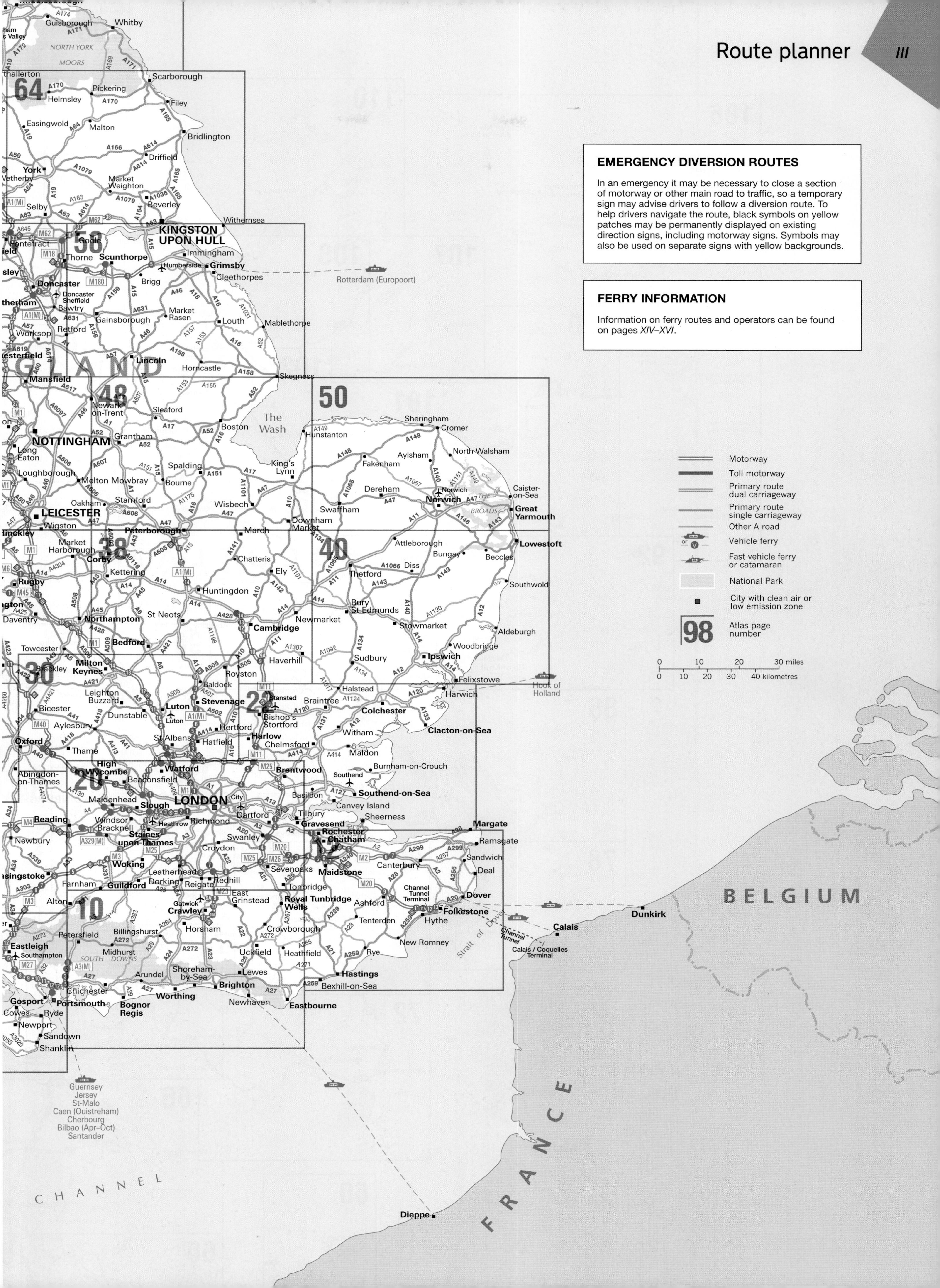

Motorway	
Toll motorway	
Primary route dual carriageway	
Primary route single carriageway	
Other A road	
Vehicle ferry	
Fast vehicle ferry or catamaran	
National Park	
City with clean air or low emission zone	
98	Atlas page number

0   10   20   30 miles
0   10   20   30   40 kilometres

64

58

48

50

38

40

30

20

28

10

KINGSTON UPON HULL

NOTTINGHAM

LEICESTER

Peterborough

Cambridge

Ipswich

Norwich

Great Yarmouth

Lowestoft

LONDON

Oxford

Reading

Southampton

Portsmouth

Brighton

Eastbourne

Hastings

Dover

Folkestone

Calais

Dunkirk

Dieppe

BELGIUM

FRANCE

CHANNEL

Rotterdam (Europoort)

Hook of Holland

Guernsey
Jersey
St-Malo
Caen (Ouistreham)
Cherbourg
Bilbao (Apr–Oct)
Santander

Channel Tunnel Terminal

Calais / Coquelles Terminal

Strait of Dover

ENGLAND

NORTH YORK MOORS

The Wash

THE BROADS

SOUTH DOWNS

SCOTLAND

Grid reference panels: 106, 110, 112, 106, 107, 108, 104, 100, 102, 101, 96, 98, 92, 94, 90, 86, 88, 80, 78, 72, 74, 66, 60, 60

Western Isles — Outer Hebrides — Inner Hebrides

Places:

Stromness, Kirkwall, St Margaret's Hope, Gills, John o' Groats, Scrabster, Thurso, Wick, Port Nis (Port of Ness), Melvich, Tongue, Scourie, Altnaharra, Helmsdale, Steòrnabhagh (Stornoway), Stornoway, The Minch, Isle of Lewis, Lairg, Bonar Bridge, Ullapool, Tain, Cullen, Taransay, Tairbeart (Tarbert), Harris, Gairloch, Alness, Cromarty, Nairn, Elgin, Keith, Huntly, Uibhist a Tuath (North Uist), Uig, Kinlochewe, Achnasheen, Dingwall, Inverness, Forres, Aberlour, Loch nam Madadh (Lochmaddy), Dunvegan, Portree, Raasay, Kyle of Lochalsh, Drumnadrochit, Grantown-on-Spey, Tomintoul, Beinn na Faoghla (Benbecula), Isle of Skye, Invermoriston, Aviemore, Uibhist a Deas (South Uist), Loch Baghasdail (Lochboisdale), Armadale, Invergarry, Newtonmore, Kingussie, CAIRNGORMS, Braemar, Ballater, Barraigh (Barra), Bàgh a' Chaisteil (Castlebay), Rùm, Eigg, Mallaig, Fort William, Pitlochry, Blairgowrie, Forfar, Coll, Tobermory, Ballachulish, Aberfeldy, Coupar Angus, Tiree, Isle of Mull, Killin, Tyndram, Lochearnhead, Crianlarich, Crieff, Perth, Dundee, Newport-on-Tay, Fionnphort, Oban, Auchterarder, St Andrews, Cupar, Colonsay, Inveraray, LOCH LOMOND AND THE TROSSACHS, Callander, Dunblane, Kinross, Glenrothes, Lochgilphead, Helensburgh, Stirling, Alloa, Dunfermline, Kirkcaldy, Port Askaig, Jura, Dunoon, Dumbarton, Greenock, Glasgow, Rosyth, Edinburgh, EDINBURGH, Falkirk, Kennacraig, Tarbert, Bute, Largs, Paisley, GLASGOW, Airdrie, Livingston, Dalkeith, Port Ellen, Islay, Ardrossan, Kilwinning, East Kilbride, Strathaven, Motherwell, Lanark, Peebles, Galashiels, Arran, Irvine, KILMARNOCK, Troon, Prestwick, Glasgow Prestwick, Ayr, Cumnock, Biggar, Selkirk, Campbeltown, Maybole, Hawick, Girvan, Thornhill, Moffat, Langholm, Cairnryan, New Galloway, Dumfries, Lockerbie, Stranraer, Newton Stewart, Castle Douglas, Annan, Longtown, Carlisle Lake District, Carlisle, Brampton, Maryport, Workington, Cockermouth, Penrith, Isle of Man, Ramsey, Peel, Douglas, Keswick, LAKE DISTRICT, Egremont, Ambleside, Ravenglass, Windermere, Kendal, Millom

NORTHERN IRELAND, Larne, BELFAST

Firth of Clyde, Firth of Forth, Moray Firth, Solway Firth, Sound of Harris, Sound of Barra

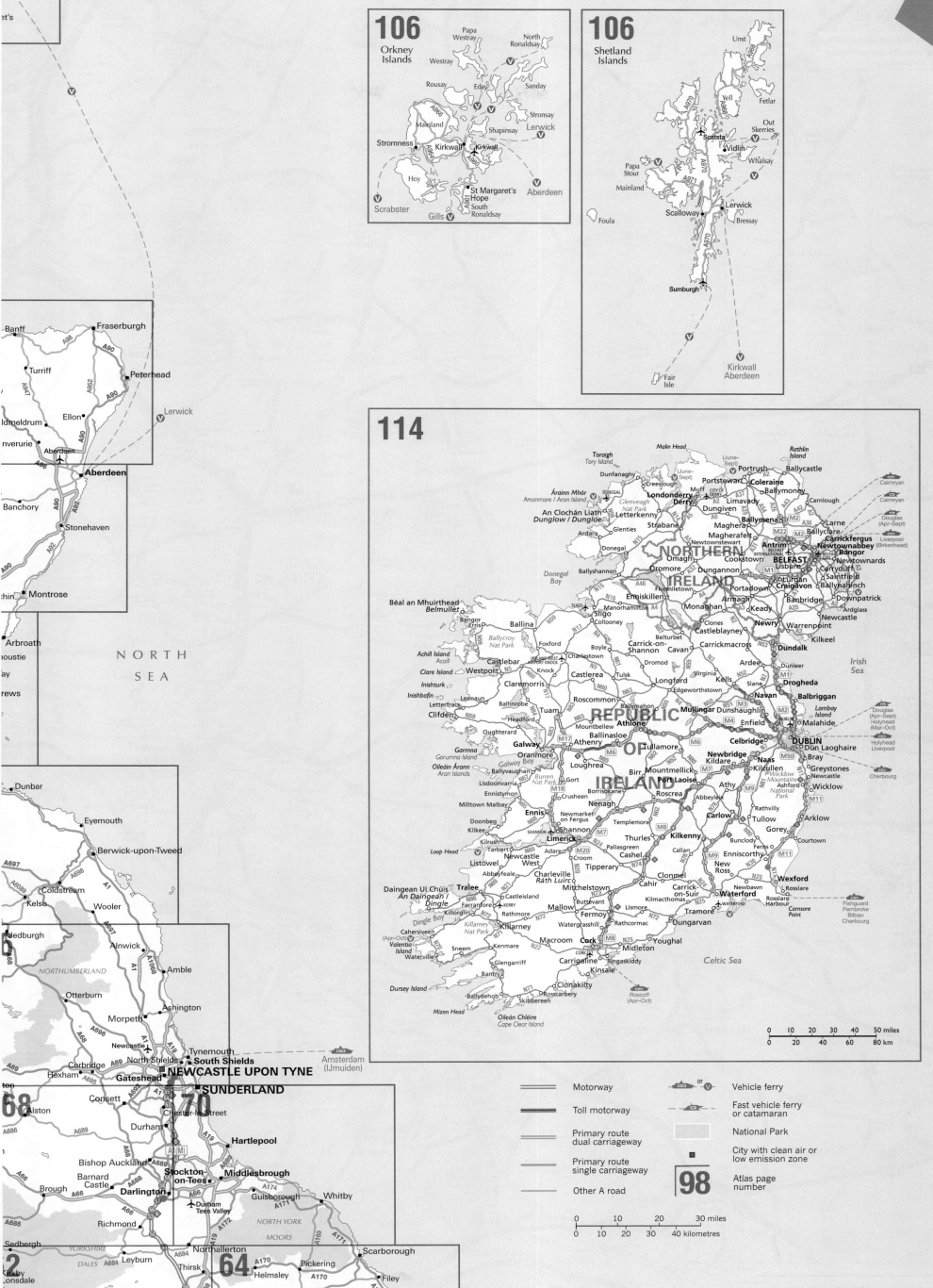

106
Orkney Islands

Papa Westray
North Ronaldsay
Westray
Rousay
Eday
Sanday
Mainland
Shapinsay
Stronsay
Lerwick
Stromness
Kirkwall
Kirkwall
Hoy
St Margaret's Hope
South Ronaldsay
Scrabster
Gills
Aberdeen

106
Shetland Islands

Unst
Yell
Fetlar
Scatsta
Vidlin
Out Skerries
Whalsay
Papa Stour
Mainland
Scalloway
Lerwick
Bressay
Foula
Sumburgh
Fair Isle
Kirkwall
Aberdeen

114

NORTHERN IRELAND

Malin Head
Toraigh / Tory Island
Rathlin Island
Ballycastle
Dunfanaghy
Portrush
Portstewart
Creeslough
(June–Sept)
Árainn Mhór / Arranmore / Aran Island
DONEGAL
Glenveagh Nat Park
Muff
CITY OF DERRY
Londonderry
Derry
Limavady
Coleraine
Ballymoney
Carnlough
Cairnryan
Cairnryan
An Clochán Liath Dunglow / Dungloe
Letterkenny
Dungiven
Ballymena
M2
Larne
Douglas (Apr–Sept)
Ardara
Glenties
Strabane
Maghera
M22
M2
Ballyclare
Liverpool (Birkenhead)
Donegal
Newtownstewart
Magherafelt
Antrim
BELFAST INTERNATIONAL
Carrickfergus
Omagh
Cookstown
Belfast
Newtownabbey
Bangor
Ballyshannon
Dromore
Dungannon
M1
Belfast
Lisburn
Newtownards
Donegal Bay
Fivemiletown
A4
Portadown
Lurgan
Craigavon
Carryduff
Saintfield
Ballynahinch
Enniskillen
A4
Monaghan
Armagh
Keady
A25
Banbridge
Ardglass
Béal an Mhuirthead / Belmullet
Manorhamilton
SLIGO
Sligo
Clones
Castleblayney
Newry
Warrenpoint
Newcastle
Downpatrick
Bangor Erris
Colooney
Belturbet
Carrickmacross
N53
Kilkeel
Ballina
Boyle
Carrick-on-Shannon
Cavan
Dundalk
Achill Island
Ballycroy Nat Park
IRELAND WEST AIRPORT KNOCK
Charlestown
Dromod
Virginia
Ardee
Dunleer
Irish Sea
Acaill
Castlebar
Knock
Tulsk
N5
Longford
Kells
Slane
Drogheda
M1
Clare Island
Westport
N5
Claremorris
Castlerea
N60
Edgeworthstown
Navan
Balbriggan
Inishturk
Roscommon
Ballymahon
Mullingar
Dunshaughlin
Lambay Island
Inishbofin
Ballinrobe
Tuam
Dunshaughlin
Letterfrack
Leenaun
Headford
Ballymore
Enfield
M4
Malahide
Clifden
N59
Oughterard
N63
Athlone
M6
DUBLIN
Dublin
Garma
REPUBLIC OF IRELAND
Ballinasloe
Tullamore
M6
Celbridge
DUBLIN
Dún Laoghaire
Gorumna Island
Galway
Oranmore
M17
Athenry
M6
Newbridge
Naas
M50
Bray
Oileán Árann / Aran Islands
Galway Bay
Loughrea
Birr
Kildare
Kilcullen
Greystones
Ballyvaughan
Mountmellick
M7
Newcastle
Wicklow Mountains National Park
Ballyvaughan
Burren Nat Park
Gort
Port Laoise
Athy
Ashford
Wicklow
Lisdoonvarna
M18
Crusheen
Roscrea
M9
Abbeyleix
N11
Rathnew
Ennistymon
Borrisokane
Nenagh
Rathdrum
Milltown Malbay
Newmarket on Fergus
Templemore
M8
Carlow
Tullow
Gorey
Doonbeg
Ennis
Thurles
Kilkenny
Courtown
Kilkee
SHANNON
Shannon
M7
Pallasgreen
Callan
M9
Enniscorthy
M11
Loop Head
Tarbert
Limerick
Adare
M20
Cashel
New Ross
Kilrush
Newcastle West
Croom
N74
Clonmel
Wexford
Listowel
Abbeyfeale
Tipperary
Cahir
Carrick-on-Suir
Waterford
Newbawn
Rosslare
Daingean Uí Chúis / An Daingean / Dingle
Tralee
Charleville Ráth Luirc
Mitchelstown
Clonmel
Waterford
Rosslare Harbour
Fishguard Pembroke Bilbao Cherbourg
Farranfore
KERRY
Castleisland
Buttevant
Lismore
Kilmacthomas
Carnsore Point
Dingle Bay
Killorglin
Rathmore
Mallow
Fermoy
Waterglasshill
Tramore
Dungarvan
Killarney Nat Park
Killarney
Rathcormac
Cahersiveen
(Apr–Oct)
Valentia Island
Macroom
Cork
Midleton
Youghal
Celtic Sea
Waterville
Sneem
Kenmare
Carrigaline
CORK
Ringaskiddy
Dursey Island
Glengarriff
Kinsale
Roscoff (Apr–Oct)
Bantry
Clonakilty
Ballydehob
Rosscarbery
Skibbereen
Mizen Head
Oileán Chléire / Cape Clear Island

0 10 20 30 40 50 miles
0 20 40 60 80 km

(Scotland mainland inset)

Banff
Fraserburgh
Turriff
A90
Peterhead
A947
A952
Ldmeldrum
Ellon
A90
nverurie
A96
Aberdeen
Banchory
A90
A92
Lerwick
Stonehaven
A90
hin
Montrose
Arbroath
oustie
ay
NORTH SEA
ews

(Northern England inset)

Dunbar
Eyemouth
A1
Berwick-upon-Tweed
A6089
A697
A698
Coldstream
A1
Kelso
Wooler
edburgh
A68
NORTHUMBERLAND
Alnwick
A1068
A697
Amble
6
Otterburn
Ashington
A696
Morpeth
A69
A1
Newcastle
A19
Tynemouth
North Shields
South Shields
Amsterdam (IJmuiden)
68
Corbridge
A69
A1
Hexham
A695
Gateshead
NEWCASTLE UPON TYNE
SUNDERLAND
on
Consett
A692
70
Chester-le-Street
Alston
A689
A19
A686
Durham
Hartlepool
A1(M)
Bishop Auckland
A68
A689
Stockton-on-Tees
Middlesbrough
A19
A174
Barnard Castle
A66
A688
A66
Darlington
Guisborough
A171
Whitby
Brough
A685
Richmond
A66
A172
A169
NORTH YORK MOORS
Sedbergh
2
YORKSHIRE DALES
A684
Northallerton
64
A170
Pickering
A170
Scarborough
Kirkby Lonsdale
A65
Leyburn
Thirsk
A19
A170
Helmsley
A64
Filey
A168
A165
Ripon
Ecc ngwold

Legend

Motorway	Vehicle ferry
Toll motorway	Fast vehicle ferry or catamaran
Primary route dual carriageway	National Park
Primary route single carriageway	City with clean air or low emission zone
Other A road	**98** Atlas page number

0 10 20 30 miles
0 10 20 30 40 kilometres

Restricted junctions

Motorway and primary route junctions which have access or exit restrictions are shown on the map pages thus: 3 56

M1 London - Leeds

Junction	Northbound	Southbound
2	Access only from A1 *(northbound)*	Exit only to A1 *(southbound)*
4	Access only from A41 *(northbound)*	Exit only to A41 *(southbound)*
6A	Access only from M25 (no link from A405)	Exit only to M25 (no link from A405)
7	Access only from A414	Exit only to A414
17	Exit only to M45	Access only from M45
19	Exit only to M6 *(northbound)*	Exit only to A14 *(southbound)*
21A	Exit only, no access	Access only, no exit
24A	Access only, no exit	Access only from A50 *(eastbound)*
35A	Exit only, no access	Access only, no exit
43	Exit only to M621	Access only from M621
48	Exit only to A1(M) *(northbound)*	Access only from A1(M) *(southbound)*

M2 Rochester - Faversham

Junction	Westbound	Eastbound
1	No exit to A2 *(eastbound)*	No access from A2 *(westbound)*

M3 Sunbury - Southampton

Junction	Northeastbound	Southwestbound
8	Access only from A303, no exit	Exit only to A303, no access
10	Exit only, no access	Access only, no exit
14	Access from M27 only, no exit	No access to M27 *(westbound)*

M4 London - South Wales

Junction	Westbound	Eastbound
1	Access only from A4 *(westbound)*	Exit only to A4 *(eastbound)*
2	Access only from A4 *(westbound)*	Access only from A4 *(eastbound)*
21	Exit only to M48	Access only from M48
23	Access only from M48	Exit only to M48
25	Exit only, no access	Access only, no exit
25A	Exit only, no access	Access only, no exit
29	Exit only to A48(M)	Access only from A48(M)
38	Exit only, no access	No restriction
39	Access only, no exit	No access or exit
42	Exit only to A483	Access only from A483

M5 Birmingham - Exeter

Junction	Northeastbound	Southwestbound
10	Access only, no exit	Exit only, no access
11A	Access only from A417 *(westbound)*	Exit only to A417 *(eastbound)*
18A	Exit only to M49	Access only from M49
18	Exit only, no access	Access only, no exit

M6 Toll Motorway

Junction	Northwestbound	Southeastbound
T1	Access only, no exit	No access or exit
T2	No access or exit	Exit only, no access
T5	Access only, no exit	Exit only to A5148 *(northbound)*, no access
T7	Exit only, no access	Access only, no exit
T8	Exit only, no access	Access only, no exit

M6 Rugby - Carlisle

Junction	Northbound	Southbound
3A	Exit only to M6 Toll	Access only from M6 Toll
4	Exit only to M42 *(southbound)* & A446	Exit only to A446
4A	Access only from M42 *(southbound)*	Exit only to M42
5	Exit only, no access	Access only, no exit
10A	Exit only to M54	Access only from M54
11A	Access only from M6 Toll	Exit only to M6 Toll
with M56 (jct 20A)	No restriction	Access only from M56 *(eastbound)*
20	Exit only to M56 *(westbound)*	Access only from M56 *(eastbound)*
24	Access only, no exit	Exit only, no access
25	Exit only, no access	Access only, no exit
30	Access only from M61	Exit only to M61
31A	Exit only, no access	Access only, no exit
45	Exit only, no access	Access only, no exit

M8 Edinburgh - Bishopton

Junction	Westbound	Eastbound
6	Exit only, no access	Access only, no exit
6A	Access only, no exit	Exit only, no access
7	Access only, no exit	Exit only, no access
7A	Exit only, no access	Access only from A725 *(northbound)*, no exit
8	No access from M73 *(southbound)* or from A8 *(eastbound)* & A89	No exit to M73 *(northbound)* or to A8 *(westbound)* & A89
9	Access only, no exit	Exit only, no access
13	Access only from M80 *(southbound)*	Exit only to M80 *(northbound)*
14	Access only, no exit	Exit only, no access
16	Exit only to A804	Access only from A879
17	Exit only to A82	No restriction
18	Access only from A82 *(eastbound)*	Exit only to A814
19	No access from A814 *(westbound)*	Exit only to A814 *(westbound)*
20	Exit only, no access	Access only, no exit
21	Access only, no exit	Exit only to A8
22	Exit only to M77 *(southbound)*	Access only from M77 *(northbound)*
23	Exit only to B768	Access only from B768
25	No access or exit from or to A8	No access or exit from or to A8
25A	Exit only, no access	Access only, no exit
28	Exit only, no access	Access only, no exit
28A	Exit only to A737	Access only from A737
29A	Exit only to A8	Access only, no exit

M9 Edinburgh - Dunblane

Junction	Northwestbound	Southeastbound
2	Access only, no exit	Exit only, no access
3	Exit only, no access	Access only, no exit
6	Access only, no exit	Exit only to A905
8	Exit only to M876 *(southwestbound)*	Access only from M876 *(northeastbound)*

M11 London - Cambridge

Junction	Northbound	Southbound
4	Access only from A406 *(eastbound)*	Exit only to A406
5	Exit only, no access	Access only, no exit
8A	Exit only, no access	No direct access, use jct 8
9	Exit only to A11	Access only from A11
13	Exit only, no access	Access only, no exit
14	Exit only, no access	Access only, no exit

M20 Swanley - Folkestone

Junction	Northwestbound	Southeastbound
2	Staggered junction; follow signs - access only	Staggered junction; follow signs - exit only
3	Exit only to M26 *(westbound)*	Access only from M26 *(eastbound)*
5	Access only from A20	For access follow signs - exit only to A20
6	No restriction	For exit follow signs
11A	Access only, no exit	Exit only, no access

M23 Hooley - Crawley

Junction	Northbound	Southbound
7	Exit only to A23 *(northbound)*	Access only from A23 *(southbound)*
10A	Access only, no exit	Exit only, no access

M25 London Orbital Motorway

Junction	Clockwise	Anticlockwise
1B	No direct access, use slip road to jct 2 Exit only	Access only, no exit
5	No exit to M26 *(eastbound)*	No access from M26
19	Exit only, no access	Access only, no exit
21	Access only from M1 *(southbound)* Exit only to M1 *(northbound)*	Access only from M1 *(southbound)* Exit only to M1 *(northbound)*
31	No exit (use slip road via jct 30), access only	No access (use slip road via jct 30), exit only

M26 Sevenoaks - Wrotham

Junction	Westbound	Eastbound
with M25 (jct 5)	Exit only to clockwise M25 *(westbound)*	Access only from anticlockwise M25 *(eastbound)*
with M20 (jct 3)	Access only from M20 *(northwestbound)*	Exit only to M20 *(southeastbound)*

M27 Cadnam - Portsmouth

Junction	Westbound	Eastbound
4	Staggered junction; follow signs - access only from M3 *(southbound)*. Exit only to M3 *(northbound)*	Staggered junction; follow signs - access only from M3 *(southbound)*. Exit only to M3 *(northbound)*
10	Exit only, no access	Access only, no exit
12	Staggered junction; follow signs - exit only to M275 *(southbound)*	Staggered junction; follow signs - access only from M275 *(northbound)*

M40 London - Birmingham

Junction	Northwestbound	Southeastbound
3	Exit only, no access	Access only, no exit
7	Exit only, no access	Access only, no exit
8	Exit only to M40/A40	Access only from M40/A40
13	Exit only, no access	Access only, no exit
14	Access only, no exit	Exit only, no access
16	Access only, no exit	Exit only, no access

M42 Bromsgrove - Measham

Junction	Northeastbound	Southwestbound
1	Access only, no exit	Exit only, no access
7	Exit only to M6 *(northwestbound)*	Access only from M6 *(northwestbound)*
7A	Exit only to M6 *(southeastbound)*	No access or exit
8	Access only from M6 *(southeastbound)*	Exit only to M6 *(northwestbound)*

M45 Coventry - M1

Junction	Westbound	Eastbound
Dunchurch (unnumbered)	Access only from A45	Exit only, no access
with M1 (jct 17)	Access only from M1 *(northbound)*	Exit only to M1 *(southbound)*

M48 Chepstow

Junction	Westbound	Eastbound
21	Access only from M4 *(westbound)*	Exit only to M4 *(eastbound)*
23	No exit to M4 *(eastbound)*	No access from M4 *(westbound)*

M53 Mersey Tunnel - Chester

Junction	Northbound	Southbound
11	Access only from M56 *(westbound)* Exit only to M56 *(eastbound)*	Access only from M56 *(westbound)* Exit only to M56 *(eastbound)*

M54 Telford - Birmingham

Junction	Westbound	Eastbound
with M6 (jct 10A)	Access only from M6 *(northbound)*	Exit only to M6 *(southbound)*

M56 Chester - Manchester

Junction	Westbound	Eastbound
1	Access only from M60 *(westbound)*	Exit only to M60 *(eastbound)* & A34 *(northbound)*
2	Exit only, no access	Access only, no exit
3	Access only, no exit	Exit only, no access
4	Exit only, no access	Access only, no exit
7	Exit only, no access	No restriction
8	Access only, no exit	No access or exit
9	No exit to M6 *(southbound)*	No access from M6 *(northbound)*
15	Exit only to M53	Access only from M53
16	No access or exit	No restriction

M57 Liverpool Outer Ring Road

Junction	Northwestbound	Southeastbound
3	Access only, no exit	Exit only, no access
5	Access only from A580 *(westbound)*	Exit only, no access

M60 Manchester Orbital

Junction	Clockwise	Anticlockwise
2	Access only, no exit	Exit only, no access
3	No access from M56	Access only from A34 *(northbound)*
4	Access only from A34 *(northbound)*. Exit only to M56	Access only from M56 *(eastbound)*. Exit only to A34 *(southbound)*
5	Access and exit only from and to A5103 *(northbound)*	Access and exit only from and to A5103 *(southbound)*
7	No direct access, use slip road to jct 8. Exit only to A56	Access only from A56. No exit, use jct 8
14	Access from A580 *(eastbound)*	Exit only to A580 *(westbound)*
16	Access only, no exit	Exit only, no access
20	Exit only, no access	Access only, no exit
22	No restriction	Exit only, no access
25	Exit only, no access	No restriction
26	No restriction	Exit only, no access
27	Access only, no exit	Exit only, no access

M61 Manchester - Preston

Junction	Northwestbound	Southeastbound
3	No access or exit	Exit only, no access
with M6 (jct 30)	Exit only to M6 *(northbound)*	Access only from M6 *(southbound)*

M62 Liverpool - Kingston upon Hull

Junction	Westbound	Eastbound
23	Access only, no exit	Exit only, no access
32A	No access to A1(M) *(southbound)*	No restriction

M65 Preston - Colne

Junction	Northeastbound	Southwestbound
9	Exit only, no access	Access only, no exit
11	Access only, no exit	Exit only, no access

M66 Bury

Junction	Northbound	Southbound
with A56	Exit only to A56 *(northbound)*	Access only from A56 *(southbound)*
1	Exit only, no access	Access only, no exit

M67 Hyde Bypass

Junction	Westbound	Eastbound
1A	Access only, no exit	Exit only, no access
2	Exit only, no access	Access only, no exit

M69 Coventry - Leicester

Junction	Northbound	Southbound
2	Access only, no exit	Exit only, no access

M73 East of Glasgow

Junction	Northbound	Southbound
1	No exit to A74 & A721	No exit to A74 & A721
2	No access from or exit to A89. No access from *(eastbound)*	No access from or exit to A89. No exit to M8 *(westbound)*

M74 and A74(M) Glasgow - Gretna

Junction	Northbound	Southbound
3	Exit only, no access	Access only, no exit
3A	Access only, no exit	Exit only, no access
4	No access from A74 & A721	Access only, no exit to A74 & A721
7	Access only, no exit	Exit only, no access
9	No access or exit	Exit only, no access
10	No restriction	Access only, no exit
11	Access only, no exit	Exit only, no access
12	Exit only, no access	Access only, no exit
18	Exit only, no access	Access only, no exit

M77 Glasgow - Kilmarnock

Junction	Northbound	Southbound
with M8 (jct 22)	No exit to M8 *(westbound)*	No access from M8 *(eastbound)*
4	Access only, no exit	Exit only, no access
6	Access only, no exit	Exit only, no access
7	Access only, no exit	No restriction
8	Exit only, no access	Exit only, no access

M80 Glasgow - Stirling

Junction	Northbound	Southbound
4A	Exit only, no access	Access only, no exit
6A	Access only, no exit	Exit only, no access
8	Exit only to M876 *(northeastbound)*	Access only from M876 *(southwestbound)*

M90 Edinburgh - Perth

Junction	Northbound	Southbound
1	No exit, access only	Exit only to A90 *(eastbound)*
2A	Exit only to A92 *(eastbound)*	Access only from A92 *(westbound)*
7	Access only, no exit	Exit only, no access
8	Exit only, no access	Access only, no exit
10	No access from A912. No exit to A912 *(southbound)*	No access from A912 *(northbound)* No exit to A912

M180 Doncaster - Grimsby

Junction	Westbound	Eastbound
1	Access only, no exit	Exit only, no access

M606 Bradford Spur

Junction	Northbound	Southbound
2	Exit only, no access	No restriction

M621 Leeds - M1

Junction	Clockwise	Anticlockwise
2A	Access only, no exit	Exit only, no access
4	No exit or access	No restriction
5	Access only, no exit	Exit only, no access
6	Exit only, no access	Access only, no exit
with M1 (jct 43)	Exit only to M1 *(southbound)*	Access only from M1 *(northbound)*

M876 Bonnybridge - Kincardine Bridge

Junction	Northeastbound	Southwestbound
with M80 (jct 5)	Access only from M80 *(northeastbound)*	Exit only to M80 *(southwestbound)*
with M9 (jct 8)	Exit only to M9 *(eastbound)*	Access only from M9 *(westbound)*

A1(M) South Mimms - Baldock

Junction	Northbound	Southbound
2	Exit only, no access	Access only, no exit
3	No restriction	Exit only, no access
5	Access only, no exit	No access or exit

A1(M) Pontefract - Bedale

Junction	Northbound	Southbound
41	No access to M62 *(eastbound)*	No restriction
43	Access only from M1 *(northbound)*	Exit only to M1 *(southbound)*

A1(M) Scotch Corner - Newcastle upon Tyne

Junction	Northbound	Southbound
57	Exit only to A66(M) *(eastbound)*	Access only from A66(M) *(westbound)*
65	No access Exit only to A194(M) & A1 *(northbound)*	No exit Access only from A194(M) & A1 *(southbound)*

A3(M) Horndean - Havant

Junction	Northbound	Southbound
1	Access only from A3	Exit only to A3
4	Exit only, no access	Access only, no exit

A38(M) Birmingham, Victoria Road (Park Circus)

Junction	Northbound	Southbound
with B4132	No exit	No access

A48(M) Cardiff Spur

Junction	Westbound	Eastbound
29	Access only from M4 *(westbound)*	Exit only to M4 *(eastbound)*
29A	Exit only to A48 *(westbound)*	Access only from A48 *(eastbound)*

A57(M) Manchester, Brook Street (A34)

Junction	Westbound	Eastbound
with A34	No exit	No access

A58(M) Leeds, Park Lane and Westgate

Junction	Northbound	Southbound
with A58	No restriction	No access

A64(M) Leeds, Clay Pit Lane (A58)

Junction	Westbound	Eastbound
with A58	No exit (to Clay Pit Lane)	No access (from Clay Pit Lane)

A66(M) Darlington Spur

Junction	Westbound	Eastbound
with A1(M) (jct 57)	Exit only to A1(M) *(southbound)*	Access only from A1(M) *(northbound)*

A74(M) Gretna - Abington

Junction	Northbound	Southbound
18	Exit only, no access	Access only, no exit

A194(M) Newcastle upon Tyne

Junction	Northbound	Southbound
with A1(M) (jct 65)	Access only from A1(M) *(northbound)*	Exit only to A1(M) *(southbound)*

A12 M25 - Ipswich

Junction	Northeastbound	Southwestbound
13	Access only, no exit	No restriction
14	Exit only, no access	Access only, no exit
20A	Exit only, no access	Access only, no exit
20B	Access only, no exit	Exit only, no access
21	No restriction	Access only, no exit
23	Exit only, no access	Access only, no exit
24	Access only, no exit	Exit only, no access
27	Exit only, no access	Access only, no exit
Dedham & Stratford St Mary (unnumbered)	Exit only	Access only

A14 M1 - Felixstowe

Junction	Westbound	Eastbound
with M1/M6 (jct19)	Exit only to M6 and M1 *(northbound)*	Access only from M6 and M1 *(southbound)*
4	Exit only, no access	Access only, no exit
21	Access only, no exit	Exit only, no access
22	Exit only, no access	Access only from A1 *(southbound)*
23	Access only, no exit	Exit only, no access
31	No restriction	Access only, no exit
34	Access only, no exit	Exit only, no access
36	Exit only to A11, access only from A1303	Access only from A11
38	Access only from A11	Exit only to A11
39	Exit only, no access	Access only, no exit
61	Access only, no exit	Exit only, no access

A55 Holyhead - Chester

Junction	Westbound	Eastbound
8A	Exit only, no access	Access only, no exit
23A	Access only, no exit	Exit only, no access
24A	Exit only, no access	No access or exit
27A	No restriction	No access or exit
33A	Exit only, no access	No access or exit
33B	Exit only, no access	Access only, no exit
36A	Exit only to A5104	Access only from A5104

Since Britain's first motorway (the Preston Bypass) opened in 1958, motorways have changed significantly. A vast increase in car journeys over the last 62 years has meant that motorways quickly filled to capacity. To combat this, the recent development of smart motorways uses technology to monitor and actively manage traffic flow and congestion.

How they work

Smart motorways utilise various active traffic management methods, monitored through a regional traffic control centre:

- Traffic flow is monitored using CCTV
- Speed limits are changed to smooth traffic flow and reduce stop-start driving
- Capacity of the motorway can be increased by either temporarily or permanently opening the hard shoulder to traffic
- Warning signs and messages alert drivers to hazards and traffic jams ahead
- Lanes can be closed in the case of an accident or emergency by displaying a red X sign

- Emergency refuge areas are located regularly along the motorway where there is no hard shoulder available

Refuge areas for emergency use only

The map shows the main motorway network with the three different types of smart motorway in operation. Since January 2022, plans for the opening of further schemes have been put on hold to allow a review of safety data and the improvement of existing schemes.

Controlled motorway
Variable speed limits without hard shoulder (the hard shoulder is used in emergencies only)

Hard shoulder running
Variable speed limits with part-time hard shoulder (the hard shoulder is open to traffic at busy times when signs permit)

All lane running
Variable speed limits with hard shoulder as permanent running lane (there is no hard shoulder); this is standard for all new motorway schemes since 2013

Standard motorway

Quick tips

- Never drive in a lane closed by a red X

- Keep to the speed limit shown on the gantries
- A solid white line indicates the hard shoulder – do not drive in it unless directed or in the case of an emergency
- A broken white line indicates a normal running lane
- Exit the smart motorway where possible if your vehicle is in difficulty. In an emergency, move onto the hard shoulder where there is one, or the nearest emergency refuge area
- Put on your hazard lights if you break down

SCOTLAND

Perth

M90 - M9 J1A–M90 J3

Stirling

M9 J1–1A

Glasgow

Edinburgh

Newcastle upon Tyne

Carlisle

ENGLAND

M62 J26–28
M62 J18–20
M62 J25–26
M62 J28–29
Bradford Leeds
M62 J29–30
Kingston upon Hull
M62 J10–12
Preston
M1 J39–42
M6 J21A–26 (due to open 2022/23)
Manchester
M1 J32–35A
Liverpool
Sheffield
M1 J31–32
M56 J6–8
M1 J28–31
M60 J8–18
Stoke-on-Trent
M1 J25–28
M6 J16–19
Derby
M6 J13–15
Nottingham
M42 J7–9
M1 J23A–25
Leicester
M6 J10A–13
M6 J4–10A
M6 J2–4
Birmingham Coventry
M1 J16–19
M5 J4A–6
Northampton Cambridge
M42 J3A–7
M1 J10–13
M1 J13–16 (due to open 2022/23)
Luton
M4 J24–28
M25 J23–27
Swansea
M4 J19–20
M25 J27–30
Cardiff
Reading LONDON
M25 J2–3
Bristol
M4 J3–12
M20 J4–7
M5 J15–17
M3 J2–4A
M25 J5–6
Folkestone
M23 J8–10
M20 J3–5
Southampton
Brighton
Exeter
Portsmouth

Plymouth

M27 J4–11

WALES

M25 J6–23

Smart motorways (*Intelligent Transport Systems* in Scotland) are the responsibility of National Highways, Transport Scotland and Transport for Wales

Since Britain's first motorway (the Preston Bypass) opened in 1958, motorways have changed significantly. A vast increase in car journeys over the last 62 years has meant that motorways quickly filled to capacity. To combat this, the recent development of smart motorways uses technology to monitor and actively manage traffic flow and congestion.

How they work

Smart motorways utilise various active traffic management methods, monitored through a regional traffic control centre:

- Traffic flow is monitored using CCTV
- Speed limits are changed to smooth traffic flow and reduce stop-start driving
- Capacity of the motorway can be increased by either temporarily or permanently opening the hard shoulder to traffic
- Warning signs and messages alert drivers to hazards and traffic jams ahead
- Lanes can be closed in the case of an accident or emergency by displaying a red X sign

- Emergency refuge areas are located regularly along the motorway where there is no hard shoulder available

Refuge areas for emergency use only

The map shows the main motorway network with the three different types of smart motorway in operation. Since January 2022, plans for the opening of further schemes have been put on hold to allow a review of safety data and the improvement of existing schemes.

Controlled motorway
Variable speed limits without hard shoulder (the hard shoulder is used in emergencies only)

Hard shoulder running
Variable speed limits with part-time hard shoulder (the hard shoulder is open to traffic at busy times when signs permit)

All lane running
Variable speed limits with hard shoulder as permanent running lane (there is no hard shoulder); this is standard for all new motorway schemes since 2013

Standard motorway

Quick tips

- Never drive in a lane closed by a red X

- Keep to the speed limit shown on the gantries
- A solid white line indicates the hard shoulder – do not drive in it unless directed or in the case of an emergency
- A broken white line indicates a normal running lane
- Exit the smart motorway where possible if your vehicle is in difficulty. In an emergency, move onto the hard shoulder where there is one, or the nearest emergency refuge area
- Put on your hazard lights if you break down

Map labels

SCOTLAND

Perth

M9
M90
M90 - M9 J1A–M90 J3

Stirling
M80
M9
M9 J1–1A
Edinburgh

M8
M80
M9
M8

Glasgow
M77
M74

A74(M)

Newcastle upon Tyne

Carlisle
ENGLAND

M6

A1(M)

M62 J26–28
M62 J18–20   M62 J25–26   M62 J28–29
Bradford   Leeds   M62 J29–30   Kingston upon Hull
M55   M62
M62 J10–12   M65   M62   M1 J39–42
Preston   M66   M62   M180
M6   M1   M1 J32–35A
M6 J21A–26 (due to open 2022/23)   M61   A1(M)   M18
Manchester   M1 J31–32
M58   M60
Liverpool   M62   M1 J28–31
M53   M56   Sheffield
M60 J8–18   M56 J6–8   M1 J25–28
M6 J16–19   Stoke-on-Trent   M1
Derby   M1 J23A–25
M6 J13–15   M42 J7–9   Nottingham
M54   M42   Leicester
M6 J10A–13   M6 Toll   M69   M6 J2–4
M6 J4–10A   M42   M6   M1 J16–19
Birmingham   Coventry   Northampton   Cambridge
M5 J4A–6   M42   M45   M1 J10–13
M5   M40   M11
M42 J3A–7
M50   M1 J13–16 (due to open 2022/23)   Luton
A1(M)
M4 J24–28   M4 J19–20   M1 J6A–10   M25 J23–27
Swansea   M48   M5   Reading   M25   M25 J27–30
M4   M25 J6–23   LONDON   M25 J2–3
Cardiff   M4   M25   M2
Bristol   M4 J3–12   M26   M20   M20 J4–7
M5 J15–17   M3   M23   M25 J5–6   Folkestone
M3 J2–4A   M20 J3–5
M23 J8–10
M5
Southampton   M27   A3(M)   Brighton
Exeter   Portsmouth

Plymouth   M27 J4–11

WALES

Smart motorways (*Intelligent Transport Systems* in Scotland) are the responsibility of National Highways, Transport Scotland and Transport for Wales

Caravan and camping sites in Britain

These pages list the top 300 AA-inspected Caravan and Camping (C & C) sites in the Pennant rating scheme. **Five Pennant Premier sites are shown in green,** Four Pennant sites are shown in blue.
Listings include addresses, telephone numbers and websites together with page and grid references to locate the sites in the atlas. The total number of pitches is also included for each site, together with the type of pitch available.
The following abbreviations are used: **C = Caravan CV = Campervan T = Tent**
To discover more about the AA-rated caravan and camping sites not included on these pages please visit **RatedTrips.com**

ENGLAND

Alders Caravan Park
Home Farm, Alne, York
YO61 1RY
Tel: 01347 838722 64 C6
alderscaravanpark.co.uk
Total Pitches: 91 (C, CV & T)

Andrewshayes Holiday Park
Dalwood, Axminster
EX13 7DY
Tel: 01404 831225 6 H5
andrewshayes.co.uk
Total Pitches: 230 (C, CV & T)

Atlantic Bays Holiday Park
Padstow, Cornwall
PL28 8PY
Tel: 01841 520855 3 M2
atlanticbaysholidaypark.co.uk
Total Pitches: 241 (C, CV & T)

Ayr Holiday Park
St Ives, Cornwall
TR26 1EJ
Tel: 01736 795855 2 E8
ayrholidaypark.co.uk
Total Pitches: 40 (C, CV & T)

Back of Beyond Touring Park
234 Ringwood Road, St Leonards, Dorset
BH24 2SB
Tel: 01202 876968 8 G8
backofbeyondtouringpark.co.uk
Total Pitches: 83 (C, CV & T)

Bagwell Farm Touring Park
Knights in the Bottom, Chickerell, Weymouth
DT3 4EA
Tel: 01305 782575 7 R8
bagwellfarm.co.uk
Total Pitches: 320 (C, CV & T)

Bardsea Leisure Park
Priory Road, Ulverston
LA12 9QE
Tel: 01229 584712 61 P4
bardsealeisure.co.uk
Total Pitches: 171 (C & CV)

Bath Chew Valley Caravan Park
Ham Lane, Bishop Sutton
BS39 5TZ
Tel: 01275 332127 17 Q5
bathchewvalley.co.uk
Total Pitches: 45 (C, CV & T)

Bay View Farm C & C Park
Croyde, Devon
EX33 1PN
Tel: 01271 890501 14 K5
bayviewfarm.co.uk
Total Pitches: 75 (C, CV & T)

Bay View Holiday Park
Bolton le Sands, Carnforth
LA5 9TN
Tel: 01524 732854 61 T6
holgates.co.uk
Total Pitches: 202 (C, CV & T)

Beacon Cottage Farm Touring Park
Beacon Drive, St Agnes
TR5 0NU
Tel: 01872 552347 2 J6
beaconcottagefarmholidays.co.uk
Total Pitches: 70 (C, CV & T)

Beaconsfield Farm Caravan Park
Battlefield, Shrewsbury
SY4 4AA
Tel: 01939 210370 45 M10
beaconsfieldholidaypark.co.uk
Total Pitches: 95 (C & CV)

Beech Croft Farm C & C Park
Beech Croft, Blackwell in the Peak, Buxton
SK17 9TQ
Tel: 01298 85330 56 H12
beechcroftfarm.co.uk
Total Pitches: 30 (C, CV & T)

Bellingham C & C Club Site
Brown Rigg, Bellingham
NE48 2JY
Tel: 01434 220175 76 G9
campingandcaravanningclub.co.uk/bellingham
Total Pitches: 68 (C, CV & T)

Beverley Park C & C Park
Goodrington Road, Paignton
TQ4 7JE
Tel: 01803 843887 6 A13
beverley-holidays.co.uk
Total Pitches: 149 (C, CV & T)

Blue Rose Caravan & Country Park
Star Carr Lane, Brandesburton
YO25 8RU
Tel: 01964 543366 65 Q10
bluerosepark.com
Total Pitches: 114 (C & CV)

Briarfields Motel & Touring Park
Gloucester Road, Cheltenham
GL51 0SX
Tel: 01242 235324 28 H3
briarfields.net
Total Pitches: 72 (C, CV & T)

Broadhembury C & C Park
Steeds Lane, Kingsnorth, Ashford
TN26 1NQ
Tel: 01233 620859 12 K8
broadhembury.co.uk
Total Pitches: 120 (C, CV & T)

Brook Lodge Farm C & C Park
Cowslip Green, Redhill, Bristol, Somerset
BS40 5RB
Tel: 01934 862311 17 N4
brooklodgefarm.com
Total Pitches: 129 (C, CV & T)

Burnham-on-Sea Holiday Village
Marine Drive, Burnham-on-Sea
TA8 1LA
Tel: 01278 783391 16 K7
haven.com/burnhamonsea
Total Pitches: 781 (C, CV & T)

Burrowhayes Farm C & C Site & Riding Stables
West Luccombe, Porlock, Minehead
TA24 8HT
Tel: 01643 862463 15 U3
burrowhayes.co.uk
Total Pitches: 139 (C, CV & T)

Burton Constable Holiday Park & Arboretum
Old Lodges, Sproatley, Hull
HU11 4LJ
Tel: 01964 562508 65 R12
burtonconstableholidaypark.co.uk
Total Pitches: 500 (C, CV & T)

Caister-on-Sea Holiday Park
Ormesby Road, Caister-on-Sea, Great Yarmouth
NR30 5NH
Tel: 01493 728931 51 T11
haven.com/caister
Total Pitches: 949 (C & CV)

Caistor Lakes Leisure Park
99a Brigg Road, Caistor
LN7 6RX
Tel: 01472 859626 58 K6
caistorlakes.co.uk
Total Pitches: 36 (C & CV)

Cakes & Ale
Abbey Lane, Theberton, Leiston
IP16 4TE
Tel: 01728 831655 41 R8
cakesandale.co.uk
Total Pitches: 255 (C, CV & T)

Calloose C & C Park
Leedstown, Hayle
TR27 5ET
Tel: 01736 850431 2 F10
calloose.co.uk
Total Pitches: 134 (C, CV & T)

Camping Caradon Touring Park
Trelawne, Looe
PL13 2NA
Tel: 01503 272388 4 G10
campingcaradon.co.uk
Total Pitches: 75 (C, CV & T)

Capesthorne Hall
Congleton Road, Siddington, Macclesfield
SK11 9JY
Tel: 01625 861221 55 T12
capesthorne.com/caravan-park
Total Pitches: 50 (C & CV)

Carlyon Bay C & C Park
Bethesda, Cypress Avenue, Carlyon Bay
PL25 3RE
Tel: 01726 812735 3 R6
carlyonbay.net
Total Pitches: 180 (C, CV & T)

Carnevas Holiday Park
Carnevas Farm, St Merryn, Cornwall
PL28 8PN
Tel: 01841 520230 3 M2
carnevasholidaypark.com
Total Pitches: 209 (C, CV & T)

Cartref C & C
Cartref, Ford Heath, Shrewsbury, Shropshire
SY5 9GD
Tel: 01743 821688 44 K11
cartrefcaravansite.co.uk
Total Pitches: 44 (C, CV & T)

Carvynick Holiday Park
Summercourt, Newquay
TR8 5AF
Tel: 01872 510716 3 M5
carvynick.co.uk
Total Pitches: 47 (C, CV & T)

Castlerigg Hall C & C Park
Castlerigg Hall, Keswick
CA12 4TE
Tel: 017687 74499 67 L8
castlerigg.co.uk
Total Pitches: 105 (C, CV & T)

Cheddar Mendip Heights C & C Club Site
Townsend, Priddy, Wells
BA5 3BP
Tel: 01749 870241 17 P6
campingandcaravanningclub.co.uk/cheddar
Total Pitches: 92 (C, CV & T)

Chy Carne Holiday Park
Kuggar, Ruan Minor, Helston, Cornwall
TR12 7LX
Tel: 01326 290200 2 J13
chycarne.co.uk
Total Pitches: 60 (C, CV & T)

Clippesby Hall
Hall Lane, Clippesby, Great Yarmouth
NR29 3BL
Tel: 01493 367800 51 R11
clippesbyhall.com
Total Pitches: 120 (C, CV & T)

Cofton Holidays
Starcross, Dawlish
EX6 8RP
Tel: 01626 890111 6 C8
coftonholidays.co.uk
Total Pitches: 532 (C, CV & T)

Concierge Camping
Ratham Estate, Ratham Lane, West Ashling, Chichester
PO18 8DL
Tel: 01243 573118 10 C9
conciergecamping.co.uk
Total Pitches: 27 (C & CV)

Coombe Touring Park
Race Plain, Netherhampton, Salisbury
SP2 8PN
Tel: 01722 328451 8 F3
coombecaravanpark.co.uk
Total Pitches: 56 (C, CV & T)

Cornish Farm Touring Park
Shoreditch, Taunton
TA3 7BS
Tel: 01823 327746 16 H12
cornishfarm.com
Total Pitches: 48 (C, CV & T)

Cosawes Park
Perranarworthal, Truro
TR3 7QS
Tel: 01872 863724 2 K9
cosawes.co.uk
Total Pitches: 59 (C, CV & T)

Cote Ghyll C & C Park
Osmotherley, Northallerton
DL6 3AH
Tel: 01609 883425 70 G13
coteghyll.com
Total Pitches: 95 (C, CV & T)

Country View Holiday Park
Sand Road, Sand Bay, Weston-super-Mare
BS22 9UJ
Tel: 01934 627595 16 K4
cvhp.co.uk
Total Pitches: 255 (C, CV & T)

Crealy Theme Park & Resort
Sidmouth Road, Clyst St Mary, Exeter
EX5 1DR
Tel: 01395 234888 6 D6
crealy.co.uk
Total Pitches: 127 (C, CV & T)

Crows Nest Caravan Park
Gristhorpe, Filey
YO14 9PS
Tel: 01723 582206 65 P3
crowsnestcaravanpark.com
Total Pitches: 263 (C, CV & T)

Deepdale Backpackers & Camping
Deepdale Farm, Burnham Deepdale
PE31 8DD
Tel: 01485 210256 50 D5
deepdalebackpackers.co.uk
Total Pitches: 80 (CV & T)

Dibles Park
Dibles Road, Warsash, Southampton, Hampshire
SO31 9SA
Tel: 01489 575232 9 Q7
diblespark.co.uk
Total Pitches: 57 (C, CV & T)

Dornafield
Dornafield Farm, Two Mile Oak, Newton Abbot
TQ12 6DD
Tel: 01803 812732 5 U7
dornafield.com
Total Pitches: 135 (C, CV & T)

East Fleet Farm Touring Park
Chickerell, Weymouth
DT3 4DW
Tel: 01305 785768 7 R9
eastfleet.co.uk
Total Pitches: 400 (C, CV & T)

Eastham Hall Holiday Park
Saltcotes Road, Lytham St Annes, Lancashire
FY8 4LS
Tel: 01253 737907 61 R14
easthamhall.co.uk
Total Pitches: 274 (C & CV)

Eden Valley Holiday Park
Lanlivery, Nr Lostwithiel
PL30 5BU
Tel: 01208 872277 3 R5
edenvalleyholidaypark.co.uk
Total Pitches: 94 (C, CV & T)

Exe Valley Caravan Site
Mill House, Bridgetown, Dulverton
TA22 9JR
Tel: 01643 851432 16 B10
exevalleycamping.co.uk
Total Pitches: 48 (C, CV & T)

Eye Kettleby Lakes
Eye Kettleby, Melton Mowbray
LE14 2TN
Tel: 01664 565900 47 T10
eyekettlebylakes.com
Total Pitches: 130 (C, CV & T)

Fen Farm Caravan Site
Moore Lane, East Mersea, Mersea Island, Colchester, Essex
CO5 8FE
Tel: 01206 383275 23 Q5
fenfarm.co.uk
Total Pitches: 180 (C, CV & T)

Fernwood Caravan Park
Lyneal, Ellesmere, Shropshire
SY12 0QF
Tel: 01948 710221 44 K7
fernwoodpark.co.uk
Total Pitches: 225 (C & CV)

Fields End Water Caravan Park & Fishery
Benwick Road, Doddington, March
PE15 0TY
Tel: 01354 740199 39 N2
fieldsendwater.co.uk
Total Pitches: 90 (C, CV & T)

Flower of May Holiday Park
Lebberston Cliff, Filey, Scarborough
YO11 3NU
Tel: 01723 584311 65 P3
flowerofmay.com
Total Pitches: 503 (C, CV & T)

Forest Glade Holiday Park
Near Kentisbeare, Cullompton, Devon
EX15 2DT
Tel: 01404 841381 6 F3
forest-glade.co.uk
Total Pitches: 124 (C, CV & T)

Freshwater Beach Holiday Park
Burton Bradstock, Bridport
DT6 4PT
Tel: 01308 897317 7 N6
freshwaterbeach.co.uk
Total Pitches: 750 (C, CV & T)

Glenfield Caravan Park
Blackmoor Lane, Bardsey, Leeds
LS17 9DZ
Tel: 01937 574657 63 S11
glenfieldcaravanpark.co.uk
Total Pitches: 31 (C, CV & T)

Globe Vale Holiday Park
Radnor, Redruth
TR16 4BH
Tel: 01209 891183 2 J8
globevale.co.uk
Total Pitches: 195 (C, CV & T)

Glororum Caravan Park
Glororum Farm, Bamburgh
NE69 7AW
Tel: 01670 860256 85 T12
northumbrianleisure.co.uk
Total Pitches: 213 (C & CV)

Golden Cap Holiday Park
Seatown, Chideock, Bridport
DT6 6JX
Tel: 01308 422139 7 M6
wdlh.co.uk
Total Pitches: 345 (C, CV & T)

Golden Coast Holiday Park
Station Road, Woolacombe
EX34 7HW
Tel: 01271 872302 15 L4
woolacombe.com
Total Pitches: 431 (C, CV & T)

Golden Sands Holiday Park
Quebec Road, Mablethorpe
LN12 1QJ
Tel: 01507 477871 59 S9
haven.com/goldensands
Total Pitches: 1672 (C, CV & T)

Golden Square C & C Park
Oswaldkirk, Helmsley
YO62 5YQ
Tel: 01439 788269 64 E4
goldensquarecaravanpark.com
Total Pitches: 150 (C, CV & T)

Golden Valley C & C Park
Coach Road, Ripley, Derbyshire
DE55 4ES
Tel: 01773 513881 47 M3
goldenvalleycaravanpark.co.uk
Total Pitches: 47 (C, CV & T)

Goosewood Holiday Park
Sutton-on-the-Forest, York
YO61 1ET
Tel: 01347 810829 64 D7
flowerofmay.com
Total Pitches: 145 (C & CV)

Greenacre Place Touring Caravan Park
Bristol Road, Edithmead, Highbridge
TA9 4HA
Tel: 01278 785227 16 K7
greenacreplace.com
Total Pitches: 10 (C & CV)

Green Acres Caravan Park
High Knells, Houghton, Carlisle
CA6 4JW
Tel: 01228 675418 75 T13
caravanpark-cumbria.com
Total Pitches: 35 (C, CV & T)

Greenhill Farm C & C Park
Greenhill Farm, New Road, Landford, Salisbury
SP5 2AZ
Tel: 01794 324117 8 K5
greenhillfarm.co.uk
Total Pitches: 160 (C, CV & T)

Greenhills Holiday Park
Crowhill Lane, Bakewell, Derbyshire
DE45 1PX
Tel: 01629 813052 56 K13
greenhillsholidaypark.co.uk
Total Pitches: 245 (C, CV & T)

Grouse Hill Caravan Park
Flask Bungalow Farm, Fylingdales, Robin Hood's Bay
YO22 4QH
Tel: 01947 880543 71 R12
grousehill.co.uk
Total Pitches: 192 (C, CV & T)

Gunvenna Holiday Park
St Minver, Wadebridge
PL27 6QN
Tel: 01208 862405 4 B5
gunvenna.com
Total Pitches: 131 (C, CV & T)

Haggerston Castle Holiday Park
Beal, Berwick-upon-Tweed
TD15 2PA
Tel: 01289 381333 85 Q10
haven.com/haggerstoncastle
Total Pitches: 1340 (C & CV)

Harbury Fields
Harbury Fields Farm, Harbury, Nr Leamington Spa
CV33 9JN
Tel: 01926 612457 37 L8
harburyfields.co.uk
Total Pitches: 59 (C & CV)

Harford Bridge Holiday Park
Peter Tavy, Tavistock
PL19 9LS
Tel: 01822 810349 5 N5
harfordbridge.co.uk
Total Pitches: 198 (C, CV & T)

Haw Wood Farm Caravan Park
Hinton, Saxmundham
IP17 3QT
Tel: 01502 359550 41 R6
hawwoodfarm.co.uk
Total Pitches: 115 (C, CV & T)

Heathfield Farm Camping
Heathfield Road, Freshwater, Isle of Wight
PO40 9SH
Tel: 01983 407822 9 L11
heathfieldcamping.co.uk
Total Pitches: 75 (C, CV & T)

Heathland Beach Holiday Park
London Road, Kessingland
NR33 7PJ
Tel: 01502 740337 41 T3
heathlandbeach.co.uk
Total Pitches: 263 (C, CV & T)

Hedley Wood C & C Park
Bridgerule, Holsworthy, Devon
EX22 7ED
Tel: 01288 381404 14 G12
hedleywood.co.uk
Total Pitches: 138 (C, CV & T)

Hendra Holiday Park
Newquay
TR8 4NY
Tel: 01637 875778 3 L4
hendra-holidays.com
Total Pitches: 865 (C, CV & T)

Herding Hill Farm Touring & Camping Site
Shield Hill, Haltwhistle, Northumberland
NE49 9NW
Tel: 01434 320175 76 E12
herdinghillfarm.co.uk
Total Pitches: 22 (C, CV & T)

Highfield Farm Touring Park
Long Road, Comberton, Cambridge
CB23 7DG
Tel: 01223 262308 39 N9
highfieldfarmtouringpark.co.uk
Total Pitches: 120 (C, CV & T)

Highlands End Holiday Park
Eype, Bridport, Dorset
DT6 6AR
Tel: 01308 422139 7 N6
wdlh.co.uk
Total Pitches: 357 (C, CV & T)

Hill of Oaks & Blakeholme
Windermere
LA12 8NR
Tel: 015395 31578 61 R2
hillofoaks.co.uk
Total Pitches: 263 (C & CV)

Hillside Caravan Park
Canvas Farm, Moor Road, Knayton, Thirsk
YO7 4BR
Tel: 01845 537349 63 U2
hillsidecaravanpark.co.uk
Total Pitches: 52 (C & CV)

Holiday Resort Unity
Coast Road, Brean Sands, Brean
TA8 2RB
Tel: 01278 751235 16 J6
hru.co.uk
Total Pitches: 1114 (C, CV & T)

Hollins Farm C & C
Far Arnside, Carnforth
LA5 0SL
Tel: 01524 701767 61 S4
holgates.co.uk
Total Pitches: 14 (C, CV & T)

Hylton Caravan Park
Eden Street, Silloth
CA7 4AY
Tel: 016973 32666 66 H2
stanwix.com
Total Pitches: 303 (C, CV & T)

Island Lodge C & C Site
Stumpy Post Cross, Kingsbridge
TQ7 4BL
Tel: 01548 852956 5 S11
islandlodgesite.co.uk
Total Pitches: 30 (C, CV & T)

Isle of Avalon Touring Caravan Park
Godney Road, Glastonbury
BA6 9AF
Tel: 01458 833618 17 N9
avaloncaravanpark.co.uk
Total Pitches: 120 (C, CV & T)

Jasmine Caravan Park
Cross Lane, Snainton, Scarborough
YO13 9BE
Tel: 01723 859240 65 L3
jasminepark.co.uk
Total Pitches: 84 (C, CV & T)

Kennford International Holiday Park
Kennford, Exeter
EX6 7YN
Tel: 01392 833046 6 B7
kennfordinternational.co.uk
Total Pitches: 87 (C, CV & T)

Killiwerris Touring Park
Penstraze, Chacewater, Truro, Cornwall
TR4 8PF
Tel: 01872 561356 2 K7
killiwerris.co.uk
Total Pitches: 17 (C & CV)

King's Lynn C & C Park
New Road, North Runcton, King's Lynn
PE33 0RA
Tel: 01553 840004 49 T10
kl-cc.co.uk
Total Pitches: 170 (C, CV & T)

Kloofs Caravan Park
Sandhurst Lane, Bexhill
TN39 4RG
Tel: 01424 842839 12 D14
kloofs.com
Total Pitches: 125 (C, CV & T)

Kneps Farm Holiday Caravan Park
River Road, Stanah, Thornton-Cleveleys, Blackpool
FY5 5LR
Tel: 01253 823632 61 R11
knepsfarm.co.uk
Total Pitches: 86 (C & CV)

Knight Stainforth Hall Caravan & Campsite
Stainforth, Settle
BD24 0DP
Tel: 01729 822200 62 G6
knightstainforth.co.uk
Total Pitches: 160 (C, CV & T)

Ladycross Plantation Caravan Park
Egton, Whitby
YO21 1UA
Tel: 01947 895502 71 P11
ladycrossplantation.co.uk
Total Pitches: 130 (C & CV)

Lady's Mile Holiday Park
Dawlish, Devon
EX7 0LX
Tel: 01626 863411 6 C9
ladysmile.co.uk
Total Pitches: 692 (C, CV & T)

Lakeland Leisure Park
Moor Lane, Flookburgh
LA11 7LT
Tel: 01539 558556 61 R5
haven.com/lakeland
Total Pitches: 977 (C, CV & T)

Lamb Cottage Caravan Park
Dalefords Lane, Whitegate, Northwich
CW8 2BN
Tel: 01606 882302 55 P13
lambcottage.co.uk
Total Pitches: 71 (C & CV)

Langstone Manor C & C Park
Moortown, Tavistock
PL19 9JZ
Tel: 01822 613371 5 N6
langstonemanor.co.uk
Total Pitches: 83 (C, CV & T)

Lanyon Holiday Park
Loscombe Lane, Four Lanes, Redruth
TR16 6LP
Tel: 01209 313474 2 H9
lanyonholidaypark.co.uk
Total Pitches: 74 (C, CV & T)

Lickpenny Caravan Site
Lickpenny Lane, Tansley, Matlock
DE4 5GF
Tel: 01629 583040 46 K2
lickpennycaravanpark.co.uk
Total Pitches: 80 (C & CV)

Lime Tree Park
Dukes Drive, Buxton
SK17 9RP
Tel: 01298 22988 56 G12
limetreeparkbuxton.com
Total Pitches: 149 (C, CV & T)

Lincoln Farm Park Oxfordshire
High Street, Standlake
OX29 7RH
Tel: 01865 300239 29 S7
lincolnfarmpark.co.uk
Total Pitches: 90 (C, CV & T)

Littlesea Holiday Park
Lynch Lane, Weymouth
DT4 9DT
Tel: 01305 774414 7 S9
haven.com/littlesea
Total Pitches: 861 (C, CV & T)

Little Trevothan C & C Park
Trevothan, Coverack, Helston, Cornwall
TR12 6SD
Tel: 01326 280260 2 K13
littletrevothan.co.uk
Total Pitches: 108 (C, CV & T)

Long Acres Touring Park
Station Road, Old Leake, Boston
PE22 9RF
Tel: 01205 871555 49 N3
long-acres.co.uk
Total Pitches: 40 (C, CV & T)

Long Hazel Park
High Street, Sparkford, Yeovil, Somerset
BA22 7JH
Tel: 01963 440002 17 R11
longhazelpark.co.uk
Total Pitches: 50 (C, CV & T)

Longnor Wood Holiday Park
Newtown, Longnor, Nr Buxton
SK17 0NG
Tel: 01298 83648 56 G14
longnorwood.co.uk
Total Pitches: 68 (C, CV & T)

Manor Wood Country Caravan Park
Manor Wood, Coddington, Chester
CH3 9EN
Tel: 01829 782990 44 K3
cheshire-caravan-sites.co.uk
Total Pitches: 66 (C, CV & T)

Marton Mere Holiday Village
Mythop Road, Blackpool
FY4 4XN
Tel: 01253 767544 61 Q13
haven.com/martonmere
Total Pitches: 782 (C & CV)

Mayfield Park
Cheltenham Road, Cirencester
GL7 7BH
Tel: 01285 831301 28 K6
mayfieldpark.co.uk
Total Pitches: 105 (C, CV & T)

Meadow Lakes Holiday Park
Hewas Water, St Austell, Cornwall
PL26 7JG
Tel: 01726 882540 3 P7
meadow-lakes.co.uk
Total Pitches: 232 (C, CV & T)

Meadowbank Holidays
Stour Way, Christchurch
BH23 2PQ
Tel: 01202 483597 8 G10
meadowbank-holidays.co.uk
Total Pitches: 221 (C & CV)

Middlewood Farm Holiday Park
Middlewood Lane, Fylingthorpe, Robin Hood's Bay, Whitby
YO22 4UF
Tel: 01947 880414 71 R12
middlewoodfarm.com
Total Pitches: 144 (C, CV & T)

Mill Farm C & C Park
Fiddington, Bridgwater, Somerset
TA5 1JQ
Tel: 01278 732286 16 H8
millfarm.biz
Total Pitches: 275 (C, CV & T)

Mill Park Touring C & C Park
Mill Lane, Berrynarbor, Ilfracombe, Devon
EX34 9SH
Tel: 01271 882647 15 N3
millpark.com
Total Pitches: 160 (C, CV & T)

Minnows Touring Park
Holbrook Lane, Sampford Peverell
EX16 7EN
Tel: 01884 821770 16 D13
minnowstouringpark.co.uk
Total Pitches: 60 (C, CV & T)

Monkey Tree Holiday Park
Hendra Croft, Scotland Road, Newquay
TR8 5QR
Tel: 01872 572032 3 L6
monkeytreeholidaypark.co.uk
Total Pitches: 700 (C, CV & T)

Moon & Sixpence
Newbourn Road, Waldringfield, Woodbridge
IP12 4PP
Tel: 01473 736650 41 N11
moonandsixpence.co.uk
Total Pitches: 275 (C & CV)

Moss Wood Caravan Park
Crimbles Lane, Cockerham
LA2 0ES
Tel: 01524 791041 61 T10
mosswood.co.uk
Total Pitches: 168 (C & CV)

Naburn Lock Caravan Park
Naburn
YO19 4RU
Tel: 01904 728697 64 E10
naburnlock.co.uk
Total Pitches: 115 (C, CV & T)

New Lodge Farm C & C Site
New Lodge Farm, Bulwick, Corby
NN17 3DU
Tel: 01780 450493 38 E1
newlodgefarm.com
Total Pitches: 72 (C, CV & T)

Newberry Valley Park
Woodlands, Combe Martin
EX34 0AT
Tel: 01271 882334 15 N3
newberryvalleypark.co.uk
Total Pitches: 112 (C, CV & T)

Newlands Holidays
Charmouth, Bridport
DT6 6RB
Tel: 01297 560259 7 L6
newlandsholidays.co.uk
Total Pitches: 330 (C, CV & T)

Ninham Country Holidays
Ninham, Shanklin, Isle of Wight
PO37 7PL
Tel: 01983 864243 9 R12
ninham-holidays.co.uk
Total Pitches: 135 (C, CV & T)

North Morte Farm C & C Park
North Morte Road, Mortehoe, Woolacombe
EX34 7EG
Tel: 01271 870381 15 L3
northmortefarm.co.uk
Total Pitches: 253 (C, CV & T)

Northam Farm Caravan & Touring Park
Brean, Burnham-on-Sea
TA8 2SE
Tel: 01278 751244 16 K5
northamfarm.co.uk
Total Pitches: 350 (C, CV & T)

Oakdown Country Holiday Park
Gatedown Lane, Weston, Sidmouth
EX10 0PT
Tel: 01297 680387 6 G6
oakdown.co.uk
Total Pitches: 170 (C, CV & T)

Old Hall Caravan Park
Capernwray, Carnforth
LA6 1AD
Tel: 01524 733276 61 U5
oldhallcaravanpark.co.uk
Total Pitches: 298 (C & CV)

Old Oaks Touring & Glamping
Wick Farm, Wick, Glastonbury
BA6 8JS
Tel: 01458 831437 17 P9
theoldoaks.co.uk
Total Pitches: 100 (C, CV & T)

Orchard Farm Holiday Village
Stonegate, Hunmanby, Filey, North Yorkshire
YO14 0PU
Tel: 01723 891582 65 Q4
orchardfarmholidayvillage.co.uk
Total Pitches: 137 (C, CV & T)

Orchard Park
Frampton Lane, Hubbert's Bridge, Boston, Lincolnshire
PE20 3QU
Tel: 01205 290328 49 L5
orchardpark.co.uk
Total Pitches: 251 (C, CV & T)

Ord House Country Park
East Ord, Berwick-upon-Tweed
TD15 2NS
Tel: 01289 305288 85 P8
maguirescountryparks.co.uk
Total Pitches: 344 (C, CV & T)

Otterington Park
Station Farm, South Otterington, Northallerton, North Yorkshire
DL7 9JB
Tel: 01609 780656 63 T2
otteringtonpark.com
Total Pitches: 67 (C, CV & T)

Oxon Hall Touring Park
Welshpool Road, Shrewsbury
SY3 5FB
Tel: 01743 340868 45 L11
morris-leisure.co.uk
Total Pitches: 165 (C, CV & T)

Park Cliffe C & C Estate
Birks Road, Tower Wood, Windermere
LA23 3PG
Tel: 015395 31344 61 R1
parkcliffe.co.uk
Total Pitches: 126 (C, CV & T)

Parkers Farm Holiday Park
Higher Mead Farm, Ashburton, Devon
TQ13 7LJ
Tel: 01364 654869 5 T6
parkersfarmholidays.co.uk
Total Pitches: 118 (C, CV & T)

Park Foot C & C Park
Howtown Road, Pooley Bridge
CA10 2NA
Tel: 017684 86309 67 Q8
parkfootullswater.co.uk
Total Pitches: 454 (C, CV & T)

Parkland C & C Site
Sorley Green Cross, Kingsbridge
TQ7 4AF
Tel: 01548 852723 5 S11
parklandsite.co.uk
Total Pitches: 50 (C, CV & T)

Pebble Bank Caravan Park
Camp Road, Wyke Regis, Weymouth
DT4 9HF
Tel: 01305 774844 7 S9
pebblebank.co.uk
Total Pitches: 120 (C, CV & T)

Perran Sands Holiday Park
Perranporth, Truro
TR6 0AQ
Tel: 01872 573551 2 K5
haven.com/perransands
Total Pitches: 1012 (C, CV & T)

Petwood Caravan Park
Off Stixwould Road, Woodhall Spa
LN10 6QH
Tel: 01526 354799 59 L14
petwoodcaravanpark.com
Total Pitches: 98 (C, CV & T)

Plough Lane Touring Caravan Site
Plough Lane, Chippenham, Wiltshire
SN15 5PS
Tel: 01249 750146 18 D5
ploughlane.co.uk
Total Pitches: 52 (C & CV)

Polladras Holiday Park
Carleen, Breage, Helston
TR13 9NX
Tel: 01736 762220 2 G10
polladrasholidaypark.co.uk
Total Pitches: 42 (C, CV & T)

Polmanter Touring Park
Halsetown, St Ives
TR26 3LX
Tel: 01736 795640 2 E9
polmanter.com
Total Pitches: 294 (C, CV & T)

Porthtowan Tourist Park
Mile Hill, Porthtowan, Truro
TR4 8TY
Tel: 01209 890256 2 H7
porthtowantouristpark.co.uk
Total Pitches: 80 (C, CV & T)

Primrose Valley Holiday Park
Filey
YO14 9RF
Tel: 01723 513771 65 Q4
haven.com/primrosevalley
Total Pitches: 1549 (C & CV)

Ranch Caravan Park
Station Road, Honeybourne, Evesham
WR11 7PR
Tel: 01386 830744 36 F12
ranch.co.uk
Total Pitches: 338 (C & CV)

Ripley Caravan Park
Knaresborough Road, Ripley, Harrogate
HG3 3AU
Tel: 01423 770050 63 R7
ripleycaravanpark.com
Total Pitches: 135 (C, CV & T)

River Dart Country Park
Holne Park, Ashburton
TQ13 7NP
Tel: 01364 652511 5 S7
riverdart.co.uk
Total Pitches: 170 (C, CV & T)

River Valley Holiday Park
London Apprentice, St Austell
PL26 7AP
Tel: 01726 73533 3 Q6
rivervalleyholidaypark.co.uk
Total Pitches: 85 (C, CV & T)

Riverside C & C Park
Marsh Lane, North Molton Road, South Molton
EX36 3HQ
Tel: 01769 579269 15 R7
exmoorriverside.co.uk
Total Pitches: 61 (C, CV & T)

Riverside Caravan Park
High Bentham, Lancaster
LA2 7FJ
Tel: 015242 61272 62 D6
riversidecaravanpark.co.uk
Total Pitches: 267 (C & CV)

Riverside Meadows Country Caravan Park
Ure Bank Top, Ripon
HG4 1JD
Tel: 01765 602964 63 S5
flowerofmay.com
Total Pitches: 349 (C)

Robin Hood C & C Park
Green Dyke Lane, Slingsby
YO62 4AP
Tel: 01653 628391 64 G5
robinhoodcaravanpark.co.uk
Total Pitches: 66 (C, CV & T)

Rose Farm Touring & Camping Park
Stepshort, Belton, Nr Great Yarmouth
NR31 9JS
Tel: 01493 738292 51 S13
rosefarmtouringpark.com
Total Pitches: 147 (C, CV & T)

Rosedale Abbey Caravan Park
Rosedale Abbey, Pickering
YO18 8SA
Tel: 01751 417272 71 M13
rosedaleabbeycaravanpark.co.uk
Total Pitches: 141 (C, CV & T)

Rudding Holiday Park
Follifoot, Harrogate
HG3 1JH
Tel: 01423 870439 63 S9
ruddingholidaypark.co.uk
Total Pitches: 143 (C, CV & T)

Run Cottage Touring Park
Alderton Road, Hollesley, Woodbridge
IP12 3RQ
Tel: 01394 411309 41 Q12
runcottage.co.uk
Total Pitches: 47 (C, CV & T)

Rutland C & C
Park Lane, Greetham, Oakham
LE15 7FN
Tel: 01572 813520 48 D11
rutlandcaravanandcamping.co.uk
Total Pitches: 130 (C, CV & T)

St Helens in the Park
Wykeham, Scarborough
YO13 9QD
Tel: 01723 862771 65 M3
sthelenscaravanpark.co.uk
Total Pitches: 260 (C, CV & T)

St Ives Bay Holiday Park
73 Loggans Road, Upton Towans, Hayle
TR27 5BH
Tel: 01736 752274 2 F9
stivesbay.co.uk
Total Pitches: 507 (C, CV & T)

Salcombe Regis C & C Park
Salcombe Regis, Sidmouth
EX10 0JH
Tel: 01395 514303 6 G7
salcombe-regis.co.uk
Total Pitches: 110 (C, CV & T)

Sand le Mere Holiday Village
Southfield Lane, Tunstall
HU12 0JF
Tel: 01964 670403 65 U13
sand-le-mere.co.uk
Total Pitches: 89 (C & CV)

Searles Leisure Resort
South Beach Road, Hunstanton
PE36 5BB
Tel: 01485 534211 49 U6
searles.co.uk
Total Pitches: 413 (C, CV & T)

Seaview Holiday Park
Preston, Weymouth
DT3 6DZ
Tel: 01305 832271 7 T8
haven.com/parks/dorset/seaview
Total Pitches: 347 (C, CV & T)

Severn Gorge Park
Bridgnorth Road, Tweedale, Telford
TF7 4JB
Tel: 01952 684789 45 R12
severngorgepark.co.uk
Total Pitches: 132 (C & CV)

Shamba Holidays
East Moors Lane, St Leonards, Ringwood
BH24 2SB
Tel: 01202 873302 8 G8
shambaholidays.co.uk
Total Pitches: 150 (C, CV & T)

Shrubbery Touring Park
Rousdon, Lyme Regis
DT7 3XW
Tel: 01297 442227 6 J6
shrubberypark.co.uk
Total Pitches: 122 (C, CV & T)

Silverdale Caravan Park
Middlebarrow Plain, Cove Road, Silverdale, Nr Carnforth
LA5 0SH
Tel: 01524 701508 61 T4
holgates.co.uk
Total Pitches: 427 (C, CV & T)

Skelwith Fold Caravan Park
Ambleside, Cumbria
LA22 0HX
Tel: 015394 32277 67 N12
skelwith.com
Total Pitches: 470 (C & CV)

Skirlington Leisure Park
Driffield, Skipsea
YO25 8SY
Tel: 01262 468213 65 R9
skirlington.com
Total Pitches: 930 (C & CV)

Sleningford Watermill Caravan Camping Park
North Stainley, Ripon
HG4 3HQ
Tel: 01765 635201 63 R4
sleningfordwatermill.co.uk
Total Pitches: 150 (C, CV & T)

Somers Wood Caravan Park
Somers Road, Meriden
CV7 7PL
Tel: 01676 522978 36 H4
somerswood.co.uk
Total Pitches: 48 (C & CV)

Southfork Caravan Park
Parrett Works, Martock, Somerset
TA12 6AE
Tel: 01935 825661 17 M13
southforkcaravans.co.uk
Total Pitches: 30 (C, CV & T)

South Lea Caravan Park
The Balk, Pocklington, York, North Yorkshire
YO42 2NX
Tel: 01759 303467 64 J10
south-lea.co.uk
Total Pitches: 97 (C, CV & T)

South Lytchett Manor C & C Park
Dorchester Road, Lytchett Minster, Poole
BH16 6JB
Tel: 01202 622577 8 D10
southlytchettmanor.co.uk
Total Pitches: 154 (C, CV & T)

South Meadows Caravan Park
South Road, Belford
NE70 7DP
Tel: 01668 213326 85 S12
southmeadows.co.uk
Total Pitches: 273 (C, CV & T)

Stanmore Hall Touring Park
Stourbridge Road, Bridgnorth
WV15 6DT
Tel: 01746 761761 35 R2
morris-leisure.co.uk
Total Pitches: 129 (C, CV & T)

Stanwix Park Holiday Centre
Greenrow, Silloth
CA7 4HH
Tel: 016973 32666 66 H2
stanwix.com
Total Pitches: 337 (C, CV & T)

Stroud Hill Park
Fen Road, Pidley, St Ives
PE28 3DE
Tel: 01487 741333 39 M5
stroudhillpark.co.uk
Total Pitches: 60 (C, CV & T)

Summers Ponds Fishery & Campsite
Chapel Road, Barns Green, Horsham
RH13 0PR
Tel: 01403 732539 10 J5
summersponds.co.uk
Total Pitches: 90 (C, CV & T)

Swiss Farm Touring & Camping
Marlow Road, Henley-on-Thames
RG9 2HY
Tel: 01491 573419 20 C6
swissfarmhenley.co.uk
Total Pitches: 148 (C, CV & T)

Tanner Farm Touring C & C Park
Tanner Farm, Goudhurst Road, Marden
TN12 9ND
Tel: 01622 832399 12 D7
tannerfarmpark.co.uk
Total Pitches: 122 (C, CV & T)

Tehidy Holiday Park
Harris Mill, Illogan, Portreath
TR16 4JQ
Tel: 01209 216489 2 H8
tehidy.co.uk
Total Pitches: 52 (C, CV & T)

Tencreek Holiday Park
Polperro Road, Looe
PL13 2JR
Tel: 01503 262447 4 G10
dolphinholidays.co.uk
Total Pitches: 355 (C, CV & T)

Teversal C & C Club Site
Silverhill Lane, Teversal
NG17 3JJ
Tel: 01623 551838 47 N1
campingandcaravanningclub.co.uk/teversal
Total Pitches: 136 (C, CV & T)

The Inside Park
Down House Estate, Blandford Forum, Dorset
DT11 9AD
Tel: 01258 453719 8 B8
theinsidepark.co.uk
Total Pitches: 125 (C & CV)

The Laurels Holiday Park
Padstow Road, Whitecross, Wadebridge
PL27 7JQ
Tel: 01208 813341 3 P2
thelaurelsholidaypark.co.uk
Total Pitches: 30 (C, CV & T)

The Old Brick Kilns
Little Barney Lane, Barney, Fakenham
NR21 0NL
Tel: 01328 878305 50 H7
old-brick-kilns.co.uk
Total Pitches: 65 (C, CV & T)

The Orchards Holiday Caravan Park
Main Road, Newbridge, Yarmouth, Isle of Wight
PO41 0TS
Tel: 01983 531331 9 N11
orchards-holiday-park.co.uk
Total Pitches: 225 (C, CV & T)

The Quiet Site
Ullswater, Watermillock
CA11 0LS
Tel: 07768 727016 67 P8
thequietsite.co.uk
Total Pitches: 151 (C, CV & T)

Thornton's Holt Camping Park
Stragglethorpe Road, Stragglethorpe, Radcliffe on Trent
NG12 2JZ
Tel: 0115 933 2125 47 R6
thorntons-holt.co.uk
Total Pitches: 155 (C, CV & T)

Thornwick Bay Holiday Village
North Marine Road, Flamborough
YO15 1AU
Tel: 01262 850569 65 S5
haven.com/parks/yorkshire/thornwick-bay
Total Pitches: 225 (C, CV & T)

Thorpe Park Holiday Centre
Cleethorpes
DN35 0PW
Tel: 01472 813395 59 P5
haven.com/thorpepark
Total Pitches: 1491 (C, CV & T)

Treago Farm Caravan Site
Crantock, Newquay
TR8 5QS
Tel: 01637 830277 2 K4
treagofarm.co.uk
Total Pitches: 100 (C, CV & T)

Treloy Touring Park
Newquay
TR8 4JN
Tel: 01637 872063 3 M4
treloy.co.uk
Total Pitches: 223 (C, CV & T)

Trencreek Holiday Park
Hillcrest, Higher Trencreek, Newquay
TR8 4NS
Tel: 01637 874210 3 L4
trencreekholidaypark.co.uk
Total Pitches: 200 (C, CV & T)

Trethem Mill Touring Park
St Just-in-Roseland, Nr St Mawes, Truro
TR2 5JF
Tel: 01872 580504 3 M9
trethem.com
Total Pitches: 84 (C, CV & T)

Trevalgan Touring Park
Trevalgan, St Ives
TR26 3BJ
Tel: 01736 791892 2 D9
trevalgantouringpark.co.uk
Total Pitches: 135 (C, CV & T)

Trevarrian Holiday Park
Mawgan Porth, Newquay, Cornwall
TR8 4AQ
Tel: 01637 860381 3 M3
trevarrian.co.uk
Total Pitches: 185 (C, CV & T)

Trevarth Holiday Park
Blackwater, Truro
TR4 8HR
Tel: 01872 560266 2 J7
trevarth.co.uk
Total Pitches: 50 (C, CV & T)

Trevedra Farm C & C Site
Sennen, Penzance
TR19 7BE
Tel: 01736 871818 2 B11
trevedrafarm.co.uk
Total Pitches: 100 (C, CV & T)

Trevella Park
Crantock, Newquay
TR8 5EW
Tel: 01637 830308 3 L5
trevella.co.uk
Total Pitches: 290 (C, CV & T)

Trevornick
Holywell Bay, Newquay
TR8 5PW
Tel: 01637 830531 2 K5
trevornick.co.uk
Total Pitches: 600 (C, CV & T)

Trewan Hall
St Columb Major, Cornwall
TR9 6DB
Tel: 01637 880261 3 N4
trewan-hall.co.uk
Total Pitches: 200 (C, CV & T)

Tudor C & C
Shepherds Patch, Slimbridge, Gloucester
GL2 7BP
Tel: 01453 890483 28 D7
tudorcaravanpark.com
Total Pitches: 75 (C, CV & T)

Twitchen House Holiday Park
Mortehoe Station Road, Mortehoe, Woolacombe
EX34 7ES
Tel: 01271 872302 15 L4
woolacombe.com
Total Pitches: 569 (C, CV & T)

Two Mills Touring Park
Yarmouth Road, North Walsham
NR28 9NA
Tel: 01692 405829 51 N8
twomills.co.uk
Total Pitches: 81 (C, CV & T)

Ulwell Cottage Caravan Park
Ulwell Cottage, Ulwell, Swanage
BH19 3DG
Tel: 01929 422823 8 E12
ulwellcottagepark.co.uk
Total Pitches: 219 (C, CV & T)

Upper Lynstone Caravan Park
Lynstone, Bude
EX23 0LP
Tel: 01288 352017 14 F11
upperlynstone.co.uk
Total Pitches: 106 (C, CV & T)

Vale of Pickering Caravan Park
Carr House Farm, Allerston, Pickering
YO18 7PQ
Tel: 01723 859280 64 K3
valeofpickering.co.uk
Total Pitches: 120 (C, CV & T)

Waldegraves Holiday Park
Mersea Island, Colchester
CO5 8SE
Tel: 01206 382898 23 P5
waldegraves.co.uk
Total Pitches: 126 (C, CV & T)

Waleswood C &C Park
Delves Lane, Waleswood, Wales Bar, Wales, South Yorkshire
S26 5RN
Tel: 07825 125328 57 Q10
waleswood.co.uk
Total Pitches: 163 (C, CV & T)

Warcombe Farm C & C Park
Station Road, Mortehoe, Woolacombe
EX34 7EJ
Tel: 01271 870690 15 L3
warcombefarm.co.uk
Total Pitches: 250 (C, CV & T)

Wareham Forest Tourist Park
North Trigon, Wareham
BH20 7NZ
Tel: 01929 551393 8 B10
warehamforest.co.uk
Total Pitches: 200 (C, CV & T)

Waren C & C Park
Waren Mill, Bamburgh
NE70 7EE
Tel: 01668 214366 85 T12
meadowhead.co.uk/parks/waren
Total Pitches: 458 (C, CV & T)

Warren Farm Holiday Centre
Brean Sands, Brean, Burnham-on-Sea
TA8 2RP
Tel: 01278 751227 16 J5
warrenfarm.co.uk
Total Pitches: 975 (C, CV & T)

Waterfoot Caravan Park
Pooley Bridge, Penrith, Cumbria
CA11 0JF
Tel: 017684 86302 67 Q8
waterfootpark.co.uk
Total Pitches: 184 (C, CV & T)

Watergate Bay Touring Park
Watergate Bay, Tregurrian
TR8 4AD
Tel: 01637 860387 3 M3
watergatebaytouringpark.co.uk
Total Pitches: 173 (C, CV & T)

Waterrow Touring Park
Wiveliscombe, Taunton
TA4 2AZ
Tel: 01984 623464 16 E11
waterrowpark.co.uk
Total Pitches: 42 (C, CV & T)

Wayfarers C & C Park
Relubbus Lane, St Hilary, Penzance
TR20 9EF
Tel: 01736 763326 2 F10
wayfarerspark.co.uk
Total Pitches: 35 (C, CV & T)

Wayside Holiday Park
Wrelton, Pickering, North Yorkshire
YO18 8PG
Tel: 01751 472608 64 H2
waysideparks.co.uk
Total Pitches: 152 (C & CV)

Wells Touring Park
Haybridge, Wells
BA5 1AJ
Tel: 01749 676869 17 P7
wellstouringpark.co.uk
Total Pitches: 56 (C, CV & T)

Westbrook Park
Little Hereford, Herefordshire
SY8 4AU
Tel: 01584 711280 35 M7
westbrookpark.co.uk
Total Pitches: 59 (C, CV & T)

Wheathill Touring Park
Wheathill, Bridgnorth
WV16 6QT
Tel: 01584 823456 35 P4
wheathillpark.co.uk
Total Pitches: 50 (C & CV)

Whitefield Forest Touring Park
Brading Road, Ryde, Isle of Wight
PO33 1QL
Tel: 01983 617069 9 S11
whitefieldforest.co.uk
Total Pitches: 90 (C, CV & T)

Whitehill Country Park
Stoke Road, Paignton, Devon
TQ4 7PF
Tel: 01803 782338 5 V9
whitehill-park.co.uk
Total Pitches: 325 (C, CV & T)

Whitemead Caravan Park
East Burton Road, Wool
BH20 6HG
Tel: 01929 462241 8 A11
whitemeadcaravanpark.co.uk
Total Pitches: 105 (C, CV & T)

Willowbank Holiday Home & Touring Park
Coastal Road, Ainsdale, Southport
PR8 3ST
Tel: 01704 571566 54 H4
willowbankcp.co.uk
Total Pitches: 315 (C & CV)

Willow Valley Holiday Park
Bush, Bude, Cornwall
EX23 9LB
Tel: 01288 353104 14 F11
willowvalley.co.uk
Total Pitches: 44 (C, CV & T)

Wilson House Holiday Park
Lancaster Road, Out Rawcliffe, Preston, Lancashire
PR3 6BN
Tel: 07807 560685 61 S11
whhp.co.uk
Total Pitches: 40 (C & CV)

Wolds View Touring Park
115 Brigg Road, Caistor
LN7 6RX
Tel: 01472 851099 58 K6
woldsviewtouringpark.co.uk
Total Pitches: 60 (C, CV & T)

Wooda Farm Holiday Park
Poughill, Bude
EX23 9HJ
Tel: 01288 352069 14 F11
wooda.co.uk
Total Pitches: 255 (C, CV & T)

Woodclose Caravan Park
High Casterton, Kirkby Lonsdale
LA6 2SE
Tel: 01524 271597 62 C4
woodclosepark.com
Total Pitches: 117 (C & CV)

Woodhall Country Park
Stixwold Road, Woodhall Spa
LN10 6UJ
Tel: 01526 353710 59 L14
woodhallcountrypark.co.uk
Total Pitches: 120 (C, CV & T)

Woodland Springs Adult Touring Park
Venton, Drewsteignton
EX6 6PG
Tel: 01647 231648 5 R2
woodlandsprings.co.uk
Total Pitches: 93 (C, CV & T)

Woodlands Grove C & C Park
Blackawton, Dartmouth
TQ9 7DQ
Tel: 01803 712598 5 U10
woodlandsgrove.com
Total Pitches: 350 (C, CV & T)

Woodovis Park
Gulworthy, Tavistock
PL19 8NY
Tel: 01822 832968 5 L6
woodovis.com
Total Pitches: 89 (C, CV & T)

Yeatheridge Farm Caravan Park
East Worlington, Crediton, Devon
EX17 4TN
Tel: 01884 860330 15 S10
yeatheridge.co.uk
Total Pitches: 122 (C, CV & T)

York Caravan Park
Stockton Lane, York, North Yorkshire
YO32 9UB
Tel: 01904 424222 64 E9
yorkcaravanpark.com
Total Pitches: 55 (C & CV)

York Meadows Caravan Park
York Road, Sheriff Hutton, York, North Yorkshire
YO60 6QP
Tel: 01347 878508 64 E6
yorkmeadowscaravanpark.com
Total Pitches: 60 (C, CV & T)

SCOTLAND

Auchenlarie Holiday Park
Gatehouse of Fleet
DG7 2EX
Tel: 01556 506200 73 N9
swalwellholidaygroup.co.uk
Total Pitches: 451 (C, CV & T)

Banff Links Caravan Park
Inverboyndie, Banff, Aberdeenshire
AB45 2JJ
Tel: 01261 812228 104 K3
banfflinkscaravanpark.co.uk
Total Pitches: 93 (C, CV & T)

Beecraigs C & C Site
Beecraigs Country Park, The Visitor Centre, Linlithgow
EH49 6PL
Tel: 01506 284516 82 K4
westlothian.gov.uk/stay-at-beecraigs
Total Pitches: 38 (C, CV & T)

Belhaven Bay C & C Park
Belhaven Bay, Dunbar, East Lothian
EH42 1TS
Tel: 01368 865956 84 H3
meadowhead.co.uk
Total Pitches: 119 (C, CV & T)

Blair Castle Caravan Park
Blair Atholl, Pitlochry
PH18 5SR
Tel: 01796 481263 97 P10
blaircastlecaravanpark.co.uk
Total Pitches: 338 (C, CV & T)

Brighouse Bay Holiday Park
Brighouse Bay, Borgue, Kirkcudbright
DG6 4TS
Tel: 01557 870267 73 Q10
gillespie-leisure.co.uk
Total Pitches: 418 (C, CV & T)

Cairnsmill Holiday Park
Largo Road, St Andrews
KY16 8NN
Tel: 01334 473604 91 Q9
cairnsmill.co.uk
Total Pitches: 256 (C, CV & T)

Craig Tara Holiday Park
Ayr
KA7 4LB
Tel: 0800 975 7579 81 L9
haven.com/craigtara
Total Pitches: 1144 (C & CV)

Craigtoun Meadows Holiday Park
Mount Melville, St Andrews
KY16 8PQ
Tel: 01334 475959 91 Q8
craigtounmeadows.co.uk
Total Pitches: 257 (C, CV & T)

Faskally Caravan Park
Pitlochry
PH16 5LA
Tel: 01796 472007 97 Q12
faskally.co.uk
Total Pitches: 430 (C, CV & T)

Glenearly Caravan Park
Dalbeattie, Dumfries & Galloway
DG5 4NE
Tel: 01556 611393 74 F13
glenearlycaravanpark.co.uk
Total Pitches: 113 (C, CV & T)

Glen Nevis C & C Park
Glen Nevis, Fort William
PH33 6SX
Tel: 01397 702191 94 G4
glen-nevis.co.uk
Total Pitches: 415 (C, CV & T)

Hoddom Castle Caravan Park
Hoddom, Lockerbie
DG11 1AS
Tel: 01576 300251 75 N11
hoddomcastle.co.uk
Total Pitches: 265 (C, CV & T)

Huntly Castle Caravan Park
The Meadow, Huntly
AB54 4UJ
Tel: 01466 794999 104 G7
huntlycastle.co.uk
Total Pitches: 130 (C, CV & T)

Invercoe C & C Park
Ballachulish, Glencoe
PH49 4HP
Tel: 01855 811210 94 F7
invercoe.co.uk
Total Pitches: 66 (C, CV & T)

Linwater Caravan Park
West Clifton, East Calder
EH53 0HT
Tel: 0131 333 3326 83 M5
linwater.co.uk
Total Pitches: 64 (C, CV & T)

Milton of Fonab Caravan Park
Bridge Road, Pitlochry
PH16 5NA
Tel: 01796 472882 97 Q12
fonab.co.uk
Total Pitches: 181 (C, CV & T)

Sands of Luce Holiday Park
Sands of Luce, Sandhead, Stranraer
DG9 9JN
Tel: 01776 830456 72 E9
sandsofluce.com
Total Pitches: 350 (C, CV & T)

Seal Shore Camping and Touring Site
Kildonan, Isle of Arran, North Ayrshire
KA27 8SE
Tel: 01770 820320 80 E8
campingarran.com
Total Pitches: 47 (C, CV & T)

Seaward Holiday Park
Dhoon Bay, Kirkudbright
DG6 4TJ
Tel: 01557 870267 73 R10
gillespie-leisure.co.uk
Total Pitches: 84 (C, CV & T)

Seton Sands Holiday Village
Longniddry
EH32 0QF
Tel: 01875 813333 83 T3
haven.com/setonsands
Total Pitches: 640 (C & CV)

Shieling Holidays Mull
Craignure, Isle of Mull, Argyll & Bute
PA65 6AY
Tel: 01680 812496 93 S11
shielingholidays.co.uk
Total Pitches: 106 (C, CV & T)

Silver Sands Holiday Park
Covesea, West Beach, Lossiemouth
IV31 6SP
Tel: 01343 813262 103 V1
silver-sands.co.uk
Total Pitches: 340 (C, CV & T)

Skye C & C Club Site
Loch Greshornish, Borve, Arnisort, Edinbane, Isle of Skye
IV51 9PS
Tel: 01470 582230 100 c4
campingandcaravanningclub.co.uk/skye
Total Pitches: 107 (C, CV & T)

Thurston Manor Leisure Park
Innerwick, Dunbar
EH42 1SA
Tel: 01368 840643 84 J4
thurstonmanor.co.uk
Total Pitches: 690 (C & CV)

Witches Craig C & C Park
Blairlogie, Stirling
FK9 5PX
Tel: 01786 474947 89 T6
witchescraig.co.uk
Total Pitches: 60 (C, CV & T)

WALES

Bron Derw Touring Caravan Park
Llanrwst
LL26 0YT
Tel: 01492 640494 53 P10
bronderw-wales.co.uk
Total Pitches: 48 (C & CV)

Bryn Gloch C & C Park
Betws Garmon, Caernarfon
LL54 7YY
Tel: 01286 650216 52 H11
bryngloch.co.uk
Total Pitches: 177 (C, CV & T)

Caerfai Bay Caravan & Tent Park
Caerfai Bay, St Davids, Haverfordwest
SA62 6QT
Tel: 01437 720274 24 C6
caerfaibay.co.uk
Total Pitches: 136 (C, CV & T)

Cenarth Falls Holiday Park
Cenarth, Newcastle Emlyn
SA38 9JS
Tel: 01239 710345 32 E12
cenarth-holipark.co.uk
Total Pitches: 119 (C, CV & T)

Daisy Bank Caravan Park
Snead, Montgomery
SY15 6EB
Tel: 01588 620471 34 H2
daisy-bank.co.uk
Total Pitches: 78 (C, CV & T)

Dinlle Caravan Park
Dinas Dinlle, Caernarfon
LL54 5TW
Tel: 01286 830324 52 F11
thornleyleisure.co.uk
Total Pitches: 349 (C, CV & T)

Eisteddfa
Eisteddfa Lodge, Pentrefelin, Criccieth
LL52 0PT
Tel: 01766 522696 42 K6
eisteddfapark.co.uk
Total Pitches: 116 (C, CV & T)

Fforest Fields C & C Park
Hundred House, Builth Wells
LD1 5RT
Tel: 01982 570406 34 D10
fforestfields.co.uk
Total Pitches: 122 (C, CV & T)

Fishguard Bay Resort
Garn Gelli, Fishguard
SA65 9ET
Tel: 01348 811415 24 G3
fishguardbay.com
Total Pitches: 102 (C, CV & T)

Greenacres Holiday Park
Black Rock Sands, Morfa Bychan, Porthmadog
LL49 9YF
Tel: 01766 512781 42 K6
haven.com/greenacres
Total Pitches: 945 (C & CV)

Hafan y Môr Holiday Park
Pwllheli
LL53 6HJ
Tel: 01758 612112 42 H6
haven.com/hafanymor
Total Pitches: 875 (C & CV)

Hendre Mynach Touring C & C Park
Llanaber Road, Barmouth
LL42 1YR
Tel: 01341 280262 43 M10
hendremynach.co.uk
Total Pitches: 241 (C, CV & T)

Home Farm Caravan Park
Marian-glas, Isle of Anglesey
LL73 8PH
Tel: 01248 410614 52 G6
homefarm-anglesey.co.uk
Total Pitches: 102 (C, CV & T)

Islawrffordd Caravan Park
Talybont, Barmouth
LL43 2AQ
Tel: 01341 247269 43 L9
islawrffordd.co.uk
Total Pitches: 306 (C & CV)

Kiln Park Holiday Centre
Marsh Road, Tenby
SA70 8RB
Tel: 01834 844121 24 K10
haven.com/kilnpark
Total Pitches: 849 (C, CV & T)

Pencelli Castle C & C Park
Pencelli, Brecon
LD3 7LX
Tel: 01874 665451 26 K3
pencelli-castle.com
Total Pitches: 80 (C, CV & T)

Penisar Mynydd Caravan Park
Caerwys Road, Rhuallt, St Asaph
LL17 0TY
Tel: 01745 582227 54 C11
penisarmynydd.co.uk
Total Pitches: 71 (C, CV & T)

Plassey Holiday Park
The Plassey, Eyton, Wrexham
LL13 0SP
Tel: 01978 780277 44 H4
plassey.com
Total Pitches: 123 (C, CV & T)

Pont Kemys C & C Park
Chainbridge, Abergavenny
NP7 9DS
Tel: 01873 880688 27 Q6
pontkemys.com
Total Pitches: 65 (C, CV & T)

Presthaven Sands Holiday Park
Gronant, Prestatyn
LL19 9TT
Tel: 01745 856471 54 C10
haven.com/presthavensands
Total Pitches: 1102 (C & CV)

Red Kite Touring Park
Van Road, Llanidloes
SY18 6NG
Tel: 01686 412122 33 T3
redkitetouringpark.co.uk
Total Pitches: 66 (C & CV)

Riverside Camping
Seiont Nurseries, Pont Rug, Caernarfon
LL55 2BB
Tel: 01286 678781 52 H10
riversidecamping.co.uk
Total Pitches: 73 (C, CV & T)

The Trotting Mare Caravan Park
Overton, Wrexham
LL13 0LE
Tel: 01978 711963 44 J6
thetrottingmare.co.uk
Total Pitches: 65 (C, CV & T)

Trawsdir Touring C & C Park
Llanaber, Barmouth
LL42 1RR
Tel: 01341 280999 43 L10
barmouthholidays.co.uk
Total Pitches: 80 (C, CV & T)

Tyddyn Isaf Caravan Park
Lligwy Bay, Dulas, Isle of Anglesey
LL70 9PQ
Tel: 01248 410203 52 G5
tyddynisaf.co.uk
Total Pitches: 136 (C, CV & T)

White Tower Caravan Park
Llandwrog, Caernarfon
LL54 5UH
Tel: 01286 830649 52 G11
whitetowerpark.co.uk
Total Pitches: 126 (C & CV)

CHANNEL ISLANDS

La Bailloterie Camping
Bailloterie Lane, Vale, Guernsey
GY3 5HA
Tel: 01481 243636 6 e2
campinginguernsey.com
Total Pitches: 109 (C, CV & T)

Traffic signs

Signs giving orders

Signs with red circles are mostly prohibitive.
Plates below signs qualify their message

 Entry to 20mph zone

 End of 20mph zone

Maximum speed

National speed limit applies

School crossing patrol

 Stop and give way

GIVE WAY Give way to traffic on major road

STOP Manually operated temporary STOP and GO signs

GO

No entry for vehicular traffic

No vehicles except bicycles being pushed

No cycling

No motor vehicles

No buses (over 8 passenger seats)

No overtaking

No towed caravans

No vehicles carrying explosives

No vehicle or combination of vehicles over length shown

4.4 m 14'6" No vehicles over height shown

2.0 m 6'6" No vehicles over width shown

 Give priority to vehicles from opposite direction

No right turn

No left turn

No U-turns

Except for loading — No goods vehicles over maximum gross weight shown (in tonnes) except for loading and unloading

WEAK BRIDGE 18T m g w — No vehicles over maximum gross weight shown (in tonnes)

P Permit holders only Parking restricted to permit holders

RED ROUTE No stopping at any time except buses No stopping during period indicated except for buses

URBAN CLEARWAY Monday to Friday am 8.00 - 9.30 pm 4.30 - 6.30 No stopping during times shown except for as long as needed to set down or pick up passengers

No waiting

No stopping (Clearway)

Signs with blue circles but no red border mostly give positive instruction.

Ahead only

Turn left ahead (right if symbol reversed)

Turn left (right if symbol reversed)

Keep left (right if symbol reversed)

Vehicles may pass either side to reach same destination

Mini-roundabout (roundabout circulation – give way to vehicles from the immediate right)

Route to be used by pedal cycles only

Segregated pedal cycle and pedestrian route

30 Minimum speed

End of minimum speed

Only Buses and cycles only

Only Trams only

Pedestrian crossing point over tramway

One-way traffic (note: compare circular 'Ahead only' sign)

With-flow bus and cycle lane

Contraflow bus lane

With-flow pedal cycle lane

Warning signs

Mostly triangular

STOP 100 yds Distance to 'STOP' line ahead

Dual carriageway ends

Road narrows on right (left if symbol reversed)

Road narrows on both sides

GIVE WAY 50 yds Distance to 'Give Way' line ahead

Crossroads

Junction on bend ahead

T-junction with priority over vehicles from the right

Staggered junction

Traffic merging from left ahead

The priority through route is indicated by the broader line.

Double bend first to left (symbol may be reversed)

Bend to right (or left if symbol reversed)

Roundabout

Uneven road

REDUCE SPEED NOW Plate below some signs

Two-way traffic crosses one-way road

Two-way traffic straight ahead

Opening or swing bridge ahead

Low-flying aircraft or sudden aircraft noise

Falling or fallen rocks

Traffic signals not in use

Traffic signals

Slippery road

10% Steep hill downwards

20% Steep hill upwards

Gradients may be shown as a ratio i.e. 20% = 1:5

Tunnel ahead

Trams crossing ahead

Level crossing with barrier or gate ahead

Level crossing without barrier or gate ahead

Level crossing without barrier

Patrol School crossing patrol ahead (some signs have amber lights which flash when crossings are in use)

Frail (or blind or disabled if shown) pedestrians likely to cross road ahead

No footway for 400 yds Pedestrians in road ahead

Zebra crossing

Safe height 16'-6" Overhead electric cable; plate indicates maximum height of vehicles which can pass safely

14'-6" 4.4 m Available width of headroom indicated

Sharp deviation of route to left (or right if chevrons reversed)

STOP when lights show Light signals ahead at level crossing, airfield or bridge

Red Green STOP Clear IF NO LIGHT - PHONE CROSSING OPERATOR Miniature warning lights at level crossings

Cattle

Wild animals

Wild horses or ponies

Accompanied horses or ponies

Cycle route ahead

Ice Risk of ice

Queues likely Traffic queues likely ahead

Humps for ½ mile Distance over which road humps extend

Hidden dip Other danger; plate indicates nature of danger

Soft verges for 2 miles Soft verges

Side winds

Hump bridge

Ford Worded warning sign

Quayside or river bank

Risk of grounding

Direction signs

Mostly rectangular

Signs on motorways - blue backgrounds

 At a junction leading directly into a motorway (junction number may be shown on a black background)

 On approaches to junctions (junction number on black background)

 Route confirmatory sign after junction

 Downward pointing arrows mean 'Get in lane' The left-hand lane leads to a different destination from the other lanes.

 The panel with the inclined arrow indicates the destinations which can be reached

Signs on primary routes - green backgrounds

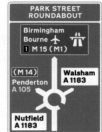 On approaches to junctions

 At the junction

 On approaches to junctions

 Route confirmatory sign after junction

On approach to a junction in Wales (bilingual)

Blue panels indicate that the motorway starts at the junction ahead. Motorways shown in brackets can also be reached along the route indicated. White panels indicate local or non-primary routes leading from the junction ahead. Brown panels show the route to tourist attractions. The name of the junction may be shown at the top of the sign. The aircraft symbol indicates the route to an airport. A symbol may be included to warn of a hazard or restriction along that route.

 Primary route forming part of a ring road

 R

Signs on non-primary and local routes - black borders

 On approaches to junctions

 At the junction

Direction to toilets with access for the disabled

Green panels indicate that the primary route starts at the junction ahead. Route numbers on a blue background show the direction to a motorway. Route numbers on a green background show the direction to a primary route.

Signs on non-primary and local routes - black borders

 150 yds Picnic site

 Wrest Park Ancient monument in the care of English Heritage

 P Saturday only Direction to a car park

 Zoo Tourist attraction

300 yds Direction to camping and caravan site

 Advisory route for lorries

 Route for pedal cycles forming part of a network

Marton 3 Recommended route for pedal cycles to place shown

 **Public library Council offices** Route for pedestrians

Emergency diversion routes

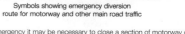 Symbols showing emergency diversion route for motorway and other main road traffic

Northtown Diversion route

In an emergency it may be necessary to close a section of motorway or other main road to traffic, so a temporary sign may advise drivers to follow a diversion route. To help drivers navigate the route, black symbols on yellow patches may be permanently displayed on existing direction signs, including motorway signs. Symbols may also be used on separate signs with yellow backgrounds.

Note: The signs shown in this road atlas are those most commonly in use and are not all drawn to the same scale. In Scotland and Wales bilingual versions of some signs are used, showing both English and Gaelic or Welsh spellings. Some older designs of signs may still be seen on the roads. A comprehensive explanation of the signing system illustrating the vast majority of road signs can be found in the AA's handbook Know Your Road Signs. Where there is a reference to a rule number, this refers to The Highway Code.

 THE HIGHWAY CODE / KNOW YOUR ROAD SIGNS

Road markings

Information signs

All retangular

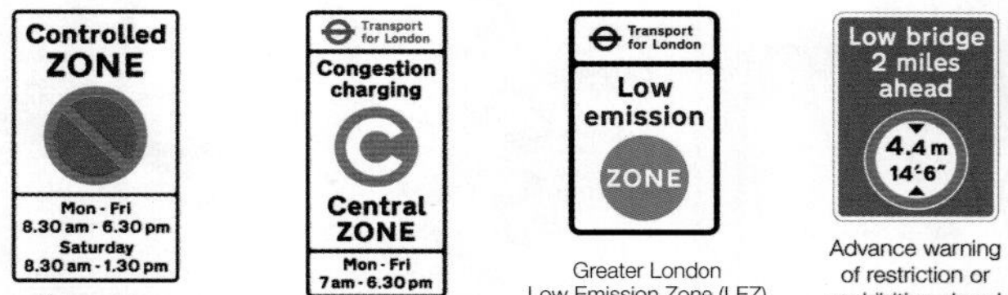
Controlled ZONE
Mon - Fri 8.30 am - 6.30 pm Saturday 8.30 am - 1.30 pm
Transport for London
Congestion charging
Central ZONE
Mon - Fri 7am - 6.30 pm
Transport for London
Low emission
ZONE
Low bridge 2 miles ahead
4.4 m 14'6"

Entrance to controlled parking zone

Entrance to congestion charging zone

Greater London Low Emission Zone (LEZ)

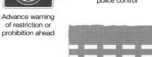

Advance warning of restriction or prohibition ahead

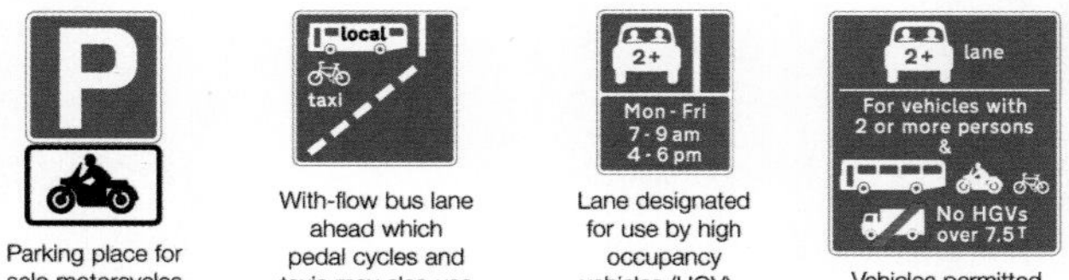
P
local
taxi
2+
Mon - Fri 7 - 9 am 4 - 6 pm
2+ lane
For vehicles with 2 or more persons
No HGVs over 7.5T

Parking place for solo motorcycles

With-flow bus lane ahead which pedal cycles and taxis may also use

Lane designated for use by high occupancy vehicles (HOV) - see rule 142

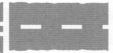

Vehicles permitted to use an HOV lane ahead

M62
Except buses

End of motorway

Start of motorway and point from which motorway regulations apply

Appropriate traffic lanes at junction ahead

Traffic on the main carriageway coming from right has priority over joining traffic

Additional traffic joining from left ahead. Traffic on main carriageway has priority over joining traffic from right hand lane of slip road

Traffic in right hand lane of slip road joining the main carriageway has prority over left hand lane

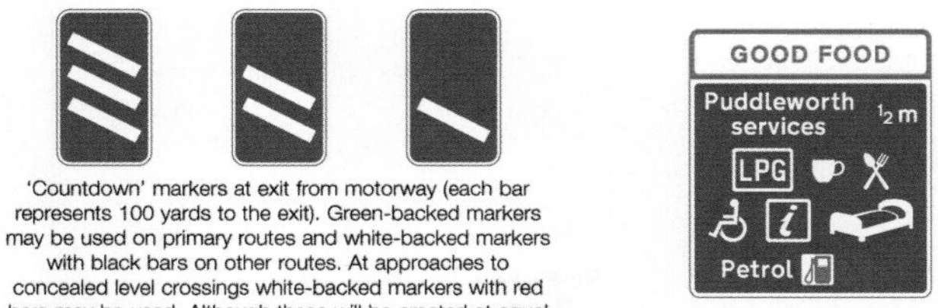
GOOD FOOD
Puddleworth services
½ m
LPG
Petrol

'Countdown' markers at exit from motorway (each bar represents 100 yards to the exit). Green-backed markers may be used on primary routes and white-backed markers with black bars on other routes. At approaches to concealed level crossings white-backed markers with red bars may be used. Although these will be erected at equal distances the bars do not represent 100 yard intervals.

Motorway service area sign showing the operator's name

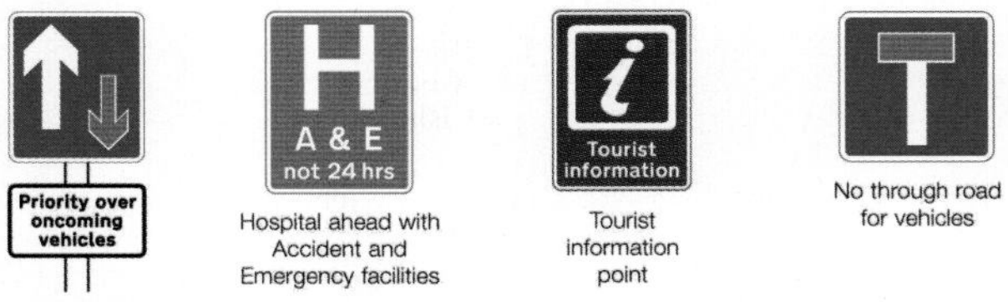
Priority over oncoming vehicles
H
A & E
not 24 hrs
Tourist information

Traffic has priority over oncoming vehicles

Hospital ahead with Accident and Emergency facilities

Tourist information point

No through road for vehicles

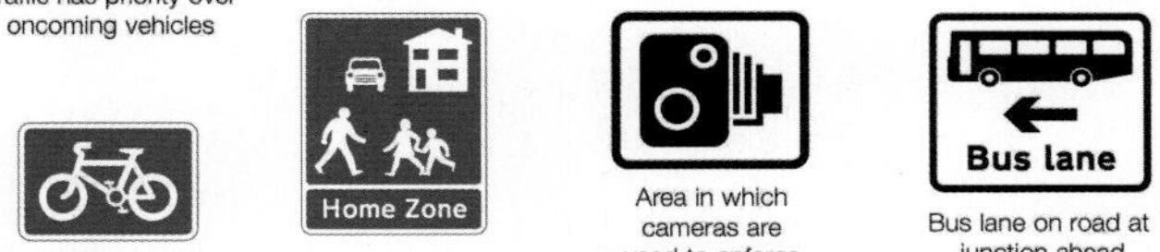
Home Zone
Bus lane

Recommended route for pedal cycles

Home Zone Entry

Area in which cameras are used to enforce traffic regulations

Bus lane on road at junction ahead

*Home Zone Entry – You are entering an area where people could be using the whole street for a range of activities. You should drive slowly and carefully and be prepared to stop to allow people time to move out of the way.

Roadworks signs

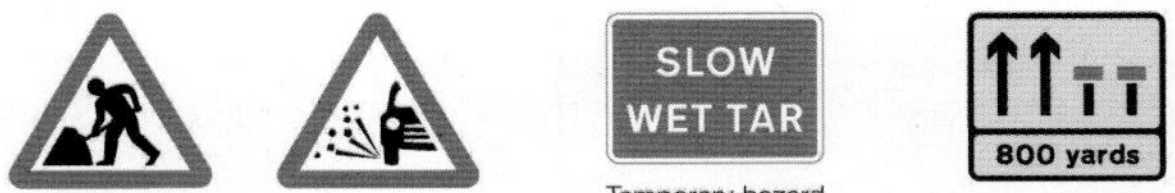
SLOW
WET TAR
800 yards

Road works

Loose chippings

Temporary hazard at roadworks

Temporary lane closure (the number and position of arrows and red bars may be varied according to lanes open and closed)

50
¾ mile ahead
Delays possible until Mar 08
1 mile
Sorry for any delay
End
Authority name

Slow-moving or stationary works vehicle blocking a traffic lane. Pass in the direction shown by the arrow.

Mandatory speed limit ahead

Roadworks 1 mile ahead

End of roadworks and any temporary restrictions including speed limits

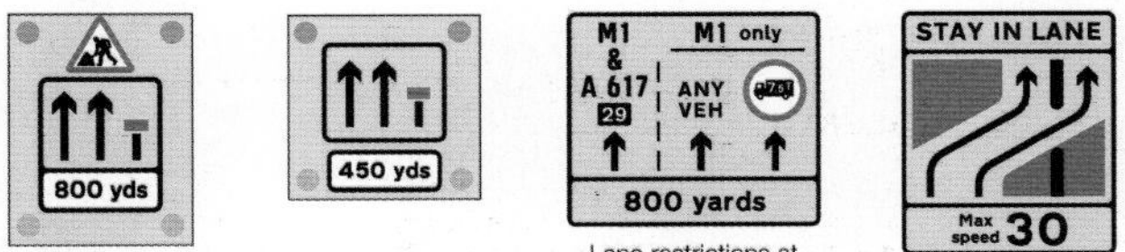
800 yds
450 yds
M1 & A 617
M1 only
29
ANY VEH
800 yards
STAY IN LANE
Max speed 30

Signs used on the back of slow-moving or stationary vehicles warning of a lane closed ahead by a works vehicle. There are no cones on the road.

Lane restrictions at roadworks ahead

One lane crossover at contraflow roadworks

Across the carriageway

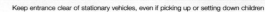

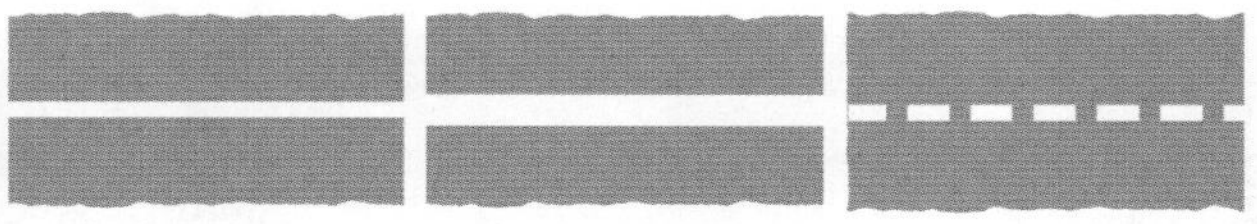

Stop line at signals or police control

Stop line at 'Stop' sign

Stop line for pedestrians at a level crossing

Give way to traffic on major road (can also be used at mini roundabouts)

Give way to traffic from the right at a roundabout

Give way to traffic from the right at a mini-roundabout

Along the carriageway

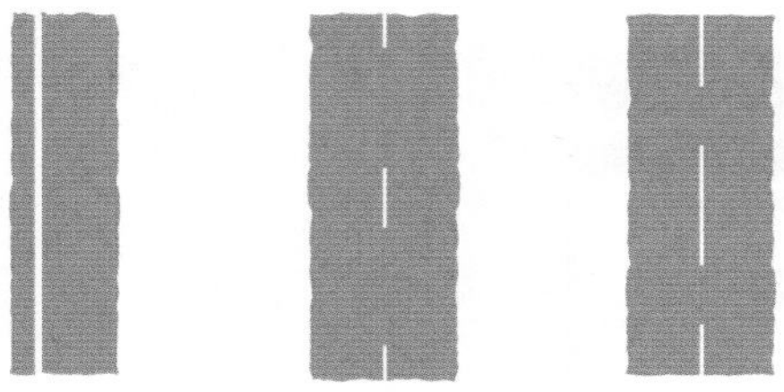

Edge line

Centre line See Rule 127

Hazard warning line See Rule 127

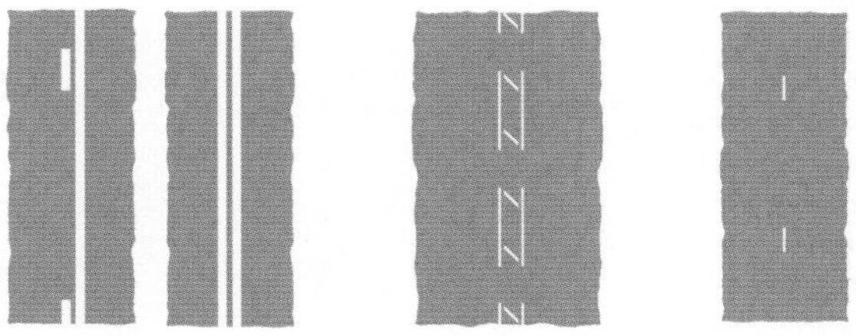

Double white lines See Rules 128 and 129

See Rule 130

Lane line See Rule 131

Along the edge of the carriageway

Waiting restrictions

Waiting restrictions indicated by yellow lines apply to the carriageway, pavement and verge. You may stop to load or unload (unless there are also loading restrictions as described below) or while passengers board or alight. Double yellow lines mean no waiting at any time, unless there are signs that specifically indicate seasonal restrictions. The times at which the restrictions apply for other road markings are shown on nearby plates or on entry signs to controlled parking zones. If no days are shown on the signs, the restrictions are in force every day including Sundays and Bank Holidays. White bay markings and upright signs (see below) indicate where parking is allowed.

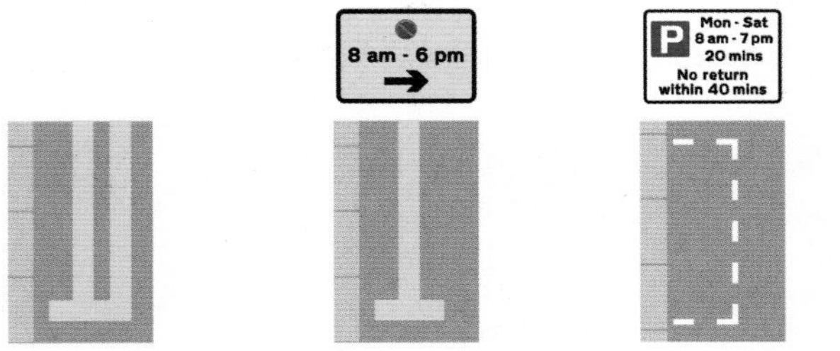
8 am - 6 pm
P
Mon - Sat 8 am - 7 pm
20 mins
No return within 40 mins

No waiting at any time

No waiting during times shown on sign

Waiting is limited to the duration specified during the days and times shown

Red Route stopping controls

Red lines are used on some roads instead of yellow lines. In London the double and single red lines used on Red Routes indicate that stopping to park, load/unload or to board and alight from a vehicle (except for a licensed taxi or if you hold a Blue Badge) is prohibited. The red lines apply to the carriageway, pavement and verge. The times that the red line prohibitions apply are shown on nearby signs, but the double red line ALWAYS means no stopping at any time. On Red Routes you may stop to park, load/unload in specially marked boxes and adjacent signs specify the times and purposes and duration allowed. A box MARKED IN RED indicates that it may only be available for the purpose specified for part of the day (e.g. between busy peak periods). A box MARKED IN WHITE means that it is available throughout the day.

RED AND SINGLE YELLOW LINES CAN ONLY GIVE A GUIDE TO THE RESTRICTIONS AND CONTROLS IN FORCE AND SIGNS, NEARBY OR AT A ZONE ENTRY, MUST BE CONSULTED.

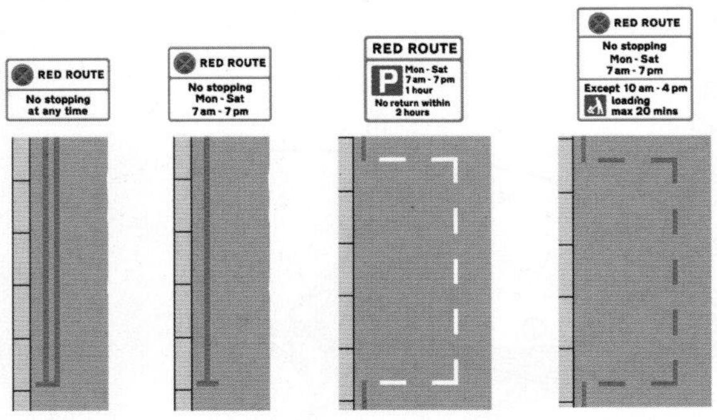
RED ROUTE
No stopping at any time
RED ROUTE
No stopping Mon - Sat 7 am - 7 pm
RED ROUTE
P
Mon - Sat 7 am - 7 pm 1 hour
No return within 2 hours
RED ROUTE
No stopping Mon - Sat 7 am - 7 pm
Except 10 am - 4 pm loading max 20 mins

No stopping at any time

No stopping during times shown on sign

Parking is limited to the duration specified during the days and times shown

Only loading may take place at the times shown for up to a maximum duration of 20 mins

On the kerb or at the edge of the carriageway

Loading restrictions on roads other than Red Routes

Yellow marks on the kerb or at the edge of the carriageway indicate that loading or unloading is prohibited at the times shown on the nearby black and white plates. You may stop while passengers board or alight. If no days are indicated on the signs the restrictions are in force every day including Sundays and Bank Holidays.

ALWAYS CHECK THE TIMES SHOWN ON THE PLATES.

Lengths of road reserved for vehicles loading and unloading are indicated by a white 'bay' marking with the words 'Loading Only' and a sign with the white on blue 'trolley' symbol. This sign also shows whether loading and unloading is restricted to goods vehicles and the times at which the bay can be used. If no times or days are shown it may be used at any time. Vehicles may not park here if they are not loading or unloading.

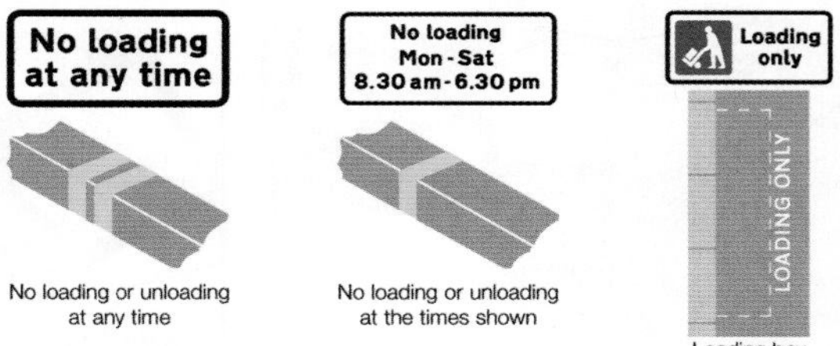
No loading at any time
No loading Mon - Sat 8.30 am - 6.30 pm
Loading only
LOADING ONLY

No loading or unloading at any time

No loading or unloading at the times shown

Loading bay

Other road markings

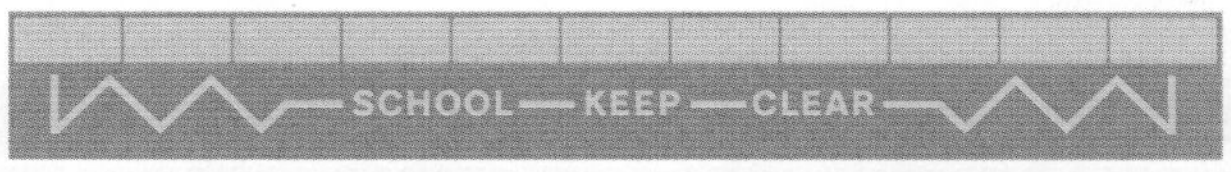
SCHOOL KEEP CLEAR

Keep entrance clear of stationary vehicles, even if picking up or setting down children

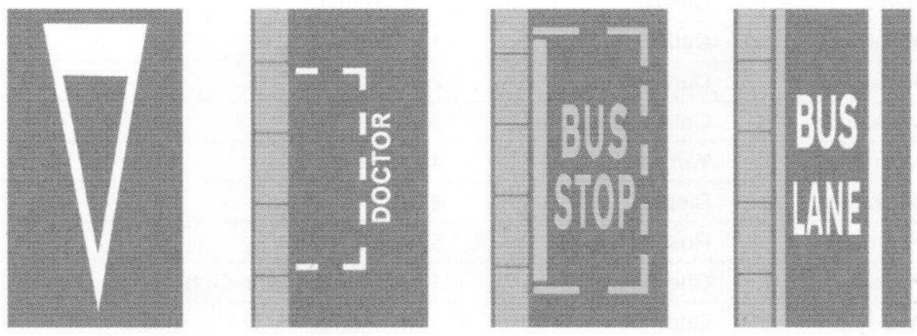
DOCTOR
BUS STOP
BUS LANE

Warning of 'Give Way' just ahead

Parking space reserved for vehicles named

See Rule 243

See Rule 141

KEEP CLEAR
CITY
A3
YORK ST

Box junction - See Rule 174

Do not block that part of the carriageway indicated

Indication of traffic lanes

Light signals controlling traffic

Traffic Light Signals

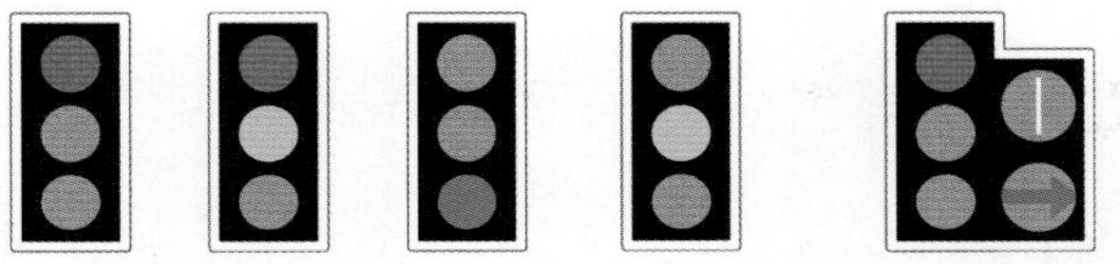

RED means 'Stop'. Wait behind the stop line on the carriageway

RED AND AMBER also means 'Stop'. Do not pass through or start until GREEN shows

GREEN means you may go on if the way is clear. Take special care if you intend to turn left or right and give way to pedestrians who are crossing

AMBER means 'Stop' at the stop line. You may go on only if the AMBER appears after you have crossed the stop line or are so close to it that to pull up might cause an accident

A GREEN ARROW may be provided in addition to the full green signal if movement in a certain direction is allowed before or after the full green phase. If the way is clear you may go but only in the direction shown by the arrow. You may do this whatever other lights may be showing. White light signals may be provided for trams

Flashing red lights

Alternately flashing red lights mean YOU MUST STOP

At level crossings, lifting bridges, airfields, fire stations, etc.

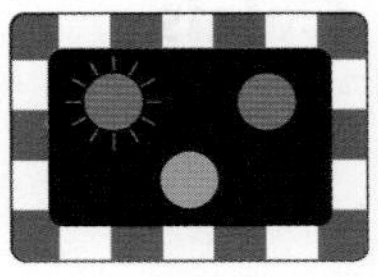

Motorway signals

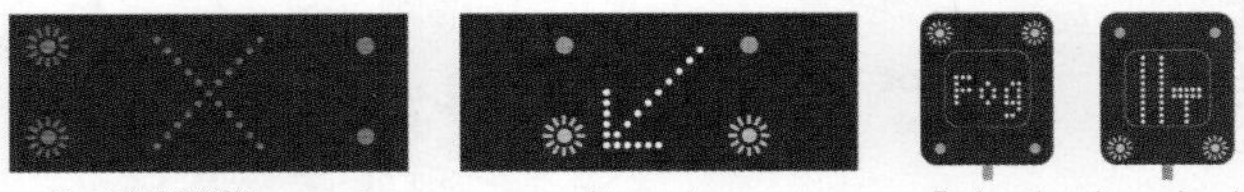
Fog

You **MUST NOT** proceed further in this lane

Change lane

Reduced visibility ahead

Lane ahead closed

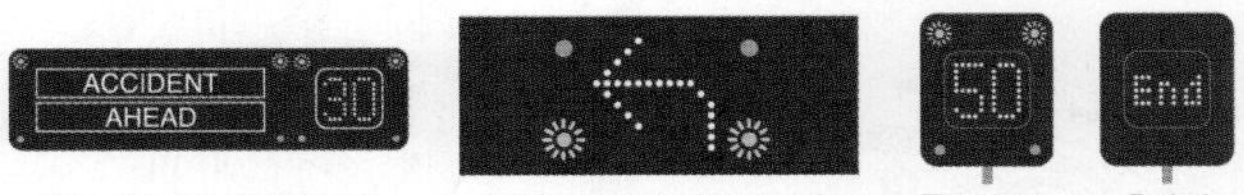
ACCIDENT
AHEAD
30
50
End

Temporary maximum speed advised and information message

Leave motorway at next exit

Temporary maximum speed advised

End of restriction

Lane control signals

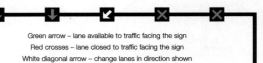

Green arrow – lane available to traffic facing the sign

Red crosses – lane closed to traffic facing the sign

White diagonal arrow – change lanes in direction shown

Channel hopping and the Isle of Wight

For business or pleasure, hopping on a ferry across to France, the Channel Islands or Isle of Wight has never been easier.

The vehicle ferry services listed in the table give you all the options, together with detailed port plans to help you navigate to and from the ferry terminals. Simply choose your preferred route, not forgetting the fast sailings (see ⛴). Bon voyage!

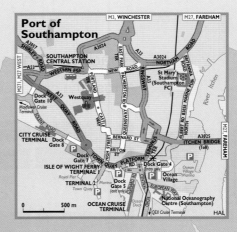

Port of Southampton

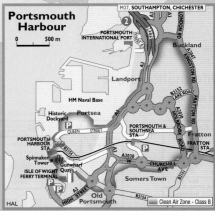

Portsmouth Harbour

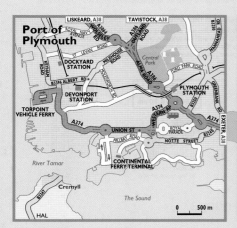

Port of Plymouth

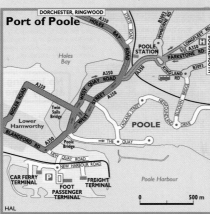

Port of Poole

ENGLISH CHANNEL AND ISLE OF WIGHT FERRY CROSSINGS

From	To	Journey time	Operator website
Dover	Calais	1 hr 30 mins	dfdsseaways.co.uk
Dover	Calais	1 hr 30 mins	poferries.com
Dover	Dunkirk	2 hrs	dfdsseaways.co.uk
Folkestone	Calais (Coquelles)	35 mins	eurotunnel.com
Lymington	Yarmouth (IOW)	40 mins	wightlink.co.uk
Newhaven	Dieppe	4 hrs	dfdsseaways.co.uk
Plymouth	Roscoff	5 hrs 30 mins	brittany-ferries.co.uk
Poole	Cherbourg	4 hrs 30 mins (Apr–Oct)	brittany-ferries.co.uk
Poole	Guernsey	3 hrs ⛴	condorferries.co.uk
Poole	Jersey	4 hrs ⛴	condorferries.co.uk
Poole	St-Malo	6 hrs 20 mins–12 hrs (via Channel Is.) ⛴	condorferries.co.uk
Portsmouth	Caen (Ouistreham)	5 hrs 45 mins–7 hrs	brittany-ferries.co.uk
Portsmouth	Cherbourg	8 hrs	brittany-ferries.co.uk
Portsmouth	Fishbourne (IOW)	45 mins	wightlink.co.uk
Portsmouth	Guernsey	7 hrs	condorferries.co.uk
Portsmouth	Jersey	8–11 hrs	condorferries.co.uk
Portsmouth	St-Malo	11 hrs	brittany-ferries.co.uk
Southampton	East Cowes (IOW)	1 hr	redfunnel.co.uk

The information listed is provided as a guide only, as services are liable to change at short notice and are weather dependent. Services shown are for vehicle ferries only, operated by conventional ferry unless indicated as a fast ferry service (⛴). Please check sailings before planning your journey.

Travelling further afield? For ferry services to Northern Spain see *brittany-ferries.co.uk*.

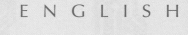

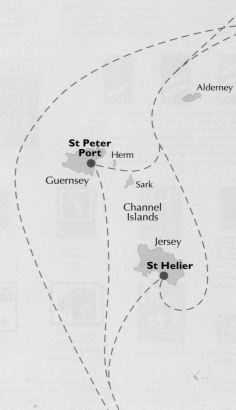

E N G L I S H

Plymouth

Roscoff

Alderney

St Peter Port
Herm

Guernsey
Sark

Channel Islands

Jersey

St Helier

St-Malo

Calais

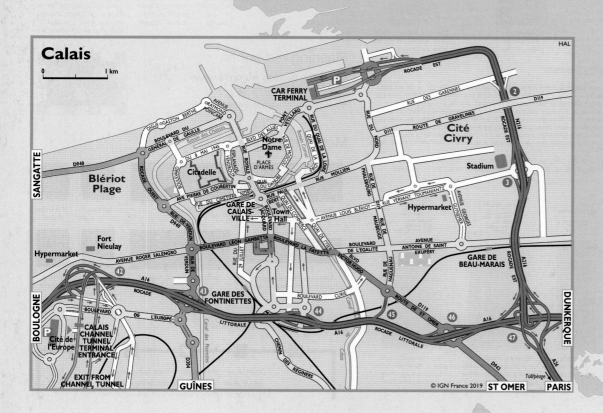

© IGN France 2019

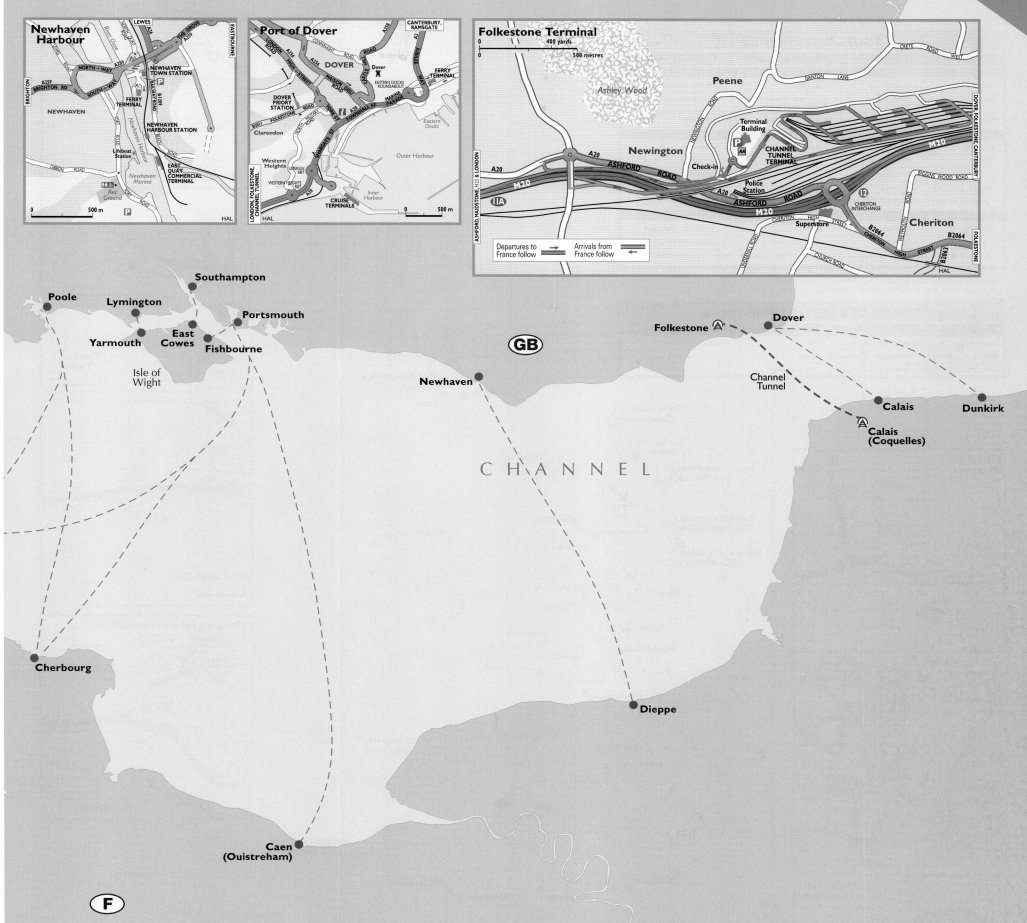

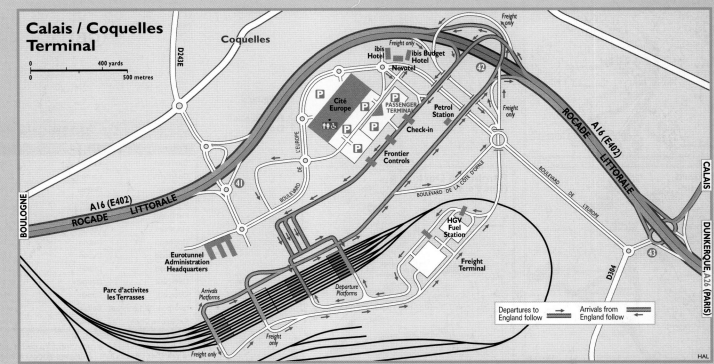

SCOTLAND FERRIES

From	To	Journey time	Operator website
Scottish Islands/west coast of Scotland			
Gourock	Dunoon	20 mins	western-ferries.co.uk
Glenelg	Skye	20 mins (Easter–Oct)	skyeferry.co.uk
Numerous and varied sailings from the west coast of Scotland to Scottish islands are provided by Caledonian MacBrayne. Please visit calmac.co.uk for all ferry information, including those of other operators.			
Orkney Islands			
Aberdeen	Kirkwall	6 hrs–7 hrs 15 mins	northlinkferries.co.uk
Gills	St Margaret's Hope	1 hr	pentlandferries.com
Scrabster	Stromness	1 hr 30 mins	northlinkferries.co.uk
Lerwick	Kirkwall	5 hrs 30 mins	northlinkferries.co.uk
Inter-island services are operated by Orkney Ferries. Please see orkneyferries.co.uk for details.			
Shetland Islands			
Aberdeen	Lerwick	12 hrs	northlinkferries.co.uk
Kirkwall	Lerwick	7 hrs 45 mins	northlinkferries.co.uk
Inter-island services are operated by Shetland Island Council Ferries. Please see shetland.gov.uk/ferries for details.			

Please note that some smaller island services are day and weather dependent. Reservations are required for some routes. Book and confirm sailing schedules by contacting the operator.

NORTH SEA FERRY CROSSINGS

From	To	Journey time	Operator website
Harwich	Hook of Holland	7–8 hrs	stenaline.co.uk
Kingston upon Hull	Rotterdam (Europoort)	11 hrs	poferries.com
Newcastle upon Tyne	Amsterdam (IJmuiden)	15 hrs 30 mins	dfdsseaways.co.uk

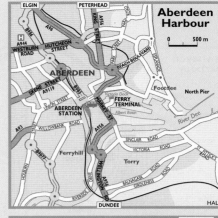

Aberdeen Harbour

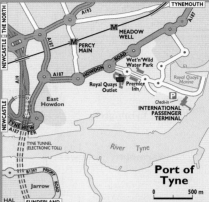

Port of Tyne

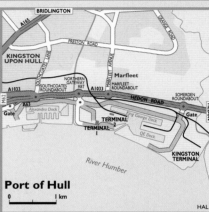

Port of Hull

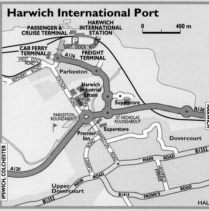

Harwich International Port

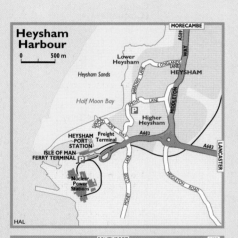

Heysham Harbour

Liverpool Docks

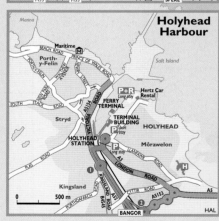

Holyhead Harbour

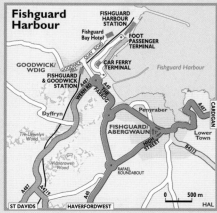

Fishguard Harbour

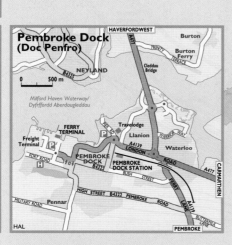

Pembroke Dock (Doc Penfro)

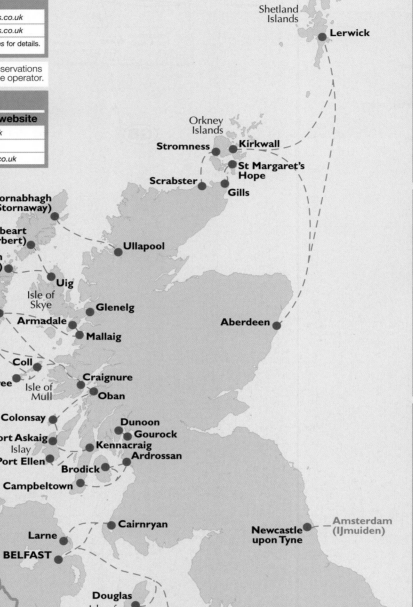

IRISH SEA FERRY CROSSINGS

From	To	Journey time		Operator website
Cairnryan	Belfast	2 hrs 15 mins		stenaline.co.uk
Cairnryan	Larne	2 hrs		poferries.com
Douglas	Belfast	2 hrs 45 mins (April–Sept)		steam-packet.com
Douglas	Dublin	2 hrs 55 mins (April–Sept)		steam-packet.com
Fishguard	Rosslare	3 hrs 15 mins		stenaline.co.uk
Heysham	Douglas	3 hrs 45 mins		steam-packet.com
Holyhead	Dublin	2 hrs (Mar–Oct)		irishferries.com
Holyhead	Dublin	3 hrs 15 mins		irishferries.com
Holyhead	Dublin	3 hrs 15 mins		stenaline.co.uk
Liverpool	Douglas	2 hrs 45 mins (Apr–Oct)		steam-packet.com
Liverpool	Dublin	8 hrs–8 hrs 30 mins		poferries.com
Liverpool (Birkenhead)	Belfast	8 hrs		stenaline.co.uk
Pembroke Dock	Rosslare	4 hrs		irishferries.com

The information listed is provided as a guide only, as services are liable to change at short notice and are weather dependent. Services shown are for vehicle ferries only, operated by conventional ferry unless indicated as a fast ferry service (🚢). Please check sailings before planning your journey.

Motoring information

M4	Motorway with number	3	Restricted primary route junctions		Narrow primary/other A/B road with passing places (Scotland)		Railway line, in tunnel
Toll T4	Toll motorway with toll station	S	Primary route service area		Road under construction		Railway station, tram stop, level crossing
6	Motorway junction with and without number	BATH	Primary route destination		Road tunnel		Preserved or tourist railway
5	Restricted motorway junctions	A1123	Other A road single/ dual carriageway	Toll	Road toll, steep gradient (arrows point downhill)		Airport (major/minor)
Fleet S R Todhills	Motorway service area, rest area	B2070	B road single/ dual carriageway	5	Distance in miles between symbols	H	Heliport
	Motorway and junction under construction		Minor road more than 4 metres wide, less than 4 metres wide	or V V	Vehicle ferry (all year, seasonal)	F	International freight terminal
A3	Primary route single/ dual carriageway		Roundabout		Fast vehicle ferry or catamaran	H	24-hour Accident & Emergency hospital
1	Primary route junction with and without number		Interchange/junction	or P P	Passenger ferry (all year, seasonal)	C	Crematorium

P+R	Park and Ride (at least 6 days per week)
	City, town, village or other built-up area
628 ▲	Height in metres
637 Lecht Summit	Mountain pass
	Snow gates (on main routes)
	National boundary
	County or administrative boundary
	City with clean air zone, low emission zone (visit www.gov.uk/guidance/ driving-in-a-clean-air-zone)

Touring information
To avoid disappointment, check opening times before visiting

	Scenic route		Industrial interest	RSPB	RSPB site		Cave or cavern		National Trust site
i	Tourist Information Centre		Aqueduct or viaduct		National Nature Reserve (England, Scotland, Wales)		Windmill, monument or memorial		National Trust for Scotland site
i	Tourist Information Centre (seasonal)		Vineyard		Local nature reserve		Beach (award winning)		English Heritage site
V	Visitor or heritage centre		Brewery or distillery		Wildlife Trust reserve		Lighthouse		Historic Scotland site
	Picnic site		Garden		Forest drive		Golf course		Cadw (Welsh heritage) site
	Caravan site (AA inspected)		Arboretum		National trail		Football stadium	★	Other place of interest
▲	Camping site (AA inspected)		Country park		Viewpoint		County cricket ground		Boxed symbols indicate attractions within urban area
	Caravan & camping site (AA inspected)		Showground		Waterfall		Rugby Union national stadium		World Heritage Site (UNESCO)
	Abbey, cathedral or priory		Theme park		Hill-fort		International athletics stadium		National Park and National Scenic Area (Scotland)
	Ruined abbey, cathedral or priory		Farm or animal centre		Roman antiquity		Horse racing, show jumping		Forest Park
	Castle		Zoological or wildlife collection		Prehistoric monument		Motor-racing circuit		Sandy beach
	Historic house or building		Bird collection	1066	Battle site with year		Air show venue		Heritage coast
	Museum or art gallery		Aquarium		Preserved or tourist railway		Ski slope (natural, artificial)		Major shopping centre

Town plans

2	Motorway and junction		Railway station		Toilet, with facilities for the less able	i	Tourist Information Centre	+	Abbey, chapel, church
4	Primary road single/ dual carriageway and numbered junction		Tramway		Building of interest	V	Visitor or heritage centre		Synagogue
37	A road single/ dual carriageway and numbered junction		London Underground station		Ruined building		Post Office		Mosque
	B road single/ dual carriageway		London Overground station		City wall		Public library		Golf course
	Local road single/ dual carriageway		Rail interchange		Cliff lift		Shopping centre		Racecourse
	Other road single/dual carriageway, minor road		Docklands Light Railway (DLR) station		Escarpment		Shopmobility		Nature reserve
	One-way, gated/ closed road	o	Light rapid transit system station		River/canal, lake		Theatre or performing arts centre		Aquarium
	Restricted access road	H	Airport, heliport		Lock, weir		Cinema		World Heritage Site (UNESCO)
	Pedestrian area	R	Railair terminal		Park/sports ground		Museum		English Heritage site
	Footpath	P+R	Park and Ride (at least 6 days per week)		Cemetery		Castle		Historic Scotland site
	Road under construction	P P	Car park, with electric charging point		Woodland		Castle mound		Cadw (Welsh heritage) site
	Road tunnel		Bus/coach station		Built-up area	•	Monument, memorial, statue		National Trust site
	Level crossing	H H	Hospital, 24-hour Accident & Emergency hospital		Beach		Viewpoint		National Trust Scotland site

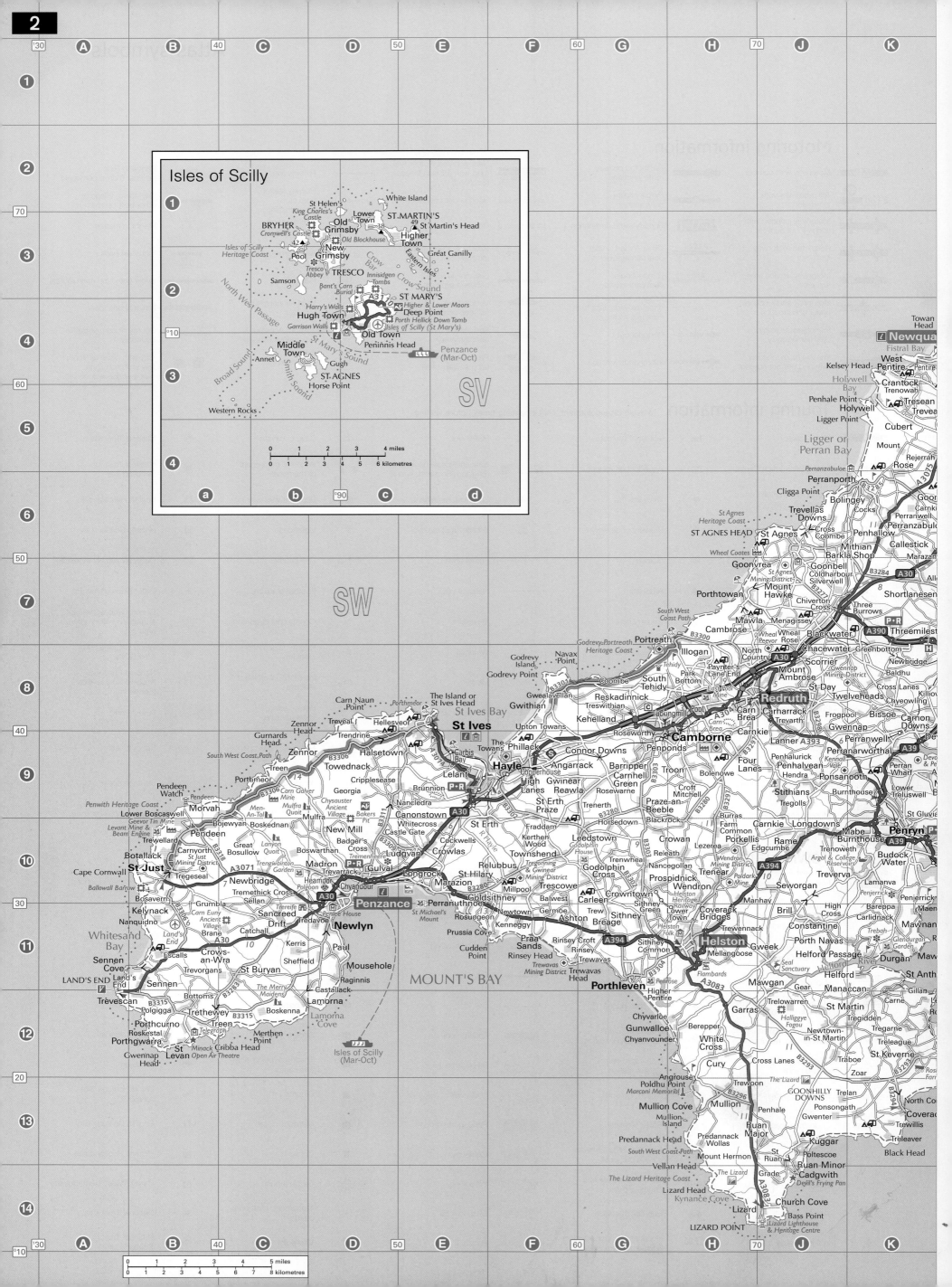

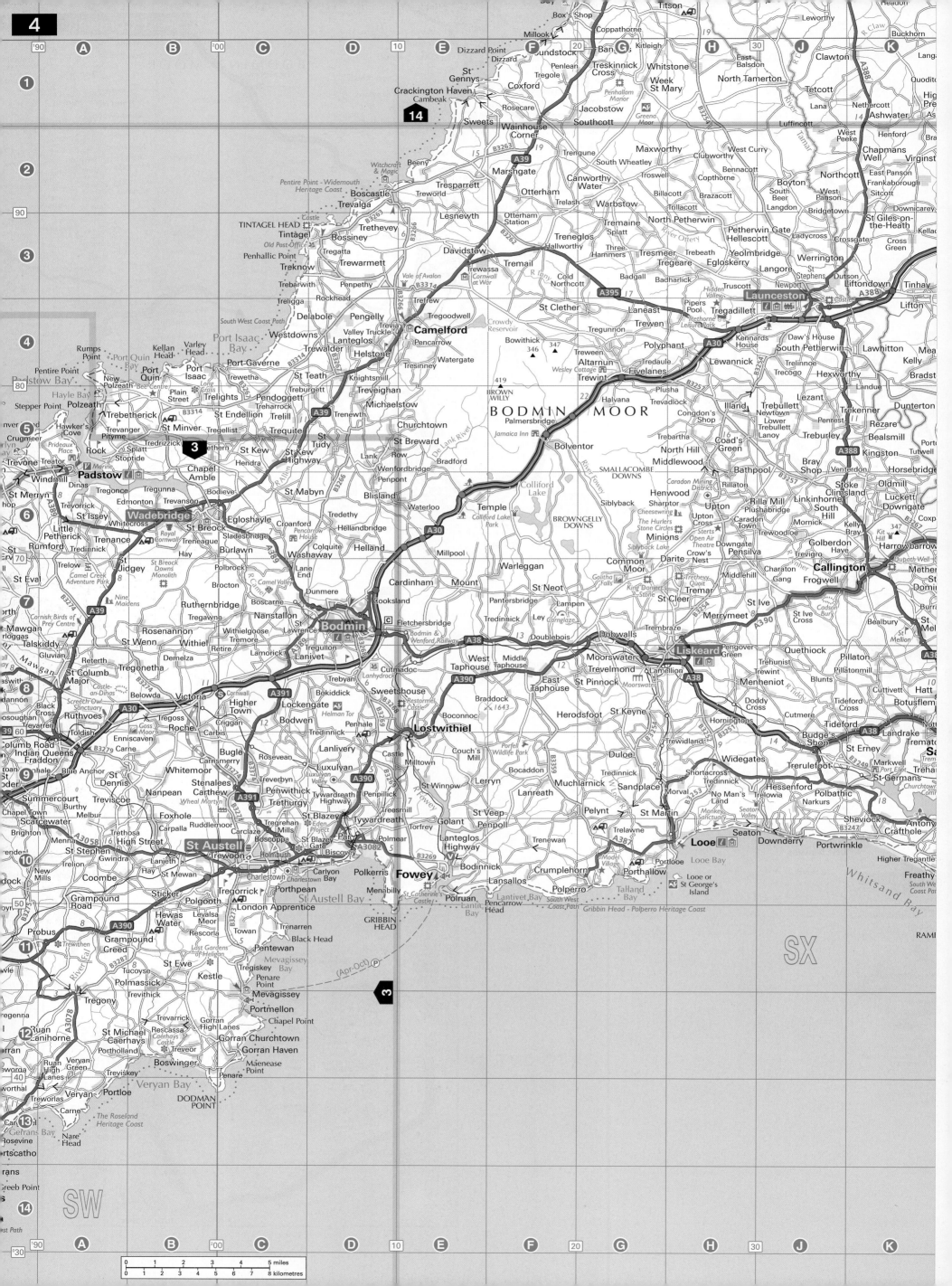

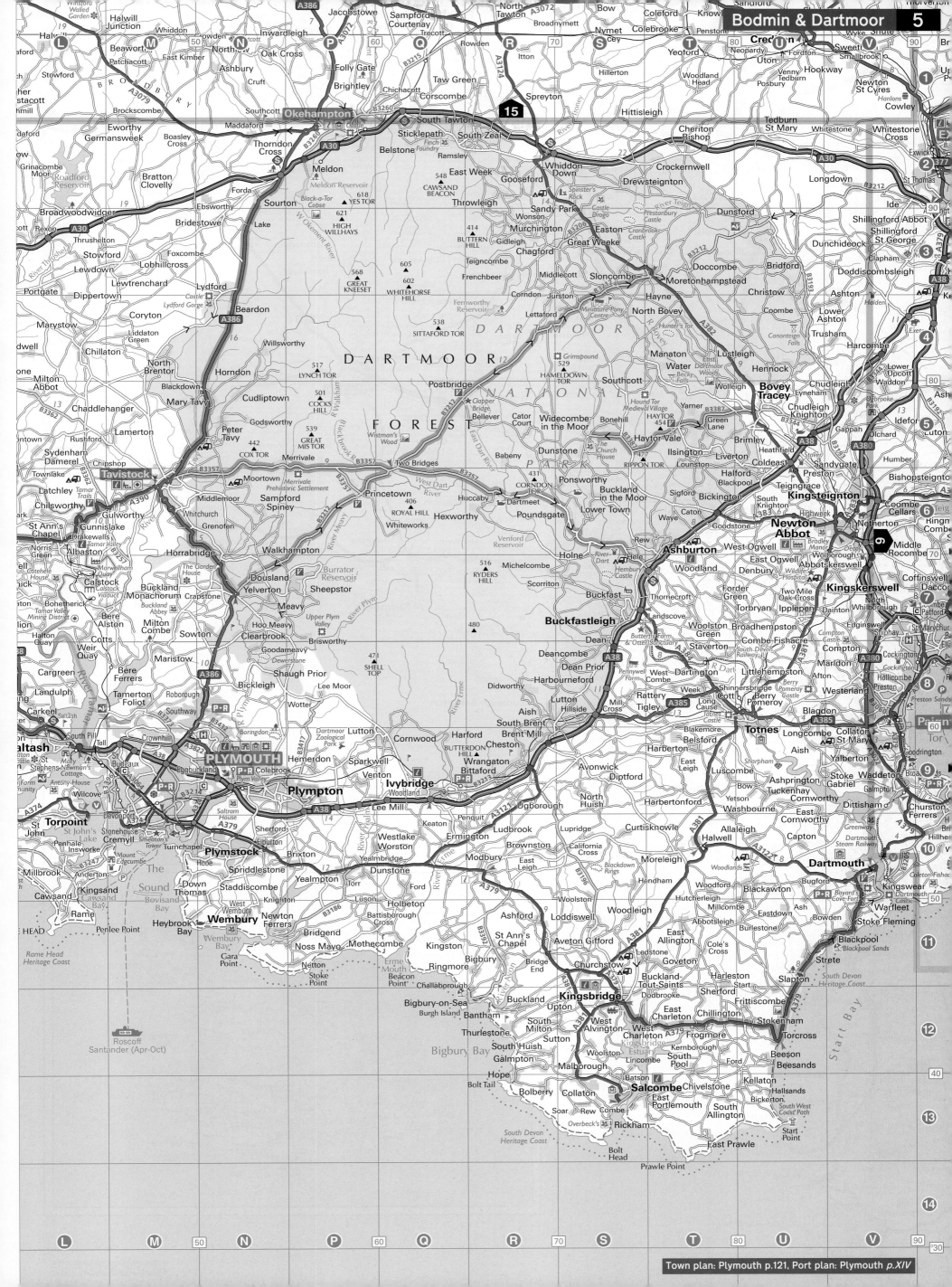

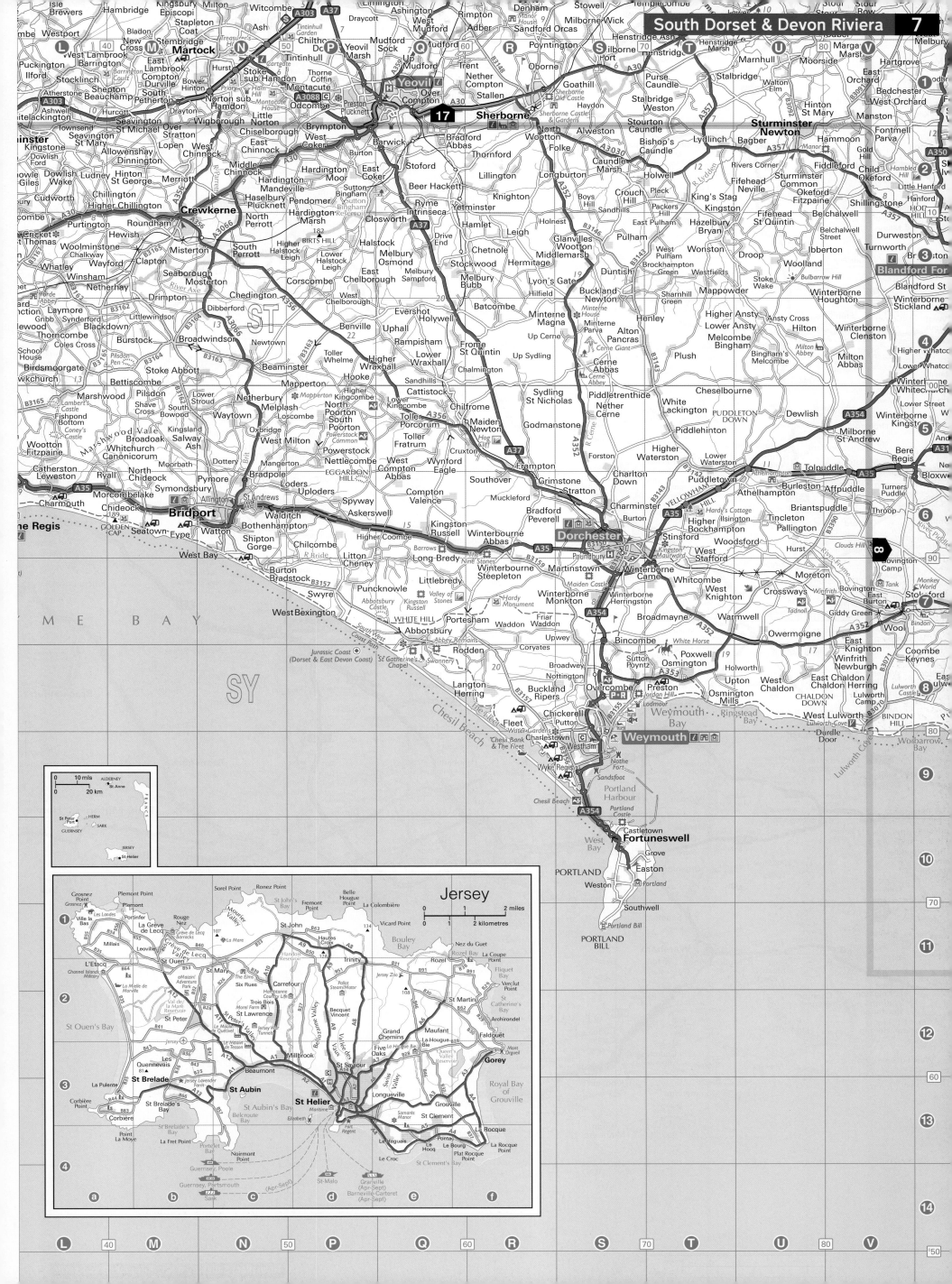

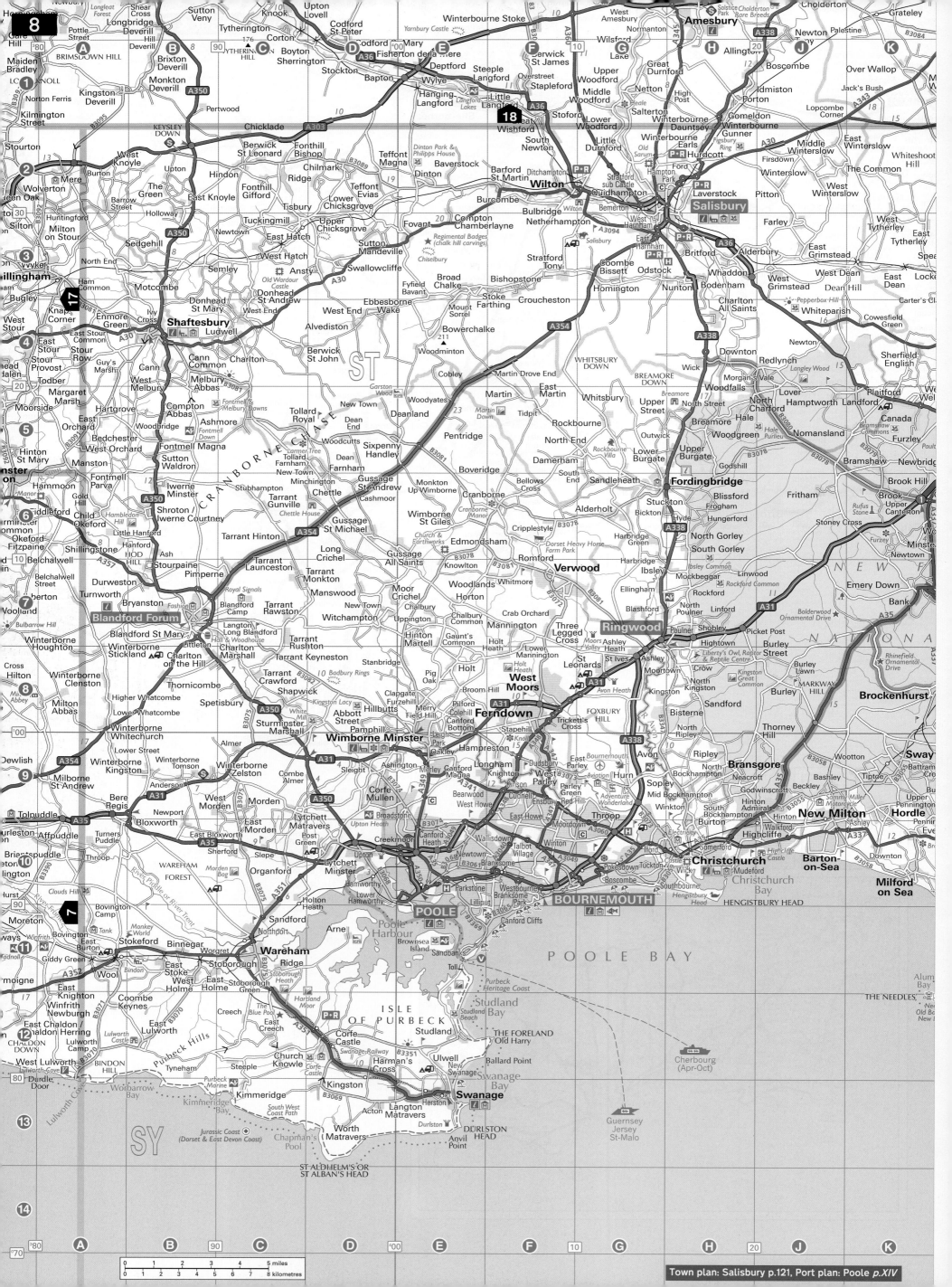

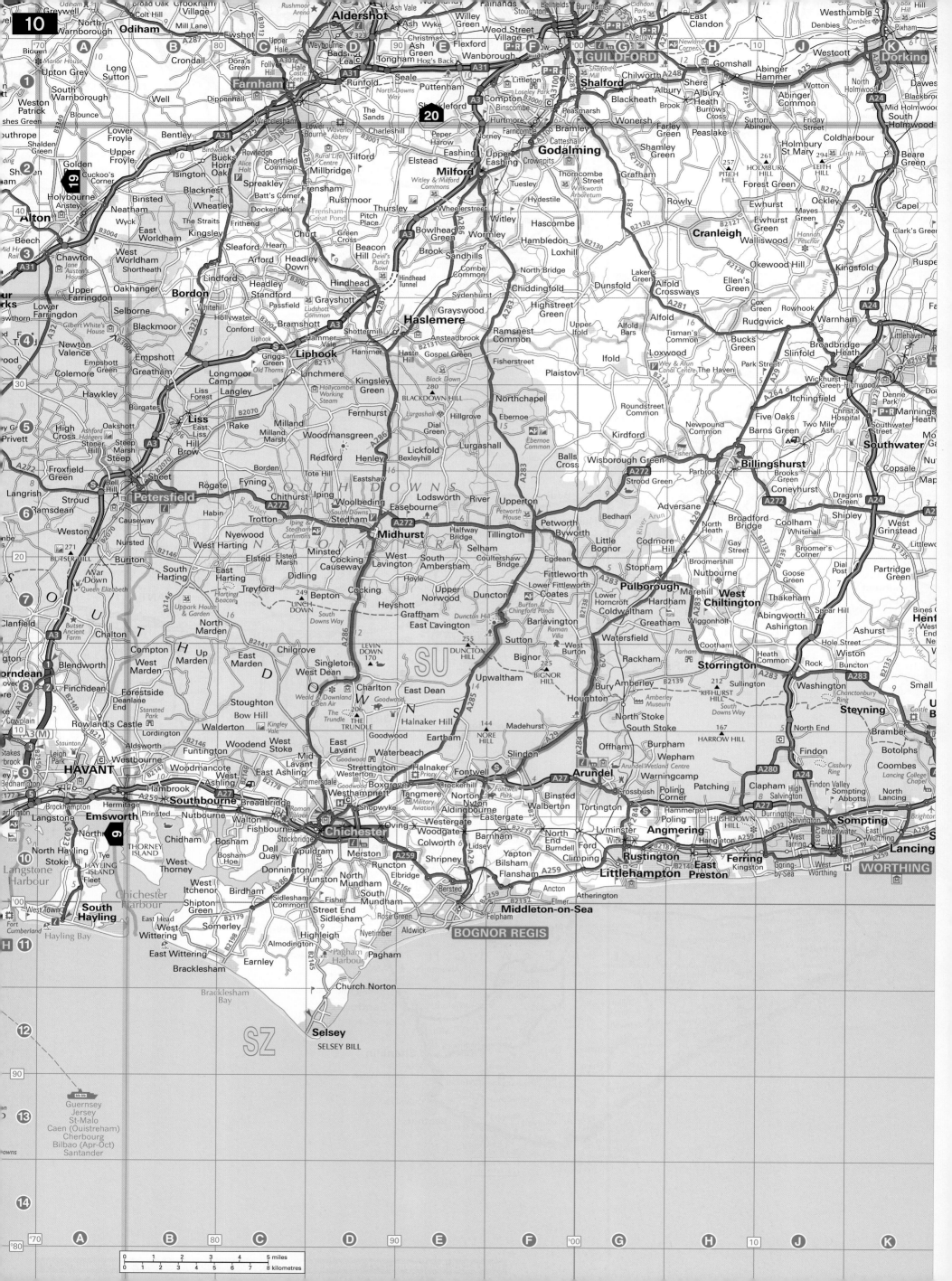

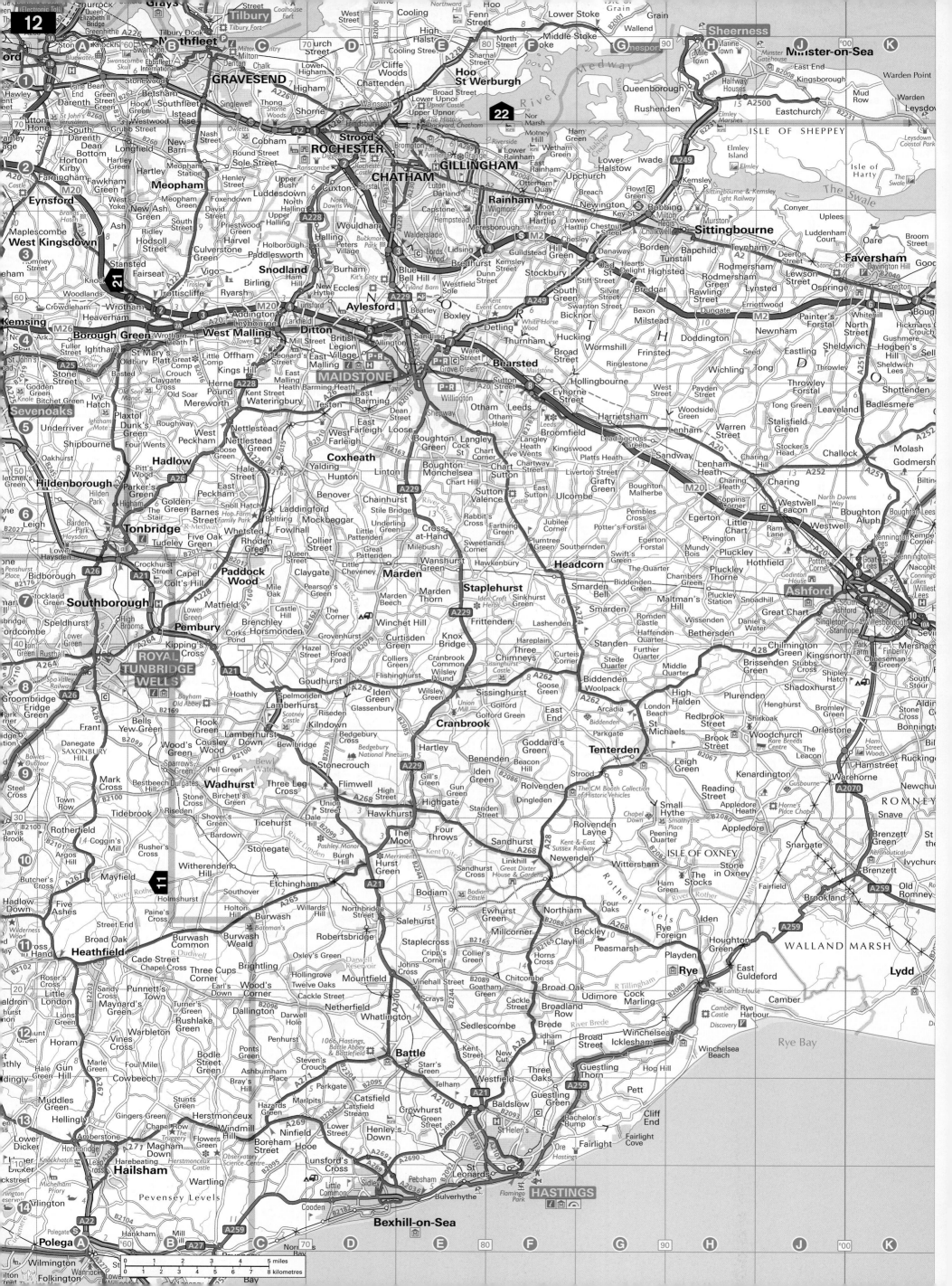

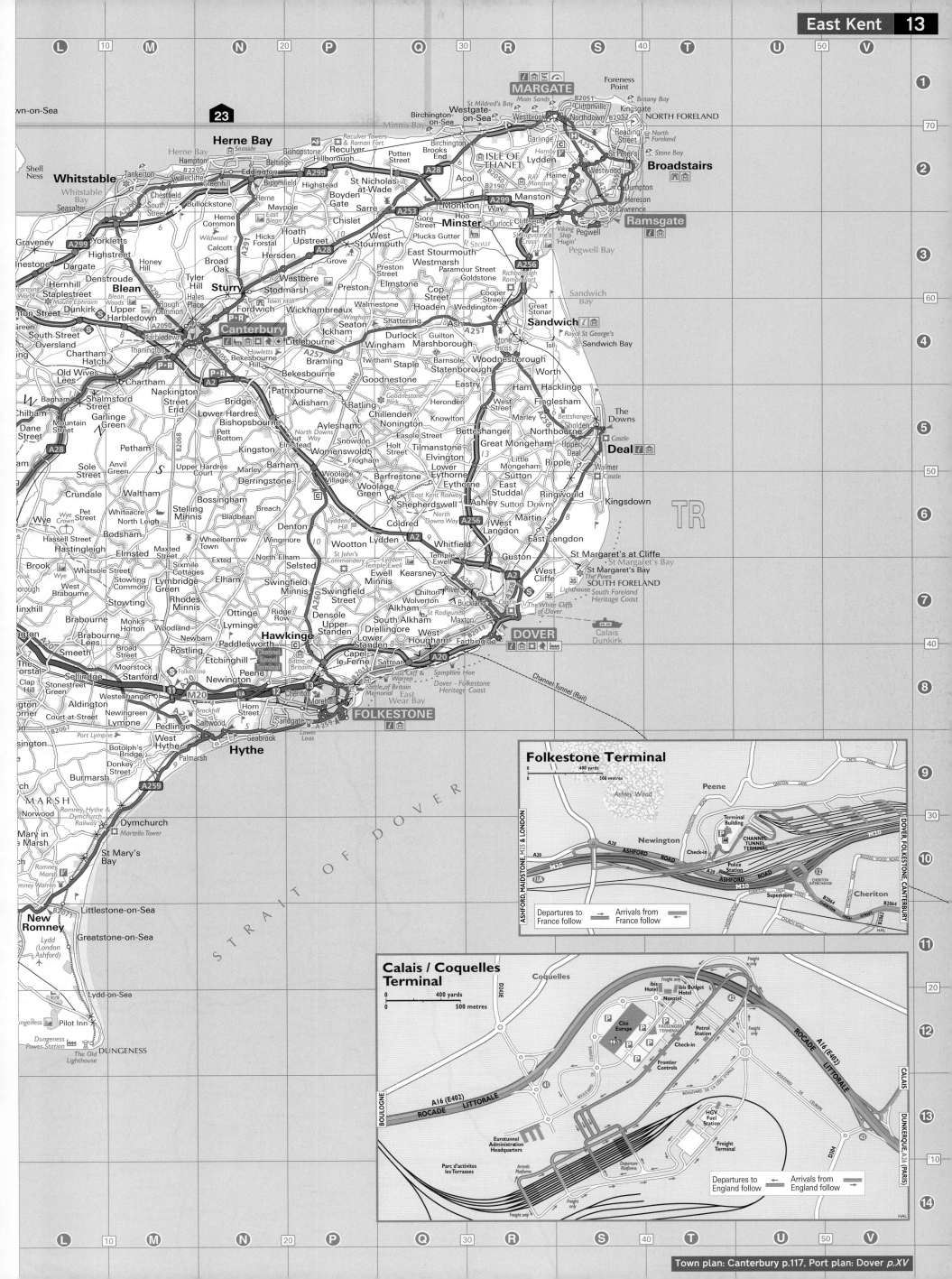

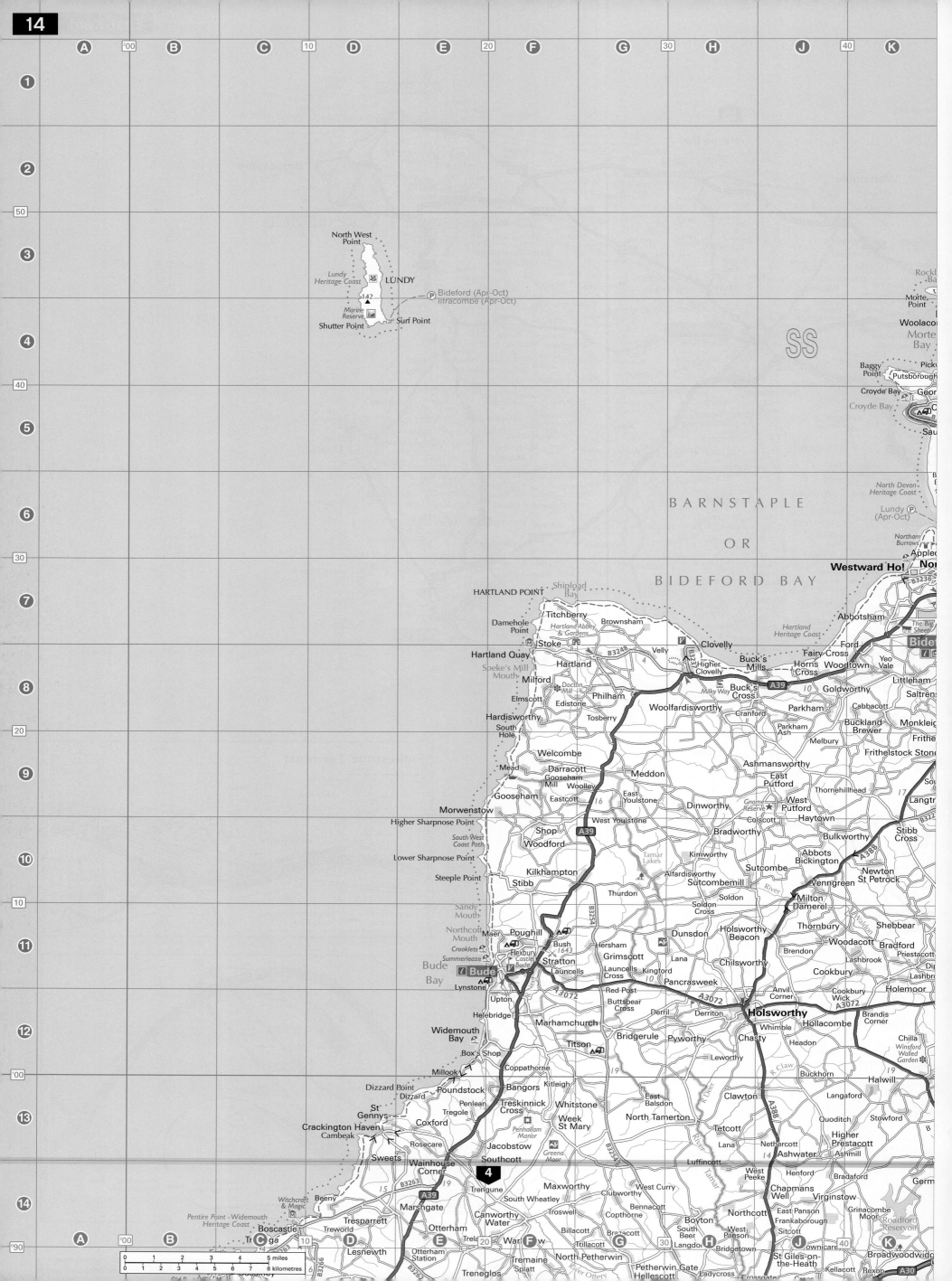

A '00 B 10 C D 20 E F G 30 H J 40 K

SS

BARNSTAPLE

OR

BIDEFORD BAY

North West
Point

Lundy
Heritage Coast
LUNDY
142

Marine
Reserve
Shutter Point
Surf Point

Bideford (Apr-Oct)
Ilfracombe (Apr-Oct)

Rockh..
Ba..

Morte
Point

Woolaco..
Morte
Bay

Baggy
Point
Putsborough
Croyde Bay
Geor
Croyde Bay
Sau

North Devon
Heritage Coast
Lundy
(Apr-Oct)
Northam
Burrows..

Westward Ho!
No..
Appled..

Shipload
Bay
HARTLAND POINT
Titchberry
Brownsham
Damehole
Point
Hartland Abbey
& Gardens
Stoke
Velly
Clovelly
Hartland
Heritage Coast
Abbotsham
The Big
Sheep
Bide

Hartland Quay
Hartland
4
Higher
Clovelly
Horns
Cross
Buck's
Mills
Fairy Cross
Woodtown
Ford
Yeo
Vale

Speke's Mill
Mouth
Milford
Docton
Mill
Buck's
Cross
A39
10
Goldworthy
Littleham
Saltren

Elmscott
Edistone
Philham
Woolfardisworthy
Cranford
Parkham
Cabbacott
Monklei..

Hardisworthy
South
Hole
Tosberry
Parkham
Ash
Buckland
Brewer
Frithe..

Mead
Welcombe
Darracott
Gooseham
Mill
Woolley
Meddon
Ashmansworthy
Melbury
Frithelstock Stone

Gooseham
Eastcott
16
East Youlstone
East
Putford
Thornehillhead
Langtr..

Morwenstow
Goosehan
West Youlstone
Dinworthy
Gnomes
Reserve
West
Putford
Haytown
So..

Higher Sharpnose Point
Shop
A39
Colscott
Stibb
Cross
Stibb..

South West
Coast Path
Woodford
Bradworthy
Bulkworthy
A388

Lower Sharpnose Point
Kimworthy
Abbots
Bickington
Newton
St Petrock

Steeple Point
Kilkhampton
Thurdon
Alfardisworthy
Sutcombe
Venngreen
Milton
Damerel

Stibb
Soldon
Sutcombemill
17

Sandy
Mouth
Tamar
Lakes
Soldon
Cross
Thornbury
Shebbear

Northcott
Mouth
Maer
Poughill
Bush
Hersham
Dunsdon
Holsworthy
Beacon
Woodacott
Bradford

Crooklets
Flexbury
Castle
1643
Grimscott
Lana
Brendon
Chilsworthy
Lashbrook
Priestacott
Di..

Summerleaze
Bude
Stratton
Launcells
Launcells
Cross
Kingford
Cookbury
Lashbro..

Bude
Bay
Bude
Launcells
Red
Post
10
Pancrasweek
Anvil
Corner
Cookbury
Wick
Holemoor

Lynstone
Upton
Buttsbear
Cross
Derril
Derriton
A3072
Holsworthy
Brandis
Corner

Helebridge
Red Post
A3072
Whimble
Hollacombe
Chilla

Widemouth
Bay
Marhamchurch
Bridgerule
Pyworthy
Chasty
Headon
Winsford
Walled
Garden

Box's Shop
Titson
Leworthy
Buckhorn
Halwill

Millook
Coppathorne
19
R Claw
Clawton
Langaford

Dizzard Point
Dizzard
Poundstock
Bangors
Kitleigh
East
Balsdon
Tetcott
Quoditch
Stowfo..

Penlean
Whitstone
North Tamerton
Lana
Higher
Prestacott

St
Gennys
Tregole
Treskinnick
Cross
Week
St Mary
Penhallam
Manor
Nethercott
Ashmill

Crackington Haven
Coxford
Jacobstow
Southcott
Greena
Moor
Luffincott
Ashwater

Cambeak
Rosecare
B3254
West
Peeke
Henford
Bradaford
Germ..

Sweets
Wainhouse
Corner
4
Trengune
Maxworthy
Clubworthy
West Curry
Chapmans
Well
Virginstow

Beeny
Marshgate
South Wheatley
Troswell
Boyton
East Panson
West
Panson
Northcott
Grinacombe
Moor
Roadford
Reservoir

Witchcraft
& Magic
B3263
A39
Canworthy
Water
Billacott
Copthorne
Frankaborough
Sitcott

Pentire Point - Widemouth
Heritage Coast
Otterham
Warbstow
Brazzacott
Trillacott
South
Beer
Bridgetown
St Giles-on-
the-Heath
Kellacott
Rexon

Boscastle
Tr..ga
Tresparrett
Treworld
Lesnewth
Otterham
Station
Warb..w
Tremaine
North Petherwin
Petherwin Gate
Hellescott
Ladycross
Crossgate
Broadwoodwidger

Trenglos
Splatt
R.. Ottery
A30

0 1 2 3 4 5 miles
0 1 2 3 4 5 6 7 8 kilometres

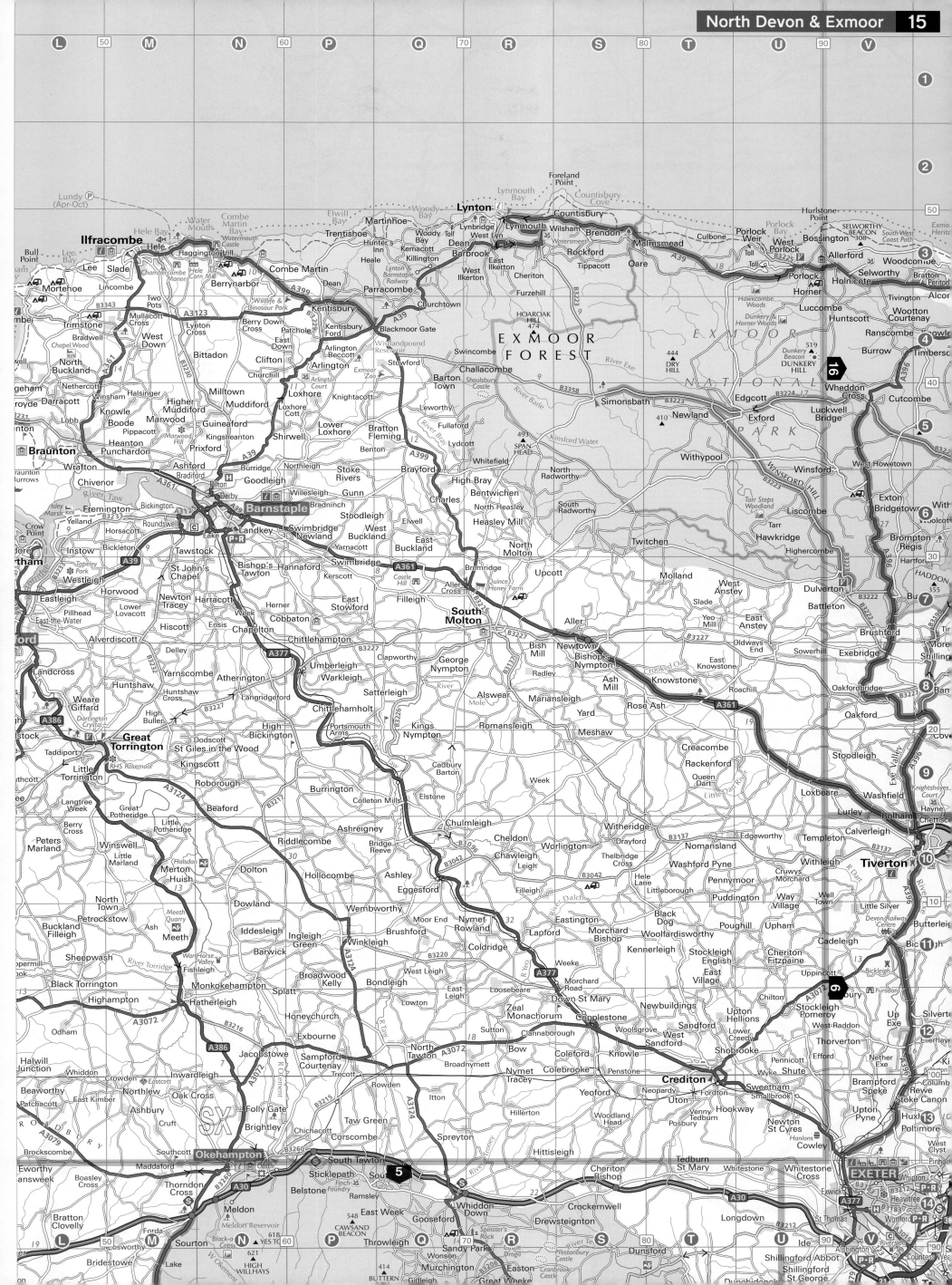

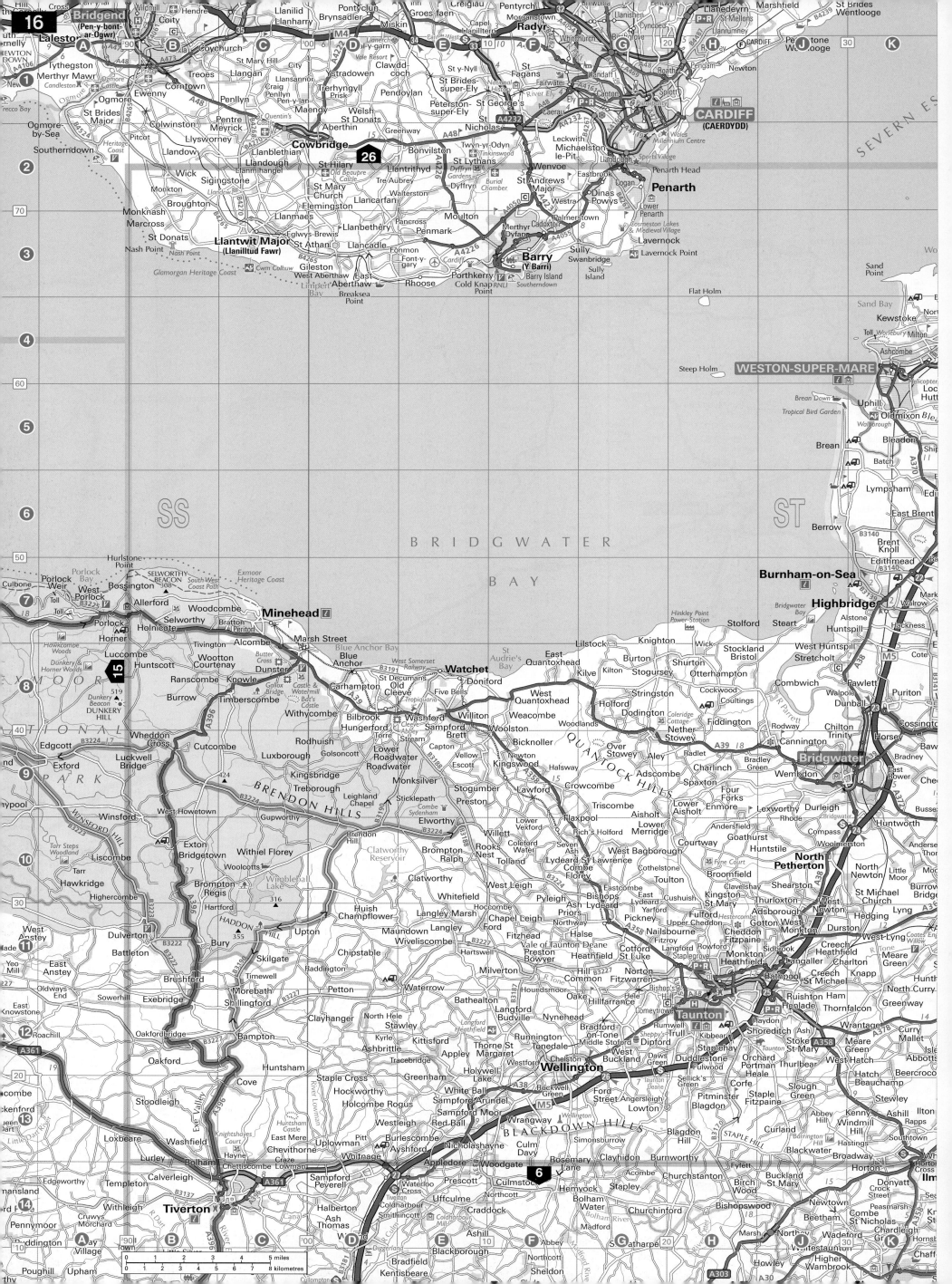

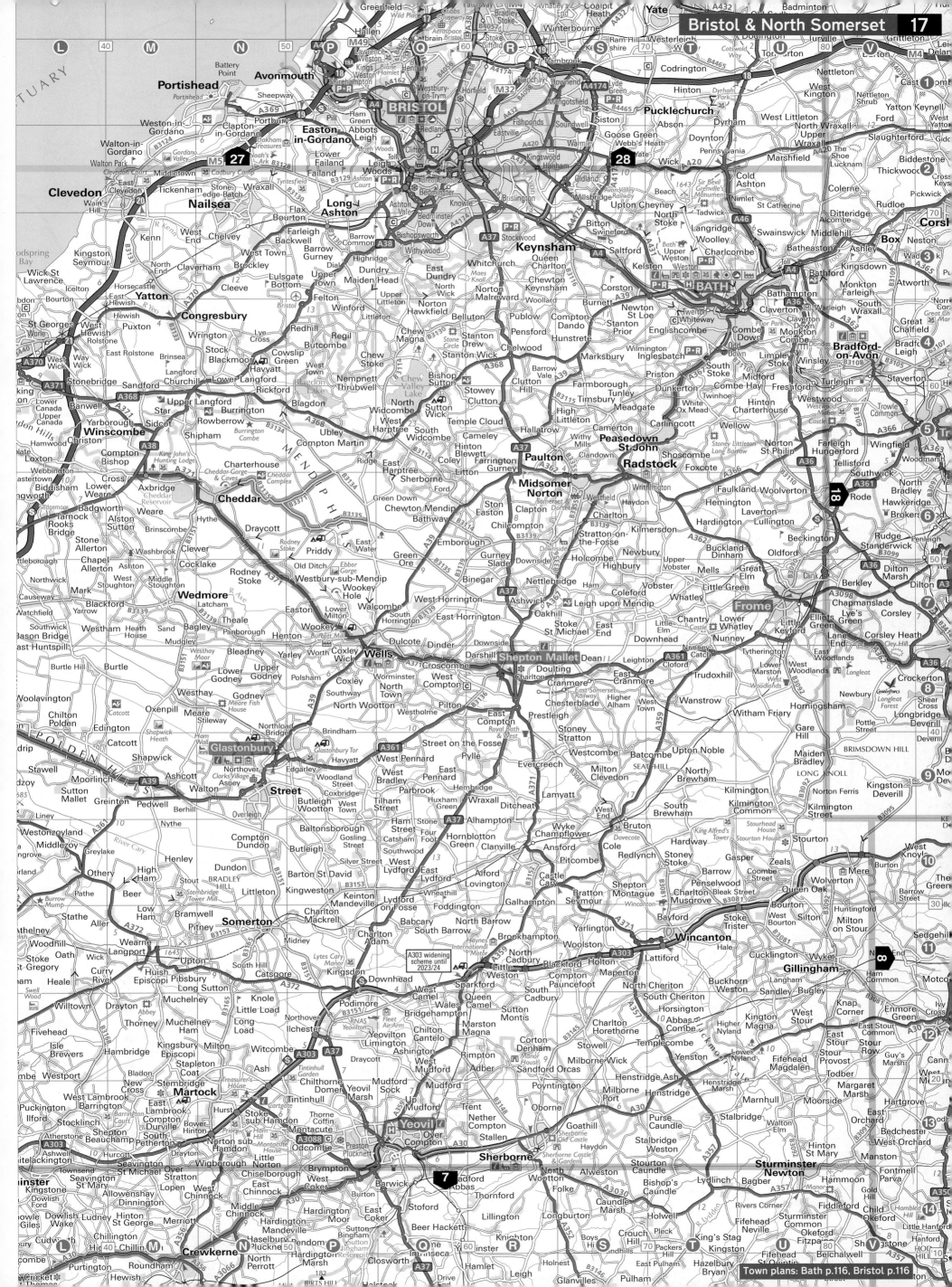

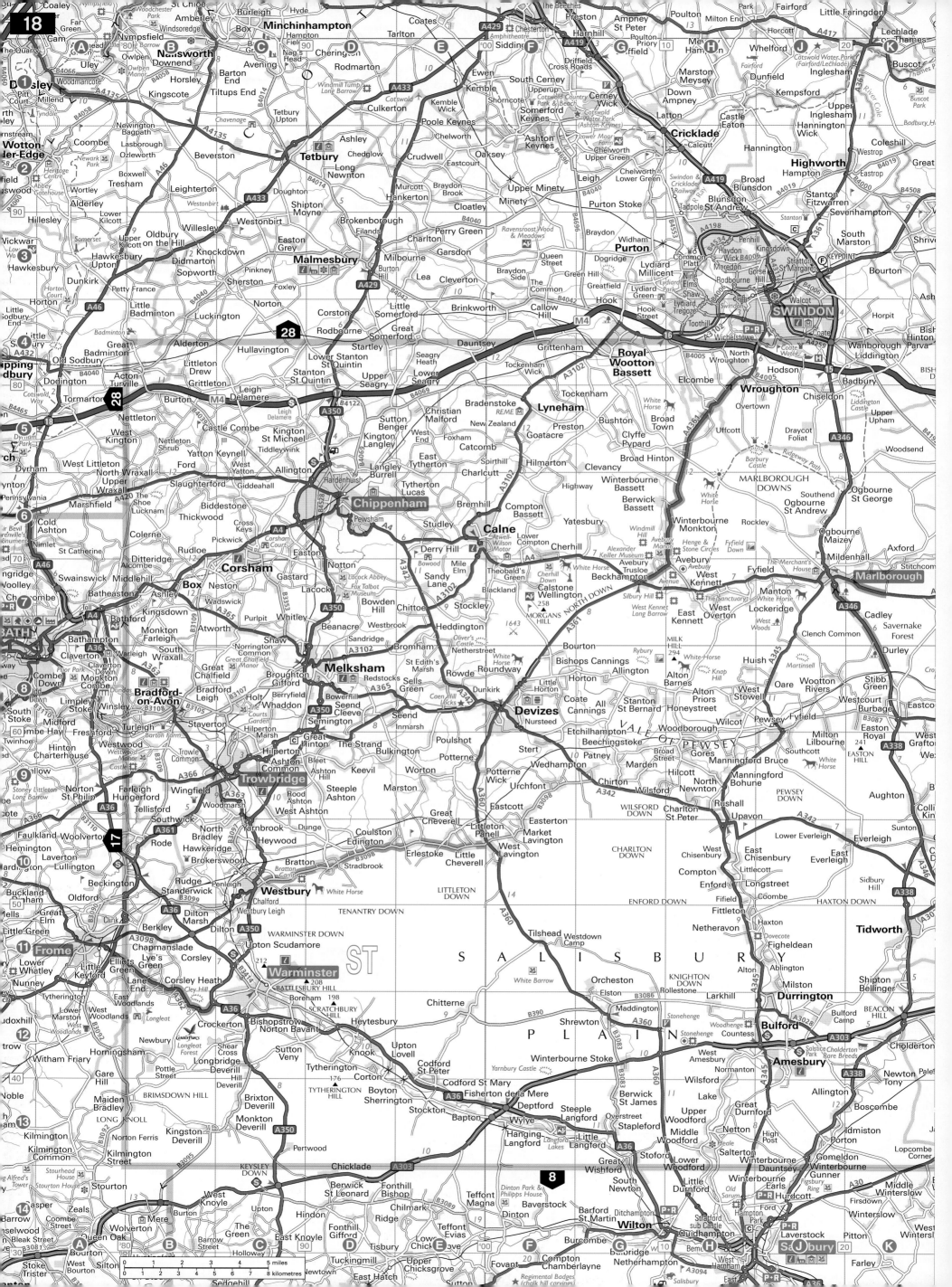

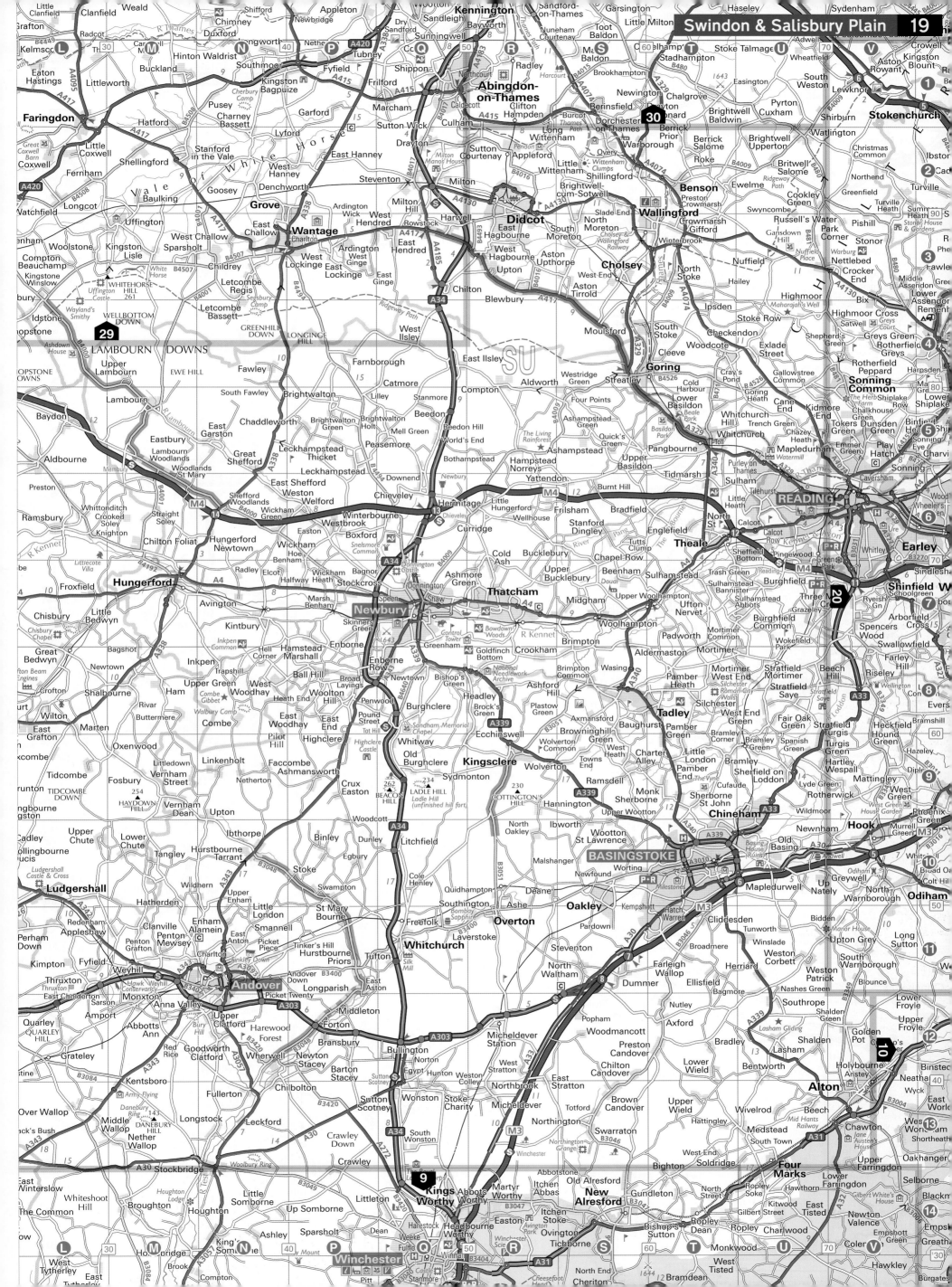

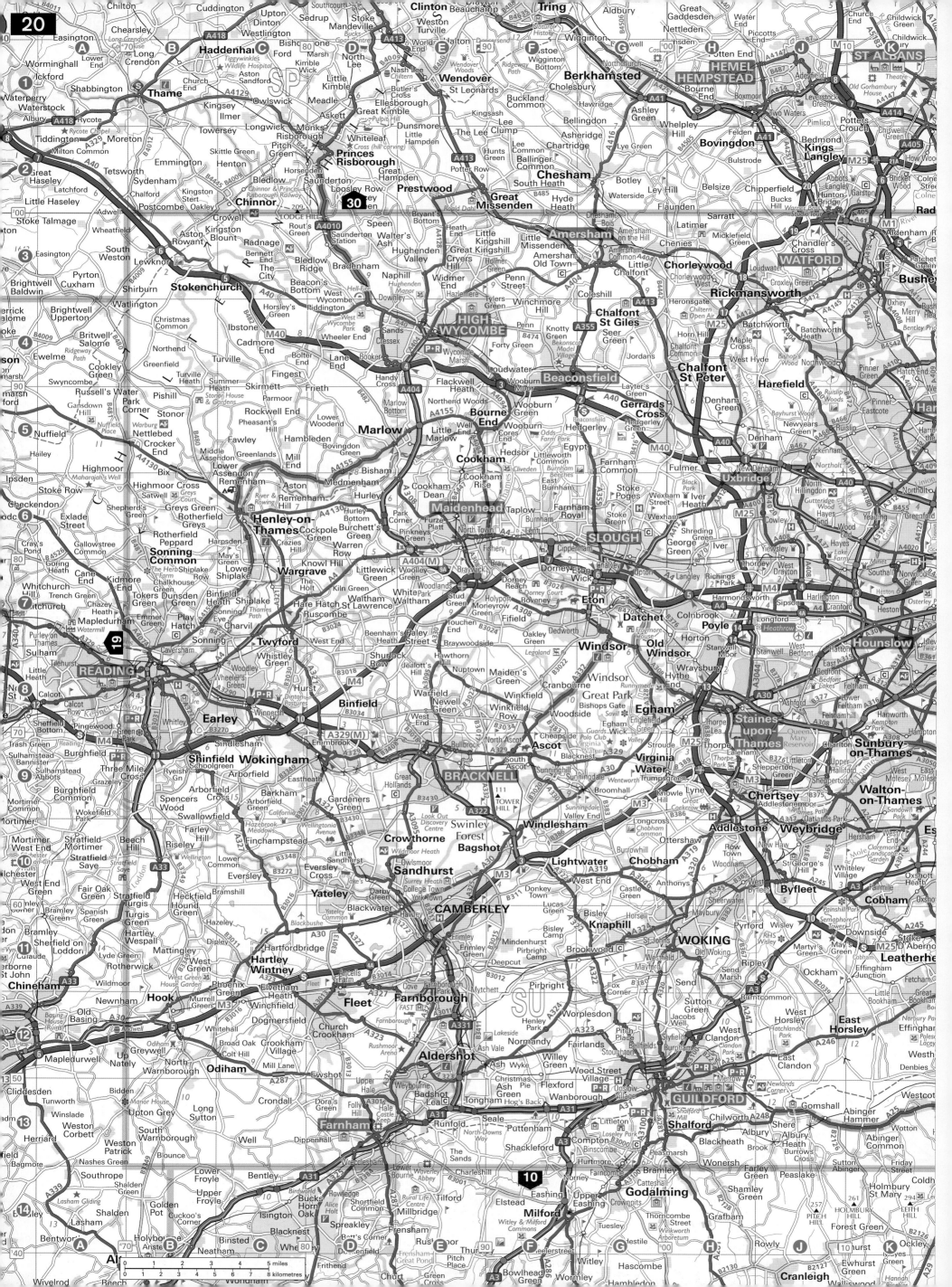

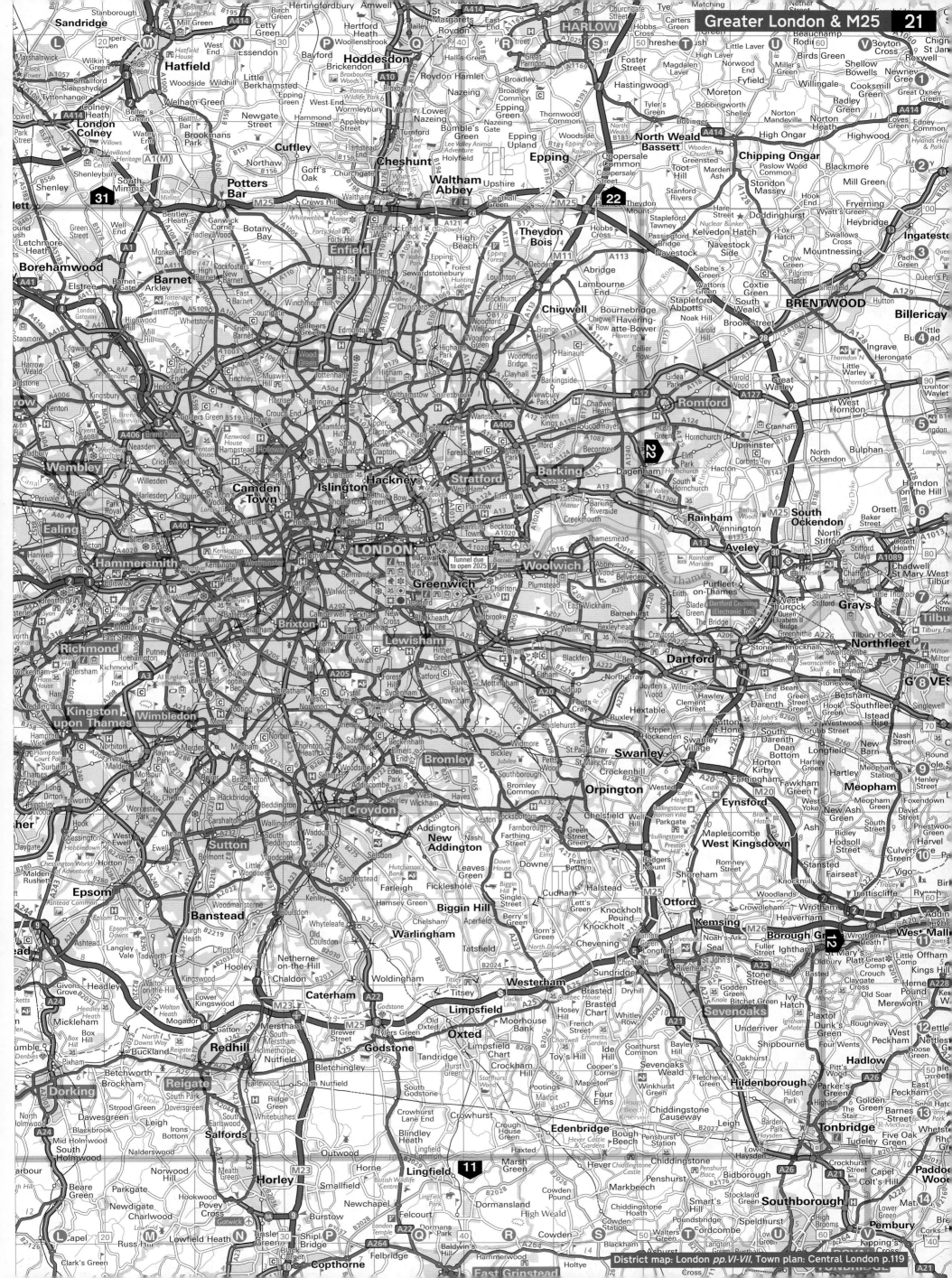

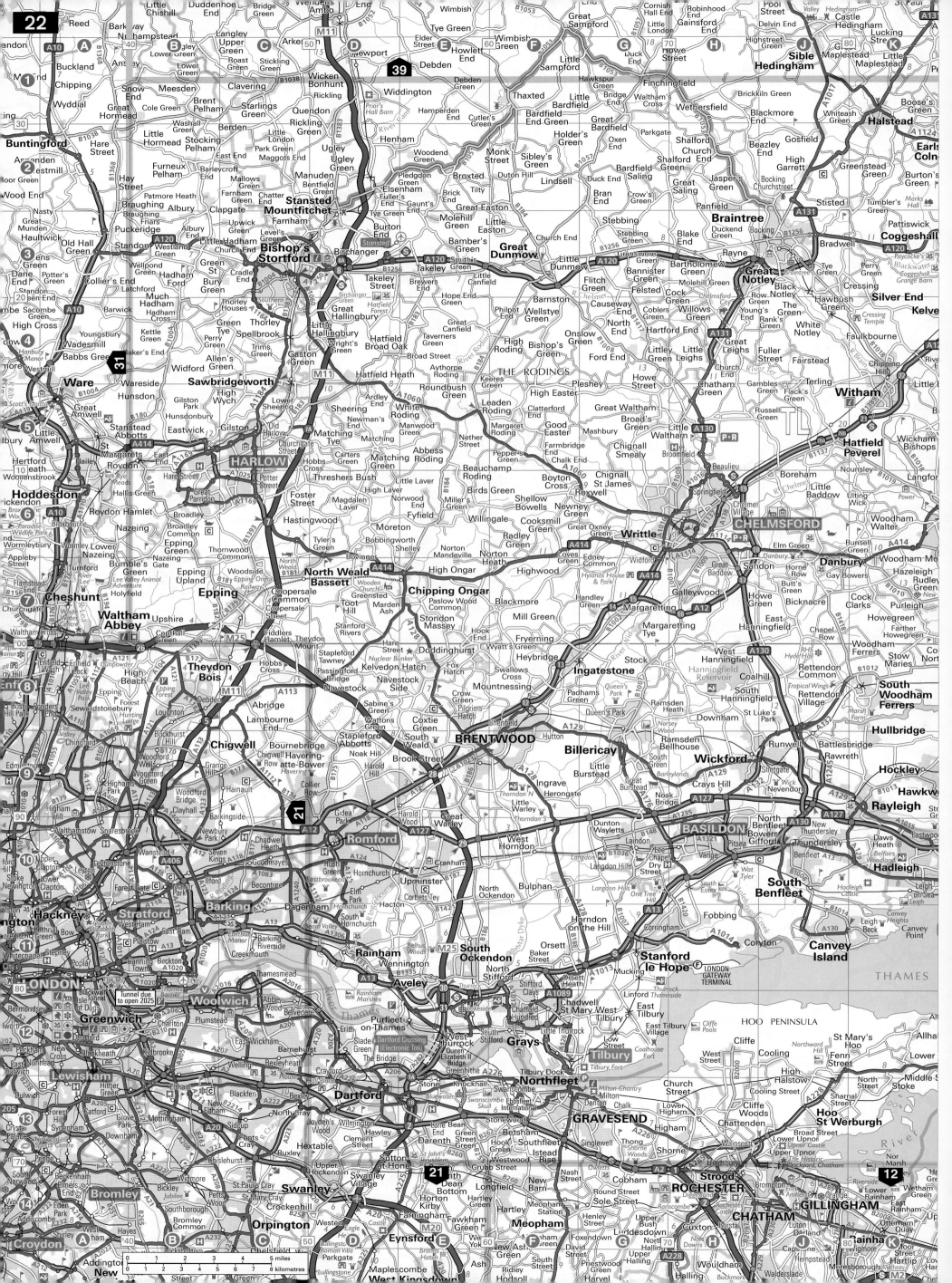

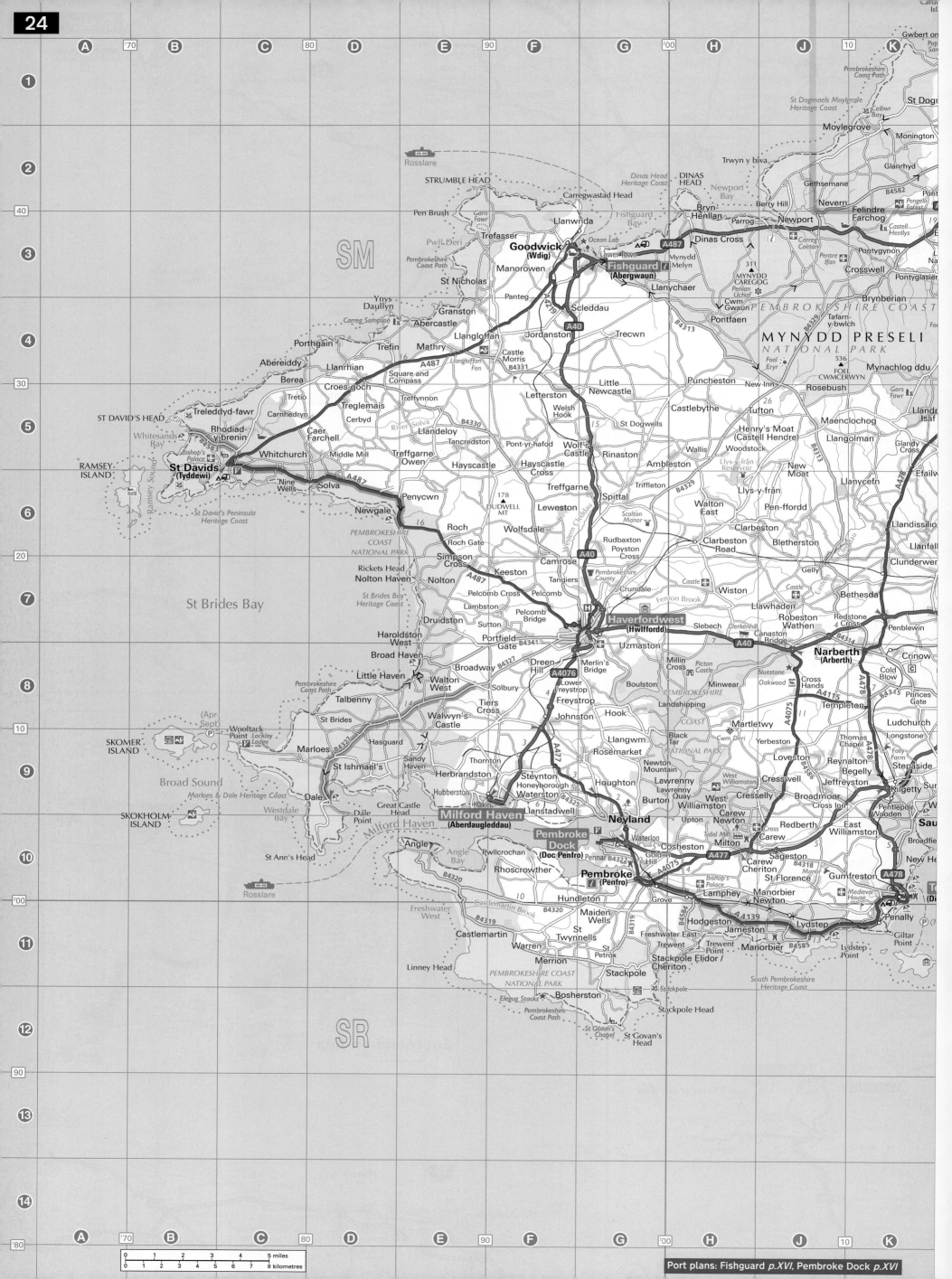

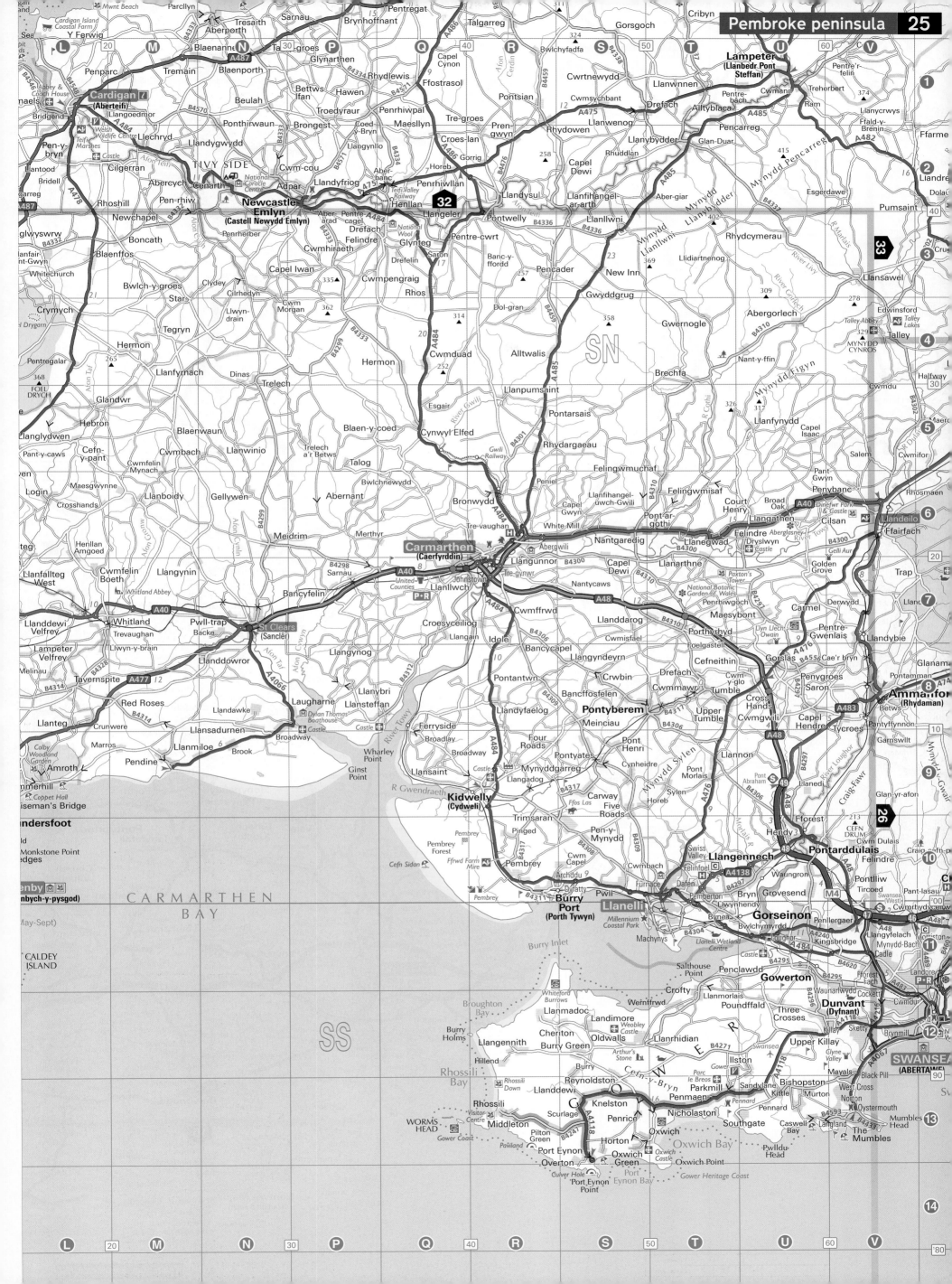

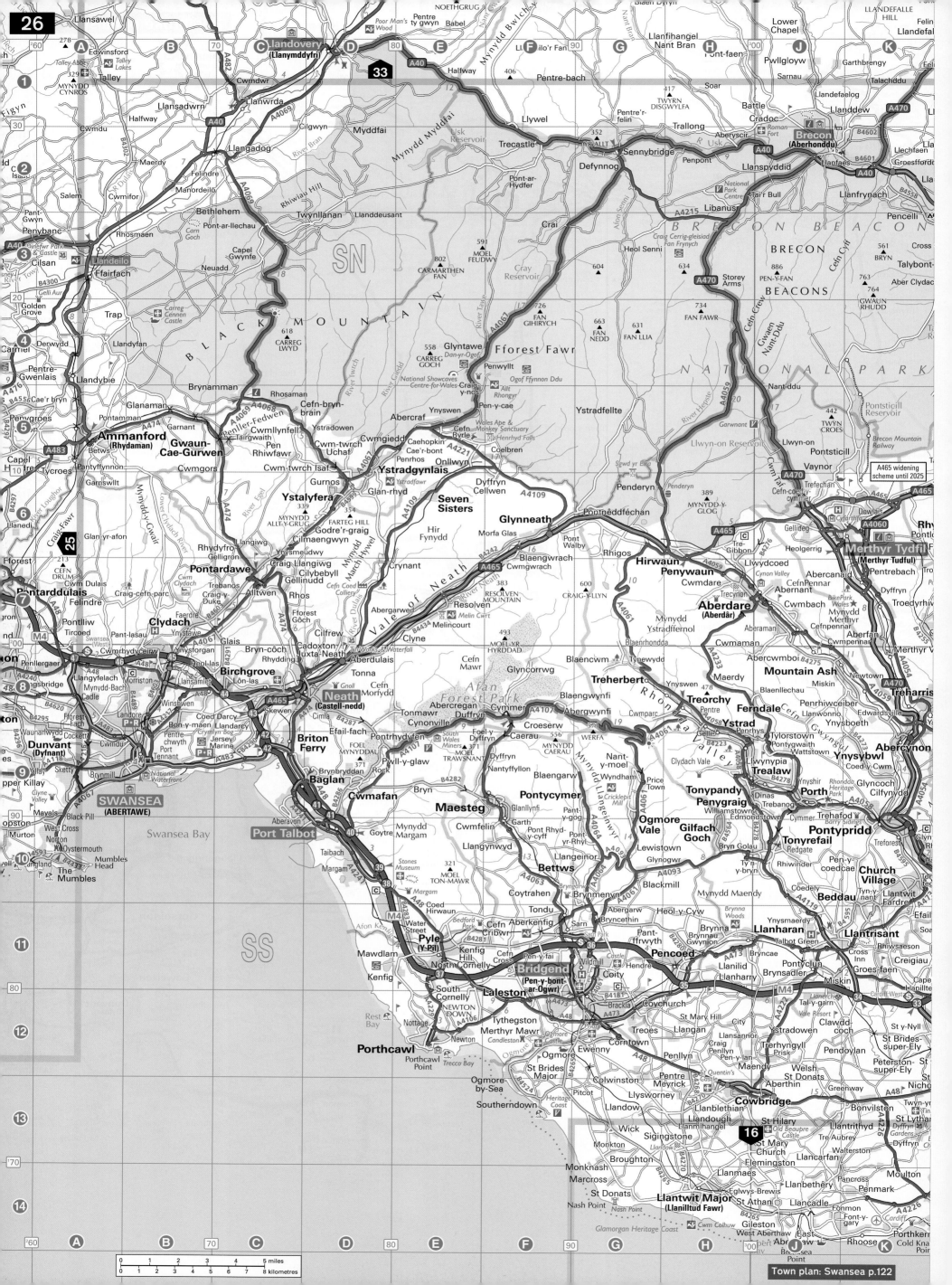

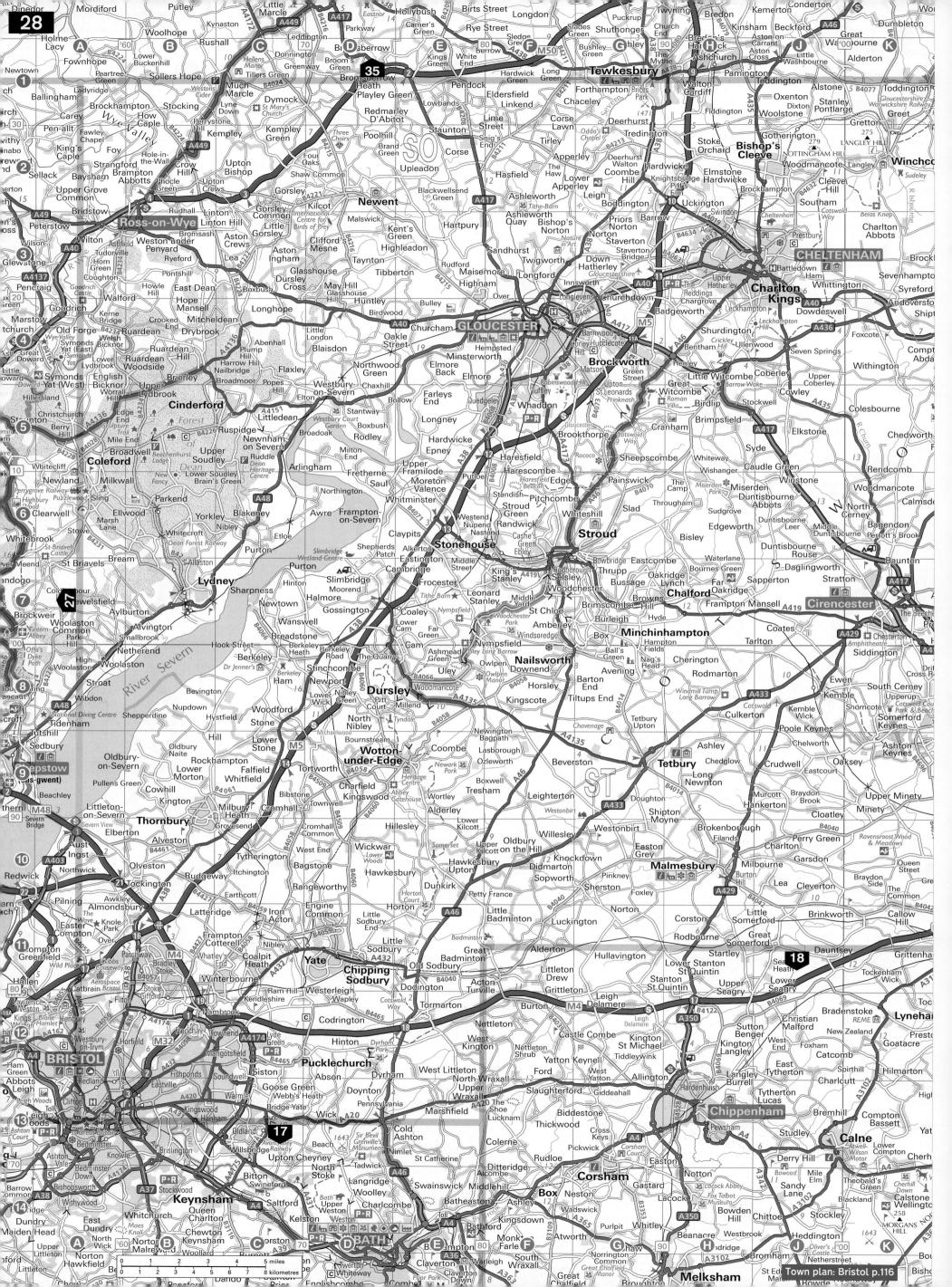

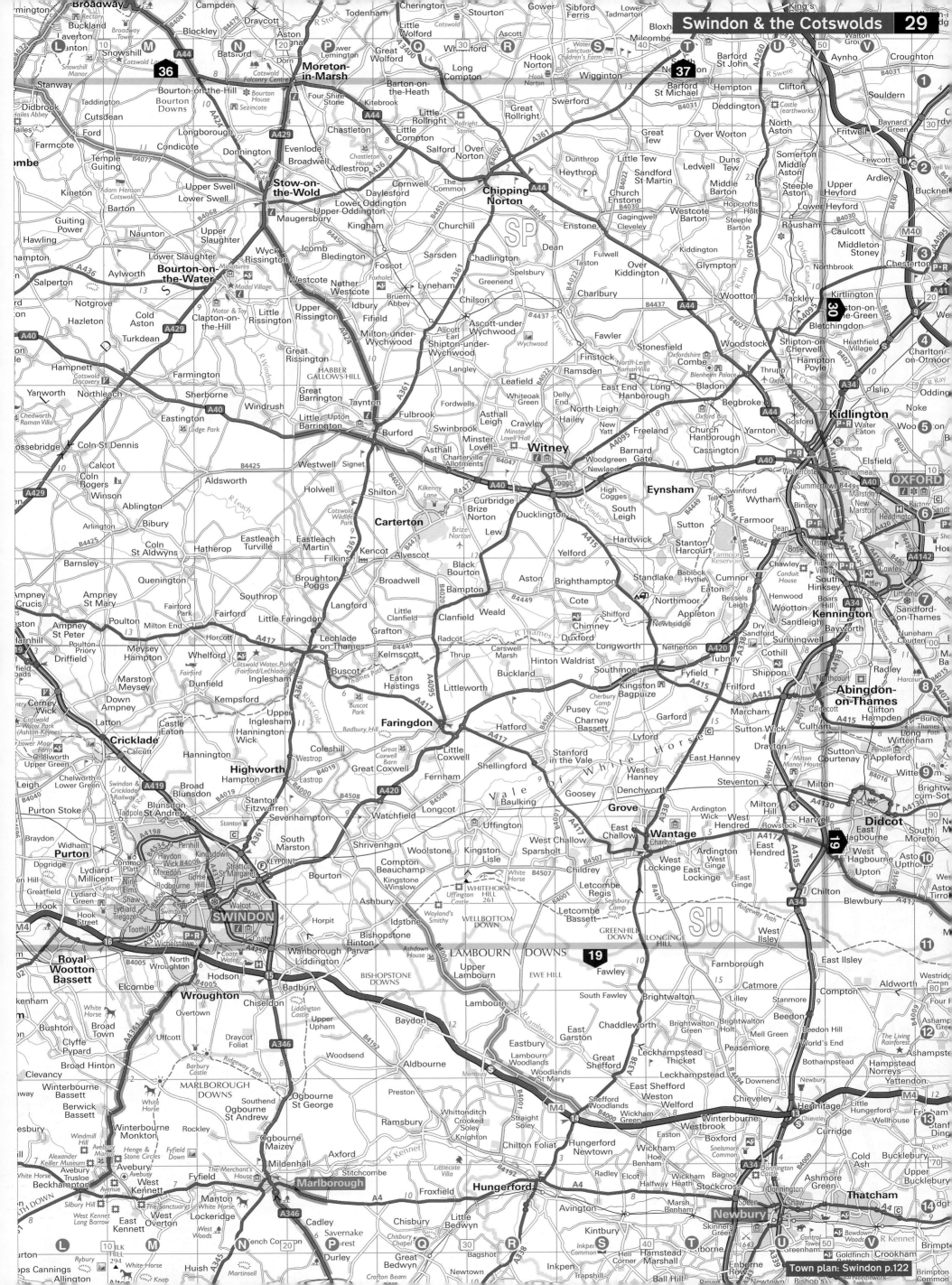

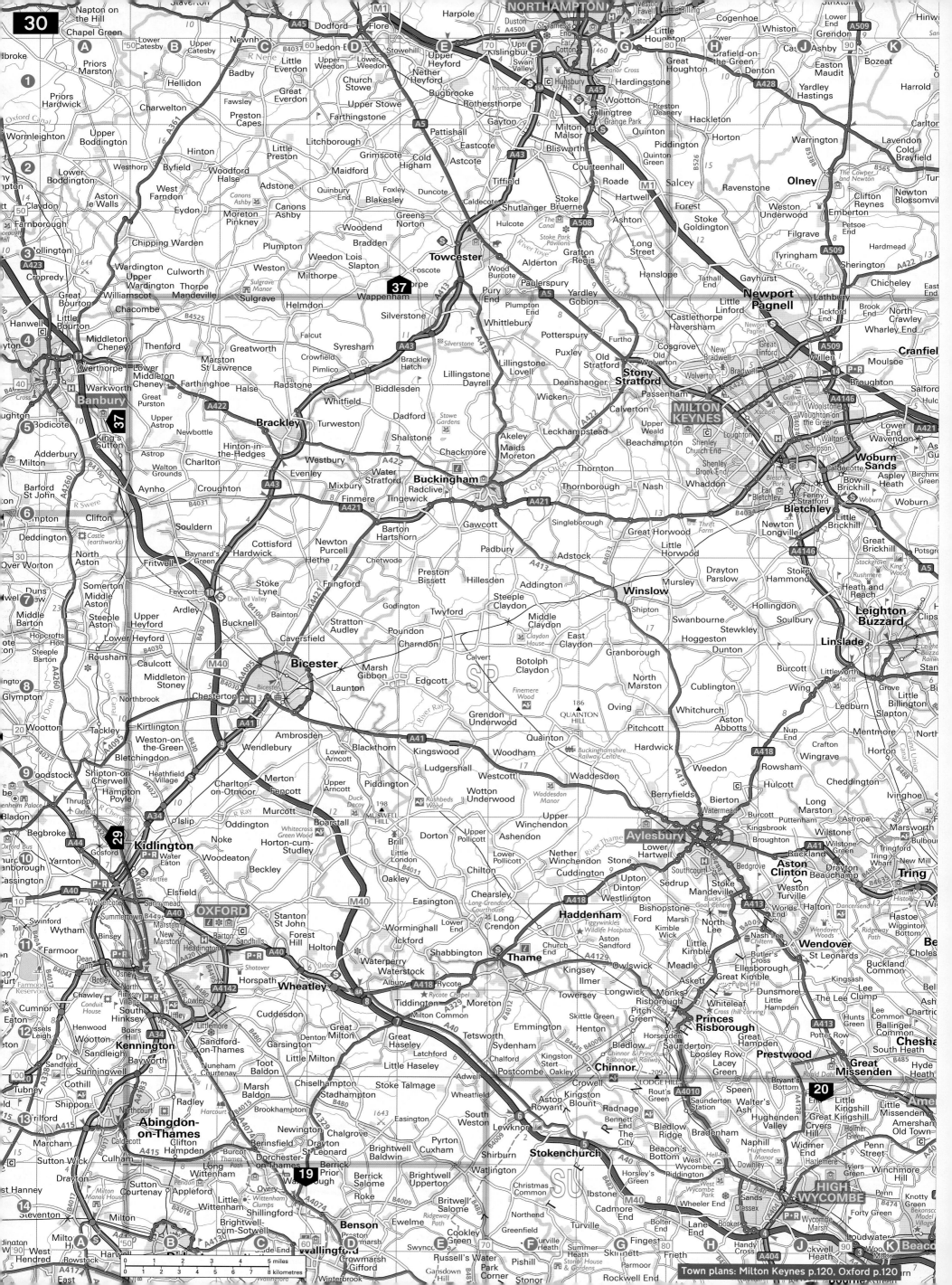

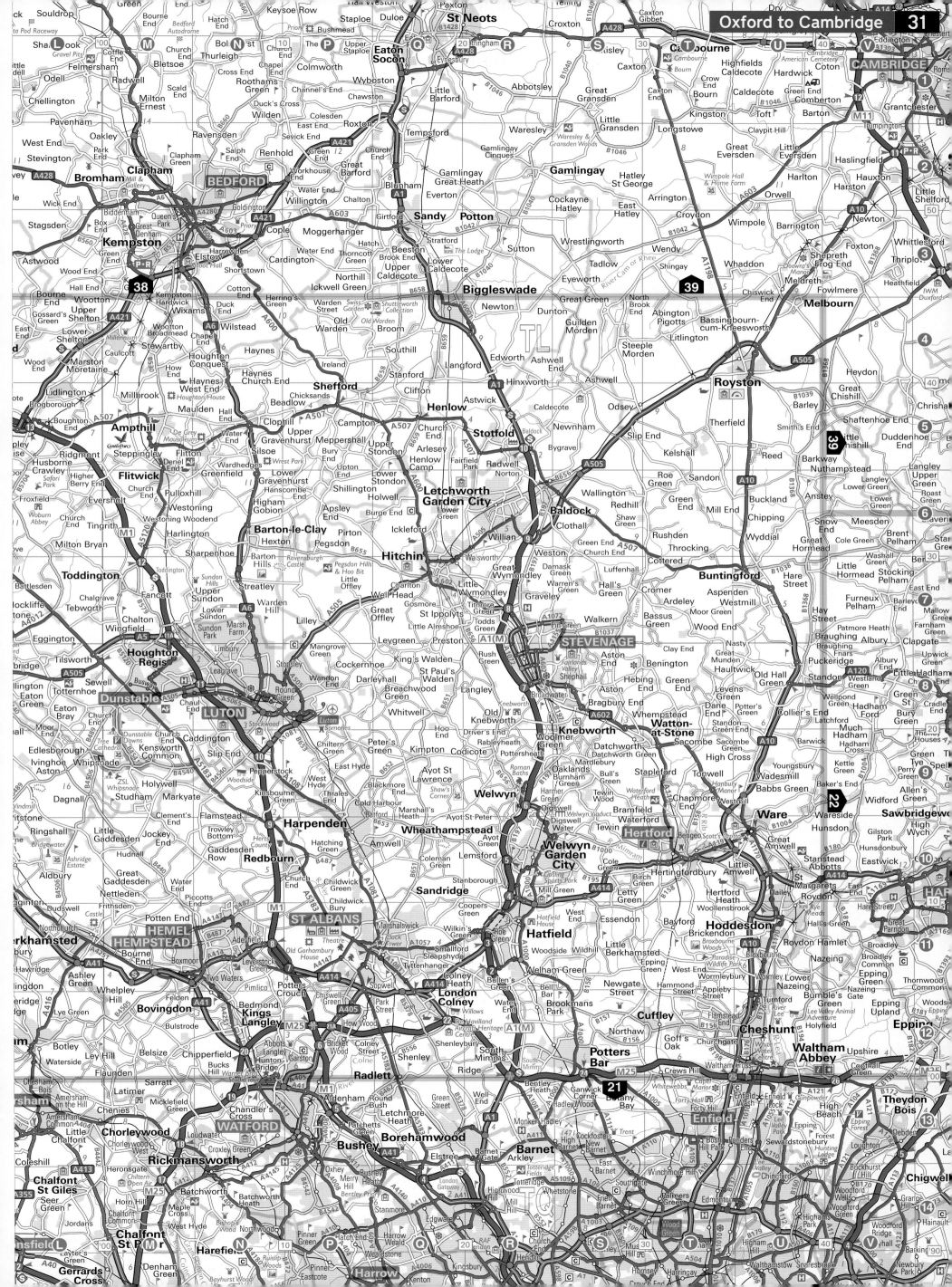

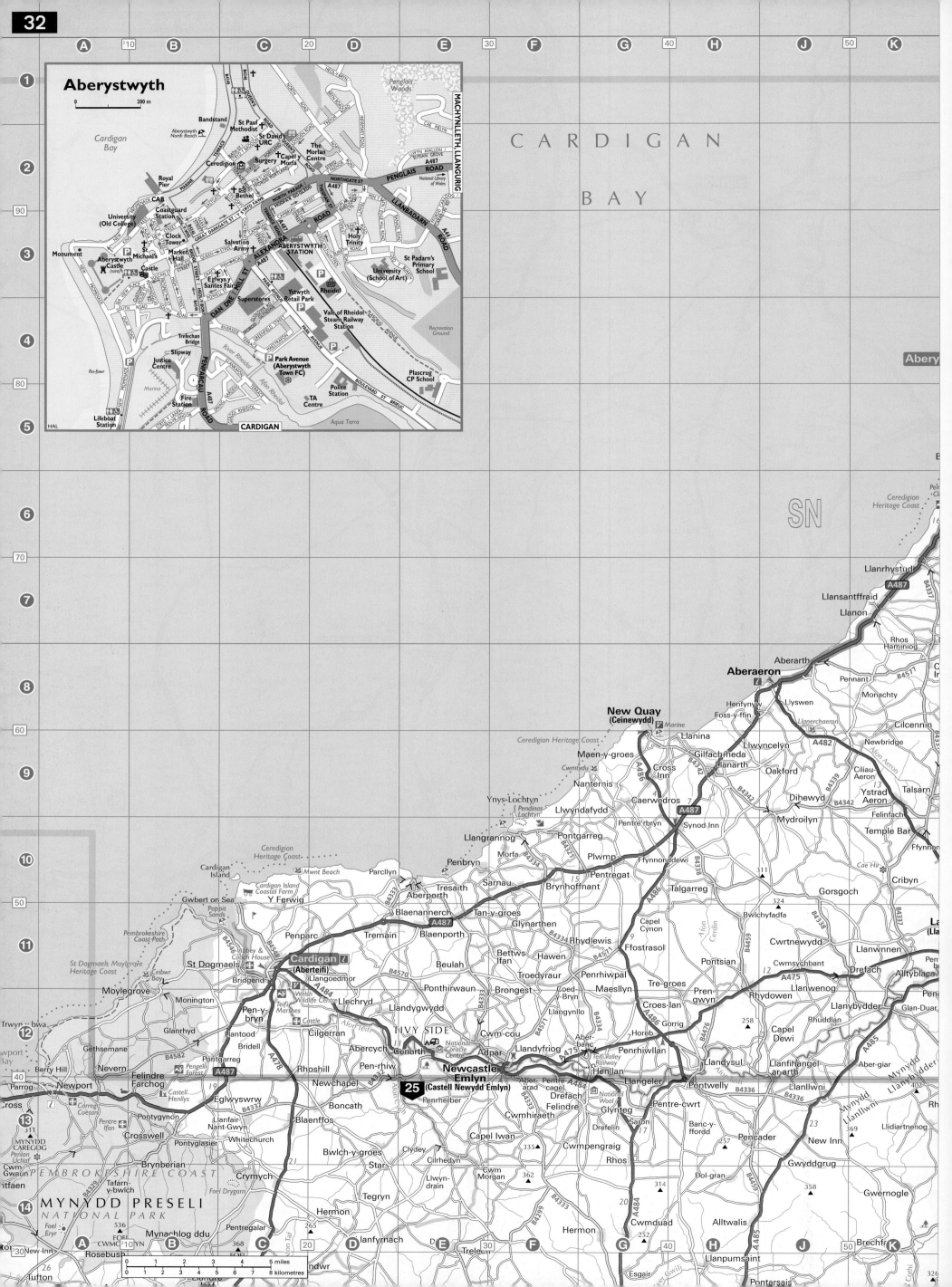

Aberystwyth

0   200 m

Cardigan Bay

Penglais Woods

St Paul Methodist
Bandstand
Aberystwyth North Beach
St David's URC
Surgery
The Morlan Centre
Ceredigion
Capel y Morfa
NORTHGATE ST
A487
National Library of Wales
Royal Pier
CAB
Coastguard Station
Bethel
A487
PENGLAIS ROAD
LLANBADARN ROAD
A44
University (Old College)
Clock Tower
Salvation Army
Holy Trinity
ABERYSTWYTH STATION
St Padarn's Primary School
Monument
Aberystwyth Castle (ruins)
Michael's
Market Hall
Eglwys y Santes Fair
University (School of Art)
Castle
Superstores
Ystwyth Retail Park
Rheidol
Trefechan Bridge
River Rheidol
Vale of Rheidol Steam Railway Station
Recreation Ground
Slipway
Justice Centre
Afon Rheidol
Park Avenue (Aberystwyth Town FC)
Plascrug CP School
Ro-fawr
Fire Station
Police Station
TA Centre
Lifeboat Station
Marina
Aqua Terra
CARDIGAN

MACHYNLLETH, LLANGURIG

HAL

CARDIGAN BAY

SN

Ceredigion Heritage Coast

Aber

Llanrhystud
A487
Llansantffraid
Llanon
Rhos Haminiog
Aberarth
Aberaeron
Pennant
Monachty
Henfynyw
Llyswen
Foss-y-ffin
Newbridge
B4571
New Quay (Ceinewydd)
Marine
Llanina
Llwyncelyn
A482
Cilcennin
Maen-y-groes
Gilfachreda
Llanarth
Oakford
B4339
Ciliau-Aeron
Cwmtydu
Cross Inn
A487
Ystrad Aeron
Ceredigion Heritage Coast
Nanternis
Caerwedros
Dihewyd
B4342
Talsarn
Ynys-Lochtyn
Llwyndafydd
Synod Inn
Mydroilyn
Felinfach
Pendinas Lochtyn
Pentre'rbryn
A487
Temple Bar
Llangrannog
Pontgarreg
Plwmp
B4321
Ffynnon
Morfa
B4334
Ffynnonddewi
Penbryn
B4338
Cae Hir
Cribyn
Parcllyn
Sarnau
Pentregat
311
Gorsgoch
Mwnt Beach
Tresaith
Brynhoffnant
Talgarreg
324
Bwlchyfadfa
Cardigan Island
Aberporth
B4334
A486
B4459
Cwrtnewydd
Cardigan Island Coastal Farm
Y Ferwig
Tan-y-groes
Glynarthen
Rhydlewis
Capel Cynon
Ffostrasol
Cwmsychbant
La (Lla
Gwbert on Sea
Blaenannerch
A487
Bettws Ifan
Afon Cerdin
A475
Llanwnnen
Poppit Sands
Penparc
Tremain
Blaenporth
Hawen
B4571
Pontsian
12
Drefach
Abbey & Coach House
Beulah
Troedyraur
Penrhiwpal
Tre-groes
Rhydowen
Llanwenog
Alltyblaca
Pembrokeshire Coast Path
St Dogmaels Moylegrove Heritage Coast
St Dogmaels
Bridgend
B4570
Ponthirwaun
Brongest
Maesllyn
Croes-lan
258
Pen
Ceibwr Bay
Llangoedmor
Cardigan (Aberteifi)
Llandygwydd
Langynllo
Prengwyn
Llandysul
Glan-Duar
Moylegrove
Monington
Pen-y-bryn
Welsh Wildlife Centre
Llechryd
B4334
Gorrig
Rhuddlan
Llanfihangel-ar-arth
Teifi Marshes
Castle
TVY SIDE
Aber-banc
Horeb
Capel Dewi
Glanrhyd
Llantood
Cilgerran
Afon Teifi
Cwm-cou
National Coracle Centre
Adpar
Llandyfriog
Penrhiwllan
Henllan
Landysul
Trwyn
bwa
Bridell
Abercych
Cenarth
Teifi Valley Railway
Penrhiwpal
Pontwelly
Llanllwni
Newport
Gethsemane
Pontgarreg
A478
Pen-rhiw
Newcastle Emlyn (Castell Newydd Emlyn)
Aber-arad
Pentre A484
Llangeler
B4336
Aber-giar
Nevern
Felindre Farchog
Pengelli Forest
A487
Rhoshill
Newchapel
Penherber
Drefach
National Wool M
Pentre-cwrt
Llanllwni
Carreg Coetan
19
25
Drefelin
New Inn
Parrog
Castell Henllys
Eglwyswrw
Boncath
Cwmhiraeth
Glynteg
Saron
Banc-y-ffordd
Pencader
Cross
Berry Hill
Pentre Ifan
B4332
17
257
23
B4459
Crosswell
Pontygynon
Llanfair-Nant-Gwyn
Blaenffos
Capel Iwan
Cwmpengraig
Gwyddgrug
Pontglasier
Whitechurch
Cwm Morgan
Rhos
358
Gwernogle
MYNYDD CAREGOG
311
Brynberian
335
Capel Iwan
Clydey
Cilrhedyn
Cwmduad
A484
Pencader
CWMC
Tafarn-y-bwlch
Foel Drygarn
Bwlch-y-groes
Star
Llwyn-drain
362
314
Pentregalar
PEMBROKESHIRE COAST
Crymych
265
20
Esgair
Foel Eryr
536
NATIONAL PARK
Hermon
Tegryn
Cwmduad
Alltwalis
MYNYDD PRESELI
Mynachlog ddu
368
Hermon
Cwmdaud
Llanpumsaint
New Inn
Rosebush
Llanfyrnach
Trelech
Brechfa
Tufton
26
A329
ndwr
Pontarsais

0   5 miles
0 1 2 3 4 5 6 7 8 kilometres

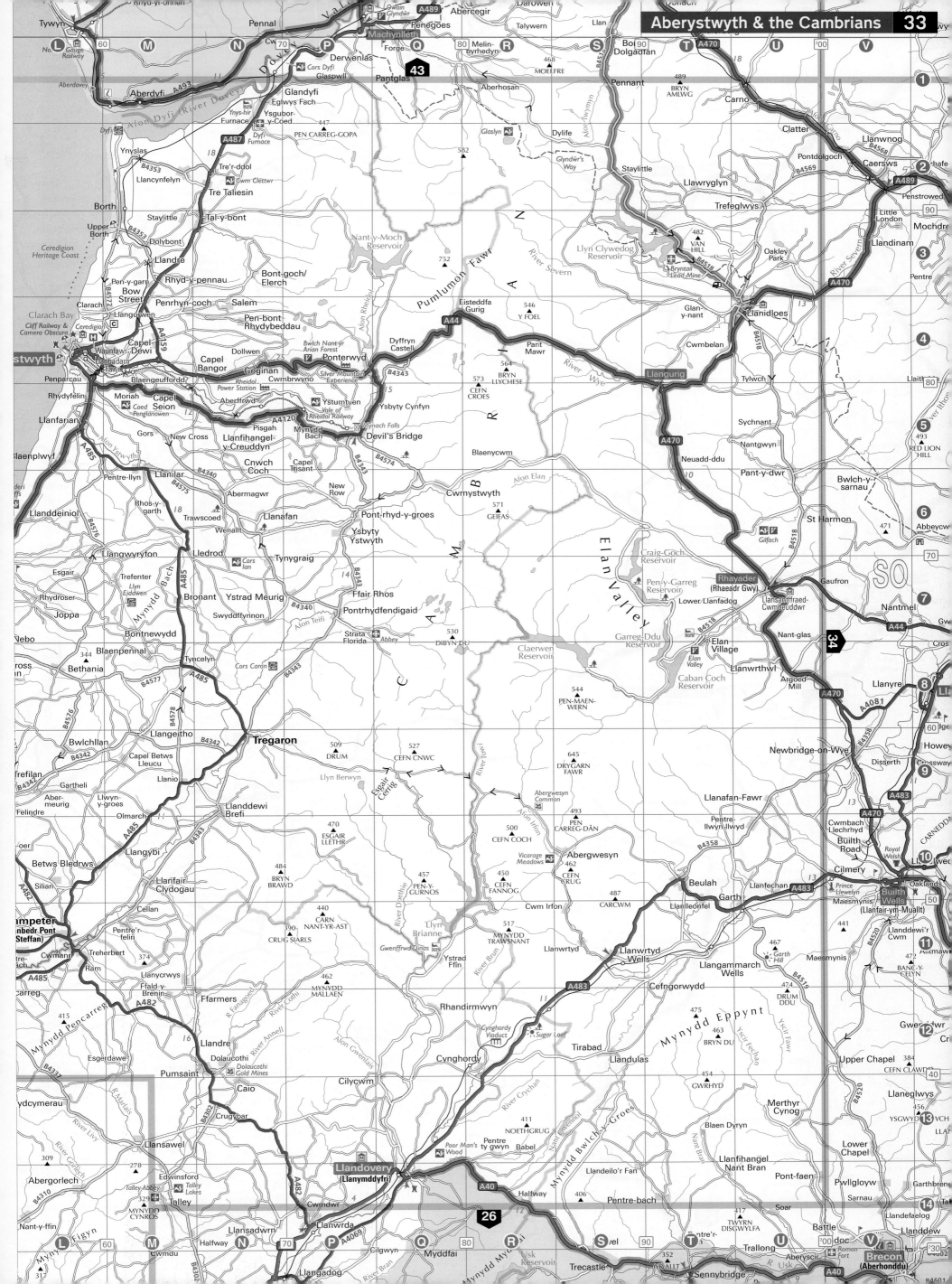

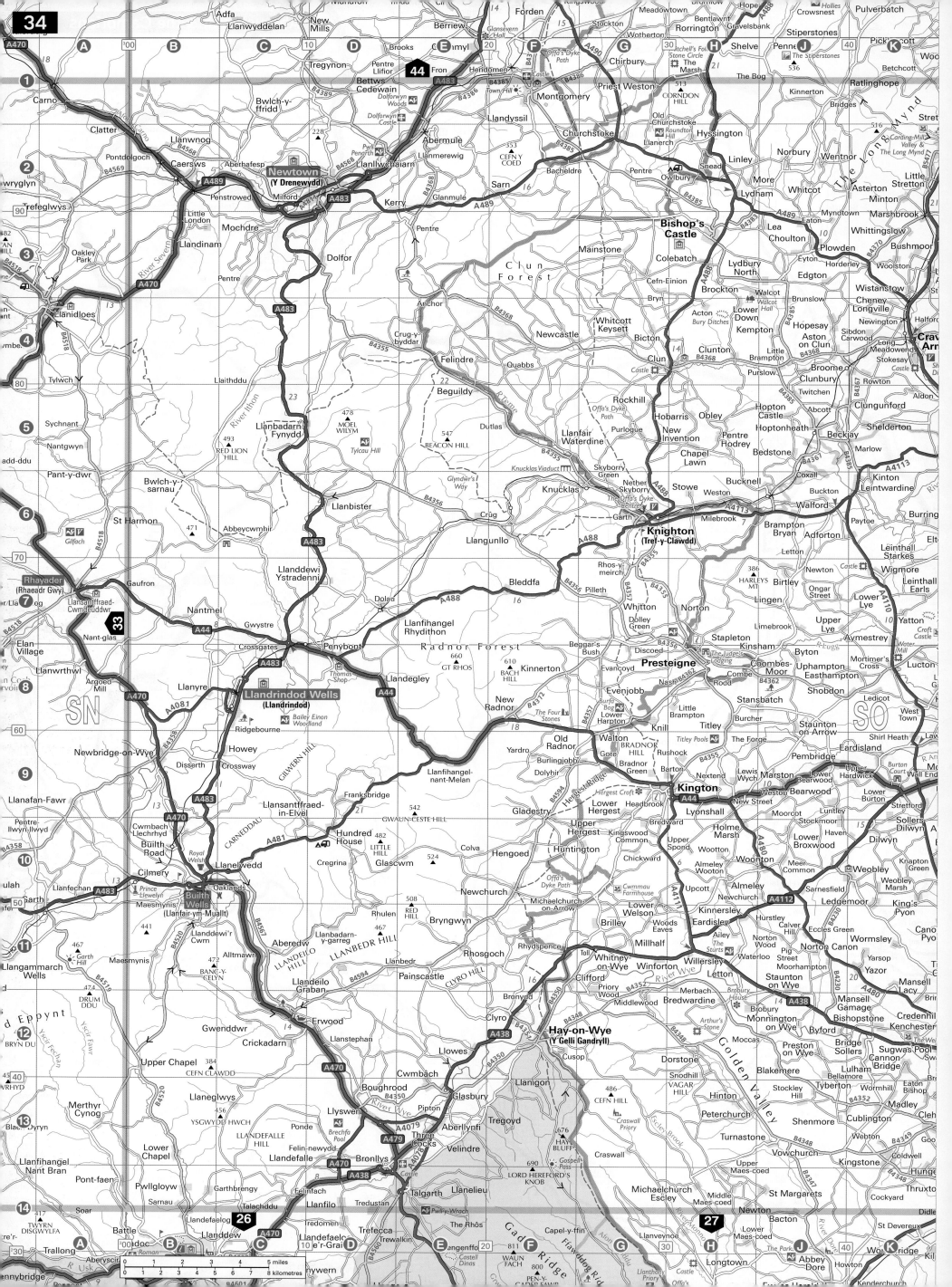

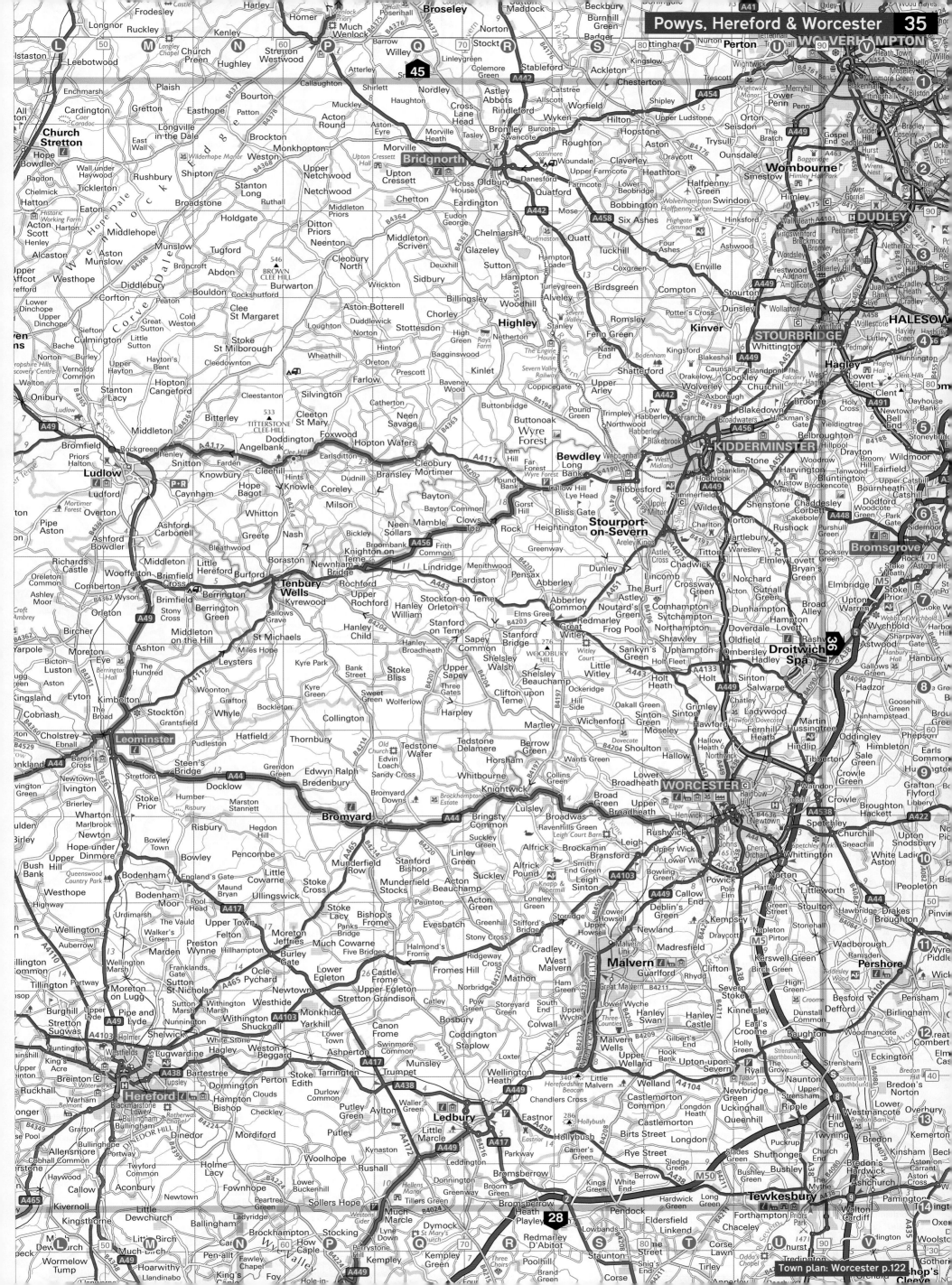

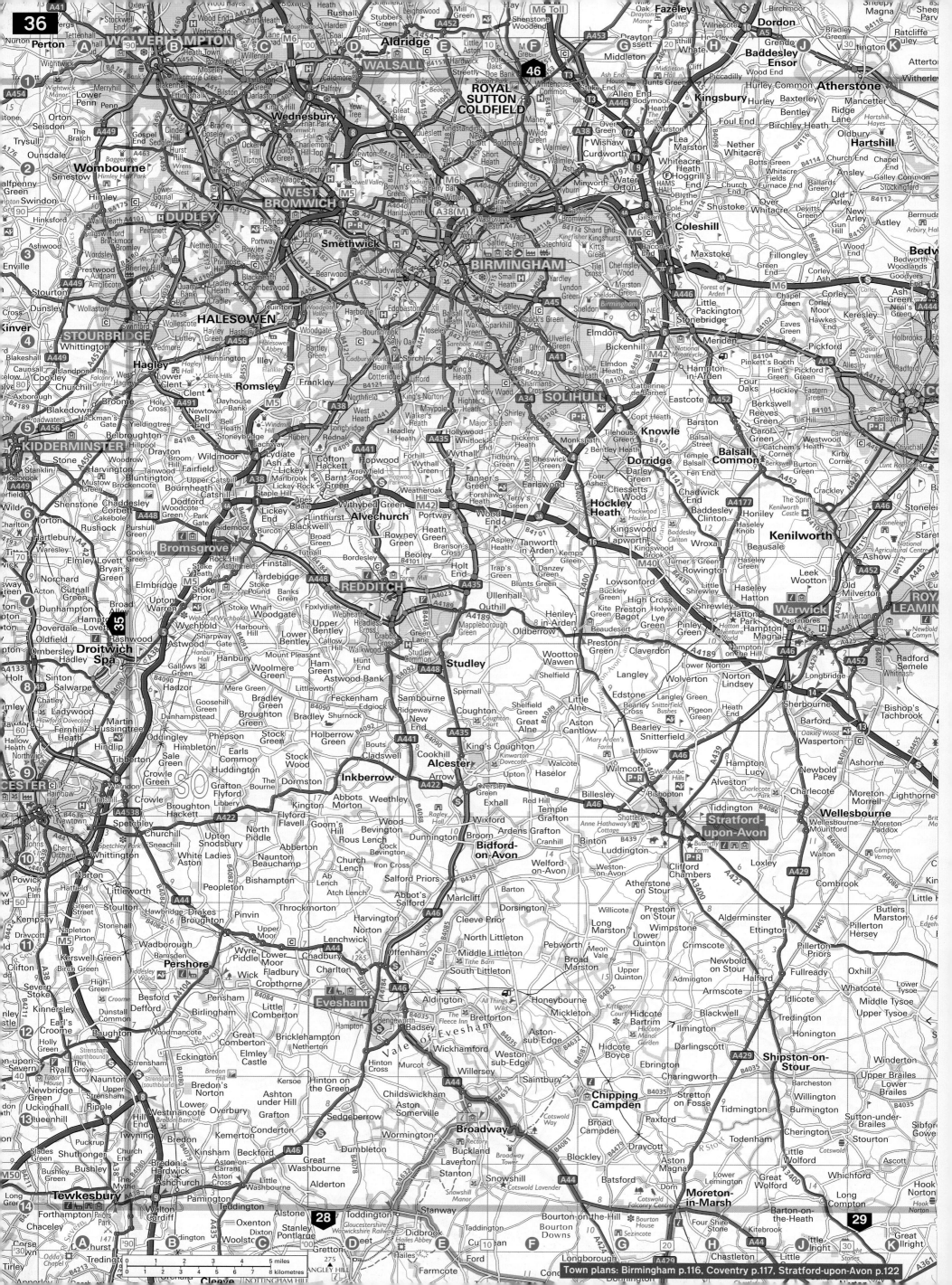

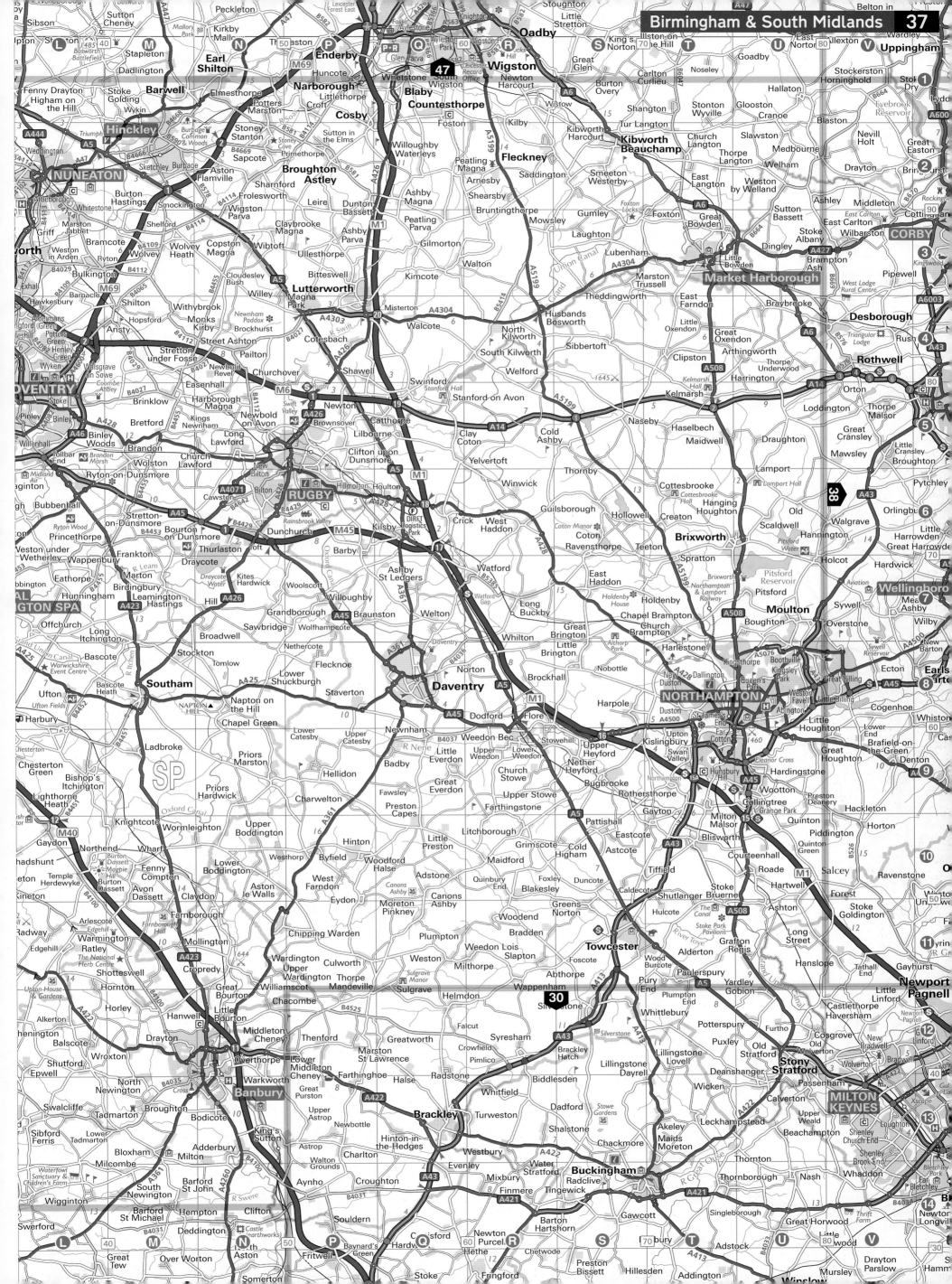

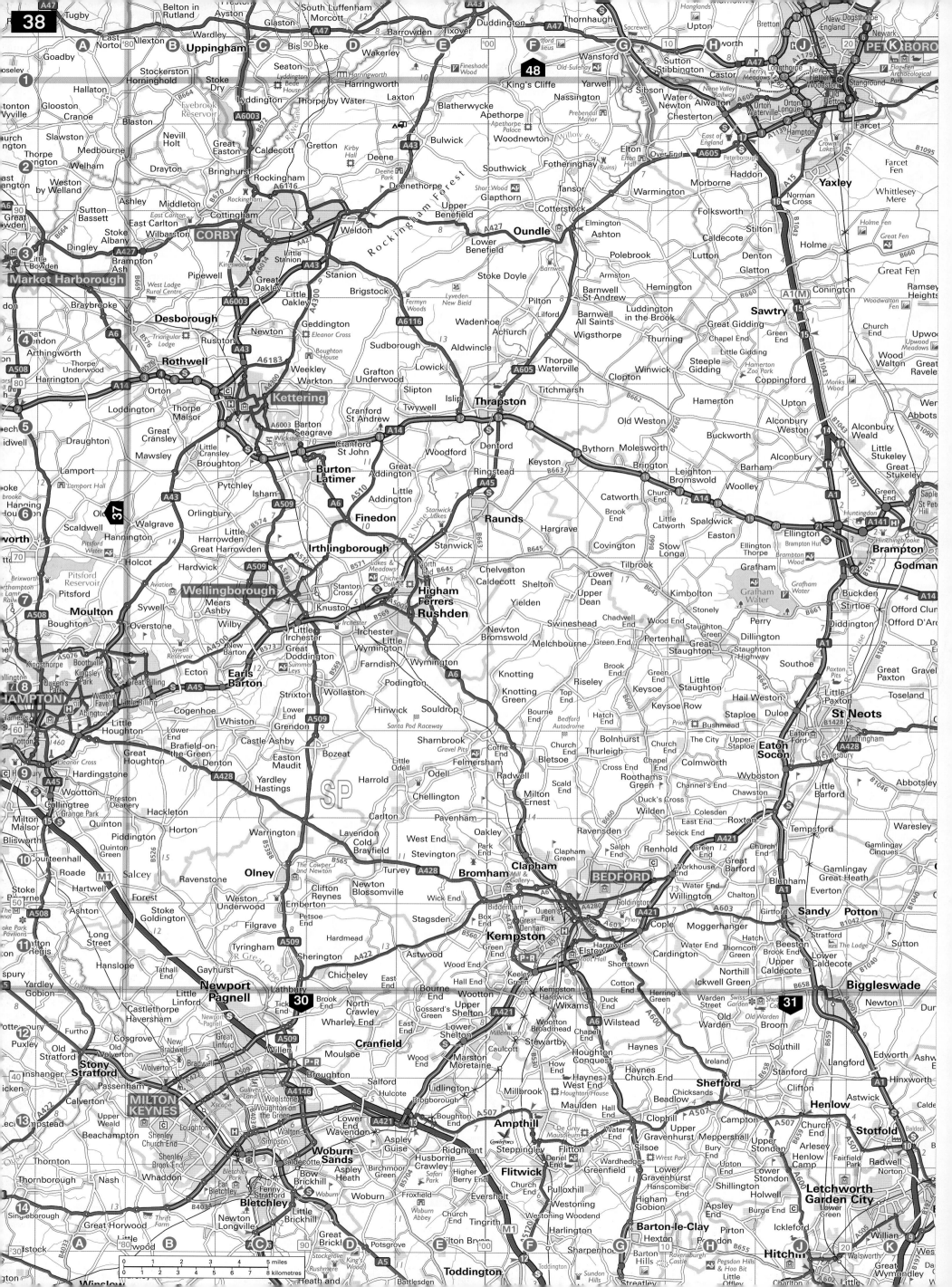

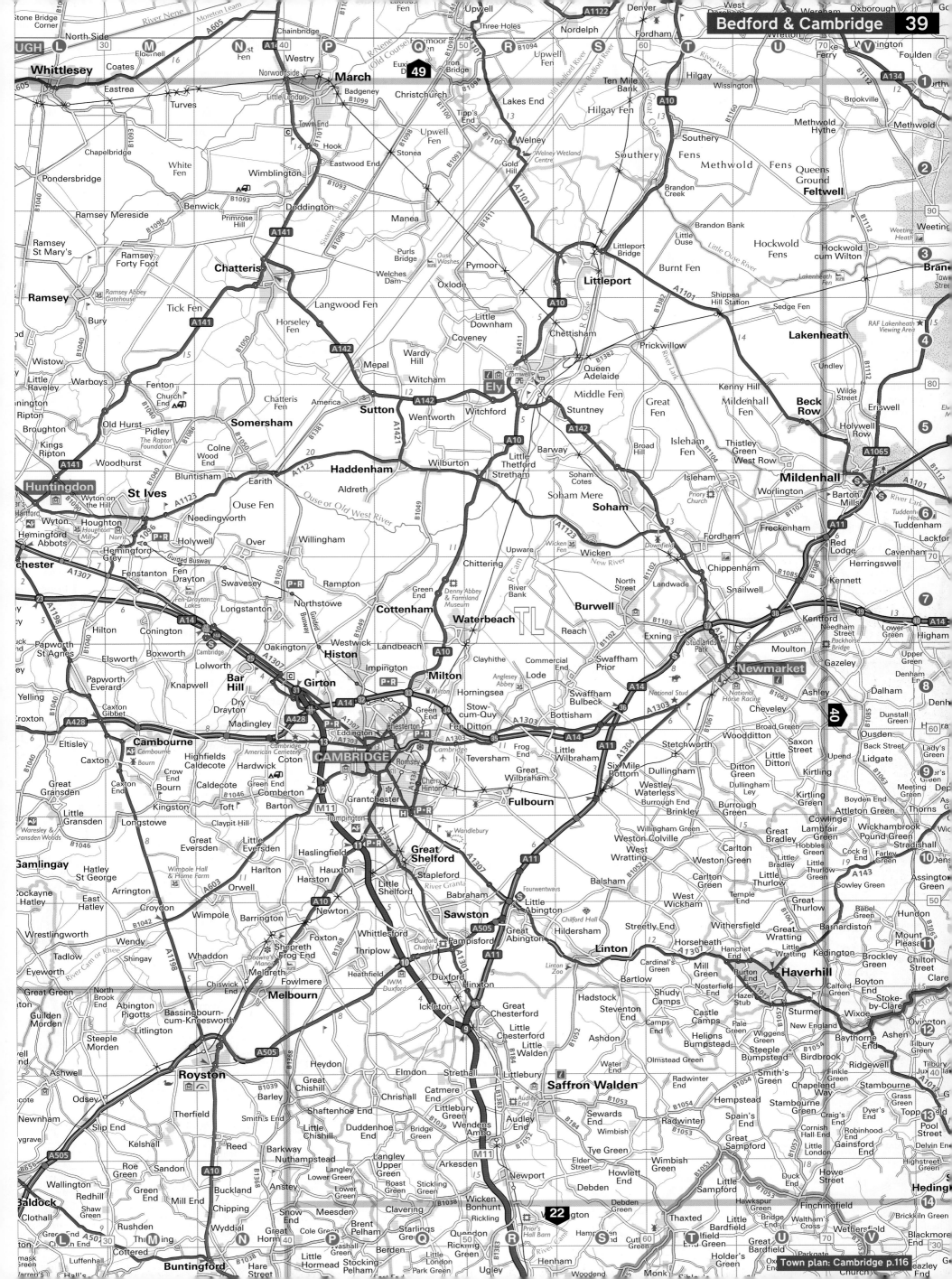

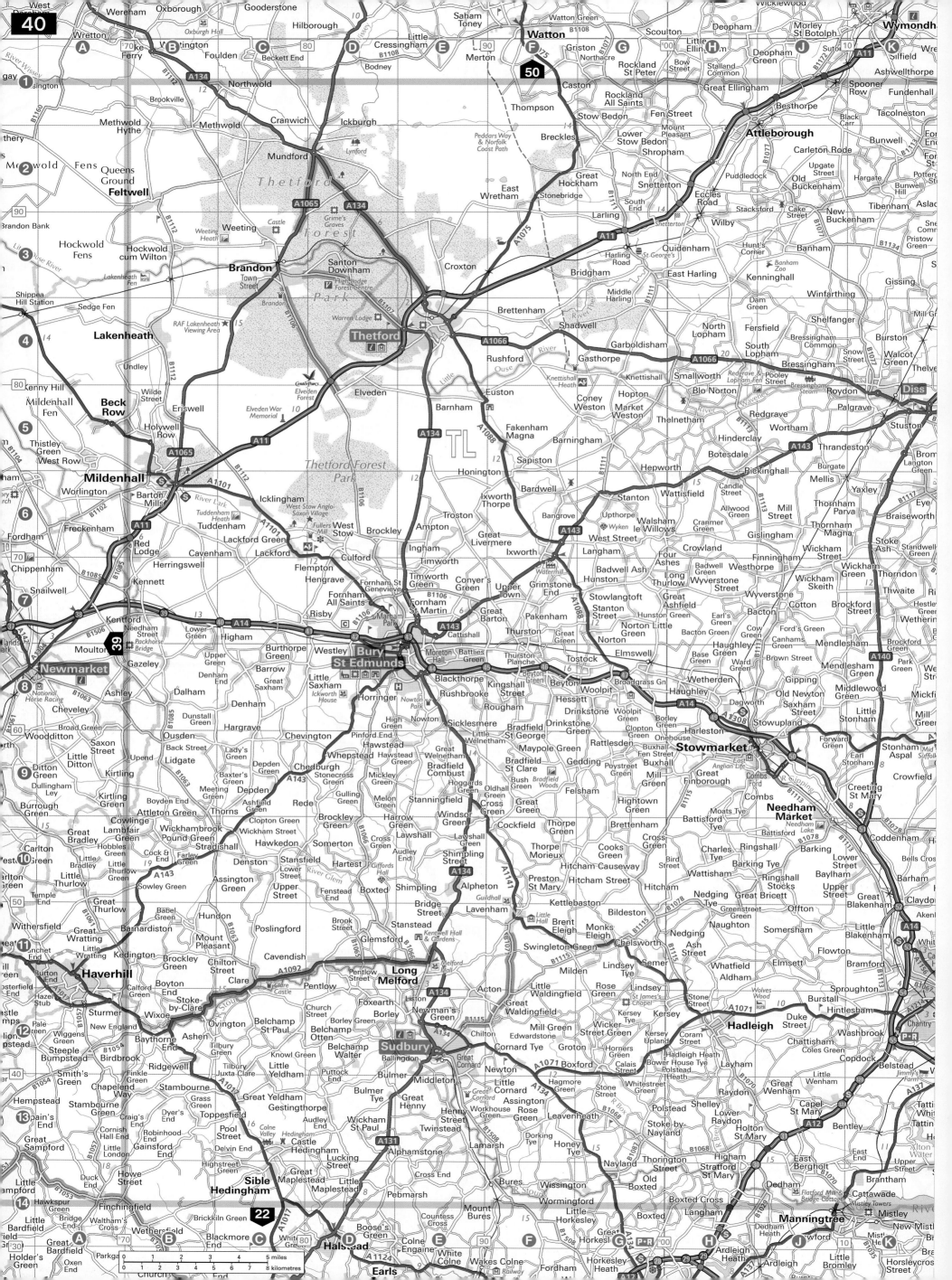

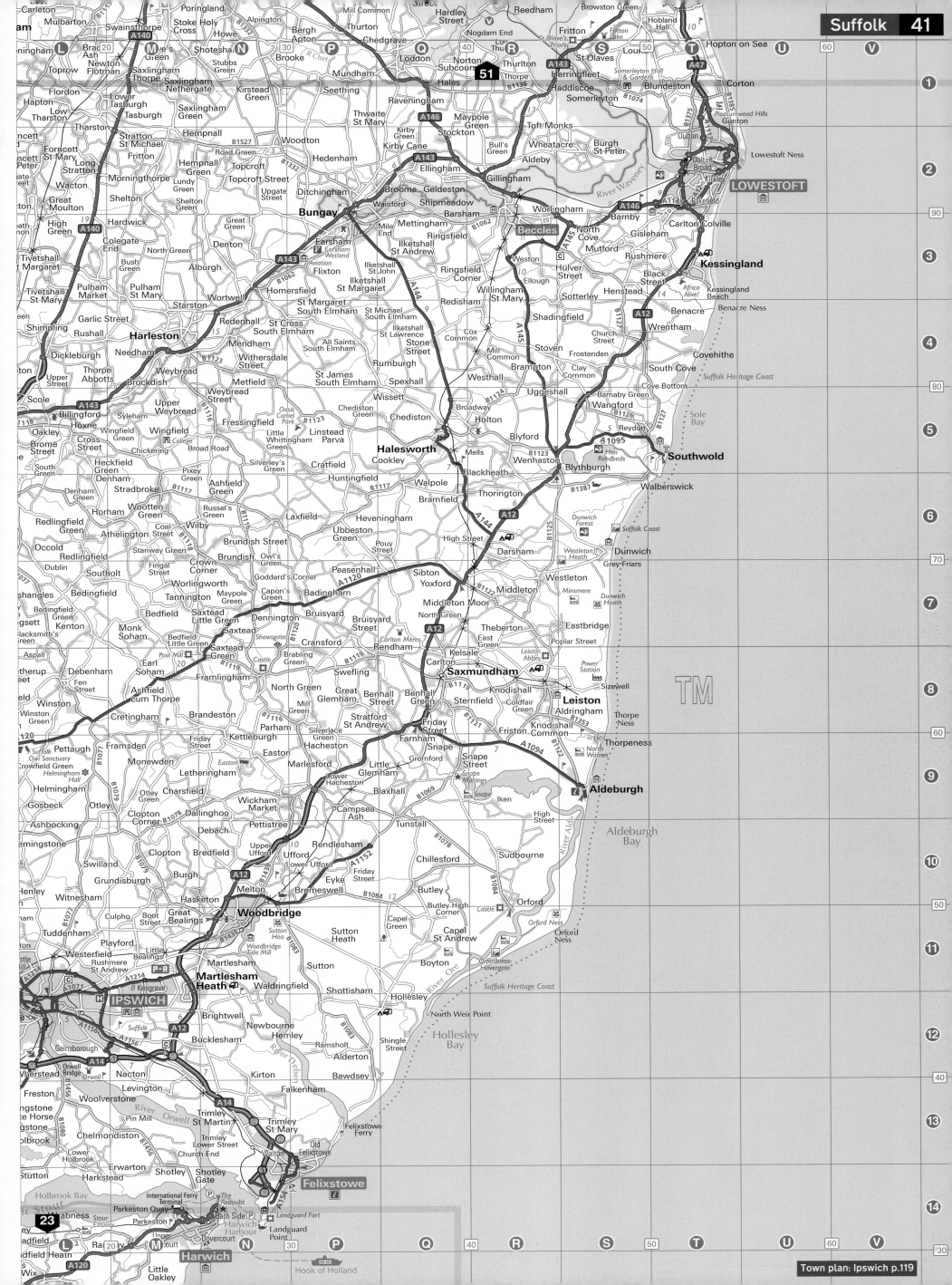

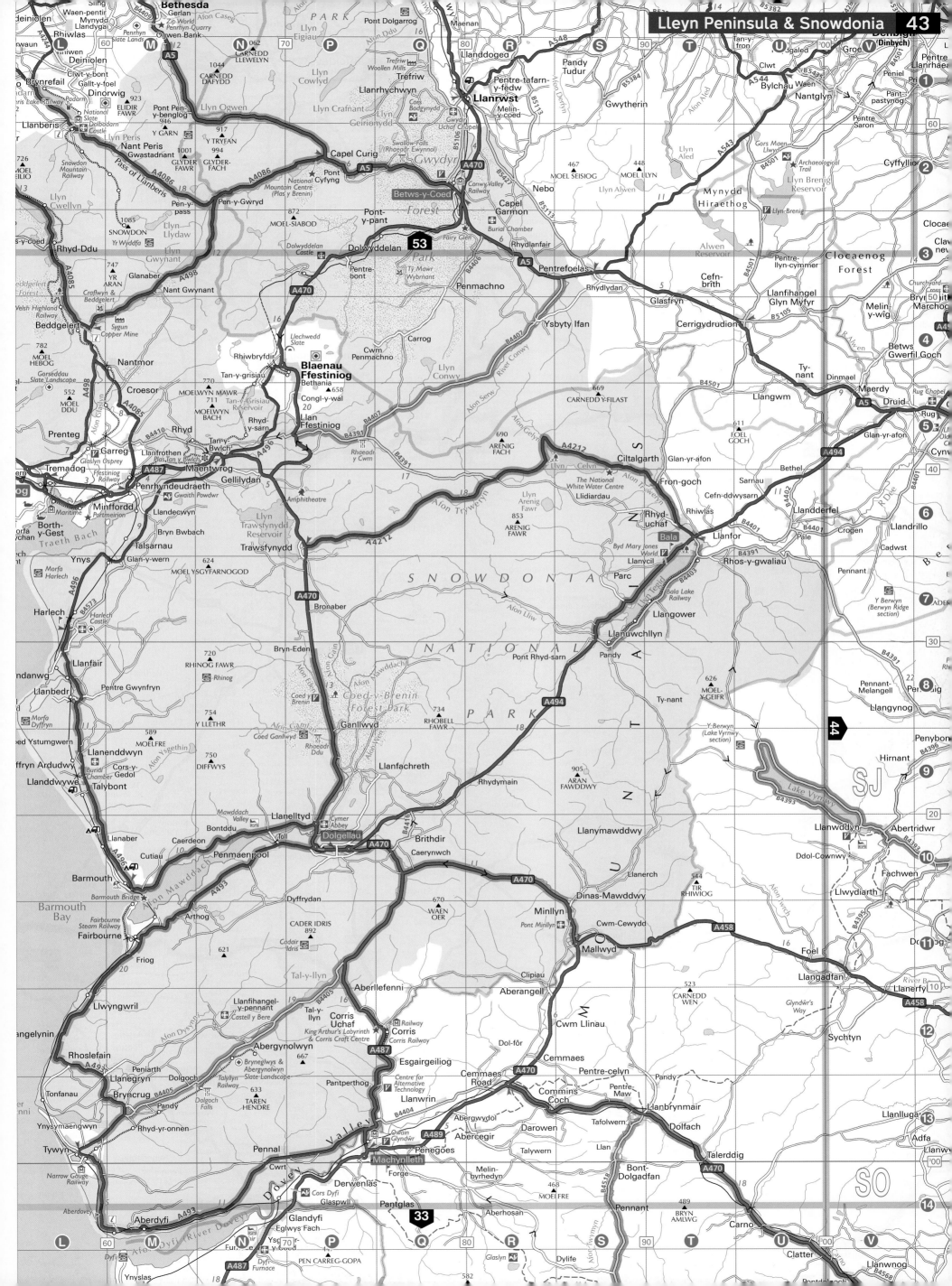

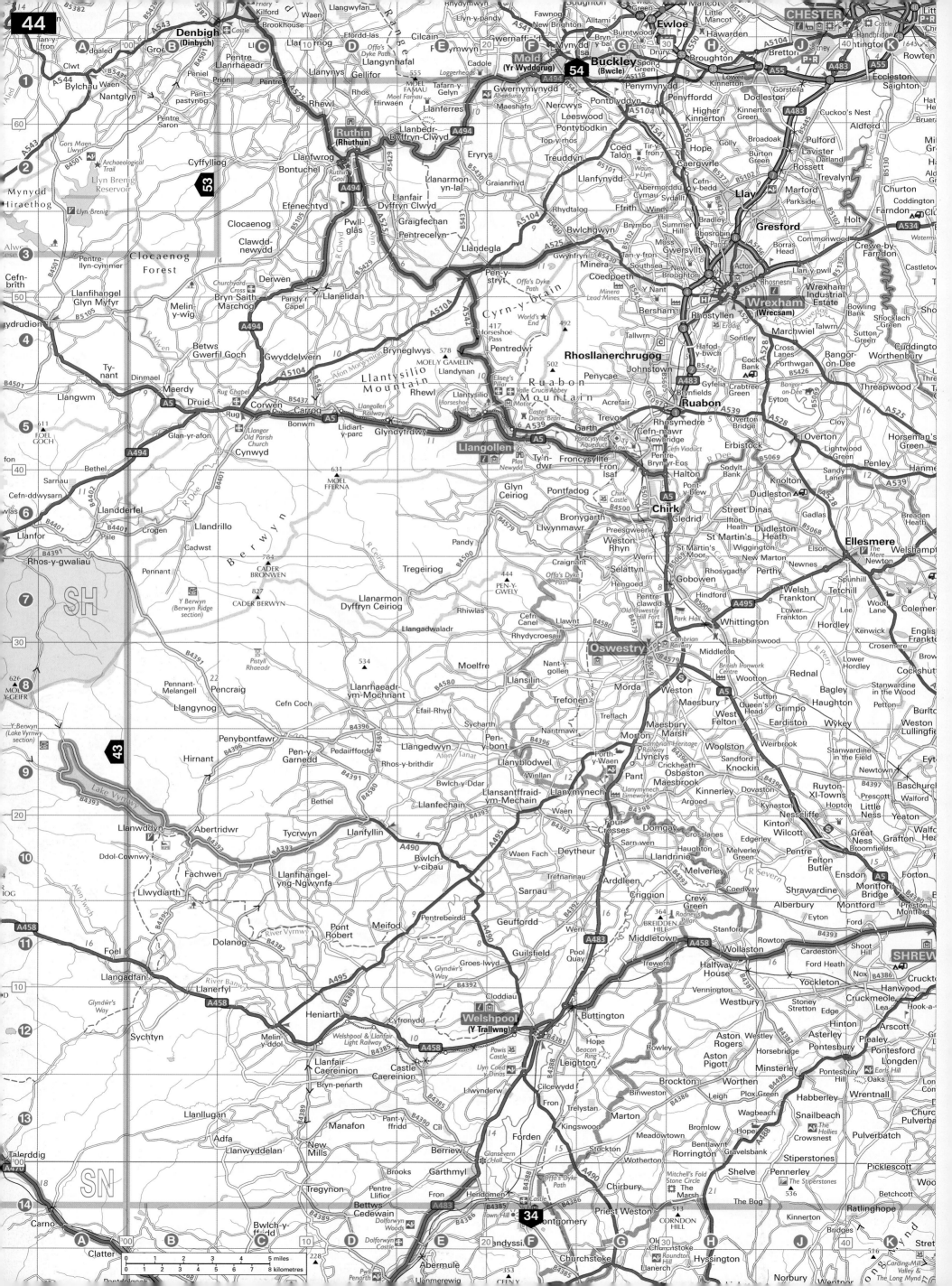

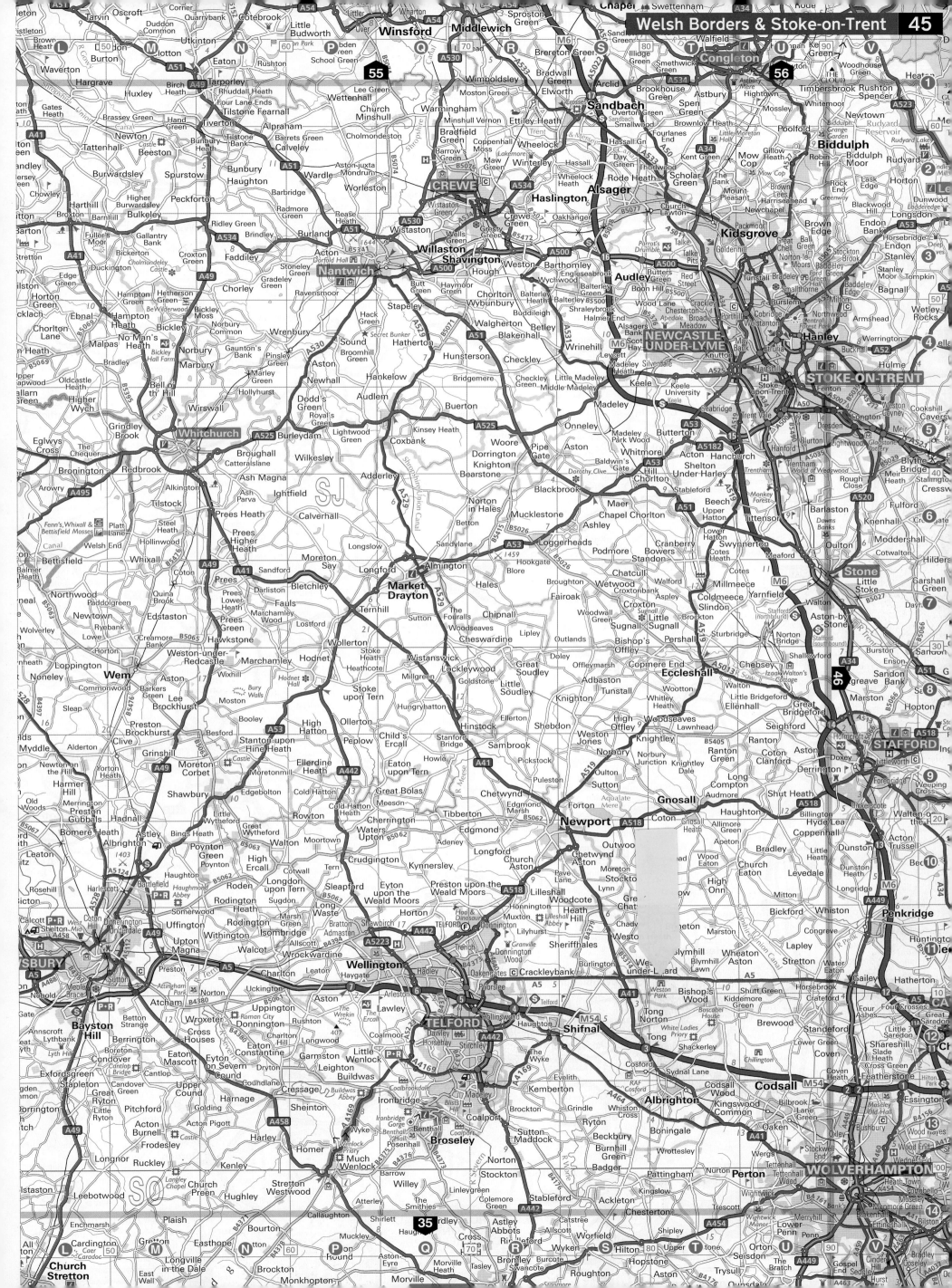

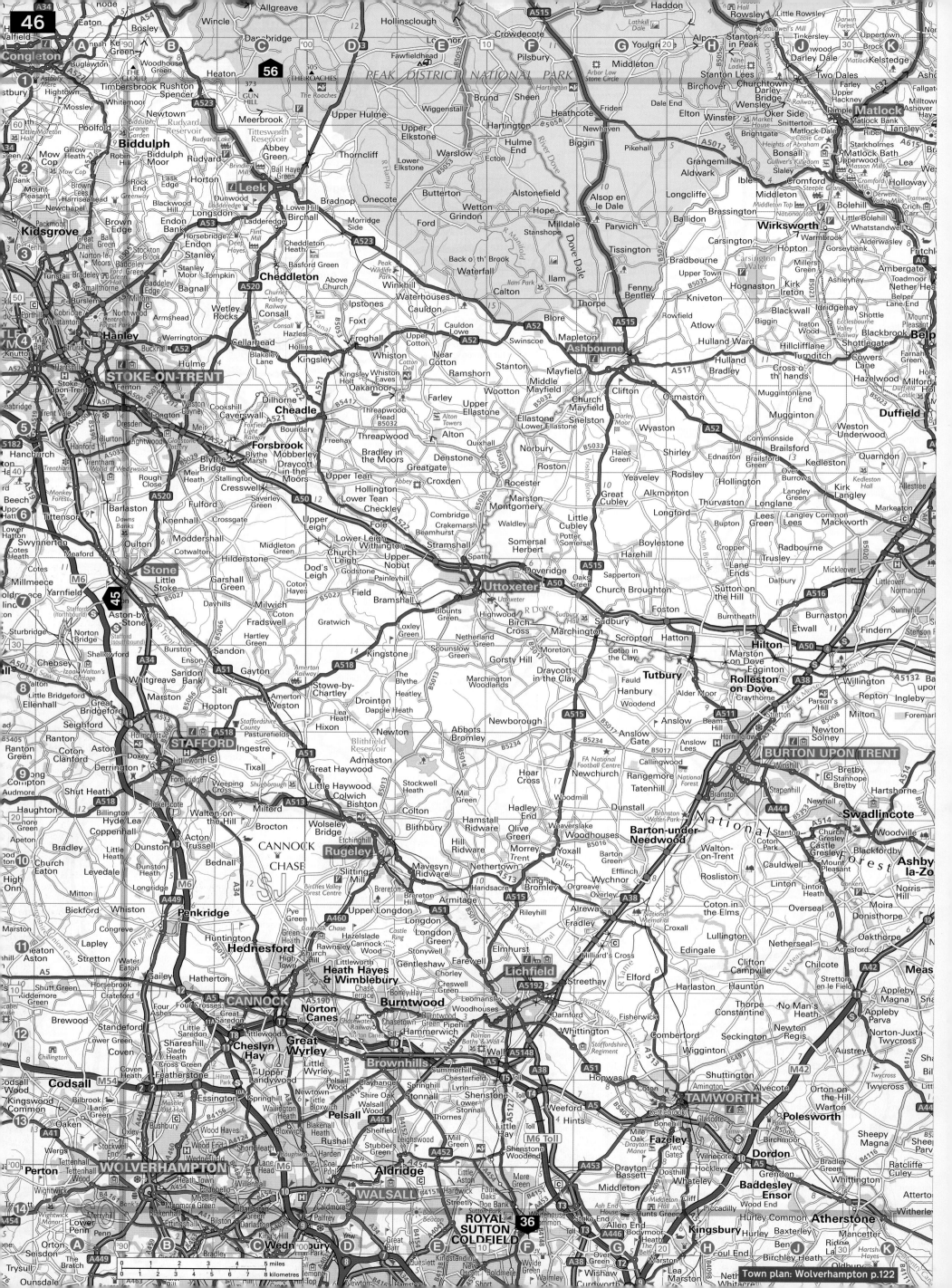

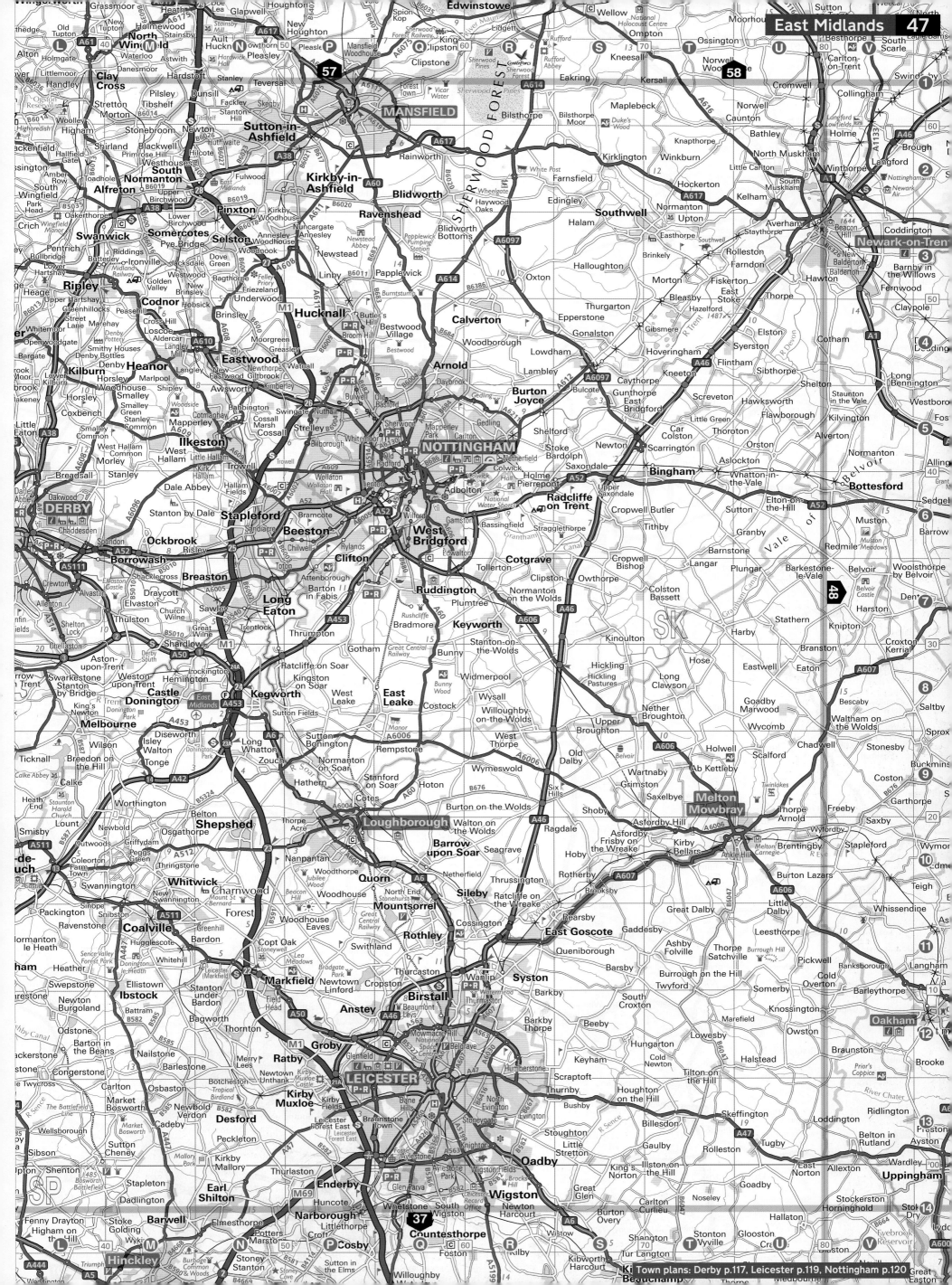

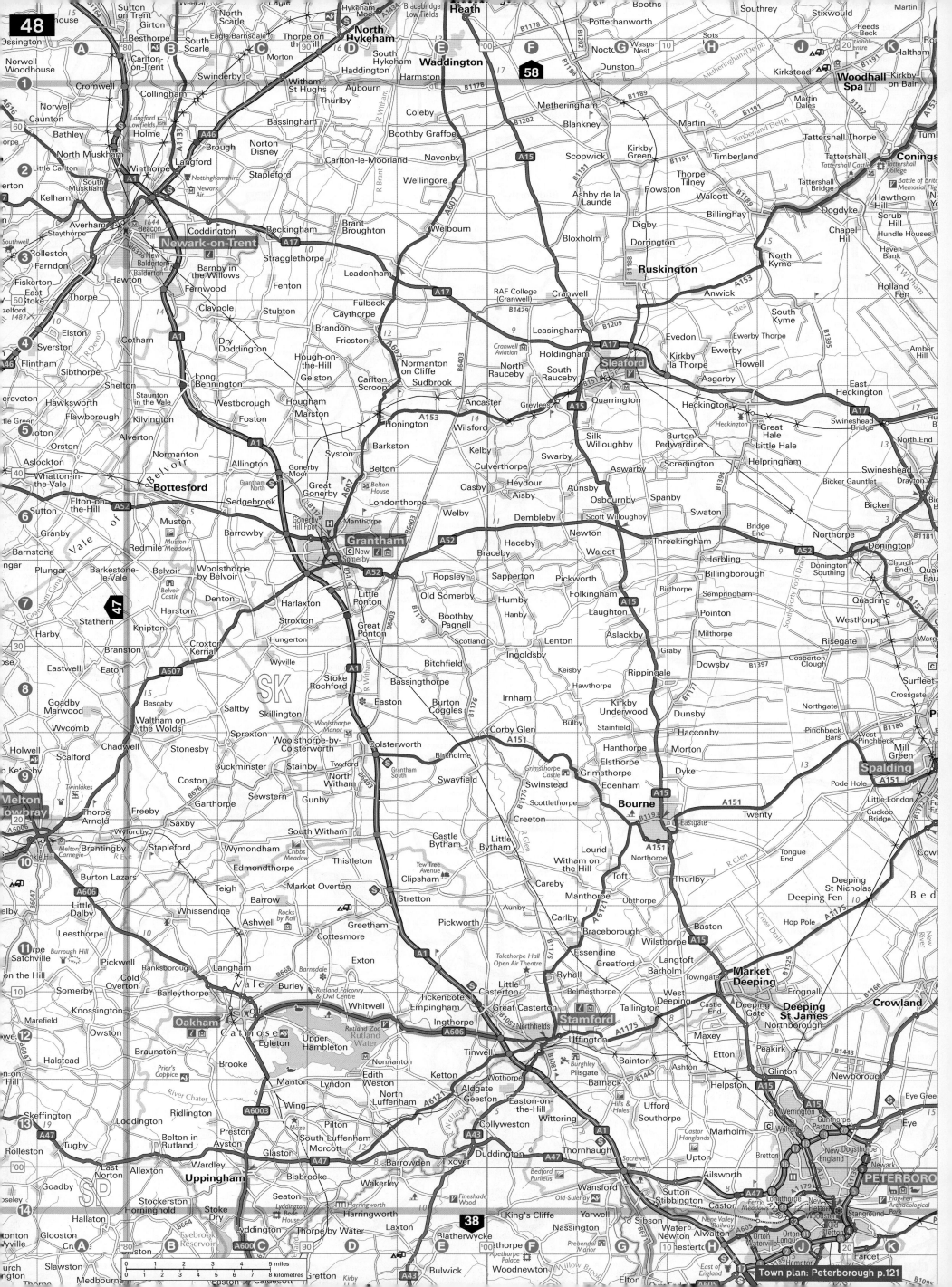

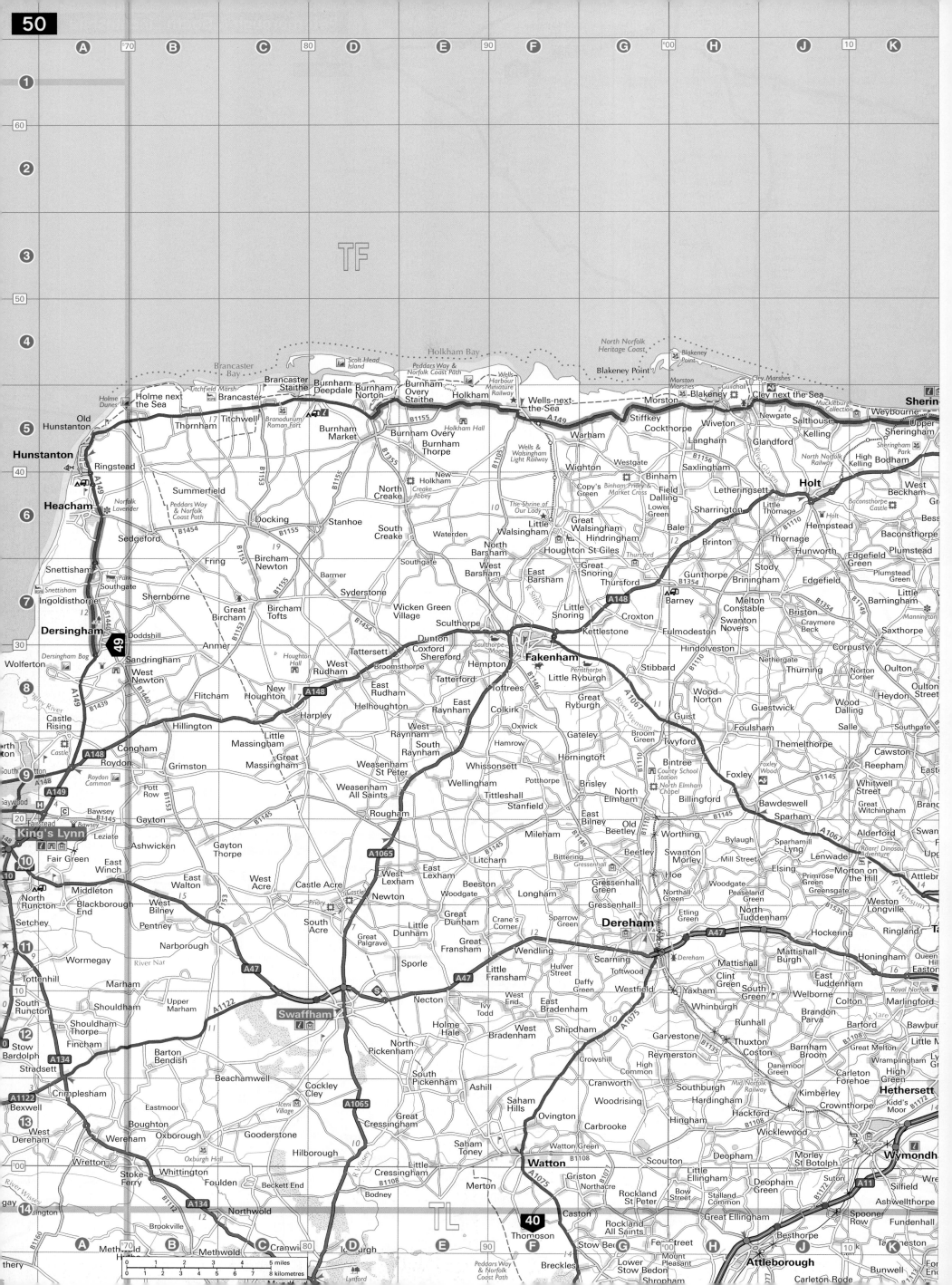

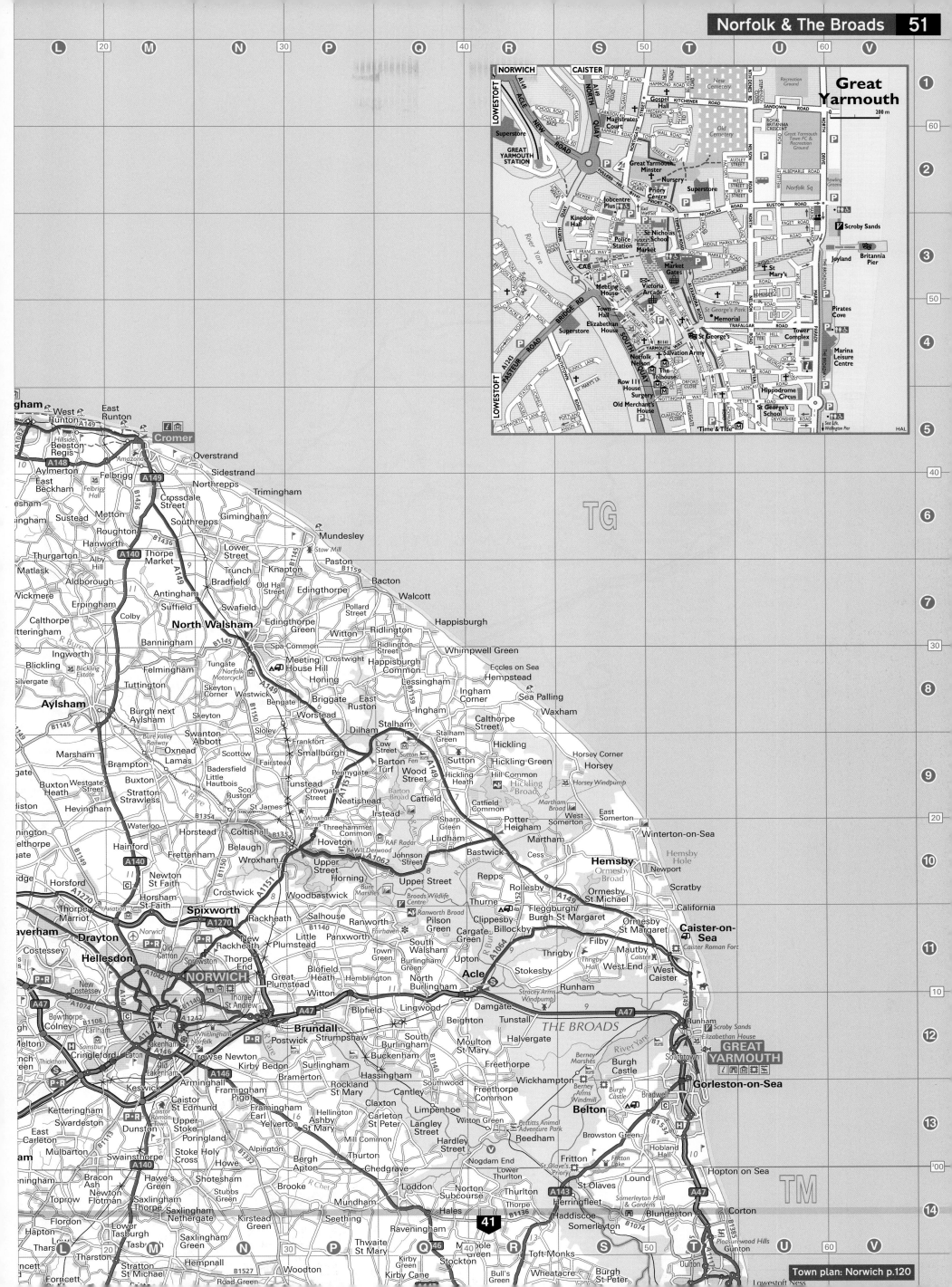

L 20 M N 30 P Q 40 R S 50 T U 60 V

NORWICH CAISTER

Great Yarmouth

200 m

Gospel Hall
New Cemetery
Recreation Ground
Magistrates Court
Superstore
GREAT YARMOUTH STATION
Great Yarmouth Minster
Jobcentre Plus
Nursery
Kingdom Hall
Superstore
Priory Centre
Police Station
St Nicholas School
Market
Old Cemetery
Royal Britannia Crescent
Great Yarmouth Town FC & Recreation Ground
Norfolk Sq
Scroby Sands
Meeting House
CAB
Market Gates
Victoria Arcade
St Mary's
Joyland
Britannia Pier
Town Hall
Elizabethan House
St George's Park
Memorial
Pirates Cove
Superstore
St George's
Salvation Army
Norfolk Nelson
The Tolhouse
Marina Leisure Centre
Row 111 House
House Surgery
Hippodrome Circus
Old Merchant's House
St George's School
'Time & Tide'
Sea Life, Wellington Pier
HAL

TG

1 / 60
2
3 / 50
4
5 / 40

gham West Runton East Runton
Cromer
Overstrand
Hillside Beeston Regis
Amazona
Sidestrand
Aylmerton Felbrigg
Northrepps
East Beckham Felbrigg Hall
Crossdale Street
Trimingham
esham Metton Roughton Southrepps Gimingham
Sustead Hanworth
Mundesley
gingham Thurgarton Alby Hill Thorpe Market Lower Street Stow Mill
Matlask Aldborough Antingham Bradfield Paston Knapton B1159
Wickmere Erpingham Colby Suffield Swafield Old Hall Street Bacton Walcott
Calthorpe North Walsham Edingthorpe Pollard Street
tteringham Ingworth Banningham B1145 Edingthorpe Green Ridlington Happisburgh
Blickling Felmingham Spa Common Witton Ridlington Street Whimpwell Green
Silvergate Blickling Estate Tungate Meeting House Hill Crostwight Happisburgh Eccles on Sea
Tuttington Norfolk Motorcycle Honing Common Hempstead
Aylsham Skeyton Corner Westwick Bengate Lessingham Sea Palling
Burgh next Aylsham Skeyton Briggate East Ruston Ingham Corner Waxham
Marsham Bure Valley Railway Swanton Abbott Sloley Worstead Ingham
Brampton Oxnead Scottow Frankfort Dilham Calthorpe Street Hickling
Buxton Lamas Badersfield Smallburgh Stalham Hickling Green Horsey Corner
Westgate Street Little Hautbois Fairstead Low Street Stalham Green Hickling Heath Horsey
Buxton Heath Stratton Strawless Sco Ruston Tunstead Pennygate Barton Turf Sutton Hill Common Horsey Windpump
Hevingham Waterloo St James Crowgate Street Wood Street Sutton Fen Hickling Broad
Neatishead Catfield Barton Broad Catfield Common East Somerton
R Bure Horstead Coltishall Threehammer Common Irstead Martham Broad West Somerton
Hainford Belaugh Wroxham Barns Sharp Green Ludham Martham Winterton-on-Sea
nington Frettenham Hoveton RAF Radar Potter Heigham Cess Hemsby Hole
elthorpe Horsham Wroxham BeWILDerwood Johnson Street Bastwick Martham
A140 St Faith A1062 Upper Street Horning Repps Ormesby Broad Hemsby Newport
idge Horsford Newton St Faith Crostwick Woodbastwick Upper Street Thurne Rollesby Ormesby St Michael Scratby
Thorpe Marriot Rackheath Salhouse Ranworth Broads Wildlife Centre Clippesby California
Aviation Spixworth New Rackheath Pilson Green Fleggburgh/ Ormesby St Margaret
averham Drayton Norwich Old Catton Thorpe End Ranworth Broad Cargate Green Burgh St Margaret Caister-on-Sea
Hellesdon A1270 Sprowston Fairhaven Town Green Billockby Caister Roman Fort
New Costessey Panxworth South Walsham Filby Mautby West End
NORWICH Great Plumstead Blofield Heath Hemblington Burlingham Green Thrigby West Caister
A47 Bowthorpe Thorpe St Andrew Witton North Burlingham Thrigby Hall West Caister
Colney Earlham A47 Blofield Lingwood **Acle** Upton Stokesby Runham
A1074 A11 B1140 Postwick Strumpshaw Damgate Stracey Arms Windpump
Melton Sainsbury's Whitlingham Norfolk South Burlingham Beighton Tunstall THE BROADS A47 Runham
nch Cringleford Eaton Lakenham Trowse Newton Buckenham Moulton St Mary Halvergate River Yare Scroby Sands
Thickthorn Kirby Bedon Surlingham Freethorpe Elizabethan House **GREAT YARMOUTH**
Keswick Armingland Bramerton Hassingham Southwood Berney Marshes Southtown
Framingham Pigot Rockland St Mary Cantley Freethorpe Common Berney Arms Windmill **Gorleston-on-Sea**
Caister St Edmund Upper Stoke Framingham Earl Claxton Wickhampton Burgh Castle
Ketteringham Caister Roman Town Yelverton Carleton St Peter Burgh Castle
Swardeston Dunston Poringland Hellington Limpenhoe Witton Green Pettitts Animal Adventure Park **Belton**
am East Carleton Stoke Holy Cross Ashby St Mary Langley Street Browston Green B1534
Mulbarton Howe Alpington Mill Common Hardley Street Reedham Hobland Hall
Bracon Ash Hawe's Green Bergh Apton Thurton Chedgrave Nogdam End St Olave's Priory Fritton Lake Hopton on Sea
Newton Flotman Shotesham Brooke R Chet Lower Thurlton Fritton Corton
Toprow Green Stubbs Green Loddon Norton Subcourse St Olaves TM
Flordon Saxlingham Thorpe Mundham Thurlton Somerleyton Hall & Gardens A47
am Hapton Saxlingham Nethergate Kirstead Green Seething Hales A143 Haddiscoe Somerleyton Blundeston
Thars Lower Tasburgh Thwaite St Mary Ravingham Herringfleet Gunton
Stratton St Michael Saxlingham Green **41** Stockton Bull's Green Burgh St Peter Pleasurewood Hills
ncett Tasburgh Hempnall Woodton Kirby Green Wheatacre Oulton
Forncett B1527 Kirby Cane Toft Monks

L 20 M N 30 P Q 46 R 40 S 50 T 60 U V
Lowestoft Ness

6 / 40
7 / 30
8 / 20
9
10 / 20
11 / 10
12
13 / '00
14

Town plan: Norwich p.120

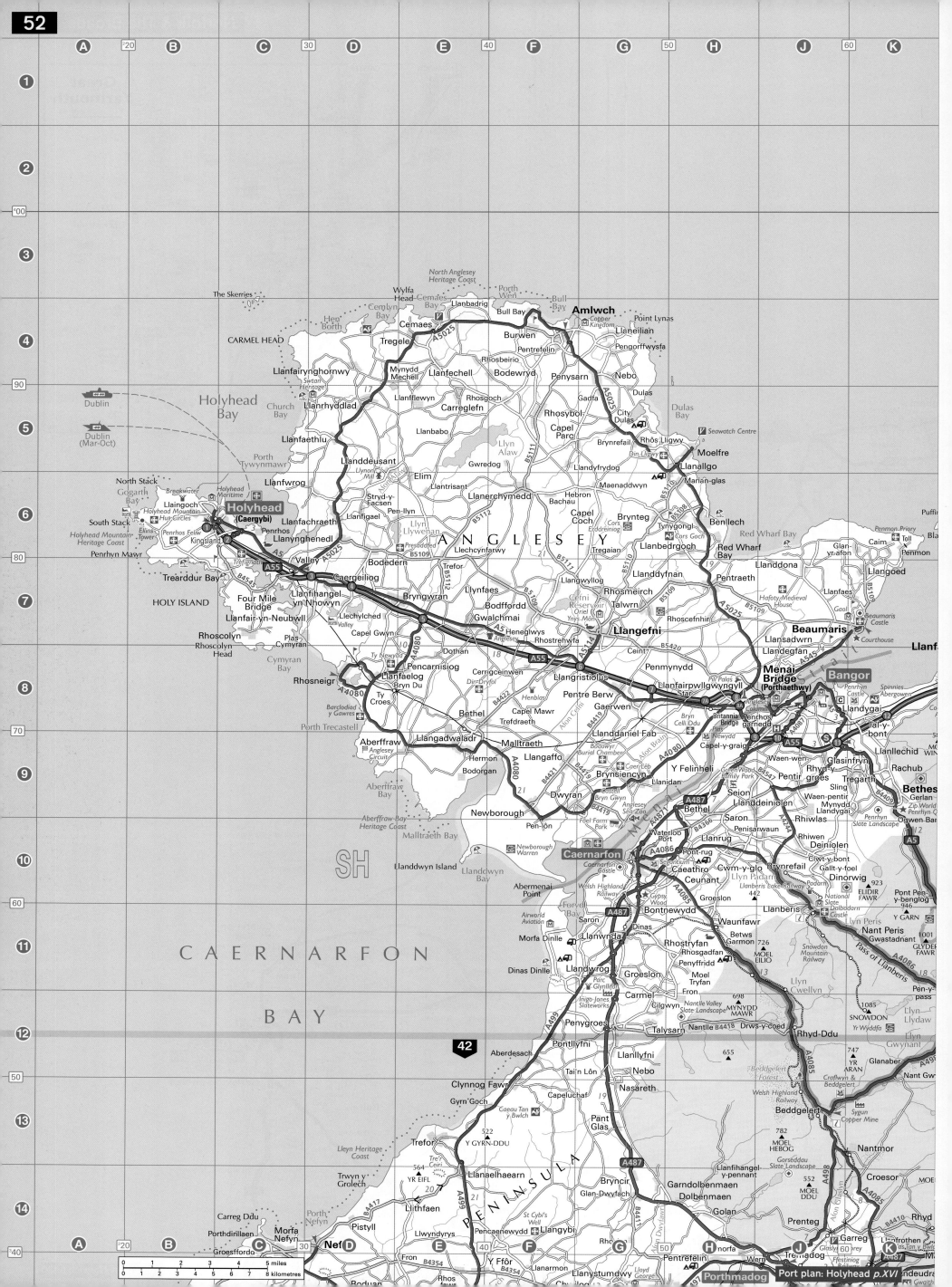

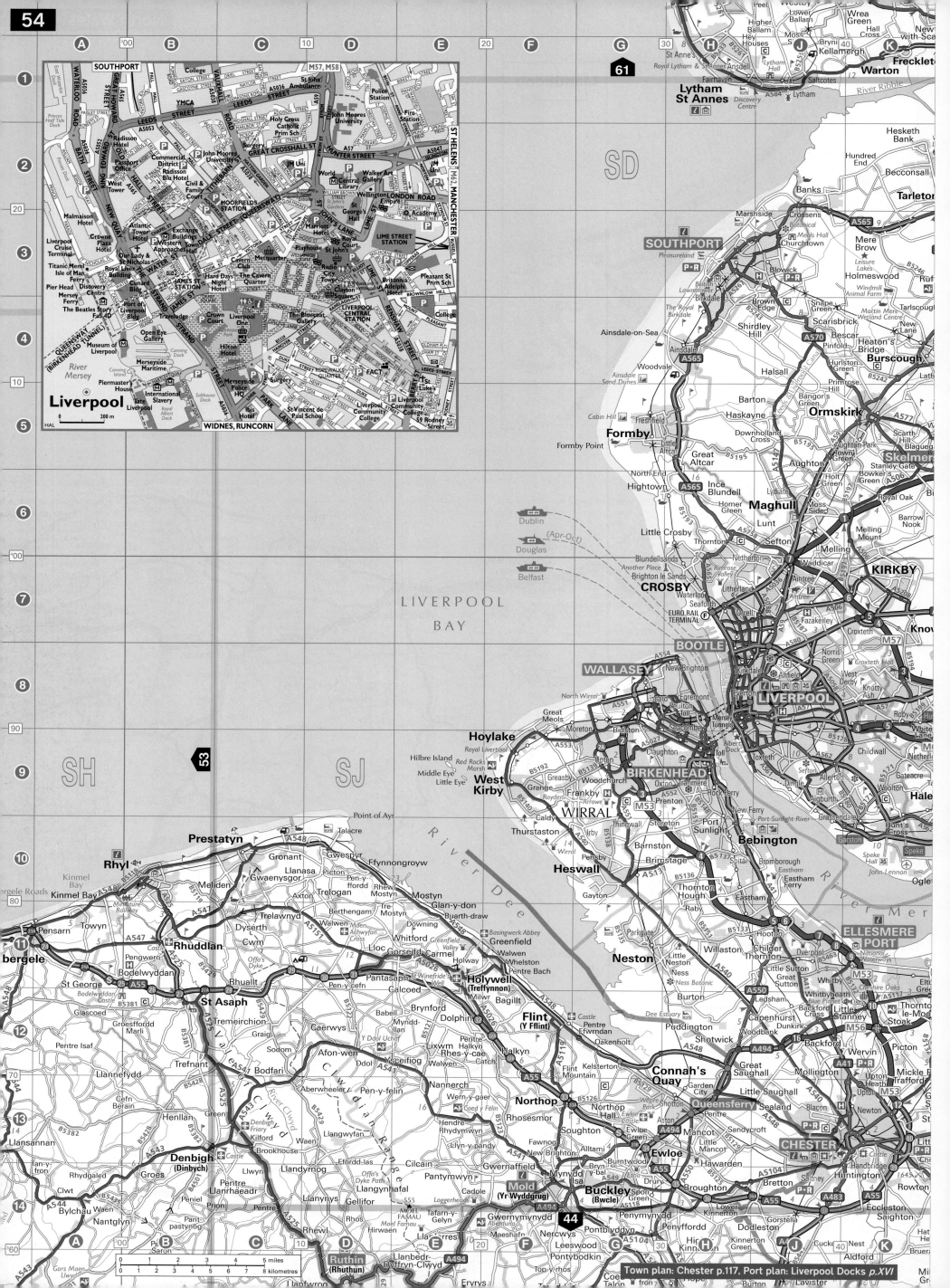

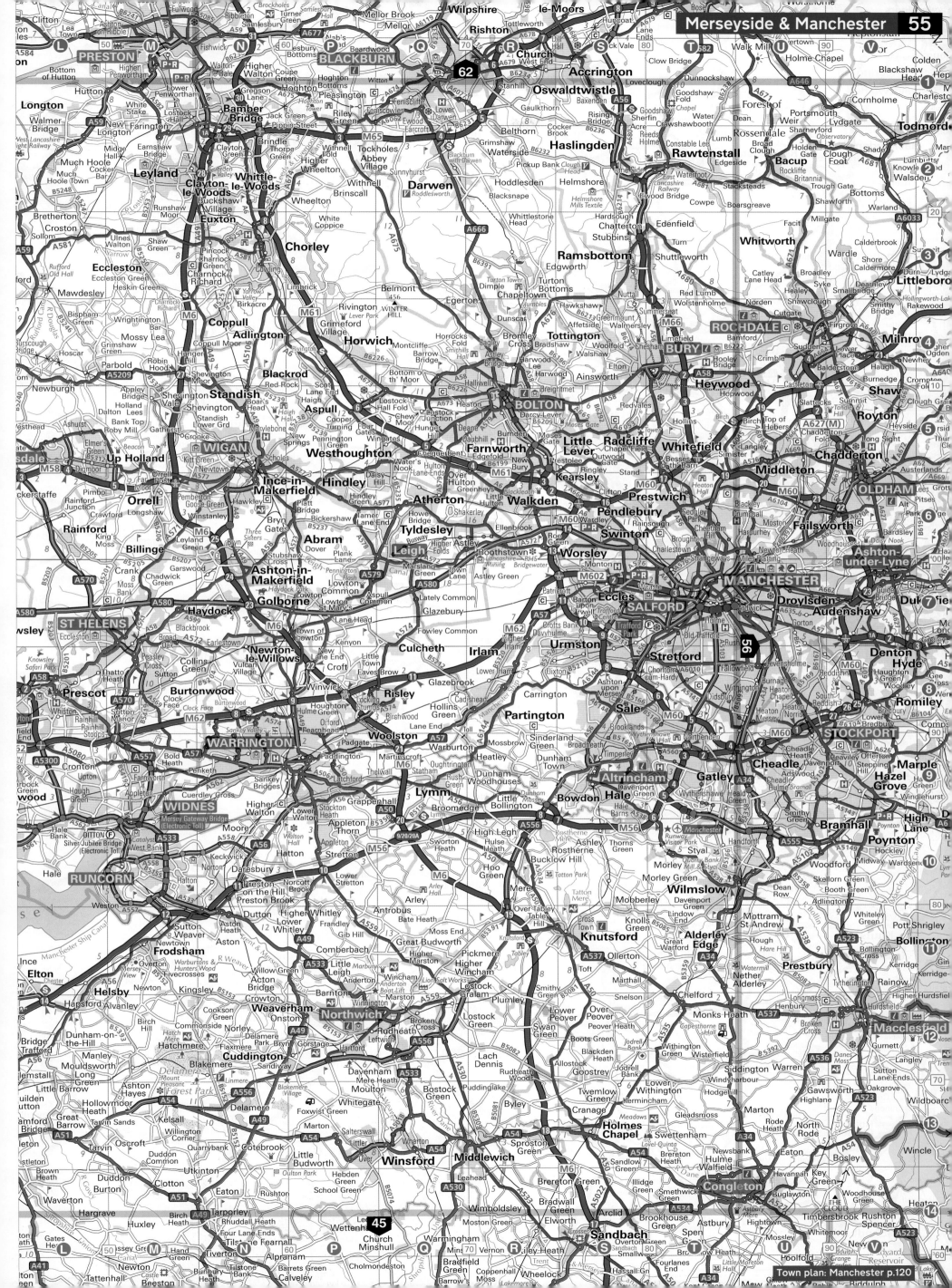

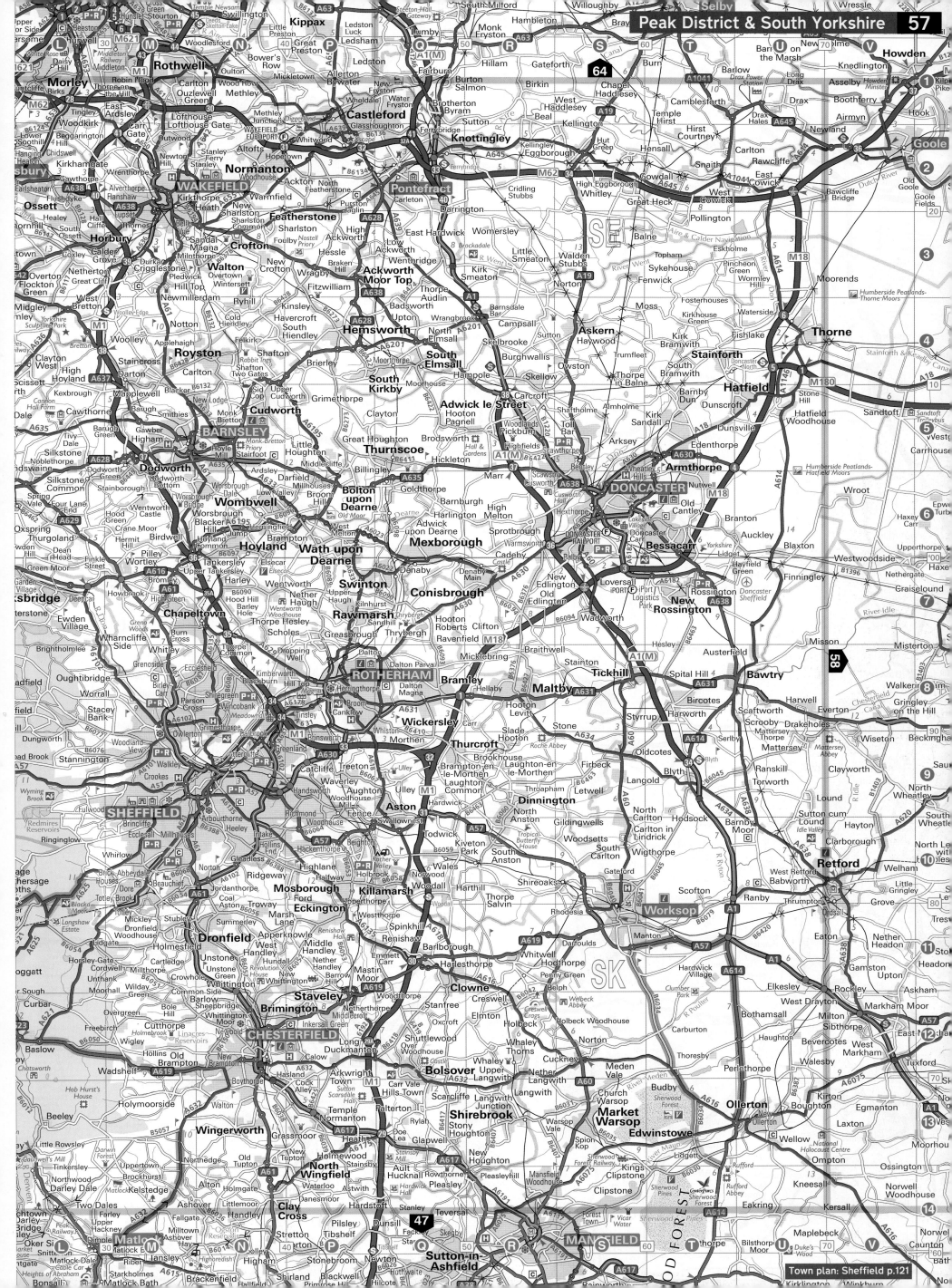

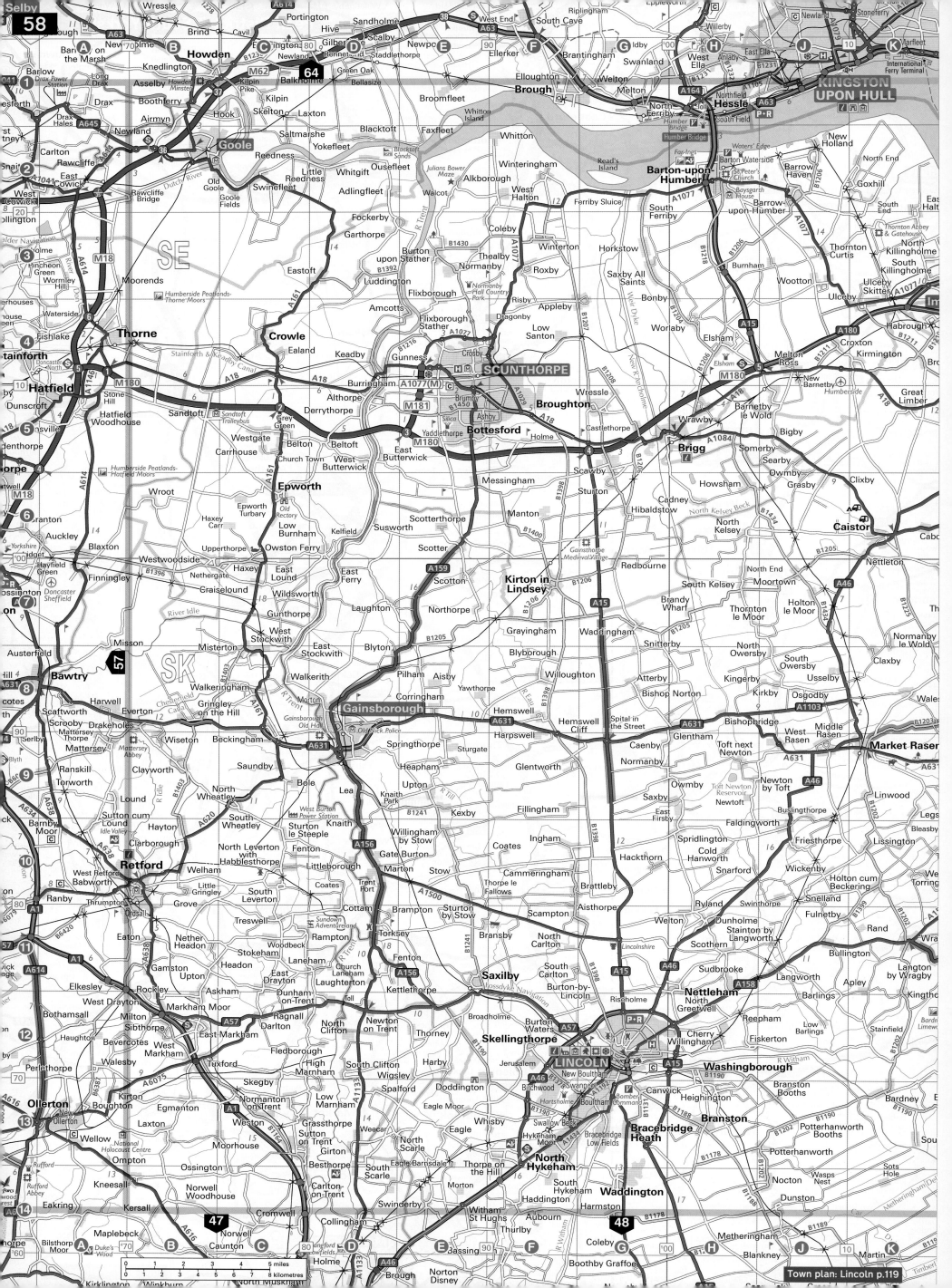

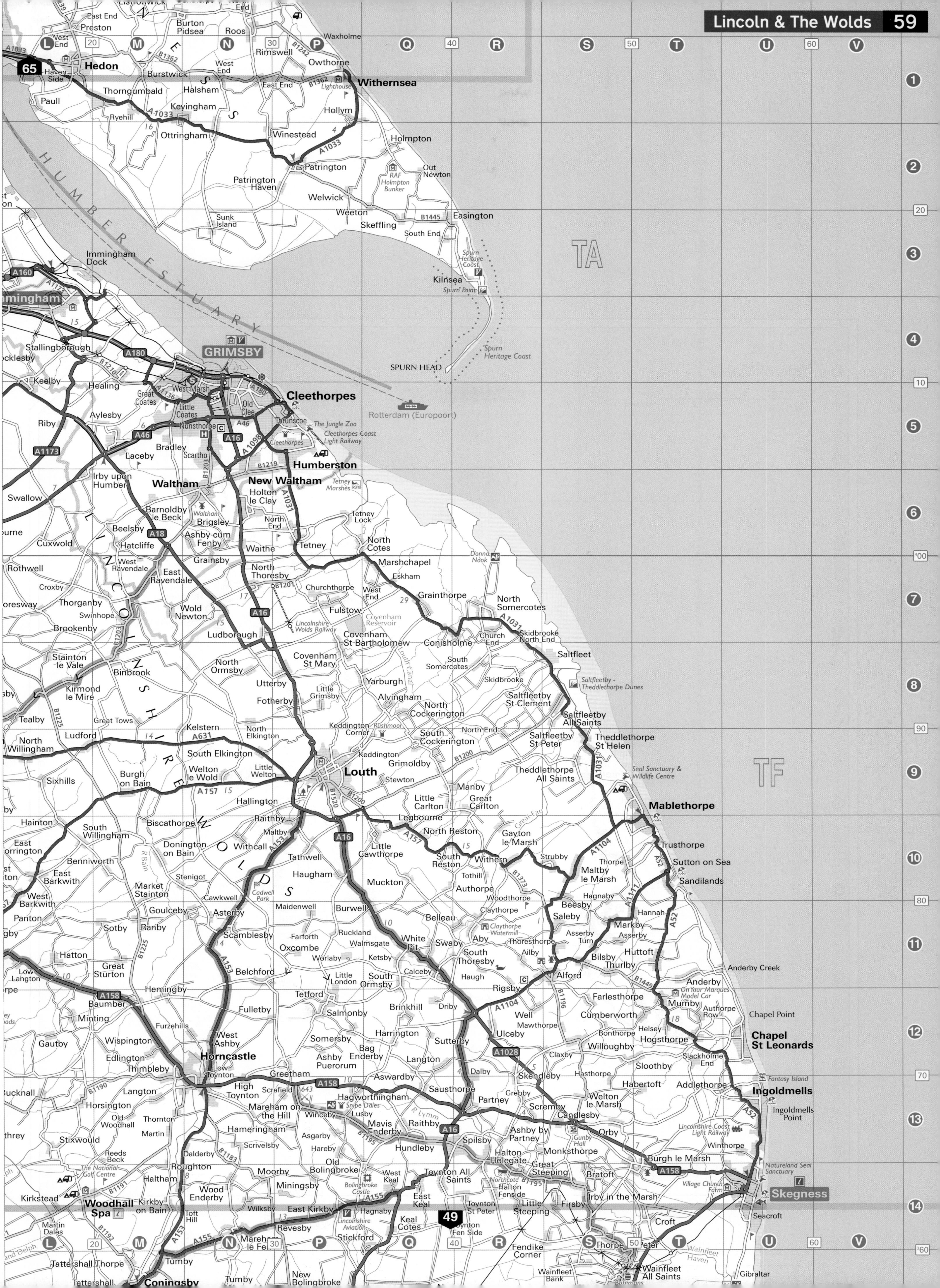
Hedon
Preston
East End
Burton Pidsea
Roos
Waxholme
Rimswell
Owthorne
Withernsea
Lighthouse
Burstwick
West End
Halsham
Thorngumbald
Paull
Keyingham
Ryehill
Ottringham
Hollym
Winestead
Holmpton
Patrington
RAF Holmpton Bunker
Out Newton
Patrington Haven
Welwick
Weeton
Skeffling
Easington
South End
Sunk Island
Immingham Dock
Immingham
HUMBER ESTUARY
TA
Spurn Heritage Coast
Kilnsea
Spurn Point
SPURN HEAD
Stallingborough
Keelby
Healing
GRIMSBY
West Marsh
Great Coates
Little Coates
Old Clee
Cleethorpes
Rotterdam (Europoort)
Riby
Aylesby
Nunsthorpe
Thrunscoe
The Jungle Zoo
Cleethorpes Coast Light Railway
Bradley
Scartho
Laceby
Humberston
Irby upon Humber
Waltham
New Waltham
Tetney Marshes
Holton le Clay
Swallow
Barnoldby le Beck
Brigsley
Tetney Lock
North End
Beelsby
Ashby cum Fenby
Cuxwold
Hatcliffe
Waithe
Tetney
North Cotes
West Ravendale
Grainsby
Marshchapel
Donna Nook
Rothwell
East Ravendale
North Thoresby
Eskham
Croxby
Churchthorpe
West End
Grainthorpe
North Somercotes
Thorganby
Swinhope
Wold Newton
Fulstow
Covenham Reservoir
Lincolnshire Wolds Railway
Brookenby
Ludborough
Covenham St Bartholomew
Conisholme
Church End
Skidbrooke North End
Saltfleet
Stainton le Vale
Binbrook
North Ormsby
Covenham St Mary
South Somercotes
Saltfleetby - Theddlethorpe Dunes
Kirmond le Mire
Utterby
Little Grimsby
Yarburgh
Skidbrooke
Fotherby
Alvingham
Saltfleetby St Clement
North Cockerington
Tealby
Great Tows
Kelstern
Keddington Corner
Rushmoor
Saltfleetby All Saints
North Elkington
South Cockerington
North End
Saltfleetby St Peter
Theddlethorpe St Helen
Ludford
North Willingham
South Elkington
Keddington
Grimoldby
Sixhills
Burgh on Bain
Welton le Wold
Little Welton
Louth
Stewton
Theddlethorpe All Saints
Seal Sanctuary & Wildlife Centre
TF
Hallington
Manby
Great Carlton
Little Carlton
Mablethorpe
Hainton
Biscathorpe
Raithby
Legbourne
South Willingham
Maltby
North Reston
Gayton le Marsh
Trusthorpe
East Torrington
Donington on Bain
Withcall
Tathwell
Little Cawthorpe
South Reston
Withern
Strubby
Thorpe
Sutton on Sea
Benniworth
Haugham
Tothill
Maltby le Marsh
Sandilands
East Barkwith
Stenigot
Muckton
Authorpe
Hagnaby
Market Stainton
Cawkwell
Cadwell Park
Woodthorpe
Beesby
Hannah
West Barkwith
Maidenwell
Burwell
Claythorpe
Saleby
Panton
Goulceby
Asterby
Belleau
Claythorpe Watermill
Markby
Asserby Turn
Asserby
Sotby
Ranby
Scamblesby
Farforth
Ruckland
Walmsgate
White Pit
Swaby
Aby
Thoresthorpe
Oxcombe
Hatton
Worlaby
Ketsby
South Thoresby
Ailby
Bilsby
Thurlby
Huttoft
Great Sturton
Belchford
Little London
South Ormsby
Calceby
Haugh
Alford
Anderby Creek
Low Langton
Rigsby
Anderby
Baumber
Hemingby
Tetford
Farlesthorpe
On Your Marques Model Car
Mumby
Minting
Fulletby
Salmonby
Brinkhill
Driby
Well
Cumberworth
Authorpe Row
Chapel Point
Furzehills
Mawthorpe
Helsey
Gautby
Wispington
West Ashby
Somersby
Harrington
Sutterby
Ulceby
Bonthorpe
Willoughby
Hogsthorpe
Chapel St Leonards
Edlington
Horncastle
Bag Enderby
Ashby Puerorum
Claxby
Slackholme End
Thimbleby
Low Toynton
Greetham
Langton
Dalby
Skendleby
Hasthorpe
Sloothby
Fantasy Island
Bucknall
Langton
High Toynton
Scrafield
Aswardby
Sausthorpe
Grebby
Habertoft
Addlethorpe
Ingoldmells
Hagworthingham
Snipe Dales
Partney
Welton le Marsh
Ingoldmells Point
Horsington
Mareham on the Hill
Lusby
Scremby
Candlesby
Old Woodhall
Thornton
Winceby
Mavis Enderby
Raithby
Gunby Hall
Orby
Lincolnshire Coast Light Railway
Martin
Hameringham
Ashby by Partney
Stixwould
Scrivelsby
Asgarby
Hareby
Hundleby
Spilsby
Winthorpe
Reeds Beck
Dalderby
Monksthorpe
Burgh le Marsh
The National Golf Centre
Roughton
Old Bolingbroke
Halton Holegate
Great Steeping
Bratoft
Natureland Seal Sanctuary
Haltham
Moorby
West Keal
Toynton All Saints
Northcote
Halton Fenside
Village Church Farm
Wood Enderby
Miningsby
Bolingbroke Castle
East Keal
Skegness
Kirkstead
Woodhall Spa
Kirkby on Bain
Wilksby
East Kirkby
Lincolnshire Aviation
Toynton St Peter
Little Steeping
Firsby
Irby in the Marsh
Croft
Seacroft
Toft Hill
Hagnaby
Keal Cotes
Toynton Fen Side
Martin Dales
Revesby
Stickford
Mareham le Fen
Fendike Corner
Thorpe
Peter
Wainfleet Haven
Tattershall Thorpe
Tumby
New Bolingbroke
Wainfleet Bank
Wainfleet All Saints
Gibraltar
Tattershall
Coningsby
LINCOLNSHIRE WOLDS
HOLDERNESS

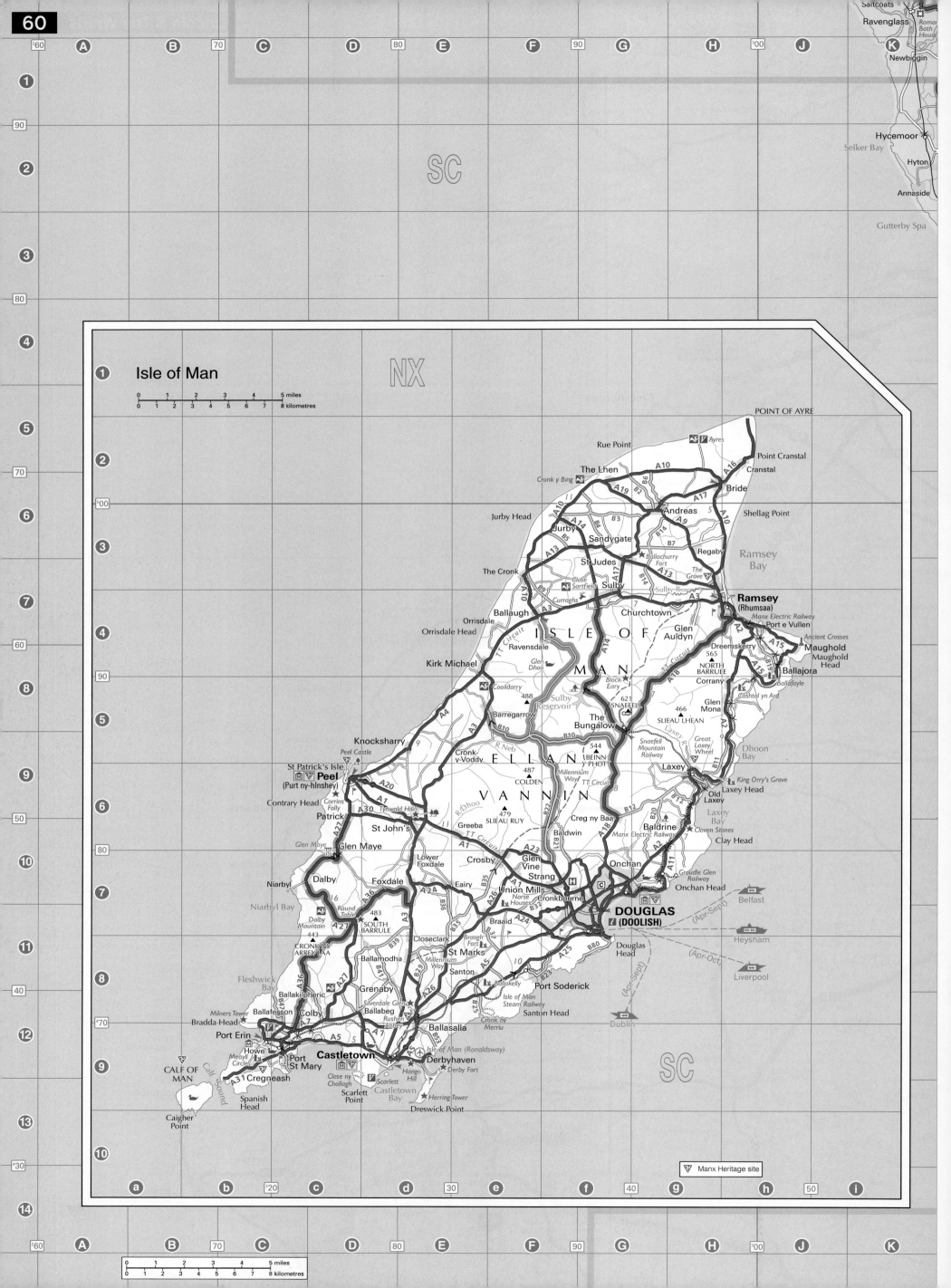

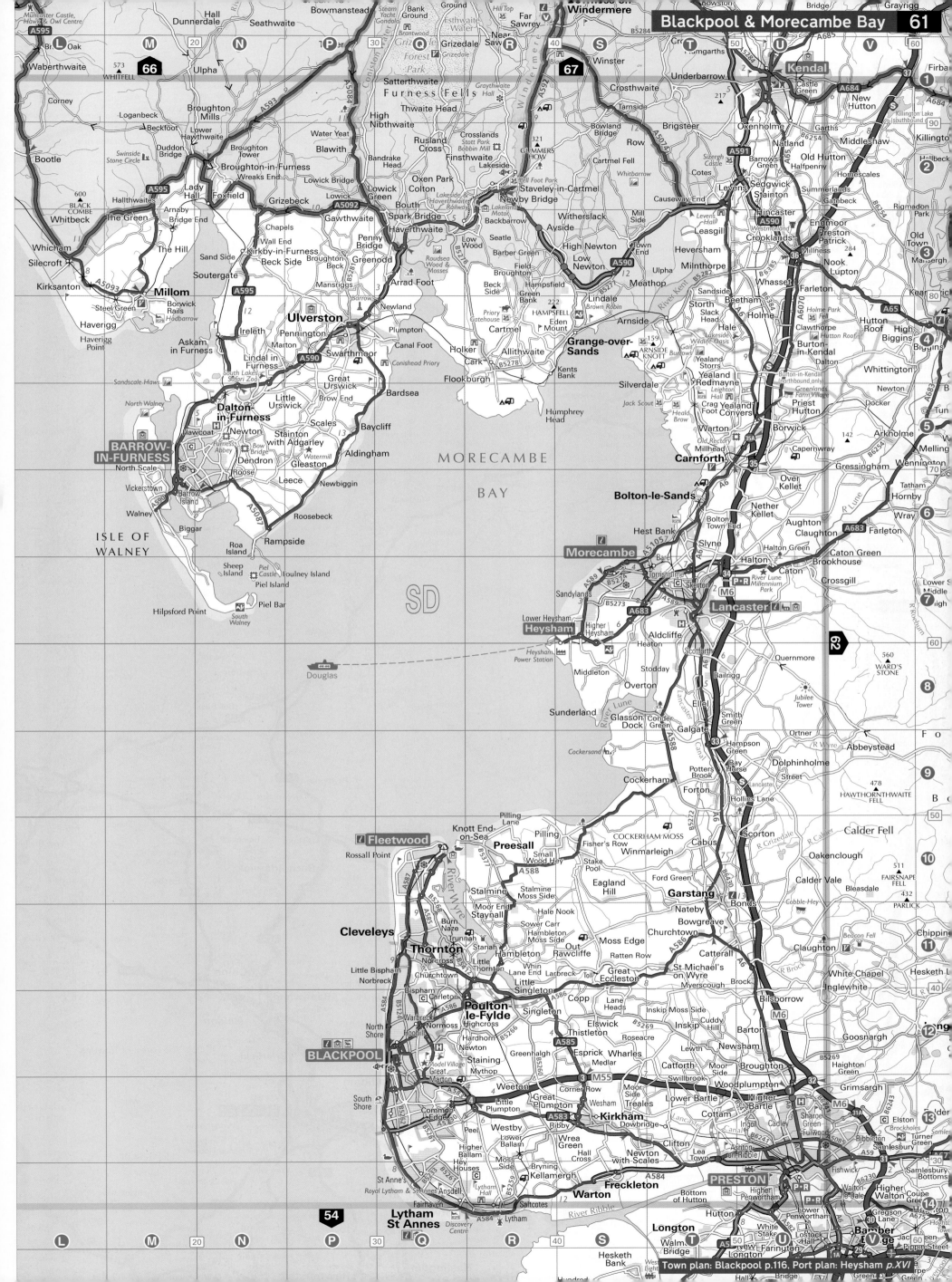

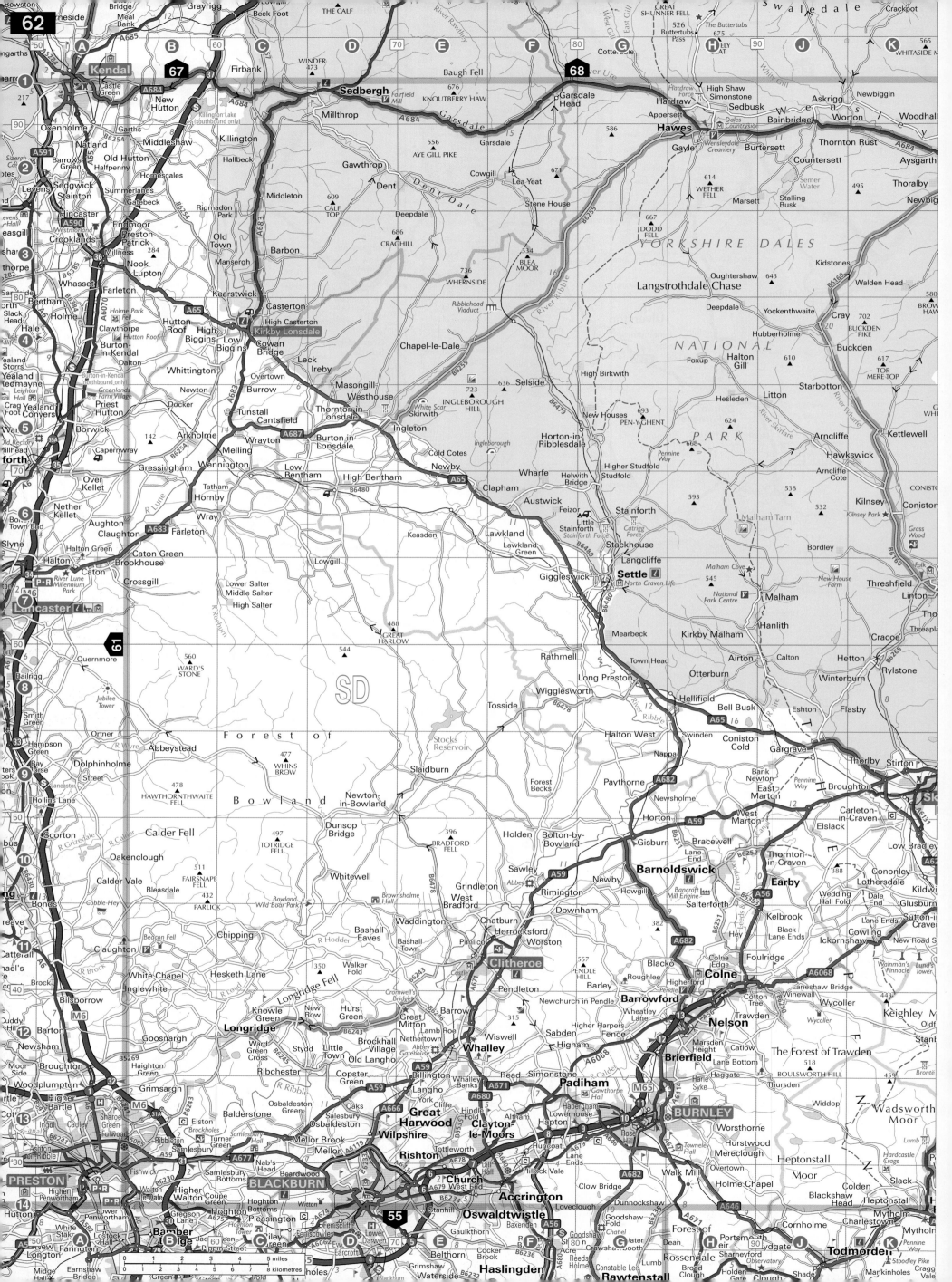

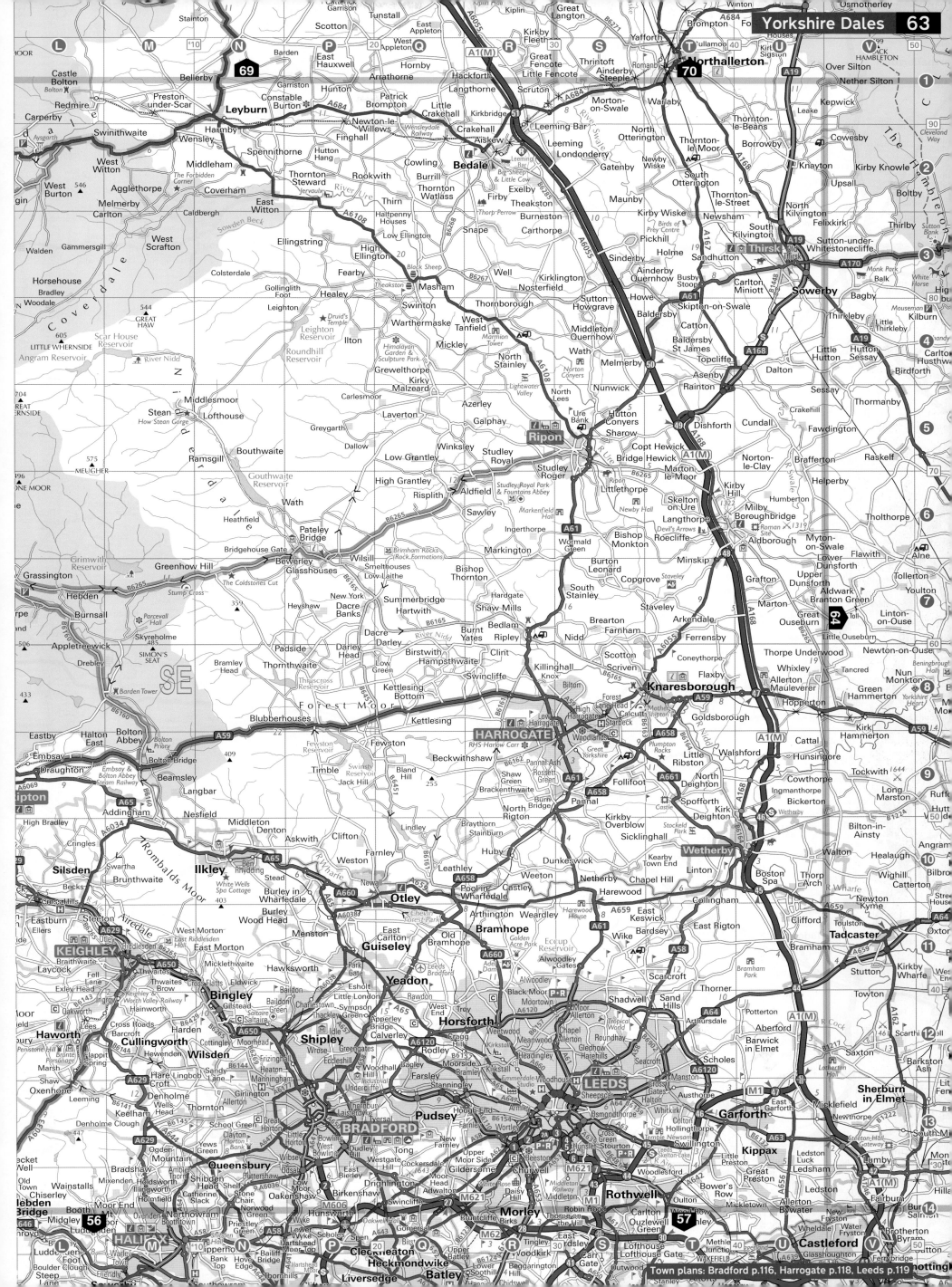

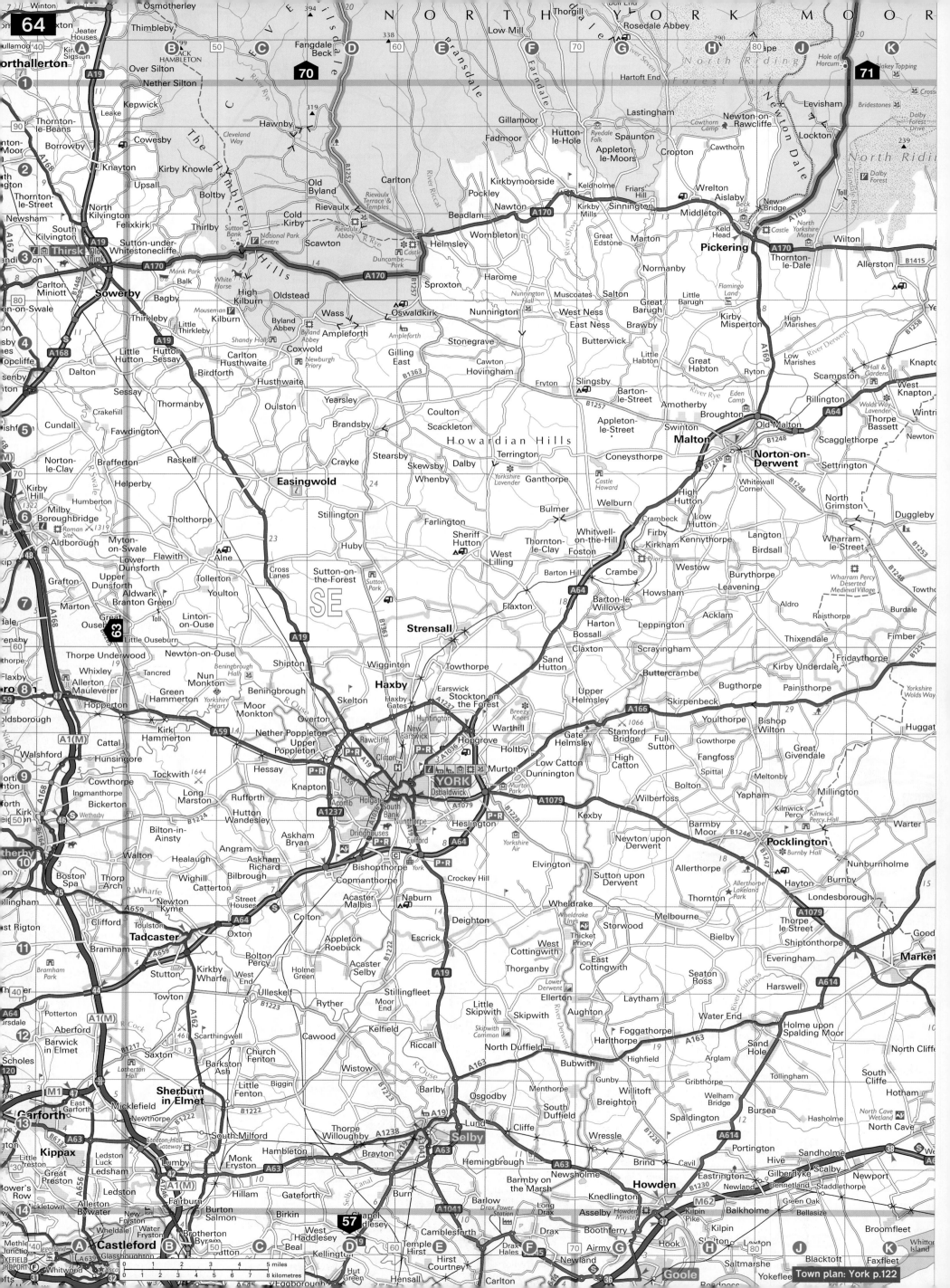

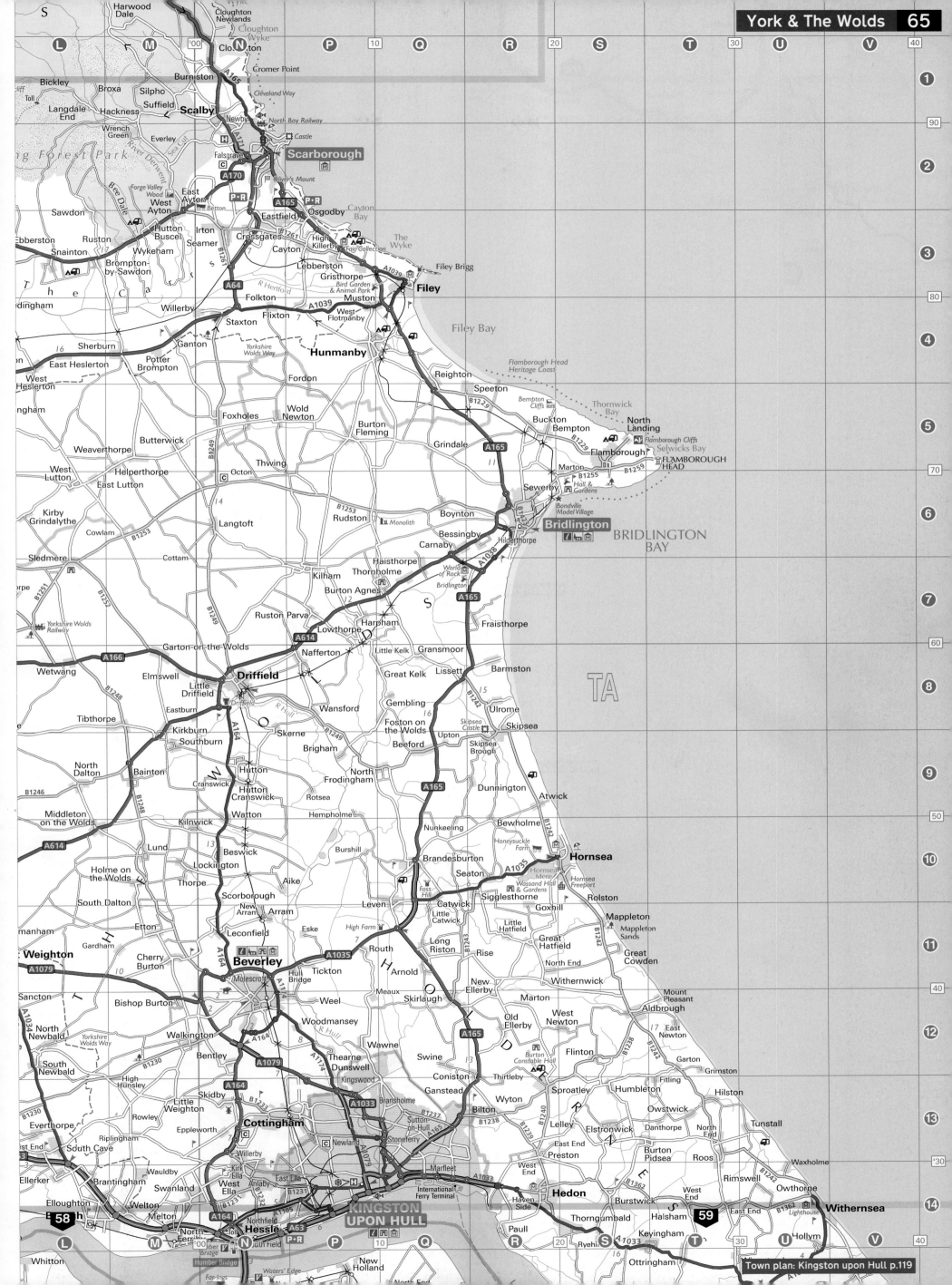

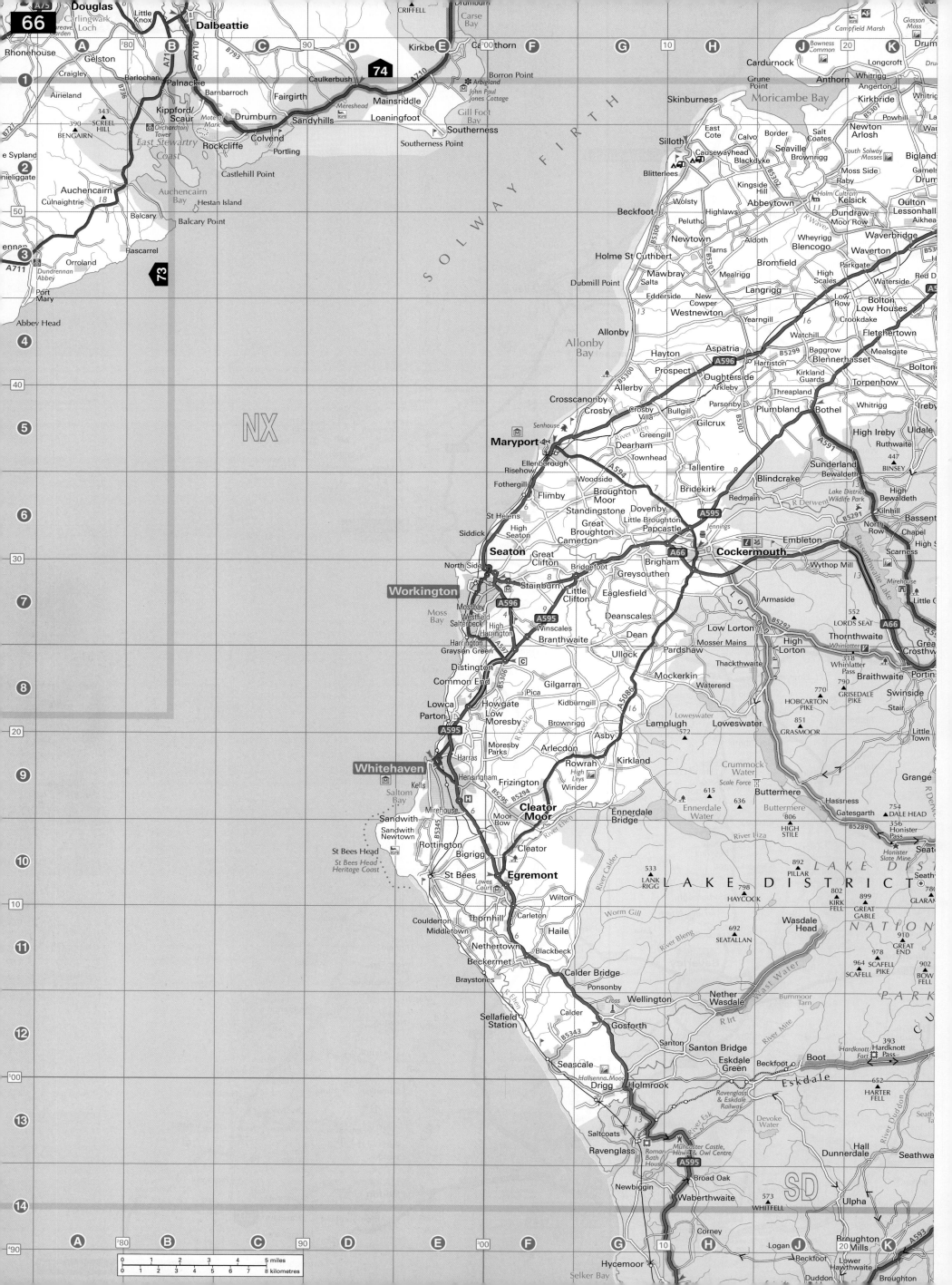

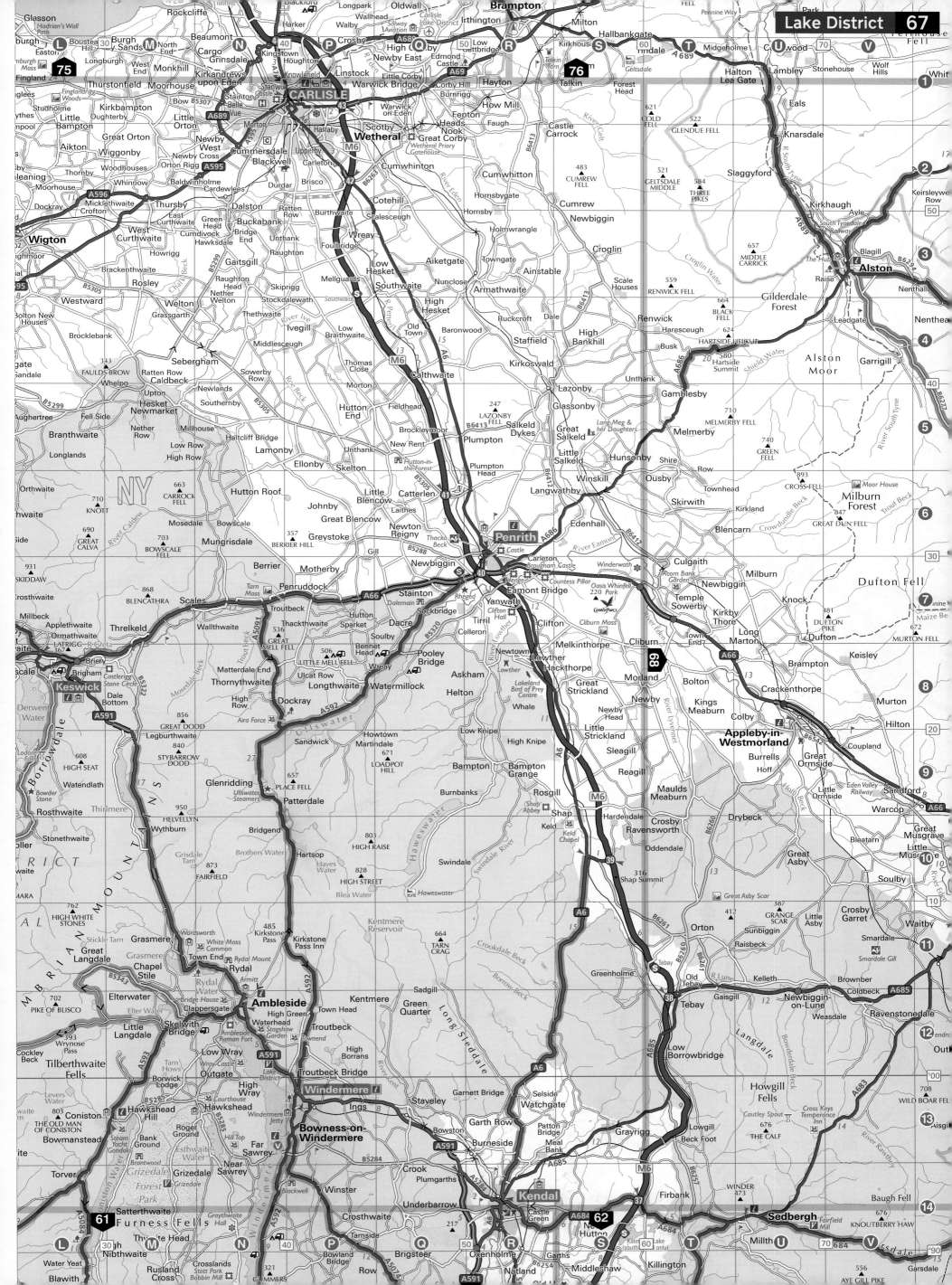

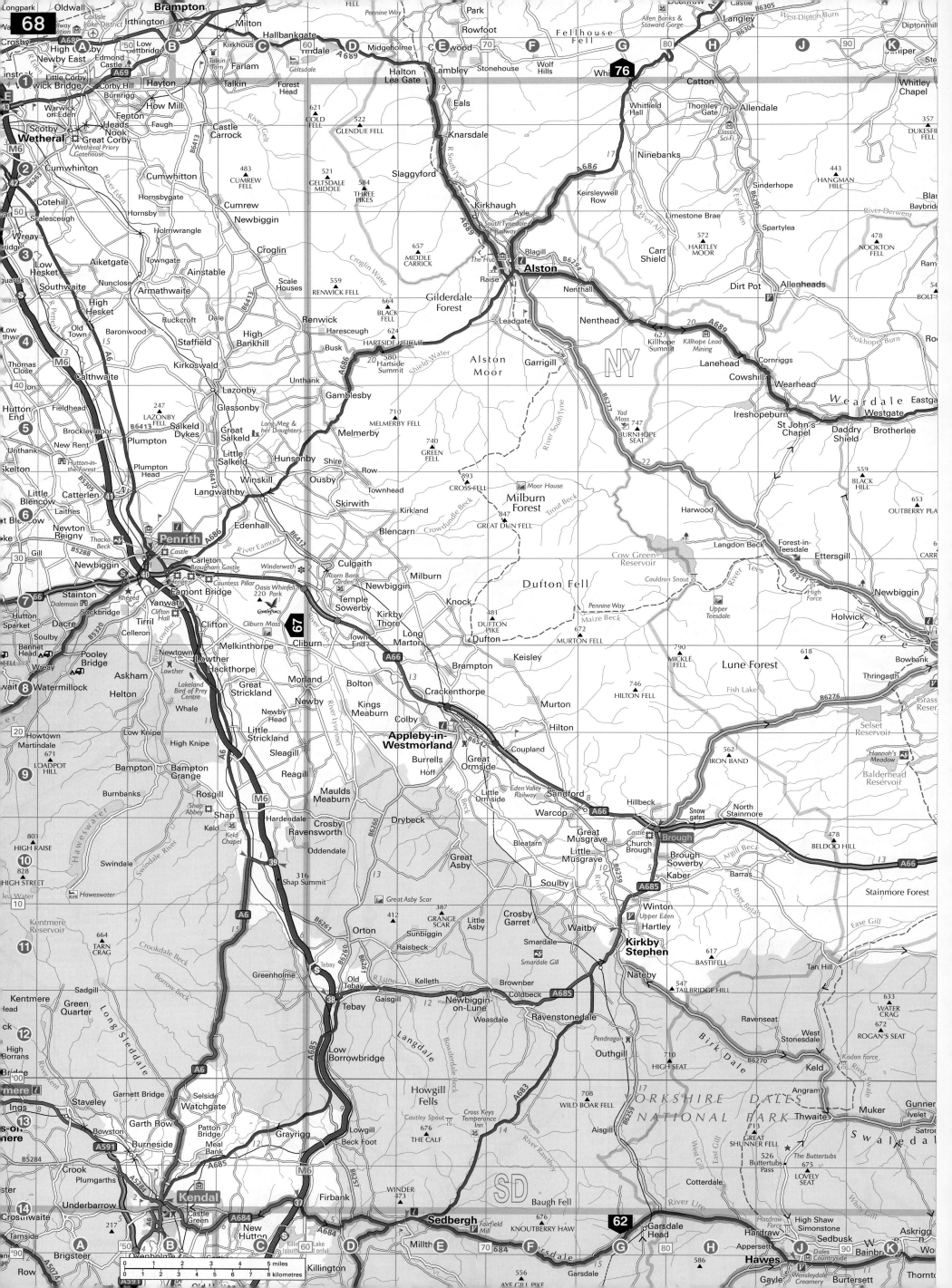

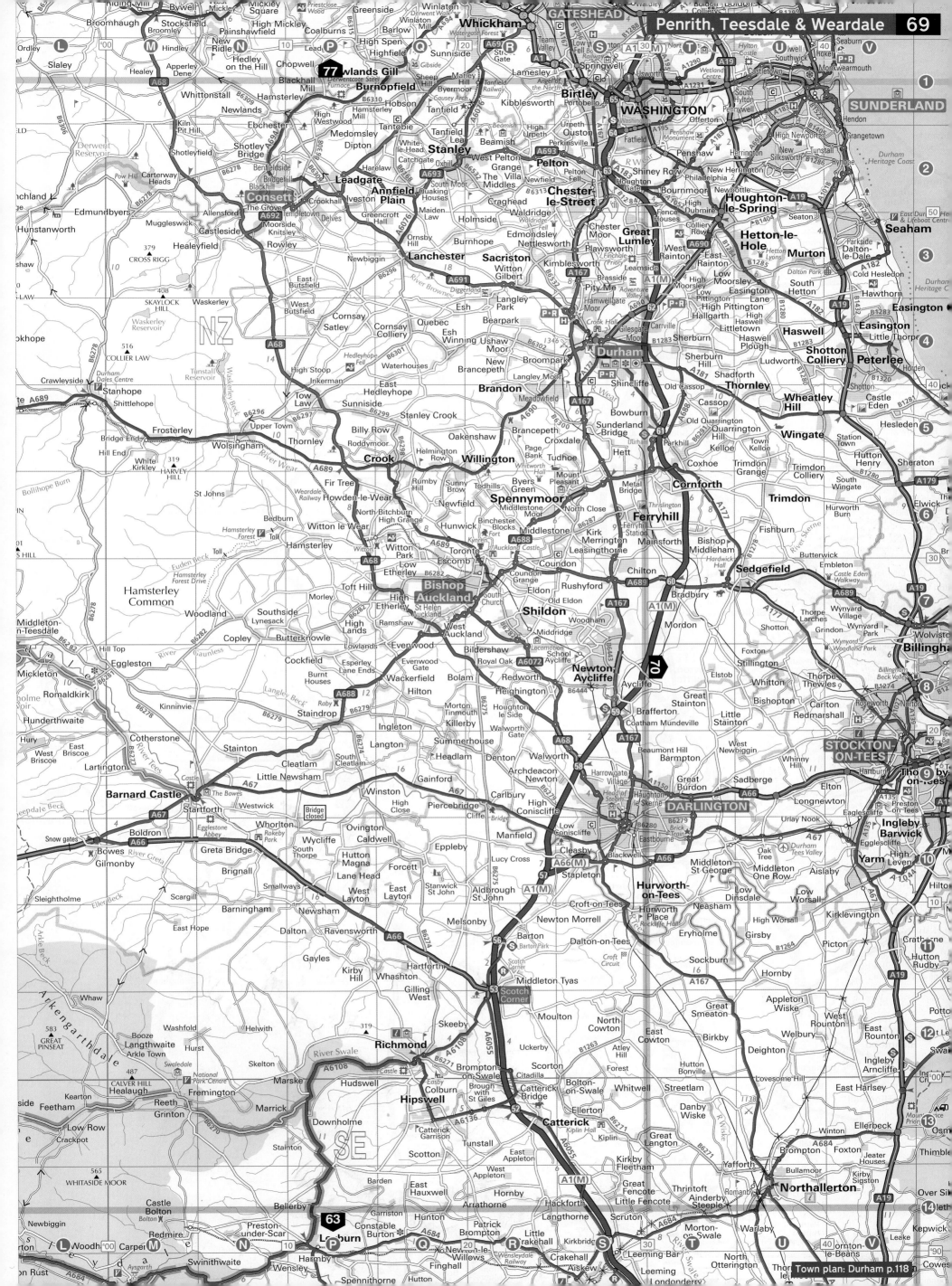

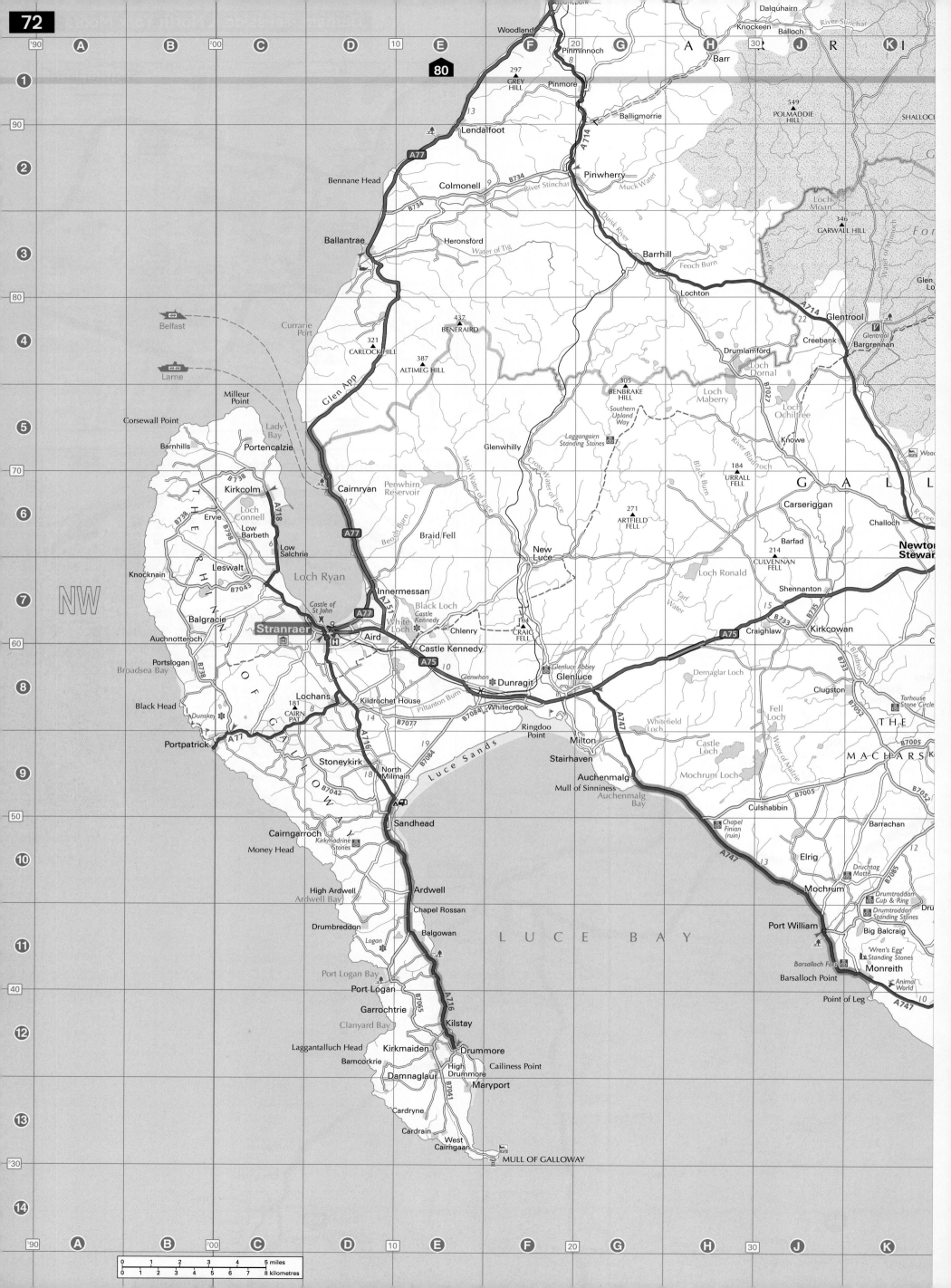

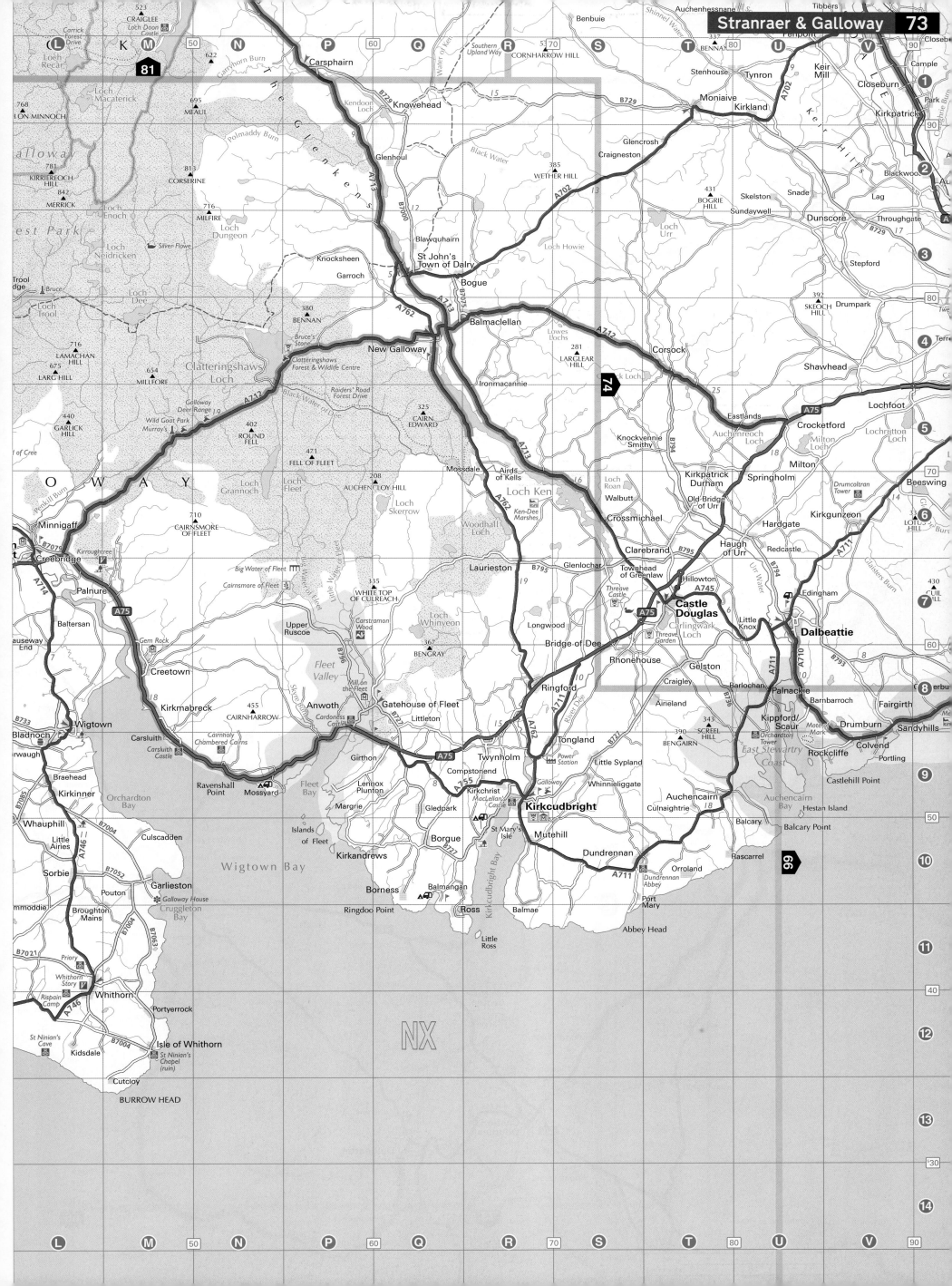

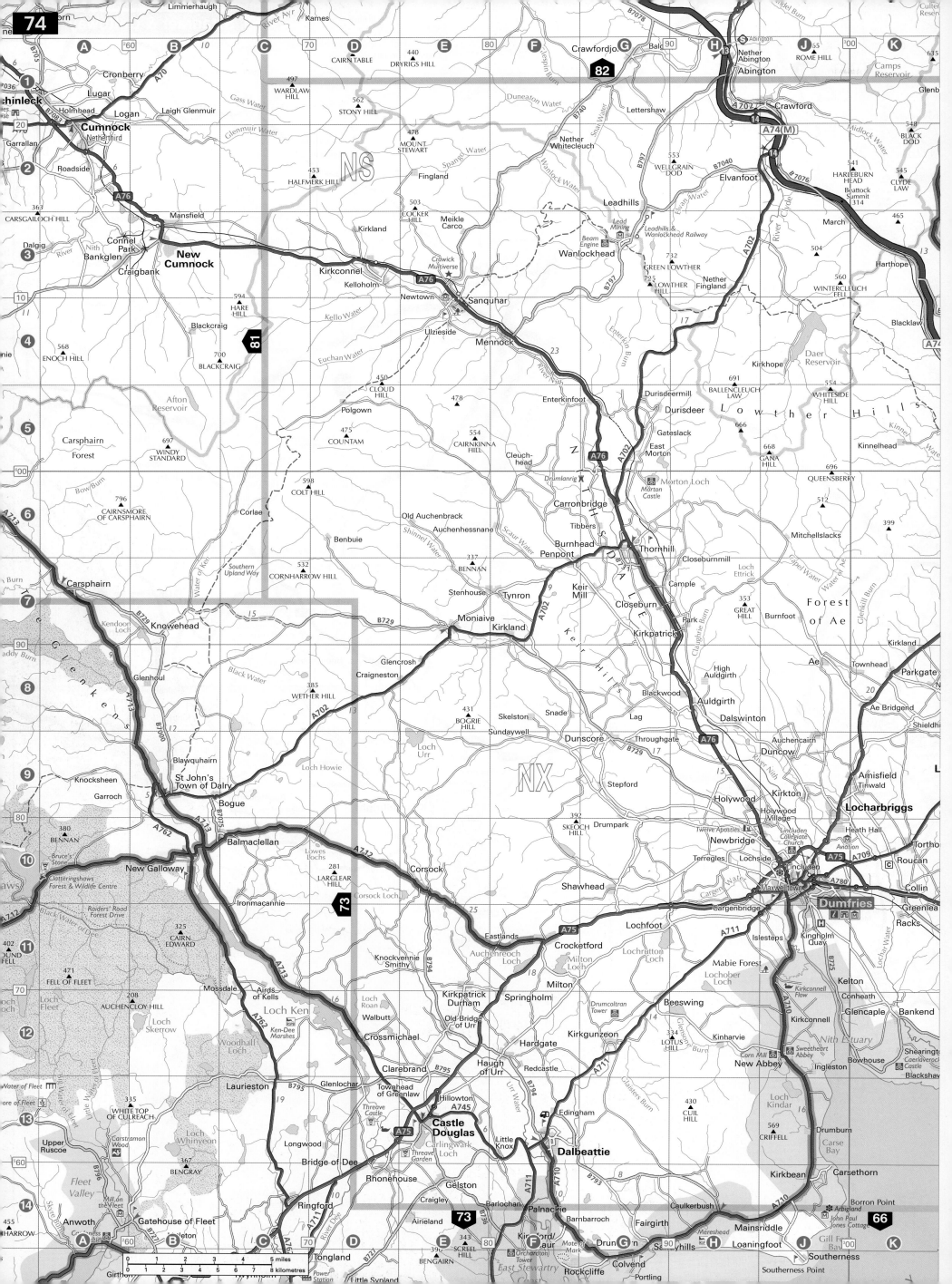

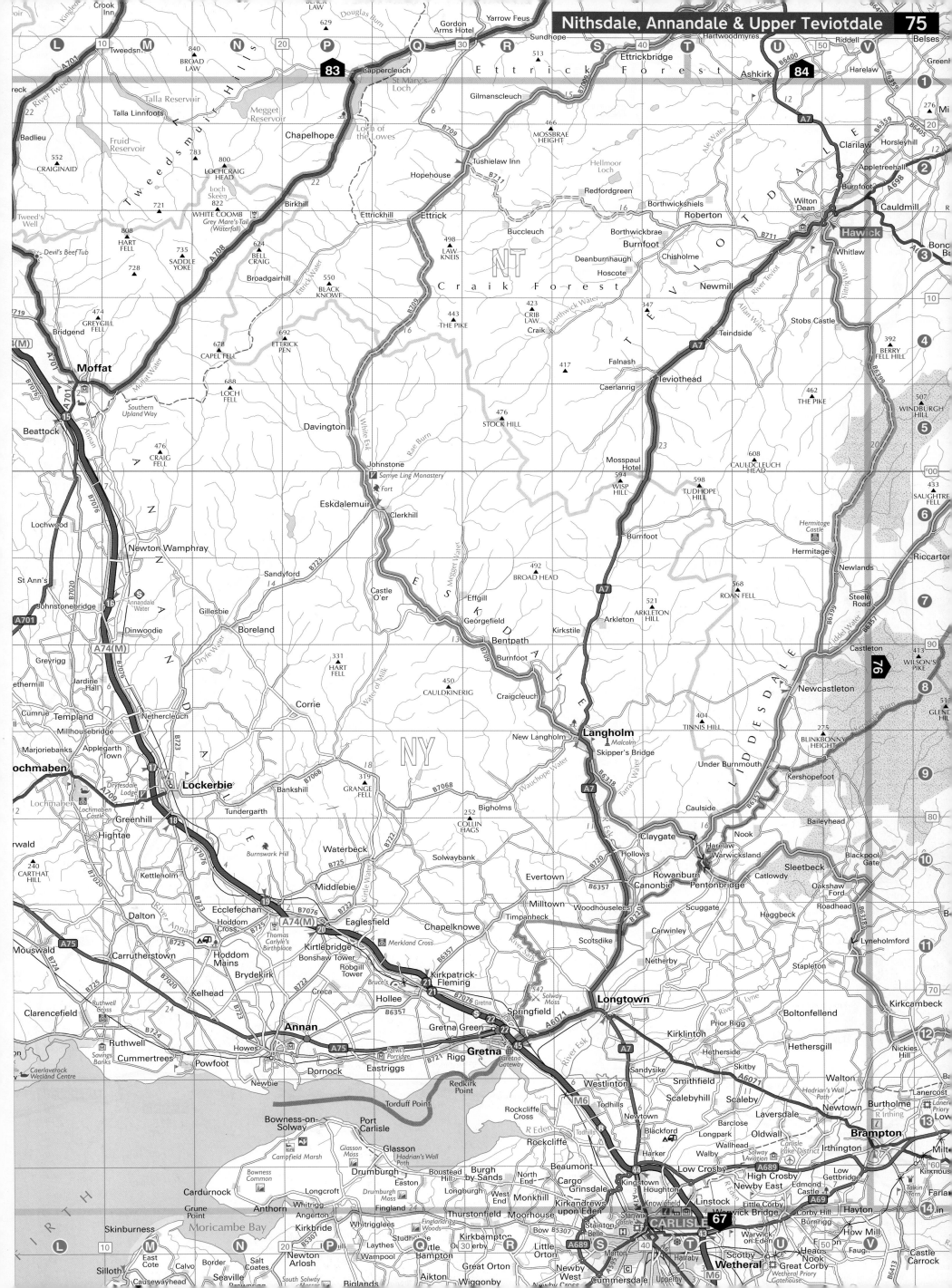

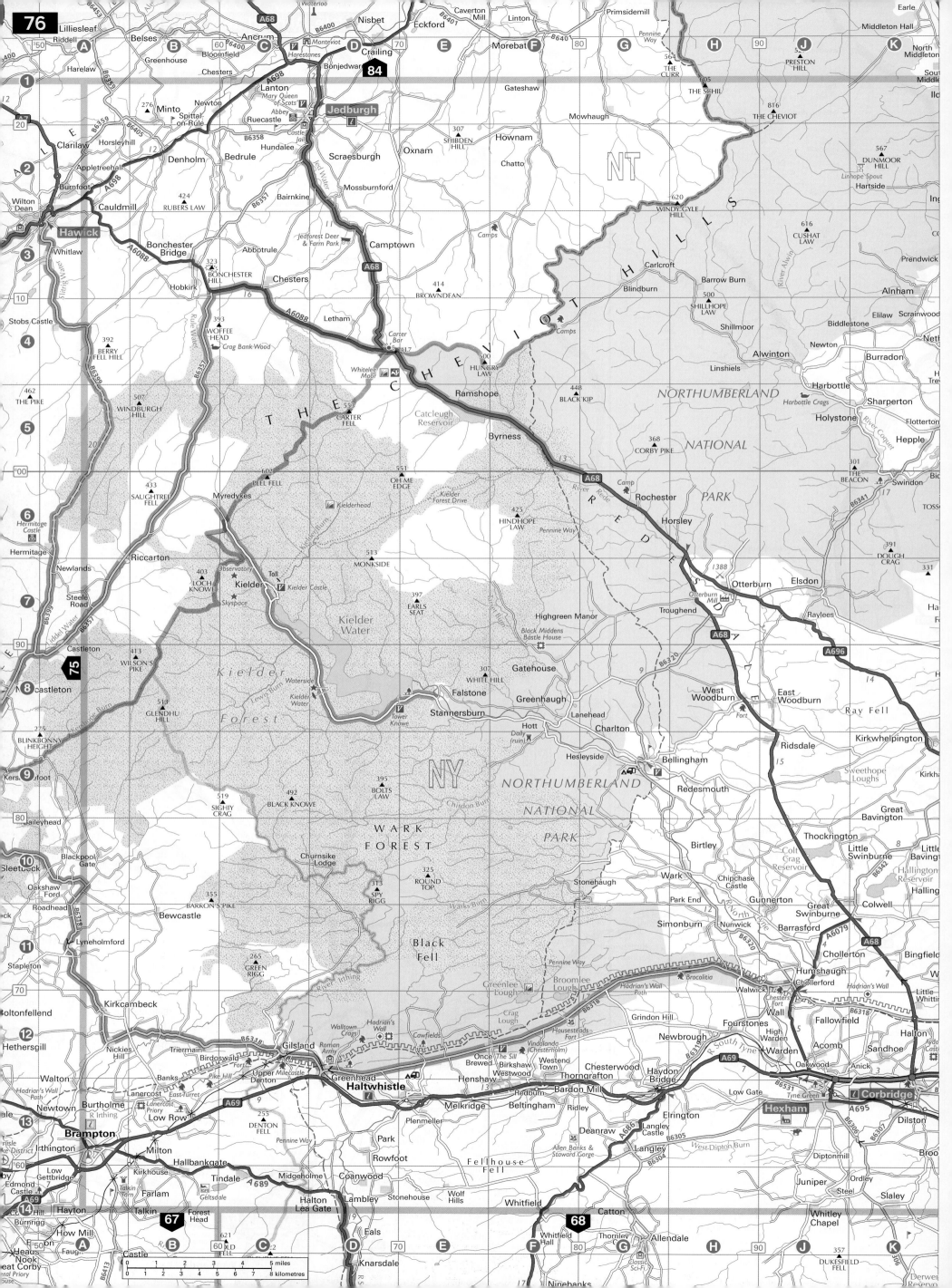

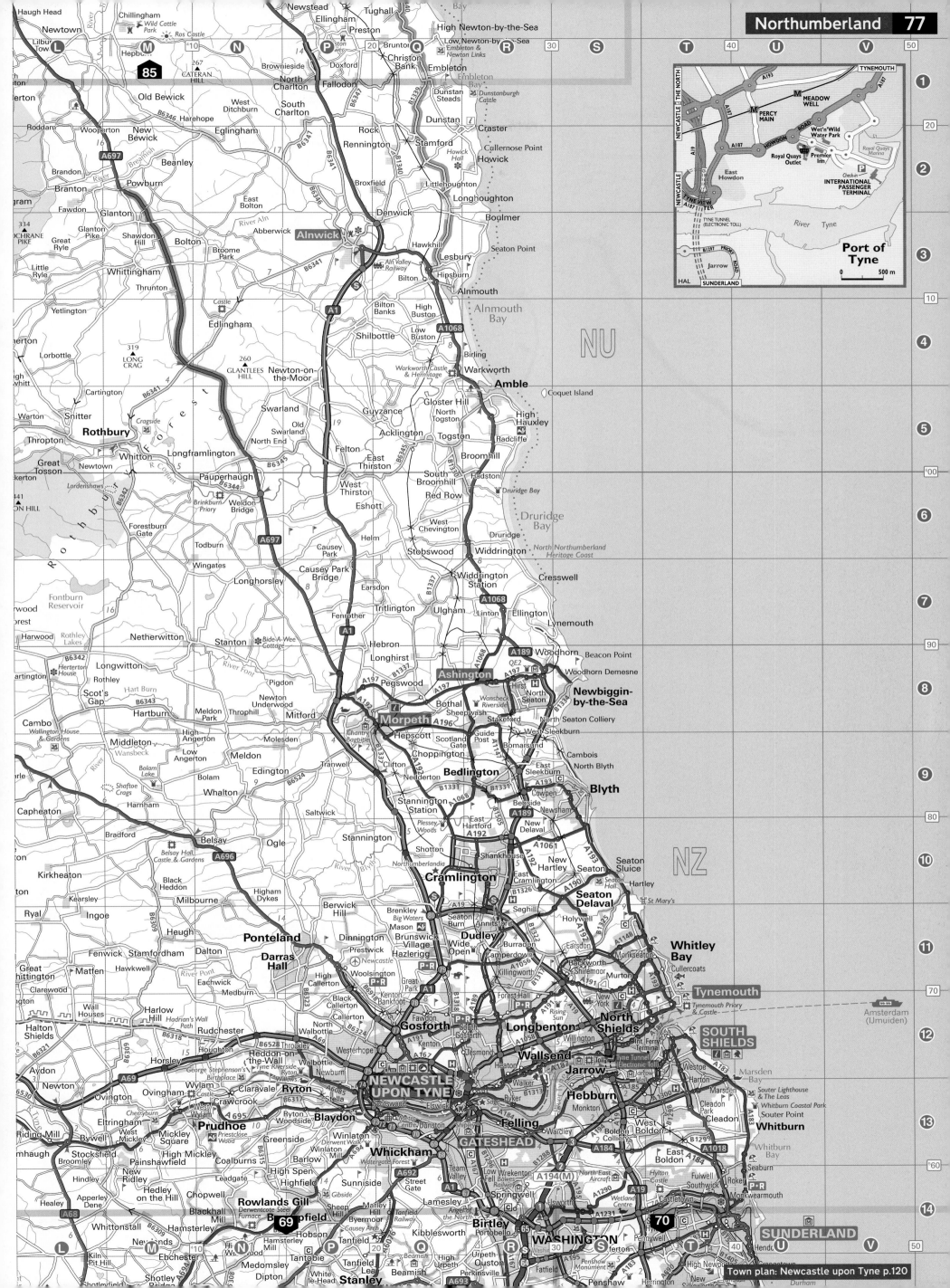

Port of Tyne

0   500 m

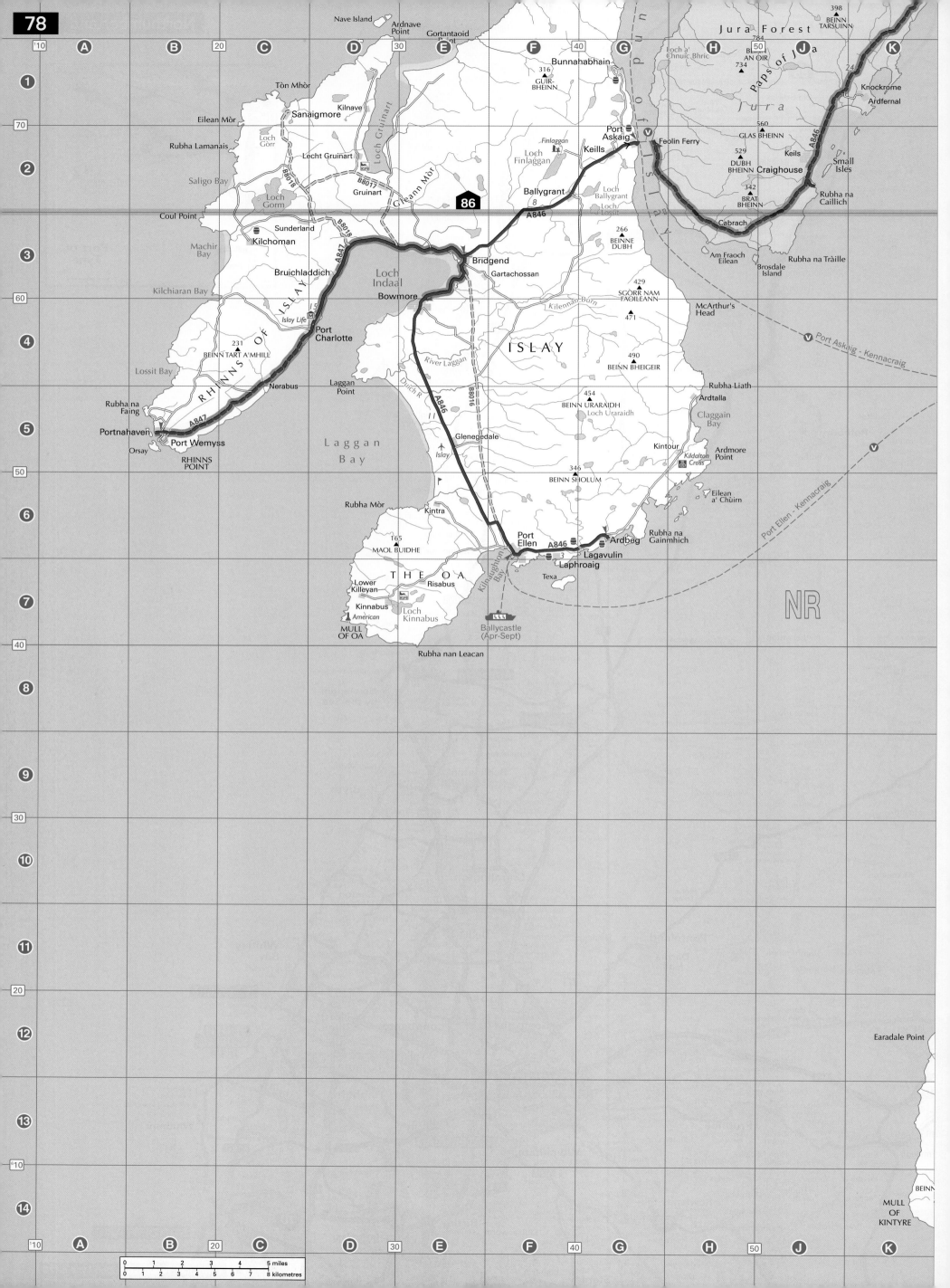

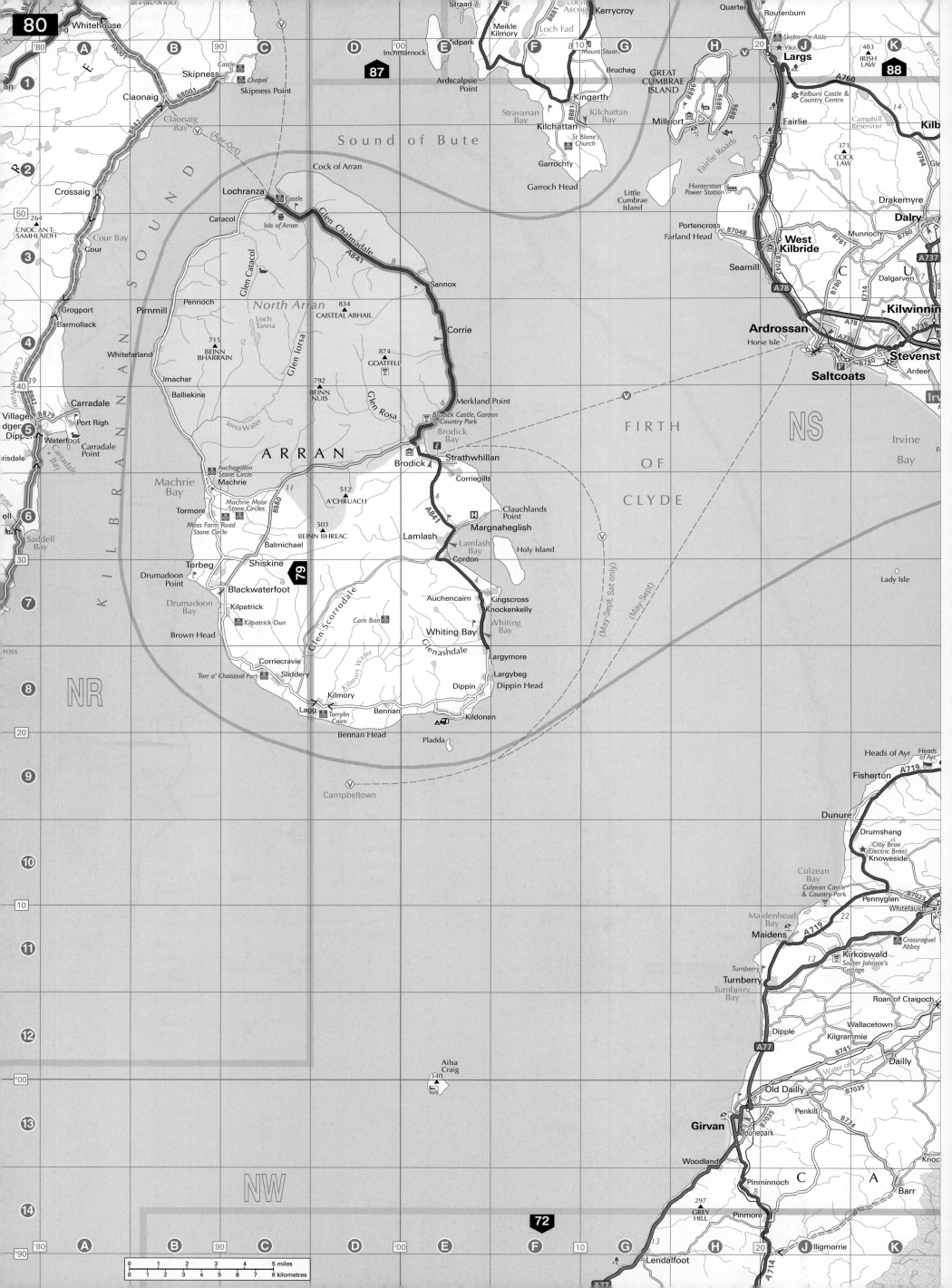

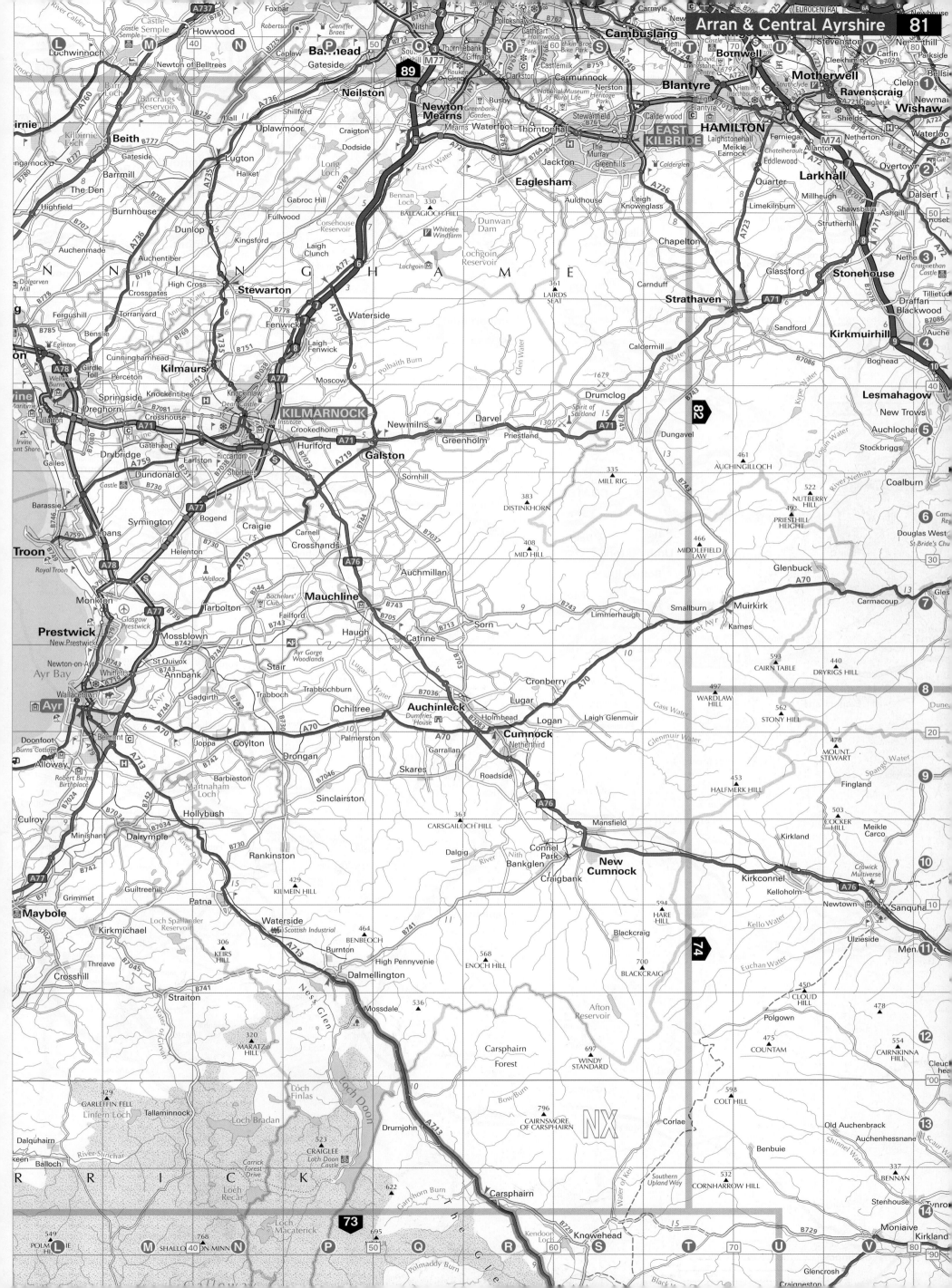

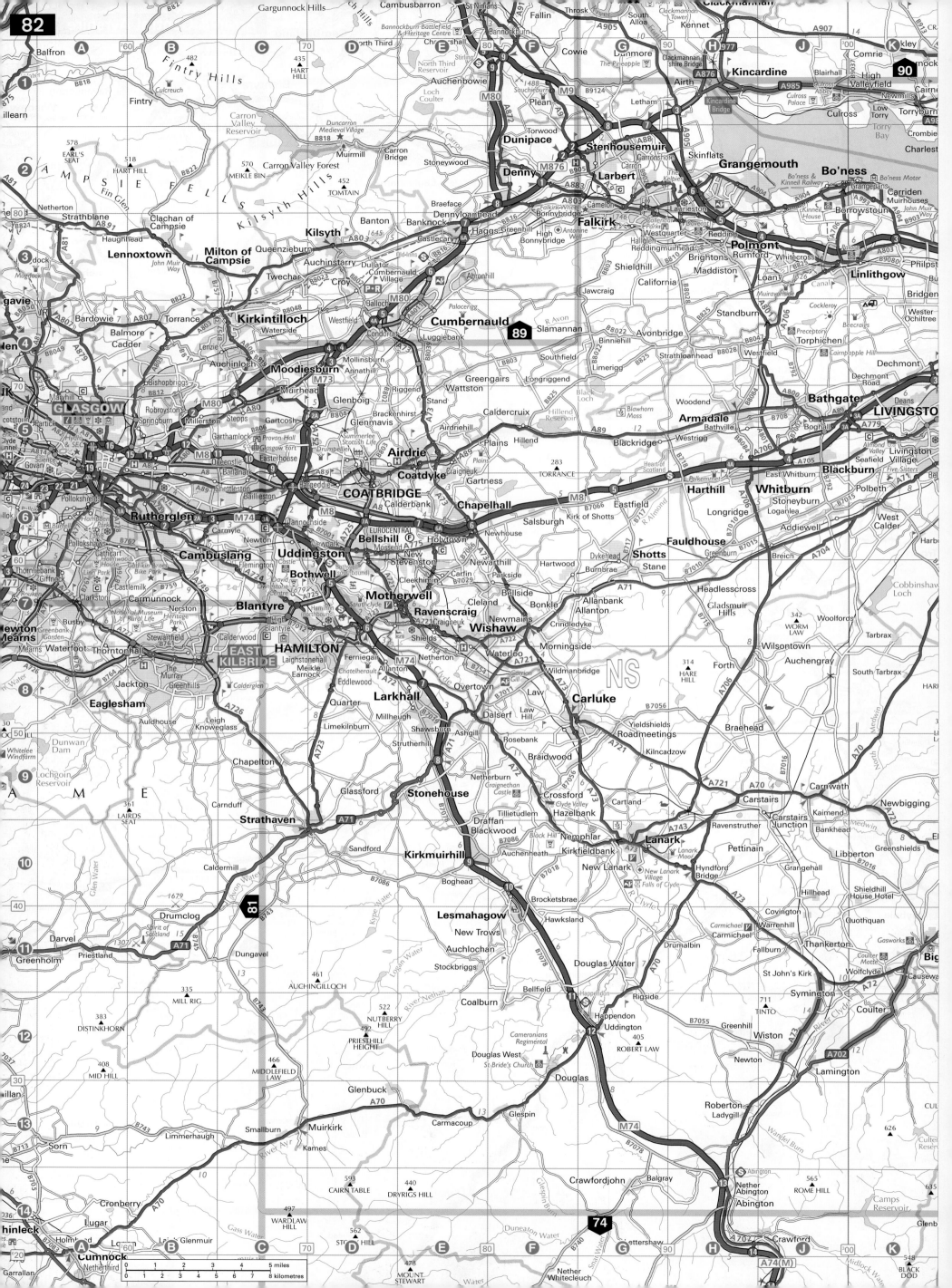

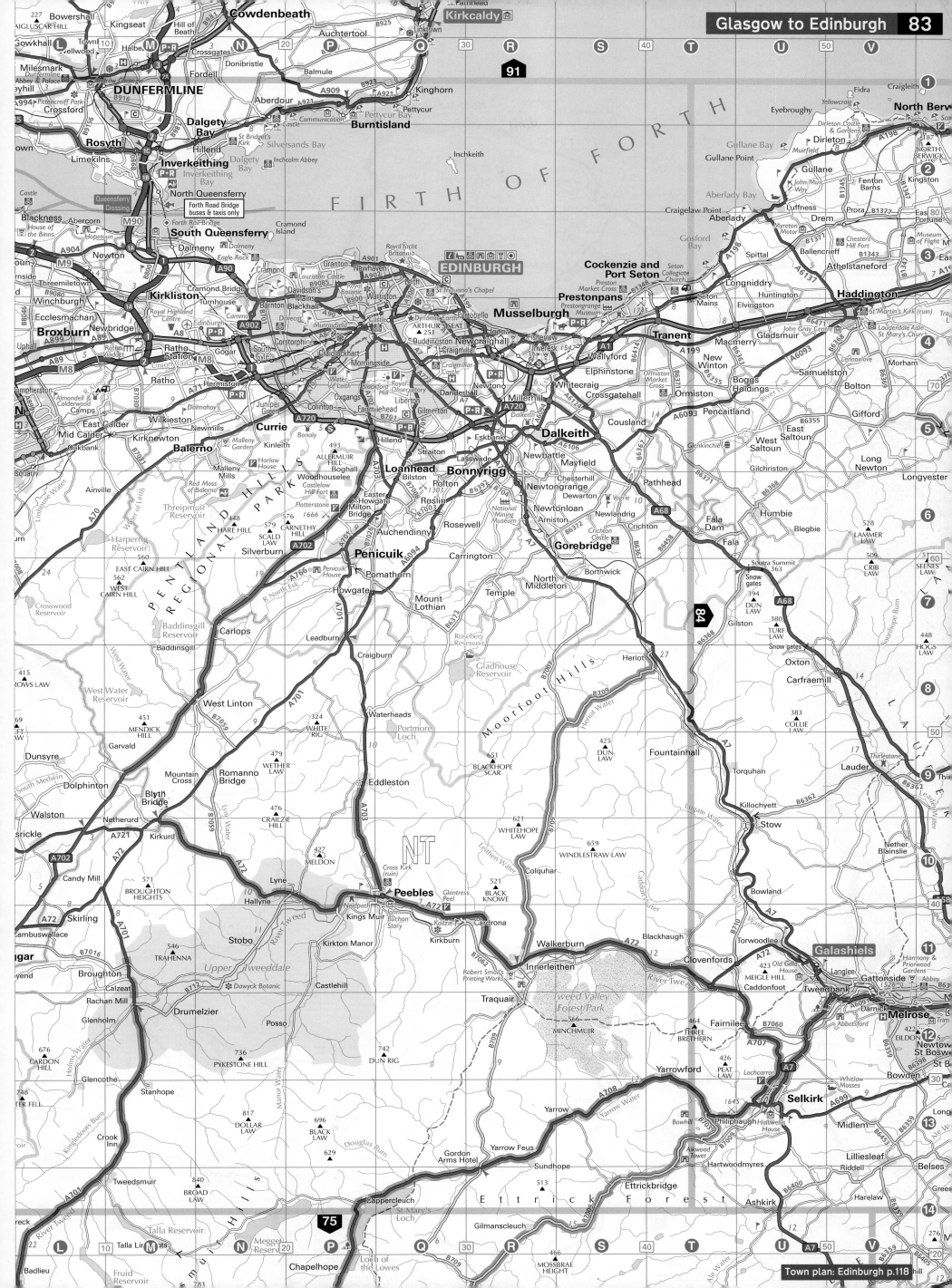

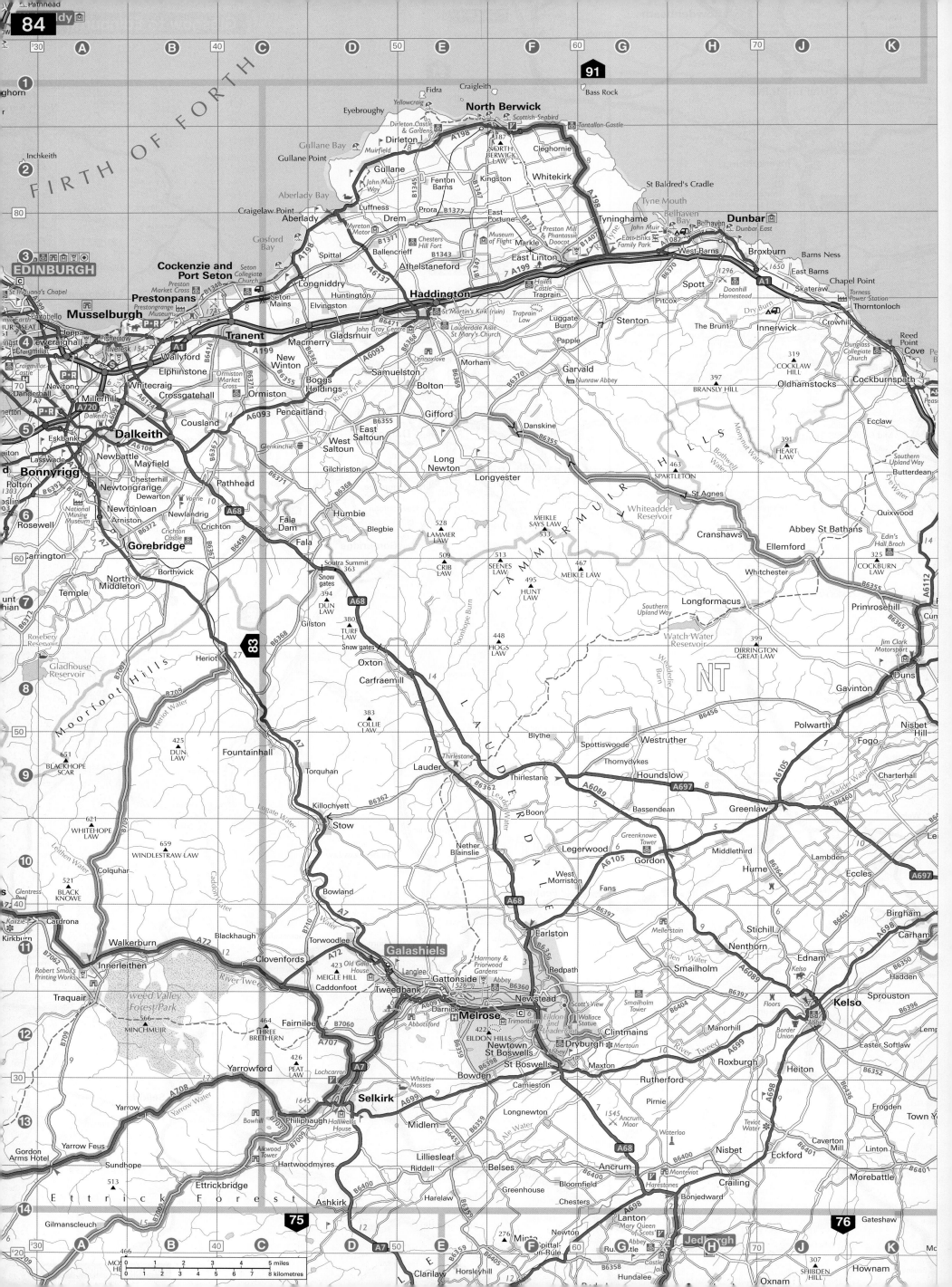

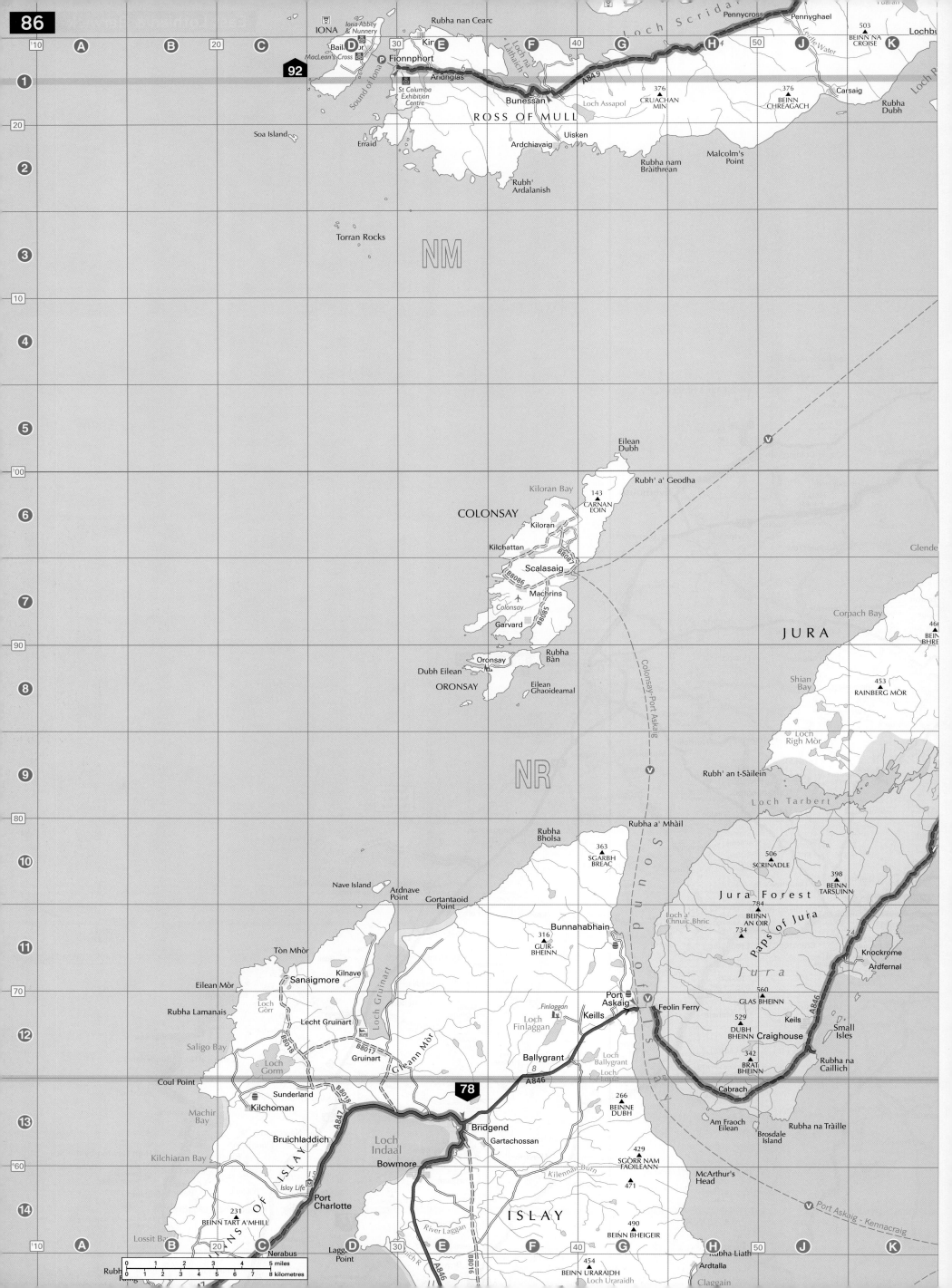

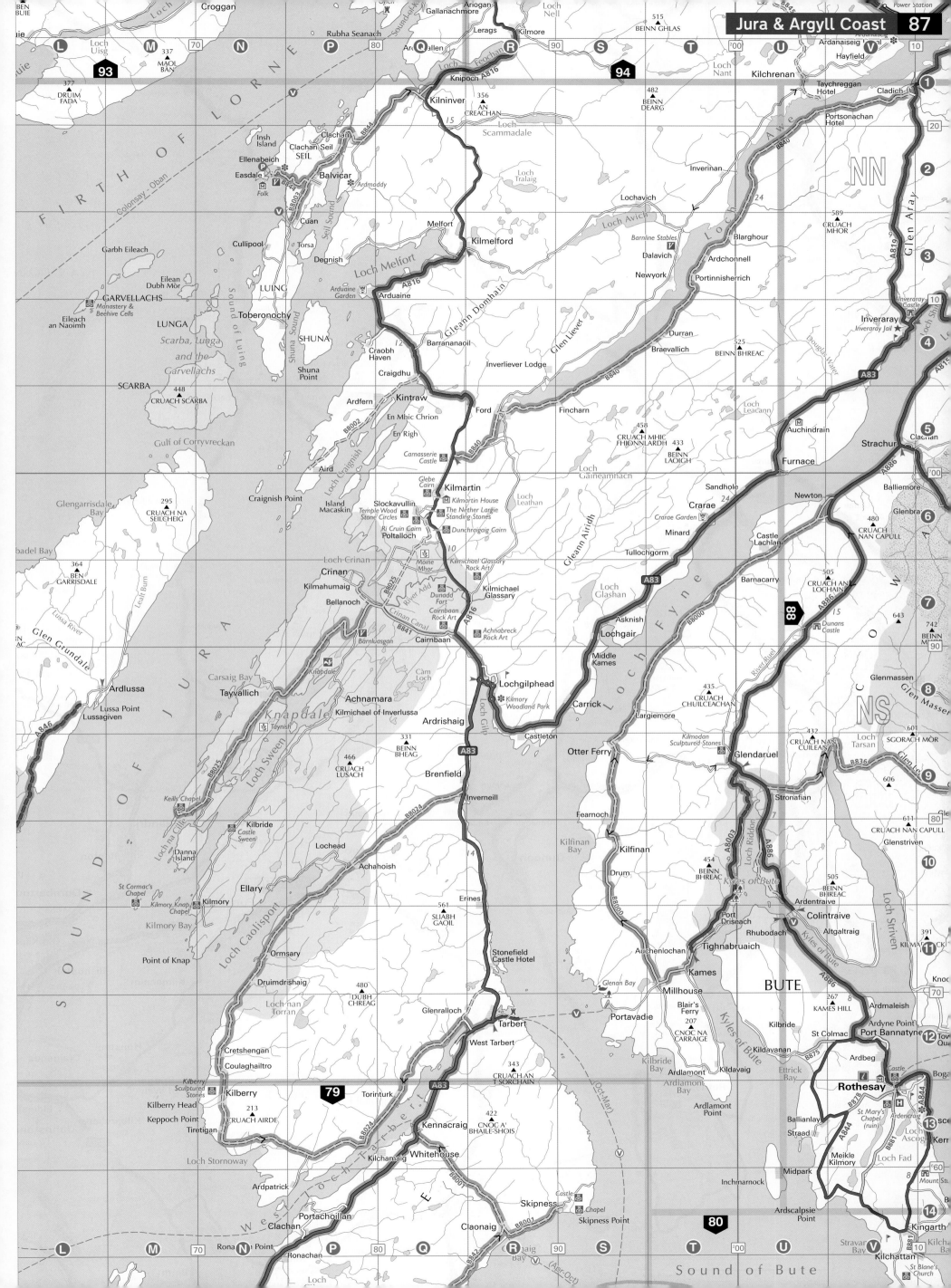

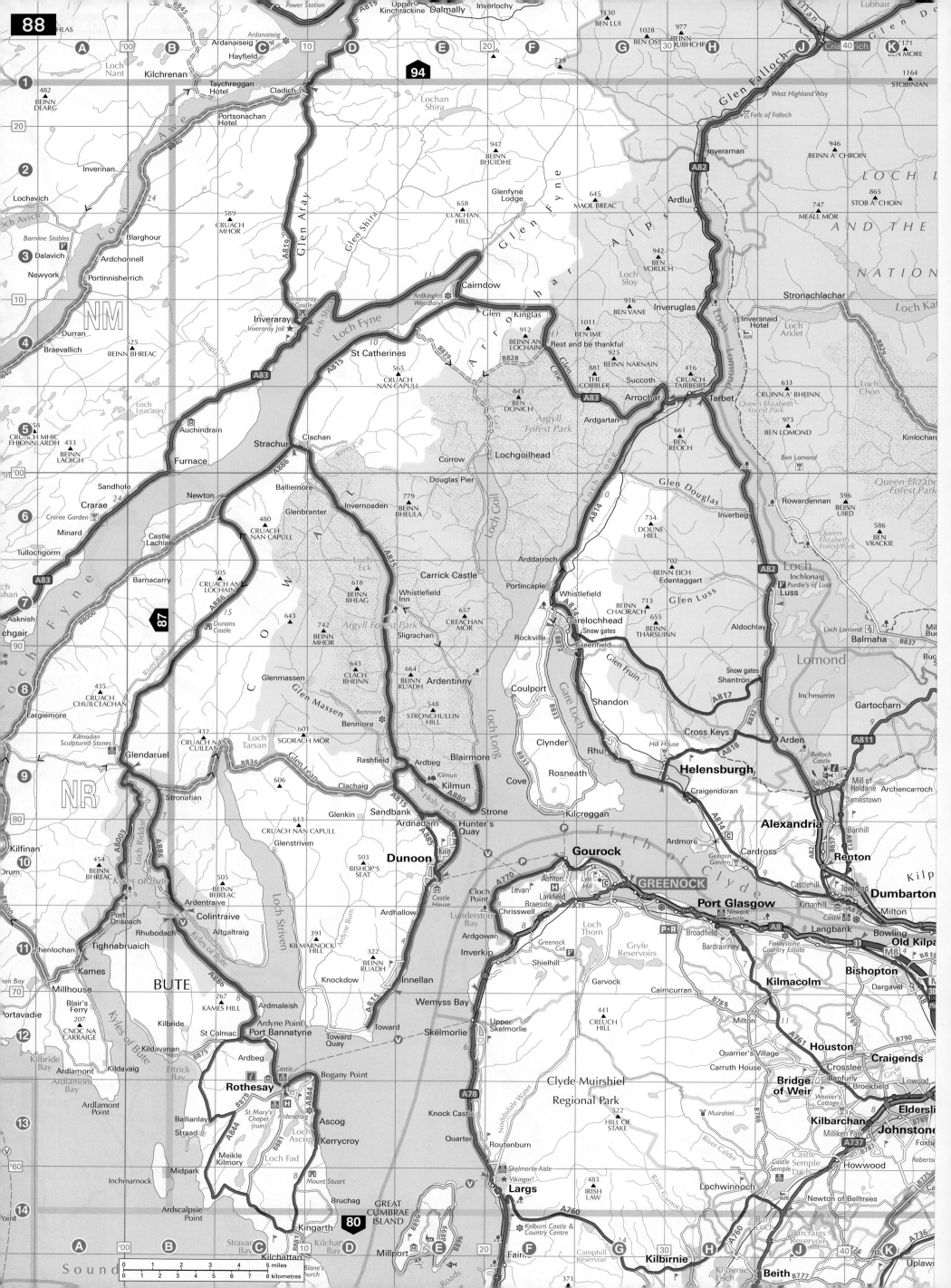

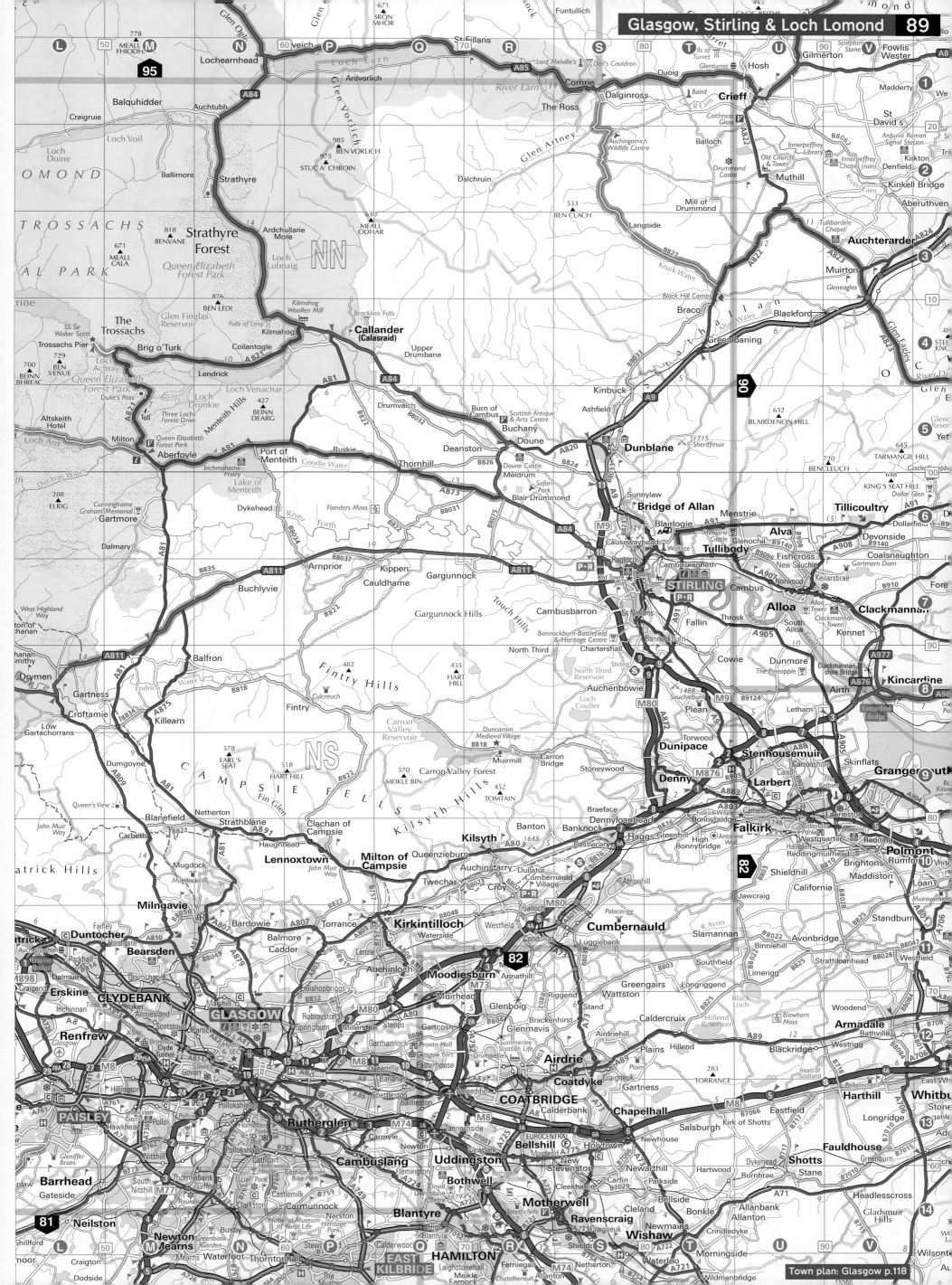

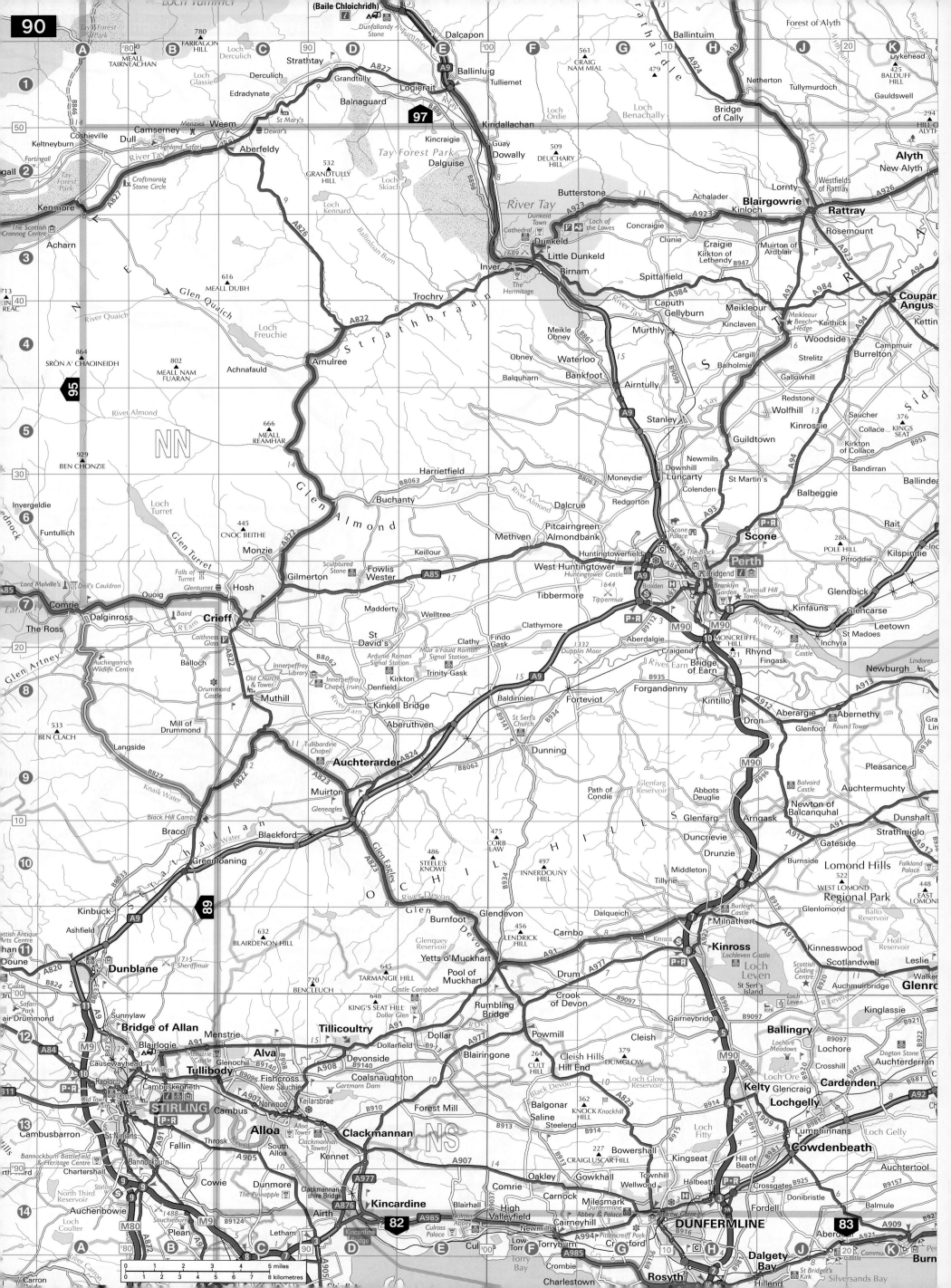

Town plan: Dundee p.117

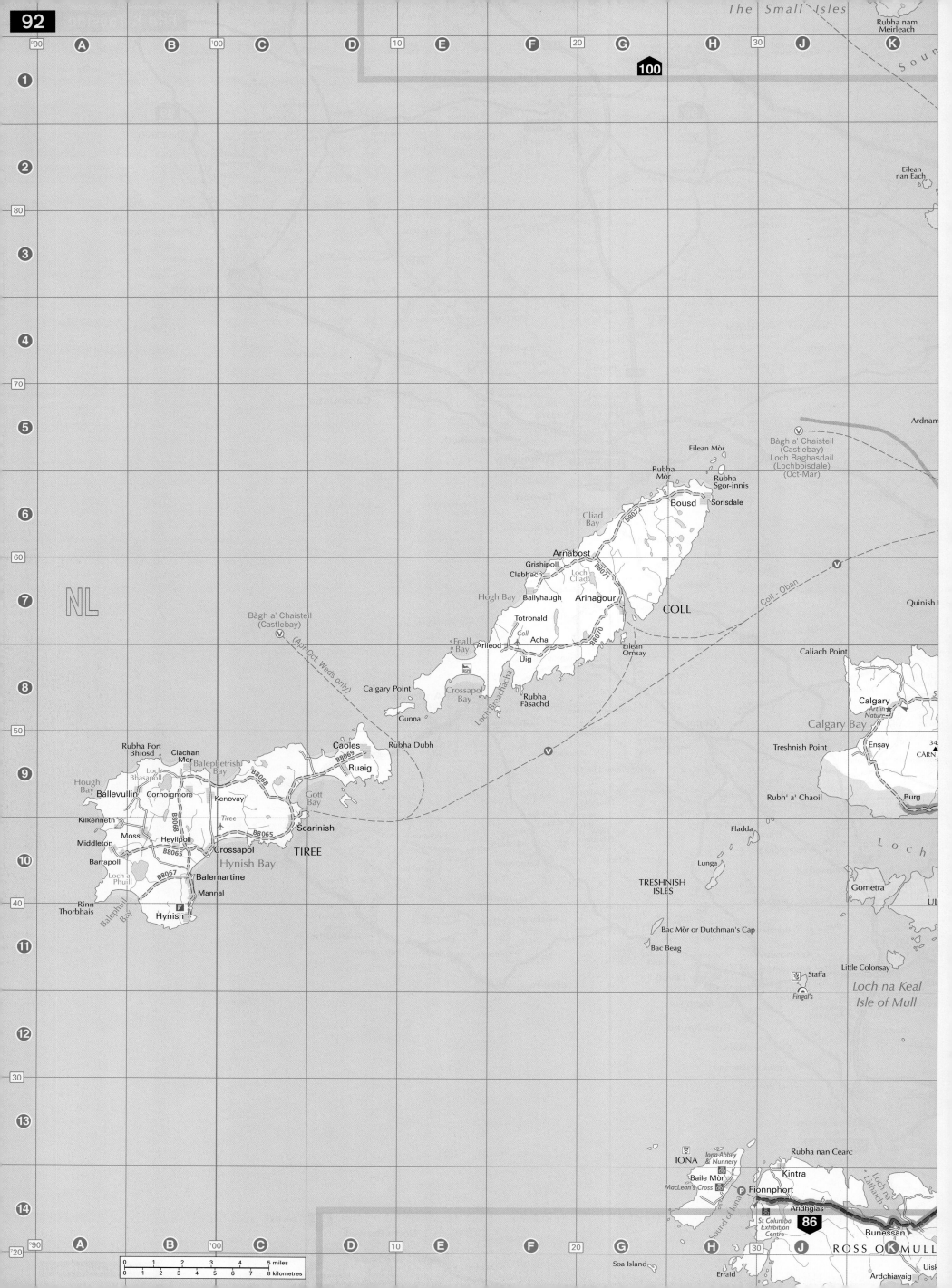

The Small Isles

Rubha nam
Meirleach

Sound

Eilean
nan Each

NL

Ardnam

Bàgh a' Chaisteil
(Castlebay)
Loch Baghasdail
(Lochboisdale)
(Oct–Mar)

Eilean Mòr

Rubha
Mòr

Rubha
Sgor-innis

Bousd   Sorisdale

Cliad
Bay

Arnabost

Grishipoll

Clabhach

Loch
Cliad

Hogh Bay   Ballyhaugh

Arinagour

COLL

Coll – Oban

Quinish

Totronald

Coll

Acha

Feall
Bay

Arileod

Uig

Eilean Ornsay

Caliach Point

Bàgh a' Chaisteil
(Castlebay)

(Apr–Oct Weds only)

Calgary Point

Crossapol
Bay

Loch Breachacha

Rubha
Fàsachd

Gunna

Calgary

Art in
Nature

Calgary Bay

Treshnish Point

Ensay

CÀRN

Rubha Port
Bhiosd

Clachan
Mor

Balephetrish
Bay

Caoles

Rubha Dubh

Ruaig

Rubh' a' Chaoil

Burg

Loch
Bhasapoll

Hough
Bay

Ballevullin

Cornoigmore

Kenovay

Tiree

Gott
Bay

Scarinish

Fladda

Lunga

Loch

Gometra

Ul

Kilkenneth

Moss   Heylipoll

Middleton

Barrapoll

Loch a'
Phuill

Crossapol

Balemartine

Mannal

TIREE

Hynish Bay

TRESHNISH
ISLES

Little Colonsay

Rinn
Thorbhais

Balephuil
Bay

Hynish

Bac Mòr or Dutchman's Cap

Bac Beag

Staffa

Fingal's

Loch na Keal

Isle of Mull

IONA

Iona Abbey
& Nunnery

Rubha nan Cearc

Baile Mòr

Kintra

MacLean's Cross

Fionnphort

Aridhglas

St Columba
Exhibition
Centre

86

ROSS OF MULL

Soa Island

Bunessan

Erraid

Ardchiavaig

All vehicles must have the relevant island permit prior to travel to The Small Isles. Services are seasonal, day & weather dependent.

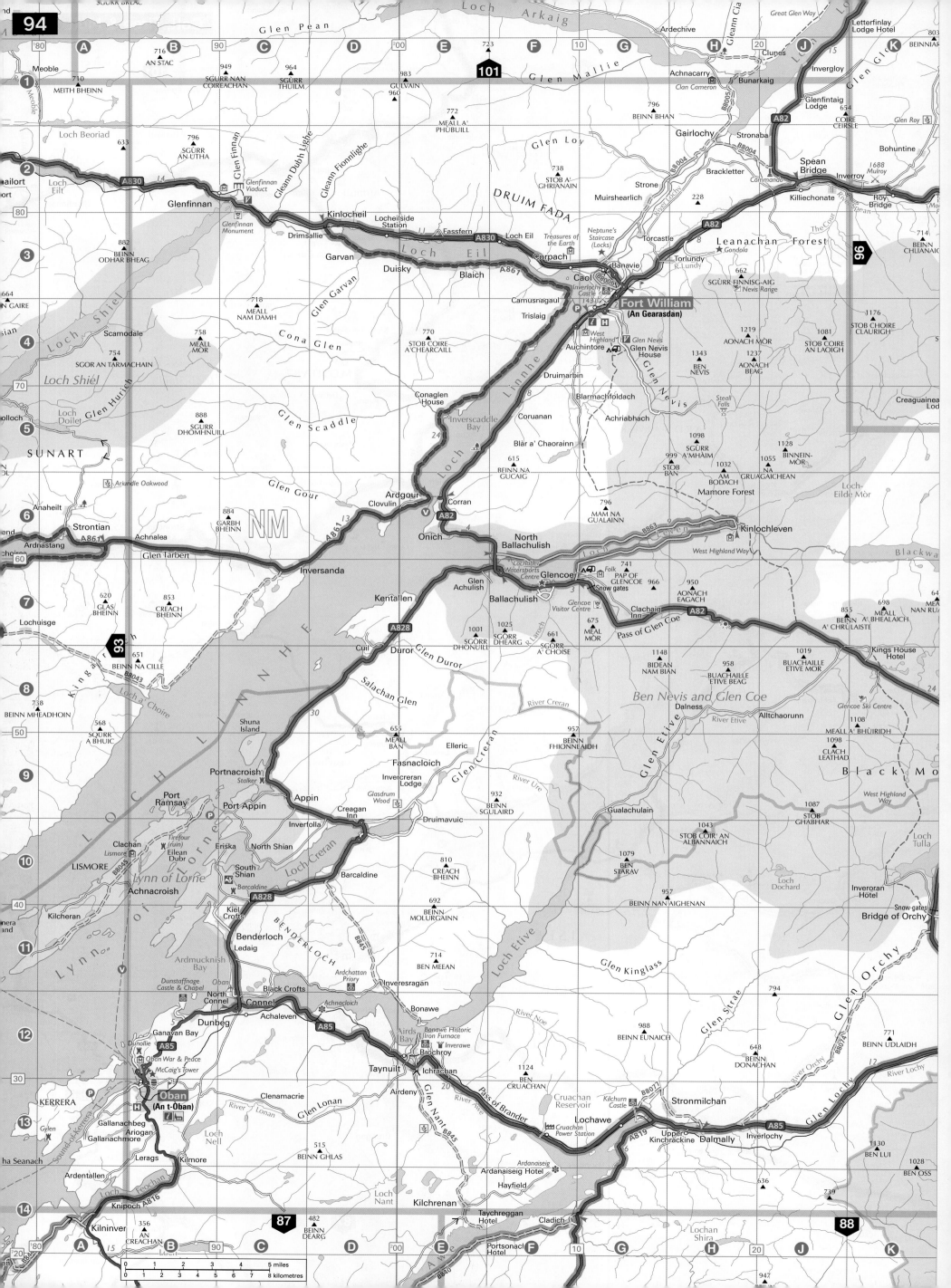

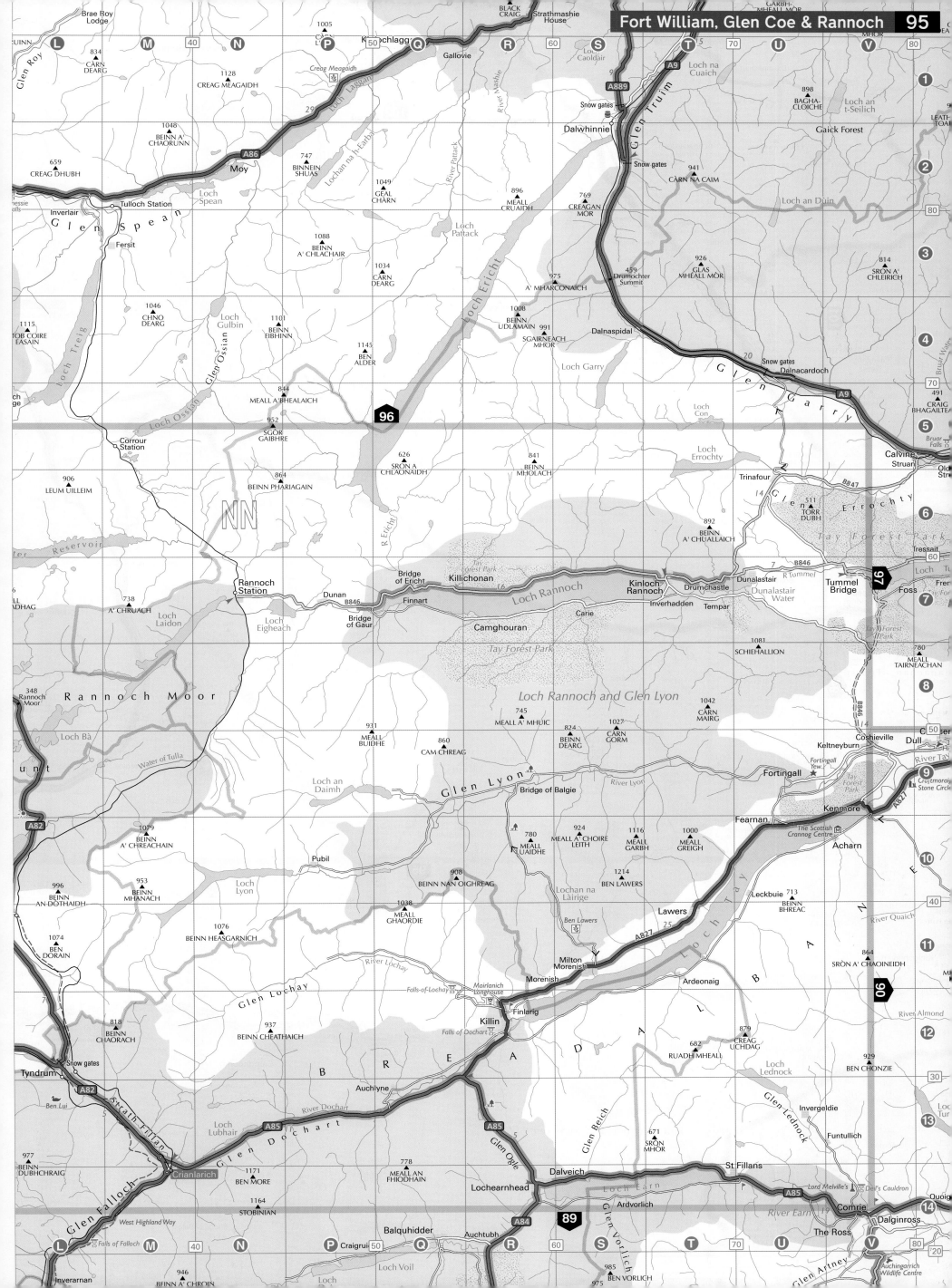

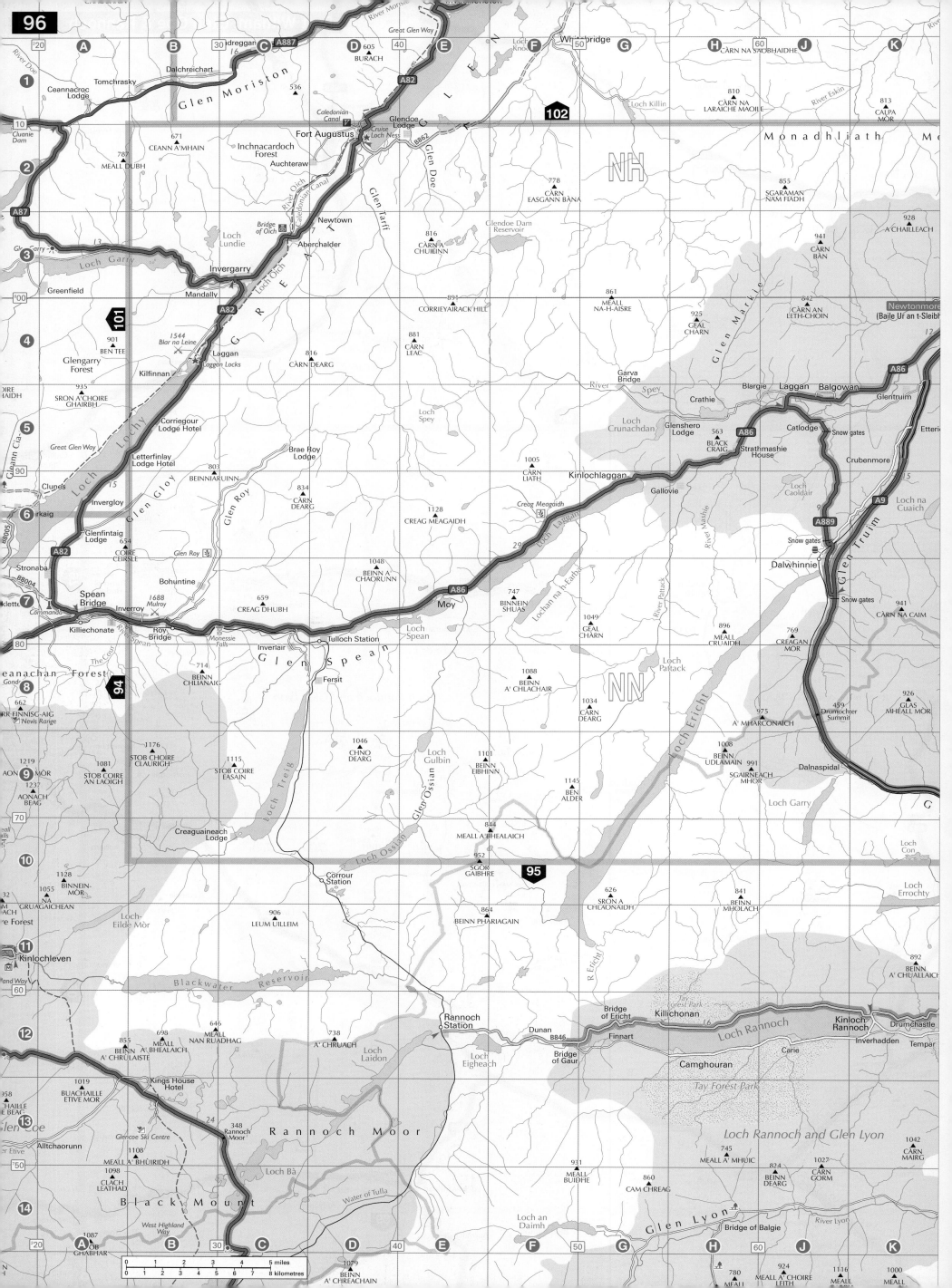

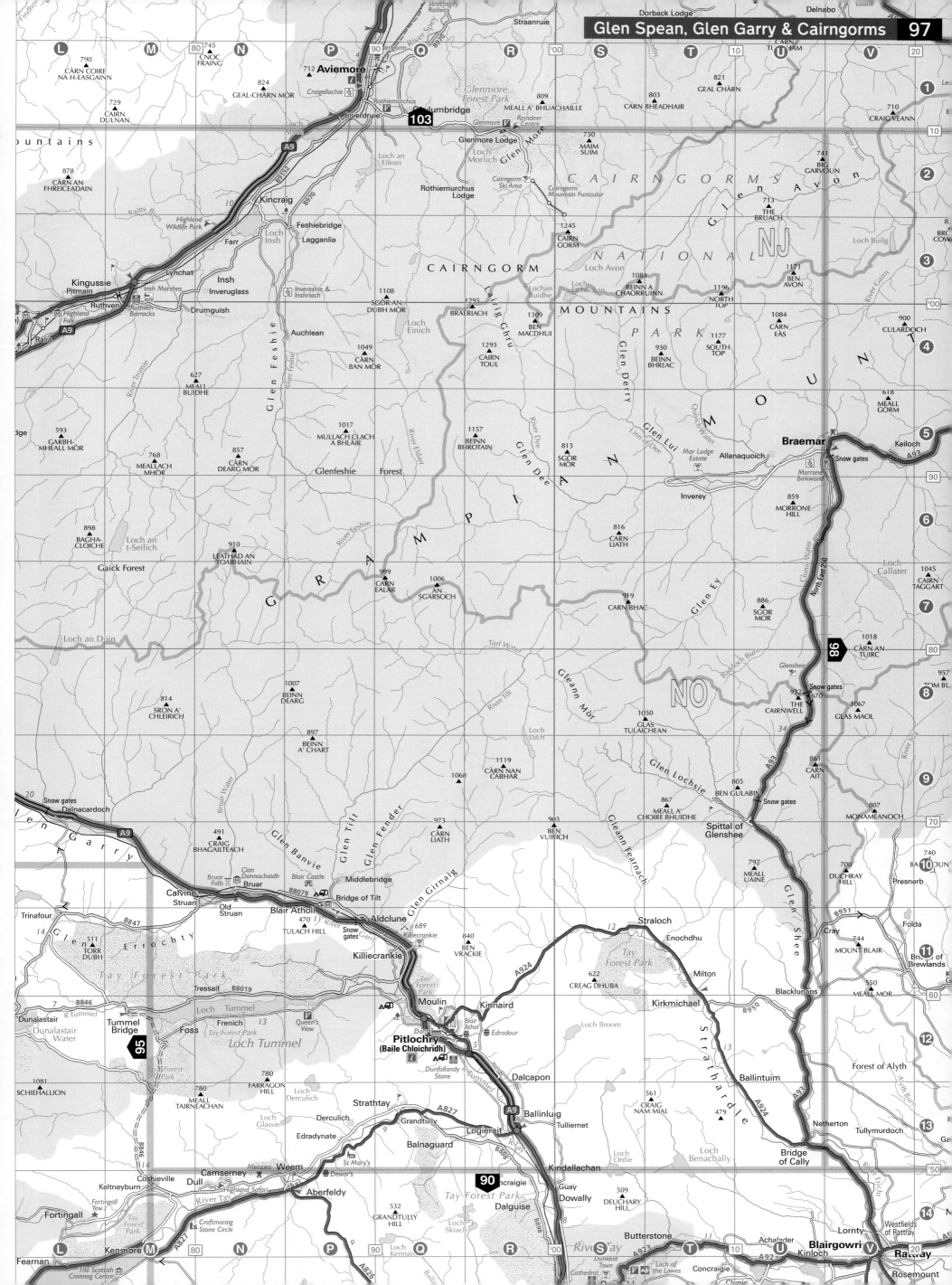

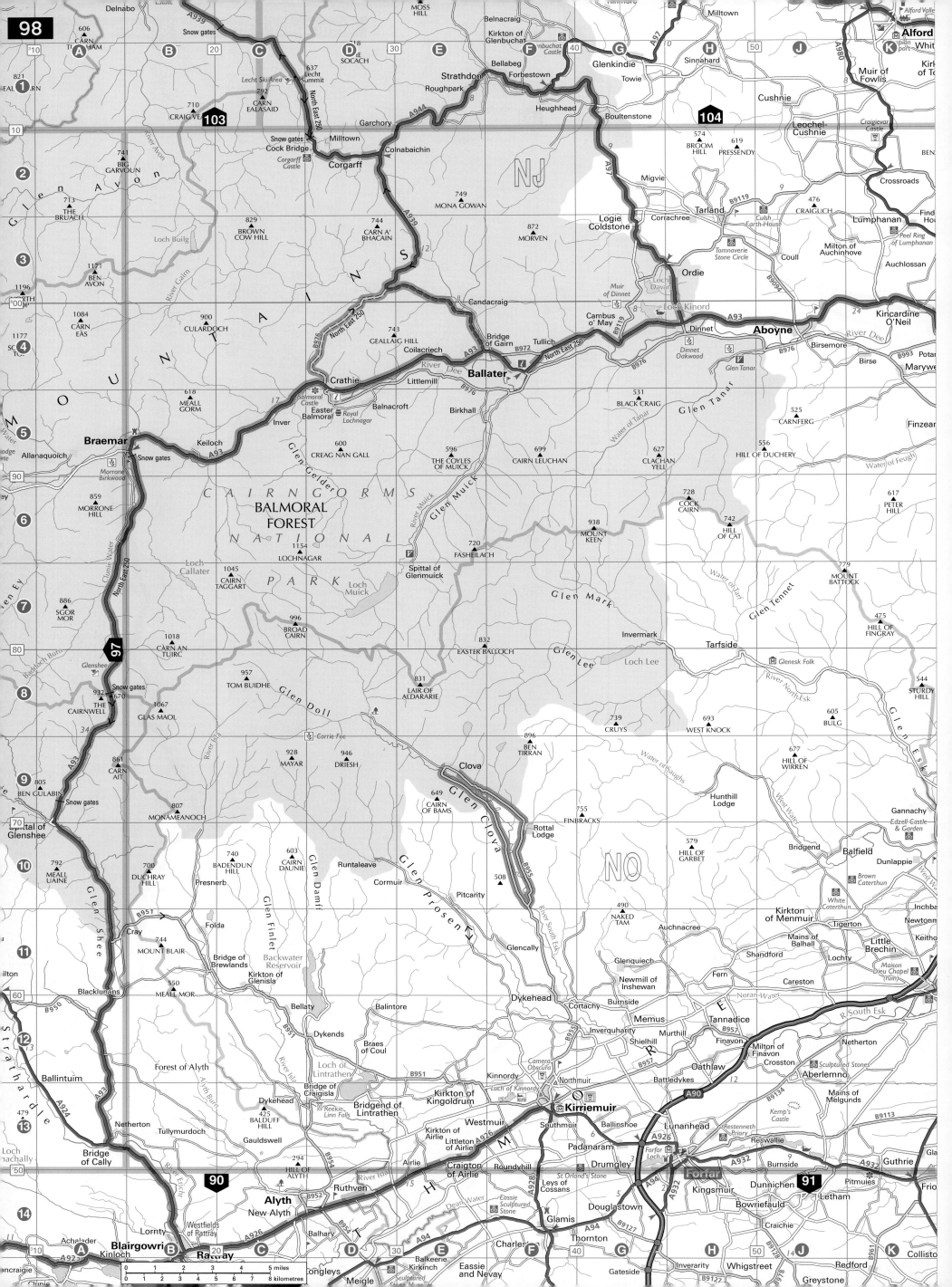

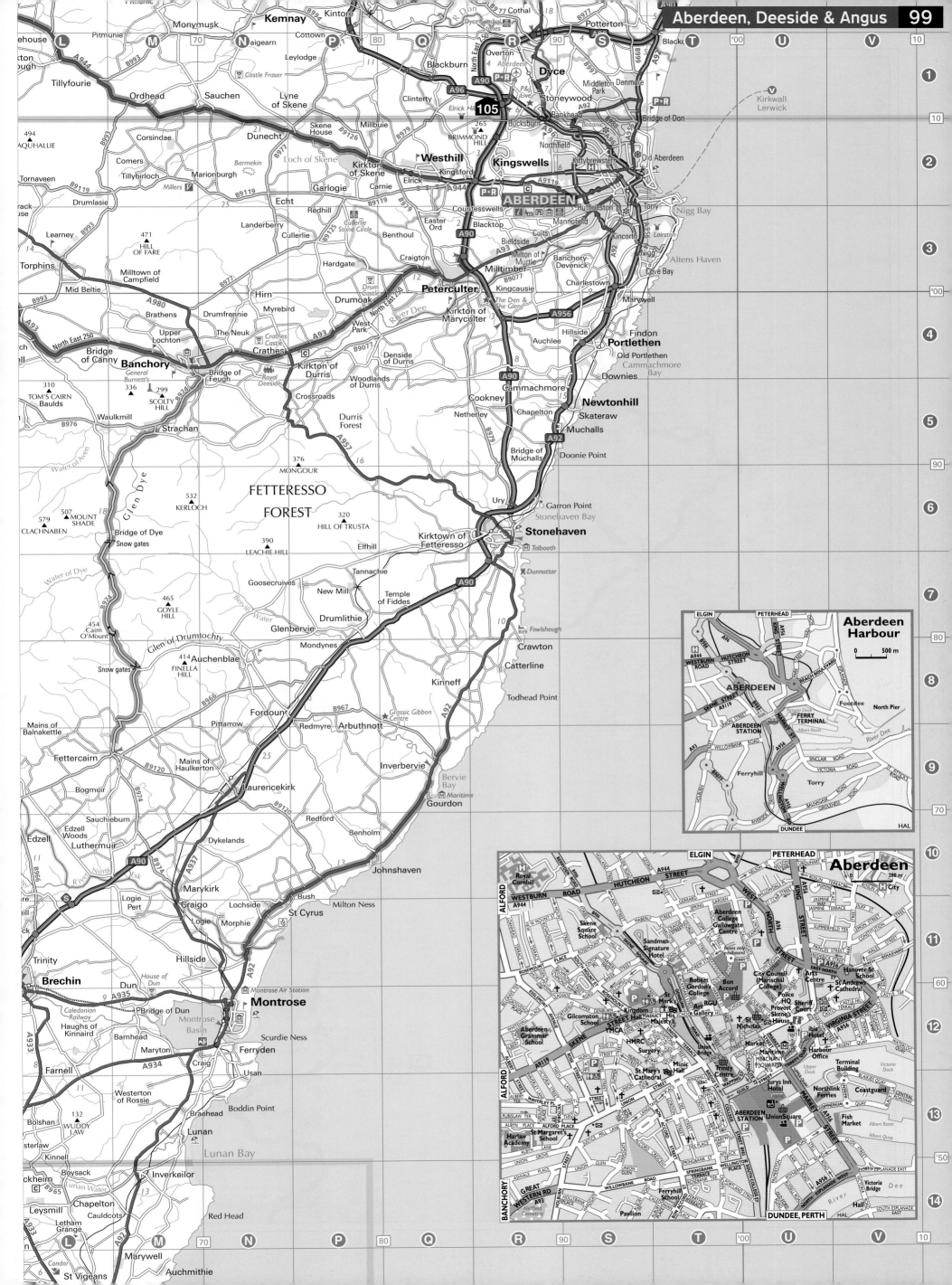

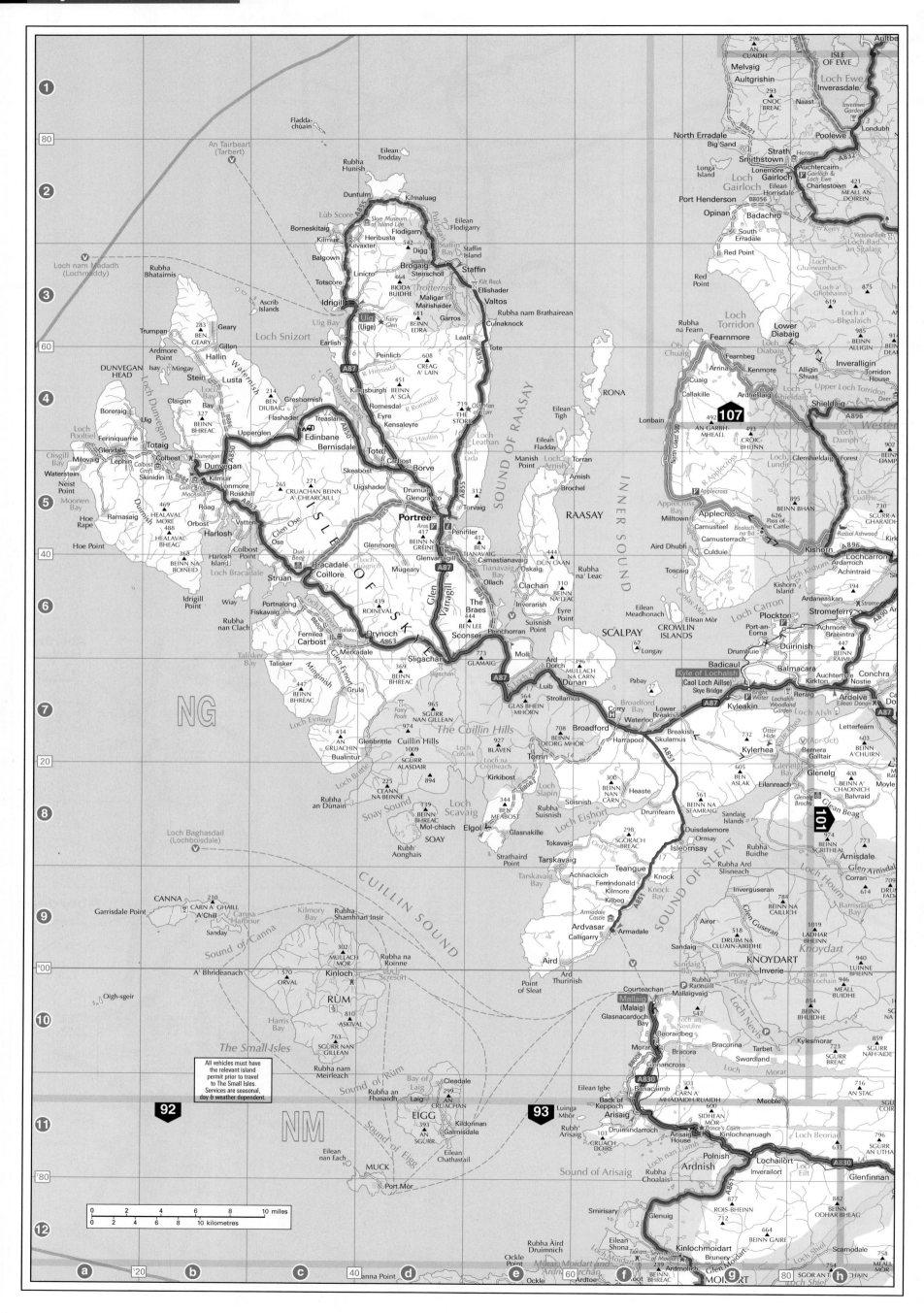

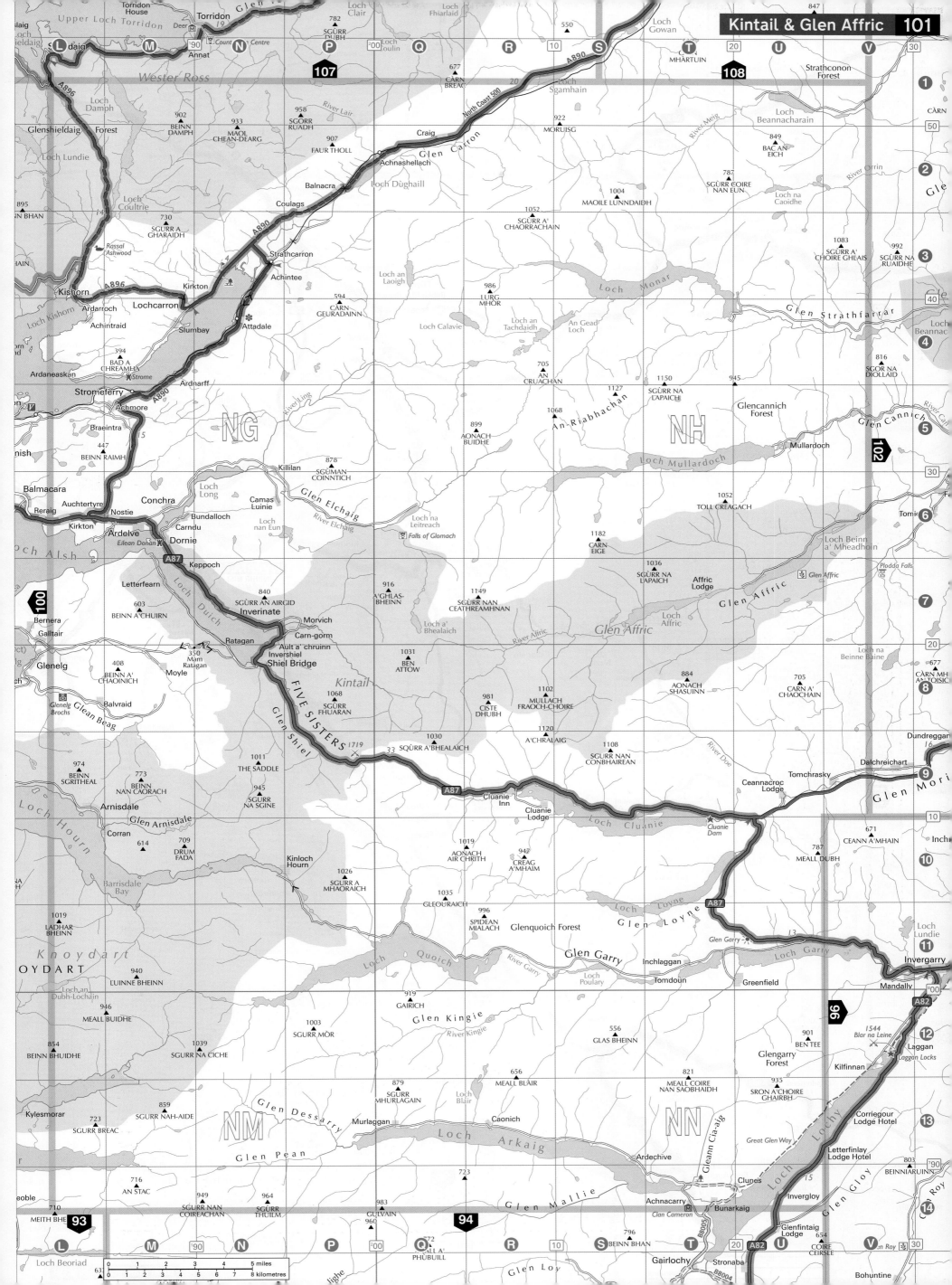

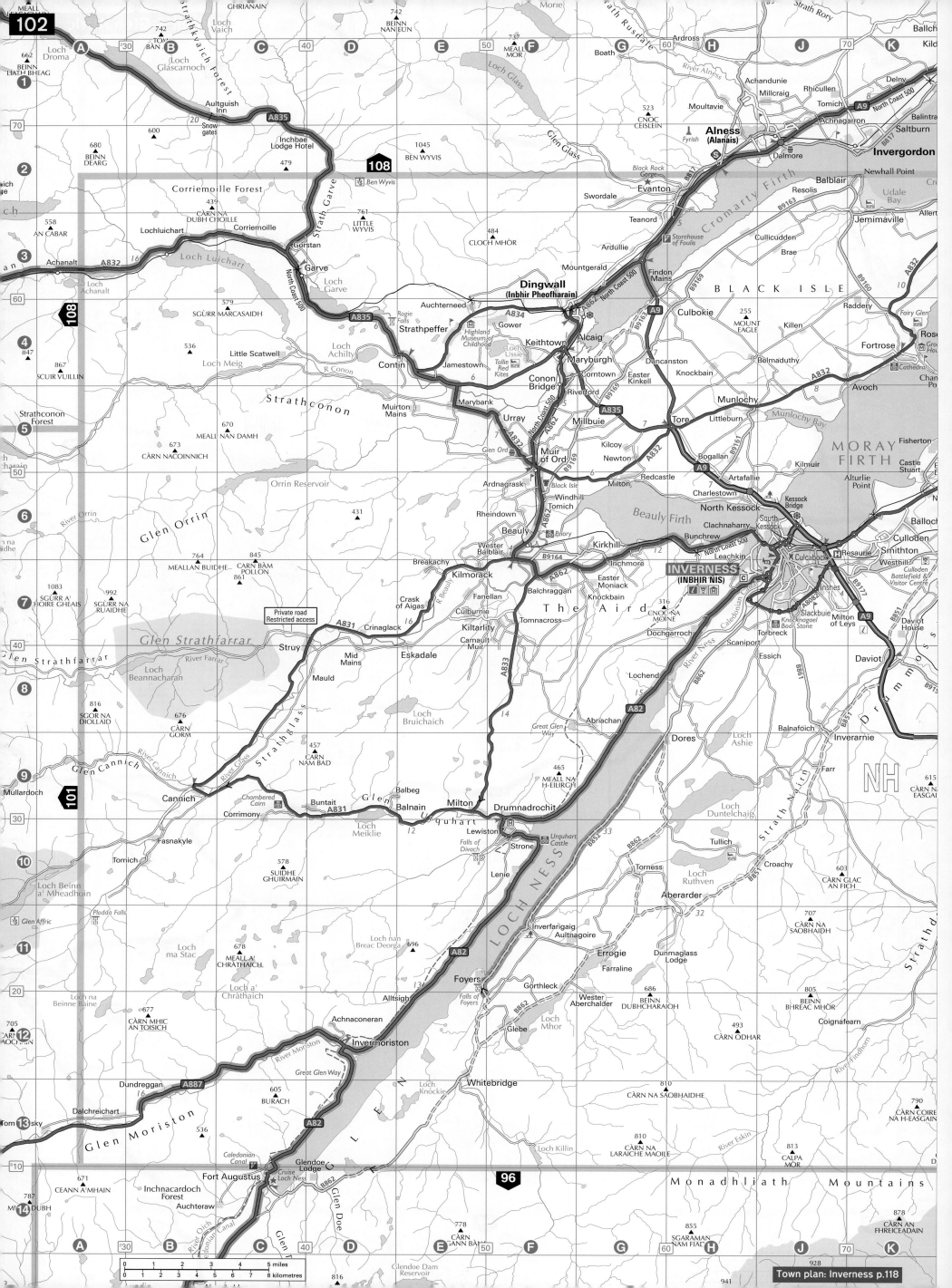

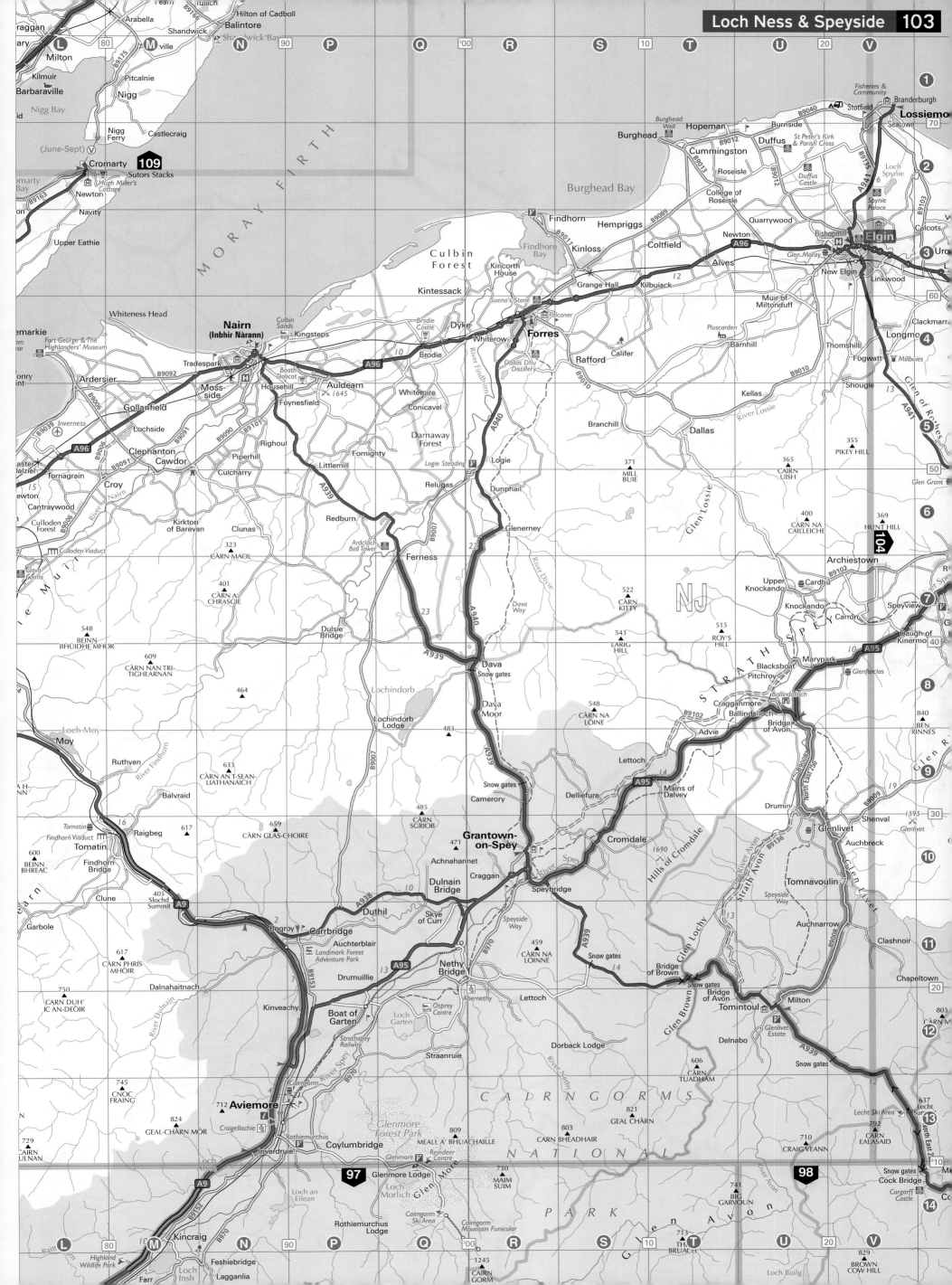

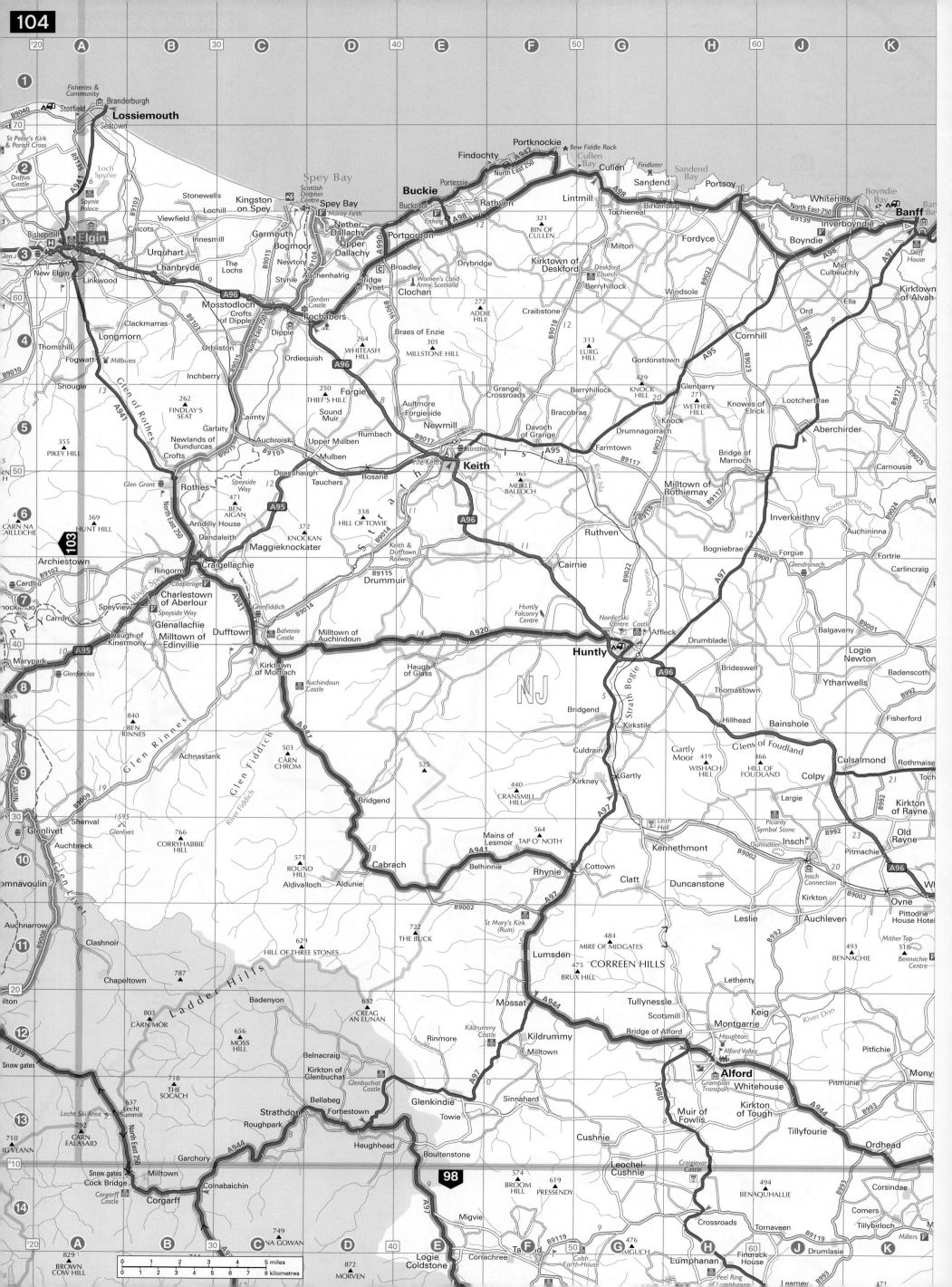

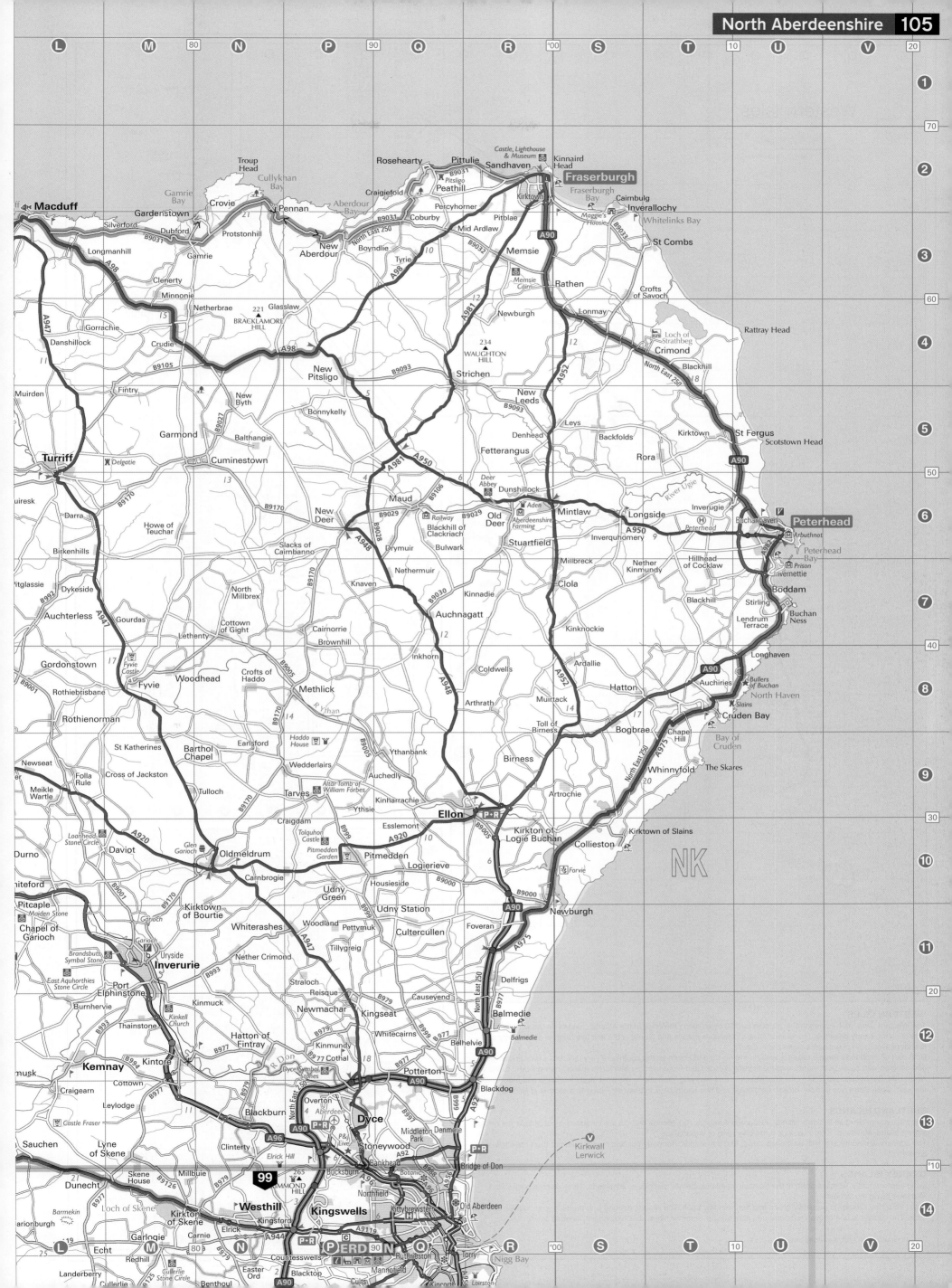

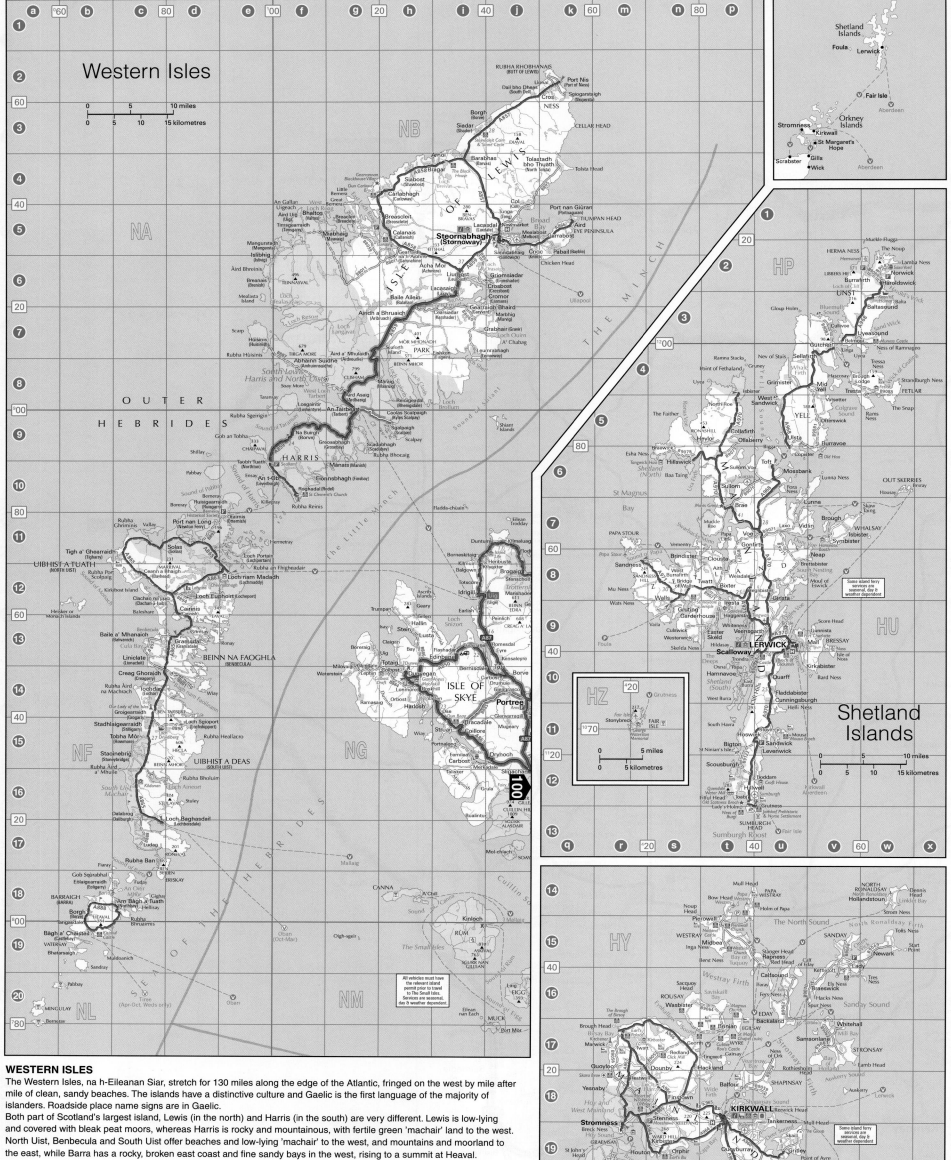

WESTERN ISLES

The Western Isles, na h-Eileanan Siar, stretch for 130 miles along the edge of the Atlantic, fringed on the west by mile after mile of clean, sandy beaches. The islands have a distinctive culture and Gaelic is the first language of the majority of islanders. Roadside place name signs are in Gaelic.

Both part of Scotland's largest island, Lewis (in the north) and Harris (in the south) are very different. Lewis is low-lying and covered with bleak peat moors, whereas Harris is rocky and mountainous, with fertile green 'machair' land to the west. North Uist, Benbecula and South Uist offer beaches and low-lying 'machair' to the west, and mountains and moorland to the east, while Barra has a rocky, broken east coast and fine sandy bays in the west, rising to a summit at Heaval.

SHETLAND ISLANDS

The most northerly of all Britain's islands, this group numbers 100, though only 15 are inhabited. Most people live on the largest island, Mainland, where Lerwick is the only town of importance.

The scenery is magnificent, with unspoiled views, and the islands' northerly position means summer days have little or no darkness.

ORKNEY ISLANDS

Lying approximately 10 miles north of the Scottish mainland, Orkney comprises 70 islands, 18 of which are inhabited, Mainland being the largest.

Apart from Hoy, Orkney is generally green and flat, with few trees. The islands abound with prehistoric antiquities and rare birds. The climate is one of even temperatures and 'twilight' summer nights, but with violent winds at times.

For information on ferry services see page XVI.

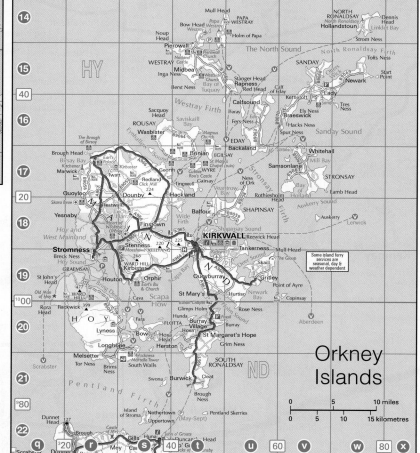

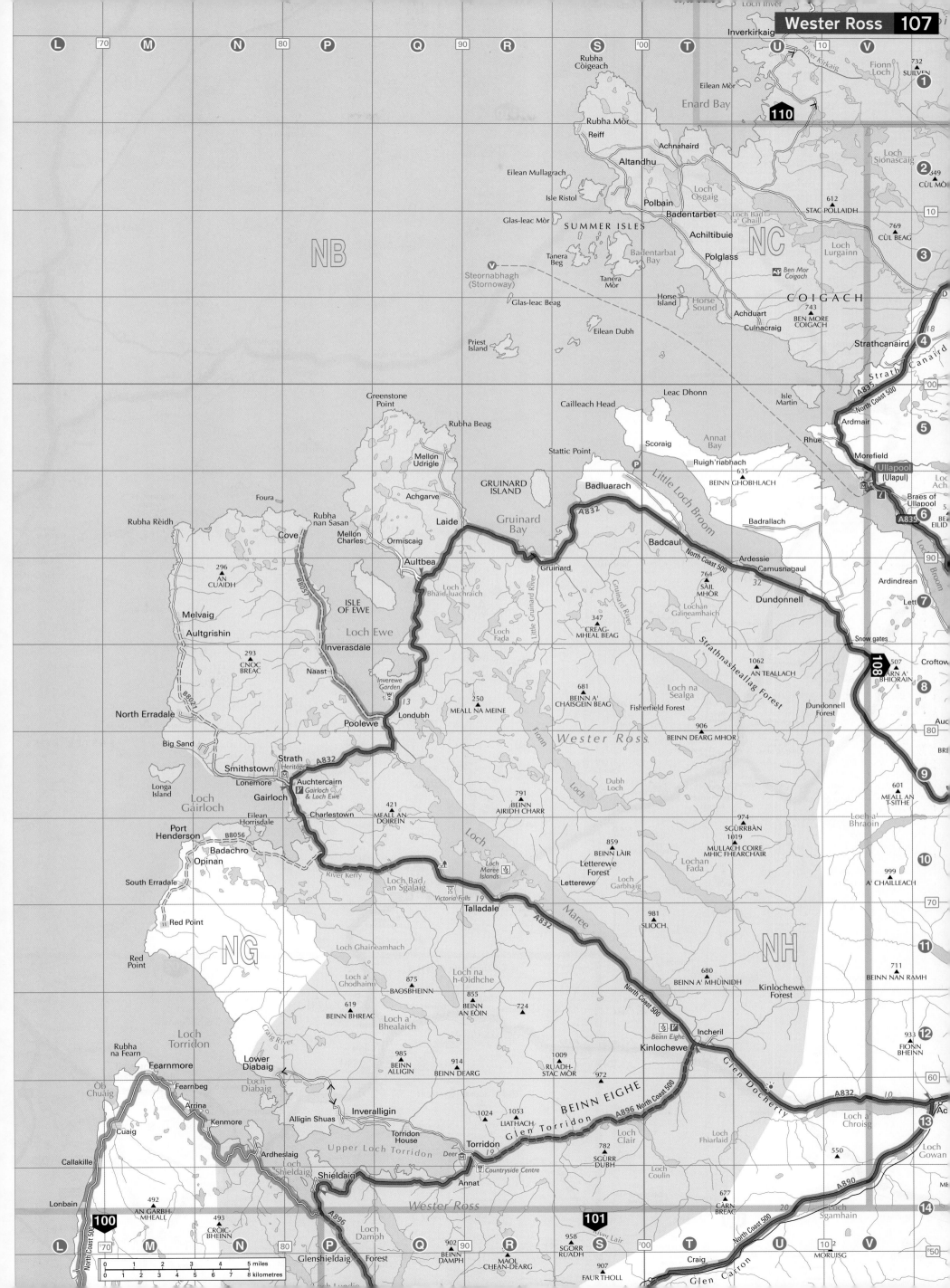

Inverkirkaig
River Kirkaig
Fionn Loch
732 SUILVEN
1
110
L 70 M N 80 P Q 90 R S T U V

Loch Inver
Loch Sionascaig

Enard Bay
Rubha Còigeach
Eilean Mòr
849 CÙL MÒ
2

Rubha Mòr
Reiff
Achnahaird
Altandhu
Loch Osgaig
Loch Lurgainn
612 STAC POLLAIDH
3

Eilean Mullagrach
Isle Ristol
Polbain
Badentarbet
769 CÙL BEAG

NB
SUMMER ISLES
Badentarbat Bay
Achiltibuie
Polglass
Ben Mor Coigach

COIGACH
743 BEN MORE COIGACH
D

Glas-leac Mòr
Tanera Beg
Tanera Mòr
Horse Island
Achduart
Culnacraig
18
4
Strathcanaird

V Steornabhagh (Stornaway)
Glas-leac Beag
Eilean Dubh
Horse Sound
A835 North Coast 500
Strath Canaird
'00

Priest Island
Cailleach Head
Leac Dhonn
Isle Martin
Ardmair
5

Greenstone Point
Rubha Beag
Scoraig
Annat Bay
Rhue
Morefield
Braes of Ullapool

Mellon Udrigle
Stattic Point
Ruigh'riabhach
Ullapool (Ùlapul)
BE EILID
6
A835

Rubha Rèidh
Foura
Cove
Rubha nan Sasan
Mellon Charles
Achgarve
Laide
GRUINARD ISLAND
Badluarach
A832
Little Loch Broom
635 BEINN GHÒBHLACH
7

Ormiscaig
Aultbea
Gruinard Bay
Gruinard
Badcaul
Ardessie
Camusnagaul
North Coast 500
Ardindrean
Lett

Melvaig
Aultgrishin
296 AN CUAIDH
ISLE OF EWE
Loch a' Bhaid-luachraich
Little Gruinard River
Gruinard River
764 SÀIL MHÒR
32 Dundonnell
Lochan Gaineamhaich

Loch Ewe
347 CREAG-MHEAL BEAG
Strathnasheallag Forest
Snow gates
108
507 ARN A' BHIORAIN
8

Inverasdale
293 CNOC BREAC
Naast
250 MEALL NA MEINE
681 BEINN A' CHAISGEIN BEAG
Fisherfield Forest
Loch na Sealga
Dundonnell Forest
1062 AN TEALLACH
Croftow
'80

North Erradale
Inverewe Garden
13
Londubh
Poolewe
Fionn
Wester Ross
906 BEINN DEARG MHOR
601 MEALL AN T-SITHE
9

Big Sand
Smithstown
Strath Heritage
A832
Loch
Dubh Loch
974 SGÙRR BÀN
1019 MULLACH COIRE MHIC FHEARCHAIR
Loch-a' Bhraoin

Longa Island
Loch Gairloch
Lonemore
Gairloch
Auchtercairn
Gairloch & Loch Ewe
421 MEALL AN DOIREIN
791 BEINN AIRIDH CHARR
859 BEINN LÀIR
Letterewe Forest
Lochan Fada
999 A' CHAILLEACH
10
'70

Port Henderson
Eilean Horrisdale
Charlestown
Letterewe
Loch Garbhaig

Badachro
Opinan
B8056
River Kerry
Loch
Loch Maree Islands
981 SLIOCH
680 BEINN A' MHÙINIDH
711 BEINN NAN RAMH
11

South Erradale
Red Point
Loch Bad an Sgalaig
Victoria Falls 19
Talladale
A832
Maree
Kinlochewe Forest

Red Point
NG
Loch Ghaineamhach
Loch na h-Oidhche
North Coast 500
933 FIONN BHEINN
12

Rubha na Fearn
Fearnmore
875 BAOSBHEINN
855 BEINN AN EÒIN
724
Incheril
Beinn Eighe
Kinlochewe
A832
'60

Òb Chuaig
Fearnbeg
619 BEINN BHREAC
Loch a' Ghodhainn
Loch a' Bhealaich
1009 RUADH-STAC MÒR
A896 North Coast 500
Glen Docherty
A832 10
Loch a' Chroisg
Ac
13

Callakille
Arrina
Kenmore
Cuaig
Lower Diabaig
Loch Diabaig
Alligin Shuas
Inveralligin
985 BEINN ALLIGIN
914 BEINN DEARG
972
BEINN EIGHE
1024 LIATHACH
1053
Glen Torridon
A896 North Coast 500
Loch Clair
Loch Fhiarlaid
Loch Coulin
550
Loch Gowan
14

Lonbain
492 AN GARBH-MHEALL
Ardheslaig
Torridon House
Torridon
Deer
Countryside Centre
19
Upper Loch Torridon
782 SGÙRR DUBH

100
493 CRÒIC-BHEINN
Loch Shieldaig
Shieldaig
Annat
A896
Wester Ross
958 SGORR RUADH
677 CÀRN BREAC
A890 North Coast 500
Loch Sgamhain
20

North Coast 500
0 1 2 3 4 5 miles
0 1 2 3 4 5 6 7 8 kilometres
Glenshieldaig Forest
902 BEINN DAMPH
MAOL CHEAN-DEARG
907 FUAR THOLL
Craig
A890 North Coast 500
Glen Carron
MORUISG
'50

101
L 70 M N 80 P Q 90 R S T U V 102

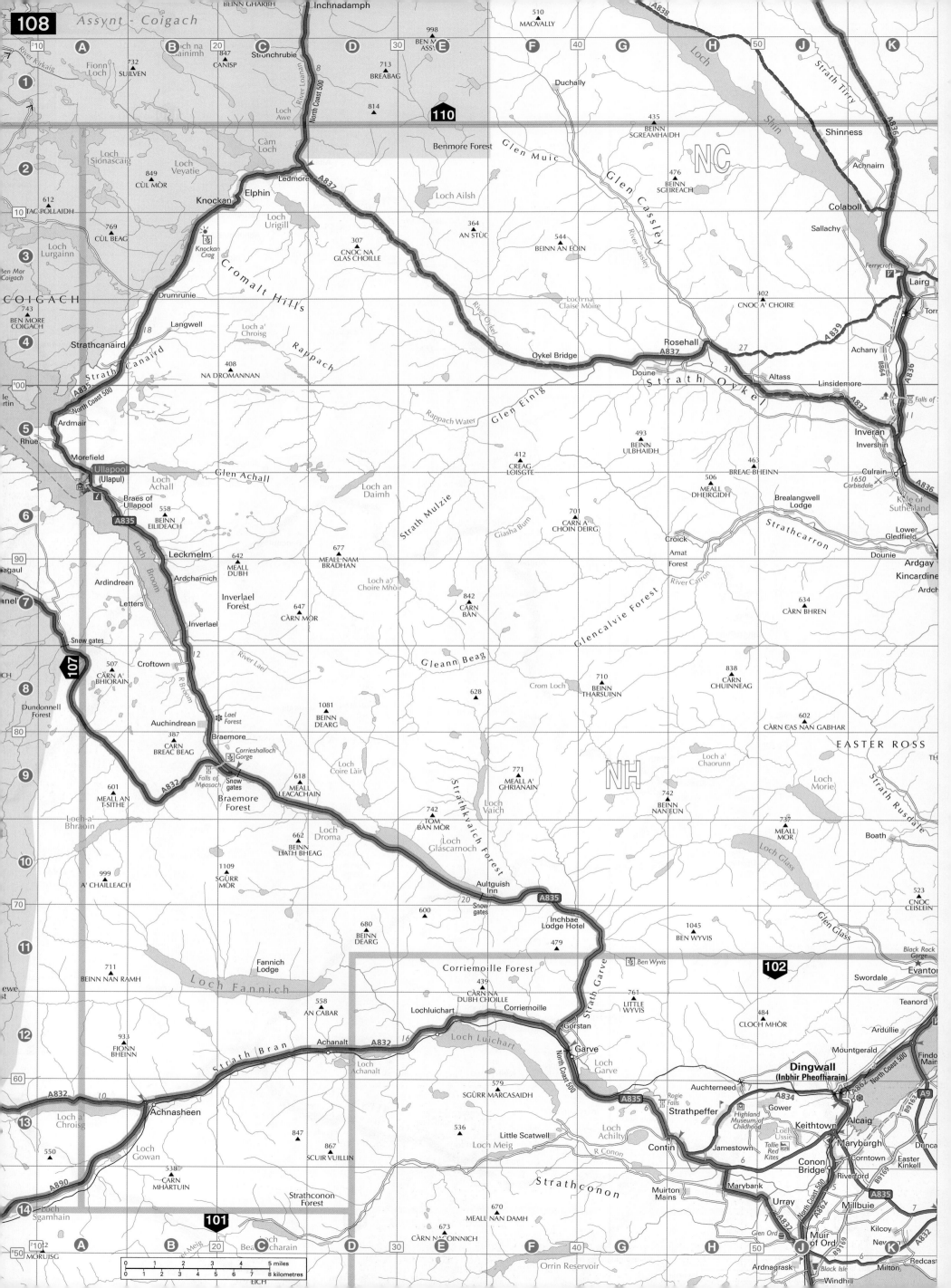

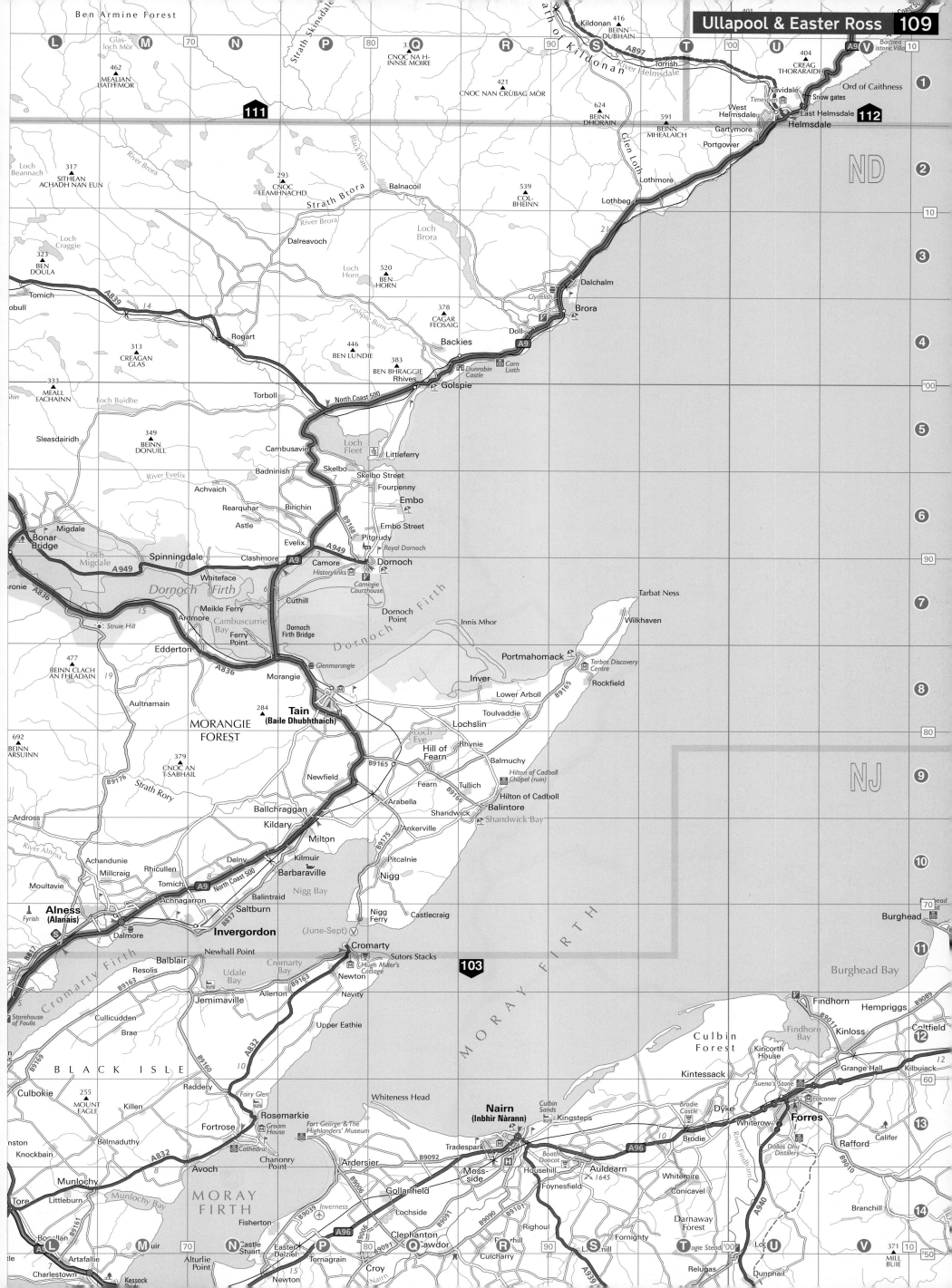

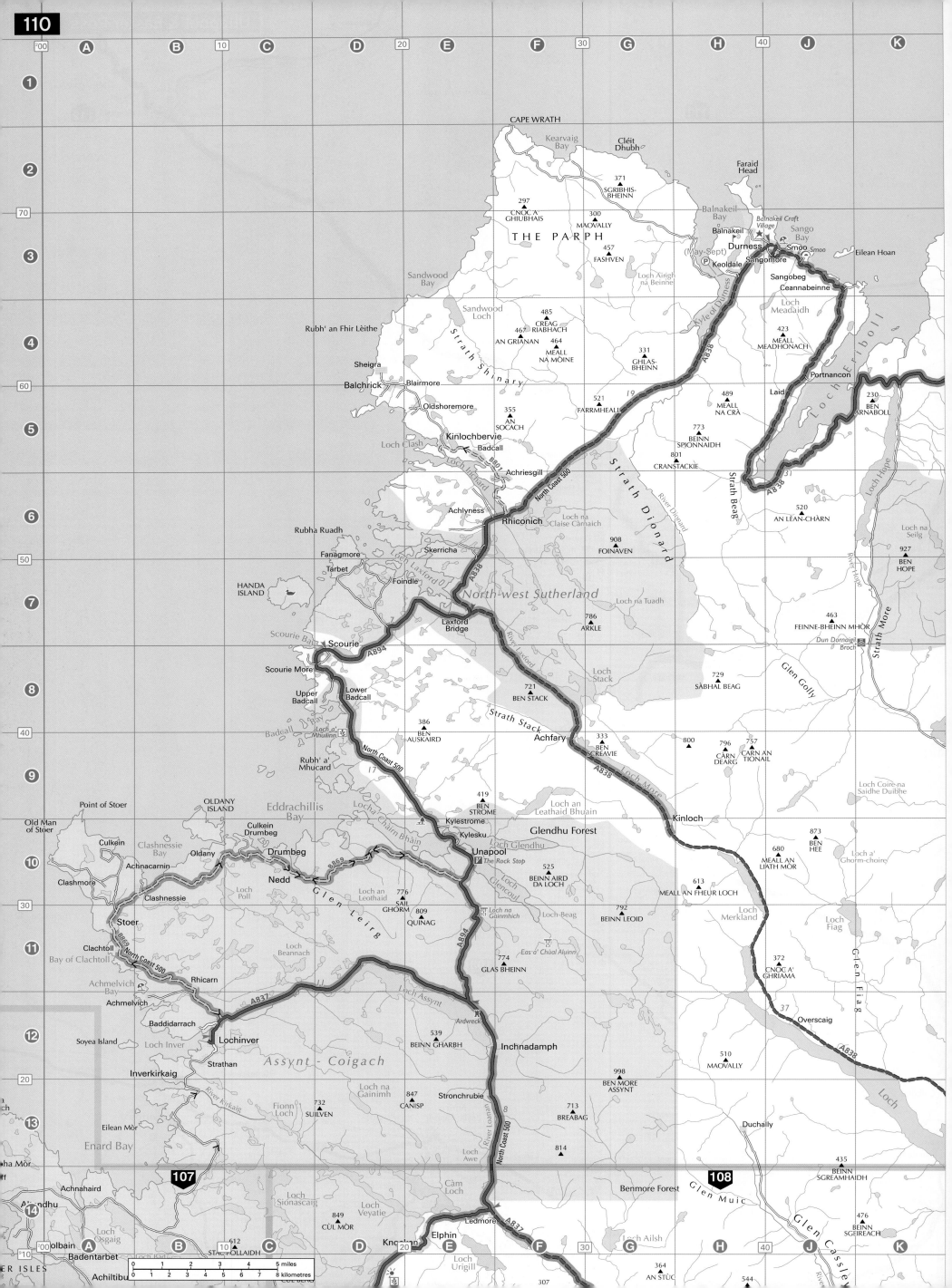

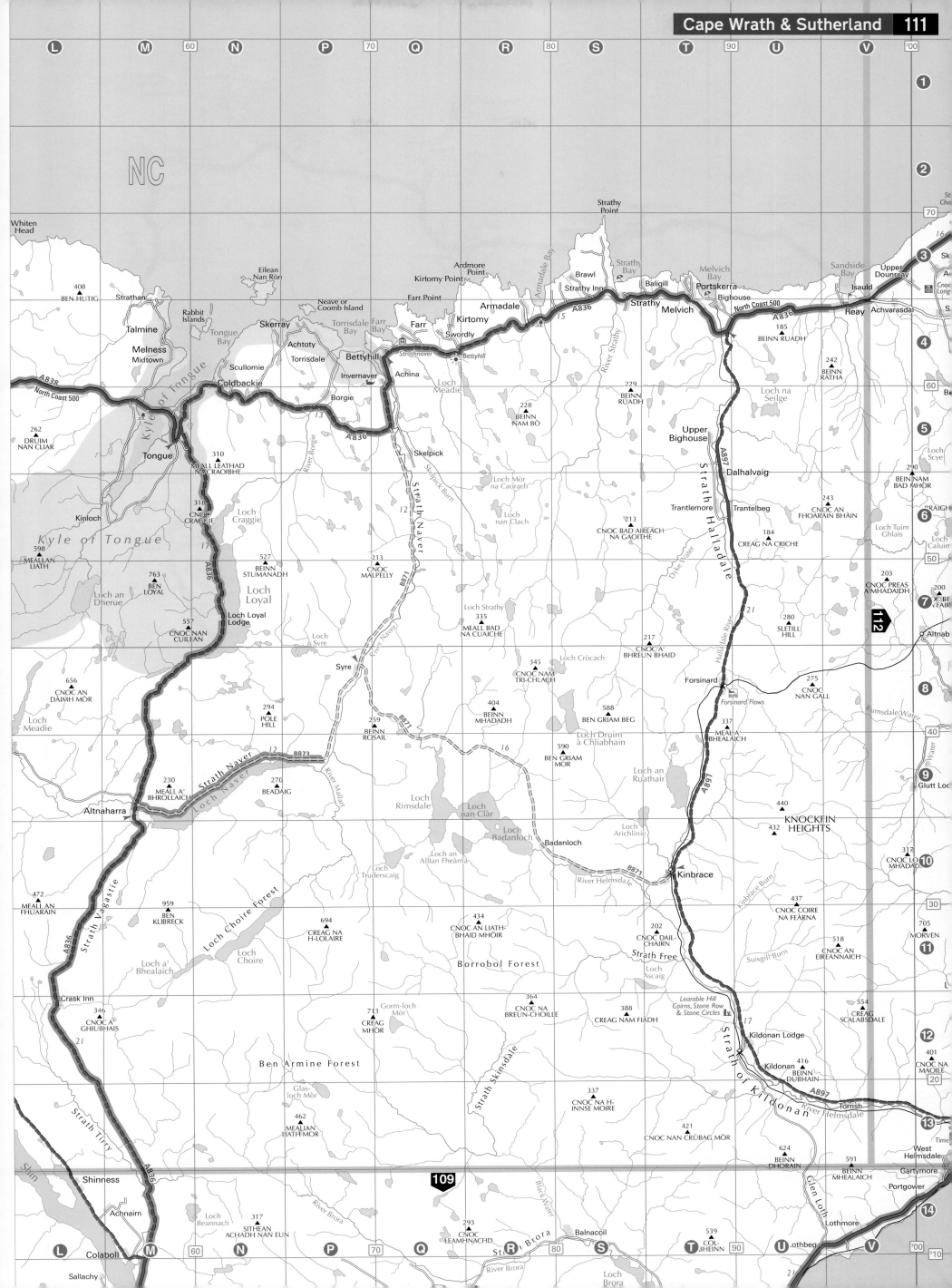

NC

Whiten Head

408 BEN-HUTIG

Strathan

Talmine

Melness
Midtown

Eilean Nan Ròn

Rabbit Islands

Skerray

Neave or Coomb Island

Torrisdale Bay

Ardmore Point

Kirtomy Point

Farr Point

Farr Bay

Farr

Swordly

Strathy Point

Strathy Bay

Brawl

Strathy Inn

Armadale

Kirtomy

Strathnaver

Bettyhill

Strathy

Baligill

Portskerra

Melvich Bay

Bighouse

North Coast 500

Strathy

Melvich

Sandside Bay

Reay

Isauld

Upper Dounreay

Achvarasdal

Tongue Bay

Achtoty

Torrisdale

Bettyhill

Invernaver

Achina

185 BEINN RUADH

North Coast 500

242 BEINN RATHA

Scullomie

Coldbackie

Borgie

Kyle of Tongue

Tongue

North Coast 500

A838

262 DRUIM NAN CLIAR

310 MEALL LEATHAD NA CRAOIBHE

Kinloch

Kyle of Tongue

318 CNOC CRAGGIE

Loch Craggie

A836

A836

Loch Meadie

228 BEINN NAM BÒ

229 BEINN RUADH

Upper Bighouse

Strath Halladale

A897

Dalhalvaig

Trantlemore

Trantlebeg

243 CNOC AN FHOARAIN BHÀIN

290 BEINN NAM BAD MHÒR

RÀIGH

Loch Tuim Ghlais

Loch Calum

Skelpick

Loch Mòr na Caorach

Loch nan Clach

213 CNOC BAD AIREACH NA GAOITHE

184 CREAG NA CRICHE

203 CNOC PREAS A'MHADAIDH

200 CNC BE A'FAIR

598 MEALLAN LIATH

763 BEN LOYAL

Loch an Dherue

Loch Loyal

527 BEINN STUMANADH

213 CNOC MALPELLY

B871

Loch Strathy

335 MEALL BAD NA CUAICHE

217 CNOC A' BHREUN BHAID

280 SLETILL HILL

112

Altnab

557 CNOC NAN CUILEAN

Loch Loyal Lodge

Loch Syre

Strath Naver

Syre

River Naver

345 CNOC NAM TRI-CHLACH

Loch Cròcach

275 CNOC NAN GALL

Forsinard

Forsinard Flows

Rumsdale Water

656 CNOC AN DÀIMH MÒR

Loch Meadie

294 POLE HILL

259 BEINN ROSAIL

B871

404 BEINN MHADADH

588 BEN GRIAM BEG

337 MEALL A' BHEALAICH

A897

Water

230 MEALL A' BHROLLAICH

Strath Naver

270 BEADAIG

B873

River Mallart

16

590 BEN GRIAM MOR

Loch Druim à Chliabhain

Loch an Ruathair

440

9 Glutt Loc

Altnaharra

Loch Naver

Loch Rimsdale

Loch nan Clàr

Loch Badanloch

Loch Arichlinie

432

KNOCKFIN HEIGHTS

317 CNOC LO MHADAD

10

472 MEALL AN FHUARAIN

Strath Vagastie

Loch an Alltan Fheàrna

Loch Truderscaig

Badanloch

B871

River Helmsdale

Kinbrace

Kinbrace Burn

A897

437 CNOC COIRE NA FEÀRNA

30

705 MORVEN

11

Crask Inn

346 CNOC A' GHIUBHAIS

21

Loch a' Bhealaich

Loch Choire

Loch Choire Forest

694 CREAG NA H-LOLAIRE

434 CNOC AN LIATH-BHAID MHÒIR

202 CNOC DAIL-CHAIRN

Strath Free

Loch Ascaig

518 CNOC AN EIREANNAICH

554 CREAG SCALABSDALE

12

959 BEN KLIBRECK

Ben Armine Forest

713 CREAG MHÒR

Gorm-loch Mòr

364 CNOC NA BREUN-CHOILLE

388 CREAG NAM FIADH

Borrobol Forest

Learable Hill Cairns, Stone Row & Stone Circles

17

Strath of Kildonan

Kildonan Lodge

401 CNOC NA MAOILE

20

Strath Tirry

Glas-loch Mòr

462 MEALLAN LIATH MÒR

Strath Skinsdale

337 CNOC NA H-INNSE MOIRE

Kildonan

416 BEINN DUBHAIN

A897

River Helmsdale

13

West Helmsdale

Shin

Crask Inn

Shinness

A836

109

421 CNOC NAN CRÙBAG MÒR

624 BEINN DHORAIN

Glen Loth

591 BEINN MHEALAICH

Torrish

Gartymore

Portgower

14

Colaboll

Achnairn

317 SITHEAN ACHADH NAN EUN

Loch Beannach

293 CNOC LEAMHNACHD

Balnacoil

539 COL- BHEINN

othbeg

Lothmore

Sallachy

River Brora

Loch Brora

21

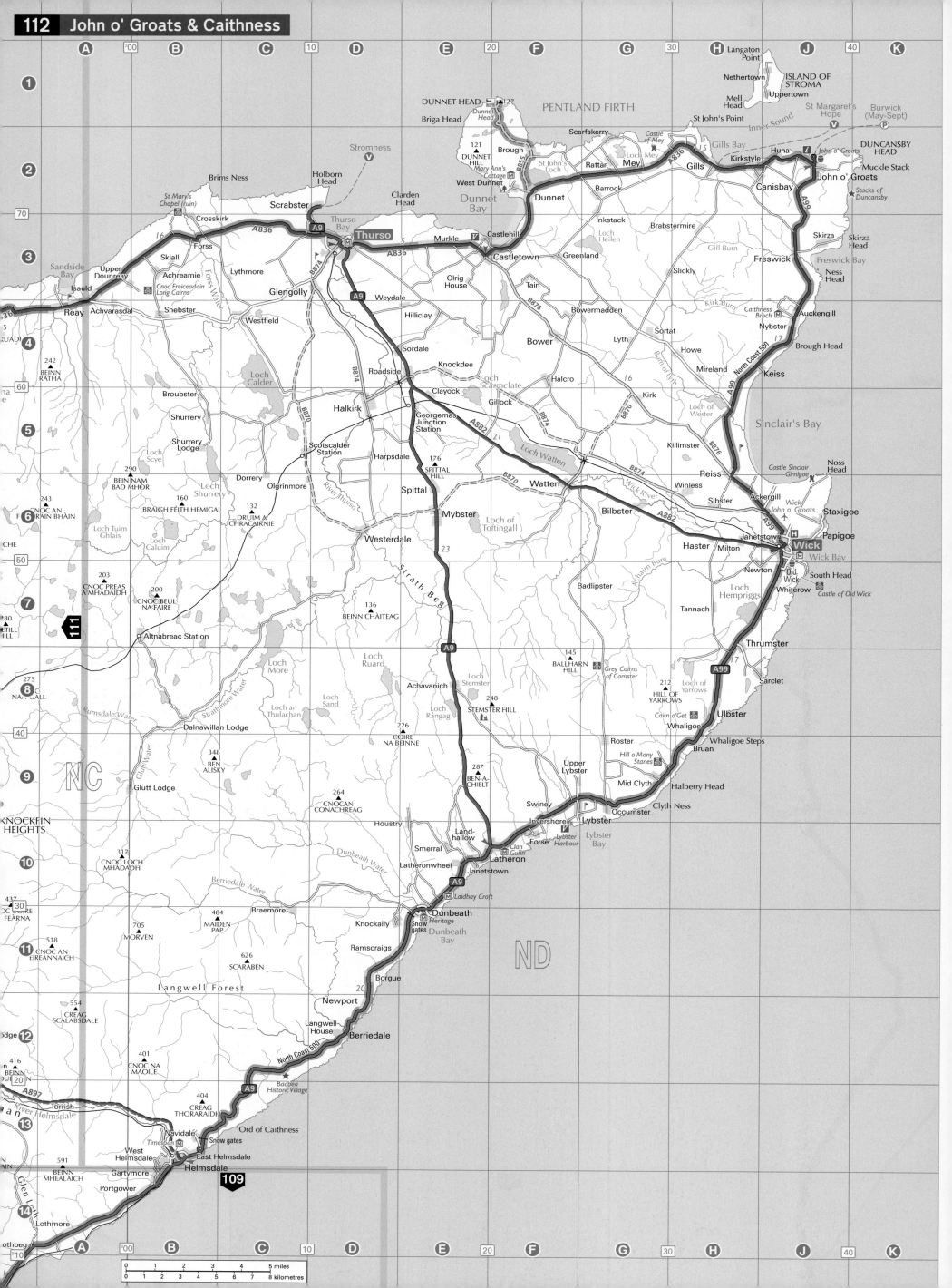

111

109

ENGLAND

- **Acorn Bank Garden** CA10 1SP Cumb 68 D7
- **Aldborough Roman Site** YO51 9ES N York 63 U6
- **Alfriston Clergy House** BN26 5TL E Susx 11 S10
- **Alton Towers** ST10 4DB Staffs 46 E5
- **Anglesey Abbey** CB25 9EJ Cambs 39 R8
- **Anne Hathaway's Cottage** CV37 9HH Warwks 36 G10
- **Antony House** PL11 2QA Cnwll 5 L9
- **Appuldurcombe House** PO38 3EW IoW 9 Q13
- **Apsley House** W1J 7NT Gt Lon 21 N7
- **Arlington Court** EX31 4LP Devon 15 P4
- **Ascott** LU7 0PS Bucks 30 J8
- **Ashby-de-la-Zouch Castle** LE65 1BR Leics 47 L10
- **Athelhampton House & Gardens** DT2 7LG Dorset 7 U6
- **Attingham Park** SY4 4TP Shrops 45 M11
- **Audley End House & Gardens** CB11 4JF Essex 39 R13
- **Avebury Manor & Garden** SN8 1RF Wilts 18 G6
- **Baconsthorpe Castle** NR25 6LN Norfk 50 K6
- **Baddesley Clinton Hall** B93 0DQ Warwks 36 H6
- **Bamburgh Castle** NE69 7DF Nthumb 85 T11
- **Barnard Castle** DL12 8PR Dur 69 M9
- **Barrington Court** TA19 0NQ Somset 17 L13
- **Basildon Park** RG8 9NR W Berk 19 T5
- **Bateman's** TN19 7DS E Susx 12 C11
- **Battle of Britain Memorial Flight Visitor Centre** LN4 4SY Lincs 48 K2
- **Beamish Museum** DH9 0RG Dur 69 R2
- **Beatrix Potter Gallery** LA22 0NS Cumb 67 N13
- **Beaulieu** SO42 7ZN Hants 9 M8
- **Belton House** NG32 2LS Lincs 48 D6
- **Belvoir Castle** NG32 1PE Leics 48 B7
- **Bembridge Windmill** PO35 5SQ IoW 9 S11
- **Beningbrough Hall & Gardens** YO30 1DD N York 64 C8
- **Benthall Hall** TF12 5RX Shrops 45 Q13
- **Berkeley Castle** GL13 9PJ Gloucs 28 C8
- **Berrington Hall** HR6 0DW Herefs 35 M8
- **Berry Pomeroy Castle** TQ9 6LJ Devon 5 U8
- **Beth Chatto Gardens** CO7 7DB Essex 23 Q3
- **Biddulph Grange Garden** ST8 7SD Staffs 45 U2
- **Bishop's Waltham Palace** SO32 1DH Hants 9 Q5
- **Blackpool Zoo** FY3 8PP Bpool 61 Q12
- **Blenheim Palace** OX20 1PX Oxon 29 T4
- **Blickling Estate** NR11 6NF Norfk 51 L8
- **Blue John Cavern** S33 8WA Derbys 56 H10
- **Bodiam Castle** TN32 5UA E Susx 12 E10
- **Bolsover Castle** S44 6PR Derbys 57 Q12
- **Boscobel House** ST19 9AR Staffs 45 T12
- **Bovington Tank Museum** BH20 6JG Dorset 8 A11
- **Bowes Castle** DL12 9LD Dur 69 L10
- **Bradford Industrial Museum** BD2 3HP W Yorks 63 P13
- **Bradley Manor** TQ12 6BN Devon 5 U6
- **Bramber Castle** BN44 3WW W Susx 10 K8
- **Brinkburn Priory** NE65 8AR Nthumb 77 N6
- **Brockhampton Estate** WR6 5TB Herefs 35 Q9
- **Brough Castle** CA17 4EJ Cumb 68 G10
- **Buckfast Abbey** TQ11 0EE Devon 5 S7
- **Buckingham Palace** SW1A 1AA Gt Lon 21 N7
- **Buckland Abbey** PL20 6EY Devon 5 M7
- **Buscot Park** SN7 8BU Oxon 29 P8
- **Byland Abbey** YO61 4BD N York 64 C4
- **Cadbury World** B30 1JR Birm 36 D4
- **Calke Abbey** DE73 7LE Derbys 47 L9
- **Canons Ashby House** NN11 3SD Nhants 37 Q10
- **Canterbury Cathedral** CT1 2EH Kent 13 N4
- **Carisbrooke Castle** PO30 1XY IoW 9 P11
- **Carlyle's House** SW3 5HL Gt Lon 21 N7
- **Castle Drogo** EX6 6PB Devon 5 S2
- **Castle Howard** YO60 7DA N York 64 G5
- **Castle Rising Castle** PE31 6AH Norfk 49 U9
- **Charlecote Park** CV35 9ER Warwks 36 J9
- **Chartwell** TN16 1PS Kent 21 S12
- **Chastleton House** GL56 0SU Oxon 29 P2
- **Chatsworth** DE45 1PP Derbys 57 L12
- **Chedworth Roman Villa** GL54 3LJ Gloucs 29 L5
- **Chessington World of Adventures** KT9 2NE Gt Lon 21 L10
- **Chester Cathedral** CH1 2HU Ches W 54 K13
- **Chester Zoo** CH2 1EU Ches W 54 K12
- **Chesters Roman Fort & Museum** NE46 4EU Nthumb 76 J11
- **Chiswick House & Gardens** W4 2RP Gt Lon 21 M7
- **Chysauster Ancient Village** TR20 8XA Cnwll 2 D10
- **Claremont Landscape Garden** KT10 9JG Surrey 20 K10
- **Claydon House** MK18 2EY Bucks 30 F7
- **Cleeve Abbey** TA23 0PS Somset 16 D8
- **Clevedon Court** BS21 6QU N Som 17 M2
- **Cliveden** SL6 0JA Bucks 20 F5
- **Clouds Hill** BH20 7NQ Dorset 7 V6
- **Clumber Park** S80 3AZ Notts 57 T12
- **Colchester Zoo** CO3 0SL Essex 23 N3
- **Coleridge Cottage** TA5 1NQ Somset 16 G9
- **Coleton Fishacre** TQ6 0EQ Devon 6 B14
- **Compton Castle** TQ3 1TA Devon 5 V8
- **Conisbrough Castle** DN12 3BU Donc 57 R7
- **Corbridge Roman Town** NE45 5NT Nthumb 76 K13
- **Corfe Castle** BH20 5EZ Dorset 8 D12
- **Corsham Court** SN13 0BZ Wilts 18 C6
- **Cotehele** PL12 6TA Cnwll 5 L7
- **Coughton Court** B49 5JA Warwks 36 E8
- **Courts Garden** BA14 6RR Wilts 18 C8
- **Cragside** NE65 7PX Nthumb 77 M5
- **Crealy Theme Park** EX5 1DR Devon 6 D6
- **Crich Tramway Village** DE4 5DP Derbys 46 K2
- **Croft Castle** HR6 9PW Herefs 34 K7
- **Croome Park** WR8 9DW Worcs 35 U12
- **Deddington Castle** OX15 0TE Oxon 29 U1
- **Didcot Railway Centre** OX11 7NJ Oxon 19 R2
- **Dover Castle** CT16 1HU Kent 13 R7
- **Drayton Manor Theme Park** B78 3SA Staffs 46 G13
- **Dudmaston Estate** WV15 6QN Shrops 35 R3
- **Dunham Massey** WA14 4SJ Traffd 55 R9
- **Dunstanburgh Castle** NE66 3TT Nthumb 77 R1
- **Dunster Castle** TA24 6SL Somset 16 C8
- **Durham Cathedral** DH1 3EH Dur 69 S4
- **Dyrham Park** SN14 8HY S Glos 28 D12
- **East Riddlesden Hall** BD20 5EL Brad 63 M11
- **Eden Project** PL24 2SG Cnwll 3 R6
- **Eltham Palace & Gardens** SE9 5QE Gt Lon 21 R8
- **Emmetts Garden** TN14 6BA Kent 21 S12
- **Exmoor Zoo** EX31 4SG Devon 15 Q4
- **Farleigh Hungerford Castle** BA2 7RS Somset 18 B9
- **Farnborough Hall** OX17 1DU Warwks 37 M11
- **Felbrigg Hall** NR11 8PR Norfk 51 L6
- **Fenton House & Garden** NW3 6SP Gt Lon 21 N5
- **Finch Foundry** EX20 2NW Devon 5 Q2
- **Finchale Priory** DH1 5SH Dur 69 S3
- **Fishbourne Roman Palace** PO19 3QR W Susx 10 C10
- **Flamingo Land** YO17 6UX N York 64 H4
- **Forde Abbey** TA20 4LU Somset 7 L3
- **Fountains Abbey & Studley Royal** HG4 3DY N York 63 R6
- **Gawthorpe Hall** BB12 8UA Lancs 62 G13
- **Gisborough Priory** TS14 6HG R & Cl 70 K9
- **Glendurgan Garden** TR11 5JZ Cnwll 2 K11
- **Goodrich Castle** HR9 6HY Herefs 28 A4
- **Great Chalfield Manor & Garden** SN12 8NH Wilts 18 C8
- **Great Coxwell Barn** SN7 7LZ Oxon 29 Q9
- **Greenway** TQ5 0ES Devon 5 V10
- **Haddon Hall** DE45 1LA Derbys 56 K13
- **Hailes Abbey** GL54 5PB Gloucs 29 L1
- **Ham House & Garden** TW10 7RS Gt Lon 21 L8
- **Hampton Court Palace** KT8 9AU Gt Lon 21 L9
- **Hanbury Hall** WR9 7EA Worcs 36 B8
- **Hardwick Hall** S44 5QJ Derbys 57 Q14
- **Hardy's Cottage** DT2 8QJ Dorset 7 T6
- **Hare Hill** SK10 4PY Ches E 56 C11
- **Hatchlands Park** GU4 7RT Surrey 20 J12
- **Heale Gardens** SP4 6NU Wilts 18 H13
- **Helmsley Castle** YO62 5AB N York 64 E3
- **Hereford Cathedral** HR1 2NG Herefs 35 M13
- **Hergest Croft Gardens** HR5 3EG Herefs 34 G9
- **Hever Castle & Gardens** TN8 7NG Kent 21 S13
- **Hidcote Manor Garden** GL55 6LR Gloucs 36 G12
- **Hill Top** LA22 0LF Cumb 67 N13
- **Hinton Ampner** SO24 0LA Hants 9 R3
- **Holkham Hall** NR23 1AB Norfk 50 E5
- **Housesteads Roman Fort** NE47 6NN Nthumb 76 F12
- **Howletts Wild Animal Park** CT4 5EL Kent 13 N4
- **Hughenden Manor** HP14 4LA Bucks 20 E3
- **Hurst Castle** SO41 0TP Hants 9 L11
- **Hylands House & Park** CM2 8WQ Essex 22 G7
- **Ickworth** IP29 5QE Suffk 40 D8
- **Ightham Mote** TN15 0NT Kent 21 U12
- **Ironbridge Gorge Museums** TF8 7DQ Wrekin 45 Q13
- **Kedleston Hall** DE22 5JH Derbys 46 K5
- **Kenilworth Castle & Elizabethan Garden** CV8 1NE Warwks 36 J6
- **Kenwood House** NW3 7JR Gt Lon 21 N5
- **Killerton** EX5 3LE Devon 6 C4
- **King John's Hunting Lodge** BS26 2AP Somset 17 M6
- **Kingston Lacy** BH21 4EA Dorset 8 D8
- **Kirby Hall** NN17 3EN Nhants 38 D2
- **Knightshayes Court** EX16 7RQ Devon 16 C13
- **Knole House** TN13 1HU Kent 21 T12
- **Knowsley Safari Park** L34 4AN Knows 55 L8
- **Lacock Abbey** SN15 2LG Wilts 18 D7
- **Lamb House** TN31 7ES E Susx 12 H11
- **Lanhydrock House** PL30 5AD Cnwll 3 R4
- **Launceston Castle** PL15 7DR Cnwll 4 J4
- **Leeds Castle** ME17 1PB Kent 12 F5
- **Legoland** SL4 4AY W&M 20 F8
- **Lindisfarne Castle** TD15 2SH Nthumb 85 S10
- **Lindisfarne Priory** TD15 2RX Nthumb 85 S10
- **Little Moreton Hall** CW12 4SD Ches E 45 T2
- **Liverpool Cathedral** L1 7AZ Lpool 54 J9
- **London Zoo ZSL** NW1 4RY Gt Lon 21 N6
- **Longleat** BA12 7NW Wilts 18 B12
- **Loseley Park** GU3 1HS Surrey 20 G13
- **Ludgershall Castle** SP11 9QR Wilts 19 L10
- **Lydford Castle** EX20 4BH Devon 5 N4
- **Lyme Park, House & Garden** SK12 2NX Ches E 56 E10
- **Lytes Cary Manor** TA11 7HU Somset 17 P11
- **Lyveden New Bield** PE8 5AT Nhant 38 E3
- **Maiden Castle** DT2 9PP Dorset 7 S7
- **Mapledurham Estate** RG4 7TR Oxon 19 U5
- **Marble Hill House** TW1 2NL Gt Lon 21 L8
- **Marwell Zoo** SO21 1JH Hants 9 Q4
- **Melford Hall** CO10 9AA Suffk 40 E11
- **Merseyside Maritime Museum** L3 4AQ Lpool 54 H9
- **Minster Lovell Hall** OX29 0RR Oxon 29 R5
- **Mompesson House** SP1 2EL Wilts 8 G3
- **Monk Bretton Priory** S71 5QD Barns 57 N5
- **Montacute House** TA15 6XP Somset 17 N13
- **Morwellham Quay** PL19 8JL Devon 5 L7
- **Moseley Old Hall** WV10 7HY Staffs 46 B13
- **Mottisfont** SO51 0LP Hants 9 L3
- **Mottistone Manor Garden** PO30 4ED IoW 9 N12
- **Mount Grace Priory** DL6 3JG N York 70 F13
- **National Maritime Museum** SE10 9NF Gt Lon 21 Q7
- **National Motorcycle Museum** B92 0ED Solhll 36 H4
- **National Portrait Gallery** WC2H 0HE Gt Lon 21 N6
- **National Railway Museum** YO26 4XJ York 64 D9
- **National Space Centre** LE4 5NS C Leic 47 Q12
- **Natural History Museum** SW7 5BD Gt Lon 21 N7
- **Needles Old Battery** PO39 0JH IoW 9 L12
- **Nene Valley Railway** PE8 6LR Cambs 38 H1
- **Netley Abbey** SO31 5FB Hants 9 P7
- **Newark Air Museum** NG24 2NY Notts 48 B2
- **Newtown Old Town Hall** PO30 4PA IoW 9 N10
- **North Leigh Roman Villa** OX29 6QB Oxon 29 S4
- **Norwich Cathedral** NR1 4DH Norfk 51 M12
- **Nostell Priory** WF4 1QE Wakefd 57 P3
- **Nunnington Hall** YO62 5UY N York 64 F4
- **Nymans House** RH17 6EB W Susx 11 M5
- **O2 Arena** SE10 0DX Gt Lon 21 Q6
- **Old Royal Naval College** SE10 9NN Gt Lon 21 Q7
- **Old Sarum** SP1 3SD Wilts 8 G2
- **Old Wardour Castle** SP3 6RR Wilts 8 C3
- **Oliver Cromwell's House** CB7 4HF Cambs 39 R4
- **Orford Castle** IP12 2ND Suffk 41 R10
- **Ormesby Hall** TS3 0SR R & Cl 70 H9
- **Osborne House** PO32 6JX IoW 9 Q9
- **Osterley Park & House** TW7 4RB Gt Lon 20 K7
- **Overbeck's** TQ8 8LW Devon 5 S13
- **Oxburgh Hall** PE33 9PS Norfk 50 B13
- **Packwood House** B94 6AT Warwks 36 G6
- **Paignton Zoo** TQ4 7EU Torbay 6 A13
- **Paycocke's House & Garden** CO6 1NS Essex 22 K3
- **Peckover House & Garden** PE13 1JR Cambs 49 Q12
- **Pendennis Castle** TR11 4LP Cnwll 3 L10
- **Petworth House & Park** GU28 0AE W Susx 10 F6
- **Pevensey Castle** BN24 5LE E Susx 11 U10
- **Peveril Castle** S33 8WQ Derbys 56 J10
- **Polesden Lacey** RH5 6BD Surrey 20 K12
- **Portland Castle** DT5 1AZ Dorset 7 S10
- **Portsmouth Historic Dockyard** PO1 3LJ C Port 9 S8
- **Powderham Castle** EX6 8JQ Devon 6 C8
- **Prior Park Landscape Garden** BA2 5AH BaNES 17 U4
- **Prudhoe Castle** NE42 6NA Nthumb 77 M13
- **Quarry Bank Mill & Styal** SK9 4LA Ches E 55 T10
- **Quebec House** TN16 1TD Kent 21 R12
- **Ramsey Abbey Gatehouse** PE26 1DH Cambs 39 L3
- **Reculver Towers & Roman Fort** CT6 6SU Kent 13 P2
- **Red House** DA6 8JF Gt Lon 21 S7
- **Restormel Castle** PL22 0EE Cnwll 4 E8
- **Richborough Roman Fort** CT13 9JW Kent 13 R3
- **Richmond Castle** DL10 4QW N York 69 Q12
- **Roche Abbey** S66 8NW Rothm 57 R9
- **Rochester Castle** ME1 1SW Medway 12 D2
- **Rockbourne Roman Villa** SP6 3PG Hants 8 G5
- **Roman Baths & Pump Room** BA1 1LZ BaNES 17 U4
- **Royal Botanic Gardens, Kew** TW9 3AB Gt Lon 21 L7
- **Royal Observatory Greenwich** SE10 8XJ Gt Lon 21 Q7
- **Rufford Old Hall** L40 1SG Lancs 55 L3
- **Runnymede** SL4 2JJ W & M 20 G8
- **Rushton Triangular Lodge** NN14 1RP Nhants 38 B4
- **Rycote Chapel** OX9 2PA Oxon 30 E12
- **St Leonard's Tower** ME19 6PE Kent 12 C4
- **St Michael's Mount** TR17 0HT Cnwll 2 E11
- **St Paul's Cathedral** EC4M 8AD Gt Lon 21 P6
- **Salisbury Cathedral** SP1 2EJ Wilts 8 G3
- **Saltram** PL7 1UH C Plym 5 N9
- **Sandham Memorial Chapel** RG20 9JT Hants 19 Q8
- **Sandringham House & Grounds** PE35 6EH Norfk 49 U8
- **Saxtead Green Post Mill** IP13 9QQ Suffk 41 N8
- **Scarborough Castle** YO11 1HY N York 65 P2
- **Science Museum** SW7 2DD Gt Lon 21 N7
- **Scotney Castle** TN3 8JN Kent 12 C8
- **Shaw's Corner** AL6 9BX Herts 31 Q9
- **Sheffield Park & Garden** TN22 3QX E Susx 11 Q6
- **Sherborne Old Castle** DT9 3SA Dorset 17 R13
- **Sissinghurst Castle Garden** TN17 2AB Kent 12 F8
- **Sizergh Castle & Garden** LA8 8AE Cumb 61 T2
- **Smallhythe Place** TN30 7NG Kent 12 G10
- **Snowshill Manor & Garden** WR12 7JU Gloucs 36 E14
- **Souter Lighthouse** SR6 7NH S Tyne 77 U13
- **Speke Hall, Garden & Estate** L24 1XD Lpool 54 K10
- **Spinnaker Tower** PO1 3TT C Port 9 S9
- **Stokesay Castle** SY7 9AH Shrops 34 K4
- **Stonehenge** SP4 7DE Wilts 18 H12
- **Stourhead** BA12 6QD Wilts 17 U10
- **Stowe Gardens** MK18 5EQ Bucks 30 E5
- **Sudbury Hall** DE6 5HT Derbys 46 G7
- **Sulgrave Manor** OX17 2SD Nhants 37 Q11
- **Sunnycroft** TF1 2DR Wrekin 45 Q11
- **Sutton Hoo** IP12 3DJ Suffk 41 N11
- **Sutton House** E9 6JQ Gt Lon 21 Q5
- **Tate Britain** SW1P 4RG Gt Lon 21 N7
- **Tate Liverpool** L3 4BB Lpool 54 H9
- **Tate Modern** SE1 9TG Gt Lon 21 P6
- **Tattershall Castle** LN4 4LR Lincs 48 K2
- **Tatton Park** WA16 6QN Ches E 55 R10
- **The British Library** NW1 2DB Gt Lon 21 N6
- **The British Museum** WC1B 3DG Gt Lon 21 N6
- **The Lost Gardens of Heligan** PL26 6EN Cnwll 3 P7
- **The Lowry** M50 3AZ Salfd 55 T7
- **The National Gallery** WC2N 5DN Gt Lon 21 N6
- **The Vyne** RG24 9HL Hants 19 T9
- **The Weir Garden** HR4 7QF Herefs 34 K12
- **Thornton Abbey & Gatehouse** DN39 6TU N Linc 58 K3
- **Thorpe Park** KT16 8PN Surrey 20 H9
- **Tilbury Fort** RM18 7NR Thurr 22 G12
- **Tintagel Castle** PL34 0HE Cnwll 4 C3
- **Tintinhull Garden** BA22 8PZ Somset 17 P13
- **Totnes Castle** TQ9 5NU Devon 5 U8
- **Tower of London** EC3N 4AB Gt Lon 21 P6
- **Townend** LA23 1LB Cumb 67 P12
- **Treasurer's House** YO1 7JL York 64 E9
- **Trelissick Garden** TR3 6QL Cnwll 3 L9
- **Trengwainton Garden** TR20 8RZ Cnwll 2 C10
- **Trerice** TR8 4PG Cnwll 3 L5
- **Twycross Zoo** CV9 3PX Leics 46 K12
- **Upnor Castle** ME2 4XG Medway 22 J13
- **Uppark House & Garden** GU31 5QR W Susx 10 B7
- **Upton House & Garden** OX15 6HT Warwks 37 L11
- **Victoria & Albert Museum** SW7 2RL Gt Lon 21 N7
- **Waddesdon Manor** HP18 0JH Bucks 30 F9
- **Wakehurst Place** RH17 6TN W Susx 11 N4
- **Wall Roman Site** WS14 0AW Staffs 46 E12
- **Wallington** NE61 4AR Nthumb 77 L9
- **Walmer Castle & Gardens** CT14 7LJ Kent 13 S6
- **Warkworth Castle & Hermitage** NE65 0UJ Nthumb 77 Q4
- **Warner Bros. Studio Tour London** WD25 7LR Herts 31 N12
- **Warwick Castle** CV34 4QU Warwks 36 J8
- **Washington Old Hall** NE38 7LE Sundld 70 D1
- **Waterperry Gardens** OX33 1LG Oxon 30 D11
- **Weeting Castle** IP27 0RQ Norfk 40 C3
- **Wenlock Priory** TF13 6HS Shrops 45 P13
- **West Midland Safari & Leisure Park** DY12 1LF Worcs 35 T5
- **West Wycombe Park** HP14 3AJ Bucks 20 D4
- **Westbury Court Garden** GL14 1PD Gloucs 28 D5
- **Westminster Abbey** SW1P 3PA Gt Lon 21 N7
- **Westonbirt Arboretum** GL8 8QS Gloucs 28 G9
- **Westwood Manor** BA15 2AF Wilts 18 B9
- **Whipsnade Zoo ZSL** LU6 2LF Beds C 31 M9
- **Whitby Abbey** YO22 4JT N York 71 R10
- **Wicksteed Park** NN15 6NJ Nhants 38 C5
- **Wightwick Manor & Gardens** WV6 8EE Wolves 45 U14
- **Wild Place Project** BS10 7TP S Gloucs 27 V11
- **Wimpole Estate** SG8 0BW Cambs 39 M10
- **Winchester Cathedral** SO23 9LS Hants 9 P3
- **Winchester City Mill** SO23 0EJ Hants 9 P3
- **Windsor Castle** SL4 1NJ W & M 20 G7
- **Winkworth Arboretum** GU8 4AD Surrey 10 F2
- **Wisley RHS Garden** GU23 6QB Surrey 20 J11
- **Woburn Safari Park** MK17 9QN Beds C 31 L6
- **Wookey Hole Caves** BA5 1BA Somset 17 P7
- **Woolsthorpe Manor** NG33 5PD Lincs 48 D9
- **Wordsworth House** CA13 9RX Cumb 66 H6
- **Wrest Park** MK45 4HR Beds C 31 N5
- **Wroxeter Roman City** SY5 6PR Shrops 45 N12
- **WWT Arundel Wetland Centre** BN18 9PB W Susx 10 G9
- **WWT Slimbridge Wetland Centre** GL2 7BT Gloucs 28 D6
- **Yarmouth Castle** PO41 0PB IoW 9 M11
- **York Minster** YO1 7HH York 64 E9

SCOTLAND

- **Aberdour Castle** KY3 0SL Fife 83 N1
- **Alloa Tower** FK10 1PP Clacks 90 C13
- **Arbroath Abbey** DD11 1EG Angus 91 T3
- **Arduaine Garden** PA34 4XQ Ag & B 87 P3
- **Bachelors' Club** KA5 5RB S Ayrs 81 N7
- **Balmoral Castle Grounds** AB35 5TB Abers 98 D5
- **Balvenie Castle** AB55 4DH Moray 104 C7
- **Bannockburn Battlefield & Heritage Centre** FK7 0LJ Stirlg 89 S7
- **Blackness Castle** EH49 7NH Falk 83 L2
- **Blair Castle** PH18 5TL P & K 97 P10
- **Bothwell Castle** G71 8BL S Lans 82 C7
- **Branklyn Garden** PH2 7BB P & K 90 H7
- **Brodick Castle, Garden & Country Park** KA27 8HY N Ayrs 80 E5
- **Brodie Castle** IV36 2TE Moray 103 Q4
- **Broughton House & Garden** DG6 4JX D & G 73 R9
- **Burleigh Castle** KY13 9GG P & K 90 H11
- **Caerlaverock Castle** DG1 4RU D & G 74 K12
- **Cardoness Castle** DG7 2EH D & G 73 P8
- **Castle Campbell & Garden** FK14 7PP Clacks 90 E12
- **Castle Fraser, Garden & Estate** AB51 7LD Abers 105 L13
- **Castle Kennedy Gardens** DG9 8SL D & G 72 E7
- **Castle Menzies** PH15 2JD P & K 90 B2
- **Corgarff Castle** AB36 8YP Abers 98 D2
- **Craigievar Castle** AB33 8JF Abers 98 K2
- **Craigmillar Castle** EH16 4SY C Edin 83 Q4
- **Crarae Garden** PA32 8YA Ag & B 87 T6
- **Crathes Castle & Garden** AB31 5QJ Abers 99 N4
- **Crichton Castle** EH37 5XA Mdloth 83 S6
- **Crossraguel Abbey** KA19 8HQ S Ayrs 80 K11
- **Culloden Battlefield** IV2 5EU Highld 102 K6
- **Culross Palace** KY12 8JH Fife 82 J1
- **Culzean Castle & Country Park** KA19 8LE S Ayrs 80 J10
- **Dallas Dhu Distillery** IV36 2RR Moray 103 R4
- **David Livingstone Centre** G72 9BY S Lans 82 C7
- **Dirleton Castle & Garden** EH39 5ER E Loth 84 E2
- **Doune Castle** FK16 6EA Stirlg 89 R5
- **Drum Castle, Garden & Estate** AB31 5EY Abers 99 P3
- **Dryburgh Abbey** TD6 0RQ Border 84 F12
- **Duff House** AB45 3SX Abers 104 K3
- **Dumbarton Castle** G82 1JJ W Duns 88 J11
- **Dundrennan Abbey** DG6 4QH D & G 73 S10
- **Dunnottar Castle** AB39 2TL Abers 99 R7
- **Dunstaffnage Castle & Chapel** PA37 1PZ Ag & B 94 B12
- **Edinburgh Castle** EH1 2NG C Edin 83 Q4
- **Edinburgh Zoo RZSS** EH12 6TS C Edin 83 P4
- **Edzell Castle & Garden** DD9 7UE Angus 98 K10
- **Eilean Donan Castle** IV40 8DX Highld 101 M6
- **Elgin Cathedral** IV30 1HU Moray 103 V3
- **Falkland Palace & Garden** KY15 7BU Fife 91 L10
- **Fort George** IV2 7TE Highld 103 L4
- **Fyvie Castle** AB53 8JS Abers 105 M8
- **Georgian House** EH2 4DR C Edin 83 P4
- **Gladstone's Land** EH1 2NT C Edin 83 Q4
- **Glamis Castle** DD8 1RJ Angus 91 N2
- **Glasgow Botanic Gardens** G12 0UE C Glas 89 N12
- **Glasgow Cathedral** G4 0QZ C Glas 89 P12
- **Glasgow Science Centre** G51 1EA C Glas 89 N12
- **Glen Grant Distillery** AB38 7BS Moray 104 B6
- **Glenluce Abbey** DG8 0AF D & G 72 F8
- **Greenbank Garden** G76 8RB E Rens 81 R1
- **Haddo House** AB41 7EQ Abers 105 P9
- **Harmony Garden** TD6 9LJ Border 84 E12
- **Hermitage Castle** TD9 0LU Border 75 U6
- **Highland Wildlife Park RZSS** PH21 1NL Highld 97 N3
- **Hill House** G84 9AJ Ag & B 88 G9
- **Hill of Tarvit Mansion & Garden** KY15 5PB Fife 91 N9
- **Holmwood** G44 3YG C Glas 89 N14
- **House of Dun** DD10 9LQ Angus 99 M12
- **House of the Binns** EH49 7NA W Loth 83 L3
- **Huntingtower Castle** PH1 3JL P & K 90 G7
- **Huntly Castle** AB54 4SH Abers 104 G7
- **Hutchesons' Hall** G1 1EJ C Glas 89 N12
- **Inchmahome Priory** FK8 3RA Stirlg 89 N5
- **Inveresk Lodge Garden** EH21 7TE E Loth 83 R4
- **Inverewe Garden & Estate** IV22 2LG Highld 107 Q8
- **Inverlochy Castle** PH33 6SN Highld 94 G3
- **Kellie Castle & Garden** KY10 2RF Fife 91 R10
- **Kildrummy Castle** AB33 8RA Abers 104 F12
- **Killiecrankie** PH16 5LG P & K 97 Q11
- **Leith Hall Garden & Estate** AB54 4NQ Abers 104 G10
- **Linlithgow Palace** EH49 7AL W Loth 82 K3
- **Lochleven Castle** KY13 8UF P & K 90 H11
- **Logan Botanic Garden** DG9 9ND D & G 72 D11
- **Malleny Garden** EH14 7AF C Edin 83 N5
- **Melrose Abbey** TD6 9LG Border 84 E12
- **National Museum of Scotland** EH1 1JF C Edin 83 Q4
- **Newark Castle** PA14 5NH Inver 88 H11
- **Palace of Holyroodhouse** EH8 8DX C Edin 83 Q4
- **Pitmedden Garden** AB41 7PD Abers 105 P10
- **Preston Mill & Phantassie Doocot** EH40 3DS E Loth 84 F3
- **Priorwood Garden** TD6 9PX Border 84 E12
- **Robert Smail's Printing Works** EH44 6HA Border 83 R11
- **Rothesay Castle** PA20 0DA Ag & B 88 C13
- **Royal Botanic Garden Edinburgh** EH3 5LR C Edin 83 P3
- **Royal Yacht Britannia** EH6 6JJ C Edin 83 Q3
- **St Andrews Aquarium** KY16 9AS Fife 91 R8
- **Scone Palace** PH2 6BD P & K 90 H6
- **Smailholm Tower** TD5 7PG Border 84 G12
- **Souter Johnnie's Cottage** KA19 8HY S Ayrs 80 J11
- **Stirling Castle** FK8 1EJ Stirlg 89 S7
- **Sweetheart Abbey** DG2 8BU D & G 74 J12
- **Tantallon Castle** EH39 5PN E Loth 84 F1
- **Tenement House** G3 6QN C Glas 89 N12
- **The Burrell Collection** G43 1AT C Glas 89 N13
- **The Falkirk Wheel** FK1 4RS Falk 82 G2
- **The Hunterian Museum** G12 8QQ C Glas 89 N12
- **Threave Castle** DG7 1TJ D & G 74 D13
- **Threave Garden** DG7 1RX D & G 74 E13
- **Tolquhon Castle** AB41 7LP Abers 105 P10
- **Traquair House** EH44 6PW Border 83 R11
- **Urquhart Castle** IV63 6XJ Highld 102 F10
- **Weaver's Cottage** PA10 2JG Rens 88 K13
- **Whithorn Priory & Museum** DG8 8PY D & G 73 L11

WALES

- **Aberconwy House** LL32 8AY Conwy 53 N7
- **Aberdulais Tin Works & Waterfall** SA10 8EU Neath 26 D8
- **Beaumaris Castle** LL58 8AP IoA 52 K7
- **Big Pit: National Coal Museum** NP4 9XP Torfn 27 N6
- **Bodnant Garden** LL28 5RE Conwy 53 P8
- **Caerleon Roman Fortress & Baths** NP18 1AE Newpt 27 Q9
- **Caernarfon Castle** LL55 2AY Gwynd 52 G10
- **Caldicot Castle & Country Park** NP26 4HU Mons 27 T10
- **Cardiff Castle** CF10 3RB Cardif 27 M12
- **Castell Coch** CF15 7JS Cardif 27 L11
- **Chirk Castle** LL14 5AF Wrexhm 44 G6
- **Colby Woodland Garden** SA67 8PP Pembks 25 L9
- **Conwy Castle** LL32 8AY Conwy 53 N7
- **Criccieth Castle** LL52 0DP Gwynd 42 K6
- **Dinefwr Park & Castle** SA19 6RT Carmth 25 V6
- **Dolaucothi Gold Mines** SA19 8US Carmth 33 N12
- **Erddig** LL13 0YT Wrexhm 44 H4
- **Ffestiniog Railway** LL49 9NF Gwynd 43 M6
- **Harlech Castle** LL46 2YH Gwynd 43 L7
- **Llanerchaeron** SA48 8DG Cerdgn 32 J8
- **National Showcaves Centre for Wales** SA9 1GJ Powys 26 E4
- **Penrhyn Castle** LL57 4HT Gwynd 52 K8
- **Plas Newydd** LL61 6DQ IoA 52 H9
- **Plas yn Rhiw** LL53 8AB Gwynd 42 D8
- **Portmeirion** LL48 6ER Gwynd 43 L6
- **Powis Castle & Garden** SY21 8RF Powys 44 F12
- **Raglan Castle** NP15 2BT Mons 27 S6
- **Sygun Copper Mine** LL55 4NE Gwynd 43 M4
- **Tintern Abbey** NP16 6SE Mons 27 U7
- **Tudor Merchant's House** SA70 7BX Pembks 24 K10
- **Tŷ Mawr Wybrnant** LL25 0HJ Conwy 43 Q3
- **Valle Crucis Abbey** LL20 8DD Denbgs 44 F5

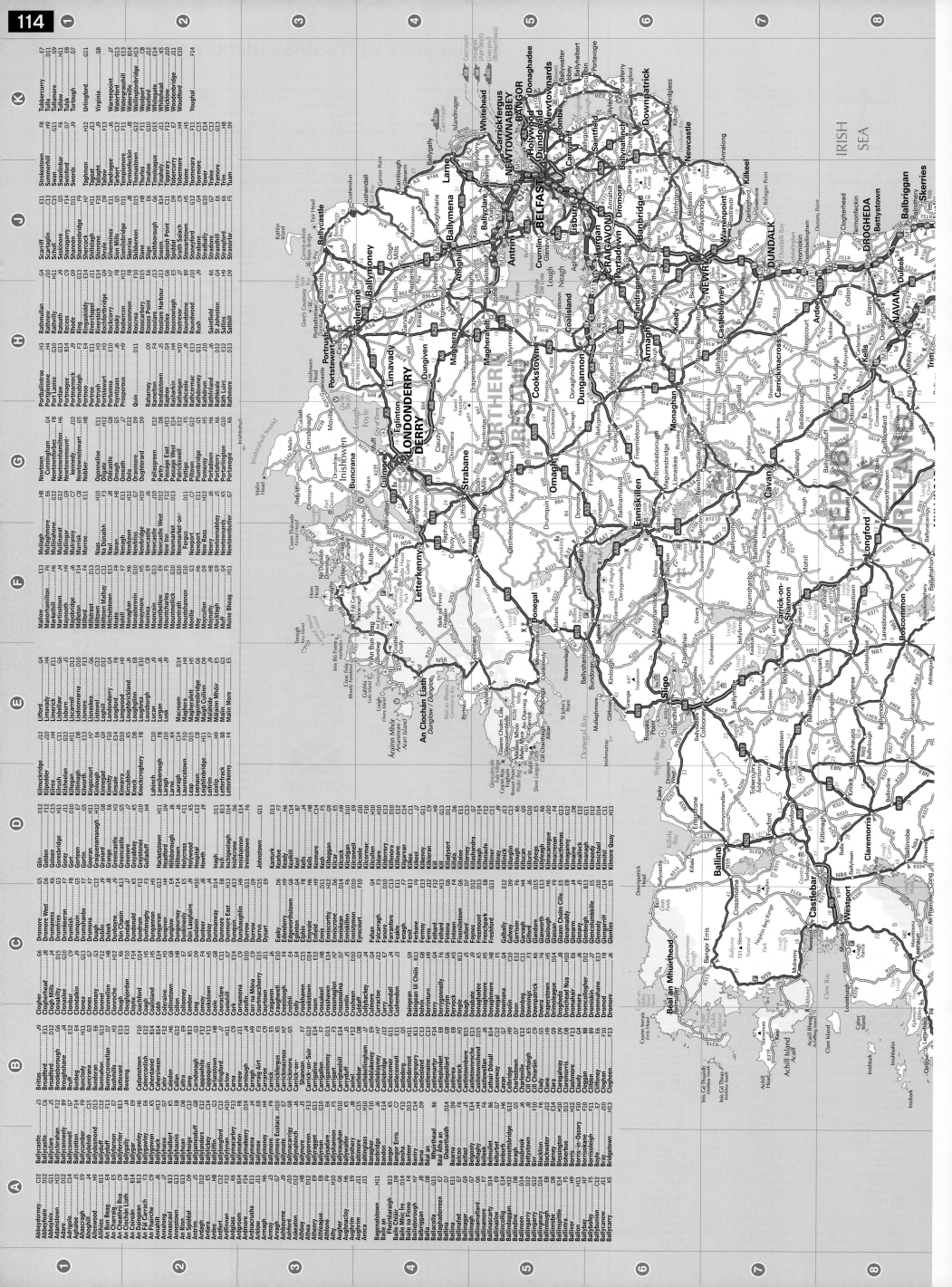

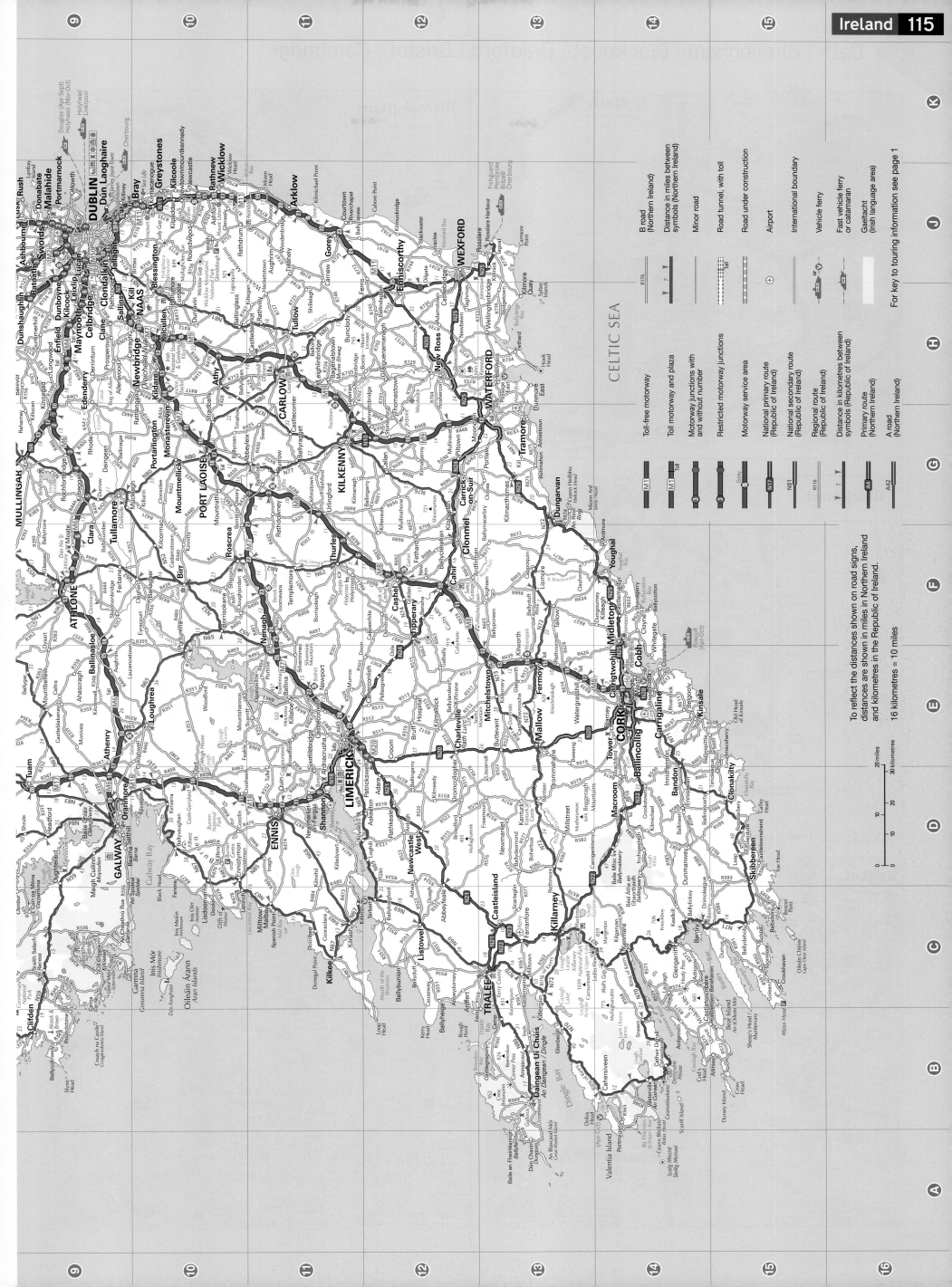

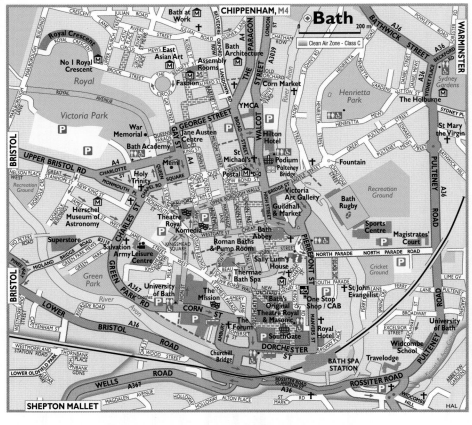

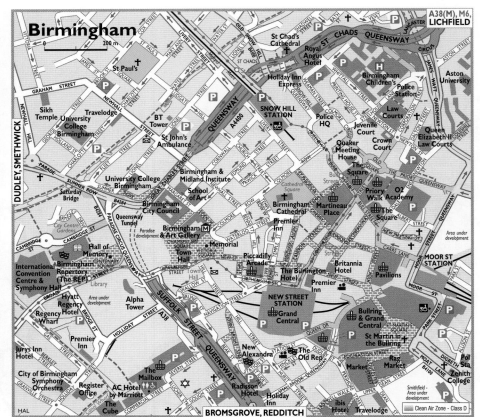

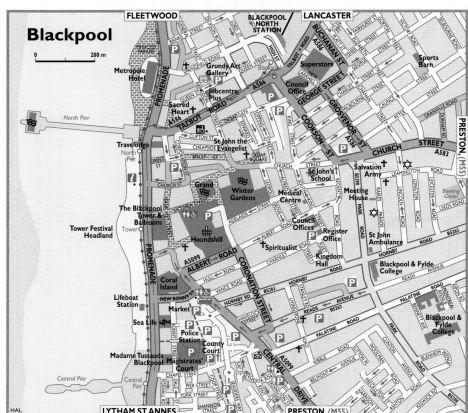

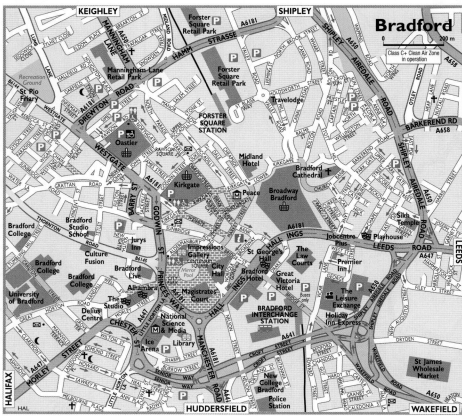

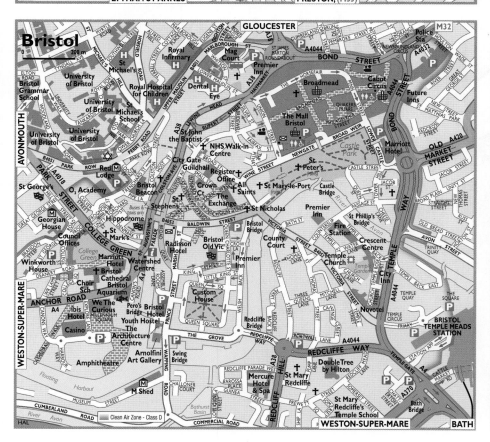

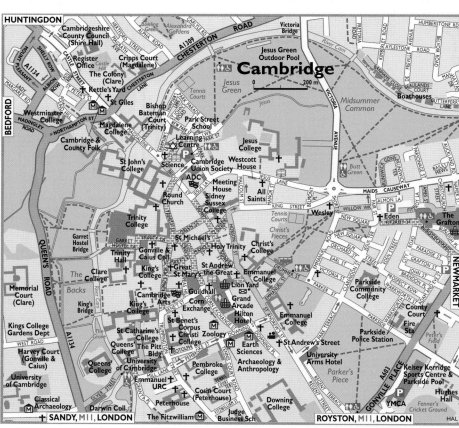

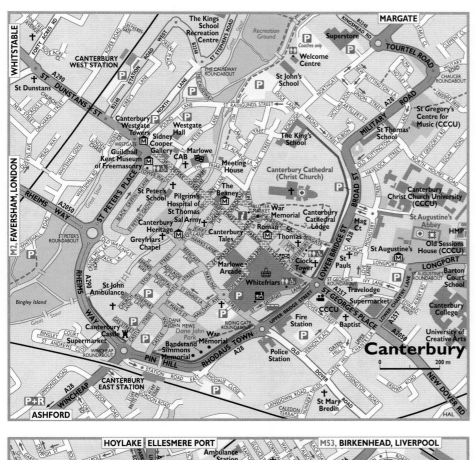

Canterbury

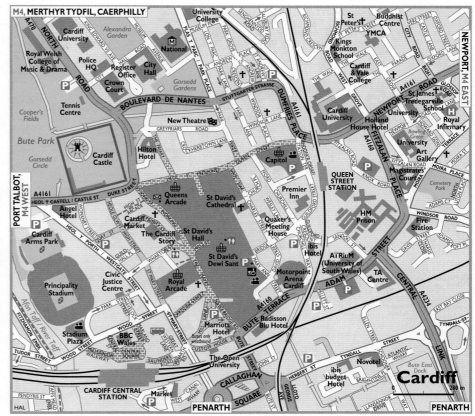

Cardiff

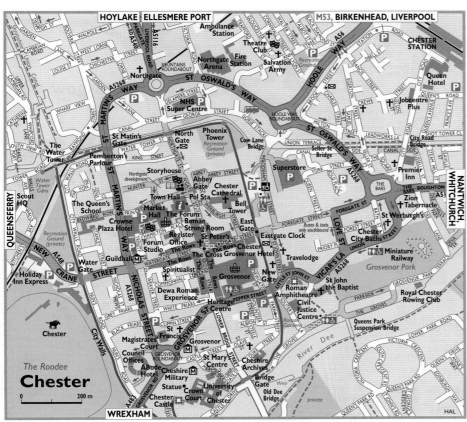

Chester

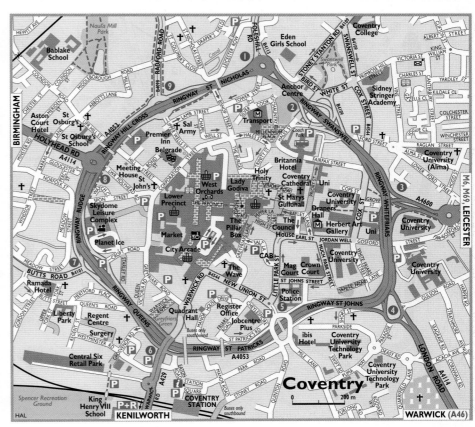

Coventry

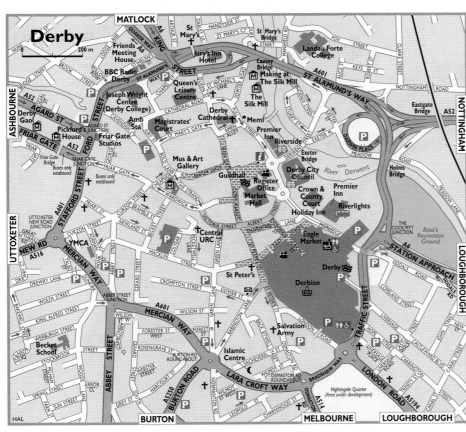

Derby

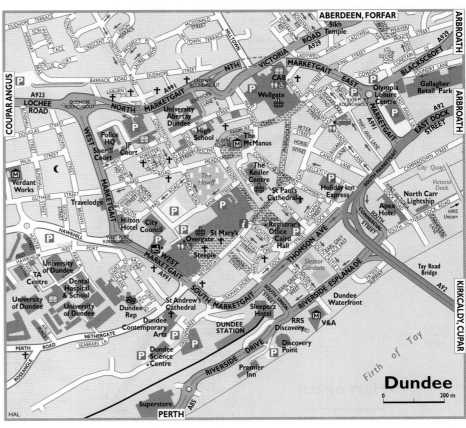

Dundee

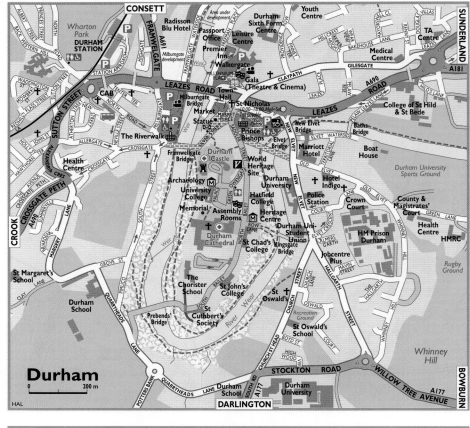

Durham

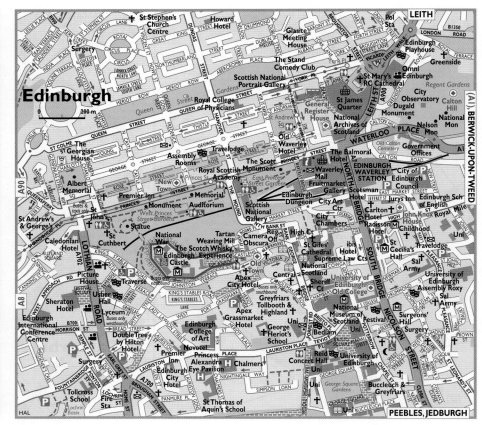

Edinburgh

Exeter

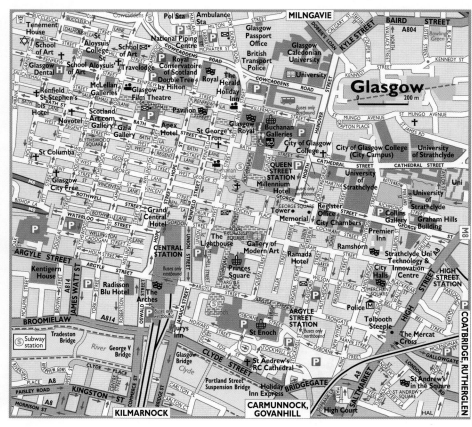

Glasgow

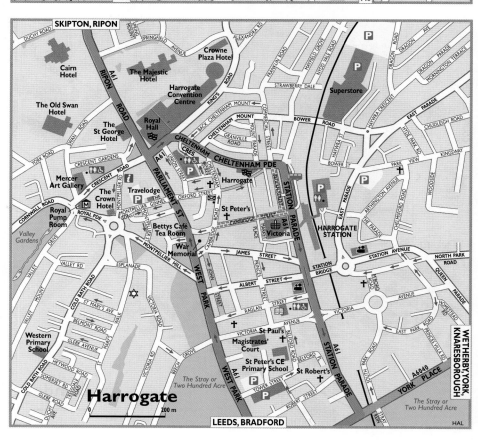

Harrogate

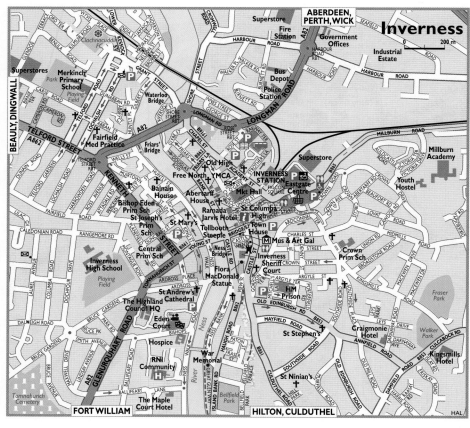

Inverness

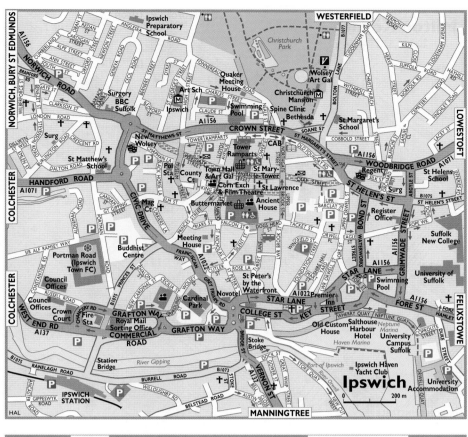

Ipswich

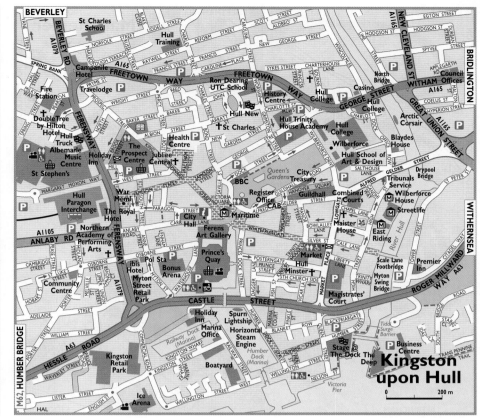

Kingston upon Hull

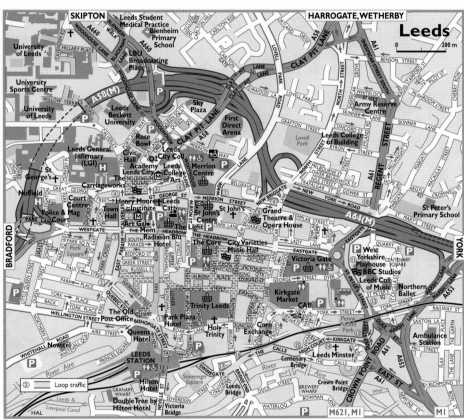

Leeds

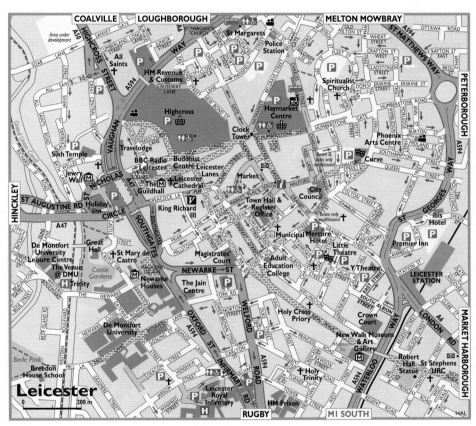

Leicester

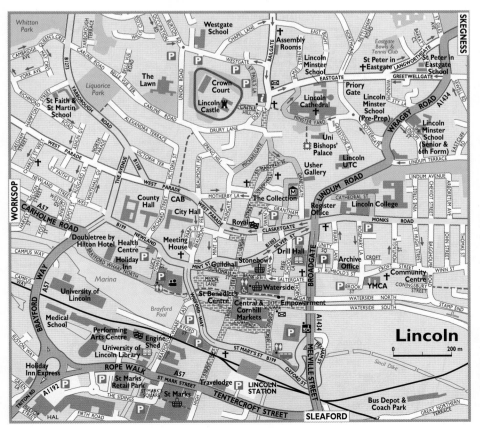

Lincoln

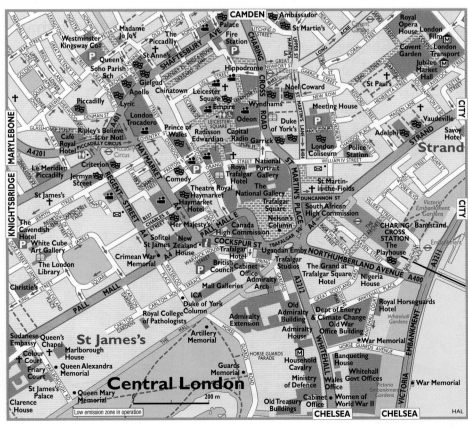

Central London

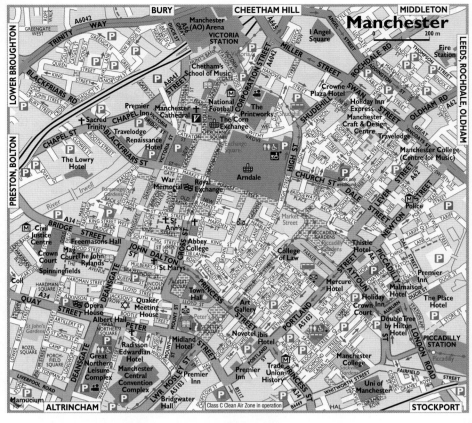

Manchester

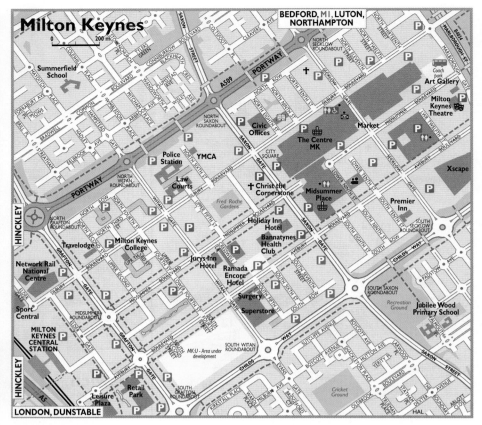

Milton Keynes

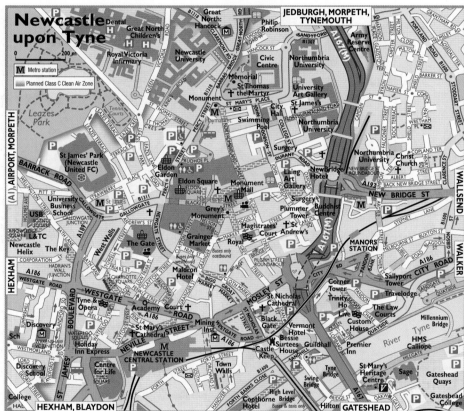

Newcastle upon Tyne

Norwich

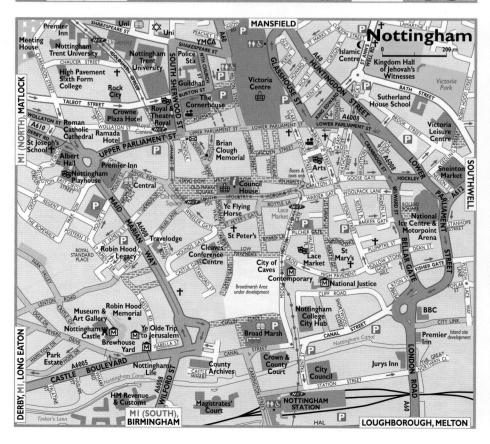

Nottingham

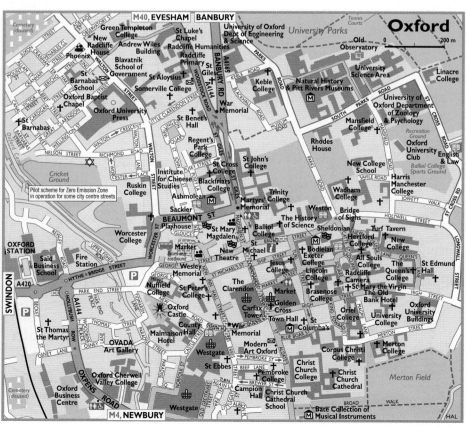

Oxford

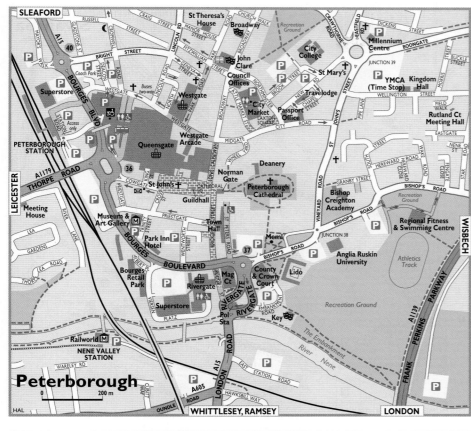

Peterborough

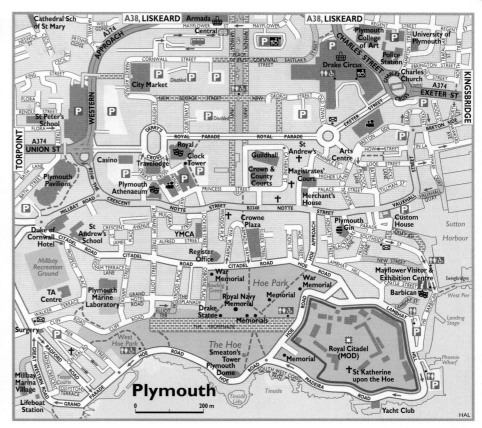

Plymouth

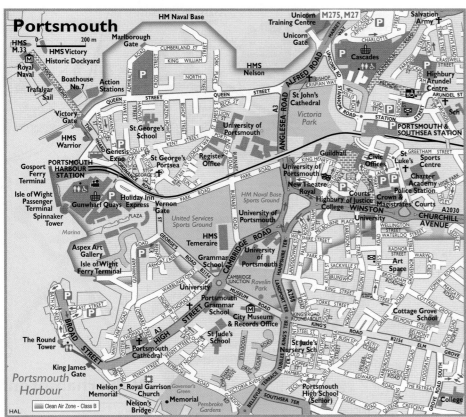

Portsmouth

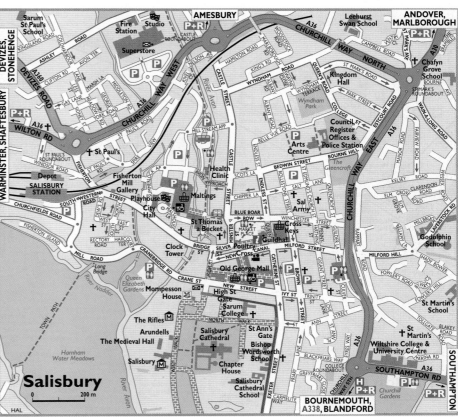

Salisbury

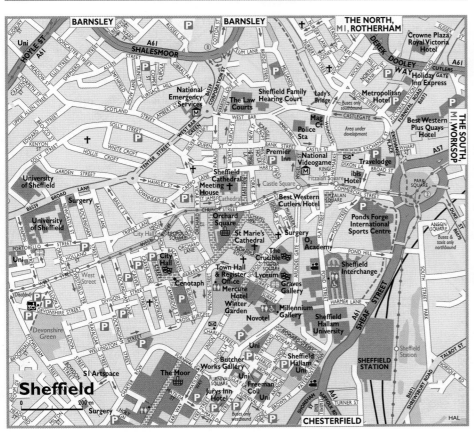

Sheffield

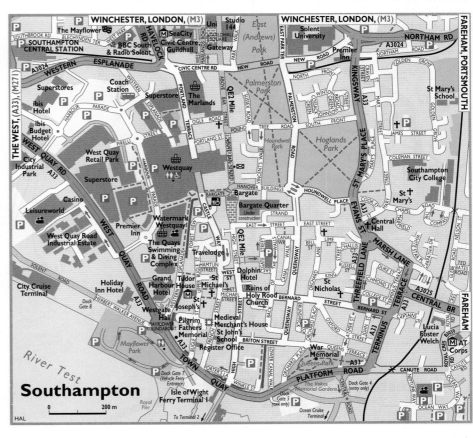

Southampton

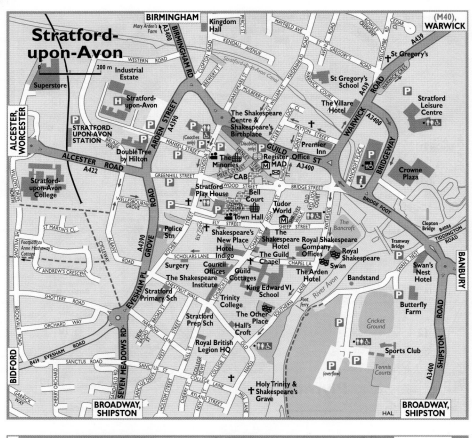

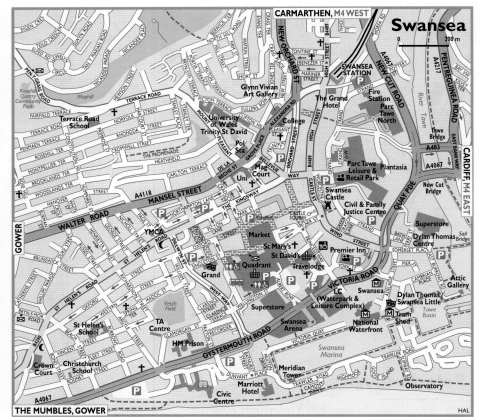

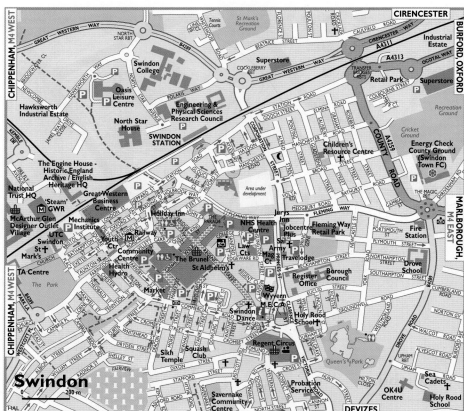

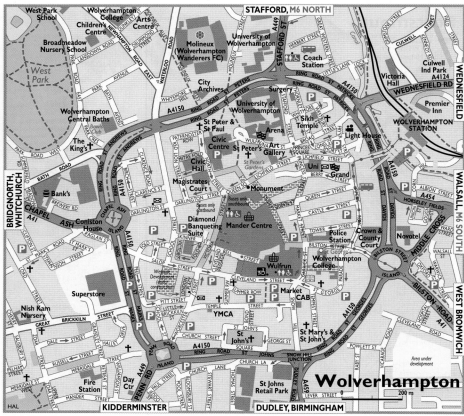

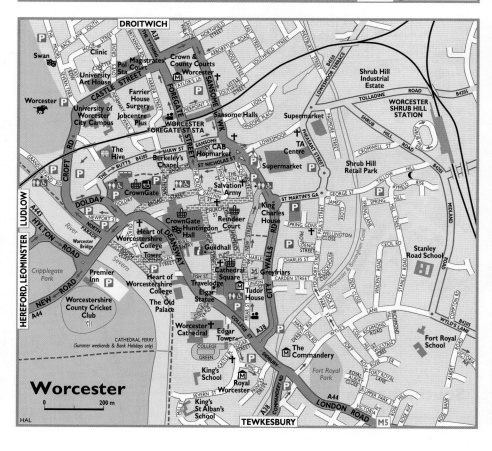

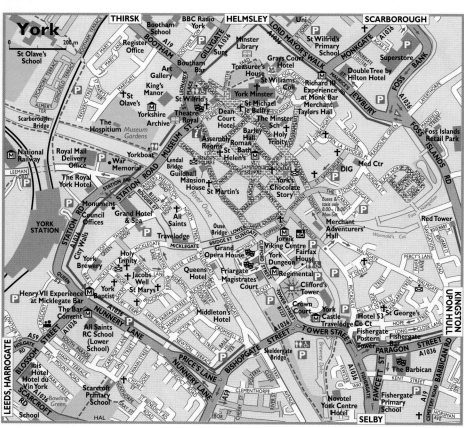

This index lists places appearing in the main map section of the atlas in alphabetical order. The reference following each name gives the atlas page number and grid reference of the square in which the place appears. The map shows counties, unitary authorities and administrative areas, together with a list of the abbreviated name forms used in the index. The top 100 places of tourist interest are indexed in **red**, World Heritage sites in green, motorway service areas in **blue**, airports in blue *italic* and National Parks in green *italic*.

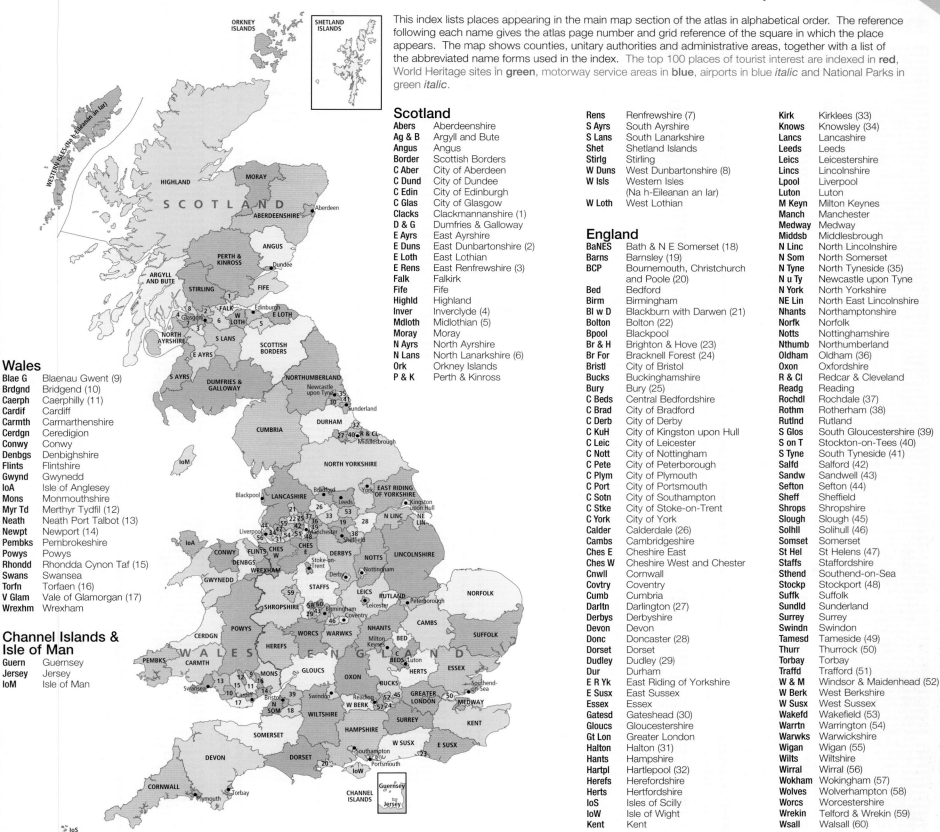

Scotland

Abers	Aberdeenshire
Ag & B	Argyll and Bute
Angus	Angus
Border	Scottish Borders
C Aber	City of Aberdeen
C Dund	City of Dundee
C Edin	City of Edinburgh
C Glas	City of Glasgow
Clacks	Clackmannanshire (1)
D & G	Dumfries & Galloway
E Ayrs	East Ayrshire
E Duns	East Dunbartonshire (2)
E Loth	East Lothian
E Rens	East Renfrewshire (3)
Falk	Falkirk
Fife	Fife
Highld	Highland
Inver	Inverclyde (4)
Mdloth	Midlothian (5)
Moray	Moray
N Ayrs	North Ayrshire
N Lans	North Lanarkshire (6)
Ork	Orkney Islands
P & K	Perth & Kinross

Rens	Renfrewshire (7)
S Ayrs	South Ayrshire
S Lans	South Lanarkshire
Shet	Shetland Islands
Stirlg	Stirling
W Duns	West Dunbartonshire (8)
W Isls	Western Isles (Na h-Eileanan an Iar)
W Loth	West Lothian

England

BaNES	Bath & N E Somerset (18)
Barns	Barnsley (19)
BCP	Bournemouth, Christchurch and Poole (20)
Bed	Bedford
Birm	Birmingham
Bl w D	Blackburn with Darwen (21)
Bolton	Bolton (22)
Bpool	Blackpool
Br & H	Brighton & Hove (23)
Br For	Bracknell Forest (24)
Bristl	City of Bristol
Bucks	Buckinghamshire
Bury	Bury (25)
C Beds	Central Bedfordshire
C Brad	City of Bradford
C Derb	City of Derby
C KuH	City of Kingston upon Hull
C Leic	City of Leicester
C Nott	City of Nottingham
C Pete	City of Peterborough
C Plym	City of Plymouth
C Port	City of Portsmouth
C Sotn	City of Southampton
C Stke	City of Stoke-on-Trent
C York	City of York
Calder	Calderdale (26)
Cambs	Cambridgeshire
Ches E	Cheshire East
Ches W	Cheshire West and Chester
Cnwll	Cornwall
Covtry	Coventry
Cumb	Cumbria
Darltn	Darlington (27)
Derbys	Derbyshire
Devon	Devon
Donc	Doncaster (28)
Dorset	Dorset
Dudley	Dudley (29)
Dur	Durham
E R Yk	East Riding of Yorkshire
E Susx	East Sussex
Essex	Essex
Gatesd	Gateshead (30)
Gloucs	Gloucestershire
Gt Lon	Greater London
Halton	Halton (31)
Hants	Hampshire
Hartpl	Hartlepool (32)
Herefs	Herefordshire
Herts	Hertfordshire
IoS	Isles of Scilly
IoW	Isle of Wight
Kent	Kent

Kirk	Kirklees (33)
Knows	Knowsley (34)
Lancs	Lancashire
Leeds	Leeds
Leics	Leicestershire
Lincs	Lincolnshire
Lpool	Liverpool
Luton	Luton
M Keyn	Milton Keynes
Manch	Manchester
Medway	Medway
Middsb	Middlesbrough
N Linc	North Lincolnshire
N Som	North Somerset
N Tyne	North Tyneside (35)
N u Ty	Newcastle upon Tyne
N York	North Yorkshire
NE Lin	North East Lincolnshire
Nhants	Northamptonshire
Norfk	Norfolk
Notts	Nottinghamshire
Nthumb	Northumberland
Oldham	Oldham (36)
Oxon	Oxfordshire
R & Cl	Redcar & Cleveland
Readg	Reading
Rochdl	Rochdale (37)
Rothm	Rotherham (38)
Rutlnd	Rutland
S Glos	South Gloucestershire (39)
S on T	Stockton-on-Tees (40)
S Tyne	South Tyneside (41)
Salfd	Salford (42)
Sandw	Sandwell (43)
Sefton	Sefton (44)
Sheff	Sheffield
Shrops	Shropshire
Slough	Slough (45)
Solhll	Solihull (46)
Somset	Somerset
St Hel	St Helens (47)
Staffs	Staffordshire
Sthend	Southend-on-Sea
Stockp	Stockport (48)
Suffk	Suffolk
Sundld	Sunderland
Surrey	Surrey
Swindn	Swindon
Tamesd	Tameside (49)
Thurr	Thurrock (50)
Torbay	Torbay
Traffd	Trafford (51)
W & M	Windsor & Maidenhead (52)
W Berk	West Berkshire
W Susx	West Sussex
Wakefd	Wakefield (53)
Warrtn	Warrington (54)
Warwks	Warwickshire
Wigan	Wigan (55)
Wilts	Wiltshire
Wirral	Wirral (56)
Wokham	Wokingham (57)
Wolves	Wolverhampton (58)
Worcs	Worcestershire
Wrekin	Telford & Wrekin (59)
Wsall	Walsall (60)

Wales

Blae G	Blaenau Gwent (9)
Brdgnd	Bridgend (10)
Caerph	Caerphilly (11)
Cardif	Cardiff
Carmth	Carmarthenshire
Cerdgn	Ceredigion
Conwy	Conwy
Denbgs	Denbighshire
Flints	Flintshire
Gwynd	Gwynedd
IoA	Isle of Anglesey
Mons	Monmouthshire
Myr Td	Merthyr Tydfil (12)
Neath	Neath Port Talbot (13)
Newpt	Newport (14)
Pembks	Pembrokeshire
Powys	Powys
Rhondd	Rhondda Cynon Taf (15)
Swans	Swansea
Torfn	Torfaen (16)
V Glam	Vale of Glamorgan (17)
Wrexhm	Wrexham

Channel Islands & Isle of Man

Guern	Guernsey
Jersey	Jersey
IoM	Isle of Man

Using the National Grid

With an Ordnance Survey National Grid reference you can pinpoint anywhere in the country in this atlas. The blue grid lines which divide the main-map pages into 5km squares for ease of indexing also match the National Grid. A National Grid reference gives two letters and some figures. An example is how to find the summit of Snowdon using its 4-figure grid reference of **SH6154**.

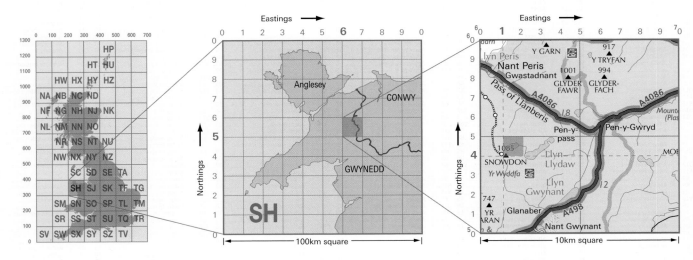

The letters **SH** indicate the 100km square of the National Grid in which Snowdon is located.

In a 4-figure grid reference the first two figures (eastings) are read along the map from left to right, the second two (northings) up the map. The figures **6** and **5**, the first and third figures of the Snowdon reference, indicate the 10km square within the **SH** square, lying above (north) and right (east) of the intersection of the vertical (easting) line **6** and horizontal (northing) line **5**.

The summit is finally pinpointed by figures **1** and **4** which locate a 1km square within the 10km square. At road atlas scales these grid lines are normally estimated by eye.

124 Abbas Combe – Ball Haye Green

A

Abbas Combe Somset 17 T12
Abberley Worcs 35 S7
Abberley Common Worcs 35 R7
Abberton Essex 23 P4
Abberton Worcs 36 C10
Abberwick Nthumb 77 N3
Abbess Roding Essex 22 E5
Abbey Devon 6 F2
Abbeycwmhir Powys 34 C6
Abbeydale Sheff 57 M10
Abbey Dore Herefs 27 R1
Abbey Green Staffs 46 C2
Abbey Hill Somset 16 J13
Abbey St Bathans Border 84 K6
Abbeystead Lancs 62 B9
Abbeytown Cumb 66 J2
Abbey Village Lancs 55 P2
Abbey Wood Gt Lon 21 S7
Abbotrule Border 76 C3
Abbots Bickington Devon 14 J10
Abbots Bromley Staffs 46 E9
Abbotsbury Dorset 7 Q7
Abbot's Chair Derbys 56 F8
Abbots Deuglie P & K 90 H9
Abbotsham Devon 14 K7
Abbotskerswell Devon 5 V7
Abbots Langley Herts 31 N12
Abbotsleigh Devon 5 U11
Abbots Leigh N Som 27 U13
Abbotsley Cambs 38 K9
Abbots Morton Worcs 36 D9
Abbots Ripton Cambs 38 K5
Abbot's Salford Warwks 36 E10
Abbotstone Hants 9 R2
Abbotswood Hants 9 M4
Abbots Worthy Hants 9 P2
Abbotts Ann Hants 19 M12
Abbott Street Dorset 8 D8
Abcott Shrops 34 J5
Abdon Shrops 35 N3
Abenhall Gloucs 28 C4
Aberaeron Cerdgn 32 J8
Aberaman Rhondd 26 J7
Aberangell Gwynd 43 R11
Aber-arad Carmth 32 F12
Aberarder Highld 102 H10
Aberargie P & K 90 J8
Aberarth Cerdgn 32 J8
Aberavon Neath 26 C10
Aber-banc Cerdgn 32 G12
Aberbargoed Caerph 27 M7
Aberbeeg Blae G 27 N7
Abercanaid Myr Td 26 K7
Abercarn Caerph 27 N9
Abercastle Pembks 24 E4
Abercegir Powys 43 R13
Aberchalder Highld 96 C3
Aberchirder Abers 104 J5
Aber Clydach Powys 27 L3
Abercorn W Loth 83 L3
Abercraf Powys 26 E5
Abercregan Neath 26 E8
Abercwmboi Rhondd 26 J8
Abercych Pembks 32 D12
Abercynon Rhondd 26 K9
Aberdalgie P & K 90 G7
Aberdare Rhondd 26 J7
Aberdaron Gwynd 42 C8
Aberdeen C Aber 99 S2
Aberdeen Airport C Aber 105 P13
Aberdesach Gwynd 42 H3
Aberdour Fife 83 N1
Aberdulais Neath 26 D8
Aberdyfi Gwynd 33 M1
Aberedw Powys 34 C11
Abereiddy Pembks 24 C4
Abererch Gwynd 42 G6
Aberfan Myr Td 26 K7
Aberfeldy P & K 90 C2
Aberffraw IoA 52 E9
Aberffrwd Cerdgn 33 N5
Aberford Leeds 63 U12
Aberfoyle Stirlg 89 M5
Abergarw Brdgnd 26 G11
Abergarwed Neath 26 E7
Abergavenny Mons 27 P5
Abergele Conwy 53 R7
Aber-giar Carmth 32 K12
Abergorlech Carmth 25 U4
Abergwesyn Powys 33 S10
Abergwili Carmth 25 R6
Abergwydol Powys 43 Q13
Abergwynfi Neath 26 F8
Abergwyngregyn Gwynd 53 L8
Abergynolwyn Gwynd 43 N12
Aberhafesp Powys 34 C2
Aberhosan Powys 33 R1
Aberkenfig Brdgnd 26 F11
Aberlady E Loth 84 D3
Aberlemno Angus 98 J12
Aberllefenni Gwynd 43 Q12
Aberllynfi Powys 34 E13
Aberlour, Charlestown of Moray 104 B7
Abermagwr Cerdgn 33 N6
Aber-meurig Cerdgn 33 L9
Abermorddu Flints 44 H2
Abermule Powys 34 E2
Abernant Carmth 25 P6
Abernant Rhondd 26 J7
Abernethy P & K 90 J8
Abernyte P & K 91 L5
Aberporth Cerdgn 32 E10
Abersoch Gwynd 42 F8
Abersychan Torfn 27 P7
Aberthin V Glam 26 J13
Abertillery Blae G 27 N7
Abertridwr Caerph 27 L10
Abertridwr Powys 44 B10
Abertysswg Caerph 27 L6
Aberuthven P & K 90 E8
Aberwheeler Denbgs 54 C13
Aberyscir Powys 26 H2
Aberystwyth Cerdgn 33 L4
Abingdon-on-Thames Oxon 29 U8
Abinger Common Surrey 20 K13
Abinger Hammer Surrey 20 J13
Abington Nhants 37 U8
Abington S Lans 82 H14
Abington Pigotts Cambs 31 T4
Abington Services S Lans 82 H14
Abingworth W Susx 10 J7
Ab Kettleby Leics 47 T9
Ab Lench Worcs 36 D10
Ablington Gloucs 29 M6
Ablington Wilts 18 J11
Abney Derbys 56 J10
Above Church Staffs 46 D3
Aboyne Abers 98 J4
Abhainn Suidhe W Isls 106 f8
Abram Wigan 55 P6
Abriachan Highld 102 G8
Abridge Essex 21 S3
Abronhill N Lans 89 S10
Abson S Glos 28 D13
Abthorpe Nhants 37 R11
Aby Lincs 59 R11
Acaster Malbis C York 64 D10
Acaster Selby N York 64 D11
Accrington Lancs 62 F14
Acha Ag & B 92 F8
Achahoish Ag & B 87 P10
Achalader P & K 90 H2
Achaleven Ag & B 94 C12
Acha Mor W Isls 106 i6
Achanalt Highld 108 D12
Achandunie Highld 109 L10
Achany Highld 108 K4
Acharacle Highld 93 R5
Acharn Highld 93 S8
Acharn P & K 95 V10
Achavanich Highld 112 E8
Achduart Highld 107 T4
Achfary Highld 110 F9
Achgarve Highld 107 Q6
A'Chill Highld 100 b9
Achiltibuie Highld 107 T3
Achina Highld 111 Q4
Achinhoan Ag & B 79 P12
Achintee Highld 101 N3
Achintraid Highld 101 L4
Achlyness Highld 110 E6
Achmelvich Highld 110 B12
Achmore Highld 101 M5
Achmore W Isls 106 i6
Achnacarnin Highld 110 A10
Achnacarry Highld 101 T14
Achnacloich Highld 100 e9
Achnaconeran Highld 102 D12
Achnacroish Ag & B 94 B10
Achnadrish Ag & B 93 M8
Achnafauld P & K 90 C4
Achnagarron Highld 109 M10
Achnaha Highld 93 M5
Achnahaird Highld 107 T2
Achnahannet Highld 103 Q10
Achnairn Highld 108 K2
Achnalea Highld 94 B6
Achnamara Ag & B 87 P8
Achnasheen Highld 108 B13
Achnashellach Highld 101 Q2
Achnastank Moray 104 B9
Achosnich Highld 93 L5
Achranich Highld 93 S9
Achreamie Highld 112 B3
Achriabhach Highld 94 G5
Achriesgill Highld 110 F6
Achtoty Highld 111 P4
Achurch Nhants 38 F4
Achvaich Highld 109 N6
Achvarasdal Highld 112 A4
Ackergill Highld 112 J6
Acklam Middsb 70 G9
Acklam N York 64 H7
Ackleton Shrops 45 S14
Acklington Nthumb 77 Q5
Ackton Wakefd 57 P2
Ackworth Moor Top Wakefd 57 P3
Acle Norfk 51 R11
Acock's Green Birm 36 F4
Acol Kent 13 R2
Acomb C York 64 D9
Acomb Nthumb 76 J12
Acombe Somset 6 G2
Aconbury Herefs 35 M14
Acre Lancs 55 S2
Acrefair Wrexhm 44 G5
Acresford Derbys 46 J11
Acton Ches E 45 P3
Acton Dorset 8 D13
Acton Gt Lon 21 M6
Acton Shrops 34 H4
Acton Staffs 45 T5
Acton Suffk 40 E11
Acton Worcs 35 T7
Acton Wrexhm 44 H3
Acton Beauchamp Herefs 35 Q10
Acton Bridge Ches W 55 N11
Acton Burnell Shrops 45 M13
Acton Green Herefs 35 Q10
Acton Pigott Shrops 45 M13
Acton Round Shrops 35 P1
Acton Scott Shrops 35 L3
Acton Trussell Staffs 46 B10
Acton Turville S Glos 18 B4
Adbaston Staffs 45 S8
Adber Dorset 17 Q12
Adbolton Notts 47 Q6
Adderbury Oxon 37 N13
Adderley Shrops 45 Q6
Adderstone Nthumb 85 S12
Addiewell W Loth 82 J6
Addingham C Brad 63 M10
Addington Bucks 30 F7
Addington Gt Lon 21 Q10
Addington Kent 12 C4
Addiscombe Gt Lon 21 P9
Addlestone Surrey 20 J10
Addlestonemoor Surrey 20 J9
Addlethorpe Lincs 59 T13
Adeney Wrekin 45 Q10
Adeyfield Herts 31 N11
Adfa Powys 44 C13
Adforton Herefs 34 K6
Adisham Kent 13 P5
Adlestrop Gloucs 29 P2
Adlingfleet E R Yk 58 D2
Adlington Ches E 56 D10
Adlington Lancs 55 P4
Admaston Staffs 46 D9
Admaston Wrekin 45 P11
Admington Warwks 36 H11
Adpar Cerdgn 32 F12
Adsborough Somset 16 J11
Adscombe Somset 16 G9
Adstock Bucks 30 F7
Adstone Nhants 37 Q10
Adswood Stockp 56 C9
Adversane W Susx 10 H6
Advie Highld 103 T9
Adwalton Leeds 63 Q14
Adwell Oxon 30 E13
Adwick le Street Donc 57 R5
Adwick upon Dearne Donc 57 Q6
Ae D & G 74 J8
Ae Bridgend D & G 74 K8
Afan Forest Park Neath 26 F8
Affetside Bury 55 S4
Affleck Abers 104 H7
Affpuddle Dorset 7 V6
Affric Lodge Highld 101 T7
Afon-wen Flints 54 D12
Afon Wen Gwynd 42 H6
Afton Devon 5 U8
Afton IoW 9 L11
Agglethorpe N York 63 M2
Aigburth Lpool 54 J9
Aike E R Yk 65 N10
Aiketgate Cumb 67 Q3
Aikhead Cumb 66 K3
Aikton Cumb 67 L2
Ailby Lincs 59 R11
Ailey Herefs 34 H11
Ailsworth C Pete 48 H14
Ainderby Quernhow N York 63 S3
Ainderby Steeple N York 63 S1
Aingers Green Essex 23 R3
Ainsdale Sefton 54 H4
Ainsdale-on-Sea Sefton 54 G4
Ainstable Cumb 67 R3
Ainsworth Bury 55 S4
Ainthorpe N York 71 M11
Aintree Sefton 54 J7
Ainville W Loth 83 M6
Aird Ag & B 87 P5
Aird D & G 72 D8
Aird Highld 100 e9
Aird W Isls 106 k5
Àird a' Mhulaidh W Isls 106 g7
Aird Asaig W Isls 106 g8
Aird Dhubh Highld 100 g5
Airdeny Ag & B 94 D13
Airdrie N Lans 82 E5
Airdriehill N Lans 82 E5
Airds of Kells D & G 73 R5
Àird Uig W Isls 106 f5
Airidh a bhruaich W Isls 106 h7
Airieland D & G 73 T8
Airlie Angus 98 E13
Airmyn E R Yk 58 B2
Airntully P & K 90 G4
Airor Highld 100 g9
Airth Falk 82 H1
Airton N York 62 J8
Aisby Lincs 48 F6
Aisby Lincs 58 E8
Aisgill Cumb 68 G13
Aish Devon 5 R8
Aish Devon 5 U9
Aisholt Somset 16 G9
Aiskew N York 63 R2
Aislaby N York 64 H2
Aislaby N York 71 Q11
Aislaby S on T 70 F10
Aisthorpe Lincs 58 F10
Aith Shet 106 t8
Akeld Nthumb 85 P13
Akeley Bucks 30 F5
Akenham Suffk 41 L11
Albaston Cnwll 5 L6
Alberbury Shrops 44 J11
Albourne W Susx 11 M7
Albourne Green W Susx 11 M7
Albrighton Shrops 45 L10
Albrighton Shrops 45 T13
Alburgh Norfk 41 N3
Albury Herts 22 B3
Albury Oxon 30 E11
Albury Surrey 20 H13
Albury End Herts 22 B3
Albury Heath Surrey 20 J13
Alby Hill Norfk 51 L7
Alcaig Highld 102 G4
Alcaston Shrops 35 L3
Alcester Warwks 36 E9
Alciston E Susx 11 S9
Alcombe Somset 16 C7
Alcombe Wilts 18 B7
Alconbury Cambs 38 J5
Alconbury Weald Cambs 38 K5
Alconbury Weston Cambs 38 J5
Aldborough N York 63 U6
Aldborough Norfk 51 L7
Aldbourne Wilts 19 L5
Aldbrough E R Yk 65 S12
Aldbrough St John N York 69 R10
Aldbury Herts 31 L10
Aldcliffe Lancs 61 T7
Aldclune P & K 97 P11
Aldeburgh Suffk 41 S9
Aldeby Norfk 41 R2
Aldenham Herts 20 K3
Alderbury Wilts 8 H3
Aldercar Derbys 47 M4
Alderford Norfk 50 K10
Alderholt Dorset 8 G6
Alderley Gloucs 28 E9
Alderley Edge Ches E 55 T11
Aldermans Green Covtry 37 L4
Aldermaston W Berk 19 S7
Alderminster Warwks 36 H11
Alder Moor Staffs 46 H8
Aldersey Green Ches W 45 L2
Aldershot Hants 20 E12
Alderton Gloucs 36 D14
Alderton Nhants 37 T11
Alderton Shrops 45 L9
Alderton Suffk 41 P12
Alderton Wilts 28 F11
Alderwasley Derbys 46 K3
Aldfield N York 63 R6
Aldford Ches W 44 K2
Aldgate Rutlnd 48 E13
Aldham Essex 23 M2
Aldham Suffk 40 J11
Aldingbourne W Susx 10 E9
Aldingham Cumb 61 P5
Aldington Kent 13 L8
Aldington Worcs 36 E12
Aldington Corner Kent 13 L8
Aldivalloch Moray 104 D10
Aldochlay Ag & B 88 J7
Aldon Shrops 34 K5
Aldoth Cumb 66 H3
Aldreth Cambs 39 P6
Aldridge Wsall 46 E13
Aldringham Suffk 41 R8
Aldro N York 64 J7
Aldsworth Gloucs 29 N6
Aldsworth W Susx 10 B9
Aldunie Moray 104 D10
Aldwark Derbys 46 H2
Aldwark N York 64 B7
Aldwick W Susx 10 E11
Aldwincle Nhants 38 F4
Aldworth W Berk 19 S5
Alexandria W Duns 88 J10
Aley Somset 16 G9
Alfardisworthy Devon 14 G10
Alfington Devon 6 F5
Alfold Surrey 10 G4
Alfold Bars W Susx 10 G4
Alfold Crossways Surrey 10 G3
Alford Abers 104 H12
Alford Lincs 59 S11
Alford Somset 17 R10
Alfreton Derbys 47 M2
Alfrick Worcs 35 R10
Alfrick Pound Worcs 35 R10
Alfriston E Susx 11 S10
Algarkirk Lincs 49 L6
Alhampton Somset 17 R10
Alkborough N Linc 58 E2
Alkerton Gloucs 28 E6
Alkerton Oxon 37 L12
Alkham Kent 13 Q7
Alkington Shrops 45 M6
Alkmonton Derbys 46 G6
Allaleigh Devon 5 U10
Allanaquoich Abers 97 U5
Allanbank N Lans 82 F7
Allanton Border 85 M8
Allanton N Lans 82 F7
Allanton S Lans 82 D8
Allaston Gloucs 28 B7
Allbrook Hants 9 P4
All Cannings Wilts 18 G8
Allendale Nthumb 68 H1
Allen End Warwks 36 G1
Allenheads Nthumb 68 J3
Allensford Dur 69 N2
Allen's Green Herts 22 C4
Allensmore Herefs 35 L13
Allenton C Derb 47 L7
Aller Devon 15 S7
Aller Somset 17 M11
Allerby Cumb 66 G5
Allercombe Devon 6 D6
Aller Cross Devon 15 R7
Allerford Somset 16 B7
Allerston N York 64 K3
Allerthorpe E R Yk 64 H10
Allerton C Brad 63 N13
Allerton Highld 103 L2
Allerton Lpool 54 J9
Allerton Bywater Leeds 63 U14
Allerton Mauleverer N York 63 U8
Allesley Covtry 36 K4
Allestree C Derb 46 K6
Allet Common Cnwll 2 K7
Allexton Leics 48 B13
Allgreave Ches E 56 E13
Allhallows Medway 22 K12
Allhallows-on-Sea Medway 22 K12
Alligin Shuas Highld 107 P13
Allimore Green Staffs 45 U10
Allington Dorset 7 N6
Allington Kent 12 E4
Allington Lincs 48 C5
Allington Wilts 18 C5
Allington Wilts 18 G8
Allington Wilts 18 K13
Allithwaite Cumb 61 R4
Alloa Clacks 90 C13
Allonby Cumb 66 G4
Allostock Ches W 55 R12
Alloway S Ayrs 81 L9
Allowenshay Somset 7 L2
All Saints South Elmham Suffk 41 P4
Allscott Shrops 35 R1
Allscott Wrekin 45 P11
All Stretton Shrops 35 L1
Alltami Flints 54 G13
Alltchaorunn Highld 94 H8
Alltmawr Powys 34 C11
Alltsigh Highld 102 E12
Alltwalis Carmth 25 R4
Alltwen Neath 26 C7
Alltyblaca Cerdgn 32 K11
Allwood Green Suffk 40 H6
Almeley Herefs 34 H10
Almeley Wooton Herefs 34 H10
Almer Dorset 8 C9
Almholme Donc 57 S5
Almington Staffs 45 R7
Almodington W Susx 10 C11
Almondbank P & K 90 G6
Almondbury Kirk 56 J4
Almondsbury S Glos 28 B11
Alne N York 64 B6
Alness Highld 109 M11
Alnham Nthumb 76 K3
Alnmouth Nthumb 77 Q3
Alnwick Nthumb 77 P3
Alperton Gt Lon 21 L6
Alphamstone Essex 40 E13
Alpheton Suffk 40 E10
Alphington Devon 6 B6
Alpington Norfk 51 N13
Alport Derbys 56 K14
Alpraham Ches E 45 N2
Alresford Essex 23 Q3
Alrewas Staffs 46 G11
Alsager Ches E 45 S2
Alsagers Bank Staffs 45 S4
Alsop en le Dale Derbys 46 G3
Alston Cumb 68 F3
Alston Devon 6 K4
Alstone Gloucs 36 C14
Alstone Somset 16 K7
Alstonefield Staffs 46 F2
Alston Sutton Somset 17 M6
Alswear Devon 15 R8
Alt Oldham 56 D6
Altandhu Highld 107 S2
Altarnun Cnwll 4 G4
Altass Highld 108 J4
Altcreich Ag & B 93 R11
Altgaltraig Ag & B 88 B11
Altham Lancs 62 F13
Althorne Essex 23 M8
Althorpe N Linc 58 D5
Altnabreac Station Highld 112 B7
Altnaharra Highld 111 M9
Altofts Wakefd 57 N2
Alton Derbys 57 N14
Alton Hants 19 V13
Alton Staffs 46 E5
Alton Wilts 18 J11
Alton Barnes Wilts 18 H8
Alton Pancras Dorset 7 T4
Alton Priors Wilts 18 H8
Alton Towers Staffs 46 E5
Altrincham Traffd 55 S9
Altskeith Hotel Stirlg 89 L5
Alva Clacks 90 C12
Alvanley Ches W 55 L12
Alvaston C Derb 47 L7
Alvechurch Worcs 36 D6
Alvecote Warwks 46 H13
Alvediston Wilts 8 D4
Alveley Shrops 35 S4
Alverdiscott Devon 15 M7
Alverstoke Hants 9 S9
Alverstone IoW 9 R11
Alverthorpe Wakefd 57 M2
Alverton Notts 47 U5
Alves Moray 103 T3
Alvescot Oxon 29 Q7
Alveston S Glos 28 B10
Alveston Warwks 36 H9
Alvingham Lincs 59 Q8
Alvington Gloucs 28 B7
Alwalton C Pete 38 H1
Alweston Dorset 7 S2
Alwinton Nthumb 76 J4
Alwoodley Leeds 63 R11
Alwoodley Gates Leeds 63 S11
Alyth P & K 90 K2
Am Bàgh a Tuath W Isls 106 c18
Ambergate Derbys 46 K3
Amber Hill Lincs 48 K4
Amberley Gloucs 28 G7
Amberley W Susx 10 G8
Amber Row Derbys 47 L2
Amberstone E Susx 11 T8
Amble Nthumb 77 R5
Amblecote Dudley 35 U3
Ambler Thorn C Brad 63 M14
Ambleside Cumb 67 N12
Ambleston Pembks 24 H5
Ambrosden Oxon 30 D9
Amcotts N Linc 58 E4
America Cambs 39 P5
Amersham Bucks 20 G3
Amersham Common Bucks 20 G3
Amersham Old Town Bucks 20 G3
Amersham on the Hill Bucks 20 G3
Amerton Staffs 46 C8
Amesbury Wilts 18 J12
Amhuinnsuidhe W Isls 106 f8
Amington Staffs 46 H13
Amisfield D & G 74 K9
Amlwch IoA 52 F4
Ammanford Carmth 26 A5
Amotherby N York 64 G5
Ampfield Hants 9 N4
Ampleforth N York 64 D4
Ampney Crucis Gloucs 29 L7
Ampney St Mary Gloucs 29 L7
Ampney St Peter Gloucs 29 L7
Amport Hants 19 M12
Ampthill C Beds 31 M5
Ampton Suffk 40 E6
Amroth Pembks 25 L9
Amulree P & K 90 C4
Amwell Herts 31 Q10
Anaheilt Highld 93 U6
Ancaster Lincs 48 E5
Ancells Farm Hants 20 D11
Anchor Shrops 34 E3
Ancroft Nthumb 85 P9
Ancrum Border 84 G14
Ancton W Susx 10 F10
Anderby Lincs 59 T11
Anderby Creek Lincs 59 U11
Andersea Somset 16 K10
Andersfield Somset 16 H10
Anderson Dorset 8 B9
Anderton Ches W 55 P11
Anderton Cnwll 5 L10
Andover Hants 19 N11
Andover Down Hants 19 N11
Andoversford Gloucs 28 K4
Andreas IoM 60 g3
Anelog Gwynd 42 C8
Anerley Gt Lon 21 P9
Anfield Lpool 54 J8
Angarrack Cnwll 2 F9
Angarrick Cnwll 2 K9
Angelbank Shrops 35 N5
Angersleigh Somset 16 G13
Angerton Cumb 66 K1
Angle Pembks 24 E10
Anglesey IoA 52 F6
Anglesey Abbey Cambs 39 R8
Angmering W Susx 10 H10
Angram N York 64 C10
Angram N York 68 J13
Angrouse Cnwll 2 H13
Anick Nthumb 76 J12
Ankerville Highld 109 Q10
Ankle Hill Leics 47 U10
Anlaby E R Yk 65 N14
Anmer Norfk 50 B8
Anmore Hants 9 T6
Annan D & G 75 N12
Annandale Water Services D & G 75 M7
Annaside Cumb 60 K2
Annat Highld 107 Q14
Annathill N Lans 82 D4
Anna Valley Hants 19 N12
Annbank S Ayrs 81 N8
Anne Hathaway's Cottage Warwks 36 G10
Annesley Notts 47 P3
Annesley Woodhouse Notts 47 N3
Annfield Plain Dur 69 Q2
Anniesland C Glas 89 M12
Annitsford N Tyne 77 R11
Annscroft Shrops 45 L12
Ansdell Lancs 61 Q14
Ansford Somset 17 R10
Ansley Warwks 36 K2
Anslow Staffs 46 H8
Anslow Gate Staffs 46 G9
Anslow Lees Staffs 46 H9
Ansteadbrook Surrey 10 E4
Anstey Hants 10 A2
Anstey Herts 39 P14
Anstey Leics 47 Q12
Anstruther Fife 91 S11
Ansty W Susx 11 M6
Ansty Warwks 37 M4
Ansty Wilts 8 D3
Ansty Cross Dorset 7 U4
An Tairbeart W Isls 106 g8
Anthill Common Hants 9 S6
Anthonys Surrey 20 H10
Anthorn Cumb 75 N14
Antingham Norfk 51 N7
An t-Ob W Isls 106 f10
Antonine Wall 89 T10
Anton's Gowt Lincs 49 M4
Antony Cnwll 5 L10
Antrobus Ches W 55 P11
Anvil Corner Devon 14 J12
Anvil Green Kent 13 M6
Anwick Lincs 48 H3
Anwoth D & G 73 P8
Aperfield Gt Lon 21 R11
Apes Dale Worcs 36 C6
Apethorpe Nhants 38 F1
Apeton Staffs 45 U10
Apley Lincs 58 K11
Apperknowle Derbys 57 N11
Apperley Gloucs 28 G2
Apperley Bridge C Brad 63 P12
Apperley Dene Nthumb 77 M14
Appersett N York 62 H1
Appin Ag & B 94 C9
Appleby N Linc 58 G4
Appleby-in-Westmorland Cumb 68 E8
Appleby Magna Leics 46 K12
Appleby Parva Leics 46 K12
Appleby Street Herts 31 T12
Applecross Highld 100 g5
Appledore Devon 6 E2
Appledore Devon 15 L6
Appledore Kent 12 J10
Appledore Heath Kent 12 J9
Appleford Oxon 19 R2
Applegarth Town D & G 75 M9
Applehaigh Wakefd 57 N4
Applemore Hants 9 M7
Appleshaw Hants 19 M11
Applethwaite Cumb 67 L7
Appleton Halton 55 M9
Appleton Oxon 29 T7
Appleton Warrtn 55 P10
Appleton-le-Moors N York 64 G2
Appleton-le-Street N York 64 G5
Appleton Roebuck N York 64 D11
Appleton Thorn Warrtn 55 P10
Appleton Wiske N York 70 E12
Appletreehall Border 75 V2
Appletreewick N York 63 M7
Appley Somset 16 E12
Appley Bridge Lancs 55 M5
Apse Heath IoW 9 R12
Apsley End C Beds 31 P6
Apuldram W Susx 10 C10
Arabella Highld 109 Q9
Arbirlot Angus 91 T3
Arborfield Wokham 20 C9
Arborfield Cross Wokham 20 C9
Arborfield Green Wokham 20 C9
Arbourthorne Sheff 57 N9
Arbroath Angus 91 T3
Arbuthnott Abers 99 P8
Arcadia Kent 12 G8
Archddu Carmth 25 R10
Archdeacon Newton Darltn 69 S9
Archencarroch W Duns 88 K9
Archiestown Moray 104 A7
Archirondel Jersey 7 f2
Arclid Ches E 45 S1
Ardallie Abers 105 S8
Ardanaiseig Hotel Ag & B 94 F14
Ardaneaskan Highld 101 L4
Ardarroch Highld 101 L4
Ardbeg Ag & B 78 G6
Ardbeg Ag & B 88 C12
Ardbeg Ag & B 88 E9
Ardcharnich Highld 108 B7
Ardchiavaig Ag & B 86 F2
Ardchonnell Ag & B 87 T3
Ardchronie Highld 109 L7
Ardchullarie More Stirlg 89 N3
Arddarroch Ag & B 88 F7
Arddleen Powys 44 G10
Ard Dorch Highld 100 e7
Ardechive Highld 101 S13
Ardeer N Ayrs 80 K4
Ardeley Herts 31 T7
Ardelve Highld 101 M6
Arden Ag & B 88 J9
Ardens Grafton Warwks 36 F10
Ardentallen Ag & B 93 U14
Ardentinny Ag & B 88 E8
Ardentraive Ag & B 88 B11
Ardeonaig Stirlg 95 T11
Ardersier Highld 103 L5
Ardessie Highld 107 U7
Ardfern Ag & B 87 Q5
Ardfernal Ag & B 86 K11
Ardgartan Ag & B 88 G5
Ardgay Highld 108 K6
Ardgour Highld 94 E6
Ardgowan Inver 88 F11
Ardhallow Ag & B 88 E11
Ardhasig W Isls 106 g8
Ardheslaig Highld 107 N13
Ardindrean Highld 108 B7
Ardingly W Susx 11 N5
Ardington Oxon 29 T10
Ardington Wick Oxon 29 T10
Ardlamont Ag & B 87 T12
Ardleigh Essex 23 Q2
Ardleigh Heath Essex 23 P1
Ardler P & K 91 L3
Ardley Oxon 30 B7
Ardley End Essex 22 D5
Ardlui Ag & B 88 H2
Ardlussa Ag & B 87 L8
Ardmair Highld 107 V5
Ardmaleish Ag & B 88 C12
Ardminish Ag & B 79 L6
Ardmolich Highld 93 S4
Ardmore Ag & B 88 H10
Ardmore Highld 109 N7
Ardnadam Ag & B 88 E9
Ardnagrask Highld 102 F6
Ardnamurchan Highld 93 P5
Ardnarff Highld 101 M4
Ardnastang Highld 93 U6
Ardpatrick Ag & B 79 P4
Ardrishaig Ag & B 87 R8
Ardross Highld 109 L10
Ardrossan N Ayrs 80 J4
Ardsley Barns 57 N5
Ardslignish Highld 93 P6
Ardtalla Ag & B 78 H5
Ardtoe Highld 93 Q4
Arduaine Ag & B 87 P3
Ardullie Highld 102 G3
Ardvasar Highld 100 f9
Ardvorlich P & K 95 S14
Ardvourlie W Isls 106 g7
Ardwell D & G 72 E10
Ardwick Manch 56 C7
Areley Kings Worcs 35 S6
Arevegaig Highld 93 R5
Arford Hants 10 C3
Arglam E R Yk 64 H12
Argoed Caerph 27 M8
Argoed Shrops 44 H9
Argoed Mill Powys 33 U8
Argos Hill E Susx 11 T5
Argyll Forest Park Ag & B 88 F5
Aribruach W Isls 106 h7
Aridhglas Ag & B 92 J14
Arileod Ag & B 92 F8
Arinagour Ag & B 92 G7
Ariogan Ag & B 94 B13
Arisaig Highld 93 R1
Arisaig House Highld 93 R2
Arkendale N York 63 T7
Arkesden Essex 39 Q14
Arkholme Lancs 62 B5
Arkleby Cumb 66 H5
Arkleton D & G 75 S7
Arkle Town N York 69 M12
Arkley Gt Lon 21 M3
Arksey Donc 57 S5
Arkwright Town Derbys 57 P12
Arle Gloucs 28 H3
Arlecdon Cumb 66 F9
Arlescote Warwks 37 L11
Arlesey C Beds 31 Q5
Arleston Wrekin 45 Q11
Arley Ches E 55 Q10
Arlingham Gloucs 28 D5
Arlington Devon 15 P4
Arlington E Susx 11 S9
Arlington Gloucs 29 M6
Arlington Beccott Devon 15 P4
Armadale Highld 100 f9
Armadale Highld 111 R4
Armadale W Loth 82 H5
Armaside Cumb 66 J7
Armathwaite Cumb 67 R3
Arminghall Norfk 51 N13
Armitage Staffs 46 E10
Armitage Bridge Kirk 56 H4
Armley Leeds 63 R13
Armscote Warwks 36 H12
Armshead Staffs 46 B4
Armston Nhants 38 G3
Armthorpe Donc 57 T6
Arnabost Ag & B 92 G6
Arnaby Cumb 61 M3
Arncliffe N York 62 J5
Arncliffe Cote N York 62 J5
Arncroach Fife 91 R10
Arndilly House Moray 104 B6
Arne Dorset 8 D11
Arnesby Leics 37 R2
Arngask P & K 90 H9
Arnisdale Highld 101 L9
Arnish Highld 100 e5
Arniston Mdloth 83 R6
Arnol W Isls 106 i4
Arnold E R Yk 65 Q11
Arnold Notts 47 Q4
Arnprior Stirlg 89 P7
Arnside Cumb 61 T4
Aros Ag & B 93 P9
Arowry Wrexhm 45 L6
Arrad Foot Cumb 61 Q3
Arram E R Yk 65 N11
Arran N Ayrs 79 S8
Arrathorne N York 69 R14
Arreton IoW 9 Q11
Arrina Highld 107 M13
Arrington Cambs 39 M10
Arrochar Ag & B 88 G5
Arrow Warwks 36 E9
Arrowfield Top Worcs 36 D6
Arscott Shrops 44 K12
Artafallie Highld 102 H6
Arthington Leeds 63 R11
Arthingworth Nhants 37 U4
Arthog Gwynd 43 M11
Arthrath Abers 105 R8
Arthursdale Leeds 63 T12
Artrochie Abers 105 S9
Arundel W Susx 10 G9
Asby Cumb 66 G8
Ascog Ag & B 88 D13
Ascot W & M 20 F9
Ascott Warwks 36 K14
Ascott Earl Oxon 29 R4
Ascott-under-Wychwood Oxon 29 R4
Asenby N York 63 T4
Asfordby Leics 47 T10
Asfordby Hill Leics 47 T10
Asgarby Lincs 48 H4
Asgarby Lincs 59 P13
Ash Devon 5 U11
Ash Devon 15 M11
Ash Dorset 8 B6
Ash Kent 12 B3
Ash Kent 13 Q4
Ash Somset 16 J12
Ash Somset 17 N12
Ash Surrey 20 F12
Ashampstead W Berk 19 S5
Ashampstead Green W Berk 19 S5
Ashbocking Suffk 41 L10
Ashbourne Derbys 46 G4
Ashbrittle Somset 16 E12
Ashburnham Place E Susx 12 C13
Ashburton Devon 5 T6
Ashbury Devon 15 M13
Ashbury Oxon 29 Q10
Ashby N Linc 58 E5
Ashby by Partney Lincs 59 R13
Ashby cum Fenby NE Lin 59 N6
Ashby de la Launde Lincs 48 G2
Ashby-de-la-Zouch Leics 47 L10
Ashby Folville Leics 47 T11
Ashby Magna Leics 37 Q2
Ashby Parva Leics 37 P3
Ashby Puerorum Lincs 59 P12
Ashby St Ledgers Nhants 37 Q7
Ashby St Mary Norfk 51 P13
Ashchurch Gloucs 36 B14
Ashcombe Devon 6 B9
Ashcombe N Som 16 K4
Ashcott Somset 17 M9
Ashdon Essex 39 S12
Ashdown Forest E Susx 11 R4
Ashe Hants 19 R10
Asheldham Essex 23 N7
Ashen Essex 40 B12
Ashendon Bucks 30 F10
Asheridge Bucks 30 K12
Ashfield Hants 9 M5
Ashfield Herefs 28 A3
Ashfield Stirlg 89 S5
Ashfield cum Thorpe Suffk 41 M8
Ashfield Green Suffk 40 C9
Ashfield Green Suffk 41 N6
Ashfold Crossways W Susx 11 L5
Ashford Devon 5 R11
Ashford Devon 15 M5
Ashford Kent 12 K7
Ashford Surrey 20 J8
Ashford Bowdler Shrops 35 M6
Ashford Carbonell Shrops 35 M6
Ashford Hill Hants 19 S8
Ashford in the Water Derbys 56 J13
Ashgill S Lans 82 E8
Ash Green Surrey 20 F13
Ash Green Warwks 36 K4
Ashill Devon 6 E2
Ashill Norfk 50 E13
Ashill Somset 16 K13
Ashingdon Essex 23 L9
Ashington BCP 8 E9
Ashington Nthumb 77 R8
Ashington Somset 17 Q12
Ashington W Susx 10 J7
Ashkirk Border 75 U1
Ashlett Hants 9 P8
Ashleworth Gloucs 28 F2
Ashleworth Quay Gloucs 28 F2
Ashley Cambs 39 U8
Ashley Ches E 55 S10
Ashley Devon 15 Q10
Ashley Dorset 8 G8
Ashley Gloucs 28 H9
Ashley Hants 8 K9
Ashley Hants 9 M2
Ashley Kent 13 R6
Ashley Nhants 37 U2
Ashley Staffs 45 S6
Ashley Wilts 18 B7
Ashley Green Bucks 31 L11
Ashleyhay Derbys 46 J3
Ashley Heath Dorset 8 G8
Ashley Moor Herefs 35 L7
Ash Magna Shrops 45 N6
Ashmansworth Hants 19 P9
Ashmansworthy Devon 14 H9
Ashmead Green Gloucs 28 E8
Ashmill Devon 14 J13
Ash Mill Devon 15 S8
Ashmore Dorset 8 C5
Ashmore Green W Berk 19 R7
Ashorne Warwks 36 K9
Ashover Derbys 57 M14
Ashover Hay Derbys 46 K1
Ashow Warwks 36 K6
Ash Parva Shrops 45 N6
Ashperton Herefs 35 P12
Ashprington Devon 5 U9
Ash Priors Somset 16 G11
Ashreigney Devon 15 P10
Ash Street Suffk 40 H11
Ashtead Surrey 21 L11
Ash Thomas Devon 6 D2
Ashton C Pete 48 H12
Ashton Cnwll 2 G11
Ashton Devon 5 V4
Ashton Hants 9 Q5
Ashton Herefs 35 M8
Ashton Inver 88 F10
Ashton Nhants 37 U11
Ashton Nhants 38 G3
Ashton Somset 17 M7
Ashton Common Wilts 18 C9
Ashton Hayes Ches W 55 M13
Ashton Hill Wilts 18 D9
Ashton-in-Makerfield Wigan 55 N7
Ashton Keynes Wilts 28 K9
Ashton-on-Ribble Lancs 61 U13
Ashton under Hill Worcs 36 C13
Ashton-under-Lyne Tamesd 56 D7
Ashton upon Mersey Traffd 55 S8
Ashton Vale Bristl 17 Q2
Ashurst Hants 9 L6
Ashurst Kent 11 S3
Ashurst Lancs 55 L5
Ashurst W Susx 10 K7
Ashurst Wood W Susx 11 Q3
Ash Vale Surrey 20 E12
Ashwater Devon 14 J13
Ashwell Herts 31 S5
Ashwell Rutlnd 48 C11
Ashwell Somset 17 L13
Ashwell End Herts 31 S4
Ashwellthorpe Norfk 50 K14
Ashwick Somset 17 R7
Ashwicken Norfk 50 B10
Ashwood Staffs 35 U3
Askam in Furness Cumb 61 N4
Askern Donc 57 S4
Askerswell Dorset 7 P6
Askett Bucks 30 H11
Askham Cumb 67 R8
Askham Notts 58 B12
Askham Bryan C York 64 D10
Askham Richard C York 64 C10
Asknish Ag & B 87 S7
Askrigg N York 62 J1
Askwith N York 63 P10
Aslackby Lincs 48 G7
Aslacton Norfk 41 L2
Aslockton Notts 47 T6
Asney Somset 17 N9
Aspall Suffk 41 L8
Aspatria Cumb 66 H4
Aspenden Herts 31 U7
Aspenshaw Derbys 56 F9
Asperton Lincs 49 L6
Aspley Staffs 45 T7
Aspley Guise C Beds 30 K5
Aspley Heath C Beds 30 K6
Aspley Heath Warwks 36 E6
Aspull Wigan 55 P5
Aspull Common Wigan 55 P7
Asselby E R Yk 64 G14
Asserby Lincs 59 S11
Asserby Turn Lincs 59 S11
Assington Suffk 40 F13
Assington Green Suffk 40 C10
Astbury Ches E 45 T1
Astcote Nhants 37 S10
Asterby Lincs 59 N11
Asterley Shrops 44 J12
Asterton Shrops 34 J2
Asthall Oxon 29 Q5
Asthall Leigh Oxon 29 R5
Astle Highld 109 N6
Astley Shrops 45 M10
Astley Warwks 36 K3
Astley Wigan 55 R6
Astley Worcs 35 S7
Astley Abbots Shrops 35 R1
Astley Bridge Bolton 55 R4
Astley Cross Worcs 35 T7
Astley Green Wigan 55 R7
Aston Birm 36 E3
Aston Ches E 45 P4
Aston Ches W 55 N11
Aston Derbys 56 J10
Aston Flints 54 H13
Aston Herefs 35 L8
Aston Herts 31 S8
Aston Oxon 29 R7
Aston Rothm 57 Q9
Aston Shrops 35 T2
Aston Shrops 45 M8
Aston Staffs 45 S5
Aston Staffs 45 U9
Aston Wokham 20 C6
Aston Wrekin 45 P12
Aston Abbotts Bucks 30 H8
Aston Botterell Shrops 35 P4
Aston-by-Stone Staffs 46 B7
Aston Cantlow Warwks 36 F8
Aston Clinton Bucks 30 J10
Aston Crews Herefs 28 C3
Aston Cross Gloucs 36 B14
Aston End Herts 31 S8
Aston-Eyre Shrops 35 Q2
Aston Fields Worcs 36 C7
Aston Flamville Leics 37 N2
Aston Heath Ches W 55 N11
Aston Ingham Herefs 28 C3
Aston juxta Mondrum Ches E 45 P2
Aston le Walls Nhants 37 N10
Aston Magna Gloucs 36 G13
Aston Munslow Shrops 35 M3
Aston-on-Carrant Gloucs 36 B14
Aston on Clun Shrops 34 J4
Aston Pigott Shrops 44 H12
Aston Rogers Shrops 44 H12
Aston Rowant Oxon 20 B3
Aston Sandford Bucks 30 G11
Aston Somerville Worcs 36 D13
Aston-sub-Edge Gloucs 36 F12
Aston Tirrold Oxon 19 S3
Aston-upon-Trent Derbys 47 M8
Aston Upthorpe Oxon 19 S3
Astrop Nhants 30 B5
Astrope Herts 30 J10
Astwick C Beds 31 R5
Astwith Derbys 57 P14
Astwood M Keyn 38 E11
Astwood Worcs 36 B7
Astwood Bank Worcs 36 D8
Aswarby Lincs 48 G6
Aswardby Lincs 59 Q12
Atcham Shrops 45 M12
Atch Lench Worcs 36 D10
Athelhampton Dorset 7 U6
Athelington Suffk 41 M6
Athelney Somset 16 K11
Athelstaneford E Loth 84 E3
Atherfield Green IoW 9 P13
Atherington Devon 15 N8
Atherington W Susx 10 G10
Atherstone Somset 17 L13
Atherstone Warwks 46 K14
Atherstone on Stour Warwks 36 H10
Atherton Wigan 55 Q6
Atley Hill N York 69 S12
Atlow Derbys 46 H4
Attadale Highld 101 N4
Attenborough Notts 47 P7
Atterby Lincs 58 G8
Attercliffe Sheff 57 N9
Atterley Shrops 45 P14
Atterton Leics 47 L14
Attingham Park Shrops 45 M11
Attleborough Norfk 40 H1
Attleborough Warwks 37 L2
Attlebridge Norfk 50 K10
Attleton Green Suffk 40 B10
Atwick E R Yk 65 R9
Atworth Wilts 18 C7
Auberrow Herefs 35 L11
Aubourn Lincs 58 F14
Auchbreck Moray 103 V10
Auchedly Abers 105 P9
Auchenblae Abers 99 N8
Auchenbowie Stirlg 89 S8
Auchencairn D & G 73 T9
Auchencairn D & G 74 J9
Auchencairn N Ayrs 80 E7
Auchencrow Border 85 M6
Auchendinny Mdloth 83 Q6
Auchengray S Lans 82 J8
Auchenhalrig Moray 104 D3
Auchenheath S Lans 82 F10
Auchenhessnane D & G 74 F6
Auchenlochan Ag & B 87 T11
Auchenmade N Ayrs 81 M3
Auchenmalg D & G 72 G9
Auchentiber N Ayrs 81 M3
Auchindrain Ag & B 88 B5
Auchindrean Highld 108 B8
Auchininna Abers 104 K6
Auchinleck E Ayrs 81 R8
Auchinloch N Lans 89 Q11
Auchinstarry N Lans 89 R10
Auchintore Highld 94 F4
Auchiries Abers 105 T8
Auchlean Highld 97 P4
Auchlee Abers 99 R4
Auchleven Abers 104 J11
Auchlochan S Lans 82 F11
Auchlossan Abers 98 K3
Auchlyne Stirlg 95 Q13
Auchmillan E Ayrs 81 Q7
Auchmithie Angus 91 U3
Auchmuirbridge Fife 90 K11
Auchnacree Angus 98 H11
Auchnagatt Abers 105 Q7
Auchnarrow Moray 103 V11
Auchnotteroch D & G 72 B7
Auchroisk Moray 104 C5
Auchterarder P & K 90 D9
Auchteraw Highld 96 D2
Auchterblair Highld 103 P11
Auchtercairn Highld 107 P9
Auchterderran Fife 90 K12
Auchterhouse Angus 91 M4
Auchterless Abers 105 L7
Auchtermuchty Fife 90 K9
Auchterneed Highld 102 E4
Auchtertool Fife 90 K13
Auchtertyre Highld 101 L6
Auchtubh Stirlg 89 N1
Auckengill Highld 112 J4
Auckley Donc 57 T6
Audenshaw Tamesd 56 D7
Audlem Ches E 45 Q5
Audley Staffs 45 S3
Audley End Essex 39 R13
Audley End Essex 40 D13
Audley End Suffk 40 E10
Audley End House & Gardens Essex 39 R13
Audmore Staffs 45 T9
Audnam Dudley 35 U3
Aughertree Cumb 67 L5
Aughton E R Yk 64 G12
Aughton Lancs 54 J5
Aughton Lancs 62 B6
Aughton Rothm 57 Q9
Aughton Wilts 18 K9
Aughton Park Lancs 54 K5
Auldearn Highld 103 P4
Aulden Herefs 35 L10
Auldgirth D & G 74 H8
Auldhouse S Lans 81 S2
Ault a' chruinn Highld 101 N7
Aultbea Highld 107 Q7
Aultgrishin Highld 107 M7
Aultguish Inn Highld 108 F10
Ault Hucknall Derbys 57 Q13
Aultmore Moray 104 E5
Aultnagoire Highld 102 F11
Aultnamain Highld 109 M8
Aunby Lincs 48 F11
Aunk Devon 6 D4
Aunsby Lincs 48 F6
Aust S Glos 28 A10
Austendike Lincs 49 L9
Austerfield Donc 57 U8
Austerlands Oldham 56 E5
Austhorpe Leeds 63 T13
Austonley Kirk 56 H5
Austrey Warwks 46 J12
Austwick N York 62 F6
Authorpe Lincs 59 Q10
Authorpe Row Lincs 59 T12
Avebury Wilts 18 H7
Avebury Wilts 18 H7
Avebury Trusloe Wilts 18 G7
Aveley Thurr 22 E11
Avening Gloucs 28 G8
Averham Notts 47 U3
Aveton Gifford Devon 5 R11
Aviemore Highld 103 N13
Avington W Berk 19 N7
Avoch Highld 102 K4
Avon Hants 8 G9
Avonbridge Falk 82 H4
Avon Dassett Warwks 37 M10
Avonmouth Bristl 27 U12
Avonwick Devon 5 S9
Awbridge Hants 9 L4
Awkley S Glos 28 A10
Awliscombe Devon 6 F4
Awre Gloucs 28 D6
Awsworth Notts 47 N5
Axborough Worcs 35 U5
Axbridge Somset 17 M6
Axford Hants 19 T12
Axford Wilts 18 K6
Axmansford Hants 19 S8
Axminster Devon 6 J5
Axmouth Devon 6 J6
Axton Flints 54 D10
Aycliffe Dur 69 S8
Aydon Nthumb 77 L12
Aylburton Gloucs 28 B7
Ayle Nthumb 68 F3
Aylesbeare Devon 6 D6
Aylesbury Bucks 30 H10
Aylesby NE Lin 59 M5
Aylesford Kent 12 D4
Aylesham Kent 13 P5
Aylestone C Leic 47 Q13
Aylestone Park C Leic 47 Q13
Aylmerton Norfk 51 L6
Aylsham Norfk 51 L8
Aylton Herefs 35 Q13
Aylworth Gloucs 29 M3
Aymestrey Herefs 34 K7
Aynho Nhants 30 B6
Ayot Green Herts 31 R10
Ayot St Lawrence Herts 31 Q9
Ayot St Peter Herts 31 R9
Ayr S Ayrs 81 L8
Aysgarth N York 63 L2
Ayshford Devon 16 D13
Ayside Cumb 61 R3
Ayston Rutlnd 48 C13
Aythorpe Roding Essex 22 E4
Ayton Border 85 N6
Azerley N York 63 R5

B

Babbacombe Torbay 6 B11
Babbington Notts 47 N5
Babbinswood Shrops 44 H8
Babbs Green Herts 31 U9
Babcary Somset 17 Q11
Babel Carmth 33 R13
Babel Green Suffk 40 B11
Babell Flints 54 E12
Babeny Devon 5 R5
Bablock Hythe Oxon 29 T7
Babraham Cambs 39 R10
Babworth Notts 57 U10
Bachau IoA 52 F6
Bache Shrops 35 L4
Bacheldre Powys 34 F2
Bachelor's Bump E Susx 12 F13
Backaland Ork 106 u16
Backbarrow Cumb 61 R3
Backe Carmth 25 N7
Backfolds Abers 105 S5
Backford Ches W 54 J12
Backford Cross Ches W 54 J12
Backies Highld 109 Q4
Back of Keppoch Highld 100 f11
Back o' th' Brook Staffs 46 E3
Back Street Suffk 40 B9
Backwell N Som 17 N3
Backworth N Tyne 77 S11
Bacon's End Solhll 36 G3
Baconsthorpe Norfk 50 K6
Bacton Herefs 27 R1
Bacton Norfk 51 P7
Bacton Suffk 40 J7
Bacton Green Suffk 40 H7
Bacup Lancs 56 C2
Badachro Highld 107 N10
Badanloch Highld 111 R10
Badbury Swindn 18 J4
Badby Nhants 37 Q9
Badcall Highld 110 E5
Badcaul Highld 107 T6
Baddeley Edge C Stke 46 B3
Baddeley Green C Stke 46 B3
Baddesley Clinton Warwks 36 H6
Baddesley Ensor Warwks 46 J14
Baddidarrach Highld 110 B12
Baddinsgill Border 83 M8
Badenscoth Abers 104 K8
Badentarbet Highld 107 T3
Badenyon Abers 104 C12
Badersfield Norfk 51 N9
Badgall Cnwll 4 G3
Badgeney Cambs 39 P1
Badger Shrops 45 S14
Badger's Cross Cnwll 2 D10
Badgers Mount Kent 21 S10
Badgeworth Gloucs 28 H4
Badgworth Somset 17 L6
Badharlick Cnwll 4 H3
Badicaul Highld 100 g7
Badingham Suffk 41 P7
Badlesmere Kent 12 K5
Badlieu Border 75 L2
Badlipster Highld 112 F7
Badluarach Highld 107 S6
Badninish Highld 109 P6
Badrallach Highld 107 U6
Badsey Worcs 36 E12
Badshot Lea Surrey 20 E13
Badsworth Wakefd 57 Q4
Badwell Ash Suffk 40 G7
Badwell Green Suffk 40 H7
Bagber Dorset 7 U2
Bagby N York 64 B3
Bag Enderby Lincs 59 Q12
Bagendon Gloucs 28 K6
Bagginswood Shrops 35 Q4
Baggrow Cumb 66 J4
Bàgh a' Chaisteil W Isls 106 b19
Bagham Kent 13 L5
Bagillt Flints 54 F11
Baginton Warwks 36 K6
Baglan Neath 26 C9
Bagley Leeds 63 Q12
Bagley Shrops 44 K8
Bagley Somset 17 N7
Bagmore Hants 19 U12
Bagnall Staffs 46 B3
Bagnor W Berk 19 Q7
Bagshot Surrey 20 F10
Bagshot Wilts 19 M7
Bagstone S Glos 28 C10
Bagthorpe Notts 47 N3
Bagworth Leics 47 M12
Bagwyllydiart Herefs 27 S2
Baildon C Brad 63 P12
Baildon Green C Brad 63 N12
Baile Ailein W Isls 106 h6
Baile a' Mhanaich W Isls 106 c13
Baile Mòr Ag & B 92 H14
Bailey Green Hants 9 T3
Baileyhead Cumb 75 V10
Bailiff Bridge Calder 56 H1
Baillieston C Glas 82 C6
Bailrigg Lancs 61 T8
Bainbridge N York 62 J1
Bainshole Abers 104 J8
Bainton C Pete 48 G12
Bainton E R Yk 65 M9
Bainton Oxon 30 C7
Baintown Fife 91 N11
Bairnkine Border 76 D2
Baker's End Herts 31 U9
Baker Street Thurr 22 F11
Bakewell Derbys 56 K13
Bala Gwynd 43 T6
Balallan W Isls 106 h6
Balbeg Highld 102 D9
Balbeggie P & K 90 J6
Balblair Highld 102 K2
Balby Donc 57 S6
Balcary D & G 73 U10
Balchraggan Highld 102 F7
Balchrick Highld 110 D4
Balcombe W Susx 11 N4
Balcombe Lane W Susx 11 N4
Balcomie Links Fife 91 T10
Baldersby N York 63 T4
Baldersby St James N York 63 T4
Balderstone Lancs 62 C13
Balderstone Rochdl 56 D4
Balderton Notts 48 B3
Baldhu Cnwll 2 K8
Baldinnie Fife 91 P9
Baldinnies P & K 90 F8
Baldock Herts 31 R6
Baldock Services Herts 31 R5
Baldovie C Dund 91 Q5
Baldrine IoM 60 g6
Baldslow E Susx 12 F13
Baldwin IoM 60 f6
Baldwinholme Cumb 67 M2
Baldwin's Gate Staffs 45 S6
Baldwin's Hill W Susx 11 P3
Bale Norfk 50 H6
Baledgarno P & K 91 L5
Balemartine Ag & B 92 B10
Balerno C Edin 83 N5
Balfarg Fife 91 L11
Balfield Angus 98 J10
Balfour Ork 106 t18
Balfron Stirlg 89 M8
Balgaveny Abers 104 K7
Balgonar Fife 90 F13
Balgowan D & G 72 E11
Balgowan Highld 96 J5
Balgown Highld 100 c3
Balgracie D & G 72 B7
Balgray S Lans 82 G14
Balham Gt Lon 21 N8
Balhary P & K 91 L2
Balholmie P & K 90 H4
Baligill Highld 111 T3
Balintore Angus 98 D12
Balintore Highld 109 R9
Balintraid Highld 109 N10
Balivanich W Isls 106 c13
Balk N York 64 B3
Balkeerie Angus 91 M3
Balkholme E R Yk 64 H14
Ballabeg IoM 60 d8
Ballachulish Highld 94 F7
Ballafesson IoM 60 c8
Ballajora IoM 60 h4
Ballakilpheric IoM 60 c8
Ballamodha IoM 60 d8
Ballantrae S Ayrs 72 D3
Ballards Gore Essex 23 M9
Ballards Green Warwks 36 J2
Ballasalla IoM 60 d8
Ballater Abers 98 F4
Ballaugh IoM 60 e4
Ballchraggan Highld 109 P9
Ballencrieff E Loth 84 D3
Ballevullin Ag & B 92 B9
Ball Green C Stke 45 U3
Ball Haye Green Staffs 46 C2

Ball Hill Hants 19 P8
Ballianlay Ag & B 88 B13
Ballidon Derbys 46 H3
Balliekine N Ayrs 79 R8
Balliemore Ag & B 88 D6
Balligmorrie S Ayrs 72 G1
Ballimore Stirlg 89 M2
Ballindalloch Moray 103 U8
Ballindean P & K 91 L6
Ballingdon Suffk 40 E12
Ballinger Common Bucks 30 K12
Ballingham Herefs 28 A1
Ballingry Fife 90 J12
Ballinluig P & K 97 R13
Ballinshoe Angus 98 G13
Ballintuim P & K 97 U12
Balloch Highld 102 K6
Balloch N Lans 89 R11
Balloch P & K 89 T2
Balloch S Ayrs 81 L13
Balloch W Duns 88 J9
Balls Cross W Susx 10 F5
Balls Green E Susx 11 R3
Ball's Green Gloucs 28 G8
Ballygown Ag & B 93 L10
Ballygrant Ag & B 86 F12
Ballyhaugh Ag & B 92 F7
Balmacara Highld 100 h7
Balmaclellan D & G 73 R4
Balmae D & G 73 R11
Balmaha Stirlg 88 K7
Balmalcolm Fife 91 M10
Balmangan D & G 73 Q10
Balmedie Abers 105 R12
Balmer Heath Shrops 44 K7
Balmerino Fife 91 N7
Balmerlawn Hants 9 L8
Balmichael N Ayrs 79 S9
Balmore E Duns 89 N11
Balmuchy Highld 109 R9
Balmule Fife 90 K14
Balmullo Fife 91 P7
Balnacoil Highld 109 Q2
Balnacra Highld 101 P2
Balnacroft Abers 98 D5
Balnafoich Highld 102 J8
Balnaguard P & K 97 Q13
Balnahard Ag & B 93 M12
Balnain Highld 102 D9
Balnakeil Highld 110 H3
Balne N York 57 S3
Balquharn P & K 90 F4
Balquhidder Stirlg 89 M1
Balsall Common Solhll 36 H5
Balsall Heath Birm 36 E4
Balsall Street Solhll 36 H5
Balscote Oxon 37 L12
Balsham Cambs 39 S10
Baltasound Shet 106 w3
Balterley Staffs 45 S3
Balterley Green Staffs 45 S3
Balterley Heath Staffs 45 R3
Baltersan D & G 73 L7
Balthangie Abers 105 N5
Baltonsborough Somset 17 P10
Balvicar Ag & B 87 P2
Balvraid Highld 101 L8
Balvraid Highld 103 M9
Balwest Cnwll 2 F10
Bamber Bridge Lancs 55 N1
Bamber's Green Essex 22 E3
Bamburgh Nthumb 85 T12
Bamburgh Castle Nthumb 85 T11
Bamford Derbys 56 K10
Bamford Rochdl 56 C4
Bampton Cumb 67 R9
Bampton Devon 16 C12
Bampton Oxon 29 R7
Bampton Grange Cumb 67 R9
Banavie Highld 94 G3
Banbury Oxon 37 N12
Bancffosfelen Carmth 25 S8
Banchory Abers 99 M4
Banchory-Devenick Abers 99 S3
Bancycapel Carmth 25 R8
Bancyfelin Carmth 25 P7
Banc-y-ffordd Carmth 25 R3
Bandirran P & K 90 K5
Bandrake Head Cumb 61 Q2
Banff Abers 104 K3
Bangor Gwynd 52 J8
Bangor-on-Dee Wrexhm 44 J4
Bangors Cnwll 14 F13
Bangor's Green Lancs 54 J5
Bangrove Suffk 40 F6
Banham Norfk 40 J3
Bank Hants 8 K7
Bankend D & G 74 K12
Bankfoot P & K 90 G4
Bankglen E Ayrs 81 R10
Bank Ground Cumb 67 M13
Bankhead C Aber 99 S2
Bankhead S Lans 82 J10
Bank Newton N York 62 J9
Banknock Falk 89 S10
Banks Cumb 76 B13
Banks Lancs 54 J2
Banks Green Worcs 36 C7
Bankshill D & G 75 N9
Bank Street Worcs 35 P8
Bank Top Calder 56 H2
Bank Top Lancs 55 M5
Banningham Norfk 51 M8
Bannister Green Essex 22 G3
Bannockburn Stirlg 89 T7
Banstead Surrey 21 N11
Bantham Devon 5 R12
Banton N Lans 89 R10
Banwell N Som 17 L5
Bapchild Kent 12 H3
Bapton Wilts 18 E13
Barabhas W Isls 106 i4
Barassie S Ayrs 81 L6
Barbaraville Highld 109 N10
Barber Booth Derbys 56 H10
Barber Green Cumb 61 R3
Barbieston S Ayrs 81 N9
Barbon Cumb 62 C3
Barbridge Ches E 45 P2
Barbrook Devon 15 R3
Barby Nhants 37 P6
Barcaldine Ag & B 94 D10
Barcheston Warwks 36 J13
Barclose Cumb 75 T13
Barcombe E Susx 11 Q8
Barcombe Cross E Susx 11 Q7
Barcroft C Brad 63 L12
Barden N York 69 P14
Barden Park Kent 21 U13
Bardfield End Green Essex 22 F1
Bardfield Saling Essex 22 G2
Bardney Lincs 58 K13
Bardon Leics 47 M11
Bardon Mill Nthumb 76 F13
Bardowie E Duns 89 N11
Bardown E Susx 12 C10
Bardrainney Inver 88 H11
Bardsea Cumb 61 Q5
Bardsey Leeds 63 T11
Bardsey Island Gwynd 42 B9
Bardsley Oldham 56 D6
Bardwell Suffk 40 F6
Bare Lancs 61 T7
Bareppa Cnwll 2 K11
Barfad D & G 72 J6
Barford Norfk 50 K12
Barford Warwks 36 J8
Barford St John Oxon 37 M14
Barford St Martin Wilts 8 F2
Barford St Michael Oxon 37 M14
Barfrestone Kent 13 Q5
Bargate Derbys 47 L4
Bargeddie N Lans 82 C6
Bargoed Caerph 27 M8
Bargrennan D & G 72 K4
Barham Cambs 38 H5
Barham Kent 13 P5
Barham Suffk 40 K10
Bar Hill Cambs 39 N8
Barholm Lincs 48 G11
Barkby Leics 47 R12
Barkby Thorpe Leics 47 R12
Barkers Green Shrops 45 M8
Barkestone-le-Vale Leics 47 U7
Barkham Wokham 20 C9
Barking Gt Lon 21 R6
Barking Suffk 40 J10
Barking Riverside Gt Lon 21 S6
Barkingside Gt Lon 21 R5
Barking Tye Suffk 40 J10
Barkisland Calder 56 G3
Barkla Shop Cnwll 2 J6
Barkston Lincs 48 D5
Barkston Ash N York 64 B12
Barkway Herts 31 U5
Barlanark C Glas 89 Q13
Barlaston Staffs 45 U6
Barlavington W Susx 10 F7
Barlborough Derbys 57 Q11
Barlby N York 64 E13
Barlestone Leics 47 M12
Barley Herts 39 P13
Barley Lancs 62 G11
Barleycroft End Herts 22 B2
Barley Hole Rothm 57 N7
Barleythorpe Rutlnd 48 B12
Barling Essex 23 M10
Barlings Lincs 58 J12
Barlochan D & G 73 U8
Barlow Derbys 57 M12
Barlow Gatesd 77 P13
Barlow N York 64 E14
Barmby Moor E R Yk 64 H10
Barmby on the Marsh E R Yk 64 F14
Barmer Norfk 50 D7
Barming Heath Kent 12 D4
Barmollack Ag & B 79 Q7
Barmouth Gwynd 43 M10
Barmpton Darltn 70 D9
Barmston E R Yk 65 R8
Barnaby Green Suffk 41 S4
Barnacarry Ag & B 87 U7
Barnack C Pete 48 G12
Barnacle Warwks 37 L4
Barnard Castle Dur 69 N9
Barnard Gate Oxon 29 T5
Barnardiston Suffk 40 B11
Barnbarroch D & G 66 B1
Barnburgh Donc 57 Q6
Barnby Suffk 41 S3
Barnby Dun Donc 57 T5
Barnby in the Willows Notts 48 C3
Barnby Moor Notts 57 U10
Barncorkrie D & G 72 D12
Barnehurst Gt Lon 21 S7
Barnes Gt Lon 21 M7
Barnes Street Kent 12 B6
Barnet Gt Lon 21 M3
Barnetby le Wold N Linc 58 J5
Barnet Gate Gt Lon 21 M3
Barney Norfk 50 G7
Barnham Suffk 40 E5
Barnham W Susx 10 F10
Barnham Broom Norfk 50 J12
Barnhead Angus 99 M12
Barnhill C Dund 91 Q5
Barnhill Ches W 45 L3
Barnhill Moray 103 T4
Barnhills D & G 72 B5
Barningham Dur 69 N10
Barningham Suffk 40 G5
Barnoldby le Beck NE Lin 59 M6
Barnoldswick Lancs 62 H10
Barnsdale Bar Donc 57 R4
Barns Green W Susx 10 J5
Barnsley Barns 57 M5
Barnsley Gloucs 29 L7
Barnsole Kent 13 Q4
Barnstaple Devon 15 N6
Barnston Essex 22 F4
Barnston Wirral 54 G10
Barnstone Notts 47 T6
Barnt Green Worcs 36 D6
Barnton C Edin 83 N4
Barnton Ches W 55 P12
Barnwell All Saints Nhants 38 F4
Barnwell St Andrew Nhants 38 G4
Barnwood Gloucs 28 G4
Baron's Cross Herefs 35 L9
Baronwood Cumb 67 R4
Barr S Ayrs 80 K14
Barra W Isls 106 b18
Barra Airport W Isls 106 c18
Barrachan D & G 72 K10
Barraigh W Isls 106 b18
Barrananaoil Ag & B 87 Q4
Barrapoll Ag & B 92 A10
Barras Cumb 68 H10
Barrasford Nthumb 76 J11
Barregarrow IoM 60 e5
Barrets Green Ches E 45 N2
Barrhead E Rens 89 L14
Barrhill S Ayrs 72 G3
Barrington Cambs 39 N11
Barrington Somset 17 L13
Barripper Cnwll 2 G9
Barrmill N Ayrs 81 M2
Barrock Highld 112 G2
Barrow Gloucs 28 G3
Barrow Lancs 62 E12
Barrow Rutlnd 48 C10
Barrow Shrops 45 Q13
Barrow Somset 17 T10
Barrow Suffk 40 C8
Barroway Drove Norfk 49 S13
Barrow Bridge Bolton 55 Q4
Barrow Burn Nthumb 76 H3
Barrowby Lincs 48 C6
Barrow Common N Som 17 P3
Barrowden Rutlnd 48 D13
Barrowford Lancs 62 H12
Barrow Gurney N Som 17 P3
Barrow Haven N Linc 58 J2
Barrow Hill Derbys 57 P11
Barrow-in-Furness Cumb 61 N6
Barrow Island Cumb 61 M6
Barrow Nook Lancs 54 K6
Barrow's Green Ches E 45 Q2
Barrows Green Cumb 61 U2
Barrow Street Wilts 8 A2
Barrow-upon-Humber N Linc 58 J2
Barrow upon Soar Leics 47 Q10
Barrow upon Trent Derbys 47 L8
Barrow Vale BaNES 17 R4
Barry Angus 91 R5
Barry V Glam 16 F3
Barry Island V Glam 16 F3
Barsby Leics 47 S11
Barsham Suffk 41 Q3
Barston Solhll 36 H5
Bartestree Herefs 35 N12
Barthol Chapel Abers 105 N9
Bartholomew Green Essex 22 H3
Barthomley Ches E 45 S3
Bartley Hants 9 L6
Bartley Green Birm 36 D4
Bartlow Cambs 39 S11
Barton Cambs 39 P9
Barton Ches W 44 K3
Barton Gloucs 29 L2
Barton Herefs 34 G9
Barton Lancs 54 J5
Barton Lancs 61 U12
Barton N York 69 R11
Barton Oxon 30 C11
Barton Torbay 6 B11
Barton Warwks 36 F10
Barton Bendish Norfk 50 B12
Barton End Gloucs 28 F8
Barton Green Staffs 46 G10
Barton Hartshorn Bucks 30 D6
Barton Hill N York 64 G7
Barton in Fabis Notts 47 P7
Barton in the Beans Leics 47 L12
Barton-le-Clay C Beds 31 N6
Barton-le-Street N York 64 G5
Barton-le-Willows N York 64 G7
Barton Mills Suffk 40 B6
Barton-on-Sea Hants 8 J10
Barton-on-the-Heath Warwks 36 J14
Barton Park Services N York 69 R11
Barton St David Somset 17 P10
Barton Seagrave Nhants 38 C5
Barton Stacey Hants 19 P12
Barton Town Devon 15 Q4
Barton Turf Norfk 51 Q9
Barton-under-Needwood Staffs 46 G10
Barton-upon-Humber N Linc 58 H2
Barton upon Irwell Salfd 55 S7
Barton Waterside N Linc 58 H2
Barugh Barns 57 M5
Barugh Green Barns 57 M5
Barvas W Isls 106 i4
Barway Cambs 39 S5
Barwell Leics 37 M1
Barwick Devon 15 N11
Barwick Herts 31 U9
Barwick Somset 7 Q2
Barwick in Elmet Leeds 63 U12
Baschurch Shrops 44 K9
Bascote Warwks 37 M8
Bascote Heath Warwks 37 L8
Base Green Suffk 40 H8
Basford Green Staffs 46 C3
Bashall Eaves Lancs 62 D11
Bashall Town Lancs 62 E11
Bashley Hants 8 J9
Basildon Essex 22 H10
Basingstoke Hants 19 T10
Baslow Derbys 57 L12
Bason Bridge Somset 16 K7
Bassaleg Newpt 27 P10
Bassendean Border 84 G9
Bassenthwaite Cumb 66 K6
Bassett C Sotn 9 N5
Bassingbourn-cum-Kneesworth Cambs 31 T4
Bassingfield Notts 47 R6
Bassingham Lincs 48 D2
Bassingthorpe Lincs 48 E8
Bassus Green Herts 31 T7
Basted Kent 12 B4
Baston Lincs 48 H11
Bastwick Norfk 51 R10
Batch Somset 16 K5
Batchworth Herts 20 J4
Batchworth Heath Herts 20 J4
Batcombe Dorset 7 R4
Batcombe Somset 17 S9
Bate Heath Ches E 55 Q11
Batford Herts 31 P9
Bath BaNES 17 T4
Bath BaNES 17 U4
Bathampton BaNES 17 U3
Bathealton Somset 16 E12
Batheaston BaNES 17 U3
Bathford BaNES 17 U3
Bathgate W Loth 82 J5
Bathley Notts 47 U2
Bathpool Cnwll 4 H6
Bathpool Somset 16 J11
Bath Side Essex 23 U1
Bathville W Loth 82 H5
Bathway Somset 17 Q6
Batley Kirk 56 K2
Batsford Gloucs 36 G14
Batson Devon 5 S13
Battersby N York 70 J11
Battersea Gt Lon 21 N7
Battisborough Cross Devon 5 P11
Battisford Suffk 40 J10
Battisford Tye Suffk 40 H10
Battle E Susx 12 E12
Battle Powys 26 J1
Battleborough Somset 16 K6
Battledown Gloucs 28 J3
Battledykes Angus 98 H12
Battlefield Shrops 45 M10
Battlesbridge Essex 22 J9
Battlesden C Beds 31 L7
Battleton Somset 16 B11
Battlies Green Suffk 40 F8
Battram Leics 47 M12
Battramsley Cross Hants 9 L9
Batt's Corner Hants 10 C2
Baughton Worcs 35 U12
Baughurst Hants 19 S8
Baulds Abers 99 L5
Baulking Oxon 29 R9
Baumber Lincs 59 M12
Baunton Gloucs 28 K7
Baveney Wood Shrops 35 Q5
Baverstock Wilts 8 E2
Bawburgh Norfk 51 L12
Bawdeswell Norfk 50 H9
Bawdrip Somset 16 K9
Bawdsey Suffk 41 P12
Bawsey Norfk 49 U9
Bawtry Donc 57 T8
Baxenden Lancs 55 S1
Baxterley Warwks 36 J1
Baxter's Green Suffk 40 C9
Bay Highld 100 b4
Bayble W Isls 106 k5
Baybridge Hants 9 Q4
Baybridge Nthumb 69 L2
Baycliff Cumb 61 P5
Baydon Wilts 19 L5
Bayford Herts 31 T11
Bayford Somset 17 T11
Bayhead W Isls 106 c12
Bay Horse Lancs 61 T9
Bayley's Hill Kent 21 T12
Baylham Suffk 40 K10
Baynard's Green Oxon 30 B7
Baysdale Abbey N York 70 K11
Baysham Herefs 27 V2
Bayston Hill Shrops 45 L12
Baythorne End Essex 40 B12
Bayton Worcs 35 Q6
Bayton Common Worcs 35 R6
Bayworth Oxon 29 U7
Beach S Glos 17 T2
Beachampton Bucks 30 G5
Beachamwell Norfk 50 C12
Beachley Gloucs 27 V9
Beachy Head E Susx 11 T11
Beacon Devon 6 G3
Beacon End Essex 23 N2
Beacon Hill Kent 12 F9
Beacon Hill Notts 48 B3
Beacon Hill Surrey 10 D3
Beacon's Bottom Bucks 20 C3
Beaconsfield Bucks 20 F4
Beaconsfield Services Bucks 20 G5
Beadlam N York 64 F3
Beadlow C Beds 31 P5
Beadnell Nthumb 85 U13
Beaford Devon 15 N9
Beal N York 57 R1
Beal Nthumb 85 R10
Bealbury Cnwll 4 K7
Bealsmill Cnwll 4 K5
Beam Hill Staffs 46 H8
Beamhurst Staffs 46 E6
Beaminster Dorset 7 N4
Beamish Dur 69 R2
Beamish - The Living Museum of the North Dur 69 R2
Beamsley N York 63 M9
Bean Kent 22 E13
Beanacre Wilts 18 D7
Beanley Nthumb 77 M2
Beardon Devon 5 N4
Beardwood Bl w D 62 D14
Beare Devon 6 C4
Beare Green Surrey 10 K2
Bearley Warwks 36 G8
Bearley Cross Warwks 36 G8
Bearpark Dur 69 R4
Bearsden E Duns 89 M11
Bearsted Kent 12 F4
Bearstone Shrops 45 R6
Bearwood BCP 8 E9
Bearwood Birm 36 D3
Bearwood Herefs 34 J9
Beattock D & G 75 L5
Beauchamp Roding Essex 22 E6
Beauchief Sheff 57 M10
Beaudesert Warwks 36 G7
Beaufort Blae G 27 M5
Beaulieu Essex 22 H6
Beaulieu Hants 9 M8
Beaulieu Road Station Hants 9 L7
Beauly Highld 102 F6
Beaumaris IoA 52 K7
Beaumaris Castle IoA 52 K7
Beaumont Cumb 75 R14
Beaumont Essex 23 S3
Beaumont Jersey 7 c3
Beaumont Hill Darltn 69 S9
Beaumont Leys C Leic 47 Q12
Beausale Warwks 36 H6
Beauworth Hants 9 R3
Beaworthy Devon 15 L13
Beazley End Essex 22 H2
Bebington Wirral 54 H10
Bebside Nthumb 77 R9
Beccles Suffk 41 R3
Becconsall Lancs 55 L2
Beckbury Shrops 45 S13
Beckenham Gt Lon 21 Q9
Beckermet Cumb 66 F11
Beckett End Norfk 50 C14
Beckfoot Cumb 61 M2
Beckfoot Cumb 66 G3
Beckfoot Cumb 66 J12
Beck Foot Cumb 68 D13
Beckford Worcs 36 C13
Beckhampton Wilts 18 G7
Beck Hole N York 71 P12
Beckingham Lincs 48 C3
Beckingham Notts 58 C9
Beckington Somset 18 B10
Beckjay Shrops 34 J5
Beckley E Susx 12 G11
Beckley Hants 8 J9
Beckley Oxon 30 C10
Beck Row Suffk 39 U5
Becks C Brad 63 L10
Beck Side Cumb 61 N3
Beck Side Cumb 61 R3
Beckton Gt Lon 21 R6
Beckwithshaw N York 63 R9
Becontree Gt Lon 21 S5
Becquet Vincent Jersey 7 d2
Bedale N York 63 R2
Bedburn Dur 69 N6
Bedchester Dorset 8 B5
Beddau Rhondd 26 K10
Beddgelert Gwynd 43 L4
Beddingham E Susx 11 Q9
Beddington Gt Lon 21 P9
Beddington Corner Gt Lon 21 N9
Bedfield Suffk 41 M7
Bedfield Little Green Suffk 41 M7
Bedford Bed 38 F11
Bedgebury Cross Kent 12 D9
Bedgrove Bucks 30 H10
Bedham W Susx 10 G6
Bedhampton Hants 9 U7
Bedingfield Suffk 41 L7
Bedingfield Green Suffk 41 L7
Bedlam N York 63 R7
Bedlington Nthumb 77 R9
Bedlinog Myr Td 26 K7
Bedminster Bristl 17 Q2
Bedminster Down Bristl 17 Q2
Bedmond Herts 31 N12
Bednall Staffs 46 C10
Bedrule Border 76 C2
Bedstone Shrops 34 J5
Bedwas Caerph 27 M10
Bedwellty Caerph 27 M7
Bedworth Warwks 37 L3
Bedworth Woodlands Warwks 36 K3
Beeby Leics 47 S12
Beech Hants 19 U13
Beech Staffs 45 U6
Beech Hill W Berk 19 U8
Beechingstoke Wilts 18 G9
Beedon W Berk 19 Q5
Beedon Hill W Berk 19 Q5
Beeford E R Yk 65 Q9
Beeley Derbys 57 L13
Beelsby NE Lin 59 M6
Beenham W Berk 19 S7
Beenham's Heath W & M 20 D7
Beeny Cnwll 4 E2
Beer Devon 6 H7
Beer Somset 17 M10
Beercrocombe Somset 16 K12
Beer Hackett Dorset 7 R2
Beesands Devon 5 U12
Beesby Lincs 59 S10
Beeson Devon 5 U12
Beeston C Beds 38 J11
Beeston Ches W 45 M2
Beeston Leeds 63 R13
Beeston Norfk 50 F10
Beeston Notts 47 P6
Beeston Regis Norfk 51 L5
Beeswing D & G 74 G12
Beetham Cumb 61 T4
Beetham Somset 6 J2
Beetley Norfk 50 G10
Began Cardif 27 N11
Begbroke Oxon 29 U5
Begdale Cambs 49 Q12
Begelly Pembks 24 K9
Beggarington Hill Leeds 57 L2
Beggar's Bush Powys 34 G8
Beguildy Powys 34 E5
Beighton Norfk 51 Q12
Beighton Sheff 57 P10
Beinn Na Faoghla W Isls 106 d13
Beith N Ayrs 81 M2
Bekesbourne Kent 13 N4
Bekesbourne Hill Kent 13 N4
Belaugh Norfk 51 N10
Belbroughton Worcs 36 B5
Belchalwell Dorset 7 U3
Belchalwell Street Dorset 7 U3
Belchamp Otten Essex 40 D12
Belchamp St Paul Essex 40 C12
Belchamp Walter Essex 40 D12
Belchford Lincs 59 N11
Belford Nthumb 85 S12
Belgrave C Leic 47 Q12
Belhaven E Loth 84 H3
Belhelvie Abers 105 Q12
Belhinnie Abers 104 F10
Bellabeg Abers 104 D13
Bellamore Herefs 34 J12
Bellanoch Ag & B 87 P7
Bellasize E R Yk 64 J14
Bellaty Angus 98 C12
Bell Bar Herts 31 S11
Bell Busk N York 62 J8
Belleau Lincs 59 R11
Bell End Worcs 36 B5
Bellerby N York 69 P14
Bellever Devon 5 R5
Belle Vue Cumb 67 N1
Belle Vue Wakefd 57 M3
Bellfield S Lans 82 F12
Bellfields Surrey 20 G12
Bell Heath Worcs 36 B5
Bell Hill Hants 9 U4
Bellingdon Bucks 30 K11
Bellingham Nthumb 76 G9
Belloch Ag & B 79 M8
Bellochantuy Ag & B 79 M9
Bell o' th' Hill Ches W 45 M4
Bellows Cross Dorset 8 F6
Bells Cross Suffk 41 L10
Bellshill N Lans 82 D6
Bellshill Nthumb 85 S12
Bellside N Lans 82 F7
Bellsquarry W Loth 83 L5
Bells Yew Green E Susx 11 U3
Belluton BaNES 17 R4
Belmaduthy Highld 102 H4
Belmesthorpe Rutlnd 48 F11
Belmont Bl w D 55 Q3
Belmont Gt Lon 21 N10
Belmont S Ayrs 81 L9
Belmont Shet 106 v3
Belnacraig Abers 104 D12
Belowda Cnwll 3 P4
Belper Derbys 46 K4
Belper Lane End Derbys 46 K4
Belph Derbys 57 R11
Belsay Nthumb 77 M10
Belses Border 84 F13
Belsford Devon 5 T9
Belsize Herts 31 M12
Belstead Suffk 40 K12
Belstone Devon 5 Q2
Belthorn Bl w D 55 R2
Beltinge Kent 13 N2
Beltingham Nthumb 76 F13
Beltoft N Linc 58 D5
Belton Leics 47 M9
Belton Lincs 48 D6
Belton N Linc 58 C5
Belton Norfk 51 S13
Belton House Lincs 48 D6
Belton in Rutland Rutlnd 48 B13
Beltring Kent 12 C6
Belvedere Gt Lon 21 S7
Belvoir Leics 48 B7
Bembridge IoW 9 S11
Bemerton Wilts 8 G2
Bempton E R Yk 65 R5
Benacre Suffk 41 T4
Benbecula W Isls 106 d13
Benbecula Airport W Isls 106 c13
Benbuie D & G 74 D6
Benderloch Ag & B 94 C11
Benenden Kent 12 F9
Benfieldside Dur 69 N2
Benfleet Essex 22 J10
Bengate Norfk 51 P8
Bengeo Herts 31 T10
Bengeworth Worcs 36 D12
Benhall Green Suffk 41 Q8
Benhall Street Suffk 41 Q8
Benholm Abers 99 Q10
Beningbrough N York 64 C8
Benington Herts 31 S8
Benington Lincs 49 N4
Benington Sea End Lincs 49 P4
Benllech IoA 52 H6
Benmore Ag & B 88 D8
Bennacott Cnwll 4 H2
Bennan N Ayrs 80 D8
Bennet Head Cumb 67 P8
Bennetland E R Yk 64 J14
Bennett End Bucks 20 C3
Ben Nevis Highld 94 H4
Benniworth Lincs 59 M10
Benover Kent 12 D6
Ben Rhydding C Brad 63 N10
Benslie N Ayrs 81 L4
Benson Oxon 19 T2
Bentfield Green Essex 22 D2
Benthall Shrops 45 Q13
Bentham Gloucs 28 H4
Benthoul C Aber 99 Q3
Bentlawnt Shrops 44 H13
Bentley Donc 57 S5
Bentley E R Yk 65 N12
Bentley Hants 10 B2
Bentley Suffk 40 K13
Bentley Warwks 36 J1
Bentley Heath Herts 21 N3
Bentley Heath Solhll 36 G5
Benton Devon 15 Q5
Bentpath D & G 75 R7
Bentwichen Devon 15 R6
Bentworth Hants 19 U12
Benvie Angus 91 M5
Benville Dorset 7 P4
Benwick Cambs 39 M2
Beoley Worcs 36 E7
Beoraidbeg Highld 100 f10
Bepton W Susx 10 D7
Berden Essex 22 C2
Berea Pembks 24 C4
Bere Alston Devon 5 L7
Bere Ferrers Devon 5 M8
Berepper Cnwll 2 H12
Bere Regis Dorset 8 A10
Bergh Apton Norfk 51 P13
Berhill Somset 17 M9
Berinsfield Oxon 30 C13
Berkeley Gloucs 28 C8
Berkeley Heath Gloucs 28 C8
Berkeley Road Gloucs 28 D7
Berkhamsted Herts 31 L11
Berkley Somset 18 B11
Berkswell Solhll 36 H5
Bermondsey Gt Lon 21 P7
Bermuda Warwks 37 L3
Bernera Highld 100 h7
Bernisdale Highld 100 d4
Berrick Prior Oxon 19 T2
Berrick Salome Oxon 19 T2
Berriedale Highld 112 D12
Berrier Cumb 67 N7
Berriew Powys 44 E13
Berrington Nthumb 85 Q10
Berrington Shrops 45 M12
Berrington Worcs 35 N7
Berrington Green Worcs 35 N7
Berrow Somset 16 J6
Berrow Worcs 35 S14
Berrow Green Worcs 35 R9
Berry Brow Kirk 56 H4
Berry Cross Devon 15 L10
Berry Down Cross Devon 15 N4
Berryfield Wilts 18 D8
Berryfields Bucks 30 G9
Berry Hill Gloucs 27 V5
Berry Hill Pembks 24 J2
Berryhillock Moray 104 G3
Berryhillock Moray 104 G5
Berrynarbor Devon 15 N3
Berry Pomeroy Devon 5 U8
Berry's Green Gt Lon 21 R11
Bersham Wrexhm 44 H4
Bersted W Susx 10 E10
Berthengam Flints 54 D11
Berwick E Susx 11 S9
Berwick Bassett Wilts 18 G6
Berwick Hill Nthumb 77 P10
Berwick St James Wilts 18 G13
Berwick St John Wilts 8 C4
Berwick St Leonard Wilts 8 C2
Berwick Station E Susx 11 S9
Berwick-upon-Tweed Nthumb 85 P8
Bescaby Leics 48 B8
Bescar Lancs 54 J4
Besford Shrops 45 N8
Besford Worcs 36 B12
Bessacarr Donc 57 T6
Bessels Leigh Oxon 29 U7
Besses o' th' Barn Bury 55 T5
Bessingby E R Yk 65 R6
Bessingham Norfk 51 L6
Bestbeech Hill E Susx 11 U4
Besthorpe Norfk 40 J1
Besthorpe Notts 58 D14
Bestwood Village Notts 47 Q4
Beswick E R Yk 65 N10
Betchcott Shrops 44 K14
Betchworth Surrey 21 M12
Bethania Cerdgn 33 L8
Bethania Gwynd 43 P5
Bethel Gwynd 43 U6
Bethel Gwynd 52 H9
Bethel IoA 52 E8
Bethel Powys 44 D9
Bethersden Kent 12 H7
Bethesda Gwynd 52 K9
Bethesda Gwynd 52 K9
Bethesda Pembks 24 J7
Bethlehem Carmth 26 B2
Bethnal Green Gt Lon 21 P6
Betley Staffs 45 S4
Betsham Kent 22 F13
Betteshanger Kent 13 R5
Bettiscombe Dorset 7 L4
Bettisfield Wrexhm 45 L6
Betton Shrops 45 Q6
Betton Strange Shrops 45 M12
Bettws Brdgnd 26 G10
Bettws Newpt 27 P9
Bettws Cedewain Powys 34 D1
Bettws Ifan Cerdgn 32 F11
Bettws-Newydd Mons 27 R6
Bettyhill Highld 111 Q4
Betws Carmth 26 A5
Betws Bledrws Cerdgn 33 L10
Betws Garmon Gwynd 52 H11
Betws Gwerfil Goch Denbgs 44 B4
Betws-y-Coed Conwy 53 N11
Betws-yn-Rhos Conwy 53 R8
Beulah Cerdgn 32 E11
Beulah Powys 33 T10
Bevendean Br & H 11 N9
Bevercotes Notts 57 U12
Beverley E R Yk 65 N12
Beverston Gloucs 28 G9
Bevington Gloucs 28 C8
Bewaldeth Cumb 66 K6
Bewcastle Cumb 76 B11
Bewdley Worcs 35 S5
Bewerley N York 63 P6
Bewholme E R Yk 65 R10
Bewlbridge Kent 12 C9
Bexhill-on-Sea E Susx 12 D14
Bexley Gt Lon 21 S8
Bexleyheath Gt Lon 21 S7
Bexleyhill W Susx 10 E5
Bexon Kent 12 G4
Bexwell Norfk 49 T13
Beyton Suffk 40 F8
Beyton Green Suffk 40 F8
Bhaltos W Isls 106 f5
Bhatarsaigh W Isls 106 b19
Bibstone S Glos 28 C9
Bibury Gloucs 29 M6
Bicester Oxon 30 C8
Bickenhill Solhll 36 G4
Bicker Lincs 48 K6
Bicker Bar Lincs 48 K6
Bicker Gauntlet Lincs 48 K6
Bickershaw Wigan 55 P6
Bickerstaffe Lancs 54 K6
Bickerton Ches E 45 M3
Bickerton Devon 5 U13
Bickerton N York 64 B9
Bickerton Nthumb 76 K5
Bickford Staffs 45 U11
Bickington Devon 5 U6
Bickington Devon 15 M6
Bickleigh Devon 5 N8
Bickleigh Devon 6 B3
Bickleton Devon 15 M6
Bickley Ches W 45 M4
Bickley Gt Lon 21 R9
Bickley N York 65 L1
Bickley Worcs 35 P6
Bickley Moss Ches W 45 M4
Bicknacre Essex 22 J7
Bicknoller Somset 16 F9
Bicknor Kent 12 G4
Bickton Hants 8 G6
Bicton Herefs 35 L8
Bicton Shrops 34 G4
Bicton Shrops 44 K10
Bidborough Kent 11 T2
Bidden Hants 20 B13
Biddenden Kent 12 G8
Biddenden Green Kent 12 G7
Biddenham Bed 38 F10
Biddestone Wilts 18 C6
Biddisham Somset 17 L6
Biddlesden Bucks 30 D5
Biddlestone Nthumb 76 K4
Biddulph Staffs 45 U2
Biddulph Moor Staffs 46 B2
Bideford Devon 15 L7
Bidford-on-Avon Warwks 36 F10
Bidston Wirral 54 G8
Bielby E R Yk 64 H11
Bieldside C Aber 99 R3
Bierley IoW 9 Q13
Bierton Bucks 30 H9
Big Balcraig D & G 72 K11
Bigbury Devon 5 R11
Bigbury-on-Sea Devon 5 R12
Bigby Lincs 58 J5
Biggar Cumb 61 M6
Biggar S Lans 82 K11
Biggin Derbys 46 G2
Biggin Derbys 46 J4
Biggin N York 64 C13
Biggin Hill Gt Lon 21 R11
Biggleswade C Beds 31 Q4
Bigholms D & G 75 R9
Bighouse Highld 111 T4
Bighton Hants 9 S2
Biglands Cumb 67 L2
Bignor W Susx 10 F8
Bigrigg Cumb 66 F10
Big Sand Highld 107 N9
Bigton Shet 106 t11
Bilborough C Nott 47 P5
Bilbrook Somset 16 D8
Bilbrook Staffs 45 U13
Bilbrough N York 64 C10
Bilbster Highld 112 G6
Bildershaw Dur 69 R8
Bildeston Suffk 40 G11
Billacott Cnwll 4 H2
Billericay Essex 22 G9
Billesdon Leics 47 T13
Billesley Warwks 36 F9
Billingborough Lincs 48 H7
Billinge St Hel 55 M6
Billingford Norfk 41 L5
Billingford Norfk 50 H9
Billingham S on T 70 G8
Billinghay Lincs 48 J3
Billingley Barns 57 P6
Billingshurst W Susx 10 H5
Billingsley Shrops 35 R4
Billington C Beds 30 K8
Billington Lancs 62 E12
Billington Staffs 45 U9
Billockby Norfk 51 R11
Billy Row Dur 69 Q5
Bilsborrow Lancs 61 U12
Bilsby Lincs 59 S11
Bilsham W Susx 10 F10
Bilsington Kent 12 K9
Bilsthorpe Notts 47 R1
Bilsthorpe Moor Notts 47 S1
Bilston Mdloth 83 Q6
Bilston Wolves 36 C1
Bilstone Leics 47 L12
Bilting Kent 13 L6
Bilton E R Yk 65 R13
Bilton N York 63 S8
Bilton Nthumb 77 Q3
Bilton Warwks 37 N6
Bilton Banks Nthumb 77 Q3
Bilton-in-Ainsty N York 64 B10
Binbrook Lincs 59 M8
Binchester Blocks Dur 69 R6
Bincombe Dorset 7 S8
Binegar Somset 17 R7
Bines Green W Susx 10 K7
Binfield Br For 20 D8
Binfield Heath Oxon 20 B7
Bingfield Nthumb 76 K11
Bingham Notts 47 T6
Bingham's Melcombe Dorset 7 U4
Bingley C Brad 63 N12
Bings Heath Shrops 45 M10
Binham Norfk 50 G6
Binley Covtry 37 L5
Binley Hants 19 P10
Binley Woods Warwks 37 L5
Binnegar Dorset 8 B11
Binniehill Falk 82 G4
Binscombe Surrey 20 G13
Binsey Oxon 29 U6
Binstead IoW 9 R10
Binsted Hants 10 B2
Binsted W Susx 10 F9
Binton Warwks 36 F10
Bintree Norfk 50 H9
Binweston Shrops 44 H13
Birch Essex 23 M4
Birch Rochdl 56 C5
Birchall Staffs 46 C3
Bircham Newton Norfk 50 C7
Bircham Tofts Norfk 50 C7
Birchanger Essex 22 D3
Birchanger Green Services Essex 22 D3
Birch Cross Staffs 46 F7
Birchencliffe Kirk 56 H3
Bircher Herefs 35 L7
Birchett's Green E Susx 12 C9
Birchfield Birm 36 E2
Birch Green Essex 23 M4
Birch Green Herts 31 S10
Birch Green Worcs 35 U11
Birchgrove Cardif 27 M12
Birchgrove Swans 26 C8
Birchgrove W Susx 11 Q5
Birch Heath Ches W 45 M1
Birch Hill Ches W 55 M12
Birchington Kent 13 R2
Birchington-on-Sea Kent 13 Q2
Birchley Heath Warwks 36 J2
Birchmoor Warwks 46 J13
Birchmoor Green C Beds 31 L6
Birchover Derbys 46 H1
Birch Services Rochdl 55 T5
Birch Vale Derbys 56 F9
Birchwood Lincs 58 F13
Birch Wood Somset 6 H2
Birchwood Warrtn 55 Q8
Bircotes Notts 57 T8
Birdbrook Essex 40 B12
Birdforth N York 64 B4
Birdham W Susx 10 C10
Birdingbury Warwks 37 M7
Birdlip Gloucs 28 H5
Birdoswald Cumb 76 C12
Birdsall N York 64 J6
Birds Edge Kirk 56 K5
Birds Green Essex 22 E6
Birdsgreen Shrops 35 S3
Birdsmoorgate Dorset 7 L4
Bird Street Suffk 40 H10
Birdwell Barns 57 M6
Birdwood Gloucs 28 D4
Birgham Border 84 K11
Birichin Highld 109 P6
Birkacre Lancs 55 N4
Birkby N York 70 D12
Birkdale Sefton 54 H4
Birkenbog Abers 104 G2
Birkenhead Wirral 54 H9
Birkenhead (Queensway) Tunnel Lpool 54 H9
Birkenhills Abers 105 L6
Birkenshaw Kirk 63 Q14
Birkhall Abers 98 E5
Birkhill Angus 91 N5
Birkhill D & G 75 P2
Birkholme Lincs 48 E9
Birkin N York 57 R1
Birks Leeds 57 L1
Birkshaw Nthumb 76 F12
Birley Herefs 35 L10
Birley Carr Sheff 57 M8
Birling Kent 12 C3
Birling Nthumb 77 Q4
Birling Gap E Susx 11 T11
Birlingham Worcs 36 B12
Birmingham Birm 36 E3
Birmingham Airport Solhll 36 G4
Birnam P & K 90 F3
Birness Abers 105 R9
Birse Abers 98 K4
Birsemore Abers 98 J4
Birstall Kirk 56 K1
Birstall Leics 47 Q12
Birstwith N York 63 Q8
Birthorpe Lincs 48 H7
Birtley Gatesd 69 S1
Birtley Herefs 34 J7
Birtley Nthumb 76 H10
Birts Street Worcs 35 S13
Bisbrooke Rutlnd 48 C14
Biscathorpe Lincs 59 M10
Biscovey Cnwll 3 R6
Bisham W & M 20 D5
Bishampton Worcs 36 C10
Bish Mill Devon 15 R7
Bishop Auckland Dur 69 R7
Bishopbridge Lincs 58 H8
Bishopbriggs E Duns 89 P11
Bishop Burton E R Yk 65 M12
Bishop Middleham Dur 70 D6
Bishopmill Moray 103 V3
Bishop Monkton N York 63 S6
Bishop Norton Lincs 58 G8
Bishopsbourne Kent 13 N5
Bishops Cannings Wilts 18 F8
Bishop's Castle Shrops 34 H3
Bishop's Caundle Dorset 7 S2
Bishop's Cleeve Gloucs 28 J2
Bishop's Frome Herefs 35 Q11
Bishops Gate Surrey 20 G8
Bishop's Green Essex 22 F4
Bishop's Green Hants 19 R8
Bishop's Hull Somset 16 H12
Bishop's Itchington Warwks 37 L9
Bishops Lydeard Somset 16 G11
Bishop's Norton Gloucs 28 F3
Bishop's Nympton Devon 15 S8
Bishop's Offley Staffs 45 S8
Bishop's Stortford Herts 22 C3
Bishop's Sutton Hants 9 S2
Bishop's Tachbrook Warwks 36 K8
Bishop's Tawton Devon 15 N7
Bishopsteignton Devon 6 B10
Bishopstoke Hants 9 P5
Bishopston Swans 25 U13
Bishopstone Bucks 30 H10
Bishopstone E Susx 11 R10
Bishopstone Herefs 34 K12
Bishopstone Kent 13 P2
Bishopstone Swindn 29 P11
Bishopstone Wilts 8 F3
Bishopstrow Wilts 18 C12
Bishop Sutton BaNES 17 Q5
Bishop's Waltham Hants 9 R5
Bishopswood Somset 6 J2
Bishop's Wood Staffs 45 T12
Bishopsworth Bristl 17 Q3
Bishop Thornton N York 63 R7
Bishopthorpe C York 64 D10
Bishopton Darltn 70 E8
Bishopton Rens 88 K11
Bishopton Warwks 36 G9
Bishop Wilton E R Yk 64 H8
Bishton Newpt 27 R10
Bishton Staffs 46 D9
Bisley Gloucs 28 H6
Bisley Surrey 20 G11
Bisley Camp Surrey 20 F11
Bispham Bpool 61 Q11
Bispham Green Lancs 55 L4
Bissoe Cnwll 2 K8
Bisterne Hants 8 G8
Bitchet Green Kent 21 U12
Bitchfield Lincs 48 E8
Bittadon Devon 15 M4
Bittaford Devon 5 R9
Bittering Norfk 50 F10
Bitterley Shrops 35 N5
Bitterne C Sotn 9 P6
Bitteswell Leics 37 P3
Bitton S Glos 17 S3
Bix Oxon 20 B6
Bixter Shet 106 t8
Blaby Leics 47 Q14
Blackadder Border 85 L8
Blackawton Devon 5 U10
Blackbeck Cumb 66 F11
Blackborough Devon 6 E3
Blackborough End Norfk 49 U10
Black Bourton Oxon 29 Q7
Blackboys E Susx 11 S6
Blackbrook Derbys 46 K4
Blackbrook St Hel 55 M7
Blackbrook Staffs 45 S6
Blackbrook Surrey 21 L13
Blackburn Abers 105 N13
Blackburn Bl w D 62 D14
Blackburn Rothm 57 N8
Blackburn W Loth 82 J5
Blackburn with Darwen Services Bl w D 55 Q2
Black Callerton N u Ty 77 P12
Black Carr Norfk 40 J1
Black Corner W Susx 11 M3
Blackcraig E Ayrs 81 S11
Black Crofts Ag & B 94 C12
Black Cross Cnwll 3 N4
Blackden Heath Ches E 55 S12
Blackdog Abers 105 R13
Black Dog Devon 15 T11
Blackdown Devon 5 N5
Blackdown Dorset 7 L4
Blackdyke Cumb 66 H2
Blacker Barns 57 M5
Blacker Hill Barns 57 N6
Blackfen Gt Lon 21 S8
Blackfield Hants 9 N8
Blackford Cumb 75 S13
Blackford P & K 90 C10
Blackford Somset 17 M7
Blackford Somset 17 S11
Blackfordby Leics 46 K10
Blackgang IoW 9 P13
Blackhall C Edin 83 P4
Blackhall Colliery Dur 70 G5
Blackhall Mill Gatesd 69 P1
Blackhall Rocks Dur 70 G5
Blackham E Susx 11 R2
Blackhaugh Border 83 T11
Blackheath Essex 23 P3
Blackheath Gt Lon 21 Q7
Blackheath Sandw 36 C3
Blackheath Suffk 41 R6
Blackheath Surrey 20 H13
Black Heddon Nthumb 77 M10
Blackhill Abers 105 T4
Blackhill Abers 105 T7
Blackhill Dur 69 N2
Blackhill of Clackriach Abers 105 Q6
Blackjack Lincs 49 L6
Blackland Wilts 18 F7
Black Lane Ends Lancs 62 J11
Blacklaw D & G 74 K4
Blackley Manch 56 C6
Blacklunans P & K 97 U11
Blackmarstone Herefs 35 M13
Blackmill Brdgnd 26 G10
Blackmoor Hants 10 B4
Black Moor Leeds 63 R12
Blackmoor N Som 17 N4
Blackmoorfoot Kirk 56 G4
Blackmoor Gate Devon 15 P4
Blackmore Essex 22 F7
Blackmore End Essex 22 H1
Blackmore End Herts 31 Q9
Black Mountains 27 P2
Blackness Falk 83 L3
Blacknest Hants 10 B2
Blacknest W & M 20 G9
Black Notley Essex 22 J3
Blacko Lancs 62 H11
Black Pill Swans 25 V12
Blackpool Bpool 61 Q12
Blackpool Devon 5 U6
Blackpool Devon 5 V11
Blackpool Gate Cumb 76 A10
Blackpool Zoo Bpool 61 Q12
Blackridge W Loth 82 G5
Blackrock Cnwll 2 H10
Blackrock Mons 27 N5
Blackrod Bolton 55 P4
Blacksboat Moray 103 U8
Blackshaw D & G 74 K12
Blackshaw Head Calder 62 K14
Blacksmith's Green Suffk 40 K7
Blacksnape Bl w D 55 R2
Blackstone W Susx 11 L7
Black Street Suffk 41 T3
Black Tar Pembks 24 G9
Blackthorn Oxon 30 D9
Blackthorpe Suffk 40 F8
Blacktoft E R Yk 58 D2
Blacktop C Aber 99 R3
Black Torrington Devon 15 L11
Blackwall Derbys 46 J4
Blackwall Tunnel Gt Lon 21 Q6
Blackwater Cnwll 2 J7
Blackwater Hants 20 D11
Blackwater IoW 9 Q11
Blackwater Somset 16 J13
Blackwaterfoot N Ayrs 79 S10
Blackwell Cumb 67 P2
Blackwell Darltn 69 S10
Blackwell Derbys 47 M2
Blackwell Derbys 56 H12
Blackwell Warwks 36 H12
Blackwell Worcs 36 C6
Blackwellsend Green Gloucs 28 E2
Blackwood Caerph 27 M8
Blackwood D & G 74 H8
Blackwood S Lans 82 E10
Blackwood Hill Staffs 46 B2
Blacon Ches W 54 J13
Bladbean Kent 13 N6
Bladnoch D & G 73 L9
Bladon Oxon 29 T5
Bladon Somset 17 M12
Blaenannerch Cerdgn 32 D11
Blaenau Ffestiniog Gwynd 43 P4
Blaenau Ffestiniog Gwynd 43 P4
Blaenavon Torfn 27 P6
Blaenavon Industrial Landscape Torfn 27 N6
Blaencwm Rhondd 26 G8
Blaen Dyryn Powys 33 T13
Blaenffos Pembks 25 L3
Blaengarw Brdgnd 26 G9
Blaengeuffordd Cerdgn 33 M4
Blaengwrach Neath 26 F6
Blaengwynfi Neath 26 F8
Blaenllechau Rhondd 26 J8
Blaenpennal Cerdgn 33 M8
Blaenplwyf Cerdgn 33 L5
Blaenporth Cerdgn 32 E11
Blaenrhondda Rhondd 26 G8
Blaenwaun Carmth 25 M5
Blaen-y-coed Carmth 25 P5
Blaen-y-cwm Blae G 27 L5
Blaenycwm Cerdgn 33 R5
Blagdon N Som 17 P5
Blagdon Somset 16 H13
Blagdon Torbay 5 V8
Blagdon Hill Somset 16 H13
Blagill Cumb 68 F3
Blaguegate Lancs 55 L5
Blaich Highld 94 E3
Blain Highld 93 R5
Blaina Blae G 27 N6
Blair Atholl P & K 97 P10
Blair Drummond Stirlg 89 R6
Blairgowrie P & K 90 J2
Blairhall Fife 82 J1
Blairingone P & K 90 E12
Blairlogie Stirlg 89 T6
Blairmore Ag & B 88 E9
Blairmore Highld 110 D5
Blair's Ferry Ag & B 87 T12
Blaisdon Gloucs 28 D4
Blakebrook Worcs 35 T5
Blakedown Worcs 35 U5
Blake End Essex 22 H3
Blakeley Lane Staffs 46 C4
Blakemere Ches W 55 N12
Blakemere Herefs 34 J12
Blakemore Devon 5 T8
Blakenall Heath Wsall 46 D13
Blakeney Gloucs 28 C6
Blakeney Norfk 50 H5
Blakenhall Ches E 45 R4
Blakenhall Wolves 36 B1
Blakeshall Worcs 35 T4
Blakesley Nhants 37 R10
Blanchland Nthumb 69 L2
Blandford Camp Dorset 8 C7
Blandford Forum Dorset 8 B7
Blandford St Mary Dorset 8 B7
Bland Hill N York 63 Q9
Blanefield Stirlg 89 M10
Blankney Lincs 48 G1
Blantyre S Lans 82 C7
Blàr a' Chaorainn Highld 94 G5
Blarghour Ag & B 87 T3
Blargie Highld 96 J5
Blarmachfoldach Highld 94 F5
Blashford Hants 8 H7
Blaston Leics 38 B1
Blatherwycke Nhants 38 E1
Blawith Cumb 61 P2
Blawquhairn D & G 73 Q3
Blaxhall Suffk 41 Q9
Blaxton Donc 57 U6
Blaydon Gatesd 77 P13
Bleadney Somset 17 N7
Bleadon N Som 16 K5
Bleak Street Somset 17 U10
Blean Kent 13 M3
Bleasby Lincs 58 K10
Bleasby Notts 47 T4
Bleasdale Lancs 62 B10
Bleatarn Cumb 68 F10
Bleathwood Herefs 35 N6
Blebocraigs Fife 91 P8
Bleddfa Powys 34 F7
Bledington Gloucs 29 P3
Bledlow Bucks 30 G12
Bledlow Ridge Bucks 20 C3
Bleet Wilts 18 C9
Blegbie E Loth 84 D6
Blencarn Cumb 68 D6
Blencogo Cumb 66 J3
Blendworth Hants 9 U6
Blenheim Palace Oxon 29 T4
Blennerhasset Cumb 66 J4
Bletchingdon Oxon 30 B9
Bletchingley Surrey 21 P12
Bletchley M Keyn 30 J6
Bletchley Shrops 45 P7
Bletchley Park Museum M Keyn 30 J6
Bletherston Pembks 24 J6
Bletsoe Bed 38 F9
Blewbury Oxon 19 R3
Blickling Norfk 51 L8
Blidworth Notts 47 Q2
Blidworth Bottoms Notts 47 Q3
Blindburn Nthumb 76 G3
Blindcrake Cumb 66 H6
Blindley Heath Surrey 21 Q13
Blisland Cnwll 4 E6
Blissford Hants 8 H6
Bliss Gate Worcs 35 R6
Blisworth Nhants 37 T10
Blithbury Staffs 46 E10
Blitterlees Cumb 66 H2
Blockley Gloucs 36 G14
Blofield Norfk 51 P12
Blofield Heath Norfk 51 P11
Blo Norton Norfk 40 H5
Bloomfield Border 84 F14
Blore Staffs 45 R7
Blore Staffs 46 F4
Blounce Hants 20 B13
Blounts Green Staffs 46 E7
Blowick Sefton 54 J3
Bloxham Oxon 37 M13
Bloxholm Lincs 48 G3
Bloxwich Wsall 46 C13
Bloxworth Dorset 8 B10
Blubberhouses N York 63 P8
Blue Anchor Cnwll 3 N5
Blue Anchor Somset 16 D8
Blue Bell Hill Kent 12 D3
Blue John Cavern Derbys 56 H10
Blundellsands Sefton 54 H7
Blundeston Suffk 41 T1
Blunham C Beds 38 J10
Blunsdon St Andrew Swindn 29 M10
Bluntington Worcs 35 V6
Bluntisham Cambs 39 N6
Blunts Cnwll 4 J8
Blunts Green Warwks 36 F7
Blurton C Stke 45 U5
Blyborough Lincs 58 F8
Blyford Suffk 41 R5
Blymhill Staffs 45 T11
Blymhill Lawn Staffs 45 T11
Blyth Notts 57 T9
Blyth Nthumb 77 S9
Blyth Bridge Border 83 M9
Blythburgh Suffk 41 R5
Blythe Border 84 F9
Blythe Bridge Staffs 46 C5
Blythe End Warwks 36 H2
Blythe Marsh Staffs 46 C5
Blyth Services Notts 57 T9
Blyton Lincs 58 E8
Boarhills Fife 91 S9
Boarhunt Hants 9 S7
Boarley Kent 12 E4
Boarsgreave Lancs 55 T2
Boarshead E Susx 11 S4
Boar's Head Wigan 55 N5
Boars Hill Oxon 29 U7
Boarstall Bucks 30 D10
Boasley Cross Devon 5 N2
Boath Highld 108 K10
Boat of Garten Highld 103 P12
Bobbing Kent 12 G2
Bobbington Staffs 35 T2
Bobbingworth Essex 22 D6
Bocaddon Cnwll 4 F9
Bocking Essex 22 J3
Bocking Churchstreet Essex 22 J2
Bockleton Worcs 35 N8
Boconnoc Cnwll 4 E8
Boddam Abers 105 U7
Boddam Shet 106 t12
Boddington Gloucs 28 G2
Bodedern IoA 52 D6
Bodelwyddan Denbgs 53 T7
Bodenham Herefs 35 M10
Bodenham Wilts 8 H3
Bodenham Moor Herefs 35 M10
Bodewryd IoA 52 F4
Bodfari Denbgs 54 C12
Bodffordd IoA 52 F7
Bodham Norfk 50 K5
Bodiam E Susx 12 E10
Bodicote Oxon 37 N13
Bodieve Cnwll 3 P2
Bodinnick Cnwll 4 E10
Bodle Street Green E Susx 11 V8
Bodmin Cnwll 3 R3
Bodmin Moor Cnwll 4 F5
Bodney Norfk 50 D14
Bodorgan IoA 52 E9
Bodsham Kent 13 M6
Boduan Gwynd 42 F6
Bodwen Cnwll 3 Q4
Bodymoor Heath Warwks 36 G1
Bogallan Highld 102 H5
Bogbrae Abers 105 S8
Bogend S Ayrs 81 N6
Boggs Holdings E Loth 84 C4
Boghall Mdloth 83 P5
Boghall W Loth 82 J5
Boghead S Lans 82 E10
Bogmoor Moray 104 D3
Bogmuir Abers 99 L9
Bogniebrae Abers 104 H6
Bognor Regis W Susx 10 E11
Bogroy Highld 103 P11
Bogue D & G 73 Q3
Bohetherick Cnwll 5 L7
Bohortha Cnwll 3 M10
Bohuntine Highld 96 B7
Bojewyan Cnwll 2 B10
Bokiddick Cnwll 3 R4
Bolam Dur 69 Q8
Bolam Nthumb 77 N9
Bolberry Devon 5 R13
Bold Heath St Hel 55 M9
Boldmere Birm 36 F2
Boldon Colliery S Tyne 77 S13
Boldre Hants 9 L9
Boldron Dur 69 M10
Bole Notts 58 C9
Bolehill Derbys 46 J2
Bole Hill Derbys 57 M12
Bolenowe Cnwll 2 H9
Bolham Devon 16 C13
Bolham Water Devon 6 G2
Bolingey Cnwll 2 K6
Bollington Ches E 56 D11
Bollington Cross Ches E 56 D11
Bollow Gloucs 28 D5
Bolney W Susx 11 M6
Bolnhurst Bed 38 G9
Bolnore W Susx 11 N6
Bolshan Angus 99 L13
Bolsover Derbys 57 Q12
Bolster Moor Kirk 56 G3
Bolsterstone Sheff 57 L7

Boltby N York 64 B2
Bolter End Bucks 20 C4
Bolton Bolton 55 R5
Bolton Cumb 68 D8
Bolton E Loth 84 E4
Bolton E R Yk 64 H9
Bolton Nthumb 77 N3
Bolton Abbey N York 63 M9
Bolton Bridge N York 63 M9
Bolton-by-Bowland Lancs 62 F10
Boltongate Cumb 67 P10
Bolton-le-Sands Lancs 61 M11
Bolton Low Houses Cumb 66 K4
Bolton New Houses Cumb 66 K4
Bolton-on-Swale N York 69 S13
Bolton Percy N York 64 C11
Bolton Town End Lancs 61 T6
Bolton upon Dearne Barns 57 Q6
Bomarsund Nthumb 77 R9
Bomere Heath Shrops 45 L10
Bonar Bridge Highld 109 L6
Bonawe Ag & B 94 E12
Bonby N Linc 58 H3
Boncath Pembks 25 M3
Bonchester Bridge Border 76 B3
Bonchurch IoW 9 R13
Bondleigh Devon 15 Q12
Bonds Lancs 61 T11
Bonehill Staffs 46 G13
Bo'ness Falk 82 K2
Boney Hay Staffs 46 D11
Bonhill W Duns 88 J10
Boningale Shrops 45 T13
Bonjedward Border 76 C2
Bonkle N Lans 82 F7
Bonnington Angus 91 S4
Bonnington Kent 13 L8
Bonnybank Fife 91 N11
Bonnybridge Falk 89 T10
Bonnykelly Abers 105 P5
Bonnyrigg Mdloth 83 R5
Bonnyton Angus 91 L2
Bonsall Derbys 46 J2
Bonshaw Tower D & G 75 P11
Bont Mons 27 R4
Bontddu Gwynd 43 N10
Bont-Dolgadfan Powys 43 R13
Bont-goch Cerdgn 33 N3
Bonthorpe Lincs 59 S12
Bontnewydd Cerdgn 33 L2
Bontnewydd Gwynd 52 G11
Bontuchel Denbgs 44 C2
Bonvilston V Glam 26 K13
Bonwm Denbgs 44 D5
Bon-y-maen Swans 26 B8
Boode Devon 15 M5
Booker Bucks 20 D4
Booley Shrops 45 N8
Boon Border 84 F9
Boon Hill Staffs 45 T4
Boorley Green Hants 9 Q6
Boosbeck R & Cl 71 L9
Boose's Green Essex 22 J10
Boot Cumb 66 J12
Booth Calder 62 J10
Boothby Graffoe Lincs 48 D2
Boothby Pagnell Lincs 48 E7
Boothferry E R Yk 58 B1
Booth Green Ches E 56 D10
Boothstown Salfd 55 Q6
Boothtown Calder 56 H1
Boothville Nhants 37 U8
Bootle Cumb 61 K3
Bootle Sefton 54 H7
Booze N York 69 M12
Boraston Shrops 35 P7
Bordeaux Guern 6 e2
Borden Kent 12 G3
Borden W Susx 10 C6
Border Cumb 66 D7
Bordesley Worcs 36 D7
Bordley N York 62 H7
Bordon Hants 10 B3
Boreham Essex 22 H6
Boreham Wilts 18 C12
Boreham Street E Susx 11 V8
Borehamwood Herts 21 N3
Boreland D & G 75 N7
Boreraig Highld 100 a4
Boreton Shrops 45 M12
Borgh W Isls 106 b18
Borgh W Isls 106 j3
Borgie Highld 111 P5
Borgue D & G 73 Q10
Borgue Highld 112 D11
Borley Essex 40 D12
Borley Green Essex 40 D12
Borley Green Suffk 40 F8
Borneskitaig Highld 100 c2
Borness D & G 73 Q10
Boroughbridge N York 63 T6
Borough Green Kent 12 B4
Borras Head Wrexhm 44 J3
Borrowash Derbys 47 M7
Borrowby N York 63 U13
Borrowby N York 71 L9
Borrowdale Cumb 67 L9
Borrowstoun Falk 82 J2
Borstal Medway 12 D2
Borth Cerdgn 33 M2
Borthwick Mdloth 83 R7
Borthwickbrae Border 75 T3
Borthwickshiels Border 75 T2
Borth-y-Gest Gwynd 43 L6
Borve Highld 100 d5
Borve W Isls 106 b18
Borve W Isls 106 i9
Borve W Isls 106 j3
Borwick Lodge Cumb 61 U5
Borwick Rails Cumb 61 M4
Bosavern Cnwll 2 B10
Bosbury Herefs 35 Q12
Boscarne Cnwll 3 Q2
Boscastle Cnwll 4 E2
Boscombe BCP 8 G10
Boscombe Wilts 18 K13
Boscoppa Cnwll 3 Q6
Bosham W Susx 10 C10
Bosham Hoe W Susx 10 C10
Bosherston Pembks 24 G12
Boskednan Cnwll 2 C10
Bosley Ches E 56 D13
Bosoughan Cnwll 3 M4
Bossall N York 64 G7
Bossiney Cnwll 4 D3
Bossingham Kent 13 M6
Bossington Somset 15 U3
Bostock Green Ches W 55 Q13
Boston Lincs 49 M5
Boston Spa Leeds 63 U10
Boswarthan Cnwll 2 C10
Boswinger Cnwll 3 P8
Botallack Cnwll 2 B10
Botany Bay Gt Lon 21 N3
Botcheston Leics 47 N13
Botesdale Suffk 40 H5
Bothal Nthumb 77 R8
Bothampstead W Berk 19 R5
Bothamsall Notts 57 U12
Bothel Cumb 66 J5
Bothenhampton Dorset 7 N6
Bothwell S Lans 82 D7
Bothwell Services (southbound) S Lans 82 D7
Botley Bucks 31 L12
Botley Hants 9 Q6
Botley Oxon 31 U6
Botolph Claydon Bucks 30 F8
Botolphs W Susx 10 K9
Botolph's Bridge Kent 13 L8
Bottesford Leics 48 B6
Bottesford N Linc 58 E5
Bottisham Cambs 39 R8
Bottomcraig Fife 91 N7
Bottom of Hutton Lancs 55 L1
Bottom o' th' Moor Bolton 55 Q4
Botton Calder 56 D2
Bottoms Cnwll 2 B12
Botts Green Warwks 36 H2
Botusfleming Cnwll 5 L8
Botwnnog Gwynd 42 E7
Bough Beech Kent 21 S13
Boughrood Powys 34 D14
Boughspring Gloucs 27 V8
Boughton Nhants 37 U7
Boughton Norfk 49 V13
Boughton Notts 57 V13
Boughton Aluph Kent 12 K6
Boughton End C Beds 31 L5
Boughton Green Kent 12 E5
Boughton Malherbe Kent 12 G6
Boughton Monchelsea Kent 12 E5
Boughton Street Kent 13 L4
Boulby R & Cl 71 N9
Boulder Clough Calder 56 F2
Bouldon Shrops 35 M3

Boulmer Nthumb 77 R3
Boulston Pembks 24 G8
Boultenstone Abers 104 E13
Boultham Lincs 58 G14
Boundary Staffs 46 C5
Bourn Cambs 39 M9
Bournbrook Birm 36 D4
Bourne Lincs 48 G8
Bournebridge Essex 22 D9
Bourne End Bed 38 E10
Bourne End Bucks 20 E5
Bourne End C Beds 31 L4
Bourne End Herts 31 M11
Bournemouth BCP 8 F10
Bournemouth Airport BCP 8 G9
Bournes Green Gloucs 28 H7
Bournes Green Sthend 23 L10
Bournheath Worcs 36 B6
Bournmoor Dur 70 D2
Bournstream Gloucs 28 D9
Bournville Birm 36 D4
Bourton Dorset 17 U10
Bourton N Som 17 L4
Bourton Oxon 29 P10
Bourton Shrops 35 N1
Bourton on Dunsmore Warwks 37 M6
Bourton-on-the-Hill Gloucs 29 N1
Bourton-on-the-Water Gloucs 29 N3
Bousd Ag & B 92 H6
Boustead Hill Cumb 75 M14
Bouth Cumb 61 Q2
Bouthwaite N York 63 N5
Bouts Worcs 36 D9
Boveney Bucks 20 F7
Boveridge Dorset 8 F6
Bovey Tracey Devon 5 U5
Bovingdon Herts 31 M12
Bovingdon Green Bucks 20 D6
Bovinger Essex 22 D6
Bovington Camp Dorset 8 M1
Bow Cumb 67 M1
Bow Devon 15 R12
Bow Gt Lon 21 Q6
Bow Ork 106 s20
Bowbank Dur 68 K8
Bow Brickhill M Keyn 30 K6
Bowbridge Gloucs 28 G6
Bowburn Dur 70 D5
Bowcombe IoW 9 P11
Bowd Devon 6 F6
Bowden Border 84 E12
Bowden Devon 5 U12
Bowden Hill Wilts 18 D7
Bowdon Traffd 55 S9
Bower Highld 112 F4
Bowerchalke Wilts 8 E4
Bowerhill Wilts 18 D8
Bower Hinton Somset 17 N13
Bower House Tye Suffk 40 G13
Bowermadden Highld 112 F4
Bowers Staffs 45 T6
Bowers Gifford Essex 22 J10
Bowershall Fife 90 G13
Bower's Row Leeds 63 U14
Bowes Dur 69 L10
Bowgreave Lancs 61 T11
Bowhouse D & G 74 K12
Bowithick Cnwll 4 F4
Bowker's Green Lancs 54 K6
Bowland Bridge Cumb 61 S2
Bowley Herefs 35 M10
Bowley Town Herts 31 P11
Bowlhead Green Surrey 10 E3
Bowling Brad 63 P13
Bowling W Duns 88 J11
Bowling Bank Wrexhm 44 J4
Bowling Green Worcs 35 T10
Bowmanstead Cumb 67 N2
Bowmore Ag & B 78 E4
Bowness-on-Solway Cumb 75 P13
Bowness-on-Windermere Cumb 67 P13
Bow of Fife Fife 91 M9
Bowriefauld Angus 91 R2
Bowscale Cumb 67 N6
Bowsden Nthumb 85 P10
Bowston Cumb 67 Q13
Bow Street Cerdgn 33 M3
Bow Street Norfk 50 H14
Bowthorpe Norfk 51 L12
Box Gloucs 28 G7
Box Wilts 18 B7
Boxbush Gloucs 28 D5
Boxbush Gloucs 28 D5
Box End Bed 38 F11
Boxford Suffk 40 G12
Boxford W Berk 19 P6
Boxgrove W Susx 10 E9
Box Hill Surrey 21 L12
Boxley Kent 12 E4
Boxmoor Herts 31 M11
Boxted Essex 40 K14
Boxted Suffk 40 D10
Boxted Cross Essex 23 P1
Boxwell Gloucs 28 F9
Boxworth Cambs 39 M8
Boyden End Suffk 40 B9
Boyden Gate Kent 13 P2
Boylestone Derbys 46 G6
Boyndie Abers 104 J3
Boyndlie Abers 105 Q3
Boynton E R Yk 65 Q6
Boysack Angus 91 T2
Boys Hill Dorset 7 S2
Boythorpe Derbys 57 N13
Boyton Cnwll 4 J2
Boyton Suffk 41 Q11
Boyton Wilts 18 D13
Boyton Cross Essex 22 F6
Boyton End Suffk 40 B12
Bozeat Nhants 38 D9
Braaid IoM 60 e7
Brabling Green Suffk 41 N8
Brabourne Kent 13 L7
Brabourne Lees Kent 13 L7
Brabstermire Highld 112 H3
Bracadale Highld 100 c6
Braceborough Lincs 48 G11
Bracebridge Heath Lincs 58 G14
Bracebridge Low Fields Lincs 58 G13
Braceby Lincs 48 F6
Bracewell Lancs 62 H11
Brackenfield Derbys 47 L2
Brackenhirst N Lans 82 D5
Brackenthwaite Cumb 67 L3
Brackenthwaite N York 63 R9
Brackla Brdgnd 26 G12
Bracklesham W Susx 10 C11
Bracketter Highld 94 H2
Brackley Nhants 30 C5
Brackley Hatch Nhants 30 D5
Bracknell Br For 20 E9
Braco P & K 89 T4
Bracobrae Moray 104 G5
Bracon Ash Norfk 51 L14
Bracora Highld 100 g10
Bracorina Highld 100 g10
Bradaford Devon 4 K2
Bradbourne Derbys 46 H3
Bradbury Dur 70 D7
Bradden Nhants 37 R11
Braddock Cnwll 4 E8
Bradeley C Stke 45 U3
Bradenham Bucks 20 D3
Bradenstoke Wilts 18 F5
Bradfield Devon 6 E3
Bradfield Essex 23 R1
Bradfield Norfk 51 N7
Bradfield Sheff 57 L7
Bradfield W Berk 19 T6
Bradfield Combust Suffk 40 E9
Bradfield Green Ches E 45 Q2
Bradfield Heath Essex 23 R1
Bradfield St Clare Suffk 40 F9
Bradfield St George Suffk 40 F9
Bradford C Brad 63 P13
Bradford Cnwll 4 E5
Bradford Devon 14 K11
Bradford Nthumb 77 M5
Bradford Nthumb 85 S10
Bradford Abbas Dorset 7 Q2
Bradford Leigh Wilts 18 B8
Bradford-on-Avon Wilts 18 B8
Bradford-on-Tone Somset 16 F12
Bradford Peverell Dorset 7 S6
Brading IoW 9 S11
Bradley Ches E 55 N11
Bradley Derbys 46 H4
Bradley Hants 19 T12
Bradley NE Lin 59 N5
Bradley N York 62 K9
Bradley Staffs 45 U10
Bradley Worcs 36 C8

Bradley Wrexhm 44 H3
Bradley Green Somset 16 J9
Bradley Green Warwks 46 J13
Bradley Green Worcs 36 C9
Bradley in the Moors Staffs 46 E5
Bradley Stoke S Glos 28 B11
Bradmore Notts 47 Q7
Bradney Somset 16 K9
Bradninch Devon 6 D3
Bradninch Devon 15 P6
Bradnop Staffs 46 D2
Bradnor Green Herefs 34 G9
Bradpole Dorset 7 N6
Bradshaw Bolton 55 R4
Bradshaw Calder 63 M14
Bradshaw Kirk 56 G4
Bradstone Devon 4 K4
Bradwall Green Ches E 55 S14
Bradwell Derbys 56 J10
Bradwell Devon 15 M4
Bradwell Essex 22 K3
Bradwell M Keyn 30 H4
Bradwell Norfk 51 T13
Bradwell-on-Sea Essex 23 P6
Bradwell Waterside Essex 23 N6
Bradworthy Devon 14 H10
Brae Highld 102 J3
Braeface Falk 89 Q9
Braehead Angus 99 M13
Braehead D & G 73 L9
Braehead S Lans 82 J8
Braemar Abers 98 B5
Braemore Highld 108 B9
Braemore Highld 112 C11
Braes of Coul Angus 98 D12
Braes of Enzie Moray 104 D5
Braes of Ullapool Highld 108 A6
Braeswick Ork 106 v16
Braevallich Ag & B 87 T4
Braewick Shet 106 s6
Brafferton Darltn 70 D8
Brafferton N York 63 U5
Brafield-on-the-Green Nhants 38 B9
Bragar W Isls 106 h4
Bragbury End Herts 31 S8
Braidwood S Lans 82 F9
Brailsford Derbys 46 J5
Brailsford Green Derbys 46 J5
Brain's Green Gloucs 28 C6
Braintree Essex 22 J3
Braiseworth Suffk 40 K6
Braishfield Hants 9 L3
Braithwaite C Brad 63 L11
Braithwaite Cumb 66 K8
Braithwaite Donc 57 T3
Braithwell Donc 57 R8
Braken Hill Wakefd 57 N3
Bramber W Susx 10 K8
Brambridge Hants 9 P4
Bramcote Notts 47 N6
Bramcote Warwks 37 M3
Bramdean Hants 9 S3
Bramerton Norfk 51 N13
Bramfield Herts 31 S9
Bramfield Suffk 41 R6
Bramford Suffk 40 K11
Bramhall Stockp 56 C9
Bramham Leeds 63 U11
Bramhope Leeds 63 R11
Bramley Hants 19 U8
Bramley Leeds 63 Q13
Bramley Rothm 57 Q8
Bramley Surrey 10 G2
Bramley Corner Hants 19 U8
Bramley Green Hants 19 U8
Bramley Head N York 63 N8
Bramling Kent 13 P4
Brampford Speke Devon 6 B5
Brampton Cambs 38 K6
Brampton Cumb 68 E8
Brampton Cumb 76 B14
Brampton Lincs 58 D11
Brampton Norfk 51 M8
Brampton Rothm 57 P6
Brampton Suffk 41 R4
Brampton Abbotts Herefs 28 B3
Brampton Ash Nhants 37 U3
Brampton Bryan Herefs 34 J6
Brampton-en-le-Morthen Rothm 57 Q9
Bramshall Staffs 46 E7
Bramshaw Hants 8 K5
Bramshill Hants 20 B10
Bramshott Hants 10 C4
Bramwell Somset 17 M11
Branault Highld 93 P4
Brancaster Norfk 50 C5
Brancaster Staithe Norfk 50 C5
Brancepeth Dur 69 S5
Branchill Moray 103 R5
Brand End Lincs 49 N4
Branderburgh Moray 104 A1
Brandesburton E R Yk 65 Q10
Brandeston Suffk 41 M8
Brand Green Gloucs 28 D2
Brandis Corner Devon 14 K12
Brandiston Norfk 50 K9
Brandon Dur 69 R4
Brandon Lincs 48 D3
Brandon Suffk 40 C3
Brandon Warwks 37 N5
Brandon Bank Norfk 39 T3
Brandon Creek Norfk 39 T2
Brandon Parva Norfk 50 J12
Brandsby N York 64 D5
Brandy Wharf Lincs 58 H7
Brane Cnwll 2 C11
Bran End Essex 22 F2
Branksome BCP 8 E10
Branksome Park BCP 8 E10
Bransbury Hants 19 P12
Bransby Lincs 58 E11
Branscombe Devon 6 H7
Bransford Worcs 35 S10
Bransgore Hants 8 H9
Bransholme C KuH 65 Q13
Branson's Cross Worcs 36 E6
Branston Leics 48 B8
Branston Lincs 58 H13
Branston Staffs 46 H9
Branston Booths Lincs 58 J13
Branstone IoW 9 R12
Brant Broughton Lincs 48 D2
Brantham Suffk 40 K14
Branthwaite Cumb 66 G8
Branthwaite Cumb 67 L5
Brantingham E R Yk 58 G1
Branton Donc 57 T5
Branton Nthumb 85 M11
Branton Green N York 63 U7
Branxholm Border 75 T3
Branxholme Border 75 T3
Branxton Nthumb 85 M11
Brassey Green Ches W 55 M14
Brassington Derbys 46 H2
Brasted Kent 21 S12
Brasted Chart Kent 21 S12
Brathens Abers 99 M4
Bratoft Lincs 59 S14
Brattleby Lincs 58 F10
Bratton Somset 16 B7
Bratton Wrekin 45 P10
Bratton Clovelly Devon 5 L2
Bratton Fleming Devon 15 P5
Bratton Seymour Somset 17 S11
Braughing Herts 31 V7
Braughing Friars Herts 22 B2
Braunston Nhants 37 P7
Braunston Rutlnd 48 B12
Braunstone Leics 47 Q13
Braunton Devon 15 L5
Brawby N York 64 G4
Brawdy Pembks 24 E6
Brawith N York 70 H11
Brawl Highld 111 T3
Braworth N York 70 H11
Bray W & M 20 F7
Braybrooke Nhants 37 U4
Braydon Wilts 29 L9
Braydon Brook Wilts 29 L9
Braydon Side Wilts 29 K10
Brayford Devon 15 Q6
Bray's Hill E Susx 12 C12
Bray Shop Cnwll 4 J6
Braystones Cumb 66 F11
Braythorn N York 63 Q10
Braythorpe N York 64 C11
Brayton N York 64 C13
Braywick W & M 20 E7
Braywoodside W & M 20 E7
Brazacott Cnwll 4 H3
Breach Kent 12 G2
Breachwood Green Herts 31 Q8
Breaden Heath Shrops 44 J6
Breadsall Derbys 47 L5
Breadstone Gloucs 28 D7
Breage Cnwll 2 G11
Breakachy Highld 102 E7

Breakish Highld 100 f7
Brealangwell Lodge Highld 108 J6
Bream Gloucs 28 B6
Breamore Hants 8 H5
Brean Somset 16 J5
Breanais W Isls 106 e6
Brearley Calder 56 F1
Brearton N York 63 S7
Breascleit W Isls 106 h5
Breaston Derbys 47 N7
Brechfa Carmth 25 T4
Brechin Angus 99 L11
Breckles Norfk 40 G2
Breckonside D & G 74 J6
Brecon Powys 26 J2
Brecon Beacons National Park Powys 26 D8
Bredbury Stockp 56 D8
Brede E Susx 12 F12
Bredenbury Herefs 35 P9
Bredfield Suffk 41 N10
Bredgar Kent 12 G3
Bredhurst Kent 12 E3
Bredicot Worcs 36 B10
Bredon Worcs 36 B13
Bredon's Hardwick Worcs 36 B13
Bredon's Norton Worcs 36 B13
Bredwardine Herefs 34 G10
Breedon on the Hill Leics 47 M9
Breich W Loth 82 H6
Breightmet Bolton 55 R5
Breighton E R Yk 64 G13
Breinton Herefs 35 L13
Breinton Common Herefs 35 M5
Bremhill Wilts 18 E6
Bremridge Devon 15 Q7
Brenchley Kent 12 C7
Brendon Devon 15 S3
Brendon Hill Somset 16 D10
Brenkley N u Ty 77 R11
Brent Cross Gt Lon 21 M5
Brent Eleigh Suffk 40 F11
Brentford Gt Lon 21 L7
Brentingby Leics 47 U10
Brent Knoll Somset 16 K6
Brent Mill Devon 5 R9
Brent Pelham Herts 22 B1
Brentwood Essex 22 E9
Brenzett Kent 12 K10
Brereton Staffs 46 D10
Brereton Green Ches E 55 S14
Brereton Heath Ches E 55 T14
Bressay Shet 106 v9
Bressingham Norfk 40 K4
Bressingham Common Norfk 40 J4
Bretby Derbys 46 J9
Bretford Warwks 37 M5
Bretforton Worcs 36 E12
Bretherdale Head Cumb 67 S12
Bretherton Lancs 54 K2
Brettabister Shet 106 u7
Brettenham Norfk 40 F4
Brettenham Suffk 40 G10
Bretton Flints 54 H13
Brewers End Essex 22 D4
Brewer Street Surrey 21 P12
Brewood Staffs 45 U11
Briantspuddle Dorset 7 V6
Brick End Essex 22 E2
Brick Houses Sheff 57 M10
Brickendon Herts 31 T11
Brickkiln Green Essex 22 H1
Bricklehampton Worcs 36 C12
Bride IoM 60 g2
Bridekirk Cumb 66 H6
Bridell Pembks 32 C12
Bridestowe Devon 5 N3
Brideswell Abers 104 H8
Bridford Devon 5 U3
Bridge Cnwll 2 H9
Bridge Kent 13 N5
Bridge End Cumb 61 M2
Bridge End Cumb 67 M3
Bridge End Devon 5 R10
Bridge End Dur 69 N5
Bridge End Essex 22 G1
Bridge End Lincs 48 H6
Bridgefoot Angus 91 N4
Bridgefoot Cumb 66 G7
Bridge Green Essex 39 Q14
Bridgehampton Somset 17 Q12
Bridge Hewick N York 63 S5
Bridgehouse Gate N York 63 N6
Bridgemary Hants 9 R8
Bridgemere Ches E 45 R4
Bridgend Abers 104 E10
Bridgend Abers 104 J8
Bridgend Ag & B 78 E4
Bridgend Angus 98 K10
Bridgend Brdgnd 26 G11
Bridgend Cerdgn 32 G10
Bridgend Cumb 67 N10
Bridgend D & G 75 L9
Bridgend Devon 5 P11
Bridgend Fife 91 M8
Bridgend Moray 104 D8
Bridgend P & K 90 H7
Bridgend W Loth 82 K3
Bridgend of Lintrathen Angus 98 C13
Bridge of Alford Abers 104 H13
Bridge of Allan Stirlg 89 S6
Bridge of Avon Moray 103 U9
Bridge of Avon Moray 103 U10
Bridge of Balgie P & K 95 S10
Bridge of Brewlands Angus 98 B11
Bridge of Brown Highld 103 U10
Bridge of Cally P & K 97 R13
Bridge of Canny Abers 99 M4
Bridge of Craigisla Angus 98 D13
Bridge of Dee D & G 74 D14
Bridge of Don C Aber 99 S2
Bridge of Dun Angus 99 M12
Bridge of Dye Abers 99 M6
Bridge of Earn P & K 90 H8
Bridge of Ericht P & K 95 V7
Bridge of Feugh Abers 99 N5
Bridge of Gairn Abers 98 E5
Bridge of Gaur P & K 95 V7
Bridge of Marnoch Abers 104 H5
Bridge of Muchalls Abers 99 S5
Bridge of Orchy Ag & B 94 K11
Bridge of Tilt P & K 97 P9
Bridge of Tynet Moray 104 D3
Bridge of Walls Shet 106 s8
Bridge of Weir Rens 88 J13
Bridge Reeve Devon 15 Q10
Bridgerule Devon 14 G12
Bridges Shrops 34 J2
Bridge Sollers Herefs 34 K12
Bridge Street Suffk 40 E11
Bridgetown Somset 16 C10
Bridge Trafford Ches W 55 L12
Bridge Yate S Glos 28 C13
Bridgham Norfk 40 G3
Bridgnorth Shrops 35 R2
Bridgwater Somset 16 J9
Bridgwater Services Somset 16 J9
Bridlington E R Yk 65 R6
Bridport Dorset 7 N6
Bridstow Herefs 27 V3
Brierfield Lancs 62 H13
Brierley Gloucs 28 B4
Brierley Herefs 35 L9
Brierley Barns 57 P4
Brierley Hill Dudley 36 B3
Brierton Hartpl 70 H6
Briery Cumb 67 L8
Brig o' Turk Stirlg 89 M4
Brigg N Linc 58 H5
Briggate Norfk 51 P8
Briggswath N York 71 Q11
Brigham Cumb 66 G6
Brigham E R Yk 65 P9
Brighouse Calder 56 H1
Brighstone IoW 9 N12
Brightgate Derbys 46 J2
Brighthampton Oxon 29 S7
Brightholmlee Sheff 57 L7
Brightley Devon 15 P13
Brightling E Susx 12 C12
Brightlingsea Essex 23 P4
Brighton Br & H 11 N10
Brighton Cnwll 3 N5
Brighton City Airport W Susx 10 K9
Brighton le Sands Sefton 54 G7
Brightons Falk 82 H3
Brightwalton W Berk 19 P5
Brightwalton Green W Berk 19 P5
Brightwalton Holt W Berk 19 P5
Brightwell Suffk 41 N12
Brightwell Baldwin Oxon 19 U2

Brightwell-cum-Sotwell Oxon 19 S2
Brignall Dur 69 N10
Brig o'Turk Stirlg 89 M4
Brigsley NE Lin 59 N6
Brigsteer Cumb 61 T2
Brigstock Nhants 38 D3
Brill Bucks 30 E10
Brill Cnwll 2 H11
Brilley Herefs 34 G11
Brimfield Herefs 35 M7
Brimington Derbys 57 P12
Brimley Devon 5 U6
Brimpsfield Gloucs 28 H5
Brimpton W Berk 19 S8
Brimpton Common W Berk 19 S8
Brimscombe Gloucs 28 G7
Brimstage Wirral 54 H10
Brincliffe Sheff 57 M9
Brind E R Yk 64 G13
Brindham Somset 17 P8
Brindister Shet 106 u8
Brindle Lancs 55 P1
Brineton Staffs 45 T11
Bringhurst Leics 37 U2
Bringsty Common Herefs 35 Q9
Brington Cambs 38 G5
Briningham Norfk 50 H7
Brinkhill Lincs 59 Q12
Brinkley Cambs 39 T10
Brinklow Warwks 37 M5
Brinkworth Wilts 18 F4
Brinscall Lancs 55 P2
Brinscombe Somset 17 L6
Brinsea N Som 17 M4
Brinsley Notts 47 M4
Brinsworth Rothm 57 P9
Brinton Norfk 50 H6
Brisco Cumb 67 P2
Brisley Norfk 50 G9
Brislington Bristl 17 T2
Brissenden Green Kent 12 J8
Bristol Bristl 27 V13
Bristol Airport N Som 17 P3
Briston Norfk 50 J7
Britannia Lancs 56 C2
Britford Wilts 8 H3
Brithdir Caerph 27 M6
Brithdir Gwynd 43 Q10
British Legion Village Kent 12 E4
Briton Ferry Neath 26 D8
Britwell Salome Oxon 19 U2
Brixham Torbay 6 B13
Brixton Devon 5 P10
Brixton Gt Lon 21 P7
Brixton Deverill Wilts 18 C12
Brixworth Nhants 37 T6
Brize Norton Oxon 29 Q6
Brize Norton Airport Oxon 29 Q6
Broad Alley Worcs 35 U7
Broad Blunsdon Swindn 29 M9
Broadbottom Tamesd 56 E8
Broadbridge W Susx 10 C9
Broadbridge Heath W Susx 10 J4
Broad Campden Gloucs 36 G13
Broad Carr Calder 56 G3
Broad Chalke Wilts 8 F3
Broad Clough Lancs 56 C2
Broadclyst Devon 6 C5
Broadfield Inver 88 K10
Broad Ford Kent 12 D8
Broadford Highld 100 f7
Broadford Bridge W Susx 10 H5
Broadgairhill Border 75 P5
Broadgrass Green Suffk 40 G8
Broad Green Cambs 39 U9
Broad Green Essex 22 K3
Broad Green Essex 23 L14
Broad Green Worcs 35 R9
Broadhaugh Border 85 M7
Broad Haven Pembks 24 E8
Broadheath Traffd 55 S9
Broadhembury Devon 6 E4
Broadhempston Devon 5 U7
Broad Hill Cambs 39 S5
Broad Hinton Wilts 18 H5
Broadholme Lincs 58 D12
Broadland Row E Susx 12 F12
Broadlay Carmth 25 Q9
Broad Layings Hants 19 P8
Broadley Lancs 56 C3
Broadley Moray 104 D3
Broadley Common Essex 22 C6
Broad Marston Worcs 36 F11
Broad Meadow Staffs 45 T4
Broadmayne Dorset 7 T7
Broadmere Hants 19 U11
Broadmoor Pembks 24 H9
Broadnymett Devon 15 R12
Broadoak Dorset 7 M5
Broad Oak Carmth 25 U6
Broad Oak Cumb 66 H14
Broad Oak Dorset 7 U7
Broad Oak E Susx 11 U6
Broad Oak E Susx 12 F12
Broad Oak Hants 9 T4
Broadoak Hants 9 U7
Broad Oak Herefs 27 T3
Broad Oak Kent 13 N3
Broadoak Wrexhm 44 H4
Broad Oak St Helens 54 K7
Broad Road Suffk 41 N6
Broad's Green Essex 22 G5
Broadsea Abers 105 R2
Broadstairs Kent 13 S2
Broadstone BCP 8 E9
Broadstone Mons 27 V6
Broadstone Shrops 35 M3
Broad Street E Susx 12 G12
Broad Street Kent 12 E4
Broad Street Kent 13 L8
Broad Street Medway 12 D2
Broad Street Green Essex 23 L5
Broad Town Wilts 18 G5
Broadwas Worcs 35 S9
Broadwater Herts 31 R8
Broadwater W Susx 10 K10
Broadwaters Worcs 35 T5
Broadway Carmth 25 N9
Broadway Pembks 24 F8
Broadway Somset 16 K13
Broadway Suffk 41 Q5
Broadway Worcs 36 E13
Broadwell Gloucs 28 A5
Broadwell Gloucs 29 P2
Broadwell Oxon 29 Q7
Broadwell Warwks 37 N7
Broadwey Dorset 7 S8
Broadwindsor Dorset 7 M4
Broadwood Kelly Devon 15 P11
Broadwoodwidger Devon 4 K3
Brobury Herefs 34 H12
Brochroy Ag & B 94 F12
Brock Lancs 61 U11
Brockamin Worcs 35 S10
Brockbridge Hants 9 S5
Brockdish Norfk 41 M4
Brockencote Worcs 35 U6
Brockenhurst Hants 8 K8
Brocketsbrae S Lans 82 F11
Brockford Street Suffk 40 K7
Brockhall Nhants 37 R8
Brockham Surrey 11 L2
Brockhampton Gloucs 28 J3
Brockhampton Hants 9 U7
Brockhampton Herefs 28 A1
Brockhampton Green Dorset 7 T4
Brockholes Kirk 56 J4
Brockhurst Derbys 57 N13
Brocklebank Cumb 67 M3
Brocklesby Lincs 58 K4
Brockley N Som 17 N3
Brockley Suffk 40 D9
Brockley Green Suffk 40 C11
Brockley Green Suffk 40 D10
Brockleymoor Cumb 67 Q6
Brockmoor Dudley 35 U3
Brockscombe Devon 15 L13
Brock's Green Hants 19 Q8
Brockton Shrops 34 J2
Brockton Shrops 35 L1
Brockton Shrops 35 N2
Brockton Shrops 35 R2
Brockton Shrops 45 S11
Brockton Staffs 45 T7
Brockweir Gloucs 27 V6
Brockwood Park Hants 9 S4
Brockworth Gloucs 28 G4
Brocton Cnwll 3 R4
Brocton Staffs 46 C10

Brodick N Ayrs 80 E5
Brodie Moray 103 Q4
Brodsworth Donc 57 R5
Brogaig Highld 100 d3
Brogborough C Beds 31 L5
Brokenborough Wilts 28 J10
Broken Cross Ches E 55 T12
Broken Cross Ches W 55 Q12
Brokerswood Wilts 18 B10
Bromborough Wirral 54 J10
Brome Suffk 40 K5
Brome Street Suffk 41 L5
Bromeswell Suffk 41 P10
Bromfield Cumb 66 J3
Bromfield Shrops 35 L5
Bromham Bed 38 F10
Bromham Wilts 18 E7
Bromley Barns 57 M7
Bromley Dudley 36 B3
Bromley Gt Lon 21 R8
Bromley Shrops 35 R1
Bromley Common Gt Lon 21 R9
Bromley Cross Bolton 55 R4
Bromley Green Kent 12 J8
Bromlow Shrops 44 H13
Brompton Medway 12 E2
Brompton N York 70 E13
Brompton-by-Sawdon N York 65 L2
Brompton-on-Swale N York 69 R13
Brompton Ralph Somset 16 E10
Brompton Regis Somset 16 C10
Bromsash Herefs 28 B3
Bromsberrow Gloucs 35 R14
Bromsberrow Heath Gloucs 35 R14
Bromsgrove Worcs 36 C6
Bromstead Heath Staffs 45 S10
Bromyard Herefs 35 Q9
Bromyard Downs Herefs 35 Q9
Bronaber Gwynd 43 P7
Broncroft Shrops 35 M3
Brongest Cerdgn 32 G12
Bronington Wrexhm 45 L6
Bronllys Powys 34 E13
Bronnant Cerdgn 33 M7
Bronwydd Carmth 25 R4
Bronydd Powys 34 F11
Bronygarth Shrops 44 G6
Brook Carmth 25 L8
Brook Hants 8 K5
Brook Hants 9 L6
Brook IoW 9 M12
Brook Kent 13 L7
Brook Surrey 10 E2
Brook Surrey 10 G3
Brooke Norfk 51 N14
Brooke Rutlnd 48 B12
Brookenby Lincs 59 L7
Brook End Bed 38 G7
Brook End C Beds 38 J11
Brook End M Keyn 38 D11
Brookfield Rens 88 K13
Brookhampton Oxon 30 D13
Brook Hill Hants 8 K5
Brookhouse Lancs 61 U7
Brookhouse Rothm 57 R9
Brookhouse Green Ches E 55 T14
Brookhouses Derbys 56 F9
Brookland Kent 12 J11
Brooklands Traffd 55 S8
Brookmans Park Herts 31 R12
Brooks Powys 34 C1
Brooksby Leics 47 S10
Brooks End Kent 13 Q2
Brooks Green W Susx 10 J5
Brook Street Essex 22 E9
Brook Street Kent 12 J8
Brook Street Suffk 40 D11
Brook Street W Susx 11 N5
Brookthorpe Gloucs 28 F5
Brookville Norfk 50 B14
Brookwood Surrey 20 G11
Broom Bed 38 J11
Broom Rothm 57 P8
Broom Warwks 36 E9
Broome Norfk 41 P2
Broome Shrops 34 K4
Broome Worcs 35 U5
Broomedge Warrtn 55 R10
Broome Park Nthumb 77 N2
Broomer's Corner W Susx 10 J6
Broomershill W Susx 10 H6
Broomfield Essex 22 H5
Broomfield Kent 12 G4
Broomfield Kent 13 N3
Broomfield Somset 16 H10
Broomfields Shrops 44 K10
Broomfleet E R Yk 58 F1
Broom Green Norfk 50 G9
Broomhall W & M 20 G9
Broomhaugh Nthumb 77 L13
Broom Hill Barns 57 P5
Broom Hill Dorset 8 E8
Broomhill Nthumb 77 Q4
Broom Hill Worcs 35 U6
Broomhill Green Ches E 45 P4
Broompark Dur 69 R4
Broom's Green Gloucs 35 R14
Broomsthorpe Norfk 50 E8
Brora Highld 109 T4
Broseley Shrops 45 Q13
Brotherlee Dur 69 L5
Brotherton N York 57 S1
Brotton R & Cl 71 L9
Broubster Highld 112 D4
Brough Cumb 68 G10
Brough Derbys 56 J10
Brough E R Yk 58 G1
Brough Highld 112 F2
Brough Notts 48 B2
Brough Shet 106 v7
Broughall Shrops 45 N5
Brough Lodge Shet 106 v3
Brough Sowerby Cumb 68 G10
Broughton Border 83 M11
Broughton Bucks 30 J10
Broughton Cambs 39 L5
Broughton Flints 54 H13
Broughton Hants 9 L2
Broughton Lancs 61 U13
Broughton M Keyn 30 J4
Broughton N Linc 58 G5
Broughton N York 62 J9
Broughton N York 64 G4
Broughton Nhants 38 B5
Broughton Oxon 37 M13
Broughton Salfd 55 T6
Broughton Staffs 45 S7
Broughton V Glam 26 G12
Broughton Astley Leics 37 P2
Broughton Beck Cumb 61 P3
Broughton Gifford Wilts 18 C8
Broughton Green Worcs 36 C8
Broughton Hackett Worcs 36 C10
Broughton-in-Furness Cumb 61 N2
Broughton Mains D & G 73 M11
Broughton Mills Cumb 61 M1
Broughton Moor Cumb 66 G6
Broughton Poggs Oxon 29 P7
Broughty Ferry C Dund 91 Q5
Bround with St Giles N York 69 R12
Brow End Cumb 61 P5
Brown Candover Hants 19 S12
Brown Edge Lancs 54 H4
Brown Edge Staffs 46 B2
Brown Heath Ches W 54 K13
Brownheath Shrops 45 L8
Brownhill Abers 105 P7
Brownhills Fife 91 R8
Brownhills Wsall 46 E13
Browninghill Green Hants 19 S9
Brownlow Heath Ches E 55 T14
Brownrigg Cumb 66 F8
Brownsham Devon 14 F8
Brownside Lancs 62 H13
Browns Hill Gloucs 28 G6
Brownsover Warwks 37 P5
Brownston Devon 5 R10
Browston Green Norfk 51 S13
Broxa N York 65 L1
Broxbourne Herts 31 T11
Broxburn E Loth 84 F3
Broxburn W Loth 82 K4
Broxfield Nthumb 77 Q1

Broxted Essex 22 E2
Broxton Ches W 45 L3
Broyle Side E Susx 11 R8
Brù W Isls 106 i5
Bruan Highld 112 H9
Bruar P & K 97 M9
Bruchag Ag & B 88 D14
Bruera Ches W 54 K13
Bruern Abbey Oxon 29 Q3
Bruichladdich Ag & B 78 D4
Bruisyard Suffk 41 P7
Bruisyard Street Suffk 41 P7
Brund Staffs 46 F1
Brundall Norfk 51 P12
Brundish Suffk 41 N7
Brundish Street Suffk 41 N6
Brunery Highld 93 R4
Brunnion Cnwll 2 E9
Brunslow Shrops 34 J4
Brunswick Village N u Ty 77 R11
Bruntcliffe Leeds 63 Q14
Brunthwaite C Brad 63 M10
Bruntingthorpe Leics 37 R3
Brunton Fife 91 M7
Brunton Nthumb 77 Q1
Brunton Wilts 18 K9
Brushford Devon 15 Q11
Brushford Somset 16 C11
Bruton Somset 17 S10
Bryan's Green Worcs 35 U7
Bryanston Dorset 8 B8
Bryant's Bottom Bucks 20 D3
Brydekirk D & G 75 N11
Bryher IoS 2 b1
Brymbo Wrexhm 44 G3
Brympton Somset 17 P13
Bryn Carmth 25 S10
Bryn Ches W 55 P12
Bryn Neath 26 E8
Bryn Shrops 34 G3
Bryn Du IoA 52 D7
Brynamman Carmth 26 C6
Brynberian Pembks 24 K3
Brynbryddan Neath 26 D8
Bryncae Rhondd 26 H11
Bryncethin Brdgnd 26 G11
Bryncir Gwynd 42 J5
Bryn-côch Neath 26 D8
Bryncroes Gwynd 42 E7
Bryncrug Gwynd 43 M13
Bryn-Eden Gwynd 43 P8
Bryneglwys Denbgs 44 D4
Brynfields Wrexhm 44 H5
Brynford Flints 54 E11
Bryn Gates Wigan 55 N6
Bryn Golau Rhondd 26 J10
Bryngwran IoA 52 E7
Bryngwyn Mons 27 R6
Bryngwyn Powys 34 E11
Bryn-Henllan Pembks 24 J3
Brynhoffnant Cerdgn 32 F10
Bryn-mawr Gwynd 42 E7
Brynmawr Blae G 27 M5
Brynmenyn Brdgnd 26 G11
Brynmill Swans 26 A9
Brynna Rhondd 26 H11
Bryn-penarth Powys 44 E13
Brynrefail Gwynd 52 J10
Brynrefail IoA 52 G5
Brynsadler Rhondd 26 K11
Bryn Saith Marchog Denbgs 44 C3
Brynsiencyn IoA 52 G8
Brynteg IoA 52 G6
Bryn-y-bal Flints 54 F14
Bryn-y-Maen Conwy 53 P7
Bualintur Highld 100 d8
Buarth-draw Flints 54 E11
Bubbenhall Warwks 37 L6
Bubwith E R Yk 64 G12
Buccleuch Border 75 R4
Buchanan Smithy Stirlg 89 L8
Buchanhaven Abers 105 U6
Buchanty P & K 90 D6
Buchany Stirlg 89 R5
Buchlyvie Stirlg 89 M6
Buckabank Cumb 67 N2
Buckden Cambs 38 J8
Buckden N York 62 J4
Buckenham Norfk 51 Q13
Buckerell Devon 6 F4
Buckfast Devon 5 S8
Buckfastleigh Devon 5 S8
Buckhaven Fife 91 N13
Buckholt Mons 27 U4
Buckhorn Weston Dorset 17 U12
Buckhurst Hill Essex 21 R4
Buckie Moray 104 E3
Buckingham Bucks 30 F6
Buckland Bucks 30 K10
Buckland Devon 5 R11
Buckland Gloucs 36 E14
Buckland Hants 9 L9
Buckland Herts 31 U6
Buckland Kent 13 R6
Buckland Oxon 29 R8
Buckland Surrey 21 M12
Buckland Brewer Devon 14 J8
Buckland Common Bucks 30 K12
Buckland Dinham Somset 17 U6
Buckland Filleigh Devon 15 L11
Buckland in the Moor Devon 5 S6
Buckland Monachorum Devon 5 M7
Buckland Newton Dorset 7 S3
Buckland Ripers Dorset 7 S8
Buckland St Mary Somset 16 H13
Buckland-Tout-Saints Devon 5 S11
Bucklebury W Berk 19 S6
Bucklers Hard Hants 9 N9
Bucklesham Suffk 41 N12
Buckley Flints 54 G13
Bucklow Hill Ches E 55 R10
Buckminster Leics 48 C9
Bucknall C Stke 46 B4
Bucknall Lincs 58 K13
Bucknell Oxon 30 C7
Bucknell Shrops 34 J6
Buckpool Moray 104 E3
Bucksburn C Aber 99 R2
Buck's Cross Devon 14 H8
Bucks Green W Susx 10 H4
Buckshaw Village Lancs 55 N2
Bucks Hill Herts 31 N12
Bucks Horn Oak Hants 10 C2
Buck's Mills Devon 14 H8
Buckton E R Yk 65 R5
Buckton Herefs 34 J6
Buckton Nthumb 85 R11
Buckworth Cambs 38 H5
Budby Notts 57 U13
Buddileigh Staffs 45 S3
Budd's Titson Cnwll 14 F12
Budge's Shop Cnwll 4 J8
Budlake Devon 6 C4
Budle Nthumb 85 T11
Budleigh Salterton Devon 6 E8
Budlett's Common E Susx 11 R6
Budock Water Cnwll 2 K10
Buerton Ches E 45 Q5
Bugbrooke Nhants 37 R9
Bugford Devon 5 U9
Buglawton Ches E 56 C14
Bugle Cnwll 3 Q5
Bugley Dorset 17 U11
Bugthorpe E R Yk 64 G8
Buildwas Shrops 45 P12
Builth Road Powys 34 B10
Builth Wells Powys 34 B10
Bulbourne Herts 30 K10
Bulbridge Wilts 8 F2
Bulby Lincs 48 F8
Buldoo Highld 112 C3
Bulford Wilts 18 H12
Bulford Camp Wilts 18 H12
Bulkeley Ches E 45 M3
Bulkington Warwks 37 L3
Bulkington Wilts 18 D9
Bulkworthy Devon 14 J10
Bullamoor N York 70 D14
Bull Bay IoA 52 F3
Bullbridge Derbys 47 L3
Bullbrook Br For 20 E9
Bullen's Green Herts 31 R11
Bulley Gloucs 28 E4
Bullgill Cumb 66 G5
Bullinghope Herefs 35 M13
Bullington Hants 19 Q12
Bullington Lincs 58 J11
Bull's Green Herts 31 S9
Bull's Green Norfk 41 R2

Bulmer Essex 40 D12
Bulmer N York 64 F6
Bulmer Tye Essex 40 D13
Bulphan Thurr 22 F10
Bulstone Devon 6 G7
Bulstrode Herts 31 M12
Bulverhythe E Susx 12 E14
Bulwark Abers 105 Q6
Bulwell C Nott 47 P5
Bulwick Nhants 38 E2
Bumble's Green Essex 22 C6
Bunacaimb Highld 100 f10
Bunarkaig Highld 101 T14
Bunbury Ches E 45 N2
Bunbury Heath Ches E 45 N2
Bunchrew Highld 102 H6
Bundalloch Highld 101 M6
Bunessan Ag & B 86 F1
Bungay Suffk 41 P3
Bunker's Hill Lincs 49 L2
Bunnahabhain Ag & B 86 E14
Bunny Notts 47 Q8
Buntingford Herts 31 U7
Bunwell Norfk 40 K2
Bunwell Hill Norfk 40 K2
Bupton Derbys 46 H6
Burbage Derbys 56 F12
Burbage Leics 37 M2
Burbage Wilts 18 K8
Burcher Herefs 34 K8
Burchett's Green W & M 20 D6
Burcombe Wilts 8 F2
Burcot Oxon 30 C13
Burcote Shrops 35 R1
Burcott Bucks 30 H8
Burcott Bucks 30 K10
Burdale N York 64 K7
Burford Oxon 29 P5
Burford Shrops 35 N7
Burg Ag & B 92 K9
Burgate Hants 8 H5
Burgates Hants 10 B5
Burge End Herts 31 P6
Burgess Hill W Susx 11 N7
Burgh Suffk 41 N10
Burgh by Sands Cumb 67 M1
Burgh Castle Norfk 51 S13
Burghclere Hants 19 Q8
Burghead Moray 103 T2
Burghfield W Berk 19 U7
Burghfield Common W Berk 19 U7
Burgh Heath Surrey 21 N11
Burgh Hill E Susx 12 D9
Burghill Herefs 35 L12
Burgh Island Devon 5 R11
Burgh le Marsh Lincs 59 T13
Burgh next Aylsham Norfk 51 M8
Burgh on Bain Lincs 59 N10
Burgh St Margaret Norfk 51 R11
Burgh St Peter Norfk 41 S2
Burghwallis Donc 57 R4
Burham Kent 12 D3
Buriton Hants 9 U4
Burland Ches E 45 P3
Burlawn Cnwll 3 P2
Burleigh Gloucs 28 G7
Burlescombe Devon 16 E13
Burleston Dorset 7 U5
Burlestone Devon 5 U11
Burley Hants 8 J8
Burley Rutlnd 48 C11
Burley Shrops 35 L4
Burley Gate Herefs 35 N11
Burley in Wharfedale C Brad 63 P10
Burley Lawn Hants 8 J8
Burley Street Hants 8 J8
Burley Wood Head C Brad 63 P11
Burlingham Green Norfk 51 Q11
Burlingjobb Powys 34 G10
Burlton Shrops 45 L8
Burmarsh Kent 13 M9
Burmington Warwks 36 J13
Burn N York 57 S1
Burnage Manch 56 C8
Burnaston Derbys 46 J7
Burnbanks Cumb 67 R9
Burnbrae N Lans 82 F7
Burn Bridge N York 63 R9
Burnby E R Yk 64 J10
Burn Cross Sheff 57 M7
Burndell W Susx 10 F10
Burnden Bolton 55 R5
Burnedge Rochdl 56 D4
Burneside Cumb 67 R13
Burness Ork 106 v15
Burneston N York 63 S2
Burnett BaNES 17 S3
Burnfoot Border 75 T4
Burnfoot Border 75 U3
Burnfoot D & G 74 K8
Burnfoot D & G 75 P7
Burnfoot P & K 90 C11
Burnham Bucks 20 F6
Burnham N Linc 58 J4
Burnham Deepdale Norfk 50 D5
Burnham Green Herts 31 S9
Burnham Market Norfk 50 D5
Burnham Norton Norfk 50 D5
Burnham-on-Crouch Essex 23 M6
Burnham-on-Sea Somset 16 K7
Burnham Overy Norfk 50 D5
Burnham Overy Staithe Norfk 50 D5
Burnham Thorpe Norfk 50 E5
Burnhead D & G 74 G7
Burnhervie Abers 105 L13
Burnhill Green Staffs 45 S13
Burnhope Dur 69 Q3
Burnhouse N Ayrs 81 L3
Burniston N York 65 N1
Burnley Lancs 62 G13
Burnmouth Border 85 M6
Burn Naze Lancs 61 R11
Burn of Cambus Stirlg 89 R5
Burnopfield Dur 69 Q2
Burnrigg Cumb 67 Q1
Burnsall N York 63 L7
Burnside Angus 98 K12
Burnside Angus 99 L13
Burnside Fife 90 J10
Burnside Moray 103 U3
Burnside W Loth 82 K3
Burnside of Duntrune Angus 91 P5
Burnt Heath Derbys 56 K12
Burntheath Derbys 46 H7
Burnt Heath Essex 23 P2
Burnt Hill W Berk 19 S6
Burnt Houses Dur 69 Q8
Burntisland Fife 83 P1
Burnt Oak E Susx 11 S5
Burnton E Ayrs 81 P11
Burntwood Staffs 46 E12
Burntwood Green Staffs 46 E12
Burnt Yates N York 63 Q7
Burpham Surrey 20 H12
Burpham W Susx 10 G9
Burradon N Tyne 77 R11
Burradon Nthumb 76 K4
Burrafirth Shet 106 w2
Burras Cnwll 2 H10
Burravoe Shet 106 u5
Burrells Cumb 68 D10
Burrelton P & K 90 K4
Burridge Devon 15 N6
Burridge Hants 9 Q6
Burrill N York 63 Q2
Burringham N Linc 58 E5
Burrington Devon 15 Q9
Burrington Herefs 34 K6
Burrington N Som 17 N5
Burrough End Cambs 39 U9
Burrough Green Cambs 39 U9
Burrough on the Hill Leics 47 U11
Burrow Somset 16 C8
Burrow-bridge Somset 16 K11
Burrowhill Surrey 20 G10
Burry Swans 25 S12
Burry Port Carmth 25 R10
Burscough Lancs 54 K4
Burscough Bridge Lancs 54 K4
Bursea E R Yk 64 H13
Burshill E R Yk 65 P10
Bursledon Hants 9 P7
Burslem C Stke 45 U4
Burstall Suffk 40 K12
Burston Devon 15 R11
Burston Norfk 40 K3
Burston Staffs 46 B7

Burston Staffs 46 B7
Burstow Surrey 11 N2
Burstwick E R Yk 65 S14
Burtersett N York 62 H2
Burtholme Cumb 76 A13
Burthorpe Green Suffk 40 C8
Burthwaite Cumb 67 P3
Burthy Cnwll 3 N5
Burtle Somset 17 L8
Burtle Hill Somset 17 L8
Burtoft Lincs 49 L6
Burton BCP 8 H10
Burton Ches W 54 H12
Burton Ches W 55 M14
Burton Dorset 7 S6
Burton Nthumb 85 T12
Burton Pembks 24 G9
Burton Somset 7 P2
Burton Somset 16 G8
Burton Wilts 17 V10
Burton Wilts 18 B5
Burton Agnes E R Yk 65 Q7
Burton Bradstock Dorset 7 N7
Burton-by-Lincoln Lincs 58 G12
Burton Coggles Lincs 48 E8
Burton Dassett Warwks 37 L10
Burton End Essex 22 D3
Burton End Suffk 39 U11
Burton Fleming E R Yk 65 P5
Burton Green Warwks 36 J5
Burton Green Wrexhm 44 H2
Burton Hastings Warwks 37 M3
Burton Hill Wilts 28 H10
Burton-in-Kendal Cumb 61 U4
Burton-in-Kendal Services Cumb 61 U4
Burton in Lonsdale N York 62 D5
Burton Joyce Notts 47 R5
Burton Latimer Nhants 38 D6
Burton Lazars Leics 47 U10
Burton Leonard N York 63 S7
Burton on the Wolds Leics 47 Q9
Burton Overy Leics 47 S14
Burton Pedwardine Lincs 48 H5
Burton Pidsea E R Yk 65 S13
Burton Salmon N York 57 Q1
Burton's Green Essex 22 K2
Burton upon Stather N Linc 58 E3
Burton upon Trent Staffs 46 H9
Burton Waters Lincs 58 F12
Burtonwood Warrtn 55 N8
Burtonwood Services Warrtn 55 N8
Burwardsley Ches W 45 M2
Burwarton Shrops 35 P3
Burwash E Susx 12 C11
Burwash Common E Susx 11 U6
Burwash Weald E Susx 11 V6
Burwell Cambs 39 S7
Burwell Lincs 59 Q11
Burwen IoA 52 F4
Burwick Ork 106 t21
Bury Bury 55 T4
Bury Cambs 39 L4
Bury Somset 16 B11
Bury W Susx 10 G8
Bury End C Beds 31 P5
Bury Green Herts 22 C3
Bury St Edmunds Suffk 40 E8
Burythorpe N York 64 H7
Busby E Rens 81 R1
Busby Stoop N York 63 T3
Buscot Oxon 29 P8
Bush Abers 99 P10
Bush Cnwll 14 F11
Bush Bank Herefs 35 L10
Bushbury Wolves 46 B13
Bushby Leics 47 S13
Bushey Herts 20 K3
Bushey Heath Herts 20 K4
Bush Green Norfk 41 M3
Bush Green Suffk 40 F9
Bush Hill Park Gt Lon 21 P3
Bushley Worcs 35 U14
Bushley Green Worcs 35 U14
Bushmead Bed 38 H8
Bushmoor Shrops 34 K3
Bushton Wilts 18 G5
Busk Cumb 68 D4
Buslingthorpe Lincs 58 J9
Bussage Gloucs 28 G7
Bussex Somset 17 L9
Butcher's Cross E Susx 11 T5
Butcombe N Som 17 P4
Bute Ag & B 88 B12
Butleigh Somset 17 P10
Butleigh Wootton Somset 17 P9
Butler's Cross Bucks 30 H11
Butler's Hill Notts 47 P4
Butlers Marston Warwks 36 K10
Butley Suffk 41 Q10
Butley High Corner Suffk 41 Q11
Buttercrambe N York 64 G8
Butterdean Border 84 K6
Butterknowle Dur 69 P7
Butterleigh Devon 6 C3
Butterley Derbys 47 M3
Buttermere Cumb 66 J9
Buttermere Wilts 19 M8
Butters Green Staffs 45 T3
Buttershaw C Brad 63 N14
Butterstone P & K 90 G2
Butterton Staffs 45 T5
Butterton Staffs 46 E2
Butterwick Dur 70 E6
Butterwick Lincs 49 N4
Butterwick N York 64 G4
Butterwick N York 65 M5
Butt Green Ches E 45 Q3
Buttington Powys 44 F12
Buttonbridge Shrops 35 R5
Buttonoak Shrops 35 S5
Buttsash Hants 9 N7
Buttsbear Cross Cnwll 14 G12
Butt's Green Essex 22 J7
Buxhall Suffk 40 H9
Buxhall Fen Street Suffk 40 H9
Buxted E Susx 11 R6
Buxton Derbys 56 G12
Buxton Norfk 51 M9
Buxton Heath Norfk 51 L9
Buxworth Derbys 56 F10
Bwlch Powys 27 M3
Bwlchgwyn Wrexhm 44 G3
Bwlchllan Cerdgn 33 L9
Bwlchnewydd Carmth 25 Q6
Bwlchtocyn Gwynd 42 F8
Bwlch-y-cibau Powys 44 E10
Bwlch-y-Ddar Powys 44 E9
Bwlchyfadfa Cerdgn 32 H11
Bwlch-y-ffridd Powys 34 C1
Bwlch-y-groes Pembks 25 M3
Bwlchymyrdd Swans 25 U11
Bwlch-y-sarnau Powys 34 B6
Byermoor Gatesd 69 Q1
Byers Green Dur 69 R6
Byfield Nhants 37 P10
Byfleet Surrey 20 J10
Byford Herefs 34 J12
Bygrave Herts 31 S5
Byker N u Ty 77 R13
Byland Abbey N York 64 C4
Bylaugh Norfk 50 H10
Bylchau Conwy 53 S10
Byley Ches W 55 R13
Bynea Carmth 25 T11
Byram N York 57 Q1
Byrness Nthumb 76 F5
Bystock Devon 6 D8
Bythorn Cambs 38 G5
Byton Herefs 34 J8
Bywell Nthumb 77 L13
Byworth W Susx 10 F6

C

Cabbacott Devon 14 K8
Cabourne Lincs 58 K6
Cabrach Ag & B 78 H3
Cabrach Moray 104 D10
Cabus Lancs 61 T10
Cackle Street E Susx 11 R5
Cackle Street E Susx 12 C12
Cackle Street E Susx 12 F12
Cadbury Devon 6 B3
Cadbury Barton Devon 15 Q9
Cadbury World Birm 36 D4
Cadder E Duns 89 P11
Caddington C Beds 31 N9
Caddonfoot Border 84 D11
Cadeby Donc 57 R6
Cadeby Leics 47 M13
Cadeleigh Devon 6 B3
Cade Street E Susx 11 U6
Cadgwith Cnwll 2 J14
Cadham Fife 91 L11
Cadishead Salfd 55 R8
Cadle Swans 25 V11
Cadley Lancs 61 U13
Cadley Wilts 18 K10
Cadley Wilts 18 K7
Cadmore End Bucks 20 C4
Cadnam Hants 9 L6
Cadney N Linc 58 H6
Cadole Flints 54 F14
Cadoxton V Glam 16 F3
Cadoxton Juxta-Neath Neath 26 D8
Cadwst Denbgs 44 B6
Caeathro Gwynd 52 H10
Caehopkin Powys 26 E5
Caenby Lincs 58 G9
Caerau Brdgnd 26 F9
Caerau Cardif 27 L12
Cae'r-bont Powys 26 E5
Cae'r bryn Carmth 25 U8
Caerdeon Gwynd 43 N10
Caer Farchell Pembks 24 C5
Caergeiliog IoA 52 D7
Caergwrle Flints 44 H2
Caerhun Conwy 53 N8
Caerlanrig Border 75 S5
Caerleon Newpt 27 Q9
Caernarfon Gwynd 52 G10
Caernarfon Castle Gwynd 52 G10
Caerphilly Caerph 27 M10
Caersws Powys 34 B2
Caerwedros Cerdgn 32 G9
Caerwent Mons 27 T9
Caerwys Flints 54 D12
Caerynwch Gwynd 43 Q10
Caggle Street Mons 27 R4
Caim IoA 52 K6
Caio Carmth 33 N13
Cairinis W Isls 106 d12
Cairnbaan Ag & B 87 Q7
Cairnbulg Abers 105 S2
Cairncross Border 85 M6
Cairncurran Inver 88 H11
Cairndow Ag & B 88 E3
Cairneyhill Fife 82 K1
Cairngarroch D & G 72 D10
Cairngorms National Park 97 T3
Cairnie Abers 104 F7
Cairnorrie Abers 105 P7
Cairnryan D & G 72 D6
Cairnty Moray 104 C5
Caister-on-Sea Norfk 51 T11
Caistor Lincs 58 K6
Caistor St Edmund Norfk 51 M13
Cakebole Worcs 35 U6
Cake Street Norfk 40 J2
Calais Street Suffk 40 G13
Calanais W Isls 106 h5
Calbourne IoW 9 N11
Calceby Lincs 59 Q11
Calcoed Flints 54 E12
Calcot Gloucs 29 L5
Calcot W Berk 19 U6
Calcot Row W Berk 19 U6
Calcots Moray 104 B3
Calcott Kent 13 N3
Calcott Shrops 44 K11
Calcutt N York 63 S8
Calcutt Wilts 29 M9
Caldbeck Cumb 67 M4
Caldbergh N York 63 M2
Caldecote Cambs 38 H3
Caldecote Cambs 39 M9
Caldecote Herts 31 R5
Caldecote Nhants 37 S10
Caldecott Nhants 38 E7
Caldecott Oxon 29 U8
Caldecott Rutlnd 38 C2
Caldecotte M Keyn 30 J5
Calder Cumb 66 F12
Calderbank N Lans 82 E6
Calder Bridge Cumb 66 F11
Calderbrook Rochdl 56 D3
Caldercruix N Lans 82 F5
Calder Grove Wakefd 57 M3
Caldermill S Lans 81 T4
Caldermore Rochdl 56 D3
Calder Vale Lancs 61 U10
Calderwood S Lans 81 T1
Caldey Island Pembks 24 K11
Caldicot Mons 27 T10
Caldmore Wsall 46 D14
Caldwell N York 69 Q10
Caldy Wirral 54 F9
Calenick Cnwll 3 L8
Calf of Man IoM 60 b9
Calford Green Suffk 40 B11
Calfsound Ork 106 u16
Calgary Ag & B 92 K8
Califer Moray 103 S4
California Falk 82 H3
California Norfk 51 T10
California Cross Devon 5 S10
Calke Derbys 47 L9
Calke Abbey Derbys 47 L9
Callakille Highld 107 L13
Callander Stirlg 89 P4
Callanish W Isls 106 h5
Callaughton Shrops 45 P14
Callerton N u Ty 77 P12
Callestick Cnwll 2 K6
Calligarry Highld 100 f9
Callington Cnwll 4 K7
Callingwood Staffs 46 G9
Callow Herefs 35 L14
Callow End Worcs 35 T10
Callow Hill Wilts 28 K11
Callow Hill Worcs 35 R6
Callow Hill Worcs 36 D8
Callows Grave Worcs 35 N7
Calmore Hants 9 L6
Calmsden Gloucs 28 K6
Calne Wilts 18 E6
Calow Derbys 57 P12
Calshot Hants 9 P8
Calstock Cnwll 5 L7
Calstone Wellington Wilts 18 F7
Calthorpe Norfk 51 L7
Calthorpe Street Norfk 51 R8
Calthwaite Cumb 67 Q4
Calton N York 62 J8
Calton Staffs 46 F4
Calveley Ches E 45 N2
Calver Derbys 56 K12
Calverhall Shrops 45 P6
Calver Hill Herefs 34 J11
Calverleigh Devon 6 B2
Calverley Leeds 63 Q12
Calver Sough Derbys 56 K12
Calvert Bucks 30 E8
Calverton M Keyn 30 G5
Calverton Notts 47 R4
Calvine P & K 97 N10
Calvo Cumb 66 H2
Calzeat Border 83 M11
Cam Gloucs 28 E8
Camasachoirce Highld 93 T6
Camasine Highld 93 T6
Camas Luinie Highld 101 N6
Camastianavaig Highld 100 e6
Camault Muir Highld 102 F7
Camber E Susx 12 J12
Camberley Surrey 20 E10
Camberwell Gt Lon 21 P7
Camblesforth N York 57 T1
Cambo Nthumb 77 L8
Cambois Nthumb 77 S9
Camborne Cnwll 2 G8
Camborne & Redruth Mining District Cnwll 2 G8
Cambourne Cambs 39 M9
Cambridge Cambs 39 Q9
Cambridge Gloucs 28 D7
Cambridge Airport Cambs 39 Q9
Cambrose Cnwll 2 H7
Cambus Clacks 90 C13
Cambusavie Highld 109 P5
Cambusbarron Stirlg 89 S7
Cambuskenneth Stirlg 89 T7
Cambuslang S Lans 89 P13
Cambus o' May Abers 98 G4
Cambuswallace S Lans 82 K11
Camden Town Gt Lon 21 N6
Cameley BaNES 17 R5
Camelford Cnwll 4 E4
Camelon Falk 82 G2
Camerory Highld 103 R9
Camer's Green Worcs 35 S13
Camerton BaNES 17 S5
Camerton Cumb 66 F6
Camghouran P & K 95 R7
Camieston Border 84 F12
Cammachmore Abers 99 S4
Cammeringham Lincs 58 F10
Camore Highld 109 P7
Campbeltown Ag & B 79 N11
Campbeltown Airport Ag & B 79 M11
Camperdown N Tyne 77 R11
Cample D & G 74 G7
Campmuir P & K 90 K4
Camps W Loth 83 L5
Campsall Donc 57 R4
Campsea Ash Suffk 41 P9
Camps End Cambs 39 T12
Campton C Beds 31 P5
Camptown Border 76 D3
Camrose Pembks 24 F6
Camserney P & K 90 B2
Camusnagaul Highld 94 F4
Camusnagaul Highld 107 U7
Camusteel Highld 100 g5
Camusterrach Highld 100 g5
Canada Hants 8 K5
Canal Foot Cumb 61 Q4
Canaston Bridge Pembks 24 J7
Candacraig Abers 98 E4
Candlesby Lincs 59 S13
Candle Street Suffk 40 H6
Candover Green Shrops 45 M12
Candy Mill Border 83 L10
Cane End Oxon 19 U5
Canewdon Essex 23 M9
Canford Bottom Dorset 8 E8
Canford Cliffs BCP 8 F11
Canford Heath BCP 8 E10
Canford Magna BCP 8 E9
Canhams Green Suffk 40 J7
Canisbay Highld 112 H2
Canklow Rothm 57 P8
Canley Covtry 36 K5
Cann Dorset 8 B4
Canna Highld 100 b9
Cann Common Dorset 8 B4
Cannich Highld 102 B9
Cannington Somset 16 J9
Canning Town Gt Lon 21 R6
Cannock Staffs 46 C11
Cannock Chase Staffs 46 C10
Cannock Wood Staffs 46 D11
Cannon Bridge Herefs 34 K12
Canonbie D & G 75 S10
Canon Frome Herefs 35 P12
Canon Pyon Herefs 35 L11
Canons Ashby Nhants 37 Q10
Canonstown Cnwll 2 E9
Canterbury Kent 13 M4
Canterbury Cathedral Kent 13 N4
Cantley Norfk 51 Q13
Cantlop Shrops 45 M12
Canton Cardif 27 M12
Cantraywood Highld 103 L6
Cantsfield Lancs 62 C5
Canvey Island Essex 22 J11
Canwick Lincs 58 G13
Canworthy Water Cnwll 4 G2
Caol Highld 94 G3
Caolas Scalpaigh W Isls 106 h9
Caoles Ag & B 92 D9
Caonich Highld 101 R13
Capel Kent 12 B7
Capel Surrey 10 K2
Capel Bangor Cerdgn 33 N4
Capel Betws Lleucu Cerdgn 33 M9
Capel Coch IoA 52 G6
Capel Curig Conwy 53 M11
Capel Cynon Cerdgn 32 G11
Capel Dewi Carmth 25 S6
Capel Dewi Cerdgn 32 J12
Capel-Dewi Cerdgn 33 M4
Capel Garmon Conwy 53 P11
Capel Green Suffk 41 Q11
Capel Gwyn Carmth 25 S6
Capel Gwyn IoA 52 D7
Capel Gwynfe Carmth 26 C3
Capel Hendre Carmth 25 U8
Capel Isaac Carmth 25 U5
Capel Iwan Carmth 25 N3
Capel-le-Ferne Kent 13 Q8
Capelles Guern 6 d2
Capel Llanilltern Cardif 26 K12
Capel Mawr IoA 52 F8
Capel Parc IoA 52 F5
Capel St Andrew Suffk 41 Q11
Capel St Mary Suffk 40 J13
Capel Seion Cerdgn 33 M5
Capel Trisant Cerdgn 33 P5
Capeluchaf Gwynd 42 H4
Capelulo Conwy 53 M7
Capel-y-ffin Powys 27 P1
Capel-y-graig Gwynd 52 H9
Capenhurst Ches W 54 J12
Capernwray Lancs 61 U5
Cape Wrath Highld 110 F1
Capheaton Nthumb 77 L9
Caplaw E Rens 88 K14
Capon's Green Suffk 41 N7
Cappercleuch Border 83 P14
Capstone Medway 12 E2
Capton Devon 5 U10
Capton Somset 16 E9
Caputh P & K 90 G3
Caradon Mining District Cnwll 4 H6
Caradon Town Cnwll 4 H6
Carbeth Stirlg 89 M10
Carbis Cnwll 3 Q5
Carbis Bay Cnwll 2 E9
Carbost Highld 100 c6
Carbost Highld 100 d5
Carbrook Sheff 57 N9
Carbrooke Norfk 50 F13
Carburton Notts 57 T12
Carclaze Cnwll 3 Q6
Car Colston Notts 47 T5
Carcroft Donc 57 R5
Cardenden Fife 90 K12
Cardeston Shrops 44 J11
Cardewlees Cumb 67 N2
Cardhu Moray 103 U7
Cardiff Cardif 27 M12
Cardiff Airport V Glam 16 E3
Cardiff Gate Services Cardif 27 N11
Cardiff West Services Cardif 26 K12
Cardigan Cerdgn 32 C11
Cardinal's Green Cambs 39 T11
Cardington Bed 38 G11
Cardington Shrops 35 M1
Cardinham Cnwll 4 E7
Cardrain D & G 72 E13
Cardrona Border 83 R11
Cardross Ag & B 88 H10
Cardryne D & G 72 E13
Cardurnock Cumb 75 N14
Careby Lincs 48 F10
Careston Angus 98 J11
Carew Pembks 24 H10
Carew Cheriton Pembks 24 H10
Carew Newton Pembks 24 H10
Carey Herefs 27 V1
Carfin N Lans 82 E7
Carfraemill Border 84 E8
Cargate Green Norfk 51 Q11
Cargenbridge D & G 74 J11
Cargill P & K 90 J4
Cargo Cumb 75 S14
Cargreen Cnwll 5 L8
Cargurrel Cnwll 3 M9
Carham Nthumb 84 K11
Carhampton Somset 16 D8
Carharrack Cnwll 2 J8
Carie P & K 95 S7
Carinish W Isls 106 d12
Carisbrooke IoW 9 P11
Cark Cumb 61 R4
Carkeel Cnwll 5 L8
Càrlabhagh W Isls 106 h4
Carland Cross Cnwll 3 M6
Carlbury Darltn 69 R9
Carlby Lincs 48 F11
Carlcroft Nthumb 76 G3
Carlecotes Barns 56 J6
Carleen Cnwll 2 G10
Carlesmoor N York 63 Q5
Carleton Cumb 66 F11
Carleton Cumb 67 P2
Carleton Cumb 67 R7
Carleton Lancs 61 Q12
Carleton Wakefd 57 Q2
Carleton Forehoe Norfk 50 J12
Carleton-in-Craven N York 62 K10
Carleton Rode Norfk 40 K2
Carleton St Peter Norfk 51 P13
Carlidnack Cnwll 2 K11
Carlincraig Abers 104 K7
Carlingcott BaNES 17 S5
Carlin How R & Cl 71 M9
Carlisle Cumb 67 P1
Carlisle Lake District Airport Cumb 75 U13
Carloggas Cnwll 3 M3
Carlops Border 83 N7
Carloway W Isls 106 h4
Carlton Barns 57 N4
Carlton Bed 38 E9
Carlton Cambs 39 T10
Carlton Leeds 57 M1
Carlton Leics 47 L13
Carlton N York 57 T2
Carlton N York 63 M3
Carlton N York 64 E2
Carlton Notts 47 R5
Carlton S on T 70 E8
Carlton Suffk 41 Q8
Carlton Colville Suffk 41 T3
Carlton Curlieu Leics 37 S1
Carlton Green Cambs 39 T10
Carlton Husthwaite N York 64 B4
Carlton-in-Cleveland N York 70 H12
Carlton in Lindrick Notts 57 S10
Carlton-le-Moorland Lincs 48 D2
Carlton Miniott N York 63 T3
Carlton-on-Trent Notts 58 C14
Carlton Scroop Lincs 48 D4
Carluke S Lans 82 F8
Carlyon Bay Cnwll 3 R6
Carmacoup S Lans 82 E13
Carmarthen Carmth 25 R6
Carmel Carmth 25 U7
Carmel Flints 54 E11
Carmel Gwynd 52 G12
Carmichael S Lans 82 H11
Carmunnock C Glas 89 N14
Carmyle C Glas 89 P13
Carmyllie Angus 91 R3
Carnaby E R Yk 65 Q6
Carnbee Fife 91 R10
Carnbo P & K 90 G11
Carn Brea Cnwll 2 H8
Carnbrogie Abers 105 P10
Carndu Highld 101 M6
Carnduff S Lans 81 T3
Carne Cnwll 2 K12
Carne Cnwll 3 N9
Carne Cnwll 3 P5
Carnell E Ayrs 81 P6
Carnewas Cnwll 3 M3
Carnforth Lancs 61 T5
Carn-gorm Highld 101 P7
Carnhedryn Pembks 24 D5
Carnhell Green Cnwll 2 G9
Carnie Abers 99 Q2
Carnkie Cnwll 2 H8
Carnkie Cnwll 2 J10
Carnkiet Cnwll 2 K6
Carno Powys 33 U1
Carnock Fife 90 F14
Carnon Downs Cnwll 2 K8
Carnousie Abers 104 K5
Carnoustie Angus 91 S5
Carnsmerry Cnwll 3 Q5
Carnwath S Lans 82 J9
Carnyorth Cnwll 2 B10
Carol Green Solhll 36 J5
Carpalla Cnwll 3 P6
Carperby N York 63 L2
Carr Rothm 57 R8
Carradale Ag & B 79 Q8
Carradale Village Ag & B 79 P8
Carrbridge Highld 103 P11
Carrbrook Tamesd 56 E6
Carrefour Jersey 7 c2
Carreglefn IoA 52 E5
Carr Gate Wakefd 57 M2
Carrhouse N Linc 58 C5
Carrick Ag & B 87 S8
Carrick Castle Ag & B 88 E7
Carriden Falk 82 K2
Carrington Lincs 49 M2
Carrington Mdloth 83 R6
Carrington Traffd 55 R8
Carrog Conwy 43 Q4
Carrog Denbgs 44 D5
Carron Falk 82 G2
Carron Moray 103 V7
Carronbridge D & G 74 G6
Carron Bridge Stirlg 89 R9
Carronshore Falk 82 G2
Carrow Hill Mons 27 S9
Carr Shield Nthumb 68 H3
Carrutherstown D & G 75 M11
Carruth House Inver 88 J12
Carr Vale Derbys 57 Q13
Carrville Dur 70 D4
Carsaig Ag & B 86 J1
Carseriggan D & G 72 J6
Carsethorn D & G 74 J14
Carshalton Gt Lon 21 N10
Carsington Derbys 46 J3
Carskey Ag & B 79 M14
Carsluith D & G 73 M9
Carsphairn D & G 81 R14
Carstairs S Lans 82 H9
Carstairs Junction S Lans 82 J9
Carswell Marsh Oxon 29 R8
Carter's Clay Hants 9 L4
Carters Green Essex 22 D5
Carterton Oxon 29 Q6
Carterway Heads Nthumb 69 M2
Carthew Cnwll 3 Q5
Carthorpe N York 63 S3
Cartington Nthumb 77 L5
Cartland S Lans 82 G9
Cartledge Derbys 57 M11
Cartmel Cumb 61 R4
Cartmel Fell Cumb 61 S2
Carway Carmth 25 S9
Carwinley Cumb 75 T11
Cashe's Green Gloucs 28 F6
Cashmoor Dorset 8 D6
Cassington Oxon 29 U5
Cassop Dur 70 D5
Castallack Cnwll 2 D11
Castel Guern 6 d3
Castell Conwy 53 N9
Castell-y-bwch Torfn 27 P9
Casterton Cumb 62 C4
Castle Cnwll 3 R5
Castle Acre Norfk 50 D10
Castle Ashby Nhants 38 C9
Castlebay W Isls 106 b19
Castle Bolton N York 63 L1
Castle Bromwich Solhll 36 F3
Castle Bytham Lincs 48 E10
Castlebythe Pembks 24 H5
Castle Caereinion Powys 44 E12
Castle Camps Cambs 39 T12
Castle Carrock Cumb 67 R1
Castlecary N Lans 89 S10
Castle Cary Somset 17 R10
Castle Combe Wilts 18 B5
Castlecraig Highld 109 Q11
Castle Donington Leics 47 M8
Castle Douglas D & G 74 E13
Castle Eaton Swindn 29 M8
Castle Eden Dur 70 F5
Castle End C Pete 48 H12
Castleford Wakefd 57 P1
Castle Frome Herefs 35 Q11
Castle Gate Cnwll 2 D10
Castle Green Cumb 61 U1
Castle Green Surrey 20 G10
Castle Gresley Derbys 46 J10
Castle Hedingham Essex 40 C13
Castlehill Border 83 P11
Castlehill Highld 112 E3
Castle Hill Kent 12 C7
Castle Hill Suffk 40 K11
Castlehill W Duns 88 J10
Castle Howard N York 64 G5
Castle Kennedy D & G 72 E8
Castle Lachlan Ag & B 87 U6
Castlemartin Pembks 24 F11
Castlemilk C Glas 89 N14
Castle Morris Pembks 24 F4
Castlemorton Worcs 35 S13
Castlemorton Common Worcs 35 S13
Castle O'er D & G 75 P7
Castle Rising Norfk 49 U9
Castleside Dur 69 N3
Castle Stuart Highld 102 K6
Castlethorpe M Keyn 30 H4
Castlethorpe N Linc 58 G5
Castleton Ag & B 87 R9
Castleton Border 75 V8
Castleton Derbys 56 J10
Castleton N York 71 L11
Castleton Newpt 27 P11
Castleton Rochdl 56 C4
Castletown Ches W 44 K3
Castletown Dorset 7 S10
Castletown Highld 112 E3
Castletown IoM 60 d9
Castletown Sundld 77 T14
Castley N York 63 R10
Caston Norfk 50 G14
Castor C Pete 48 H14
Caswell Bay Swans 25 U13
Catacol N Ayrs 79 S6
Cat and Fiddle Derbys 56 F12
Catbrain S Glos 28 A11
Catbrook Mons 27 U7
Catch Flints 54 F12
Catchall Cnwll 2 C11
Catchem's Corner Solhll 36 J5
Catchgate Dur 69 Q2
Catcliffe Rothm 57 P9
Catcomb Wilts 18 F5
Catcott Somset 17 L9
Caterham Surrey 21 P11
Catfield Norfk 51 Q9
Catfield Common Norfk 51 R9
Catford Gt Lon 21 Q8
Catforth Lancs 61 T12
Cathcart C Glas 89 N13
Cathedine Powys 27 L2
Catherine-de-Barnes Solhll 36 G4
Catherine Slack C Brad 63 M14
Catherington Hants 9 T6
Catherston Leweston Dorset 7 L6
Catherton Shrops 35 Q5
Catisfield Hants 9 R7
Catley Herefs 35 Q12
Catley Lane Head Rochdl 56 C3
Catlodge Highld 96 J5
Catlow Lancs 62 H12
Catlowdy Cumb 75 U10
Catmere End Essex 39 Q13
Catmore W Berk 19 Q4
Caton Devon 5 T6
Caton Lancs 61 U7
Caton Green Lancs 62 B6
Cator Court Devon 5 R5
Catrine E Ayrs 81 Q7
Cat's Ash Newpt 27 R9
Catsfield E Susx 12 D13
Catsfield Stream E Susx 12 D13
Catsgore Somset 17 P11
Catsham Somset 17 Q10
Catshill Worcs 36 C6
Catstree Shrops 35 R1
Cattadale Ag & B 79 M13
Cattal N York 63 U9
Cattawade Suffk 40 K14
Catterall Lancs 61 T11
Catteralslane Shrops 45 N5
Catterick N York 69 R13
Catterick Bridge N York 69 R13
Catterick Garrison N York 69 Q13
Catterlen Cumb 67 Q6
Catterline Abers 99 R8
Catterton N York 64 C10
Catteshall Surrey 10 F2
Catthorpe Leics 37 Q5
Cattishall Suffk 40 E7
Cattistock Dorset 7 Q5
Catton N York 63 T4
Catton Nthumb 76 G14
Catwick E R Yk 65 Q10
Catworth Cambs 38 G6
Caudle Green Gloucs 28 H5
Caulcott C Beds 31 M4
Caulcott Oxon 30 B8
Cauldcots Angus 91 U2
Cauldhame Stirlg 89 P7
Cauldmill Border 76 A2
Cauldon Staffs 46 E4
Cauldon Lowe Staffs 46 E4
Cauldwell Derbys 46 J10
Caulkerbush D & G 66 D1
Caulside D & G 75 T9
Caundle Marsh Dorset 7 S2
Caunsall Worcs 35 U4
Caunton Notts 47 T1
Causeway Hants 9 U4
Causeway End Cumb 61 T2
Causeway End D & G 73 L8
Causeway End Essex 22 G4
Causewayend S Lans 82 K11
Causewayhead Cumb 66 H2
Causewayhead Stirlg 89 T6
Causeyend Abers 105 Q12
Causey Park Nthumb 77 P7
Causey Park Bridge Nthumb 77 P7
Cavendish Suffk 40 D11
Cavenham Suffk 40 C6
Caversfield Oxon 30 C7
Caversham Readg 20 B8
Caverswall Staffs 46 C5
Caverton Mill Border 84 J13
Cavil E R Yk 64 H13
Cawdor Highld 103 M5
Cawkwell Lincs 59 N11
Cawood N York 64 D12
Cawsand Cnwll 5 L10
Cawston Norfk 50 K9
Cawston Warwks 37 N6
Cawthorn N York 64 H2
Cawthorne Barns 57 L5
Cawton N York 64 E4
Caxton Cambs 39 M9
Caxton End Cambs 39 M9
Caxton Gibbet Cambs 39 L8
Caynham Shrops 35 N6
Caythorpe Lincs 48 D4
Caythorpe Notts 47 S4
Cayton N York 65 P3
Ceannabeinne Highld 110 J3
Ceann a Bhaigh W Isls 106 c12
Ceannacroc Lodge Highld 101 U9
Cearsiadar W Isls 106 i7
Ceciliford Mons 27 U7
Cefn Newpt 27 P10
Cefn Berain Conwy 53 S9
Cefn-brîth Conwy 43 T3
Cefn-bryn-brain Carmth 26 C5
Cefn Byrle Powys 26 E5
Cefn Canel Powys 44 F7
Cefn Coch Powys 44 D8
Cefn-coed-y-cymmer Myr Td 26 J6
Cefn Cribwr Brdgnd 26 F11
Cefn Cross Brdgnd 26 F11
Cefn-ddwysarn Gwynd 43 U6
Cefn-Einion Shrops 34 G3
Cefneithin Carmth 25 U8
Cefngorwydd Powys 33 T11
Cefn-mawr Wrexhm 44 G5
Cefnpennar Rhondd 26 J7
Cefn-y-bedd Flints 44 H2
Cefn-y-pant Carmth 25 L5
Ceint IoA 52 G7
Cellan Cerdgn 33 M11
Cellardyke Fife 91 S11
Cellarhead Staffs 46 C4
Celleron Cumb 67 Q7
Celynen Caerph 27 N8
Cemaes IoA 52 E4
Cemmaes Powys 43 R12
Cemmaes Road Powys 43 R13
Cenarth Cerdgn 32 E12
Cerbyd Pembks 24 D5
Ceres Fife 91 P9
Cerne Abbas Dorset 7 S4
Cerney Wick Gloucs 29 L8
Cerrigceinwen IoA 52 F8
Cerrigydrudion Conwy 43 U4
Cess Norfk 51 R10
Ceunant Gwynd 52 H10
Chaceley Gloucs 28 G1
Chacewater Cnwll 2 K8
Chackmore Bucks 30 E5
Chacombe Nhants 37 N12
Chadbury Worcs 36 D11
Chadderton Oldham 56 D5
Chadderton Fold Oldham 56 D5
Chaddesden C Derb 47 L6
Chaddesley Corbett Worcs 35 U6
Chaddlehanger Devon 5 M5
Chaddleworth W Berk 19 P5
Chadlington Oxon 29 R3
Chadshunt Warwks 36 K10
Chadwell Leics 47 U9
Chadwell Shrops 45 S11
Chadwell End Bed 38 G7
Chadwell Heath Gt Lon 21 S5
Chadwell St Mary Thurr 22 F12
Chadwick Worcs 35 T7
Chadwick End Solhll 36 H6
Chadwick Green St Hel 55 M7
Chaffcombe Somset 7 L2
Chafford Hundred Thurr 22 F12
Chagford Devon 5 S3
Chailey E Susx 11 P7
Chainbridge Cambs 49 P13
Chainhurst Kent 12 D6
Chalbury Dorset 8 E7
Chalbury Common Dorset 8 E7
Chaldon Surrey 21 P11
Chaldon Herring Dorset 7 U8
Chale IoW 9 P13
Chale Green IoW 9 P13
Chalfont Common Bucks 20 H4
Chalfont St Giles Bucks 20 G4
Chalfont St Peter Bucks 20 H4
Chalford Gloucs 28 G7
Chalford Oxon 30 F12
Chalford Wilts 18 C10
Chalgrave C Beds 31 M7
Chalgrove Oxon 30 D13
Chalk Kent 22 G13
Chalk End Essex 22 F5
Chalkhouse Green Oxon 20 B7
Chalkway Somset 7 L3
Chalkwell Kent 12 G3
Challaborough Devon 5 R12
Challacombe Devon 15 Q4
Challoch D & G 72 K6
Challock Kent 12 K5
Chalmington Dorset 7 Q4
Chalton C Beds 31 M7
Chalton C Beds 38 H10
Chalton Hants 9 U5
Chalvey Slough 20 G7
Chalvington E Susx 11 S9
Chambers Green Kent 12 H7
Chandler's Cross Herts 20 J3
Chandlers Cross Worcs 35 S13
Chandler's Ford Hants 9 N5
Channel's End Bed 38 H9
Channel Tunnel Terminal Kent 13 N8
Chantry Somset 17 T7
Chantry Suffk 40 K12
Chapel Cumb 66 K6
Chapel Fife 91 L13
Chapel Allerton Leeds 63 S12
Chapel Allerton Somset 17 M6
Chapel Amble Cnwll 3 P1
Chapel Brampton Nhants 37 T7
Chapelbridge Cambs 39 L2
Chapel Chorlton Staffs 45 T6
Chapel Cross E Susx 11 U6
Chapel End Bed 38 H9
Chapel End C Beds 31 N4
Chapel End Cambs 38 H4
Chapel End Warwks 36 K2
Chapelend Way Essex 40 B13
Chapel-en-le-Frith Derbys 56 G10
Chapel Field Bury 55 S5
Chapelgate Lincs 49 P9
Chapel Green Warwks 36 J3
Chapel Green Warwks 37 N8
Chapel Haddlesey N York 57 S1
Chapelhall N Lans 82 E6
Chapel Hill Abers 105 T8
Chapel Hill Lincs 48 K3
Chapel Hill Mons 27 U8
Chapel Hill N York 63 S10
Chapelhope Border 75 P2
Chapelknowe D & G 75 R11
Chapel Lawn Shrops 34 H5
Chapel-le-Dale N York 62 E4
Chapel Leigh Somset 16 F11
Chapel Milton Derbys 56 G10
Chapel of Garioch Abers 105 L11
Chapel Rossan D & G 72 E11
Chapel Row E Susx 11 U8
Chapel Row Essex 22 J7
Chapel Row W Berk 19 S7
Chapels Cumb 61 N3
Chapel St Leonards Lincs 59 U12
Chapel Stile Cumb 67 M11
Chapelton Abers 99 R5
Chapelton Angus 91 T2
Chapelton Devon 15 N7
Chapelton S Lans 82 C9
Chapeltown Bl w D 55 R3
Chapel Town Cnwll 3 M5
Chapeltown Moray 104 A11
Chapeltown Sheff 57 N7
Chapmanslade Wilts 18 B11
Chapmans Well Devon 4 K2
Chapmore End Herts 31 T9
Chappel Essex 23 L2
Charaton Cnwll 4 J7
Chard Somset 6 K3
Chard Junction Somset 6 K4
Chardleigh Green Somset 6 K2
Chardstock Devon 6 K4
Charfield S Glos 28 D9
Chargrove Gloucs 28 H4
Charing Kent 12 J6
Charing Heath Kent 12 H6
Charing Hill Kent 12 J5
Charingworth Gloucs 36 G13
Charlbury Oxon 29 S4
Charlcombe BaNES 17 T3
Charlcutt Wilts 18 E5
Charlecote Warwks 36 J9
Charlemont Sandw 36 D2
Charles Devon 15 Q6
Charleshill Surrey 10 D2
Charleston Angus 91 N2
Charlestown C Aber 99 S3
Charlestown C Brad 63 P12
Charlestown Calder 56 E1
Charlestown Cnwll 3 Q6
Charlestown Cnwll 3 Q6
Charlestown Derbys 56 F8
Charlestown Dorset 7 S9
Charlestown Fife 83 L2
Charlestown Highld 102 H6
Charlestown Highld 107 P10
Charlestown Salfd 55 T6
Charlestown of Aberlour Moray 104 B7
Charles Tye Suffk 40 H10
Charlesworth Derbys 56 F8
Charlinch Somset 16 H9
Charlottetown Fife 91 L9
Charlton Gt Lon 21 R7
Charlton Hants 19 N11
Charlton Herts 31 Q7
Charlton Nhants 30 B5
Charlton Nthumb 76 G9
Charlton Oxon 29 T10
Charlton Somset 16 J11
Charlton Somset 17 R8
Charlton Somset 17 S6
Charlton Surrey 20 J9
Charlton W Susx 10 D8
Charlton Wilts 8 C4
Charlton Wilts 28 J10
Charlton Worcs 35 T6
Charlton Worcs 36 D11
Charlton Wrekin 45 N11
Charlton Abbots Gloucs 28 K3
Charlton Adam Somset 17 P11
Charlton All Saints Wilts 8 H4
Charlton Down Dorset 7 S5
Charlton Hill Shrops 45 N12
Charlton Horethorne Somset 17 S12
Charlton Kings Gloucs 28 J3
Charlton Mackrell Somset 17 P11
Charlton Marshall Dorset 8 C8
Charlton Musgrove Somset 17 T11
Charlton-on-Otmoor Oxon 30 C9
Charlton on the Hill Dorset 8 B8
Charlton St Peter Wilts 18 H9
Charlwood Hants 9 T2
Charlwood Surrey 11 L2
Charminster Dorset 7 S6
Charmouth Dorset 7 L6
Charndon Bucks 30 E8
Charney Bassett Oxon 29 S9
Charnock Green Lancs 55 N3
Charnock Richard Lancs 55 N3
Charnock Richard Services Lancs 55 M3
Charsfield Suffk 41 N9
Chart Corner Kent 12 E5
Charter Alley Hants 19 S9
Charterhall Border 84 K9
Charterhouse Somset 17 N5
Chartershall Stirlg 89 S7
Charterville Allotments Oxon 29 R5
Chartham Kent 13 M5
Chartham Hatch Kent 13 M4
Chart Hill Kent 12 E6
Chartridge Bucks 30 K12
Chart Sutton Kent 12 F6
Chartway Street Kent 12 F5
Charvil Wokham 20 C7
Charwelton Nhants 37 P9
Chase Terrace Staffs 46 D12
Chasetown Staffs 46 D12
Chastleton Oxon 29 P2
Chasty Devon 14 H12
Chatburn Lancs 62 F11
Chatcull Staffs 45 S7
Chatham Caerph 27 N10
Chatham Medway 12 E2
Chatham Green Essex 22 H4
Chathill Nthumb 85 T13
Chatley Worcs 35 U8
Chatsworth House Derbys 57 L12
Chattenden Medway 22 J13
Chatter End Essex 22 C2
Chatteris Cambs 39 N3
Chatterton Lancs 55 S3
Chattisham Suffk 40 J12
Chatto Border 76 F2
Chatton Nthumb 85 R13
Chaul End C Beds 31 N8
Chawleigh Devon 15 R10
Chawley Oxon 29 U7
Chawston Bed 38 J9
Chawton Hants 19 V13
Chaxhill Gloucs 28 D5
Chazey Heath Oxon 19 U5
Cheadle Staffs 46 D5
Cheadle Stockp 56 C9
Cheadle Heath Stockp 56 C9
Cheadle Hulme Stockp 56 C9
Cheam Gt Lon 21 M10
Cheapside W & M 20 F9
Chearsley Bucks 30 F10
Chebsey Staffs 45 U8
Checkendon Oxon 19 U4
Checkley Ches E 45 R4
Checkley Herefs 35 N13
Checkley Staffs 46 D6
Checkley Green Ches E 45 R4
Chedburgh Suffk 40 C9
Cheddar Somset 17 N6
Cheddington Bucks 30 K9
Cheddleton Staffs 46 C3
Cheddleton Heath Staffs 46 C3
Cheddon Fitzpaine Somset 16 H11
Chedglow Wilts 28 H9
Chedgrave Norfk 51 Q14
Chedington Dorset 7 N3
Chediston Suffk 41 Q5
Chediston Green Suffk 41 Q5
Chedworth Gloucs 29 L5
Chedzoy Somset 16 K9
Cheeseman's Green Kent 12 K8
Cheetham Hill Manch 55 T6
Cheldon Devon 15 R10
Chelford Ches E 55 T12
Chellaston C Derb 47 L7
Chellington Bed 38 E9
Chelmarsh Shrops 35 R3
Chelmer Village Essex 22 H6
Chelmick Shrops 35 L2
Chelmondiston Suffk 41 M13
Chelmorton Derbys 56 H13
Chelmsford Essex 22 H6
Chelmsley Wood Solhll 36 G3
Chelsea Gt Lon 21 N7
Chelsfield Gt Lon 21 S10
Chelsham Surrey 21 Q11
Chelston Somset 16 G12
Chelsworth Suffk 40 G11
Cheltenham Gloucs 28 H3
Chelveston Nhants 38 E7
Chelvey N Som 17 N3
Chelwood BaNES 17 R4
Chelwood Common E Susx 11 Q5
Chelwood Gate E Susx 11 Q4
Chelworth Wilts 28 J9
Chelworth Lower Green Wilts 29 L9
Chelworth Upper Green Wilts 29 L9
Cheney Longville Shrops 34 K4
Chenies Bucks 20 H3
Chepstow Mons 27 U9
Chequerbent Bolton 55 Q5
Chequers Corner Norfk 49 Q12
Cherhill Wilts 18 F6
Cherington Gloucs 28 H8
Cherington Warwks 36 J13
Cheriton Devon 15 R3
Cheriton Hants 9 R3
Cheriton Kent 13 P8
Cheriton Pembks 24 G11
Cheriton Swans 25 S12
Cheriton Bishop Devon 5 T2
Cheriton Fitzpaine Devon 15 U11
Cherrington Wrekin 45 Q10
Cherry Burton E R Yk 65 M11
Cherry Hinton Cambs 39 Q9
Cherry Orchard Worcs 35 U10
Cherry Willingham Lincs 58 H12
Chertsey Surrey 20 H9
Cherwell Valley Services Oxon 30 B7
Cheselbourne Dorset 7 U5
Chesham Bucks 31 L12
Chesham Bury 55 T4
Chesham Bois Bucks 20 G3
Cheshunt Herts 31 U12
Chesil Beach Dorset 7 R9
Chesley Kent 12 G3
Cheslyn Hay Staffs 46 C12
Chessetts Wood Warwks 36 G6
Chessington Gt Lon 21 L10
Chessington World of Adventures Gt Lon 21 L10
Chester Ches W 54 K13
Chesterblade Somset 17 S8
Chesterfield Derbys 57 N12
Chesterfield Staffs 46 E12
Chesterhill Mdloth 83 S6
Chester-le-Street Dur 69 S2
Chester Moor Dur 69 S3
Chesters Border 76 C3
Chesters Border 84 G14
Chester Services Ches W 55 L12
Chesterton Cambs 38 H1
Chesterton Cambs 39 Q8
Chesterton Gloucs 28 K7
Chesterton Oxon 30 C8
Chesterton Shrops 35 S1
Chesterton Staffs 45 T4
Chesterton Green Warwks 37 L9
Chesterwood Nthumb 76 G12
Chester Zoo Ches W 54 K12
Chestfield Kent 13 M2
Chestnut Street Kent 12 G3
Cheston Devon 5 R9
Cheswardine Shrops 45 R7
Cheswick Nthumb 85 Q9
Cheswick Green Solhll 36 F5
Chetnole Dorset 7 R3
Chettiscombe Devon 6 C2
Chettisham Cambs 39 R4
Chettle Dorset 8 D6
Chetton Shrops 35 Q2
Chetwode Bucks 30 D7
Chetwynd Wrekin 45 R9
Chetwynd Aston Wrekin 45 S10
Cheveley Cambs 39 U8
Chevening Kent 21 S11
Cheverton IoW 9 P12
Chevington Suffk 40 C9
Cheviot Hills 76 F4
Chevithorne Devon 16 C13
Chew Magna BaNES 17 Q4
Chew Moor Bolton 55 Q5
Chew Stoke BaNES 17 Q4
Chewton Keynsham BaNES 17 S3
Chewton Mendip Somset 17 Q6
Chichacott Devon 15 P13
Chicheley M Keyn 38 D11
Chichester W Susx 10 D10
Chickerell Dorset 7 R8
Chickering Suffk 41 M5
Chicklade Wilts 8 C2
Chicksands C Beds 31 P5
Chickward Herefs 34 G10
Chidden Hants 9 T5
Chiddingfold Surrey 10 F3
Chiddingly E Susx 11 S8
Chiddingstone Kent 11 S2
Chiddingstone Causeway Kent 21 T13
Chiddingstone Hoath Kent 11 R2
Chideock Dorset 7 M6
Chidham W Susx 10 B10
Chidswell Kirk 57 L2
Chieveley W Berk 19 Q6
Chieveley Services W Berk 19 Q6
Chignall St James Essex 22 G5
Chignall Smealy Essex 22 G5
Chigwell Essex 21 R4
Chigwell Row Essex 21 S4
Chilbolton Hants 19 N12
Chilcomb Hants 9 Q3
Chilcombe Dorset 7 P6
Chilcompton Somset 17 R6
Chilcote Leics 46 J11
Childer Thornton Ches W 54 J11
Child Okeford Dorset 8 A6
Childrey Oxon 29 S10
Child's Ercall Shrops 45 Q8
Childswickham Worcs 36 E13
Childwall Lpool 54 K9
Childwick Bury Herts 31 P10
Childwick Green Herts 31 P10
Chilfrome Dorset 7 Q5
Chilgrove W Susx 10 C8
Chilham Kent 13 L5
Chilla Devon 14 K12
Chillaton Devon 5 L4
Chillenden Kent 13 Q5
Chillerton IoW 9 P12
Chillesford Suffk 41 Q10
Chillingham Nthumb 85 R13
Chillington Devon 5 T12
Chillington Somset 7 L2
Chilmark Wilts 8 D2
Chilmington Green Kent 12 J7
Chilson Oxon 29 R4
Chilsworthy Cnwll 5 L6
Chilsworthy Devon 14 H11
Chiltern Green C Beds 31 P9
Chiltern Hills 20 C3
Chilthorne Domer Somset 17 P13
Chilton Bucks 30 E10
Chilton Devon 15 U12
Chilton Dur 69 S7
Chilton Kent 13 Q7
Chilton Oxon 29 U10
Chilton Suffk 40 E12
Chilton Candover Hants 19 S12
Chilton Cantelo Somset 17 Q12
Chilton Foliat Wilts 19 M6
Chilton Polden Somset 17 L8
Chilton Street Suffk 40 C11
Chilton Trinity Somset 16 J9
Chilwell Notts 47 P6
Chilworth Hants 9 N5
Chilworth Surrey 20 H13
Chimney Oxon 29 S7
Chineham Hants 19 U9
Chingford Gt Lon 21 Q4
Chinley Derbys 56 F10
Chinnor Oxon 30 G12
Chipchase Castle Nthumb 76 H10
Chipnall Shrops 45 R7
Chippenham Cambs 39 U7
Chippenham Wilts 18 D6
Chipperfield Herts 31 M12
Chipping Herts 31 U6
Chipping Lancs 62 C11
Chipping Campden Gloucs 36 G13
Chipping Hill Essex 22 K4
Chipping Norton Oxon 29 R2
Chipping Ongar Essex 22 E7
Chipping Sodbury S Glos 28 D11
Chipping Warden Nhants 37 N11
Chipshop Devon 5 L5
Chipstable Somset 16 D11
Chipstead Kent 21 T11
Chipstead Surrey 21 N11
Chirbury Shrops 44 G14
Chirk Wrexhm 44 G6
Chirnside Border 85 M7
Chirnsidebridge Border 85 M7
Chirton Wilts 18 G9
Chisbury Wilts 19 L7
Chiselborough Somset 7 N2
Chiseldon Swindn 18 J4
Chiselhampton Oxon 30 C13
Chiserley Calder 63 L14
Chisholme Border 75 T3
Chislehurst Gt Lon 21 R8
Chislet Kent 13 P3
Chiswell Green Herts 31 P12
Chiswick Gt Lon 21 M7
Chiswick End Cambs 39 N11
Chisworth Derbys 56 E8
Chitcombe E Susx 12 F11
Chithurst W Susx 10 C6
Chittering Cambs 39 Q7
Chitterne Wilts 18 E12
Chittlehamholt Devon 15 Q8
Chittlehampton Devon 15 P7
Chittoe Wilts 18 E7
Chivelstone Devon 5 T13
Chivenor Devon 15 M6
Chiverton Cross Cnwll 2 J7
Chlenry D & G 72 E7
Chobham Surrey 20 G10
Cholderton Wilts 18 K12
Cholesbury Bucks 30 K11
Chollerford Nthumb 76 J11
Chollerton Nthumb 76 J11
Cholmondeston Ches E 45 P2
Cholsey Oxon 19 S3
Cholstrey Herefs 35 L9
Chop Gate N York 70 J13
Choppington Nthumb 77 R9
Chopwell Gatesd 77 N14
Chorley Ches E 45 N3
Chorley Lancs 55 N3
Chorley Shrops 35 Q4
Chorley Staffs 46 E11
Chorleywood Herts 20 H3
Chorleywood West Herts 20 H3
Chorlton Ches E 45 R3
Chorlton-cum-Hardy Manch 55 T8
Chorlton Lane Ches W 45 L4
Choulton Shrops 34 J3
Chowley Ches W 45 L2
Chrishall Essex 39 P13
Chrisswell Inver 88 F11
Christchurch BCP 8 H10
Christchurch Cambs 39 Q1
Christchurch Gloucs 27 V5
Christchurch Newpt 27 Q10
Christian Malford Wilts 18 E5
Christleton Ches W 54 K13
Christmas Common Oxon 20 B4
Christmas Pie Surrey 20 F13
Christon N Som 17 L5
Christon Bank Nthumb 85 U14
Christow Devon 5 U3
Christ's Hospital W Susx 10 J5
Chuck Hatch E Susx 11 R4
Chudleigh Devon 5 V5
Chudleigh Knighton Devon 5 U5
Chulmleigh Devon 15 Q10
Chunal Derbys 56 F8
Church Lancs 62 E14
Churcham Gloucs 28 E4
Church Aston Wrekin 45 R10
Church Brampton Nhants 37 T7
Church Brough Cumb 68 G10
Church Broughton Derbys 46 H7
Church Cove Cnwll 2 J14
Church Crookham Hants 20 D12
Churchdown Gloucs 28 G4
Church Eaton Staffs 45 T10
Church End Bed 38 G9
Church End Bed 38 H9
Church End Bucks 30 F11
Church End C Beds 31 L6
Church End C Beds 31 L8
Church End C Beds 31 M6
Church End C Beds 31 M9
Church End C Beds 31 Q5
Church End C Beds 38 J10
Church End Cambs 38 G6
Church End Cambs 38 K4
Church End Cambs 39 M5
Church End Essex 22 F3
Church End Essex 22 H2
Church End Essex 22 H4
Churchend Essex 23 P9
Church End Gloucs 35 U13
Church End Gt Lon 21 M4
Church End Herts 22 B3
Church End Herts 31 P10
Church End Herts 31 S6
Church End Lincs 48 K7
Church End Lincs 59 R7
Church End Suffk 41 M13
Church End Warwks 36 H2
Church End Warwks 36 J2
Church Enstone Oxon 29 S2
Church Fenton N York 64 C12
Churchfield Sandw 36 D2
Churchgate Herts 31 T12
Churchgate Street Essex 22 C5
Church Green Devon 6 G5
Church Gresley Derbys 46 J10
Church Hanborough Oxon 29 T5
Church Hill Staffs 46 D11
Church Houses N York 71 L13
Churchill Devon 6 J4
Churchill Devon 15 N4
Churchill N Som 17 M5
Churchill Oxon 29 Q3
Churchill Worcs 35 U5
Churchill Worcs 36 B10
Churchinford Somset 6 H2
Church Knowle Dorset 8 C12
Church Laneham Notts 58 D11
Church Langton Leics 37 T2
Church Lawford Warwks 37 N5
Church Lawton Ches E 45 T2
Church Leigh Staffs 46 D6
Church Lench Worcs 36 D10
Church Mayfield Staffs 46 G5
Church Minshull Ches E 45 Q1
Church Norton W Susx 10 D11
Churchover Warwks 37 P4
Church Preen Shrops 45 M14
Church Pulverbatch Shrops 44 K13
Churchstanton Somset 6 G2
Churchstoke Powys 34 G2
Churchstow Devon 5 S11
Church Stowe Nhants 37 R9
Church Street Essex 40 C12
Church Street Kent 22 H13
Church Street Suffk 41 S4
Church Stretton Shrops 35 L2
Churchthorpe Lincs 59 P7
Churchtown Bpool 61 Q11
Churchtown Cnwll 4 D5
Churchtown Derbys 57 L14
Churchtown Devon 15 Q4
Churchtown IoM 60 g4
Churchtown Lancs 61 T11
Church Town N Linc 58 C5
Churchtown Sefton 54 J3
Church Village Rhondd 26 K10
Church Warsop Notts 57 S13
Church Wilne Derbys 47 M7
Churnsike Lodge Nthumb 76 D10
Churston Ferrers Torbay 6 B13
Churt Surrey 10 D3
Churton Ches W 44 K2
Churwell Leeds 63 R14
Chwilog Gwynd 42 H6
Chyandour Cnwll 2 D10
Chyanvounder Cnwll 2 H12
Chyeowling Cnwll 2 K8
Chyvarloe Cnwll 2 H12
Cîl Powys 44 E13
Cilcain Flints 54 E13
Cilcennin Cerdgn 32 K8
Cilcewydd Powys 44 F13
Cilfrew Neath 26 D7
Cilfynydd Rhondd 26 K9
Cilgerran Pembks 32 C12
Cilgwyn Carmth 26 C2
Cilgwyn Gwynd 52 G12
Ciliau-Aeron Cerdgn 32 K9
Cilmaengwyn Neath 26 C6
Cilmery Powys 34 B10
Cilrhedyn Pembks 25 N4
Cilsan Carmth 25 U6
Ciltalgarth Gwynd 43 S5
Cilycwm Carmth 33 Q13
Cimla Neath 26 D8
Cinderford Gloucs 28 C5
Cinder Hill Wolves 36 B2
Cippenham Slough 20 G6
Cirencester Gloucs 28 K7
Citadilla N York 69 R13
City Gt Lon 21 P6
City V Glam 26 H12
City Airport Gt Lon 21 R6
City Dulas IoA 52 G5

Clabhach Ag & B 92 F7
Clachaig Ag & B 88 D9
Clachaig Inn Highld 94 G7
Clachan Ag & B 79 H4
Clachan Ag & B 88 C5
Clachan Ag & B 94 B10
Clachan Highld 100 e6
Clachan-a-Luib W Isls 106 d12
Clachan Mor Ag & B 92 H9
Clachan na Luib W Isls 106 d12
Clachan of Campsie E Duns 89 P10
Clachan-Seil Ag & B 87 P2
Clachnaharry Highld 102 H6
Clachtoll Highld 110 A11
Clacket Lane Services Surrey 21 R12
Clackmannan Clacks 90 D13
Clackmannanshire Bridge Fife 90 D14
Clackmarras Moray 104 A4
Clacton-on-Sea Essex 23 J4
Cladich Ag & B 88 C1
Cladswell Worcs 36 E9
Claggan Highld 93 S9
Claigan Highld 100 A4
Clandown BaNES 17 S5
Clanfield Hants 9 S7
Clanfield Oxon 29 Q7
Cannaborough Devon 15 J10
Clanville Hants 19 M11
Clanville Somset 17 N5
Claonaig Ag & B 79 R4
Clapgate Dorset 8 E8
Clapgate Herts 22 B3
Clapham Bed 38 F10
Clapham Devon 6 A7
Clapham Gt Lon 21 M7
Clapham N York 62 E6
Clapham W Susx 10 H9
Clapham Green Bed 38 F10
Clap Hill Kent 13 L8
Clappersgate Cumb 67 N12
Clapton Somset 7 M3
Clapton Somset 17 R6
Clapton-in-Gordano N Som 27 T13
Clapton-on-the-Hill Gloucs 29 N5
Clapworthy Devon 15 Q8
Clarach Cerdgn 33 M4
Claravale Gatesd 77 N13
Clarbeston Pembks 24 J6
Clarbeston Road Pembks 24 J6
Clarborough Notts 58 B10
Clare Suffk 40 C11
Clarebrand D & G 74 E12
Clarencefield D & G 75 L12
Clarewood Nthumb 76 K11
Clarilaw Border 76 A2
Clark's Green Surrey 10 K2
Clarkston E Rens 89 N13
Clashmore Highld 109 N7
Clashmore Highld 110 A10
Clashnessie Highld 110 A10
Clashnoir Moray 104 A11
Clathy P & K 90 F7
Clatt Abers 104 H10
Clatter Powys 33 J3
Clatterford End Essex 22 F5
Clatworthy Somset 16 E10
Claughton Lancs 61 U11
Claughton Lancs 62 B6
Claughton Wirral 54 H9
Claverdon Warwks 36 H8
Claverham N Som 17 N3
Clavering Essex 22 C1
Claverley Shrops 35 S2
Claverton BaNES 17 U4
Claverton Down BaNES 17 U4
Clawdd-coch V Glam 26 K12
Clawdd-newydd Denbgs 44 C3
Clawthorpe Cumb 61 U4
Clawton Devon 14 J13
Claxby Lincs 58 K8
Claxby Lincs 59 S12
Claxton N York 64 G8
Claxton Norfk 51 P13
Claybrooke Magna Leics 37 N4
Clay Common Suffk 41 S4
Clay Coton Nhants 37 Q5
Clay Cross Derbys 57 N14
Claydon Oxon 37 N11
Claydon Suffk 40 K10
Clay End Herts 31 S8
Claygate D & G 75 S10
Claygate Kent 12 D7
Claygate Surrey 21 L10
Claygate Cross Kent 12 B4
Clayhall Gt Lon 21 R5
Clayhanger Devon 16 D12
Clayhanger Wsall 46 D13
Clayhidon Devon 16 G13
Clayhill E Susx 12 F11
Clayhill Hants 9 L7
Clayhithe Cambs 39 R8
Clayock Highld 112 E5
Claypit Hill Cambs 39 N10
Claypits Gloucs 28 E6
Claypole Lincs 48 B4
Claythorpe Lincs 59 R11
Clayton C Brad 63 N13
Clayton Donc 57 R5
Clayton S Yorks 57 Q5
Clayton W Susx 11 M8
Clayton Green Lancs 55 N2
Clayton-le-Moors Lancs 62 T13
Clayton-le-Woods Lancs 55 N2
Clayton West Kirk 57 L4
Clayworth Notts 58 B9
Cleadale Highld 100 d13
Cleadon S Tyne 77 T13
Cleadon Park S Tyne 77 T13
Clearbrook Devon 5 N7
Clearwell Gloucs 27 V7
Cleasby N York 69 S10
Cleat Ork 106 t21
Cleatlam Dur 69 P9
Cleator Cumb 66 F10
Cleator Moor Cumb 66 F10
Cleckheaton Kirk 56 J1
Cleedownton Shrops 35 N4
Cleehill Shrops 35 N5
Cleekhimin N Lans 82 E7
Clee St Margaret Shrops 35 N4
Cleestanton Shrops 35 N5
Cleethorpes NE Lin 59 P5
Cleeton St Mary Shrops 35 P5
Cleeve N Som 17 N3
Cleeve Oxon 19 U4
Cleeve Hill Gloucs 28 J2
Cleeve Prior Worcs 36 E11
Cleghornie E Loth 84 F2
Clehonger Herefs 35 L13
Cleish P & K 90 G12
Cleland N Lans 82 E7
Clement's End C Beds 31 M10
Clement Street Kent 22 D13
Clench Common Wilts 18 J7
Clenchwarton Norfk 49 S9
Clenerty Abers 105 M4
Clent Worcs 36 B5
Cleobury Mortimer Shrops 35 Q5
Cleobury North Shrops 35 P3
Cleongart Ag & B 79 M9
Clephanton Highld 103 N5
Clerkhill D & G 75 Q6
Cleuch-head D & G 74 G5
Clevancy Wilts 18 G5
Clevedon N Som 27 T2
Cleveley Oxon 29 T3
Cleveleys Lancs 61 Q11
Cleverton Wilts 28 H10
Clewer Somset 17 M6
Clewer next the Sea Norfk 50 H5
Cliburn Cumb 68 D8
Cliddesden Hants 19 T11
Cliff Warwks 36 J1
Cliffe Lancs 62 E13
Cliffe Medway 22 H12
Cliffe N York 64 E1
Cliffe N York 69 R9
Cliff End E Susx 12 G13
Cliffe Woods Medway 22 H13
Clifford Herefs 34 F11
Clifford Leeds 63 U11
Clifford Chambers Warwks 36 G10
Clifford's Mesne Gloucs 28 D3
Cliffsend Kent 13 R2
Clifton Bristl 27 V13
Clifton C Beds 31 Q5
Clifton C York 64 D9
Clifton Calder 56 H2
Clifton Cumb 67 Q7
Clifton Derbys 46 G4
Clifton Donc 57 R7
Clifton Lancs 61 T13
Clifton N York 63 P11
Clifton Nthumb 77 Q9
Clifton Oxon 37 M13
Clifton Salfd 55 S6
Clifton Worcs 35 T11
Clifton Campville Staffs 46 J11
Clifton Hampden Oxon 30 B13
Clifton Reynes M Keyn 38 D10
Clifton upon Dunsmore Warwks 37 P5
Clifton upon Teme Worcs 35 R8
Cliftonville Kent 13 S1
Climping W Susx 10 F10
Climpy S Lans 82 H7
Clink Somset 17 U7
Clint N York 63 R8
Clinterty C Aber 105 N13
Clint Green Norfk 50 H11
Clintmains Border 84 G12
Clipiau Gwynd 43 R11
Clippesby Norfk 51 R11
Clipsham Rutlnd 48 E10
Clipston Nhants 37 T4
Clipston Notts 47 R7
Clipstone C Beds 30 K7
Clipstone Notts 57 S14
Clitheroe Lancs 62 E11
Clive Shrops 45 M9
Cliveden Bucks 20 F5
Clixby Lincs 58 K5
Cloatley Wilts 28 J9
Clocaenog Denbgs 44 C3
Clochan Moray 104 E3
Clock Face St Hel 55 M8
Cloddiau Powys 44 F12
Clodock Herefs 27 Q2
Clola Abers 105 S7
Clophill C Beds 31 N5
Clopton Nhants 38 G4
Clopton Suffk 41 M10
Clopton Corner Suffk 41 M10
Clopton Green Suffk 40 C10
Clopton Green Suffk 40 G9
Clos du Valle Guern 6 e1
Closeburn D & G 74 G7
Closeburnmill D & G 74 G7
Closeclark IoM 60 d7
Closworth Somset 7 Q2
Clothall Herts 31 S6
Clotton Ches W 55 M14
Cloudesley Bush Warwks 37 N3
Clough Oldham 56 D5
Clough Foot Calder 56 E1
Clough Head Calder 56 G3
Cloughton N York 71 T14
Cloughton Newlands N York 71 T13
Clousta Shet 106 t8
Clova Angus 98 E9
Clovelly Devon 14 H8
Cloverhords Border 84 D11
Clovulin Highld 94 E6
Clow Bridge Lancs 62 G14
Clowne Derbys 57 Q11
Clows Top Worcs 35 R6
Cloy Wrexhm 44 H5
Cluanie Inn Highld 101 R9
Cluanie Lodge Highld 101 R9
Clubworthy Cnwll 4 H2
Clugston D & G 72 K8
Clun Shrops 34 H4
Clunas Highld 103 N6
Clunbury Shrops 34 J4
Clunderwen Carmth 24 K7
Clune Highld 103 L10
Clunes Highld 101 S12
Clungunford Shrops 34 J5
Clunie P & K 90 H3
Clunton Shrops 34 H4
Clutton BaNES 17 R5
Clutton Ches W 45 L2
Clutton Hill BaNES 17 R5
Clwt Conwy 53 S10
Clwt-y-bont Gwynd 52 J10
Clydach Mons 27 N5
Clydach Swans 26 B7
Clydach Vale Rhondd 26 H9
Clydebank W Duns 89 L11
Clydey Pembks 25 M3
Clyffe Pypard Wilts 18 G5
Clynder Ag & B 88 F9
Clyne Neath 26 E7
Clynnog Fawr Gwynd 42 H4
Clyro Powys 34 F11
Clyst Honiton Devon 6 C6
Clyst Hydon Devon 6 D4
Clyst St George Devon 6 C7
Clyst St Lawrence Devon 6 D4
Clyst St Mary Devon 6 C6
Cnoc W Isls 106 j5
Cnwch Coch Cerdgn 33 N6
Coad's Green Cnwll 4 H5
Coal Aston Derbys 57 N11
Coalbrookvale Blae G 27 N6
Coalburn S Lans 82 G11
Coalburns Gatesd 77 N13
Coaley Gloucs 28 E7
Coalhill Essex 22 J8
Coalmoor Wrekin 45 Q12
Coalpit Heath S Glos 28 C11
Coal Pool Wsall 46 D14
Coalport Wrekin 45 Q12
Coalsnaughton Clacks 90 D12
Coal Street Suffk 41 M6
Coaltown of Balgonie Fife 91 L12
Coaltown of Wemyss Fife 91 M12
Coalville Leics 47 M11
Coanwood Nthumb 76 D14
Coat Somset 17 M12
Coatbridge N Lans 82 D5
Coatdyke N Lans 82 D5
Coate Swindn 29 M11
Coate Wilts 18 F8
Coates Cambs 49 M14
Coates Gloucs 28 J7
Coates Lincs 58 E10
Coates Notts 58 D10
Coates W Susx 10 F7
Coatham R & Cl 70 J7
Coatham Mundeville Darltn 69 S8
Cobbaton Devon 15 P7
Coberley Gloucs 28 J4
Cobhall Common Herefs 35 L13
Cobham Kent 12 C2
Cobham Surrey 20 K10
Cobham Services Surrey 20 K11
Coblers Green Essex 22 G4
Cobley Dorset 8 F5
Cobnash Herefs 35 L8
Cobo Guern 6 d2
Cobridge C Stke 45 U4
Coburby Abers 105 Q3
Cock Alley Derbys 57 P12
Cockayne N York 70 K13
Cockayne Hatley C Beds 39 L11
Cock Bank Wrexhm 44 H4
Cock Bevington Warwks 36 E10
Cock Bridge Abers 98 D2
Cockburnspath Border 84 K4
Cock Clarks Essex 22 K7
Cock & End Suffk 40 B10
Cockenzie and Port Seton E Loth 83 T3
Cocker Bar Lancs 55 L1
Cocker Brook Lancs 62 D13
Cockerham Lancs 61 S9
Cockermouth Cumb 66 H6
Cockernhoe Herts 31 P8
Cockersdale Leeds 63 Q13
Cockett Swans 26 A9
Cockfield Dur 69 P8
Cockfield Suffk 40 E10
Cockfosters Gt Lon 21 N3
Cocking W Susx 10 D7
Cocking Causeway W Susx 10 D7
Cockington Torbay 6 A12
Cocklake Somset 17 M7
Cockle Beck Cumb 66 K12
Cockley Cley Norfk 50 B12
Cock Marling E Susx 12 G12
Cockpole Green Wokham 20 C6
Cocks Cnwll 2 K6
Cockshutford Shrops 35 N3
Cockshutt Shrops 45 L8
Cockthorpe Norfk 50 F5
Cockwells Cnwll 2 E10
Cockwood Devon 6 C8
Cockyard Derbys 56 F11
Cockyard Herefs 34 K14
Coddenham Suffk 40 K10
Coddington Ches W 45 L2
Coddington Herefs 35 R12
Coddington Notts 48 B2
Codford St Mary Wilts 18 E13
Codford St Peter Wilts 18 E13
Codicote Herts 31 R9
Codmore Hill W Susx 10 H6
Codnor Derbys 47 M4
Codrington S Glos 28 D12
Codsall Staffs 45 U13
Codsall Wood Staffs 45 T13
Coed Darcy Neath 26 C8
Coedely Rhondd 26 J11
Coed Hirwaun Neath 26 E11
Coedkernew Newpt 27 P11
Coed Morgan Mons 27 R5
Coedpoeth Wrexhm 44 G3
Coed Talon Flints 44 G2
Coedway Powys 44 H11
Coed-y-Bryn Cerdgn 32 G11
Coed-y-caerau Newpt 27 R9
Coed-y-Cwm Rhondd 26 K9
Coed-y-paen Mons 27 Q8
Coed-yr-ynys Powys 27 M2
Coed Ystumgwern Gwynd 43 L9
Coelbren Powys 26 F5
Coffinswell Devon 6 A12
Coffle End Bed 38 F9
Cofton Devon 6 C8
Cofton Hackett Worcs 36 D5
Cogan V Glam 27 M13
Cogenhoe Nhants 38 B8
Cogges Oxon 29 S6
Coggeshall Essex 23 L3
Coggin's Mill E Susx 11 T5
Coignafearn Highld 102 K12
Coilacriech Abers 98 E4
Coilantogle Stirlg 89 N4
Coillore Highld 100 c6
Col W Isls 106 j5
Colaboll Highld 108 K2
Colan Cnwll 3 M4
Colaton Raleigh Devon 6 E6
Colbost Highld 100 b5
Colburn N York 69 Q13
Colby Cumb 68 E8
Colby IoM 60 d8
Colby Norfk 51 M7
Colchester Essex 23 N2
Colchester Zoo Essex 23 N3
Cold Ash W Berk 19 R7
Cold Ashby Nhants 37 S5
Cold Ashton S Glos 28 E13
Cold Aston Gloucs 29 M5
Coldbackie Highld 111 N4
Coldbeck Cumb 68 F12
Cold Blow Pembks 24 K8
Cold Brayfield M Keyn 38 D10
Coldean Br & H 11 N9
Coldeast Devon 5 U6
Colden Common Hants 9 P4
Coldfair Green Suffk 41 R8
Coldham Cambs 49 P13
Cold Hanworth Lincs 58 H10
Coldharbour Cnwll 2 K7
Coldharbour Devon 6 E2
Coldharbour Gloucs 27 V7
Cold Harbour Herts 31 P9
Cold Harbour Oxon 19 T5
Coldharbour Surrey 10 J2
Cold Hatton Wrekin 45 P9
Cold Hatton Heath Wrekin 45 P9
Cold Hesledon Dur 70 F3
Cold Hiendley Wakefd 57 N4
Cold Higham Nhants 37 S10
Coldingham Border 85 M5
Cold Kirby N York 64 C2
Coldmeece Staffs 45 U7
Cold Newton Leics 47 T12
Cold Northcott Cnwll 4 G3
Cold Norton Essex 23 L7
Cold Overton Leics 48 B11
Coldred Kent 13 Q6
Coldridge Devon 15 Q11
Coldstream Border 85 L11
Coldwaltham W Susx 10 G7
Coldwell Herefs 34 K13
Cold Weston Shrops 35 N4
Coldwells Abers 105 T8
Cole Somset 17 S10
Colebatch Shrops 34 H3
Colebrook Devon 6 D3
Colebrooke Devon 15 S13
Coleby Lincs 48 E1
Coleby N Linc 58 E3
Cole End Warwks 36 H3
Coleford Devon 15 S12
Coleford Gloucs 28 A5
Coleford Somset 17 S7
Coleford Water Somset 16 F10
Colegate End Norfk 41 L3
Cole Green Herts 31 S10
Cole Green Herts 22 B1
Cole Henley Hants 19 Q9
Colehill Dorset 8 E8
Coleman Green Herts 31 Q10
Coleman's Hatch E Susx 11 Q4
Colemere Shrops 44 K7
Colemore Hants 9 U3
Colemore Green Shrops 45 R14
Colenden P & K 90 H6
Coleorton Leics 47 M11
Colerne Wilts 18 B6
Colesbourne Gloucs 28 K5
Cole's Cross Devon 5 T11
Coles Cross Dorset 7 L4
Colesden Bed 38 H9
Coles Green Suffk 40 K12
Coleshill Bucks 20 F3
Coleshill Oxon 29 P9
Coleshill Warwks 36 H3
Colestocks Devon 6 E4
Coley BaNES 17 Q5
Colgate W Susx 11 L4
Colinsburgh Fife 91 Q11
Colinton C Edin 83 P5
Colintraive Ag & B 88 B11
Colkirk Norfk 50 F8
Coll W Isls 106 j5
Collace P & K 90 K5
Collafirth Shet 106 u6
Coll Airport Ag & B 92 F7
Collaton Devon 5 P11
Collaton St Mary Torbay 5 V8
College of Roseisle Moray 103 V2
College Town Br For 20 E10
Collessie Fife 91 L9
Colleton Mills Devon 15 Q9
Collier Row Gt Lon 22 D9
Collier's End Herts 31 U8
Collier's Green Kent 12 E8
Colliers Green Kent 12 E8
Collier Street Kent 12 D6
Colliery Row Sundld 70 D3
Collieston Abers 105 S10
Collin D & G 74 K11
Collingbourne Ducis Wilts 18 K9
Collingbourne Kingston Wilts 18 K9
Collingham Leeds 63 T10
Collingham Notts 58 C14
Collington Herefs 35 P8
Collingtree Nhants 37 U9
Collins Green Warrtn 55 M8
Collins Green Worcs 35 R9
Colliston Angus 91 T2
Colliton Devon 6 E4
Collyweston Nhants 48 E13
Colmonell S Ayrs 72 E4
Colmworth Bed 38 H9
Colnabaichin Abers 98 D2
Colnbrook Slough 20 H7
Colne Cambs 39 N5
Colne Lancs 62 H11
Colne Edge Lancs 62 H11
Colne Engaine Essex 22 K1
Colney Norfk 51 L12
Colney Heath Herts 31 R11
Colney Street Herts 31 Q11
Coln Rogers Gloucs 29 L6
Coln St Aldwyns Gloucs 29 M6
Coln St Dennis Gloucs 29 L5
Colonsay Ag & B 86 f5
Colonsay Airport Ag & B 86 F7
Colpy Abers 104 J8
Colquhar Border 83 R10
Colscott Devon 14 J10
Colsterdale N York 63 N2
Colsterworth Lincs 48 D9
Colston Bassett Notts 47 S7
Coltfield Moray 103 T3
Colt Hill Hants 20 C12
Coltishall Norfk 51 N10
Colton Cumb 61 Q2
Colton Leeds 63 T13
Colton N York 64 C11
Colton Norfk 50 K12
Colton Staffs 46 D9
Colt's Hill Kent 12 C6
Columbjohn Devon 6 C5
Colva Powys 34 E10
Colvend D & G 74 F14
Colwall Herefs 35 S12
Colwell Nthumb 76 K11
Colwich Staffs 46 D9
Colwick Notts 47 R5
Colwinston V Glam 26 G12
Colworth W Susx 10 E10
Colwyn Bay Conwy 53 Q7
Colyford Devon 6 H6
Colyton Devon 6 H6
Combe Herefs 34 J8
Combe Oxon 29 T4
Combe W Berk 19 N8
Combe Almer Dorset 8 D9
Combe Common Surrey 10 E3
Combe Down BaNES 17 U4
Combe Fishacre Devon 5 U7
Combe Florey Somset 16 G10
Combe Hay BaNES 17 T5
Combeinteignhead Devon 6 B9
Combe Martin Devon 15 N3
Combe Raleigh Devon 6 G4
Comberbach Ches W 55 P11
Comberford Staffs 46 G12
Comberton Cambs 39 N9
Comberton Herefs 35 L7
Combe St Nicholas Somset 6 K2
Combpyne Devon 6 J6
Combridge Staffs 46 E6
Combrook Warwks 36 K10
Combs Derbys 56 F11
Combs Suffk 40 H9
Combs Ford Suffk 40 H9
Combwich Somset 16 J8
Comers Abers 99 M2
Comeytrowe Somset 16 H12
Comhampton Worcs 35 T7
Commercial End Cambs 39 S8
Commins Coch Powys 43 R13
Common Edge Bpool 61 Q13
Common End Cumb 66 F8
Commonmoor Cnwll 4 G7
Common Moor Cnwll 4 G7
Common Platt Wilts 29 L10
Commonside Ches W 55 M12
Commonside Derbys 46 H5
Common Side Derbys 57 M11
Commonwood Shrops 45 L8
Commonwood Wrexhm 44 J3
Compass Somset 16 J10
Compstall Stockp 56 E8
Compton Devon 5 V8
Compton Hants 9 M3
Compton Hants 9 P3
Compton Staffs 35 T3
Compton Surrey 20 F13
Compton W Berk 19 R4
Compton W Susx 9 U7
Compton Wilts 18 J10
Compton Abbas Dorset 8 B5
Compton Abdale Gloucs 29 L4
Compton Bassett Wilts 18 G6
Compton Beauchamp Oxon 29 Q10
Compton Bishop Somset 17 L5
Compton Chamberlayne Wilts 8 E3
Compton Dando BaNES 17 R4
Compton Dundon Somset 17 N10
Compton Durville Somset 17 M13
Compton Greenfield S Glos 27 V11
Compton Martin BaNES 17 P5
Compton Pauncefoot Somset 17 R11
Compton Valence Dorset 7 Q6
Comrie Fife 90 F14
Comrie P & K 89 S1
Conaglen House Highld 94 E5
Conchra Highld 101 M6
Concraigie P & K 90 G3
Conder Green Lancs 61 T9
Conderton Worcs 36 C13
Condicote Gloucs 29 N2
Condorrat N Lans 89 R11
Condover Shrops 45 L12
Coney Hill Gloucs 28 G4
Coneyhurst W Susx 10 J6
Coneysthorpe N York 64 G5
Coney Weston Suffk 40 G5
Conford Hants 10 C4
Congdon's Shop Cnwll 4 H5
Congerstone Leics 47 L12
Congham Norfk 50 B9
Congleton Ches E 45 U1
Congl-y-wal Gwynd 43 P4
Congresbury N Som 17 M4
Congreve Staffs 46 B11
Conheath D & G 74 K12
Conicavel Moray 103 Q5
Coningsby Lincs 48 K2
Conington Cambs 38 J6
Conington Cambs 39 M7
Conisbrough Donc 57 R7
Conisholme Lincs 59 T7
Coniston Cumb 67 M13
Coniston E R Yk 65 R12
Coniston Cold N York 62 J9
Conistone N York 62 K6
Connah's Quay Flints 54 G13
Connel Ag & B 94 C12
Connel Park E Ayrs 81 R10
Connor Downs Cnwll 2 F9
Conon Bridge Highld 102 F4
Cononley N York 62 K10
Cononsyth Angus 91 S2
Consall Staffs 46 C4
Consett Dur 69 P2
Constable Burton N York 63 P1
Constable Lee Lancs 55 T2
Constantine Cnwll 2 J11
Constantine Bay Cnwll 3 M2
Contin Highld 102 E4
Conwy Conwy 53 N7
Conyer Kent 12 K2
Conyer's Green Suffk 40 E7
Cooden E Susx 12 D14
Cookbury Devon 14 K11
Cookbury Wick Devon 14 J11
Cookham W & M 20 E6
Cookham Dean W & M 20 E6
Cookham Rise W & M 20 E6
Cookhill Worcs 36 E9
Cookley Suffk 41 P5
Cookley Worcs 35 T4
Cookley Green Oxon 19 U3
Cookney Abers 99 R5
Cooksbridge E Susx 11 P8
Cooks Green Suffk 40 G10
Cook's Green Essex 23 S3
Cookshill Staffs 46 B5
Cooksmill Green Essex 22 F6
Cookson Green Ches W 55 N12
Coolham W Susx 10 J6
Cooling Medway 22 H13
Cooling Street Medway 22 H13
Coombe Cnwll 3 L4
Coombe Cnwll 3 M8
Coombe Cnwll 4 G7
Coombe Cnwll 14 F10
Coombe Devon 6 D6
Coombe Devon 6 E6
Coombe Gloucs 28 D8
Coombe Hants 9 S4
Coombe Bissett Wilts 8 G3
Coombe Cellars Devon 6 B9
Coombe Cross Hants 9 T4
Coombe Hill Gloucs 28 G3
Coombe Keynes Dorset 8 A12
Coombe Pafford Torbay 6 B11
Coombes W Susx 10 K9
Coombes-Moor Herefs 34 J8
Coombe Street Somset 17 U10
Coombeswood Dudley 36 C3
Copdock Suffk 40 K12
Copford Essex 23 M3
Copford Green Essex 23 M3
Copgrove N York 63 S7
Copister Shet 106 u6
Cople Bed 38 H10
Copley Dur 69 N7
Coplow Dale Derbys 56 J11
Copmanthorpe C York 64 D10
Copmere End Staffs 45 T8
Copp Lancs 61 S12
Coppathorne Cnwll 14 F11
Coppenhall Staffs 46 B10
Coppenhall Moss Ches E 45 R2
Copperhouse Cnwll 2 F9
Coppicegate Shrops 35 R4
Coppingford Cambs 38 J5
Coppins Corner Kent 12 J6
Copplestone Devon 15 S12
Coppull Lancs 55 N3
Coppull Moor Lancs 55 N3
Copsale W Susx 10 K6
Copster Green Lancs 62 D13
Copston Magna Warwks 37 N3
Cop Street Kent 13 Q4
Copt Heath Solhll 36 G5
Copt Hewick N York 63 S5
Copthall Green Essex 22 C7
Copthorne Cnwll 4 H4
Copthorne W Susx 11 M3
Copt Oak Leics 47 N11
Copy's Green Norfk 50 F6
Copythorne Hants 9 L6
Coram Street Suffk 40 H12
Corbets Tey Gt Lon 22 E10
Corbière Jersey 7 a3
Corbridge Nthumb 76 K13
Corby Nhants 38 C3
Corby Glen Lincs 48 E9
Corby Hill Cumb 67 Q1
Cordon N Ayrs 80 E6
Cordwell Derbys 57 M11
Coreley Shrops 35 P6
Cores End Bucks 20 F5
Corfe Somset 16 H12
Corfe Castle Dorset 8 D12
Corfe Mullen Dorset 8 D9
Corfton Shrops 35 L3
Corgarff Abers 98 D2
Corhampton Hants 9 S4
Corlae D & G 81 T13
Corley Warwks 36 K4
Corley Ash Warwks 36 J4
Corley Moor Warwks 36 J4
Corley Services Warwks 36 K4
Cornabus Ag & B 78 E6
Cornard Tye Suffk 40 F12
Corndon Devon 5 R3
Corner Row Lancs 61 S13
Corney Cumb 66 J13
Cornforth Dur 70 D6
Cornhill Abers 104 H4
Cornhill-on-Tweed Nthumb 85 M11
Cornholme Calder 56 D1
Cornish Hall End Essex 39 U13
Cornoigmore Ag & B 92 B9
Cornriggs Dur 68 J4
Cornsay Dur 69 P4
Cornsay Colliery Dur 69 P4
Corntown Highld 102 G4
Corntown V Glam 26 G12
Cornwall Airport Newquay Cnwll 3 M4
Cornwell Oxon 29 Q3
Cornwood Devon 5 P9
Cornworthy Devon 5 U9
Corpach Highld 94 F3
Corpusty Norfk 50 K8
Corrachree Abers 98 H3
Corran Highld 94 E6
Corran Highld 101 L9
Corranbuie Ag & B 79 Q5
Corrany IoM 60 g5
Corrie D & G 75 P7
Corrie N Ayrs 80 E4
Corriecravie N Ayrs 79 S11
Corriegills N Ayrs 80 E5
Corriemoille Highld 102 B3
Corrimony Highld 102 C9
Corringham Lincs 58 E8
Corringham Thurr 22 H11
Corris Gwynd 43 Q13
Corris Uchaf Gwynd 43 Q13
Corrow Ag & B 88 E5
Corry Highld 100 f7
Corscombe Devon 15 P13
Corscombe Dorset 7 P3
Corse Gloucs 28 E3
Corse Lawn Gloucs 28 F2
Corsham Wilts 18 B6
Corsindae Abers 99 M2
Corsley Wilts 18 B11
Corsley Heath Wilts 18 B11
Corsock D & G 74 E10
Corston BaNES 17 T3
Corston Wilts 28 H11
Corstorphine C Edin 83 N4
Cortachy Angus 98 E13
Corton Suffk 41 T2
Corton Wilts 18 D12
Corton Denham Somset 17 R12
Coruanan Highld 94 F5
Corwen Denbgs 44 C5
Coryates Dorset 7 Q7
Coryton Devon 5 L4
Coryton Thurr 22 J11
Cosby Leics 37 P1
Coseley Dudley 36 B2
Cosford Shrops 45 S12
Cosgrove Nhants 30 B4
Cosham C Port 9 S7
Cosheston Pembks 24 H9
Coshieville P & K 95 U8
Cossall Notts 47 N5
Cossington Leics 47 R11
Cossington Somset 17 L8
Costa Ork 106 s17
Costessey Norfk 51 L11
Costock Notts 47 Q8
Coston Leics 48 B9
Cote Oxon 29 R7
Cote Somset 17 L7
Cotebrook Ches W 55 N13
Cotehill Cumb 67 Q2
Cotes Cumb 61 R2
Cotes Leics 47 Q9
Cotes Staffs 45 T7
Cotesbach Leics 37 Q4
Cotford St Luke Somset 16 G11
Cotgrave Notts 47 R6
Cotham Notts 48 B4
Cothelstone Somset 16 G10
Cotherstone Dur 69 M9
Cothill Oxon 29 U8
Cotleigh Devon 6 H4
Cotmanhay Derbys 47 M5
Coton Cambs 39 N9
Coton Nhants 37 S6
Coton Shrops 45 M7
Coton Staffs 45 U9
Coton Staffs 46 C7
Coton Clanford Staffs 45 U9
Coton Hayes Staffs 45 U9
Coton Hill Shrops 45 L11
Coton in the Clay Staffs 46 F8
Coton in the Elms Derbys 46 H10
Coton Park Derbys 46 J10
Cott Devon 5 U8
Cottam E R Yk 65 M7
Cottam Lancs 61 U13
Cottam Notts 58 D11
Cottenham Cambs 39 P7
Cotterdale N York 68 H13
Cottered Herts 31 T7
Cotteridge Birm 36 D5
Cotterstock Nhants 38 F2
Cottesbrooke Nhants 37 T6
Cottesmore Rutlnd 48 D11
Cotteylands Devon 16 C13
Cottingham E R Yk 65 P13
Cottingham Nhants 38 B2
Cottingley C Brad 63 N12
Cottisford Oxon 30 C6
Cotton Suffk 40 J7
Cotton End Bed 38 G11
Cotton Tree Lancs 62 J11
Cottown Abers 104 K10
Cottown Abers 105 M8
Cottown of Gight Abers 105 M7
Cotts Devon 5 L7
Cotwall Wrekin 45 P10
Cotwalton Staffs 45 U6
Couch's Mill Cnwll 4 F9
Coughton Herefs 28 A3
Coughton Warwks 36 E8
Coulaghailtro Ag & B 79 P5
Coulags Highld 101 N3
Coulderton Cumb 66 E11
Coull Abers 98 K3
Coulport Ag & B 88 F9
Coulsdon Gt Lon 21 N11
Coulston Wilts 18 E9
Coulter S Lans 82 K12
Coultershaw Bridge W Susx 10 E6
Coultings Somset 16 H8
Coulton N York 64 F4
Coultra Fife 91 N7
Cound Shrops 45 N12
Coundon Dur 69 R7
Coundon Grange Dur 69 R7
Countersett N York 62 K2
Countess Wilts 18 H12
Countess Cross Essex 23 L1
Countesthorpe Leics 37 Q2
Countisbury Devon 15 R3
Coupar Angus P & K 90 K3
Coup Green Lancs 55 N1
Coupland Cumb 68 F9
Coupland Nthumb 85 N12
Cour Ag & B 79 R6
Courance D & G 75 L8
Court-at-Street Kent 13 L8
Courteachan Highld 100 f10
Courteenhall Nhants 37 U10
Court Henry Carmth 25 U6
Courtsend Essex 23 P9
Courtway Somset 16 H10
Cousland Mdloth 83 S5
Cousley Wood E Susx 12 C8
Cove Ag & B 88 F9
Cove Border 84 K4
Cove Devon 16 C13
Cove Hants 20 E11
Cove Highld 107 P6
Cove Bay C Aber 99 S3
Cove Bottom Suffk 41 S4
Covehithe Suffk 41 T4
Coven Staffs 46 B12
Coveney Cambs 39 Q4
Covenham St Bartholomew Lincs 59 P8
Covenham St Mary Lincs 59 P8
Coven Heath Staffs 46 B12
Coventry Covtry 36 K5
Coverack Cnwll 2 K13
Coverack Bridges Cnwll 2 G10
Coverham N York 63 N2
Covington Cambs 38 G6
Covington S Lans 82 J11
Cowan Bridge Lancs 62 C5
Cowbeech E Susx 11 U8
Cowbit Lincs 49 L10
Cowbridge V Glam 26 H13
Cowdale Derbys 56 G12
Cowden Kent 11 R3
Cowdenbeath Fife 90 H13
Cowden Pound Kent 11 R3
Cowden Station Kent 11 R3
Cowers Lane Derbys 46 K4
Cowes IoW 9 P9
Cowesby N York 64 B2
Cowesfield Green Wilts 8 K3
Cowfold W Susx 10 K6
Cowgill Cumb 62 F2
Cowhill S Glos 28 B9
Cowie Abers 99 R6
Cowie Stirlg 89 T8
Cowlam E R Yk 65 L6
Cowley Devon 6 B5
Cowley Gloucs 28 J5
Cowley Gt Lon 20 J6
Cowley Oxon 30 B12
Cowling Lancs 55 N3
Cowling N York 62 K11
Cowling N York 63 Q2
Cowlinge Suffk 40 B10
Cowmes Kirk 56 J3
Cowpe Lancs 55 T2
Cowpen Nthumb 77 R9
Cowpen Bewley S on T 70 G7
Cowplain Hants 9 T6
Cowshill Dur 68 J4
Cowslip Green N Som 17 N4
Cowthorpe N York 63 U9
Coxall Herefs 34 J6
Coxbank Ches E 45 Q5
Coxbench Derbys 47 L5
Coxbridge Somset 17 P9
Cox Common Suffk 41 Q4
Coxford Norfk 50 D8
Coxgreen Staffs 35 T4
Coxgreen Sundld 70 D2
Coxheath Kent 12 D5
Coxhoe Dur 70 D5
Coxley Somset 17 P8
Coxley Wick Somset 17 P8
Coxpark Cnwll 5 L6
Coxtie Green Essex 22 E8
Coxwold N York 64 C4
Coychurch Brdgnd 26 G11
Coylton S Ayrs 81 N9
Coylumbridge Highld 97 P3
Coytrahen Brdgnd 26 F10
Crabbs Cross Worcs 36 D7
Crab Orchard Dorset 8 F7
Crabtree W Susx 10 K6
Crabtree Green Wrexhm 44 J4
Crackenthorpe Cumb 68 E8
Crackington Haven Cnwll 14 D13
Crackley Staffs 45 T3
Crackleybank Shrops 45 S11
Crackpot N York 69 L13
Cracoe N York 62 K7
Craddock Devon 6 F2
Cradle End Herts 22 B3
Cradley Dudley 36 B3
Cradley Herefs 35 R11
Cradley Heath Sandw 36 C3
Cradoc Powys 26 J1
Crafthole Cnwll 4 K10
Crag Foot Lancs 61 T5
Craggan Moray 103 S10
Cragganmore Moray 103 T9
Cragg Hill Leeds 63 Q12
Cragg Vale Calder 56 F2
Craghead Dur 69 R2
Cragside House & Garden Nthumb 77 M5
Crai Powys 26 F2
Craibstone Moray 104 F4
Craichie Angus 98 H13
Craig Angus 99 M12
Craig Highld 101 Q3
Craigbank E Ayrs 81 R10
Craigburn Border 83 P7
Craig-cefn-parc Swans 26 B7
Craigcleuch D & G 75 R8
Craigdam Abers 105 M8
Craigdhu Ag & B 87 N3
Craigearn Abers 105 L12
Craigellachie Moray 104 B7
Craigend P & K 90 H7
Craigend Rens 88 K12
Craigendoran Ag & B 88 G9
Craigends Rens 88 K12
Craigenputtock D & G 74 E9
Craighat Stirlg 88 K9
Craighlaw D & G 72 J7
Craighouse Ag & B 86 J12
Craigie P & K 90 H4
Craigie S Ayrs 81 N6
Craigiefold Abers 105 Q3
Craigley D & G 74 E12
Craig Llangiwg Neath 26 C6
Craiglockhart C Edin 83 P4
Craigmillar C Edin 83 Q4
Craignant Shrops 44 G6
Craigneuk N Lans 82 D6
Craigneuk N Lans 82 E7
Craignure Ag & B 93 S11
Craigo Angus 99 M11
Craigrothie Fife 91 M9
Craigruie Stirlg 95 M14
Craig's End Essex 40 C13
Craigton Angus 91 R1
Craigton C Aber 99 R3
Craigton E Rens 89 M14
Craigton of Airlie Angus 98 E13
Craig-y-Duke Neath 26 C6
Craig-y-nos Powys 26 F4
Craik Border 75 Q4
Crail Fife 91 T10
Crailing Border 84 H13
Crailinghall Border 84 H13
Craiselound N Linc 58 C6
Crakehall N York 63 Q1
Crakemarsh Staffs 46 E6
Crambe N York 64 G7
Crambeck N York 64 G6
Cramlington Nthumb 77 R10
Cramond C Edin 83 N3
Cramond Bridge C Edin 83 N3
Crampmoor Hants 9 M4
Cranage Ches E 55 R13
Cranberry Staffs 45 U6
Cranborne Dorset 8 F6
Cranbourne Br For 20 G8
Cranbrook Devon 6 D5
Cranbrook Kent 12 E8
Cranbrook Common Kent 12 E8
Crane Moor S Yorks 57 M5
Crane's Corner Norfk 50 F11
Cranfield C Beds 38 E11
Cranford Gt Lon 20 K7
Cranford St Andrew Nhants 38 D5
Cranford St John Nhants 38 D5
Cranham Gloucs 28 G5
Cranham Gt Lon 22 E10
Crank St Hel 55 M7
Cranleigh Surrey 10 H3
Cranmer Green Suffk 40 H6
Cranmore IoW 9 M10
Cranmore Somset 17 S8
Cranoe Leics 37 U2
Cransford Suffk 41 P8
Cranshaws Border 84 H6
Cranstal IoM 60 h2
Cranswick E R Yk 65 N9
Crantock Cnwll 2 K4
Cranwell Lincs 48 F4
Cranwich Norfk 40 C2
Cranworth Norfk 50 G12
Craobh Haven Ag & B 87 P4
Crapstone Devon 5 N6
Crarae Ag & B 87 T6
Crask Inn Highld 111 L12
Crask of Aigas Highld 102 E7
Craster Nthumb 77 R2
Craswall Herefs 34 G13
Crateford Staffs 46 B12
Cratfield Suffk 41 P5
Crathes Abers 99 N4
Crathie Abers 98 D4
Crathie Highld 96 H5
Crathorne N York 70 G10
Craven Arms Shrops 34 K3
Crawcrook Gatesd 77 N13
Crawford Lancs 54 K6
Crawford S Lans 74 J1
Crawfordjohn S Lans 82 G13
Crawick D & G 74 E1
Crawley Hants 9 N2
Crawley Oxon 29 R5
Crawley W Susx 11 M3
Crawley Down W Susx 11 N3
Crawleyside Dur 69 L4
Crawshawbooth Lancs 55 T1
Crawton Abers 99 R8
Craxe's Green Essex 23 M4
Cray N York 62 J4
Cray P & K 97 U11
Crayford Gt Lon 22 D12
Crayke N York 64 D5
Craymere Beck Norfk 50 J6
Crays Hill Essex 22 H9
Cray's Pond Oxon 19 T4
Craythorne Staffs 46 H8
Craze Lowman Devon 6 C2
Crazies Hill Wokham 20 C6
Creacombe Devon 15 U9
Creagan Inn Ag & B 94 D10
Creag Ghoraidh W Isls 106 c14
Creagorry W Isls 106 c14
Creaguaineach Lodge Highld 96 C10
Creamore Bank Shrops 45 M7
Creaton Nhants 37 T6
Creca D & G 75 P11
Credenhill Herefs 35 L12
Crediton Devon 15 T12
Creebank D & G 72 J5
Creebridge D & G 73 L6
Creech Somset 7 L4
Creech Heathfield Somset 16 J11
Creech St Michael Somset 16 J11
Creed Cnwll 3 N7
Creekmoor BCP 8 E10
Creekmouth Gt Lon 22 C11
Creeting St Mary Suffk 40 J9
Creeton Lincs 48 F8
Creetown D & G 73 L7
Cregneash IoM 60 b9
Cregny-baa IoM 60 f6
Cregrina Powys 34 D10
Creich Fife 91 M7
Creigiau Cardif 26 K11
Cremyll Cnwll 5 L10
Cressage Shrops 45 N12
Cressbrook Derbys 56 J12
Cresselly Pembks 24 J9
Cressex Bucks 20 D4
Cressing Essex 22 J3
Cresswell Nthumb 77 S9
Cresswell Pembks 24 J8
Cresswell Staffs 46 B6
Creswell Derbys 57 R12
Creswell Green Staffs 46 E11
Cretingham Suffk 41 M9
Cretshengan Ag & B 79 P5
Crewe Ches E 45 R2
Crewe-by-Farndon Ches W 45 L3
Crewe Green Ches E 45 S2
Crew Green Powys 44 H11
Crewkerne Somset 7 M3
Crews Hill Gt Lon 21 Q3
Crewton C Derb 47 L6
Crianlarich Stirlg 95 M13
Cribbs Causeway S Glos 27 V11
Cribyn Cerdgn 32 K10
Criccieth Gwynd 42 K6
Crich Derbys 46 K2
Crich Carr Derbys 46 K2
Crichton Mdloth 83 S6
Crick Mons 27 T9
Crick Nhants 37 Q6
Crickadarn Powys 34 C12
Cricket St Thomas Somset 7 L3
Crickham Somset 17 M7
Crickheath Shrops 44 G9
Crickhowell Powys 27 M3
Cricklade Wilts 29 L9
Cricklewood Gt Lon 21 M5
Cridling Stubbs N York 57 R1
Crieff P & K 90 C7
Criggan Cnwll 3 Q4
Criggion Powys 44 G11
Crigglestone Wakefd 57 M3
Crimble Rochdl 56 C4
Crimond Abers 105 T5
Crimplesham Norfk 49 U13
Crimscote Warwks 36 H11
Crinaglack Highld 102 E8
Crinan Ag & B 87 P7
Cringleford Norfk 51 L12
Cringles C Brad 63 L10
Crinow Pembks 24 K8
Cripplesease Cnwll 2 E9
Cripplestyle Dorset 8 F6
Cripp's Corner E Susx 12 E11
Croanford Cnwll 3 Q2
Crockenhill Kent 21 S10
Crocker End Oxon 20 B5
Crockerhill W Susx 10 E9
Crockernwell Devon 5 S2
Crocker's Ash Herefs 27 U5
Crockerton Wilts 18 C12
Crocketford D & G 74 F11
Crockey Hill C York 64 E10
Crockham Hill Kent 21 R12
Crockhurst Street Kent 12 B7
Crockleford Heath Essex 23 P2
Crockwell Essex 23 P2
Croeserw Neath 26 F9
Croes-goch Pembks 24 E4
Croes-lan Cerdgn 32 G12
Croesor Gwynd 43 M4
Croesyceiliog Carmth 25 R7
Croesyceiliog Torfn 27 Q8
Croes-y-mwyalch Torfn 27 Q9
Croes-y-pant Mons 27 Q7
Croft Leics 37 P2
Croft Lincs 59 S14
Croft Warrtn 55 P8
Croftamie Stirlg 88 K9
Croftmalloch W Loth 82 H5
Croft Mitchell Cnwll 2 H9
Crofton Cumb 67 M2
Crofton Wakefd 57 N3
Crofton Wilts 19 L8
Croft-on-Tees N York 69 S11
Croftown Highld 108 A7
Crofts Moray 104 B6
Crofts Bank Traffd 55 S7
Crofts of Dipple Moray 104 C4
Crofts of Haddo Abers 105 M8
Crofts of Savoch Abers 105 S5
Crofty Swans 25 T11
Croggan Ag & B 93 S12
Croglin Cumb 68 C3
Croick Highld 108 G5
Cromarty Highld 102 K3
Crombie Fife 90 F14
Cromdale Highld 103 S10
Cromer Herts 31 S7
Cromer Norfk 51 M5
Cromford Derbys 46 J2
Cromhall S Glos 28 C9
Cromhall Common S Glos 28 C10
Cromor W Isls 106 j6
Crompton Fold Oldham 56 D5
Cromwell Notts 58 B14
Cronberry E Ayrs 81 R8
Crondall Hants 20 C13
Cronk-y-Voddy IoM 60 e5
Cronton Knows 55 L9
Crook Cumb 67 P13
Crook Dur 69 Q5
Crookdake Cumb 66 J3
Crooked End Gloucs 28 B4
Crooked Holme Cumb 76 B14
Crooked Soley Wilts 19 M6
Crookes Sheff 57 M9
Crookhall Dur 69 P2
Crookham Nthumb 85 N11
Crookham W Berk 19 R8
Crookham Village Hants 20 C12
Crook Inn Border 83 N14
Crooklands Cumb 61 U3
Crook of Devon P & K 90 F11
Cropper Derbys 46 H6
Cropredy Oxon 37 N11
Cropston Leics 47 Q11
Cropthorne Worcs 36 C11
Cropton N York 64 H2
Cropwell Bishop Notts 47 S6
Cropwell Butler Notts 47 S6
Cros W Isls 106 k2
Crosbost W Isls 106 i6
Crosby Cumb 66 G5
Crosby IoM 60 e7
Crosby N Linc 58 E4
Crosby Sefton 54 H7
Crosby Garrett Cumb 68 F11
Crosby Ravensworth Cumb 68 E10
Crosby Villa Cumb 66 G5
Croscombe Somset 17 Q8
Crosemere Shrops 44 K8
Crosland Edge Kirk 56 H4
Crosland Hill Kirk 56 H4
Cross Somset 17 M6
Crossaig Ag & B 79 R6
Crossapol Ag & B 92 B10
Cross Ash Mons 27 S4
Cross-at-Hand Kent 12 E6
Crossbush W Susx 10 G9
Crosscanonby Cumb 66 G4
Cross Coombe Cnwll 2 K7
Crossdale Street Norfk 51 M6
Cross End Bed 38 F9
Cross End Essex 40 E14
Crossens Sefton 54 J3
Cross Flatts C Brad 63 N11
Crossford Fife 83 L1
Crossford S Lans 82 F10
Crossgate Cnwll 4 H4
Crossgate Lincs 48 K8
Crossgate Staffs 46 B6
Crossgatehall E Loth 83 S4
Crossgates E Ayrs 81 M4
Crossgates Fife 90 H14
Crossgates N York 65 M3
Crossgates Powys 34 C8
Cross Gates Leeds 63 T13
Crossgill Lancs 61 U7
Cross Green Devon 4 J4
Cross Green Leeds 63 S13
Cross Green Staffs 46 B12
Cross Green Suffk 40 E9
Cross Green Suffk 40 F10
Cross Green Suffk 40 G10
Crosshands Carmth 25 U8
Cross Hands Pembks 24 J6
Crosshands E Ayrs 81 N6
Cross Hill Derbys 47 M4
Crosshill Fife 90 H12
Crosshill S Ayrs 81 L11
Cross Hills N York 63 L10
Crosshouse E Ayrs 81 M5
Cross Houses Shrops 45 M12
Cross Houses Shrops 35 M1
Cross in Hand E Susx 11 T6
Cross Inn Cerdgn 32 J8
Cross Inn Cerdgn 33 L6
Cross Inn Pembks 24 K9
Cross Inn Rhondd 26 K11
Cross Keys Ag & B 88 H6
Cross Keys Wilts 18 B6
Crosskeys Caerph 27 N8
Crosskirk Highld 112 B3
Crosslands Cumb 61 Q2
Cross Lane IoW 9 Q11
Cross Lane Head Shrops 35 R1
Cross Lanes Cnwll 2 H12
Cross Lanes N York 64 D7
Cross Lanes Wrexhm 44 J4
Crosslee Rens 88 K12
Crossley Kirk 56 K3
Crossmichael D & G 74 E12
Cross Oak Powys 27 L2
Cross of Jackston Abers 105 L9
Cross o' th' hands Derbys 46 J4
Crosspost W Susx 11 M6
Crossroads Abers 99 N5
Crossroads Abers 99 P4
Cross Roads C Brad 63 M12
Cross Street Suffk 41 L5
Crosston Angus 98 J12
Cross Town Ches E 55 S11
Crossway Mons 27 S5
Crossway Powys 34 C9
Crossway Green Mons 27 U9
Crossway Green Worcs 35 T7
Crossways Dorset 7 U7
Crosswell Pembks 24 K3
Crosthwaite Cumb 61 R1
Croston Lancs 55 L3
Crostwick Norfk 51 N11
Crostwight Norfk 51 P8
Crouch Kent 12 B4
Crouch Kent 13 L2
Croucheston Wilts 8 F3
Crouch End Gt Lon 21 N5
Crouch Hill Dorset 7 S3
Crough House Green Kent 21 R13
Croughton Nhants 30 B6
Crovie Abers 105 M2
Crow Hants 8 H8
Crow Edge Barns 56 K6
Crow End Cambs 39 M9
Crowan Cnwll 2 G9
Crowborough E Susx 11 S5
Crowborough Warren E Susx 11 S4
Crowcombe Somset 16 F9
Crowdecote Derbys 56 H13
Crowden Derbys 56 G6
Crowden Devon 15 M13
Crowdhill Hants 9 P5
Crowell Oxon 20 B3
Crowfield Nhants 37 R11
Crowfield Suffk 40 K9
Crowfield Green Suffk 40 K9
Crowgate Street Norfk 51 P9
Crow Green Essex 22 E8
Crowhill E Loth 84 H3
Crow Hill Herefs 28 B3
Crowhole Derbys 57 M11
Crowhurst E Susx 12 D13
Crowhurst Surrey 21 P13
Crowhurst Lane End Surrey 21 P13
Crowland Lincs 48 K11
Crowland Suffk 40 G6
Crowlas Cnwll 2 E10
Crowle N Linc 58 C4
Crowle Worcs 36 B9
Crowle Green Worcs 36 B9
Crowmarsh Gifford Oxon 19 T3
Crown Corner Suffk 41 N6
Crownhill C Plym 5 M9
Crownpits Surrey 10 F2
Crownthorpe Norfk 50 J12
Crowntown Cnwll 2 G10
Crows-an-Wra Cnwll 2 B11
Crow's Green Essex 22 G2
Crow's Nest Cnwll 4 G7
Crowsnest Shrops 44 J12
Crowthorne Wokham 20 D10
Crowton Ches W 55 N12
Croxall Staffs 46 H11
Croxby Lincs 59 L7
Croxdale Dur 69 S5
Croxden Staffs 46 E6
Croxley Green Herts 20 H3
Croxteth Lpool 54 K7
Croxton Cambs 39 L8
Croxton N Linc 58 J4
Croxton Norfk 40 E4
Croxton Norfk 50 D6
Croxton Staffs 45 S7
Croxton Green Ches E 45 N3
Croxton Kerrial Leics 48 B8
Croy Highld 103 M6
Croy N Lans 89 R10
Croyde Devon 14 K5
Croydon Cambs 39 M11
Croydon Gt Lon 21 P9
Crubenmore Highld 96 K5
Cruckmeole Shrops 44 K12
Cruckton Shrops 44 K11
Cruden Bay Abers 105 U8
Crudgington Wrekin 45 P10
Crudwell Wilts 28 J9
Cruft Devon 5 L2
Crug Powys 34 D5
Crugmeer Cnwll 3 N1
Crugybar Carmth 33 N12
Crug-y-byddar Powys 34 D4
Crumlin Caerph 27 N7
Crumplehorn Cnwll 4 F10
Crumpsall Manch 55 T6
Crundale Kent 13 L6
Crundale Pembks 24 G7
Crunwere Pembks 25 L8
Cruwys Morchard Devon 15 U10
Crux Easton Hants 19 P9

Cruxton Dorset 7 R5
Crwbin Carmth 25 S8
Cryers Hill Bucks 20 E3
Crymych Pembks 25 L4
Crynant Neath 26 D7
Crystal Palace Gt Lon 21 P8
Cuaig Highld 107 M13
Cuan Ag & B 87 P3
Cubbington Warwks 36 K7
Cubert Cnwll 2 K5
Cubley Barns 56 K6
Cublington Bucks 30 H8
Cublington Herefs 34 K13
Cuckfield W Susx 11 N5
Cucklington Somset 17 U11
Cuckney Notts 57 S12
Cuckoo Bridge Lincs 48 K9
Cuckoo's Corner Hants 10 A2
Cuckoo's Nest Ches W 44 J1
Cuddesdon Oxon 30 C12
Cuddington Bucks 30 F10
Cuddington Ches W 55 N12
Cuddington Heath Ches W 45 L4
Cuddy Hill Lancs 61 T12
Cudham Gt Lon 21 R11
Cudliptown Devon 5 N5
Cudnell BCP 8 F9
Cudworth Barns 57 N5
Cudworth Somset 7 L2
Cuerdley Cross Warrtn 55 M9
Cufaude Hants 19 U9
Cuffley Herts 31 T12
Cuil Highld 94 D7
Culbokie Highld 102 H4
Culbone Somset 15 T3
Culburnie Highld 102 E7
Culcabock Highld 102 J7
Culcharry Highld 103 N5
Culcheth Warrtn 55 Q8
Culdrain Abers 104 G9
Culduie Highld 100 g5
Culford Suffk 40 D6
Culgaith Cumb 68 D7
Culham Oxon 30 B13
Culkein Highld 110 A10
Culkein Drumbeg Highld 110 C10
Culkerton Gloucs 28 H8
Cullen Moray 104 G2
Cullercoats N Tyne 77 T11
Cullerlie Abers 99 P3
Cullicudden Highld 102 H3
Cullingworth C Brad 63 M12
Cuillin Hills Highld 100 d7
Cullipool Ag & B 87 N3
Cullivoe Shet 106 v3
Culloden Highld 102 K6
Cullompton Devon 6 D3
Cullompton Services Devon 6 D3
Culm Davy Devon 16 F13
Culmington Shrops 35 L4
Culmstock Devon 6 F2
Culnacraig Highld 107 U4
Culnaightrie D & G 73 T9
Culnaknock Highld 100 e3
Culpho Suffk 41 M11
Culrain Highld 108 K6
Culross Fife 82 J1
Culroy S Ayrs 81 L10
Culsalmond Abers 104 K9
Culscadden D & G 73 M10
Culshabbin D & G 72 J9
Culswick Shet 106 s9
Cultercullen Abers 105 Q11
Cults C Aber 99 R3
Culverstone Green Kent 12 B3
Culverthorpe Lincs 48 F5
Culworth Nhants 37 P11
Culzean Castle & Country Park S Ayrs 80 J10
Cumbernauld N Lans 89 S11
Cumbernauld Village N Lans 89 S10
Cumberworth Lincs 59 T12
Cumdivock Cumb 67 M3
Cuminestown Abers 105 N5
Cumledge Border 84 K7
Cummersdale Cumb 67 N2
Cummertrees D & G 75 M12
Cummingston Moray 103 T2
Cumnock E Ayrs 81 R8
Cumnor Oxon 29 U7
Cumrew Cumb 67 S2
Cumrue D & G 75 L8
Cumwhinton Cumb 67 Q2
Cumwhitton Cumb 67 R2
Cundall N York 63 U5
Cunninghamhead N Ayrs 81 M4
Cunningsburgh Shet 106 u10
Cupar Fife 91 N9
Cupar Muir Fife 91 N9
Curbar Derbys 57 L12
Curbridge Hants 9 Q6
Curbridge Oxon 29 R6
Curdridge Hants 9 Q6
Curdworth Warwks 36 G2
Curland Somset 16 J13
Curridge W Berk 19 Q6
Currie C Edin 83 N5
Curry Mallet Somset 16 K12
Curry Rivel Somset 17 L11
Curteis Corner Kent 12 G8
Curtisden Green Kent 12 D7
Curtisknowle Devon 5 S10
Cury Cnwll 2 H12
Cushnie Abers 104 G13
Cushuish Somset 16 G10
Cusop Herefs 34 F12
Cusworth Donc 57 R6
Cutcloy D & G 73 M13
Cutcombe Somset 16 B9
Cutgate Rochdl 56 C4
Cuthill Highld 109 P7
Cutiau Gwynd 43 M10
Cutler's Green Essex 22 E1
Cutmadoc Cnwll 3 R4
Cutmere Cnwll 4 J8
Cutnall Green Worcs 35 U7
Cutsdean Gloucs 29 L1
Cutthorpe Derbys 57 M12
Cuttivett Cnwll 4 K8
Cuxham Oxon 30 E13
Cuxton Medway 12 D2
Cuxwold Lincs 59 L6
Cwm Blae G 27 M6
Cwm Denbgs 54 C11
Cwmafan Neath 26 D9
Cwmaman Rhondd 26 J8
Cwmann Carmth 33 L11
Cwmavon Torfn 27 P6
Cwmbach Carmth 25 N5
Cwmbach Carmth 25 S10
Cwmbâch Powys 34 E13
Cwmbach Rhondd 26 J7
Cwmbach Llechrhyd Powys 34 B10
Cwmbelan Powys 33 T4
Cwmbran Torfn 27 P9
Cwmbrwyno Cerdgn 33 P4
Cwm Capel Carmth 25 S10
Cwmcarn Caerph 27 N9
Cwmcarvan Mons 27 T6
Cwm-celyn Blae G 27 N6
Cwm-Cewydd Gwynd 43 S11
Cwm-cou Cerdgn 32 E12
Cwm Crawnon Powys 27 L4
Cwmdare Rhondd 26 H7
Cwmdu Carmth 26 A1
Cwmdu Powys 27 M3
Cwmdu Swans 26 A9
Cwmduad Carmth 25 Q4
Cwm Dulais Swans 25 V10
Cwmdwr Carmth 33 P14
Cwmfelin Brdgnd 26 F10
Cwmfelin Myr Td 26 K7
Cwmfelin Boeth Carmth 25 L7
Cwmfelinfach Caerph 27 M9
Cwmfelin Mynach Carmth 25 M6
Cwmffrwd Carmth 25 R7
Cwmgiedd Powys 26 D5
Cwmgorse Carmth 26 C5
Cwm Gwaun Pembks 24 H4
Cwmgwili Carmth 25 U8
Cwmgwrach Neath 26 F7
Cwmhiraeth Carmth 25 P3
Cwmifor Carmth 26 B2
Cwm Irfon Powys 33 S11
Cwmisfael Carmth 25 S7
Cwm Llinau Powys 43 R12
Cwmllynfell Neath 26 C5
Cwmmawr Carmth 25 T8
Cwm Morgan Carmth 25 N4
Cwmparc Rhondd 26 G8
Cwmpengraig Carmth 25 Q3
Cwm Penmachno Conwy 43 Q4
Cwmpennar Rhondd 26 J7
Cwmrhos Powys 27 M3
Cwmrhydyceirw Swans 26 B8
Cwmsychbant Cerdgn 32 J11
Cwmtillery Blae G 27 N6
Cwm-twrch Isaf Powys 26 D5
Cwm-twrch Uchaf Powys 26 D5
Cwm-y-glo Carmth 25 U8
Cwm-y-glo Gwynd 52 J10
Cwmyoy Mons 27 P3
Cwmystwyth Cerdgn 33 Q6
Cwrt Gwynd 43 N14
Cwrtnewydd Cerdgn 32 J11
Cwrt-y-gollen Powys 27 N4
Cyfarthfa Castle Museum Myr Td 26 J6
Cyffylliog Denbgs 44 C2
Cyfronydd Powys 44 D12
Cylibebyll Neath 26 C7
Cymau Flints 44 G2
Cymmer Neath 26 F8
Cymmer Rhondd 26 J9
Cyncoed Cardif 27 M11
Cynghordy Carmth 33 R12
Cynheidre Carmth 25 S9
Cynonville Neath 26 E8
Cynwyd Denbgs 44 C5
Cynwyl Elfed Carmth 25 Q5

D

Daccombe Devon 6 B11
Dacre Cumb 67 Q7
Dacre N York 63 P7
Dacre Banks N York 63 P7
Daddry Shield Dur 68 J5
Dadford Bucks 30 E5
Dadlington Leics 47 M14
Dafen Carmth 25 T10
Daffy Green Norfk 50 G12
Dagenham Gt Lon 22 D11
Daglingworth Gloucs 28 J6
Dagnall Bucks 31 L9
Dagworth Suffk 40 H8
Dail bho Dheas W Isls 106 j2
Dailly S Ayrs 80 K12
Dainton Devon 5 V7
Dairsie Fife 91 P8
Daisy Hill Bolton 55 Q6
Daisy Hill Leeds 63 R14
Dalabrog W Isls 106 c16
Dalavich Ag & B 87 T3
Dalbeattie D & G 74 F13
Dalbury Derbys 46 J7
Dalby IoM 60 c7
Dalby Lincs 59 R13
Dalby N York 64 E5
Dalcapon P & K 97 R13
Dalchalm Highld 109 S3
Dalchreichart Highld 102 A13
Dalchruin P & K 89 R2
Dalcrue P & K 90 F6
Dalderby Lincs 59 N13
Dalditch Devon 6 D8
Dale Cumb 67 R4
Dale Pembks 24 D9
Dale Abbey Derbys 47 M6
Dale Bottom Cumb 67 L8
Dale End Derbys 46 H1
Dale End N York 62 K10
Dale Hill E Susx 12 D9
Dalehouse N York 71 N9
Dalelia Highld 93 S5
Dalgarven N Ayrs 80 K3
Dalgety Bay Fife 83 N2
Dalgig E Ayrs 81 R10
Dalginross P & K 89 S1
Dalguise P & K 90 E2
Dalhalvaig Highld 111 T6
Dalham Suffk 40 B8
Daliburgh W Isls 106 c16
Dalkeith Mdloth 83 R5
Dallas Moray 103 T5
Dallinghoo Suffk 41 N9
Dallington E Susx 11 V7
Dallington Nhants 37 T8
Dallow N York 63 P5
Dalmally Ag & B 94 H13
Dalmary Stirlg 89 M6
Dalmellington E Ayrs 81 P11
Dalmeny C Edin 83 M3
Dalmore Highld 109 M11
Dalmuir W Duns 89 L11
Dalnabreck Highld 93 S5
Dalnacardoch P & K 97 L9
Dalnahaitnach Highld 103 N12
Dalnaspidal P & K 96 J9
Dalnawillan Lodge Highld 112 B8
Dalness Highld 94 H8
Dalqueich P & K 90 G11
Dalquhairn S Ayrs 81 L13
Dalreavoch Highld 109 P3
Dalry N Ayrs 80 K3
Dalrymple E Ayrs 81 M10
Dalserf S Lans 82 E8
Dalsmeran Ag & B 79 L13
Dalston Cumb 67 N2
Dalston Gt Lon 21 P6
Dalswinton D & G 74 H8
Dalton Cumb 61 U4
Dalton D & G 75 M11
Dalton Lancs 55 L5
Dalton N York 63 U4
Dalton N York 69 P11
Dalton Nthumb 77 N11
Dalton Rothm 57 Q8
Dalton-in-Furness Cumb 61 N5
Dalton-le-Dale Dur 70 F3
Dalton Magna Rothm 57 Q8
Dalton-on-Tees N York 69 S11
Dalton Parva Rothm 57 Q8
Dalton Piercy Hartpl 70 G6
Dalveich Stirlg 95 S14
Dalwhinnie Highld 96 J7
Dalwood Devon 6 H4
Damask Green Herts 31 S7
Damerham Hants 8 G5
Damgate Norfk 51 R12
Dam Green Norfk 40 H3
Damnaglaur D & G 72 E12
Danaway Kent 12 G3
Danbury Essex 22 J6
Danby N York 71 M11
Danby Bottom N York 71 L12
Danby Wiske N York 70 D13
Dandaleith Moray 104 B6
Danderhall Mdloth 83 R5
Danebridge Ches E 56 E13
Dane End Herts 31 T8
Danegate E Susx 11 T4
Danehill E Susx 11 Q5
Dane Hills C Leic 47 Q13
Danemoor Green Norfk 50 J12
Danesford Shrops 35 R2
Danesmoor Derbys 57 P14
Dane Street Kent 13 L5
Daniel's Water Kent 12 J7
Danshillock Abers 105 L4
Danskine E Loth 84 F5
Danthorpe E R Yk 65 T13
Danzey Green Warwks 36 F7
Dapple Heath Staffs 46 D8
Darby Green Hants 20 D10
Darcy Lever Bolton 55 R5
Dardy Powys 27 N4
Darenth Kent 22 E13
Daresbury Halton 55 N10
Darfield Barns 57 P6
Darfoulds Notts 57 S11
Dargate Kent 13 L3
Dargavel Rens 88 K11
Darite Cnwll 4 H7
Darland Medway 12 E2
Darland Wrexhm 44 J2
Darlaston Wsall 36 C1
Darlaston Green Wsall 36 C1
Darley N York 63 Q8
Darley Abbey C Derb 47 L6
Darley Bridge Derbys 46 J1
Darley Dale Derbys 57 L14
Darley Green Solhll 36 G6
Darleyhall Herts 31 P8
Darley Head N York 63 P8
Darlingscott Warwks 36 H12
Darlington Darltn 69 S10
Darliston Shrops 45 N7
Darlton Notts 58 C12
Darnford Staffs 46 F12
Darnick Border 84 E12
Darowen Powys 43 R13
Darra Abers 105 L6
Darracott Devon 14 F9
Darracott Devon 15 L5
Darras Hall Nthumb 77 P11
Darrington Wakefd 57 Q3
Darsham Suffk 41 R7
Darshill Somset 17 R8
Dartford Kent 22 D13
Dartford Crossing Kent 22 E12
Dartington Devon 5 T8
Dartmeet Devon 5 R6
Dartmoor National Park Devon 5 R5
Dartmouth Devon 5 V10
Darton Barns 57 M4
Darvel E Ayrs 81 R5
Darwell Hole E Susx 12 C12
Darwen Bl w D 55 Q2
Datchet W & M 20 G7
Datchworth Herts 31 S9
Datchworth Green Herts 31 S9
Daubhill Bolton 55 R5
Daugh of Kinermony Moray 104 A7
Dauntsey Wilts 18 E4
Dava Highld 103 R8
Davenham Ches W 55 Q12
Davenport Stockp 56 D9
Davenport Green Ches E 55 T11
Davenport Green Traffd 55 T9
Daventry Nhants 37 Q8
Davidson's Mains C Edin 83 P3
Davidstow Cnwll 4 F3
David Street Kent 12 B3
Davington D & G 75 P5
Davington Hill Kent 12 K3
Daviot Abers 105 L10
Daviot Highld 102 K8
Daviot House Highld 102 K7
Davis's Town E Susx 11 S7
Davoch of Grange Moray 104 F5
Davyhulme Traffd 55 S7
Daw End Wsall 46 D13
Dawesgreen Surrey 21 M13
Dawley Wrekin 45 Q12
Dawlish Devon 6 C9
Dawlish Warren Devon 6 C9
Dawn Conwy 53 Q8
Daws Green Somset 16 G12
Daws Heath Essex 22 K10
Daw's House Cnwll 4 J4
Dawsmere Lincs 49 P7
Daybrook Notts 47 Q4
Day Green Ches E 45 S2
Dayhills Staffs 46 C7
Dayhouse Bank Worcs 36 C5
Daylesford Gloucs 29 P2
Ddol Flints 54 D12
Ddol-Cownwy Powys 44 B10
Deal Kent 13 S5
Dean Cumb 66 G7
Dean Devon 5 S8
Dean Devon 15 P3
Dean Devon 15 R3
Dean Dorset 8 D5
Dean Hants 9 N2
Dean Hants 9 R5
Dean Lancs 56 C1
Dean Oxon 29 R3
Dean Somset 17 S8
Dean Bottom Kent 21 U9
Deanburnhaugh Border 75 S3
Deancombe Devon 5 S8
Dean Court Oxon 29 U6
Deane Bolton 55 Q5
Deane Hants 19 R10
Dean End Dorset 8 D5
Dean Head Barns 57 L6
Deanhead Kirk 56 F3
Deanland Dorset 8 D5
Deanlane End W Susx 9 U6
Dean Prior Devon 5 S8
Deanraw Nthumb 76 G13
Dean Row Ches E 56 C10
Deans W Loth 82 K5
Deanscales Cumb 66 G7
Deanshanger Nhants 30 G5
Deanshaugh Moray 104 D5
Deanston Stirlg 89 R5
Dean Street Kent 12 D5
Dearham Cumb 66 G5
Dearnley Rochdl 56 D3
Debach Suffk 41 M10
Debden Essex 21 R3
Debden Essex 39 S14
Debden Green Essex 22 E1
Debenham Suffk 41 L8
Deblin's Green Worcs 35 T11
Dechmont W Loth 82 K4
Dechmont Road W Loth 82 K5
Deddington Oxon 29 U1
Dedham Essex 40 J14
Dedham Heath Essex 23 Q1
Dedworth W & M 20 F7
Deene Nhants 38 D2
Deenethorpe Nhants 38 E2
Deepcar Sheff 57 L7
Deepcut Surrey 20 F11
Deepdale Cumb 62 E3
Deepdale N York 62 H4
Deeping Gate C Pete 48 H12
Deeping St James Lincs 48 J12
Deeping St Nicholas Lincs 48 K10
Deerhurst Gloucs 28 G1
Deerhurst Walton Gloucs 28 G2
Deerton Street Kent 12 J3
Defford Worcs 36 B12
Defynnog Powys 26 G2
Deganwy Conwy 53 N7
Degnish Ag & B 87 P3
Deighton C York 64 E11
Deighton N York 70 E12
Deiniolen Gwynd 52 J10
Delabole Cnwll 4 D4
Delamere Ches W 55 N13
Delamere Park Ches W 55 N12
Delfrigs Abers 105 R11
Delley Devon 15 M8
Delliefure Highld 103 S9
Dell Quay W Susx 10 C10
Delly End Oxon 29 S5
Delnabo Moray 103 U12
Delny Highld 109 N10
Delph Oldham 56 E5
Delves Dur 69 P3
Delvin End Essex 40 C13
Dembleby Lincs 48 F6
Demelza Cnwll 3 P4
Denaby Donc 57 Q7
Denaby Main Donc 57 Q7
Denbies Surrey 20 K12
Denbigh Denbgs 54 C13
Denbrae Fife 91 N8
Denbury Devon 5 U7
Denby Derbys 47 L4
Denby Bottles Derbys 47 L4
Denby Dale Kirk 56 K5
Denchworth Oxon 29 S9
Dendron Cumb 61 N5
Denel End C Beds 31 M5
Denfield P & K 90 E8
Denford Nhants 38 E5
Dengie Essex 23 N7
Denham Bucks 20 H5
Denham Suffk 40 C8
Denham Suffk 41 L6
Denham End Suffk 40 C8
Denham Green Bucks 20 H5
Denham Green Suffk 41 L6
Denhead Abers 105 R5
Denhead Fife 91 Q9
Denhead of Gray C Dund 91 M5
Denholm Border 76 B2
Denholme C Brad 63 M13
Denholme Clough C Brad 63 M13
Denio Gwynd 42 G6
Denmead Hants 9 T6
Denmore C Aber 105 Q13
Denne Park W Susx 10 K5
Dennington Suffk 41 N7
Denny Falk 89 T9
Dennyloanhead Falk 89 T9
Den of Lindores Fife 91 L8
Denshaw Oldham 56 E4
Denside of Durris Abers 99 Q4
Densole Kent 13 P7
Denston Suffk 40 C10
Denstone Staffs 46 E5
Denstroude Kent 13 M3
Dent Cumb 62 E2
Denton Cambs 38 J3
Denton Darltn 69 R9
Denton E Susx 11 R10
Denton Kent 13 P6
Denton Kent 22 G13
Denton Lincs 48 C7
Denton N York 63 N10
Denton Nhants 38 B9
Denton Norfk 41 N3
Denton Oxon 30 C12
Denton Tamesd 56 D7
Denver Norfk 49 T13
Denwick Nthumb 77 Q3
Deopham Norfk 50 H13
Deopham Green Norfk 50 H14
Depden Suffk 40 C9
Depden Green Suffk 40 C9
Deptford Gt Lon 21 Q7
Deptford Wilts 18 F13
Derby C Derb 47 L6
Derby Devon 15 N6
Derbyhaven IoM 60 d9
Derculich P & K 97 P13
Dereham Norfk 50 G11
Deri Caerph 27 L7
Derril Devon 14 H12
Derringstone Kent 13 P6
Derrington Staffs 45 U9
Derriton Devon 14 H12
Derry Hill Wilts 18 E6
Derrythorpe N Linc 58 D5
Dersingham Norfk 49 U7
Dervaig Ag & B 93 L8
Derwen Denbgs 44 C3
Derwenlas Powys 43 P14
Derwent Valley Mills Derbys 46 K2
Derwent Water Cumb 67 L8
Derwydd Carmth 25 V7
Desborough Nhants 38 B4
Desford Leics 47 N13
Detchant Nthumb 85 R11
Detling Kent 12 E4
Deuxhill Shrops 35 Q3
Devauden Mons 27 T8
Devil's Bridge Cerdgn 33 P5
Devitts Green Warwks 36 J2
Devizes Wilts 18 F8
Devonport C Plym 5 M10
Devonside Clacks 90 D12
Devoran Cnwll 2 K9
Devoran & Perran Cnwll 2 K9
Dewarton Mdloth 83 S6
Dewlish Dorset 7 U5
Dewsbury Kirk 56 K2
Dewsbury Moor Kirk 56 K2
Deytheur Powys 44 F10
Dial N Som 17 P3
Dial Green W Susx 10 E5
Dial Post W Susx 10 K7
Dibberford Dorset 7 N4
Dibden Hants 9 N7
Dibden Purlieu Hants 9 N7
Dickens Heath Solhll 36 F5
Dickleburgh Norfk 41 L4
Didbrook Gloucs 29 L1
Didcot Oxon 19 R2
Diddington Cambs 38 J7
Diddlebury Shrops 35 M3
Didley Herefs 27 T1
Didling W Susx 10 C7
Didmarton Gloucs 28 F10
Didsbury Manch 55 T8
Didworthy Devon 5 R8
Digby Lincs 48 G3
Digg Highld 100 d3
Diggle Oldham 56 F5
Digmoor Lancs 55 L5
Digswell Herts 31 R9
Digswell Water Herts 31 S10
Dihewyd Cerdgn 32 J9
Dilham Norfk 51 P8
Dilhorne Staffs 46 C5
Dill Hall Lancs 62 F14
Dillington Cambs 38 H7
Dilston Nthumb 76 K13
Dilton Wilts 18 C11
Dilton Marsh Wilts 18 B11
Dilwyn Herefs 34 K10
Dimple Bolton 55 R3
Dimple Derbys 46 J1
Dinas Carmth 25 N4
Dinas Cnwll 3 N2
Dinas Gwynd 42 E6
Dinas Gwynd 52 G11
Dinas Rhondd 26 J9
Dinas Cross Pembks 24 H3
Dinas Dinlle Gwynd 52 F11
Dinas-Mawddwy Gwynd 43 S10
Dinas Powys V Glam 16 G2
Dinder Somset 17 Q8
Dinedor Herefs 35 M13
Dingestow Mons 27 T5
Dingle Lpool 54 J9
Dingleden Kent 12 F9
Dingley Nhants 37 U3
Dingwall Highld 102 F4
Dinmael Conwy 44 B5
Dinnet Abers 98 H4
Dinnington N u Ty 77 Q11
Dinnington Rothm 57 R9
Dinnington Somset 7 M2
Dinorwig Gwynd 52 J10
Dinorwig Slate Landscape Gwynd 52 J10
Dinton Bucks 30 G10
Dinton Wilts 8 E2
Dinwoodie D & G 75 M7
Dinworthy Devon 14 H9
Dipford Somset 16 H12
Dipley Hants 20 B11
Dippen Ag & B 79 Q8
Dippenhall Surrey 20 D13
Dippermill Devon 14 K11
Dippertown Devon 5 L4
Dippin N Ayrs 80 E8
Dipple Moray 104 C4
Dipple S Ayrs 80 J12
Diptford Devon 5 S9
Dipton Dur 69 Q2
Diptonmill Nthumb 76 J13
Dirleton E Loth 84 E2
Dirt Pot Nthumb 68 J3
Discoed Powys 34 G8
Diseworth Leics 47 N9
Dishforth N York 63 T5
Disley Ches E 56 E10
Diss Norfk 40 K4
Disserth Powys 34 B9
Distington Cumb 66 F8
Ditchampton Wilts 8 F2
Ditcheat Somset 17 R9
Ditchingham Norfk 41 P2
Ditchling E Susx 11 N7
Ditherington Shrops 45 M11
Ditteridge Wilts 18 B7
Dittisham Devon 5 V9
Ditton Kent 12 D4
Ditton Green Cambs 39 U9
Ditton Priors Shrops 35 P3
Dixton Gloucs 28 J1
Dixton Mons 27 U5
Dizzard Cnwll 14 E13
Dobcross Oldham 56 E5
Dobwalls Cnwll 4 G7
Doccombe Devon 5 T3
Dochgarroch Highld 102 H7
Dockenfield Surrey 10 C2
Docker Lancs 62 B5
Docking Norfk 50 C6
Docklow Herefs 35 N9
Dockray Cumb 67 L3
Dockray Cumb 67 N8
Dodbrooke Devon 5 S12
Doddinghurst Essex 22 E8
Doddington Cambs 39 P2
Doddington Kent 12 H4
Doddington Lincs 58 E12
Doddington Nthumb 85 P12
Doddington Shrops 35 P5
Doddiscombsleigh Devon 5 V3
Dodd's Green Ches E 45 P5
Doddshill Norfk 49 U7
Doddy Cross Cnwll 4 J8
Dodford Nhants 37 R8
Dodford Worcs 36 B6
Dodington S Glos 28 E11
Dodington Somset 16 G8
Dodleston Ches W 44 J1
Dodscott Devon 15 M9
Dodside E Rens 81 Q2
Dod's Leigh Staffs 46 D7
Dodworth Barns 57 M5
Dodworth Bottom Barns 57 M6
Dodworth Green Barns 57 M6
Doe Bank Birm 46 F14
Doe Lea Derbys 57 Q13
Dogdyke Lincs 48 K2
Dogley Lane Kirk 56 J4
Dogmersfield Hants 20 C12
Dogridge Wilts 29 L10
Dogsthorpe C Pete 48 J13
Dog Village Devon 6 C5
Dolanog Powys 44 C11
Dolau Powys 34 D7
Dolaucothi Carmth 33 N12
Dolbenmaen Gwynd 42 K5
Doley Staffs 45 R8
Dolfach Powys 43 T13
Dolfor Powys 34 D3
Dol-fôr Powys 43 R12
Dolgarrog Conwy 53 N9
Dolgellau Gwynd 43 P10
Dolgoch Gwynd 43 N13
Dol-gran Carmth 25 R4
Doll Highld 109 R4
Dollar Clacks 90 E12
Dollarfield Clacks 90 E12
Dolley Green Powys 34 G7
Dollwen Cerdgn 33 N4
Dolphin Flints 54 E12
Dolphinholme Lancs 61 U9
Dolphinton S Lans 83 M9
Dolton Devon 15 N10
Dolwen Conwy 53 Q8
Dolwyddelan Conwy 43 P3
Dolybont Cerdgn 33 M3
Dolyhir Powys 34 F9
Domgay Powys 44 G10
Donaldson's Lodge Nthumb 85 M10
Doncaster Donc 57 S6
Doncaster Carr Donc 57 S6
Doncaster North Services Donc 57 U4
Doncaster Sheffield Airport Donc 57 U7
Donhead St Andrew Wilts 8 C4
Donhead St Mary Wilts 8 C4
Donibristle Fife 90 J14
Doniford Somset 16 E8
Donington Lincs 48 K6
Donington on Bain Lincs 59 M10
Donington Park Services Leics 47 N8
Donington Southing Lincs 48 K7
Donisthorpe Leics 46 K11
Donkey Street Kent 13 M9
Donkey Town Surrey 20 F10
Donnington Gloucs 29 N2
Donnington Herefs 35 R14
Donnington Shrops 45 N12
Donnington W Berk 19 Q7
Donnington W Susx 10 D10
Donnington Wrekin 45 R11
Donnington Wood Wrekin 45 R11
Donyatt Somset 6 K2
Doomsday Green W Susx 10 K5
Doonfoot S Ayrs 81 L9
Dora's Green Hants 20 D13
Dorback Lodge Highld 103 S12
Dorchester Dorset 7 S6
Dorchester-on-Thames Oxon 19 S2
Dordon Warwks 46 J13
Dore Sheff 57 M10
Dores Highld 102 G9
Dorking Surrey 21 L13
Dorking Tye Suffk 40 F13
Dormansland Surrey 11 Q2
Dormans Park Surrey 11 P2
Dormington Herefs 35 N12
Dormston Worcs 36 C9
Dorn Gloucs 36 H14
Dorney Bucks 20 F7
Dorney Reach Bucks 20 F7
Dornie Highld 101 M6
Dornoch Highld 109 P7
Dornock D & G 75 P12
Dorrery Highld 112 C6
Dorridge Solhll 36 G6
Dorrington Lincs 48 G3
Dorrington Shrops 45 L13
Dorrington Shrops 45 R5
Dorsington Warwks 36 F11
Dorstone Herefs 34 H12
Dorton Bucks 30 E10
Dosthill Staffs 46 H14
Dothan IoA 52 E8
Dottery Dorset 7 N5
Doublebois Cnwll 4 F8
Doughton Gloucs 28 G9
Douglas IoM 60 f7
Douglas S Lans 82 F12
Douglas and Angus C Dund 91 P5
Douglas Pier Ag & B 88 E6
Douglastown Angus 91 P2
Douglas Water S Lans 82 G11
Douglas West S Lans 82 F12
Doulting Somset 17 R8
Dounby Ork 106 r17
Doune Highld 108 G4
Doune Stirlg 89 R5
Dounepark S Ayrs 80 H13
Dounie Highld 108 K6
Dousland Devon 5 N7
Dovaston Shrops 44 J9
Dove Dale Derbys 46 F3
Dove Green Notts 47 N3
Dove Holes Derbys 56 G11
Dovenby Cumb 66 G6
Dover Kent 13 R7
Dover Wigan 55 P6
Dover Castle Kent 13 R7
Dovercourt Essex 23 T1
Doverdale Worcs 35 U7
Doveridge Derbys 46 F7
Doversgreen Surrey 21 N13
Dowally P & K 90 F2
Dowbridge Lancs 61 S13
Dowdeswell Gloucs 28 K4
Dowlais Myr Td 26 K6
Dowland Devon 15 N10
Dowlish Ford Somset 7 L2
Dowlish Wake Somset 7 L2
Down Ampney Gloucs 29 L8
Downderry Cnwll 4 J10
Downe Gt Lon 21 R10
Downend Gloucs 28 F8
Downend IoW 9 Q11
Downend S Glos 28 C12
Downend W Berk 19 Q5
Downfield C Dund 91 N5
Downgate Cnwll 4 H6
Downgate Cnwll 4 K6
Downham Essex 22 H8
Downham Gt Lon 21 Q8
Downham Lancs 62 F11
Downham Market Norfk 49 T13
Down Hatherley Gloucs 28 G3
Downhead Somset 17 Q11
Downhead Somset 17 S7
Downhill Cnwll 3 M3
Downhill P & K 90 G6
Downholland Cross Lancs 54 J5
Downholme N York 69 P13
Downicarey Devon 4 K2
Downies Abers 99 S5
Downing Flints 54 E11
Downley Bucks 20 D3
Down St Mary Devon 15 R12
Downside Somset 17 R6
Downside Somset 17 R8
Downside Surrey 20 K11
Down Thomas Devon 5 N10
Downton Hants 8 K10
Downton Wilts 8 H4
Dowsby Lincs 48 H8
Dowsdale Lincs 49 L11
Doxey Staffs 45 U9
Doxford Nthumb 85 T14
Doynton S Glos 28 D13
Draethen Caerph 27 N10
Draffan S Lans 82 E9
Dragonby N Linc 58 F4
Dragons Green W Susx 10 J6
Drakeholes Notts 58 B8
Drakelow Worcs 35 T4
Drakemyre N Ayrs 80 K2
Drakes Broughton Worcs 36 B11
Drakewalls Cnwll 5 L6
Draughton N York 63 L9
Draughton Nhants 37 U5
Drax N York 57 U1
Drax Hales N York 57 U1
Draycote Warwks 37 M6
Draycot Foliat Swindn 18 J5
Draycott Derbys 47 M7
Draycott Gloucs 36 G13
Draycott Shrops 35 T2
Draycott Somset 17 N6
Draycott Somset 17 Q12
Draycott Worcs 35 U11
Draycott in the Clay Staffs 46 G8
Draycott in the Moors Staffs 46 C5
Drayford Devon 15 S10
Drayton C Port 9 T7
Drayton Leics 38 B2
Drayton Lincs 48 K6
Drayton Norfk 51 L11
Drayton Oxon 29 U9
Drayton Oxon 37 M12
Drayton Somset 17 M12
Drayton Somset 17 N13
Drayton Worcs 36 B5
Drayton Bassett Staffs 46 G13
Drayton Beauchamp Bucks 30 K10
Drayton Manor Park Staffs 46 G13
Drayton Parslow Bucks 30 H7
Drayton St Leonard Oxon 30 C13
Drebley N York 63 M8
Dreemskerry IoM 60 h4
Dreen Hill Pembks 24 F8
Drefach Carmth 25 Q3
Drefach Carmth 25 T8
Drefach Cerdgn 32 J11
Drefelin Carmth 25 Q3
Dreghorn N Ayrs 81 M5
Drellingore Kent 13 P7
Drem E Loth 84 E3
Dresden C Stke 46 B5
Drewsteignton Devon 5 S2
Driby Lincs 59 Q12
Driffield E R Yk 65 N8
Driffield Gloucs 29 L8
Driffield Cross Roads Gloucs 29 L8
Drift Cnwll 2 C11
Drigg Cumb 66 G13
Drighlington Leeds 63 Q14
Drimnin Highld 93 P8
Drimpton Dorset 7 M4
Drimsallie Highld 94 D3
Dringhouses C York 64 D10
Drinkstone Suffk 40 G8
Drinkstone Green Suffk 40 G8
Drive End Dorset 7 Q3
Driver's End Herts 31 R8
Drointon Staffs 46 D8
Droitwich Spa Worcs 35 U8
Dron P & K 90 H8
Dronfield Derbys 57 N11
Dronfield Woodhouse Derbys 57 M11
Drongan E Ayrs 81 N9
Dronley Angus 91 M4
Droop Dorset 7 U3
Dropping Well Rothm 57 N8
Droxford Hants 9 S5
Droylsden Tamesd 56 D7
Druid Denbgs 44 B5
Druidston Pembks 24 E7
Druimarbin Highld 94 F4
Druimavuic Ag & B 94 E9
Druimdrishaig Ag & B 87 N11
Druimindarroch Highld 93 R2
Drum Ag & B 87 S10
Drum P & K 90 F11
Drumalbin S Lans 82 H11
Drumbeg Highld 110 C10
Drumblade Abers 104 H7
Drumbreddon D & G 72 D11
Drumbuie Highld 100 g6
Drumburgh Cumb 75 Q14
Drumburn D & G 66 C2
Drumburn D & G 74 J13
Drumchapel C Glas 89 M11
Drumchastle P & K 95 T7
Drumclog S Lans 81 S5
Drumeldrie Fife 91 P11
Drumelzier Border 83 M12
Drumfearn Highld 100 f8
Drumfrennie Abers 99 N4
Drumgley Angus 98 G13
Drumguish Highld 97 M4
Drumin Moray 103 U9
Drumjohn D & G 81 Q13
Drumlamford S Ayrs 72 H4
Drumlasie Abers 99 L2
Drumleaning Cumb 67 L2
Drumlemble Ag & B 79 M12
Drumlithie Abers 99 P7
Drummoddie D & G 72 K10
Drummore D & G 72 E12
Drummuir Moray 104 D7
Drumnadrochit Highld 102 F9
Drumnagorrach Moray 104 G5
Drumoak Abers 99 P4
Drumpark D & G 74 G10
Drumrunie Highld 108 B3
Drumshang S Ayrs 80 K10
Drumuie Highld 100 d5
Drumuillie Highld 103 P11
Drumvaich Stirlg 89 Q5
Drunzie P & K 90 H10
Druridge Nthumb 77 R6
Drury Flints 54 G14
Drws-y-coed Gwynd 52 H12
Drybeck Cumb 68 E9
Drybridge Moray 104 E3
Drybridge N Ayrs 81 M5
Drybrook Gloucs 28 B4
Dryburgh Border 84 F12
Dry Doddington Lincs 48 C4
Dry Drayton Cambs 39 N8
Dryhill Kent 21 S12
Drymen Stirlg 89 L8
Drymuir Abers 105 Q6
Drynoch Highld 100 d6
Dry Sandford Oxon 29 U7
Dryslwyn Carmth 25 U6
Dry Street Essex 22 G10
Dryton Shrops 45 N12
Dubford Abers 105 M3
Dublin Suffk 41 L7
Duchally Highld 110 H13
Duck End Bed 31 N4
Duck End Cambs 38 K8
Duck End Essex 22 G2
Duck End Essex 39 U14
Duckend Green Essex 22 H3
Duckington Ches W 45 L3
Ducklington Oxon 29 S6
Duck's Cross Bed 38 H9
Duddenhoe End Essex 39 Q13
Duddingston C Edin 83 Q4
Duddington Nhants 48 E13
Duddlestone Somset 16 H12
Duddleswell E Susx 11 R5
Duddlewick Shrops 35 Q4
Duddo Nthumb 85 N10
Duddon Ches W 55 M14
Duddon Bridge Cumb 61 M2
Duddon Common Ches W 55 M13
Dudleston Shrops 44 H6
Dudleston Heath Shrops 44 J6
Dudley Dudley 36 B2
Dudley N Tyne 77 R11
Dudley Hill C Brad 63 P13
Dudley Port Sandw 36 C2
Dudnill Shrops 35 P6
Dudsbury Dorset 8 F9
Dudswell Herts 31 L11
Duffield Derbys 46 K5
Duffryn Neath 26 E8
Dufftown Moray 104 C7
Duffus Moray 103 U2
Dufton Cumb 68 E7
Duggleby N York 64 K6
Duirinish Highld 100 g6
Duisdalemore Highld 100 g8
Duisky Highld 94 E3
Dukestown Blae G 27 L5
Duke Street Suffk 40 J12
Dukinfield Tamesd 56 D7
Dulas IoA 52 G5
Dulcote Somset 17 Q8
Dulford Devon 6 E3
Dull P & K 90 B2
Dullatur N Lans 89 R10
Dullingham Cambs 39 T9
Dullingham Ley Cambs 39 T9
Dulnain Bridge Highld 103 Q11
Duloe Bed 38 J8
Duloe Cnwll 4 G9
Dulsie Bridge Highld 103 P7
Dulverton Somset 16 B11
Dulwich Gt Lon 21 P8
Dumbarton W Duns 88 K10
Dumbleton Gloucs 36 D13
Dumfries D & G 74 J10
Dumgoyne Stirlg 89 M9
Dummer Hants 19 S11
Dumpton Kent 13 S2
Dun Angus 99 M12
Dunalastair P & K 95 U7
Dunan Highld 100 e7
Dunan P & K 95 P7
Dunaverty Ag & B 79 M14
Dunball Somset 16 K8
Dunbar E Loth 84 H3
Dunbeath Highld 112 E11
Dunbeg Ag & B 94 B12
Dunblane Stirlg 89 S5
Dunbog Fife 91 L8
Dunbridge Hants 9 L3
Duncanston Highld 102 G4
Duncanstone Abers 104 H10
Dunchideock Devon 6 A7
Dunchurch Warwks 37 N6
Duncote Nhants 37 S10
Duncow D & G 74 J9
Duncrievie P & K 90 H10
Duncton W Susx 10 F7
Dundee C Dund 91 P5
Dundee Airport C Dund 91 N6
Dundon Somset 17 N10
Dundonald S Ayrs 81 M6
Dundonnell Highld 107 U7
Dundraw Cumb 66 K3
Dundreggan Highld 102 B13
Dundrennan D & G 73 S10
Dundry N Som 17 Q3
Dunecht Abers 99 P2
Dunfermline Fife 83 L1
Dunfield Gloucs 29 M8
Dunford Bridge Barns 56 J6
Dungate Kent 12 H4
Dungavel S Lans 81 T5
Dunge Wilts 18 C10
Dungeness Kent 13 L12
Dungworth Sheff 57 L9
Dunham Massey Traffd 55 R9
Dunham-on-the-Hill Ches W 55 L12
Dunham-on-Trent Notts 58 D12
Dunhampstead Worcs 36 B8
Dunhampton Worcs 35 T7
Dunham Town Traffd 55 R9
Dunham Woodhouses Traffd 55 R9
Dunholme Lincs 58 H11
Dunino Fife 91 R9
Dunipace Falk 89 T9
Dunkeld P & K 90 F3
Dunkerton BaNES 17 T5
Dunkeswell Devon 6 F3
Dunkeswick N York 63 S10
Dunkirk Ches W 54 J12
Dunkirk Kent 13 L4
Dunkirk S Glos 28 E10
Dunkirk Wilts 18 E8
Dunk's Green Kent 12 B5
Dunlappie Angus 98 K10
Dunley Hants 19 Q10
Dunley Worcs 35 S7
Dunlop E Ayrs 81 N3
Dunmaglass Highld 102 G11
Dunmere Cnwll 3 Q3
Dunmore Falk 90 C14
Dunnet Highld 112 F2
Dunnichen Angus 91 R2
Dunning P & K 90 F9
Dunnington C York 64 F9
Dunnington E R Yk 65 R9
Dunnington Warwks 36 E10
Dunnockshaw Lancs 62 G14
Dunn Street Kent 12 E3
Dunoon Ag & B 88 E10
Dunphail Moray 103 R6
Dunragit D & G 72 F8
Duns Border 84 K8
Dunsa Derbys 56 K12
Dunsby Lincs 48 H8
Dunscar Bolton 55 R4
Dunscore D & G 74 G9
Dunscroft Donc 57 T5
Dunsdale R & Cl 70 K9
Dunsden Green Oxon 20 B7
Dunsdon Devon 14 H11
Dunsfold Surrey 10 G3
Dunsford Devon 5 U3
Dunshalt Fife 90 K9
Dunshillock Abers 105 R6
Dunsill Notts 47 N1
Dunsley N York 71 Q10
Dunsley Staffs 35 U4
Dunsmore Bucks 30 J11
Dunsop Bridge Lancs 62 D10
Dunstable C Beds 31 M8
Dunstall Staffs 46 G9
Dunstall Common Worcs 35 U12
Dunstall Green Suffk 40 B8
Dunstan Nthumb 77 Q2
Dunstan Steads Nthumb 77 Q1
Dunster Somset 16 C8
Duns Tew Oxon 29 U2
Dunston Gatesd 77 Q13
Dunston Lincs 58 J14
Dunston Norfk 51 M13
Dunston Staffs 46 B10
Dunstone Devon 5 P10
Dunstone Devon 5 S5
Dunston Heath Staffs 46 B10
Dunsville Donc 57 T5
Dunswell E R Yk 65 P12
Dunsyre S Lans 83 L9
Dunterton Devon 4 K5
Dunthrop Oxon 29 S2
Duntisbourne Abbots Gloucs 28 J6
Duntisbourne Leer Gloucs 28 J6
Duntisbourne Rouse Gloucs 28 J6
Duntish Dorset 7 S3
Duntocher W Duns 89 L11
Dunton Bucks 30 H8
Dunton C Beds 31 R4
Dunton Norfk 50 E7
Dunton Bassett Leics 37 P2
Dunton Green Kent 21 T11
Dunton Wayletts Essex 22 G9
Duntulm Highld 100 d2
Dunure S Ayrs 80 K9
Dunvant Swans 25 U12
Dunvegan Highld 100 b5
Dunwich Suffk 41 S6
Dunwood Staffs 46 B2
Durdar Cumb 67 P2
Durgan Cnwll 2 K11
Durgates E Susx 12 B9
Durham Dur 69 S4
Durham Cathedral Dur 69 S4
Durham Services Dur 70 D5
Durham Tees Valley Airport S on T 70 E10
Durisdeer D & G 74 G5
Durisdeermill D & G 74 G5
Durkar Wakefd 57 M3
Durleigh Somset 16 J9
Durley Hants 9 Q5
Durley Wilts 18 K8
Durley Street Hants 9 Q5
Durlock Kent 13 Q4
Durlock Kent 13 R3
Durlow Common Herefs 35 P13
Durn Rochdl 56 D3
Durness Highld 110 J3
Durno Abers 105 L10
Duror Highld 94 D7
Durran Ag & B 87 T4
Durrington W Susx 10 J9
Durrington Wilts 18 J12
Dursley Gloucs 28 E8
Dursley Cross Gloucs 28 C3
Durston Somset 16 J11
Durweston Dorset 8 B7
Duston Nhants 37 T8
Duthil Highld 103 P11
Dutlas Powys 34 F5
Duton Hill Essex 22 F2
Dutson Cnwll 4 J3
Dutton Ches W 55 N11
Duxford Cambs 39 Q11
Duxford Oxon 29 S8
Duxford IWM Cambs 39 Q11
Dwygyfylchi Conwy 53 M7
Dwyran IoA 52 F9
Dyce C Aber 105 P13
Dyer's End Essex 40 B13
Dyfatty Carmth 25 S10
Dyffrydan Gwynd 43 N11
Dyffryn Brdgnd 26 F9
Dyffryn Myr Td 26 K7
Dyffryn V Glam 16 E2
Dyffryn Ardudwy Gwynd 43 L9
Dyffryn Castell Cerdgn 33 Q4
Dyffryn Cellwen Neath 26 F5
Dyke Lincs 48 H9
Dyke Moray 103 Q4
Dykehead Angus 98 C13
Dykehead Angus 98 F12
Dykehead N Lans 82 G7
Dykehead Stirlg 89 N6
Dykelands Abers 99 N10
Dykends Angus 98 D12
Dykeside Abers 105 L7
Dykes of Gray C Dund 91 M5
Dylife Powys 33 S2
Dymchurch Kent 13 M10
Dymock Gloucs 28 D1
Dyrham S Glos 28 D12
Dysart Fife 91 M13
Dyserth Denbgs 54 C11

E

Eachway Worcs 36 C5
Eachwick Nthumb 77 N11
Eagland Hill Lancs 61 S10
Eagle Lincs 58 E13
Eagle Barnsdale Lincs 58 E13
Eagle Moor Lincs 58 E13
Eaglescliffe S on T 70 F9
Eaglesfield Cumb 66 G7
Eaglesfield D & G 75 P11
Eaglesham E Rens 81 R2
Eagley Bolton 55 R4
Eairy IoM 60 d7
Eakring Notts 47 S1
Ealand N Linc 58 C4
Ealing Gt Lon 21 L6
Eals Nthumb 68 E1
Eamont Bridge Cumb 67 R7
Earby Lancs 62 J10
Earcroft Bl w D 55 Q2
Eardington Shrops 35 R2
Eardisland Herefs 34 K9
Eardisley Herefs 34 H11
Eardiston Shrops 44 J8
Eardiston Worcs 35 Q7
Earith Cambs 39 N5
Earle Nthumb 85 P13
Earlestown St Hel 55 N7
Earley Wokham 20 B8
Earlham Norfk 51 L12
Earlish Highld 100 c3
Earls Barton Nhants 38 C8
Earls Colne Essex 23 L2
Earls Common Worcs 36 C9
Earl's Croome Worcs 35 U12
Earlsditton Shrops 35 P5
Earlsdon Covtry 36 K5
Earl's Down E Susx 11 U7
Earlsferry Fife 91 Q11
Earlsfield Gt Lon 21 N8
Earlsford Abers 105 N9
Earl's Green Suffk 40 H7
Earlsheaton Kirk 57 L2
Earl Shilton Leics 47 N14
Earl Soham Suffk 41 M8
Earl Sterndale Derbys 56 G13
Earlston Border 84 F11
Earlston E Ayrs 81 N5
Earl Stonham Suffk 40 K9
Earlswood Surrey 21 N13
Earlswood Warwks 36 F6
Earlswood Common Mons 27 T9
Earnley W Susx 10 C11
Earnshaw Bridge Lancs 55 M2
Earsdon N Tyne 77 S11
Earsdon Nthumb 77 P7
Earsham Norfk 41 P3
Earswick C York 64 E8
Eartham W Susx 10 E9
Earthcott S Glos 28 C10
Easby N York 70 J11
Easdale Ag & B 87 N2
Easebourne W Susx 10 D6
Easenhall Warwks 37 N5
Eashing Surrey 10 E2
Easington Bucks 30 E10
Easington Dur 70 F4
Easington E R Yk 59 Q3
Easington Nthumb 85 S12
Easington Oxon 30 E13
Easington R & Cl 71 M9
Easington Colliery Dur 70 F4
Easington Lane Sundld 70 E3
Easingwold N York 64 C6
Easole Street Kent 13 Q5
Eassie and Nevay Angus 91 M3
East Aberthaw V Glam 16 D3
East Allington Devon 5 T11
East Anstey Devon 15 U7
East Anton Hants 19 N11
East Appleton N York 69 R13
East Ardsley Leeds 57 M1
East Ashey IoW 9 R11
East Ashling W Susx 10 C9
East Aston Hants 19 P11
East Ayton N York 65 M2
East Balsdon Cnwll 14 G13
East Bank Blae G 27 N6
East Barkwith Lincs 59 L10
East Barming Kent 12 D5
East Barnby N York 71 P10
East Barnet Gt Lon 21 N3
East Barns E Loth 84 J3
East Barsham Norfk 50 F7
East Beckham Norfk 51 L6
East Bedfont Gt Lon 20 J8
East Bergholt Suffk 40 J14
East Bierley Kirk 63 P14
East Bilney Norfk 50 G10
East Blatchington E Susx 11 R10
East Bloxworth Dorset 8 B10
East Boldon S Tyne 77 T13
East Boldre Hants 9 M8
East Bolton Nthumb 77 N2
Eastbourne Darltn 70 D10
Eastbourne E Susx 11 U11
East Bower Somset 16 K9
East Bradenham Norfk 50 F12
East Brent Somset 16 K6
Eastbridge Suffk 41 S7
East Bridgford Notts 47 S5
East Briscoe Dur 69 L9
Eastbrook V Glam 16 G2
East Buckland Devon 15 Q6
East Budleigh Devon 6 E8
Eastburn C Brad 63 L11
Eastburn E R Yk 65 M8
East Burnham Bucks 20 G6
East Burton Dorset 8 A11
Eastbury W Berk 19 M5
East Butsfield Dur 69 P3
East Butterwick N Linc 58 D5
Eastby N York 63 L9
East Calder W Loth 83 L5
East Carleton Norfk 51 L13
East Carlton Leeds 63 Q11
East Carlton Nhants 38 B3
East Chaldon Dorset 7 U8
East Challow Oxon 29 S10
East Charleton Devon 5 T12
East Chelborough Dorset 7 Q3
East Chiltington E Susx 11 P7
East Chinnock Somset 7 N2
East Chisenbury Wilts 18 H10
East Cholderton Hants 19 L11
Eastchurch Kent 23 N13
East Clandon Surrey 20 J12
East Claydon Bucks 30 F7
East Clevedon N Som 17 M2
East Coker Somset 7 P2
Eastcombe Gloucs 28 G7
Eastcombe Somset 16 G10
East Compton Somset 17 R8
East Cornworthy Devon 5 U9
East Cote Cumb 66 H1
Eastcote Gt Lon 20 K5
Eastcote Nhants 37 S10
Eastcote Solhll 36 G5
Eastcott Cnwll 14 G9
Eastcott Wilts 18 F9
East Cottingwith E R Yk 64 G11
Eastcourt Wilts 18 K8
Eastcourt Wilts 28 J9
East Cowes IoW 9 Q9
East Cowick E R Yk 57 U2
East Cowton N York 70 D12
East Cramlington Nthumb 77 R10
East Cranmore Somset 17 S8
East Creech Dorset 8 C12
East Curthwaite Cumb 67 M3
East Dean E Susx 11 T11
East Dean Gloucs 28 C3
East Dean Hants 8 K3
East Dean W Susx 10 E8
Eastdown Devon 5 U11
East Down Devon 15 P4
East Drayton Notts 58 C11
East Dulwich Gt Lon 21 P7
East Dundry N Som 17 Q3
East Ella C KuH 65 P14
East End Bed 38 H9
East End C Beds 31 L4
East End E R Yk 59 N1
East End E R Yk 65 R13
East End Essex 22 B5
Eastend Essex 23 M9
East End Hants 9 M9
East End Hants 19 P8
East End Herts 22 C2
East End Kent 12 F8
East End Kent 23 N13
East End M Keyn 30 K4
East End Oxon 29 S4
East End Somset 17 S7
East End Suffk 40 K13
Easter Balmoral Abers 98 D5
Easter Compton S Glos 27 V11
Easter Dalziel Highld 103 L5
Eastergate W Susx 10 E9
Easterhouse C Glas 82 C5
Easter Howgate Mdloth 83 P6
Easter Kinkell Highld 102 G4
Easter Moniack Highld 102 G7
Eastern Green Covtry 36 J5
Easter Ord Abers 99 Q3
Easter Pitkierie Fife 91 S10
Easter Skeld Shet 106 t9
Easter Softlaw Border 84 K12
Easterton Wilts 18 F10
Eastertown Somset 16 K6
East Everleigh Wilts 18 K10
East Farleigh Kent 12 D5
East Farndon Nhants 37 T4
East Ferry Lincs 58 D7
Eastfield N Lans 82 G6
Eastfield N York 65 N3
East Firsby Lincs 58 H9
East Fortune E Loth 84 E3
East Garforth Leeds 63 U13
East Garston W Berk 19 N5
Eastgate Dur 69 L5
Eastgate Lincs 48 H10
Eastgate Norfk 50 K9
East Ginge Oxon 29 T10
East Goscote Leics 47 R11
East Grafton Wilts 19 L8
East Green Suffk 41 R7
East Grimstead Wilts 8 J3
East Grinstead W Susx 11 P3
East Guldeford E Susx 12 H11
East Haddon Nhants 37 S7
East Hagbourne Oxon 19 R3
East Halton N Linc 58 K3
East Ham Gt Lon 21 R6
Eastham Wirral 54 J10
Eastham Ferry Wirral 54 J10
Easthampton Herefs 34 K8
East Hanney Oxon 29 T9
East Hanningfield Essex 22 J7
East Hardwick Wakefd 57 Q3
East Harling Norfk 40 G3
East Harlsey N York 70 F13
East Harnham Wilts 8 G3
East Harptree BaNES 17 Q5
East Hartford Nthumb 77 R10
East Harting W Susx 10 B7
East Hatch Wilts 8 C3
East Hatley Cambs 39 L10
East Hauxwell N York 69 Q14
East Haven Angus 91 S4
Eastheath Wokham 20 C9
East Heckington Lincs 48 J5
East Hedleyhope Dur 69 Q4
East Helmsdale Highld 112 B13
East Hendred Oxon 29 U10
East Heslerton N York 65 L4
East Hewish N Som 17 L4
East Hoathly E Susx 11 S7
East Holme Dorset 8 B11
East Hope Dur 69 M11
Easthope Shrops 35 N1
Easthorpe Essex 23 M3
Easthorpe Notts 47 T3
East Horrington Somset 17 Q7
East Horsley Surrey 20 J12
East Horton Nthumb 85 Q12
East Howe BCP 8 F9
East Huntspill Somset 16 K7

130 East Hyde – Frampton-on-Severn

East Hyde C Beds 31 P9
East Ilkerton Devon 15 R3
East Ilsley W Berk 19 Q4
Eastington Devon 15 R11
Eastington Gloucs 28 E6
Eastington Gloucs 29 M5
East Keal Lincs 59 Q14
East Kennett Wilts 18 H7
East Keswick Leeds 63 T11
East Kilbride S Lans 81 S2
East Kimber Devon 15 L13
East Kirkby Lincs 49 M1
East Knighton Dorset 7 V7
East Knowstone Devon 15 T8
East Knoyle Wilts 8 B2
East Lambrook Somset 17 M13
Eastlands D & G 74 F11
East Langdon Kent 13 R6
East Langton Leics 37 T2
East Lavant W Susx 10 D9
East Lavington W Susx 10 E7
East Layton N York 69 Q11
Eastleach Martin Gloucs 29 P7
Eastleach Turville Gloucs 29 N6
East Leake Notts 47 Q8
East Learmouth Nthumb 85 M11
East Leigh Devon 5 R10
East Leigh Devon 5 T9
Eastleigh Devon 15 L7
East Leigh Devon 15 Q11
Eastleigh Hants 9 P5
East Lexham Norfk 50 E10
Eastling Kent 12 J4
East Linton E Loth 84 F3
East Liss Hants 10 B5
East Lockinge Oxon 29 T10
East Lound N Linc 58 C7
East Lulworth Dorset 8 B12
East Lutton N York 65 L6
East Lydeard Somset 16 G11
East Lydford Somset 17 Q10
East Malling Kent 12 D4
East Malling Heath Kent 12 C4
East Marden W Susx 10 C8
East Markham Notts 58 B12
East Martin Hants 8 F5
East Marton N York 62 J9
East Meon Hants 9 T4
East Mere Devon 16 C13
East Mersea Essex 23 P5
East Midlands Airport Leics 47 N8
East Molesey Surrey 20 K9
Eastmoor Norfk 50 B13
East Morden Dorset 8 C10
East Morton C Brad 63 M11
East Morton D & G 74 G5
East Ness N York 64 F4
East Newton E R Yk 65 T12
Eastney C Port 9 T9
Eastnor Herefs 35 R13
East Norton Leics 47 U13
Eastoft N Linc 58 D3
East Ogwell Devon 5 U6
Easton Cambs 38 H6
Easton Cumb 75 Q14
Easton Devon 5 S3
Easton Dorset 7 S10
Easton Hants 9 Q2
Easton Lincs 48 D8
Easton Norfk 50 K11
Easton Somset 17 P7
Easton Suffk 41 N9
Easton W Berk 19 P6
Easton Wilts 18 C6
Easton Grey Wilts 28 G10
Easton-in-Gordano N Som 27 U12
Easton Maudit Nhants 38 C9
Easton-on-the-Hill Nhants 48 F13
Easton Royal Wilts 18 K8
East Orchard Dorset 8 A5
East Ord Nthumb 85 P8
East Panson Devon 4 K2
East Parley BCP 8 F9
East Peckham Kent 12 C6
East Pennard Somset 17 Q9
East Portlemouth Devon 5 T13
East Prawle Devon 5 T13
East Preston W Susx 10 H10
East Pulham Dorset 7 T3
East Putford Devon 14 J9
East Quantoxhead Somset 16 F8
East Rainham Medway 12 F2
East Rainton Sundld 70 D3
East Ravendale NE Lin 59 M7
East Raynham Norfk 50 E8
Eastrea Cambs 39 L1
Eastriggs D & G 75 P12
East Rigton Leeds 63 T11
Eastrington E R Yk 64 H14
East Rolstone N Som 17 L4
Eastrop Swindn 29 P9
East Rounton N York 70 F12
East Rudham Norfk 50 D8
East Runton Norfk 51 L5
East Ruston Norfk 51 P8
Eastry Kent 13 R5
East Saltoun E Loth 84 D5
Eastshaw W Susx 10 D6
East Sheen Gt Lon 21 M8
East Shefford W Berk 19 N6
East Sleekburn Nthumb 77 R9
East Somerton Norfk 51 S10
East Stockwith Lincs 58 C8
East Stoke Dorset 8 B11
East Stoke Notts 47 U4
East Stour Dorset 17 V12
East Stour Common Dorset 17 V12
East Stourmouth Kent 13 Q3
East Stowford Devon 15 P7
East Stratton Hants 19 R12
East Studdal Kent 13 R6
East Sutton Kent 12 F6
East Taphouse Cnwll 4 F8
East-the-Water Devon 15 L7
East Thirston Nthumb 77 P5
East Tilbury Thurr 22 G12
East Tilbury Village Thurr 22 G12
East Tisted Hants 9 U2
East Torrington Lincs 58 K10
East Tuddenham Norfk 50 J11
East Tytherley Hants 8 K3
East Tytherton Wilts 18 E6
East Village Devon 15 T11
Eastville Bristl 28 B13
Eastville Lincs 49 P2
East Wall Shrops 35 M2
East Walton Norfk 50 B10
East Water Somset 17 P6
East Week Devon 5 R2
Eastwell Leics 47 U8
East Wellow Hants 9 L4
East Wemyss Fife 91 M12
East Whitburn W Loth 82 J5
Eastwick Herts 22 B5
East Wickham Gt Lon 21 S7
East Williamston Pembks 24 J10
East Winch Norfk 49 U10
East Winterslow Wilts 8 J2
East Wittering W Susx 10 B11
East Witton N York 63 N2
Eastwood Notts 47 N4
Eastwood Sthend 22 K10
East Woodburn Nthumb 76 J8
Eastwood End Cambs 39 P2
East Woodhay Hants 19 P8
East Woodlands Somset 17 U8
East Worldham Hants 10 B3
East Worthing W Susx 10 K10
East Wretham Norfk 40 F2
East Youlstone Devon 14 G9
Eathorpe Warwks 37 L7
Eaton Ches E 56 C13
Eaton Ches W 55 N14
Eaton Leics 47 U8
Eaton Norfk 51 M12
Eaton Notts 58 B11
Eaton Oxon 29 T7
Eaton Shrops 34 J3
Eaton Shrops 35 M3
Eaton Bishop Herefs 34 K13
Eaton Bray C Beds 31 L8
Eaton Constantine Shrops 45 N12
Eaton Ford Cambs 38 J9
Eaton Green C Beds 31 L8
Eaton Hastings Oxon 29 Q8
Eaton Mascott Shrops 45 M12
Eaton Socon Cambs 38 J9
Eaton upon Tern Shrops 45 Q9
Eaves Brow Warrtn 55 P8
Eaves Green Solhll 36 J4
Ebberston N York 64 K3
Ebbesborne Wake Wilts 8 D4
Ebbw Vale Blae G 27 M6
Ebchester Dur 69 P1
Ebdon N Som 17 L4
Ebernoe W Susx 10 F5
Ebford Devon 6 C7
Ebley Gloucs 28 F6
Ebnal Ches W 45 L4
Ebnall Herefs 35 L9
Ebrington Gloucs 36 G12
Ebsworthy Devon 5 N2
Ecchinswell Hants 19 Q9
Ecclaw Border 84 K5
Ecclefechan D & G 75 N11
Eccles Border 84 K10
Eccles Kent 12 D3
Eccles Salfd 55 S7
Ecclesall Sheff 57 M10
Ecclesfield Sheff 57 N8
Eccles Green Herefs 34 J11
Eccleshall Staffs 45 T8
Eccleshill C Brad 63 P12
Ecclesmachan W Loth 83 L4
Eccles on Sea Norfk 51 R8
Eccles Road Norfk 40 H3
Eccleston Ches W 44 K1
Eccleston Lancs 55 M3
Eccleston St Hel 55 L7
Eccleston Green Lancs 55 M3
Echt Abers 99 N2
Eckford Border 84 J13
Eckington Derbys 57 P11
Eckington Worcs 36 B12
Ecton Nhants 38 B8
Ecton Staffs 46 E2
Edale Derbys 56 H9
Eday Ork 106 u16
Eday Airport Ork 106 u16
Edburton W Susx 11 L8
Edderside Cumb 66 H3
Edderton Highld 109 N8
Eddington Cambs 39 P9
Eddington Kent 13 N2
Eddleston Border 83 P9
Eddlewood S Lans 82 D8
Edenbridge Kent 21 R13
Edenfield Lancs 55 T3
Edenhall Cumb 67 S6
Edenham Lincs 48 G9
Eden Mount Cumb 61 S4
Eden Park Gt Lon 21 Q9
Eden Project Cnwll 3 Q6
Edensor Derbys 56 K13
Edentaggart Ag & B 88 H7
Edenthorpe Donc 57 T5
Edern Gwynd 42 E6
Edgarley Somset 17 P9
Edgbaston Birm 36 E4
Edgcott Bucks 30 E8
Edgcott Somset 15 T5
Edgcumbe Cnwll 2 J10
Edge Gloucs 28 F6
Edge Shrops 44 J12
Edgebolton Shrops 45 N9
Edge End Gloucs 28 A5
Edgefield Norfk 50 J7
Edgefield Green Norfk 50 J7
Edgefold Bolton 55 R5
Edge Green Ches W 45 L3
Edgehill Warwks 37 L11
Edgerley Shrops 44 J10
Edgerton Kirk 56 H3
Edgeside Lancs 55 T2
Edgeworth Gloucs 28 H6
Edgeworthy Devon 15 T10
Edginswell Torbay 6 A11
Edgiock Worcs 36 D8
Edgmond Wrekin 45 R10
Edgmond Marsh Wrekin 45 R9
Edgton Shrops 34 J3
Edgware Gt Lon 21 L4
Edgworth Bl w D 55 R3
Edinbane Highld 100 c4
Edinburgh C Edin 83 Q4
Edinburgh Airport C Edin 83 M4
Edinburgh Castle C Edin 83 Q4
Edinburgh Old & New Town C Edin 83 Q4
Edinburgh Royal Botanic Gardens C Edin 83 P3
Edinburgh Zoo RZSS C Edin 83 P4
Edingale Staffs 46 H11
Edingham D & G 74 F13
Edingley Notts 47 S2
Edingthorpe Norfk 51 P7
Edingthorpe Green Norfk 51 P7
Edington Border 85 M7
Edington Nthumb 77 P9
Edington Somset 17 L9
Edington Wilts 18 D10
Edingworth Somset 17 L6
Edistone Devon 14 G8
Edithmead Somset 16 K7
Edith Weston Rutlnd 48 D12
Edlesborough Bucks 31 L9
Edlingham Nthumb 77 N4
Edlington Lincs 59 M12
Edmond Castle Cumb 75 U14
Edmondsham Dorset 8 F6
Edmondsley Dur 69 R3
Edmondstown Rhondd 26 J9
Edmondthorpe Leics 48 C10
Edmonton Cnwll 3 P2
Edmonton Gt Lon 21 P4
Edmundbyers Dur 69 M2
Ednam Border 84 J11
Ednaston Derbys 46 H5
Edney Common Essex 22 G7
Edradynate P & K 97 P13
Edrom Border 85 L7
Edstaston Shrops 45 M7
Edstone Warwks 36 G8
Edvin Loach Herefs 35 Q9
Edwalton Notts 47 Q6
Edwardstone Suffk 40 F12
Edwardsville Myr Td 26 K8
Edwinsford Carmth 33 M14
Edwinstowe Notts 57 T13
Edworth C Beds 31 R4
Edwyn Ralph Herefs 35 P9
Edzell Angus 99 L10
Edzell Woods Abers 99 L10
Efail-fach Neath 26 D8
Efail Isaf Rhondd 26 K11
Efailnewydd Gwynd 42 G6
Efail-Rhyd Powys 44 E8
Efailwen Carmth 24 K5
Efenechtyd Denbgs 44 D2
Effgill D & G 75 R7
Effingham Surrey 20 K12
Effingham Junction Surrey 20 K11
Efflinch Staffs 46 G10
Efford Devon 15 U12
Egbury Hants 19 P10
Egdean W Susx 10 F6
Egerton Bolton 55 R4
Egerton Kent 12 H6
Egerton Forstal Kent 12 G6
Eggborough N York 57 S2
Eggbuckland C Plym 5 N9
Eggesford Devon 15 Q10
Eggington C Beds 31 L7
Egginton Derbys 46 J8
Egglescliffe S on T 70 F10
Eggleston Dur 69 L8
Egham Surrey 20 H8
Egham Wick Surrey 20 G8
Egleton Rutlnd 48 C12
Eglingham Nthumb 77 N2
Egloshayle Cnwll 3 Q2
Egloskerry Cnwll 4 H3
Eglwysbach Conwy 53 P8
Eglwys-Brewis V Glam 16 D3
Eglwys Cross Wrexhm 45 L5
Eglwys Fach Cerdgn 33 N1
Eglwyswrw Pembks 24 K3
Egmanton Notts 58 B13
Egremont Cumb 66 F10
Egremont Wirral 54 H8
Egton N York 71 P11
Egton Bridge N York 71 P12
Egypt Bucks 20 G5
Egypt Hants 19 Q12
Eigg Highld 93 M1
Eight Ash Green Essex 23 M2
Eilanreach Highld 100 h8
Eilean Donan Castle Highld 101 M6
Eisgein W Isls 106 i7
Eishken W Isls 106 i7
Eisteddfa Gurig Cerdgn 33 Q4
Elan Valley Powys 33 S7
Elan Village Powys 33 T8
Elberton S Glos 28 B10
Elbridge W Susx 10 E10
Elburton C Plym 5 N10
Elcombe Swindn 18 H4
Elcot W Berk 19 N7
Eldernell Cambs 49 M14
Eldersfield Worcs 28 E1
Elderslie Rens 88 K13
Elder Street Essex 39 S14
Eldon Dur 69 R7
Eldwick C Brad 63 N11
Elerch Cerdgn 33 N3
Elfhill Abers 99 Q6
Elford Nthumb 85 T12
Elford Staffs 46 G11
Elgin Moray 103 V3
Elgol Highld 100 e8
Elham Kent 13 N7
Elie Fife 91 Q11
Elilaw Nthumb 76 K4
Elim IoA 52 E6
Eling Hants 9 M6
Elkesley Notts 57 U11
Elkstone Gloucs 28 J5
Ella Abers 104 J4
Ellacombe Torbay 6 B12
Elland Calder 56 H2
Elland Lower Edge Calder 56 H2
Ellary Ag & B 87 N10
Ellastone Staffs 46 F5
Ellel Lancs 61 T8
Ellemford Border 84 J6
Ellenabeich Ag & B 87 N2
Ellenborough Cumb 66 F5
Ellenbrook Salfd 55 R6
Ellenhall Staffs 45 T8
Ellen's Green Surrey 10 H3
Ellerbeck N York 70 F13
Ellerby N York 71 N10
Ellerdine Heath Wrekin 45 P9
Ellerhayes Devon 6 C4
Elleric Ag & B 94 E9
Ellerker E R Yk 65 L14
Ellers N York 63 L11
Ellerton E R Yk 64 G12
Ellerton N York 69 S13
Ellerton Shrops 45 R8
Ellesborough Bucks 30 H11
Ellesmere Shrops 44 J7
Ellesmere Port Ches W 54 K11
Ellingham Hants 8 G7
Ellingham Norfk 41 Q2
Ellingham Nthumb 85 T13
Ellingstring N York 63 P3
Ellington Cambs 38 J6
Ellington Nthumb 77 R7
Ellington Thorpe Cambs 38 J6
Elliots Green Somset 17 U7
Ellisfield Hants 19 T11
Ellishader Highld 100 e3
Ellistown Leics 47 M11
Ellon Abers 105 R9
Ellonby Cumb 67 P5
Ellough Suffk 41 R3
Elloughton E R Yk 65 L14
Ellwood Gloucs 28 A6
Elm Cambs 49 Q12
Elmbridge Worcs 36 B7
Elmdon Essex 39 Q13
Elmdon Solhll 36 G4
Elmdon Heath Solhll 36 G4
Elmer W Susx 10 F10
Elmers End Gt Lon 21 Q9
Elmer's Green Lancs 55 M5
Elmesthorpe Leics 37 N1
Elm Green Essex 22 J6
Elmhurst Staffs 46 F11
Elmley Castle Worcs 36 C12
Elmley Lovett Worcs 35 U7
Elmore Gloucs 28 E4
Elmore Back Gloucs 28 E4
Elm Park Gt Lon 22 D10
Elmscott Devon 14 F8
Elmsett Suffk 40 J11
Elms Green Worcs 35 R7
Elmstead Heath Essex 23 Q3
Elmstead Market Essex 23 Q3
Elmstead Row Essex 23 Q3
Elmsted Kent 13 M7
Elmstone Kent 13 Q3
Elmstone Hardwicke Gloucs 28 H2
Elmswell E R Yk 65 M8
Elmswell Suffk 40 G8
Elmton Derbys 57 R12
Elphin Highld 108 C2
Elphinstone E Loth 83 S4
Elrick Abers 99 Q2
Elrig D & G 72 J10
Elrington Nthumb 76 H13
Elsdon Nthumb 76 J7
Elsecar Barns 57 N7
Elsenham Essex 22 D2
Elsfield Oxon 30 B10
Elsham N Linc 58 H4
Elsing Norfk 50 J10
Elslack N York 62 J10
Elson Hants 9 S8
Elson Shrops 44 J6
Elsrickle S Lans 83 L10
Elstead Surrey 10 E2
Elsted W Susx 10 C7
Elsted Marsh W Susx 10 C6
Elsthorpe Lincs 48 G9
Elstob Dur 70 D8
Elston Lancs 62 B13
Elston Notts 47 U4
Elston Wilts 18 G12
Elstone Devon 15 Q9
Elstow Bed 38 G11
Elstree Herts 21 L3
Elstronwick E R Yk 65 S13
Elswick Lancs 61 S12
Elswick N u Ty 77 Q13
Elsworth Cambs 39 M8
Elterwater Cumb 67 M12
Eltham Gt Lon 21 R8
Eltisley Cambs 39 L9
Elton Bury 55 S4
Elton Cambs 38 G2
Elton Ches W 55 L11
Elton Derbys 46 H1
Elton Gloucs 28 D5
Elton Herefs 35 L6
Elton S on T 70 F9
Elton Green Ches W 55 L12
Elton-on-the-Hill Notts 47 U6
Eltringham Nthumb 77 M13
Elvanfoot S Lans 74 J2
Elvaston Derbys 47 M7
Elveden Suffk 40 D4
Elvetham Heath Hants 20 D11
Elvingston E Loth 84 D4
Elvington C York 64 G10
Elvington Kent 13 Q5
Elwell Devon 15 Q6
Elwick Hartpl 70 G6
Elwick Nthumb 85 S11
Elworth Ches E 45 R1
Elworthy Somset 16 E10
Ely Cambs 39 R4
Ely Cardif 27 L12
Emberton M Keyn 38 C11
Embleton Cumb 66 J6
Embleton Dur 70 F7
Embleton Nthumb 85 U14
Embo Highld 109 Q6
Emborough Somset 17 R6
Embo Street Highld 109 Q6
Embsay N York 63 L9
Emery Down Hants 8 K7
Emley Kirk 56 K4
Emley Moor Kirk 56 K4
Emmbrook Wokham 20 C9
Emmer Green Readg 20 B7
Emmett Carr Derbys 57 Q11
Emmington Oxon 30 F12
Emneth Norfk 49 Q12
Emneth Hungate Norfk 49 R12
Empingham Rutlnd 48 D12
Empshott Hants 10 B4
Empshott Green Hants 9 U2
Emsworth Hants 10 B9
Enborne W Berk 19 P7
Enborne Row W Berk 19 P8
Enchmarsh Shrops 35 M1
Enderby Leics 47 P14
Endmoor Cumb 61 U3
Endon Staffs 46 B3
Endon Bank Staffs 46 B3
Enfield Gt Lon 21 Q3
Enfield Lock Gt Lon 21 Q3
Enfield Wash Gt Lon 21 Q3
Enford Wilts 18 H10
Engine Common S Glos 28 C11
England's Gate Herefs 35 M10
Englefield W Berk 19 T6
Englefield Green Surrey 20 G8
Engleseabrook Ches E 45 S3
English Bicknor Gloucs 28 A4
Englishcombe BaNES 17 T4
English Frankton Shrops 45 L8
Engollan Cnwll 3 M2
Enham Alamein Hants 19 N11
Enmore Somset 16 H9
Enmore Green Dorset 8 B4
Ennerdale Bridge Cumb 66 G9
Enniscaven Cnwll 3 P5
Enochdhu P & K 97 T11
Ensay Ag & B 92 K9
Ensbury BCP 8 F9
Ensdon Shrops 44 K10
Ensis Devon 15 N7
Enson Staffs 46 B8
Enstone Oxon 29 S3
Enterkinfoot D & G 74 G5
Enterpen N York 70 G11
Enville Staffs 35 T3
Eochar W Isls 106 c14
Eòlaigearraidh W Isls 106 c18
Eoligarry W Isls 106 c18
Epney Gloucs 28 E5
Epperstone Notts 47 S4
Epping Essex 22 C7
Epping Green Essex 22 B6
Epping Green Herts 31 S11
Epping Upland Essex 22 B7
Eppleby N York 69 Q10
Eppleworth E R Yk 65 N13
Epsom Surrey 21 M10
Epwell Oxon 37 L12
Epworth N Linc 58 C6
Epworth Turbary N Linc 58 C6
Erbistock Wrexhm 44 J5
Erdington Birm 36 F2
Eridge Green E Susx 11 T3
Eridge Station E Susx 11 S4
Erines Ag & B 87 R10
Eriska Ag & B 94 C10
Eriskay W Isls 106 c18
Eriswell Suffk 40 B5
Erith Gt Lon 22 D12
Erlestoke Wilts 18 E10
Ermington Devon 5 Q10
Erpingham Norfk 51 L7
Erriottwood Kent 12 H4
Errogie Highld 102 G11
Errol P & K 90 K7
Erskine Rens 89 L11
Erskine Bridge Rens 89 L11
Ervie D & G 72 C6
Erwarton Suffk 41 M14
Erwood Powys 34 C12
Eryholme N York 70 D11
Eryrys Denbgs 44 F2
Escalls Cnwll 2 B11
Escomb Dur 69 Q6
Escott Somset 16 E9
Escrick N York 64 E11
Esgair Carmth 25 Q5
Esgair Cerdgn 33 L7
Esgairgeiliog Powys 43 Q12
Esgerdawe Carmth 33 M12
Esgyryn Conwy 53 P7
Esh Dur 69 Q4
Esher Surrey 20 K10
Esholt C Brad 63 P11
Eshott Nthumb 77 Q6
Eshton N York 62 J8
Esh Winning Dur 69 Q4
Eskadale Highld 102 E7
Eskbank Mdloth 83 R5
Eskdale Green Cumb 66 H12
Eskdalemuir D & G 75 Q6
Eske E R Yk 65 P11
Eskham Lincs 59 Q7
Eskholme Donc 57 T3
Esperley Lane Ends Dur 69 P8
Esprick Lancs 61 S12
Essendine Rutlnd 48 F11
Essendon Herts 31 S11
Essich Highld 102 H8
Essington Staffs 46 C13
Esslemont Abers 105 Q10
Eston R & Cl 70 H9
Etal Nthumb 85 N11
Etchilhampton Wilts 18 F8
Etchingham E Susx 12 D10
Etchinghill Kent 13 N8
Etchinghill Staffs 46 D10
Etchingwood E Susx 11 S6
Etling Green Norfk 50 H11
Etloe Gloucs 28 C6
Eton W & M 20 G7
Eton Wick W & M 20 F7
Etruria C Stke 45 U4
Etteridge Highld 96 K5
Ettersgill Dur 68 J7
Ettiley Heath Ches E 45 R1
Ettingshall Wolves 36 B1
Ettington Warwks 36 J11
Etton C Pete 48 H12
Etton E R Yk 65 M11
Ettrick Border 75 Q3
Ettrickbridge Border 83 S14
Ettrickhill Border 75 Q3
Etwall Derbys 46 J7
Eudon George Shrops 35 Q3
Euston Suffk 40 E5
Euximoor Drove Cambs 49 Q14
Euxton Lancs 55 N3
Evancoyd Powys 34 G8
Evanton Highld 102 H2
Evedon Lincs 48 G4
Evelith Shrops 45 R12
Evelix Highld 109 P6
Evenjobb Powys 34 G8
Evenley Nhants 30 C6
Evenlode Gloucs 29 P2
Evenwood Dur 69 Q8
Evenwood Gate Dur 69 Q8
Evercreech Somset 17 R9
Everingham E R Yk 64 J11
Everleigh Wilts 18 K10
Everley N York 65 M2
Eversholt C Beds 31 L6
Evershot Dorset 7 Q4
Eversley Hants 20 C10
Eversley Cross Hants 20 C10
Everthorpe E R Yk 65 L13
Everton C Beds 38 K10
Everton Hants 8 K10
Everton Lpool 54 H8
Everton Notts 57 U8
Evertown D & G 75 S10
Evesbatch Herefs 35 Q11
Evesham Worcs 36 D12
Evington C Leic 47 R13
Ewden Village Sheff 57 L7
Ewell Surrey 21 M10
Ewell Minnis Kent 13 Q7
Ewelme Oxon 19 T2
Ewen Gloucs 28 K8
Ewenny V Glam 26 G12
Ewerby Lincs 48 H4
Ewerby Thorpe Lincs 48 H4
Ewhurst Surrey 10 H2
Ewhurst Green E Susx 12 E11
Ewhurst Green Surrey 10 H3
Ewloe Flints 54 H13
Ewloe Green Flints 54 G13
Ewood Bl w D 55 Q1
Ewood Bridge Lancs 55 S2
Eworthy Devon 14 K13
Ewshot Hants 20 D13
Ewyas Harold Herefs 27 R2
Exbourne Devon 15 P12
Exbury Hants 9 N8
Exceat E Susx 11 S11
Exebridge Somset 16 B12
Exelby N York 63 R2
Exeter Devon 6 B6
Exeter Airport Devon 6 C6
Exeter Services Devon 6 C6
Exford Somset 15 U5
Exfordsgreen Shrops 45 L12
Exhall Warwks 36 F9
Exhall Warwks 37 L3
Exlade Street Oxon 19 U4
Exley Head C Brad 63 L11
Exminster Devon 6 B7
Exmoor National Park 15 U5
Exmouth Devon 6 D8
Exning Suffk 39 T7
Exted Kent 13 N7
Exton Devon 6 C7
Exton Hants 9 S4
Exton Rutlnd 48 D11
Exton Somset 16 B10
Exwick Devon 6 B6
Eyam Derbys 56 K11
Eydon Nhants 37 P11
Eye C Pete 48 K13
Eye Herefs 35 L8
Eye Suffk 40 K6
Eye Green C Pete 48 K13
Eyemouth Border 85 N6
Eyeworth C Beds 39 L11
Eyhorne Street Kent 12 F5
Eyke Suffk 41 P10
Eynesbury Cambs 38 J9
Eynsford Kent 21 T9
Eynsham Oxon 29 T6
Eype Dorset 7 M6
Eyre Highld 100 d4
Eythorne Kent 13 Q6
Eyton Herefs 35 L8
Eyton Shrops 34 J3
Eyton Shrops 44 J11
Eyton Shrops 44 K9
Eyton Wrexhm 44 J5
Eyton on Severn Shrops 45 N12
Eyton upon the Weald Moors Wrekin 45 Q11

F

Faccombe Hants 19 N9
Faceby N York 70 G12
Fachwen Powys 44 B10
Facit Lancs 56 C3
Fackley Notts 47 N1
Faddiley Ches E 45 N3
Fadmoor N York 64 F2
Faerdre Swans 26 B7
Faifley W Duns 89 L11
Failand N Som 17 P2
Failford S Ayrs 81 P7
Failsworth Oldham 56 C6
Fairbourne Gwynd 43 M11
Fairburn N York 64 B14
Fairfield Derbys 56 G12
Fairfield Kent 12 J10
Fairfield Worcs 36 B5
Fairfield Park Herts 31 R6
Fairford Gloucs 29 N7
Fairford Park Gloucs 29 N7
Fairgirth D & G 66 C1
Fair Green Norfk 49 U10
Fairhaven Lancs 61 Q14
Fair Isle Shet 106 r11
Fair Isle Airport Shet 106 r11
Fairlands Surrey 20 G12
Fairlie N Ayrs 80 J2
Fairlight E Susx 12 G13
Fairlight Cove E Susx 12 G13
Fairmile Devon 6 E5
Fairmile Surrey 20 K10
Fairmilehead C Edin 83 P5
Fairnilee Border 84 D12
Fair Oak Hants 9 P5
Fairoak Staffs 45 S7
Fair Oak Green Hants 19 U8
Fairseat Kent 12 B3
Fairstead Essex 22 J4
Fairstead Norfk 49 T9
Fairstead Norfk 51 N9
Fairwarp E Susx 11 R5
Fairwater Cardif 27 L12
Fairy Cross Devon 14 K8
Fakenham Norfk 50 F8
Fakenham Magna Suffk 40 F5
Fala Mdloth 84 C6
Fala Dam Mdloth 84 C6
Falcut Nhants 30 C4
Faldingworth Lincs 58 J10
Faldouët Jersey 7 f2
Falfield S Glos 28 C9
Falkenham Suffk 41 N13
Falkirk Falk 82 G2
Falkirk Wheel Falk 82 G2
Falkland Fife 91 L10
Fallburn S Lans 82 J11
Fallgate Derbys 47 L1
Fallin Stirlg 89 T7
Fallodon Nthumb 85 T14
Fallowfield Manch 56 C8
Fallowfield Nthumb 76 J12
Falmer E Susx 11 P9
Falmouth Cnwll 3 L10
Falnash Border 75 S4
Falsgrave N York 65 N2
Falstone Nthumb 76 E8
Fanagmore Highld 110 D7
Fancott C Beds 31 M7
Fanellan Highld 102 E7
Fangdale Beck N York 70 J14
Fangfoss E R Yk 64 H9
Fanmore Ag & B 93 L10
Fannich Lodge Highld 108 C11
Fans Border 84 G10
Far Bletchley M Keyn 30 J6
Farcet Cambs 38 K2
Far Cotton Nhants 37 U9
Farden Shrops 35 N5
Fareham Hants 9 R7
Farewell Staffs 46 E11
Far Forest Worcs 35 R5
Farforth Lincs 59 P11
Far Green Gloucs 28 E7
Faringdon Oxon 29 Q9
Farington Lancs 55 M1
Farlam Cumb 76 B14
Farleigh N Som 17 N3
Farleigh Surrey 21 Q10
Farleigh Hungerford Somset 18 B9
Farleigh Wallop Hants 19 T11
Farlesthorpe Lincs 59 S12
Farleton Cumb 61 U3
Farleton Lancs 62 B6
Farley Derbys 46 J1
Farley Staffs 46 E5
Farley Wilts 8 J3
Farley Green Suffk 40 B10
Farley Green Surrey 20 J13
Farley Hill Wokham 20 B10
Farleys End Gloucs 28 E5
Farlington C Port 9 T7
Farlington N York 64 E6
Farlow Shrops 35 P4
Farmborough BaNES 17 S4
Farmbridge End Essex 22 F5
Farmcote Gloucs 29 L2
Farmcote Shrops 35 S2
Farmington Gloucs 29 M4
Farmoor Oxon 29 U6
Far Moor Wigan 55 M6
Farms Common Cnwll 2 H10
Farm Town Leics 47 L10
Farmtown Moray 104 G5
Farnah Green Derbys 46 K4
Farnborough Gt Lon 21 R10
Farnborough Hants 20 E12
Farnborough W Berk 19 P4
Farnborough Warwks 37 M11
Farnborough Park Hants 20 E11
Farncombe Surrey 10 F2
Farndish Bed 38 D8
Farndon Ches W 44 K3
Farndon Notts 47 U3
Farne Islands Nthumb 85 U11
Farnell Angus 99 L12
Farnham Dorset 8 D5
Farnham Essex 22 C3
Farnham N York 63 S7
Farnham Suffk 41 Q8
Farnham Surrey 20 D13
Farnham Common Bucks 20 G5
Farnham Green Essex 22 C2
Farnham Royal Bucks 20 G6
Farningham Kent 21 T9
Farnley Leeds 63 R13
Farnley N York 63 Q10
Farnley Tyas Kirk 56 J4
Farnsfield Notts 47 S2
Farnworth Bolton 55 R5
Farnworth Halton 55 M9
Far Oakridge Gloucs 28 H7
Farr Highld 97 N3
Farr Highld 102 J9
Farr Highld 111 Q4
Farraline Highld 102 G11
Farringdon Devon 6 D6
Farrington Gurney BaNES 17 R5
Far Sawrey Cumb 67 N13
Farsley Leeds 63 Q12
Farther Howegreen Essex 22 K7
Farthing Green Kent 12 F6
Farthinghoe Nhants 30 B5
Farthingloe Kent 13 Q7
Farthingstone Nhants 37 R10
Farthing Street Gt Lon 21 R10
Fartown Kirk 56 J3
Farway Devon 6 G5
Fasnacloich Ag & B 94 E9
Fasnakyle Highld 102 B10
Fassfern Highld 94 E3
Fatfield Sundld 70 D2
Faugh Cumb 67 R2
Fauld Staffs 46 G8
Fauldhouse W Loth 82 H6
Faulkbourne Essex 22 J4
Faulkland Somset 17 T6
Fauls Shrops 45 N7
Faversham Kent 12 K3
Fawdington N York 63 U5
Fawdon N u Ty 77 Q12
Fawdon Nthumb 77 L2
Fawfieldhead Staffs 56 G14
Fawkham Green Kent 21 U9
Fawler Oxon 29 S4
Fawley Bucks 20 C5
Fawley Hants 9 P8
Fawley W Berk 19 N4
Fawley Chapel Herefs 28 A2
Fawnog Flints 54 F13
Fawsley Nhants 37 Q9
Faxfleet E R Yk 58 E2
Faygate W Susx 11 L4
Fazakerley Lpool 54 J7
Fazeley Staffs 46 H13
Fearby N York 63 P3
Fearn Highld 109 Q9
Fearnan P & K 95 U10
Fearnbeg Highld 107 M13
Fearnhead Warrtn 55 P8
Fearnmore Highld 107 M12
Fearnoch Ag & B 87 S10
Featherstone Staffs 46 B12
Featherstone Wakefd 57 P3
Feckenham Worcs 36 D8
Feering Essex 23 L3
Feetham N York 69 L13
Feizor N York 62 F6
Felbridge Surrey 11 P3
Felbrigg Norfk 51 M6
Felcourt Surrey 11 P2
Felden Herts 31 M12
Felindre Carmth 25 Q3
Felindre Carmth 25 U6
Felindre Carmth 26 C2
Felindre Cerdgn 33 L9
Felindre Powys 27 M3
Felindre Powys 34 E4
Felindre Swans 26 A7
Felindre Farchog Pembks 24 K3
Felinfach Cerdgn 32 K9
Felinfach Powys 34 C14
Felinfoel Carmth 25 T10
Felingwmisaf Carmth 25 T6
Felingwmuchaf Carmth 25 T6
Felin-newydd Powys 34 D13
Felixkirk N York 64 B3
Felixstowe Suffk 41 P14
Felixstowe Ferry Suffk 41 P13
Felkington Nthumb 85 N10
Felkirk Wakefd 57 N4
Felling Gatesd 77 R13
Fell Lane C Brad 63 L11
Fell Side Cumb 67 M5
Felmersham Bed 38 E9
Felmingham Norfk 51 N8
Felpham W Susx 10 E11
Felsham Suffk 40 F9
Felsted Essex 22 G3
Feltham Gt Lon 20 K8
Felthamhill Surrey 20 J8
Felthorpe Norfk 51 L10
Felton Herefs 35 N11
Felton N Som 17 P3
Felton Nthumb 77 P5
Felton Butler Shrops 44 J10
Feltwell Norfk 40 B2
Fenay Bridge Kirk 56 J3
Fence Lancs 62 G12
Fence Rothm 57 P9
Fence Houses Sundld 70 D3
Fencott Oxon 30 C9
Fendike Corner Lincs 49 Q1
Fen Ditton Cambs 39 Q8
Fen Drayton Cambs 39 M7
Fen End Lincs 48 K9
Fen End Solhll 36 H6
Fenham Nthumb 85 R10
Feniscliffe Bl w D 55 Q1
Feniscowles Bl w D 55 P1
Feniton Devon 6 E5
Feniton Court Devon 6 F5
Fenn Green Shrops 35 S4
Fenn Street Medway 22 J12
Fenny Bentley Derbys 46 G4
Fenny Bridges Devon 6 F5
Fenny Compton Warwks 37 M10
Fenny Drayton Leics 37 L1
Fenny Stratford M Keyn 30 J6
Fenrother Nthumb 77 P7
Fenstanton Cambs 39 M7
Fenstead End Suffk 40 D10
Fen Street Norfk 40 G1
Fen Street Suffk 41 L8
Fenton C Stke 45 U5
Fenton Cambs 39 M5
Fenton Cumb 67 R1
Fenton Lincs 48 C3
Fenton Lincs 58 D11
Fenton Notts 58 C10
Fenton Nthumb 85 P12
Fenton Barns E Loth 84 E2
Fenwick Donc 57 S3
Fenwick E Ayrs 81 P4
Fenwick Nthumb 77 M11
Fenwick Nthumb 85 R10
Feock Cnwll 3 L9
Feolin Ferry Ag & B 86 G12
Fergushill N Ayrs 81 L4
Feriniquarrie Highld 100 a4
Fermain Bay Guern 6 e3
Fern Angus 98 H11
Ferndale Rhondd 26 H8
Ferndown Dorset 8 F8
Ferness Highld 103 Q6
Fernham Oxon 29 Q9
Fernhill Heath Worcs 35 U9
Fernhurst W Susx 10 D5
Fernie Fife 91 M8
Ferniegair S Lans 82 D8
Fernilea Highld 100 c6
Fernilee Derbys 56 F11
Fernwood Notts 48 B3
Ferrensby N York 63 T7
Ferriby Sluice N Linc 58 G2
Ferrindonald Highld 100 f9
Ferring W Susx 10 H10
Ferrybridge Wakefd 57 Q2
Ferrybridge Services Wakefd 57 Q2
Ferryden Angus 99 N12
Ferryhill Dur 69 S6
Ferryhill Station Dur 69 S6
Ferry Point Highld 109 N7
Ferryside Carmth 25 Q8
Fersfield Norfk 40 J4
Fersit Highld 96 D8
Feshiebridge Highld 97 P3
Fetcham Surrey 20 K11
Fetlar Shet 106 w4
Fetterangus Abers 105 R5
Fettercairn Abers 99 M9
Fewcott Oxon 30 B7
Fewston N York 63 P9
Ffairfach Carmth 26 A3
Ffair Rhos Cerdgn 33 P7
Ffald-y-Brenin Carmth 33 M12
Ffarmers Carmth 33 M12
Ffawyddog Powys 27 N4
Ffestiniog Railway Gwynd 43 M6
Ffordd-las Denbgs 54 D14
Fforest Carmth 25 U10
Fforest Gôch Neath 26 C7
Ffostrasol Cerdgn 32 G11
Ffrith Flints 44 G2
Ffynnonddewi Cerdgn 32 G10
Ffynnongroyw Flints 54 D10
Ffynnon-oer Cerdgn 32 K10
Fickleshole Surrey 21 Q10
Fiddington Gloucs 28 H1
Fiddington Somset 16 H8
Fiddleford Dorset 7 V2
Fiddlers Green Cnwll 3 L5
Fiddlers Hamlet Essex 22 C7
Field Staffs 46 D7
Field Broughton Cumb 61 R3
Field Dalling Norfk 50 H6
Fieldhead Cumb 67 Q5
Field Head Leics 47 N12
Fifehead Magdalen Dorset 17 U12
Fifehead Neville Dorset 7 U2
Fifehead St Quintin Dorset 7 U2
Fife Keith Moray 104 E5
Fifield Oxon 29 P4
Fifield W & M 20 F7
Figheldean Wilts 18 J11
Filands Wilts 28 H10
Filby Norfk 51 S11
Filey N York 65 Q3
Filgrave M Keyn 38 C11
Filkins Oxon 29 P7
Filleigh Devon 15 Q7
Filleigh Devon 15 R10
Fillingham Lincs 58 F9
Fillongley Warwks 36 J3
Filmore Hill Hants 9 T3
Filton S Glos 28 B12
Fimber E R Yk 64 K7
Finavon Angus 98 H12
Finberry Kent 12 K8
Fincham Norfk 49 U12
Finchampstead Wokham 20 C10
Fincharn Ag & B 87 S5
Finchdean Hants 9 U6
Finchingfield Essex 39 U14
Finchley Gt Lon 21 N4
Findern Derbys 46 K7
Findhorn Moray 103 R3
Findhorn Bridge Highld 103 M10
Findochty Moray 104 F2
Findo Gask P & K 90 F8
Findon Abers 99 S4
Findon W Susx 10 J9
Findon Mains Highld 102 H3
Findon Valley W Susx 10 J9
Findrack House Abers 99 L3
Finedon Nhants 38 D6
Fingal Street Suffk 41 M7
Fingask P & K 90 J8
Fingest Bucks 20 C4
Finghall N York 63 P2
Fingland Cumb 67 L1
Fingland D & G 74 E2
Finglesham Kent 13 R5
Fingringhoe Essex 23 P3
Finkle Green Essex 40 B12
Finkle Street Barns 57 M7
Finlarig Stirlg 95 R12
Finmere Oxon 30 D6
Finnart P & K 95 Q7
Finningham Suffk 40 J7
Finningley Donc 57 U7
Finsbay W Isls 106 f10
Finstall Worcs 36 C6
Finsthwaite Cumb 61 R2
Finstock Oxon 29 S4
Finstown Ork 106 s18
Fintry Abers 105 M5
Fintry Stirlg 89 P8
Finzean Abers 99 L5
Fionnphort Ag & B 92 J14
Fionnsbhagh W Isls 106 f10
Firbank Cumb 68 D14
Firbeck Rothm 57 S9
Firby N York 63 R2
Firby N York 64 G6
Firgrove Rochdl 56 D4
Firle E Susx 11 R9
Firsby Lincs 59 S14
Firsdown Wilts 8 J2
Fir Tree Dur 69 P6
Fishbourne IoW 9 R10
Fishbourne W Susx 10 C10
Fishbourne Roman Palace W Susx 10 C10
Fishburn Dur 70 E6
Fishcross Clacks 90 C12
Fisher W Susx 10 D10
Fisherford Abers 104 K8
Fisherrow E Loth 83 R4
Fisher's Pond Hants 9 P4
Fisher's Row Lancs 61 S10
Fisherstreet W Susx 10 E4
Fisherton Highld 102 K5
Fisherton S Ayrs 80 K9
Fisherton de la Mere Wilts 18 F13
Fisherwick Staffs 46 G12
Fishery W & M 20 E6
Fishguard Pembks 24 G3
Fishlake Donc 57 U4
Fishleigh Devon 15 M11
Fishmere End Lincs 49 L6
Fishnish Pier Ag & B 93 R10
Fishpond Bottom Dorset 7 L5
Fishponds Bristl 28 B12
Fishtoft Lincs 49 N5
Fishtoft Drove Lincs 49 M4
Fishwick Lancs 62 B14
Fiskavaig Highld 100 c6
Fiskerton Lincs 58 H12
Fiskerton Notts 47 T3
Fitling E R Yk 65 T13
Fittleton Wilts 18 H11
Fittleworth W Susx 10 G7
Fitton End Cambs 49 P11
Fitz Shrops 44 K10
Fitzhead Somset 16 F11
Fitzroy Somset 16 G11
Fitzwilliam Wakefd 57 P3
Five Ash Down E Susx 11 R6
Five Ashes E Susx 11 T5
Five Bells Somset 16 E8
Five Bridges Herefs 35 P11
Fivecrosses Ches W 55 M11
Fivehead Somset 17 L12
Fivelanes Cnwll 4 G4
Five Lanes Mons 27 S9
Five Oak Green Kent 12 B6
Five Oaks Jersey 7 e3
Five Oaks W Susx 10 H5
Five Roads Carmth 25 S9
Five Wents Kent 12 F5
Flack's Green Essex 22 J5
Flackwell Heath Bucks 20 E5
Fladbury Worcs 36 C11
Fladdabister Shet 106 u10
Flagg Derbys 56 H13
Flamborough E R Yk 65 S5
Flamborough Head E R Yk 65 T5
Flamingo Land Theme Park N York 64 H4
Flamstead Herts 31 N10
Flamstead End Herts 31 T12
Flansham W Susx 10 F10
Flanshaw Wakefd 57 M2
Flappit Spring C Brad 63 M12
Flasby N York 62 J8
Flash Staffs 56 F13
Flashader Highld 100 c4
Flaunden Herts 31 M12
Flawborough Notts 47 U5
Flawith N York 64 B6
Flax Bourton N Som 17 P3
Flaxby N York 63 T8
Flaxley Gloucs 28 C4
Flaxmere Ches W 55 N12
Flaxpool Somset 16 F9
Flaxton N York 64 F7
Fleckney Leics 37 R2
Flecknoe Warwks 37 P8
Fledborough Notts 58 D12
Fleet Dorset 7 R8
Fleet Hants 9 U8
Fleet Hants 20 D12
Fleet Lincs 49 N9
Fleetend Hants 9 Q7
Fleet Hargate Lincs 49 N9
Fleet Services Hants 20 C11
Fleetwood Lancs 61 Q10
Flegburgh Norfk 51 R11
Flemingston V Glam 16 D3
Flemington S Lans 89 Q14
Flempton Suffk 40 D7
Fletchersbridge Cnwll 4 E7
Fletcher's Green Kent 21 T13
Fletchertown Cumb 66 K4
Fletching E Susx 11 Q6
Fleur-de-lis Caerph 27 M8
Flexbury Cnwll 14 F11
Flexford Surrey 20 F13
Flimby Cumb 66 F6
Flimwell E Susx 12 D9
Flint Flints 54 F12
Flintham Notts 47 T4
Flint Mountain Flints 54 F12
Flinton E R Yk 65 S12
Flint's Green Solhll 36 J4
Flishinghurst Kent 12 E8
Flitcham Norfk 50 B8
Flitch Green Essex 22 G3
Flitton C Beds 31 N5
Flitwick C Beds 31 M6
Flixborough N Linc 58 E4
Flixborough Stather N Linc 58 E4
Flixton N York 65 N4
Flixton Suffk 41 P3
Flixton Traffd 55 R8
Flockton Kirk 56 K4
Flockton Green Kirk 57 L3
Flodden Nthumb 85 N11
Flodigarry Highld 100 d2
Flookburgh Cumb 61 R4
Flordon Norfk 41 L1
Flore Nhants 37 R8
Flotterton Nthumb 76 K5
Flowers Green E Susx 11 U8
Flowton Suffk 40 J11
Flushdyke Wakefd 57 L2
Flushing Cnwll 3 L10
Fluxton Devon 6 E6
Flyford Flavell Worcs 36 C9
Fobbing Thurr 22 H11
Fochabers Moray 104 C4
Fochriw Caerph 27 L6
Fockerby N Linc 58 D3
Foddington Somset 17 Q11
Foel Powys 43 U11
Foelgastell Carmth 25 T8
Foel y Dyffryn Brdgnd 26 F9
Foggathorpe E R Yk 64 H12
Fogo Border 84 K9
Fogwatt Moray 104 A4
Foindle Highld 110 D7
Folda Angus 98 B11
Fole Staffs 46 D6
Foleshill Covtry 37 L4
Folke Dorset 7 S2
Folkestone Kent 13 P8
Folkestone Services Kent 13 M8
Folkingham Lincs 48 G7
Folkington E Susx 11 T10
Folksworth Cambs 38 H3
Folkton N York 65 P4
Folla Rule Abers 105 L9
Follifoot N York 63 S9
Folly Gate Devon 15 N13
Folly Hill Surrey 20 D13
Fonmon V Glam 16 D3
Fonthill Bishop Wilts 8 C2
Fonthill Gifford Wilts 8 C2
Fontmell Magna Dorset 8 B5
Fontmell Parva Dorset 8 A6
Fontwell W Susx 10 E9
Font-y-gary V Glam 16 E3
Foolow Derbys 56 J11
Foots Cray Gt Lon 21 S8
Forbestown Abers 104 D13
Forcett N York 69 Q10
Ford Ag & B 87 R5
Ford Bucks 30 G11
Ford Derbys 57 P10
Ford Devon 5 Q10
Ford Devon 5 T12
Ford Devon 14 K8
Ford Gloucs 29 L2
Ford Nthumb 85 N11
Ford Shrops 44 K11
Ford Somset 16 E11
Ford Somset 17 Q6
Ford Staffs 46 E3
Ford W Susx 10 F10
Ford Wilts 8 H2
Ford Wilts 18 B5
Forda Devon 5 N2
Fordcombe Kent 11 S2
Fordell Fife 90 J14
Forden Powys 44 F13
Ford End Essex 22 G4
Forder Green Devon 5 T7
Ford Green Lancs 61 T10
Fordham Cambs 39 T6
Fordham Essex 23 M2
Fordham Norfk 49 T14
Fordham Heath Essex 23 M2
Ford Heath Shrops 44 K11
Fordingbridge Hants 8 G6
Fordon E R Yk 65 N4
Fordoun Abers 99 N8
Ford's Green Suffk 40 J7
Fordstreet Essex 23 M2
Ford Street Somset 16 G13
Fordton Devon 15 T13
Fordwells Oxon 29 R5
Fordwich Kent 13 N4
Fordyce Abers 104 H3
Forebridge Staffs 46 B9
Foremark Derbys 46 K8
Forest Guern 6 d4
Forest N York 69 S12
Forest Becks Lancs 62 F9
Forestburn Gate Nthumb 77 M6
Forest Chapel Ches E 56 E12
Forest Coal Pit Mons 27 P3
Forest Gate Gt Lon 21 R5
Forest Green Surrey 10 J2
Forest Hall N Tyne 77 R12
Forest Head Cumb 76 B14
Forest Hill Gt Lon 21 Q8
Forest Hill Oxon 30 C11
Forest-in-Teesdale Dur 68 J6
Forest Lane Head N York 63 S8
Forest Mill Clacks 90 E13
Forest of Bowland Lancs 62 C9
Forest of Dean Gloucs 28 B5
Forest Row E Susx 11 Q4
Forest Side IoW 9 P11
Forestside W Susx 10 B8
Forest Town Notts 47 Q1
Forfar Angus 98 H13
Forgandenny P & K 90 G8
Forge Powys 43 Q14
Forge Hammer Torfn 27 P8
Forge Side Torfn 27 N6
Forgie Moray 104 D5
Forgieside Moray 104 D5
Forgue Abers 104 J6
Forhill Worcs 36 E5
Formby Sefton 54 H5
Forncett End Norfk 40 K2
Forncett St Mary Norfk 41 L2
Forncett St Peter Norfk 41 L2
Fornham All Saints Suffk 40 D7
Fornham St Martin Suffk 40 E7
Fornham St Genevieve Suffk 40 D7
Fornighty Highld 103 P5
Forres Moray 103 R4
Forsbrook Staffs 46 C5
Forse Highld 112 F10
Forshaw Heath Warwks 36 E6
Forsinard Highld 111 T8
Forss Highld 112 B3
Forston Dorset 7 S5
Fort Augustus Highld 96 D2
Forteviot P & K 90 G8
Forth S Lans 82 H8
Forthampton Gloucs 28 G1
Fort Hommet Guern 6 c2
Forth Rail Bridge C Edin 83 M3
Forth Road Bridge Fife 83 M3
Fortingall P & K 95 U9
Forton Hants 19 P12
Forton Lancs 61 T9
Forton Shrops 44 K10
Forton Somset 6 K3
Forton Staffs 45 S9
Fort Richmond Guern 6 c2
Fortrie Abers 104 K6
Fortrose Highld 102 K4
Fortuneswell Dorset 7 S10
Fort William Highld 94 G4
Forty Green Bucks 20 F4
Forty Hill Gt Lon 21 P3
Forward Green Suffk 40 K9
Fosbury Wilts 19 M9
Foscot Oxon 29 P3
Foscote Nhants 37 S11
Fosdyke Lincs 49 M7
Fosdyke Bridge Lincs 49 M7
Foss P & K 97 M12
Fossebridge Gloucs 29 L5
Foss-y-ffin Cerdgn 32 H8
Fosterhouses Donc 57 U4
Foster Street Essex 22 C6
Foston Derbys 46 G7
Foston Leics 37 R2
Foston Lincs 48 C5
Foston N York 64 F6
Foston on the Wolds E R Yk 65 Q8
Fotherby Lincs 59 P8
Fothergill Cumb 66 F6
Fotheringhay Nhants 38 G2
Foul Anchor Cambs 49 Q10
Foulbridge Cumb 67 P3
Foulby Wakefd 57 N3
Foulden Border 85 N7
Foulden Norfk 50 C14
Foul End Warwks 36 H2
Foul Mile E Susx 11 U7
Foulness Island Essex 23 N9
Foulridge Lancs 62 H11
Foulsham Norfk 50 H9
Fountainhall Border 84 C9
Four Ashes Solhll 36 G5
Four Ashes Staffs 35 T3
Four Ashes Staffs 46 B12
Four Ashes Suffk 40 H6
Four Cabots Guern 6 d3
Four Crosses Powys 44 G10
Four Crosses Staffs 46 C12
Four Elms Kent 21 S13
Four Foot Somset 17 Q10
Four Forks Somset 16 H9
Four Gates Bolton 55 P5
Four Gotes Cambs 49 Q10
Four Lane End Barns 57 L6
Four Lane Ends Ches W 45 N1
Four Lanes Cnwll 2 H9
Fourlanes End Ches E 45 T2
Four Marks Hants 19 U13
Four Mile Bridge IoA 52 C7
Four Oaks Birm 46 F14
Four Oaks E Susx 12 G11
Four Oaks Gloucs 28 C2
Four Oaks Solhll 36 H4
Fourpenny Highld 109 Q6
Four Points W Berk 19 S5
Four Roads Carmth 25 R9
Four Shire Stone Warwks 29 P1
Fourstones Nthumb 76 H12
Four Throws Kent 12 E10
Four Wents Kent 12 B3
Fovant Wilts 8 E3
Foveran Abers 105 R11
Fowey Cnwll 4 E10
Fowley Common Warrtn 55 Q7
Fowlhall Kent 12 C6
Fowlis Angus 91 M5
Fowlis Wester P & K 90 D7
Fowlmere Cambs 39 P11
Fownhope Herefs 35 N14
Foxbar Rens 89 L13
Foxcombe Devon 5 M3
Fox Corner Surrey 20 G12
Foxcote Gloucs 28 K4
Foxcote Somset 17 T5
Foxdale IoM 60 d7
Foxearth Essex 40 D12
Foxendown Kent 12 B2
Foxfield Cumb 61 N2
Foxham Wilts 18 E5
Fox Hatch Essex 22 E8
Foxhills Hants 9 L6
Foxhole Cnwll 3 P6
Foxholes N York 65 N5
Foxhunt Green E Susx 11 S7
Foxley Nhants 37 R10
Foxley Norfk 50 H9
Foxley Wilts 28 G10
Foxlydiate Worcs 36 D7
Fox Street Essex 23 P2
Foxt Staffs 46 D4
Foxton Cambs 39 P11
Foxton Dur 70 E8
Foxton Leics 37 T3
Foxton N York 70 F13
Foxup N York 62 H4
Foxwist Green Ches W 55 P13
Foxwood Shrops 35 P5
Foy Herefs 28 A2
Foyers Highld 102 E11
Foynesfield Highld 103 N5
Fraddam Cnwll 2 F10
Fraddon Cnwll 3 N5
Fradley Staffs 46 G11
Fradswell Staffs 46 C7
Fraisthorpe E R Yk 65 R7
Framfield E Susx 11 R6
Framingham Earl Norfk 51 N13
Framingham Pigot Norfk 51 N13
Framlingham Suffk 41 N8
Frampton Dorset 7 R5
Frampton Lincs 49 M6
Frampton Cotterell S Glos 28 C11
Frampton Mansell Gloucs 28 H7
Frampton-on-Severn Gloucs 28 D6

G

Frampton West End Lincs 49 M5
Framsden Suff 41 L9
Framwellgate Moor Dur...69 S4
Franche Worcs 35 C5
Franche Ches W 55 P11
Frankby Wirral 54 F9
Frankfort Norfk 51 N8
Franklands Gate Herefs ..35 M11
Frankley Worcs 36 C4
Frankton Warwks 37 N6
Fransbridge Powys 23 Q3
Frant E Susx 11 T3
Fraserburgh Abers 105 R2
Frating Essex 23 Q3
Frating Green Essex 23 Q3
Fratton C Port 9 T8
Freathy Cnwll 4 K10
Freckenham Suffk 39 U6
Freckleton Lancs 61 S14
Freebirch Derbys 57 M12
Freeby Leics 48 B9
Freefolk Hants 19 Q11
Freehay Staffs 46 D5
Freeland Oxon 29 T5
Freethorpe Norfk 51 R13
Freethorpe Common
  Norfk 51 R13
Freiston Lincs 49 N5
Fremington Devon 15 M6
Fremington N York 69 M13
Frenchay S Glos 28 B12
Frenchbeer Devon 5 R3
French Street Kent 21 S12
Frenich P & K 97 N12
Frensham Surrey 10 C2
Freshbrook Swindn 29 N11
Freshfield Sefton 54 G5
Freshford Wilts 17 U4
Freshwater IoW 9 L11
Freshwater Bay IoW 9 L11
Freshwater East Pembks ..24 H11
Fressingfield Suffk 41 M5
Freston Suffk 23 L2
Freswick Highld 112 J3
Frethorne Gloucs 28 D5
Frettenham Norfk 51 N10
Freuchie Fife 91 L10
Freystrop Pembks 24 F8
Friar Park Sandw 36 D2
Friar's Gate E Susx 11 R4
Friar's Hill N York 64 G2
Friar Waddon Dorset 7 R7
Friday Bridge Cambs 49 Q13
Friday Street Suffk 41 M9
Friday Street Suffk 41 P10
Friday Street Surrey 20 K13
Fridaythorpe E R Yk 64 K8
Friden Derbys 46 G1
Friendly Calder 56 G2
Friern Barnet Gt Lon 21 N5
Friesthorpe Lincs 58 J10
Frieston Lincs 48 D4
Frieth Bucks 20 C4
Friezeland Notts 47 N3
Frilford Oxon 29 T8
Frilsham W Berk 19 R6
Frimley Surrey 20 E11
Frimley Green Surrey 20 E11
Frindsbury Medway 12 D2
Fring Norfk 50 B7
Fringford Oxon 30 D7
Frinsted Kent 12 F4
Frinton-on-Sea Essex 23 T3
Friockheim Angus 91 S2
Friog Gwynd 43 M11
Frisby on the Wreake
  Leics 47 S10
Friskney Lincs 49 Q2
Friskney Eaudike Lincs ..49 Q2
Friston E Susx 11 S11
Friston Suffk 41 R8
Fritchley Derbys 47 L3
Fritham Hants 8 J6
Frith Bank Lincs 49 M4
Frith Common Worcs 35 Q7
Frithelstock Devon 15 L9
Frithelstock Stone Devon .15 L9
Frithend Hants 10 B3
Frithsden Herts 31 M11
Frithville Lincs 49 M3
Frittenden Kent 12 F7
Frittiscombe Devon 5 U12
Fritton Norfk 41 N2
Fritton Norfk 51 S13
Fritwell Oxon 30 B7
Frizinghall C Brad 63 N12
Frizington Cumb 66 F9
Frocester Gloucs 28 E7
Frodesley Shrops 45 M13
Frodsham Ches W 55 M11
Frogden Border 84 K13
Frog End Cambs 39 R9
Froggatt Derbys 56 K11
Froghall Staffs 46 D4
Frogham Hants 8 H6
Frogham Kent 13 Q5
Frogmore Devon 5 T12
Frognall Lincs 48 J11
Frogpool Cnwll 2 K8
Frog Pool Worcs 35 T7
Frogwell Cnwll 4 J7
Frolesworth Leics 37 P2
Frome Somset 17 U7
Frome St Quintin Dorset ..7 Q4
Fromes Hill Herefs 35 Q11
Fron Gwynd 42 G6
Fron Gwynd 52 H10
Fron Powys 34 E14
Fron Powys 44 E14
Fron Powys 44 F13
Froncysyllte Wrexhm 44 G5
Fron-goch Gwynd 43 T6
Fron Isaf Wrexhm 44 G5
Frostenden Suffk 41 S4
Frosterley Dur 69 M5
Froxfield C Beds 31 L6
Froxfield Wilts 19 L7
Froxfield Green Hants 9 U4
Fryern Hill Hants 9 N4
Fryerning Essex 22 F7
Fryton N York 64 F5
Fulanary Highld 93 Q9
Fulbeck Lincs 48 D3
Fulbourn Cambs 39 R9
Fulbrook Oxon 29 Q5
Fulflood Hants 9 P3
Fulford C York 64 E9
Fulford Somset 16 H11
Fulford Staffs 46 B6
Fulham Gt Lon 21 N7
Fulking W Susx 11 L8
Fullaby Lincs 59 Q12
Fuller's End Essex 22 D2
Fuller's Moor Ches W 45 L3
Fullerton Hants 19 N12
Fuller Street Essex 22 H4
Fuller Street Kent 11 S2
Fullready Warwks 36 J11
Full Sutton E R Yk 64 G8
Fullwood E Ayrs 81 N2
Fulmer Bucks 20 G5
Fulmodeston Norfk 50 G7
Fulnetby Lincs 58 J11
Fulney Lincs 49 L9
Fulstone Kirk 56 J5
Fulstow Lincs 59 P6
Fulwell Oxon 29 S3
Fulwell Sundld 77 T14
Fulwood Lancs 61 U13
Fulwood Notts 47 N2
Fulwood Sheff 57 M10
Fulwood Somset 16 H12
Fundenhall Norfk 41 L1
Funtington W Susx 10 C9
Funtley Hants 9 R7
Funtullich P & K 95 T6
Furley Devon 6 J4
Furnace Ag & B 87 T6
Furnace Carmth 25 T9
Furnace Cerdgn 33 N3
Furnace End Warwks 36 H2
Furner's Green E Susx ...11 Q6
Furness Vale Derbys 56 F10
Further Quarter Kent 12 G8
Furtho Nhants 30 G4
Furzehill Devon 15 R3
Furzehill Dorset 8 E8
Furzehills Lincs 59 M12
Furzley Corner Hants 9 L5
Furze Platt W & M 20 E6
Fyfett Somset 6 H2
Fyfield Essex 22 E6
Fyfield Hants 19 L11
Fyfield Oxon 29 T8
Fyfield Wilts 18 H7
Fyfield Wilts 18 J7
Fyfield Bavant Wilts 8 E3
Fylingthorpe N York 71 R11
Fyning W Susx 10 C5
Fyvie Abers 105 M8

132 Gyfelia – Hinton Martell

Gyfelia Wrexhm 44 H4
Gyrn Goch Gwynd 42 H4

H

Habberley Shrops 44 J13
Habberley Worcs 35 T5
Habergham Lancs 62 G13
Habertoft Lincs 59 T13
Habin W Susx 10 C6
Habrough NE Lin 58 K4
Hacconby Lincs 48 H8
Haceby Lincs 48 F6
Hacheston Suffk 41 P9
Hackbridge Gt Lon 21 N9
Hackenthorpe Sheff 57 P10
Hackford Norfk 50 J13
Hackforth N York 69 R14
Hack Green Ches E 45 P4
Hackland Ork 106 s17
Hackleton Nhants 38 B9
Hacklinge Kent 13 R5
Hackman's Gate Worcs 35 U5
Hackness N York 65 M1
Hackness Somset 16 K7
Hackney Gt Lon 21 P6
Hackthorn Lincs 58 G10
Hackthorpe Cumb 67 R8
Hacton Gt Lon 22 E10
Hadden Border 84 K11
Haddenham Bucks 30 F11
Haddenham Cambs 39 Q5
Haddington E Loth 84 E4
Haddington Lincs 58 F14
Haddiscoe Norfk 41 R1
Haddon Cambs 38 H2
Hade Edge Kirk 56 H6
Hadfield Derbys 56 F7
Hadham Cross Herts 22 B4
Hadham Ford Herts 22 B3
Hadleigh Essex 22 K10
Hadleigh Suffk 40 H12
Hadleigh Heath Suffk 40 G12
Hadley Worcs 35 U8
Hadley Wrekin 45 Q11
Hadley End Staffs 46 F9
Hadley Wood Gt Lon 21 N3
Hadlow Kent 12 B5
Hadlow Down E Susx 11 S6
Hadnall Shrops 45 M9
Hadrian's Wall 76 K12
Hadstock Essex 39 S12
Hadston Nthumb 77 R5
Hadzor Worcs 36 B8
Haffenden Quarter Kent 12 G7
Hafodunos Conwy 53 Q9
Hafod-y-bwch Wrexhm 44 H4
Hafod-y-coed Blae G 27 N7
Hafodyrynys Caerph 27 N8
Haggate Lancs 62 H12
Haggbeck Cumb 75 U11
Haggersta Shet 106 t9
Haggerston Nthumb 85 Q10
Haggington Hill Devon 15 N3
Haggs Falk 89 S10
Hagley Herefs 35 N12
Hagley Worcs 36 B4
Hagmore Green Suffk 40 G13
Hagnaby Lincs 59 P14
Hagnaby Lincs 59 S11
Hagworthingham Lincs 59 P13
Haigh Wigan 55 P5
Haighton Green Lancs 62 B13
Haile Cumb 66 F11
Hailes Gloucs 28 K1
Hailey Herts 31 U10
Hailey Oxon 19 T3
Hailey Oxon 29 S5
Hailsham E Susx 11 T9
Hail Weston Cambs 38 J8
Hainault Gt Lon 21 S4
Haine Kent 13 S2
Hainford Norfk 51 M10
Hainton Lincs 59 L10
Hainworth C Brad 63 M12
Haisthorpe E R Yk 65 Q7
Hakin Pembks 24 E9
Halam Notts 47 S3
Halbeath Fife 90 H14
Halberton Devon 6 D2
Halcro Highld 112 F4
Hale Cumb 61 U4
Hale Halton 55 L10
Hale Hants 8 H5
Hale Somset 17 T11
Hale Surrey 20 D13
Hale Traffd 55 S9
Hale Bank Halton 55 L10
Hale Barns Traffd 55 S9
Hale Green E Susx 11 T8
Hale Nook Lancs 61 R11
Hales Norfk 41 Q1
Hales Staffs 45 R7
Halesgate Lincs 49 M8
Hales Green Derbys 46 G5
Halesowen Dudley 36 C4
Hales Place Kent 13 M4
Hale Street Kent 12 C6
Halesville Essex 23 M9
Halesworth Suffk 41 Q5
Halewood Knows 55 L9
Halford Devon 5 U6
Halford Shrops 34 K4
Halford Warwks 36 J11
Halfpenny Cumb 61 U2
Halfpenny Green Staffs 35 T2
Halfpenny Houses N York 63 Q3
Halfway Carmth 26 A1
Halfway Carmth 33 R14
Halfway Sheff 57 P10
Halfway W Berk 19 P7
Halfway Bridge W Susx 10 E6
Halfway House Shrops 44 H11
Halfway Houses Kent 23 M13
Halifax Calder 56 G1
Halket E Ayrs 81 N2
Halkirk Highld 112 D5
Halkyn Flints 54 F12
Hall E Rens 81 N2
Hallam Fields Derbys 47 N6
Halland E Susx 11 R7
Hallaton Leics 37 U1
Hallatrow BaNES 17 R5
Hallbankgate Cumb 76 B14
Hallbeck Cumb 62 C2
Hall Cliffe Wakefd 57 L3
Hall Cross Lancs 61 S13
Hall Dunnerdale Cumb 66 K13
Hallen S Glos 27 V11
Hall End Bed 38 F11
Hall End C Beds 31 N5
Hallfield Gate Derbys 47 L2
Hallgarth Dur 70 D4
Hallglen Falk 82 G3
Hall Green Birm 36 F4
Hallin Highld 100 b4
Halling Medway 12 D3
Hallington Lincs 59 P9
Hallington Nthumb 76 K10
Halliwell Bolton 55 Q4
Halloughton Notts 47 S3
Hallow Worcs 35 T9
Hallow Heath Worcs 35 T9
Hallsands Devon 5 U13
Hall's Green Essex 22 B6
Hall's Green Herts 31 S7
Hallthwaites Cumb 61 M2
Hallworthy Cnwll 4 F3
Hallyne Border 83 N10
Halmer End Staffs 45 S4
Halmond's Frome Herefs 35 Q11
Halmore Gloucs 28 D7
Halnaker W Susx 10 E9
Halsall Lancs 54 J4
Halse Nhants 30 C4
Halse Somset 16 F11
Halsetown Cnwll 2 E9
Halsham E R Yk 59 N1
Halsinger Devon 15 M5
Halstead Essex 22 K1
Halstead Kent 21 S10
Halstead Leics 47 U12
Halstock Dorset 7 P3
Halsway Somset 16 F9
Haltcliff Bridge Cumb 67 N5
Haltham Lincs 59 M14
Haltoft End Lincs 49 N4
Halton Bucks 30 J11
Halton Halton 55 M10
Halton Lancs 61 U7
Halton Leeds 63 T13
Halton Nthumb 76 K12
Halton Wrexhm 44 H6
Halton East N York 63 L9
Halton Fenside Lincs 59 R14
Halton Gill N York 62 H4
Halton Green Lancs 61 U6
Halton Holegate Lincs 59 R13
Halton Lea Gate Nthumb 76 C14
Halton Quay Cnwll 5 L7
Halton Shields Nthumb 77 L12
Halton West N York 62 G9
Haltwhistle Nthumb 76 E13
Halvana Cnwll 4 G5
Halvergate Norfk 51 R12
Halwell Devon 5 T10
Halwill Devon 14 K13
Halwill Junction Devon 14 K12
Ham Devon 6 H4
Ham Gloucs 28 C8
Ham Gloucs 28 J3
Ham Gt Lon 21 L8
Ham Kent 13 R5
Ham Somset 16 J11
Ham Somset 17 S7
Ham Wilts 19 M8
Hambleden Bucks 20 C5
Hambledon Hants 9 S6
Hambledon Surrey 10 F3
Hamble-le-Rice Hants 9 P7
Hambleton Lancs 61 R11
Hambleton N York 64 D13
Hambleton Moss Side Lancs 61 R11
Hambridge Somset 17 L12
Hambrook S Glos 28 B12
Hambrook W Susx 10 B9
Ham Common Dorset 17 V11
Hameringham Lincs 59 P13
Hamerton Cambs 38 H5
Ham Green Herefs 35 S12
Ham Green Kent 12 F2
Ham Green Kent 12 G10
Ham Green N Som 27 U12
Ham Green Worcs 36 D8
Ham Hill Kent 12 C3
Hamilton S Lans 82 D7
Hamilton Services (northbound) S Lans 82 D7
Hamlet Dorset 7 Q3
Hammer W Susx 10 D4
Hammerpot W Susx 10 H9
Hammersmith Gt Lon 21 M7
Hammer Vale Hants 10 D4
Hammerwich Staffs 46 E12
Hammerwood E Susx 11 Q3
Hammond Street Herts 31 T12
Hammoon Dorset 7 V2
Hamnavoe Shet 106 t10
Hampden Park E Susx 11 U10
Hamperden End Essex 22 E1
Hampnett Gloucs 29 L4
Hampole Donc 57 R4
Hampreston Dorset 8 F9
Hampsfield Cumb 61 S3
Hampson Green Lancs 61 T9
Hampstead Gt Lon 21 N5
Hampstead Norreys W Berk 19 R5
Hampsthwaite N York 63 R8
Hampton C Pete 38 J2
Hampton Devon 6 J5
Hampton Gt Lon 20 K9
Hampton Kent 13 N2
Hampton Shrops 35 R3
Hampton Swindn 29 N9
Hampton Worcs 36 D12
Hampton Bishop Herefs 35 N13
Hampton Court Palace Gt Lon 21 L9
Hampton Fields Gloucs 28 G8
Hampton Green Ches W 45 M4
Hampton Heath Ches W 45 M4
Hampton-in-Arden Solhll 36 H4
Hampton Loade Shrops 35 R3
Hampton Lovett Worcs 35 U7
Hampton Lucy Warwks 36 J9
Hampton Magna Warwks 36 J7
Hampton on the Hill Warwks 36 J8
Hampton Park Wilts 8 H2
Hampton Poyle Oxon 30 B9
Hampton Wick Gt Lon 21 L9
Hamptworth Wilts 8 J5
Hamrow Norfk 50 F9
Hamsey E Susx 11 Q8
Hamsey Green Surrey 21 Q11
Hamstall Ridware Staffs 46 F10
Hamstead Birm 36 E2
Hamstead IoW 9 N10
Hamstead Marshall W Berk 19 P7
Hamsterley Dur 69 P1
Hamsterley Dur 69 P6
Hamsterley Mill Dur 69 P1
Hamstreet Kent 12 K9
Ham Street Somset 17 Q10
Hamwood N Som 17 L5
Hamworthy BCP 8 D10
Hanbury Staffs 46 G8
Hanbury Worcs 36 C8
Hanby Lincs 48 F7
Hanchet End Suffk 39 T11
Hanchurch Staffs 45 T5
Handa Island Highld 110 C7
Handale R & Cl 71 M9
Hand and Pen Devon 6 D5
Handbridge Ches W 54 K13
Handcross W Susx 11 M5
Handforth Ches E 56 C10
Hand Green Ches W 45 M1
Handley Ches W 45 L2
Handley Derbys 47 L1
Handley Green Essex 22 G7
Handsacre Staffs 46 E10
Handsworth Birm 36 D3
Handsworth Sheff 57 P9
Handy Cross Bucks 20 E4
Hanford C Stke 45 U5
Hanford Dorset 8 A6
Hanging Heaton Kirk 57 L2
Hanging Houghton Nhants 37 U6
Hanging Langford Wilts 18 F13
Hangleton Br & H 11 M9
Hangleton W Susx 10 H10
Hanham S Glos 17 R2
Hankelow Ches E 45 Q4
Hankerton Wilts 28 J9
Hankham E Susx 11 U9
Hanley C Stke 45 U4
Hanley Broadheath Worcs 35 Q7
Hanley Castle Worcs 35 T12
Hanley Child Worcs 35 Q7
Hanley Swan Worcs 35 T12
Hanley William Worcs 35 Q7
Hanlith N York 62 H7
Hanmer Wrexhm 45 L6
Hannaford Devon 15 P7
Hannah Lincs 59 S11
Hannington Hants 19 R9
Hannington Nhants 38 B6
Hannington Swindn 29 N9
Hannington Wick Swindn 29 N8
Hanscombe End C Beds 31 P6
Hanslope M Keyn 38 B11
Hanthorpe Lincs 48 G9
Hanwell Gt Lon 21 L7
Hanwell Oxon 37 M12
Hanwood Shrops 44 K12
Hanworth Gt Lon 20 K8
Hanworth Norfk 51 L6
Happendon S Lans 82 G12
Happendon Services S Lans 82 G12
Happisburgh Norfk 51 Q7
Happisburgh Common Norfk 51 Q8
Hapsford Ches W 55 L12
Hapton Lancs 62 F13
Hapton Norfk 41 L1
Harberton Devon 5 T9
Harbertonford Devon 5 T9
Harbledown Kent 13 M4
Harborne Birm 36 D4
Harborough Magna Warwks 37 N5
Harbottle Nthumb 76 J5
Harbourneford Devon 5 S8
Harbours Hill Worcs 36 C7
Harbridge Hants 8 G6
Harbridge Green Hants 8 G6
Harburn W Loth 82 K6
Harbury Warwks 37 L9
Harby Leics 47 T7
Harby Notts 58 E12
Harcombe Devon 6 A8
Harcombe Devon 6 G6
Harcombe Bottom Devon 6 K5
Harden C Brad 63 M12
Harden Wsall 46 D13
Hardendale Cumb 67 S10
Hardenhuish Wilts 18 D6
Hardgate Abers 99 P3
Hardgate D & G 74 F12
Hardgate N York 63 R7
Hardgate W Duns 89 M11
Hardham W Susx 10 G7
Hardhorn Lancs 61 R12
Hardingham Norfk 50 H13
Hardingstone Nhants 37 U9
Hardington Somset 17 T6
Hardington Mandeville Somset 7 P2
Hardington Marsh Somset 7 P3
Hardington Moor Somset 7 P2
Hardisworthy Devon 14 F8
Hardley Hants 9 N8
Hardley Street Norfk 51 Q13
Hardmead M Keyn 38 D11
Hardraw N York 62 H1
Hardsough Lancs 55 S2
Hardstoft Derbys 57 P14
Hardway Hants 9 S8
Hardway Somset 17 T10
Hardwick Bucks 30 H9
Hardwick Cambs 39 N9
Hardwick Nhants 38 B7
Hardwick Norfk 41 M3
Hardwick Oxon 29 S6
Hardwick Oxon 30 C7
Hardwick Rothm 57 Q9
Hardwick Wsall 46 E14
Hardwicke Gloucs 28 E5
Hardwicke Gloucs 28 H2
Hardwick Hall Derbys 57 Q14
Hardwick Village Notts 57 T11
Hardy's Green Essex 23 M3
Harebeating E Susx 11 T8
Hareby Lincs 59 P13
Hare Croft C Brad 63 M12
Harefield Gt Lon 20 J4
Hare Green Essex 23 R2
Hare Hatch Wokham 20 D7
Harehill Derbys 46 G6
Harehills Leeds 63 S13
Harehope Nthumb 77 M1
Harelaw Border 84 E14
Harelaw D & G 75 T10
Harelaw Dur 69 Q2
Hareplain Kent 12 F8
Haresceugh Cumb 68 D4
Harescombe Gloucs 28 F5
Haresfield Gloucs 28 F5
Harestock Hants 9 P2
Hare Street Essex 22 B6
Hare Street Essex 22 D7
Hare Street Herts 31 U7
Harewood Leeds 63 S10
Harewood End Herefs 27 U2
Harford Devon 5 Q9
Hargate Norfk 40 K2
Hargatewall Derbys 56 H11
Hargrave Ches W 45 L1
Hargrave Nhants 38 F6
Hargrave Suffk 40 C9
Harker Cumb 75 S13
Harkstead Suffk 41 L14
Harlaston Staffs 46 H11
Harlaxton Lincs 48 C7
Harlech Gwynd 43 L7
Harlech Castle Gwynd 43 L7
Harlescott Shrops 45 L10
Harlesden Gt Lon 21 M6
Harlesthorpe Derbys 57 Q11
Harleston Devon 5 T11
Harleston Norfk 41 M4
Harleston Suffk 40 H8
Harlestone Nhants 37 T8
Harle Syke Lancs 62 H12
Harley Rothm 57 N7
Harley Shrops 45 N13
Harling Road Norfk 40 G3
Harlington C Beds 31 M6
Harlington Donc 57 Q6
Harlington Gt Lon 20 J7
Harlosh Highld 100 b5
Harlow Essex 22 B5
Harlow Carr RHS N York 63 R9
Harlow Hill Nthumb 77 M12
Harlthorpe E R Yk 64 G12
Harlton Cambs 39 N10
Harlyn Cnwll 3 M1
Harman's Cross Dorset 8 D12
Harmby N York 63 N2
Harmer Green Herts 31 S9
Harmer Hill Shrops 45 L9
Harmondsworth Gt Lon 20 J7
Harmston Lincs 48 E1
Harnage Shrops 45 N13
Harnham Nthumb 77 M9
Harnhill Gloucs 29 L7
Harold Hill Gt Lon 22 D9
Haroldston West Pembks 24 E7
Haroldswick Shet 106 w2
Harold Wood Gt Lon 22 E9
Harome N York 64 E3
Harpenden Herts 31 P10
Harpford Devon 6 E6
Harpham E R Yk 65 P7
Harpley Norfk 50 C8
Harpley Worcs 35 Q8
Harpole Nhants 37 S8
Harpsdale Highld 112 D5
Harpsden Oxon 20 C6
Harpswell Lincs 58 F9
Harpurhey Manch 56 C6
Harpur Hill Derbys 56 G12
Harraby Cumb 67 P2
Harracott Devon 15 N7
Harrapool Highld 100 f7
Harras Cumb 66 E9
Harrietfield P & K 90 E6
Harrietsham Kent 12 G5
Harringay Gt Lon 21 P5
Harrington Cumb 66 E7
Harrington Lincs 59 Q12
Harrington Nhants 37 U4
Harringworth Nhants 38 D1
Harris W Isls 106 f9
Harriseahead Staffs 45 U2
Harriston Cumb 66 J4
Harrogate N York 63 S8
Harrold Bed 38 D9
Harrop Dale Oldham 56 F5
Harrow Gt Lon 21 L5
Harrowbarrow Cnwll 5 L6
Harrowden Bed 38 G11
Harrowgate Village Darltn 69 S9
Harrow Green Suffk 40 E10
Harrow Hill Gloucs 28 C4
Harrow on the Hill Gt Lon 21 L5
Harrow Weald Gt Lon 21 L4
Harston Cambs 39 P10
Harston Leics 48 B7
Harswell E R Yk 64 J11
Hart Hartpl 70 G5
Hartburn Nthumb 77 M8
Hartburn S on T 70 F9
Hartest Suffk 40 D10
Hartfield E Susx 11 R3
Hartford Cambs 39 L6
Hartford Ches W 55 P12
Hartford Somset 16 C11
Hartfordbridge Hants 20 C11
Hartford End Essex 22 G4
Hartforth N York 69 Q11
Hartgrove Dorset 8 A5
Harthill Ches W 45 L2
Harthill N Lans 82 H6
Harthill Rothm 57 Q10
Harthope D & G 74 K3
Hartington Derbys 46 F1
Hartington Nthumb 77 L8
Hartland Devon 14 G8
Hartland Quay Devon 14 F8
Hartlebury Worcs 35 T6
Hartlepool Hartpl 70 H6
Hartley Cumb 68 G11
Hartley Kent 12 B2
Hartley Kent 12 E9
Hartley Nthumb 77 S10
Hartley Green Kent 12 B2
Hartley Green Staffs 46 C8
Hartley Wespall Hants 19 U9
Hartley Wintney Hants 20 C11
Hartlip Kent 12 F3
Hartoft End N York 71 M14
Harton N York 64 G7
Harton S Tyne 77 T12
Harton Shrops 35 L3
Hartpury Gloucs 28 E3
Hartshead Kirk 56 J2
Hartshead Moor Services Calder 56 J2
Hartshead Moor Top Kirk 56 J1
Hartshill C Stke 45 U4
Hartshill Warwks 36 K2
Hartshorne Derbys 46 K9
Hartside Nthumb 76 K2
Hartsop Cumb 67 P10
Hart Station Hartpl 70 G5
Hartswell Somset 16 E11
Hartwell Nhants 37 U10
Hartwith N York 63 Q7
Hartwood N Lans 82 F7
Hartwoodmyres Border 84 C14
Harvel Kent 12 C3
Harvington Worcs 35 U6
Harvington Worcs 36 E11
Harwell Notts 57 U8
Harwell Oxon 29 U10
Harwich Essex 23 U1
Harwood Bolton 55 R4
Harwood Dur 68 H6
Harwood Nthumb 77 L7
Harwood Dale N York 71 S13
Harwood Lee Bolton 55 R4
Harworth Notts 57 T8
Hasbury Dudley 36 C4
Hascombe Surrey 10 G3
Haselbech Nhants 37 T5
Haselbury Plucknett Somset 7 N2
Haseley Warwks 36 H7
Haseley Green Warwks 36 H7
Haseley Knob Warwks 36 H6
Haselor Warwks 36 F9
Hasfield Gloucs 28 F2
Hasguard Pembks 24 E9
Hasholme E R Yk 64 J13
Haskayne Lancs 54 J5
Hasketon Suffk 41 M10
Hasland Derbys 57 N13
Haslemere Surrey 10 E4
Haslingden Lancs 55 S2
Haslingfield Cambs 39 P10
Haslington Ches E 45 R2
Hassall Ches E 45 S2
Hassall Green Ches E 45 S2
Hassell Street Kent 13 L6
Hassingham Norfk 51 Q12
Hassness Cumb 66 J9
Hassocks W Susx 11 N7
Hassop Derbys 56 K12
Haste Hill Surrey 10 E4
Haster Highld 112 H6
Hasthorpe Lincs 59 S13
Hastingleigh Kent 13 L6
Hastings E Susx 12 F14
Hastings Somset 16 K13
Hastingwood Essex 22 C6
Hastoe Herts 30 K11
Haswell Dur 70 E4
Haswell Plough Dur 70 E4
Hatch C Beds 38 J11
Hatch Beauchamp Somset 16 K12
Hatch End Bed 38 G8
Hatch End Gt Lon 20 K4
Hatchet Gate Hants 9 M8
Hatching Green Herts 31 P10
Hatchmere Ches W 55 N12
Hatch Warren Hants 19 T11
Hatcliffe NE Lin 59 M6
Hatfield Donc 57 U5
Hatfield Herefs 35 N9
Hatfield Herts 31 R11
Hatfield Worcs 35 U10
Hatfield Broad Oak Essex 22 D4
Hatfield Heath Essex 22 D4
Hatfield Peverel Essex 22 J5
Hatfield Woodhouse Donc 57 U5
Hatford Oxon 29 R9
Hatherden Hants 19 M10
Hatherleigh Devon 15 M12
Hathern Leics 47 P9
Hatherop Gloucs 29 N6
Hathersage Derbys 56 K10
Hathersage Booths Derbys 56 K10
Hatherton Ches E 45 Q4
Hatherton Staffs 46 C11
Hatley St George Cambs 39 L10
Hatt Cnwll 4 K8
Hattersley Tamesd 56 E8
Hattingley Hants 19 T13
Hatton Abers 105 T8
Hatton Angus 91 Q3
Hatton Derbys 46 H7
Hatton Gt Lon 20 J7
Hatton Lincs 59 L11
Hatton Shrops 35 L2
Hatton Warrtn 55 N10
Hatton Warwks 36 H7
Hatton Heath Ches W 45 L1
Hatton of Fintray Abers 105 N12
Hatton Park Warwks 36 J7
Haugh E Ayrs 81 P7
Haugh Lincs 59 R11
Haugh Rochdl 56 D4
Haugham Lincs 59 P10
Haughhead E Duns 89 P10
Haugh Head Nthumb 85 Q13
Haughley Suffk 40 H8
Haughley Green Suffk 40 H8
Haugh of Glass Moray 104 E8
Haugh of Urr D & G 74 F12
Haughs of Kinnaird Angus 99 L12
Haughton Ches E 45 N2
Haughton Notts 57 U12
Haughton Powys 44 H10
Haughton Shrops 35 Q1
Haughton Shrops 44 J8
Haughton Shrops 45 N10
Haughton Shrops 45 R12
Haughton Staffs 45 U9
Haughton Green Tamesd 56 D8
Haughton le Skerne Darltn 70 D9
Haultwick Herts 31 T8
Haunton Staffs 46 H11
Hautes Croix Jersey 7 d1
Hauxton Cambs 39 P10
Havannah Ches E 56 C14
Havant Hants 9 U7
Haven Herefs 34 K10
Haven Bank Lincs 48 K3
Haven Side E R Yk 65 R14
Havenstreet IoW 9 R10
Havercroft Wakefd 57 N4
Haverfordwest Pembks 24 G7
Haverhill Suffk 39 U11
Haverigg Cumb 61 M4
Havering-atte-Bower Gt Lon 22 D9
Haversham M Keyn 30 H4
Haverthwaite Cumb 61 Q3
Haverton Hill S on T 70 G8
Havyatt N Som 17 N4
Havyatt Somset 17 P9
Hawarden Flints 54 H13
Hawbridge Worcs 36 B11
Hawbush Green Essex 22 J3
Hawcoat Cumb 61 N5
Hawen Cerdgn 32 F11
Hawes N York 62 H2
Hawe's Green Norfk 51 M14
Hawford Worcs 35 T8
Hawick Border 75 V3
Hawkchurch Devon 6 K4
Hawkedon Suffk 40 C10
Hawkenbury Kent 12 F6
Hawkeridge Wilts 18 C10
Hawkerland Devon 6 E7
Hawker's Cove Cnwll 3 N1
Hawkesbury S Glos 28 E10
Hawkesbury Warwks 37 L4
Hawkesbury Upton S Glos 28 E10
Hawkes End Covtry 36 J4
Hawk Green Stockp 56 E9
Hawkhead Rens 89 M13
Hawkhill Nthumb 77 Q3
Hawkhurst Kent 12 E9
Hawkhurst Common E Susx 11 S7
Hawkinge Kent 13 P8
Hawkley Hants 9 U3
Hawkley Wigan 55 N6
Hawkridge Somset 15 U6
Hawksdale Cumb 67 N3
Hawkshaw Bury 55 S3
Hawkshead Cumb 67 N13
Hawkshead Hill Cumb 67 M13
Hawksland S Lans 82 F11
Hawkspur Green Essex 22 G1
Hawkstone Shrops 45 N7
Hawkswick N York 62 K5
Hawksworth Leeds 63 P11
Hawksworth Notts 47 U5
Hawkwell Essex 23 L9
Hawkwell Nthumb 77 M11
Hawley Hants 20 E11
Hawley Kent 22 D13
Hawling Gloucs 29 L3
Hawnby N York 64 C2
Haworth C Brad 63 L12
Hawridge Bucks 30 K11
Hawstead Suffk 40 E9
Hawstead Green Suffk 40 E9
Hawthorn Dur 70 F3
Hawthorn Hants 9 T2
Hawthorn Rhondd 26 K10
Hawthorn Hill Br For 20 E8
Hawthorn Hill Lincs 48 K2
Hawthorpe Lincs 48 F8
Hawton Notts 47 U3
Haxby C York 64 E8
Haxby Gates C York 64 E8
Haxey N Linc 58 C7
Haxey Carr N Linc 58 C6
Haxted Surrey 21 R13
Haxton Wilts 18 H11
Hay Cnwll 3 P2
Hay Cnwll 3 P6
Haydock St Hel 55 N7
Haydon BaNES 17 S6
Haydon Dorset 17 S13
Haydon Somset 16 J12
Haydon Bridge Nthumb 76 G13
Haydon Wick Swindn 29 M10
Haye Cnwll 4 K6
Hayes Gt Lon 20 J6
Hayes Gt Lon 21 R9
Hayes End Gt Lon 20 J6
Hayfield Ag & B 94 F14
Hayfield Derbys 56 F9
Hayfield Green Donc 57 U7
Haygate Wrekin 45 P11
Hay Green Norfk 49 R10
Hayhillock Angus 91 R3
Hayle Cnwll 2 F9
Hayle Port Cnwll 2 F9
Hayley Green Dudley 36 C4
Hayling Island Hants 9 U8
Haymoor Green Ches E 45 Q3
Hayne Devon 5 T3
Hayne Devon 16 C13
Haynes C Beds 31 N4
Haynes Church End C Beds 31 N4
Haynes West End C Beds 31 N4
Hay-on-Wye Powys 34 F12
Hayscastle Pembks 24 E5
Hayscastle Cross Pembks 24 F5
Hay Street Herts 31 U7
Hayton Cumb 66 H4
Hayton Cumb 75 V14
Hayton E R Yk 64 J10
Hayton Notts 58 B10
Hayton's Bent Shrops 35 M4
Haytor Vale Devon 5 T5
Haytown Devon 14 J10
Haywards Heath W Susx 11 N6
Haywood Donc 57 S4
Haywood Herefs 35 L14
Haywood Oaks Notts 47 R2
Hazards Green E Susx 12 C13
Hazelbank S Lans 82 F9
Hazelbury Bryan Dorset 7 T3
Hazeleigh Essex 22 K7
Hazeley Hants 20 B11
Hazelford Notts 47 T4
Hazel Grove Stockp 56 D9
Hazelhurst Tamesd 56 E6
Hazelslade Staffs 46 D11
Hazel Street Kent 12 C8
Hazel Stub Suffk 39 U12
Hazelton Walls Fife 91 M7
Hazelwood Derbys 46 K4
Hazlemere Bucks 20 E3
Hazlerigg N u Ty 77 Q11
Hazles Staffs 46 D4
Hazleton Gloucs 29 L4
Heacham Norfk 49 U6
Headbourne Worthy Hants 9 P2
Headbrook Herefs 34 G9
Headcorn Kent 12 F7
Headingley Leeds 63 R12
Headington Oxon 30 B11
Headlam Dur 69 Q9
Headlesscross N Lans 82 H7
Headless Cross Worcs 36 D7
Headley Hants 10 C3
Headley Hants 19 R8
Headley Surrey 21 M12
Headley Down Hants 10 C3
Headley Heath Worcs 36 E5
Headon Devon 14 J12
Headon Notts 58 B11
Heads Nook Cumb 67 R2
Heage Derbys 47 L3
Healaugh N York 64 C10
Healaugh N York 69 M13
Heald Green Stockp 55 T9
Heale Devon 15 P3
Heale Somset 16 H12
Heale Somset 17 L11
Healey N York 63 P3
Healey Nthumb 77 L14
Healey Rochdl 56 C3
Healey Wakefd 57 L3
Healeyfield Dur 69 N3
Healing NE Lin 59 M4
Heamoor Cnwll 2 D10
Heanor Derbys 47 M4
Heanton Punchardon Devon 15 M5
Heapham Lincs 58 E9
Hearn Hants 10 C3
Heart of Scotland Services N Lans 82 H6
Hearts Delight Kent 12 G3
Heasley Mill Devon 15 R6
Heaste Highld 100 f8
Heath Derbys 57 P13
Heath Wakefd 57 N2
Heath and Reach C Beds 30 K7
Heath Common W Susx 10 J7
Heathcote Derbys 46 F1
Heathcote Shrops 45 Q8
Heath End Bucks 20 E3
Heath End Hants 19 P8
Heath End Leics 47 L9
Heath End Warwks 36 H8
Heather Leics 47 L11
Heathfield Cambs 39 Q11
Heathfield Devon 5 U5
Heathfield E Susx 11 T6
Heathfield N York 63 N6
Heathfield Somset 16 G11
Heathfield Village Oxon 30 B9
Heath Green Worcs 36 E6
Heath Hall D & G 74 J10
Heath Hayes & Wimblebury Staffs 46 D11
Heath Hill Shrops 45 S11
Heath House Somset 17 M7
Heathrow Airport Gt Lon 20 J7
Heathstock Devon 6 H4
Heathton Shrops 35 T2
Heath Town Wolves 46 B14
Heathwaite N York 70 G12
Heatley Staffs 46 E8
Heatley Warrtn 55 R9
Heaton Bolton 55 Q5
Heaton C Brad 63 N12
Heaton Lancs 61 S7
Heaton N u Ty 77 R12
Heaton Staffs 56 E14
Heaton Chapel Stockp 56 C8
Heaton Mersey Stockp 56 C8
Heaton Norris Stockp 56 C8
Heaton's Bridge Lancs 54 K4
Heaverham Kent 21 U11
Heaviley Stockp 56 D9
Heavitree Devon 6 B6
Hebburn S Tyne 77 S13
Hebden N York 63 L7
Hebden Bridge Calder 56 E1
Hebden Green Ches W 55 P13
Hebing End Herts 31 T8
Hebron Carmth 25 L5
Hebron IoA 52 G6
Hebron Nthumb 77 P8
Heckfield Hants 20 B10
Heckfield Green Suffk 41 L5
Heckfordbridge Essex 23 M3
Heckington Lincs 48 H5
Heckmondwike Kirk 56 K2
Heddington Wilts 18 E7
Heddon-on-the-Wall Nthumb 77 N12
Hedenham Norfk 41 P2
Hedge End Hants 9 P6
Hedgerley Bucks 20 G5
Hedgerley Green Bucks 20 G5
Hedging Somset 16 K11
Hedley on the Hill Nthumb 77 M14
Hednesford Staffs 46 C11
Hedon E R Yk 65 R14
Hedsor Bucks 20 F5
Heeley Sheff 57 N10
Hegdon Hill Herefs 35 N10
Heglibister Shet 106 t8
Heighington Darltn 69 R8
Heighington Lincs 58 H13
Heightington Worcs 35 S6
Heiton Border 84 J12
Hele Devon 5 S6
Hele Devon 6 C4
Hele Devon 15 M3
Hele Somset 16 G12
Helebridge Cnwll 14 F12
Hele Lane Devon 15 S10
Helensburgh Ag & B 88 G9
Helenton S Ayrs 81 M6
Helford Cnwll 2 K11
Helford Passage Cnwll 2 K11
Helhoughton Norfk 50 E8
Helions Bumpstead Essex 39 U12
Hellaby Rothm 57 R8
Helland Cnwll 3 R2
Hellandbridge Cnwll 3 R2
Hell Corner W Berk 19 N8
Hellescott Cnwll 4 H3
Hellesdon Norfk 51 M11
Hellesveor Cnwll 2 E8
Hellidon Nhants 37 P9
Hellifield N York 62 H8
Hellingly E Susx 11 T8
Hellington Norfk 51 P13
Helm Nthumb 77 P6
Helmdon Nhants 30 C4
Helme Kirk 56 G4
Helmingham Suffk 41 L9
Helmington Row Dur 69 Q5
Helmsdale Highld 112 B13
Helmshore Lancs 55 S2
Helmsley N York 64 E3
Helperby N York 63 U6
Helperthorpe N York 65 M5
Helpringham Lincs 48 H5
Helpston C Pete 48 H12
Helsby Ches W 55 L11
Helsey Lincs 59 T12
Helston Cnwll 2 H11
Helstone Cnwll 4 D4
Helton Cumb 67 R8
Helwith N York 69 N12
Helwith Bridge N York 62 G6
Hemblington Norfk 51 P11
Hembridge Somset 17 Q9
Hemel Hempstead Herts 31 N11
Hemerdon Devon 5 P9
Hemingbrough N York 64 F13
Hemingby Lincs 59 M12
Hemingfield Barns 57 N6
Hemingford Abbots Cambs 39 L6
Hemingford Grey Cambs 39 L6
Hemingstone Suffk 40 K10
Hemington Leics 47 N8
Hemington Nhants 38 G3
Hemington Somset 17 T6
Hemley Suffk 41 N12
Hemlington Middsb 70 H10
Hempholme E R Yk 65 P9
Hempnall Norfk 41 M2
Hempnall Green Norfk 41 M2
Hempriggs Moray 103 T3
Hempstead Essex 39 T13
Hempstead Medway 12 E3
Hempstead Norfk 50 K6
Hempstead Norfk 51 R8
Hempsted Gloucs 28 F4
Hempton Norfk 50 F8
Hempton Oxon 29 T1
Hemsby Norfk 51 S10
Hemswell Lincs 58 F8
Hemswell Cliff Lincs 58 F9
Hemsworth Wakefd 57 P4
Hemyock Devon 6 F2
Henbury Bristl 27 V12
Henbury Ches E 56 C12
Hendham Devon 5 S10
Hendomen Powys 44 F14
Hendon Gt Lon 21 M5
Hendon Sundld 70 F1
Hendra Cnwll 2 J9
Hendra Cnwll 3 Q1
Hendre Brdgnd 26 G11
Hendre Flints 54 E13
Hendy Carmth 25 U10
Heneglwys IoA 52 F7
Henfield W Susx 11 L7
Henford Devon 4 K2
Henfynyw Cerdgn 32 J8
Henghurst Kent 12 J8
Hengoed Caerph 27 M9
Hengoed Powys 34 F10
Hengoed Shrops 44 G7
Hengrave Suffk 40 D7
Henham Essex 22 D2
Heniarth Powys 44 D12
Henlade Somset 16 J12
Henley Dorset 7 S4
Henley Gloucs 28 H4
Henley Shrops 35 L3
Henley Shrops 35 M5
Henley Somset 17 M10
Henley Suffk 41 L10
Henley W Susx 10 D5
Henley Green Covtry 37 L4
Henley-in-Arden Warwks 36 G7
Henley-on-Thames Oxon 20 C6
Henley Park Surrey 20 F12
Henley's Down E Susx 12 D13
Henley Street Kent 12 C2
Henllan Cerdgn 32 G12
Henllan Denbgs 53 T9
Henllan Amgoed Carmth 25 L7
Henllys Torfn 27 P9
Henlow C Beds 31 Q5
Henlow Camp C Beds 31 Q5
Hennock Devon 5 U4
Henny Street Essex 40 E13
Henryd Conwy 53 N8
Henry's Moat (Castell Hendre) Pembks 24 H5
Hensall N York 57 S2
Henshaw Nthumb 76 F13
Hensingham Cumb 66 E9
Henstead Suffk 41 S3
Hensting Hants 9 P4
Henstridge Somset 17 T13
Henstridge Ash Somset 17 T12
Henstridge Marsh Somset 17 T12
Henton Oxon 30 G12
Henton Somset 17 N7
Henwick Worcs 35 T9
Henwood Cnwll 4 H6
Henwood Oxon 29 U7
Heolgerrig Myr Td 26 J6
Heol-las Swans 26 B8
Heol Senni Powys 26 G3
Heol-y-Cyw Brdgnd 26 G11
Hepburn Nthumb 85 R14
Hepple Nthumb 76 K5
Hepscott Nthumb 77 Q9
Heptonstall Calder 62 K14
Hepworth Kirk 56 J5
Hepworth Suffk 40 G6
Herbrandston Pembks 24 E9
Hereford Herefs 35 M13
Hereson Kent 13 S2
Heribusta Highld 100 c2
Heriot Border 83 T8
Hermiston C Edin 83 N4
Hermitage Border 75 V6
Hermitage Dorset 7 S3
Hermitage W Berk 19 R6
Hermitage W Susx 10 B9
Hermit Hill Barns 57 M6
Hermon Carmth 25 Q4
Hermon IoA 52 E9
Hermon Pembks 25 M4
Herne Kent 13 N2
Herne Bay Kent 13 N2
Herne Common Kent 13 N2
Herne Hill Gt Lon 21 P8
Herne Pound Kent 12 C5
Herner Devon 15 N7
Hernhill Kent 13 L3
Herodsfoot Cnwll 4 G8
Heronden Kent 13 Q5
Herongate Essex 22 F9
Heronsford S Ayrs 72 E3
Heronsgate Herts 20 H4
Herriard Hants 19 U11
Herringfleet Suffk 51 S14
Herring's Green Bed 31 N4
Herringswell Suffk 40 B6
Herringthorpe Rothm 57 P8
Herrington Sundld 70 E2
Hersden Kent 13 P3
Hersham Cnwll 14 G11
Hersham Surrey 20 K10
Herstmonceux E Susx 11 U8
Herston Dorset 8 E13
Herston Ork 106 t20
Hertford Herts 31 T10
Hertford Heath Herts 31 U10
Hertingfordbury Herts 31 T10
Hesketh Bank Lancs 54 K2
Hesketh Lane Lancs 62 C11
Hesket Newmarket Cumb 67 M5
Heskin Green Lancs 55 M3
Hesleden Dur 70 F5
Hesleden N York 62 H5
Hesley Donc 57 T8
Hesleyside Nthumb 76 G9
Heslington C York 64 E9
Hessay C York 64 C9
Hessenford Cnwll 4 J9
Hessett Suffk 40 F8
Hessle E R Yk 58 H1
Hessle Wakefd 57 P3
Hest Bank Lancs 61 T6
Hestley Green Suffk 41 L7
Heston Gt Lon 20 K7
Heston Services Gt Lon 20 K7
Hestwall Ork 106 r18
Heswall Wirral 54 G10
Hethe Oxon 30 C7
Hethersett Norfk 50 K13
Hethersgill Cumb 75 U12
Hetherside Cumb 75 T12
Hetherson Green Ches W 45 M3
Hethpool Nthumb 85 M13
Hett Dur 69 S5
Hetton N York 62 K8
Hetton-le-Hole Sundld 70 E3
Hetton Steads Nthumb 85 Q11
Heugh Nthumb 77 M11
Heughhead Abers 104 D13
Heugh Head Border 85 M6
Heveningham Suffk 41 P6
Hever Kent 21 S13
Heversham Cumb 61 T3
Hevingham Norfk 51 L9
Hewas Water Cnwll 3 P7
Hewelsfield Gloucs 27 V7
Hewenden C Brad 63 M12
Hewish N Som 17 M4
Hewish Somset 7 M3
Hewood Dorset 7 L4
Hexham Nthumb 76 J13
Hextable Kent 22 D13
Hexthorpe Donc 57 S6
Hexton Herts 31 P6
Hexworthy Cnwll 4 K4
Hexworthy Devon 5 R6
Hey Lancs 62 H11
Heybridge Essex 22 F8
Heybridge Essex 23 L6
Heybridge Basin Essex 23 L6
Heybrook Bay Devon 5 M11
Heydon Cambs 39 P13
Heydon Norfk 50 K8
Heydour Lincs 48 F6
Hey Houses Lancs 61 Q14
Heylipoll Ag & B 92 B10
Heylor Shet 106 s5
Heyrod Tamesd 56 E7
Heysham Lancs 61 S7
Heyshaw N York 63 P7
Heyshott W Susx 10 D7
Heyside Oldham 56 D5
Heytesbury Wilts 18 D12
Heythrop Oxon 29 S2
Heywood Rochdl 56 C4
Heywood Wilts 18 C10
Hibaldstow N Linc 58 G6
Hickleton Donc 57 Q5
Hickling Norfk 51 R9
Hickling Notts 47 S8
Hickling Green Norfk 51 R9
Hickling Heath Norfk 51 R9
Hickling Pastures Notts 47 S8
Hickmans Green Kent 13 L4
Hicks Forstal Kent 13 N3
Hickstead W Susx 11 M6
Hidcote Bartrim Gloucs 36 G12
Hidcote Boyce Gloucs 36 G12
High Ackworth Wakefd 57 P3
Higham Barns 57 M5
Higham Derbys 47 L2
Higham Kent 12 B6
Higham Kent 22 H13
Higham Lancs 62 G12
Higham Suffk 40 B7
Higham Suffk 40 H13
Higham Dykes Nthumb 77 N10
Higham Ferrers Nhants 38 E7
Higham Gobion C Beds 31 P6
Higham Hill Gt Lon 21 Q4
Higham on the Hill Leics 37 L1
Highampton Devon 15 L12
Highams Park Gt Lon 21 Q4
High Angerton Nthumb 77 M8
High Ardwell D & G 72 D10
High Auldgirth D & G 74 H8
High Bankhill Cumb 67 S4
High Barnet Gt Lon 21 N3
High Beach Essex 21 R3
High Bentham N York 62 D6
High Bewaldeth Cumb 66 K6
High Bickington Devon 15 P8
High Biggins Cumb 62 C4
High Birkwith N York 62 G4
High Blantyre S Lans 82 C7
High Bonnybridge Falk 89 T10
High Borrans Cumb 67 P12
High Bradley N York 63 L10
High Bray Devon 15 Q6
Highbridge Hants 9 P4
Highbridge Somset 16 K7
Highbrook W Susx 11 P4
High Brooms Kent 11 T2
High Bullen Devon 15 M8
Highburton Kirk 56 J4
Highbury Gt Lon 21 P5
Highbury Somset 17 S7
High Buston Nthumb 77 Q4
High Callerton Nthumb 77 P11
High Casterton Cumb 62 C4
High Catton E R Yk 64 G9
Highclere Hants 19 P9
Highcliffe BCP 8 J10
High Close Dur 69 Q9
High Cogges Oxon 29 S6
High Common Norfk 50 G12
High Coniscliffe Darltn 69 R9
High Crosby Cumb 75 U14
High Cross Cnwll 2 J11
High Cross E Ayrs 81 N3
High Cross Hants 9 U3
High Cross Herts 31 U9
Highcross Lancs 61 Q12
High Cross W Susx 11 L7
High Cross Warwks 36 H7
High Drummore D & G 72 E12
High Dubmire Sundld 70 D3
High Easter Essex 22 F5
High Eggborough N York 57 S2
High Ellington N York 63 P3
Higher Alham Somset 17 S8
Higher Ansty Dorset 7 U4
Higher Ballam Lancs 61 R13
Higher Bartle Lancs 61 U13
Higher Berry End C Beds 31 L6
Higher Bockhampton Dorset 7 T6
Higher Brixham Torbay 6 B14
Higher Burrowton Devon 6 D5
Higher Burwardsley Ches W 45 M2
High Ercall Wrekin 45 N10
Higher Chillington Somset 7 L2
Higher Clovelly Devon 14 H8
Highercombe Somset 16 B10
Higher Coombe Dorset 7 P6
Higher Disley Ches E 56 E10
Higher Folds Wigan 55 Q6
Higherford Lancs 62 H11
Higher Gabwell Devon 6 B11
Higher Halstock Leigh Dorset 7 P3
Higher Harpers Lancs 62 G12
Higher Heysham Lancs 61 S7
Higher Hurdsfield Ches E 56 D12
Higher Irlam Salfd 55 R7
Higher Kingcombe Dorset 7 P5
Higher Kinnerton Flints 44 H1
Higher Marston Ches W 55 Q11
Higher Muddiford Devon 15 N5
Higher Nyland Dorset 17 T12
Higher Ogden Rochdl 56 E4
Higher Pentire Cnwll 2 H11
Higher Penwortham Lancs 61 U14
Higher Prestacott Devon 14 J13
Higher Studfold N York 62 G5
Higher Town Cnwll 3 L8
Higher Town Cnwll 3 Q4
Higher Town IoS 2 c1
Higher Tregantle Cnwll 5 L10
Higher Walton Lancs 55 N1
Higher Walton Warrtn 55 N9
Higher Wambrook Somset 6 J3
Higher Waterston Dorset 7 T5
Higher Whatcombe Dorset 8 A8
Higher Wheelton Lancs 55 P2
Higher Whitley Ches W 55 P10
Higher Wincham Ches W 55 Q11
Higher Wraxhall Dorset 7 Q4
Higher Wych Ches W 45 L5
High Etherley Dur 69 Q7
High Ferry Lincs 49 N4
Highfield E R Yk 64 G12
Highfield Gatesd 77 N14
Highfield N Ayrs 81 L2
Highfields Donc 57 R5
Highfields Caldecote Cambs 39 N9
High Flats Kirk 56 K5
High Garrett Essex 22 J2
Highgate E Susx 11 Q4
Highgate Gt Lon 21 N5
Highgate Kent 12 E9
High Grange Dur 69 Q6
High Grantley N York 63 Q6
High Green Cumb 67 P12
High Green Kirk 56 K4
High Green Norfk 41 L3
High Green Norfk 50 K12
High Green Sheff 57 M7
High Green Shrops 35 R4
High Green Suffk 40 E8
High Green Worcs 35 U11
Highgreen Manor Nthumb 76 G7
High Halden Kent 12 G8
High Halstow Medway 22 J12
High Ham Somset 17 M10
High Harrington Cumb 66 F7
High Harrogate N York 63 S8
High Haswell Dur 70 E4
High Hatton Shrops 45 P9
High Hauxley Nthumb 77 R5
High Hawsker N York 71 R11
High Hesket Cumb 67 Q4
High Hoyland Barns 57 L5
High Hunsley E R Yk 65 M12
High Hurstwood E Susx 11 R5
High Hutton N York 64 H6
High Ireby Cumb 66 K5
High Kelling Norfk 50 K5
High Kilburn N York 64 C4
High Killerby N York 65 P3
High Knipe Cumb 67 R9
High Lands Dur 69 P7
Highlane Ches E 56 C13
Highlane Derbys 57 P10
High Lane Stockp 56 E9
High Lanes Cnwll 2 F9
High Laver Essex 22 D6
Highlaws Cumb 66 H3
Highleadon Gloucs 28 E3
High Legh Ches E 55 R10
Highleigh W Susx 10 C11
High Leven S on T 70 G10
Highley Shrops 35 R4
High Littleton BaNES 17 R5
High Lorton Cumb 66 J7
High Marishes N York 64 J4
High Marnham Notts 58 D12
High Melton Donc 57 R6
High Mickley Nthumb 77 M13
Highmoor Cumb 67 L3
Highmoor Oxon 20 B6
Highmoor Cross Oxon 20 B6
Highmoor Hill Mons 27 T10
High Moorsley Sundld 70 D3
Highnam Gloucs 28 E3
High Newport Sundld 70 E2
High Newton Cumb 61 S3
High Newton-by-the-Sea Nthumb 85 U13
High Nibthwaite Cumb 61 P2
High Offley Staffs 45 S8
High Ongar Essex 22 E7
High Onn Staffs 45 T10
High Park Corner Essex 23 P3
High Pennyvenie E Ayrs 81 P11
High Pittington Dur 70 D4
High Post Wilts 18 J13
Highridge N Som 17 Q3
High Roding Essex 22 F4
High Row Cumb 67 N5
High Row Cumb 67 N8
High Salter Lancs 62 C7
High Salvington W Susx 10 J9
High Scales Cumb 66 J3
High Seaton Cumb 66 F6
High Shaw N York 62 H1
High Side Cumb 66 K6
High Spen Gatesd 77 N14
Highstead Kent 13 P2
Highsted Kent 12 H3
High Stoop Dur 69 P4
High Street Cnwll 3 P6
High Street Kent 12 D9
Highstreet Kent 13 L3
High Street Suffk 41 R6
High Street Suffk 41 R9
Highstreet Green Essex 40 C14
Highstreet Green Surrey 10 F3
Hightae D & G 75 L10
Highter's Heath Birm 36 E5
High Throston Hartpl 70 G6
Hightown Ches E 45 U1
Hightown Hants 8 H8
Hightown Sefton 54 H6
High Town Staffs 46 C11
Hightown Green Suffk 40 G9
High Toynton Lincs 59 N13
High Trewhitt Nthumb 77 L4
High Urpeth Dur 69 R2
High Valleyfield Fife 82 K1
High Warden Nthumb 76 J12
Highway Herefs 35 L11
Highway Wilts 18 F6
Highweek Devon 5 U6
High Westwood Dur 69 P1
Highwood Essex 22 F7
Highwood Staffs 46 E7
Highwood W Susx 10 K4
Highwood Hill Gt Lon 21 M4
High Woolaston Gloucs 28 A8
High Worsall N York 70 E11
Highworth Swindn 29 P9
High Wray Cumb 67 N13
High Wych Herts 22 C5
High Wycombe Bucks 20 E4
Hilborough Norfk 50 D13
Hilcote Derbys 47 N2
Hilcott Wilts 18 H9
Hildenborough Kent 21 U13
Hilden Park Kent 21 U13
Hildersham Cambs 39 R11
Hilderstone Staffs 46 C7
Hilderthorpe E R Yk 65 R6
Hilfield Dorset 7 R3
Hilgay Norfk 49 T14
Hill S Glos 28 B8
Hill Warwks 37 N7
Hillam N York 64 C14
Hillbeck Cumb 68 G9
Hillborough Kent 13 P2
Hill Brow Hants 10 B5
Hillbutts Dorset 8 D8
Hill Chorlton Staffs 45 S6
Hillclifflane Derbys 46 J4
Hill Common Norfk 51 R9
Hill Common Somset 16 F11
Hill Deverill Wilts 18 C12
Hilldyke Lincs 49 M4
Hill End Dur 69 M5
Hillend Fife 83 M2
Hill End Fife 90 F12
Hill End Gloucs 36 B13
Hillend Mdloth 83 Q5
Hillend N Lans 82 F5
Hillend Swans 25 R12
Hillersland Gloucs 27 V5
Hillerton Devon 15 R13
Hillesden Bucks 30 E7
Hillesley Gloucs 28 E10
Hillfarrance Somset 16 G12
Hill Green Kent 12 F3
Hillgrove W Susx 10 E5
Hillhampton Herefs 35 N11
Hillhead Abers 104 H8
Hillhead Devon 6 B14
Hill Head Hants 9 Q8
Hillhead S Lans 82 J10
Hillhead of Cocklaw Abers 105 T7
Hilliard's Cross Staffs 46 G11
Hilliclay Highld 112 E4
Hillingdon Gt Lon 20 J6
Hillington C Glas 89 M13
Hillington Norfk 50 B8
Hillis Corner IoW 9 P10
Hillmorton Warwks 37 P6
Hillock Vale Lancs 62 F14
Hill of Beath Fife 90 J13
Hill of Fearn Highld 109 Q9
Hillowton D & G 74 E13
Hillpool Worcs 35 U5
Hillpound Hants 9 R5
Hill Ridware Staffs 46 E10
Hillside Abers 99 S4
Hillside Angus 99 N11
Hillside Devon 5 S8
Hill Side Kirk 56 J3
Hill Side Worcs 35 S8
Hills Town Derbys 57 Q13
Hillstreet Hants 9 L5
Hillswick Shet 106 s6
Hill Top Dur 69 L8
Hill Top Hants 9 N8
Hill Top Kirk 56 G4
Hill Top Rothm 57 N8
Hill Top Sandw 36 C2
Hill Top Wakefd 57 M3
Hillwell Shet 106 t12
Hilmarton Wilts 18 F5
Hilperton Wilts 18 C9
Hilperton Marsh Wilts 18 C9
Hilsea C Port 9 T8
Hilston E R Yk 65 T13
Hiltingbury Hants 9 N4
Hilton Border 85 M8
Hilton Cambs 39 L7
Hilton Cumb 68 F8
Hilton Derbys 46 H7
Hilton Dorset 7 U4
Hilton Dur 69 Q8
Hilton S on T 70 G10
Hilton Shrops 35 S1
Hilton of Cadboll Highld 109 R9
Hilton Park Services Staffs 46 C13
Himbleton Worcs 36 B9
Himley Staffs 35 U2
Hincaster Cumb 61 U3
Hinchley Wood Surrey 21 L9
Hinckley Leics 37 M2
Hinderclay Suffk 40 H5
Hinderwell N York 71 N9
Hindford Shrops 44 H7
Hindhead Surrey 10 D3
Hindhead Tunnel Surrey 10 D3
Hindle Fold Lancs 62 E13
Hindley Nthumb 77 L14
Hindley Wigan 55 P6
Hindley Green Wigan 55 P6
Hindlip Worcs 35 U9
Hindolveston Norfk 50 H8
Hindon Wilts 8 C2
Hindringham Norfk 50 G6
Hingham Norfk 50 H13
Hinksford Staffs 35 U3
Hinstock Shrops 45 Q8
Hintlesham Suffk 40 J12
Hinton Gloucs 28 C7
Hinton Hants 8 J9
Hinton Herefs 34 H13
Hinton Nhants 37 P10
Hinton S Glos 28 D12
Hinton Shrops 35 Q4
Hinton Shrops 44 K12
Hinton Admiral Hants 8 J9
Hinton Ampner Hants 9 S3
Hinton Blewett BaNES 17 Q5
Hinton Charterhouse BaNES 17 U5
Hinton Cross Worcs 36 D12
Hinton-in-the-Hedges Nhants 30 C5
Hinton Marsh Hants 9 R3
Hinton Martell Dorset 8 E7

Hinton on the Green Worcs 36 D12
Hinton Parva Swindn 29 P11
Hinton St George Somset 7 M2
Hinton St Mary Dorset 17 U13
Hinton Waldrist Oxon 29 S8
Hints Shrops 35 P6
Hints Staffs 46 G13
Hinwick Bed 38 D8
Hinxhill Kent 12 K7
Hinxton Cambs 39 Q11
Hinxworth Herts 31 R4
Hipperholme Calder 56 H1
Hipsburn Nthumb 77 Q3
Hipswell N York 69 Q13
Hirn Abers 99 N3
Hirnant Powys 44 B9
Hirst Nthumb 77 R8
Hirst Courtney N York 57 T2
Hirwaen Denbgs 44 D1
Hirwaun Rhondd 26 H6
Hiscott Devon 15 M7
Histon Cambs 39 P8
Hitcham Suffk 40 G10
Hitcham Causeway Suffk 40 G10
Hitcham Street Suffk 40 G10
Hitchin Herts 31 Q7
Hither Green Gt Lon 21 Q8
Hittisleigh Devon 15 R13
Hive E R Yk 64 J13
Hixon Staffs 46 D8
Hoaden Kent 13 Q4
Hoar Cross Staffs 46 F9
Hoarwithy Herefs 27 U2
Hoath Kent 13 P3
Hoathly Kent 12 C8
Hobarris Shrops 34 H5
Hobbles Green Suffk 40 B10
Hobbs Cross Essex 21 S3
Hobbs Cross Essex 22 C5
Hobkirk Border 76 B3
Hobland Hall Norfk 51 T13
Hobsick Notts 47 N4
Hobson Dur 69 Q1
Hoby Leics 47 S10
Hoccombe Somset 16 F11
Hockering Norfk 50 J11
Hockerton Notts 47 T2
Hockley Ches E 56 D10
Hockley Covtry 36 J5
Hockley Essex 22 K9
Hockley Staffs 46 H13
Hockley Heath Solhll 36 G6
Hockliffe C Beds 31 L7
Hockwold cum Wilton Norfk 40 B3
Hockworthy Devon 16 D13
Hoddesdon Herts 31 U11
Hoddlesden Bl w D 55 R2
Hoddom Cross D & G 75 N11
Hoddom Mains D & G 75 N11
Hodgehill Ches E 55 T13
Hodgeston Pembks 24 H11
Hodnet Shrops 45 P8
Hodsock Notts 57 T9
Hodsoll Street Kent 12 B3
Hodson Swindn 18 J4
Hodthorpe Derbys 57 R11
Hoe Hants 9 R5
Hoe Norfk 50 G10
Hoe Benham W Berk 19 P7
Hoe Gate Hants 9 S6
Hoff Cumb 68 E9
Hogben's Hill Kent 12 K4
Hoggards Green Suffk 40 E9
Hoggeston Bucks 30 H8
Hoggrill's End Warwks 36 H2
Hog Hill E Susx 12 G12
Hoghton Lancs 55 P1
Hoghton Bottoms Lancs 55 P1
Hognaston Derbys 46 H3
Hogsthorpe Lincs 59 T12
Holbeach Lincs 49 N9
Holbeach Bank Lincs 49 N8
Holbeach Clough Lincs 49 N8
Holbeach Drove Lincs 49 M11
Holbeach Hurn Lincs 49 N8
Holbeach St Johns Lincs 49 N10
Holbeach St Mark's Lincs 49 N7
Holbeach St Matthew Lincs 49 P7
Holbeck Notts 57 R12
Holbeck Woodhouse Notts 57 R12
Holberrow Green Worcs 36 D9
Holbeton Devon 5 Q10
Holborn Gt Lon 21 P6
Holborough Kent 12 C3
Holbrook Derbys 47 L5
Holbrook Sheff 57 P10
Holbrook Suffk 41 L13
Holbrook Moor Derbys 47 L4
Holbrooks Covtry 36 K4
Holburn Nthumb 85 Q11
Holbury Hants 9 N8
Holcombe Devon 6 C10
Holcombe Somset 17 S7
Holcombe Rogus Devon 16 E13
Holcot Nhants 37 U7
Holden Lancs 62 F10
Holdenby Nhants 37 S7
Holden Gate Calder 56 C2
Holder's Green Essex 22 F2
Holdgate Shrops 35 N3
Holdingham Lincs 48 G4
Holditch Dorset 6 K4
Holdsworth Calder 63 M14
Holehouse Derbys 56 F8
Hole-in-the-Wall Herefs 28 B2
Holemoor Devon 14 K11
Hole Street W Susx 10 J8
Holford Somset 16 G8
Holgate C York 64 D9
Holker Cumb 61 R4
Holkham Norfk 50 E5
Hollacombe Devon 14 J12
Holland Fen Lincs 48 K4
Holland Lees Lancs 55 M5
Holland-on-Sea Essex 23 S4
Hollandstoun Ork 106 w14
Hollee D & G 75 Q12
Hollesley Suffk 41 Q12
Hollicombe Torbay 6 A12
Hollingbourne Kent 12 F4
Hollingbury Br & H 11 N9
Hollingdon Bucks 30 J7
Hollingrove E Susx 12 C11
Hollingthorpe Leeds 63 T13
Hollington Derbys 46 H6
Hollington Staffs 46 E6
Hollingworth Tamesd 56 F7
Hollins Bury 55 T5
Hollins Derbys 57 M12
Hollins Staffs 46 C4
Hollinsclough Staffs 56 G13
Hollins End Sheff 57 N10
Hollins Green Warrtn 55 Q8
Hollins Lane Lancs 61 T9
Hollinswood Wrekin 45 R12
Hollinwood Shrops 45 M6
Hollocombe Devon 15 P10
Holloway Derbys 46 K2
Holloway Gt Lon 21 P5
Holloway Wilts 8 B2
Hollowell Nhants 37 S6
Hollowmoor Heath Ches W 55 L13
Hollows D & G 75 S10
Hollybush Caerph 27 M7
Hollybush E Ayrs 81 M9
Hollybush Herefs 35 S13
Holly End Norfk 49 Q12
Holly Green Worcs 35 U12
Hollyhurst Ches E 45 N5
Hollym E R Yk 59 P1
Hollywater Hants 10 C4
Hollywood Worcs 36 E5
Holmbridge Kirk 56 H5
Holmbury St Mary Surrey 10 J2
Holmbush Cnwll 3 Q6
Holmcroft Staffs 46 B9
Holme Cambs 38 J3
Holme Cumb 61 U4
Holme Kirk 56 H5
Holme N Linc 58 F5
Holme N York 63 T3
Holme Notts 48 B2
Holme Chapel Lancs 62 H14
Holme Green N York 64 D11
Holme Hale Norfk 50 E12
Holme Lacy Herefs 35 N13
Holme Marsh Herefs 34 H10
Holme next the Sea Norfk 50 B5
Holme on the Wolds E R Yk 65 M10
Holme Pierrepont Notts 47 R6
Holmer Herefs 35 M12
Holmer Green Bucks 20 F3
Holme St Cuthbert Cumb 66 H3
Holmes Chapel Ches E 55 S13
Holmesfield Derbys 57 M11
Holmes Hill E Susx 11 S8
Holmeswood Lancs 54 K3
Holmethorpe Surrey 21 N12
Holme upon Spalding Moor E R Yk 64 J12
Holmewood Derbys 57 P13
Holmfield Calder 63 M14
Holmfirth Kirk 56 H5
Holmgate Derbys 57 N14
Holmhead E Ayrs 81 R8
Holmpton E R Yk 59 Q2
Holmrook Cumb 66 G13
Holmshurst E Susx 12 B10
Holmside Dur 69 R3
Holmwrangle Cumb 67 R3
Holne Devon 5 S7
Holnest Dorset 7 S3
Holnicote Somset 16 B7
Holsworthy Devon 14 H12
Holsworthy Beacon Devon 14 J11
Holt Dorset 8 E8
Holt Norfk 50 J6
Holt Wilts 18 C8
Holt Worcs 35 T8
Holt Wrexhm 44 K3
Holtby C York 64 F9
Holt End Worcs 36 E7
Holt Fleet Worcs 35 T8
Holt Green Lancs 54 J5
Holt Heath Dorset 8 F8
Holt Heath Worcs 35 T8
Holton Oxon 30 D11
Holton Somset 17 S11
Holton Suffk 41 R5
Holton cum Beckering Lincs 58 K10
Holton Heath Dorset 8 C10
Holton Hill E Susx 12 C10
Holton le Clay Lincs 59 N6
Holton le Moor Lincs 58 J7
Holton St Mary Suffk 40 J13
Holt Street Kent 13 Q5
Holtye E Susx 11 R3
Holway Flints 54 E11
Holwell Dorset 7 S2
Holwell Herts 31 Q6
Holwell Leics 47 T9
Holwell Oxon 29 P6
Holwick Dur 68 K7
Holworth Dorset 7 U8
Holybourne Hants 10 A2
Holy Cross Worcs 36 B5
Holyfield Essex 31 U12
Holyhead IoA 52 B6
Holy Island IoA 52 C6
Holy Island Nthumb 85 S10
Holy Island Nthumb 85 S10
Holymoorside Derbys 57 M13
Holyport W & M 20 E7
Holystone Nthumb 76 K5
Holytown N Lans 82 E6
Holywell C Beds 31 M9
Holywell Cambs 39 M6
Holywell Cnwll 2 K5
Holywell Dorset 7 Q4
Holywell Flints 54 E11
Holywell Nthumb 77 S11
Holywell Warwks 36 H7
Holywell Green Calder 56 G3
Holywell Lake Somset 16 F12
Holywell Row Suffk 40 B5
Holywood D & G 74 H9
Holywood Village D & G 74 J10
Homer Shrops 45 P13
Homer Green Sefton 54 H6
Homersfield Suffk 41 N3
Homescales Cumb 62 B2
Hom Green Herefs 28 A3
Homington Wilts 8 G3
Honeyborough Pembks 24 F9
Honeybourne Worcs 36 F12
Honeychurch Devon 15 P12
Honey Hill Kent 13 M3
Honeystreet Wilts 18 H8
Honey Tye Suffk 40 G13
Honiley Warwks 36 H6
Honing Norfk 51 P8
Honingham Norfk 50 K11
Honington Lincs 48 D5
Honington Suffk 40 F6
Honington Warwks 36 J12
Honiton Devon 6 G4
Honley Kirk 56 H4
Honnington Wrekin 45 R10
Hoo Kent 13 Q3
Hoobrook Worcs 35 T6
Hood Green Barns 57 M6
Hood Hill Rothm 57 N7
Hooe C Plym 5 N10
Hooe E Susx 12 C13
Hoo End Herts 31 Q8
Hoo Green Ches E 55 R10
Hoohill Bpool 61 Q12
Hook Cambs 39 P2
Hook Devon 6 K3
Hook E R Yk 58 C1
Hook Gt Lon 21 L10
Hook Hants 9 Q7
Hook Hants 20 B12
Hook Pembks 24 G8
Hook Wilts 29 L11
Hook-a-Gate Shrops 45 L12
Hook Bank Worcs 35 T12
Hooke Dorset 7 P4
Hook End Essex 22 E7
Hookgate Staffs 45 R6
Hook Green Kent 12 C8
Hook Green Kent 22 F13
Hook Norton Oxon 37 L14
Hook Street Gloucs 28 C8
Hook Street Wilts 29 L11
Hookway Devon 15 U13
Hookwood Surrey 11 M2
Hooley Surrey 21 N11
Hooley Bridge Rochdl 56 C4
Hoo Meavy Devon 5 N7
Hoo St Werburgh Medway 22 J13
Hooton Ches W 54 J11
Hooton Levitt Rothm 57 R8
Hooton Pagnell Donc 57 Q5
Hooton Roberts Rothm 57 Q7
Hopcrofts Holt Oxon 29 U2
Hope Derbys 56 J10
Hope Devon 5 R12
Hope Flints 44 H2
Hope Powys 44 G12
Hope Shrops 44 H13
Hope Staffs 46 F3
Hope Bagot Shrops 35 N6
Hope Bowdler Shrops 35 L2
Hope End Green Essex 22 E3
Hopehouse Border 75 Q2
Hopeman Moray 103 T2
Hope Mansell Herefs 28 B4
Hopesay Shrops 34 J4
Hopetown Wakefd 57 N2
Hope under Dinmore Herefs 35 M10
Hopgrove C York 64 E9
Hopperton N York 63 U8
Hop Pole Lincs 48 J11
Hopsford Warwks 37 M4
Hopstone Shrops 35 S2
Hopton Derbys 46 J3
Hopton Shrops 44 J9
Hopton Staffs 46 B8
Hopton Suffk 40 G5
Hopton Cangeford Shrops 35 M4
Hopton Castle Shrops 34 J5
Hoptonheath Shrops 34 J5
Hopton on Sea Norfk 51 T14
Hopton Wafers Shrops 35 P5
Hopwas Staffs 46 G13
Hopwood Rochdl 56 C5
Hopwood Worcs 36 D5
Hopwood Park Services Worcs 36 D6
Horam E Susx 11 T7
Horbling Lincs 48 H6
Horbury Wakefd 57 L3
Horcott Gloucs 29 N7
Horden Dur 70 F4
Horderley Shrops 34 K3
Hordle Hants 8 K9
Hordley Shrops 44 J7
Horeb Carmth 25 S9
Horeb Cerdgn 32 G12
Horfield Bristl 28 A12
Horham Suffk 41 M6
Horkesley Heath Essex 23 N2
Horkstow N Linc 58 G3
Horley Oxon 37 M12
Horley Surrey 11 M2
Hornblotton Green Somset 17 Q10
Hornby Lancs 62 B6
Hornby N York 69 R14
Hornby N York 70 E11
Horncastle Lincs 59 N13
Hornchurch Gt Lon 22 D10
Horncliffe Nthumb 85 N9
Horndean Border 85 N9
Horndean Hants 9 U6
Horndon Devon 5 N4
Horndon on the Hill Thurr 22 G11
Horne Surrey 11 N2
Horner Somset 16 B7
Horne Row Essex 22 J7
Horners Green Suffk 40 G12
Horney Common E Susx 11 R5
Horn Hill Bucks 20 H4
Horning Norfk 51 P10
Horninghold Leics 38 B1
Horninglow Staffs 46 H8
Horningsea Cambs 39 Q8
Horningsham Wilts 18 B12
Horningtoft Norfk 50 F9
Horningtops Cnwll 4 H8
Hornsbury Somset 6 K2
Hornsby Cumb 67 R2
Hornsbygate Cumb 67 R2
Horns Cross Devon 14 J8
Horns Cross E Susx 12 F11
Hornsea E R Yk 65 R10
Hornsey Gt Lon 21 P5
Horn's Green Gt Lon 21 S11
Horn Street Kent 13 N8
Hornton Oxon 37 L11
Horpit Swindn 29 P11
Horrabridge Devon 5 N7
Horringer Suffk 40 D8
Horringford IoW 9 Q11
Horrocks Fold Bolton 55 R4
Horrocksford Lancs 62 F11
Horsacott Devon 15 M6
Horsebridge Devon 5 L5
Horsebridge E Susx 11 T8
Horsebridge Hants 9 L2
Horsebridge Shrops 44 J12
Horsebridge Staffs 46 C3
Horsebrook Staffs 45 U11
Horsecastle N Som 17 M3
Horsedown Cnwll 2 G10
Horsehay Wrekin 45 Q12
Horseheath Cambs 39 T11
Horsehouse N York 63 L3
Horsell Surrey 20 G11
Horseman's Green Wrexhm 44 K5
Horsenden Bucks 30 G12
Horsey Norfk 51 S9
Horsey Somset 16 K9
Horsey Corner Norfk 51 S9
Horsford Norfk 51 L10
Horsforth Leeds 63 Q12
Horsham W Susx 10 K4
Horsham Worcs 35 R9
Horsham St Faith Norfk 51 M10
Horsington Lincs 59 L13
Horsington Somset 17 T12
Horsley Derbys 47 L5
Horsley Gloucs 28 F8
Horsley Nthumb 76 G6
Horsley Nthumb 77 M12
Horsley Cross Essex 23 R2
Horsleycross Street Essex 23 R2
Horsley-Gate Derbys 57 M11
Horsleyhill Border 76 A2
Horsley's Green Bucks 20 C4
Horsley Woodhouse Derbys 47 L5
Horsmonden Kent 12 D7
Horspath Oxon 30 C11
Horstead Norfk 51 N10
Horsted Keynes W Susx 11 P5
Horton Bucks 30 K9
Horton Dorset 8 E7
Horton Lancs 62 H9
Horton Nhants 38 B10
Horton S Glos 28 E11
Horton Shrops 45 L8
Horton Somset 6 K2
Horton Staffs 46 B2
Horton Surrey 21 L10
Horton Swans 25 S13
Horton W & M 20 H7
Horton Wilts 18 F8
Horton Wrekin 45 Q11
Horton Cross Somset 16 K13
Horton-cum-Studley Oxon 30 C10
Horton Green Ches W 45 L4
Horton Heath Hants 9 P5
Horton-in-Ribblesdale N York 62 G5
Horton Kirby Kent 21 U9
Horwich Bolton 55 P4
Horwich End Derbys 56 F10
Horwood Devon 15 M7
Hoscar Lancs 55 L4
Hoscote Border 75 S3
Hose Leics 47 T8
Hosey Hill Kent 21 S12
Hosh P & K 90 C7
Hoswick Shet 106 u11
Hotham E R Yk 64 K13
Hothfield Kent 12 J7
Hoton Leics 47 Q9
Hott Nthumb 76 F8
Hough Ches E 45 R3
Hough Ches E 56 C11
Hougham Lincs 48 C5
Hough End Leeds 63 Q13
Hough Green Halton 55 L9
Hough-on-the-Hill Lincs 48 D4
Houghton Cambs 39 L6
Houghton Cumb 75 T14
Houghton Hants 9 L2
Houghton Nthumb 77 N12
Houghton Pembks 24 G9
Houghton W Susx 10 G8
Houghton Conquest C Beds 31 M4
Houghton Gate Dur 70 D2
Houghton Green E Susx 12 H11
Houghton Green Warrtn 55 P8
Houghton le Side Darltn 69 R8
Houghton-le-Spring Sundld 70 D3
Houghton on the Hill Leics 47 S13
Houghton Regis C Beds 31 M8
Houghton St Giles Norfk 50 F6
Houlton Warwks 37 Q6
Hound Green Hants 20 B11
Houndslow Border 84 G9
Houndsmoor Somset 16 F11
Houndwood Border 85 L6
Hounslow Gt Lon 20 K7
Househill Highld 103 N4
Houses Hill Kirk 56 J3
Housieside Abers 105 P10
Houston Rens 88 K12
Houstry Highld 112 E10
Houton Ork 106 s19
Hove Br & H 11 M10
Hove Edge Calder 56 H2
Hoveringham Notts 47 S4
Hoveton Norfk 51 P10
Hovingham N York 64 F4
Howbrook Barns 57 M7
How Caple Herefs 28 B1
Howden E R Yk 64 G14
Howden-le-Wear Dur 69 Q6
Howe Highld 112 H4
Howe IoM 60 b9
Howe N York 63 T3
Howe Norfk 51 N14
Howe Bridge Wigan 55 Q6
Howe Green Essex 22 H7
Howegreen Essex 22 K7
Howell Lincs 48 H4
How End C Beds 31 M4
Howe of Teuchar Abers 105 M6
Howes D & G 75 N12
Howe Street Essex 22 G5
Howe Street Essex 39 U14
Howey Powys 34 C9
Howgate Cumb 66 E8
Howgate Mdloth 83 P7
Howgill Lancs 62 G10
Howick Nthumb 77 R2
Howle Wrekin 45 Q9
Howle Hill Herefs 28 B3
Howlett End Essex 39 S14
Howley Somset 6 J3
How Mill Cumb 67 R1
Howmore W Isls 106 c15
Hownam Border 76 F2
Howrigg Cumb 67 M3
Howsham N Linc 58 H6
Howsham N York 64 G7
Howtel Nthumb 85 M12
Howt Green Kent 12 G2
Howton Herefs 27 S2
Howtown Cumb 67 P9
How Wood Herts 31 P12
Howwood Rens 88 J13
Hoxa Ork 106 t20
Hoxne Suffk 41 L5
Hoy Ork 106 r20
Hoylake Wirral 54 F9
Hoyland Barns 57 N6
Hoyland Common Barns 57 N6
Hoylandswaine Barns 57 L6
Hoyle W Susx 10 E7
Hoyle Mill Barns 57 N5
Hubberholme N York 62 J4
Hubberston Pembks 24 E9
Hubbert's Bridge Lincs 49 L5
Huby N York 63 R10
Huby N York 64 D6
Huccaby Devon 5 R6
Hucclecote Gloucs 28 G4
Hucking Kent 12 F4
Hucknall Notts 47 P4
Huddersfield Kirk 56 H3
Huddington Worcs 36 B9
Hudnall Herts 31 M10
Hudswell N York 69 P12
Huggate E R Yk 64 K8
Hugglescote Leics 47 M11
Hughenden Valley Bucks 20 E3
Hughley Shrops 45 N14
Hugh Town IoS 2 c2
Huish Devon 15 M10
Huish Wilts 18 H8
Huish Champflower Somset 16 E11
Huish Episcopi Somset 17 M11
Hùisinis W Isls 106 e7
Huisinish W Isls 106 e7
Hulcote C Beds 30 K5
Hulcote Nhants 37 T11
Hulcott Bucks 30 J9
Hulham Devon 6 D8
Hulland Derbys 46 H4
Hulland Ward Derbys 46 J4
Hullavington Wilts 18 C4
Hull Bridge E R Yk 65 P11
Hullbridge Essex 22 K8
Hull, Kingston upon C KuH 65 P14
Hulme Manch 55 T7
Hulme Staffs 46 B4
Hulme Warrtn 55 P8
Hulme End Staffs 46 F2
Hulme Walfield Ches E 55 T13
Hulse Heath Ches E 55 R10
Hulton Lane Ends Bolton 55 Q5
Hulverstone IoW 9 M12
Hulver Street Norfk 50 F11
Hulver Street Suffk 41 S3
Humber Devon 6 A9
Humber Herefs 35 M9
Humber Bridge N Linc 58 H2
Humberside Airport N Linc 58 J4
Humberston NE Lin 59 P5
Humberstone C Leic 47 R12
Humberton N York 63 U6
Humbie E Loth 84 D6
Humbleton E R Yk 65 S13
Humbleton Nthumb 85 P13
Humby Lincs 48 F7
Hume Border 84 J10
Humshaugh Nthumb 76 J11
Huna Highld 112 J2
Huncoat Lancs 62 F13
Huncote Leics 47 P14
Hundalee Border 76 C2
Hundall Derbys 57 N11
Hunderthwaite Dur 69 L8
Hundleby Lincs 59 Q13
Hundle Houses Lincs 48 K3
Hundleton Pembks 24 G10
Hundon Suffk 40 B11
Hundred End Lancs 54 K2
Hundred House Powys 34 D10
Hungarton Leics 47 S12
Hungerford Hants 8 H6
Hungerford Somset 16 D8
Hungerford W Berk 19 M7
Hungerford Newtown W Berk 19 N6
Hunger Hill Bolton 55 Q5
Hunger Hill Lancs 55 M4
Hungerstone Herefs 34 K13
Hungerton Lincs 48 C8
Hungryhatton Shrops 45 Q8
Hunmanby N York 65 P4
Hunningham Warwks 37 L7
Hunnington Worcs 36 C4
Hunsbury Hill Nhants 37 T9
Hunsdon Herts 22 B5
Hunsdonbury Herts 22 B5
Hunsingore N York 63 U9
Hunslet Leeds 63 S13
Hunsonby Cumb 67 S5
Hunstanton Norfk 49 U5
Hunstanworth Dur 68 K3
Hunsterson Ches E 45 Q4
Hunston Suffk 40 G7
Hunston W Susx 10 D10
Hunston Green Suffk 40 G7
Hunstrete BaNES 17 R4
Hunsworth Kirk 56 J1
Hunt End Worcs 36 D8
Hunter's Inn Devon 15 Q3
Hunter's Quay Ag & B 88 E10
Huntham Somset 16 K11
Hunthill Lodge Angus 98 H9
Huntingdon Cambs 38 K6
Huntingfield Suffk 41 P6
Huntingford Dorset 17 V11
Huntington C York 64 E8
Huntington Ches W 54 K14
Huntington E Loth 84 D4
Huntington Herefs 34 G10
Huntington Herefs 35 L12
Huntington Staffs 46 C11
Huntingtowerfield P & K 90 G6
Huntley Gloucs 28 D4
Huntly Abers 104 G8
Hunton Hants 19 Q12
Hunton Kent 12 D6
Hunton N York 63 P1
Hunton Bridge Herts 31 N12
Hunt's Corner Norfk 40 J3
Huntscott Somset 16 B8
Hunt's Cross Lpool 54 K9
Hunts Green Bucks 30 J12
Hunts Green Warwks 36 G1
Huntsham Devon 16 D12
Huntshaw Devon 15 M8
Huntshaw Cross Devon 15 M8
Huntspill Somset 16 K7
Huntstile Somset 16 J10
Huntworth Somset 16 K10
Hunwick Dur 69 Q6
Hunworth Norfk 50 J6
Hurcott Somset 17 L13
Hurdcott Wilts 8 H2
Hurdsfield Ches E 56 D12
Hurley W & M 20 D6
Hurley Warwks 36 H1
Hurley Bottom W & M 20 D6
Hurley Common Warwks 36 H1
Hurlford E Ayrs 81 P5
Hurlston Green Lancs 54 J4
Hurn BCP 8 G9
Hurn's End Lincs 49 P4
Hursley Hants 9 N3
Hurst Dorset 7 U6
Hurst N York 69 M12
Hurst Somset 17 N13
Hurst Wokham 20 C8
Hurstbourne Priors Hants 19 P11
Hurstbourne Tarrant Hants 19 N10
Hurst Green E Susx 12 D10
Hurst Green Essex 23 Q4
Hurst Green Lancs 62 D12
Hurst Green Surrey 21 R12
Hurst Hill Dudley 36 B2
Hurstley Herefs 34 J11
Hurstpierpoint W Susx 11 M7
Hurst Wickham W Susx 11 M7
Hurstwood Lancs 62 H13
Hurtiso Ork 106 u19
Hurtmore Surrey 20 F13
Hurworth Burn Dur 70 F6
Hurworth-on-Tees Darltn 70 D11
Hurworth Place Darltn 69 S11
Hury Dur 69 L9
Husbands Bosworth Leics 37 R4
Husborne Crawley C Beds 31 L5
Husthwaite N York 64 C5
Hutcherleigh Devon 5 T10
Hut Green N York 57 S2
Huthwaite Notts 47 N2
Huttoft Lincs 59 T11
Hutton Border 85 N8
Hutton Cumb 67 P7
Hutton E R Yk 65 N9
Hutton Essex 22 F8
Hutton Lancs 55 L1
Hutton N Som 17 L5
Hutton Bonville N York 70 D12
Hutton Buscel N York 65 M3
Hutton Conyers N York 63 S5
Hutton Cranswick E R Yk 65 N9
Hutton End Cumb 67 Q5
Hutton Hang N York 63 P2
Hutton Henry Dur 70 F5
Hutton-le-Hole N York 64 G1
Hutton Lowcross R & Cl 70 J10
Hutton Magna Dur 69 P10
Hutton Mulgrave N York 71 P11
Hutton Roof Cumb 62 B4
Hutton Roof Cumb 67 N6
Hutton Rudby N York 70 G11
Hutton Sessay N York 64 B4
Hutton Wandesley N York 64 C9
Huxham Devon 6 B5
Huxham Green Somset 17 Q9
Huxley Ches W 45 M1
Huyton Knows 54 K8
Hycemoor Cumb 60 K2
Hyde Gloucs 28 G7
Hyde Hants 8 H6
Hyde Tamesd 56 D8
Hyde Heath Bucks 30 K12
Hyde Lea Staffs 46 B10
Hydestile Surrey 10 F2
Hykeham Moor Lincs 58 F13
Hylands House & Park Essex 22 G7
Hyndford Bridge S Lans 82 H10
Hynish Ag & B 92 B11
Hyssington Powys 34 H2
Hystfield Gloucs 28 C8
Hythe Essex 23 P2
Hythe Hants 9 N7
Hythe Kent 13 N9
Hythe Somset 17 M6
Hythe End W & M 20 H8
Hyton Cumb 60 K2

I

Ibberton Dorset 7 U3
Ible Derbys 46 H2
Ibsley Hants 8 H7
Ibstock Leics 47 M12
Ibstone Bucks 20 C4
Ibthorpe Hants 19 N10
Iburndale N York 71 Q11
Ibworth Hants 19 S10
Icelton N Som 17 L3
Ichrachan Ag & B 94 E12
Ickburgh Norfk 40 D1
Ickenham Gt Lon 20 J5
Ickford Bucks 30 D11
Ickham Kent 13 P4
Ickleford Herts 31 Q6
Icklesham E Susx 12 G12
Ickleton Cambs 39 Q12
Icklingham Suffk 40 C6
Ickornshaw N York 62 K11
Ickwell Green C Beds 38 J11
Icomb Gloucs 29 P3
Idbury Oxon 29 P4
Iddesleigh Devon 15 N11
Ide Devon 6 A6
Ideford Devon 6 A9
Ide Hill Kent 21 S12
Iden E Susx 12 H11
Iden Green Kent 12 D8
Iden Green Kent 12 F9
Idle C Brad 63 P12
Idless Cnwll 3 L7
Idlicote Warwks 36 J12
Idmiston Wilts 18 J13
Idole Carmth 25 R7
Idridgehay Derbys 46 J4
Idrigill Highld 100 c3
Idstone Oxon 29 Q11
Iffley Oxon 30 B12
Ifield W Susx 11 M3
Ifold W Susx 10 G4
Iford BCP 8 G10
Iford E Susx 11 Q9
Ifton Mons 27 T10
Ifton Heath Shrops 44 H6
Ightfield Shrops 45 N6
Ightham Kent 21 U11
Iken Suffk 41 R9
Ilam Staffs 46 F3
Ilchester Somset 17 P12
Ilderton Nthumb 77 L1
Ilford Gt Lon 21 R5
Ilford Somset 17 L13
Ilfracombe Devon 15 M3
Ilkeston Derbys 47 N5
Ilketshall St Andrew Suffk 41 Q3
Ilketshall St John Suffk 41 Q3
Ilketshall St Lawrence Suffk 41 Q4
Ilketshall St Margaret Suffk 41 P3
Ilkley C Brad 63 N10
Illand Cnwll 4 H5
Illey Dudley 36 C4
Illidge Green Ches E 55 S14
Illingworth Calder 63 M14
Illogan Cnwll 2 H8
Illston on the Hill Leics 47 T14
Ilmer Bucks 30 G11
Ilmington Warwks 36 H12
Ilminster Somset 7 L2
Ilsington Devon 5 T5
Ilsington Dorset 7 U6
Ilston Swans 25 U12
Ilton N York 63 P4
Ilton Somset 17 L13
Imachar N Ayrs 79 R7
Immingham NE Lin 59 L4
Immingham Dock NE Lin 59 L3
Impington Cambs 39 P8
Ince Ches W 55 L11
Ince Blundell Sefton 54 H6
Ince-in-Makerfield Wigan 55 N6
Inchbae Lodge Hotel Highld 108 G11
Inchbare Angus 99 L10
Inchberry Moray 104 C4
Incheril Highld 107 T12
Inchinnan Rens 89 L12
Inchlaggan Highld 101 T11
Inchmichael P & K 90 K6
Inchmore Highld 102 G6
Inchnadamph Highld 110 F12
Inchture P & K 91 L6
Inchyra P & K 90 J7
Indian Queens Cnwll 3 N5
Ingatestone Essex 22 F8
Ingbirchworth Barns 56 K5
Ingerthorpe N York 63 R6
Ingestre Staffs 46 C9
Ingham Lincs 58 F10
Ingham Norfk 51 Q8
Ingham Suffk 40 E6
Ingham Corner Norfk 51 Q8
Ingleborough Norfk 49 Q10
Ingleby Derbys 46 K8
Ingleby Arncliffe N York 70 F12
Ingleby Barwick S on T 70 F10
Ingleby Cross N York 70 G12
Ingleby Greenhow N York 70 J11
Ingleigh Green Devon 15 P11
Inglesbatch BaNES 17 T4
Inglesham Swindn 29 P8
Ingleston D & G 74 J12
Ingleton Dur 69 Q8
Ingleton N York 62 D5
Inglewhite Lancs 61 U12
Ingmanthorpe N York 63 U9
Ingoe Nthumb 77 L11
Ingol Lancs 61 U13
Ingoldisthorpe Norfk 49 U7
Ingoldmells Lincs 59 U13
Ingoldsby Lincs 48 F8
Ingram Nthumb 77 L2
Ingrave Essex 22 F9
Ingrow C Brad 63 M12
Ings Cumb 67 P13
Ingst S Glos 28 A10
Ingthorpe Rutlnd 48 E12
Ingworth Norfk 51 L8
Inkberrow Worcs 36 D9
Inkerman Dur 69 P5
Inkersall Green Derbys 57 P12
Inkhorn Abers 105 Q8
Inkpen W Berk 19 N8
Inkstack Highld 112 G2
Inmarsh Wilts 18 D8
Innellan Ag & B 88 E11
Innerleithen Border 83 R11
Innerleven Fife 91 N11
Innermessan D & G 72 D7
Innerwick E Loth 84 J4
Innesmill Moray 104 B3
Innsworth Gloucs 28 G3
Insch Abers 104 J10
Insh Highld 97 N3
Inshes Highld 102 J7
Inskip Lancs 61 T12
Inskip Moss Side Lancs 61 T12
Instow Devon 15 L6
Insworke Cnwll 5 L10
Intake Sheff 57 N10
Inver Abers 98 C5
Inver Highld 109 R8
Inver P & K 90 F3
Inverailort Highld 93 T2
Inveralligin Highld 107 P13
Inverallochy Abers 105 S2
Inveran Highld 108 K5
Inveraray Ag & B 88 C4
Inverarish Highld 100 e6
Inverarity Angus 91 Q3
Inverarnan Stirlg 88 H2
Inverarnie Highld 102 J9
Inverasdale Highld 107 P8
Inverbeg Ag & B 88 H6
Inverbervie Abers 99 Q9
Inverboyndie Abers 104 K3
Invercreran Lodge Ag & B 94 E9
Inverdruie Highld 103 N13
Inveresk E Loth 83 R4
Inveresragan Ag & B 94 D11
Inverey Abers 97 T6
Inverfarigaig Highld 102 F11
Inverfolla Ag & B 94 D10
Invergarry Highld 96 C3
Invergeldie P & K 95 U13
Invergloy Highld 101 U14
Invergordon Highld 109 N11
Invergowrie P & K 91 M5
Inverguseran Highld 100 g9
Inverhadden P & K 95 T7
Inverie Highld 100 g9
Inverinan Ag & B 87 T2
Inverinate Highld 101 N7
Inverkeilor Angus 91 U2
Inverkeithing Fife 83 M2
Inverkeithny Abers 104 J6
Inverkip Inver 88 F11
Inverkirkaig Highld 110 B13
Inverlael Highld 108 B7
Inverlair Highld 96 C8
Inverliever Lodge Ag & B 87 R4
Inverlochy Ag & B 94 H13
Invermark Angus 98 G7
Invermoriston Highld 102 D12
Invernaver Highld 111 Q4
Inverneill Ag & B 87 Q9
Inverness Highld 102 J6
Inverness Airport Highld 103 L5
Invernettie Abers 105 U7
Invernoaden Ag & B 88 D6
Inveroran Hotel Ag & B 94 K10
Inverquharity Angus 98 G12
Inverquhomery Abers 105 S6
Inverroy Highld 96 B7
Inversanda Highld 94 C7
Invershiel Highld 101 N8
Invershin Highld 108 K5
Invershore Highld 112 F9
Inversnaid Hotel Stirlg 88 H4
Inverugie Abers 105 T6
Inveruglas Ag & B 88 H4
Inveruglass Highld 97 N3
Inverurie Abers 105 M11
Inwardleigh Devon 15 N13
Inworth Essex 23 L4
Iochdar W Isls 106 c14
Iona Ag & B 92 H13
Iping W Susx 10 D6
iPort Logistics Park Donc 57 T7
Ipplepen Devon 5 U7
Ipsden Oxon 19 T3
Ipstones Staffs 46 D4
Ipswich Suffk 41 L12
Irby Wirral 54 G10
Irby in the Marsh Lincs 59 S14
Irby upon Humber NE Lin 59 L6
Irchester Nhants 38 D7
Ireby Cumb 66 K5
Ireby Lancs 62 D4
Ireland C Beds 31 P4
Ireleth Cumb 61 N4
Ireshopeburn Dur 68 J5
Ireton Wood Derbys 46 J4
Irlam Salfd 55 R8
Irnham Lincs 48 F8
Iron Acton S Glos 28 C11
Iron Bridge Cambs 49 Q14
Ironbridge Wrekin 45 Q13
Ironbridge Gorge Wrekin 45 Q13
Iron Cross Warwks 36 E10
Ironmacannie D & G 73 R4
Irons Bottom Surrey 21 M13
Ironville Derbys 47 M3
Irstead Norfk 51 Q9
Irthington Cumb 75 U13
Irthlingborough Nhants 38 D6
Irton N York 65 N3
Irvine N Ayrs 81 L5
Isauld Highld 112 A3
Isbister Shet 106 t4
Isbister Shet 106 v7
Isfield E Susx 11 Q7
Isham Nhants 38 C6
Isington Hants 10 B2
Islandpool Worcs 35 U4
Islay Ag & B 78 F4
Islay Airport Ag & B 78 E5
Isle Abbotts Somset 17 L12
Isle Brewers Somset 17 L12
Isleham Cambs 39 T6
Isle of Dogs Gt Lon 21 Q7
Isle of Grain Medway 23 L12
Isle of Lewis W Isls 106 i5
Isle of Man IoM 60 f5
Isle of Man Ronaldsway Airport IoM 60 d9
Isle of Mull Ag & B 93 Q11
Isle of Purbeck Dorset 8 E12
Isle of Sheppey Kent 12 J2
Isle of Skye Highld 100 d6
Isle of Thanet Kent 13 R2
Isle of Walney Cumb 61 M6
Isle of Whithorn D & G 73 M12
Isle of Wight IoW 9 Q11
Isleornsay Highld 100 g8
Isles of Scilly IoS 2 c2
Isles of Scilly St Mary's Airport IoS 2 c2
Islesteps D & G 74 J11
Islet Village Guern 6 e2
Isleworth Gt Lon 21 L7
Isley Walton Leics 47 M9
Islibhig W Isls 106 f6
Islington Gt Lon 21 P6
Islip Nhants 38 E5
Islip Oxon 30 B10
Islivig W Isls 106 f6
Isombridge Wrekin 45 P11
Istead Rise Kent 22 F13
Itchen Abbas Hants 9 Q2
Itchen Stoke Hants 9 R2
Itchingfield W Susx 10 J5
Itchington S Glos 28 C10
Itteringham Norfk 50 K7
Itton Devon 15 Q13
Itton Mons 27 T8
Itton Common Mons 27 T8
Ivegill Cumb 67 P4
Ivelet N York 68 K13
Iver Bucks 20 H6
Iver Heath Bucks 20 H6
Iveston Dur 69 P2
Ivinghoe Bucks 30 K9
Ivinghoe Aston Bucks 31 L9
Ivington Herefs 35 L9
Ivington Green Herefs 35 L9
Ivybridge Devon 5 Q9
Ivychurch Kent 12 K10
Ivy Cross Dorset 8 B4
Ivy Hatch Kent 21 U12
Ivy Todd Norfk 50 E12
Iwade Kent 12 H2
Iwerne Courtney Dorset 8 B6
Iwerne Minster Dorset 8 B6
Ixworth Suffk 40 F6
Ixworth Thorpe Suffk 40 F6

J

Jack Green Lancs 55 N1
Jack Hill N York 63 P9
Jack-in-the-Green Devon 6 D5
Jack's Bush Hants 19 L13
Jacksdale Notts 47 M3
Jackson Bridge Kirk 56 J5
Jackton S Lans 81 R2
Jacobstow Cnwll 14 E13
Jacobstowe Devon 15 N12
Jacobs Well Surrey 20 G12
Jameston Pembks 24 J11
Jamestown Highld 102 E4
Jamestown W Duns 88 J9
Janetstown Highld 112 E10
Janetstown Highld 112 J6
Jardine Hall D & G 75 M8
Jarrow S Tyne 77 S13
Jarvis Brook E Susx 11 S5
Jasper's Green Essex 22 H2
Jawcraig Falk 89 T10
Jaywick Essex 23 S5
Jealott's Hill Br For 20 E8
Jeater Houses N York 70 F14
Jedburgh Border 76 C1
Jeffreyston Pembks 24 J9
Jemimaville Highld 102 K2
Jerbourg Guern 6 e4
Jersey Jersey 7 d2
Jersey Airport Jersey 7 b2
Jersey Marine Neath 26 C9
Jerusalem Lincs 58 F12
Jesmond N u Ty 77 R12
Jevington E Susx 11 T10
Jingle Street Mons 27 T5
Jockey End Herts 31 M10
Jodrell Bank Ches E 55 S12
Jodrell Bank Ches E 55 S12
Johnby Cumb 67 P6
John Lennon Airport Lpool 54 K10
John o' Groats Highld 112 J2
Johns Cross E Susx 12 D11
Johnshaven Abers 99 P10
Johnson Street Norfk 51 Q10
Johnston Pembks 24 F8
Johnstone D & G 75 P5
Johnstone Rens 88 K13
Johnstonebridge D & G 75 M7
Johnstown Carmth 25 Q7
Johnstown Wrexhm 44 H4
Joppa C Edin 83 R4
Joppa Cerdgn 33 L7
Joppa S Ayrs 81 N9
Jordans Bucks 20 G4
Jordanston Pembks 24 F4
Jordanthorpe Sheff 57 N10
Joyden's Wood Kent 22 D13
Jubilee Corner Kent 12 F6
Jump Barns 57 N6
Jumper's Town E Susx 11 R4
Juniper Nthumb 76 J14
Juniper Green C Edin 83 N5
Jura Ag & B 86 J9
Jurassic Coast Devon 6 K7
Jurby IoM 60 f3
Jurston Devon 5 R4

K

Kaber Cumb 68 G10
Kaimend S Lans 82 J9
Kames Ag & B 87 T11
Kames E Ayrs 82 C13
Kea Cnwll 3 L8
Keadby N Linc 58 D4
Keal Cotes Lincs 49 N1
Kearby Town End N York 63 S10
Kearsley Bolton 55 S6
Kearsley Nthumb 77 L10
Kearsney Kent 13 Q7
Kearstwick Cumb 62 C4
Kearton N York 69 L13
Keasden N York 62 E6
Keaton Devon 5 Q10
Keckwick Halton 55 N10
Keddington Lincs 59 P9
Keddington Corner Lincs 59 Q9
Kedington Suffk 40 B11
Kedleston Derbys 46 K5
Keelby Lincs 59 L4
Keele Staffs 45 T4
Keele Services Staffs 45 T5
Keele University Staffs 45 T4
Keeley Green Bed 38 F11
Keelham C Brad 63 M13
Keeres Green Essex 22 E5
Keeston Pembks 24 F7
Keevil Wilts 18 D9
Kegworth Leics 47 N8
Kehelland Cnwll 2 G8
Keig Abers 104 J12
Keighley C Brad 63 M11
Keilarsbrae Clacks 90 C13
Keillour P & K 90 E6
Keiloch Abers 98 B5
Keils Ag & B 86 J12
Keinton Mandeville Somset 17 P10
Keir Mill D & G 74 G7
Keirsleywell Row Nthumb 68 G2
Keisby Lincs 48 F8
Keisley Cumb 68 F8
Keiss Highld 112 H4
Keith Moray 104 E5
Keithick P & K 90 K4
Keithock Angus 99 L11
Keithtown Highld 102 F4
Kelbrook Lancs 62 J11
Kelby Lincs 48 F5
Keld Cumb 67 S10
Keld N York 68 J12
Keld Head N York 64 H3
Keldholme N York 64 G2
Kelfield N Linc 58 D6
Kelfield N York 64 D12
Kelham Notts 47 U2
Kelhead D & G 75 M12
Kellacott Devon 5 L3
Kellamergh Lancs 61 S14
Kellas Angus 91 Q4
Kellas Moray 103 U5
Kellaton Devon 5 U13
Kelleth Cumb 68 E11
Kelling Norfk 50 J5
Kellingley N York 57 R2
Kellington N York 57 S2
Kelloe Dur 70 D5
Kelloholm D & G 74 D3
Kells Cumb 66 E9
Kelly Devon 4 K4
Kelly Bray Cnwll 4 K6
Kelmarsh Nhants 37 T5
Kelmscott Oxon 29 P8
Kelsale Suffk 41 Q7
Kelsall Ches W 55 M13
Kelshall Herts 31 T5
Kelsick Cumb 66 J2
Kelso Border 84 J12
Kelstedge Derbys 57 M14
Kelstern Lincs 59 M9
Kelsterton Flints 54 G12
Kelston BaNES 17 T3
Keltneyburn P & K 95 V9
Kelton D & G 74 J11
Kelty Fife 90 H13
Kelvedon Essex 23 L4
Kelvedon Hatch Essex 22 E8
Kelynack Cnwll 2 B11
Kemacott Devon 15 Q3
Kemback Fife 91 P9
Kemberton Shrops 45 R13
Kemble Gloucs 28 J8
Kemble Wick Gloucs 28 J8
Kemerton Worcs 36 C13
Kemeys Commander Mons 27 Q7
Kemnay Abers 105 L12
Kempe's Corner Kent 12 K6
Kempley Gloucs 28 C2
Kempley Green Gloucs 28 C2
Kempsey Worcs 35 T11
Kempsford Gloucs 29 N8
Kemps Green Warwks 36 F6
Kempshott Hants 19 T10
Kempston Bed 38 F11
Kempston Hardwick Bed 31 M4
Kempton Shrops 34 J4
Kemp Town Br & H 11 N10
Kemsing Kent 21 U11
Kemsley Kent 12 H2
Kemsley Street Kent 12 F3
Kenardington Kent 12 J9
Kenchester Herefs 34 K12
Kencot Oxon 29 Q7
Kendal Cumb 67 R14
Kenderchurch Herefs 27 S2
Kendleshire S Glos 28 C12
Kenfig Brdgnd 26 E11
Kenfig Hill Brdgnd 26 E11
Kenilworth Warwks 36 J6
Kenley Gt Lon 21 P10
Kenley Shrops 45 N13
Kenmore Highld 107 N13
Kenmore P & K 95 V9
Kenn Devon 6 B7
Kenn N Som 17 M3
Kennacraig Ag & B 79 Q3
Kennall Vale Cnwll 2 J9
Kennards House Cnwll 4 H4
Kenneggy Cnwll 2 F11
Kennerleigh Devon 15 T11
Kennet Clacks 90 D13
Kennethmont Abers 104 G10
Kennett Cambs 39 U7
Kennford Devon 6 B7
Kenninghall Norfk 40 H3
Kennington Kent 12 K6
Kennington Oxon 30 B12
Kennington Lees Kent 12 K6
Kennoway Fife 91 N11
Kenny Somset 16 K13
Kenny Hill Suffk 39 U5
Kennythorpe N York 64 H6
Kenovay Ag & B 92 B9
Kensaleyre Highld 100 d4
Kensington Gt Lon 21 N7
Kensington Palace Gt Lon 21 N6
Kensworth Common C Beds 31 M9
Kentallen Highld 94 E7
Kentchurch Herefs 27 S2
Kentford Suffk 40 B7
Kent Green Ches E 45 T2
Kentisbeare Devon 6 E3
Kentisbury Devon 15 P4
Kentisbury Ford Devon 15 P4
Kentish Town Gt Lon 21 N6
Kentmere Cumb 67 Q12
Kenton Devon 6 C8
Kenton Gt Lon 21 L5
Kenton N u Ty 77 Q12
Kenton Suffk 41 L7
Kenton Bankfoot N u Ty 77 Q12
Kentra Highld 93 R5
Kents Bank Cumb 61 R4
Kentsboro Hants 19 M13
Kent's Green Gloucs 28 D3
Kent's Oak Hants 9 L4
Kent Street E Susx 12 E12
Kent Street Kent 12 C5
Kenwick Shrops 44 K7
Kenwyn Cnwll 3 L7
Kenyon Warrtn 55 P7
Keoldale Highld 110 H3
Keppoch Highld 101 M7
Kepwick N York 64 B1
Keresley Covtry 36 K4
Kermincham Ches E 55 T13
Kernborough Devon 5 T12
Kerne Bridge Herefs 28 A4
Kerrera Ag & B 93 U13
Kerridge Ches E 56 D11
Kerridge-end Ches E 56 D11
Kerris Cnwll 2 C11
Kerry Powys 34 D2
Kerrycroy Ag & B 88 D13
Kersall Notts 47 T1
Kersbrook Devon 6 E8
Kerscott Devon 15 P7
Kersey Suffk 40 H12
Kersey Tye Suffk 40 G12
Kersey Upland Suffk 40 G12
Kershader W Isls 106 i7
Kershopefoot Cumb 75 U9
Kersoe Worcs 36 C12
Kerswell Devon 6 E3
Kerswell Green Worcs 35 U11
Kerthen Wood Cnwll 2 F10
Kesgrave Suffk 41 M11
Kessingland Suffk 41 T3
Kessingland Beach Suffk 41 T3
Kestle Cnwll 3 P7
Kestle Mill Cnwll 3 L5
Keston Gt Lon 21 R10
Keswick Cumb 67 L8
Keswick Norfk 51 M13
Ketsby Lincs 59 Q11
Kettering Nhants 38 C5
Ketteringham Norfk 51 L13
Kettins P & K 90 K4
Kettlebaston Suffk 40 G10
Kettlebridge Fife 91 M10
Kettlebrook Staffs 46 H13
Kettleburgh Suffk 41 N8
Kettle Green Herts 22 B4
Kettleholm D & G 75 M10
Kettleness N York 71 P9
Kettleshulme Ches E 56 E11
Kettlesing N York 63 Q8
Kettlesing Bottom N York 63 Q8
Kettlestone Norfk 50 G7
Kettlethorpe Lincs 58 D11
Kettletoft Ork 106 v16
Kettlewell N York 62 K5
Ketton Rutlnd 48 E13
Kew Gt Lon 21 L7
Kew Royal Botanic Gardens Gt Lon 21 L7
Kewstoke N Som 16 K4
Kexbrough Barns 57 M5
Kexby C York 64 G9
Kexby Lincs 58 E9
Key Green Ches E 56 C14
Key Green N York 71 P12
Keyham Leics 47 S12
Keyhaven Hants 9 L10
Keyingham E R Yk 59 M1
Keymer W Susx 11 N7
Keynsham BaNES 17 S3
Keysoe Bed 38 G8
Keysoe Row Bed 38 G8
Keyston Cambs 38 F5
Key Street Kent 12 G3
Keyworth Notts 47 R7
Kibbear Somset 16 H12
Kibblesworth Gatesd 69 R1
Kibworth Beauchamp Leics 37 S2
Kibworth Harcourt Leics 37 S2
Kidbrooke Gt Lon 21 R7
Kidburngill Cumb 66 G8
Kiddemore Green Staffs 45 U12
Kidderminster Worcs 35 T5
Kiddington Oxon 29 T3
Kidd's Moor Norfk 50 K13
Kidlington Oxon 29 U5
Kidmore End Oxon 19 U5
Kidsdale D & G 73 L12
Kidsgrove Staffs 45 T3
Kidstones N York 62 K3
Kidwelly Carmth 25 R9
Kiel Crofts Ag & B 94 C11
Kielder Nthumb 76 C7
Kielder Forest 76 C8
Kiells Ag & B 86 G12
Kilbarchan Rens 88 K13
Kilbeg Highld 100 f9
Kilberry Ag & B 79 N3
Kilbirnie N Ayrs 81 L2
Kilbride Ag & B 87 N10
Kilbride Ag & B 88 B12
Kilbuiack Moray 103 S3
Kilburn Derbys 47 L4
Kilburn Gt Lon 21 M6
Kilburn N York 64 C4
Kilby Leics 37 R1
Kilchamaig Ag & B 79 Q3
Kilchattan Ag & B 80 G2
Kilchattan Ag & B 86 F6
Kilcheran Ag & B 93 U11
Kilchoan Highld 93 M6
Kilchoman Ag & B 78 C3
Kilchrenan Ag & B 94 E14
Kilconquhar Fife 91 Q11
Kilcot Gloucs 28 C2
Kilcoy Highld 102 G5
Kilcreggan Ag & B 88 F9
Kildale N York 70 K11
Kildalloig Ag & B 79 P12
Kildary Highld 109 P10
Kildavaig Ag & B 87 T12
Kildavanan Ag & B 88 B12
Kildonan Highld 111 U12
Kildonan N Ayrs 80 E8
Kildonan Lodge Highld 111 U12
Kildonnan Highld 93 M1
Kildrochet House D & G 72 D8
Kildrummy Abers 104 F12
Kildwick N York 63 L10
Kilfinan Ag & B 87 S10
Kilfinnan Highld 96 B4
Kilford Denbgs 54 C13
Kilgetty Pembks 24 K9
Kilgrammie S Ayrs 80 K12
Kilgwrrwg Common Mons 27 T8
Kilham E R Yk 65 P7
Kilham Nthumb 85 M12
Kilkenneth Ag & B 92 A10
Kilkenzie Ag & B 79 M11
Kilkerran Ag & B 79 N12
Kilkhampton Cnwll 14 G10
Killamarsh Derbys 57 Q10
Killay Swans 25 V12
Killearn Stirlg 89 M8
Killen Highld 102 J4
Killerby Darltn 69 Q9
Killerton Devon 6 C4
Killichonan P & K 95 Q7
Killiechonate Highld 94 J2
Killiechronan Ag & B 93 N10
Killiecrankie P & K 97 Q11
Killilan Highld 101 N5
Killimster Highld 112 H5
Killin Stirlg 95 R12
Killinghall N York 63 R8
Killington Cumb 62 C2
Killington Devon 15 Q3
Killington Lake Services Cumb 62 B1
Killingworth N Tyne 77 R11
Killiow Cnwll 3 L8
Killochyett Border 84 D9
Kilmacolm Inver 88 J11
Kilmahog Stirlg 89 P4
Kilmahumaig Ag & B 87 P7
Kilmaluag Highld 100 d2
Kilmany Fife 91 N7
Kilmarnock E Ayrs 81 N5
Kilmartin Ag & B 87 Q6
Kilmaurs E Ayrs 81 N4
Kilmelford Ag & B 87 R3
Kilmersdon Somset 17 S6
Kilmeston Hants 9 R3
Kilmichael Ag & B 79 M11
Kilmichael Glassary Ag & B 87 R7
Kilmichael of Inverlussa Ag & B 87 P8
Kilmington Devon 6 J5
Kilmington Wilts 17 U9
Kilmington Common Wilts 17 U9
Kilmington Street Wilts 17 U9
Kilmorack Highld 102 E7
Kilmore Ag & B 94 B13
Kilmore Highld 100 f9
Kilmory Ag & B 87 N11
Kilmory Highld 93 N5
Kilmory N Ayrs 80 D8
Kilmuir Highld 100 b5
Kilmuir Highld 100 c2
Kilmuir Highld 102 J6
Kilmuir Highld 109 P10
Kilmun Ag & B 88 E9
Kilnave Ag & B 86 D11
Kilncadzow S Lans 82 G9
Kilndown Kent 12 D8
Kiln Green Wokham 20 D7
Kilnhill Cumb 66 K6
Kilnhurst Rothm 57 Q7
Kilninver Ag & B 87 Q1
Kiln Pit Hill Nthumb 69 M1
Kilnsea E R Yk 59 R3
Kilnsey N York 62 K6
Kilnwick E R Yk 65 M10
Kilnwick Percy E R Yk 64 J9
Kilnwood Vale W Susx 11 L4
Kiloran Ag & B 86 F6

Kilpatrick N Ayrs 79 S10
Kilpeck Herefs 27 S1
Kilpin E R Yk 58 C1
Kilpin Pike E R Yk 58 C1
Kilrenny Fife 91 S11
Kilsby Nhants 37 Q6
Kilspindie P & K 90 K6
Kilstay D & G 72 E12
Kilsyth N Lans 89 R10
Kiltarlity Highld 102 F7
Kilton R & Cl 71 M9
Kilton Somset 16 G8
Kilton Thorpe R & Cl 71 L9
Kilvaxter Highld 100 c3
Kilve Somset 16 F8
Kilvington Notts 48 B5
Kilwinning N Ayrs 81 L4
Kimberley Norfk 50 J13
Kimberley Notts 47 N5
Kimberworth Rothm 57 P8
Kimblesworth Dur 69 S3
Kimble Wick Bucks 30 H11
Kimbolton Cambs 38 H7
Kimbolton Herefs 35 M8
Kimcote Leics 37 Q3
Kimmeridge Dorset 8 C13
Kimmerston Nthumb 85 P11
Kimpton Hants 19 L11
Kimpton Herts 31 Q9
Kimworthy Devon 14 H10
Kinbrace Highld 111 T10
Kinbuck Stirlg 89 S4
Kincaple Fife 91 Q8
Kincardine Fife 90 D14
Kincardine Highld 109 L7
Kincardine Bridge Fife 82 H1
Kincardine O'Neil Abers 98 K4
Kinclaven P & K 90 J4
Kincorth C Aber 99 S3
Kincorth House Moray 103 R3
Kincraig Highld 97 N2
Kincraigie P & K 90 E2
Kindallachan P & K 90 E2
Kinerarach Ag & B 79 M5
Kineton Gloucs 29 L2
Kineton Warwks 36 K10
Kinfauns P & K 90 J7
Kingarth Ag & B 80 F1
Kingcausie Abers 99 R4
Kingcoed Mons 27 S6
Kingerby Lincs 58 J8
Kingford Devon 14 G11
Kingham Oxon 29 Q3
Kingholm Quay D & G 74 J11
Kinghorn Fife 83 Q1
Kinglassie Fife 90 K12
Kingoodie P & K 91 M6
King's Acre Herefs 35 L12
Kingsand Cnwll 5 L10
Kingsash Bucks 30 J11
Kingsbarns Fife 91 S9
Kingsborough Kent 23 N13
Kingsbridge Devon 5 S12
Kingsbridge Somset 16 C9
Kingsbridge Swans 25 U11
King's Bromley Staffs 46 F10
Kingsbrook Bucks 30 H10
Kingsburgh Highld 100 c4
Kingsbury Gt Lon 21 L5
Kingsbury Warwks 36 H1
Kingsbury Episcopi Somset 17 M12
King's Caple Herefs 27 V2
Kingsclere Hants 19 R9
King's Cliffe Nhants 38 F1
Kings Clipstone Notts 57 T14
Kingscote Gloucs 28 F8
Kingscott Devon 15 M9
King's Coughton Warwks 36 E9
Kingscross N Ayrs 80 E7
Kingsdon Somset 17 P11
Kingsdown Kent 13 S6
Kingsdown Swindn 29 N10
Kingsdown Wilts 18 B7
Kingseat Abers 105 Q12
Kingseat Fife 90 H13
Kingsey Bucks 30 F11
Kingsfold W Susx 10 K3
Kingsford C Aber 99 R2
Kingsford E Ayrs 81 N3
Kingsford Worcs 35 T4
Kingsgate Kent 13 S1
Kings Green Gloucs 35 S14
Kingshall Street Suffk 40 F8
Kingsheanton Devon 15 N5
King's Heath Birm 36 E4
Kings Hill Kent 12 C4
King's Hill Wsall 36 C1
Kings House Hotel Highld 94 K8
Kingshurst Solhll 36 G3
Kingside Hill Cumb 66 J2
Kingskerswell Devon 6 A11
Kingskettle Fife 91 M10
Kingsland Dorset 7 N5
Kingsland Herefs 34 K8
Kingsland IoA 52 C6
Kings Langley Herts 31 N12
Kingsley Ches W 55 N12
Kingsley Hants 10 B3
Kingsley Staffs 46 D4
Kingsley Green W Susx 10 D4
Kingsley Holt Staffs 46 D4
Kingsley Park Nhants 37 U8
Kingslow Shrops 45 S14
King's Lynn Norfk 49 T9
Kings Meaburn Cumb 68 D8
Kingsmead Hants 9 R6
King's Mills Guern 6 c3
King's Moss St Hel 55 M6
Kingsmuir Angus 91 Q2
Kings Muir Border 83 Q11
Kingsmuir Fife 91 R10
Kings Newnham Warwks 37 N5
King's Newton Derbys 47 L8
Kingsnorth Kent 12 K8
King's Norton Birm 36 E5
King's Norton Leics 47 S13
Kings Nympton Devon 15 Q9
King's Pyon Herefs 34 K10
Kings Ripton Cambs 39 L5
King's Somborne Hants 9 M2
King's Stag Dorset 7 T2
King's Stanley Gloucs 28 F7
King's Sutton Nhants 37 N13
Kingstanding Birm 36 E2
Kingsteignton Devon 5 V6
Kingsteps Highld 103 P4
King Sterndale Derbys 56 G12
Kingsthorne Herefs 27 T1
Kingsthorpe Nhants 37 U8
Kingston Cambs 39 M9
Kingston Cnwll 4 K5
Kingston Devon 5 Q11
Kingston Devon 6 E7
Kingston Dorset 7 U3
Kingston Dorset 8 D13
Kingston E Loth 84 E2
Kingston Hants 8 G8
Kingston IoW 9 P12
Kingston Kent 13 N5
Kingston W Susx 10 H10
Kingston Bagpuize Oxon 29 T8
Kingston Blount Oxon 20 B3
Kingston by Sea W Susx 11 L9
Kingston Deverill Wilts 18 B13
Kingstone Herefs 34 K13
Kingstone Somset 7 L2
Kingstone Staffs 46 E8
Kingstone Winslow Oxon 29 Q10
Kingston Lacy House & Gardens Dorset 8 D8
Kingston Lisle Oxon 29 R10
Kingston near Lewes E Susx 11 P9
Kingston on Soar Notts 47 P8
Kingston on Spey Moray 104 C2
Kingston Russell Dorset 7 Q6
Kingston St Mary Somset 16 H11
Kingston Seymour N Som 17 M3
Kingston Stert Oxon 30 F12
Kingston upon Hull C KuH 65 P14
Kingston upon Thames Gt Lon 21 L9
Kingstown Cumb 75 S14
King's Walden Herts 31 Q8
Kingswear Devon 5 V10
Kingswells C Aber 99 R2
Kings Weston Bristl 27 U12
Kingswinford Dudley 35 U3
Kingswood Bucks 30 E9
Kingswood C KuH 65 P13
Kingswood Gloucs 28 D9
Kingswood Kent 12 F5
Kingswood Powys 44 F13
Kingswood S Glos 28 B13
Kingswood Somset 16 F9
Kingswood Surrey 21 M11
Kingswood Warwks 36 G6
Kingswood Brook Warwks 36 G6
Kingswood Common Herefs 34 G10
Kingswood Common Staffs 45 T13
Kings Worthy Hants 9 P2
Kingthorpe Lincs 58 K11
Kington Herefs 34 G9
Kington S Glos 28 B9
Kington Worcs 36 C9
Kington Langley Wilts 18 D5
Kington Magna Dorset 17 U12
Kington St Michael Wilts 18 D5
Kingussie Highld 97 M3
Kingweston Somset 17 P10
Kinharrachie Abers 105 Q9
Kinharvie D & G 74 H12
Kinkell Bridge P & K 90 D8
Kinknockie Abers 105 S7
Kinleith C Edin 83 N5
Kinlet Shrops 35 R4
Kinloch Highld 100 d10
Kinloch Highld 110 G10
Kinloch Highld 111 M6
Kinloch P & K 90 H3
Kinlochard Stirlg 89 L5
Kinlochbervie Highld 110 E5
Kinlocheil Highld 94 D3
Kinlochewe Highld 107 T12
Kinloch Hourn Highld 101 P10
Kinlochlaggan Highld 96 G6
Kinlochleven Highld 94 H6
Kinlochmoidart Highld 93 S4
Kinlochnanuagh Highld 93 S2
Kinloch Rannoch P & K 95 T7
Kinloss Moray 103 S3
Kinmel Bay Conwy 53 S6
Kinmuck Abers 105 N12
Kinmundy Abers 105 P12
Kinnabus Ag & B 78 D7
Kinnadie Abers 105 R7
Kinnaird P & K 97 R12
Kinneff Abers 99 Q8
Kinnelhead D & G 74 K5
Kinnell Angus 99 L13
Kinnerley Shrops 44 H9
Kinnersley Herefs 34 H11
Kinnersley Worcs 35 U12
Kinnerton Powys 34 F8
Kinnerton Shrops 34 J1
Kinnerton Green Flints 44 H1
Kinnesswood P & K 90 J11
Kinninvie Dur 69 N8
Kinnordy Angus 98 F12
Kinoulton Notts 47 S7
Kinross P & K 90 H11
Kinrossie P & K 90 J5
Kinross Services P & K 90 H11
Kinsbourne Green Herts 31 P9
Kinsey Heath Ches E 45 Q5
Kinsham Herefs 34 J7
Kinsham Worcs 36 B13
Kinsley Wakefd 57 P4
Kinson BCP 8 F9
Kintail Highld 101 P8
Kintbury W Berk 19 N7
Kintessack Moray 103 R3
Kintillo P & K 90 H8
Kinton Herefs 34 K6
Kinton Shrops 44 J10
Kintore Abers 105 M12
Kintour Ag & B 78 H5
Kintra Ag & B 78 E6
Kintra Ag & B 92 J13
Kintraw Ag & B 87 Q5
Kintyre Ag & B 79 N8
Kinveachy Highld 103 P12
Kinver Staffs 35 T4
Kiplin N York 69 S13
Kippax Leeds 63 U13
Kippen Stirlg 89 P7
Kippford D & G 66 B2
Kipping's Cross Kent 12 B7
Kirbister Ork 106 s19
Kirby Bedon Norfk 51 N12
Kirby Bellars Leics 47 T10
Kirby Cane Norfk 41 Q2
Kirby Corner Covtry 36 J5
Kirby Cross Essex 23 T3
Kirby Fields Leics 47 P13
Kirby Green Norfk 41 Q2
Kirby Grindalythe N York 65 L6
Kirby Hill N York 63 T6
Kirby Hill N York 69 P11
Kirby Knowle N York 64 B2
Kirby-le-Soken Essex 23 T3
Kirby Misperton N York 64 H4
Kirby Muxloe Leics 47 P13
Kirby Sigston N York 70 F14
Kirby Underdale E R Yk 64 J8
Kirby Wiske N York 63 T3
Kirdford W Susx 10 G5
Kirk Highld 112 G5
Kirkabister Shet 106 u10
Kirkandrews D & G 73 Q10
Kirkandrews upon Eden Cumb 75 S14
Kirkbampton Cumb 67 M1
Kirkbean D & G 74 J14
Kirk Bramwith Donc 57 T4
Kirkbride Cumb 66 K1
Kirkbridge N York 63 R1
Kirkbuddo Angus 91 R3
Kirkburn Border 83 Q11
Kirkburn E R Yk 65 M8
Kirkburton Kirk 56 J4
Kirkby Knows 54 K7
Kirkby Lincs 58 J8
Kirkby N York 70 H11
Kirkby Fleetham N York 69 S14
Kirkby Green Lincs 48 G2
Kirkby-in-Ashfield Notts 47 P2
Kirkby-in-Furness Cumb 61 N3
Kirkby la Thorpe Lincs 48 G4
Kirkby Lonsdale Cumb 62 C4
Kirkby Malham N York 62 H7
Kirkby Mallory Leics 47 N13
Kirkby Malzeard N York 63 Q5
Kirkby Mills N York 64 G2
Kirkbymoorside N York 64 F2
Kirkby on Bain Lincs 48 K1
Kirkby Overblow N York 63 S10
Kirkby Stephen Cumb 68 G11
Kirkby Thore Cumb 68 D7
Kirkby Underwood Lincs 48 G8
Kirkby Wharf N York 64 C11
Kirkby Woodhouse Notts 47 N3
Kirkcaldy Fife 91 L13
Kirkcambeck Cumb 76 A12
Kirkchrist D & G 73 R9
Kirkcolm D & G 72 C6
Kirkconnel D & G 74 D3
Kirkconnell D & G 74 J12
Kirkcowan D & G 72 J7
Kirkcudbright D & G 73 R9
Kirkdale Lpool 54 H8
Kirk Deighton N York 63 T9
Kirk Ella E R Yk 65 N14
Kirkfieldbank S Lans 82 G10
Kirkgunzeon D & G 74 G12
Kirk Hallam Derbys 47 N5
Kirkham Lancs 61 S13
Kirkham N York 64 G6
Kirkhamgate Wakefd 57 L2
Kirk Hammerton N York 64 B8
Kirkharle Nthumb 77 L9
Kirkhaugh Nthumb 68 E3
Kirkheaton Kirk 56 J3
Kirkheaton Nthumb 77 L10
Kirkhill Highld 102 G6
Kirkhope S Lans 74 J4
Kirkhouse Cumb 76 B14
Kirkhouse Green Donc 57 T4
Kirkibost Highld 100 e8
Kirkinch P & K 91 M3
Kirkinner D & G 73 L9
Kirkintilloch E Duns 89 Q11
Kirk Ireton Derbys 46 J3
Kirkland Cumb 66 G9
Kirkland Cumb 68 D6
Kirkland D & G 74 D3
Kirkland D & G 74 F7
Kirkland D & G 74 K8
Kirkland Guards Cumb 66 J4
Kirk Langley Derbys 46 J6
Kirkleatham R & Cl 70 J8
Kirklevington S on T 70 F11
Kirkley Suffk 41 T2
Kirklington N York 63 S3
Kirklington Notts 47 S2
Kirklinton Cumb 75 T12
Kirkliston C Edin 83 M4
Kirkmabreck D & G 73 M8
Kirkmaiden D & G 72 E12
Kirk Merrington Dur 69 S6
Kirk Michael IoM 60 e4
Kirkmichael P & K 97 T12
Kirkmichael S Ayrs 81 L11
Kirkmuirhill S Lans 82 E10
Kirknewton Nthumb 85 N12
Kirknewton W Loth 83 M5
Kirkney Abers 104 G9
Kirk of Shotts N Lans 82 F6
Kirkoswald Cumb 67 S4
Kirkoswald S Ayrs 80 J11
Kirkpatrick D & G 74 H7
Kirkpatrick Durham D & G 74 E11
Kirkpatrick-Fleming D & G 75 Q11
Kirk Sandall Donc 57 T5
Kirksanton Cumb 61 L3
Kirk Smeaton N York 57 R3
Kirkstall Leeds 63 R12
Kirkstead Lincs 48 J1
Kirkstile Abers 104 G8
Kirkstile D & G 75 S7
Kirkstone Pass Inn Cumb 67 P11
Kirkstyle Highld 112 H2
Kirkthorpe Wakefd 57 N2
Kirkton Abers 104 J10
Kirkton D & G 74 J9
Kirkton Fife 91 N6
Kirkton Highld 101 L6
Kirkton Highld 101 N3
Kirkton P & K 90 E8
Kirkton Manor Border 83 P11
Kirkton of Airlie Angus 98 E13
Kirkton of Auchterhouse Angus 91 M4
Kirkton of Barevan Highld 103 M6
Kirkton of Collace P & K 90 J5
Kirkton of Durris Abers 99 P4
Kirkton of Glenbuchat Abers 104 D12
Kirkton of Glenisla Angus 98 C11
Kirkton of Kingoldrum Angus 98 E12
Kirkton of Lethendy P & K 90 H3
Kirkton of Logie Buchan Abers 105 R10
Kirkton of Maryculter Abers 99 R4
Kirkton of Menmuir Angus 98 J11
Kirkton of Monikie Angus 91 R4
Kirkton of Rayne Abers 104 K9
Kirkton of Skene Abers 99 Q2
Kirkton of Tealing Angus 91 P4
Kirkton of Tough Abers 104 J13
Kirktown Abers 105 R2
Kirktown Abers 105 T5
Kirktown of Alvah Abers 104 K3
Kirktown of Bourtie Abers 105 N10
Kirktown of Deskford Moray 104 G3
Kirktown of Fetteresso Abers 99 R6
Kirktown of Mortlach Moray 104 C8
Kirktown of Slains Abers 105 S10
Kirkurd Border 83 M10
Kirkwall Ork 106 t18
Kirkwall Airport Ork 106 t19
Kirkwhelpington Nthumb 76 K9
Kirk Yetholm Border 85 L13
Kirmington N Linc 58 K4
Kirmond le Mire Lincs 59 L8
Kirn Ag & B 88 E10
Kirriemuir Angus 98 F13
Kirstead Green Norfk 41 N1
Kirtlebridge D & G 75 P11
Kirtling Cambs 39 U9
Kirtling Green Cambs 39 U9
Kirtlington Oxon 29 U4
Kirtomy Highld 111 Q4
Kirton Lincs 49 M6
Kirton Notts 57 U13
Kirton Suffk 41 N12
Kirton End Lincs 49 L5
Kirtonhill W Duns 88 J10
Kirton Holme Lincs 49 L5
Kirton in Lindsey N Linc 58 F7
Kirwaugh D & G 73 L9
Kishorn Highld 101 L4
Kislingbury Nhants 37 S9
Kitebrook Warwks 29 P1
Kite Green Warwks 36 G7
Kites Hardwick Warwks 37 N7
Kitleigh Cnwll 14 F13
Kitt Green Wigan 55 M5
Kittisford Somset 16 E12
Kittle Swans 25 U13
Kitt's Green Birm 36 G3
Kittybrewster C Aber 99 S2
Kitwood Hants 9 T2
Kivernoll Herefs 27 T1
Kiveton Park Rothm 57 Q10
Knaith Lincs 58 D10
Knaith Park Lincs 58 D9
Knap Corner Dorset 17 V12
Knaphill Surrey 20 G11
Knapp Somset 16 K11
Knapp Hill Hants 9 N4
Knapthorpe Notts 47 T2
Knapton C York 64 D9
Knapton N York 64 K4
Knapton Norfk 51 P7
Knapton Green Herefs 34 K10
Knapwell Cambs 39 M8
Knaresborough N York 63 T8
Knarsdale Nthumb 68 E2
Knaven Abers 105 P7
Knayton N York 63 U2
Knebworth Herts 31 S8
Knedlington E R Yk 64 G14
Kneesall Notts 58 B14
Kneeton Notts 47 T4
Knelston Swans 25 S13
Knenhall Staffs 46 B6
Knettishall Suffk 40 G4
Knightacott Devon 15 Q5
Knightcote Warwks 37 M10
Knightley Staffs 45 T8
Knightley Dale Staffs 45 T9
Knighton BCP 8 F9
Knighton C Leic 47 R13
Knighton Devon 5 N11
Knighton Dorset 7 R2
Knighton Powys 34 G6
Knighton Somset 16 G8
Knighton Staffs 45 R5
Knighton Staffs 45 S8
Knighton Wilts 19 L6
Knighton on Teme Worcs 35 P7
Knightsbridge Gloucs 28 G2
Knightsmill Cnwll 4 D4
Knightwick Worcs 35 R9
Knill Herefs 34 G8
Knipoch Ag & B 93 U14
Knipton Leics 48 B7
Knitsley Dur 69 P3
Kniveton Derbys 46 H3
Knock Cumb 68 E7
Knock Highld 100 f9
Knock Moray 104 G5
Knock W Isls 106 j5
Knockally Highld 112 D11
Knockan Highld 108 C2
Knockando Moray 103 U7
Knockbain Highld 102 G7
Knockbain Highld 102 H4
Knock Castle N Ayrs 88 E13
Knockdee Highld 112 E4
Knockdow Ag & B 88 D11
Knockdown Wilts 28 F10
Knockeen S Ayrs 81 L13
Knockenkelly N Ayrs 80 E7
Knockentiber E Ayrs 81 N5
Knockhall Kent 22 E13
Knockholt Kent 21 S11
Knockholt Pound Kent 21 S11
Knockin Shrops 44 H9
Knockinlaw E Ayrs 81 N5
Knockmill Kent 21 U10
Knocknain D & G 72 B7
Knockrome Ag & B 86 K11
Knocksharry IoM 60 d5
Knocksheen D & G 73 P3
Knockvennie Smithy D & G 74 E11
Knodishall Suffk 41 R8
Knodishall Common Suffk 41 R8
Knole Somset 17 N11
Knole Park S Glos 28 A11
Knolls Green Ches E 55 T11
Knolton Wrexhm 44 J6
Knook Wilts 18 D12
Knossington Leics 48 B12
Knott End-on-Sea Lancs 61 R10
Knotting Bed 38 F8
Knotting Green Bed 38 F8
Knottingley Wakefd 57 R2
Knotty Ash Lpool 54 K8
Knotty Green Bucks 20 F4
Knowbury Shrops 35 N5
Knowe D & G 72 J5
Knowehead D & G 73 Q1
Knoweside S Ayrs 80 K10
Knowes of Elrick Abers 104 J5
Knowle Bristl 17 R2
Knowle Devon 6 D3
Knowle Devon 6 E8
Knowle Devon 15 L5
Knowle Devon 15 S12
Knowle Shrops 35 N6
Knowle Solhll 36 G5
Knowle Somset 16 C8
Knowle Cross Devon 6 D5
Knowlefield Cumb 75 T14
Knowle Green Lancs 62 C12
Knowle Hill Surrey 20 G9
Knowle St Giles Somset 6 K2
Knowle Village Hants 9 R7
Knowle Wood Calder 56 D2
Knowl Green Essex 40 C12
Knowl Hill W & M 20 D7
Knowlton Dorset 8 E7
Knowlton Kent 13 Q5
Knowsley Knows 54 K7
Knowsley Safari Park Knows 55 L8
Knowstone Devon 15 T8
Knox N York 63 R8
Knox Bridge Kent 12 E7
Knoydart Highld 100 h9
Knucklas Powys 34 G6
Knuston Nhants 38 D7
Knutsford Ches E 55 S11
Knutsford Services Ches E 55 R11
Knutton Staffs 45 T4
Krumlin Calder 56 G3
Kuggar Cnwll 2 J13
Kyleakin Highld 100 g7
Kyle of Lochalsh Highld 100 g7
Kylerhea Highld 100 g7
Kylesku Highld 110 E10
Kylesmorar Highld 100 h10
Kyles Scalpay W Isls 106 h9
Kylestrome Highld 110 E10
Kynaston Herefs 35 P13
Kynaston Shrops 44 J9
Kynnersley Wrekin 45 Q10
Kyre Green Worcs 35 P8
Kyre Park Worcs 35 P8
Kyrewood Worcs 35 N7
Kyrle Somset 16 E12

L

La Bellieuse Guern 6 d3
Lacasaigh W Isls 106 i6
Lacasdal W Isls 106 j5
Laceby NE Lin 59 M5
Lacey Green Bucks 30 H12
Lach Dennis Ches W 55 R12
Lackenby R & Cl 70 J9
Lackford Suffk 40 C6
Lackford Green Suffk 40 C6
Lacock Wilts 18 D7
Ladbroke Warwks 37 M9
Ladderedge Staffs 46 C3
Laddingford Kent 12 C6
Lade Bank Lincs 49 N3
Ladock Cnwll 3 M6
Lady Ork 106 v15
Ladybank Fife 91 M10
Ladycross Cnwll 4 J3
Ladygill S Lans 82 H13
Lady Hall Cumb 61 M2
Ladykirk Border 85 M9
Ladyridge Herefs 28 A1
Lady's Green Suffk 40 C9
Ladywood Birm 36 E3
Ladywood Worcs 35 U8
La Fontenelle Guern 6 e1
La Fosse Guern 6 d4
Lag D & G 74 G8
Laga Highld 93 Q6
Lagavulin Ag & B 78 G6
Lagg N Ayrs 80 D8
Laggan Highld 96 B4
Laggan Highld 96 J5
Lagganlia Highld 97 P3
La Greve Guern 6 e2
La Grève de Lecq Jersey 7 b1
La Hougue Bie Jersey 7 e3
La Houguette Guern 6 b3
Laid Highld 110 J5
Laide Highld 107 R6
Laig Highld 100 d11
Laigh Clunch E Ayrs 81 P3
Laigh Fenwick E Ayrs 81 P4
Laigh Glenmuir E Ayrs 81 S8
Laighstonehall S Lans 82 D8
Laindon Essex 22 G10
Lairg Highld 108 K3
Laisterdyke C Brad 63 P13
Laithes Cumb 67 Q6
Lake Devon 5 N3
Lake Devon 15 N6
Lake IoW 9 R12
Lake Wilts 18 H13
Lake District Cumb 66 K10
Lake District National Park Cumb 66 K10
Lakenham Norfk 51 M12
Lakenheath Suffk 40 B4
Laker's Green Surrey 10 G3
Lakes End Norfk 39 R1
Lakeside Cumb 61 R2
Laleham Surrey 20 J9
Laleston Brdgnd 26 F12
Lamanva Cnwll 2 K10
Lamarsh Essex 40 E13
Lamas Norfk 51 M9
Lambden Border 84 J10
Lamberhurst Kent 12 C8
Lamberhurst Down Kent 12 C8
Lamberton Border 85 P7
Lambeth Gt Lon 21 P7
Lambfair Green Suffk 40 B10
Lambley Notts 47 R4
Lambley Nthumb 76 D14
Lambourn W Berk 19 M5
Lambourne End Essex 21 S4
Lambourn Woodlands W Berk 19 M5
Lamb Roe Lancs 62 E12
Lambs Green W Susx 11 L3
Lambston Pembks 24 F7
Lamellion Cnwll 4 G8
Lamerton Devon 5 M5
Lamesley Gatesd 77 R14
Lamington S Lans 82 J12
Lamlash N Ayrs 80 E6
Lamonby Cumb 67 P5
Lamorick Cnwll 3 Q4
Lamorna Cnwll 2 C12
Lamorran Cnwll 3 M8
Lampen Cnwll 4 F7
Lampeter Cerdgn 33 L11
Lampeter Velfrey Pembks 25 L8
Lamphey Pembks 24 H10
Lamplugh Cumb 66 G8
Lamport Nhants 37 U6
Lamyatt Somset 17 S9
Lana Devon 14 H11
Lana Devon 14 H13
Lanark S Lans 82 G10
Lancaster Lancs 61 T7
Lancaster Services Lancs 61 U9
Lancaut Gloucs 27 U8
Lanchester Dur 69 Q3
Lancing W Susx 10 K10
L'Ancresse Guern 6 e1
Landbeach Cambs 39 Q7
Landcross Devon 15 L8
Landerberry Abers 99 N3
Landford Wilts 8 K5
Land-hallow Highld 112 E10
Landimore Swans 25 S12
Landkey Devon 15 N6
Landore Swans 26 B8
Landrake Cnwll 4 K8
Landscove Devon 5 T7
Land's End Cnwll 2 A11
Land's End Airport Cnwll 2 B11
Landshipping Pembks 24 H8
Landue Cnwll 4 K5
Landulph Cnwll 5 L8
Landwade Suffk 39 T7
Lane Cnwll 3 L4
Laneast Cnwll 4 G4
Lane Bottom Lancs 62 H12
Lane End Bucks 20 D4
Lane End Cnwll 3 Q3
Lane End Hants 9 R3
Lane End Kent 22 E13
Lane End Lancs 62 H10
Lane End Warrtn 55 Q8
Lane End Wilts 18 B11
Lane Ends Derbys 46 H7
Lane Ends Lancs 62 F13
Lane Ends N York 62 K11
Lane Green Staffs 45 U13
Laneham Notts 58 D11
Lanehead Dur 68 H4
Lane Head Dur 69 P10
Lanehead Nthumb 76 F8
Lane Head Wigan 55 P7
Lane Head Wsall 46 C13
Lane Heads Lancs 61 S12
Lanercost Cumb 76 B13
Laneshaw Bridge Lancs 62 J11
Lane Side Lancs 55 S2
Langaford Devon 14 K13
Langal Highld 93 S5
Langaller Somset 16 J11
Langar Notts 47 T7
Langbank Rens 88 J11
Langbar N York 63 M9
Langbaurgh N York 70 J10
Langcliffe N York 62 G7
Langdale End N York 65 L1
Langdon Cnwll 4 J3
Langdon Beck Dur 68 J6
Langdon Hills Essex 22 G10
Langdown Hants 9 N7
Langdyke Fife 91 M11
Langenhoe Essex 23 P4
Langford C Beds 31 Q4
Langford Devon 6 D4
Langford Essex 22 K6
Langford N Som 17 N4
Langford Notts 48 B2
Langford Oxon 29 P7
Langford Somset 16 H11
Langford Budville Somset 16 F12
Langham Dorset 17 U11
Langham Essex 23 P1
Langham Norfk 50 H5
Langham Rutlnd 48 B11
Langham Suffk 40 G7
Langho Lancs 62 E13
Langholm D & G 75 S9
Langland Swans 25 V13
Langlee Border 84 E11
Langley Ches E 56 D12
Langley Derbys 47 M4
Langley Gloucs 28 K2
Langley Hants 9 N8
Langley Herts 31 R8
Langley Kent 12 F5
Langley Nthumb 76 G13
Langley Oxon 29 Q4
Langley Rochdl 56 C5
Langley Slough 20 H7
Langley Somset 16 E11
Langley W Susx 10 C5
Langley Warwks 36 G8
Langley Burrell Wilts 18 D5
Langley Castle Nthumb 76 G13
Langley Common Derbys 46 J6
Langley Green Derbys 46 J6
Langley Green Essex 23 L3
Langley Green Warwks 36 G8
Langley Heath Kent 12 F5
Langley Lower Green Essex 39 P14
Langley Marsh Somset 16 E11
Langley Mill Derbys 47 M4
Langley Moor Dur 69 S4
Langley Park Dur 69 R3
Langley Street Norfk 51 Q13
Langley Upper Green Essex 39 P14
Langley Vale Surrey 21 M11
Langney E Susx 11 U10
Langold Notts 57 S9
Langore Cnwll 4 H3
Langport Somset 17 M11
Langrick Lincs 49 L4
Langridge BaNES 17 T3
Langridgeford Devon 15 N8
Langrigg Cumb 66 J3
Langrish Hants 9 U4
Langsett Barns 56 K6
Langside P & K 89 S3
Langstone Hants 9 U8
Langstone Newpt 27 R10
Langthorne N York 63 Q1
Langthorpe N York 63 T6
Langthwaite N York 69 M12
Langtoft E R Yk 65 N6
Langtoft Lincs 48 H11
Langton Dur 69 Q9
Langton Lincs 59 M13
Langton Lincs 59 Q12
Langton N York 64 H6
Langton by Wragby Lincs 58 K11
Langton Green Kent 11 S3
Langton Green Suffk 40 K6
Langton Herring Dorset 7 R8
Langton Long Blandford Dorset 8 C7
Langton Matravers Dorset 8 E13
Langtree Devon 15 L9
Langtree Week Devon 15 L9
Langwathby Cumb 67 S6
Langwell Highld 108 B4
Langwell House Highld 112 D12
Langwith Derbys 57 R13
Langwith Junction Derbys 57 R13
Langworth Lincs 58 J11
Lanhydrock House & Gardens Cnwll 3 R4
Lanivet Cnwll 3 Q4
Lanjeth Cnwll 3 P6
Lank Cnwll 3 R1
Lanlivery Cnwll 3 R5
Lanner Cnwll 2 J9
Lanoy Cnwll 4 H5
Lanreath Cnwll 4 F9
Lansallos Cnwll 4 F10
Lanteglos Cnwll 4 D4
Lanteglos Highway Cnwll 4 E10
Lanton Border 76 C1
Lanton Nthumb 85 N12
La Passee Guern 6 d2
Lapford Devon 15 R11
Laphroaig Ag & B 78 F6
Lapley Staffs 45 U11
La Pulente Jersey 7 a3
Lapworth Warwks 36 G6
Larachbeg Highld 93 R9
Larbert Falk 82 G2
Larbreck Lancs 61 S11
Largie Abers 104 J9
Largiemore Ag & B 87 S8
Largoward Fife 91 Q10
Largs N Ayrs 88 F14
Largybeg N Ayrs 80 E8
Largymore N Ayrs 80 E8
Larkbeare Devon 6 E5
Larkfield Inver 88 F10
Larkfield Kent 12 D4
Larkhall S Lans 82 E8
Larkhill Wilts 18 H12
Larling Norfk 40 G3
La Rocque Jersey 7 f4
La Rousaillerie Guern 6 d2
Lartington Dur 69 M9
Lasborough Gloucs 28 F9
Lasham Hants 19 U12
Lashbrook Devon 14 K11
Lashbrook Devon 14 K11
Lashenden Kent 12 F7
Lask Edge Staffs 46 B2
Lasswade Mdloth 83 R5
Lastingham N York 64 G1
Latcham Somset 17 M7
Latchford Herts 31 U8
Latchford Oxon 30 E12
Latchford Warrtn 55 P9
Latchingdon Essex 23 L7
Latchley Cnwll 5 L6
Lately Common Warrtn 55 Q7
Lathbury M Keyn 30 J4
Latheron Highld 112 F10
Latheronwheel Highld 112 E10
Lathom Lancs 55 L4
Lathones Fife 91 Q10
Latimer Bucks 20 H3
Latteridge S Glos 28 C11
Lattiford Somset 17 S11
Latton Wilts 29 L8
Lauder Border 84 E9
Laugharne Carmth 25 P8
Laughterton Lincs 58 D11
Laughton E Susx 11 R8
Laughton Leics 37 S3
Laughton Lincs 48 G7
Laughton Lincs 58 D7
Laughton Common Rothm 57 R9
Laughton-en-le-Morthen Rothm 57 R9
Launcells Cnwll 14 F11
Launcells Cross Cnwll 14 G11
Launceston Cnwll 4 J4
Launton Oxon 30 D8
Laurencekirk Abers 99 N9
Laurieston D & G 73 R7
Laurieston Falk 82 H3
Lavendon M Keyn 38 D10
Lavenham Suffk 40 F11
Lavernock V Glam 16 G3
Laversdale Cumb 75 U13
Laverstock Wilts 8 H2
Laverstoke Hants 19 Q11
Laverton Gloucs 36 E13
Laverton N York 63 Q5
Laverton Somset 17 U6
La Villette Guern 6 d3
Lavister Wrexhm 44 J2
Law S Lans 82 F8
Lawers P & K 95 T11
Lawford Essex 23 Q1
Lawford Somset 16 F9
Law Hill S Lans 82 F8
Lawhitton Cnwll 4 K4
Lawkland N York 62 F6
Lawkland Green N York 62 F6
Lawley Wrekin 45 Q12
Lawnhead Staffs 45 T8
Lawrence Weston Bristl 27 U12
Lawrenny Pembks 24 H9
Lawrenny Quay Pembks 24 H9
Lawshall Suffk 40 E10
Lawshall Green Suffk 40 E10
Lawton Herefs 34 K9
Laxay W Isls 106 i6
Laxdale W Isls 106 j5
Laxey IoM 60 g6
Laxfield Suffk 41 N6
Laxford Bridge Highld 110 E7
Laxo Shet 106 u7
Laxton E R Yk 58 C1
Laxton Nhants 38 E1
Laxton Notts 58 B13
Laycock C Brad 63 L11
Layer Breton Essex 23 M4
Layer-de-la-Haye Essex 23 N3
Layer Marney Essex 23 M4
Layham Suffk 40 H12
Laymore Dorset 7 L4
Layter's Green Bucks 20 G4
Laytham E R Yk 64 G12
Laythes Cumb 66 K1
Lazenby R & Cl 70 J9
Lazonby Cumb 67 R5
Lea Derbys 46 K2
Lea Herefs 28 C3
Lea Lincs 58 D9
Lea Shrops 34 J3
Lea Shrops 44 K12
Lea Wilts 28 J10
Leachkin Highld 102 H7
Leadburn Border 83 P7
Leadenham Lincs 48 D3
Leaden Roding Essex 22 E5
Leadgate Cumb 68 F4
Leadgate Dur 69 P2
Leadgate Nthumb 77 N14
Leadhills S Lans 74 G2
Leadingcross Green Kent 12 G5
Leadmill Derbys 56 K10
Leafield Oxon 29 R4
Leagrave Luton 31 N8
Leahead Ches W 55 Q14
Lea Heath Staffs 46 D8
Leake N York 63 U1
Leake Common Side Lincs 49 N3
Lealholm N York 71 N11
Lealholm Side N York 71 N11
Lealt Highld 100 e3
Leam Derbys 56 K11
Lea Marston Warwks 36 H2
Leamington Hastings Warwks 37 M7
Leamington Spa Warwks 36 K7
Leamside Dur 70 D3
Leap Cross E Susx 11 T8
Learney Abers 99 L3
Leasgill Cumb 61 T3
Leasingham Lincs 48 G4
Leasingthorne Dur 69 S6
Leatherhead Surrey 21 L11
Leathley N York 63 Q10
Leaton Shrops 45 L10
Leaton Wrekin 45 P11
Lea Town Lancs 61 T13
Leaveland Kent 12 K5
Leavenheath Suffk 40 G13
Leavening N York 64 H7
Leaves Green Gt Lon 21 R10
Lea Yeat Cumb 62 F2
Lebberston N York 65 P3
Le Bigard Guern 6 c4
Le Bourg Guern 6 d4
Le Bourg Jersey 7 f4
Lechlade on Thames Gloucs 29 P8
Lecht Gruinart Ag & B 86 D12
Leck Lancs 62 C4
Leckbuie P & K 95 U10
Leckford Hants 19 N13
Leckhampstead Bucks 30 F5
Leckhampstead W Berk 19 P5
Leckhampstead Thicket W Berk 19 P5
Leckhampton Gloucs 28 H4
Leckmelm Highld 108 B7
Leckwith V Glam 27 M13
Leconfield E R Yk 65 N11
Ledaig Ag & B 94 C11
Ledburn Bucks 30 K8
Ledbury Herefs 35 R13
Leddington Gloucs 35 Q14
Ledgemoor Herefs 34 K10
Ledicot Herefs 34 K8
Ledmore Highld 108 C2
Ledsham Ches W 54 J12
Ledsham Leeds 64 B14
Ledston Leeds 63 U14
Ledstone Devon 5 S11
Ledston Luck Leeds 63 U13
Ledwell Oxon 29 T2
Lee Devon 15 L3
Lee Gt Lon 21 Q7
Lee Hants 9 M5
Lee Shrops 44 K7
Leebotwood Shrops 45 L14
Lee Brockhurst Shrops 45 M8
Leece Cumb 61 N6
Lee Chapel Essex 22 G10
Lee Clump Bucks 30 K12
Lee Common Bucks 30 K12
Leeds Kent 12 F5
Leeds Leeds 63 R13
Leeds Bradford Airport Leeds 63 Q11
Leeds Castle Kent 12 F5
Leeds Skelton Lake Services Leeds 63 T13
Leedstown Cnwll 2 G10
Lee Green Ches E 45 Q1
Leek Staffs 46 C2
Leek Wootton Warwks 36 J7
Lee Mill Devon 5 P9
Leeming C Brad 63 L13
Leeming N York 63 R2
Leeming Bar N York 63 R2
Leeming Bar Rest Area N York 63 R2
Lee Moor Devon 5 P8
Lee-on-the-Solent Hants 9 R8
Lees C Brad 63 L12
Lees Derbys 46 J6
Lees Oldham 56 E6
Lees Green Derbys 46 J6
Leesthorpe Leics 47 U11
Leeswood Flints 44 G1
Leetown P & K 90 K7
Leftwich Ches W 55 Q12
Legar Powys 27 N4
Legbourne Lincs 59 Q10
Legburthwaite Cumb 67 M9
Legerwood Border 84 F10
Legoland W & M 20 F8
Le Gron Guern 6 c3
Legsby Lincs 58 K9
Le Haguais Jersey 7 e4
Le Hocq Jersey 7 e4
Leicester C Leic 47 Q13
Leicester Forest East Leics 47 P13
Leicester Forest East Services Leics 47 P13
Leigh Devon 15 R10
Leigh Dorset 7 R3
Leigh Gloucs 28 G2
Leigh Kent 21 T13
Leigh Shrops 44 H13
Leigh Surrey 21 M13
Leigh Wigan 55 Q7
Leigh Wilts 29 L9
Leigh Worcs 35 S10
Leigh Beck Essex 22 K11
Leigh Delamere Wilts 18 C5
Leigh Delamere Services Wilts 18 C5
Leigh Green Kent 12 H9
Leigh Knoweglass S Lans 81 S2
Leighland Chapel Somset 16 D9
Leigh-on-Sea Sthend 22 K10
Leigh Park Dorset 8 E9
Leigh Park Hants 9 U7
Leigh Sinton Worcs 35 S10
Leighswood Wsall 46 E13
Leighterton Gloucs 28 F9
Leighton N York 63 P4
Leighton Powys 44 F12
Leighton Shrops 45 P12
Leighton Somset 17 T8
Leighton Bromswold Cambs 38 H5
Leighton Buzzard C Beds 30 K7
Leigh upon Mendip Somset 17 S7
Leigh Woods N Som 27 V13
Leinthall Earls Herefs 34 K7
Leinthall Starkes Herefs 34 K7
Leintwardine Herefs 34 K6
Leire Leics 37 P3
Leiston Suffk 41 R8
Leith C Edin 83 Q3
Leitholm Border 84 K10
Lelant Cnwll 2 E9
Lelley E R Yk 65 S13
Lem Hill Worcs 35 R5
Lempitlaw Border 84 K12
Lemreway W Isls 106 i7
Lemsford Herts 31 R10
Lenchwick Worcs 36 D11
Lendalfoot S Ayrs 72 E1
Lendrick Stirlg 89 N4
Lendrum Terrace Abers 105 U7
Lenham Kent 12 G5
Lenham Heath Kent 12 H6
Lenie Highld 102 F10
Lennel Border 85 M10
Lennox Plunton D & G 73 Q9
Lennoxtown E Duns 89 P10
Lent Bucks 20 F6
Lenton C Nott 47 Q6
Lenton Lincs 48 F7
Lenwade Norfk 50 J10
Lenzie E Duns 89 Q11
Leochel-Cushnie Abers 104 G13
Leomansley Staffs 46 F12
Leominster Herefs 35 L9
Leonard Stanley Gloucs 28 F7
Leoville Jersey 7 b1
Lepe Hants 9 N9
Lephin Highld 100 a5
Leppington N York 64 H7
Lepton Kirk 56 K3
Lerags Ag & B 94 B13
L'Erée Guern 6 b3
Lerryn Cnwll 4 E9
Lerwick Shet 106 u9
Les Arquêts Guern 6 b3
Lesbury Nthumb 77 Q3
Les Hubits Guern 6 e3
Leslie Abers 104 H11
Leslie Fife 91 L11
Les Lohiers Guern 6 c3
Lesmahagow S Lans 82 F11
Les Murchez Guern 6 c4
Lesnewth Cnwll 4 E2
Les Nicolles Guern 6 d4
Les Quartiers Guern 6 d2
Les Quennevais Jersey 7 b3
Les Sages Guern 6 c3
Lessingham Norfk 51 Q8
Lessonhall Cumb 66 K2
Lestowder Cnwll 2 K12
Les Villets Guern 6 c4
Leswalt D & G 72 C7
L'Etacq Jersey 7 a2
Letchmore Heath Herts 21 L3
Letchworth Garden City Herts 31 R6
Letcombe Bassett Oxon 29 S11
Letcombe Regis Oxon 29 S10
Letham Angus 91 R2
Letham Border 76 D4
Letham Falk 82 G1
Letham Fife 91 M9
Letham Grange Angus 91 T2
Lethenty Abers 104 H11
Lethenty Abers 105 N7
Letheringham Suffk 41 N9
Letheringsett Norfk 50 J6
Lettaford Devon 5 S4
Letterewe Highld 107 S10
Letterfearn Highld 101 M7
Letterfinlay Lodge Hotel Highld 96 B5
Letters Highld 108 B7
Lettershaw S Lans 74 G1
Letterston Pembks 24 F5
Lettoch Highld 103 R12
Lettoch Highld 103 T9
Letton Herefs 34 H11
Letton Herefs 34 J6
Lett's Green Kent 21 S11
Letty Green Herts 31 S10
Letwell Rothm 57 S9
Leuchars Fife 91 Q7
Leumrabhagh W Isls 106 i7
Leurbost W Isls 106 i6
Levalsa Meor Cnwll 3 Q7
Levan Inver 88 F10
Levedale Staffs 45 U10
Level's Green Essex 22 C3
Leven E R Yk 65 Q10
Leven Fife 91 N11
Levens Cumb 61 T2
Levens Green Herts 31 U8
Levenshulme Manch 56 C8
Levenwick Shet 106 u11
Leverburgh W Isls 106 f10
Leverington Cambs 49 P11
Leverstock Green Herts 31 N11
Leverton Lincs 49 P4
Le Villocq Guern 6 d2
Levington Suffk 41 M13
Levisham N York 64 J1
Lew Oxon 29 R6
Lewannick Cnwll 4 H4
Lewdown Devon 5 M3
Lewes E Susx 11 Q8
Leweston Pembks 24 F6
Lewisham Gt Lon 21 Q8
Lewiston Highld 102 F10
Lewistown Brdgnd 26 G10
Lewis Wych Herefs 34 H9
Lewknor Oxon 20 B3
Leworthy Devon 14 H12
Leworthy Devon 15 Q5
Lewson Street Kent 12 J3
Lewth Lancs 61 T12
Lewtrenchard Devon 5 M3
Lexden Essex 23 N2
Lexworthy Somset 16 J9
Ley Cnwll 4 F7
Leybourne Kent 12 C4
Leyburn N York 63 N1
Leycett Staffs 45 S4
Leygreen Herts 31 Q8
Ley Hill Bucks 31 L12
Leyland Lancs 55 M2
Leyland Green St Hel 55 N6
Leylodge Abers 105 M13
Leys Abers 105 S5
Leys P & K 91 L4
Leysdown-on-Sea Kent 23 P13
Leysmill Angus 91 T2
Leys of Cossans Angus 91 N2
Leysters Herefs 35 N8
Leyton Gt Lon 21 Q5
Leytonstone Gt Lon 21 Q5
Lezant Cnwll 4 J5
Lezerea Cnwll 2 H10
Leziate Norfk 49 U10
Lhanbryde Moray 104 B3
Libanus Powys 26 H2
Libberton S Lans 82 J10
Libbery Worcs 36 C9
Liberton C Edin 83 Q5
Lichfield Staffs 46 F12
Lickey Worcs 36 C5
Lickey End Worcs 36 C6
Lickey Rock Worcs 36 C6
Lickfold W Susx 10 E5
Liddaton Green Devon 5 M4
Liddesdale Highld 93 T7
Liddington Swindn 18 K4
Lidgate Derbys 57 M11
Lidgate Suffk 40 B9
Lidget Donc 57 U6
Lidgett Notts 57 T13
Lidham Hill E Susx 12 F12
Lidlington C Beds 31 L5
Lidsey W Susx 10 E10
Lidsing Kent 12 E3
Liff Angus 91 M5
Lifford Birm 36 E4
Lifton Devon 4 K3
Liftondown Devon 4 K3
Lighthorne Warwks 36 K9
Lighthorne Heath Warwks 37 L9
Lightwater Surrey 20 F10
Lightwater Valley Theme Park N York 63 R4
Lightwood C Stke 46 B5
Lightwood Green Ches E 45 P5
Lightwood Green Wrexhm 44 J5
Lilbourne Nhants 37 Q5
Lilburn Tower Nthumb 85 Q14
Lilford Nhants 38 F4
Lilleshall Wrekin 45 R10
Lilley Herts 31 P7
Lilley W Berk 19 P5
Lilliesleaf Border 84 E13
Lillingstone Dayrell Bucks 30 F5
Lillingstone Lovell Bucks 30 F4
Lillington Dorset 7 R2
Lilliput BCP 8 E11
Lilstock Somset 16 G7
Lilyhurst Shrops 45 R11
Limbrick Lancs 55 P3
Limbury Luton 31 N8
Limebrook Herefs 34 J7
Limefield Bury 55 T4
Limekilnburn S Lans 82 D8
Limekilns Fife 83 L2
Limerigg Falk 82 G4
Limerstone IoW 9 N12
Limestone Brae Nthumb 68 G3
Lime Street Worcs 28 F1
Limington Somset 17 P12
Limmerhaugh E Ayrs 81 S7
Limpenhoe Norfk 51 Q13
Limpley Stoke Wilts 17 U4
Limpsfield Surrey 21 R12
Limpsfield Chart Surrey 21 R12
Linby Notts 47 P3
Linchmere W Susx 10 D4
Lincluden D & G 74 J10
Lincoln Lincs 58 G12
Lincomb Worcs 35 T7
Lincombe Devon 5 S12
Lincombe Devon 15 L3
Lindale Cumb 61 S3
Lindal in Furness Cumb 61 N4
Lindfield W Susx 11 N5
Lindford Hants 10 C3
Lindley Kirk 56 H3
Lindley N York 63 Q10
Lindores Fife 91 L8
Lindow End Ches E 55 T11
Lindridge Worcs 35 Q7
Lindsell Essex 22 F2
Lindsey Suffk 40 G11
Lindsey Tye Suffk 40 G11
Liney Somset 17 L9
Linford Hants 8 H7
Linford Thurr 22 G12
Lingbob C Brad 63 M12
Lingdale R & Cl 71 L9
Lingen Herefs 34 J7
Lingfield Surrey 11 P2
Lingfield Common Surrey 11 P2
Lingwood Norfk 51 Q12
Liniclate W Isls 106 c14
Linicro Highld 100 c3
Linkend Worcs 28 F1
Linkenholt Hants 19 N9
Linkhill Kent 12 F10
Linkinhorne Cnwll 4 J6
Linktown Fife 91 L13
Linkwood Moray 104 A3
Linley Shrops 34 J2
Linley Green Herefs 35 Q10
Linleygreen Shrops 45 Q14
Linlithgow W Loth 82 J3
Linshiels Nthumb 76 H4
Linsidemore Highld 108 J5
Linslade C Beds 30 K7
Linstead Parva Suffk 41 P5
Linstock Cumb 75 T14
Linthurst Worcs 36 C6
Linthwaite Kirk 56 H4
Lintlaw Border 85 L7
Lintmill Moray 104 G2
Linton Border 84 K13
Linton Cambs 39 S11
Linton Derbys 46 J10
Linton Herefs 28 C2
Linton Kent 12 E5
Linton Leeds 63 T10
Linton N York 62 K7
Linton Nthumb 77 R7
Linton Heath Derbys 46 J10
Linton Hill Herefs 28 C3
Linton-on-Ouse N York 64 B7
Linwood Hants 8 H7
Linwood Lincs 58 K9
Linwood Rens 88 K13
Lionacleit W Isls 106 c14
Lional W Isls 106 k2
Lions Green E Susx 11 T7
Liphook Hants 10 C4
Lipley Shrops 45 R7
Liscard Wirral 54 G8
Liscombe Somset 15 U6
Liskeard Cnwll 4 H8
Lismore Ag & B 93 U10
Liss Hants 10 B5
Lissett E R Yk 65 Q8
Liss Forest Hants 10 B5
Lissington Lincs 58 K10
Liston Essex 40 E12
Lisvane Cardif 27 M11
Liswerry Newpt 27 Q10
Litcham Norfk 50 E10
Litchborough Nhants 37 R10
Litchfield Hants 19 Q10
Litherland Sefton 54 H7
Litlington Cambs 31 T4
Litlington E Susx 11 S10
Little Abington Cambs 39 R11
Little Addington Nhants 38 E6
Little Airies D & G 73 L10
Little Almshoe Herts 31 R7
Little Alne Warwks 36 F8
Little Altcar Sefton 54 H5
Little Amwell Herts 31 U10
Little Asby Cumb 68 E11
Little Aston Staffs 46 E14
Little Atherfield IoW 9 P13
Little Ayton N York 70 J10
Little Baddow Essex 22 J6
Little Badminton S Glos 28 F11
Little Bampton Cumb 67 L1
Little Bardfield Essex 22 G1
Little Barford Bed 38 J9
Little Barningham Norfk 50 K7
Little Barrington Gloucs 29 P5
Little Barrow Ches W 55 L13
Little Barugh N York 64 H4
Little Bavington Nthumb 76 K10
Little Bealings Suffk 41 M11
Littlebeck N York 71 Q12
Little Bedwyn Wilts 19 L7
Little Bentley Essex 23 R2
Little Berkhamsted Herts 31 S11
Little Billing Nhants 38 B8
Little Billington C Beds 30 K8
Little Birch Herefs 27 U1
Little Bispham Bpool 61 Q11
Little Blakenham Suffk 40 K11
Little Blencow Cumb 67 Q6
Little Bloxwich Wsall 46 D13
Little Bognor W Susx 10 G6
Little Bolehill Derbys 46 J3
Little Bollington Ches E 55 R9
Little Bookham Surrey 20 K12
Littleborough Devon 15 T10
Littleborough Notts 58 D10
Littleborough Rochdl 56 D3
Littlebourne Kent 13 P4
Little Bourton Oxon 37 N12
Little Bowden Leics 37 T3
Little Bradley Suffk 39 U10
Little Brampton Herefs 34 H8
Little Brampton Shrops 34 J4
Little Braxted Essex 22 K5
Little Brechin Angus 98 K11
Littlebredy Dorset 7 Q7
Little Brickhill M Keyn 30 K6
Little Bridgeford Staffs 45 U8
Little Brington Nhants 37 S8
Little Bromley Essex 23 Q2
Little Broughton Cumb 66 G6
Little Budworth Ches W 55 N13
Littleburn Highld 102 H5
Little Burstead Essex 22 G9
Littlebury Essex 39 R13
Littlebury Green Essex 39 Q13
Little Bytham Lincs 48 F10
Little Canfield Essex 22 E3
Little Carlton Lincs 59 Q9
Little Carlton Notts 47 U2
Little Casterton Rutlnd 48 F12
Little Catwick E R Yk 65 Q11
Little Catworth Cambs 38 H6
Little Cawthorpe Lincs 59 Q10
Little Chalfont Bucks 20 G3
Little Chart Kent 12 H6
Little Chesterford Essex 39 R12
Little Cheveney Kent 12 D7
Little Cheverell Wilts 18 E10
Little Chishill Cambs 39 P13
Little Clacton Essex 23 S4
Little Clanfield Oxon 29 Q7
Little Clifton Cumb 66 G7
Little Coates NE Lin 59 M5
Little Comberton Worcs 36 C12
Little Common E Susx 12 D14
Little Comp Kent 12 B4
Little Compton Warwks 29 Q1
Little Corby Cumb 67 Q1
Little Cornard Suffk 40 F13
Littlecott Wilts 18 H10
Little Cowarne Herefs 35 P10
Little Coxwell Oxon 29 Q9
Little Crakehall N York 63 Q1
Little Cransley Nhants 38 B5
Little Cressingham Norfk 50 E13
Little Crosby Sefton 54 H6
Little Crosthwaite Cumb 66 K7
Little Cubley Derbys 46 G6
Little Dalby Leics 47 U11
Littledean Gloucs 28 C5
Little Dewchurch Herefs 27 U1
Little Ditton Cambs 39 U9
Little Doward Herefs 27 U4
Littledown Hants 19 M9
Little Downham Cambs 39 R4
Little Driffield E R Yk 65 N8
Little Dunham Norfk 50 E11
Little Dunkeld P & K 90 F3
Little Dunmow Essex 22 G3
Little Durnford Wilts 8 G2
Little Easton Essex 22 F3
Little Eaton Derbys 47 L5
Little Ellingham Norfk 50 H14
Little Elm Somset 17 T7
Little Everdon Nhants 37 Q9
Little Eversden Cambs 39 N10
Little Faringdon Oxon 29 P7
Little Fencote N York 69 S14
Little Fenton N York 64 C12
Littleferry Highld 109 Q5
Little Fransham Norfk 50 F11
Little Gaddesden Herts 31 L10
Little Garway Herefs 27 S3
Little Gidding Cambs 38 H4
Little Glemham Suffk 41 P9
Little Gorsley Herefs 28 C3
Little Gransden Cambs 39 L9
Little Green Notts 47 T5
Little Green Somset 17 T7
Little Grimsby Lincs 59 P8
Little Gringley Notts 58 B10
Little Habton N York 64 G4

Little Hadham *Herts*...22 B3
Little Hale *Lincs*...48 H5
Little Hallam *Derbys*...47 N5
Little Hallingbury *Essex*...22 C4
Little Hampden *Bucks*...20 D6
Little Hampton *W Susx*...10 G10
Little Hanford *Dorset*...14 A6
Little Harrowden *Nhants*...38 C6
Little Haseley *Oxon*...30 D12
Little Hatfield *E R Yk*...65 R11
Little Hautbois *Norfk*...51 N9
Little Haven *Pembks*...24 E8
Littlehaven *W Susx*...10 K4
Little Hay *Staffs*...46 F13
Little Hayfield *Derbys*...55 R6
Little Haywood *Staffs*...46 D9
Little Heath *W Berk*...19 U6
Little Heath *Staffs*...45 U10
Little Hereford *Herefs*...35 N7
Little Horkesley *Essex*...23 N1
Little Hormead *Herts*...22 B2
Little Horsted *E Susx*...11 R7
Little Horton *Wilts*...18 F8
Little Horwood *Bucks*...30 G7
Little Houghton *Barns*...57 P5
Little Houghton *Nhants*...38 B9
Littlehoughton *Nthumb*...77 Q2
Little Hucklow *Derbys*...56 J11
Little Hulton *Salfd*...55 R6
Little Hungerford *W Berk*...19 R6
Little Hutton *N York*...64 B4
Little Irchester *Nhants*...38 D7
Little Kelk *E R Yk*...65 P8
Little Keyford *Somset*...17 U7
Little Kimble *Bucks*...30 H11
Little Kineton *Warwks*...36 K10
Little Kingshill *Bucks*...20 E3
Little Knox *D & G*...74 F13
Little Langdale *Cumb*...67 M12
Little Langford *Wilts*...18 F13
Little Laver *Essex*...22 D6
Little Leigh *Ches W*...55 P11
Little Leighs *Essex*...22 H4
Little Lever *Bolton*...55 S5
Little Linford *M Keyn*...30 H4
Little Load *Somset*...17 N12
Little London *Bucks*...30 D10
Little London *E Susx*...11 U7
Little London *Essex*...22 C2
Little London *Gloucs*...28 D4
Little London *Hants*...19 N11
Little London *Hants*...19 T9
Little London *Leeds*...63 Q13
Little London *Lincs*...49 P12
Little London *Lincs*...59 N10
Little London *Norfk*...49 S9
Little London *Powys*...34 B3
Little Longstone *Derbys*...56 J12
Little Madeley *Staffs*...45 S4
Little Malvern *Worcs*...35 S12
Little Mancot *Flints*...54 H13
Little Maplestead *Essex*...40 D14
Little Marcle *Herefs*...35 Q13
Little Marland *Devon*...15 M10
Little Marlow *Bucks*...20 E6
Little Massingham *Norfk*...50 B9
Little Melton *Norfk*...51 L12
Littlemill *Abers*...98 E4
Littlemill *Highld*...103 P5
Little Mill *Mons*...27 Q7
Little Milton *Oxon*...30 D12
Little Missenden *Bucks*...20 F3
Little Mongeham *Kent*...13 R5
Littlemoor *Derbys*...57 N14
Little Moor *Somset*...16 J10
Littlemore *Oxon*...30 B12
Little Musgrave *Cumb*...68 G10
Little Ness *Shrops*...44 K10
Little Neston *Ches W*...54 G11
Little Newcastle *Pembks*...24 G5
Little Newsham *Dur*...69 P9
Little Norton *Somset*...17 N13
Little Oakley *Essex*...23 T2
Little Oakley *Nhants*...38 C3
Little Odell *Bed*...38 E9
Little Offley *Herts*...31 P7
Little Ormside *Cumb*...68 F9
Little Orton *Cumb*...67 N1
Little Ouse *Cambs*...39 T4
Little Ouseburn *N York*...63 U7
Littleover *C Derb*...46 K7
Little Oxendon *Nhants*...37 T4
Little Packington *Warwks*...36 H4
Little Pattenden *Kent*...12 D6
Littleport *Lancs*...61 R13
Little Plumstead *Norfk*...51 P11
Little Ponton *Lincs*...48 D7
Littleport *Cambs*...39 S4
Littleport Bridge *Cambs*...39 S3
Little Posbrook *Hants*...9 Q8
Little Potheridge *Devon*...15 M10
Little Preston *Nhants*...37 Q10
Little Preston *Leeds*...63 T13
Littler *Ches W*...55 P13
Little Raveley *Cambs*...39 L5
Little Reedness *E R Yk*...58 D2
Little Ribston *N York*...63 T9
Little Rissington *Gloucs*...29 N4
Little Rollright *Oxon*...29 Q1
Little Rowsley *Derbys*...57 L13
Little Ryburgh *Norfk*...50 F8
Little Ryle *Nthumb*...77 L3
Little Ryton *Shrops*...45 L13
Little Salkeld *Cumb*...67 S5
Little Sampford *Essex*...39 U14
Little Sandhurst *Br For*...20 D10
Little Saredon *Staffs*...46 B12
Little Saughall *Ches W*...54 J13
Little Saxham *Suffk*...40 D8
Little Scatwell *Highld*...102 C4
Little Shelford *Cambs*...39 P10
Little Shrewley *Warwks*...36 H7
Little Silver *Devon*...6 B3
Little Singleton *Lancs*...61 R13
Little Skipwith *N York*...64 F12
Little Smeaton *N York*...57 R3
Little Snoring *Norfk*...50 G7
Little Sodbury *S Glos*...28 E11
Little Sodbury End *S Glos*...28 D11
Little Somborne *Hants*...9 M2
Little Somerford *Wilts*...28 J10
Little Soudley *Shrops*...45 R8
Little Stainforth *N York*...62 H7
Little Stainton *Darltn*...70 D8
Little Stanion *Nhants*...38 C3
Little Stanney *Ches W*...54 J12
Little Staughton *Bed*...38 H8
Little Steeping *Lincs*...59 R14
Little Stoke *Staffs*...46 B6
Littlestone-on-Sea *Kent*...13 L11
Little Stonham *Suffk*...40 K8
Little Stretton *Leics*...47 S13
Little Stretton *Shrops*...45 L2
Little Strickland *Cumb*...67 S9
Little Stukeley *Cambs*...38 K5
Little Sugnall *Staffs*...45 T7
Little Sutton *Ches W*...54 J11
Little Sutton *Shrops*...35 M4
Little Swinburne *Nthumb*...76 J10
Little Sypland *D & G*...73 S9
Little Tew *Oxon*...29 S3
Little Tey *Essex*...23 L3
Little Thetford *Cambs*...39 R5
Little Thirkleby *N York*...64 B4
Little Thornage *Norfk*...50 J6
Little Thornton *Lancs*...61 R11
Littlethorpe *Leics*...37 P1
Littlethorpe *N York*...63 S6
Little Thorpe *Dur*...70 F4
Little Thurlow *Suffk*...39 U10
Little Thurlow Green *Suffk*...39 U10
Little Thurrock *Thurr*...22 F12
Littleton *BaNES*...17 Q4
Littleton *Ches W*...54 K13
Littleton *D & G*...73 Q8
Littleton *Hants*...9 P2
Littleton *Somset*...17 N10
Littleton *Surrey*...20 H9
Littleton *Surrey*...20 J12
Littleton Drew *Wilts*...18 B4
Littleton-on-Severn...28 A10
  S Glos
Littleton Pannell *Wilts*...18 F10
Little Torrington *Devon*...15 L9
Little Totham *Essex*...23 L5
Littletown *Dur*...70 D4
Little Town *Lancs*...62 D12
Little Town *Warrtn*...55 N8
Little Twycross *Leics*...46 K12
Little Urswick *Cumb*...61 P5
Little Wakering *Essex*...23 M10
Little Walden *Essex*...39 R12
Little Waldingfield *Suffk*...40 F11
Little Walsingham *Norfk*...50 F6

Little Waltham *Essex*...22 H5
Little Warley *Essex*...22 F9
Little Washbourne *Gloucs*...36 C14
Little Weighton *E R Yk*...65 M13
Little Welnetham *Suffk*...40 E9
Little Welton *Lincs*...59 P9
Little Wenham *Suffk*...40 J13
Little Wenlock *Wrekin*...45 P12
Little Weston *Somset*...17 R11
Little Whitefield *IoW*...9 R11
Little Whittingham Green...41 N5
  Suffk
Little Whittington *Nthumb*...76 K12
Littlewick Green *W & M*...20 D7
Little Wilbraham *Cambs*...39 R9
Littlewindsor *Dorset*...7 N4
Little Witcombe *Gloucs*...28 H4
Little Witley *Worcs*...35 S8
Little Wittenham *Oxon*...19 S2
Little Wolford *Warwks*...36 J14
Littleworth *Bucks*...30 J8
Littleworth *Oxon*...29 R8
Littleworth *Staffs*...46 D11
Littleworth *Worcs*...35 U11
Littleworth *W Susx*...10 K6
Littleworth Common *Bucks*...20 F6
Little Wratting *Suffk*...39 U11
Little Wymington *Bed*...38 E8
Little Wymondley *Herts*...31 R8
Little Wyrley *Staffs*...46 D12
Little Wytheford *Shrops*...45 N10
Little Yeldham *Essex*...40 C14
Littley Green *Essex*...22 G4
Litton *Derbys*...56 J11
Litton *N York*...62 J6
Litton *Somset*...17 Q6
Litton Cheney *Dorset*...7 P6
Liurbost *W Isls*...106 i6
Liverpool *Lpool*...54 H8
Liversedge *Kirk*...56 K1
Liverton *Devon*...5 U5
Liverton *R & Cl*...71 L9
Liverton Mines *R & Cl*...71 L9
Liverton Street *Kent*...12 G6
Livingston *W Loth*...82 K5
Livingston Village *W Loth*...82 K5
Lixwm *Flints*...54 E12
Lizard *Cnwll*...2 J14
Llaingoch *IoA*...52 B6
Llaithddu *Powys*...34 B3
Llan *Powys*...43 S13
Llanaber *Gwynd*...43 M10
Llanaelhaearn *Gwynd*...42 G4
Llanafan *Cerdgn*...33 N6
Llanafan-Fawr *Powys*...33 U9
Llanafan-fechan *Powys*...33 U9
Llanallgo *IoA*...52 H5
Llanarmon *Gwynd*...42 H5
Llanarmon Dyffryn...44 E7
  Ceiriog *Wrexhm*
Llanarmon-yn-Ial *Denbgs*...44 E1
Llanarth *Cerdgn*...32 H9
Llanarth *Mons*...27 R5
Llanarthne *Carmth*...25 T7
Llanasa *Flints*...54 D10
Llanbabo *IoA*...52 E5
Llanbadarn Fawr *Cerdgn*...33 M4
Llanbadarn Fynydd *Powys*...34 C5
Llanbadarn-y-garreg...34 D11
  Powys
Llanbadoc *Mons*...27 R8
Llanbadrig *IoA*...52 F4
Llanbeder *Newpt*...27 R9
Llanbedr *Gwynd*...43 L8
Llanbedr *Powys*...27 N3
Llanbedr *Powys*...34 D11
Llanbedr-Dyffryn-Clwyd...44 D2
  Denbgs
Llanbedrgoch *IoA*...52 H6
Llanbedrog *Gwynd*...42 F7
Llanbedr-y-Cennin *Conwy*...53 M10
Llanberis *Gwynd*...52 J10
Llanbethery *V Glam*...16 E3
Llanbister *Powys*...34 D6
Llanblethian *V Glam*...26 H13
Llanboidy *Carmth*...25 M6
Llanbradach *Caerph*...27 L9
Llanbrynmair *Powys*...43 S13
Llancadle *V Glam*...16 E3
Llancarfan *V Glam*...16 F2
Llancloudy *Herefs*...27 T3
Llancynfelyn *Cerdgn*...33 M2
Llandaff *Cardif*...27 L12
Llandanwg *Gwynd*...43 L8
Llandarcy *Neath*...26 C8
Llandawke *Carmth*...25 N8
Llanddaniel Fab *IoA*...52 G8
Llanddarog *Carmth*...25 T7
Llanddeiniol *Cerdgn*...33 L6
Llanddeiniolen *Gwynd*...52 H9
Llandderfel *Gwynd*...43 U6
Llanddeusant *Carmth*...26 E2
Llanddeusant *IoA*...52 D5
Llanddew *Powys*...26 K1
Llanddewi *Swans*...25 R13
Llanddewi Brefi *Cerdgn*...33 N9
Llanddewi'r Cwm *Powys*...34 B11
Llanddewi Rhydderch...27 R5
  Mons
Llanddewi Velfrey *Pembks*...24 K7
Llanddewi Ystradenni...34 D7
  Powys
Llanddoged *Conwy*...53 P1
Llanddona *IoA*...52 H7
Llanddowror *Carmth*...25 M8
Llanddulas *Conwy*...53 R7
Llanddwywe *Gwynd*...43 L9
Llanddyfnan *IoA*...52 G7
Llandecwyn *Gwynd*...43 M7
Llandefaelog *Powys*...26 K1
Llandefaelog-Tre'r-Graig...26 K14
  Powys
Llandefalle *Powys*...34 D13
Llandegai *Gwynd*...52 J8
Llandegfan *IoA*...52 H8
Llandegla *Denbgs*...44 E2
Llandegley *Powys*...34 D8
Llandegveth *Mons*...27 Q8
Llandegwning *Gwynd*...42 E7
Llandeilo *Carmth*...26 B3
Llandeilo Graban *Powys*...34 C12
Llandeilo'r Fan *Powys*...33 S14
Llandeloy *Pembks*...24 E6
Llandenny *Mons*...27 S7
Llandevaud *Newpt*...27 R9
Llandevenny *Mons*...27 R10
Llandinabo *Herefs*...27 U2
Llandinam *Powys*...33 U3
Llandissilio *Pembks*...24 K6
Llandogo *Mons*...27 U6
Llandough *V Glam*...26 H13
Llandough *V Glam*...27 M13
Llandovery *Carmth*...33 S14
Llandow *V Glam*...26 G13
Llandre *Carmth*...33 N12
Llandre *Cerdgn*...33 M3
Llandre Isaf *Pembks*...24 K5
Llandrillo *Denbgs*...44 B6
Llandrillo-yn-Rhôs *Conwy*...53 P6
Llandrindod Wells *Powys*...34 C8
Llandrinio *Powys*...44 G10
Llandudno *Conwy*...53 N6
Llandudno Junction...53 N7
  Conwy
Llandulas *Powys*...33 S12
Llandwrog *Gwynd*...52 G11
Llandybie *Carmth*...25 V7
Llandyfaelog *Carmth*...25 R8
Llandyfan *Carmth*...26 B4
Llandyfriog *Cerdgn*...32 F12
Llandyfrydog *IoA*...52 F5
Llandygai *Gwynd*...52 J8
Llandygwydd *Cerdgn*...32 E12
Llandynan *Denbgs*...44 F5
Llandyrnog *Denbgs*...54 C14
Llandysilio *Powys*...44 G10
Llandyssil *Powys*...34 E1
Llandysul *Cerdgn*...32 H11
Llanedeyrn *Cardif*...27 M11
Llaneglwys *Powys*...34 C13
Llanegryn *Gwynd*...43 M11
Llanegwad *Carmth*...25 U6
Llanelian-yn-Rhôs *Conwy*...53 Q7
Llanelidan *Denbgs*...44 D3
Llanelieu *Powys*...34 E14
Llanellen *Mons*...27 Q5
Llanelli *Carmth*...25 S10
Llanelltyd *Gwynd*...43 P10
Llanelly *Mons*...27 N4
Llanelly Hill *Mons*...27 N4
Llanelwedd *Powys*...34 B10
Llanenddwyn *Gwynd*...43 L9
Llanengan *Gwynd*...42 E8
Llanerch *Powys*...34 J2
Llanerchymedd *IoA*...52 F6
Llanerfyl *Powys*...44 B12
Llanfabon *Caerph*...27 L8
Llanfachraeth *IoA*...52 D6
Llanfachreth *Gwynd*...43 Q9
Llanfaelog *IoA*...52 D8

Llanfaelrhys *Gwynd*...42 D8
Llanfaenor *Mons*...27 S4
Llanfaes *IoA*...52 K7
Llanfaes *Powys*...26 K2
Llanfaethlu *IoA*...52 D5
Llanfair *Gwynd*...43 L8
Llanfair Caereinion *Powys*...44 D12
Llanfair Clydogau *Cerdgn*...33 M10
Llanfair Dyffryn Clwyd...44 D2
  Denbgs
Llanfairfechan *Conwy*...53 L8
Llanfair Kilgeddin *Mons*...27 R6
Llanfair-Nant-Gwyn...25 L3
  Pembks
Llanfairpwllgwyngyll *IoA*...52 H8
Llanfair Talhaiarn *Conwy*...53 R8
Llanfair Waterdine *Shrops*...34 F5
Llanfair-yn-Neubwll *IoA*...52 D7
Llanfallteg *Carmth*...25 L6
Llanfallteg West *Carmth*...25 L6
Llanfarian *Cerdgn*...33 L5
Llanfechain *Powys*...44 E9
Llanfechell *IoA*...52 E4
Llanferres *Denbgs*...44 E1
Llan Ffestiniog *Gwynd*...43 P5
Llanfflewyn *IoA*...52 E5
Llanfigael *IoA*...52 E6
Llanfihangel-ar-arth...25 S3
  Carmth
Llanfihangel Glyn Myfyr...43 U4
  Conwy
Llanfihangel Nant Bran...33 T14
  Powys
Llanfihangel-nant-Melan...34 E9
  Powys
Llanfihangel Rhydithon...34 D7
  Powys
Llanfihangel Rogiet *Mons*...27 T10
Llanfihangel Tal-y-llyn...26 K2
  Powys
Llanfihangel-uwch-Gwili...25 T5
  Carmth
Llanfihangel-y-Creuddyn...33 N5
  Cerdgn
Llanfihangel-yng-...44 C10
  Ngwynfa *Powys*
Llanfihangel yn Nhowyn...52 D7
  IoA
Llanfihangel-y-pennant...43 M12
  Gwynd
Llanfihangel-y-pennant...43 N12
  Gwynd
Llanfilo *Powys*...34 D14
Llanfoist *Mons*...27 P5
Llanfor *Gwynd*...43 U6
Llanfrechfa *Torfn*...27 Q8
Llanfrothen *Gwynd*...43 M5
Llanfrynach *Powys*...26 K2
Llanfwrog *Denbgs*...44 D2
Llanfwrog *IoA*...52 D6
Llanfyllin *Powys*...44 D9
Llanfynydd *Carmth*...25 U5
Llanfynydd *Flints*...44 G2
Llanfyrnach *Pembks*...25 L4
Llangadfan *Powys*...44 B11
Llangadog *Carmth*...26 C2
Llangadwaladr *IoA*...52 E9
Llangadwaladr *Powys*...44 E7
Llangaffo *IoA*...52 F9
Llangain *Carmth*...25 R7
Llangammarch Wells...33 T11
  Powys
Llangan *V Glam*...26 H12
Llangarron *Herefs*...27 U3
Llangasty-Talyllyn *Powys*...27 L2
Llangathen *Carmth*...25 U6
Llangattock *Powys*...27 N4
Llangattock Lingoed *Mons*...27 R3
Llangattock-Vibon-Avel...27 T4
  Mons
Llangedwyn *Powys*...44 E8
Llangefni *IoA*...52 G7
Llangeinor *Brdgnd*...26 G10
Llangeitho *Cerdgn*...33 M9
Llangeler *Carmth*...25 Q3
Llangelynin *Gwynd*...43 L11
Llangendeirne *Carmth*...25 S8
Llangennech *Carmth*...25 T9
Llangennith *Swans*...25 R12
Llangenny *Powys*...27 N4
Llangernyw *Conwy*...53 Q9
Llangian *Gwynd*...42 E8
Llangiwg *Neath*...26 C6
Llanglydwen *Carmth*...25 L5
Llangoed *IoA*...52 K7
Llangoedmor *Cerdgn*...32 D11
Llangollen *Denbgs*...44 F5
Llangolman *Pembks*...24 K5
Llangors *Powys*...27 L2
Llangorwen *Cerdgn*...33 M4
Llangovan *Mons*...27 T6
Llangower *Gwynd*...43 T7
Llangrannog *Cerdgn*...32 F10
Llangristiolus *IoA*...52 F8
Llangrove *Herefs*...27 U4
Llangua *Mons*...27 R2
Llangunllo *Powys*...34 F6
Llangunnor *Carmth*...25 S6
Llangurig *Powys*...33 T5
Llangwm *Conwy*...43 U3
Llangwm *Mons*...27 S8
Llangwm *Pembks*...24 G9
Llangwnnadl *Gwynd*...42 D7
Llangwyfan *Denbgs*...54 D14
Llangwyllog *IoA*...52 F7
Llangwyryfon *Cerdgn*...33 M7
Llangybi *Cerdgn*...33 M9
Llangybi *Gwynd*...42 H4
Llangybi *Mons*...27 R8
Llangyfelach *Swans*...26 A8
Llangynhafal *Denbgs*...54 D14
Llangynidr *Powys*...27 M3
Llangynin *Carmth*...25 N7
Llangynllo *Cerdgn*...32 G11
Llangynog *Carmth*...25 P7
Llangynog *Powys*...44 C8
Llangynwyd *Brdgnd*...26 F10
Llanhamlach *Powys*...26 K2
Llanharan *Rhondd*...26 J11
Llanharry *Rhondd*...26 J11
Llanhennock *Mons*...27 R9
Llanhilleth *Blae G*...27 N7
Llanidloes *Powys*...33 T4
Llaniestyn *Gwynd*...42 E7
Llanigon *Powys*...34 F14
Llanilar *Cerdgn*...33 M5
Llanilid *Rhondd*...26 H11
Llanina *Cerdgn*...32 H9
Llanio *Cerdgn*...33 M8
Llanishen *Cardif*...27 M11
Llanishen *Mons*...27 T7
Llanllawddog *Carmth*...25 S5
Llanllechid *Gwynd*...52 K9
Llanlleonfel *Powys*...33 U10
Llanllowell *Mons*...27 R8
Llanllugan *Powys*...44 C12
Llanllwch *Carmth*...25 R7
Llanllwchaiarn *Powys*...34 D2
Llanllwni *Carmth*...25 S3
Llanllyfni *Gwynd*...42 H3
Llanllywel *Mons*...27 R8
Llanmadoc *Swans*...25 R12
Llanmaes *V Glam*...16 C3
Llanmartin *Newpt*...27 R10
Llanmerewig *Powys*...34 E2
Llanmihangel *V Glam*...16 C2
Llanmiloe *Carmth*...25 M9
Llanmorlais *Swans*...25 S12
Llannefydd *Conwy*...53 S8
Llannon *Carmth*...25 T9
Llannor *Gwynd*...42 G5
Llanon *Cerdgn*...32 K7
Llanover *Mons*...27 Q6
Llanpumsaint *Carmth*...25 R5
Llanreithan *Pembks*...24 E5
Llanrhaeadr *Denbgs*...53 T14
Llanrhaeadr-ym-...44 D8
  Mochnant *Powys*
Llanrhian *Pembks*...24 D4
Llanrhidian *Swans*...25 S12
Llanrhychwyn *Conwy*...53 N10
Llanrhyddlad *IoA*...52 D5
Llanrhystud *Cerdgn*...32 K7
Llanrothal *Herefs*...27 T4
Llanrug *Gwynd*...52 H10
Llanrumney *Cardif*...27 N11
Llanrwst *Conwy*...53 N10
Llansadurnen *Carmth*...25 N8
Llansadwrn *Carmth*...26 B1
Llansadwrn *IoA*...52 H7
Llansaint *Carmth*...25 Q9
Llansamlet *Swans*...26 B8
Llansanffraid Glan Conwy...53 P7
  Conwy
Llansannan *Conwy*...53 R9
Llansannor *V Glam*...26 H12
Llansantffraed *Powys*...27 L2
Llansantffraed-...33 N9
  Cwmdeuddwr *Powys*
Llansantffraed-in-Elvel...34 C10
  Powys
Llansantffraid *Cerdgn*...32 K7
Llansantffraid-ym-...44 F9
  Mechain *Powys*

Llansawel *Carmth*...25 V3
Llansilin *Powys*...44 F8
Llansoy *Mons*...27 S7
Llanspyddid *Powys*...26 J2
Llanstadwell *Pembks*...24 F10
Llansteffan *Carmth*...25 Q8
Llanstephan *Powys*...34 D12
Llantarnam *Torfn*...27 Q8
Llanteg *Pembks*...25 L8
Llanthewy Skirrid *Mons*...27 P2
Llanthony *Mons*...27 P3
Llantilio-Crossenny *Mons*...27 R5
Llantilio Pertholey *Mons*...27 Q4
Llantood *Pembks*...32 C12
Llantrisant *IoA*...52 E6
Llantrisant *Mons*...27 R8
Llantrisant *Rhondd*...26 J11
Llantrithyd *V Glam*...16 E2
Llantwit Fardre *Rhondd*...26 K10
Llantwit Major *V Glam*...16 C3
Llantysilio *Denbgs*...44 E5
Llanuwchllyn *Gwynd*...43 S7
Llanvaches *Newpt*...27 S9
Llanvair Discoed *Mons*...27 S9
Llanvapley *Mons*...27 R5
Llanvetherine *Mons*...27 R4
Llanveynoe *Herefs*...27 Q1
Llanvihangel Crucorney...27 Q3
  Mons
Llanvihangel Gobion *Mons*...27 Q6
Llanvihangel-Ystern-...27 S5
  Llewern *Mons*
Llanwarne *Herefs*...27 U2
Llanwddyn *Powys*...44 B10
Llanwenarth *Mons*...27 P5
Llanwenog *Cerdgn*...32 J11
Llanwern *Newpt*...27 R10
Llanwinio *Carmth*...25 N5
Llanwnda *Gwynd*...52 G11
Llanwnda *Pembks*...24 F3
Llanwnnen *Cerdgn*...32 K11
Llanwnog *Powys*...33 U3
Llanwonno *Rhondd*...26 J8
Llanwrda *Carmth*...26 C1
Llanwrin *Powys*...43 Q13
Llanwrthwl *Powys*...33 U8
Llanwrtyd *Powys*...33 S11
Llanwrtyd Wells *Powys*...33 S11
Llanwyddelan *Powys*...44 C12
Llanyblodwel *Shrops*...44 F9
Llanybri *Carmth*...25 P8
Llanybydder *Carmth*...32 K12
Llanycefn *Pembks*...24 J6
Llanychaer *Pembks*...24 F4
Llanycil *Gwynd*...43 T7
Llanycrwys *Carmth*...33 M11
Llanymawddwy *Gwynd*...43 S10
Llanymynech *Powys*...44 G9
Llanynghenedl *IoA*...52 D6
Llanynys *Denbgs*...54 D14
Llan-y-pwll *Wrexhm*...44 H3
Llanyre *Powys*...34 B8
Llanystumdwy *Gwynd*...42 J6
Llanywern *Powys*...44 F6
Llawhaden *Pembks*...24 J7
Llawnt *Shrops*...44 F7
Llawryglyn *Powys*...33 T3
Llay *Wrexhm*...44 H2
Llechcynfarwy *IoA*...52 E6
Llechfaen *Powys*...26 K2
Llechrhyd *Caerph*...27 L5
Llechryd *Cerdgn*...32 D12
Llechylched *IoA*...52 D7
Lledrod *Cerdgn*...33 M6
Llidiardau *Gwynd*...43 S6
Llidiartnenog *Carmth*...25 U4
Llidiart-y-parc *Denbgs*...44 D5
Llithfaen *Gwynd*...42 G4
Lloc *Flints*...54 D11
Llowes *Powys*...34 E12
Llwydcoed *Rhondd*...26 H6
Llwydiarth *Powys*...44 C10
Llwyn *Denbgs*...44 C4
Llwyncelyn *Cerdgn*...32 H9
Llwyndafydd *Cerdgn*...32 G9
Llwynderw *Powys*...44 F13
Llwyn-drain *Pembks*...25 M4
Llwyn-du *Mons*...27 N4
Llwyngwril *Gwynd*...43 L11
Llwynhendy *Carmth*...25 T10
Llwynmawr *Wrexhm*...44 F6
Llwyn-on *Powys*...26 J5
Llwyn-y-brain *Carmth*...25 L7
Llwyn-y-groes *Cerdgn*...33 L9
Llwynypia *Rhondd*...26 H9
Llynclys *Shrops*...44 G8
Llynfaes *IoA*...52 F7
Llŷn Peninsula *Gwynd*...42 F6
Llyn-y-pandy *Flints*...54 F13
Llysfaen *Conwy*...53 Q7
Llyswen *Powys*...34 D13
Llysworney *V Glam*...26 H13
Llyswen *Powys*...34 D13
Llysworney *V Glam*...16 C2
Llys-y-frân *Pembks*...24 H6
Llywel *Powys*...33 S13
Load Brook *Sheff*...57 L9
Loan *Falk*...82 H3
Loanend *Nthumb*...85 N9
Loanhead *Mdloth*...83 Q5
Loaningfoot *D & G*...74 J13
Loans *S Ayrs*...81 L6
Lobb *Devon*...15 L5
Lobhillcross *Devon*...5 M3
Lochailort *Highld*...93 T2
Lochaline *Highld*...93 R10
Lochans *D & G*...72 D8
Locharbriggs *D & G*...74 J9
Lochavich *Ag & B*...87 U14
Lochawe *Ag & B*...94 G13
Loch Baghasdail *W Isls*...106 c17
Lochboisdale *W Isls*...106 c17
Lochbuie *Ag & B*...93 Q13
Lochcarron *Highld*...101 M4
Lochdon *Ag & B*...93 S12
Lochdonhead *Ag & B*...93 S12
Lochead *Ag & B*...87 N9
Lochearnhead *Stirlg*...95 R14
Lochee *C Dund*...91 M5
Loch Eil *Highld*...94 E3
Locheilside Station *Highld*...94 D3
Lochend *Highld*...102 G8
Locheport *W Isls*...106 d12
Loch Euphort *W Isls*...106 d12
Lochfoot *D & G*...74 H11
Lochgair *Ag & B*...87 S7
Lochgarthside *Highld*...96 H2
Lochgelly *Fife*...90 K13
Lochgilphead *Ag & B*...87 S8
Lochgoilhead *Ag & B*...88 F5
Loch Head *D & G*...72 J10
Lochieheads *Fife*...91 L9
Lochill *Moray*...104 B3
Lochindorb Lodge *Highld*...103 R9
Lochinver *Highld*...110 B10
Loch Loyal Lodge *Highld*...111 N5
Lochluichart *Highld*...102 D3
Lochmaben *D & G*...75 L9
Lochmaddy *W Isls*...106 e12
Loch nam Madadh *W Isls*...106 e12
Loch Ness *Highld*...102 F10
Lochore *Fife*...90 J12
Loch Portain *W Isls*...106 e11
Lochportain *W Isls*...106 e11
Lochranza *N Ayrs*...79 S5
Loch Sgioporta *W Isls*...106 d15
Loch Sheldaig *Highld*...107 Q8
Lochside *Abers*...99 N4
Lochside *D & G*...74 J10
Lochside *Highld*...103 M5
Lochskipport *W Isls*...106 d15
Lochslin *Highld*...109 Q8
Lochton *S Ayrs*...72 G4
Lochty *Angus*...98 J12
Lochty *Fife*...91 R10
Lochuisge *Highld*...93 U6
Lochwinnoch *Rens*...88 J14
Lochwood *D & G*...75 L6
Lockengate *Cnwll*...3 Q4
Lockerbie *D & G*...75 M9
Lockeridge *Wilts*...18 H7
Lockerley *Hants*...8 K3
Locking *N Som*...17 L5
Locking Stumps *Warrtn*...55 P8
Lockington *E R Yk*...65 M10
Lockington *Leics*...47 N8
Lockleywood *Shrops*...45 Q8
Locksbottom *Gt Lon*...21 R10
Locksgreen *IoW*...9 N10
Lockton *N York*...64 K2
Loddington *Leics*...47 U13
Loddington *Nhants*...38 B5
Loddiswell *Devon*...5 S11
Loddon *Norfk*...51 Q14
Lode *Cambs*...39 R8
Lode Heath *Solhll*...36 G4
Loders *Dorset*...7 N6
Lodsworth *W Susx*...10 D6
Lofthouse *Leeds*...57 M1
Lofthouse *N York*...63 N5
Lofthouse Gate *Wakefd*...57 M2
Loftus *R & Cl*...71 L9
Logan *E Ayrs*...81 R8
Loganbeck *Cumb*...61 L1
Loganlea *W Loth*...82 J6

Loggerheads *Staffs*...45 R6
Logie *Angus*...99 M11
Logie *Fife*...91 P7
Logie *Fife*...91 L9
Logie Coldstone *Abers*...98 G3
Logie Newton *Abers*...104 K8
Logie Pert *Angus*...99 M11
Logierait *P & K*...97 R13
Logierieve *Abers*...105 Q9
Login *Carmth*...25 L6
Lolworth *Cambs*...39 M8
Lonbain *Highld*...100 U11
Londesborough *E R Yk*...64 K10
London *Gt Lon*...21 P6
London Apprentice *Cnwll*...3 Q6
London Ashford Airport...13 L11
  Kent
London Beach *Kent*...12 G8
London City Airport *Gt Lon*...21 R6
London Colney *Herts*...31 Q12
Londonderry *N York*...63 Q2
London Gateway Services...31 R11
  Gt Lon
London Gatwick Airport...11 M2
  W Susx
London Heathrow Airport...20 J7
  Gt Lon
London Luton Airport...31 P8
  Luton
London Oxford Airport...29 U4
  Oxon
London Southend Airport...23 L10
  Essex
London Stansted Airport...22 E3
  Essex
London Zoo ZSL *Gt Lon*...21 N6
Londonthorpe *Lincs*...48 D6
Lonemore *Highld*...107 N9
Long Ashton *N Som*...17 P3
Long Bank *Worcs*...35 S6
Long Bennington *Lincs*...48 B5
Longbenton *N Tyne*...77 R12
Longborough *Gloucs*...29 N2
Long Bredy *Dorset*...7 P6
Longbridge *Birm*...36 D5
Longbridge *Warwks*...36 J8
Longbridge Deverill *Wilts*...18 C12
Long Buckby *Nhants*...37 R7
Longburgh *Cumb*...67 N1
Longburton *Dorset*...7 R2
Long Cause *Devon*...5 U8
Long Clawson *Leics*...47 U8
Longcliffe *Derbys*...56 K14
Longcombe *Devon*...5 U9
Long Common *Hants*...9 Q5
Long Compton *Staffs*...45 T9
Long Compton *Warwks*...36 J14
Longcot *Oxon*...29 Q9
Long Crendon *Bucks*...30 E11
Long Crichel *Dorset*...8 D6
Longcroft *Cumb*...75 N14
Longcross *Surrey*...20 G9
Longden *Shrops*...44 K12
Long Ditton *Surrey*...21 L9
Longdon *Staffs*...46 D11
Longdon *Worcs*...35 T13
Longdon Green *Staffs*...46 D11
Longdon upon Tern *Wrekin*...45 P10
Longdown *Devon*...5 V2
Longdowns *Cnwll*...2 J10
Long Drax *N York*...64 E14
Long Duckmanton *Derbys*...57 P12
Long Eaton *Derbys*...47 N7
Longfield *Kent*...22 F13
Longford *Covtry*...37 L4
Longford *Derbys*...46 H6
Longford *Gloucs*...28 F3
Longford *Gt Lon*...20 J7
Longford *Kent*...21 T11
Longford *Shrops*...45 Q7
Longford *Wrekin*...45 R9
Longforgan *P & K*...91 L5
Longformacus *Border*...84 G9
Longframlington *Nthumb*...77 N5
Long Green *Ches W*...54 J11
Long Green *Worcs*...35 T13
Longham *Dorset*...8 F9
Longham *Norfk*...50 F10
Long Hanborough *Oxon*...29 T5
Longhaven *Abers*...105 U8
Long Hedges *Lincs*...49 N4
Longhirst *Nthumb*...77 Q8
Longhope *Gloucs*...28 C4
Longhope *Ork*...106 s20
Longhorsley *Nthumb*...77 N7
Longhoughton *Nthumb*...77 Q2
Long Itchington *Warwks*...37 M7
Longlands *Cumb*...67 L5
Longlane *Derbys*...46 H6
Long Lane *Wrekin*...45 P10
Longlane *W Berk*...19 Q5
Long Lawford *Warwks*...37 N5
Longleat Safari &...18 B12
  Adventure Park *Wilts*
Longlevens *Gloucs*...28 F3
Longley *Calder*...56 H4
Longley Green *Worcs*...35 R10
Long Load *Somset*...17 M12
Longmanhill *Abers*...105 M3
Long Marston *Herts*...30 J10
Long Marston *N York*...64 C9
Long Marston *Warwks*...36 G11
Long Marton *Cumb*...68 E8
Long Meadowend *Shrops*...34 K4
Long Melford *Suffk*...40 E11
Longmoor Camp *Hants*...10 B4
Longmorn *Moray*...104 B4
Longmoss *Ches E*...56 C12
Long Newnton *Gloucs*...28 H9
Longnewton *Border*...84 F13
Long Newton *E Loth*...84 D5
Longnewton *S on T*...70 D9
Longney *Gloucs*...28 E5
Longniddry *E Loth*...84 C4
Longnor *Shrops*...45 L13
Longnor *Staffs*...56 G13
Longparish *Hants*...19 P11
Longpark *Cumb*...75 T14
Long Preston *N York*...62 G9
Longridge *Lancs*...62 C12
Longridge *Staffs*...46 B10
Longridge *W Loth*...82 H6
Longriggend *N Lans*...82 G4
Long Riston *E R Yk*...65 R11
Longrock *Cnwll*...2 E10
Longsdon *Staffs*...46 B2
Longshaw *Wigan*...55 M5
Longside *Abers*...105 T6
Long Sight *Oldham*...56 D5
Longslow *Shrops*...45 Q7
Longstanton *Cambs*...39 M8
Longstock *Hants*...19 M13
Longstone *Pembks*...25 L9
Longstowe *Cambs*...39 M10
Long Stratton *Norfk*...51 L14
Long Street *M Keyn*...30 H4
Longstreet *Wilts*...18 H10
Long Sutton *Hants*...20 B13
Long Sutton *Lincs*...49 P9
Long Sutton *Somset*...17 N12
Longthorpe *C Pete*...38 J1
Long Thurlow *Suffk*...40 J7
Longthwaite *Cumb*...67 P8
Longton *C Stke*...46 B5
Longton *Lancs*...55 L1
Longtown *Cumb*...75 T13
Longtown *Herefs*...27 Q2
Longueville *Jersey*...7 e3
Longville in the Dale...45 M14
  Shrops
Long Waste *Wrekin*...45 P10
Long Whatton *Leics*...47 N9
Longwick *Bucks*...30 F12
Long Wittenham *Oxon*...19 R2
Longwitton *Nthumb*...77 M8
Longwood *D & G*...73 S8
Longworth *Oxon*...29 S8
Longyester *E Loth*...84 E6
Lonmay *Abers*...105 S4
Lonmore *Highld*...100 b5
Loose *Kent*...12 E5
Loosebeare *Devon*...15 R11
Loosegate *Lincs*...49 M9
Loosley Row *Bucks*...20 D3
Lootcherbrae *Abers*...104 J5
Lopcombe Corner *Wilts*...9 N11
Lopen *Somset*...7 N2
Loppington *Shrops*...45 L8
Lorbottle *Nthumb*...77 L4
Lordington *W Susx*...10 B9
Lords Wood *Medway*...12 E3
Lornty *P & K*...90 J2
Loscoe *Derbys*...47 M4
Loscombe *Dorset*...7 N5
Losgaintir *W Isls*...106 f9
Lossiemouth *Moray*...104 B2
Lostford *Shrops*...45 Q7
Lostock Gralam *Ches W*...55 Q12

Lostock Green *Ches W*...55 Q12
Lostock Hall *Lancs*...55 M1
Lostock Hall Fold *Bolton*...55 Q5
Lostock Junction *Bolton*...55 Q5
Lostwithiel *Cnwll*...4 E9
Lothbeg *Highld*...109 S2
Lothersdale *N York*...62 K10
Lothmore *Highld*...109 S2
Loudwater *Bucks*...20 F4
Loughborough *Leics*...47 P10
Loughor *Swans*...25 T11
Loughton *Essex*...21 R4
Loughton *M Keyn*...30 H5
Loughton *Shrops*...35 N3
Lound *Lincs*...48 G11
Lound *Notts*...57 U9
Lound *Suffk*...51 T1
Lounston *Devon*...5 U5
Louth *Lincs*...59 Q9
Love Clough *Lancs*...62 G14
Lovedean *Hants*...9 T6
Lover *Wilts*...8 J3
Loversall *Donc*...57 S7
Loves Green *Essex*...22 F6
Lovesome Hill *N York*...70 D13
Loveston *Pembks*...24 J9
Lovington *Somset*...17 Q10
Low Ackworth *Wakefd*...57 Q3
Low Angerton *Nthumb*...77 M9
Lowbands *Gloucs*...35 S14
Low Barbeth *D & G*...72 C6
Low Barlings *Lincs*...58 J12
Low Bell End *N York*...71 M13
Low Bentham *N York*...62 C6
Low Biggins *Cumb*...62 C4
Low Borrowbridge *Cumb*...68 D12
Low Bradfield *Sheff*...57 L8
Low Bradley *N York*...63 L10
Low Braithwaite *Cumb*...67 P4
Low Burnham *N Linc*...58 C5
Low Buston *Nthumb*...77 Q4
Lowca *Cumb*...66 E8
Low Catton *E R Yk*...64 G9
Low Crosby *Cumb*...67 Q1
Low Crosby *Cumb*...75 T14
Lowdham *Notts*...47 S4
Lowe *Shrops*...45 M7
Lowe Hill *Staffs*...46 C2
Low Ellington *N York*...63 P3
Lower Aisholt *Somset*...16 H9
Lower Ansty *Dorset*...7 U4
Lower Apperley *Gloucs*...28 G2
Lower Arboll *Highld*...109 R8
Lower Arncott *Oxon*...30 C9
Lower Ashton *Devon*...5 V3
Lower Assendon *Oxon*...20 B6
Lower Ballam *Lancs*...61 R13
Lower Bartle *Lancs*...61 T13
Lower Basildon *W Berk*...19 U5
Lower Bearwood *Herefs*...34 J9
Lower Beeding *W Susx*...11 L5
Lower Benefield *Nhants*...38 E3
Lower Bentley *Worcs*...36 C7
Lower Beobridge *Shrops*...35 S2
Lower Birchwood *Derbys*...47 M3
Lower Boddington *Nhants*...37 N10
Lower Bourne *Surrey*...10 C2
Lower Brailes *Warwks*...36 K13
Lower Breakish *Highld*...100 f7
Lower Bredbury *Stockp*...56 D8
Lower Broadheath *Worcs*...35 T9
Lower Broxwood *Herefs*...34 J10
Lower Buckenham *Norfk*...51 P14
Lower Bullingham *Herefs*...35 M13
Lower Burgate *Hants*...8 H5
Lower Burrowton *Devon*...6 D5
Lower Burton *Herefs*...34 K10
Lower Caldecote *C Beds*...38 J11
Lower Cam *Gloucs*...28 D7
Lower Canada *N Som*...17 L4
Lower Catesby *Nhants*...37 P8
Lower Chapel *Powys*...34 C14
Lower Chicksgrove *Wilts*...8 D2
Lower Chute *Wilts*...19 L9
Lower Clapton *Gt Lon*...21 P5
Lower Clent *Worcs*...36 B5
Lower Common *Hants*...19 U13
Lower Creedy *Devon*...15 T12
Lower Crossings *Derbys*...56 F10
Lower Cumberworth *Kirk*...56 K5
Lower Darwen *Bl w D*...55 Q1
Lower Dean *Bed*...38 G7
Lower Denby *Kirk*...56 K5
Lower Diabaig *Highld*...107 N13
Lower Dicker *E Susx*...11 T8
Lower Dinchope *Shrops*...35 L4
Lower Down *Shrops*...34 H4
Lower Dunsforth *N York*...63 U7
Lower Egleton *Herefs*...35 P11
Lower Elkstone *Staffs*...46 D2
Lower Ellastone *Staffs*...46 F5
Lower End *Bucks*...30 D9
Lower End *Nhants*...38 C8
Lower Everleigh *Wilts*...18 J10
Lower Exbury *Hants*...9 P9
Lower Eythorne *Kent*...13 Q6
Lower Failand *N Som*...17 N2
Lower Farringdon *Hants*...10 B3
Lower Feltham *Gt Lon*...20 J8
Lower Fittleworth *W Susx*...10 G7
Lower Foxdale *IoM*...60 d7
Lower Frankton *Shrops*...44 J7
Lower Freystrop *Pembks*...24 G8
Lower Froyle *Hants*...20 B13
Lower Gabwell *Devon*...6 B11
Lower Gledfield *Highld*...108 K6
Lower Godney *Somset*...17 N8
Lower Gornal *Dudley*...36 B2
Lower Gravenhurst *C Beds*...31 Q5
Lower Green *Herts*...31 S5
Lower Green *Kent*...11 U3
Lower Green *Kent*...12 B7
Lower Green *Norfk*...50 G6
Lower Green *Staffs*...45 U12
Lower Green *Suffk*...40 C7
Lower Hacheston *Suffk*...41 P9
Lower Halliford *Surrey*...20 J9
Lower Halstow *Kent*...12 F2
Lower Hamworthy *BCP*...8 D10
Lower Hardres *Kent*...13 N5
Lower Harpton *Herefs*...34 G8
Lower Hartlip *Kent*...12 F3
Lower Hartshay *Derbys*...47 L3
Lower Hartwell *Bucks*...30 G10
Lower Hawthwaite *Cumb*...61 N2
Lower Haysden *Kent*...21 U13
Lower Hergest *Herefs*...34 G9
Lower Heyford *Oxon*...29 U3
Lower Heysham *Lancs*...61 R8
Lower Higham *Kent*...22 H13
Lower Holbrook *Suffk*...41 L13
Lower Hordley *Shrops*...44 J8
Lower Horncroft *W Susx*...10 G7
Lower Horsebridge *E Susx*...11 T8
Lower Houses *Kirk*...56 J4
Lower Irlam *Salfd*...55 R8
Lower Kilburn *Derbys*...47 L5
Lower Kilcott *Gloucs*...28 E10
Lower Killeyan *Ag & B*...78 B7
Lower Kingcombe *Dorset*...7 P5
Lower Kingswood *Surrey*...21 M12
Lower Kinnerton *Ches W*...54 H14
Lower Langford *N Som*...17 N4
Lower Largo *Fife*...91 P11
Lower Leigh *Staffs*...46 D6
Lower Lemington *Gloucs*...36 H14
Lower Llanfadog *Powys*...33 U7
Lower Lovacott *Devon*...15 M7
Lower Loxhore *Devon*...15 P5
Lower Lydbrook *Gloucs*...28 A4
Lower Lye *Herefs*...34 K7
Lower Machen *Newpt*...27 N10
Lower Maes-coed *Herefs*...27 Q1
Lower Mannington *Dorset*...8 F7
Lower Marston *Somset*...17 U8
Lower Meend *Gloucs*...27 V7
Lower Merridge *Somset*...16 H10
Lower Middleton Cheney...37 N12
  Nhants
Lower Milton *Somset*...17 P7
Lower Moor *Worcs*...36 C11
Lower Morton *S Glos*...28 B9
Lower Nazeing *Essex*...31 U12
Lower Norton *Warwks*...36 H8
Lower Nyland *Dorset*...17 U12
Lower Penarth *V Glam*...16 G3
Lower Penn *Staffs*...35 U2
Lower Pennington *Hants*...9 L9
Lower Peover *Ches E*...55 R12
Lower Place *Rochdl*...56 D4
Lower Pollicott *Bucks*...30 F10
Lower Quinton *Warwks*...36 G11

Lulworth Camp *Dorset*...8 A12
Lumb *Calder*...56 F2
Lumb *Lancs*...55 T2
Lumby *N York*...64 B13
Lumloch *E Duns*...89 P12
Lumphanan *Abers*...98 K3
Lumphinnans *Fife*...90 J13
Lumsden *Abers*...104 F11
Lunan *Angus*...91 U2
Lunanhead *Angus*...98 H13
Luncarty *P & K*...90 G6
Lund *E R Yk*...65 L10
Lund *N York*...64 G13
Lundie *Angus*...91 L4
Lundin Links *Fife*...91 P11
Lundin Mill *Fife*...91 P11
Lundy *Devon*...14 C2
Lunga *Ag & B*...87 N4
Lunna *Shet*...106 v7
Lunsford *Kent*...12 D4
Lunsford's Cross *E Susx*...12 D13
Lunt *Sefton*...54 H6
Luppitt *Devon*...6 H4
Lupridge *Devon*...5 S10
Lupset *Wakefd*...57 M3
Lupton *Cumb*...62 B3
Lurgashall *W Susx*...10 E5
Lurley *Devon*...16 B13
Lusby *Lincs*...59 P13
Luscombe *Devon*...5 T9
Luss *Ag & B*...88 J7
Lussagiven *Ag & B*...87 L8
Lusta *Highld*...100 b4
Lustleigh *Devon*...5 T4
Luston *Herefs*...35 L8
Luthermuir *Abers*...99 M11
Luthrie *Fife*...91 M8
Lutley *Dudley*...36 B4
Luton *Devon*...6 B9
Luton *Devon*...6 D3
Luton *Luton*...31 P9
Luton *Medway*...12 E2
Luton Airport *Luton*...31 P8
Lutterworth *Leics*...37 P4
Lutton *Devon*...5 P9
Lutton *Lincs*...49 P8
Lutton *Nhants*...38 H3
Luxborough *Somset*...16 C9
Luxulyan *Cnwll*...3 R5
Luxulyan Valley *Cnwll*...3 R5
Luzley *Tamesd*...56 E7
Lybster *Highld*...112 G9
Lydbury North *Shrops*...34 J3
Lydcott *Devon*...15 Q5
Lydd *Kent*...12 K11
Lydd Airport *Kent*...13 L11
Lydden *Kent*...13 Q6
Lydden *Kent*...13 S3
Lyddington *Rutlnd*...38 C1
Lydd-on-Sea *Kent*...13 L12
Lydeard St Lawrence...16 F10
  Somset
Lyde Green *Hants*...20 B11
Lyde Green *S Glos*...28 C12
Lydford *Devon*...5 N4
Lydford on Fosse *Somset*...17 Q10
Lydgate *Calder*...56 D1
Lydgate *Rochdl*...56 E5
Lydham *Shrops*...34 J2
Lydiard Green *Wilts*...29 L10
Lydiard Millicent *Wilts*...29 L10
Lydiard Tregoze *Swindn*...29 M11
Lydiate *Sefton*...54 J5
Lydiate Ash *Worcs*...36 C5
Lydlinch *Dorset*...7 T2
Lydney *Gloucs*...28 B6
Lydstep *Pembks*...24 J11
Lye *Dudley*...36 B4
Lye Cross *N Som*...17 N4
Lye Green *E Susx*...11 T4
Lye Green *Warwks*...36 G7
Lye Head *Worcs*...35 S6
Lye's Green *Wilts*...18 B12
Lyford *Oxon*...29 S8
Lymbridge Green *Kent*...13 M7
Lyme Regis *Dorset*...6 K6
Lyminge *Kent*...13 N7
Lymington *Hants*...9 L9
Lyminster *W Susx*...10 G9
Lymm *Warrtn*...55 Q9
Lymore *Hants*...9 L10
Lympne *Kent*...13 M8
Lympsham *Somset*...16 K6
Lympstone *Devon*...6 C7
Lynbridge *Devon*...15 R3
Lynch *Somset*...15 U3
Lynchat *Highld*...97 L4
Lyndhurst *Hants*...9 L7
Lyndon *Rutlnd*...48 C13
Lyne *Border*...83 P10
Lyne *Surrey*...20 H9
Lyneal *Shrops*...44 K7
Lyne Down *Herefs*...35 Q14
Lyneham *Devon*...5 V5
Lyneham *Oxon*...29 Q4
Lyneham *Wilts*...18 F5
Lyneholmford *Cumb*...76 B12
Lynemouth *Nthumb*...77 R7
Lyne of Skene *Abers*...105 M13
Lyness *Ork*...106 s20
Lyng *Norfk*...50 J10
Lyng *Somset*...16 K11
Lynn *Staffs*...46 E13
Lynn *Wrekin*...45 S10
Lynsted *Kent*...12 H3
Lynstone *Cnwll*...14 F11
Lynton *Devon*...15 R3
Lyon's Gate *Dorset*...7 R4
Lyonshall *Herefs*...34 H10
Lytchett Matravers *Dorset*...8 D9
Lytchett Minster *Dorset*...8 D10
Lyth *Highld*...112 G4
Lytham *Lancs*...61 R14
Lytham St Annes *Lancs*...54 J1
Lythbank *Shrops*...45 L12
Lythe *N York*...71 P10
Lythmore *Highld*...112 C3

M

Maaruig *W Isls*...106 h8
Mabe Burnthouse *Cnwll*...2 J10
Mablethorpe *Lincs*...59 T10
Macclesfield *Ches E*...56 D12
Macduff *Abers*...105 L3
Macharioch *Ag & B*...79 N14
Machan *Carmth*...25 U4
Machrie *N Ayrs*...79 R8
Machrihanish *Ag & B*...79 L11
Machrins *Ag & B*...86 f4
Machroes *Gwynd*...42 F8
Machynlleth *Powys*...43 P13
Machynys *Carmth*...25 T10
Mackworth *Derbys*...46 K6
Macmerry *E Loth*...84 C4
Maddaford *Devon*...15 N14
Madderty *P & K*...90 D7
Maddington *Wilts*...18 H12
Maddiston *Falk*...82 H3
Madehurst *W Susx*...10 F8
Madeley *Staffs*...45 S4
Madeley *Wrekin*...45 Q13
Madeley Heath *Staffs*...45 S4
Madeley Park Wood *Staffs*...45 S5
Madford *Devon*...6 F3
Madingley *Cambs*...39 N8
Madley *Herefs*...34 K13
Madresfield *Worcs*...35 T11
Madron *Cnwll*...2 D10
Maenaddwyn *IoA*...52 G5
Maen-y-groes *Cerdgn*...32 G9
Maenclochog *Pembks*...24 J5
Maendy *V Glam*...26 J12
Maenporth *Cnwll*...2 K11
Maentwrog *Gwynd*...43 N5
Maer *Cnwll*...14 F11
Maer *Staffs*...45 S5
Maerdy *Carmth*...26 A3
Maerdy *Conwy*...43 U3
Maerdy *Rhondd*...26 H8
Maesbrook *Shrops*...44 G9
Maesbury *Shrops*...44 H8
Maesbury Marsh *Shrops*...44 H8
Maesgwynne *Carmth*...25 M6
Maeshafn *Denbgs*...44 F1
Maesllyn *Cerdgn*...32 G11
Maesmynis *Powys*...34 B11
Maesteg *Brdgnd*...26 F9
Maesybont *Carmth*...25 U6
Maesycwmmer *Caerph*...27 M9

Magdalen Laver Essex 22 D6
Maggieknockater Moray 104 G6
Maggots End Essex 22 C2
Magham Down E Susx 11 U8
Maghull Sefton 54 K5
Magor Mons 27 S10
Magor Services Mons 27 S10
Maidenbower W Susx 11 M3
Maiden Bradley Wilts 18 B13
Maidencombe Torbay 6 B11
Maidenhayne Devon 6 J5
Maiden Head N Som 17 N4
Maidenhead W & M 20 E6
Maiden Law Dur 69 Q3
Maiden Newton Dorset 7 Q5
Maidens S Ayrs 80 J11
Maiden's Green Br For 20 F8
Maidenwell Lincs 59 P11
Maids Moreton Bucks 30 F5
Maidstone Kent 12 E4
Maidstone Services Kent 12 F4
Maidwell Nhants 37 T5
Mail Shet 106 u10
Maindee Newpt 27 Q10
Mainland Ork 106 s18
Mainland Shet 106 u8
Mainsforth Dur 70 D6
Mains of Balhall Angus 98 J11
Mains of Balnakettle Abers 99 L9
Mains of Dalvey Moray 103 T9
Mains of Haulkerton Abers 99 N9
Mains of Lesmoir Abers 104 F10
Mains of Melgunds Angus 98 J12
Mainsriddle D & G 66 D1
Mainstone Shrops 34 G3
Maisemore Gloucs 28 F3
Major's Green Worcs 36 F5
Makeney Derbys 47 L5
Malborough Devon 5 S13
Malcoff Derbys 56 G10
Malden Rushett Gt Lon 21 L10
Maldon Essex 22 L6
Malham N York 62 J7
Maligar Highld 100 d3
Mallaig Highld 100 f10
Mallaigvaig Highld 100 f10
Malleny Mills C Edin 83 N5
Mallows Green Essex 22 C2
Malltraeth IoA 52 F9
Mallwyd Gwynd 43 S11
Malmesbury Wilts 28 H10
Malmsmead Devon 15 S3
Malpas Ches W 45 L4
Malpas Cnwll 3 L8
Malpas Newpt 27 Q9
Malshanger Hants 19 S10
Malswick Gloucs 28 D3
Maltby Lincs 59 P10
Maltby Rothm 57 R8
Maltby S on T 70 G10
Maltby le Marsh Lincs 59 S10
Malting Green Essex 23 N3
Maltman's Hill Kent 12 H7
Malton N York 64 H5
Malvern Worcs 35 S11
Malvern Hills 35 S12
Malvern Link Worcs 35 S12
Malvern Wells Worcs 35 S12
Mamble Worcs 35 Q6
Mamhilad Mons 27 Q7
Manaccan Cnwll 2 K12
Manafon Powys 44 D13
Manais W Isls 106 g10
Manaton Devon 5 T4
Manby Lincs 59 Q9
Mancetter Warwks 36 K1
Manchester Manch 55 T8
Manchester Airport Manch 55 T10
Mancot Flints 54 H13
Mandally Highld 96 B3
Manea Cambs 39 Q3
Maney Birm 36 F1
Manfield N York 69 R10
Mangersta W Isls 106 f5
Mangerton Dorset 7 N5
Mangotsfield S Glos 28 C12
Mangrove Green Herts 31 P8
Manhay Cnwll 2 H10
Manish W Isls 106 g10
Mankinholes Calder 56 E2
Manley Ches W 55 M12
Manmoel Caerph 27 M7
Mannal Ag & B 92 B10

Manningford Bohune Wilts 18 H9
Manningford Bruce Wilts 18 H9
Manningham C Brad 63 N12
Mannings Heath W Susx 11 L5
Mannington Dorset 8 F7
Manningtree Essex 23 R1
Mannofield C Aber 99 R3
Manorbier Pembks 24 J11
Manorbier Newton Pembks 24 H10
Manordeilo Carmth 26 B2
Manorhill Border 84 H12
Manorowen Pembks 24 F3
Manor Park Gt Lon 21 R6
Mansell Gamage Herefs 34 J12
Mansell Lacy Herefs 34 K11
Mansergh Cumb 62 C3
Mansfield E Ayrs 81 R8
Mansfield Notts 47 P1
Mansfield Woodhouse Notts 57 R14
Mansriggs Cumb 61 P3
Manston Dorset 17 V13
Manston Kent 13 R2
Manston Leeds 63 T13
Manswood Dorset 8 D7
Manthorpe Lincs 48 G10
Manthorpe Lincs 48 D9
Manton N Linc 58 G5
Manton Notts 57 S11
Manton Rutlnd 48 C13
Manton Wilts 18 J7
Manuden Essex 22 C2
Maperton Somset 17 S11
Maplebeck Notts 47 T1
Maple Cross Herts 20 H4
Mapledurham Oxon 19 U5
Mapledurwell Hants 19 U10
Maplehurst W Susx 10 K6
Maplescombe Kent 21 T10
Mapperley Derbys 47 M5
Mapperley Park C Nott 47 R5
Mapperton Dorset 7 P5
Mappleborough Green Warwks 36 E7
Mappleton E R Yk 65 T11
Mapplewell Barns 57 M4
Mappowder Dorset 7 T3
Maraig W Isls 106 h8
Marazanvose Cnwll 2 K6
Marazion Cnwll 2 D11
Marbhig W Isls 106 j7
Marbury Ches E 45 N4
March Cambs 39 P1
March S Lans 74 J3
Marcham Oxon 29 U8
Marchamley Shrops 45 N8
Marchamley Wood Shrops 45 N7
Marchington Staffs 46 F7
Marchington Woodlands Staffs 46 F8
Marchwiel Wrexhm 44 H4
Marchwood Hants 9 M6
Marcross V Glam 16 B3
Marden Herefs 35 M11
Marden Kent 12 D7
Marden Wilts 18 G9
Marden Ash Essex 22 D7
Marden Beech Kent 12 D7
Marden's Hill E Susx 11 S4
Marden Thorn Kent 12 E7
Mardlebury Herts 31 S9
Mardy Mons 27 Q4
Marefield Leics 47 T12
Mareham le Fen Lincs 49 L1
Mareham on the Hill Lincs 59 N13
Marehay Derbys 47 L4
Marehill W Susx 10 H7
Maresfield E Susx 11 R6
Marfleet C KuH 65 Q14
Marford Wrexhm 44 H2
Margam Neath 26 D11
Margaret Marsh Dorset 17 V13
Margaret Roding Essex 22 E5
Margaretting Essex 22 F7
Margaretting Tye Essex 22 G7
Margate Kent 13 R1
Margnaheglish N Ayrs 80 E6
Margrie D & G 73 Q9
Margrove Park R & Cl 71 L9
Marham Norfk 50 B12
Marhamchurch Cnwll 14 F12
Marholm C Pete 48 H13

Marian-glas IoA 52 H6
Mariansleigh Devon 15 R8
Marine Town Kent 23 M13
Marionburgh Abers 99 M2
Marishader Highld 100 d3
Maristow Devon 5 M8
Marjoriebanks D & G 75 L9
Markbeech Kent 11 R2
Markby Lincs 59 S11
Mark Causeway Somset 17 L7
Mark Cross E Susx 11 T4
Markeaton C Derb 46 K6
Market Bosworth Leics 47 M13
Market Deeping Lincs 48 H11
Market Drayton Shrops 45 Q7
Market Harborough Leics 37 U3
Market Lavington Wilts 18 F10
Market Overton Rutlnd 48 C10
Market Rasen Lincs 58 K9
Market Stainton Lincs 59 M11
Market Warsop Notts 57 S13
Market Weighton E R Yk 64 K11
Market Weston Suffk 40 G5
Markfield Leics 47 N12
Markham Caerph 27 M7
Markham Moor Notts 58 B12
Markinch Fife 91 L11
Markington N York 63 R6
Markle E Loth 84 F3
Marksbury BaNES 17 S4
Mark's Corner IoW 9 P10
Marks Tey Essex 23 M3
Markwell Cnwll 4 K9
Markyate Herts 31 N9
Marlborough Wilts 18 J7
Marlbrook Herefs 35 M10
Marlbrook Worcs 36 C6
Marlcliff Warwks 36 E10
Marldon Devon 6 V8
Marle Green E Susx 11 T7
Marlesford Suffk 41 P9
Marley Kent 13 R5
Marley Green Ches E 45 N4
Marley Hill Gatesd 77 Q14
Marlingford Norfk 50 K12
Marloes Pembks 24 C9
Marlow Bucks 20 D5
Marlow Herefs 34 K5
Marlow Bottom Bucks 20 D5
Marlpit Hill Kent 21 R13
Marlpits E Susx 11 R5
Marlpool Derbys 47 M4
Marnhull Dorset 17 U13
Marple Stockp 56 E9
Marple Bridge Stockp 56 E9
Marr Donc 57 R5
Marrick N York 69 N13
Marros Carmth 25 M9
Marsden S Tyne 77 T13
Marsden Kirk 56 G4
Marsden Height Lancs 62 H12
Marsett N York 62 J2
Marsh Bucks 30 H11
Marsh C Brad 63 L12
Marsh Devon 6 J2
Marshall's Heath Herts 31 Q10
Marshalswick Herts 31 Q11
Marsham Norfk 51 L9
Marsh Baldon Oxon 30 C13
Marsh Benham W Berk 19 P7
Marshborough Kent 13 R4
Marshbrook Shrops 34 K3
Marshchapel Lincs 59 Q7
Marsh Farm Luton 31 N7
Marshfield Newpt 27 N11
Marshfield S Glos 28 E13
Marshgate Cnwll 4 F2
Marsh Gibbon Bucks 30 D8
Marsh Green Devon 6 D6
Marsh Green Kent 11 R2
Marsh Green Wrekin 45 P10
Marshland St James Norfk 49 R12
Marsh Lane Derbys 57 P11
Marske N York 69 N11
Marske-by-the-Sea R & Cl 70 K8
Marsland Green Wigan 55 Q7
Marston Ches W 55 Q11
Marston Herefs 34 J9
Marston Lincs 48 C4
Marston Oxon 30 B11
Marston Staffs 45 U9
Marston Staffs 46 B8
Marston Warwks 36 H2
Marston Wilts 18 E9
Marston Doles Warwks 37 N9
Marston Green Solhll 36 G3
Marston Jabbet Warwks 37 L3
Marston Magna Somset 17 Q12
Marston Meysey Wilts 29 M8
Marston Montgomery Derbys 46 F6
Marston Moretaine C Beds 31 L4
Marston on Dove Derbys 46 H8
Marston St Lawrence Nhants 30 B4
Marston Stannett Herefs 35 N9
Marston Trussell Nhants 37 S4
Marstow Herefs 27 V4
Marsworth Bucks 30 K10
Marten Wilts 19 L8
Marthall Ches E 55 T11
Martham Norfk 51 S10
Martin Hants 8 F5
Martin Kent 13 R6
Martin Lincs 48 H2
Martin Lincs 59 M13
Martindale Cumb 67 P9
Martin Dales Lincs 48 J1
Martin Drove End Hants 8 F4
Martinhoe Devon 15 Q3
Martin Hussingtree Worcs 35 U8
Martinscroft Warrtn 55 Q9
Martinstown Dorset 7 S7
Martlesham Suffk 41 M11
Martlesham Heath Suffk 41 M11
Martletwy Pembks 24 H8
Martley Worcs 35 S8
Martock Somset 17 M12
Marton Ches E 56 C13
Marton Cumb 61 N4
Marton E R Yk 65 R12
Marton E R Yk 65 S10
Marton Lincs 58 D10
Marton Middsb 70 H9
Marton N York 64 G3
Marton N York 64 E5
Marton Shrops 44 G12
Marton Warwks 37 M7
Marton-le-Moor N York 63 T5
Martyr's Green Surrey 20 J11
Martyr Worthy Hants 9 Q2
Marwick Ork 106 r17
Marwood Devon 15 M5
Marybank Highld 102 E5
Maryburgh Highld 102 F4
Maryhill C Glas 89 N12
Marykirk Abers 99 M10
Maryland Mons 27 U6
Marylebone Gt Lon 21 N6
Marylebone Wigan 55 M5
Maryport Cumb 66 F6
Maryport D & G 72 E13
Marystow Devon 5 L4
Mary Tavy Devon 5 N5
Maryton Angus 99 M13
Marywell Abers 98 K4
Marywell Abers 99 R4
Marywell Angus 91 U2
Masham N York 63 Q3
Mashbury Essex 22 G5
Masongill N York 62 D4
Mastin Moor Derbys 57 Q12

Maud Abers 105 Q6
Maufant Jersey 7 e2
Maugersbury Gloucs 29 P2
Maughold IoM 60 h4
Mauld Highld 102 D8
Maulden C Beds 31 N5
Maulds Meaburn Cumb 68 D9
Maunby N York 63 T2
Maund Bryan Herefs 35 N10
Maundown Somset 16 E11
Mautby Norfk 51 S11
Mavesyn Ridware Staffs 46 D10
Mavis Enderby Lincs 59 Q13
Mawbray Cumb 66 G3
Mawdesley Lancs 55 L4
Mawdlam Brdgnd 26 E11
Mawgan Cnwll 2 J11
Maw Green Ches E 45 R2
Mawla Cnwll 2 J7
Mawnan Cnwll 2 K11
Mawnan Smith Cnwll 2 K11
Mawsley Nhants 38 B5
Mawthorpe Lincs 59 S12
Maxey C Pete 48 H12
Maxstoke Warwks 36 H3
Maxted Street Kent 13 M7
Maxton Border 84 G12
Maxton Kent 13 R7
Maxwelltown D & G 74 J10
Maxworthy Cnwll 4 H2
Mayals Swans 25 V13
May Bank Staffs 45 U4
Maybole S Ayrs 80 K11
Maybury Surrey 20 H11
Mayes Green Surrey 10 K3
Mayfield E Susx 11 T5
Mayfield Mdloth 83 S5
Mayfield Staffs 46 G4
Mayford Surrey 20 G11
Mayland Essex 23 M7
Maylandsea Essex 23 M7
Maynard's Green E Susx 11 T7
Maypole Br & H 36 E5
Maypole Kent 13 P2
Maypole Mons 27 T4
Maypole Green Norfk 41 R1
Maypole Green Suffk 40 F8
Maypole Green Suffk 41 N7
May's Green Oxon 20 B6
May's Green Surrey 20 K11
Mead Devon 14 F9
Meadgate BaNES 17 S5
Meadle Bucks 30 H11
Meadowfield Dur 69 R5
Meadowtown Shrops 44 H13
Meadwell Devon 5 L4
Meaford Staffs 45 U6
Mealabost W Isls 106 j5
Meal Bank Cumb 67 R13
Mealrigg Cumb 66 H3
Mealsgate Cumb 66 K4
Meanwood Leeds 63 R12
Mearbeck N York 62 H7
Meare Somset 17 M7
Meare Green Somset 16 J11
Meare Green Somset 16 K11
Mears Ashby Nhants 38 B7
Measham Leics 46 K11
Meath Green Surrey 11 M2
Meathop Cumb 61 R3
Meaux E R Yk 65 Q12
Meavag W Isls 106 f5
Meavy Devon 5 N7
Medbourne Leics 38 B2
Meddon Devon 14 G9
Meden Vale Notts 57 S13
Medhurst Row Kent 21 S13
Medlam Lincs 49 M2
Medmenham Bucks 20 D5
Mednow Dur 69 P2
Medstead Hants 19 U13
Medstead Services Medway 12 E2
Meerbrook Staffs 46 C1
Meer Common Herefs 34 J10
Meesden Herts 22 C1
Meeson Wrekin 45 Q9
Meeth Devon 15 M11
Meeting Green Suffk 40 B9
Meeting House Hill Norfk 51 P8
Meidrim Carmth 25 N6
Meifod Powys 44 E11
Meigle P & K 91 L3
Meikle Carco D & G 74 E10
Meikle Earnock S Lans 82 D8
Meikle Ferry Highld 109 N7
Meikle Kilmany Fife 91 M6
Meikle Obney P & K 90 F4
Meikle Wartle Abers 105 L8
Meinciau Carmth 25 S8
Meir C Stke 46 B5
Meir Heath Staffs 46 B5
Melbost W Isls 106 j5
Melbourn Cambs 39 N11
Melbourne Derbys 47 L8
Melbourne E R Yk 64 H10
Melbury Devon 14 J9
Melbury Abbas Dorset 8 B3
Melbury Bubb Dorset 7 Q3
Melbury Osmond Dorset 7 Q3
Melbury Sampford Dorset 7 Q3
Melchbourne Bed 38 F7
Melcombe Bingham Dorset 7 U4
Meldon Devon 15 P2
Meldon Nthumb 77 P8
Meldon Park Nthumb 77 N8
Meldreth Cambs 39 N11
Meldrum Stirlg 89 R6
Melfort Ag & B 87 Q3
Meliden Denbgs 53 S6
Melin-byrhedyn Powys 43 R14
Melincourt Neath 26 E8
Melin-y-coed Conwy 53 P10
Melin-y-ddol Powys 44 C12
Melin-y-wig Denbgs 44 C4
Melkinthorpe Cumb 67 R7
Melkridge Nthumb 76 E13
Melksham Wilts 18 D8
Mellangoose Cnwll 2 H11
Mell Green W Berk 19 Q5
Mellguards Cumb 67 P3
Melling Lancs 62 B5
Melling Sefton 54 J6
Melling Mount Sefton 54 K6
Mellis Suffk 40 K6
Mellon Charles Highld 107 P6
Mellon Udrigle Highld 107 P6
Mellor Lancs 62 C13
Mellor Stockp 56 E9
Mellor Brook Lancs 62 C13
Mells Somset 17 T7
Melmerby Cumb 67 S4
Melmerby N York 63 R3
Melmerby N York 69 M13
Melness Highld 111 N4
Melon Green Suffk 40 D9
Melplash Dorset 7 N5
Melrose Border 84 E12
Melsetter Ork 106 r21
Melsonby N York 69 R11
Meltham Kirk 56 H4
Meltham Mills Kirk 56 H4
Melton E R Yk 65 N14
Melton Suffk 41 N10
Meltonby E R Yk 64 H9
Melton Constable Norfk 50 H6
Melton Mowbray Leics 47 U10
Melton Ross N Linc 58 J4
Melvaig Highld 107 M7
Melverley Shrops 44 H10
Melverley Green Shrops 44 H10
Melvich Highld 111 T4
Membury Devon 6 J4
Membury Services W Berk 19 M5
Memsie Abers 105 R3
Memus Angus 98 G12
Menabilly Cnwll 3 R6
Menagissey Cnwll 2 J7
Menai Bridge IoA 52 J8
Mendham Suffk 41 N4
Mendip Hills 17 P5
Mendlesham Suffk 40 K8
Mendlesham Green Suffk 40 J8
Menheniot Cnwll 4 H8
Menithwood Worcs 35 R7
Menna Cnwll 3 N6
Mennock D & G 74 F5
Menston C Brad 63 P11
Menstrie Clacks 90 C12
Menthorpe N York 64 G12
Mentmore Bucks 30 K9
Meoble Highld 100 h11
Meole Brace Shrops 45 L11
Meols Wirral 54 F8
Meonstoke Hants 9 S5
Meopham Kent 12 C2
Meopham Green Kent 12 C2
Meopham Station Kent 12 C2

Mepal Cambs 39 P4
Meppershall C Beds 31 P5
Merbach Herefs 34 H12
Mere Ches E 55 R10
Mere Wilts 8 B2
Mere Brow Lancs 54 K3
Mereclough Lancs 62 H13
Mere Green Birm 36 F1
Mere Green Worcs 36 C8
Mere Heath Ches W 55 Q12
Meresborough Medway 12 F3
Mereworth Kent 12 C5
Mergie Abers 99 P6
Merley BCP 8 E9
Merlin's Bridge Pembks 24 F8
Merrington Shrops 45 L9
Merrion Pembks 24 F11
Merriott Somset 7 M2
Merrivale Devon 5 N5
Merrow Surrey 20 H12
Merry Field Hill Dorset 8 E8
Merry Hill Herts 20 K4
Merryhill Wolves 35 U2
Merry Lees Leics 47 N12
Mersea Island Essex 23 P4
Mersey Gateway Bridge Halton 55 M10
Mersham Kent 13 L8
Merstham Surrey 21 N12
Merston W Susx 10 D10
Merstone IoW 9 Q11
Merther Cnwll 3 L8
Merthyr Carmth 25 Q6
Merthyr Cynog Powys 33 J13
Merthyr Dyfan V Glam 16 F3
Merthyr Mawr Brdgnd 26 F12
Merthyr Tydfil Myr Td 26 K6
Merthyr Vale Myr Td 26 K8
Merton Devon 15 M10
Merton Gt Lon 21 N9
Merton Norfk 50 F14
Merton Oxon 30 C9
Meshaw Devon 15 S9
Messing Essex 23 M4
Messingham N Linc 58 F5
Metfield Suffk 41 N4
Metheringham Lincs 48 G1
Methil Fife 91 N12
Methleigh Cnwll 2 H11
Methley Leeds 57 M1
Methley Junction Leeds 57 N1
Methlick Abers 105 P8
Methven P & K 90 F6
Methwold Norfk 40 B2
Methwold Hythe Norfk 40 B2
Mettingham Suffk 41 Q3
Metton Norfk 51 M6
Mevagissey Cnwll 3 Q8
Mexborough Donc 57 Q6
Mey Highld 112 G2
Meysey Hampton Gloucs 29 M7
Miabhag W Isls 106 f5
Michaelchurch Herefs 27 U2
Michaelchurch Escley Herefs 34 H14
Michaelchurch-on-Arrow Powys 34 F10
Michaelston-le-Pit V Glam 16 F2
Michaelstone-y-Fedw Newpt 27 N11
Michaelstow Cnwll 4 D5
Michaelwood Services Gloucs 28 D8
Michelcombe Devon 5 R7
Micheldever Hants 19 R13
Micheldever Station Hants 19 R12
Michelmersh Hants 9 L3
Mickfield Suffk 40 K8
Micklebring Donc 57 R8
Mickleby N York 71 P10
Micklefield Leeds 64 B13
Micklefield Green Herts 20 H3
Mickleham Surrey 21 L12
Mickleover C Derb 46 K7
Micklethwaite C Brad 63 N11
Micklethwaite Cumb 67 M2
Mickleton Dur 69 L8
Mickleton Gloucs 36 G11
Mickletown Leeds 57 N1
Mickle Trafford Ches W 54 K13
Mickley Derbys 57 M11
Mickley N York 63 R4
Mickley Green Suffk 40 D9
Mickley Square Nthumb 77 M13
Mid Ardlaw Abers 105 Q2
Midbea Ork 106 t15
Mid Beltie Abers 99 L3
Mid Bockhampton BCP 8 H9
Mid Calder W Loth 83 L5
Mid Clyth Highld 112 G9
Mid Culbeuchly Abers 104 K3
Middle Assendon Oxon 20 B6
Middle Aston Oxon 29 U2
Middle Barton Oxon 29 U3
Middlebie D & G 75 P10
Middle Chinnock Somset 7 N2
Middle Claydon Bucks 30 F7
Middlecliffe Barns 57 P5
Middlecott Devon 5 S2
Middlecroft Derbys 57 P12
Middle Duntisbourne Gloucs 28 J6
Middleham N York 63 P2
Middle Handley Derbys 57 P11
Middle Harling Norfk 40 G3
Middlehill Cnwll 4 G7
Middlehill Wilts 18 B7
Middlehope Shrops 35 L3
Middle Kames Ag & B 87 T8
Middle Littleton Worcs 36 E11
Middle Madeley Staffs 45 S4
Middle Maes-coed Herefs 34 H14
Middlemarsh Dorset 7 R4
Middle Mayfield Staffs 46 G4
Middle Mill Pembks 24 D6
Middlemoor Devon 5 M6
Middle Quarter Kent 12 G8
Middle Rasen Lincs 58 J9
Middle Rocombe Devon 6 B11
Middlesbrough Middsb 70 G9
Middlesceugh Cumb 67 N3
Middleshaw Cumb 62 C2
Middlesmoor N York 63 L5
Middle Stoford Somset 16 G12
Middle Stoke Medway 12 H1
Middlestone Dur 69 S5
Middlestone Moor Dur 69 S5
Middlestown Wakefd 57 L3
Middle Street Gloucs 28 E7
Middle Taphouse Cnwll 4 F8
Middlethird Border 84 H10
Middleton Ag & B 92 B10
Middleton Derbys 46 H1
Middleton Derbys 56 J14
Middleton Essex 40 E13
Middleton Hants 19 Q11
Middleton Herefs 35 M7
Middleton Lancs 61 S8
Middleton Leeds 63 S14
Middleton N York 63 N9
Middleton N York 64 G3
Middleton Nhants 38 C3
Middleton Norfk 49 U11
Middleton Nthumb 77 N8
Middleton Nthumb 85 S11
Middleton P & K 90 H9
Middleton Rochdl 56 C5
Middleton Shrops 34 K6
Middleton Shrops 35 N6
Middleton Suffk 41 R7
Middleton Swans 25 R13
Middleton Warwks 36 G2
Middleton Cheney Nhants 37 N12
Middleton Green Staffs 46 C6
Middleton Hall Nthumb 85 P13
Middleton-in-Teesdale Dur 68 K7
Middleton Moor Suffk 41 R7
Middleton One Row Darltn 70 E10
Middleton-on-Leven N York 70 G11
Middleton-on-Sea W Susx 10 F10
Middleton on the Hill Herefs 35 M8
Middleton on the Wolds E R Yk 65 L10
Middleton Park C Aber 105 Q13
Middleton Priors Shrops 35 Q2
Middleton Quernhow N York 63 S4
Middleton St George Darltn 70 D10
Middleton Scriven Shrops 35 Q3
Middleton Stoney Oxon 30 B8
Middleton Tyas N York 69 R11
Middletown Cumb 66 E11
Middle Town IoS 2 c1
Middletown N Som 17 N2

Middletown Powys 44 H11
Middle Tysoe Warwks 36 K12
Middle Wallop Hants 19 L13
Middlewich Ches E 55 R13
Middle Winterslow Wilts 8 K2
Middlewood Cnwll 4 H5
Middle Woodford Wilts 8 H2
Middlewood Green Suffk 40 J8
Middle Yard Gloucs 28 F7
Middlezoy Somset 17 L10
Middridge Dur 69 R7
Midford BaNES 17 T4
Midge Hall Lancs 55 M2
Midgeholme Cumb 76 B14
Midgham W Berk 19 S7
Midgley Calder 56 F1
Midgley Wakefd 57 L4
Mid Holmwood Surrey 21 L13
Midhopestones Sheff 57 L7
Midhurst W Susx 10 D6
Mid Lavant W Susx 10 D9
Midlem Border 84 E13
Mid Mains Highld 102 D8
Midney Somset 17 N11
Midpark Ag & B 88 B14
Midsomer Norton BaNES 17 S6
Midtown Highld 111 N4
Midville Lincs 49 N2
Midway Ches E 56 D10
Mid Yell Shet 106 v4
Migdale Highld 109 L6
Migvie Abers 98 G2
Milborne Port Somset 17 S12
Milborne St Andrew Dorset 7 V5
Milborne Wick Somset 17 S12
Milbourne Nthumb 77 N10
Milbourne Wilts 28 H10
Milbury Heath S Glos 28 C9
Milby N York 63 U6
Milcombe Oxon 37 M14
Milden Suffk 40 F11
Mildenhall Suffk 39 U5
Mildenhall Wilts 18 K7
Mile Elm Wilts 18 E7
Mile End Gloucs 27 V5
Mile End Suffk 41 P3
Mileham Norfk 50 F10
Mile Oak Br & H 11 M9
Mile Oak Kent 12 C7
Miles Hope Herefs 35 N8
Milesmark Fife 90 F14
Miles Platting Manch 56 C7
Mile Town Kent 23 M13
Milfield Nthumb 85 N12
Milford Derbys 46 K4
Milford Devon 14 F8
Milford Powys 34 C1
Milford Staffs 46 B9
Milford Surrey 10 E2
Milford Haven Pembks 24 F9
Milford on Sea Hants 8 K10
Milkwall Gloucs 27 V6
Milland W Susx 10 C5
Milland Marsh W Susx 10 C5
Mill Bank Calder 56 F2
Millbeck Cumb 67 L8
Millbreck Abers 105 R6
Millbridge Surrey 10 C2
Millbrook C Beds 31 M5
Millbrook Cnwll 5 L10
Millbrook Jersey 7 c3
Millbrook Sotn 9 M6
Millbuie Abers 105 N13
Millbuie Highld 102 G5
Millcombe Devon 5 U11
Mill Common Norfk 51 P13
Mill Common Suffk 41 R4
Millcorner E Susx 12 F11
Millcraig Highld 109 M10
Mill Cross Devon 5 S8
Milldale Staffs 46 F2
Mill End Bucks 20 C5
Mill End Cambs 39 T9
Mill End Herts 31 U6
Millerhill Mdloth 83 R5
Miller's Dale Derbys 56 H12
Millers Green Derbys 46 J3
Millerston C Glas 89 P12
Millgate Lancs 56 C3
Mill Green Cambs 39 T11
Mill Green Essex 22 F7
Mill Green Herts 31 R11
Mill Green Lincs 49 L8
Mill Green Norfk 40 K4
Mill Green Shrops 45 Q8
Mill Green Staffs 46 E10
Mill Green Suffk 40 F8
Mill Green Suffk 40 F11
Mill Green Suffk 40 J6
Mill Green Suffk 40 K7
Mill Green W & M 20 E7
Millhalf Herefs 34 G11
Millhayes Devon 6 H3
Millhayes Devon 6 J4
Millheugh S Lans 82 D8
Mill Hill E Susx 11 U9
Mill Hill Gt Lon 21 M4
Millhouse Ag & B 87 T11
Millhouse Cumb 67 M5
Millhousebridge D & G 75 M8
Millhouse Green Barns 56 K6
Millhouses Barns 57 M5
Millhouses Sheff 57 M10
Milliken Park Rens 88 K13
Millin Cross Pembks 24 G8
Millington E R Yk 64 K9
Mill Lane Hants 20 C11
Millmeece Staffs 45 T7
Millness D & G 75 P9
Mill of Drummond P & K 89 T7
Mill of Haldane W Duns 88 K10
Millom Cumb 61 M3
Millook Cnwll 14 E13
Millpool Cnwll 4 F6
Millport N Ayrs 80 H2
Millthorpe Derbys 57 M11
Millthrop Cumb 62 D1
Milltimber C Aber 99 R3
Milltown Abers 98 D2
Milltown Abers 104 F11
Milltown Cnwll 4 F8
Milltown D & G 75 S11
Milltown Derbys 57 M14
Milltown Devon 15 N5
Milltown of Auchindoun Moray 104 D7
Milltown of Campfield Abers 99 M3
Milltown of Edinvillie Moray 104 ...
Milltown of Rothiemay Moray 104 G6
Milnathort P & K 90 H11
Milngavie E Duns 89 N11
Milnrow Rochdl 56 D4
Milnthorpe Cumb 61 T3
Milnthorpe Wakefd 57 M3
Milovaig Highld 100 a4
Milson Shrops 35 P6
Milstead Kent 12 G4
Milston Wilts 18 J11
Milthorpe Lincs 48 H7
Milthorpe Nhants 37 Q11
Milton C Stke 46 B3
Milton Cambs 39 Q8
Milton Cumb 76 B13
Milton D & G 72 K8
Milton D & G 74 G10
Milton Derbys 46 K8
Milton Highld 102 E5
Milton Highld 102 F7
Milton Highld 102 K6
Milton Highld 109 N11
Milton Highld 112 E4
Milton Inver 88 G11
Milton Kent 12 D2
Milton Moray 104 F3
Milton N Som 16 K4
Milton Newpt 27 Q10
Milton Notts 58 B12
Milton Oxon 29 U2
Milton Oxon 37 M14
Milton P & K 90 C5
Milton Pembks 24 H9
Milton Port 89 N11
Milton Somset 17 M11
Milton Stirlg 89 L5
Milton W Duns 88 K11
Milton Abbas Dorset 7 V4
Milton Abbot Devon 5 L5
Milton Bridge Mdloth 83 P6
Milton Bryan C Beds 31 L6
Milton Clevedon Somset 17 S9
Milton Combe Devon 5 M7
Milton Damerel Devon 14 J10
Milton End Gloucs 28 D5
Milton Ernest Bed 38 F9
Milton Green Ches W 45 L2
Milton Hill Oxon 29 U9
Milton Keynes M Keyn 30 J5
Milton Lilbourne Wilts 18 J8
Milton Malsor Nhants 37 T9
Milton Morenish P & K 95 S11
Milton of Auchinhove Abers 99 ...
Milton of Balgonie Fife 91 M11
Milton of Buchanan Stirlg 88 K7
Milton of Campsie E Duns 89 P10
Milton of Finavon Angus 98 H12
Milton of Leys Highld 102 J7
Milton of Murtle C Aber 99 R3
Milton on Stour Dorset 17 U11
Milton Regis Kent 12 F3
Milton Street E Susx 11 S10
Milton-under-Wychwood Oxon 29 Q4

Milverton Somset 16 F11
Milverton Warwks 36 K7
Milwich Staffs 46 C7
Milwr Flints 54 E12
Minard Ag & B 87 T6
Minchington Dorset 8 D6
Minchinhampton Gloucs 28 G7
Mindenhurst Surrey 20 F11
Mindrum Nthumb 85 M12
Minehead Somset 16 C7
Minera Wrexhm 44 G3
Minety Wilts 28 K9
Minffordd Gwynd 43 L6
Mingarrypark Highld 93 R5
Miningsby Lincs 59 P14
Minions Cnwll 4 H6
Minishant S Ayrs 81 L10
Minllyn Gwynd 43 S11
Minnes Abers 105 R10
Minngearraidh W Isls 106 c16
Minnigaff D & G 73 L6
Minnonie Abers 105 M3
Minshull Vernon Ches E 45 Q1
Minskip N York 63 T7
Minstead Hants 9 L6
Minsted W Susx 10 D6
Minster Kent 13 R2
Minster Kent 23 N13
Minsterley Shrops 44 J12
Minster Lovell Oxon 29 R5
Minster-on-Sea Kent 23 N13
Minsterworth Gloucs 28 E4
Minterne Magna Dorset 7 R4
Minterne Parva Dorset 7 R4
Minting Lincs 59 L12
Mintlaw Abers 105 R6
Minto Border 84 F14
Minton Shrops 34 K2
Minwear Pembks 24 H7
Minworth Birm 36 G2
Mirbister Ork 106 s18
Mirehouse Cumb 66 E9
Mireland Highld 112 H5
Mirfield Kirk 56 K3
Miserden Gloucs 28 H6
Miskin Rhondd 26 K11
Misson Notts 57 U7
Misterton Leics 37 Q4
Misterton Notts 58 C7
Misterton Somset 7 N3
Mistley Essex 23 R1
Mistley Heath Essex 23 R1
Mitcham Gt Lon 21 N9
Mitcheldean Gloucs 28 C4
Mitchell Cnwll 3 L5
Mitchellslacks D & G 74 K6
Mitchel Troy Mons 27 T5
Mitford Nthumb 77 P8
Mithian Cnwll 2 J6
Mitton Staffs 45 U10
Mixbury Oxon 30 D6
Mixenden Calder 63 M14
Moats Tye Suffk 40 H9
Mobberley Ches E 55 S11
Mobberley Staffs 46 D5
Moccas Herefs 34 J12
Mochdre Conwy 53 P7
Mochdre Powys 34 C3
Mochrum D & G 72 J10
Mockbeggar Hants 8 H7
Mockbeggar Kent 12 D6
Mockerkin Cumb 66 G9
Modbury Devon 5 R10
Moddershall Staffs 45 U6
Modsarie Highld 111 P4
Moelfre IoA 52 H6
Moelfre Powys 44 E8
Moel Tryfan Gwynd 52 H11
Moel-y-crio Flints 54 E13
Moffat D & G 75 L4
Mogador Surrey 21 M12
Moggerhanger C Beds 38 J11
Moira Leics 46 K10
Molash Kent 12 K5
Mol-chlach Highld 100 d8
Mold Flints 54 F13
Molehill Green Essex 22 E3
Molehill Green Essex 22 G3
Molescroft E R Yk 65 N10
Molesden Nthumb 77 P9
Molesworth Cambs 38 F5
Moll Highld 100 e6
Molland Devon 15 U7
Mollington Ches W 54 J12
Mollington Oxon 37 M11
Mollinsburn N Lans 89 Q11
Monachty Cerdgn 32 K8
Monevechadan Ag & B 88 F5
Monewden Suffk 41 M9
Moneydie P & K 90 F6
Moneyrow Green W & M 20 E7
Moniaive D & G 74 E6
Monifieth Angus 91 Q5
Monikie Angus 91 Q4
Monimail Fife 91 L9
Monington Pembks 32 B11
Monk Bretton Barns 57 N5
Monken Hadley Gt Lon 21 N3
Monk Fryston N York 64 B14
Monkhide Herefs 35 P12
Monkhill Cumb 67 M1
Monkhopton Shrops 35 P2
Monkland Herefs 34 K9
Monknash V Glam 16 B2
Monkokehampton Devon 15 N11
Monkseaton N Tyne 77 S11
Monks Eleigh Suffk 40 G11
Monk's Gate W Susx 11 L5
Monk's Heath Ches E 55 T12
Monk Sherborne Hants 19 T9
Monkshill Abers 105 M6
Monksilver Somset 16 E9
Monks Kirby Warwks 37 N4
Monk Soham Suffk 41 M7
Monkspath Solhll 36 F5
Monks Risborough Bucks 30 H12
Monksthorpe Lincs 59 R13
Monk Street Essex 22 F2
Monkswood Mons 27 Q6
Monkton Devon 6 G4
Monkton Kent 13 Q2
Monkton S Ayrs 81 L7
Monkton S Tyne 77 S13
Monkton V Glam 16 B3
Monkton Combe BaNES 17 T4
Monkton Deverill Wilts 18 B13
Monkton Farleigh Wilts 18 B7
Monkton Heathfield Somset 16 J11
Monkton Up Wimborne Dorset 8 E6
Monkton Wyld Dorset 6 K5
Monkwearmouth Sundld 77 T14
Monkwood Hants 9 T2
Monmore Green Wolves 36 B1
Monmouth Mons 27 U5
Monnington on Wye Herefs 34 J12
Monreith D & G 72 J10
Montacute Somset 17 N12
Montford Shrops 44 K10
Montford Bridge Shrops 44 K10
Montgarrie Abers 104 J12
Montgarswood E Ayrs 81 P7
Montgomery Powys 44 F13
Montpelier Bristl 27 V12
Montrave Fife 91 M11
Montrose Angus 99 N13
Mont Saint Guern 6 c2
Monxton Hants 19 M12
Monyash Derbys 56 H13
Monymusk Abers 104 K12
Monzie P & K 90 C6
Moodiesburn N Lans 89 Q11
Moonzie Fife 91 M8
Moor Allerton Leeds 63 R12
Moorbath Dorset 7 M5
Moorby Lincs 59 N13
Moor Crichel Dorset 8 D7
Moordown BCP 8 F9
Moore Halton 55 N10
Moor End C Beds 31 M8

Moor End Calder 63 M14
Moor End Devon 15 Q11
Moorend Gloucs 28 D6
Moor End N York 64 H11
Moorends Donc 57 U3
Moorgreen Hants 9 P5
Moorgreen Notts 47 N4
Moorhall Derbys 57 M12
Moorhampton Herefs 34 J12
Moorhead C Brad 63 P12
Moorhouse Cumb 67 M1
Moorhouse Notts 58 C13
Moorhouse Bank Surrey 21 R12
Moorland Somset 16 K10
Moorlinch Somset 17 L9
Moor Monkton N York 64 C9
Moor Row Cumb 66 F10
Moor Row Cumb 67 L3
Moorsholm R & Cl 71 L9
Moorside Dorset 17 U13
Moor Side Lincs 49 L2
Moor Side Lincs 49 L1
Moorside Oldham 56 D5
Moorswater Cnwll 4 G8
Moor Street Medway 12 F2
Moorthorpe Wakefd 57 Q4
Moortown Devon 5 N6
Moortown Hants 8 H7
Moortown IoW 9 N12
Moortown Leeds 63 R12
Moortown Lincs 58 J7
Moortown Wrekin 45 P10
Morangie Highld 109 P8
Morar Highld 100 f10
Morborne Cambs 38 H2
Morchard Bishop Devon 15 S11
Morchard Road Devon 15 S11
Morcombelake Dorset 7 M5
Morcott Rutlnd 48 D13
Morda Shrops 44 G8
Morden Dorset 8 C9
Morden Gt Lon 21 N9
Mordiford Herefs 35 N13
Mordon Dur 70 D7
More Shrops 34 H2
Morebath Devon 16 C11
Morebattle Border 84 K13
Morecambe Lancs 61 S7
Moredon Swindn 29 M10
Morefield Highld 107 V5
Morehall Kent 13 N8
Moreleigh Devon 5 S10
Morenish P & K 95 S11
Moresby Parks Cumb 66 E9
Morestead Hants 9 Q3
Moreton Dorset 7 V7
Moreton Herefs 35 M8
Moreton Oxon 30 E12
Moreton Staffs 45 S10
Moreton Wirral 54 G9
Moreton Corbet Shrops 45 N9
Moreton Hall Suffk 40 E8
Moretonhampstead Devon 5 T3
Moreton-in-Marsh Gloucs 29 P1
Moreton Jeffries Herefs 35 P11
Moreton Morrell Warwks 36 K9
Moreton on Lugg Herefs 35 M12
Moreton Paddox Warwks 36 K10
Moreton Pinkney Nhants 37 P11
Moreton Say Shrops 45 P7
Moreton Valence Gloucs 28 E6
Morfa Cerdgn 32 F10
Morfa Bychan Gwynd 42 K6
Morfa Dinlle Gwynd 52 F11
Morfa Glas Neath 26 F7
Morfa Nefyn Gwynd 42 E5
Morganstown Cardif 27 L11
Morgan's Vale Wilts 8 H4
Moriah Cerdgn 33 M5
Morland Cumb 67 S7
Morley Ches E 55 T10
Morley Derbys 47 L5
Morley Dur 69 Q7
Morley Leeds 63 R14
Morley Green Ches E 55 T10
Morley St Botolph Norfk 50 J14
Mornick Cnwll 4 J7
Morningside C Edin 83 P4
Morningside N Lans 82 G7
Morningthorpe Norfk 41 M2
Morpeth Nthumb 77 Q8
Morphie Abers 99 N11
Morrey Staffs 46 F10
Morridge Side Staffs 46 D3
Morriston Swans 26 B8
Morston Norfk 50 H5
Mortehoe Devon 15 L3
Morthen Rothm 57 Q9
Mortimer W Berk 19 T8
Mortimer Common W Berk 19 T8
Mortimer's Cross Herefs 34 K8
Mortimer West End Hants 19 T8
Mortlake Gt Lon 21 M7
Morton Cumb 67 N2
Morton Derbys 57 N14
Morton Lincs 48 G9
Morton Lincs 58 D8
Morton Norfk 50 K10
Morton Notts 47 U2
Morton Shrops 44 G9
Morton-on-Swale N York 63 S1
Morton on the Hill Norfk 50 K10
Morton Tinmouth Dur 69 Q8
Morvah Cnwll 2 C9
Morval Cnwll 4 H9
Morvich Highld 101 N8
Morville Shrops 35 Q2
Morville Heath Shrops 35 R2
Morwellham Quay Devon 5 L6
Morwenstow Cnwll 14 E9
Mosborough Sheff 57 P9
Moscow E Ayrs 81 N4
Mose Shrops 35 S2
Mosedale Cumb 67 M6
Moseley Birm 36 E4
Moseley Wolves 36 B1
Moseley Worcs 35 U9
Moses Gate Bolton 55 R5
Moss Ag & B 92 B10
Moss Donc 57 T3
Moss Wrexhm 44 H3
Mossat Abers 104 G12
Mossbank Shet 106 u6
Moss Bank St Hel 55 M7
Mossbay Cumb 66 E7
Mossblown S Ayrs 81 M7
Mossbrow Traffd 55 R9
Mossburnford Border 76 D2
Mossdale D & G 73 R3
Mossdale E Ayrs 81 P11
Moss Edge Lancs 61 S11
Mossend N Lans 82 E6
Mosser Mains Cumb 66 H8
Mossley Ches E 45 U1
Mossley Tamesd 56 E6
Moss Nook Manch 55 T10
Moss-side Highld 103 N4
Moss Side Cumb 66 H2
Moss Side Lancs 61 R13
Moss Side Sefton 54 J5
Mosstodloch Moray 104 C4
Mossy Lea Lancs 55 M4
Mosterton Dorset 7 M3
Moston Manch 56 C6
Moston Shrops 45 N8
Moston Green Ches E 45 R1
Mostyn Flints 54 E11
Motcombe Dorset 17 V12
Mothecombe Devon 5 Q11
Motherby Cumb 67 P7
Motherwell N Lans 82 E7
Mottingham Gt Lon 21 R8
Mottisfont Hants 9 L3
Mottistone IoW 9 N12
Mottram in Longdendale Tamesd 56 E7
Mottram St Andrew Ches E 56 C11
Mouldsworth Ches W 55 M12
Moulin P & K 97 Q12
Moulsecoomb Br & H 11 N9
Moulsford Oxon 19 S4
Moulsham Essex 22 H6
Moulsoe M Keyn 38 D11
Moultavie Highld 109 L10
Moulton Ches W 55 Q13
Moulton Lincs 49 M9
Moulton N York 69 R11

Moulton Nhants 37 U7
Moulton Suffk 39 U8
Moulton V Glam 16 E3
Moulton Chapel Lincs 49 L10
Moulton St Mary Norfk 51 Q12
Moulton Seas End Lincs 49 M8
Mount Cnwll 4 E7
Mount Kirk 56 G3
Mountain C Brad 63 M13
Mountain Ash Rhondd 26 J8
Mountain Cross Border 83 N9
Mountain Street Kent 13 L5
Mount Ambrose Cnwll 2 J8
Mount Bures Essex 23 M1
Mountfield E Susx 12 D11
Mountgerald Highld 102 F4
Mount Hawke Cnwll 2 J7
Mountjoy Cnwll 3 M4
Mount Lothian Mdloth 83 Q7
Mountnessing Essex 22 F8
Mounton Mons 27 U8
Mount Pleasant Ches E 45 T3
Mount Pleasant Derbys 46 J10
Mount Pleasant Derbys 47 L4
Mount Pleasant Dur 69 R4
Mount Pleasant E R Yk 65 T12
Mount Pleasant Norfk 40 G2
Mount Pleasant Suffk 40 B11
Mountsorrel Leics 47 Q11
Mount Sorrel Wilts 8 E4
Mount Tabor Calder 56 G1
Mousehole Cnwll 2 C11
Mouswald D & G 75 L10
Mow Cop Ches E 45 U2
Mowhaugh Border 76 K2
Mowmacre Hill C Leic 47 Q12
Mowsley Leics 37 R3
Moy Highld 96 E2
Moy Highld 103 L9
Moyle Highld 101 M8
Moylegrove Pembks 32 B11
Muasdale Ag & B 79 M7
Muchalls Abers 99 S5
Much Birch Herefs 27 T1
Much Cowarne Herefs 35 P11
Much Dewchurch Herefs 27 T1
Muchelney Somset 17 M11
Muchelney Ham Somset 17 M11
Much Hadham Herts 22 B4
Much Hoole Lancs 55 L1
Much Hoole Town Lancs 55 L2
Muchlarnick Cnwll 4 G9
Much Marcle Herefs 35 Q13
Much Wenlock Shrops 45 P13
Muck Highld 93 L6
Mucking Thurr 22 G11
Muckleburgh Collection Norfk 50 K5
Muckleford Dorset 7 R6
Mucklestone Staffs 45 R6
Muckley Shrops 45 P13
Muckton Lincs 59 Q10
Muddiford Devon 15 N5
Muddles Green E Susx 11 S8
Mudford BCP 8 F10
Mudford Somset 17 Q13
Mudford Sock Somset 17 Q13
Mudgley Somset 17 N7
Mugdock Stirlg 89 N11
Mugeary Highld 100 d6
Mugginton Derbys 46 J5
Muggintonlane End Derbys 46 J5
Mugglewick Dur 69 M3
Muirden Abers 105 M5
Muirdrum Angus 91 R4
Muirhead Angus 91 M5
Muirhead Fife 91 L10
Muirhead N Lans 89 Q12
Muirhouses Falk 82 K2
Muirkirk E Ayrs 81 S7
Muirmill Stirlg 89 R9
Muir of Fowlis Abers 104 J12
Muir of Miltonduff Moray 103 V4
Muir of Ord Highld 102 F6
Muirshearlich Highld 94 F2
Muirtack Abers 105 R8
Muirton P & K 90 G6
Muirton Mains Highld 102 E5
Muirton of Ardblair P & K 90 H3
Muker N York 68 K13
Mulbarton Norfk 51 L13
Mulben Moray 104 C5
Mulfra Cnwll 2 D10
Mullacott Cross Devon 15 M3
Mulldonach D & G
Mullion Cnwll 2 H13
Mullion Cove Cnwll 2 H13
Mumby Lincs 59 S12
Munderfield Row Herefs 35 Q9
Munderfield Stocks Herefs 35 Q9
Mundesley Norfk 51 P6
Mundford Norfk 50 C14
Mundham Norfk 51 P14
Mundon Essex 23 L7
Mundy Bois Kent 12 H7
Munerigie Highld 101 S11
Mungrisdale Cumb 67 M6
Munlochy Highld 102 H5
Munnoch N Ayrs 80 K3
Munsley Herefs 35 Q12
Munslow Shrops 35 L3
Murchington Devon 5 S3
Murcot Worcs 36 E12
Murcott Oxon 30 C9
Murkle Highld 112 F4
Murlaggan Highld 101 Q13
Murrell Green Hants 20 B11
Murroes Angus 91 Q5
Murrow Cambs 49 N12
Mursley Bucks 30 H7
Murston Kent 12 H3
Murthill Angus 98 H12
Murthly P & K 90 G4
Murton C York 64 E9
Murton Cumb 68 F8
Murton Dur 70 E3
Murton Nthumb 85 P9
Murton Swans 25 U13
Musbury Devon 6 K6
Muscoates N York 64 F3
Musselburgh E Loth 83 R4
Muston Leics 48 B6
Muston N York 65 P4
Mustow Green Worcs 35 U6
Muswell Hill Gt Lon 21 N5
Mutehill D & G 73 R10
Muthill P & K 90 B7
Mutterton Devon 6 D4
Muxton Wrekin 45 R10
Mybster Highld 112 E6
Myddfai Carmth 26 E2
Myddle Shrops 45 L9
Mydroilyn Cerdgn 32 J9
Myerscough Lancs 61 T12
Mylor Cnwll 3 L9
Mylor Bridge Cnwll 3 L9
Mynachlog ddu Pembks 24 K4
Mynydd-bach Mons 27 U9
Mynydd-bach Swans 25 V11
Mynydd Buch Cerdgn 33 N6
Mynydd-Garreg Carmth 25 R8
Mynydd Isa Flints 54 F14
Mynydd Llandygai Gwynd 52 K9
Mynydd Mechell IoA 52 E4
Mynyddygarreg Carmth 25 R8
Mynytho Gwynd 42 F7
Myrebird Abers 99 N4
Myredykes Border 76 C5
Mytchett Surrey 20 F11
Mytham Bridge Derbys 56 K10
Mythop Lancs 61 R13
Mytholm Calder 56 F1
Mytholmroyd Calder 56 F1
Myton-on-Swale N York 63 U6

N

Naast Highld 107 P8
Nab's Head Lancs 62 C14
Na Buirgh W Isls 106 f9
Naburn C York 64 D10
Naccolt Kent 13 L7
Nackington Kent 13 N5
Nacton Suffk 41 M12
Nafferton E R Yk 65 N8
Nag's Head Gloucs 28 G8
Nailbridge Gloucs 28 C4
Nailsbourne Somset 16 H11
Nailsea N Som 17 N3
Nailstone Leics 47 M13
Nailsworth Gloucs 28 G8
Nairn Highld 103 N4

Nalderswood Surrey...21 M13
Nancegollan Cnwll...2 G10
Nancledra Cnwll...2 D9
Nanhoron Gwynd...42 E7
Nannerch Flints...54 E13
Nanpantan Leics...47 P10
Nanpean Cnwll...3 P5
Nanquidno Cnwll...2 B9
Nanstallon Cnwll...3 Q3
Nant-ddu Cnwll...26 J5
Nanternis Cerdgn...35 G9
Nantgaredig Carmth...25 S6
Nantgarw Rhondd...27 N8
Nant-glas Powys...33 U7
Nantglyn Denbgs...53 T10
Nantgwyn Powys...33 U5
Nant Gwynant Gwynd...43 M3
Nantlle Gwynd...52 H12
Nantlle Valley Slate Landscape Gwynd...52 H12
Nantmawr Shrops...44 G9
Nantmel Powys...34 B7
Nantmor Gwynd...43 M4
Nant Peris Gwynd...52 K11
Nantwich Ches E...45 Q3
Nant-y-Bwch Blae G...27 L5
Nantycaws Carmth...25 S7
Nant-y-derry Mons...27 Q6
Nant-y-ffin Carmth...25 U5
Nantyffyllon Brdgnd...26 F9
Nantyglo Blae G...27 M5
Nant-y-gollen Shrops...44 G8
Nant-y-moel Brdgnd...26 G9
Nant-y-pandy Conwy...53 L8
Naphill Bucks...20 D3
Napleton Worcs...35 U11
Nappa N York...62 H9
Napton on the Hill Warwks...37 N8
Narberth Pembks...24 K7
Narborough Leics...47 P1
Narborough Norfk...50 B11
Narkurs Cnwll...4 J9
Nasareth Gwynd...42 J4
Naseby Nhants...37 S5
Nash Bucks...30 G6
Nash Gt Lon...21 R10
Nash Herefs...34 H8
Nash Newpt...27 Q11
Nash Shrops...35 P6
Nash End Worcs...35 S5
Nashes Green Hants...19 U11
Nash Lee Bucks...30 H11
Nash Street Kent...12 C8
Nassington Nhants...38 G1
Nastend Gloucs...28 E6
Nasty Herts...31 U8
Nateby Cumb...68 G11
Nateby Lancs...61 T11
National Memorial Arboretum Staffs...46 F10
National Motor Museum (Beaulieu) Hants...9 M8
National Space Centre C Leic...47 Q12
Natland Cumb...61 U2
Naughton Suffk...40 H11
Naunton Gloucs...29 M3
Naunton Worcs...35 U13
Naunton Beauchamp Worcs...36 C10
Navenby Lincs...48 E2
Navestock Essex...22 D8
Navestock Side Essex...22 E8
Navidale Highld...112 B13
Navity Highld...103 L3
Nawton N York...64 F3
Nayland Suffk...40 G14
Nazeing Essex...22 B6
Nazeing Gate Essex...22 B6
Neacroft Hants...8 H9
Neal's Green Warwks...36 K4
Neap Shet...106 v8
Near Cotton Staffs...46 E4
Near Sawrey Cumb...67 N13
Neasden Gt Lon...21 M5
Neasham Darltn...70 D10
Neath Neath...26 D8
Neatham Hants...10 A2
Neatishead Norfk...51 P9
Nebo Cerdgn...32 K6
Nebo Conwy...53 P11
Nebo Gwynd...42 J3
Nebo IoA...52 G4
Necton Norfk...50 D12
Nedd Highld...110 C10
Nedderton Nthumb...77 Q9
Nedging Suffk...40 G11
Nedging Tye Suffk...40 H11
Needham Norfk...41 M4
Needham Market Suffk...40 J9
Needham Street Suffk...39 U7
Needingworth Cambs...39 N6
Neen Savage Shrops...35 Q5
Neen Sollars Shrops...35 Q6
Neenton Shrops...35 P3
Nefyn Gwynd...42 F5
Neilston E Rens...81 P1
Nelson Caerph...27 L8
Nelson Lancs...62 H12
Nemphlar S Lans...82 G10
Nempnett Thrubwell BaNES...17 P4
Nenthall Cumb...68 G3
Nenthead Cumb...68 G4
Nenthorn Border...84 H11
Neopardy Devon...15 T2
Nep Town W Susx...11 L7
Nerabus Ag & B...78 C4
Nercwys Flints...54 F1
Nerston S Lans...81 S1
Nesbit Nthumb...85 P12
Nesfield N York...63 M10
Ness Ches W...54 H11
Nesscliffe Shrops...44 J10
Neston Ches W...54 G11
Neston Wilts...18 C7
Netchwood Shrops...35 P2
Nether Abington S Lans...82 H14
Nether Alderley Ches E...55 T11
Netheravon Wilts...18 H11
Nether Blainslie Border...84 E10
Netherbrae Abers...105 M4
Nether Broughton Leics...47 S8
Netherburn S Lans...82 F9
Netherbury Dorset...7 N5
Netherby Cumb...75 S11
Nether Cerne Dorset...7 S5
Nethercleuch D & G...75 M8
Nether Compton Dorset...17 R13
Nethercote Warwks...37 P8
Nethercott Devon...15 L5
Nethercott Oxon...29 U4
Nether Crimond Abers...105 N11
Nether Dallachy Moray...104 D2
Netherend Gloucs...28 A7
Nether Exe Devon...6 B4
Netherfield E Susx...12 D12
Netherfield Leics...47 Q10
Netherfield Notts...47 R5
Nether Fingland S Lans...74 H3
Nethergate N Linc...58 E5
Nethergate Norfk...50 H8
Netherhampton Wilts...8 G3
Nether Handley Derbys...57 P11
Nether Haugh Rothm...57 P7
Netherhay Dorset...7 M3
Nether Headon Notts...58 B11
Nether Heyford Nhants...37 S9
Nether Kellet Lancs...61 U6
Nether Kinmundy Abers...105 T6
Netherland Green Staffs...46 F7
Nether Langwith Notts...57 R12
Netherlaw D & G...73 S11
Netherley Abers...99 R5
Nethermill D & G...75 K9
Nethermuir Abers...105 P7
Netherne-on-the-Hill Surrey...21 N11
Netheroyd Hill Kirk...56 H3
Nether Padley Derbys...56 K11
Nether Poppleton C York...64 D9
Netherseal Derbys...46 J11
Nether Silton N York...64 B1
Nether Skyborry Shrops...34 G5
Nether Stowey Somset...16 G9
Netherstreet Wilts...18 E7
Netherthird E Ayrs...81 R9
Netherthong Kirk...56 H5
Netherthorpe Derbys...57 Q11
Netherton Angus...98 A10
Netherton Devon...5 V6
Netherton Dudley...36 B3
Netherton Hants...19 M9
Netherton Herefs...27 V3
Netherton Kirk...56 H4
Netherton N Lans...82 E6
Netherton Nthumb...76 K6
Netherton Oxon...29 U8
Netherton P & K...97 U13
Netherton Sefton...54 J7
Netherton Shrops...35 S4
Netherton Stirlg...89 N10
Netherton Wakefd...57 L3
Netherton Worcs...36 C12
Nethertown Cumb...66 E11
Nethertown Highld...112 J1
Nethertown Lancs...62 E12
Nethertown Staffs...46 F10
Netherurd Border...83 M10
Nether Wallop Hants...19 M13
Nether Wasdale Cumb...66 H12
Nether Welton Cumb...67 N3
Nether Westcote Gloucs...29 P3
Nether Whitacre Warwks...36 H2
Nether Whitecleuch S Lans...74 F2
Nether Winchendon Bucks...30 F10
Netherwitton Nthumb...77 M7
Nethy Bridge Highld...103 R11
Netley Hants...9 P7
Netley Marsh Hants...9 L6
Nettacott Devon...6 B5
Nettlebed Oxon...19 U3
Nettlebridge Somset...17 R7
Nettlecombe Dorset...7 P6
Nettlecombe IoW...9 Q13
Nettleden Herts...31 N10
Nettleham Lincs...58 H11
Nettlestead Kent...12 C5
Nettlestead Green Kent...12 C5
Nettlestone IoW...9 S10
Nettlesworth Dur...69 S3
Nettleton Lincs...58 K6
Nettleton Wilts...18 B5
Nettleton Shrub Wilts...18 B5
Netton Devon...5 P11
Netton Wilts...18 H13
Neuadd Carmth...26 C3
Neuadd-ddu Powys...33 T5
Nevendon Essex...22 J9
Nevern Pembks...24 K2
Nevill Holt Leics...38 B2
New Abbey D & G...74 J12
New Aberdour Abers...105 P3
New Addington Gt Lon...21 Q10
Newall Leeds...63 P10
New Alresford Hants...9 R2
New Alyth P & K...90 K2
Newark C Pete...48 K14
Newark Ork...106 w15
Newark-on-Trent Notts...47 U2
New Arley Warwks...36 J3
New Arram E R Yk...65 N11
Newarthill N Lans...82 E7
New Ash Green Kent...12 C8
New Balderton Notts...48 B3
New Barn Kent...12 B2
Newbarn Kent...13 M7
New Barnet Gt Lon...21 N3
New Barnetby N Linc...58 J4
New Barton Nhants...38 C8
Newbattle Mdloth...83 R5
New Bewick Nthumb...77 M1
Newbiggin Cumb...61 Q3
Newbiggin Cumb...66 G14
Newbiggin Cumb...67 Q7
Newbiggin Cumb...67 S3
Newbiggin Cumb...68 D7
Newbiggin Dur...69 P3
Newbiggin Dur...69 N1
Newbiggin N York...62 K1
Newbiggin N York...63 L2
Newbiggin-by-the-Sea Nthumb...77 S8
Newbigging Angus...91 L3
Newbigging Angus...91 P4
Newbigging Angus...91 N4
Newbigging S Lans...82 K9
Newbigging-on-Lune Cumb...62 F1
New Bilton Warwks...37 N5
Newbold Derbys...57 N12
Newbold Leics...47 M10
Newbold on Avon Warwks...37 N5
Newbold on Stour Warwks...36 H11
Newbold Pacey Warwks...36 J9
Newbold Revel Warwks...37 M4
Newbold Verdon Leics...47 M13
Newborough C Pete...48 K12
Newborough IoA...52 F8
Newborough Staffs...46 F8
Newbottle Nhants...30 B5
Newbottle Sundld...70 D2
Newbourne Suffk...41 N12
New Bradwell M Keyn...30 H4
New Brampton Derbys...57 N12
New Brancepeth Dur...69 R4
Newbridge C Edin...83 M4
Newbridge Caerph...27 N8
Newbridge Cerdgn...32 K9
Newbridge Cnwll...2 C10
Newbridge Cnwll...4 K8
Newbridge D & G...74 J10
Newbridge Hants...8 K5
Newbridge IoW...9 N11
New Bridge N York...64 J2
Newbridge Oxon...29 T7
Newbridge Wrexhm...44 G5
Newbridge Green Worcs...35 T13
Newbridge-on-Usk Mons...27 R9
Newbridge-on-Wye Powys...34 B9
New Brighton Flints...54 G13
New Brighton Hants...9 S8
New Brighton Wirral...54 H8
New Brinsley Notts...47 N3
Newbrough Nthumb...76 H12
New Broughton Wrexhm...44 H3
New Buckenham Norfk...40 J2
Newbuildings Devon...15 S12
Newburgh Abers...105 R10
Newburgh Abers...105 N7
Newburgh Fife...90 K8
Newburgh Lancs...55 L4
Newburn N u Ty...77 P12
Newbury Somset...17 S7
Newbury W Berk...19 Q7
Newbury Park Gt Lon...21 R5
Newby Cumb...67 R7
Newby Lancs...62 G10
Newby N York...62 E6
Newby N York...62 H5
Newby N York...70 H10
Newby Bridge Cumb...61 R2
Newby Cross Cumb...67 N2
Newby East Cumb...75 U14
Newby Head Cumb...67 R7
New Byth Abers...105 N5
Newby West Cumb...67 N2
Newby Wiske N York...63 S2
Newcastle Mons...27 S4
Newcastle Shrops...34 G4
Newcastle Airport Nthumb...77 P11
Newcastle Emlyn Carmth...32 F12
Newcastleton Border...75 U8
Newcastle-under-Lyme Staffs...45 T4
Newcastle upon Tyne N u Ty...77 Q13
Newchapel Pembks...25 M3
Newchapel Staffs...45 U2
Newchapel Surrey...11 P2
Newchapel Surrey...21 Q13
Newchurch Blae G...27 N8
Newchurch Carmth...25 P5
Newchurch Herefs...34 G10
Newchurch IoW...9 R11
Newchurch Kent...13 L9
Newchurch Lancs...62 G13
Newchurch Lancs...62 D14
Newchurch Mons...27 U8
Newchurch Powys...34 F10
Newchurch Staffs...46 F9
Newchurch in Pendle Lancs...62 G12
New Costessey Norfk...51 L11
New Cowper Cumb...66 H3
Newcraighall C Edin...83 R4
New Crofton Wakefd...57 N3
New Cross Cerdgn...33 M5
New Cross Gt Lon...21 Q7
New Cross Somset...17 M13
New Cumnock E Ayrs...81 S10
New Deer Abers...105 N6
New Delaval Nthumb...77 S10
New Denham Bucks...20 H5
Newdigate Surrey...11 K2
New Duston Nhants...37 T8
New Earswick C York...64 E8
New Eastwood Notts...47 N4
New Edlington Donc...57 R7
New Elgin Moray...104 A3
New Ellerby E R Yk...65 R12
Newell Green Br For...20 E8
New Eltham Gt Lon...21 R8
New End Worcs...36 E8
Newenden Kent...12 F10
New England C Pete...48 J13
New England Essex...40 B12
Newent Gloucs...28 D2
New Farnley Leeds...63 R13
New Ferry Wirral...54 H9
Newfield Dur...69 Q5
Newfield Dur...69 R2
Newfield Highld...109 N9
New Fletton C Pete...48 J14
New Forest National Park...8 K7
Newfound Hants...19 S9
New Fryston Wakefd...57 P2
Newgale Pembks...24 E6
New Galloway D & G...73 Q4
New Gilston Fife...91 P10
New Grimsby IoS...2 b1
Newhall Ches E...45 P4
Newhall Derbys...46 J9
Newham Nthumb...85 T13
New Hartley Nthumb...77 S10
Newhaven C Edin...83 Q3
Newhaven E Susx...11 Q10
Newhaven Derbys...46 G1
New Hedges Pembks...24 K10
New Herrington Sundld...70 D2
Newhey Rochdl...56 D4
New Holkham Norfk...50 E6
New Holland N Linc...58 J2
Newholm N York...71 Q10
New Houghton Derbys...57 Q13
New Houghton Norfk...50 C8
Newhouse N Lans...82 E6
New Houses N York...62 G5
New Hutton Cumb...61 U1
New Hythe Kent...12 D4
Newick E Susx...11 Q6
Newingreen Kent...13 M8
Newington Kent...13 M8
Newington Kent...12 G2
Newington Oxon...30 D13
Newington Shrops...34 K4
Newington Bagpath Gloucs...28 F9
New Inn Carmth...25 S3
New Inn Cerdgn...32 J10
New Inn Mons...27 Q8
New Inn Torfn...27 Q8
New Invention Shrops...34 G5
Newland C KuH...65 M13
Newland Cumb...61 Q4
Newland E R Yk...64 H13
Newland Gloucs...27 V6
Newland N York...57 U1
Newland Oxon...29 S6
Newland Somset...15 T5
Newland Worcs...35 S11
Newlandrig Mdloth...83 S6
Newlands Border...75 V7
Newlands Cumb...67 M5
Newlands Nthumb...69 N1
Newlands of Dundurcas Moray...104 B6
New Lane Lancs...54 K4
New Lane End Warrtn...55 P8
New Langholm D & G...75 S9
New Leake Lincs...49 P2
New Leeds Abers...105 R5
New Lodge Barns...57 N5
New Longton Lancs...55 L1
New Luce D & G...72 F7
Newlyn Cnwll...2 D11
Newmachar Abers...105 P12
New Malden Gt Lon...21 M9
Newman's End Essex...22 D5
Newman's Green Suffk...40 E12
New Marske R & Cl...70 K8
New Marston Oxon...30 B11
New Marton Shrops...44 H7
New Mill Abers...99 M7
New Mill Cnwll...2 D10
New Mill Herts...30 K10
Newmill Moray...104 E5
New Mill Wilts...18 H8
New Mills Cnwll...3 M6
New Mills Derbys...56 F9
Newmills Fife...90 E15
New Mills Mons...27 U6
Newmills Mons...27 U6
New Mills Powys...44 C13
New Mistley Essex...23 R1
New Moat Pembks...24 H5
Newney Green Essex...22 G6
Newnham Gloucs...28 C5
Newnham Hants...20 B12
Newnham Herts...31 R5
Newnham Kent...12 H4
Newnham Nhants...37 Q9
Newnham Worcs...35 P7
Newnham Bridge Worcs...35 P7
Newnham on Severn Gloucs...28 C5
New Ollerton Notts...57 U13
New Oscott Birm...36 E2
New Pitsligo Abers...105 N4
Newport Cnwll...4 J3
Newport Dorset...8 B9
Newport E R Yk...64 J13
Newport Essex...39 R14
Newport Gloucs...28 D8
Newport Highld...112 C12
Newport IoW...9 P11
Newport Newpt...27 Q10
Newport Pembks...24 J3
Newport Wrekin...45 R10
Newport-on-Tay Fife...91 P6
Newport Pagnell M Keyn...30 J4
Newport Pagnell Services M Keyn...30 J4
Newpound Common W Susx...10 H5
New Prestwick S Ayrs...81 L8
New Quay Cerdgn...32 G9
New Quay Essex...23 P3
Newquay Cnwll...3 L4
Newquay Zoo Cnwll...3 L4
New Rackheath Norfk...51 N11
New Radnor Powys...34 F8
New Rent Cumb...67 Q5
New Ridley Nthumb...77 M14
New Road Side N York...62 K11
New Romney Kent...13 L11
New Rossington Donc...57 T7
New Row Cerdgn...33 Q6
New Row Lancs...62 C12
New Sauchie Clacks...90 C13
Newsbank Ches E...55 T13
Newseat Abers...105 L9
Newsham Lancs...61 U12
Newsham N York...63 R1
Newsham N York...69 P10
Newsham Nthumb...77 S10
New Sharlston Wakefd...57 N3
Newsholme E R Yk...64 H14
Newsholme Lancs...62 G9
New Shoreston Nthumb...85 T12
New Silksworth Sundld...70 D2
New Skelton R & Cl...71 L9
Newsome Kirk...56 H4
New Somerby Lincs...48 D6
New Springs Wigan...55 N5
Newstead Border...84 F12
Newstead Notts...47 P3
Newstead Nthumb...85 T13
New Stevenston N Lans...82 E6
New Street Herefs...34 H9
New Swannington Leics...47 M11
Newthorpe N York...57 P1
Newthorpe Notts...47 N4
Newtimber W Susx...11 M8
Newton Ag & B...88 E7
Newton Border...84 G13
Newton Brdgnd...26 E11
Newton C Beds...31 R4
Newton Cambs...39 P11
Newton Cambs...49 P11
Newton Cardif...27 N12
Newton Ches W...54 K13
Newton Ches W...55 M11
Newton Ches W...55 N12
Newton Cumb...61 P5
Newton Derbys...47 M2
Newton Herefs...34 H14
Newton Herefs...35 M11
Newton Highld...102 J6
Newton Highld...102 K5
Newton Highld...112 H9
Newton Lancs...55 M3
Newton Lancs...61 T11
Newton Lancs...62 C8
Newton Lincs...48 F6
Newton Mons...27 U2
Newton Moray...104 B3
Newton N York...57 U1
Newton Nhants...38 C4
Newton Norfk...50 D10
Newton Notts...47 S5
Newton Nthumb...76 K13
Newton Nthumb...77 L13
Newton S Lans...82 D1
Newton S Lans...89 Q13
Newton Sandw...36 D3
Newton Shrops...44 K7
Newton Shrops...45 M7
Newton Staffs...46 D8
Newton Suffk...40 F12
Newton W Loth...83 L3
Newton Warwks...37 P5
Newton Wilts...8 J4
Newton Abbot Devon...5 V5
Newton Arlosh Cumb...66 K1
Newton Aycliffe Dur...69 S8
Newton Bewley Hartlpl...70 G7
Newton Blossomville M Keyn...38 D10
Newton Bromswold Nhants...38 E7
Newton Burgoland Leics...47 L12
Newton by Toft Lincs...58 H9
Newton Ferrers Devon...5 P11
Newton Ferry W Isls...106 d11
Newton Flotman Norfk...41 M14
Newton Green Mons...27 U9
Newton Harcourt Leics...37 R1
Newton Heath Manch...56 C6
Newtonhill Abers...99 S5
Newton Hill Wakefd...57 M2
Newton-in-Bowland Lancs...62 D9
Newton Kyme N York...63 U11
Newton-le-Willows N York...63 Q2
Newton-le-Willows St Hel...55 N7
Newtonloan Mdloth...83 R6
Newton Longville Bucks...30 H6
Newton Mearns E Rens...81 Q2
Newtonmill Angus...99 L11
Newtonmore Highld...97 L4
Newton Morrell N York...69 S11
Newton Mountain Pembks...24 G9
Newton Mulgrave N York...71 N9
Newton of Balcanquhal P & K...90 H9
Newton of Balcormo Fife...91 R11
Newton of Belltrees Rens...88 J14
Newton-on-Ayr S Ayrs...81 L8
Newton-on-Ouse N York...64 C8
Newton-on-Rawcliffe N York...64 J1
Newton on the Hill Shrops...44 K9
Newton-on-the-Moor Nthumb...77 P4
Newton on Trent Lincs...58 C13
Newton Poppleford Devon...6 E7
Newton Purcell Oxon...30 D6
Newton Regis Warwks...46 J12
Newton Reigny Cumb...67 Q6
Newton St Cyres Devon...15 U3
Newton St Faith Norfk...51 M10
Newton St Loe BaNES...17 T4
Newton St Petrock Devon...14 K10
Newton Solney Derbys...46 J8
Newton Stacey Hants...19 P12
Newton Stewart D & G...73 L6
Newton Toney Wilts...18 K12
Newton Tracey Devon...15 M7
Newton under Roseberry R & Cl...70 J10
Newton Underwood Nthumb...77 N8
Newton upon Derwent E R Yk...64 G9
Newton Valence Hants...10 U2
Newton Wamphray D & G...75 N7
Newton with Scales Lancs...61 T13
Newtown BCP...8 C10
Newtown Ches W...55 M11
Newtown Ches W...55 L12
Newtown Cnwll...2 F11
Newtown Cnwll...4 H5
Newtown Cumb...66 H5
Newtown Cumb...67 Q1
Newtown Cumb...75 T13
Newtown D & G...74 F9
Newtown Derbys...56 E10
Newtown Devon...6 E5
Newtown Devon...15 S7
Newtown Dorset...7 N4
Newtown Dorset...7 P4
Newtown Dorset...8 D5
Newtown Gloucs...28 B8
Newtown Hants...9 R8
Newtown Hants...9 Q6
Newtown Hants...9 L4
Newtown Hants...19 R6
Newtown Hants...19 P9
Newtown Herefs...35 M10
Newtown Herefs...35 N13
Newtown Highld...96 F5
Newtown IoM...60 e7
Newtown IoW...9 N10
Newtown Nthumb...77 L5
Newtown Nthumb...85 M12
Newtown Poole...8 D10
Newtown Powys...34 D2
Newtown Rhondd...26 J6
Newtown Shrops...44 K8
Newtown Shrops...45 M6
Newtown Somset...6 H2
Newtown Staffs...45 U13
Newtown Staffs...46 C13
Newtown Wigan...55 M5
Newtown Wilts...8 C3
Newtown Wilts...18 C11
Newtown Worcs...35 U10
Newtown-in-St Martin Cnwll...2 J12
Newtown Linford Leics...47 P12
Newtown St Boswells Border...84 F12
Newtown Unthank Leics...47 N13
Newton Tredegar Caerph...27 L7
New Trows S Lans...82 F12
New Tupton Derbys...57 N13
Newtyle Angus...91 L3
New Walsoken Cambs...49 Q12
New Waltham NE Lin...59 N6
New Whittington Derbys...57 N11
New Winton E Loth...84 C4
New Yatt Oxon...29 S5
Newyears Green Gt Lon...20 J5
Newyork Ag & B...87 T3
New York Lincs...48 K2
New York N Tyne...77 S11
New York N York...63 P7
New Zealand Wilts...18 E6
Nextend Herefs...34 H9
Neyland Pembks...24 G9
Niarbyl IoM...60 c7
Nibley Gloucs...28 C6
Nibley S Glos...28 C11
Nibley Green Gloucs...28 D8
Nicholashayne Devon...6 F2
Nicholaston Swans...25 T13
Nickies Hill Cumb...76 A12
Nidd N York...63 S7
Nigg C Aber...99 S3
Nigg Highld...109 Q9
Nigg Ferry Highld...109 P10
Nimlet BaNES...17 T2
Ninebanks Nthumb...68 G2
Nine Elms Swindn...29 M10
Nine Wells Pembks...24 C5
Ninfield E Susx...12 D13
Ningwood IoW...9 M11
Nisbet Border...84 H13
Nisbet Hill Border...84 K8
Niton IoW...9 Q13
Nitshill C Glas...89 N13
Noah's Ark Kent...21 U11
Noak Bridge Essex...22 G9
Noak Hill Gt Lon...22 D9
Noblethorpe Barns...57 L5
Nobold Shrops...44 K11
Nobottle Nhants...37 S8
Nocton Lincs...58 H14
Nogdam End Norfk...51 Q13
Noke Oxon...30 B10
Nolton Pembks...24 E6
Nolton Haven Pembks...24 E6
No Man's Heath Ches W...45 L4
No Man's Heath Warwks...46 J12
No Man's Land Cnwll...4 H9
Nomansland Devon...15 U10
Nomansland Wilts...8 K4
Noneley Shrops...44 K8
Nonington Kent...13 P5
Nook Cumb...61 U3
Nook Cumb...75 U11
Norbiton Gt Lon...21 L9
Norbreck Bpool...61 Q11
Norbridge Herefs...35 R12
Norbury Ches E...45 M4
Norbury Derbys...46 G5
Norbury Gt Lon...21 N9
Norbury Shrops...34 J2
Norbury Staffs...45 S9
Norbury Common Ches E...45 M4
Norbury Junction Staffs...45 S9
Norchard Worcs...35 T7
Norcott Brook Ches W...55 P10
Norcross Lancs...61 Q11
Nordelph Norfk...49 R13
Norden Rochdl...56 C4
Nordley Shrops...35 Q1
Norfolk Broads Norfk...51 S12
Norham Nthumb...85 N10
Norland Town Calder...56 G2
Norley Ches W...55 M12
Norleywood Hants...9 M9
Normanby Lincs...58 F9
Normanby N Linc...58 E3
Normanby N York...64 F3
Normanby R & Cl...70 J9
Normanby le Wold Lincs...58 K7
Norman Cross Cambs...38 J2
Normandy Surrey...20 F12
Norman's Bay E Susx...12 C14
Norman's Green Devon...6 E4
Normanton C Derb...46 K6
Normanton Leics...48 B5
Normanton Notts...47 U3
Normanton Rutlnd...48 C13
Normanton Wakefd...57 M2
Normanton Wilts...18 H12
Normanton le Heath Leics...47 L11
Normanton on Cliffe Lincs...48 D4
Normanton on Soar Notts...47 P9
Normanton on the Wolds Notts...47 R7
Normanton on Trent Notts...58 C13
Normoss Lancs...61 Q12
Norney Surrey...10 F2
Norrington Common Wilts...18 C8
Norris Green Cnwll...5 L7
Norris Green Lpool...54 J8
Norris Hill Leics...46 K10
Norristhorpe Kirk...56 K2
Northacre Norfk...50 G13
Northall Bucks...30 K8
Northallerton N York...70 E14
Northall Green Norfk...50 G11
Northam C Sotn...9 N6
Northam Devon...14 K7
Northampton Nhants...37 T8
Northampton Worcs...35 T7
Northampton Services Nhants...37 T9
North Anston Rothm...57 R10
North Ascot Br For...20 F9
North Aston Oxon...29 U2
Northaw Herts...31 S12
Northay Somset...6 J3
North Baddesley Hants...9 M4
North Ballachulish Highld...94 H6
North Barrow Somset...17 R10
North Barsham Norfk...50 F6
Northbay W Isls...106 c18
North Benfleet Essex...22 J10
North Berwick E Loth...84 F2
North Bersted W Susx...10 E10
North Bitchburn Dur...69 Q6
North Blyth Nthumb...77 S9
North Boarhunt Hants...9 S6
North Bockhampton BCP...8 H9
Northborough C Pete...48 J12
North Bovey Devon...5 S4
North Bradley Wilts...18 C9
North Brentor Devon...5 M4
North Brewham Somset...17 T9
Northbrook Hants...19 R13
North Brook End Cambs...31 N4
North Buckland Devon...14 K4
North Burlingham Norfk...51 Q12
North Cadbury Somset...17 R11
North Carlton Lincs...58 F12
North Carlton Notts...57 S10
North Cave E R Yk...64 K13
North Cerney Gloucs...28 K6
North Chailey E Susx...11 P6
Northchapel W Susx...10 F4
North Charford Hants...8 H5
North Charlton Nthumb...85 T14
North Cheam Gt Lon...21 M9
North Cheriton Somset...17 S11
North Chideock Dorset...7 M6
Northchurch Herts...31 L11
North Cliffe E R Yk...64 K12
North Clifton Notts...58 D12
North Cockerington Lincs...59 Q8
North Connel Ag & B...94 C11
North Cornelly Brdgnd...26 E11
North Corner Cnwll...2 K13
North Cotes Lincs...59 P6
Northcott Devon...4 H2
Northcott Devon...6 F3
North Country Cnwll...2 H7
Northcourt Oxon...29 U8
North Cove Suffk...41 S3
North Cowton N York...69 S11
North Crawley M Keyn...30 K4
North Cray Gt Lon...21 S8
North Creake Norfk...50 E6
North Curry Somset...16 K11
North Dalton E R Yk...65 L9
North Deighton N York...63 T9
Northdown Kent...13 S1
North Downs...10 H1
North Duffield N York...64 F12
Northedge Derbys...57 M13
North Elkington Lincs...59 N8
North Elmham Norfk...50 G9
North Elmsall Wakefd...57 Q4
Northend BaNES...17 T4
North End C Port...9 S7
North End Cumb...75 R14
North End Dorset...17 V12
North End E R Yk...65 R12
North End Essex...22 F4
North End Essex...22 G1
North End Hants...9 T9
North End Hants...19 Q5
North End Leics...47 Q11
North End Lincs...48 K4
North End Lincs...59 N6
North End N Linc...58 K1
North End N Som...17 M4
North End Nhants...38 D7
North End Norfk...40 H2
North End Nthumb...77 S4
North End Sefton...54 H5
North End W Susx...10 H9
North End W Susx...10 K10
Northend Warwks...37 L10
North Erradale Highld...107 M8
North Evington C Leic...47 R13
North Fambridge Essex...23 L8
North Featherstone Wakefd...57 P2
North Ferriby E R Yk...58 F1
Northfield Birm...36 D5
Northfield C Aber...99 R2
Northfield E R Yk...65 N14
Northfields Lincs...48 F12
Northfleet Kent...22 F13
North Frodingham E R Yk...65 Q9
Northgate Lincs...48 K9
North Gorley Hants...8 G6
North Green Suffk...41 M6
North Green Suffk...41 N7
North Green Suffk...41 P8
North Greetwell Lincs...58 H12
North Grimston N York...64 K6
North Halling Medway...12 D2
North Hayling Hants...9 U8
North Hazelrigg Nthumb...85 R12
North Heasley Devon...15 R6
North Heath W Susx...10 H6
North Hele Devon...16 C13
North Hill Cnwll...4 H5
North Hillingdon Gt Lon...20 K6
North Hinksey Village Oxon...29 U6
North Holmwood Surrey...10 K2
North Huish Devon...5 S9
North Hush Cnwll...4 H2
Northiam E Susx...12 F11
Northill C Beds...38 H11
Northington Gloucs...28 D5
Northington Hants...19 S13
North Kelsey Lincs...58 H6
North Kelsey Moor Lincs...58 J6
North Kessock Highld...102 J6
North Killingholme Lincs...58 K3
North Kilvington N York...63 U2
North Kilworth Leics...37 R4
North Kingston Hants...8 H8
North Kyme Lincs...48 J3
North Lancing W Susx...10 K9
Northlands Lincs...49 L2
Northleach Gloucs...29 M5
North Lee Bucks...30 H11
North Lees N York...63 S5
Northleigh Devon...6 G5
Northleigh Devon...15 Q6
North Leigh Kent...13 N6
North Leigh Oxon...29 S5
North Leverton with Habblesthorpe Notts...58 C10
North Littleton Worcs...36 E11
North Lopham Norfk...40 H4
North Luffenham Rutlnd...48 D13
North Marden W Susx...10 C7
North Marston Bucks...30 F8
North Middleton Mdloth...83 S7
North Middleton Nthumb...85 P14
North Millbrex Abers...105 M6
North Milmain D & G...72 D9
North Molton Devon...15 R7
North Moreton Oxon...19 T3
Northmoor Oxon...29 T7
Northmoor Green or Moorland Somset...16 K9
North Mundham W Susx...10 D10
North Muskham Notts...47 U2
North Newbald E R Yk...65 L13
North Newington Oxon...37 M13
North Newnton Wilts...18 H9
North Newton Somset...16 J10
Northney Hants...9 U8
North Nibley Gloucs...28 D8
Northolt Gt Lon...20 K6
Northop Flints...54 F13
Northop Hall Flints...54 F13
North Ormesby Middsb...70 H9
North Ormsby Lincs...59 N8
Northorpe Lincs...48 G8
Northorpe Lincs...48 K9
Northorpe Lincs...58 E7
Northorpe Kirk...56 K3
North Otterington N York...63 T2
North Owersby Lincs...58 H8
Northowram Calder...56 G1
North Perrott Somset...7 N3
North Petherton Somset...16 J10
North Petherwin Cnwll...4 H4
North Pickenham Norfk...50 E12
North Piddle Worcs...36 C10
North Poorton Dorset...7 P5
Northport Dorset...8 B10
North Poulner Hants...8 H8
North Queensferry Fife...83 M2
North Radworthy Devon...15 R6
North Rauceby Lincs...48 F4
Northrepps Norfk...51 M6
North Reston Lincs...59 Q10
North Rigton N York...63 R10
North Rode Ches E...56 C13
North Roe Shet...106 t5
North Row Cumb...66 K6
North Runcton Norfk...49 T10
North Scale Cumb...61 N6
North Scarle Lincs...58 D13
North Seaton Nthumb...77 R8
North Seaton Colliery Nthumb...77 R8
North Shian Ag & B...94 C10
North Shields N Tyne...77 T12
North Shoebury Sthend...23 M10
North Shore Bpool...61 Q12
North Side C Pete...49 L14
North Skelton R & Cl...71 L9
North Somercotes Lincs...59 R7
North Stainley N York...63 R4
North Stainmore Cumb...68 H10
North Stifford Thurr...22 F12
North Stoke BaNES...17 T4
North Stoke Oxon...19 U4
North Stoke W Susx...10 G8
Northstowe Cambs...39 N7
North Street Cambs...39 S7
North Street Hants...9 T9
North Street Kent...12 K4
North Street Medway...12 K2
North Street W Berk...19 U6
North Sunderland Nthumb...85 U12
North Tamerton Cnwll...14 H13
North Tawton Devon...15 Q12
North Thoresby Lincs...59 N7
North Third Stirlg...89 S7
North Togston Nthumb...77 Q5
North Tolsta W Isls...106 j5
North Town Devon...15 M11
North Town Somset...17 Q8
North Town W & M...20 E6
North Tuddenham Norfk...50 H11
North Uist W Isls...106 c11
Northumberland National Park...76 F9
North Walbottle N u Ty...77 P12
North Walsham Norfk...51 N7
North Waltham Hants...19 S11
North Warnborough Hants...20 B12
North Weald Bassett Essex...22 C6
North Wheatley Notts...58 C10
North Whilborough Devon...5 V7
North Wick BaNES...17 Q4
Northwick S Glos...27 U10
Northwick Somset...16 K7
Northwick Worcs...35 T9
North Widcombe BaNES...17 Q5
North Willingham Lincs...58 K9
North Wingfield Derbys...57 P13
North Witham Lincs...48 E9
Northwold Norfk...50 B14
Northwood Derbys...56 K14
Northwood Gt Lon...20 J4
Northwood IoW...9 P10
Northwood Shrops...44 K7
Northwood Green Gloucs...28 D5
North Wootton Dorset...17 S13
North Wootton Norfk...49 T9
North Wootton Somset...17 Q8
North Wraxall Wilts...18 B5
North Wroughton Swindn...18 H4
North York Moors National Park...71 M12
Norton Donc...57 S3
Norton E Susx...11 R10
Norton Gloucs...28 G3
Norton Halton...55 M10
Norton Herts...31 R5
Norton IoW...9 L11
Norton Mons...27 T3
Norton N Som...17 L5
Norton Nhants...37 R8
Norton Notts...57 R12
Norton Powys...34 H7
Norton S on T...70 F8
Norton Sheff...57 N10
Norton Shrops...34 K3
Norton Shrops...35 P1
Norton Shrops...45 M12
Norton Suffk...40 F7
Norton Swans...25 U13
Norton W Susx...10 D10
Norton W Susx...10 E11
Norton Wilts...18 C4
Norton Worcs...35 U10
Norton Worcs...36 E11
Norton Bavant Wilts...18 D12
Norton Bridge Staffs...45 U7
Norton Canes Staffs...46 D12
Norton Canon Herefs...34 J11
Norton Disney Lincs...48 C2
Norton Ferris Wilts...17 U9
Norton Fitzwarren Somset...16 G11
Norton Green IoW...9 L11
Norton Green St Hel...55 M7
Norton Hawkfield BaNES...17 Q4
Norton Heath Essex...22 F6
Norton in Hales Shrops...45 R6
Norton-Juxta-Twycross Leics...47 L12
Norton-le-Clay N York...63 U5
Norton Lindsey Warwks...36 H8
Norton Little Green Suffk...40 G7
Norton Malreward BaNES...17 R4
Norton Mandeville Essex...22 D6
Norton-on-Derwent N York...64 H5
Norton St Philip Somset...17 U5
Norton Subcourse Norfk...51 R14
Norton sub Hamdon Somset...7 N2
Norton Wood Herefs...34 J11
Norwell Notts...47 U1
Norwell Woodhouse Notts...58 B14
Northleigh Devon...15 P6
Norwich Norfk...51 M12
Norwich Airport Norfk...51 M11
Norwick Shet...106 w2
Norwood Clacks...90 C10
Norwood Derbys...57 Q10
Norwood Kent...13 L9
Norwood End Essex...22 E6
Norwood Green Calder...56 H1
Norwood Green Gt Lon...20 K7
Norwood Hill Surrey...11 L2
Norwoodside Cambs...49 P14
Noseley Leics...47 T14
Noss Mayo Devon...5 P11
Nosterfield N York...63 R3
Nosterfield End Cambs...39 T12
Nostie Highld...101 M6
Notgrove Gloucs...29 L4
Nottage Brdgnd...26 E12
Notter Cnwll...4 K8
Nottingham C Nott...47 Q6
Nottington Dorset...7 S8
Notton Wakefd...57 M4
Notton Wilts...18 D7
Nouard's Green Worcs...35 S8
Nowton Suffk...40 E8
Nox Shrops...44 K11
Nuffield Oxon...19 U4
Nunburnholme E R Yk...64 K10
Nuncargate Notts...47 P3
Nunclose Cumb...67 Q3
Nuneaton Warwks...37 L2
Nuneham Courtenay Oxon...30 C13
Nunhead Gt Lon...21 Q7
Nunkeeling E R Yk...65 Q10
Nun Monkton N York...64 B8
Nunney Somset...17 T8
Nunney Catch Somset...17 T8
Nunnington N York...64 F4
Nunnington Herefs...35 N12
Nunnykirk Nthumb...77 M7
Nunsthorpe NE Lin...59 M6
Nunthorpe C York...64 E8
Nunthorpe Middsb...70 H10
Nunthorpe Village Middsb...70 H10
Nunton Wilts...8 H3
Nunwick N York...63 S5
Nunwick Nthumb...76 H11
Nupdown S Glos...28 B8
Nup End Herts...31 S9
Nupend Gloucs...28 E6
Nuptown Br For...20 E8
Nursling Hants...9 L5
Nursted Hants...10 B5
Nurston V Glam...16 E3
Nutbourne W Susx...10 B9
Nutbourne W Susx...10 H7
Nutfield Surrey...21 P12
Nuthall Notts...47 P5
Nuthampstead Herts...39 P14
Nuthurst W Susx...10 K5
Nuthurst Warwks...36 G6
Nutley E Susx...11 Q5
Nutley Hants...19 T12
Nutwell Donc...57 T5
Nybster Highld...112 H4
Nyetimber W Susx...10 D11
Nyewood W Susx...10 C6
Nymans W Susx...11 M4
Nymet Rowland Devon...15 R11
Nymet Tracey Devon...15 R11
Nympsfield Gloucs...28 F7
Nynehead Somset...16 F11
Nythe Somset...17 L9
Nyton W Susx...10 E9
Oad Street Kent...12 G3
Oakall Green Worcs...35 T8
Oakamoor Staffs...46 D5
Oakbank W Loth...83 L5
Oak Cross Devon...15 N13
Oakdale Caerph...27 M8
Oakdale Poole...8 D10
Oake Somset...16 F11
Oaken Staffs...45 U13
Oakenclough Lancs...61 U10
Oakengates Wrekin...45 Q11
Oakenholt Flints...54 G12
Oakenshaw Dur...69 R5
Oakenshaw Kirk...56 J1
Oakerthorpe Derbys...47 L2
Oakes Kirk...56 H3
Oakford Cerdgn...32 H9
Oakford Devon...16 C11
Oakfordbridge Devon...16 C11
Oakgrove Ches E...56 C13
Oakham Rutlnd...48 C12
Oakhanger Ches E...45 R3
Oakhanger Hants...10 B3
Oakhill Somset...17 R7
Oakhurst Kent...21 T12
Oakington Cambs...39 P8
Oaklands Herts...31 R10
Oakle Street Gloucs...28 E4
Oakley Bed...38 F10
Oakley BCP...8 D10
Oakley Bucks...30 D10
Oakley Fife...90 E15
Oakley Hants...19 R10
Oakley Oxon...30 E11
Oakley Poole...8 D9
Oakley Suffk...41 L5
Oakley Green W & M...20 F7
Oakley Park Powys...33 T3
Oakridge Lynch Gloucs...28 H7
Oaks Lancs...62 E13
Oaksey Wilts...28 J9
Oaks Green Derbys...46 F7
Oakshaw Ford Cumb...75 V10
Oakshott Hants...10 B5
Oakthorpe Leics...46 K11
Oak Tree Darltn...70 D10
Oakwood C Derb...47 L6
Oakwoodhill Surrey...10 J4
Oakworth Brad...63 L12
Oare Kent...13 L3
Oare Somset...15 T3
Oare W Berk...19 S6
Oare Wilts...18 H8
Oareford Somset...15 T3
Oasby Lincs...48 F6
Oath Somset...16 K11
Oathlaw Angus...98 H12
Oatlands N York...63 S9
Oban Ag & B...94 B13
Oban Airport Ag & B...94 C11
Obley Shrops...34 G5
Obney P & K...90 E4
Oborne Dorset...17 S13
Obthorpe Lincs...48 G11
Occlestone Green Ches W...55 Q14
Occold Suffk...41 L6
Occumster Highld...112 G9
Ochiltree E Ayrs...81 Q8
Ochr-y-foel Denbgs...53 S7
Ochtermuthill P & K...89 S3
Ochtertyre P & K...89 S2
Ockbrook Derbys...47 M6
Ocker Hill Sandw...36 C2
Ockeridge Worcs...35 S8
Ockham Surrey...20 J11
Ockle Highld...93 P4
Ockley Surrey...10 J3
Ocle Pychard Herefs...35 N11
Octon E R Yk...65 N6
Odcombe Somset...17 P13
Odd Down BaNES...17 T4
Oddendale Cumb...68 D10
Oddingley Worcs...36 B9
Oddington Gloucs...29 P3
Oddington Oxon...30 C9
Odell Bed...38 E9
Odham Devon...15 L12
Odie Ork...106 v17
Odiham Hants...20 B12
Odsal Brad...63 P14
Odsey Cambs...31 Q5
Odstock Wilts...8 G3
Odstone Leics...47 L12
Offchurch Warwks...37 L7
Offenham Worcs...36 E11
Offerton Stockp...56 D9
Offham E Susx...11 P8
Offham Kent...12 C4
Offham W Susx...10 G9
Offleymarsh Staffs...45 S8
Offord Cluny Cambs...38 K7
Offord D'Arcy Cambs...38 K8
Offton Suffk...40 H11
Offwell Devon...6 G5
Ogbourne Maizey Wilts...18 J6
Ogbourne St Andrew Wilts...18 J6
Ogbourne St George Wilts...18 K5
Ogden Calder...63 L13
Ogle Nthumb...77 N10
Oglet Lpool...54 K9
Ogmore V Glam...26 F12
Ogmore-by-Sea V Glam...26 F12
Ogmore Vale Brdgnd...26 G8
Ogwen Bank Gwynd...53 M10
Okeford Fitzpaine Dorset...8 B6
Okehampton Devon...15 N13
Okehampton Camp Devon...15 N13
Oker Side Derbys...56 K14
Okewood Hill Surrey...10 J3
Olchard Devon...5 V4
Old Nhants...37 T6
Old Aberdeen C Aber...99 S2
Old Alresford Hants...9 R2
Oldany Highld...110 B10
Old Arley Warwks...36 J2
Old Auchenbrack D & G...74 E5
Old Basford C Nott...47 Q5
Old Basing Hants...19 U10
Old Beetley Norfk...50 G10
Oldberrow Warwks...36 F7
Old Bewick Nthumb...85 R14
Old Bolingbroke Lincs...59 Q13
Old Bramhope Leeds...63 Q11
Old Brampton Derbys...57 M12
Old Bridge of Urr D & G...74 F12
Old Buckenham Norfk...40 J2
Old Burghclere Hants...19 Q9
Oldbury Kent...21 T11
Oldbury Sandw...36 C3
Oldbury Shrops...35 R2
Oldbury Warwks...36 K2
Oldbury-on-Severn S Glos...28 B9
Oldbury on the Hill Gloucs...28 F10
Old Byland N York...64 D2
Old Cantley Donc...57 T6
Old Cassop Dur...70 D5
Oldcastle Mons...27 R2
Oldcastle Heath Ches W...45 L4
Old Churchstoke Powys...34 G2
Old Clee NE Lin...59 N6
Old Cleeve Somset...16 E8
Old Colwyn Conwy...53 Q7
Oldcotes Notts...57 S9
Old Coulsdon Gt Lon...21 P11
Old Dailly S Ayrs...80 J13
Old Dalby Leics...47 S9
Old Dam Derbys...56 H11
Old Deer Abers...105 R6
Old Ditch Somset...17 Q7
Old Edlington Donc...57 R7
Old Eldon Dur...69 S6
Old Ellerby E R Yk...65 R12
Oldfield Worcs...35 T8
Oldfield C Brad...63 L12
Old Fletton C Pete...38 J1
Oldford Somset...17 U7
Old Forge Herefs...27 V4
Old Furnace Herefs...27 U3
Old Glossop Derbys...56 F8
Old Goole E R Yk...58 B2
Old Grimsby IoS...2 b1
Oldhall Green Suffk...40 E9
Old Hall Street Norfk...51 P7
Oldham Oldham...56 D6
Oldhamstocks E Loth...84 K4
Old Harlow Essex...22 C5
Old Heath Essex...23 P3
Old Heathfield E Susx...11 U6
Old Hunstanton Norfk...49 U4
Old Hurst Cambs...39 L5
Old Hutton Cumb...62 B2
Old Inns Services S Lans...89 S10
Old Kea Cnwll...3 L8
Old Kilpatrick W Duns...89 L11
Old Knebworth Herts...31 R8
Old Lakenham Norfk...51 M12
Oldland S Glos...28 C13
Old Langho Lancs...62 E13
Old Laxey IoM...60 g6
Old Leake Lincs...49 P3
Old Malton N York...64 H5
Oldmeldrum Abers...105 M10
Old Micklefield Leeds...57 P1
Old Milverton Warwks...36 K7
Oldmixon N Som...16 K5
Old Newton Suffk...40 H8
Old Oxted Surrey...21 Q12
Old Quarrington Dur...70 D5
Old Radford C Nott...47 Q5
Old Radnor Powys...34 G9
Old Rayne Abers...104 K10
Old Romney Kent...12 K11
Old Shoreham W Susx...10 K9
Oldshoremore Highld...110 E5
Old Soar Kent...12 C5
Old Sodbury S Glos...28 E11
Old Somerby Lincs...48 E6
Oldstead N York...64 C3
Old Stratford Nhants...30 G4
Old Struan P & K...97 N10
Old Swarland Nthumb...77 P4
Old Swinford Dudley...35 U4
Old Tebay Cumb...68 D11
Old Thirsk N York...63 U3
Old Town Calder...56 E1
Old Town Cumb...62 B3
Old Town E Susx...11 U11
Old Town IoS...2 c2
Old Trafford Traffd...55 T7
Old Tupton Derbys...57 N14
Oldwalls Swans...25 S12
Old Warden C Beds...38 H11
Oldways End Somset...15 U8
Old Weston Cambs...38 G5
Old Wick Highld...112 H6
Old Windsor W & M...20 G8
Old Wives Lees Kent...13 L4
Old Woking Surrey...20 H11
Old Woodhall Lincs...59 L14
Old Woods Shrops...44 K9
Olgrinmore Highld...112 C6
Oliver's Battery Hants...9 P3
Ollaberry Shet...106 t5
Ollach Highld...100 e6
Ollerton Ches E...55 S12
Ollerton Notts...57 T13
Ollerton Shrops...45 P8
Olmarch Cerdgn...33 M9
Olmstead Green Cambs...39 T12
Olney M Keyn...38 C10
Olrig House Highld...112 E3
Olton Solhll...36 F4
Olveston S Glos...28 B10
Ombersley Worcs...35 T8
Ompton Notts...57 U13
Once Brewed Nthumb...76 E12
Onchan IoM...60 f7
Onecote Staffs...46 D2
Onen Mons...27 S4
Ongar Street Herefs...34 J7
Onibury Shrops...34 K5
Onich Highld...94 H6
Onllwyn Neath...26 E6
Onneley Staffs...45 S4
Onslow Green Essex...22 F4
Onslow Village Surrey...20 G13
Onston Ches W...55 N12
Openwoodgate Derbys...47 L4
Opinan Highld...107 M7
Orbliston Moray...104 C4
Orbost Highld...100 b5
Orby Lincs...59 S13
Orchard Portman Somset...16 H12
Orcheston Wilts...18 G12
Orcop Herefs...27 T2
Orcop Hill Herefs...27 T2
Ord Abers...104 H3
Ordhead Abers...105 L12
Ordie Abers...98 H3
Ordiequish Moray...104 C5
Ore E Susx...12 F13
Oreleton Common Herefs...35 M7
Oreton Shrops...35 P4
Orford Suffk...41 S11
Orford Warrtn...55 P8
Organford Dorset...8 C10
Orgreave Staffs...46 F11
Orkney Islands Ork...106 s18
Orkney Neolithic Ork...106 s19
Orlestone Kent...12 K9
Orleton Herefs...35 L7
Orleton Worcs...35 Q7
Orlingbury Nhants...38 B6
Ormathwaite Cumb...67 L7
Ormesby R & Cl...70 H9
Ormesby St Margaret Norfk...51 S11
Ormesby St Michael Norfk...51 S11
Ormiscaig Highld...107 Q6
Ormiston E Loth...84 C5
Ormsaigmore Highld...93 N5
Ormsary Ag & B...87 N10
Ormskirk Lancs...54 K5
Ornsby Hill Dur...69 Q3
Oronsay Ag & B...86 F5
Orphir Ork...106 s19
Orpington Gt Lon...21 S9
Orrell Sefton...54 H7
Orrell Wigan...55 M5
Orrell Post Wigan...55 M5
Orrisdale IoM...60 e3
Orroland D & G...73 T11
Orsett Thurr...22 F11
Orslow Staffs...45 T10
Orston Notts...47 U5
Orthwaite Cumb...67 L5
Orthwaite Cumb...67 L5

Ortner Lancs 61 U9
Orton Cumb 68 D11
Orton Nhants 38 B5
Orton Staffs 35 U1
Orton Longueville C Pete 38 J1
Orton-on-the-Hill Leics 46 K13
Orton Rigg Cumb 67 M2
Orton Waterville C Pete 38 J1
Orwell Cambs 39 N10
Osbaldeston Lancs 62 C13
Osbaldeston Green Lancs 62 C13
Osbaldwick C York 64 E9
Osbaston Leics 47 M13
Osbaston Shrops 44 H9
Osborne IoW 9 Q10
Osborne House IoW 9 Q10
Osbournby Lincs 48 G6
Oscroft Ches W 55 M13
Ose Highld 100 c5
Osgathorpe Leics 47 M10
Osgodby Lincs 58 J8
Osgodby N York 64 E13
Osgodby N York 65 P3
Oskaig Highld 100 e6
Oskamull Ag & B 93 M10
Osmaston Derbys 46 G5
Osmington Dorset 7 T8
Osmington Mills Dorset 7 T8
Osmondthorpe Leeds 63 S13
Osmotherley N York 70 G13
Osney Oxon 29 U6
Ospringe Kent 12 K3
Ossett Wakefd 57 L2
Ossington Notts 58 C14
Ostend Essex 23 M8
Osterley Gt Lon 21 L7
Oswaldkirk N York 64 E4
Oswaldtwistle Lancs 55 R1
Oswestry Shrops 44 G8
Otairnis W Isls 106 e11
Otford Kent 21 T11
Otham Kent 12 E5
Otham Hole Kent 12 F5
Othery Somset 17 L10
Otley Leeds 63 Q10
Otley Suffk 41 M9
Otley Green Suffk 41 M9
Otterbourne Hants 9 P4
Otterburn N York 62 H8
Otterburn Nthumb 76 H7
Otter Ferry Ag & B 87 S9
Otterham Cnwll 4 F2
Otterhampton Somset 16 H8
Otterham Quay Kent 12 F2
Otterham Station Cnwll 4 F3
Otternish W Isls 106 e11
Ottershaw Surrey 20 H10
Otterswick Shet 106 v5
Otterton Devon 6 E7
Otterwood Hants 9 N8
Ottery St Mary Devon 6 F5
Ottinge Kent 13 N7
Ottringham E R Yk 59 N2
Oughterby Cumb 67 L1
Oughtershaw N York 62 H3
Oughterside Cumb 66 H4
Oughtibridge Sheff 57 M8
Oughtrington Warrtn 55 Q9
Oulston N York 64 C5
Oulton Cumb 66 K2
Oulton Leeds 63 T14
Oulton Norfk 50 K8
Oulton Staffs 45 S9
Oulton Staffs 46 B6
Oulton Suffk 41 T2
Oulton Broad Suffk 41 T2
Oulton Street Norfk 51 L8
Oundle Nhants 38 F3
Ounsdale Staffs 35 U2
Our Dynamic Earth C Edin 83 Q4
Ousby Cumb 68 D6
Ousden Suffk 40 B9
Ousefleet E R Yk 58 D2
Ouston Dur 69 S2
Outchester Nthumb 85 S12
Out Elmstead Kent 13 P5
Outgate Cumb 67 N13
Outhgill Cumb 68 G12
Outhill Warwks 36 F7
Outlands Staffs 45 S7
Outlane Kirk 56 G3
Out Newton E R Yk 59 Q2
Out Rawcliffe Lancs 61 S11
Out Skerries Shet 106 w6
Outwell Norfk 49 R13
Outwick Hants 8 G5
Outwood Surrey 21 P13
Outwood Wakefd 57 M2
Outwood Gate Bury 55 S5
Outwoods Leics 47 M10
Outwoods Staffs 45 S10
Ouzlewell Green Leeds 57 M1
Ovenden Calder 56 G1
Over Cambs 39 N6
Over Ches W 55 P13
Over Gloucs 28 F4
Over S Glos 28 A11
Over Burrows Derbys 46 J6
Overbury Worcs 36 C13
Overcombe Dorset 7 S8
Over Compton Dorset 17 Q13
Over End Cambs 38 G2
Overgreen Derbys 57 M12
Over Green Warwks 36 G2
Over Haddon Derbys 56 K13
Over Hulton Bolton 55 Q6
Over Kellet Lancs 61 U6
Over Kiddington Oxon 29 T3
Overleigh Somset 17 N9
Overley Staffs 46 G10
Over Monnow Mons 27 U5
Over Norton Oxon 29 R2
Over Peover Ches E 55 S12
Overpool Ches W 54 J11
Overscaig Highld 110 J12
Overseal Derbys 46 J10
Over Silton N York 70 F14
Oversland Kent 13 L4
Oversley Green Warwks 36 E9
Overstone Nhants 37 U7
Over Stowey Somset 16 G9
Overstrand Norfk 51 M5
Over Stratton Somset 17 M13
Overstreet Wilts 18 G13
Over Tabley Ches E 55 R11
Overthorpe Nhants 37 N12
Overton C Aber 105 P13
Overton Ches W 55 M11
Overton Hants 19 R11
Overton Lancs 61 S8
Overton N York 64 D8
Overton Shrops 35 M6
Overton Swans 25 S13
Overton Wakefd 57 L3
Overton Wrexhm 44 J5
Overton Bridge Wrexhm 44 J5
Overton Green Ches E 45 T1
Overtown Lancs 62 C4
Overtown Lancs 62 H14
Overtown N Lans 82 F8
Overtown Swindn 18 J5
Overtown Wakefd 57 N3
Over Wallop Hants 19 L13
Over Whitacre Warwks 36 J2
Over Woodhouse Derbys 57 Q12
Over Worton Oxon 29 T2
Overy Oxon 19 S2
Oving Bucks 30 G8
Oving W Susx 10 E10
Ovingdean Br & H 11 P10
Ovingham Nthumb 77 M13
Ovington Dur 69 P10
Ovington Essex 40 C12
Ovington Hants 9 R2
Ovington Norfk 50 F13
Ovington Nthumb 77 M13
Ower Hants 9 L5
Ower Hants 9 P8
Owermoigne Dorset 7 U7
Owlbury Shrops 34 H2
Owlerton Sheff 57 M9
Owlpen Gloucs 28 E8
Owl's Green Suffk 41 N7
Owlsmoor Br For 20 D10
Owlswick Bucks 30 G11
Owmby Lincs 58 H9
Owmby Lincs 58 J6
Owslebury Hants 9 Q4
Owston Donc 57 S4
Owston Leics 47 U12
Owston Ferry N Linc 58 D6
Owstwick E R Yk 65 T13
Owthorne E R Yk 65 U14
Owthorpe Notts 47 S7
Owton Manor Hartpl 70 G7
Oxborough Norfk 50 B13
Oxbridge Dorset 7 N5
Oxcombe Lincs 59 P11
Oxcroft Derbys 57 Q12
Oxen End Essex 22 G2
Oxenholme Cumb 61 U2
Oxenhope C Brad 63 L13
Oxen Park Cumb 61 Q2
Oxenpill Somset 17 M8
Oxenton Gloucs 28 J1
Oxenwood Wilts 19 M9
Oxford Oxon 30 B11
Oxford Airport Oxon 29 U4
Oxford Services Oxon 30 D12
Oxgangs C Edin 83 P5
Oxhey Herts 20 K3
Oxhill Dur 69 Q2
Oxhill Warwks 36 K11
Oxley Wolves 46 B13
Oxley Green Essex 23 M5
Oxley's Green E Susx 12 C11
Oxlode Cambs 39 Q3
Oxnam Border 76 D2
Oxnead Norfk 51 M9
Oxshott Surrey 20 K10
Oxshott Heath Surrey 20 K10
Oxspring Barns 57 L6
Oxted Surrey 21 Q12
Oxton Border 84 D8
Oxton N York 64 C11
Oxton Notts 47 R3
Oxton Wirral 54 H9
Oxwich Swans 25 S13
Oxwich Green Swans 25 S13
Oxwick Norfk 50 F8
Oykel Bridge Highld 108 F4
Oyne Abers 104 K10
Oystermouth Swans 25 V13
Ozleworth Gloucs 28 E9

P

Pabail W Isls 106 k5
Packers Hill Dorset 7 T2
Packington Leics 47 L11
Packmoor C Stke 45 U3
Packmores Warwks 36 J7
Padanaram Angus 98 G13
Padbury Bucks 30 F6
Paddington Gt Lon 21 N6
Paddington Warrtn 55 P9
Paddlesworth Kent 12 C3
Paddlesworth Kent 13 N8
Paddock Wood Kent 12 C7
Paddolgreen Shrops 45 M7
Padfield Derbys 56 F7
Padgate Warrtn 55 P9
Padhams Green Essex 22 F8
Padiham Lancs 62 F13
Padside N York 63 P8
Padstow Cnwll 3 N1
Padworth W Berk 19 T7
Page Bank Dur 69 R5
Pagham W Susx 10 D11
Paglesham Essex 23 M9
Paignton Torbay 6 A12
Pailton Warwks 37 N4
Paine's Cross E Susx 11 U6
Painleyhill Staffs 46 D7
Painscastle Powys 34 E11
Painshawfield Nthumb 77 M13
Painsthorpe E R Yk 64 J8
Painswick Gloucs 28 G6
Painter's Forstal Kent 12 J4
Paisley Rens 89 L13
Pakefield Suffk 41 T2
Pakenham Suffk 40 F7
Pale Gwynd 43 U6
Pale Green Essex 39 U12
Palestine Hants 19 L12
Paley Street W & M 20 E7
Palfrey Wsall 36 D1
Palgrave Suffk 40 K5
Pallington Dorset 7 U6
Palmarsh Kent 13 M9
Palmersbridge Cnwll 4 F5
Palmers Green Gt Lon 21 P4
Palmerston E Ayrs 81 Q9
Palmerstown V Glam 16 F3
Palnackie D & G 73 U8
Palnure D & G 73 M7
Palterton Derbys 57 Q13
Pamber End Hants 19 T9
Pamber Green Hants 19 T9
Pamber Heath Hants 19 T8
Pamington Gloucs 36 B14
Pamphill Dorset 8 D8
Pampisford Cambs 39 Q11
Panborough Somset 17 N7
Panbride Angus 91 S4
Pancrasweek Devon 14 G11
Pancross V Glam 16 D3
Pandy Caerph 27 M10
Pandy Gwynd 43 M13
Pandy Gwynd 43 S8
Pandy Mons 27 Q3
Pandy Powys 43 T13
Pandy Wrexhm 44 E6
Pandy Wrexhm 44 H3
Pandy'r Capel Denbgs 44 C3
Pandy Tudur Conwy 53 Q10
Panfield Essex 22 H2
Pangbourne W Berk 19 T5
Pangdean W Susx 11 M8
Panks Bridge Herefs 35 P11
Pannal N York 63 S9
Pannal Ash N York 63 R9
Pant Shrops 44 G9
Pantasaph Flints 54 E11
Panteg Pembks 24 F4
Pantersbridge Cnwll 4 F7
Pant-ffrwyth Brdgnd 26 G11
Pant Glas Gwynd 42 J4
Pantglas Powys 43 Q14
Pant-Gwyn Carmth 25 U5
Pant-lasau Swans 26 B7
Pant Mawr Powys 33 R4
Panton Lincs 59 L11
Pant-pastynog Denbgs 53 T10
Pantperthog Gwynd 43 P13
Pantside Caerph 27 N8
Pant-y-caws Carmth 24 K5
Pant-y-dwr Powys 33 U6
Pant-y-ffridd Powys 44 E13
Pantyffynnon Carmth 25 V8
Pantygaseg Torfn 27 P8
Pantygelli Mons 27 Q4
Pant-y-gog Brdgnd 26 G9
Pantymwyn Flints 54 E14
Panxworth Norfk 51 Q11
Papa Stour Shet 106 r7
Papa Stour Airport Shet 106 r8
Papa Westray Ork 106 t14
Papa Westray Airport Ork 106 t14
Papcastle Cumb 66 H6
Papigoe Highld 112 J6
Papple E Loth 84 F4
Papplewick Notts 47 P3
Papworth Everard Cambs 39 L8
Papworth St Agnes Cambs 39 L8
Par Cnwll 3 R6
Paramour Street Kent 13 Q3
Parbold Lancs 55 L4
Parbrook Somset 17 Q9
Parbrook W Susx 10 H5
Parc Gwynd 43 S7
Parcllyn Cerdgn 32 D10
Parc Seymour Newpt 27 S9
Pardown Hants 19 S11
Pardshaw Cumb 66 G8
Parham Suffk 41 P8
Park D & G 74 H7
Park Nthumb 76 D13
Park Bottom Cnwll 2 H8
Park Bridge Tamesd 56 D6
Park Corner E Susx 11 S3
Park Corner Oxon 19 U3
Park Corner W & M 20 E6
Park End Bed 38 E10
Parkend Gloucs 28 B6
Park End Nthumb 76 H10
Parker's Green Kent 12 B6
Parkeston Essex 23 T1
Parkeston Quay Essex 41 M14
Park Farm Kent 12 K8
Parkgate Ches W 54 G11
Parkgate Cumb 66 K3
Parkgate D & G 74 K8
Parkgate E Susx 12 D13
Parkgate Essex 22 G2
Park Gate Hants 9 Q7
Parkgate Kent 12 G9
Parkgate Kent 21 T10
Park Gate Leeds 63 P11
Parkgate Surrey 11 L2
Park Gate Worcs 36 B6
Park Green Essex 22 C2
Park Green Suffk 40 K8
Parkhall W Duns 89 L11
Parkham Devon 14 J8
Parkham Ash Devon 14 J8
Park Head Derbys 47 L3
Parkhill Dur 70 D5
Park Hill Gloucs 27 V8
Parkhouse Mons 27 U7
Parkmill Swans 25 T13
Park Royal Gt Lon 21 L6
Parkside Dur 70 F3
Parkside N Lans 82 F7
Parkside Wrexhm 44 J2
Parkstone BCP 8 E10
Park Street Herts 31 P12
Park Street W Susx 10 J4
Parkway Herefs 35 R13
Parley Green BCP 8 G9
Parmoor Bucks 20 C5
Parracombe Devon 15 Q3
Parrog Pembks 24 J3
Parsonby Cumb 66 H5
Parson Cross Sheff 57 M8
Parson Drove Cambs 49 N12
Parson's Heath Essex 23 P2
Parson's Hill Derbys 46 J8
Partick C Glas 89 M12
Partington Traffd 55 R8
Partney Lincs 59 R13
Parton Cumb 66 E8
Partridge Green W Susx 10 K7
Partrishow Powys 27 P3
Parwich Derbys 46 G3
Paslow Wood Common Essex 22 E7
Passenham Nhants 30 G5
Passfield Hants 10 C4
Passingford Bridge Essex 22 D8
Paston C Pete 48 J13
Paston Norfk 51 P7
Pasturefields Staffs 46 C9
Patchacott Devon 15 L13
Patcham Br & H 11 N9
Patchetts Green Herts 20 K3
Patching W Susx 10 H9
Patchole Devon 15 P4
Patchway S Glos 28 B11
Pateley Bridge N York 63 P6
Paternoster Heath Essex 23 M4
Pathe Somset 17 L10
Pathhead Fife 91 L13
Pathhead Mdloth 83 S6
Pathlow Warwks 36 G9
Path of Condie P & K 90 G9
Patmore Heath Herts 22 B2
Patna E Ayrs 81 N10
Patney Wilts 18 G9
Patrick IoM 60 c6
Patrick Brompton N York 63 Q1
Patricroft Salfd 55 S7
Patrington E R Yk 59 P2
Patrington Haven E R Yk 59 P2
Patrixbourne Kent 13 N4
Patterdale Cumb 67 N9
Pattingham Staffs 45 T14
Pattishall Nhants 37 S10
Pattiswick Green Essex 22 K3
Patton Shrops 35 N1
Patton Bridge Cumb 67 S13
Paul Cnwll 2 D11
Paulerspury Nhants 37 T11
Paull E R Yk 59 L1
Paulton BaNES 17 S5
Paultons Park Hants 9 L5
Paunton Herefs 35 Q10
Pauperhaugh Nthumb 77 N6
Pave Lane Wrekin 45 S10
Pavenham Bed 38 E9
Pawlett Somset 16 J8
Pawston Nthumb 85 M12
Paxford Gloucs 36 G13
Paxton Border 85 N8
Payden Street Kent 12 H5
Payhembury Devon 6 E4
Paynter's Lane End Cnwll 2 H8
Paythorne Lancs 62 G9
Paytoe Herefs 34 K6
Peacehaven E Susx 11 Q10
Peak Dale Derbys 56 G11
Peak District National Park 56 J8
Peak Forest Derbys 56 H11
Peak Hill Lincs 49 L10
Peakirk C Pete 48 J12
Pearson's Green Kent 12 C7
Peartree Green Herefs 35 N14
Peasedown St John BaNES 17 T5
Peasehill Derbys 47 M4
Peaseland Green Norfk 50 J10
Peasemore W Berk 19 Q5
Peasenhall Suffk 41 Q7
Pease Pottage W Susx 11 M4
Pease Pottage Services W Susx 11 M4
Peaslake Surrey 10 H2
Peasley Cross St Hel 55 M8
Peasmarsh E Susx 12 G11
Peasmarsh Somset 6 K2
Peasmarsh Surrey 20 G13
Peathill Abers 105 Q2
Peat Inn Fife 91 Q10
Peatling Magna Leics 37 Q2
Peatling Parva Leics 37 Q3
Peaton Shrops 35 M3
Pebmarsh Essex 40 E14
Pebsham E Susx 12 E14
Pebworth Worcs 36 F11
Pecket Well Calder 62 K14
Peckforton Ches E 45 M2
Peckham Gt Lon 21 P7
Peckleton Leics 47 N13
Pedairffordd Powys 44 D9
Pedlinge Kent 13 M8
Pedmore Dudley 36 B4
Pedwell Somset 17 M9
Peebles Border 83 Q10
Peel IoM 60 c6
Peel Lancs 61 R13
Peel Common Hants 9 R8
Peene Kent 13 N8
Peening Quarter Kent 12 G10
Peggs Green Leics 47 M10
Pegsdon C Beds 31 P6
Pegswood Nthumb 77 Q8
Pegwell Kent 13 S3
Peinchorran Highld 100 e6
Peinlich Highld 100 d4
Pelcomb Pembks 24 F7
Pelcomb Bridge Pembks 24 F7
Pelcomb Cross Pembks 24 F7
Peldon Essex 23 N4
Pell Green E Susx 12 B9
Pelsall Wsall 46 D13
Pelsall Wood Wsall 46 D13
Pelton Dur 69 S2
Pelton Fell Dur 69 S2
Pelutho Cumb 66 H3
Pelynt Cnwll 4 G9
Pemberton Carmth 25 T10
Pemberton Wigan 55 N6
Pembles Cross Kent 12 G6
Pembrey Carmth 25 R10
Pembridge Herefs 34 J9
Pembroke Pembks 24 G10
Pembroke Dock Pembks 24 G10
Pembrokeshire Coast National Park Pembks 24 D6
Pembury Kent 12 B7
Pen-allt Herefs 27 V2
Penallt Mons 27 U5
Penally Pembks 24 K11
Penare Cnwll 3 P8
Penarth V Glam 16 G2
Penblewin Pembks 24 K7
Pen-bont Rhydybeddau Cerdgn 33 N4
Penbryn Cerdgn 32 E10
Pencader Carmth 25 R3
Pencaenewydd Gwynd 42 H5
Pencaitland E Loth 84 C5
Pencarnisiog IoA 52 E8
Pencarreg Carmth 32 K11
Pencarrow Cnwll 4 E4
Pencelli Powys 26 K2
Penclawdd Swans 25 T11
Pencoed Brdgnd 26 H11
Pencombe Herefs 35 N10
Pencoyd Herefs 27 U2
Pencraig Herefs 27 V3
Pencraig Powys 44 B8
Pendeen Cnwll 2 B10
Penderyn Rhondd 26 G6
Pendine Carmth 25 M9
Pendlebury Salfd 55 S6
Pendleton Lancs 62 F12
Pendock Worcs 35 S14
Pendoggett Cnwll 4 C5
Pendomer Somset 7 P2
Pendoylan V Glam 26 K12
Penegoes Powys 43 Q13
Penelewey Cnwll 3 L8
Pen-ffordd Pembks 24 J6
Pengam Caerph 27 M8
Pengam Cardif 27 N12
Penge Gt Lon 21 Q8
Pengelly Cnwll 4 D4
Pengenffordd Powys 27 M2
Pengorffwysfa IoA 52 G4
Pengover Green Cnwll 4 H7
Pen-groes-oped Mons 27 Q6
Pengwern Denbgs 53 T7
Penhale Cnwll 2 H13
Penhale Cnwll 3 N5
Penhale Cnwll 3 R4
Penhale Cnwll 5 L10
Penhallow Cnwll 2 K6
Penhalurick Cnwll 2 J9
Penhalvean Cnwll 2 J9
Penhill Swindn 29 N10
Penhow Newpt 27 S9
Penhurst E Susx 12 C12
Peniarth Gwynd 43 M12
Penicuik Mdloth 83 P7
Peniel Carmth 25 R6
Peniel Denbgs 53 T10
Penifiler Highld 100 d5
Peninver Ag & B 79 P11
Penisarwaun Gwynd 52 J10
Penistone Barns 56 K6
Penjerrick Cnwll 2 K10
Penketh Warrtn 55 N9
Penkill S Ayrs 80 J13
Penkridge Staffs 46 B11
Penlean Cnwll 14 F13
Penleigh Wilts 18 C10
Penley Wrexhm 44 K5
Penllergaer Swans 25 V11
Pen-llyn IoA 52 E6
Penllyn V Glam 26 H12
Pen-lôn IoA 52 F9
Penmachno Conwy 43 Q3
Penmaen Caerph 27 M8
Penmaen Swans 25 T13
Penmaenan Conwy 53 M7
Penmaenmawr Conwy 53 M7
Penmaenpool Gwynd 43 N10
Penmark V Glam 16 E3
Penmon IoA 52 K6
Penmorfa Gwynd 42 K5
Penmynydd IoA 52 H8
Penn Bucks 20 F4
Penn Wolves 35 U1
Pennal Gwynd 43 N13
Pennan Abers 105 N2
Pennant Cerdgn 32 K8
Pennant Denbgs 44 B7
Pennant Powys 43 S14
Pennant-Melangell Powys 44 B8
Pennar Pembks 24 G10
Pennard Swans 25 U13
Pennerley Shrops 44 J14
Pennicott Devon 15 U12
Pennines 62 K12
Pennington Cumb 61 P4
Pennington Hants 9 L9
Pennington Green Wigan 55 P5
Pennorth Powys 27 L2
Penn Street Bucks 20 F3
Pennsylvania S Glos 28 D13
Penny Bridge Cumb 61 Q3
Pennycross Ag & B 93 N13
Pennygate Norfk 51 P9
Pennyghael Ag & B 93 N13
Pennyglen S Ayrs 80 K10
Penny Green Derbys 57 R11
Penny Hill Lincs 49 N8
Pennymoor Devon 15 U10
Pennywell Sundld 70 E1
Penparc Cerdgn 32 D11
Penparcau Cerdgn 33 L4
Penpedairheol Caerph 27 L8
Penpedairheol Mons 27 Q7
Penpergwm Mons 27 Q5
Penperlleni Mons 27 Q7
Penpethy Cnwll 4 D3
Penpillick Cnwll 3 R5
Penpol Cnwll 3 L9
Penpoll Cnwll 4 E10
Penponds Cnwll 2 G9
Penpont Cnwll 3 R2
Penpont D & G 74 F7
Penpont Powys 26 H2
Penquit Devon 5 Q10
Penrest Cnwll 4 J5
Penrherber Carmth 25 N3
Pen-rhiw Pembks 32 D12
Penrhiwceiber Rhondd 26 K8
Pen Rhiwfawr Neath 26 C5
Penrhiwgoch Carmth 25 U7
Penrhiwllan Cerdgn 32 G12
Penrhiwpal Cerdgn 32 F11
Penrhos Gwynd 42 F7
Penrhos IoA 52 C6
Penrhos Mons 27 S5
Penrhos Powys 26 E5
Penrhos garnedd Gwynd 52 J8
Penrhyn Bay Conwy 53 P6
Penrhyn-coch Cerdgn 33 M4
Penrhyndeudraeth Gwynd 43 M6
Penrhyn-side Conwy 53 P6
Penrhyn Slate Landscape Gwynd 52 K9
Penrhys Rhondd 26 J9
Penrice Swans 25 S13
Penrioch N Ayrs 79 R7
Penrith Cumb 67 R6
Penrose Cnwll 3 M2
Penruddock Cumb 67 P7
Penryn Cnwll 2 K10
Pensarn Conwy 53 S7
Pensax Worcs 35 R7
Pensby Wirral 54 G10
Penselwood Somset 17 U10
Pensford BaNES 17 R4
Pensham Worcs 36 B12
Penshaw Sundld 70 D2
Penshurst Kent 11 S2
Penshurst Station Kent 21 T13
Pensilva Cnwll 4 H6
Pensnett Dudley 36 B3
Penstone Devon 15 S12
Penstrowed Powys 34 C2
Pentewan Cnwll 3 Q7
Pentir Gwynd 52 J9
Pentire Cnwll 2 K4
Pentlepoir Pembks 24 K9
Pentlow Essex 40 D12
Pentlow Street Essex 40 D11
Pentney Norfk 50 B11
Pentonbridge Cumb 75 T10
Penton Grafton Hants 19 M11
Penton Mewsey Hants 19 M11
Pentraeth IoA 52 H7
Pentre Denbgs 54 C14
Pentre Flints 54 H13
Pentre Mons 27 Q6
Pentre Mons 27 S7
Pentre Powys 34 C3
Pentre Powys 34 E3
Pentre Powys 34 G2
Pentre Rhondd 26 H8
Pentre Shrops 44 J10
Pentre Wrexhm 44 G5
Pentre-bâch Cerdgn 33 L11
Pentre Bach Flints 54 F11
Pentrebach Myr Td 26 K7
Pentre-bach Powys 33 T14
Pentrebeirdd Powys 44 E11
Pentre Berw IoA 52 G8
Pentre-bont Conwy 43 P3
Pentre-cagel Carmth 32 F12
Pentrecelyn Denbgs 44 D3
Pentre-celyn Powys 43 S12
Pentre-chwyth Swans 26 B9
Pentre-clawdd Shrops 44 G7
Pentre-cwrt Carmth 25 Q3
Pentredwr Denbgs 44 E4
Pentrefelin Gwynd 42 K6
Pentrefelin IoA 52 F4
Pentre Ffwrndan Flints 54 G12
Pentrefoelas Conwy 43 S3
Pentregalar Pembks 25 L4
Pentregat Cerdgn 32 G10
Pentre-Gwenlais Carmth 25 V7
Pentre Gwynfryn Gwynd 43 L8
Pentre Halkyn Flints 54 F12
Pentre Hodrey Shrops 34 H5
Pentre Isaf Conwy 53 S8
Pentre Llanrhaeadr Denbgs 54 C14
Pentre Llifior Powys 44 E14
Pentre-llwyn-llwyd Powys 33 U10
Pentre-llyn Cerdgn 33 M5
Pentre-llyn-cymmer Conwy 43 U3
Pentre-Maw Powys 43 S13
Pentre Meyrick V Glam 26 H12
Pentre-piod Torfn 27 P7
Pentre-poeth Newpt 27 P10
Pentre'rbryn Cerdgn 32 G10
Pentre'r-felin Cerdgn 33 M11
Pentre'r Felin Conwy 53 P9
Pentre'r-felin Powys 26 G1
Pentre Saron Denbgs 53 T10
Pentre-tafarn-y-fedw Conwy 53 P10
Pentre ty gwyn Carmth 33 R13
Pentrich Derbys 47 L3
Pentridge Dorset 8 E5
Pen-twyn Caerph 27 N7
Pentwyn Cardif 27 N11
Pen-twyn Mons 27 U6
Pen-twyn Torfn 27 P7
Pentwynmaur Caerph 27 M8
Pentyrch Cardif 27 L11
Penwithick Cnwll 3 Q5
Penwood Hants 19 P8
Penwyllt Powys 26 F4
Penybanc Carmth 25 V6
Penybont Powys 34 D8
Pen-y-bont Powys 44 F9
Penybontfawr Powys 44 C9
Pen-y-bryn Pembks 32 C12
Pen-y-cae Powys 26 E5
Penycae Wrexhm 44 G4
Pen-y-cae-mawr Mons 27 S8
Penycaerau Gwynd 42 C8
Pen-y-cefn Flints 54 D11
Pen-y-clawdd Mons 27 T6
Pen-y-coedcae Rhondd 26 K10
Penycwn Pembks 24 E6
Pen-y-fai Brdgnd 26 F11
Pen-y-felin Flints 54 E13
Penyffordd Flints 44 H1
Pen-y-ffordd Flints 54 D10
Penyffridd Gwynd 52 H11
Pen-y-garn Cerdgn 33 M3
Pen-y-Garnedd Powys 44 D9
Pen-y-graig Gwynd 42 D7
Penygraig Rhondd 26 J9
Penygroes Carmth 25 U8
Penygroes Gwynd 52 G12
Penygroeslon Gwynd 42 D7
Pen-y-Gwryd Gwynd 53 L11
Pen-y-lan V Glam 26 H12
Pen-y-Mynydd Carmth 25 S10
Penymynydd Flints 44 H1
Pen-y-pass Gwynd 52 K11
Pen-yr-Heol Mons 27 S5
Penysarn IoA 52 G4
Pen-y-stryt Denbgs 44 F3
Penywaun Rhondd 26 H7
Penzance Cnwll 2 D10
Peopleton Worcs 36 B10
Peover Heath Ches E 55 S12
Peper Harow Surrey 10 E2
Peplow Shrops 45 P9
Pepper's Green Essex 22 F5
Pepperstock C Beds 31 N9
Perceton N Ayrs 81 M4
Percyhorner Abers 105 R2
Perelle Guern 6 c3
Perham Down Wilts 19 L11
Periton Somset 16 C7
Perivale Gt Lon 21 L6
Perkins Village Devon 6 D6
Perkinsville Dur 69 S2
Perlethorpe Notts 57 T12
Perranarworthal Cnwll 2 K9
Perranporth Cnwll 2 K6
Perranuthnoe Cnwll 2 E11
Perranwell Cnwll 2 K6
Perranwell Cnwll 2 K9
Perran Wharf Cnwll 2 K9
Perranzabuloe Cnwll 2 K6
Perrott's Brook Gloucs 28 K6
Perry Birm 36 E2
Perry Cambs 38 H7
Perry Barr Birm 36 E2
Perry Green Essex 22 K3
Perry Green Herts 22 B4
Perry Green Wilts 28 J10
Perrystone Hill Herefs 28 B2
Perry Street Somset 6 K3
Pershall Staffs 45 T8
Pershore Worcs 36 B11
Pertenhall Bed 38 G7
Perth P & K 90 H7
Perthy Shrops 44 J7
Perton Herefs 35 N12
Perton Staffs 45 U14
Pertwood Wilts 18 C13
Peterborough C Pete 48 J14
Peterborough Services Cambs 38 H2
Peterchurch Herefs 34 H13
Peterculter C Aber 99 Q3
Peterhead Abers 105 U6
Peterlee Dur 70 F4
Petersfield Hants 9 U4
Peter's Green Herts 31 P9
Petersham Gt Lon 21 L8
Peters Marland Devon 15 L10
Peterstone Wentlooge Newpt 27 P12
Peterston-super-Ely V Glam 26 K12
Peterstow Herefs 27 V3
Peters Village Kent 12 D3
Peter Tavy Devon 5 N5
Petham Kent 13 M5
Petherwin Gate Cnwll 4 H3
Petrockstow Devon 15 M11
Petsoe End M Keyn 38 C11
Pet Street Kent 13 L6
Pett E Susx 12 G13
Pettaugh Suffk 41 L9
Pett Bottom Kent 13 N5
Petterden Angus 91 P4
Pettinain S Lans 82 J10
Pettistree Suffk 41 P9
Petton Devon 16 D12
Petton Shrops 44 K8
Petts Wood Gt Lon 21 S9
Pettycur Fife 83 Q1
Petty France S Glos 28 E10
Pettymuk Abers 105 Q11
Petworth W Susx 10 F6
Pevensey E Susx 11 U9
Pevensey Bay E Susx 11 V10
Pewsey Wilts 18 J8
Pewsham Wilts 18 D6
Pheasant's Hill Bucks 20 C5
Phepson Worcs 36 B9
Philadelphia Sundld 70 D2
Philham Devon 14 G8
Philiphaugh Border 84 C13
Phillack Cnwll 2 F9
Philleigh Cnwll 3 M9
Philpot End Essex 22 F4
Philpstoun W Loth 83 L3
Phocle Green Herefs 28 B2
Phoenix Green Hants 20 C11
Pibsbury Somset 17 M11
Pica Cumb 66 F8
Piccadilly Warwks 46 H14
Piccotts End Herts 31 M11
Pickburn Donc 57 R5
Pickering N York 64 H3
Picket Piece Hants 19 N11
Picket Post Hants 8 H7
Picket Twenty Hants 19 N11
Pickford Covtry 36 J4
Pickford Green Covtry 36 J4
Pickhill N York 63 S3
Picklescott Shrops 44 K14
Pickmere Ches E 55 Q11
Pickney Somset 16 G11
Pickstock Wrekin 45 R9
Pickup Bank Bl w D 55 R2
Pickwell Devon 15 L4
Pickwell Leics 47 U11
Pickwick Wilts 18 C6
Pickworth Lincs 48 F7
Pickworth RutInd 48 E11
Picton Ches W 54 K12
Picton Flints 54 D10
Picton N York 70 F11
Piddinghoe E Susx 11 Q10
Piddington Bucks 20 D4
Piddington Nhants 38 B10
Piddington Oxon 30 D9
Piddlehinton Dorset 7 T5
Piddletrenthide Dorset 7 T5
Pidley Cambs 39 M5
Piercebridge Darltn 69 R9
Pierowall Ork 106 t15
Piff's Elm Gloucs 28 H2
Pigdon Nthumb 77 P8
Pigeon Green Warwks 36 H8
Pig Oak Dorset 8 E8
Pig Street Herefs 34 J11
Pikehall Derbys 46 G2
Pilford Dorset 8 E8
Pilgrims Hatch Essex 22 E8
Pilham Lincs 58 E8
Pill N Som 27 U12
Pillaton Cnwll 4 K8
Pillatonmill Cnwll 4 K8
Pillerton Hersey Warwks 36 J11
Pillerton Priors Warwks 36 J11
Pilleth Powys 34 G7
Pilley Barns 57 M6
Pilley Hants 9 L9
Pilley Bailey Hants 9 L9
Pillgwenlly Newpt 27 Q10
Pillhead Devon 15 L7
Pilling Lancs 61 S10
Pilling Lane Lancs 61 R10
Pilning S Glos 27 V10
Pilot Inn Kent 13 L12
Pilsbury Derbys 56 H14
Pilsdon Dorset 7 M5
Pilsgate C Pete 48 G12
Pilsley Derbys 47 M1
Pilsley Derbys 56 K12
Pilson Green Norfk 51 Q11
Piltdown E Susx 11 Q6
Pilton Devon 15 N6
Pilton Nhants 38 F4
Pilton RutInd 48 D13
Pilton Somset 17 Q8
Pilton Green Swans 25 R13
Pimbo Lancs 55 L6
Pimlico Herts 31 N11
Pimlico Lancs 62 E11
Pimlico Nhants 30 D4
Pimperne Dorset 8 C7
Pinchbeck Lincs 48 K8
Pinchbeck Bars Lincs 48 J8
Pincheon Green Donc 57 U3
Pinchinthorpe R & Cl 70 J10
Pincock Lancs 55 M3
Pinfold Lancs 54 J4
Pinford End Suffk 40 D9
Pinged Carmth 25 R10
Pingewood W Berk 19 U7
Pin Green Herts 31 S7
Pinhoe Devon 6 C6
Pinkett's Booth Covtry 36 J4
Pinkney Wilts 28 G10
Pinkneys Green W & M 20 E6
Pinley Covtry 37 L5
Pinley Green Warwks 36 H7
Pin Mill Suffk 41 M13
Pinminnoch S Ayrs 80 H14
Pinmore S Ayrs 72 G1
Pinn Devon 6 F7
Pinner Gt Lon 20 K5
Pinner Green Gt Lon 20 K4
Pinsley Green Ches E 45 N4
Pinvin Worcs 36 C11
Pinwherry S Ayrs 72 G2
Pinxton Derbys 47 N3
Pipe and Lyde Herefs 35 M12
Pipe Aston Herefs 35 L6
Pipe Gate Shrops 45 R5
Pipehill Staffs 46 E12
Piperdam Angus 91 M5
Piperhill Highld 103 N5
Pipers Pool Cnwll 4 H4
Pipewell Nhants 38 B3
Pippacott Devon 15 M5
Pippin Street Lancs 55 N2
Pipton Powys 34 E13
Pirbright Surrey 20 F11
Pirbright Camp Surrey 20 F11
Pirnie Border 84 H13
Pirnmill N Ayrs 79 R7
Pirton Herts 31 P6
Pirton Worcs 35 U11
Pisgah Cerdgn 33 N5
Pishill Oxon 20 B5
Pistyll Gwynd 42 F5
Pitblae Abers 105 R3
Pitcairngreen P & K 90 G6
Pitcalnie Highld 109 Q10
Pitcaple Abers 105 L10
Pitcarity Angus 98 E10
Pitchcombe Gloucs 28 G6
Pitchcott Bucks 30 G8
Pitcher Row Lincs 49 L7
Pitchford Shrops 45 M13
Pitch Green Bucks 30 G12
Pitch Place Surrey 10 D3
Pitch Place Surrey 20 G12
Pitchroy Moray 103 U8
Pitcombe Somset 17 S10
Pitcot V Glam 26 F13
Pitcox E Loth 84 G3
Pitfichie Abers 104 K12
Pitglassie Abers 104 K7
Pitgrudy Highld 109 P6
Pitlessie Fife 91 M10
Pitlochry P & K 97 Q12
Pitmachie Abers 104 K10
Pitmain Highld 97 L3
Pitmedden Abers 105 P10
Pitmedden Garden Abers 105 P10
Pitminster Somset 16 H13
Pitmuies Angus 91 S2
Pitmunie Abers 104 K13
Pitney Somset 17 N11
Pitroddie P & K 90 K6
Pitscottie Fife 91 P9
Pitsea Essex 22 H10
Pitses Oldham 56 D6
Pitsford Nhants 37 U7
Pitstone Bucks 30 K9
Pitt Devon 16 D13
Pitt Hants 9 P3
Pittarrow Abers 99 N9
Pitt Court Gloucs 28 D8
Pittenweem Fife 91 S11
Pitteuchar Fife 91 L12
Pittodrie House Hotel Abers 104 K11
Pitton Wilts 8 J2
Pitt's Wood Kent 12 B6
Pittulie Abers 105 R2
Pityme Cnwll 3 P1
Pity Me Dur 69 S3
Pivington Kent 12 H6
Pixey Green Suffk 41 M5
Pixham Surrey 21 L12
Plains N Lans 82 E5
Plain Street Cnwll 4 B5
Plaish Shrops 35 M1
Plaistow Gt Lon 21 R6
Plaistow W Susx 10 G4
Plaitford Hants 8 K5
Plank Lane Wigan 55 P7
Plas Cymyran IoA 52 C7
Plastow Green Hants 19 R8
Platt Bridge Wigan 55 P6
Platt Lane Shrops 45 M6
Platts Heath Kent 12 G5
Plawsworth Dur 69 S3
Plaxtol Kent 12 B5
Playden E Susx 12 H11
Playford Suffk 41 M11
Play Hatch Oxon 20 B7
Playing Place Cnwll 3 L8
Playley Green Gloucs 28 E1
Plealey Shrops 44 K12
Plean Stirlg 89 T8
Pleasance Fife 90 K9
Pleasington Bl w D 55 P1
Pleasley Derbys 57 R14
Pleasleyhill Notts 57 R14
Pleasurewood Hills Suffk 41 T1
Pleck Dorset 7 T2
Pledgdon Green Essex 22 E2
Pledwick Wakefd 57 M3
Pleinheaume Guern 6 d2
Plemont Jersey 7 a1
Plemstall Ches W 55 L12
Plenmeller Nthumb 76 E13
Pleshey Essex 22 G5
Plockton Highld 100 h6
Plowden Shrops 34 J3
Plox Green Shrops 44 J13
Pluckley Kent 12 H6
Pluckley Station Kent 12 H7
Pluckley Thorne Kent 12 H7
Plucks Gutter Kent 13 Q3
Plumbland Cumb 66 J5
Plumgarths Cumb 67 Q14
Plumley Ches E 55 R12
Plump Hill Gloucs 28 C4
Plumpton Cumb 61 Q4
Plumpton Cumb 67 Q5
Plumpton E Susx 11 P8
Plumpton Nhants 37 Q11
Plumpton End Nhants 30 F4
Plumpton Green E Susx 11 P7
Plumpton Head Cumb 67 R5
Plumstead Gt Lon 21 R7
Plumstead Norfk 50 K7
Plumstead Green Norfk 50 K6
Plumtree Notts 47 R7
Plumtree Green Kent 12 F6
Plungar Leics 47 U7
Plurenden Kent 12 H8
Plush Dorset 7 T4
Plusha Cnwll 4 H4
Plushabridge Cnwll 4 J6
Plwmp Cerdgn 32 G10
Plymouth C Plym 5 M10
Plympton C Plym 5 N9
Plymstock C Plym 5 N10
Plymtree Devon 6 E4
Pockley N York 64 E2
Pocklington E R Yk 64 J10
Pode Hole Lincs 48 K9
Podimore Somset 17 P12
Podington Bed 38 D8
Podmore Staffs 45 S6
Point Clear Essex 23 R5
Pointon Lincs 48 H7
Pokesdown BCP 8 G10
Polbain Highld 107 S2
Polbathic Cnwll 4 J9
Polbeth W Loth 82 K6
Polbrock Cnwll 3 Q3
Poldark Mine Cnwll 2 H10
Polebrook Nhants 38 G3
Pole Elm Worcs 35 T10
Polegate E Susx 11 T10
Pole Moor Kirk 56 G3
Polesden Lacey Surrey 20 K12
Polesworth Warwks 46 J13
Polgigga Cnwll 2 B12
Polglass Highld 107 T3
Polgooth Cnwll 3 P6
Polgown D & G 74 D5
Poling W Susx 10 G10
Poling Corner W Susx 10 G9
Polkerris Cnwll 3 R6
Pollard Street Norfk 51 P7
Pollington E R Yk 57 T3
Polloch Highld 93 T5
Pollok C Glas 89 M13
Pollokshaws C Glas 89 N13
Pollokshields C Glas 89 N13
Polmassick Cnwll 3 P7
Polmear Cnwll 3 R6
Polmont Falk 82 H3
Polnish Highld 93 T2
Polperro Cnwll 4 G10
Polruan Cnwll 4 E10
Polsham Somset 17 P8
Polstead Suffk 40 G13
Polstead Heath Suffk 40 G12
Poltalloch Ag & B 87 Q6
Poltescoe Cnwll 2 J13
Poltimore Devon 6 C5
Polton Mdloth 83 Q6
Polwarth Border 84 J8
Polyphant Cnwll 4 H4
Polzeath Cnwll 4 A5
Pomathorn Mdloth 83 P7
Pomeroy Derbys 56 H13
Ponde Powys 34 D13
Pondersbridge Cambs 39 L2
Ponders End Gt Lon 21 Q3
Ponsanooth Cnwll 2 K9
Ponsonby Cumb 66 G11
Ponsongath Cnwll 2 K13
Ponsworthy Devon 5 S6
Pont Abraham Services Carmth 25 U9
Pontac Jersey 7 e4
Pontamman Carmth 26 A5
Pontantwn Carmth 25 R8
Pontardawe Neath 26 C7
Pontarddulais Swans 25 U10
Pont-ar-gothi Carmth 25 T6
Pont-ar-Hydfer Powys 26 F2
Pont-ar-llechau Carmth 26 C3
Pontarsais Carmth 25 R5
Pontblyddyn Flints 44 G1
Pont Cyfyng Conwy 53 M11
Pontcysyllte Aqueduct Wrexhm 44 G5
Pont Dolgarrog Conwy 53 N9
Pontdolgoch Powys 34 B2
Pont-Ebbw Newpt 27 P10
Pontefract Wakefd 57 Q2
Ponteland Nthumb 77 P11
Ponterwyd Cerdgn 33 P4
Pontesbury Shrops 44 J12
Pontesbury Hill Shrops 44 J12
Pontesford Shrops 44 K12
Pontfadog Wrexhm 44 F6
Pontfaen Pembks 24 H4
Pont-faen Powys 33 U14
Pontgarreg Cerdgn 32 F10
Pontgarreg Pembks 32 B12
Pont Henri Carmth 25 S9
Ponthir Torfn 27 Q9
Ponthirwaun Cerdgn 32 E11
Pontllanfraith Caerph 27 M8
Pontlliw Swans 25 V10
Pontllyfni Gwynd 42 H3
Pontlottyn Caerph 27 L6
Pont Morlais Carmth 25 T9
Pontnêddféchan Neath 26 G6
Pontnewydd Torfn 27 P8
Pontnewynydd Torfn 27 P7
Pont Pen-y-benglog Gwynd 53 L10
Pontrhydfendigaid Cerdgn 33 P7
Pont Rhyd-sarn Gwynd 43 S8
Pont Rhyd-y-cyff Brdgnd 26 F10
Pontrhydyfen Neath 26 D9
Pont-rhyd-y-groes Cerdgn 33 P6
Pontrhydyrun Torfn 27 P8
Pontrilas Herefs 27 R2
Pont Robert Powys 44 D11
Pont-rug Gwynd 52 H10
Ponts Green E Susx 12 C12
Pontshill Herefs 28 B3
Pontsian Cerdgn 32 H11
Pontsticill Myr Td 26 K5
Pont Walby Neath 26 F6
Pontwelly Carmth 32 H12
Pontyates Carmth 25 S9
Pontyberem Carmth 25 T8
Pont-y-blew Wrexhm 44 H6
Pontybodkin Flints 44 G2
Pontyclun Rhondd 26 J11
Pontycymer Brdgnd 26 G9
Pontyglasier Pembks 24 K3
Pontygwaith Rhondd 26 J9
Pontygynon Pembks 24 K3
Pontymister Caerph 27 N9
Pont-y-pant Conwy 53 N12
Pontypool Torfn 27 P7
Pontypridd Rhondd 26 K10
Pont-yr-hafod Pembks 24 F5
Pont-yr-Rhyl Brdgnd 26 G10
Pontywaun Caerph 27 N9
Pool Cnwll 2 H8
Pool IoS 2 b2
Poole BCP 8 E10
Poole Keynes Gloucs 28 J8
Poolewe Highld 107 Q8
Pooley Bridge Cumb 67 Q8
Pooley Street Norfk 40 J4
Poolfold Staffs 45 U2
Pool Head Herefs 35 N10
Poolhill Gloucs 28 D2
Pool in Wharfedale Leeds 63 Q10
Pool of Muckhart Clacks 90 F11
Pool Quay Powys 44 G11
Pool Street Essex 40 C13
Pootings Kent 21 S13
Popes Hill Gloucs 28 C5
Popham Hants 19 S12
Poplar Gt Lon 21 Q6
Poplar Street Suffk 41 R7
Porchfield IoW 9 N10
Poringland Norfk 51 N13
Porkellis Cnwll 2 H10
Porlock Somset 15 U3
Porlock Weir Somset 15 U3
Portachoillan Ag & B 79 P4
Port-an-Eorna Highld 100 g6
Port Appin Ag & B 94 C9
Port Askaig Ag & B 86 G12
Portavadie Ag & B 87 S12
Port Bannatyne Ag & B 88 C12
Portbury N Som 27 U12
Port Carlisle Cumb 75 P13
Port Charlotte Ag & B 78 D4
Portchester Hants 9 S7
Port Clarence S on T 70 G8
Port Driseach Ag & B 87 T11
Port Ellen Ag & B 78 F6
Port Elphinstone Abers 105 M11
Portencalzie D & G 72 C5
Portencross N Ayrs 80 H3
Port Erin IoM 60 b9
Portesham Dorset 7 R7
Portessie Moray 104 E2
Port e Vullen IoM 60 h4
Port Eynon Swans 25 S13
Portfield Gate Pembks 24 F7
Portgate Devon 5 L3
Port Gaverne Cnwll 4 C4
Port Glasgow Inver 88 H11
Portgordon Moray 104 D3
Portgower Highld 109 U2
Porth Cnwll 3 L4
Porth Rhondd 26 J9
Porthallow Cnwll 2 K12
Porthallow Cnwll 4 G10
Porthcawl Brdgnd 26 E12
Porthcothan Cnwll 3 M2
Porthcurno Cnwll 2 B12
Porthdinllaen Gwynd 42 E5
Port Henderson Highld 107 N10
Porthgain Pembks 24 D4
Porthgwarra Cnwll 2 B12
Porthill Staffs 45 T4
Porthkea Cnwll 3 L8
Porthkerry V Glam 16 E3
Porthleven Cnwll 2 G11
Porthmadog Gwynd 43 L6
Porthmadog Gwynd 43 L6
Porthmeor Cnwll 2 C9
Porth Navas Cnwll 2 K11
Portholland Cnwll 3 P8
Porthoustock Cnwll 3 L12
Porthpean Cnwll 3 Q6
Porthtowan Cnwll 2 H7
Porthwgan Wrexhm 44 J4
Porthyrhyd Carmth 25 T7
Porth-y-Waen Shrops 44 G9
Portincaple Ag & B 88 F7
Portinfer Jersey 7 a1
Portington E R Yk 64 H13
Portinnisherrich Ag & B 87 T3
Portinscale Cumb 67 L8
Port Isaac Cnwll 4 B4
Portishead N Som 27 T12
Portknockie Moray 104 F2
Portland Dorset 7 S10
Portlethen Abers 99 S4
Portling D & G 66 C2
Portloe Cnwll 3 N9
Port Logan D & G 72 D11
Portlooe Cnwll 4 G10
Portmahomack Highld 109 S8
Port Mary D & G 73 S10
Portmeirion Gwynd 43 L6
Portmellon Cnwll 3 Q8
Port Mòr Highld 93 L3
Portmore Hants 9 L9
Port Mulgrave N York 71 N9
Portnacroish Ag & B 94 C9
Portnaguran W Isls 106 k5
Portnahaven Ag & B 78 B5
Portnalong Highld 100 c6
Portnancon Highld 110 J4
Port nan Giùran W Isls 106 k5
Port nan Long W Isls 106 d11
Port Nis W Isls 106 k2
Portobello C Edin 83 R4
Portobello Gatesd 69 S1
Portobello Wolves 46 C14
Port of Menteith Stirlg 89 N5
Port of Ness W Isls 106 k2
Porton Wilts 18 J13
Portontown Devon 5 L5
Portpatrick D & G 72 B9
Port Quin Cnwll 4 B4
Port Ramsay Ag & B 94 B9
Portreath Cnwll 2 H7
Portreath Harbour Cnwll 2 H7
Portree Highld 100 d5
Port Righ Ag & B 79 Q8
Port St Mary IoM 60 c9
Portscatho Cnwll 3 M9
Portsea C Port 9 S8
Portskerra Highld 111 T3
Portskewett Mons 27 T10
Portslade Br & H 11 M9
Portslade-by-Sea Br & H 11 M9
Portslogan D & G 72 B8
Portsmouth C Port 9 S9
Portsmouth Calder 56 D1
Portsmouth Arms Devon 15 P9
Portsmouth Dockyard C Port 9 S8
Port Soderick IoM 60 e8
Port Solent C Port 9 S7
Portsonachan Hotel Ag & B 88 B1
Portsoy Abers 104 H2
Port Sunlight Wirral 54 H10
Portswood C Sotn 9 N6
Port Talbot Neath 26 D10
Port Tennant Swans 26 B9
Portuairk Highld 93 L5
Portway Herefs 35 L12
Portway Herefs 35 L13
Portway Sandw 36 C3
Portway Worcs 36 E6
Port Wemyss Ag & B 78 B5
Port William D & G 72 J11
Portwrinkle Cnwll 4 K10
Portyerrock D & G 73 M12
Posbury Devon 15 T13
Posenhall Shrops 45 Q13
Poslingford Suffk 40 C11
Posso Border 83 P12
Postbridge Devon 5 R5
Postcombe Oxon 30 F12
Post Green Dorset 8 D10
Postling Kent 13 M8
Postwick Norfk 51 N12
Potarch Abers 99 L4
Potsgrove C Beds 31 L6
Potten End Herts 31 M11
Potten Street Kent 13 Q2
Potter Brompton N York 65 M4
Pottergate Street Norfk 41 L2
Potterhanworth Lincs 58 J13
Potterhanworth Booths Lincs 58 J13
Potter Heigham Norfk 51 R10
Potterne Wilts 18 E9
Potterne Wick Wilts 18 E9
Potter Row Bucks 30 K12
Potters Bar Herts 31 R12
Potters Brook Lancs 61 T9
Potters Corner Kent 12 J7
Potter's Cross Staffs 35 T4
Potters Crouch Herts 31 P11
Potter's Forstal Kent 12 G6
Potters Green Covtry 37 L4
Potter's Green E Susx 11 S6
Potter's Green Herts 31 U8
Pottersheath Herts 31 R9
Potters Marston Leics 37 N1
Potter Somersal Derbys 46 F6
Potterspury Nhants 30 G4
Potter Street Essex 22 C6
Potterton Abers 105 Q12
Potterton Leeds 63 U12
Potthorpe Norfk 50 F9
Pottle Street Wilts 18 B12
Potto N York 70 G12
Potton C Beds 38 K11
Pott Row Norfk 50 B9
Pott's Green Essex 23 M3
Pott Shrigley Ches E 56 D11
Poughill Cnwll 14 F11
Poughill Devon 15 U11
Poulner Hants 8 H7
Poulshot Wilts 18 E9
Poulton Gloucs 29 L7
Poulton Wirral 54 H8
Poulton-le-Fylde Lancs 61 Q12
Poulton Priory Gloucs 29 L8
Pound Bank Worcs 35 R6
Poundbury Dorset 7 S6
Poundffald Swans 25 U12
Poundgate E Susx 11 R5
Pound Green E Susx 11 S6
Pound Green Suffk 40 B10
Pound Green Worcs 35 S5
Pound Hill W Susx 11 M3
Poundon Bucks 30 D7
Poundsbridge Kent 11 S2
Poundsgate Devon 5 S6
Poundstock Cnwll 14 F13
Pound Street Hants 19 Q8
Pounsley E Susx 11 S6
Pouton D & G 73 M10
Pouy Street Suffk 41 Q6
Povey Cross Surrey 11 M2
Powburn Nthumb 77 M2
Powderham Devon 6 C8
Powerstock Dorset 7 P5
Powfoot D & G 75 M12
Pow Green Herefs 35 R12
Powhill Cumb 66 K1
Powick Worcs 35 T10
Powmill P & K 90 F12
Poxwell Dorset 7 T8
Poyle Slough 20 H7
Poynings W Susx 11 M8
Poyntington Dorset 17 S12
Poynton Ches E 56 D10
Poynton Wrekin 45 N10
Poynton Green Wrekin 45 N10
Poyston Cross Pembks 24 G7
Poystreet Green Suffk 40 G9
Praa Sands Cnwll 2 F11
Pratt's Bottom Gt Lon 21 S10
Praze-an-Beeble Cnwll 2 G9
Predannack Wollas Cnwll 2 H13
Prees Shrops 45 N7
Preesall Lancs 61 R10
Prees Green Shrops 45 N7
Preesgweene Shrops 44 G6
Prees Heath Shrops 45 N6
Prees Higher Heath Shrops 45 N6
Prees Lower Heath Shrops 45 N7
Prendwick Nthumb 77 L3
Pren-gwyn Cerdgn 32 H12
Prenteg Gwynd 43 L5
Prenton Wirral 54 H9
Prescot Knows 55 L8
Prescott Devon 6 E2
Prescott Shrops 35 Q4
Prescott Shrops 44 K9
Presnerb Angus 98 B10
Pressen Nthumb 85 L11
Prestatyn Denbgs 54 C10
Prestbury Ches E 56 C11
Prestbury Gloucs 28 J3
Presteigne Powys 34 H8
Prestleigh Somset 17 R8
Prestolee Bolton 55 S5
Preston Border 84 K7
Preston Br & H 11 N9
Preston Devon 5 V6
Preston Dorset 7 T8
Preston E R Yk 65 R13
Preston Gloucs 28 K7
Preston Herts 31 Q8
Preston Kent 12 K3
Preston Kent 13 P3
Preston Lancs 61 U14
Preston Nthumb 85 T13
Preston RutInd 48 C13
Preston Shrops 45 M11
Preston Somset 16 E9
Preston Torbay 6 A12
Preston Wilts 18 F5
Preston Wilts 19 L6
Preston Bagot Warwks 36 G7
Preston Bissett Bucks 30 E7
Preston Bowyer Somset 16 F11
Preston Brockhurst Shrops 45 M9
Preston Brook Halton 55 N10
Preston Candover Hants 19 T12
Preston Capes Nhants 37 Q10
Preston Crowmarsh Oxon 19 T2
Preston Deanery Nhants 37 U9
Preston Green Warwks 36 G7
Preston Gubbals Shrops 45 L10
Preston Montford Shrops 44 K11
Preston on Stour Warwks 36 H11
Preston on Tees S on T 70 F9
Preston on the Hill Halton 55 N10
Preston on Wye Herefs 34 J12

Prestonpans E Loth....83 S4
Preston Patrick Cumb....61 U3
Preston Plucknett Somset....17 P13
Preston St Mary Suff....40 F10
Preston Street Kent....13 Q3
Preston-under-Scar
N York....63 M1
Preston upon the Weald
Moors Wrekin....45 Q10
Preston Wynne Herefs....35 N11
Prestwich Bury....55 T6
Prestwick Nthumb....77 P11
Prestwick S Ayrs....81 M7
Prestwick Airport S Ayrs....81 M7
Prestwood Bucks....30 J12
Prestwood Staffs....35 U3
Price Town Brdgnd....26 G9
Prickwillow Cambs....39 S4
Priddy Somset....17 P6
Priestacott Devon....14 K11
Priestcliffe Derbys....56 H12
Priestcliffe Ditch Derbys....56 H12
Priest Hutton Lancs....61 U5
Priestland E Ayrs....81 Q6
Priestley Green Calder....56 H1
Priest Weston Shrops....34 G13
Priestwood Green Kent....12 C3
Primethorpe Leics....37 P2
Primrose Green Norfk....50 J10
Primrosehill Border....84 K7
Primrose Hill Cambs....39 N3
Primrose Hill Dudley....36 B3
Primrose Hill Dudley....36 B3
Primrose Hill Lancs....54 J6
Primrose Hill Lancs....54 B7
Primsidemill Border....85 L13
Prince of Wales Bridge
Princes Gate Pembks....24 K8
Princes Risborough Bucks....30 H12
Princethorpe Warwks....37 M6
Princetown Devon....5 P6
Prinsted W Susx....10 B10
Prion Denbgs....44 C1
Prior Rigg Cumb....75 U12
Priors Halton Shrops....35 L5
Priors Hardwick Warwks....37 N9
Priorslee Wrekin....45 Q11
Priors Marston Warwks....37 N9
Priors Norton Gloucs....28 G3
Priors Park Gloucs....28 G1
Priory Wood Herefs....34 G11
Prisk V Glam....26 J12
Priston BaNES....17 S4
Pristow Green Norfk....40 K3
Prittlewell Sthend....23 L10
Privett Hants....9 T3
Prixford Devon....15 N5
Probus Cnwll....3 M7
Prora E Loth....84 E3
Prospect Cumb....66 H4
Prospidnick Cnwll....2 G10
Prudhoe Nthumb....77 M13
Prussia Cove Cnwll....2 F11
Publ P & K....90 B7
Puddow Norfk....51 R4
Puckeridge Herts....31 U8
Puckington Somset....17 L13
Puckrup Gloucs....28 C12
Puddinglake Ches W....55 S13
Puddington Ches W....54 H12
Puddington Devon....15 U10
Puddledock Norfk....40 H2
Puddletown Dorset....7 U6
Pudleston Herefs....35 N9
Pudsey Leeds....63 Q13
Pulborough W Susx....10 G7
Puleston Wrekin....45 R9
Pulford Ches W....44 J2
Pulham Dorset....7 T3
Pulham Market Norfk....41 L3
Pulham St Mary Norfk....41 M3
Pullens Green S Glos....28 B9
Pulloxhill C Beds....31 N5
Pumpherston W Loth....83 L5
Pumsaint Carmth....33 N12
Puncheston Pembks....24 H5
Puncknowle Dorset....7 P7
Punnett's Town E Susx....11 U6
Purbrook Hants....9 S7
Purfleet-on-Thames Thurr....22 E12
Purleigh Essex....22 K8
Purley Gt Lon....21 P10
Purley on Thames W Berk....19 U5
Purlpit Wilts....18 C7
Purls Bridge Cambs....39 Q3
Purse Caundle Dorset....17 S13
Purslow Shrops....34 J4
Purston Jaglin Wakefd....57 P3
Purtington Somset....7 L3
Purton Gloucs....28 C6
Purton Gloucs....28 C7
Purton Wilts....29 L9
Purton Stoke Wilts....29 L9
Pury End Nhants....37 T11
Pusey Oxon....29 R8
Putley Herefs....35 P13
Putley Green Herefs....35 P13
Putney Gt Lon....21 N8
Putsborough Devon....14 L4
Puttenham Herts....30 J10
Puttenham Surrey....10 F2
Puttock End Essex....40 D12
Putton Dorset....7 S8
Putts Corner Devon....6 F5
Puxley Nhants....30 G4
Puxton N Som....17 M4
Pwll Carmth....25 S10
Pwllcrochan Pembks....24 F10
Pwll-du Mons....27 P6
Pwll-glâs Denbgs....44 D2
Pwllgloyw Powys....34 B14
Pwllheli Gwynd....42 G6
Pwllmeyric Mons....27 V9
Pwll-trap Carmth....25 N7
Pwll-y-glaw Neath....26 D9
Pydew Conwy....53 P7
Pye Bridge Derbys....47 M3
Pyecombe W Susx....11 M8
Pye Corner Newpt....27 Q10
Pye Green Staffs....46 C11
Pyleigh Somset....16 F10
Pyle Somset....7 ....
Pymoor Cambs....39 Q3
Pymore Dorset....7 N6
Pyrford Surrey....20 H11
Pyrton Oxon....30 E13
Pytchley Nhants....38 B6
Pyworthy Devon....14 H12

Q

Quabbs Shrops....34 F4
Quadring Lincs....48 K7
Quadring Eaudike Lincs....48 K7
Quainton Bucks....30 F8
Quaker's Yard Myr Td....26 K8
Quaking Houses Dur....69 Q2
Quantock Hills Somset....16 G9
Quarff Shet....106 u10
Quarley Hants....19 L12
Quarndon Derbys....46 K5
Quarr Hill IoW....9 R10
Quarrier's Village Inver....88 J12
Quarrington Lincs....48 G5
Quarrington Hill Dur....70 D5
Quarry Bank Dudley....36 B3
Quarrywood Moray....103 U3
Quarter N Ayrs....88 E13
Quarter S Lans....82 D8
Quatford Shrops....35 S2
Quatt Shrops....35 S3
Quebec Dur....69 Q4
Quedgeley Gloucs....28 F5
Queen Adelaide Cambs....39 S4
Queenborough Kent....23 M13
Queen Camel Somset....17 Q12
Queen Charlton BaNES....17 R3
Queen Dart Devon....15 T9
Queen Elizabeth Forest
Park Stirlg....89 M5
Queen Elizabeth II Bridge
Thurr....22 E12
Queenhill Worcs....35 U13
Queen Oak Dorset....17 U10
Queen's Bower IoW....9 R12
Queensbury C Brad....63 N13
Queensferry Flints....54 H13
Queen's Head Shrops....44 H8
Queenslie C Glas....89 Q12
Queen's Park Bed....38 F11
Queen's Park Nhants....37 U8

R

Raasay Highld....100 e5
Rabbit's Cross Kent....12 E6
Rableyheath Herts....31 R9
Raby Cumb....66 J2
Raby Wirral....54 H11
Rachan Mill Border....83 M12
Rachub Gwynd....52 K9
Rackenford Devon....15 U9
Rackham W Susx....10 G8
Rackheath Norfk....51 N11
Racks D & G....74 K11
Rackwick Ork....106 t20
Radbourne Derbys....46 J6
Radcliffe Bury....55 S5
Radcliffe Nthumb....77 R5
Radcliffe on Trent Notts....47 R6
Radclive Bucks....30 E6
Radcot Oxon....29 Q8
Raddery Highld....102 K4
Raddington Somset....16 E11
Radernie Fife....91 Q10
Radford Covtry....36 K4
Radford Semele Warwks....36 L8
Radlet Somset....16 H9
Radlett Herts....31 Q12
Radley Devon....15 R8
Radley Oxon....30 B13
Radley Green Essex....22 F6
Radmore Green Ches E....45 N2
Radnage Bucks....20 C3
Radstock BaNES....17 S6
Radstone Nhants....30 C4
Radway Warwks....37 L11
Radwell Bed....38 F9
Radwell Herts....31 R6
Radwinter Essex....39 T13
Radwinter End Essex....39 T13
Radyr Cardif....27 L11
RAF College (Cranwell)
Lincs....48 F4
Rafford Moray....103 R4
RAF Museum Cosford
Shrops....45 S12
RAF Museum Hendon
Gt Lon....21 M4
Ragdale Leics....47 S10
Ragdon Shrops....35 L2
Raginnis Cnwll....2 D11
Raglan Mons....27 S6
Ragnall Notts....58 D12
Rainbow Hill Worcs....35 U9
Rainford St Hel....54 L6
Rainford Junction St Hel....55 L6
Rainham Gt Lon....22 D11
Rainham Medway....12 F2
Rainhill St Hel....55 L8
Rainhill Stoops St Hel....55 M8
Rainow Ches E....56 D11
Rainsough Bury....55 T6
Rainton N York....63 S3
Rainworth Notts....47 Q2
Raisbeck Cumb....68 D11
Raise Cumb....68 E3
Raisthorpe N York....64 K7
Rait P & K....90 K6
Raithby Lincs....59 Q11
Raithby Lincs....59 R13
Raithwaite N York....71 Q10
Rake Hants....10 C5
Rakewood Rochdl....56 D4
Ralia Highld....97 L5
Ram Carmth....33 L11
Ramasaig Highld....100 a5
Rame Cnwll....2 L11
Rame Cnwll....5 L11
Ram Hill S Glos....28 C12
Ram Lane Kent....12 J6
Rampisham Dorset....7 Q4
Rampside Cumb....61 N6
Rampton Cambs....39 P8
Rampton Notts....58 D11
Ramsbottom Bury....55 S3
Ramsbury Wilts....19 L6
Ramscraigs Highld....112 D11
Ramsdean Hants....9 U4
Ramsdell Hants....19 S9
Ramsden Oxon....29 S4
Ramsden Bellhouse Essex....22 H8
Ramsden Heath Essex....22 H8
Ramsey Cambs....39 N3
Ramsey Essex....23 T1
Ramsey IoM....60 h4
Ramsey Forty Foot Cambs....39 N3
Ramsey Heights Cambs....38 M4
Ramsey Island Essex....23 M6
Ramsey Mereside Cambs....39 L3
Ramsey St Mary's Cambs....39 L3
Ramsgate Kent....13 S2
Ramsgill N York....63 N5
Ramshaw Dur....69 L3
Ramsholt Suff....41 P12
Ramshope Nthumb....76 J4
Ramshorn Staffs....46 E4
Ramsnest Common Surrey....10 E4
Ranby Lincs....59 M11
Ranby Notts....57 U10
Rand Lincs....58 K11
Randwick Gloucs....28 F6
Ranfurly Rens....88 J12
Rangemore Staffs....46 G9
Rangeworthy S Glos....28 C10
Rankinston E Ayrs....81 P10
Rank's Green Essex....22 H4
Rannoch Station P & K....95 N7
Ranscombe Somset....16 B8
Ranskill Notts....57 U9
Ranton Staffs....45 U9
Ranton Green Staffs....45 U9
Ranworth Norfk....51 Q11
Raploch Stirlg....89 S7
Rapness Ork....106 u15
Rapps Somset....16 K13
Rascarrel D & G....73 T10
Rashfield Ag & B....88 D7
Rashwood Worcs....36 B7
Raskelf N York....64 B5
Rassau Blae G....27 M5
Rastrick Calder....56 H2
Ratagan Highld....101 N8
Ratby Leics....47 P12
Ratcliffe Culey Leics....36 K14
Ratcliffe on Soar Notts....47 N8
Ratcliffe on the Wreake
Leics....47 R11
Rathen Abers....105 R3
Rathillet Fife....91 N7
Rathmell N York....62 H8
Ratho C Edin....83 M4
Ratho Station C Edin....83 M4
Rathven Moray....104 E2
Ratlake Hants....9 N4
Ratley Warwks....37 L11
Ratling Kent....13 P5
Ratlinghope Shrops....35 K2
Ratten Row Cumb....67 M3
Ratten Row Cumb....67 M4
Ratten Row Lancs....61 S11
Rattery Devon....5 S8
Rattlesden Suff....40 G9
Ratton Village E Susx....11 T10
Rattray P & K....90 H3
Raughton Cumb....67 N3
Raughton Head Cumb....67 N3
Raunds Nhants....38 E6
Ravenfield Rothm....57 Q7

Ravenglass Cumb....66 G13
Ravenhills Green Worcs....35 R10
Raveningham Norfk....41 Q1
Ravenscar N York....71 S12
Ravenscraig N Lans....82 E7
Ravensdale IoM....60 f4
Ravensden Bed....38 G10
Ravenseat N York....68 J12
Ravenshead Notts....47 Q3
Ravensmoor Ches E....45 P3
Ravensthorpe Kirk....56 K2
Ravensthorpe Nhants....37 S6
Ravenstone Leics....47 M11
Ravenstone M Keyn....38 B10
Ravenstonedale Cumb....68 F12
Ravenstruther S Lans....82 H9
Ravensworth N York....69 P11
Raw N York....71 R11
Rawcliffe E R Yk....64 D9
Rawcliffe C York....64 D9
Rawcliffe Bridge E R Yk....57 U2
Rawdon Leeds....63 Q12
Rawling Street Kent....12 H4
Rawmarsh Rothm....57 P7
Rawnsley Staffs....46 D11
Rawreth Essex....22 J9
Rawridge Devon....6 H3
Rawtenstall Lancs....55 T2
Raydon Suff....40 H13
Raylees Nthumb....76 K7
Rayleigh Essex....22 K9
Raymond's Hill Devon....6 K5
Raynes Park Gt Lon....21 M9
Reach Cambs....39 S8
Read Lancs....62 F13
Reading W Berk....20 B8
Reading Services W Berk....19 U7
Reading Street Kent....12 H9
Reading Street Kent....13 S2
Reagill Cumb....68 D9
Rearquhar Highld....109 N6
Rearsby Leics....47 S11
Rease Heath Ches E....45 P3
Reay Highld....111 V4
Reculver Kent....13 P2
Red Ball Devon....16 E13
Redberth Pembks....24 J10
Redbourn Herts....31 P10
Redbourne N Linc....58 G7
Redbrook Gloucs....27 V5
Redbrook Wrexhm....45 M5
Redbrook Street Kent....12 H8
Redburn Highld....103 P6
Redburn Nthumb....76 F13
Redcar R & C....70 K8
Redcastle D & G....74 F12
Redcastle Highld....102 G6
Red Dial Cumb....67 L3
Redding Falk....82 H3
Reddingmuirhead Falk....82 H3
Reddish Stockp....56 C8
Redditch Worcs....36 D7
Rede Suff....40 D9
Redenhall Norfk....41 M4
Redenham Hants....19 M11
Redesmouth Nthumb....76 H9
Redford Abers....99 P9
Redford Angus....91 S3
Redford W Susx....10 D5
Redfordgreen Border....75 S2
Redgate Rhondd....26 J9
Redgorton P & K....90 G6
Redgrave Suff....40 H5
Redhill Abers....99 P3
Redhill Herts....31 T6
Redhill N Som....17 N4
Redhill Surrey....21 N12
Redhouse Ag & B....79 Q5
Redisham Suff....41 R4
Redland Bristl....28 A12
Redland Ork....106 s17
Redlingfield Suff....41 L6
Redlingfield Green Suff....41 L6
Red Lumb Rochdl....55 T3
Redlynch Somset....17 T10
Redlynch Wilts....8 H4
Redmain Cumb....66 H6
Redmarley Worcs....35 S7
Redmarley D'Abitot Gloucs....28 E1
Redmarshall S on T....70 E8
Redmile Leics....48 B6
Redmire N York....63 L1
Redmyre Abers....99 P7
Rednal Birm....36 D5
Rednal Shrops....44 J8
Redpath Border....84 F12
Red Point Highld....107 M9
Red Post Cnwll....14 G11
Red Rice Hants....19 M11
Red Rock Wigan....55 N5
Red Roses Carmth....25 N8
Red Row Nthumb....77 R6
Redruth Cnwll....2 H8
Redstocks Wilts....18 D8
Redstone P & K....90 J5
Redstone Cross Pembks....24 J7
Red Street Staffs....45 T3
Redvales Bury....55 T5
Red Wharf Bay IoA....52 H5
Redwick Newpt....27 T11
Redwick S Glos....27 U10
Redworth Darltn....69 R8
Reed Herts....31 U5
Reedham Norfk....51 R13
Reedness E R Yk....58 C2
Reeds Beck Lincs....59 M13
Reeds Holme Lancs....55 T2
Reepham Lincs....58 H12
Reepham Norfk....50 J9
Reeth N York....69 M13
Reeves Green Solhll....36 J5
Regaby IoM....60 h3
Regil N Som....17 P4
Reiff Highld....107 V3
Reigate Surrey....21 N12
Reinheninch Highld....106 h4...
Reinigeadal W Isls....106 h8
Reisque Abers....105 P12
Reiss Highld....112 H6
Rejerrah Cnwll....2 K5
Releath Cnwll....2 H10
Relubbus Cnwll....2 F10
Relugas Moray....103 Q6
Remenham Wokham....20 C6
Remenham Hill Wokham....20 C6
Rempstone Notts....47 Q8
Rendcomb Gloucs....28 K6
Rendham Suff....41 P7
Rendlesham Suff....41 P9
Renfrew Rens....89 M12
Renhold Bed....38 G10
Renishaw Derbys....57 Q11
Rennington Nthumb....77 Q2
Renton W Duns....88 J10
Renwick Cumb....67 S4
Repps Norfk....51 R10
Repton Derbys....46 K8
Reraig Highld....100 h7
Rescassa Cnwll....3 P7
Rescorla Cnwll....3 Q5
Resipole Burnt Highld....93 S6
Reskadinnick Cnwll....2 G8
Resolis Highld....102 J2
Resolven Neath....26 E7
Rest and be thankful
Ag & B....88 F4
Reston Border....85 M6
Restronguet Cnwll....2 K9
Reswallie Angus....98 J13
Reterth Cnwll....3 N4
Retford Notts....57 U11
Retire Cnwll....3 Q3
Rettendon Essex....22 J8
Rettendon Village Essex....22 J8
Retyn Cnwll....3 M5
Revesby Lincs....59 M14
Rew Devon....5 S14
Rew Devon....5 T6
Rew Street IoW....9 P10
Rewe Devon....6 B5
Rexon Devon....5 L2
Reydon Suff....41 S5
Reymerston Norfk....50 H12
Reynalton Pembks....24 J9
Reynoldston Swans....25 S13
Rezare Cnwll....4 K5
Rhadyr Mons....27 R7
Rhandirmwyn Carmth....33 R12
Rheindown Highld....102 F6
Rhenigidale W Isls....106 h8
Rhes-y-cae Flints....54 E12
Rhewl Denbgs....44 D1
Rhewl Denbgs....44 E2
Rhewl Mostyn Flints....54 D10
Rhicarn Highld....110 B11
Rhiconich Highld....110 G6
Rhicullen Highld....109 N10
Rhigos Rhondd....26 G6
Rhireavach Highld....107 V6
Rhives Highld....109 Q4
Rhiwbina Cardif....27 M11

Rhiwbryfdir Gwynd....43 N4
Rhiwderyn Newpt....27 P10
Rhiwen Gwynd....52 J10
Rhiwinder Rhondd....26 J9
Rhiwlas Gwynd....43 T6
Rhiwlas Gwynd....52 J9
Rhiwlas Powys....44 D6
Rhiwsaeson Rhondd....26 K11
Rhode Somset....16 J10
Rhoden Green Kent....12 C6
Rhodesia Notts....57 S11
Rhode Minnis Kent....13 N7
Rhodiad-y-brenin Pembks....24 C5
Rhonehouse D & G....74 D14
Rhoose V Glam....16 E4
Rhos Carmth....25 Q3
Rhos Neath....26 C7
Rhosaman Carmth....25 E4
Rhosbeirio IoA....52 F4
Rhoscefnhir IoA....52 H7
Rhoscolyn IoA....52 C7
Rhoscrowther Pembks....24 F10
Rhosesmor Flints....54 F13
Rhos-fawr Gwynd....42 G6
Rhosgadfan Gwynd....52 H11
Rhosgoch IoA....52 G5
Rhosgoch Powys....34 E11
Rhos Haminiog Cerdgn....32 K8
Rhoshill Pembks....32 C12
Rhoshirwaun Gwynd....42 D8
Rhoslan Gwynd....42 K5
Rhoslefain Gwynd....43 M11
Rhosllanerchrugog
Wrexhm....44 G4
Rhôs Lligwy IoA....52 G5
Rhosmaen Carmth....26 A2
Rhosmeirch IoA....52 G7
Rhosneigr IoA....52 D7
Rhôs-on-Sea Conwy....53 P6
Rhosrobin Wrexhm....44 H3
Rhossili Swans....25 Q13
Rhostrehwfa IoA....52 G7
Rhostryfan Gwynd....52 G11
Rhostyllen Wrexhm....44 H4
Rhosybol IoA....52 G5
Rhos-y-brithdir Powys....44 E9
Rhosygadfa Shrops....44 H7
Rhos-y-gwaliau Gwynd....43 T7
Rhos-y-llan Gwynd....42 E6
Rhosymedre Wrexhm....44 G5
Rhos-y-meirch Powys....34 G7
Rhu Ag & B....88 G9
Rhuallt Denbgs....54 C11
Rhubodach Ag & B....88 B11
Rhuddall Heath Ches W....45 N1
Rhuddlan Cerdgn....32 K11
Rhuddlan Denbgs....53 T7
Rhue Highld....107 V5
Rhulen Powys....34 D11
Rhunahaorine Ag & B....79 N6
Rhyd Gwynd....43 M5
Rhydargaeau Carmth....25 R5
Rhydcymerau Carmth....33 L13
Rhydd Worcs....35 T11
Rhyd-Ddu Gwynd....52 J12
Rhydding Neath....26 C8
Rhydlanfair Conwy....53 P12
Rhydlewis Cerdgn....32 G11
Rhydlios Gwynd....42 C7
Rhydlydan Conwy....53 Q13
Rhydowen Cerdgn....32 J11
Rhydroser Cerdgn....33 L7
Rhydspence Herefs....34 F11
Rhydtalog Flints....44 F2
Rhyd-uchaf Gwynd....43 T6
Rhyd-y-clafdy Gwynd....42 F6
Rhydycroesau Shrops....44 F7
Rhydyfelin Cerdgn....33 L5
Rhyd-y-felin Rhondd....26 K10
Rhyd-y-foel Conwy....53 R7
Rhyd-y-fro Neath....26 C6
Rhydygwystl Gwynd....42 K6
Rhydymain Gwynd....43 R9
Rhyd-y-meirch Mons....27 Q6
Rhydymwyn Flints....54 E13
Rhyd-yr-onnen Gwynd....43 M13
Rhyd-y-sarn Gwynd....43 N5
Rhyl Denbgs....53 T6
Rhymney Caerph....27 L5
Rhynd P & K....90 J7
Rhynie Abers....104 F11
Ribbesford Worcs....35 S6
Ribbleton Lancs....61 U13
Ribby Lancs....61 S13
Ribchester Lancs....62 D13
Riber Derbys....46 K2
Riby Lincs....59 L5
Riccall N York....64 E12
Riccarton Border....75 V6
Riccarton E Ayrs....81 N5
Richards Castle Herefs....35 L7
Richings Park Bucks....20 H7
Richmond Gt Lon....21 L8
Richmond N York....69 Q12
Rich's Holford Somset....16 F10
Rickarton Abers....99 R6
Rickerscote Staffs....46 B9
Rickford N Som....17 N5
Rickham Devon....5 S13
Rickinghall Suff....40 H5
Rickling Essex....22 C1
Rickling Green Essex....22 D2
Rickmansworth Herts....20 H3
Riddell Border....84 E14
Riddlecombe Devon....15 P10
Riddlesden C Brad....63 L11
Ridge BaNES....17 Q5
Ridge Dorset....8 C11
Ridge Herts....31 R11
Ridge Wilts....8 C2
Ridgebourne Powys....34 C8
Ridge Green Surrey....21 P13
Ridge Lane Warwks....36 J2
Ridge Row Kent....13 P7
Ridgeway Derbys....57 P9
Ridgeway Worcs....36 D8
Ridgeway Cross Herefs....35 R11
Ridgewell Essex....40 B13
Ridgewood E Susx....11 R6
Ridgmont C Beds....31 L5
Riding Mill Nthumb....77 L13
Ridley Kent....12 B3
Ridley Nthumb....76 F13
Ridley Green Ches E....45 M3
Ridlington Norfk....51 Q7
Ridlington Rutlnd....48 B13
Ridlington Street Norfk....51 Q7
Ridsdale Nthumb....76 J9
Rievaulx N York....64 D2
Rigg D & G....75 P12
Riggend N Lans....82 D4
Righoul Highld....103 M5
Rigmadon Park Cumb....62 C3
Rigsby Lincs....59 R11
Rigside S Lans....82 G11
Riley Green Lancs....55 P1
Rileyhill Staffs....46 F11
Rilla Mill Cnwll....4 H6
Rillaton Cnwll....4 H6
Rillington N York....64 K5
Rimington Lancs....62 G11
Rimpton Somset....17 R12
Rimswell E R Yk....59 S1
Rinaston Pembks....24 G5
Ringford D & G....73 R8
Ringinglow Sheff....57 L9
Ringland Norfk....50 K11
Ringles Cross E Susx....11 R6
Ringlestone Kent....12 F4
Ringley Bolton....55 S5
Ringmer E Susx....11 Q8
Ringmore Devon....5 R11
Ringmore Devon....5 V10
Ring's End Cambs....49 N13
Ringsfield Suff....41 R4
Ringsfield Corner Suff....41 R3
Ringshall Herts....30 K10
Ringshall Suff....40 H10
Ringshall Stocks Suff....40 J10
Ringstead Nhants....38 E6
Ringstead Norfk....50 C5
Ringwood Hants....8 H7
Ringwould Kent....13 R6
Rinmore Abers....104 F13
Rinsey Cnwll....2 F11
Ripe E Susx....11 S8
Ripley Derbys....47 L3
Ripley Hants....8 H9
Ripley N York....63 R7
Ripley Surrey....20 J11
Riplingham E R Yk....65 M13
Ripon N York....63 S5
Rippingale Lincs....48 G9
Ripple Kent....13 R6
Ripple Worcs....35 U13

Ripponden Calder....56 F3
Risabus Ag & B....78 E7
Risbury Herefs....35 N10
Risby N Linc....58 G3
Risby Suff....40 B7
Risca Caerph....27 N9
Rise E R Yk....65 R11
Riseden E Susx....12 C8
Riseden Kent....12 D8
Risegate Lincs....48 K8
Riseholme Lincs....58 F11
Risehow Cumb....66 F6
Riseley Bed....38 F8
Riseley Wokham....20 B10
Rishangles Suff....41 L7
Rishton Lancs....62 E13
Rishworth Calder....56 F3
Rising Bridge Lancs....55 T2
Risley Derbys....47 M6
Risley Warrtn....55 Q8
Risplith N York....63 R6
Rivar Wilts....19 M8
Rivenhall Essex....22 K4
Rivenhall End Essex....22 K4
River Kent....13 Q7
River W Susx....10 E6
River Bank Cambs....39 R7
Rivers Corner Dorset....7 U3
Riverford Highld....102 G5
Riverhead Kent....21 T11
Rivington Lancs....55 P4
Rivington Services Lancs....55 P4
Roachill Devon....15 U8
Roade Nhants....37 U10
Roadhead Cumb....75 V11
Roadmeetings S Lans....82 F9
Roadside E Ayrs....81 R9
Roadside Highld....112 E4
Roadwater Somset....16 D9
Roag Highld....100 b5
Roa Island Cumb....61 N6
Roan of Craigoch S Ayrs....80 K11
Roast Green Essex....39 Q14
Roath Cardif....27 M12
Roberton Border....75 T3
Roberton S Lans....82 H13
Robertsbridge E Susx....12 D11
Roberttown Kirk....56 J2
Robeston Wathen Pembks....24 H7
Robgill Tower D & G....75 P11
Robin Hill Staffs....46 B2
Robin Hood Lancs....55 M4
Robin Hood Leeds....57 L1
Robinhood End Essex....40 B13
Robin Hood's Bay N York....71 S11
Roborough Devon....5 N8
Roborough Devon....15 M9
Roby Knows....54 K8
Roby Mill Lancs....55 L5
Rocester Staffs....46 F6
Roch Pembks....24 E6
Rochdale Rochdl....56 C4
Roche Cnwll....3 P4
Rochester Medway....12 D2
Rochester Nthumb....76 G6
Rochford Essex....23 L9
Rochford Worcs....35 P7
Rock Cnwll....3 N1
Rock Nthumb....77 Q1
Rock W Susx....10 K7
Rock Worcs....35 S6
Rockbeare Devon....6 D6
Rockcliffe Cumb....75 R13
Rockcliffe D & G....66 B2
Rockcliffe Cross Cumb....75 R13
Rock End Staffs....45 S4
Rockend Torbay....6 B13
Rock Ferry Wirral....54 H9
Rockfield Highld....109 S8
Rockfield Mons....27 T5
Rockford Devon....15 R3
Rockford Hants....8 H7
Rockgreen Shrops....35 M5
Rockhampton S Glos....28 C9
Rockhead Cnwll....4 C4
Rockhill Shrops....34 H5
Rockingham Nhants....38 C2
Rockland All Saints Norfk....40 G1
Rockland St Mary Norfk....51 P13
Rockland St Peter Norfk....40 G1
Rockley Notts....58 B12
Rockville Ag & B....88 F7
Rockwell End Bucks....20 C5
Rockwell Green Somset....16 F12
Rodborough Gloucs....28 F6
Rodbourne Swindn....29 M10
Rodbourne Wilts....28 H10
Rodd Herefs....34 H8
Roddam Nthumb....77 N1
Rodden Dorset....7 S8
Roddymoor Dur....69 R5
Rode Somset....18 B9
Rode Heath Ches E....45 T2
Rode Heath Ches E....56 C13
Rodel W Isls....106 f11
Roden Wrekin....45 N10
Rodhuish Somset....16 D9
Rodington Wrekin....45 N11
Rodington Heath Wrekin....45 N11
Rodley Gloucs....28 D5
Rodmarton Gloucs....28 H7
Rodmell E Susx....11 Q9
Rodmersham Kent....12 H3
Rodmersham Green Kent....12 H3
Rodney Stoke Somset....17 N6
Rodsley Derbys....46 H5
Rodway Somset....16 H9
Roe Cross Tamesd....56 E7
Roe Green Herts....31 S5
Roe Green Herts....31 R11
Roe Green Salfd....55 S6
Roehampton Gt Lon....21 M8
Roffey W Susx....10 K4
Rogart Highld....109 N4
Rogate W Susx....10 C5
Roger Ground Cumb....67 P13
Rogerstone Newpt....27 P10
Roghadal W Isls....106 f11
Rogiet Mons....27 T10
Roker Sundld....70 E1
Rollesby Norfk....51 S10
Rolleston Leics....47 U13
Rolleston Notts....47 U3
Rolleston on Dove Staffs....46 H9
Rolston E R Yk....65 T11
Rolstone N Som....17 L4
Rolvenden Kent....12 F9
Rolvenden Layne Kent....12 G9
Romaldkirk Dur....69 L8
Roman Baths & Pump
Room BaNES....17 T4
Romanby N York....70 D14
Romanno Bridge Border....83 N9
Romansleigh Devon....15 S8
Romden Castle Kent....12 H7
Romesdal Highld....100 d4
Romford Dorset....8 F7
Romford Gt Lon....22 D10
Romiley Stockp....56 D8
Romney Street Kent....21 U10
Romsey Cambs....39 Q9
Romsey Hants....9 L4
Romsley Shrops....35 S4
Romsley Worcs....36 B5
Rona Highld....100 f3
Ronachan Ag & B....79 N6
Rood Ashton Wilts....18 C9
Rookhope Dur....68 K4
Rookley IoW....9 Q12
Rookley Green IoW....9 Q12
Rooks Bridge Somset....17 L6
Rooks Nest Somset....16 E10
Rookwith N York....63 Q2
Roos E R Yk....65 T13
Roose Cumb....61 N6
Roosebeck Cumb....61 N6
Roothams Green Bed....38 G9
Ropley Hants....9 S2
Ropley Dean Hants....9 S2
Ropley Soke Hants....9 S2
Ropsley Lincs....48 E6
Rora Abers....105 S5
Rorrington Shrops....34 H13
Rosarie Moray....104 D6
Rose Cnwll....2 K5
Roseacre Kent....12 E4
Roseacre Lancs....61 S13
Rose Ash Devon....15 T8
Rosebank S Lans....82 F10
Rosebush Pembks....24 H5
Rosecare Cnwll....4 E3
Rosecliston Cnwll....3 L5
Rosedale Abbey N York....71 L13
Roseden Nthumb....85 R14
Rose Green Essex....23 M3
Rose Green Suff....40 F12
Rose Green Suff....40 G13
Rose Green W Susx....10 E11
Rosehall Highld....108 K5
Rosehearty Abers....105 R3

Rosehearty Abers....105 Q2
Rose Hill E Susx....11 Q7
Rose Hill Lancs....62 G13
Rosehill Shrops....45 L10
Rosehill Shrops....45 R7
Roseisle Moray....103 U2
Roselands E Susx....11 U10
Rosemarket Pembks....24 G9
Rosemarkie Highld....102 K4
Rosemary Lane Devon....6 G2
Rosemount P & K....90 G3
Rosenannon Cnwll....3 N3
Rosenithon Cnwll....3 L12
Roser's Cross E Susx....11 S6
Rosevean Cnwll....3 Q5
Rosevine Cnwll....3 M9
Rosewarne Cnwll....2 G9
Rosewell Mdloth....83 Q6
Roseworth S on T....70 F8
Roseworthy Cnwll....2 G9
Rosgill Cumb....67 R9
Roskestal Cnwll....2 B11
Roskhill Highld....100 b5
Roskorwell Cnwll....3 L11
Rosley Cumb....67 M3
Roslin Mdloth....83 Q6
Rosliston Derbys....46 J10
Rosneath Ag & B....88 G9
Ross D & G....73 R11
Ross Nthumb....85 S11
Rossett Wrexhm....44 J2
Rossett Green N York....63 R9
Rossie Ochill P & K....90 F8
Rossie Priory P & K....91 L4
Rossington Donc....57 T7
Ross-on-Wye Herefs....28 A3
Roster Highld....112 G9
Rostherne Ches E....55 R10
Rosthwaite Cumb....67 L9
Rothbury Nthumb....77 N5
Rotherby Leics....47 S10
Rotherfield E Susx....11 S5
Rotherfield Greys Oxon....20 B6
Rotherfield Peppard
Oxon....20 B6
Rotherham Rothm....57 P8
Rothersthorpe Nhants....37 T9
Rotherwick Hants....20 B11
Rothes Moray....104 B6
Rothesay Ag & B....88 C13
Rothiebrisbane Abers....105 L8
Rothienorman Abers....105 L8
Rothiemurchus Lodge
Highld....97 R3
Rothley Leics....47 Q11
Rothley Nthumb....77 M8
Rothmaise Abers....104 K9
Rothwell Leeds....57 M1
Rothwell Lincs....58 K6
Rothwell Nhants....38 B4
Rotsea E R Yk....65 P9
Rottal Lodge Angus....98 F10
Rottingdean Br & H....11 N10
Rottington Cumb....66 E10
Roucan D & G....74 K10
Rougham Norfk....50 E9
Rougham Suff....40 F8
Rough Close Staffs....46 B6
Rough Common Kent....13 M4
Roughlee Lancs....62 G11
Roughpark Abers....104 C13
Roughton Lincs....59 M14
Roughton Norfk....51 M6
Roughton Shrops....35 S2
Roughway Kent....12 B5
Roundbush Essex....23 L7
Round Bush Herts....31 P12
Roundbush Green Essex....22 E5
Round Green Luton....31 N8
Roundham Somset....7 M3
Roundhay Leeds....63 S12
Round Street Kent....12 C2
Roundstreet Common
W Susx....10 H5
Roundswell Devon....15 M6
Roundway Wilts....18 F8
Roundyhill Angus....98 F13
Rousay Ork....106 s16
Rousdon Devon....6 J6
Rousham Oxon....29 U3
Rous Lench Worcs....36 D10
Routenburn N Ayrs....88 E13
Routh E R Yk....65 P11
Rout's Green Bucks....20 C3
Row Cnwll....4 C6
Row Cumb....61 S2
Row Cumb....68 D6
Rowanburn D & G....75 T11
Rowardennan Stirlg....88 H6
Rowarth Derbys....56 F9
Row Ash Hants....9 Q6
Rowberrow Somset....17 N5
Rowborough IoW....9 N12
Rowde Wilts....18 E8
Rowden Devon....15 Q12
Rowen Conwy....53 N8
Rowfoot Nthumb....76 D13
Row Green Essex....22 H3
Rowhedge Essex....23 P3
Rowhook W Susx....10 J4
Rowington Warwks....36 H7
Rowland Derbys....56 K12
Rowland's Castle Hants....9 U6
Rowlands Gill Gatesd....77 P14
Rowledge Surrey....10 C2
Rowley Dur....69 N3
Rowley E R Yk....65 M12
Rowley Shrops....44 H12
Rowley Hill Kirk....56 J4
Rowley Regis Sandw....36 C3
Rowly Surrey....10 G2
Rowner Hants....9 R8
Rowney Green Worcs....36 D6
Rownhams Hants....9 M5
Rownhams Services Hants....9 M5
Rowrah Cumb....66 G10
Rowsham Bucks....30 J9
Rowsley Derbys....57 L13
Rowstock Oxon....29 T9
Rowston Lincs....48 H2
Rowthorne Derbys....57 Q14
Rowton Ches W....54 K13
Rowton Shrops....35 L1
Rowton Shrops....44 J8
Rowton Wrekin....45 Q10
Row Town Surrey....20 J10
Roxburgh Border....84 H12
Roxby N Linc....58 F3
Roxby N York....71 M9
Roxton Bed....38 J10
Roxwell Essex....22 F6
Royal Leamington Spa
Warwks....36 K7
Royal Oak Darltn....69 R8
Royal Oak Lancs....54 K5
Royal's Green Ches E....45 P4
Royal Sutton Coldfield
Birm....36 F2
Royal Tunbridge Wells
Kent....11 T3
Royal Wootton Bassett
Wilts....29 L11
Royal Yacht Britannia
C Edin....83 Q3
Roy Bridge Highld....96 B2
Roydhouse Kirk....56 K4
Roydon Essex....22 C6
Roydon Norfk....40 K4
Roydon Norfk....50 B9
Roydon Hamlet Essex....22 C6
Royston Barns....57 N4
Royston Herts....31 T4
Royton Oldham....56 D5
Rozel Jersey....7 e2
Ruabon Wrexhm....44 H4
Ruaig Ag & B....92 D10
Ruan High Lanes Cnwll....3 M8
Ruan Lanihorne Cnwll....3 M7
Ruan Major Cnwll....2 H13
Ruan Minor Cnwll....2 J13
Ruardean Gloucs....28 B4
Ruardean Hill Gloucs....28 B4
Ruardean Woodside
Gloucs....28 B4
Rubery Birm....36 C5
Rubha Ban W Isls....106 c17
Ruckcroft Cumb....67 R4
Ruckhall Herefs....35 L13
Ruckinge Kent....12 K8
Ruckland Lincs....59 P11
Ruckley Shrops....45 M13
Rudby N York....70 F11
Rudchester Nthumb....77 N12
Ruddington Notts....47 Q7
Ruddlemoor Cnwll....3 Q5
Rudford Gloucs....28 E3
Rudge Somset....18 B10
Rudgeway S Glos....28 B10
Rudgwick W Susx....10 H4
Rudhall Herefs....28 B2

Rudheath Ches W....55 Q12
Rudheath Woods Ches E....55 R12
Rudley Green Essex....23 L7
Rudloe Wilts....18 B6
Rudry Caerph....27 N10
Rudston E R Yk....65 P6
Rudyard Staffs....46 C2
Ruecastle Border....84 G13
Rufford Lancs....55 L3
Rufford Abbey Notts....57 T14
Rufforth C York....64 D9
Rug Denbgs....44 D4
Rugby Warwks....37 P5
Rugby Services Warwks....37 P5
Rugeley Staffs....46 D10
Ruigh'riabhach Highld....107 T5
Ruisigarry W Isls....106 e10
Ruishton Somset....16 J11
Ruislip Gt Lon....20 J5
Rùm Highld....100 c10
Rumbach Moray....104 D5
Rumbling Bridge P & K....90 E12
Rumburgh Suff....41 Q4
Rumby Hill Dur....69 R5
Rumford Cnwll....3 M2
Rumford Falk....82 H4
Rumney Cardif....27 N12
Rumwell Somset....16 G12
Runcorn Halton....55 M10
Runcton W Susx....10 D10
Runcton Holme Norfk....49 T12
Runfold Surrey....20 D13
Runhall Norfk....50 J12
Runham Norfk....51 S11
Runham Norfk....51 T12
Runnington Somset....16 F12
Runsell Green Essex....22 J6
Runshaw Moor Lancs....55 M3
Runswick N York....71 P9
Runtaleave Angus....98 E10
Runwell Essex....22 J9
Ruscombe Wokham....20 C7
Rush Green Essex....23 S3
Rush Green Gt Lon....22 D10
Rush Green Herts....31 R8
Rushall Herefs....35 P13
Rushall Norfk....41 L3
Rushall Wilts....18 H9
Rushall Wsall....46 D14
Rushbrooke Suff....40 E8
Rushbury Shrops....35 M2
Rushden Herts....31 T5
Rushden Nhants....38 D8
Rusher's Cross E Susx....11 U5
Rushford Devon....5 L5
Rushford Norfk....40 F4
Rushlake Green E Susx....11 U7
Rushmere Suff....41 S3
Rushmere St Andrew
Suff....41 L11
Rushmoor Surrey....10 D2
Rushock Herefs....34 H9
Rushock Worcs....35 U6
Rusholme Manch....55 T7
Rushton Ches W....55 N14
Rushton Nhants....38 B4
Rushton Shrops....45 P13
Rushton Spencer Staffs....46 C1
Rushwick Worcs....35 T10
Rushyford Dur....69 S6
Ruskie Stirlg....89 N5
Ruskington Lincs....48 G3
Rusland Cross Cumb....61 Q2
Rusper W Susx....11 L3
Ruspidge Gloucs....28 C5
Russell Green Essex....22 H5
Russell's Water Oxon....20 B5
Russ Hill Surrey....11 L2
Rusthall Kent....11 T3
Rustington W Susx....10 H10
Ruston N York....65 M3
Ruston Parva E R Yk....65 P7
Ruswarp N York....71 Q10
Rutherford Border....84 G12
Rutherglen S Lans....89 P13
Ruthernbridge Cnwll....3 Q3
Ruthin Denbgs....44 D2
Ruthrieston C Aber....99 S3
Ruthven Abers....104 H6
Ruthven Angus....91 L2
Ruthven Highld....96 K3
Ruthven Highld....103 M10
Ruthvoes Cnwll....3 N3
Ruthwaite Cumb....67 L5
Ruthwell D & G....74 K12
Ruxley Corner Gt Lon....21 S8
Ruxton Green Herefs....27 U4
Ruyton-XI-Towns Shrops....44 J9
Ryal Nthumb....77 L11
Ryall Dorset....7 M6
Ryall Worcs....35 U12
Ryarsh Kent....12 C4
Rycote Oxon....30 D11
Rydal Cumb....67 N11
Ryde IoW....9 R10
Rye E Susx....12 H11
Ryebank Shrops....45 M7
Ryecroft Gate Staffs....46 C1
Ryeford Herefs....28 A3
Rye Foreign E Susx....12 G11
Rye Harbour E Susx....12 H12
Ryehill E R Yk....59 N1
Ryeish Green Wokham....20 B9
Ryhall Rutlnd....48 F11
Ryhill Wakefd....57 N4
Ryhope Sundld....70 E2
Rylah Derbys....57 Q13
Ryland Lincs....58 H11
Rylands Notts....47 P6
Rylstone N York....62 K8
Ryme Intrinseca Dorset....7 Q2
Ryther N York....64 D12
Ryton Gatesd....77 N13
Ryton Shrops....45 S13
Ryton Warwks....37 L5
Ryton N York....64 H4
Ryton-on-Dunsmore
Warwks....37 L5

S

Sabden Lancs....62 F12
Sabine's Green Essex....22 D8
Sacombe Herts....31 T9
Sacombe Green Herts....31 T9
Sacriston Dur....69 R3
Sadberge Darltn....70 D9
Saddell Ag & B....79 P8
Saddington Leics....37 S2
Saddlebow Norfk....49 T10
Saddlescombe W Susx....11 L8
Sadgill Cumb....67 Q11
Saffron Walden Essex....39 R13
Sageston Pembks....24 J10
Saham Hills Norfk....50 F13
Saham Toney Norfk....50 E13
Saighton Ches W....54 K14
St Abbs Border....85 N5
St Agnes Border....84 H6
St Agnes Cnwll....2 J6
St Agnes Mining District
Cnwll....2 J7
St Albans Herts....31 P11
St Allen Cnwll....3 L6
St Andrew Guern....7 b2
St Andrews Fife....91 R8
St Andrews Botanic
Garden Fife....91 Q8
St Andrews Major V Glam....27 L13
St Andrews Well Dorset....7 N6
St Ann's D & G....74 J7
St Ann's Chapel Cnwll....5 L5
St Ann's Chapel Devon....5 R11
St Anthony-in-Meneage
Cnwll....2 K11
St Anthony's Hill E Susx....11 U10
St Arvans Mons....27 V8
St Asaph Denbgs....53 T8
St Athan V Glam....16 D3
St Aubin Jersey....7 c3
St Austell Cnwll....3 Q5
St Bees Cumb....66 E10
St Blazey Cnwll....3 R5
St Blazey Gate Cnwll....3 R5
St Boswells Border....84 F12
St Brelade Jersey....7 b3
St Brelade's Bay Jersey....7 b3
St Breock Cnwll....3 P2
St Breward Cnwll....4 D6
St Briavels Gloucs....27 V7
St Brides Pembks....24 D8
St Brides Major V Glam....26 F13

St Brides Netherwent
Mons....27 S10
St Brides-super-Ely
V Glam....26 K12
St Brides Wentlooge
Newpt....27 P11
St Budeaux C Plym....5 M9
Saintbury Gloucs....36 F13
St Buryan Cnwll....2 C11
St Catherine BaNES....17 U3
St Catherines Ag & B....88 D4
St Chloe Gloucs....28 F7
St Clears Carmth....25 N7
St Cleer Cnwll....4 G7
St Clement Cnwll....3 M8
St Clether Cnwll....4 G4
St Colmac Ag & B....88 B12
St Columb Major Cnwll....3 N4
St Columb Minor Cnwll....3 N4
St Columb Road Cnwll....3 N5
St Combs Abers....105 S3
St Cross South Elmham
Suff....41 N4
St Cyrus Abers....99 N10
St David's P & K....90 C7
St Davids Pembks....24 C5
St Davids Cathedral
Pembks....24 C5
St Day Cnwll....2 J8
St Decumans Somset....16 E8
St Dennis Cnwll....3 P5
St Devereux Herefs....27 S1
St Dogmaels Pembks....32 C11
St Dogwells Pembks....24 G5
St Donats V Glam....16 B3
St Edith's Marsh Wilts....18 E8
St Endellion Cnwll....4 B5
St Enoder Cnwll....3 M5
St Erme Cnwll....3 L7
St Erney Cnwll....4 K9
St Erth Cnwll....2 F9
St Erth Praze Cnwll....2 F9
St Ervan Cnwll....3 M2
St Eval Cnwll....3 M3
St Ewe Cnwll....3 P6
St Fagans Cardif....27 L12
St Fagans: National
History Museum Cardif....27 M2
St Fergus Abers....105 T5
St Fillans P & K....95 U13
St Florence Pembks....24 J10
St Gennys Cnwll....14 D13
St George Conwy....53 S7
St George's N Som....17 L4
St Georges V Glam....26 K12
St George's Hill Surrey....20 J10
St Germans Cnwll....4 J9
St Giles in the Wood
Devon....15 M9
St Giles-on-the-Heath
Devon....4 K2
St Gluvias Cnwll....2 K10
St Harmon Powys....33 U6
St Helen Auckland Dur....69 Q7
St Helens Cumb....66 F6
St Helen's E Susx....12 F13
St Helens IoW....9 S11
St Helens St Hel....55 M7
St Helier Jersey....7 d3
St Helier Gt Lon....21 N9
St Hilary Cnwll....2 E10
St Hilary V Glam....26 J13
Saint Hill Devon....6 E3
Saint Hill W Susx....11 N3
St Illtyd Blae G....27 N7
St Ippolyts Herts....31 Q7
St Ishmael's Pembks....24 D9
St Issey Cnwll....3 N2
St Ive Cnwll....4 J7
St Ives Cambs....39 M6
St Ives Cnwll....2 E8
St Ives Dorset....8 H8
St James Norfk....51 N9
St James South Elmham
Suff....41 P4
St Jidgey Cnwll....3 N3
St John Cnwll....5 L10
St John Jersey....7 e1
St Johns Dur....69 L5
St John's IoM....60 c6
St John's Kent....21 S11
St Johns Surrey....20 G11
St John's Worcs....35 T10
St John's Chapel Devon....15 M7
St John's Chapel Dur....68 K4
St John's Fen End Norfk....49 R11
St John's Highway Norfk....49 R11
St John's Kirk S Lans....82 J11
St John's Town of Dalry
D & G....73 R3
St John's Wood Gt Lon....21 N6
St Judes IoM....60 g3
St Just Cnwll....2 B10
St Just-in-Roseland
Cnwll....3 L9...

Actually this is "St Just Mining District Cnwll 2 B10"
St Katherines Abers....105 M9
St Keverne Cnwll....2 K12
St Kew Cnwll....4 B5
St Kew Highway Cnwll....4 B5
St Keyne Cnwll....4 G8
St Lawrence Cnwll....3 R4
St Lawrence Essex....23 N6
St Lawrence IoW....9 Q13
St Lawrence Jersey....7 d2
St Lawrence Kent....13 S3
St Leonards Bucks....30 K11
St Leonards Dorset....8 G8
St Leonards E Susx....12 E14
St Leonard's Street Kent....12 C4
St Levan Cnwll....2 B12
St Lythans V Glam....27 L13
St Mabyn Cnwll....4 C6
St Madoes P & K....90 J6
St Margarets Herefs....34 J13
St Margarets Herts....31 T10
St Margaret's at Cliffe
Kent....13 S7
St Margaret's Hope Ork....106 t20
St Margaret South
Elmham Suff....41 P4
St Marks IoM....60 d7
St Martin Cnwll....2 J12
St Martin Cnwll....4 H9
St Martin Guern....7 b2
St Martin Jersey....7 f1
St Martin's P & K....90 J5
St Martins Shrops....44 H6
St Mary Jersey....7 c1
St Mary Bourne Hants....19 P10
St Marychurch Torbay....6 B11
St Mary Church V Glam....16 D2
St Mary Cray Gt Lon....21 S9
St Mary Hill V Glam....26 H12
St Mary in the Marsh Kent....13 L9
St Mary's IoS....2 c2
St Mary's Ork....106 t19
St Mary's Bay Kent....13 L9
St Mary's Hoo Medway....22 K12
St Maughans Mons....27 T4
St Maughans Green Mons....27 T4
St Mawes Cnwll....3 L9
St Mawgan Cnwll....3 M3
St Mellion Cnwll....4 K7
St Mellons Cardif....27 N11
St Merryn Cnwll....3 M2
St Mewan Cnwll....3 P5
St Michael Caerhays Cnwll....3 P7
St Michael Church Somset....16 K10
St Michael Penkevil Cnwll....3 M8
St Michaels Kent....12 G8
St Michaels Worcs....35 N7
St Michael's on Wyre
Lancs....61 S11
St Michael South
Elmham Suff....41 P4
St Minver Cnwll....4 B5
St Monans Fife....91 S11
St Neot Cnwll....4 F7
St Neots Cambs....38 J9
St Newlyn East Cnwll....3 L5
St Nicholas Pembks....24 E4
St Nicholas V Glam....26 K12
St Nicholas-at-Wade Kent....13 Q2
St Ninians Stirlg....89 S7
St Olaves Norfk....51 S14
St Osyth Essex....23 R4
St Owen's Cross Herefs....27 U3
St Paul's Cray Gt Lon....21 S9
St Paul's Walden Herts....31 Q8
St Peter Jersey....7 b2
St Peter Port Guern....7 e3
St Peter's Guern....7 a2
St Peter's Kent....13 S2
St Peter's Hill Cambs....38 K6

St Petrox Pembks 24 G11
St Pinnock Cnwll 4 G8
St Quivox S Ayrs 81 M8
St Ruan Cnwll 2 J13
St Sampson Guern 6 e2
St Saviour Guern 6 c3
St Saviour Jersey 7 d3
St Stephen Cnwll 3 N6
St Stephens Cnwll 4 J3
St Stephens Cnwll 5 L9
St Teath Cnwll 4 D4
St Thomas Devon 6 B6
St Margaret's Bay Kent 13 S7
St Tudy Cnwll 3 R1
St Twynnells Pembks 24 G11
St Veep Cnwll 4 E9
St Vigeans Angus 91 T3
St Wenn Cnwll 3 P4
St Weonards Herefs 27 T3
St Winnow Cnwll 4 E9
St y-Nyll V Glam 26 K12
Salcombe Devon 5 S13
Salcombe Regis Devon 6 G7
Salcott-cum-Virley Essex 23 M5
Sale Traffd 55 S8
Saleby Lincs 59 S11
Sale Green Worcs 36 B9
Salehurst E Susx 12 E11
Salem Carmth 25 V5
Salem Cerdgn 33 N4
Salen Ag & B 93 P10
Salen Highld 93 R6
Salesbury Lancs 62 D13
Salford C Beds 30 K5
Salford Oxon 29 Q2
Salford Salfd 55 T7
Salford Priors Warwks 36 E10
Salfords Surrey 21 N13
Salhouse Norfk 51 P11
Saline Fife 90 F13
Salisbury Wilts 8 G2
Salisbury Plain Wilts 18 G12
Salkeld Dykes Cumb 67 R5
Sallachy Highld 108 J3
Salle Norfk 50 K9
Salmonby Lincs 59 P12
Salperton Gloucs 29 L3
Salph End Bed 38 G10
Salsburgh N Lans 82 F6
Salt Staffs 46 C8
Salta Cumb 66 G3
Saltaire C Brad 63 N12
Saltaire C Brad 63 N12
Saltash Cnwll 5 L9
Saltburn Highld 109 N10
Saltburn-by-the-Sea R & Cl 71 L8
Saltby Leics 48 C8
Salt Coates Cumb 66 J2
Saltcoats Cumb 66 G13
Saltcoats N Ayrs 80 J4
Saltcotes Lancs 61 R14
Saltdean Br & H 11 P10
Salterbeck Cumb 66 E7
Salterforth Lancs 62 H10
Salterswall Ches W 55 P13
Salterton Wilts 18 H13
Saltfleet Lincs 59 S8
Saltfleetby All Saints Lincs 59 S8
Saltfleetby St Clement Lincs 59 S8
Saltfleetby St Peter Lincs 59 R9
Saltford BaNES 17 S3
Salthouse Norfk 50 J5
Saltley Birm 36 F3
Saltmarsh Newpt 27 Q11
Saltmarshe E R Yk 58 C2
Saltney Flints 54 J14
Salton N York 64 G4
Saltrens Devon 15 L8
Saltwick Nthumb 77 P9
Saltwood Kent 13 N8
Salvington W Susx 10 J9
Salwarpe Worcs 35 U8
Salway Ash Dorset 7 N5
Sambourne Warwks 36 E8
Sambrook Wrekin 45 R9
Samlesbury Lancs 62 B13
Samlesbury Bottoms Lancs 62 C14
Sampford Arundel Somset 16 F13
Sampford Brett Somset 16 E8
Sampford Courtenay Devon 15 P12
Sampford Moor Somset 16 F13
Sampford Peverell Devon 6 D2
Sampford Spiney Devon 5 N6
Samsonlane Ork 106 v17
Samson's Corner Essex 23 Q4
Samuelston E Loth 84 D4
Sanaigmore Ag & B 86 C11
Sancreed Cnwll 2 C11
Sancton E R Yk 64 K12
Sand Somset 17 M7
Sandaig Highld 100 g9
Sandale Cumb 66 K4
Sandal Magna Wakefd 57 M3
Sanday Ork 106 v15
Sanday Airport Ork 106 v15
Sandbach Ches E 45 S1
Sandbach Services Ches E 45 S1
Sandbank Ag & B 88 E9
Sandbanks BCP 8 E11
Sandend Abers 104 H2
Sanderstead Gt Lon 21 P10
Sandford Cumb 68 F9
Sandford Devon 15 T12
Sandford Dorset 8 C11
Sandford Hants 8 H8
Sandford IoW 9 Q12
Sandford N Som 17 M5
Sandford S Lans 82 D10
Sandford Shrops 44 H9
Sandford Shrops 45 N7
Sandford-on-Thames Oxon 30 B12
Sandford Orcas Dorset 17 R12
Sandford St Martin Oxon 29 T2
Sandgate Kent 13 P8
Sandhaven Abers 105 R2
Sandhead D & G 72 D10
Sandhill Rothm 57 P7
Sandhills Dorset 7 Q4
Sandhills Dorset 7 S2
Sand Hills Leeds 63 T12
Sandhills Oxon 30 C11
Sandhills Surrey 10 E3
Sandhoe Nthumb 76 K12
Sandhole Ag & B 87 U6
Sand Hole E R Yk 64 J12
Sandholme E R Yk 64 J13
Sandholme Lincs 49 M6
Sandhurst Br For 20 D10
Sandhurst Gloucs 28 F3
Sandhurst Kent 12 F10
Sandhurst Cross Kent 12 E10
Sandhutton N York 63 T3
Sand Hutton N York 64 F8
Sandiacre Derbys 47 N6
Sandilands Lincs 59 T10
Sandiway Ches W 55 P12
Sandleheath Hants 8 G5
Sandleigh Oxon 29 U7
Sandley Dorset 17 U12
Sandling Kent 12 E4
Sandlow Green Ches E 55 S13
Sandness Shet 106 r8
Sandon Essex 22 H7
Sandon Herts 31 T6
Sandon Staffs 46 B8
Sandon Bank Staffs 46 B8
Sandown IoW 9 R12
Sandplace Cnwll 4 H9
Sandridge Herts 31 Q10
Sandridge Wilts 18 D7
Sandringham Norfk 49 U8
Sands Bucks 20 D4
Sandsend N York 71 Q10
Sand Side Cumb 61 N3
Sandside Cumb 61 T3
Sandtoft N Linc 58 B5
Sandway Kent 12 G5
Sandwich Kent 13 R4
Sandwich Bay Kent 13 S4
Sandwick Cumb 67 P9
Sandwick Shet 106 u11
Sandwick W Isls 106 j5
Sandwith Cumb 66 E10
Sandwith Newtown Cumb 66 E10
Sandy C Beds 38 J11
Sandy Bank Lincs 49 L2
Sandycroft Flints 54 H13
Sandy Cross E Susx 11 T6
Sandy Cross Herefs 35 Q9
Sandyford D & G 75 P7
Sandygate Devon 5 V6
Sandygate IoM 60 f3
Sandy Haven Pembks 24 E9
Sandyhills D & G 66 C1
Sandylands Lancs 61 S7
Sandy Lane C Brad 63 N12
Sandylane Staffs 45 R6
Sandylane Swans 25 U13
Sandy Lane Wilts 18 E7
Sandy Lane Wrexhm 44 K5
Sandy Park Devon 5 S3
Sandysike Cumb 75 S12
Sandyway Herefs 27 T2
Sangobeg Highld 110 J3
Sangomore Highld 110 J3
Sankey Bridges Warrtn 55 N9
Sankyn's Green Worcs 35 S7
Sanna Highld 93 L5
Sanndabhaig W Isls 106 j5
Sannox N Ayrs 80 E3
Sanquhar D & G 74 E4
Santon Cumb 66 H12
Santon IoM 60 e8
Santon Bridge Cumb 66 H12
Santon Downham Suffk 40 D3
Sapcote Leics 37 N2
Sapey Common Herefs 35 R8
Sapiston Suffk 40 F5
Sapley Cambs 38 K6
Sapperton Derbys 46 G7
Sapperton Gloucs 28 H7
Sapperton Lincs 48 F7
Saracen's Head Lincs 49 M8
Sarclet Highld 112 H8
Sarisbury Hants 9 Q7
Sarn Brdgnd 26 G11
Sarn Powys 34 F2
Sarnau Carmth 25 P7
Sarnau Cerdgn 32 F10
Sarnau Gwynd 43 U6
Sarnau Powys 34 B14
Sarnau Powys 44 F10
Sarn Bach Gwynd 42 F8
Sarnesfield Herefs 34 J10
Sarn Mellteyrn Gwynd 42 D7
Sarn Park Services Brdgnd 26 G11
Sarn-wen Powys 44 G10
Saron Carmth 25 Q3
Saron Carmth 25 V8
Saron Gwynd 52 G11
Saron Gwynd 52 H9
Sarratt Herts 20 H3
Sarre Kent 13 Q2
Sarsden Oxon 29 Q3
Sarson Hants 19 M12
Satley Dur 69 P4
Satmar Kent 13 Q8
Satron N York 68 K13
Satterleigh Devon 15 Q8
Satterthwaite Cumb 61 Q1
Satwell Oxon 20 B6
Sauchen Abers 105 L13
Saucher P & K 90 J5
Sauchieburn Abers 99 M10
Saul Gloucs 28 D6
Saundby Notts 58 C9
Saundersfoot Pembks 24 K10
Saunderton Bucks 30 G12
Saunderton Station Bucks 20 D3
Saunton Devon 15 L5
Sausthorpe Lincs 59 Q13
Saverley Green Staffs 46 C6
Savile Town Kirk 56 K2
Sawbridge Warwks 37 P7
Sawbridgeworth Herts 22 C5
Sawdon N York 65 L3
Sawley Derbys 47 N7
Sawley Lancs 62 F10
Sawley N York 63 Q6
Sawston Cambs 39 Q11
Sawtry Cambs 38 J4
Saxby Leics 48 B10
Saxby Lincs 58 H9
Saxby All Saints N Linc 58 G3
Saxelbye Leics 47 S9
Saxham Street Suffk 40 J8
Saxilby Lincs 58 E11
Saxlingham Norfk 50 H6
Saxlingham Green Norfk 41 M1
Saxlingham Nethergate Norfk 41 M1
Saxlingham Thorpe Norfk 41 M1
Saxmundham Suffk 41 Q8
Saxondale Notts 47 S6
Saxon Street Cambs 39 U9
Saxtead Suffk 41 N7
Saxtead Green Suffk 41 N8
Saxtead Little Green Suffk 41 M7
Saxthorpe Norfk 50 K7
Saxton N York 64 B12
Sayers Common W Susx 11 M7
Scackleton N York 64 E5
Scadabay W Isls 106 g9
Scadabhagh W Isls 106 g9
Scafell Pike Cumb 66 K11
Scaftworth Notts 57 U8
Scagglethorpe N York 64 J5
Scalasaig Ag & B 86 F7
Scalby E R Yk 64 J14
Scalby N York 65 N1
Scald End Bed 38 F9
Scaldwell Nhants 37 U6
Scaleby Cumb 75 T13
Scalebyhill Cumb 75 T13
Scale Houses Cumb 67 S3
Scales Cumb 61 P5
Scales Cumb 67 M7
Scalesceugh Cumb 67 P3
Scalford Leics 47 U9
Scaling N York 71 M10
Scaling Dam R & Cl 71 M10
Scalloway Shet 106 u10
Scalpay Highld 100 f6
Scalpay W Isls 106 h9
Scamblesby Lincs 59 N11
Scammonden Kirk 56 G3
Scamodale Highld 93 U4
Scampston N York 64 K4
Scampton Lincs 58 G11
Scaniport Highld 102 H8
Scapegoat Hill Kirk 56 G3
Scarba Ag & B 87 M5
Scarborough N York 65 N2
Scarcewater Cnwll 3 N6
Scarcliffe Derbys 57 Q13
Scarcroft Leeds 63 T11
Scarfskerry Highld 112 G2
Scargill Dur 69 N10
Scarinish Ag & B 92 C10
Scarisbrick Lancs 54 J4
Scarness Cumb 66 K6
Scarning Norfk 50 G11
Scarrington Notts 47 T5
Scarth Hill Lancs 54 K5
Scarthingwell N York 64 B12
Scartho NE Lin 59 N5
Scatsta Airport Shet 106 t6
Scaur D & G 66 B2
Scawby N Linc 58 G5
Scawsby Donc 57 R6
Scawthorpe Donc 57 S5
Scawton N York 64 C3
Scayne's Hill W Susx 11 P6
Scethrog Powys 27 L2
Scholar Green Ches E 45 T2
Scholes Kirk 56 J1
Scholes Kirk 56 J5
Scholes Leeds 63 T12
Scholes Rothm 57 N7
Scholes Wigan 55 N5
School Aycliffe Dur 69 S8
School Green C Brad 63 N13
School Green Ches W 55 P14
Schoolgreen Wokham 20 B9
School House Dorset 7 L4
Scissett Kirk 56 K4
Scleddau Pembks 24 F4
Scofton Notts 57 T10
Scole Norfk 41 L5
Scone P & K 90 H6
Sconser Highld 100 e6
Scoonie Fife 91 N11
Scopwick Lincs 48 G2
Scoraig Highld 107 T5
Scorborough E R Yk 65 N10
Scorrier Cnwll 2 J8
Scorriton Devon 5 S7
Scorton Lancs 61 U10
Scorton N York 69 S12
Sco Ruston Norfk 51 N9
Scotby Cumb 67 P1
Scotch Corner N York 69 R11
Scotch Corner Rest Area N York 69 R11
Scotforth Lancs 61 T8
Scot Hay Staffs 45 S4
Scothern Lincs 58 H11
Scotland Lincs 48 F7
Scotland Gate Nthumb 77 R9
Scotlandwell P & K 90 J11
Scot Lane End Bolton 55 P5
Scotscalder Station Highld 112 C5
Scotsdike Cumb 75 S11
Scot's Gap Nthumb 77 L8
Scotsmill Abers 104 H12
Scotstoun C Glas 89 M12
Scotswood N u Ty 77 Q13
Scotter Lincs 58 E6
Scotterthorpe Lincs 58 E6
Scottish Seabird Centre E Loth 84 F1
Scottlethorpe Lincs 48 G9
Scotton Lincs 58 E7
Scotton N York 63 S8
Scotton N York 69 Q13
Scottow Norfk 51 N9
Scott Willoughby Lincs 48 G6
Scoulton Norfk 50 G13
Scounslow Green Staffs 46 E8
Scourie Highld 110 D8
Scourie More Highld 110 C8
Scousburgh Shet 106 t12
Scouthead Oldham 56 E5
Scrabster Highld 112 D2
Scraesburgh Border 76 D2
Scrafield Lincs 59 P13
Scrainwood Nthumb 76 K4
Scrane End Lincs 49 N5
Scraptoft Leics 47 R12
Scratby Norfk 51 T10
Scrayingham N York 64 G8
Scrays E Susx 12 E12
Scredington Lincs 48 G5
Scremby Lincs 59 R13
Scremerston Nthumb 85 Q9
Screveton Notts 47 T5
Scrivelsby Lincs 59 N13
Scriven N York 63 S8
Scrooby Notts 57 U8
Scropton Derbys 46 G7
Scrub Hill Lincs 48 K2
Scruton N York 63 R1
Scuggate Cumb 75 T11
Scullomie Highld 111 N4
Sculthorpe Norfk 50 E7
Scunthorpe N Linc 58 E4
Scurlage Swans 25 S13
Sea Somset 6 K2
Seaborough Dorset 7 M3
Seabridge Staffs 45 T5
Seabrook Kent 13 N8
Seaburn Sundld 77 U14
Seacombe Wirral 54 H8
Seacroft Leeds 63 T12
Seacroft Lincs 49 S1
Seadyke Lincs 49 M6
Seafield W Loth 82 K5
Seaford E Susx 11 R11
Seaforth Sefton 54 H7
Seagrave Leics 47 R10
Seagry Heath Wilts 18 E4
Seaham Dur 70 F3
Seahouses Nthumb 85 U12
Seal Kent 21 U11
Sealand Flints 54 J13
Seale Surrey 20 E13
Seamer N York 65 N3
Seamer N York 70 G10
Seamill N Ayrs 80 J3
Sea Palling Norfk 51 R8
Searby Lincs 58 J5
Seasalter Kent 13 L3
Seascale Cumb 66 F12
Seathwaite Cumb 66 K10
Seathwaite Cumb 66 K13
Seatle Cumb 61 R3
Seatoller Cumb 66 K10
Seaton Cnwll 4 J10
Seaton Cumb 66 F6
Seaton Devon 6 H6
Seaton Dur 70 E3
Seaton E R Yk 65 R10
Seaton Kent 13 P4
Seaton Nthumb 77 S10
Seaton Rutlnd 48 D14
Seaton Burn N Tyne 77 Q11
Seaton Carew Hartpl 70 H7
Seaton Delaval Nthumb 77 S10
Seaton Ross E R Yk 64 H11
Seaton Sluice Nthumb 77 S10
Seatown Dorset 7 M6
Seatown Moray 104 A1
Seave Green N York 70 J12
Seaview IoW 9 S10
Seaville Cumb 66 J2
Seavington St Mary Somset 7 M2
Seavington St Michael Somset 17 M13
Sebastopol Torfn 27 P8
Sebergham Cumb 67 N4
Seckington Warwks 46 J12
Second Severn Crossing Mons 27 U10
Sedbergh Cumb 62 D1
Sedbury Gloucs 27 U9
Sedbusk N York 62 H1
Sedgeberrow Worcs 36 D13
Sedgebrook Lincs 48 C6
Sedge Fen Suffk 39 U4
Sedgefield Dur 70 E7
Sedgeford Norfk 50 B6
Sedgehill Wilts 8 B3
Sedgemoor Services Somset 17 L6
Sedgley Dudley 36 B2
Sedgley Park Bury 55 T6
Sedgwick Cumb 61 U2
Sedlescombe E Susx 12 E12
Sedrup Bucks 30 H10
Seed Kent 12 H4
Seend Wilts 18 D8
Seend Cleeve Wilts 18 D8
Seer Green Bucks 20 G4
Seething Norfk 41 P1
Sefton Sefton 54 J6
Seghill Nthumb 77 R11
Seighford Staffs 45 U8
Seion Gwynd 52 H9
Seisdon Staffs 35 T1
Selattyn Shrops 44 G7
Selborne Hants 9 U2
Selby N York 64 E13
Selham W Susx 10 E6
Selhurst Gt Lon 21 P9
Selkirk Border 84 D13
Sellack Herefs 27 V2
Sellafield Station Cumb 66 F12
Sellafirth Shet 106 v4
Sellan Cnwll 2 C10
Sellick's Green Somset 16 H13
Sellindge Kent 13 L8
Selling Kent 12 K4
Sells Green Wilts 18 D8
Selly Oak Birm 36 D4
Selmeston E Susx 11 S9
Selsdon Gt Lon 21 Q10
Selsey W Susx 10 D12
Selsfield Common W Susx 11 N4
Selside Cumb 67 R13
Selside N York 62 F4
Selsley Gloucs 28 F7
Selsted Kent 13 P7
Selston Notts 47 N3
Selworthy Somset 16 B7
Semer Suffk 40 G11
Semington Wilts 18 C8
Semley Wilts 8 B3
Sempringham Lincs 48 H7
Send Surrey 20 H11
Send Marsh Surrey 20 H11
Senghenydd Caerph 27 L9
Sennen Cnwll 2 B11
Sennen Cove Cnwll 2 B11
Sennybridge Powys 26 G2
Serlby Notts 57 T9
Sessay N York 64 B4
Setchey Norfk 49 T11
Setley Hants 9 L8
Seton Mains E Loth 84 C3
Settle N York 62 G7
Settrington N York 64 J5
Seven Ash Somset 16 G10
Sevenhampton Gloucs 28 K3
Sevenhampton Swindn 29 P9
Seven Kings Gt Lon 21 S5
Sevenoaks Kent 21 T11
Sevenoaks Weald Kent 21 T12
Seven Sisters Neath 26 E6
Seven Springs Gloucs 28 J4
Seven Star Green Essex 23 M2
Severn Beach S Glos 27 U11
Severn Bridge S Glos 27 V9
Severn Stoke Worcs 35 U12
Severn View Services S Glos 27 V10
Sevick End Bed 38 G10
Sevington Kent 12 K7
Sewards End Essex 39 S13
Sewardstonebury Essex 21 Q3
Sewell C Beds 31 L8
Sewerby E R Yk 65 R6
Seworgan Cnwll 2 J10
Sewstern Leics 48 C9
Sexhow N York 70 G11
Sgalpaigh W Isls 106 h9
Sgiogarstaigh W Isls 106 k2
Shabbington Bucks 30 E11
Shackerley Shrops 45 T12
Shackerstone Leics 47 L12
Shacklecross Derbys 47 M7
Shackleford Surrey 20 F13
Shade Calder 56 D2
Shader W Isls 106 i3
Shadforth Dur 70 D4
Shadingfield Suffk 41 R4
Shadoxhurst Kent 12 J8
Shadwell Leeds 63 S12
Shadwell Norfk 40 F4
Shaftenhoe End Herts 39 P13
Shaftesbury Dorset 8 B4
Shaftholme Donc 57 S5
Shafton Barns 57 N4
Shafton Two Gates Barns 57 N4
Shakerley Wigan 55 Q6
Shalbourne Wilts 19 M8
Shalcombe IoW 9 M11
Shalden Hants 19 U12
Shalden Green Hants 19 V12
Shaldon Devon 6 B10
Shalfleet IoW 9 N11
Shalford Essex 22 H2
Shalford Surrey 20 H13
Shalford Green Essex 22 H2
Shallowford Staffs 45 U8
Shalmsford Street Kent 13 L5
Shalstone Bucks 30 D5
Shamley Green Surrey 10 G2
Shandford Angus 98 H11
Shandon Ag & B 88 G8
Shandwick Highld 109 R9
Shangton Leics 37 T1
Shankhouse Nthumb 77 R10
Shanklin IoW 9 R12
Shantron Ag & B 88 H8
Shap Cumb 67 S9
Shapinsay Ork 106 u18
Shapwick Dorset 8 C8
Shapwick Somset 17 M9
Shard End Birm 36 G3
Shardlow Derbys 47 M7
Shareshill Staffs 46 B12
Sharlston Wakefd 57 N3
Sharlston Common Wakefd 57 N3
Sharmans Cross Solhll 36 F5
Sharnal Street Medway 22 J13
Sharnbrook Bed 38 E9
Sharneyford Lancs 56 C2
Sharnford Leics 37 N2
Sharnhill Green Dorset 7 T3
Sharoe Green Lancs 61 U13
Sharow N York 63 S5
Sharpenhoe C Beds 31 N6
Sharperton Nthumb 76 K5
Sharp Green Norfk 51 Q9
Sharpness Gloucs 28 C7
Sharpthorne W Susx 11 P4
Sharptor Cnwll 4 H6
Sharpway Gate Worcs 36 C7
Sharrington Norfk 50 H6
Shatterford Worcs 35 S4
Shatterling Kent 13 Q4
Shatton Derbys 56 K10
Shaugh Prior Devon 5 N8
Shave Cross Dorset 7 M5
Shavington Ches E 45 Q3
Shaw C Brad 63 L12
Shaw Oldham 56 D5
Shaw Swindn 29 M10
Shaw W Berk 19 Q7
Shaw Wilts 18 C7
Shawbirch Wrekin 45 P11
Shawbost W Isls 106 h4
Shawbury Shrops 45 N9
Shawclough Rochdl 56 C4
Shaw Common Gloucs 28 C2
Shawdon Hill Nthumb 77 M3
Shawell Leics 37 P4
Shawford Hants 9 P3
Shawforth Lancs 56 C2
Shaw Green Herts 31 T6
Shaw Green Lancs 55 M3
Shaw Green N York 63 R9
Shawhead D & G 74 G10
Shaw Mills N York 63 R7
Shawsburn S Lans 82 E8
Shear Cross Wilts 18 C12
Shearington D & G 74 K12
Shearsby Leics 37 R2
Shearston Somset 16 J10
Shebbear Devon 14 K11
Shebdon Staffs 45 S8
Shebster Highld 112 B4
Shedfield Hants 9 R6
Sheen Staffs 46 F1
Sheepbridge Derbys 57 N12
Sheep Hill Dur 69 Q1
Sheepridge Kirk 56 J3
Sheepscar Leeds 63 S13
Sheepscombe Gloucs 28 G5
Sheepstor Devon 5 P7
Sheepwash Devon 15 L11
Sheepwash Nthumb 77 R8
Sheepway N Som 27 T12
Sheepy Magna Leics 46 K13
Sheepy Parva Leics 46 K13
Sheering Essex 22 D5
Sheerness Kent 23 M13
Sheerwater Surrey 20 H10
Sheet Hants 10 B6
Sheffield Cnwll 2 D11
Sheffield Sheff 57 N9
Sheffield Bottom W Berk 19 T7
Sheffield Green E Susx 11 Q5
Sheffield Park E Susx 11 Q6
Shefford C Beds 31 P5
Shefford Woodlands W Berk 19 N6
Sheigra Highld 110 D4
Sheinton Shrops 45 P13
Shelderton Shrops 34 K5
Sheldon Birm 36 G4
Sheldon Derbys 56 J13
Sheldon Devon 6 F3
Sheldwich Kent 12 K4
Sheldwich Lees Kent 12 K4
Shelf Calder 63 N14
Shelfanger Norfk 40 K4
Shelfield Warwks 36 F8
Shelfield Wsall 46 D13
Shelfield Green Warwks 36 F8
Shelford Notts 47 S5
Shelford Warwks 37 M3
Shellacres Nthumb 85 M10
Shelley Essex 22 E6
Shelley Kirk 56 K4
Shelley Suffk 40 H13
Shelley Far Bank Kirk 56 K4
Shellingford Oxon 29 R9
Shellow Bowells Essex 22 F6
Shelsley Beauchamp Worcs 35 R8
Shelsley Walsh Worcs 35 R8
Shelton Bed 38 F7
Shelton Norfk 41 M2
Shelton Notts 47 U5
Shelton Shrops 45 L11
Shelton Green Norfk 41 M2
Shelton Lock C Derb 47 L7
Shelton Under Harley Staffs 45 T6
Shelve Shrops 44 H14
Shelwick Herefs 35 M12
Shenfield Essex 22 F8
Shenington Oxon 37 L12
Shenley Herts 31 Q12
Shenley Brook End M Keyn 30 H5
Shenleybury Herts 31 Q12
Shenley Church End M Keyn 30 H5
Shenmore Herefs 34 J13
Shennanton D & G 72 J7
Shenstone Staffs 46 F13
Shenstone Worcs 35 U6
Shenstone Woodend Staffs 46 F13
Shenton Leics 47 L14
Shenval Moray 103 V10
Shepeau Stow Lincs 49 M11
Shephall Herts 31 S8
Shepherd's Bush Gt Lon 21 M6
Shepherd's Green Oxon 20 B6
Shepherds Patch Gloucs 28 D7
Shepherdswell Kent 13 Q6
Shepley Kirk 56 J5
Shepperdine S Glos 28 B8
Shepperton Surrey 20 J9
Shepperton Green Surrey 20 J9
Shepreth Cambs 39 N11
Shepshed Leics 47 N10
Shepton Beauchamp Somset 17 M13
Shepton Mallet Somset 17 R8
Shepton Montague Somset 17 S10
Shepway Kent 12 E5
Sheraton Dur 70 F5
Sherborne Dorset 17 R13
Sherborne Gloucs 29 N5
Sherborne Somset 17 Q5
Sherborne St John Hants 19 T9
Sherbourne Warwks 36 J8
Sherburn Dur 70 D4
Sherburn N York 65 M4
Sherburn Hill Dur 70 D4
Sherburn in Elmet N York 64 B13
Shere Surrey 20 J13
Shereford Norfk 50 E8
Sherfield English Hants 8 K4
Sherfield on Loddon Hants 19 U9
Sherfin Lancs 55 S1
Sherford Devon 5 N10
Sherford Devon 5 T12
Sherford Dorset 8 C10
Sheriffhales Shrops 45 S11
Sheriff Hutton N York 64 F6
Sheringham Norfk 51 L5
Sherington M Keyn 38 C11
Shermanbury W Susx 11 L7
Shernborne Norfk 50 B7
Sherrington Wilts 18 E13
Sherston Wilts 28 G10
Sherwood C Nott 47 Q5
Sherwood Forest Notts 47 R1
Shetland Islands Shet 106 u8
Shettleston C Glas 89 P13
Shevington Wigan 55 M5
Shevington Moor Wigan 55 M4
Shevington Vale Wigan 55 M5
Sheviock Cnwll 4 K9
Shibden Head C Brad 63 M14
Shide IoW 9 Q11
Shidlaw Nthumb 85 L11
Shiel Bridge Highld 101 N8
Shieldaig Highld 107 P14
Shieldhill D & G 74 K8
Shieldhill Falk 82 G3
Shieldhill House Hotel S Lans 82 K10
Shields N Lans 82 E7
Shielfoot Highld 93 R4
Shielhill Angus 98 G12
Shielhill Inver 88 F11
Shifford Oxon 29 S7
Shifnal Shrops 45 R12
Shilbottle Nthumb 77 P4
Shildon Dur 69 R7
Shillford E Rens 81 P1
Shillingford Devon 16 C12
Shillingford Oxon 19 S2
Shillingford Abbot Devon 6 B7
Shillingford St George Devon 6 B7
Shillingstone Dorset 8 A6
Shillington C Beds 31 P6
Shillmoor Nthumb 76 H4
Shilton Oxon 29 Q6
Shilton Warwks 37 M4
Shimpling Norfk 41 L4
Shimpling Suffk 40 E10
Shimpling Street Suffk 40 E10
Shincliffe Dur 69 S4
Shiney Row Sundld 70 D2
Shinfield Wokham 20 B9
Shingay Cambs 39 M11
Shingle Street Suffk 41 Q12
Shinnersbridge Devon 5 T8
Shinness Highld 108 J2
Shipbourne Kent 21 U12
Shipdham Norfk 50 G12
Shipham Somset 17 M5
Shiphay Torbay 6 A11
Shiplake Oxon 20 C7
Shiplake Row Oxon 20 B7
Shiplate N Som 17 L5
Shipley C Brad 63 P12
Shipley Derbys 47 M5
Shipley Shrops 35 T1
Shipley W Susx 10 J6
Shipley Bridge Surrey 11 N2
Shipley Hatch Kent 12 K8
Shipmeadow Suffk 41 Q2
Shippea Hill Station Cambs 39 T4
Shippon Oxon 29 U8
Shipston-on-Stour Warwks 36 J12
Shipton Bucks 30 G7
Shipton Gloucs 28 K4
Shipton N York 64 D8
Shipton Shrops 35 N2
Shipton Bellinger Hants 18 K11
Shipton Gorge Dorset 7 N6
Shipton Green W Susx 10 C11
Shipton Moyne Gloucs 28 G10
Shipton-on-Cherwell Oxon 29 U4
Shiptonthorpe E R Yk 64 K11
Shipton-under-Wychwood Oxon 29 Q4
Shirburn Oxon 30 E13
Shirdley Hill Lancs 54 J4
Shire Cumb 68 D5
Shirebrook Derbys 57 R13
Shiregreen Sheff 57 N8
Shirehampton Bristl 27 U12
Shiremoor N Tyne 77 S11
Shirenewton Mons 27 T9
Shire Oak Wsall 46 E13
Shireoaks Notts 57 S10
Shirkoak Kent 12 H8
Shirland Derbys 47 M2
Shirlett Shrops 45 P14
Shirley C Sotn 9 N6
Shirley Derbys 46 H5
Shirley Gt Lon 21 Q9
Shirley Solhll 36 F5
Shirl Heath Herefs 34 K9
Shirrell Heath Hants 9 R6
Shirwell Devon 15 P5
Shiskine N Ayrs 79 S10
Shittlehope Dur 69 M5
Shobdon Herefs 34 K8
Shobley Hants 8 H7
Shobrooke Devon 15 U12
Shoby Leics 47 S9
Shocklach Ches W 44 K4
Shocklach Green Ches W 44 K4
Shoeburyness Sthend 23 M10
Sholden Kent 13 S5
Sholing C Sotn 9 P6
Shoot Hill Shrops 44 K11
Shop Cnwll 3 M2
Shop Cnwll 14 F10
Shopwyke W Susx 10 D9
Shore Rochdl 56 D3
Shoreditch Gt Lon 21 P6
Shoreditch Somset 16 H12
Shoreham Kent 21 T10
Shoreham-by-Sea W Susx 11 L9
Shoreswood Nthumb 85 N9
Shorley Hants 9 R3
Shorncote Gloucs 28 K8
Shorne Kent 22 G13
Shortacross Cnwll 4 H9
Shortbridge E Susx 11 R6
Shortfield Common Surrey 10 C2
Shortgate E Susx 11 R7
Short Heath Birm 36 E2
Shortheath Hants 10 B3
Short Heath Wsall 46 C13
Shortlanesend Cnwll 3 L7
Shortlees E Ayrs 81 N5
Shortstown Bed 38 G11
Shorwell IoW 9 P12
Shoscombe BaNES 17 T5
Shotesham Norfk 51 M14
Shotgate Essex 22 J9
Shotley Suffk 41 M13
Shotley Bridge Dur 69 N2
Shotleyfield Nthumb 69 N2
Shotley Gate Suffk 41 M14
Shottenden Kent 12 K5
Shottermill Surrey 10 D4
Shottery Warwks 36 G10
Shotteswell Warwks 37 M11
Shottisham Suffk 41 P12
Shottle Derbys 46 K4
Shottlegate Derbys 46 K4
Shotton Dur 70 E7
Shotton Dur 70 F5
Shotton Flints 54 H13
Shotton Nthumb 77 Q10
Shotton Nthumb 85 L12
Shotton Colliery Dur 70 E4
Shotts N Lans 82 G7
Shotwick Ches W 54 H12
Shougle Moray 103 V4
Shouldham Norfk 49 U12
Shouldham Thorpe Norfk 49 U12
Shoulton Worcs 35 T9
Shover's Green E Susx 12 C9
Shraleybrook Staffs 45 S4
Shrawardine Shrops 44 J10
Shrawley Worcs 35 T7
Shreding Green Bucks 20 H6
Shrewley Warwks 36 H7
Shrewsbury Shrops 45 L11
Shrewton Wilts 18 G12
Shripney W Susx 10 E10
Shrivenham Oxon 29 P10
Shropham Norfk 40 G2
Shroton Dorset 8 B6
Shrub End Essex 23 N3
Shucknall Herefs 35 N12
Shudy Camps Cambs 39 T12
Shuna Ag & B 87 P4
Shurdington Gloucs 28 H4
Shurlock Row W & M 20 D8
Shurnock Worcs 36 D8
Shurrery Highld 112 B5
Shurrery Lodge Highld 112 B5
Shurton Somset 16 H8
Shustoke Warwks 36 H2
Shute Devon 6 J5
Shute Devon 15 U12
Shutford Oxon 37 L12
Shut Heath Staffs 45 U9
Shuthonger Gloucs 35 U13
Shutlanger Nhants 37 T11
Shutterton Devon 6 C9
Shutt Green Staffs 45 U12
Shuttington Warwks 46 J12
Shuttlewood Derbys 57 Q12
Shuttleworth Bury 55 T3
Siabost W Isls 106 h4
Siadar W Isls 106 i3
Sibbertoft Nhants 37 S4
Sibdon Carwood Shrops 34 K4
Sibford Ferris Oxon 37 L13
Sibford Gower Oxon 37 L13
Sible Hedingham Essex 40 C14
Sibley's Green Essex 22 F2
Siblyback Cnwll 4 G6
Sibsey Lincs 49 N3
Sibsey Fenside Lincs 49 M3
Sibson Cambs 38 G1
Sibson Leics 47 L13
Sibster Highld 112 H6
Sibthorpe Notts 47 U4
Sibthorpe Notts 58 B12
Sibton Suffk 41 Q7
Sicklesmere Suffk 40 E8
Sicklinghall N York 63 T10
Sidbrook Somset 16 J11
Sidbury Devon 6 F6
Sidbury Shrops 35 Q3
Sid Cop Barns 57 N5
Sidcot N Som 17 M5
Sidcup Gt Lon 21 S8
Siddick Cumb 66 F6
Siddington Ches E 55 T12
Siddington Gloucs 28 K8
Sidemoor Worcs 36 C6
Sidestrand Norfk 51 N6
Sidford Devon 6 F6
Sidlesham W Susx 10 D11
Sidlesham Common W Susx 10 D11
Sidley E Susx 12 D14
Sidmouth Devon 6 F7
Siefton Shrops 35 L4
Sigford Devon 5 T6
Sigglesthorne E R Yk 65 R10
Sigingstone V Glam 16 C2
Signet Oxon 29 P5
Silchester Hants 19 T8
Sileby Leics 47 R10
Silecroft Cumb 61 L3
Silfield Norfk 50 K14
Silian Cerdgn 33 L10
Silkstead Hants 9 N4
Silkstone Barns 57 L5
Silkstone Common Barns 57 L6
Silk Willoughby Lincs 48 G5
Silloth Cumb 66 H2
Silpho N York 65 M1
Silsden C Brad 63 L10
Silsoe C Beds 31 N5
Silton Dorset 17 U11
Silverburn Mdloth 83 P6
Silverdale Lancs 61 T5
Silverdale Staffs 45 T4
Silver End Essex 22 K4
Silverford Abers 105 M3
Silvergate Norfk 51 L8
Silver Jubilee Bridge Halton 55 M10
Silverlace Green Suffk 41 P8
Silverley's Green Suffk 41 N5
Silverstone Nhants 30 E4
Silver Street Kent 12 G3
Silver Street Somset 17 P10
Silverton Devon 6 C4
Silverwell Cnwll 2 J7
Silvington Shrops 35 P5
Simister Bury 55 T5
Simmondley Derbys 56 F8
Simonburn Nthumb 76 H11
Simonsbath Somset 15 S5
Simonsburrow Devon 16 F13
Simonstone Lancs 62 F13
Simonstone N York 62 H1
Simprim Border 85 L9
Simpson M Keyn 30 J5
Simpson Cross Pembks 24 E7
Sinclair's Hill Border 85 L8
Sinclairston E Ayrs 81 P9
Sinderby N York 63 S3
Sinderhope Nthumb 68 H2
Sinderland Green Traffd 55 R9
Sindlesham Wokham 20 C9
Sinfin C Derb 46 K7
Singleborough Bucks 30 G6
Single Street Gt Lon 21 R11
Singleton Kent 12 K7
Singleton Lancs 61 R12
Singleton W Susx 10 D8
Singlewell Kent 22 G13
Sinkhurst Green Kent 12 F7
Sinnahard Abers 104 F13
Sinnington N York 64 G2
Sinope Leics 47 M10
Sinton Worcs 35 T8
Sinton Worcs 35 T8
Sinton Green Worcs 35 T8
Sipson Gt Lon 20 J7
Sirhowy Blae G 27 L5
Sissinghurst Kent 12 E8
Siston S Glos 28 C12
Sitcott Devon 4 K2
Sithney Cnwll 2 G11
Sithney Common Cnwll 2 G11
Sithney Green Cnwll 2 G11
Sittingbourne Kent 12 H3
Six Ashes Shrops 35 S3
Six Bells Blae G 27 N7
Six Hills Leics 47 R9
Sixhills Lincs 59 L9
Six Mile Bottom Cambs 39 S9
Sixmile Cottages Kent 13 M7
Sixpenny Handley Dorset 8 D5
Six Rues Jersey 7 c2
Sizewell Suffk 41 S8
Skaill Ork 106 u19
Skara Brae Ork 106 r18
Skares E Ayrs 81 Q9
Skateraw Abers 99 S5
Skateraw E Loth 84 J3
Skeabost Highld 100 d5
Skeeby N York 69 Q12
Skeffington Leics 47 T13
Skeffling E R Yk 59 Q3
Skegby Notts 47 N1
Skegby Notts 58 C13
Skegness Lincs 59 U14
Skelbo Highld 109 P5
Skelbo Street Highld 109 P6
Skelbrooke Donc 57 R4
Skeldyke Lincs 49 M6
Skellingthorpe Lincs 58 F12
Skellorn Green Ches E 56 D10
Skellow Donc 57 R4
Skelmanthorpe Kirk 56 K4
Skelmersdale Lancs 55 L5
Skelmorlie N Ayrs 88 E12
Skelpick Highld 111 Q5
Skelston D & G 74 F8
Skelton C York 64 D8
Skelton Cumb 67 P5
Skelton E R Yk 58 C1
Skelton N York 69 N12
Skelton R & Cl 71 L9
Skelton on Ure N York 63 T6
Skelwith Bridge Cumb 67 M12
Skendleby Lincs 59 R13
Skene House Abers 105 M13
Skenfrith Mons 27 T3
Skerne E R Yk 65 N8
Skerray Highld 111 P4
Skerricha Highld 110 E6
Skerton Lancs 61 T7
Sketchley Leics 37 M2
Sketty Swans 25 V12
Skewen Neath 26 C8
Skewsby N York 64 E5
Skeyton Norfk 51 M8
Skeyton Corner Norfk 51 N8
Skiall Highld 112 B3
Skidbrooke Lincs 59 R8
Skidbrooke North End Lincs 59 R7
Skidby E R Yk 65 N13
Skigersta W Isls 106 k2
Skilgate Somset 16 C11
Skillington Lincs 48 C8
Skinburness Cumb 66 H1
Skinflats Falk 82 H2
Skinidin Highld 100 b5
Skinners Green W Berk 19 P7
Skinningrove R & Cl 71 M9
Skipness Ag & B 79 S4
Skipper's Bridge D & G 75 S9
Skiprigg Cumb 67 N3
Skipsea E R Yk 65 R9
Skipsea Brough E R Yk 65 R9
Skipton N York 62 K9
Skipton-on-Swale N York 63 T4
Skipwith N York 64 F12
Skirbeck Lincs 49 M5
Skirlaugh E R Yk 65 Q12
Skirling Border 83 L11
Skirmett Bucks 20 C4
Skirpenbeck E R Yk 64 G8
Skirwith Cumb 68 D6
Skirwith N York 62 E5
Skirza Highld 112 J3
Skitby Cumb 75 T12
Skittle Green Bucks 30 G12
Skokholm Island Pembks 24 B10
Skomer Island Pembks 24 B9
Skulamus Highld 100 f7
Skyborry Green Shrops 34 G6
Skye Green Essex 23 L3
Skye of Curr Highld 103 Q11
Skyreholme N York 63 M7
Slack Calder 62 K14
Slackbuie Highld 102 J7
Slackcote Oldham 56 E5
Slack Head Cumb 61 T4
Slackholme End Lincs 59 T12
Slacks of Cairnbanno Abers 105 N6
Slad Gloucs 28 G6
Slade Devon 6 F3
Slade Devon 15 M3
Slade Devon 15 T7
Slade End Oxon 19 S2
Slade Green Gt Lon 22 D12
Slade Heath Staffs 46 B12
Slade Hooton Rothm 57 R9
Sladesbridge Cnwll 3 Q2
Slades Green Worcs 35 T14
Slaggyford Nthumb 68 E2
Slaidburn Lancs 62 E9
Slaithwaite Kirk 56 G4
Slaley Derbys 46 J2
Slaley Nthumb 76 K14
Slamannan Falk 82 G4
Slapton Bucks 30 K8
Slapton Devon 5 U11
Slapton Nhants 37 R11
Slattocks Rochdl 56 C5
Slaugham W Susx 11 M5
Slaughterford Wilts 18 B6
Slawston Leics 37 U2
Sleaford Hants 10 C3
Sleaford Lincs 48 G4
Sleagill Cumb 67 S9
Sleap Shrops 45 L8
Sleapford Wrekin 45 P10
Sleapshyde Herts 31 Q11
Sleasdairidh Highld 109 L5
Slebech Pembks 24 H7
Sledge Green Worcs 35 T14
Sledmere E R Yk 65 L7
Sleetbeck Cumb 75 V10
Sleight Dorset 8 D9
Sleightholme Dur 69 L10
Sleights N York 71 Q11
Slepe Dorset 8 C10
Slickly Highld 112 G3
Sliddery N Ayrs 79 S11
Sligachan Highld 100 d7
Sligrachan Ag & B 88 E7
Slimbridge Gloucs 28 D7
Slindon Staffs 45 T7
Slindon W Susx 10 F9
Slinfold W Susx 10 J4
Sling Gloucs 28 A6
Sling Gwynd 52 K9
Slingsby N York 64 F5
Slip End C Beds 31 N9
Slip End Herts 31 S5
Slipton Nhants 38 E5
Slitting Mill Staffs 46 D10
Slockavullin Ag & B 87 Q6
Sloley Norfk 51 N9
Sloncombe Devon 5 S3
Sloothby Lincs 59 S12
Slough Slough 20 G7
Slough Green Somset 16 J13
Slough Green W Susx 11 M5
Slumbay Highld 101 M4
Slyfield Surrey 20 G12
Slyne Lancs 61 T6
Smailholm Border 84 G11
Smallbridge Rochdl 56 D3
Smallbrook Devon 15 U13
Smallbrook Gloucs 28 A7
Smallburgh Norfk 51 P9
Smallburn E Ayrs 82 C13
Smalldale Derbys 56 G11
Smalldale Derbys 56 J10
Small Dole W Susx 11 L8
Smalley Derbys 47 M5
Smalley Common Derbys 47 M5
Smalley Green Derbys 47 M5
Smallfield Surrey 11 N2
Smallford Herts 31 Q11
Small Heath Birm 36 F3
Small Hythe Kent 12 G9
Smallridge Devon 6 K4
Smallthorne C Stke 45 U3
Smallways N York 69 P10
Smallwood Ches E 45 T1
Small Wood Hey Lancs 61 R10
Smallworth Norfk 40 H4
Smannell Hants 19 N11
Smardale Cumb 68 F11
Smarden Kent 12 G7
Smarden Bell Kent 12 G7
Smart's Hill Kent 11 S2
Smeafield Nthumb 85 R11
Smeatharpe Devon 6 G2
Smeeth Kent 13 L8
Smeeton Westerby Leics 37 S2
Smelthouses N York 63 P7
Smerral Highld 112 E10
Smestow Staffs 35 U2
Smethwick Sandw 36 D3
Smethwick Green Ches E 55 T14
Smirisary Highld 93 Q3
Smisby Derbys 46 K10
Smith End Green Worcs 35 S10
Smithfield Cumb 75 T12
Smith Green Lancs 61 T8
Smithies Barns 57 M5
Smithincott Devon 6 E2
Smith's End Herts 39 P13
Smith's Green Essex 22 E3
Smith's Green Essex 39 U12
Smithstown Highld 107 N9
Smithton Highld 102 K6
Smithy Bridge Rochdl 56 D3
Smithy Green Ches E 55 R12
Smithy Green Stockp 56 C9
Smithy Houses Derbys 47 L4
Smockington Leics 37 N3
Smoo Highld 110 J3
Smythe's Green Essex 23 M4
Snade D & G 74 F8
Snailbeach Shrops 44 J13
Snailwell Cambs 39 T7
Snainton N York 65 L3
Snaith E R Yk 57 T2
Snake Pass Inn Derbys 56 H8
Snape N York 63 R3
Snape Suffk 41 Q9
Snape Green Lancs 54 J4
Snape Street Suffk 41 Q9
Snaresbrook Gt Lon 21 R5
Snarestone Leics 46 K12
Snarford Lincs 58 H10
Snargate Kent 12 J10
Snave Kent 12 K10
Sneachill Worcs 36 B10
Snead Powys 34 H2
Sneath Common Norfk 41 L3
Sneaton N York 71 Q11
Sneatonthorpe N York 71 R11
Snelland Lincs 58 J10
Snelson Ches E 55 T12
Snelston Derbys 46 G5
Snetterton Norfk 40 G2
Snettisham Norfk 49 U7
Snibston Leics 47 M11
Snig's End Gloucs 28 E2
Snitter Nthumb 77 L5
Snitterby Lincs 58 G8
Snitterfield Warwks 36 H9
Snitterton Derbys 46 J1
Snitton Shrops 35 N5
Snoadhill Kent 12 H7
Snodhill Herefs 34 H12
Snodland Kent 12 D3
Snoll Hatch Kent 12 C6
Snowden Hill Barns 57 L6
Snowdon Gwynd 52 K12
Snowdon Kent 13 P5
Snowdonia National Park 43 R8
Snow End Herts 22 B1
Snowshill Gloucs 36 E14
Snow Street Norfk 40 J4
Soake Hants 9 T6
Soar Cardif 26 K11
Soar Devon 5 S13
Soar Powys 26 H1
Soay Highld 100 d8
Soberton Hants 9 S5
Soberton Heath Hants 9 S6
Sockbridge Cumb 67 Q7
Sockburn Darltn 70 D11
Sodom Denbgs 54 C12
Sodylt Bank Shrops 44 H6
Soham Cambs 39 S6
Soham Cotes Cambs 39 S5
Solas W Isls 106 d11
Solbury Pembks 24 E8
Soldon Devon 14 H10
Soldon Cross Devon 14 H10
Soldridge Hants 19 U13
Sole Street Kent 12 C2
Sole Street Kent 13 L6
Solihull Solhll 36 G5
Sollas W Isls 106 d11
Sollers Dilwyn Herefs 34 K9
Sollers Hope Herefs 35 P14
Sollom Lancs 55 L3
Solva Pembks 24 D6
Solwaybank D & G 75 R10
Somerby Leics 47 U11
Somerby Lincs 58 J5
Somercotes Derbys 47 M3
Somerford BCP 8 H10
Somerford Keynes Gloucs 28 K8
Somerley W Susx 10 C11
Somerleyton Suffk 41 S1
Somersal Herbert Derbys 46 F6
Somersby Lincs 59 P12
Somersham Cambs 39 N5
Somersham Suffk 40 J11
Somerton Oxon 29 U2
Somerton Somset 17 N11
Somerton Suffk 40 D10
Somerwood Shrops 45 N11
Sompting W Susx 10 K9
Sompting Abbotts W Susx 10 K9
Sonning Wokham 20 C7
Sonning Common Oxon 20 B6
Sonning Eye Oxon 20 B7
Sontley Wrexhm 44 H4
Sopley Hants 8 H9
Sopwell Herts 31 Q11
Sopworth Wilts 28 F10
Sorbie D & G 73 L10
Sordale Highld 112 D4
Sorisdale Ag & B 92 H6
Sorn E Ayrs 81 R7
Sornhill E Ayrs 81 Q6
Sortat Highld 112 G4
Sotby Lincs 59 M11
Sots Hole Lincs 58 K14
Sotterley Suffk 41 R4
Soughton Flints 54 F13
Soulbury Bucks 30 J7
Soulby Cumb 67 Q7
Soulby Cumb 68 F10
Souldern Oxon 30 B6
Souldrop Bed 38 E8
Sound Ches E 45 P4
Sound Muir Moray 104 D5
Soundwell S Glos 28 C12
Sourton Devon 5 N2
Soutergate Cumb 61 N3
South Acre Norfk 50 D11
South Alkham Kent 13 P7
Southall Gt Lon 20 K7
South Allington Devon 5 T13
South Alloa Falk 90 C13
Southam Gloucs 28 J2
Southam Warwks 37 M8
South Ambersham W Susx 10 E6
Southampton C Sotn 9 N6
Southampton Airport Hants 9 P5
South Anston Rothm 57 R10
South Ascot W & M 20 F9
South Ashford Kent 12 K7
South Baddesley Hants 9 M9
South Bank C York 64 D9
South Bank R & Cl 70 H8
South Barrow Somset 17 R11
South Beddington Gt Lon 21 N10
South Beer Cnwll 4 J2
South Benfleet Essex 22 J10
South Bockhampton BCP 8 H9
Southborough Gt Lon 21 R9
Southborough Kent 11 T2
Southbourne BCP 8 G10
Southbourne W Susx 10 B9
South Bowood Dorset 7 M5
South Bramwith Donc 57 T4
South Brent Devon 5 R8
South Brewham Somset 17 T9
South Broomhill Nthumb 77 Q6
Southburgh Norfk 50 H12
South Burlingham Norfk 51 Q12
Southburn E R Yk 65 M9
South Cadbury Somset 17 R11
South Carlton Lincs 58 F11
South Carlton Notts 57 S10
South Cave E R Yk 65 L13
South Cerney Gloucs 28 K8
South Chailey E Susx 11 P7
South Chard Somset 6 K3
South Charlton Nthumb 77 P1
South Cheriton Somset 17 S12
South Church Dur 69 R7
Southchurch Sthend 23 M10
South Cleatlam Dur 69 P9
South Cliff N York 65 N2
South Cliffe E R Yk 64 K12
South Clifton Notts 58 D12
South Cockerington Lincs 59 Q9
South Cornelly Brdgnd 26 E11
Southcott Cnwll 14 E13
Southcott Devon 5 T4
Southcott Devon 14 K9
Southcott Devon 15 M13
Southcott Wilts 18 J9
Southcourt Bucks 30 H10
South Cove Suffk 41 S4
South Creake Norfk 50 E6
South Crosland Kirk 56 H4
South Croxton Leics 47 S11
South Dalton E R Yk 65 M10
South Darenth Kent 21 U9
South Dell W Isls 106 j2
South Downs National Park 11 P9
South Duffield N York 64 F13
South Earlswood Surrey 21 N13
Southease E Susx 11 Q9
South Elkington Lincs 59 N9
South Elmsall Wakefd 57 Q4
Southend Ag & B 79 M14
South End E R Yk 59 Q3
South End Hants 8 G5
South End Herefs 35 R12
South End N Linc 58 K2
South End Norfk 40 G2
Southend Wilts 18 J6
Southend Airport Essex 23 L10
Southend-on-Sea Sthend 23 L10
Southernby Cumb 67 N5
Southernden Kent 12 G6
Southerndown V Glam 26 F13
Southerness D & G 66 E2
South Erradale Highld 107 M10
Southerton Devon 6 E6
Southery Norfk 39 T2
South Fambridge Essex 23 L9
South Fawley W Berk 19 N4
South Ferriby N Linc 58 G2
South Field E R Yk 58 H1
Southfield Falk 82 F4
Southfleet Kent 22 F13
Southford IoW 9 Q13
Southgate Gt Lon 21 N4
Southgate Norfk 49 U7
Southgate Norfk 50 E6
Southgate Norfk 50 K9
Southgate Swans 25 U13
South Godstone Surrey 21 Q13
South Gorley Hants 8 H6
South Gosforth N u Ty 77 Q12
South Green Essex 22 G9
South Green Essex 23 P4
South Green Kent 12 G3
South Green Norfk 50 J11
South Green Suffk 41 L5
South Gyle C Edin 83 N4
South Hanningfield Essex 22 H8
South Harting W Susx 10 B7
South Hayling Hants 9 U9
South Hazelrigg Nthumb 85 R12
South Heath Bucks 30 K12
South Heighton E Susx 11 Q10
South Hetton Dur 70 E3
South Hiendley Wakefd 57 N4
South Hill Cnwll 4 J6
South Hill Somset 17 N11
South Hinksey Oxon 30 B12
South Hole Devon 14 F8
South Holmwood Surrey 10 K2
South Hornchurch Gt Lon 22 D11
South Horrington Somset 17 Q7
South Huish Devon 5 R12
South Hykeham Lincs 58 F14
South Hylton Sundld 70 E1
Southill C Beds 31 Q4
Southington Hants 19 R11
South Kelsey Lincs 58 H7
South Kessock Highld 102 J6
South Killingholme N Linc 58 K3
South Kilvington N York 63 U3
South Kilworth Leics 37 R4
South Kirkby Wakefd 57 P4
South Knighton Devon 5 U6
South Kyme Lincs 48 J4
Southleigh Devon 6 H6
South Leigh Oxon 29 S6
South Leverton Notts 58 C10
South Littleton Worcs 36 E11
South Lopham Norfk 40 H4
South Luffenham Rutlnd 48 D13
South Lynn Norfk 49 T10
South Malling E Susx 11 Q8
South Marston Swindn 29 N10
South Merstham Surrey 21 N12

South Middleton Nthumb 85 P14
South Milford N York 64 B13
South Milton Devon 5 S12
South Mimms Herts 31 R12
South Mimms Services Herts 31 R12
Southminster Essex 23 N8
South Molton Devon 15 R7
South Moor Dur 69 Q2
Southmoor Oxon 29 S8
South Moreton Oxon 19 S3
Southmuir Angus 98 F13
South Mundham W Susx 10 D10
South Muskham Notts 47 U2
South Newbald E R Yk 65 L12
South Newington Oxon 37 M14
South Newton Wilts 8 F2
South Nitshill C Glas 89 M14
South Normanton Derbys 47 M2
South Norwood Gt Lon 21 P9
South Nutfield Surrey 21 P13
South Ockendon Thurr 22 E11
Southoe Cambs 38 J8
Southolt Suffk 41 L7
South Ormsby Lincs 59 Q11
Southorpe C Pete 48 G13
South Ossett Wakefd 57 L3
South Otterington N York 63 T2
Southover Dorset 7 R6
Southover E Susx 12 C10
South Owersby Lincs 58 J8
Southowram Calder 56 H2
South Park Surrey 21 M13
South Perrott Dorset 7 N3
South Petherton Somset 17 M13
South Petherwin Cnwll 4 J4
South Pickenham Norfk 50 E13
South Pill Cnwll 5 L9
South Pool Devon 5 T12
South Poorton Dorset 7 P5
Southport Sefton 54 H3
South Queensferry C Edin 83 M3
South Radworthy Devon 15 R6
South Rauceby Lincs 48 F4
South Raynham Norfk 50 E9
South Reddish Stockp 56 C8
Southrepps Norfk 51 N6
South Reston Lincs 59 R10
Southrey Lincs 58 K13
South Ronaldsay Ork 106 t21
Southrop Gloucs 29 N7
Southrope Hants 19 U12
South Runcton Norfk 49 T12
South Scarle Notts 58 D14
Southsea C Port 9 T9
Southsea Wrexhm 44 H3
South Shian Ag & B 94 C10
South Shields S Tyne 77 T12
South Shore Bpool 61 Q13
Southside Dur 69 P7
South Somercotes Lincs 59 R8
South Stainley N York 63 S7
South Stifford Thurr 22 E12
South Stoke BaNES 17 T4
South Stoke Oxon 19 S4
South Stoke W Susx 10 G9
South Stour Kent 12 K8
South Street Kent 12 B3
South Street Kent 13 L4
South Street Kent 13 M2
South Tarbrax S Lans 82 K8
South Tawton Devon 5 R2
South Tehidy Cnwll 2 H8
South Thoresby Lincs 59 R11
South Thorpe Dur 69 P10
South Town Hants 19 U13
Southtown Norfk 51 T12
Southtown Somset 16 K13
South Uist W Isls 106 d15
Southwaite Cumb 67 P3
Southwaite Services Cumb 67 P3
South Walsham Norfk 51 Q11
Southwark Gt Lon 21 P7
South Warnborough Hants 20 B13
Southwater W Susx 10 K5
Southwater Street W Susx 10 K5
Southway C Plym 5 M8
Southway Somset 17 P8
South Weald Essex 22 E9
Southwell Dorset 7 S10
Southwell Notts 47 S3
South Weston Oxon 20 B3
South Wheatley Cnwll 4 G2
South Wheatley Notts 58 C9
Southwick Hants 9 S7
Southwick Nhants 38 F2
Southwick Somset 17 L7
Southwick Sundld 77 T14
Southwick W Susx 11 L9
Southwick Wilts 18 B9
South Widcombe BaNES 17 Q5
South Wigston Leics 47 Q14
South Willingham Lincs 59 L10
South Wingate Dur 70 F6
South Wingfield Derbys 47 L2
South Witham Lincs 48 D10
Southwold Suffk 41 T5
South Wonston Hants 19 Q13
Southwood Norfk 51 Q12
Southwood Somset 17 Q10
South Woodham Ferrers Essex 22 K8
South Wootton Norfk 49 T9
South Wraxall Wilts 18 B8
South Zeal Devon 5 R2
Sovereign Harbour E Susx 11 U10
Sowerby Calder 56 F2
Sowerby N York 63 U3
Sowerby Bridge Calder 56 G2
Sowerby Row Cumb 67 N4
Sower Carr Lancs 61 R11
Sowerhill Somset 15 U8
Sowhill Torfn 27 P7
Sowley Green Suffk 40 B10
Sowood Calder 56 G3
Sowton Devon 5 N7
Sowton Devon 6 C6
Soyland Town Calder 56 F2
Spa Common Norfk 51 N7
Spain's End Essex 39 U13
Spalding Lincs 48 K9
Spaldington E R Yk 64 H13
Spaldwick Cambs 38 H6
Spalford Notts 58 D13
Spanby Lincs 48 G6
Spanish Green Hants 19 U9
Sparham Norfk 50 J10
Sparhamill Norfk 50 J10
Spark Bridge Cumb 61 Q3
Sparket Cumb 67 P7
Sparkford Somset 17 R11
Sparkhill Birm 36 F4
Sparkwell Devon 5 P9
Sparrow Green Norfk 50 F11
Sparrowpit Derbys 56 G10
Sparrows Green E Susx 12 B9
Sparsholt Hants 9 N2
Sparsholt Oxon 29 R10
Spartylea Nthumb 68 J3
Spath Staffs 46 E6
Spaunton N York 64 G2
Spaxton Somset 16 H9
Spean Bridge Highld 94 J2
Spear Hill W Susx 10 J7
Spearywell Hants 9 L3
Speen Bucks 20 D3
Speen W Berk 19 Q7
Speeton N York 65 R5
Speke Lpool 54 K10
Speldhurst Kent 11 T2
Spellbrook Herts 22 C4
Spelmonden Kent 12 D8
Spelsbury Oxon 29 R3
Spen Kirk 56 J1
Spencers Wood Wokham 20 B9
Spen Green Ches E 45 T1
Spennithorne N York 63 N2
Spennymoor Dur 69 S6
Spernall Warwks 36 E8
Spetchley Worcs 35 U10
Spetisbury Dorset 8 C8
Spexhall Suffk 41 Q4
Spey Bay Moray 104 D2
Speybridge Highld 103 R10
Speyview Moray 104 B7
Spilsby Lincs 59 R13
Spindlestone Nthumb 85 T12
Spinkhill Derbys 57 Q11
Spinningdale Highld 109 M7
Spion Kop Notts 57 S13
Spirthill Wilts 18 E5
Spital Wirral 54 H10
Spital Hill Donc 57 T8
Spital in the Street Lincs 58 G8
Spithurst E Susx 11 Q7
Spittal E Loth 84 D3
Spittal E R Yk 64 H9
Spittal Highld 112 E6
Spittal Nthumb 85 Q8
Spittal Pembks 24 G6
Spittalfield P & K 90 H3
Spittal of Glenmuick Abers 98 E6
Spittal of Glenshee P & K 97 U10
Spittal-on-Rule Border 76 B2
Spixworth Norfk 51 M10
Splatt Cnwll 3 N1
Splatt Cnwll 4 G3
Splatt Devon 15 P11
Splayne's Green E Susx 11 Q6
Splott Cardif 27 N12
Spofforth N York 63 T9
Spondon C Derb 47 M6
Spon Green Flints 54 G14
Spooner Row Norfk 40 J1
Sporle Norfk 50 D11
Spott E Loth 84 H3
Spottiswoode Border 84 G9
Spratton Nhants 37 T7
Spreakley Surrey 10 C2
Spreyton Devon 15 Q13
Spriddlestone Devon 5 N10
Spridlington Lincs 58 H10
Springburn C Glas 89 P12
Springfield D & G 75 R12
Springfield Essex 22 H6
Springfield Fife 91 M9
Springhill Staffs 46 C13
Springhill Staffs 46 E12
Springholm D & G 74 F11
Springside N Ayrs 81 M5
Springthorpe Lincs 58 E9
Spring Vale Barns 57 L6
Springwell Sundld 77 R14
Sproatley E R Yk 65 R13
Sproston Green Ches W 55 R13
Sprotbrough Donc 57 R6
Sproughton Suffk 40 K12
Sprouston Border 84 K11
Sprowston Norfk 51 N11
Sproxton Leics 48 C9
Sproxton N York 64 E3
Spunhill Shrops 44 K7
Spurstow Ches E 45 N2
Spyway Dorset 7 P6
Square and Compass Pembks 24 D4
Stableford Shrops 45 S14
Stableford Staffs 45 T6
Stacey Bank Sheff 57 L8
Stackhouse N York 62 G6
Stackpole Pembks 24 G11
Stackpole Elidor Pembks 24 G11
Stacksford Norfk 40 J2
Stacksteads Lancs 56 C2
Staddiscombe C Plym 5 N10
Staddlethorpe E R Yk 64 J14
Staden Derbys 56 G12
Stadhampton Oxon 30 D13
Stadhlaigearraidh W Isls 106 c15
Staffield Cumb 67 R4
Staffin Highld 100 d3
Stafford Staffs 46 B9
Stafford Services (northbound) Staffs 45 U7
Stafford Services (southbound) Staffs 45 U7
Stagsden Bed 38 E11
Stainborough Barns 57 M6
Stainburn Cumb 66 F7
Stainburn N York 63 R10
Stainby Lincs 48 D9
Staincross Barns 57 M4
Staindrop Dur 69 P8
Staines-upon-Thames Surrey 20 H8
Stainfield Lincs 48 G9
Stainfield Lincs 58 K12
Stainforth Donc 57 T4
Stainforth N York 62 G6
Staining Lancs 61 Q12
Stainland Calder 56 G3
Stainsacre N York 71 R11
Stainsby Derbys 57 Q13
Stainton Cumb 61 U2
Stainton Cumb 67 N1
Stainton Cumb 67 Q7
Stainton Donc 57 S8
Stainton Dur 69 N9
Stainton Middsb 70 G10
Stainton N York 69 P13
Stainton by Langworth Lincs 58 J11
Staintondale N York 71 S13
Stainton le Vale Lincs 59 L8
Stainton with Adgarley Cumb 61 N5
Stair Cumb 66 K8
Stair E Ayrs 81 N8
Stairfoot Barns 57 N5
Stairhaven D & G 72 G9
Staithes N York 71 N9
Stakeford Nthumb 77 R8
Stake Pool Lancs 61 S10
Stakes Hants 9 T7
Stalbridge Dorset 17 T13
Stalbridge Weston Dorset 17 T13
Stalham Norfk 51 Q8
Stalham Green Norfk 51 Q9
Stalisfield Green Kent 12 J5
Stalland Common Norfk 50 H14
Stallen Dorset 17 R13
Stallingborough NE Lin 59 L4
Stalling Busk N York 62 J2
Stallington Staffs 46 B6
Stalmine Lancs 61 R10
Stalmine Moss Side Lancs 61 R10
Stalybridge Tamesd 56 E7
Stambourne Essex 40 B13
Stambourne Green Essex 39 U13
Stamford Lincs 48 F12
Stamford Nthumb 77 Q2
Stamford Bridge Ches W 55 L13
Stamford Bridge E R Yk 64 G8
Stamfordham Nthumb 77 M11
Stamford Hill Gt Lon 21 P5
Stanah Lancs 61 R11
Stanborough Herts 31 R10
Stanbridge C Beds 31 L8
Stanbridge Dorset 8 E8
Stanbury C Brad 63 L12
Stand Bury 55 S5
Stand N Lans 82 E5
Standburn Falk 82 H4
Standeford Staffs 46 B12
Standen Kent 12 G7
Standen Street Kent 12 F9
Standerwick Somset 18 B10
Standford Hants 10 C4
Standingstone Cumb 66 G6
Standish Gloucs 28 E6
Standish Wigan 55 N4
Standish Lower Ground Wigan 55 N5
Standlake Oxon 29 S7
Standon Hants 9 N3
Standon Herts 31 U8
Standon Staffs 45 T6
Standon Green End Herts 31 U9
Standwell Green Suffk 40 K7
Stane N Lans 82 G7
Stanfield Norfk 50 F9
Stanford C Beds 31 Q4
Stanford Kent 13 M8
Stanford Shrops 44 H11
Stanford Bishop Herefs 35 Q10
Stanford Bridge Worcs 35 R7
Stanford Bridge Wrekin 45 R9
Stanford Dingley W Berk 19 S6
Stanford in the Vale Oxon 29 R9
Stanford le Hope Thurr 22 G11
Stanford on Avon Nhants 37 Q5
Stanford on Soar Notts 47 P9
Stanford on Teme Worcs 35 R7
Stanford Rivers Essex 22 D7
Stanfree Derbys 57 Q12
Stanghow R & Cl 71 L9
Stanground C Pete 38 K1
Stanhill Lancs 62 E14
Stanhoe Norfk 50 D6
Stanhope Border 83 M13
Stanhope Dur 69 L5
Stanhope Kent 12 K7
Stanhope Bretby Derbys 46 J9
Stanion Nhants 38 D3
Stanklin Worcs 35 U6
Stanley Derbys 47 M5
Stanley Dur 69 Q2
Stanley Notts 47 N1
Stanley P & K 90 H5
Stanley Shrops 35 R4
Stanley Staffs 46 B3
Stanley Wakefd 57 M2
Stanley Common Derbys 47 M5
Stanley Crook Dur 69 Q5
Stanley Ferry Wakefd 57 N2
Stanley Gate Lancs 54 K5
Stanley Moor Staffs 46 B3
Stanley Pontlarge Gloucs 28 K1
Stanmer Br & H 11 N9
Stanmore Gt Lon 21 L4
Stanmore Hants 9 P3
Stanmore W Berk 19 Q5
Stannersburn Nthumb 76 E8
Stanningfield Suffk 40 E9
Stanningley Leeds 63 Q13
Stannington Nthumb 77 Q10
Stannington Sheff 57 M9
Stannington Station Nthumb 77 Q9
Stansbatch Herefs 34 H8
Stansfield Suffk 40 C10
Stanshope Staffs 46 F3
Stanstead Suffk 40 D11
Stanstead Abbotts Herts 31 U10
Stansted Kent 12 B3
Stansted Airport Essex 22 E3
Stansted Mountfitchet Essex 22 D2
Stanton Derbys 46 J10
Stanton Gloucs 36 E14
Stanton Mons 27 Q3
Stanton Nthumb 77 N7
Stanton Staffs 46 F4
Stanton Suffk 40 G6
Stanton by Bridge Derbys 47 L8
Stanton by Dale Derbys 47 N6
Stanton Cross Nhants 38 D7
Stanton Drew BaNES 17 Q4
Stanton Fitzwarren Swindn 29 N9
Stanton Harcourt Oxon 29 T6
Stanton Hill Notts 47 N1
Stanton in Peak Derbys 56 K14
Stanton Lacy Shrops 35 L5
Stanton Lees Derbys 57 L14
Stanton Long Shrops 35 N2
Stanton-on-the-Wolds Notts 47 R7
Stanton Prior BaNES 17 S4
Stanton St Bernard Wilts 18 G8
Stanton St John Oxon 30 C11
Stanton St Quintin Wilts 18 D5
Stanton Street Suffk 40 G7
Stanton under Bardon Leics 47 N11
Stanton upon Hine Heath Shrops 45 N9
Stanton Wick BaNES 17 R4
Stantway Gloucs 28 D5
Stanwardine in the Field Shrops 44 K9
Stanwardine in the Wood Shrops 44 K8
Stanway Essex 23 M3
Stanway Gloucs 29 L1
Stanway Green Essex 23 N3
Stanway Green Suffk 41 M6
Stanwell Surrey 20 J8
Stanwell Moor Surrey 20 H8
Stanwick Nhants 38 E6
Stanwick St John N York 69 Q10
Stanwix Cumb 67 P1
Staoinebrig W Isls 106 c15
Stape N York 71 N14
Stapehill Dorset 8 F8
Stapeley Ches E 45 Q4
Stapenhill Staffs 46 J9
Staple Kent 13 Q4
Staple Cross Devon 16 D12
Staplecross E Susx 12 E11
Staplefield W Susx 11 M5
Staple Fitzpaine Somset 16 J13
Stapleford Cambs 39 Q10
Stapleford Herts 31 T9
Stapleford Leics 48 B10
Stapleford Lincs 48 C2
Stapleford Notts 47 N6
Stapleford Wilts 18 G13
Stapleford Abbotts Essex 22 D9
Stapleford Tawney Essex 22 D8
Staplegrove Somset 16 H11
Staplehay Somset 16 H12
Staple Hill Worcs 36 C6
Staplehurst Kent 12 E7
Staplers IoW 9 Q11
Staplestreet Kent 13 L3
Stapleton Cumb 75 V11
Stapleton Herefs 34 H7
Stapleton Leics 47 M14
Stapleton N York 69 S10
Stapleton Shrops 45 L13
Stapleton Somset 17 N12
Stapley Somset 6 G2
Staploe Bed 38 J8
Staplow Herefs 35 Q12
Star Fife 91 M11
Star IoA 52 H8
Star Pembks 25 M4
Star Somset 17 M5
Starbeck N York 63 S8
Starbotton N York 62 K5
Starcross Devon 6 C8
Stareton Warwks 36 K6
Starkholmes Derbys 46 K2
Starlings Green Essex 22 C1
Starr's Green E Susx 12 E12
Starston Norfk 41 M4
Start Devon 5 U12
Startforth Dur 69 M9
Startley Wilts 18 D4
Statenborough Kent 13 R4
Statham Warrtn 55 Q9
Stathe Somset 17 L11
Stathern Leics 47 U7
Station Town Dur 70 F5
Staughton Green Cambs 38 H7
Staughton Highway Cambs 38 H8
Staunton Gloucs 27 V5
Staunton Gloucs 28 E2
Staunton in the Vale Notts 48 B5
Staunton on Arrow Herefs 34 J8
Staunton on Wye Herefs 34 J12
Staveley Cumb 67 Q13
Staveley Derbys 57 P12
Staveley N York 63 T7
Staveley-in-Cartmel Cumb 61 R2
Staverton Devon 5 T8
Staverton Gloucs 28 G3
Staverton Nhants 37 P8
Staverton Wilts 18 C8
Staverton Bridge Gloucs 28 G3
Stawell Somset 17 L9
Stawley Somset 16 E12
Staxigoe Highld 112 J6
Staxton N York 65 N4
Staylittle Cerdgn 33 M3
Staylittle Powys 33 S2
Staynall Lancs 61 R11
Staythorpe Notts 47 U3
Stead C Brad 63 N10
Stean N York 63 M5
Stearsby N York 64 E5
Steart Somset 16 J7
Stebbing Essex 22 G3
Stebbing Green Essex 22 G3
Stechford Birm 36 F3
Stede Quarter Kent 12 G8
Stedham W Susx 10 D6
Steel Nthumb 76 J14
Steel Cross E Susx 11 S4
Steelend Fife 90 F13
Steele Road Border 76 A7
Steel Green Cumb 61 M4
Steel Heath Shrops 45 M6
Steen's Bridge Herefs 35 M9
Steep Hants 9 U3
Steephill IoW 9 Q13
Steep Lane Calder 56 F2
Steeple Dorset 8 C12
Steeple Essex 23 M7
Steeple Ashton Wilts 18 D9
Steeple Aston Oxon 29 U2
Steeple Barton Oxon 29 T3
Steeple Bumpstead Essex 39 U12
Steeple Claydon Bucks 30 F7
Steeple Gidding Cambs 38 H4
Steeple Langford Wilts 18 F13
Steeple Morden Cambs 31 S4
Steep Marsh Hants 10 B5
Steeton C Brad 63 L11
Stein Highld 100 b4
Stella Gatesd 77 P13
Stelling Minnis Kent 13 M6
Stembridge Somset 17 M12
Stenalees Cnwll 3 Q5
Stenhouse D & G 74 F7
Stenhousemuir Falk 82 G2
Stenigot Lincs 59 M10
Stenness Ork 106 s18
Stenscholl Highld 100 d3
Stenson Fields Derbys 46 K7
Stenton E Loth 84 G4
Steornabhagh W Isls 106 j5
Stepaside Pembks 24 K9
Stepford D & G 74 G9
Stepney Gt Lon 21 Q6
Stepping Hill Stockp 56 D9
Steppingley C Beds 31 M5
Stepps N Lans 89 Q12
Sternfield Suffk 41 Q8
Stert Wilts 18 F9
Stetchworth Cambs 39 T9
Stevenage Herts 31 R7
Steven's Crouch E Susx 12 D12
Stevenston N Ayrs 80 K4
Steventon Hants 19 R11
Steventon Oxon 29 U9
Steventon End Essex 39 S12
Stevington Bed 38 E10
Stewartby Bed 31 M4
Stewartfield S Lans 81 S1
Stewarton Ag & B 79 M12
Stewarton E Ayrs 81 N3
Stewkley Bucks 30 J7
Stewley Somset 16 K13
Stewton Lincs 59 Q9
Steyne Cross IoW 9 S11
Steyning W Susx 10 K8
Steynton Pembks 24 F9
Stibb Cnwll 14 F10
Stibbard Norfk 50 G8
Stibb Cross Devon 14 K10
Stibb Green Wilts 18 K8
Stibbington Cambs 48 G14
Stichill Border 84 J11
Sticker Cnwll 3 P6
Stickford Lincs 49 N1
Sticklepath Devon 5 Q2
Sticklepath Somset 16 D9
Stickling Green Essex 39 Q14
Stickney Lincs 49 M2
Stiffkey Norfk 50 G5
Stifford Clays Thurr 22 F11
Stifford's Bridge Herefs 35 R11
Stiff Street Kent 12 G3
Stile Bridge Kent 12 E6
Stileway Somset 17 N8
Stilligarry W Isls 106 c15
Stillingfleet N York 64 D11
Stillington N York 64 D6
Stillington S on T 70 E8
Stilton Cambs 38 J3
Stinchcombe Gloucs 28 D8
Stinsford Dorset 7 T6
Stiperstones Shrops 44 J13
Stirchley Birm 36 E4
Stirchley Wrekin 45 Q12
Stirling Abers 105 U7
Stirling Stirlg 89 S7
Stirling Castle Stirlg 89 S7
Stirling Services Stirlg 89 T8
Stirtloe Cambs 38 J7
Stirton N York 62 K9
Stisted Essex 22 K3
Stitchcombe Wilts 18 K7
Stithians Cnwll 2 J9
Stivichall Covtry 36 K5
Stixwould Lincs 59 L13
St Michaels Fife 91 P7
Stoak Ches W 54 K12
Stobo Border 83 N11
Stoborough Dorset 8 C11
Stoborough Green Dorset 8 C11
Stobs Castle Border 75 V4
Stobswood Nthumb 77 Q6
Stock Essex 22 G8
Stock N Som 17 N4
Stockbridge Hants 19 N13
Stockbridge W Susx 10 D10
Stockbriggs S Lans 82 E11
Stockbury Kent 12 F3
Stockcross W Berk 19 P7
Stockdalewath Cumb 67 N3
Stocker's Head Kent 12 J5
Stockerston Leics 48 B14
Stock Green Worcs 36 C9
Stocking Herefs 28 B1
Stockingford Warwks 36 K2
Stocking Pelham Herts 22 C2
Stockland Devon 6 H4
Stockland Bristol Somset 16 H8
Stockland Green Kent 11 T2
Stockleigh English Devon 15 U11
Stockleigh Pomeroy Devon 15 U12
Stockley Wilts 18 E7
Stockley Hill Herefs 34 J13
Stocklinch Somset 17 L13
Stockmoor Herefs 34 J10
Stockport Stockp 56 C8
Stocksbridge Sheff 57 L7
Stocksfield Nthumb 77 M13
Stockton Herefs 35 M8
Stockton Norfk 41 Q2
Stockton Shrops 44 G13
Stockton Shrops 45 R14
Stockton Warwks 37 M8
Stockton Wilts 18 E13
Stockton Wrekin 45 S10
Stockton Brook Staffs 46 B3
Stockton Heath Warrtn 55 P9
Stockton-on-Tees S on T 70 F9
Stockton on Teme Worcs 35 R7
Stockton on the Forest C York 64 F8
Stockwell Gloucs 28 H5
Stockwell End Wolves 45 U13
Stockwell Heath Staffs 46 E9
Stockwood Bristl 17 R3
Stockwood Dorset 7 Q3
Stock Wood Worcs 36 D9
Stodday Lancs 61 T8
Stodmarsh Kent 13 P3
Stody Norfk 50 J6
Stoer Highld 110 A11
Stoford Somset 7 Q2
Stoford Wilts 18 G13
Stogumber Somset 16 E9
Stogursey Somset 16 H8
Stoke Covtry 37 L5
Stoke Devon 14 F8
Stoke Hants 9 U8
Stoke Hants 19 P10
Stoke Medway 22 K13
Stoke Abbott Dorset 7 N4
Stoke Albany Nhants 38 B3
Stoke Ash Suffk 40 K6
Stoke Bardolph Notts 47 R5
Stoke Bliss Worcs 35 Q8
Stoke Bruerne Nhants 37 T11
Stoke-by-Clare Suffk 40 B12
Stoke-by-Nayland Suffk 40 G13
Stoke Canon Devon 6 B5
Stoke Charity Hants 19 Q13
Stoke Climsland Cnwll 4 K6
Stoke Cross Herefs 35 P10
Stoke D'Abernon Surrey 20 K11
Stoke Doyle Nhants 38 F3
Stoke Dry Rutlnd 38 C1
Stoke Edith Herefs 35 P12
Stoke End Warwks 36 G1
Stoke Farthing Wilts 8 F3
Stoke Ferry Norfk 50 B13
Stoke Fleming Devon 5 V11
Stokeford Dorset 8 B11
Stoke Gabriel Devon 5 V9
Stoke Gifford S Glos 28 B12
Stoke Golding Leics 37 L1
Stoke Goldington M Keyn 38 B11
Stoke Green Bucks 20 G6
Stokeham Notts 58 C11
Stoke Hammond Bucks 30 J7
Stoke Heath Shrops 45 Q8
Stoke Heath Worcs 36 B7
Stoke Holy Cross Norfk 51 M13
Stokeinteignhead Devon 6 B10
Stoke Lacy Herefs 35 P11
Stoke Lyne Oxon 30 C7
Stoke Mandeville Bucks 30 H10
Stokenchurch Bucks 20 C3
Stoke Newington Gt Lon 21 P5
Stokenham Devon 5 U12
Stoke-on-Trent C Stke 45 U4
Stoke Orchard Gloucs 28 H2
Stoke Poges Bucks 20 G6
Stoke Pound Worcs 36 C7
Stoke Prior Herefs 35 M9
Stoke Prior Worcs 36 B7
Stoke Rivers Devon 15 P5
Stoke Rochford Lincs 48 D8
Stoke Row Oxon 19 U4
Stoke St Gregory Somset 16 K11
Stoke St Mary Somset 16 J12
Stoke St Michael Somset 17 S7
Stoke St Milborough Shrops 35 N4
Stokesay Shrops 34 K4
Stokesby Norfk 51 R11
Stokesley N York 70 H11
Stoke sub Hamdon Somset 17 N13
Stoke Talmage Oxon 30 E13
Stoke Trister Somset 17 T11
Stoke upon Tern Shrops 45 P8
Stoke-upon-Trent C Stke 45 U4
Stoke Wake Dorset 7 U3
Stoke Wharf Worcs 36 C7
Stolford Somset 16 H7
Stondon Massey Essex 22 E7
Stone Bucks 30 G10
Stone Gloucs 28 C8
Stone Kent 22 E13
Stone Rothm 57 S9
Stone Somset 17 Q10
Stone Staffs 46 B7
Stone Worcs 35 U5
Stonea Cambs 39 Q2
Stone Allerton Somset 17 L6
Ston Easton Somset 17 R6
Stonebridge N Som 17 L5
Stonebridge Norfk 40 F2
Stonebridge Warwks 36 H4
Stone Bridge Corner C Pete 49 L13
Stonebroom Derbys 47 M2
Stone Chair Calder 63 N14
Stone Cross E Susx 11 S5
Stone Cross E Susx 11 U10
Stone Cross E Susx 12 B9
Stone Cross Kent 11 S3
Stone Cross Kent 12 K8
Stone Cross Kent 13 R4
Stonecross Green Suffk 40 D9
Stonecrouch Kent 12 D9
Stone-edge-Batch N Som 17 N2
Stoneferry C KuH 65 Q13
Stonefield Castle Hotel Ag & B 87 R11
Stonegate E Susx 12 C10
Stonegate N York 71 N11
Stonegrave N York 64 F4
Stonehall Worcs 35 U11
Stonehaugh Nthumb 76 F10
Stonehaven Abers 99 R6
Stonehenge Wilts 18 H12
Stone Hill Donc 57 U5
Stonehouse C Plym 5 M10
Stone House Cumb 62 F2
Stonehouse Gloucs 28 F6
Stonehouse Nthumb 76 D14
Stonehouse S Lans 82 E9
Stone in Oxney Kent 12 H10
Stoneleigh Warwks 36 K6
Stoneley Green Ches E 45 P3
Stonely Cambs 38 H7
Stoner Hill Hants 9 U3
Stonesby Leics 48 B9
Stonesfield Oxon 29 S4
Stones Green Essex 23 S2
Stone Street Kent 21 U12
Stone Street Suffk 40 G13
Stone Street Suffk 40 H12
Stone Street Suffk 41 Q4
Stonestreet Green Kent 13 L8
Stonethwaite Cumb 67 L10
Stonewells Moray 104 B2
Stonewood Kent 22 E13
Stoneybridge W Isls 106 c15
Stoneybridge Worcs 36 B5
Stoneyburn W Loth 82 J6
Stoney Cross Hants 8 K6
Stoneygate C Leic 47 R13
Stoneyhills Essex 23 N8
Stoneykirk D & G 72 D9
Stoney Middleton Derbys 56 K11
Stoney Stanton Leics 37 N2
Stoney Stoke Somset 17 T10
Stoney Stratton Somset 17 S9
Stoney Stretton Shrops 44 J12
Stoneywood C Aber 105 P13
Stoneywood Falk 89 S9
Stonham Aspal Suffk 40 K9
Stonnall Staffs 46 E13
Stonor Oxon 20 B5
Stonton Wyville Leics 37 T1
Stonybreck Shet 106 r11
Stony Cross Herefs 35 M7
Stony Cross Herefs 35 R11
Stonyford Hants 9 L5
Stony Houghton Derbys 57 Q13
Stony Stratford M Keyn 30 G4
Stonywell Staffs 46 E11
Stoodleigh Devon 15 Q6
Stoodleigh Devon 16 B13
Stopham W Susx 10 G7
Stopsley Luton 31 P8
Stoptide Cnwll 3 N1
Storeton Wirral 54 H10
Storeyard Green Herefs 35 R12
Storey Arms Powys 26 H3
Stornoway W Isls 106 j5
Stornoway Airport W Isls 106 j5
Storridge Herefs 35 S11
Storrington W Susx 10 H8
Storth Cumb 61 T4
Storwood E R Yk 64 G11
Stotfield Moray 104 A1
Stotfold C Beds 31 R5
Stottesdon Shrops 35 Q4
Stoughton Leics 47 R13
Stoughton Surrey 20 G12
Stoughton W Susx 10 C8
Stoulton Worcs 36 B11
Stourbridge Dudley 35 U4
Stourhead Wilts 17 U10
Stourpaine Dorset 8 B7
Stourport-on-Severn Worcs 35 T6
Stour Provost Dorset 17 U12
Stour Row Dorset 17 V12
Stourton Leeds 63 S13
Stourton Staffs 35 U4
Stourton Warwks 36 J13
Stourton Wilts 17 U10
Stourton Caundle Dorset 17 T13
Stout Somset 17 M10
Stove Shet 106 u11
Stoven Suffk 41 R4
Stow Border 84 D10
Stow Lincs 58 E10
Stow Bardolph Norfk 49 T12
Stow Bedon Norfk 40 G1
Stowbridge Norfk 49 T12
Stow-cum-Quy Cambs 39 R8
Stowe Gloucs 27 V6
Stowe Shrops 34 H6
Stowe-by-Chartley Staffs 46 D8
Stowehill Nhants 37 R9
Stowell Somset 17 S12
Stowey BaNES 17 Q5
Stowford Devon 5 L3
Stowford Devon 6 F7
Stowford Devon 14 K13
Stowford Devon 15 Q4
Stowlangtoft Suffk 40 G7
Stow Longa Cambs 38 H6
Stow Maries Essex 22 K8
Stowmarket Suffk 40 H9
Stow-on-the-Wold Gloucs 29 N2
Stowting Kent 13 M7
Stowting Common Kent 13 M7
Stowupland Suffk 40 J8
Straad Ag & B 88 B13
Straanruie Highld 103 Q12
Strachan Abers 99 M5
Strachur Ag & B 88 C5
Stradbroke Suffk 41 M6
Stradbrook Wilts 18 D10
Stradishall Suffk 40 C10
Stradsett Norfk 49 U12
Stragglethorpe Lincs 48 D3
Stragglethorpe Notts 47 S6
Straight Soley Wilts 19 M6
Straiton Mdloth 83 Q5
Straiton S Ayrs 81 M12
Straloch Abers 105 P11
Straloch P & K 97 S11
Stramshall Staffs 46 E6
Strang IoM 60 f7
Strangeways Salfd 55 T7
Strangford Herefs 28 A2
Stranraer D & G 72 D7
Strata Florida Cerdgn 33 P7
Stratfield Mortimer W Berk 19 U8
Stratfield Saye Hants 19 U8
Stratfield Turgis Hants 19 U9
Stratford C Beds 38 J11
Stratford Gt Lon 21 Q6
Stratford St Andrew Suffk 41 Q8
Stratford St Mary Suffk 40 H14
Stratford sub Castle Wilts 8 G2
Stratford Tony Wilts 8 F3
Stratford-upon-Avon Warwks 36 H9
Strath Highld 107 N9
Strathan Highld 110 B12
Strathan Highld 111 M4
Strathaven S Lans 82 D10
Strathblane Stirlg 89 N10
Strathcanaird Highld 108 B4
Strathcarron Highld 101 N3
Strathcoil Ag & B 93 R12
Strathdon Abers 104 D13
Strathkinness Fife 91 Q8
Strathloanhead W Loth 82 H4
Strathmashie House Highld 96 H5
Strathmiglo Fife 90 K10
Strathpeffer Highld 102 E4
Strathtay P & K 97 Q13
Strathwhillan N Ayrs 80 E5
Strathy Highld 111 S4
Strathy Inn Highld 111 S3
Strathyre Stirlg 89 N2
Stratton Cnwll 14 F11
Stratton Dorset 7 S6
Stratton Gloucs 28 K7
Stratton Audley Oxon 30 D7
Stratton-on-the-Fosse Somset 17 S6
Stratton St Margaret Swindn 29 N10
Stratton St Michael Norfk 41 M2
Stratton Strawless Norfk 51 M9
Stream Somset 16 E9
Streat E Susx 11 P7
Streatham Gt Lon 21 P8
Streatley C Beds 31 N7
Streatley W Berk 19 S4
Street Devon 6 G7
Street Lancs 61 U9
Street N York 71 M12
Street Somset 17 N9
Street Ashton Warwks 37 N4
Street Dinas Shrops 44 H6
Street End E Susx 11 U6
Street End Kent 13 M5
Street End W Susx 10 D11
Street Gate Gatesd 77 Q14
Streethay Staffs 46 F11
Street Houses N York 64 C10
Streetlam N York 70 D13
Street Lane Derbys 47 L4
Streetly Wsall 46 E14
Streetly End Cambs 39 T11
Street on the Fosse Somset 17 R9
Strefford Shrops 34 K3
Strelitz P & K 90 J4
Strelley Notts 47 P5
Strensall C York 64 E7
Strensham Worcs 36 B12
Strensham Services (northbound) Worcs 35 U12
Strensham Services (southbound) Worcs 36 B12
Stretcholt Somset 16 J8
Strete Devon 5 U11
Stretford Herefs 34 K9
Stretford Herefs 35 M9
Stretford Traffd 55 S8
Strethall Essex 39 Q13
Stretham Cambs 39 R6
Strettington W Susx 10 D9
Stretton Ches W 44 K3
Stretton Derbys 47 L1
Stretton Rutlnd 48 D10
Stretton Staffs 45 U11
Stretton Staffs 46 J8
Stretton Warrtn 55 P10
Stretton en le Field Leics 46 K11
Stretton Grandison Herefs 35 P12
Stretton-on-Dunsmore Warwks 37 M6
Stretton on Fosse Warwks 36 H13
Stretton Sugwas Herefs 35 L12
Stretton under Fosse Warwks 37 N4
Stretton Westwood Shrops 45 N14
Strichen Abers 105 Q4
Strines Stockp 56 E9
Stringston Somset 16 G8
Strixton Nhants 38 D8
Stroat Gloucs 27 V8
Strollamus Highld 100 e7
Stroma Highld 112 J1
Stromeferry Highld 101 M5
Stromness Ork 106 r19
Stronaba Highld 94 J2
Stronachlachar Stirlg 88 K3
Stronafian Ag & B 87 U9
Stronchrubie Highld 110 E13
Strone Ag & B 88 E9
Strone Highld 94 G2
Strone Highld 102 F10
Stronmilchan Ag & B 94 H13
Stronsay Ork 106 v17
Stronsay Airport Ork 106 v17
Strontian Highld 93 U6
Strood Kent 12 G9
Strood Medway 12 D2
Strood Green Surrey 21 M13
Strood Green W Susx 10 G6
Stroud Gloucs 28 G6
Stroud Hants 9 U4
Stroude Surrey 20 H9
Stroud Green Essex 23 L9
Stroud Green Gloucs 28 F6
Stroxton Lincs 48 D7
Struan Highld 100 c6
Struan P & K 97 N10
Strubby Lincs 59 S10
Strumpshaw Norfk 51 P12
Strutherhill S Lans 82 E9
Struthers Fife 91 N10
Struy Highld 102 D7
Stryd-y-Facsen IoA 52 D6
Stuartfield Abers 105 R6
Stubbers Green Wsall 46 D13
Stubbington Hants 9 R8
Stubbins Lancs 55 S3
Stubbs Cross Kent 12 J8
Stubbs Green Norfk 51 N14
Stubhampton Dorset 8 C6
Stubley Derbys 57 M11
Stubshaw Cross Wigan 55 N7
Stubton Lincs 48 C4
Stuckton Hants 8 H6
Studfold N York 62 G6
Stud Green W & M 20 E7
Studham C Beds 31 M9
Studholme Cumb 67 L1
Studland Dorset 8 E12
Studlands Park Suffk 39 T7
Studley Warwks 36 E8
Studley Wilts 18 E6
Studley Common Warwks 36 E8
Studley Roger N York 63 R6
Studley Royal N York 63 R5
Studley Royal Park & Fountains Abbey N York 63 R6
Stuntney Cambs 39 S5
Stunts Green E Susx 11 U8
Sturbridge Staffs 45 T7
Sturgate Lincs 58 E9
Sturmer Essex 39 U12
Sturminster Common Dorset 7 U2
Sturminster Marshall Dorset 8 D8
Sturminster Newton Dorset 7 U2
Sturry Kent 13 N3
Sturton N Linc 58 G6
Sturton by Stow Lincs 58 E10
Sturton le Steeple Notts 58 C10
Stuston Suffk 40 K5
Stutton N York 64 B11
Stutton Suffk 41 L14
Styal Ches E 55 T10
Stydd Lancs 62 D12
Stynie Moray 104 C3
Styrrup Notts 57 T8
Succoth Ag & B 88 G4
Suckley Worcs 35 R10
Suckley Green Worcs 35 R10
Sudborough Nhants 38 E4
Sudbourne Suffk 41 R10
Sudbrook Lincs 48 E5
Sudbrook Mons 27 U10
Sudbrooke Lincs 58 H11
Sudbury Derbys 46 G7
Sudbury Gt Lon 21 L5
Sudbury Suffk 40 E12
Sudden Rochdl 56 C4
Sudgrove Gloucs 28 H6
Suffield N York 65 M1
Suffield Norfk 51 M7
Sugdon Wrekin 45 P10
Sugnall Staffs 45 S7
Sugwas Pool Herefs 35 L12
Suisnish Highld 100 e8
Sulby IoM 60 f4
Sulgrave Nhants 30 C4
Sulham W Berk 19 T6
Sulhamstead W Berk 19 T7
Sulhamstead Abbots W Berk 19 T7
Sulhamstead Bannister W Berk 19 T7
Sullington W Susx 10 H8
Sullom Shet 106 t6
Sullom Voe Shet 106 u6
Sully V Glam 16 G3
Sumburgh Airport Shet 106 t12
Summerbridge N York 63 Q7
Summercourt Cnwll 3 M5
Summerfield Norfk 50 C6
Summerfield Worcs 35 T6
Summer Heath Bucks 20 B4
Summerhill Pembks 25 L9
Summerhill Staffs 46 E12
Summer Hill Wrexhm 44 H3
Summerhouse Darltn 69 R9
Summerlands Cumb 61 U2
Summerley Derbys 57 N11
Summersdale W Susx 10 D9
Summerseat Bury 55 S4
Summertown Oxon 30 B11
Summit Oldham 56 D5
Summit Rochdl 56 D3
Sunbiggin Cumb 68 E11
Sunbury-on-Thames Surrey 20 K9
Sundaywell D & G 74 F9
Sunderland Ag & B 78 C3
Sunderland Cumb 66 J5
Sunderland Lancs 61 S8
Sunderland Sundld 70 E1
Sunderland Bridge Dur 69 S5
Sundhope Border 83 R13
Sundon Park Luton 31 N7
Sundridge Kent 21 S11
Sunk Island E R Yk 59 N3
Sunningdale W & M 20 G9
Sunninghill W & M 20 F9
Sunningwell Oxon 29 U7
Sunniside Dur 69 P5
Sunniside Gatesd 77 Q14
Sunny Brow Dur 69 Q6
Sunnyhill C Derb 46 K7
Sunnyhurst Bl w D 55 Q2
Sunnylaw Stirlg 89 S6
Sunnymead Oxon 30 B11
Sunton Wilts 18 K10
Surbiton Gt Lon 21 L9
Surfleet Lincs 49 L8
Surfleet Seas End Lincs 49 L8
Surlingham Norfk 51 P12
Surrex Essex 23 L3
Sustead Norfk 51 L6
Susworth Lincs 58 D6
Sutcombe Devon 14 H10
Sutcombemill Devon 14 H10
Suton Norfk 50 J14
Sutterby Lincs 59 Q12
Sutterton Lincs 49 L6
Sutton C Beds 38 K11
Sutton C Pete 48 G14
Sutton Cambs 39 P5
Sutton Devon 5 S12
Sutton Devon 15 R12
Sutton Donc 57 S4
Sutton E Susx 11 R11
Sutton Gt Lon 21 N10
Sutton Kent 13 R6
Sutton N York 57 Q1
Sutton Norfk 51 Q9
Sutton Notts 47 U6
Sutton Oxon 29 T6
Sutton Pembks 24 F7
Sutton Shrops 35 R3
Sutton Shrops 44 J8
Sutton Shrops 45 M11
Sutton Shrops 45 Q7
Sutton St Hel 55 M8
Sutton Staffs 45 S9
Sutton Suffk 41 P11
Sutton W Susx 10 F7
Sutton Abinger Surrey 20 K13
Sutton-at-Hone Kent 21 U9
Sutton Bassett Nhants 37 U2
Sutton Benger Wilts 18 D5
Sutton Bingham Somset 7 P2
Sutton Bonington Notts 47 P9
Sutton Bridge Lincs 49 Q9
Sutton Cheney Leics 47 M13
Sutton Coldfield Birm 36 F1
Sutton Courtenay Oxon 19 R2
Sutton Crosses Lincs 49 P9
Sutton cum Lound Notts 57 U10
Sutton Fields Notts 47 N8
Sutton Green Surrey 20 H12
Sutton Green Wrexhm 44 K4
Sutton Heath Suffk 41 P11
Sutton Howgrave N York 63 S4
Sutton-in-Ashfield Notts 47 N2
Sutton-in-Craven N York 63 L11
Sutton in the Elms Leics 37 P2
Sutton Lane Ends Ches E 56 D12
Sutton Maddock Shrops 45 R13
Sutton Mallet Somset 17 L9
Sutton Mandeville Wilts 8 D3
Sutton Manor St Hel 55 M8
Sutton Marsh Herefs 35 N12
Sutton Montis Somset 17 R12
Sutton-on-Hull C KuH 65 Q13
Sutton on Sea Lincs 59 T10
Sutton-on-the-Forest N York 64 D7
Sutton on the Hill Derbys 46 H7
Sutton on Trent Notts 58 C13
Sutton Poyntz Dorset 7 T8
Sutton St Edmund Lincs 49 N11
Sutton St James Lincs 49 N10
Sutton St Nicholas Herefs 35 M11
Sutton Scotney Hants 19 Q13
Sutton Street Kent 12 F4
Sutton-under-Brailes Warwks 36 K13
Sutton-under-Whitestonecliffe N York 64 B3
Sutton upon Derwent E R Yk 64 G10
Sutton Valence Kent 12 F6
Sutton Veny Wilts 18 D12
Sutton Waldron Dorset 8 B5
Sutton Weaver Ches W 55 M11
Sutton Wick BaNES 17 Q5
Sutton Wick Oxon 29 U9
Swaby Lincs 59 Q11
Swadlincote Derbys 46 J10
Swaffham Norfk 50 D12
Swaffham Bulbeck Cambs 39 S8
Swaffham Prior Cambs 39 S8
Swafield Norfk 51 N7
Swainby N York 70 G12
Swainshill Herefs 35 L12
Swainsthorpe Norfk 51 M13
Swainswick BaNES 17 U3
Swalcliffe Oxon 37 L13
Swalecliffe Kent 13 M2
Swallow Lincs 59 L6
Swallow Beck Lincs 58 F13
Swallowcliffe Wilts 8 D3
Swallowfield Wokham 20 B10
Swallownest Rothm 57 Q9
Swallows Cross Essex 22 F8
Swampton Hants 19 P10
Swanage Dorset 8 E13
Swanbourne Bucks 30 H7
Swanbridge V Glam 16 G3
Swancote Shrops 35 R2
Swan Green Ches W 55 R12
Swanland E R Yk 65 M14
Swanley Kent 21 T9
Swanley Village Kent 21 T9
Swanmore Hants 9 R5
Swannington Leics 47 M10
Swannington Norfk 50 K10
Swanpool Lincs 58 G13
Swanscombe Kent 22 F13
Swansea Swans 26 B9
Swansea Airport Swans 25 U12
Swansea West Services Swans 26 A8
Swan Street Essex 23 L2
Swanton Abbot Norfk 51 N8
Swanton Morley Norfk 50 H10
Swanton Novers Norfk 50 H7
Swanton Street Kent 12 G4
Swan Valley Nhants 37 T9
Swan Village Sandw 36 C2
Swanwick Derbys 47 M3
Swanwick Hants 9 Q7
Swarby Lincs 48 F5
Swardeston Norfk 51 M13
Swarkestone Derbys 47 L8
Swarland Nthumb 77 P5
Swarraton Hants 19 S13
Swartha C Brad 63 M10
Swarthmoor Cumb 61 P4
Swaton Lincs 48 H6
Swavesey Cambs 39 N7
Sway Hants 8 K9
Swayfield Lincs 48 E9
Swaythling C Sotn 9 N5
Sweet Green Worcs 35 P8
Sweetham Devon 15 U13
Sweethaws E Susx 11 S5
Sweetlands Corner Kent 12 E6
Sweets Cnwll 14 E13
Sweetshouse Cnwll 3 R4
Swefling Suffk 41 P8
Swepstone Leics 47 L11
Swerford Oxon 29 S1
Swettenham Ches E 55 T13
Swffryd Blae G 27 N8
Swift's Green Kent 12 G7
Swilland Suffk 41 L10
Swillbrook Lancs 61 T13
Swillington Leeds 63 T13
Swimbridge Devon 15 P6
Swimbridge Newland Devon 15 P6
Swinbrook Oxon 29 Q5
Swincliffe Kirk 63 Q14
Swincliffe N York 63 Q8
Swincombe Devon 15 Q4
Swindale Cumb 67 R10
Swinden N York 62 H9
Swinderby Lincs 58 E14
Swindon Gloucs 28 H2
Swindon Nthumb 76 K6
Swindon Staffs 35 U2
Swindon Swindn 29 M11
Swine E R Yk 65 Q12
Swinefleet E R Yk 58 C2
Swineford S Glos 17 S3
Swineshead Bed 38 G7
Swineshead Lincs 48 K5
Swineshead Bridge Lincs 48 K5
Swiney Highld 112 F9
Swinford Leics 37 Q5
Swinford Oxon 29 T6
Swingate Notts 47 P5
Swingfield Minnis Kent 13 P7
Swingfield Street Kent 13 P7
Swingleton Green Suffk 40 G11
Swinhoe Nthumb 85 U13
Swinhope Lincs 59 M7
Swinithwaite N York 63 L2
Swinmore Common Herefs 35 Q12
Swinscoe Staffs 46 F4
Swinside Cumb 66 K8
Swinstead Lincs 48 F9
Swinthorpe Lincs 58 J10
Swinton Border 85 L9
Swinton N York 63 Q4
Swinton N York 64 H5
Swinton Rothm 57 Q7
Swinton Salfd 55 S6
Swiss Valley Carmth 25 T10
Swithland Leics 47 Q11
Swordale Highld 102 G2
Swordland Highld 100 g10
Swordly Highld 111 Q4
Sworton Heath Ches E 55 Q10
Swyddffynnon Cerdgn 33 N7
Swyncombe Oxon 19 U2
Swynnerton Staffs 45 U6
Swyre Dorset 7 P7
Sycharth Powys 44 F8
Sychnant Powys 33 U5
Sychtyn Powys 43 U12
Sydallt Wrexhm 44 H2
Syde Gloucs 28 J5
Sydenham Gt Lon 21 Q8
Sydenham Oxon 30 F12
Sydenham Damerel Devon 5 L5
Sydenhurst Surrey 10 F4
Syderstone Norfk 50 D7
Sydling St Nicholas Dorset 7 R5
Sydmonton Hants 19 Q9
Sydnal Lane Shrops 45 T12
Syerston Notts 47 T4
Syke Rochdl 56 C3
Sykehouse Donc 57 T3
Syleham Suffk 41 M5
Sylen Carmth 25 T9
Symbister Shet 106 v7
Symington S Ayrs 81 M6
Symington S Lans 82 J11
Symondsbury Dorset 7 M6
Symonds Yat (East) Herefs 27 V4
Symonds Yat (West) Herefs 27 V4
Sympson Green C Brad 63 P12
Synderford Dorset 7 L4
Synod Inn Cerdgn 32 H10
Syre Highld 111 P8
Syreford Gloucs 28 K3
Syresham Nhants 30 D4
Syston Leics 47 R11
Syston Lincs 48 D5
Sytchampton Worcs 35 T7
Sywell Nhants 38 B7

T

Tabley Hill Ches E 55 R11
Tackley Oxon 29 U4
Tacolneston Norfk 40 K1
Tadcaster N York 64 B11
Taddington Derbys 56 H12
Taddington Gloucs 29 L1
Taddiport Devon 15 L9
Tadley Hants 19 T8
Tadlow Cambs 39 L11
Tadmarton Oxon 37 L13
Tadpole Swindn 29 M9
Tadwick BaNES 17 T2
Tadworth Surrey 21 M11
Tafarnaubach Blae G 27 L5
Tafarn-y-bwlch Pembks 24 J4
Tafarn-y-Gelyn Denbgs 44 E1
Taff's Well Rhondd 27 L11
Tafolwern Powys 43 S13
Taibach Neath 26 D10
Tain Highld 109 P8
Tain Highld 112 F3
Tai'n Lôn Gwynd 42 H3
Tai'r Bull Powys 26 H2
Tairgwaith Neath 26 C5
Takeley Essex 22 E3
Takeley Street Essex 22 D3
Talachddu Powys 34 C14
Talacre Flints 54 D10
Talaton Devon 6 E5
Talbenny Pembks 24 D8
Talbot Green Rhondd 26 J11
Talbot Village BCP 8 F10
Taleford Devon 6 E5
Talerddig Powys 43 T13
Talgarreg Cerdgn 32 H10
Talgarth Powys 34 E14
Talisker Highld 100 c6
Talke Staffs 45 T3
Talke Pits Staffs 45 T3
Talkin Cumb 67 S1
Talladale Highld 107 R10
Talla Linnfoots Border 75 M1
Tallaminnock S Ayrs 81 N13
Tallarn Green Wrexhm 44 K5
Tallentire Cumb 66 H5
Talley Carmth 33 M14
Tallington Lincs 48 G12
Tallwrn Wrexhm 44 G4
Talmine Highld 111 M4
Talog Carmth 25 P5
Talsarn Cerdgn 32 K9
Talsarnau Gwynd 43 M6
Talskiddy Cnwll 3 N3
Talwrn IoA 52 G7
Talwrn Wrexhm 44 J4
Tal-y-bont Cerdgn 33 N3
Tal-y-Bont Conwy 53 N9
Talybont Gwynd 43 L9
Tal-y-bont Gwynd 52 K8
Talybont-on-Usk Powys 27 L3
Tal-y-Cafn Conwy 53 N8
Tal-y-coed Mons 27 S4
Tal-y-garn Rhondd 26 J12
Tal-y-llyn Gwynd 43 P12
Talysarn Gwynd 52 G12
Tal-y-Waun Torfn 27 P7
Talywern Powys 43 R13
Tamar Valley Mining District Devon 5 L7
Tamer Lane End Wigan 55 P6
Tamerton Foliot C Plym 5 M8
Tamworth Staffs 46 H13
Tamworth Green Lincs 49 N5
Tamworth Services Warwks 46 H13
Tancred N York 64 B8
Tancredston Pembks 24 E5
Tandridge Surrey 21 Q12
Tanfield Dur 69 Q1
Tanfield Lea Dur 69 Q2
Tangasdale W Isls 106 b18
Tangiers Pembks 24 G7
Tangley Hants 19 M10
Tangmere W Susx 10 E9
Tan Hill N York 68 J11
Tankerness Ork 106 u19
Tankersley Barns 57 M7
Tankerton Kent 13 M2
Tannach Highld 112 H7
Tannachie Abers 99 P7
Tannadice Angus 98 H12
Tanner's Green Worcs 36 E6
Tannington Suffk 41 M7
Tannochside N Lans 82 D6
Tansley Derbys 46 K2
Tansor Nhants 38 G2
Tantobie Dur 69 Q2
Tanton N York 70 H10
Tanwood Worcs 36 B6
Tanworth in Arden Warwks 36 F6
Tan-y-Bwlch Gwynd 43 N5
Tan-y-fron Conwy 53 S10
Tan-y-fron Wrexhm 44 G3
Tan-y-grisiau Gwynd 43 N4
Tan-y-groes Cerdgn 32 E11
Taobh Tuath W Isls 106 e10
Taplow Bucks 20 F6
Tarbert Ag & B 79 M5
Tarbert Ag & B 87 R12
Tarbert W Isls 106 g8
Tarbet Ag & B 88 H5
Tarbet Highld 100 g10
Tarbet Highld 110 D7
Tarbock Green Knows 55 L9
Tarbolton S Ayrs 81 N7
Tarbrax S Lans 82 K7
Tardebigge Worcs 36 C7
Tarfside Angus 98 H8
Tarland Abers 98 H3
Tarleton Lancs 55 L2
Tarlscough Lancs 54 K4
Tarlton Gloucs 28 J8
Tarnock Somset 17 L6
Tarns Cumb 66 H3
Tarnside Cumb 61 S1
Tarporley Ches W 55 N14
Tarr Somset 15 U6
Tarrant Crawford Dorset 8 C8
Tarrant Gunville Dorset 8 C6
Tarrant Hinton Dorset 8 C6
Tarrant Keyneston Dorset 8 C8
Tarrant Launceston Dorset 8 C7
Tarrant Monkton Dorset 8 C7
Tarrant Rawston Dorset 8 C7
Tarrant Rushton Dorset 8 C7
Tarring Neville E Susx 11 Q10
Tarrington Herefs 35 P12
Tarskavaig Highld 100 e8
Tarves Abers 105 P9
Tarvin Ches W 55 L13
Tarvin Sands Ches W 55 L13
Tasburgh Norfk 41 M1

Tasley Shrops 35 Q2
Taston Oxon 29 S3
Tatenhill Staffs 46 H9
Tathall End M Keyn 38 B11
Tatham Lancs 62 C6
Tathwell Lincs 59 P10
Tatsfield Surrey 21 R11
Tattenhall Ches W 45 L2
Tatterford Norfk 50 E8
Tattersett Norfk 50 D8
Tattershall Lincs 48 K2
Tattershall Bridge Lincs 48 J2
Tattershall Thorpe Lincs 48 K2
Tattingstone Suffk 40 K13
Tattingstone White Horse Suffk 40 K13
Tatton Park Ches E 55 R10
Tatworth Somset 6 K3
Tauchers Moray 104 D6
Taunton Somset 16 H12
Taunton Deane Services Somset 16 G12
Taverham Norfk 51 L11
Taverners Green Essex 22 E4
Tavernspite Pembks 25 L8
Tavistock Devon 5 M6
Tavistock Devon 5 M6
Taw Green Devon 15 Q13
Tawstock Devon 15 N7
Taxal Derbys 56 F11
Tay Bridge C Dund 91 P6
Taychreggan Hotel Ag & B 88 B1
Tay Forest Park P & K 97 M11
Tayinloan Ag & B 79 M6
Taynton Gloucs 28 D3
Taynton Oxon 29 P5
Taynuilt Ag & B 94 E12
Tayport Fife 91 Q6
Tayvallich Ag & B 87 N8
Tealby Lincs 59 L8
Tealing Angus 91 P4
Team Valley Gatesd 77 Q14
Teangue Highld 100 f9
Teanord Highld 102 G3
Tebay Cumb 68 D12
Tebay Services Cumb 68 D11
Tebworth C Beds 31 L7
Tedburn St Mary Devon 5 U2
Teddington Gloucs 36 C14
Teddington Gt Lon 21 L8
Tedstone Delamere Herefs 35 Q9
Tedstone Wafer Herefs 35 Q9
Teesport R & Cl 70 H8
Teesside Park S on T 70 G9
Teeton Nhants 37 S6
Teffont Evias Wilts 8 D2
Teffont Magna Wilts 8 D2
Tegryn Pembks 25 M4
Teigh Rutlnd 48 C10
Teigncombe Devon 5 R3
Teigngrace Devon 5 V6
Teignmouth Devon 6 B10
Teindside Border 75 T4
Telford Wrekin 45 Q12
Telford Services Shrops 45 R12
Telham E Susx 12 E13
Tellisford Somset 18 B9
Telscombe E Susx 11 Q10
Telscombe Cliffs E Susx 11 Q10
Tempar P & K 95 T7
Templand D & G 75 L8
Temple Cnwll 4 E6
Temple Mdloth 83 R7
Temple Balsall Solhll 36 H5
Temple Bar Cerdgn 32 K10
Temple Cloud BaNES 17 R5
Templecombe Somset 17 T12
Temple End Suffk 39 U10
Temple Ewell Kent 13 Q7
Temple Grafton Warwks 36 F9
Temple Guiting Gloucs 29 L2
Temple Herdewyke Warwks 37 L10
Temple Hirst N York 57 T2
Temple Normanton Derbys 57 P13
Temple of Fiddes Abers 99 Q7
Temple Sowerby Cumb 68 D7
Templeton Devon 15 U10
Templeton Pembks 24 K8
Templetown Dur 69 P2
Tempsford C Beds 38 J10
Tenbury Wells Worcs 35 N7
Tenby Pembks 24 K10
Tendring Essex 23 R3
Tendring Green Essex 23 R2
Tendring Heath Essex 23 R2
Ten Mile Bank Norfk 39 S1
Tenpenny Heath Essex 23 Q3
Tenterden Kent 12 G9
Terling Essex 22 J4
Tern Wrekin 45 P10
Ternhill Shrops 45 P7
Terregles D & G 74 H10
Terrington N York 64 F5
Terrington St Clement Norfk 49 S9
Terrington St John Norfk 49 R11
Terry's Green Warwks 36 F6
Teston Kent 12 D5
Testwood Hants 9 M6
Tetbury Gloucs 28 G9
Tetbury Upton Gloucs 28 G8
Tetchill Shrops 44 J7
Tetcott Devon 14 H13
Tetford Lincs 59 P12
Tetney Lincs 59 P6
Tetney Lock Lincs 59 P6
Tetsworth Oxon 30 E12
Tettenhall Wolves 45 U13
Tettenhall Wood Wolves 45 U14
Teversal Notts 47 N1
Teversham Cambs 39 Q9
Teviothead Border 75 T4
Tewin Herts 31 S10
Tewin Wood Herts 31 S9
Tewkesbury Gloucs 35 U14
Teynham Kent 12 J3
Thackley C Brad 63 P12
Thackthwaite Cumb 66 H8
Thackthwaite Cumb 67 P7
Thainstone Abers 105 M12
Thakeham W Susx 10 J7
Thame Oxon 30 F11
Thames Ditton Surrey 21 L9
Thamesmead Gt Lon 21 S6
Thamesport Medway 23 L13
Thanington Kent 13 M4
Thankerton S Lans 82 J11
Tharston Norfk 41 L2
Thatcham W Berk 19 R7
Thatto Heath St Hel 55 M8
Thaxted Essex 22 F1
Theakston N York 63 S2
Thealby N Linc 58 E3
Theale Somset 17 N7
Theale W Berk 19 T6
Thearne E R Yk 65 P12
The Bank Ches E 45 T2
The Beeches Gloucs 28 K7
Theberton Suffk 41 R7
The Blythe Staffs 46 D8
The Bog Shrops 44 J14
The Bourne Worcs 36 C9
The Braes Highld 100 e6
The Bratch Staffs 35 U2
The Bridge Kent 22 D12
The Broad Herefs 35 L8
The Broads 51 S12
The Brunt E Loth 84 H4
The Bryn Mons 27 Q6
The Bungalow IoM 60 f5
The Burf Worcs 35 T7
The Camp Gloucs 28 H6
The Chequer Wrexhm 45 L5
The City Bed 38 H9
The City Bucks 20 C3
The Common Oxon 29 Q2
The Common Wilts 8 J2
The Common Wilts 28 K10
The Corner Kent 12 D7
The Cronk IoM 60 e3
Theddingworth Leics 37 S3
Theddlethorpe All Saints Lincs 59 S9
Theddlethorpe St Helen Lincs 59 S9
The Deep C KuH 65 P14
The Den N Ayrs 81 L2
The Forge Herefs 34 H9
The Forstal Kent 12 K8
The Fouralls Shrops 45 Q7
The Green Cumb 61 M3
The Green Essex 22 J4
The Green N York 71 N11
The Green Wilts 8 B2
The Grove Dur 69 N2
The Grove Worcs 35 U12
The Haven W Susx 10 H4
The Haw Gloucs 28 F2
The Hendre Mons 27 T5
The Hill Cumb 61 M3
The Holt Wokham 20 D7
The Hundred Herefs 35 M8
Thelbridge Cross Devon 15 S10
The Leacon Kent 12 J9
The Lee Bucks 30 K12
The Lhen IoM 60 f2
Thelnetham Suffk 40 H5
The Lochs Moray 104 C3
Thelveton Norfk 41 L4
Thelwall Warrtn 55 Q9
The Marsh Powys 44 H14
Themelthorpe Norfk 50 J9
The Middles Dur 69 R2
The Moor Kent 12 E10
The Mumbles Swans 25 V13
The Murray S Lans 81 S2
The Mythe Gloucs 35 U14
The Narth Mons 27 U6
The Neuk Abers 99 N4
Thenford Nhants 30 B4
Theobald's Green Wilts 18 F7
The Quarry Gloucs 28 D8
The Quarter Kent 12 G7
The Reddings Gloucs 28 H3
Therfield Herts 31 T5
The Rhôs Powys 27 M1
The Ross P & K 89 S1
The Sands Surrey 20 E13
The Shoe Wilts 18 B6
The Smithies Shrops 45 Q14
The Spring Warwks 36 J6
The Square Torfn 27 P8
The Stair Kent 12 B6
The Stocks Kent 12 H10
The Straits Hants 10 B3
The Strand Wilts 18 D9
Thetford Norfk 40 E4
Thetford Forest Park 40 D3
Thethwaite Cumb 67 N4
The Towans Cnwll 2 F9
The Vauld Herefs 35 M11
The Wyke Shrops 45 R12
Theydon Bois Essex 21 R3
Theydon Mount Essex 21 S3
Thicket Priory N York 64 F11
Thickwood Wilts 18 B6
Thimbleby Lincs 59 M12
Thimbleby N York 70 F13
Thingwall Wirral 54 G10
Thirkleby N York 64 B4
Thirlby N York 64 B3
Thirlestane Border 84 F9
Thirn N York 63 Q2
Thirsk N York 63 U3
Thirtleby E R Yk 65 R13
Thistleton Lancs 61 S12
Thistleton Rutlnd 48 D10
Thistley Green Suffk 39 U5
Thixendale N York 64 J7
Thockrington Nthumb 76 K10
Tholomas Drove Cambs 49 P12
Tholthorpe N York 64 B6
Thomas Chapel Pembks 24 K9
Thomas Close Cumb 67 P4
Thomastown Abers 104 H8
Thompson Norfk 40 F1
Thomshill Moray 103 V4
Thong Kent 22 G13
Thongsbridge Kirk 56 J5
Thoralby N York 63 L2
Thoresby Notts 57 T12
Thoresthorpe Lincs 59 S11
Thoresway Lincs 59 L7
Thorganby Lincs 59 M7
Thorganby N York 64 F11
Thorgill N York 71 M13
Thorington Suffk 41 R6
Thorington Street Suffk 40 H13
Thorlby N York 62 K9
Thorley Herts 22 C4
Thorley IoW 9 M11
Thorley Houses Herts 22 C3
Thorley Street IoW 9 M11
Thormanby N York 64 B5
Thornaby-on-Tees S on T 70 G9
Thornage Norfk 50 J6
Thornborough Bucks 30 F6
Thornborough N York 63 R4
Thornbury C Brad 63 P13
Thornbury Devon 14 K11
Thornbury Herefs 35 P9
Thornbury S Glos 28 B9
Thornby Cumb 67 L2
Thornby Nhants 37 S5
Thorncliff Staffs 46 D2
Thorncombe Dorset 7 L4
Thorncombe Street Surrey 10 F2
Thorncott Green C Beds 38 J11
Thorncross IoW 9 N12
Thorndon Suffk 40 K7
Thorndon Cross Devon 5 N2
Thorne Donc 57 U4
Thorne Coffin Somset 17 P13
Thornecroft Devon 5 T7
Thornehillhead Devon 14 K9
Thorner Leeds 63 T11
Thornes Staffs 46 E13
Thornes Wakefd 57 M3
Thorne St Margaret Somset 16 F12
Thorney Bucks 20 H7
Thorney C Pete 49 L13
Thorney Notts 58 E12
Thorney Somset 17 M12
Thorney Hill Hants 8 J9
Thorney Island W Susx 10 B10
Thorney Toll Cambs 49 M13
Thornfalcon Somset 16 J12
Thornford Dorset 7 R2
Thorngrafton Nthumb 76 F12
Thorngrove Somset 17 L10
Thorngumbald E R Yk 59 M1
Thornham Norfk 50 B5
Thornham Magna Suffk 40 K6
Thornham Parva Suffk 40 K6
Thornhaugh C Pete 48 G13
Thornhill C Sotn 9 P6
Thornhill Caerph 27 M11
Thornhill Cumb 66 F11
Thornhill D & G 74 G6
Thornhill Derbys 56 J10
Thornhill Kirk 57 L3
Thornhill Stirlg 89 Q5
Thornhill Lees Kirk 56 K3
Thornhills Calder 56 J2
Thornholme E R Yk 65 Q7
Thornicombe Dorset 8 B8
Thornington Nthumb 85 M12
Thornley Dur 69 P5
Thornley Dur 70 E5
Thornley Gate Nthumb 68 H1
Thornliebank E Rens 89 N14
Thorns Suffk 40 B9
Thornsett Derbys 56 F9
Thorns Green Ches E 55 S10
Thornthwaite Cumb 66 K7
Thornthwaite N York 63 P8
Thornton Angus 91 N2
Thornton Bucks 30 F5
Thornton C Brad 63 M13
Thornton E R Yk 64 H10
Thornton Fife 91 L12
Thornton Lancs 61 Q11
Thornton Leics 47 N12
Thornton Lincs 59 M13
Thornton Middsb 70 G10
Thornton Nthumb 85 P9
Thornton Pembks 24 F9
Thornton Sefton 54 H6
Thornton Curtis N Linc 58 J3
Thorntonhall S Lans 81 R1
Thornton Heath Gt Lon 21 P9
Thornton Hough Wirral 54 H10
Thornton-in-Craven N York 62 J10
Thornton in Lonsdale N York 62 D5
Thornton-le-Beans N York 63 T1
Thornton-le-Clay N York 64 F6
Thornton-le-Dale N York 64 J3
Thornton le Moor Lincs 58 H7
Thornton-le-Moor N York 63 T2
Thornton-le-Moors Ches W 54 K12
Thornton-le-Street N York 63 U2
Thorntonloch E Loth 84 K4
Thornton Rust N York 62 K2
Thornton Steward N York 63 P2
Thornton Watlass N York 63 Q2
Thornwood Common Essex 22 C7
Thornydykes Border 84 G9
Thornythwaite Cumb 67 N8
Thoroton Notts 47 U5
Thorp Arch Leeds 63 U10
Thorpe Derbys 46 G3
Thorpe E R Yk 65 M10
Thorpe Lincs 59 S10
Thorpe N York 63 L7
Thorpe Norfk 51 R14
Thorpe Notts 47 U4
Thorpe Surrey 20 H9
Thorpe Abbotts Norfk 41 L5
Thorpe Acre Leics 47 P10
Thorpe Arnold Leics 47 U9
Thorpe Audlin Wakefd 57 Q3
Thorpe Bassett N York 64 K5
Thorpe Bay Sthend 23 M10
Thorpe by Water Rutlnd 38 C1
Thorpe Common Rothm 57 N7
Thorpe Constantine Staffs 46 J12
Thorpe End Norfk 51 N11
Thorpe Green Essex 23 S3
Thorpe Green Lancs 55 N2
Thorpe Green Suffk 40 F10
Thorpe Hesley Rothm 57 N7
Thorpe in Balne Donc 57 S4
Thorpe Langton Leics 37 T2
Thorpe Larches Dur 70 E7
Thorpe Lea Surrey 20 H8
Thorpe le Fallows Lincs 58 F10
Thorpe-le-Soken Essex 23 S3
Thorpe le Street E R Yk 64 J11
Thorpe Malsor Nhants 38 B5
Thorpe Mandeville Nhants 30 B4
Thorpe Market Norfk 51 M6
Thorpe Marriot Norfk 51 L10
Thorpe Morieux Suffk 40 F10
Thorpeness Suffk 41 S9
Thorpe on the Hill Leeds 57 M1
Thorpe on the Hill Lincs 58 F13
Thorpe Park Surrey 20 H9
Thorpe St Andrew Norfk 51 N12
Thorpe St Peter Lincs 49 Q1
Thorpe Salvin Rothm 57 R10
Thorpe Satchville Leics 47 T11
Thorpe Thewles S on T 70 E8
Thorpe Tilney Lincs 48 H2
Thorpe Underwood N York 64 B8
Thorpe Underwood Nhants 37 U4
Thorpe Waterville Nhants 38 F4
Thorpe Willoughby N York 64 D13
Thorpland Norfk 49 T12
Thorrington Essex 23 Q4
Thorverton Devon 6 B4
Thrales End C Beds 31 P9
Thrandeston Suffk 40 K5
Thrapston Nhants 38 E5
Threapland Cumb 66 J5
Threapland N York 62 K7
Threapwood Ches W 44 K5
Threapwood Staffs 46 D5
Threapwood Head Staffs 46 D5
Threave S Ayrs 81 L11
Three Ashes Herefs 27 U3
Three Bridges W Susx 11 M3
Three Burrows Cnwll 2 K7
Three Chimneys Kent 12 F8
Three Cocks Powys 34 E13
Three Crosses Swans 25 U12
Three Cups Corner E Susx 11 U6
Three Gates Worcs 35 Q8
Threehammer Common Norfk 51 P10
Three Hammers Cnwll 4 G3
Three Holes Norfk 49 R13
Threekingham Lincs 48 G6
Three Leg Cross E Susx 12 C9
Three Legged Cross Dorset 8 F7
Three Mile Cross Wokham 20 B9
Threemilestone Cnwll 2 K7
Threemiletown W Loth 83 L3
Three Oaks E Susx 12 F13
Threlkeld Cumb 67 M7
Threshers Bush Essex 22 C6
Threshfield N York 62 K7
Thrigby Norfk 51 S11
Thringarth Dur 68 K8
Thringstone Leics 47 M10
Thrintoft N York 70 D14
Thriplow Cambs 39 P11
Throapham Rothm 57 R9
Throckenhalt Lincs 49 N12
Throcking Herts 31 T6
Throckley N u Ty 77 P12
Throckmorton Worcs 36 C10
Throop BCP 8 G9
Throop Dorset 8 A10
Throphill Nthumb 77 N8
Thropton Nthumb 77 L5
Throsk Stirlg 90 C13
Througham Gloucs 28 H6
Throughgate D & G 74 G9
Throwleigh Devon 5 R2
Throwley Kent 12 J4
Throwley Forstal Kent 12 J5
Thrumpton Notts 47 P7
Thrumpton Notts 58 B10
Thrumster Highld 112 H7
Thrunscoe NE Lin 59 P5
Thrunton Nthumb 77 M3
Thrup Oxon 29 Q8
Thrupp Gloucs 28 G7
Thrupp Oxon 29 U4
Thrushelton Devon 5 L3
Thrussington Leics 47 S10
Thruxton Hants 19 L11
Thruxton Herefs 34 K14
Thrybergh Rothm 57 Q7
Thulston Derbys 47 M7
Thundersley Essex 22 J10
Thurcaston Leics 47 Q11
Thurcroft Rothm 57 Q9
Thurdon Cnwll 14 G10
Thurgarton Norfk 51 L7
Thurgarton Notts 47 S4
Thurgoland Barns 57 L6
Thurlaston Leics 47 P14
Thurlaston Warwks 37 N6
Thurlbear Somset 16 J12
Thurlby Lincs 48 D1
Thurlby Lincs 48 G10
Thurlby Lincs 59 S11
Thurleigh Bed 38 G9
Thurlestone Devon 5 R12
Thurloxton Somset 16 J10
Thurlstone Barns 56 K6
Thurlton Norfk 51 R14
Thurlwood Ches E 45 T2
Thurmaston Leics 47 R12
Thurnby Leics 47 R13
Thurne Norfk 51 R10
Thurnham Kent 12 F4
Thurning Nhants 38 G4
Thurning Norfk 50 J8
Thurnscoe Barns 57 Q5
Thurrock Services Thurr 22 E12
Thursby Cumb 67 M2
Thursden Lancs 62 J13
Thursford Norfk 50 G7
Thursley Surrey 10 E3
Thurso Highld 112 D3
Thurstaston Wirral 54 F10
Thurston Suffk 40 F7
Thurston Clough Oldham 56 E5
Thurstonfield Cumb 67 M1
Thurstonland Kirk 56 J4
Thurston Planche Suffk 40 F8
Thurton Norfk 51 P13
Thurvaston Derbys 46 H6
Thuxton Norfk 50 H12
Thwaite N York 68 J13
Thwaite Suffk 40 K7
Thwaite Head Cumb 61 Q1
Thwaites C Brad 63 M11
Thwaite St Mary Norfk 41 P1
Thwaites Brow C Brad 63 M11
Thwing E R Yk 65 N5
Tibbermore P & K 90 F7
Tibbers D & G 74 G6
Tibberton Gloucs 28 E3
Tibberton Worcs 36 B9
Tibberton Wrekin 45 Q9
Tibenham Norfk 40 K3
Tibshelf Derbys 47 M1
Tibshelf Services Derbys 47 M1
Tibthorpe E R Yk 65 M8
Ticehurst E Susx 12 C9
Tichborne Hants 9 R2
Tickencote Rutlnd 48 E12
Tickenham N Som 17 N2
Tickford End M Keyn 30 J4
Tickhill Donc 57 S8
Ticklerton Shrops 35 L2
Ticknall Derbys 47 L9
Tickton E R Yk 65 P11
Tidbury Green Solhll 36 F5
Tidcombe Wilts 19 L9
Tiddington Oxon 30 D12
Tiddington Warwks 36 H9
Tiddleywink Wilts 18 C5
Tidebrook E Susx 11 U4
Tideford Cnwll 4 K9
Tideford Cross Cnwll 4 J8
Tidenham Gloucs 27 V8
Tideswell Derbys 56 J11
Tidmarsh W Berk 19 T6
Tidmington Warwks 36 J13
Tidpit Hants 8 F5
Tidworth Wilts 18 K11
Tiers Cross Pembks 24 F8
Tiffield Nhants 37 T10
Tigerton Angus 98 J11
Tigh a' Ghearraidh W Isls 106 c11
Tigharry W Isls 106 c11
Tighnabruaich Ag & B 87 T11
Tigley Devon 5 T8
Tilbrook Cambs 38 G7
Tilbury Thurr 22 F12
Tilbury Dock Thurr 22 F12
Tilbury Green Essex 40 B12
Tilbury Juxta Clare Essex 40 C12
Tile Cross Birm 36 G3
Tile Hill Covtry 36 J5
Tilehouse Green Solhll 36 G5
Tilehurst Readg 19 U6
Tilford Surrey 10 D2
Tilgate W Susx 11 M4
Tilgate Forest Row W Susx 11 M4
Tilham Street Somset 17 Q9
Tillers Green Gloucs 35 Q14
Tillicoultry Clacks 90 D12
Tillietudlem S Lans 82 F9
Tillingham Essex 23 N7
Tillington Herefs 35 L12
Tillington W Susx 10 F6
Tillington Common Herefs 35 L11
Tillybirloch Abers 99 M2
Tillyfourie Abers 104 J13
Tillygreig Abers 105 P11
Tillyrie P & K 90 H10
Tilmanstone Kent 13 R5
Tilney All Saints Norfk 49 S10
Tilney High End Norfk 49 S10
Tilney St Lawrence Norfk 49 R11
Tilshead Wilts 18 F11
Tilstock Shrops 45 M6
Tilston Ches W 45 L3
Tilstone Bank Ches W 45 N2
Tilstone Fearnall Ches W 45 N1
Tilsworth C Beds 31 L8
Tilton on the Hill Leics 47 T12
Tiltups End Gloucs 28 F8
Tilty Essex 22 E2
Timberland Lincs 48 H2
Timbersbrook Ches E 56 C14
Timberscombe Somset 16 C8
Timble N York 63 P9
Timewell Devon 16 C11
Timpanheck D & G 75 R11
Timperley Traffd 55 S9
Timsbury BaNES 17 S5
Timsbury Hants 9 L4
Timsgarry W Isls 106 f5
Timsgearraidh W Isls 106 f5
Timworth Suffk 40 E7
Timworth Green Suffk 40 E7
Tincleton Dorset 7 U6
Tindale Cumb 76 C14
Tingewick Bucks 30 E6
Tingley Leeds 57 L1
Tingrith C Beds 31 M6
Tingwall Airport Shet 106 u9
Tingwell Ork 106 t17
Tinhay Devon 4 K3
Tinker's Hill Hants 19 P11
Tinkersley Derbys 57 L14
Tinsley Sheff 57 P8
Tinsley Green W Susx 11 M3
Tintagel Cnwll 4 D3
Tintern Mons 27 U7
Tintinhull Somset 17 N13
Tintwistle Derbys 56 F7
Tinwald D & G 74 K9
Tinwell Rutlnd 48 F12
Tippacott Devon 15 S3
Tipp's End Norfk 39 R1
Tiptoe Hants 8 K9
Tipton Sandw 36 C2
Tipton Green Sandw 36 C2
Tipton St John Devon 6 E6
Tiptree Essex 23 L4
Tiptree Heath Essex 23 L4
Tirabad Powys 33 S12
Tircoed Swans 25 V10
Tiree Ag & B 92 C10
Tiree Airport Ag & B 92 C10
Tiretigan Ag & B 79 N3
Tirley Gloucs 28 F2
Tiroran Ag & B 93 M13
Tirphil Caerph 27 L7
Tirril Cumb 67 R7
Tir-y-fron Flints 44 G2
Tisbury Wilts 8 C3
Tisman's Common W Susx 10 H4
Tissington Derbys 46 G3
Titchberry Devon 14 F7
Titchfield Hants 9 Q7
Titchfield Common Hants 9 Q7
Titchmarsh Nhants 38 F5
Titchwell Norfk 50 C5
Tithby Notts 47 S6
Tithebarn Devon 6 C6
Titley Herefs 34 H8
Titmore Green Herts 31 R7
Titsey Surrey 21 R12
Titson Cnwll 14 F12
Tittensor Staffs 45 U6
Tittleshall Norfk 50 E9
Titton Worcs 35 T7
Tiverton Ches W 45 N1
Tiverton Devon 6 C2
Tivetshall St Margaret Norfk 41 L3
Tivetshall St Mary Norfk 41 L3
Tivington Somset 16 B7
Tivy Dale Barns 57 L5
Tixall Staffs 46 C9
Tixover Rutlnd 48 E13
Toab Shet 106 t12
Toadhole Derbys 47 L2
Toadmoor Derbys 46 K3
Tobermory Ag & B 93 N7
Toberonochy Ag & B 87 N4
Tobha Mòr W Isls 106 c15
Tocher Abers 104 K9
Tochieneal Moray 104 G2
Tockenham Wilts 18 F5
Tockenham Wick Wilts 18 F4
Tocketts R & Cl 70 K9
Tockholes Bl w D 55 Q2
Tockington S Glos 28 B10
Tockwith N York 64 B9
Todber Dorset 17 U13
Todburn Nthumb 77 N6
Toddington C Beds 31 M7
Toddington Gloucs 28 K1
Toddington Services C Beds 31 M7
Todds Green Herts 31 R7
Todenham Gloucs 36 H13
Todhills Angus 91 P4
Todhills Cumb 75 S13
Todhills Dur 69 R6
Todhills Rest Area Cumb 75 S13
Todmorden Calder 56 D2
Todwick Rothm 57 Q10
Toft Cambs 39 N9
Toft Ches E 55 S11
Toft Lincs 48 G10
Toft Shet 106 u6
Toft Warwks 37 N6
Toft Hill Dur 69 Q7
Toft Hill Lincs 48 K1
Toft Monks Norfk 41 R2
Toft next Newton Lincs 58 H9
Toftrees Norfk 50 E8
Toftwood Norfk 50 G11
Togston Nthumb 77 Q5
Tokavaig Highld 100 f8
Tokers Green Oxon 20 B7
Tolastadh bho Thuath W Isls 106 k4
Toldish Cnwll 3 N5
Tolland Somset 16 F10
Tollard Farnham Dorset 8 D5
Tollard Royal Wilts 8 C5
Toll Bar Donc 57 S5
Tollbar End Covtry 37 L5
Toller Fratrum Dorset 7 Q5
Toller Porcorum Dorset 7 Q5
Tollerton N York 64 C7
Tollerton Notts 47 R7
Toller Whelme Dorset 7 P4
Tollesbury Essex 23 N5
Tolleshunt D'Arcy Essex 23 M5
Tolleshunt Knights Essex 23 M5
Tolleshunt Major Essex 23 M5
Tollingham E R Yk 64 J12
Toll of Birness Abers 105 S9
Tolpuddle Dorset 7 U6
Tolworth Gt Lon 21 L9
Tomatin Highld 103 M10
Tomchrasky Highld 101 V9
Tomdoun Highld 101 T11
Tomich Highld 102 B10
Tomich Highld 102 F6
Tomich Highld 109 L3
Tomich Highld 109 M10
Tomintoul Moray 103 U12
Tomlow Warwks 37 N8
Tomnacross Highld 102 F7
Tomnavoulin Moray 103 V10
Tompkin Staffs 46 B3
Ton Mons 27 Q7
Ton Mons 27 R8
Tonbridge Kent 21 U13
Tondu Brdgnd 26 F11
Tonedale Somset 16 F12
Tonfanau Gwynd 43 L13
Tong C Brad 63 Q13
Tong Kent 12 J4
Tong Shrops 45 S12
Tong W Isls 106 j5
Tonge Leics 47 M9
Tong Green Kent 12 J5
Tongham Surrey 20 E13
Tongland D & G 73 R9
Tong Norton Shrops 45 S12
Tongue Highld 111 M5
Tongue End Lincs 48 J10
Tongwynlais Cardif 27 L11
Tonmawr Neath 26 E8
Tonna Neath 26 D8
Ton-teg Rhondd 26 K10
Tonwell Herts 31 T9
Tonypandy Rhondd 26 H9
Tonyrefail Rhondd 26 J10
Toot Baldon Oxon 30 C12
Toot Hill Essex 22 D7
Toothill Hants 9 M5
Toothill Swindn 29 M11
Tooting Gt Lon 21 N8
Tooting Bec Gt Lon 21 N8
Topcliffe N York 63 T4
Topcroft Norfk 41 N2
Topcroft Street Norfk 41 N2
Top End Bed 38 F8
Topham Donc 57 T3
Top of Hebers Rochdl 56 C5
Toppesfield Essex 40 B13
Toprow Norfk 51 L14
Topsham Devon 6 C7
Top-y-rhos Flints 44 G2
Torbeg N Ayrs 79 R10
Torboll Highld 109 P5
Torbreck Highld 102 H7
Torbryan Devon 5 U7
Torcastle Highld 94 G3
Torcross Devon 5 U12
Tore Highld 102 H5
Torfrey Cnwll 4 E10
Torinturk Ag & B 79 Q3
Torksey Lincs 58 D11
Torlundy Highld 94 G3
Tormarton S Glos 28 E12
Tormore N Ayrs 79 R9
Tornagrain Highld 103 L5
Tornaveen Abers 99 L2
Torness Highld 102 G10
Toronto Dur 69 Q6
Torpenhow Cumb 66 K5
Torphichen W Loth 82 J4
Torphins Abers 99 L3
Torpoint Cnwll 5 L9
Torquay Torbay 6 B12
Torquhan Border 84 C9
Torr Devon 5 P10
Torran Highld 100 e5
Torrance E Duns 89 P11
Torranyard N Ayrs 81 M4
Torre Somset 16 D9
Torridon Highld 107 R13
Torridon House Highld 107 Q13
Torrin Highld 100 e7
Torrisdale Ag & B 79 P8
Torrisdale Highld 111 P4
Torrish Highld 111 V13
Torrisholme Lancs 61 T7
Torrobull Highld 108 K4
Torry C Aber 99 S2
Torryburn Fife 82 K1
Torteval Guern 6 b4
Torthorwald D & G 74 K10
Tortington W Susx 10 G9
Torton Worcs 35 T6
Tortworth S Glos 28 D9
Torvaig Highld 100 d5
Torver Cumb 67 L14
Torwood Falk 89 T9
Torwoodlee Border 84 D11
Torworth Notts 57 U9
Tosberry Devon 14 G8
Toscaig Highld 100 g6
Toseland Cambs 38 K8
Tosside Lancs 62 F8
Tostock Suffk 40 G8
Totaig Highld 100 b4
Tote Highld 100 d5
Tote Highld 100 e3
Tote Hill W Susx 10 D6
Totford Hants 19 S13
Tothill Lincs 59 R10
Totland IoW 9 L11
Totley Sheff 57 M11
Totley Brook Sheff 57 M10
Totnes Devon 5 U8
Toton Notts 47 P7
Totronald Ag & B 92 F7
Totscore Highld 100 c3
Tottenham Gt Lon 21 P4
Tottenhill Norfk 49 T11
Totteridge Gt Lon 21 M4
Totternhoe C Beds 31 L8
Tottington Bury 55 S4
Tottleworth Lancs 62 E13
Totton Hants 9 M6
Touchen End W & M 20 E7
Toulston N York 64 B11
Toulton Somset 16 G10
Toulvaddie Highld 109 R8
Tovil Kent 12 E5
Towan Cnwll 3 M2
Towan Cnwll 3 Q7
Toward Ag & B 88 D12
Toward Quay Ag & B 88 D12
Towcester Nhants 37 S11
Towednack Cnwll 2 D9
Tower of London Gt Lon 21 P6
Towersey Oxon 30 F11
Towie Abers 104 E13
Tow Law Dur 69 P5
Town End Cambs 39 P1
Town End Cumb 61 S3
Town End Cumb 67 M11
Town End Cumb 68 D7
Townend W Duns 88 J10
Towngate Cumb 67 R3
Towngate Lincs 48 H11
Town Green Lancs 54 K5
Town Green Norfk 51 Q11
Townhead Barns 56 J6
Townhead Cumb 66 G5
Town Head Cumb 67 P12
Townhead Cumb 68 D6
Townhead D & G 74 K8
Town Head N York 62 G8
Townhead of Greenlaw D & G 74 D13
Townhill Fife 90 H14
Town Kelloe Dur 70 E5
Townlake Devon 5 L6
Town Lane Wigan 55 Q7
Town Littleworth E Susx 11 Q7
Town of Lowton Wigan 55 P7
Town Row E Susx 11 T4
Towns End Hants 19 S9
Townsend Somset 7 L2
Townshend Cnwll 2 F10
Town Street Suffk 40 C3
Townwell S Glos 28 D9
Town Yetholm Border 85 L13
Towthorpe C York 64 E8
Towthorpe E R Yk 64 K7
Towton N York 64 B12
Towyn Conwy 53 S7
Toxteth Lpool 54 J9
Toynton All Saints Lincs 59 Q14
Toynton Fen Side Lincs 49 N1
Toynton St Peter Lincs 59 R14
Toy's Hill Kent 21 S12
Trabboch E Ayrs 81 N8
Trabbochburn E Ayrs 81 P8
Traboe Cnwll 2 J12
Tracebridge Somset 16 E12
Tradespark Highld 103 N4
Trafford Park Traffd 55 S7
Trallong Powys 26 H2
Tranent E Loth 83 T4
Tranmere Wirral 54 H9
Trantelbeg Highld 111 T6
Trantlemore Highld 111 T6
Tranwell Nthumb 77 P9
Trap Carmth 26 B4
Traprain E Loth 84 F3
Trap's Green Warwks 36 F7
Trapshill W Berk 19 N8
Traquair Border 83 R12
Trash Green W Berk 19 U7
Trawden Lancs 62 J12
Trawscoed Cerdgn 33 N6
Trawsfynydd Gwynd 43 P6
Trealaw Rhondd 26 J9
Treales Lancs 61 S13
Trearddur Bay IoA 52 C7
Treator Cnwll 3 N1
Tre Aubrey V Glam 16 D2
Trebanog Rhondd 26 J9
Trebanos Neath 26 C7
Trebartha Cnwll 4 H5
Trebarwith Cnwll 4 D3
Trebeath Cnwll 4 H3
Trebetherick Cnwll 4 A5
Treborough Somset 16 D9
Trebudannon Cnwll 3 M4
Trebullett Cnwll 4 J5
Treburgett Cnwll 4 D5
Treburley Cnwll 4 J5
Treburrick Cnwll 3 M2
Trebyan Cnwll 3 R4
Trecastle Powys 26 F2
Trecogo Cnwll 4 J4
Trecott Devon 15 P12
Trecwn Pembks 24 G4
Trecynon Rhondd 26 H7
Tredaule Cnwll 4 G4
Tredavoe Cnwll 2 D11
Tredegar Blae G 27 L6
Tredethy Cnwll 3 R2
Tredington Gloucs 28 H2
Tredington Warwks 36 J12
Tredinnick Cnwll 3 N2
Tredinnick Cnwll 3 Q5
Tredinnick Cnwll 4 F7
Tredinnick Cnwll 4 G9
Tredinnick Cnwll 4 H9
Tredomen Powys 27 L1
Tredrizzick Cnwll 4 B5
Tredunnock Mons 27 R9
Tredustan Powys 27 L1
Treen Cnwll 2 B12
Treen Cnwll 2 C9
Treesmill Cnwll 3 R5
Treeton Rothm 57 P9
Trefasser Pembks 24 E3
Trefdraeth IoA 52 F8
Trefecca Powys 27 L1
Trefechan Myr Td 26 J6
Trefeglwys Powys 33 U2
Trefenter Cerdgn 33 M7
Treffgarne Pembks 24 G6
Treffgarne Owen Pembks 24 E5
Treffynnon Pembks 24 E5
Trefil Blae G 27 L5
Trefilan Cerdgn 32 K9
Trefin Pembks 24 D4
Treflach Shrops 44 G8
Trefnannau Powys 44 F10
Trefnant Denbgs 54 C12
Trefonen Shrops 44 G8
Trefor Gwynd 42 G4
Trefor IoA 52 E6
Treforest Rhondd 26 K10
Trefrew Cnwll 4 E4
Trefriw Conwy 53 N10
Tregadillett Cnwll 4 H4
Tre-gagle Mons 27 U6
Tregaian IoA 52 G6
Tregare Mons 27 S5
Tregarne Cnwll 2 K12
Tregaron Cerdgn 33 N9
Tregarth Gwynd 52 K9
Tregaswith Cnwll 3 M4
Tregatta Cnwll 4 D3
Tregawne Cnwll 3 Q3
Tregeare Cnwll 4 G3
Tregeiriog Wrexhm 44 E7
Tregele IoA 52 E4
Tregellist Cnwll 4 C5
Tregenna Cnwll 3 M8
Tregeseal Cnwll 2 B10
Tregew Cnwll 3 L10
Tre-Gibbon Rhondd 26 H6
Tregidden Cnwll 2 K12
Tregiskey Cnwll 3 Q7
Treglemais Pembks 24 D5
Tregole Cnwll 14 E13
Tregolls Cnwll 2 J9
Tregonce Cnwll 3 N2
Tregonetha Cnwll 3 P4
Tregonning & Gwinear Mining District Cnwll 2 F10
Tregony Cnwll 3 N8
Tregoodwell Cnwll 4 E4
Tregorrick Cnwll 3 Q6
Tregoss Cnwll 3 P4
Tregoyd Powys 34 E13
Tregrehan Mills Cnwll 3 Q6
Tre-groes Cerdgn 32 H12
Tregullon Cnwll 3 R4
Tregunna Cnwll 3 P2
Tregunnon Cnwll 4 G4
Tregurrian Cnwll 3 M3
Tregynon Powys 44 C14
Tre-gynwr Carmth 25 R7
Trehafod Rhondd 26 J9
Trehan Cnwll 5 L9
Treharris Myr Td 26 K8
Treharrock Cnwll 4 C5
Trehemborne Cnwll 3 M2
Treherbert Carmth 33 L11
Treherbert Rhondd 26 G8
Trehunist Cnwll 4 J8
Trekenner Cnwll 4 J5
Treknow Cnwll 4 D3
Trelan Cnwll 2 J13
Trelash Cnwll 4 F2
Trelassick Cnwll 3 M6
Trelawne Cnwll 4 G10
Trelawnyd Flints 54 C11
Treleague Cnwll 2 K12
Treleaver Cnwll 2 K13
Trelech Carmth 25 N4
Trelech a'r Betws Carmth 25 P5
Treleddyd-fawr Pembks 24 C5
Trelew Cnwll 3 L9
Trelewis Myr Td 27 L8
Treligga Cnwll 4 C4
Trelights Cnwll 4 B5
Trelill Cnwll 4 C5
Trelinnoe Cnwll 4 J4
Trelion Cnwll 3 N6
Trelissick Cnwll 3 L9
Trellech Mons 27 U6
Trelleck Grange Mons 27 T7
Trelogan Flints 54 D10
Trelow Cnwll 3 N3
Trelowarren Cnwll 2 J12
Trelowia Cnwll 4 H9
Treluggan Cnwll 3 M9
Trelystan Powys 44 G13
Tremadog Gwynd 43 L6
Tremail Cnwll 4 F3
Tremain Cerdgn 32 D11
Tremaine Cnwll 4 G3
Tremar Cnwll 4 H7
Trematon Cnwll 4 K9
Trembraze Cnwll 4 H7
Tremeirchion Denbgs 54 C12
Tremethick Cross Cnwll 2 C10
Tremore Cnwll 3 Q4
Tre-Mostyn Flints 54 D11
Trenance Cnwll 3 L12
Trenance Cnwll 3 M3
Trenance Cnwll 3 N2
Trenarren Cnwll 3 Q7
Trench Wrekin 45 Q11
Trench Green Oxon 19 U5
Trendeal Cnwll 3 M6
Trendrine Cnwll 2 D9
Treneague Cnwll 3 P2
Trenear Cnwll 2 H10
Treneglos Cnwll 4 G3
Trenerth Cnwll 2 G9
Trenewan Cnwll 4 F10
Trenewth Cnwll 4 D5
Trengune Cnwll 4 F2
Treninnick Cnwll 3 L4
Trenowah Cnwll 2 K5
Trenoweth Cnwll 2 K10
Trent Dorset 17 Q13
Trentham C Stke 45 U5
Trentishoe Devon 15 P3
Trentlock Derbys 47 N7
Trent Port Lincs 58 D10
Trent Vale C Stke 45 U5
Trenwheal Cnwll 2 G10
Treoes V Glam 26 G12
Treorchy Rhondd 26 H8
Trequite Cnwll 4 C5
Tre'r-ddol Cerdgn 33 N2
Trerhyngyll V Glam 26 J12
Trerulefoot Cnwll 4 J9
Tresaith Cerdgn 32 E10
Tresawle Cnwll 3 M7
Tresco IoS 2 b2
Trescott Staffs 35 U1
Trescowe Cnwll 2 F10
Tresean Cnwll 2 K5
Tresham Gloucs 28 E9
Treshnish Isles Ag & B 92 G10
Tresillian Cnwll 3 M7
Tresinney Cnwll 4 E4
Treskinnick Cross Cnwll 14 F13
Tresmeer Cnwll 4 G3
Tresparrett Cnwll 4 E2
Tressait P & K 97 N11
Tresta Shet 106 t8
Tresta Shet 106 w4
Treswell Notts 58 C11
Treswithian Cnwll 2 G8
Tre Taliesin Cerdgn 33 N2
Trethevey Cnwll 4 D3
Trethewey Cnwll 2 B12
Trethomas Caerph 27 M10
Trethosa Cnwll 3 N6
Trethurgy Cnwll 3 Q5
Tretio Pembks 24 C5
Tretire Herefs 27 U3
Tretower Powys 27 M3
Treuddyn Flints 44 G2
Trevadlock Cnwll 4 H5
Trevalga Cnwll 4 D2
Trevalyn Wrexhm 44 J2
Trevanger Cnwll 4 B5
Trevanson Cnwll 3 P2
Trevarrack Cnwll 2 D10
Trevarren Cnwll 3 N4
Trevarrian Cnwll 3 M3
Trevarrick Cnwll 3 P8
Trevarth Cnwll 2 J8
Trevaughan Carmth 25 M7
Tre-vaughan Carmth 25 Q6
Treveal Cnwll 2 D8
Treveal Cnwll 2 K5
Treveighan Cnwll 4 D5
Trevellas Downs Cnwll 2 J6
Trevelmond Cnwll 4 G8
Trevemper Cnwll 3 L5
Treveor Cnwll 3 P8
Treverbyn Cnwll 3 M7
Treverbyn Cnwll 3 Q5
Treverva Cnwll 2 K10
Trevescan Cnwll 2 B12
Trevethin Torfn 27 P7
Trevia Cnwll 4 D4
Trevigro Cnwll 4 J7
Trevilla Cnwll 3 L9
Trevilson Cnwll 3 L5
Treviscoe Cnwll 3 N5
Treviskey Cnwll 3 N8
Trevithick Cnwll 3 M4
Trevithick Cnwll 3 P7
Trevoll Cnwll 3 L5
Trevone Cnwll 3 M1
Trevor Wrexhm 44 G5
Trevorgans Cnwll 2 C11
Trevorrick Cnwll 3 N2
Trevose Cnwll 3 M1
Trew Cnwll 2 G11
Trewalder Cnwll 4 D4
Trewalkin Powys 27 M1
Trewarmett Cnwll 4 D3
Trewassa Cnwll 4 E3
Trewavas Cnwll 2 F11
Trewavas Mining District Cnwll 2 F11
Treween Cnwll 4 G4
Trewellard Cnwll 2 B10
Trewen Cnwll 4 H4
Trewennack Cnwll 2 H11
Trewent Pembks 24 H11
Trewern Powys 44 G11
Trewetha Cnwll 4 C4
Trewethern Cnwll 3 Q1
Trewidland Cnwll 4 H9
Trewillis Cnwll 2 K13
Trewint Cnwll 4 G4
Trewint Cnwll 4 H8
Trewithian Cnwll 3 M9
Trewoodloe Cnwll 4 J6
Trewoon Cnwll 2 H13
Trewoon Cnwll 3 P6
Treworga Cnwll 3 M8
Treworgan Cnwll 3 L7
Treworlas Cnwll 3 M9
Treworld Cnwll 4 E2
Treworthal Cnwll 3 M9
Tre-wyn Mons 27 Q3
Treyarnon Cnwll 3 M2
Treyford W Susx 10 C7
Trickett's Cross Dorset 8 F8
Triermain Cumb 76 B12
Triffleton Pembks 24 G6
Trillacott Cnwll 4 H3
Trimdon Dur 70 E6
Trimdon Colliery Dur 70 E5
Trimdon Grange Dur 70 E5
Trimingham Norfk 51 N6
Trimley Lower Street Suffk 41 N13
Trimley St Martin Suffk 41 N13
Trimley St Mary Suffk 41 N13
Trimpley Worcs 35 S5
Trimsaran Carmth 25 S10
Trims Green Herts 22 C4
Trimstone Devon 15 M4
Trinafour P & K 95 U6
Trinant Caerph 27 N8
Tring Herts 30 K10
Tringford Herts 30 K10
Tring Wharf Herts 30 K10
Trinity Angus 99 L11
Trinity Jersey 7 d2
Trinity Gask P & K 90 E8
Triscombe Somset 16 G9
Trislaig Highld 94 F4
Trispen Cnwll 3 L6
Tritlington Nthumb 77 Q7
Troan Cnwll 3 M5
Trochry P & K 90 E3
Troedrhiwfuwch Caerph 27 L7
Troedyraur Cerdgn 32 F11
Troedyrhiw Myr Td 26 K7
Trofarth Conwy 53 Q8
Trois Bois Jersey 7 c2
Troon Cnwll 2 H9
Troon S Ayrs 81 L6
Tropical World Roundhay Park Leeds 63 S12
Trossachs Stirlg 89 M4
Trossachs Pier Stirlg 89 L4
Troston Suffk 40 E6
Troswell Cnwll 4 H2
Trotshill Worcs 35 U9
Trottiscliffe Kent 12 B3
Trotton W Susx 10 C6
Troughend Nthumb 76 H7
Trough Gate Lancs 56 C2
Troutbeck Cumb 67 N7
Troutbeck Cumb 67 P12
Troutbeck Bridge Cumb 67 P12
Troway Derbys 57 N11
Trowbridge Wilts 18 C9
Trowell Notts 47 N6
Trowell Services Notts 47 N5
Trowle Common Wilts 18 B9
Trowley Bottom Herts 31 N10
Trowse Newton Norfk 51 M12
Troy Leeds 63 Q12
Trudoxhill Somset 17 T8
Trull Somset 16 H12
Trumfleet Donc 57 T4
Trumpan Highld 100 b3
Trumpet Herefs 35 Q13
Trumpington Cambs 39 P10
Trumpsgreen Surrey 20 G9
Trunch Norfk 51 N7
Trunnah Lancs 61 Q11
Truro Cnwll 3 L8
Truscott Cnwll 4 H3
Trusham Devon 5 V4
Trusley Derbys 46 J6
Trusthorpe Lincs 59 T10
Trysull Staffs 35 U2
Tubney Oxon 29 T8
Tuckenhay Devon 5 U9
Tuckhill Shrops 35 S3
Tuckingmill Cnwll 2 H8
Tuckingmill Wilts 8 C3
Tuckton BCP 8 G10
Tucoyse Cnwll 3 P7
Tuddenham Suffk 40 B6
Tuddenham Suffk 41 L11
Tudeley Kent 12 B6
Tudhoe Dur 69 S5
Tudorville Herefs 28 A3
Tudweiliog Gwynd 42 D6
Tuesley Surrey 10 F2
Tuffley Gloucs 28 F5
Tufton Hants 19 Q11
Tufton Pembks 24 H5
Tugby Leics 47 U13
Tugford Shrops 35 N3
Tughall Nthumb 85 U13
Tullibody Clacks 90 C12
Tullich Abers 98 F4
Tullich Highld 102 H10
Tullich Highld 109 R9
Tulliemet P & K 97 S13
Tulloch Abers 105 N9
Tullochgorm Ag & B 87 T6
Tulloch Station Highld 96 D7
Tullymurdoch P & K 98 B13
Tullynessle Abers 104 H12
Tulse Hill Gt Lon 21 P8
Tumble Carmth 25 T8
Tumbler's Green Essex 22 K2
Tumby Lincs 48 K2
Tumby Woodside Lincs 49 L2
Tummel Bridge P & K 95 V7
Tunbridge Wells Kent 11 T3
Tundergarth D & G 75 N9
Tunga W Isls 106 j5
Tungate Norfk 51 N8
Tunley BaNES 17 S5
Tunstall C Stke 45 U3
Tunstall E R Yk 65 U13
Tunstall Kent 12 G3
Tunstall Lancs 62 C5
Tunstall N York 69 R13
Tunstall Norfk 51 R12
Tunstall Staffs 45 S8
Tunstall Suffk 41 Q9
Tunstall Sundld 70 E2
Tunstead Derbys 56 H12
Tunstead Norfk 51 N9
Tunstead Milton Derbys 56 F10
Tunworth Hants 19 U11
Tupsley Herefs 35 M12
Turgis Green Hants 19 U9
Turkdean Gloucs 29 M4
Tur Langton Leics 37 T2
Turleigh Wilts 18 B8
Turleygreen Shrops 35 S3
Turn Lancs 55 T3
Turnastone Herefs 34 J13
Turnberry S Ayrs 80 J11
Turnchapel C Plym 5 M10
Turnditch Derbys 46 J4
Turner Green Lancs 62 C13
Turner's Green E Susx 11 U7
Turner's Green Warwks 36 G7
Turners Hill W Susx 11 N3
Turners Puddle Dorset 8 A10
Turnford Herts 31 U12
Turnhouse C Edin 83 N4
Turnworth Dorset 7 V3
Turriff Abers 105 L5
Turton Bottoms Bl w D 55 R3
Turves Cambs 39 M1
Turvey Bed 38 D10
Turville Bucks 20 C4
Turville Heath Bucks 20 B4
Turweston Bucks 30 D5
Tushielaw Inn Border 75 R2
Tutbury Staffs 46 H8
Tutnall Worcs 36 C6
Tutshill Gloucs 27 U9
Tuttington Norfk 51 M8
Tutts Clump W Berk 19 S6
Tutwell Cnwll 4 K5
Tuxford Notts 58 B12
Twatt Ork 106 r17
Twatt Shet 106 t8
Twechar E Duns 89 Q10
Tweedbank Border 84 E12
Tweedmouth Nthumb 85 P8
Tweedsmuir Border 83 M14
Twelveheads Cnwll 2 K8
Twelve Oaks E Susx 12 C11
Twemlow Green Ches E 55 S13
Twenty Lincs 48 J9
Twerton BaNES 17 T4
Twickenham Gt Lon 21 L8
Twigworth Gloucs 28 F3
Twineham W Susx 11 M7
Twineham Green W Susx 11 M6
Twinhoe BaNES 17 U5
Twinstead Essex 40 E13
Twitchen Devon 15 S6
Twitchen Shrops 34 J5
Twitham Kent 13 Q4
Two Bridges Devon 5 Q6
Two Dales Derbys 57 L14
Two Gates Staffs 46 H13
Two Mile Ash W Susx 10 J5
Two Mile Oak Cross Devon 5 U7
Two Pots Devon 15 M4
Two Waters Herts 31 N11
Twycross Leics 46 K13
Twycross Zoo Leics 46 K12
Twyford Bucks 30 E7
Twyford Hants 9 P4
Twyford Leics 47 T11
Twyford Lincs 48 D9
Twyford Norfk 50 H9
Twyford Wokham 20 C7
Twyford Common Herefs 35 M13
Twyn-carno Caerph 27 L6
Twynholm D & G 73 R9
Twyning Gloucs 35 U13
Twynllanan Carmth 26 D3
Twyn-yr-Odyn V Glam 27 L13
Twyn-y-Sheriff Mons 27 S6
Twywell Nhants 38 E5
Tyberton Herefs 34 J13
Tyburn Birm 36 F2
Tycroes Carmth 25 V8
Ty Croes IoA 52 D8
Tycrwyn Powys 44 D10
Tydd Gote Lincs 49 Q10
Tydd St Giles Cambs 49 P10
Tydd St Mary Lincs 49 P10
Tye Hants 9 U8
Tye Green Essex 22 D3
Tye Green Essex 22 J3
Tye Green Essex 39 S13
Tyersal C Brad 63 P13
Tyldesley Wigan 55 Q6
Tyler Hill Kent 13 M3
Tylers Green Bucks 20 F4
Tyler's Green Essex 22 D6
Tylers Green Surrey 21 Q12
Tylorstown Rhondd 26 J8
Tylwch Powys 33 U4
Ty-nant Conwy 43 U5
Ty-nant Gwynd 43 T8
Tyncelyn Cerdgn 33 M8
Tyndrum Stirlg 95 L12
Ty'n-dwr Denbgs 44 F5
Tyneham Dorset 8 B12
Tynemouth N Tyne 77 T12
Tyne Tunnel S Tyne 77 S12
Tynewydd Rhondd 26 G8
Tyninghame E Loth 84 G3
Tynron D & G 74 F7
Ty'n-y-bryn Rhondd 26 J10
Ty'n-y-coedcae Caerph 27 M10
Tynygongl IoA 52 H6
Tynygraig Cerdgn 33 N7
Ty'n-y-Groes Conwy 53 N8
Tyn-y-nant Rhondd 26 K10
Tyrie Abers 105 Q3
Tyringham M Keyn 38 C11
Tyseley Birm 36 F4
Tythegston Brdgnd 26 F12
Tytherington Ches E 56 D11
Tytherington S Glos 28 C10
Tytherington Somset 17 U8
Tytherington Wilts 18 D12
Tytherleigh Devon 6 K4
Tytherton Lucas Wilts 18 D6
Tyttenhanger Herts 31 Q11
Tywardreath Cnwll 3 R6
Tywardreath Highway Cnwll 3 R5
Tywyn Conwy 53 N7
Tywyn Gwynd 43 L13

U

Ubbeston Green Suffk 41 P6
Ubley BaNES 17 P5
Uckerby N York 69 R12
Uckfield E Susx 11 R6
Uckinghall Worcs 35 U13
Uckington Gloucs 28 H3
Uckington Shrops 45 N11
Uddingston S Lans 82 C6
Uddington S Lans 82 G12
Udimore E Susx 12 G12
Udny Green Abers 105 P10
Udny Station Abers 105 Q11
Uffcott Wilts 18 H5
Uffculme Devon 6 E2
Uffington Lincs 48 G12
Uffington Oxon 29 R10
Uffington Shrops 45 M11
Ufford C Pete 48 G13
Ufford Suffk 41 N10
Ufton Warwks 37 L8
Ufton Nervet W Berk 19 T7
Ugadale Ag & B 79 P10
Ugborough Devon 5 R9
Uggeshall Suffk 41 R4
Ugglebarnby N York 71 Q11
Ughill Sheff 57 L8
Ugley Essex 22 D2
Ugley Green Essex 22 D2
Ugthorpe N York 71 N10
Uibhist A Deas W Isls 106 d15
Uibhist A Tuath W Isls 106 c11
Uig Ag & B 92 F8
Uig Highld 100 a4
Uig Highld 100 c3
Uig W Isls 106 f5
Uigshader Highld 100 d5
Uisken Ag & B 86 F2
Ulbster Highld 112 H8
Ulcat Row Cumb 67 P8
Ulceby Lincs 59 R12
Ulceby N Linc 58 K4
Ulceby Skitter N Linc 58 K3
Ulcombe Kent 12 F6
Uldale Cumb 66 K5
Uley Gloucs 28 E8
Ulgham Nthumb 77 Q7
Ullapool Highld 108 A6
Ullenhall Warwks 36 F7
Ullenwood Gloucs 28 H4
Ulleskelf N York 64 C12
Ullesthorpe Leics 37 P3
Ulley Rothm 57 Q9
Ullingswick Herefs 35 N11
Ullock Cumb 66 G8
Ullswater Cumb 67 P8
Ullswater Steamers Cumb 67 N9
Ulnes Walton Lancs 55 M3
Ulpha Cumb 61 T3
Ulpha Cumb 66 J14
Ulrome E R Yk 65 R8
Ulsta Shet 106 u5
Ulting Wick Essex 22 K6
Ulva Ag & B 92 K10
Ulverley Green Solhll 36 F4
Ulverston Cumb 61 P4
Ulwell Dorset 8 E12
Ulzieside D & G 74 E4
Umberleigh Devon 15 P8
Unapool Highld 110 E10
Underbarrow Cumb 61 T1
Under Burnmouth Border 75 U9

Undercliffe C Brad....63 P13
Underdale Shrops....45 M11
Underling Green Kent....12 E9
Underriver Kent....21 U12
Underwood Newpt....27 R10
Undley Suffk....39 U4
Undy Mons....27 S10
Union Mills IoM....60 f7
Union Street E Susx....12 D9
Unst Shet....106 v3
Unstone Derbys....57 N11
Unstone Green Derbys....57 N11
Unthank Cumb....67 N3
Unthank Cumb....Q5
Unthank Derbys....57 M11
Unthank Derbys....57 M11
Unthank Nthumb....85 P9
Upavon Wilts....18 H10
Up Cerne Dorset....7 S4
Upchurch Kent....12 F2
Upcott Devon....15 S7
Upcott Herefs....34 H10
Up Exe Devon....6 B4
Upgate Norfk....50 K10
Upgate Street Norfk....40 J2
Upgate Street Norfk....41 N2
Uphall Dorset....7 P4
Uphall W Loth....83 L4
Upham Hants....9 Q4
Upham Hants....15 U11
Uphampton Herefs....34 J8
Uphampton Worcs....35 T7
Uphill N Som....16 K5
Up Holland Lancs....55 M5
Uplawmoor E Rens....81 N1
Upleadon Gloucs....28 E2
Upleatham R & Cl....70 K9
Uplees Kent....12 K3
Uploders Dorset....7 P6
Uplowman Devon....16 D13
Uplyme Devon....6 K6
Up Marden W Susx....10 B8
Upminster Gt Lon....22 E11
Up Mudford Somset....17 Q13
Up Nately Hants....19 U10
Upottery Devon....6 H3
Upper Affcot Shrops....34 K4
Upper Arley Worcs....35 S4
Upper Arncott Oxon....30 D9
Upper Astrop Nhants....30 B5
Upper Badcall Highld....110 D8
Upper Basildon W Berk....19 S5
Upper Batley Kirk....56 K1
Upper Beeding W Susx....11 K8
Upper Benefield Nhants....38 E2
Upper Bentley Worcs....36 C7
Upper Bighouse Highld....111 T5
Upper Birchwood Derbys....47 M2
Upper Boat Rhondd....27 L11
Upper Boddington Nhants....37 N10
Upper Borth Cerdgn....33 M3
Upper Brailes Warwks....36 K13
Upper Breinton Herefs....34 L12
Upper Broadheath Worcs....35 T9
Upper Broughton Notts....47 S8
Upper Bucklebury W Berk....19 R7
Upper Burgate Hants....8 H5
Upper Bush Medway....12 C2
Upperby Cumb....67 P2
Upper Caldecote C Beds....38 J11
Upper Canada N Som....17 L5
Upper Canterton Hants....8 K6
Upper Catesby Nhants....37 P9
Upper Catshill Worcs....36 C6
Upper Chapel Powys....34 B12
Upper Cheddon Somset....16 H11
Upper Chicksgrove Wilts....8 D3
Upper Chute Wilts....19 L10
Upper Clapton Gt Lon....21 P5
Upper Clatford Hants....19 N12
Upper Coberley Gloucs....28 J4
Upper Cotton Staffs....46 E4
Upper Cound Shrops....45 N12
Upper Cudworth Barns....57 N5
Upper Cumberworth Kirk....56 K5
Upper Dallachy Moray....104 D3
Upper Deal Kent....13 S5
Upper Denby Kirk....56 K5
Upper Denton Cumb....76 C12
Upper Dicker E Susx....11 T9
Upper Dinchope Shrops....34 K4
Upper Dounreay Highld....112 B3
Upper Dovercourt Essex....23 T1
Upper Drumbane Stirlg....89 P5
Upper Dunsforth N York....64 B7
Upper Eashing Surrey....10 F2
Upper Eathie Highld....103 L3
Upper Egleton Herefs....35 P12
Upper Elkstone Staffs....46 E2
Upper Ellastone Staffs....46 F5
Upper End Derbys....56 G11
Upper Enham Hants....19 N11
Upper Farmcote Shrops....35 S2
Upper Farringdon Hants....19 V13
Upper Framilode Gloucs....28 D5
Upper Froyle Hants....10 B2
Upperglen Highld....100 c4
Upper Godney Somset....17 N8
Upper Gravenhurst C Beds....31 P5
Upper Green Mons....27 Q4
Upper Green Suffk....40 B8
Upper Green W Berk....19 N8
Upper Grove Common Herefs....27 V2
Upper Hackney Derbys....46 J1
Upper Hale Surrey....20 D13
Upper Halliford Surrey....20 J9
Upper Halling Medway....12 C3
Upper Hambleton Rutlnd....48 D12
Upper Harbledown Kent....13 M4
Upper Hardres Court Kent....13 N5
Upper Hardwick Herefs....34 K9
Upper Hartfield E Susx....11 R3
Upper Hartshay Derbys....47 L3
Upper Hatherley Gloucs....28 H3
Upper Hatton Staffs....45 T6
Upper Haugh Rothm....57 P7
Upper Hayton Shrops....35 M4
Upper Heaton Kirk....56 J3
Upper Helmsley N York....64 F8
Upper Hergest Herefs....34 G10
Upper Heyford Nhants....37 S9
Upper Heyford Oxon....29 U3
Upper Hill Herefs....35 L9
Upper Hockenden Kent....21 T9
Upper Hopton Kirk....56 J3
Upper Howsell Worcs....35 S11
Upper Hulme Staffs....46 D1
Upper Ifold Surrey....10 G4
Upper Inglesham Swindn....29 P8
Upper Kilcott Gloucs....28 E9
Upper Killay Swans....25 U12
Upper Kinchrackine Ag & B....94 H13
Upper Knockando Moray....103 U7
Upper Lambourn W Berk....19 M4
Upper Landywood Staffs....46 C12
Upper Langford N Som....17 N5
Upper Langwith Derbys....57 R12
Upper Largo Fife....91 P11
Upper Leigh Staffs....46 D6
Upper Littleton N Som....17 Q4
Upper Lochton Abers....99 M4
Upper Longdon Staffs....46 E11
Upper Ludstone Shrops....35 T2
Upper Lybster Highld....112 G9
Upper Lydbrook Gloucs....28 B4
Upper Lye Herefs....34 J7
Upper Maes-coed Herefs....34 H14
Upper Marham Norfk....50 B12
Upper Midhope Sheff....56 K6
Uppermill Oldham....56 E5
Upper Milton Worcs....35 T5
Upper Minety Wilts....28 K8
Upper Moor Worcs....36 C11
Upper Moor Side Leeds....63 Q13
Upper Mulben Moray....104 C5
Upper Netchwood Shrops....35 P2
Upper Nobut Staffs....46 D7
Upper Norwood W Susx....10 E7
Upper Oddington Gloucs....29 P2
Upper Padley Derbys....56 K11
Upper Pennington Hants....9 L8
Upper Pollicott Bucks....30 F10
Upper Poppleton C York....64 D9
Upper Quinton Warwks....36 G11
Upper Ratley Hants....9 L4
Upper Rissington Gloucs....29 P4
Upper Rochford Worcs....35 P7
Upper Ruscoe D & G....73 Q8
Upper Sapey Herefs....35 Q8
Upper Saxondale Notts....47 T5
Upper Seagry Wilts....28 J11
Upper Shelton C Beds....31 L4
Upper Sheringham Norfk....51 L5
Upper Skelmorlie N Ayrs....88 F12
Upper Slaughter Gloucs....29 N3
Upper Soudley Gloucs....28 C5
Upper Spond Herefs....34 H10
Upper Standen Kent....13 P7
Upper Staploe Bed....38 H8
Upper Stoke Norfk....51 N13

Upper Stondon C Beds....31 P5
Upper Stowe Nhants....37 R9
Upper Street Hants....8 H5
Upper Street Norfk....51 N10
Upper Street Norfk....51 P10
Upper Street Suffk....40 K14
Upper Street Suffk....40 K13
Upper Strensham Worcs....35 U13
Upper Sundon C Beds....31 M7
Upper Swell Gloucs....29 N2
Upper Tankersley Barns....57 M7
Upper Tean Staffs....46 D6
Upperthong Kirk....56 H5
Upperthorpe N Linc....57 Q10
Upperton W Susx....10 F6
Upper Threapwood Ches W....44 K4
Upperton Derbys....47 L2
Upper Town Derbys....46 H3
Upper Town Dur....69 N5
Upper Town Herefs....35 N11
Upper Town N Som....17 P3
Upper Town Suffk....40 F7
Upper Tumble Carmth....25 T8
Upper Tysoe Warwks....36 K12
Upper Ufford Suffk....41 N10
Upperup Gloucs....28 K8
Upper Upham Wilts....18 K5
Upper Upnor Medway....22 J13
Upper Victoria Angus....91 R4
Upper Vobster Somset....17 T7
Upper Wardington Oxon....37 N11
Upper Weald M Keyn....30 H5
Upper Weedon Nhants....37 R9
Upper Welland Worcs....35 S12
Upper Wellingham E Susx....11 Q8
Upper Weston BaNES....17 T3
Upper Weybread Suffk....41 M5
Upper Wick Worcs....35 T10
Upper Wield Hants....9 T2
Upper Winchendon Bucks....30 F10
Upperwood Derbys....46 H2
Upper Woodford Wilts....18 H13
Upper Woolhampton W Berk....19 S7
Upper Wootton Hants....19 S10
Upper Wraxall Wilts....18 B6
Upper Wyche Worcs....35 S12
Uppincott Devon....6 B3
Uppingham Rutlnd....48 C1
Uppington Dorset....8 E6
Uppington Shrops....45 N12
Upsall N York....64 B2
Upsettlington Border....85 M9
Upshire Essex....22 B7
Up Somborne Hants....9 M2
Upstreet Kent....13 P3
Up Sydling Dorset....7 R4
Upthorpe Suffk....40 G6
Upton Bucks....30 G10
Upton C Pete....48 H13
Upton Cambs....38 J5
Upton Ches W....54 K13
Upton Cnwll....14 F12
Upton Cnwll....2 M5
Upton Cumb....67 M5
Upton Devon....6 E4
Upton Devon....7 S7
Upton Dorset....7 S7
Upton Dorset....8 D10
Upton E R Yk....65 R11
Upton Halton....55 L9
Upton Hants....9 M5
Upton Hants....19 N9
Upton Leics....47 L14
Upton Lincs....58 E9
Upton Nhants....37 T9
Upton Norfk....51 Q11
Upton Notts....47 U2
Upton Notts....58 B11
Upton Oxon....19 R3
Upton Pembks....24 H10
Upton Pembks....24 J9
Upton R & Cl....71 M9
Upton Slough....20 G7
Upton Somset....16 C11
Upton Somset....17 N11
Upton Wakefd....57 Q4
Upton Warwks....36 F9
Upton Wirral....54 G10
Upton Bishop Herefs....28 C2
Upton Cheyney S Glos....17 S2
Upton Cressett Shrops....35 Q2
Upton Crews Herefs....28 B2
Upton Cross Cnwll....4 J6
Upton End C Beds....31 P6
Upton Grey Hants....19 U11
Upton Heath Ches W....54 K13
Upton Hellions Devon....15 T12
Upton Lovell Wilts....18 D12
Upton Magna Shrops....45 N11
Upton Noble Somset....17 T9
Upton Pyne Devon....6 B5
Upton St Leonards Gloucs....28 G4
Upton Scudamore Wilts....18 C11
Upton Snodsbury Worcs....36 B10
Upton Towans Cnwll....2 F9
Upton-upon-Severn Worcs....35 U12
Upton Warren Worcs....36 B7
Upwaltham W Susx....10 E8
Upware Cambs....39 R6
Upwell Norfk....49 Q13
Upwey Dorset....7 S8
Upwick Green Herts....22 C3
Upwood Cambs....39 L4
Urchfont Wilts....18 F9
Urdimarsh Herefs....35 M11
Ure Bank N York....63 S5
Urlay Nook S on T....70 F10
Urmston Traffd....55 S8
Urquhart Moray....104 B3
Urquhart Castle Highld....102 F10
Urra N York....70 J12
Urray Highld....102 F5
Ury Abers....99 P6
Uryside Abers....105 M11
Usan Angus....99 M11
Ushaw Moor Dur....69 R4
Usk Mons....27 R7
Usselby Lincs....58 J8
Usworth Sundld....77 S14
Utkinton Ches W....55 M13
Utley C Brad....63 M11
Uton Devon....15 T13
Utterby Lincs....59 P8
Uttoxeter Staffs....46 E7
Uwchmynydd Gwynd....42 C8
Uxbridge Gt Lon....20 J6
Uyeasound Shet....106 v3
Uzmaston Pembks....24 G8

Vale Guern....6 e2
Valley IoA....52 C7
Valley End Surrey....20 G10
Valley Truckle Cnwll....4 D4
Valtos Highld....100 e3
Valtos W Isls....106 h5
Vange Essex....22 H10
Varteg Torfn....27 P6
Vatsetter Shet....106 v5
Vatten Highld....100 b5
Vaynor Myr Td....26 J5
Vazon Bay Guern....6 c3
Veensgarth Shet....106 u9
Velindre Powys....34 E13
Vellow Somset....16 E9
Velly Devon....14 F8
Venngreen Devon....14 J10
Vennington Shrops....44 H12
Venn Ottery Devon....6 E6
Venny Tedburn Devon....15 T13
Ventnor IoW....9 R13
Venton Devon....5 P9
Vernham Dean Hants....19 M9
Vernham Street Hants....19 M9
Vernolds Common Shrops....35 L4
Verwood Dorset....8 F7
Veryan Cnwll....3 N9
Veryan Green Cnwll....3 N8
Vicarage Devon....6 H7
Vickerstown Cumb....61 M6
Victoria Barns....57 M5
Victoria Blae G....27 M6
Victoria Cnwll....3 P4
Vidlin Shet....106 u7
Viewfield Moray....104 A3
Viewpark N Lans....82 D6
Vigo Kent....12 B3
Village de Putron Guern....6 e3
Ville la Bas Jersey....7 a1
Vinehall Street E Susx....12 E11
Vines Cross E Susx....11 T7

Virginia Water Surrey....20 H9
Virginstow Devon....4 J2
Vobster Somset....17 T7
Voe Shet....106 u7
Vowchurch Herefs....34 J13
Vulcan Village St Hel....55 N8

W

Waberthwaite Cumb....66 H1
Wackerfield Dur....69 Q8
Wacton Norfk....41 L2
Wadborough Worcs....36 B11
Waddesdon Bucks....30 F9
Waddeton Devon....6 A13
Waddicar Sefton....54 J7
Waddingham Lincs....58 G7
Waddington Lancs....62 E11
Waddington Lincs....58 G14
Waddon Devon....6 A7
Waddon Gt Lon....21 P9
Wadebridge Cnwll....3 P2
Wadeford Somset....6 K2
Wadenhoe Nhants....38 F4
Wadesmill Herts....31 U9
Wadhurst E Susx....12 B9
Wadshelf Derbys....57 M12
Wadswick Wilts....18 B7
Wadworth Donc....57 S7
Waen Denbgs....53 S10
Waen Denbgs....54 D13
Waen Fach Powys....44 F10
Waen-pentir Gwynd....52 J9
Waen-wen Gwynd....52 J9
Wagbeach Shrops....44 J13
Wainfelin Torfn....27 P6
Wainfleet All Saints Lincs....49 Q2
Wainfleet Bank Lincs....49 Q2
Wainfleet St Mary Lincs....49 Q2
Wainford Norfk....41 R3
Wainhouse Corner Cnwll....14 E13
Wainscott Medway....22 H13
Wain's Hill N Som....17 L2
Wainstalls Calder....63 L14
Waitby Cumb....68 G11
Wakefield Wakefd....57 M2
Wake Green Birm....36 E4
Wakehurst Place W Susx....11 N4
Wakerley Nhants....48 E14
Wakes Colne Essex....23 L2
Walberswick Suffk....41 S5
Walberton W Susx....10 F9
Walbottle N u Ty....77 P12
Walbutt D & G....74 D12
Walby Cumb....67 T13
Walcombe Somset....17 Q7
Walcot Lincs....48 G7
Walcot Lincs....58 G2
Walcot N Linc....58 E2
Walcot Shrops....45 N11
Walcot Swindn....29 N11
Walcote Leics....37 Q3
Walcot Green Norfk....40 K4
Walcott Lincs....48 H2
Walcott Norfk....51 Q7
Walden N York....63 L2
Walden Head N York....62 K3
Walden Stubbs N York....57 S3
Walderslade Medway....12 E3
Walderton W Susx....10 B8
Walditch Dorset....7 N6
Waldley Derbys....46 F6
Waldridge Dur....69 S3
Waldringfield Suffk....41 N11
Waldron E Susx....11 S7
Wales Rothm....57 Q10
Wales Somset....17 Q11
Walesby Lincs....58 K9
Walesby Notts....57 U12
Walford Herefs....28 A3
Walford Herefs....34 J7
Walford Shrops....44 K9
Walford Staffs....45 T7
Walford Heath Shrops....44 K10
Walgherton Ches E....45 Q4
Walgrave Nhants....37 U6
Walhampton Hants....9 L8
Walkden Salfd....55 R6
Walker N u Ty....77 R13
Walkerburn Border....83 R11
Walker Fold Lancs....62 D11
Walkeringham Notts....58 C8
Walkerith Lincs....58 C8
Walkern Herts....31 S8
Walker's Green Herefs....35 M11
Walker's Heath Birm....36 E5
Walkerton Fife....90 K11
Walkford BCP....8 J10
Walkhampton Devon....5 N7
Walkington E R Yk....65 M12
Walkley Sheff....57 M9
Walk Mill Lancs....62 H13
Walkwood Worcs....36 D8
Wall Nthumb....76 J12
Wall Staffs....46 E12
Wallacetown S Ayrs....80 K12
Wallacetown S Ayrs....81 L8
Wallands Park E Susx....11 Q8
Wallasey Wirral....54 G8
Wallasey (Kingsway) Tunnel Wirral....54 H8
Wall End Cumb....61 N3
Wall End Herefs....34 K8
Wallend Medway....23 L12
Waller's Green Herefs....35 Q13
Wallhead Cumb....67 R1
Wall Heath Dudley....35 U3
Wall Houses Nthumb....77 L12
Wallingford Oxon....19 T3
Wallington Gt Lon....21 N9
Wallington Hants....9 R7
Wallington Herts....31 S6
Wallington Heath Wsall....46 C13
Wallis Pembks....24 H5
Wallisdown BCP....8 F10
Walliswood Surrey....10 J3
Walls Shet....106 s9
Wallsend N Tyne....77 R12
Wall under Haywood Shrops....35 M2
Wallyford E Loth....83 S4
Walmer Kent....13 S5
Walmer Bridge Lancs....55 L1
Walmersley Bury....55 T4
Walmestone Kent....13 Q4
Walmley Birm....36 F2
Walmley Ash Birm....36 F2
Walney Cumb....61 M6
Walpole Suffk....41 Q6
Walpole Cross Keys Norfk....49 R10
Walpole Highway Norfk....49 R11
Walpole St Andrew Norfk....49 R10
Walpole St Peter Norfk....49 R10
Walrow Somset....16 K7
Walsall Wsall....46 D14
Walsall Wood Wsall....46 D13
Walsden Calder....56 D2
Walsgrave on Sowe Covtry....37 L4
Walsham le Willows Suffk....40 H6
Walshaw Bury....55 S4
Walshford N York....63 U9
Walsoken Norfk....49 Q11
Walston S Lans....82 K9
Walsworth Herts....31 Q6
Walter's Ash Bucks....20 D3
Walters Green Kent....11 S2
Walterston V Glam....16 E2
Walterstone Herefs....27 Q2
Waltham Kent....13 M6
Waltham NE Lin....59 M6
Waltham Abbey Essex....31 U12
Waltham Chase Hants....9 R5
Waltham on the Wolds Leics....47 U9
Waltham St Lawrence W & M....20 D7
Waltham's Cross Essex....22 J1
Walthamstow Gt Lon....21 P5
Walton C Pete....48 J13
Walton Cumb....76 B13
Walton Derbys....57 N13
Walton Leeds....63 U11
Walton Leics....37 Q3
Walton M Keyn....30 J5
Walton Powys....34 G9
Walton Shrops....35 L5
Walton Somset....17 N9
Walton Staffs....45 U6
Walton Staffs....45 T8
Walton Suffk....41 P13
Walton W Susx....10 B9
Walton Wakefd....57 M3
Walton Warwks....36 J10
Walton Wrekin....45 N11

Walton Cardiff Gloucs....28 H1
Walton East Pembks....24 H6
Walton Elm Dorset....17 U13
Walton Grounds Nhants....30 B6
Walton Highway Norfk....49 Q11
Walton-in-Gordano N Som....27 S13
Walton-le-Dale Lancs....55 N1
Walton-on-Thames Surrey....20 K9
Walton-on-the-Hill Staffs....46 C9
Walton-on-the-Hill Surrey....21 M11
Walton-on-the-Naze Essex....23 U3
Walton on the Wolds Leics....47 Q10
Walton Park N Som....17 L2
Walton West Pembks....24 E8
Walwen Flints....54 E11
Walwen Flints....54 F12
Walwen Flints....54 F11
Walwick Nthumb....76 J11
Walworth Darltn....69 R9
Walworth Gt Lon....21 P7
Walworth Gate Darltn....69 R8
Walwyn's Castle Pembks....24 E8
Wambrook Somset....6 K3
Wampool Cumb....66 K2
Wanborough Surrey....20 F13
Wanborough Swindn....29 P10
Wandon End Herts....31 P8
Wandsworth Gt Lon....21 N8
Wangford Suffk....41 S5
Wanlip Leics....47 Q11
Wanlockhead D & G....74 H3
Wannock E Susx....11 T10
Wansford C Pete....48 G14
Wansford E R Yk....65 P8
Wanshurst Green Kent....12 E6
Wanstead Gt Lon....21 R6
Wanstrow Somset....17 T8
Wanswell Gloucs....28 C7
Wantage Oxon....29 S10
Wapley S Glos....28 D12
Wappenbury Warwks....37 L7
Wappenham Nhants....37 R11
Warbleton E Susx....11 U7
Warborough Oxon....19 S2
Warboys Cambs....39 M4
Warbreck Bpool....61 Q12
Warbstow Cnwll....14 F2
Warburton Traffd....55 R9
Warcop Cumb....68 F9
Warden Kent....23 P13
Warden Nthumb....76 J12
Ward End Birm....36 F3
Warden Street C Beds....31 P4
Ward Green Suffk....40 J8
Ward Green Cross Lancs....62 C12
Wardhedges C Beds....31 N5
Wardington Oxon....37 N11
Wardle Ches E....45 Q2
Wardle Rochdl....56 D4
Wardley Gatesd....77 S13
Wardley Rutlnd....48 B13
Wardley Salfd....55 S6
Wardlow Derbys....56 J12
Wardsend Ches E....56 D10
Wardy Hill Cambs....39 Q4
Ware Herts....31 U10
Ware Kent....13 Q3
Wareham Dorset....8 C11
Warehorne Kent....12 K8
Warenford Nthumb....85 T13
Waren Mill Nthumb....85 T12
Warenton Nthumb....85 T12
Wareside Herts....31 U9
Waresley Cambs....39 L10
Waresley Worcs....35 T6
Ware Street Kent....12 E4
Warfield Br For....20 E8
Warfleet Devon....5 V11
Wargate Lincs....48 K6
Wargrave Wokham....20 C7
Warham Herefs....35 L13
Warham Norfk....50 F5
Wark Nthumb....76 H10
Wark Nthumb....85 L11
Warkleigh Devon....15 P8
Warkton Nhants....38 C5
Warkworth Nhants....37 N12
Warkworth Nthumb....77 Q4
Warlaby N York....63 S1
Warland Calder....56 D2
Warleggan Cnwll....4 E7
Warleigh BaNES....17 U4
Warley Town Calder....56 G2
Warlingham Surrey....21 Q11
Warmanbie D & G....75 P12
Warmbrook Derbys....46 J3
Warmfield Wakefd....57 N2
Warmingham Ches E....45 R1
Warmington Nhants....38 G2
Warmington Warwks....37 M11
Warminster Wilts....18 C12
Warmley S Glos....28 C13
Warmsworth Donc....57 S6
Warmwell Dorset....7 U7
Warndon Worcs....35 U9
Warnford Hants....9 S4
Warnham W Susx....10 K4
Warningcamp W Susx....10 G9
Warninglid W Susx....11 L5
Warren Ches E....56 C12
Warren Pembks....24 F11
Warren Row W & M....20 D6
Warren Street Kent....12 H5
Warrington M Keyn....38 B9
Warrington Warrtn....55 P9
Warriston C Edin....83 Q3
Warsash Hants....9 P7
Warse Highld....112 H2
Warslow Staffs....46 E2
Warsop Vale Notts....57 R13
Warter E R Yk....64 K9
Warthermaske N York....63 R3
Warthill N York....64 F8
Wartling E Susx....11 U9
Wartnaby Leics....47 T10
Warton Lancs....61 T7
Warton Lancs....61 R4
Warton Nthumb....77 L5
Warton Warwks....46 J13
Warwick Warwks....36 J8
Warwick Bridge Cumb....67 Q1
Warwick Castle Warwks....36 J8
Warwick-on-Eden Cumb....67 Q1
Warwick Services Warwks....36 K8
Wasbister Ork....106 s16
Wasdale Head Cumb....66 K11
Wash Derbys....56 G10
Washall Green Herts....22 C1
Washaway Cnwll....3 Q3
Washbourne Devon....5 T10
Washbrook Suffk....40 K12
Washfield Devon....16 C13
Washfold N York....69 N12
Washford Somset....16 E8
Washford Pyne Devon....15 T10
Washingborough Lincs....58 H12
Washington Sundld....70 C1
Washington W Susx....10 J8
Washington Services Gatesd....69 S1
Washwood Heath Birm....36 F3
Wasing W Berk....19 S8
Waskerley Dur....69 M3
Wasperton Warwks....36 J9
Wasps Nest Lincs....58 J14
Wass N York....64 D4
Wast Water Cumb....66 K11
Watchet Somset....16 E8
Watchfield Oxon....29 Q9
Watchfield Somset....16 K7
Watchgate Cumb....67 R13
Watcombe Torbay....6 B11
Watendlath Cumb....67 L9
Water Devon....5 U4
Water Lancs....55 T2
Waterbeach Cambs....39 Q7
Waterbeach W Susx....10 D9
Waterbeck D & G....75 P11
Water Eaton Oxon....30 B10
Water Eaton Staffs....45 U11
Water End Bed....38 G11
Waterend Cumb....66 J8
Water End C Beds....31 N5
Water End E R Yk....64 K11
Water End Essex....39 S12
Water End Herts....31 N10
Water End Herts....31 Q12
Waterfall Staffs....46 E3
Waterfoot Ag & B....79 N11
Waterfoot E Rens....81 R2
Waterfoot Lancs....55 T2
Waterford Herts....31 T10
Water Fryston Wakefd....57 Q1
Watergate Cnwll....4 D4
Waterhead Cumb....67 N12
Waterheads Border....83 P8
Waterhouses Dur....69 Q4
Waterhouses Staffs....46 E3
Wateringbury Kent....12 C4
Waterlane Gloucs....28 H6
Waterloo Cnwll....4 E5
Waterloo Derbys....57 P14
Waterloo Herefs....34 H11
Waterloo Highld....100 f7
Waterloo N Lans....82 F8
Waterloo Norfk....51 N9
Waterloo P & K....90 G6
Waterloo Pembks....24 G10
Waterloo Sefton....54 H7
Waterloo Cross Devon....16 E2
Waterloo Port Gwynd....52 G10
Waterlooville Hants....9 T7
Watermead Bucks....30 H9
Watermillock Cumb....67 P8
Water Newton Cambs....38 H1
Water Orton Warwks....36 G2
Waterperry Oxon....30 D11
Waterrow Somset....16 E11
Watersfield W Susx....10 G8
Waterside Bl w D....55 R2
Waterside Bucks....30 K12
Waterside Cumb....66 K3
Waterside Donc....57 U4
Waterside E Ayrs....81 N2
Waterside E Ayrs....81 R8
Waterside E Duns....89 Q10
Water's Nook Bolton....55 P5
Waterstein Highld....100 a5
Waterstock Oxon....30 D11
Waterston Pembks....24 F9
Water Stratford Bucks....30 E6
Waters Upton Wrekin....45 P10
Water Yeat Cumb....61 Q2
Watford Herts....20 K3
Watford Nhants....37 R7
Watford Gap Services Nhants....37 R7
Wath N York....63 R6
Wath N York....63 P3
Wath upon Dearne Rothm....57 P6
Watlington Norfk....49 S11
Watlington Oxon....19 U2
Watnall Notts....47 P4
Watten Highld....112 F6
Wattisfield Suffk....40 H6
Wattisham Suffk....40 H10
Watton Dorset....7 N6
Watton E R Yk....65 N9
Watton Norfk....50 F13
Watton-at-Stone Herts....31 T9
Watton Green Norfk....50 F13
Wattons Green Essex....22 E8
Wattston N Lans....82 E4
Wattstown Rhondd....26 J8
Wattsville Caerph....27 N8
Wauldby E R Yk....65 M14
Waulkmill Abers....99 L5
Waunarlwydd Swans....26 A8
Waun Fach Powys....27 M1
Waunfawr Cerdgn....33 M4
Waunfawr Gwynd....52 J11
Waungron Swans....25 U10
Waunlwyd Blae G....27 M6
Wavendon M Keyn....30 K5
Waverbridge Cumb....66 K3
Waverton Ches W....54 K14
Waverton Cumb....66 K3
Wavertree Lpool....54 J9
Wawne E R Yk....65 P12
Waxham Norfk....51 S9
Waxholme E R Yk....59 U1
Way Kent....13 R2
Wayford Somset....7 M3
Waye Devon....5 T6
Waytown Dorset....7 N5
Way Village Devon....15 U10
Way Wick N Som....17 L4
Weacombe Somset....16 F8
Weald Oxon....29 R7
Wealdstone Gt Lon....21 L5
Weardley Leeds....63 S10
Weare Somset....17 M6
Weare Giffard Devon....15 L8
Wearhead Dur....68 J5
Wearne Somset....17 M11
Weasdale Cumb....68 D11
Weasenham All Saints Norfk....50 D9
Weasenham St Peter Norfk....50 E9
Weaste Salfd....55 S7
Weatheroak Hill Worcs....36 E6
Weaverham Ches W....55 P12
Weaverslake Staffs....46 F10
Weaverthorpe N York....65 M5
Webbington Somset....17 L5
Webb's Heath S Glos....28 C13
Webheath Worcs....36 D7
Webton Herefs....34 K13
Wedderlairs Abers....105 P9
Wedding Hall Fold N York....63 M11
Weddington Warwks....37 L2
Wedhampton Wilts....18 G9
Wedmore Somset....17 M7
Wednesbury Sandw....36 C1
Wednesfield Wolves....46 C13
Weecar Notts....58 C13
Weedon Bucks....30 H9
Weedon Bec Nhants....37 R9
Weedon Lois Nhants....37 R11
Weeford Staffs....46 F13
Week Devon....5 U5
Week Devon....15 Q9
Week Somset....16 B10
Weeke Hants....9 P2
Weekley Nhants....38 C4
Week St Mary Cnwll....14 F12
Weel E R Yk....65 P12
Weeley Essex....23 R3
Weeley Heath Essex....23 R3
Weem P & K....90 C3
Weeping Cross Staffs....46 B9
Weethley Warwks....36 E9
Weeting Norfk....39 U3
Weeton E R Yk....59 U1
Weeton Lancs....61 R13
Weeton N York....63 R10
Weetwood Leeds....63 R12
Weir Lancs....56 C2
Weir Quay Devon....5 L7
Weisdale Shet....106 t8
Welborne Norfk....50 J12
Welbourn Lincs....48 E2
Welburn N York....64 G6
Welbury N York....70 F12
Welby Lincs....48 E6
Welches Dam Cambs....39 Q3
Welcombe Devon....14 E9
Weldon Nhants....38 D3
Weldon Bridge Nthumb....77 N5
Welford Nhants....37 S4
Welford W Berk....19 P6
Welford-on-Avon Warwks....36 G10
Welham Leics....37 U2
Welham Notts....58 B10
Welham Bridge E R Yk....64 J13
Welham Green Herts....31 S11
Well Hants....20 B13
Well Lincs....59 R12
Well N York....63 R2
Welland Worcs....35 S12
Wellbank Angus....91 N4
Well End Bucks....20 E6
Well End Herts....21 M3
Wellesbourne Warwks....36 J9
Wellesbourne Mountford Warwks....36 J9
Well Head Herts....31 Q7
Well Hill Kent....21 S10
Wellhouse W Berk....19 R6
Welling Gt Lon....21 S7
Wellingborough Nhants....38 B8
Wellingham Norfk....50 E9
Wellingore Lincs....48 E2
Wellington Cumb....66 G11
Wellington Herefs....35 L11
Wellington Somset....16 F12
Wellington Wrekin....45 P11
Wellington Heath Herefs....35 R12
Wellington Marsh Herefs....35 L11
Wellow BaNES....17 T5
Wellow IoW....9 M11
Wellow Notts....57 U13
Wellpond Green Herts....22 B3
Wells Somset....17 P7
Wellsborough Leics....47 L12
Wells Green Ches E....45 Q3
Wells Head C Brad....63 M13
Wells-next-the-Sea Norfk....50 F5
Wellstye Green Essex....22 F4
Well Town Devon....6 B3
Welltree P & K....90 E8
Wellwood Fife....90 G14
Welney Norfk....39 R1
Welshampton Shrops....44 K7
Welsh Bicknor Herefs....28 A4
Welsh End Shrops....45 M6
Welsh Frankton Shrops....44 H7

Welsh Hook Pembks....24 F5
Welsh Newton Herefs....27 U4
Welshpool Powys....44 F12
Welsh St Donats V Glam....16 D2
Welton Cumb....67 N3
Welton E R Yk....58 G1
Welton Lincs....58 H11
Welton Nhants....37 Q7
Welton le Marsh Lincs....59 S13
Welton le Wold Lincs....59 N9
Welwick E R Yk....59 P2
Welwyn Herts....31 R9
Welwyn Garden City Herts....31 R9
Wem Shrops....45 M8
Wembdon Somset....16 J9
Wembley Gt Lon....21 L5
Wembury Devon....5 N11
Wembworthy Devon....15 R11
Wemyss Bay Inver....88 E12
Wenallt Cerdgn....33 N6
Wendens Ambo Essex....39 R13
Wendlebury Oxon....30 C9
Wendling Norfk....50 F11
Wendover Bucks....30 J11
Wendron Cnwll....2 H10
Wendron Mining District Cnwll....2 H10
Wendy Cambs....39 M11
Wenfordbridge Cnwll....4 R1
Wenhaston Suffk....41 R5
Wennington Cambs....38 K5
Wennington Gt Lon....22 D11
Wennington Lancs....62 C5
Wensley Derbys....46 J1
Wensley N York....63 M2
Wentbridge Wakefd....57 Q3
Wentnor Shrops....34 J2
Wentworth Cambs....39 Q5
Wentworth Rothm....57 N7
Wentworth Castle Barns....57 M6
Wenvoe V Glam....16 F2
Weobley Herefs....34 K10
Weobley Marsh Herefs....34 K10
Wepham W Susx....10 G9
Wereham Norfk....49 U13
Wergs Wolves....45 U13
Wern Gwynd....42 K6
Wern Powys....27 L4
Wern Powys....44 F11
Wernffrwd Swans....25 T12
Wern-Gifford Mons....27 Q3
Wern-y-gaer Flints....54 F13
Werrington C Pete....48 J13
Werrington Cnwll....4 J3
Werrington Staffs....46 B4
Wervin Ches W....54 K12
Wesham Lancs....61 S13
Wessington Derbys....46 K2
Westacott Devon....15 N6
West Acre Norfk....50 B10
West Allerdean Nthumb....85 P9
West Alvington Devon....5 S12
West Amesbury Wilts....18 H12
West Anstey Devon....15 U7
West Appleton N York....69 R14
West Ashby Lincs....59 N13
West Ashford Devon....15 M5
West Ashling W Susx....10 C9
West Ashton Wilts....18 C9
West Auckland Dur....69 Q7
West Ayton N York....65 M3
West Bagborough Somset....16 G10
West Bank Bl e G....27 N6
West Barkwith Lincs....58 K10
West Barnby N York....71 P10
West Barns E Loth....84 G3
West Barsham Norfk....50 F7
West Bay Dorset....7 N6
West Beckham Norfk....51 L6
West Bedfont Surrey....20 J8
West Bergholt Essex....23 N2
West Bexington Dorset....7 P7
West Bilney Norfk....49 U11
West Blatchington Br & H....11 N9
West Boldon S Tyne....77 T13
Westborough Lincs....48 C4
Westbourne BCP....8 F10
Westbourne W Susx....10 B9
West Bourton Dorset....17 U11
West Bowling C Brad....63 P13
West Bradenham Norfk....50 G12
West Bradford Lancs....62 E11
West Bradley Somset....17 Q9
West Bretton Wakefd....57 L4
West Bridgford Notts....47 Q6
West Briscoe Dur....69 L9
West Bromwich Sandw....36 D2
Westbrook Kent....13 R1
Westbrook W Berk....19 P6
Westbrook Wilts....18 D7
West Buckland Devon....15 Q6
West Buckland Somset....16 G12
West Burrafirth Shet....106 s8
West Burton N York....63 L2
West Burton W Susx....10 F7
Westbury Bucks....30 E6
Westbury Shrops....44 J12
Westbury Wilts....18 C10
Westbury Leigh Wilts....18 C10
Westbury-on-Severn Gloucs....28 D5
Westbury-on-Trym Bristl....28 A12
Westbury-sub-Mendip Somset....17 P7
West Butsfield Dur....69 P4
West Butterwick N Linc....58 D5
Westby Lancs....61 R13
West Byfleet Surrey....20 H10
West Cairngaam D & G....73 B10
West Caister Norfk....51 T11
West Calder W Loth....82 K6
West Camel Somset....17 Q11
West Chaldon Dorset....7 U8
West Challow Oxon....29 S10
West Charleton Devon....5 S12
West Chelborough Dorset....7 Q4
West Chevington Nthumb....77 Q6
West Chiltington W Susx....10 H7
West Chinnock Somset....7 N2
West Chisenbury Wilts....18 H10
West Clandon Surrey....20 H12
West Cliffe Kent....13 R7
Westcliff-on-Sea Sthend....23 L11
West Clyst Devon....6 C5
West Coker Somset....7 P2
Westcombe Somset....17 S9
West Compton Somset....17 Q8
West Compton Abbas Dorset....7 Q6
Westcote Gloucs....29 P3
Westcote Barton Oxon....29 U3
Westcott Bucks....30 F9
Westcott Devon....6 D4
Westcott Surrey....20 K13
West Cottingwith N York....64 F11
West Cowick E R Yk....57 T2
West Cross Swans....25 V13
West Curry Cnwll....14 H13
West Curthwaite Cumb....67 M3
Westdean E Susx....11 S11
West Dean W Susx....10 D8
West Dean Wilts....8 K3
West Deeping Lincs....48 H12
West Derby Lpool....54 J8
West Dereham Norfk....49 T13
West Ditchburn Nthumb....77 N2
West Down Devon....15 M4
Westdowns Cnwll....4 C4
West Drayton Gt Lon....20 J7
West Drayton Notts....58 B12
West Dunnet Highld....112 G2
West Ella E R Yk....65 N14
West End Bed....38 D9
West End BCP....8 F9
West End Caerph....27 N9
West End Cumb....67 L2
West End E R Yk....64 J13
West End E R Yk....65 P13
West End E R Yk....65 R13
West End Gloucs....28 D8
West End Hants....9 P5
West End Herts....31 S10
West End Lancs....55 Q3
West End Leeds....63 Q12
West End Lincs....59 P6
West End N Som....17 N3
West End N York....63 P9
West End Norfk....51 T12
West End Norfk....51 N12
West End Oxon....19 R6
West End S Glos....28 D11
West End Somset....17 Q8
West End Surrey....20 F11
West End Surrey....20 K10
West End W & M....20 D7
West End Wilts....8 C4
West End Wilts....18 E5
West End Wilts....28 J11
West End Green Hants....19 U8
Wester Aberchalder Highld....102 G11
Wester Balblair Highld....102 H6
Westerdale Highld....112 D6
Westerdale N York....71 L11
Westerfield Suffk....41 L11
Westergate W Susx....10 E9
Westerham Kent....21 R12
Westerhope N u Ty....77 P12
Westerland Devon....6 A12
Wester Ochiltree W Loth....82 K4
Wester Pitkierie Fife....91 S10
Wester Ross Highld....107 Q9
Westerton W Susx....10 D9
Westerton of Rossie Angus....99 M13
Westerwick Shet....106 s9
West Ewell Surrey....21 M10
West Farleigh Kent....12 E3
West Farndon Nhants....37 P10
West Felton Shrops....44 H8
Westfield BaNES....17 S6
Westfield Cumb....66 F7
Westfield E Susx....12 F12
Westfield Highld....112 C4
Westfield N Lans....89 S10
Westfield Norfk....50 G12
Westfield Surrey....20 H11
Westfield W Loth....82 H4
Westfields Dorset....7 S3
Westfields of Rattray P & K....90 H2
Westfield Sole Kent....12 E3
West Firle E Susx....11 Q9
West Flotmanby N York....65 P4
Westford Somset....16 F12
Westgate Dur....68 K5
Westgate N Linc....58 C5
Westgate Norfk....50 G5
Westgate Hill C Brad....63 Q14
Westgate-on-Sea Kent....13 R1
Westgate Street Norfk....51 L9
West Grafton Wilts....18 K8
West Grimstead Wilts....8 J3
West Grinstead W Susx....10 K6
West Haddlesey N York....57 S1
West Haddon Nhants....37 R6
West Hagbourne Oxon....19 R3
West Hagley Worcs....35 U4
Westhall Suffk....41 R4
West Hallam Derbys....47 M5
West Hallam Common Derbys....47 M5
Westham Dorset....7 S9
West Ham Gt Lon....21 R6
Westham E Susx....11 U10
Westham Somset....17 L7
Westhampnett W Susx....10 D9
West Handley Derbys....57 N11
West Hanney Oxon....29 T9
West Hanningfield Essex....22 H8
West Harnham Wilts....8 G3
West Harptree BaNES....17 Q5
West Harting W Susx....10 B7
West Hatch Somset....16 H12
West Hatch Wilts....8 C3
West Haven Angus....91 S4
Westhay Somset....17 M8
Westhead Lancs....54 K5
West Head Norfk....49 S12
West Heath Birm....36 D5
West Heath Hants....19 S9
West Helmsdale Highld....112 B13
West Hendred Oxon....29 T10
West Hesterton N York....65 L4
West Hewish N Som....17 L4
Westhide Herefs....35 N12
Westhill Abers....99 Q2
Westhill Highld....102 K6
West Hoathly W Susx....11 P4
West Holme Dorset....8 B11
Westholme Somset....17 Q8
Westhope Herefs....35 L10
Westhope Shrops....35 L3
West Horndon Essex....22 F10
West Horrington Somset....17 Q7
West Horsley Surrey....20 J12
West Horton Nthumb....85 R12
West Hougham Kent....13 P7
Westhoughton Bolton....55 P5
West Houses Lincs....49 L2
Westhouse N York....62 D5
Westhouses Derbys....47 M1
West Howe BCP....8 F9
West Howetown Somset....16 B9
Westhumble Surrey....20 K12
West Huntingtower P & K....90 G7
West Huntspill Somset....16 K8
West Hyde C Beds....31 N8
West Hyde Herts....20 H4
West Hythe Kent....13 M8
West Ilkerton Devon....15 R3
West Ilsley W Berk....19 Q4
West Itchenor W Susx....10 B10
West Keal Lincs....59 P14
West Kennett Wilts....18 H7
West Kilbride N Ayrs....80 J2
West Kingsdown Kent....21 U10
West Kington Wilts....18 B5
West Kirby Wirral....54 F10
West Knapton N York....64 K5
West Knighton Dorset....7 T7
West Knoyle Wilts....8 B2
West Kyloe Nthumb....85 R10
West Lambrook Somset....17 M13
West Langdon Kent....13 R6
West Langwell Highld....109 N4
West Lavington W Susx....10 D6
West Lavington Wilts....18 F10
West Layton N York....69 Q10
West Leake Notts....47 P8
West Learmouth Nthumb....85 M12
West Lees N York....70 G11
West Leigh Devon....15 R12
Westleigh Devon....15 L7
Westleigh Devon....16 D13
West Leigh Somset....16 F10
Westleigh Wigan....55 Q6
Westleton Suffk....41 R7
West Lexham Norfk....50 D10
Westley Shrops....44 J12
Westley Suffk....40 D8
Westley Waterless Cambs....39 T9
West Lilling N York....64 F7
Westlington Bucks....30 F10
West Linton Border....83 N8
Westlinton Cumb....75 R13
West Littleton S Glos....28 E12
West Lockinge Oxon....29 T10
West Lulworth Dorset....8 A12
West Lutton N York....65 L6
West Lydford Somset....17 Q10
West Lyng Somset....16 K11
West Lynn Norfk....49 T10
West Malling Kent....12 C4
West Malvern Worcs....35 S11
West Marden W Susx....10 B8
West Markham Notts....58 B12
Westmarsh Kent....13 Q3
West Marsh NE Lin....59 N5
West Marton N York....62 J10
West Melbury Dorset....8 C3
West Melton Rothm....57 P6
West Meon Hants....9 S4
West Meon Hut Hants....9 S4
West Meon Woodlands Hants....9 S3
West Mersea Essex....23 P4
Westmeston E Susx....11 N8
West Midland Safari Park Worcs....35 T6
West Milton Dorset....7 P5
Westminster Gt Lon....21 N7
Westminster Abbey & Palace Gt Lon....21 N7
West Molesey Surrey....20 K9
West Monkton Somset....16 J11
West Moors Dorset....8 F8
West Morden Dorset....8 C9
West Morriston Border....84 F10
West Morton C Brad....63 M11
West Mudford Somset....17 Q12
Westmuir Angus....98 H13
West Ness N York....64 F4
West Newbiggin Darltn....70 D9
West Newton E R Yk....65 S12
West Newton Norfk....49 T9
West Newton Somset....16 J11
West Norwood Gt Lon....21 P8

Westoe S Tyne....77 T12
Westo Ogwell Devon....5 U6
Weston BaNES....17 T3
Weston Ches E....45 S3
Weston Ches E....45 R4
Weston Devon....6 F4
Weston Devon....6 G7
Weston Dorset....7 S10
Weston Halton....55 M10
Weston Hants....10 A4
Weston Herefs....34 J9
Weston Herts....31 S6
Weston Lincs....49 L9
Weston N York....63 P10
Weston Nhants....37 Q11
Weston Notts....58 B13
Weston Shrops....44 K8
Weston Shrops....45 M5
Weston Shrops....35 M3
Weston Staffs....46 C8
Weston W Berk....19 N6
Weston-in-Gordano N Som....27 S13
Westoning Woodend C Beds....31 M6
Weston Jones Staffs....45 S9
Weston Longville Norfk....50 K10
Weston Lullingfields Shrops....44 K8
Weston-on-Avon Warwks....36 G10
Weston-on-the-Green Oxon....30 B9
Weston Park Staffs....45 T11
Weston Patrick Hants....19 U11
Weston Rhyn Shrops....44 G6
Weston-super-Mare N Som....16 K4
Weston Turville Bucks....30 J10
Weston-under-Lizard Staffs....45 T11
Weston under Penyard Herefs....28 B3
Weston-under-Redcastle Shrops....45 N8
Weston under Wetherley Warwks....37 L7
Weston Underwood Derbys....46 J5
Weston Underwood M Keyn....38 C10
Weston-upon-Trent Derbys....47 M8
Westonzoyland Somset....17 L10
West Orchard Dorset....17 V13
West Overton Wilts....18 H7
Westow N York....64 H6
West Panson Devon....14 J13
West Park Abers....99 P4
West Peckham Kent....12 B5
West Peeke Devon....14 J13
West Pelton Dur....69 R2
West Pennard Somset....17 P9
West Pentire Cnwll....2 K4
West Perry Cambs....38 H7
West Pinchbeck Lincs....48 K9
Westport Somset....17 L12
West Porlock Somset....16 B7
West Pulham Dorset....7 T4
West Putford Devon....14 J9
West Quantoxhead Somset....16 F8
West Rainton Dur....70 D3
West Rasen Lincs....58 J9
West Ravendale NE Lin....59 M7
Westray Ork....106 t15
Westray Airport Ork....106 t14
West Raynham Norfk....50 F8
West Retford Notts....57 U10
Westridge Green W Berk....19 R5
Westrigg W Loth....82 H5
Westrop Swindn....29 P9
West Rounton N York....70 F12
West Row Suffk....39 T5
West Rudham Norfk....50 D8
West Runton Norfk....51 L5
Westruther Border....84 F8
West Saltoun E Loth....84 D5
Westry Cambs....49 N13
West Sandford Devon....15 T12
West Sandwick Shet....106 u5
West Scrafton N York....63 L3
Westside Ork....106 s17
West Sleekburn Nthumb....77 R9
West Somerton Norfk....51 S10
West Stafford Dorset....7 T7
West Stockwith Notts....58 C7
West Stoke W Susx....10 C9
West Stonesdale N York....68 J12
West Stoughton Somset....17 M7
West Stour Dorset....17 U12
West Stourmouth Kent....13 Q3
West Stow Suffk....40 D6
West Stowell Wilts....18 H8
West Stratton Hants....19 S12
West Street Kent....12 J4
West Street Kent....12 K3
West Street Kent....13 R2
West Street Medway....22 J13
West Street Suffk....40 G5
West Tanfield N York....63 R4
West Taphouse Cnwll....4 E7
West Tarbert Ag & B....87 Q12
West Tarring W Susx....10 J10
West Thirston Nthumb....77 P5
West Thorney W Susx....10 B10
West Thorpe Notts....47 R8
West Thurrock Thurr....22 E12
West Tilbury Thurr....22 G12
West Tisted Hants....9 T3
West Torrington Lincs....58 K10
West Town BaNES....17 P4
West Town Hants....9 U9
West Town Herefs....34 K8
West Town N Som....17 N3
West Town Somset....17 R8
West Tytherley Hants....8 K2
West Tytherton Wilts....18 E6
Westvale Knows....54 K7
Westville Notts....47 P5
West Walton Norfk....49 Q11
Westward Cumb....67 L3
Westward Ho! Devon....14 K7
Westwell Kent....12 J6
Westwell Oxon....29 Q6
Westwell Leacon Kent....12 J6
West Wellow Hants....8 K5
West Wembury Devon....5 N11
West Wemyss Fife....91 M13
Westwick Cambs....39 P7
Westwick Dur....69 N9
West Wick N Som....17 L4
Westwick Norfk....51 N8
West Wickham Cambs....39 S11
West Wickham Gt Lon....21 Q9
West Williamston Pembks....24 H9
West Winch Norfk....49 T11
West Winterslow Wilts....8 J2
West Wittering W Susx....10 B11
West Witton N York....63 M2
Westwood Devon....6 D5
Westwood Kent....13 R2
Westwood Nthumb....76 J12
Westwood Notts....47 N3
Westwood Wilts....18 B9
West Woodburn Nthumb....76 J8
West Woodhay W Berk....19 N8
Westwood Heath Covtry....36 J5
West Woodlands Somset....17 T8
Westwoodside N Linc....58 C6
West Worldham Hants....10 A3
West Worthing W Susx....10 J10
West Wratting Cambs....39 S10
West Wycombe Bucks....20 D3
West Wylam Nthumb....77 N13
West Yatton Wilts....18 B5
West Yoke Kent....12 B2
West Youlstone Cnwll....14 F9
Wetham Green Kent....12 F2
Wetheral Cumb....67 Q2
Wetherby Leeds....63 U10
Wetherby Services N York....63 U9
Wetherden Suffk....40 H8
Wetheringsett Suffk....41 L7
Wethersfield Essex....22 H1
Wetherup Street Suffk....41 L7
Wetley Rocks Staffs....46 C4
Wettenhall Ches E....45 P1
Wetton Staffs....46 F2
Wetwang E R Yk....65 L8
Wetwood Staffs....45 S7
Wexcombe Wilts....19 L9
Wexham Slough....20 G6

Wexham Street Bucks 20 G6
Weybourne Norfk 50 K5
Weybourne Surrey 20 E13
Weybread Suffk 41 M4
Weybread Street Suffk 41 M5
Weybridge Surrey 20 J10
Weycroft Devon 6 K5
Weydale Highld 112 E4
Weyhill Hants 19 M11
Weymouth Dorset 7 S9
Whaddon Bucks 30 H6
Whaddon Cambs 39 N11
Whaddon Gloucs 28 F5
Whaddon Wilts 8 H3
Whaddon Wilts 18 C8
Whale Cumb 67 R8
Whaley Derbys 57 R12
Whaley Bridge Derbys 56 F10
Whaley Thorns Derbys 57 R12
Whaligoe Highld 112 H8
Whalley Lancs 62 E12
Whalley Banks Lancs 62 E12
Whalsay Shet 106 v7
Whalton Nthumb 77 N9
Whaplode Lincs 49 M9
Whaplode Drove Lincs 49 M11
Wharf Warwks 37 M10
Wharfe N York 62 F6
Wharles Lancs 61 S12
Wharley End C Beds 30 K4
Wharncliffe Side Sheff 57 L8
Wharram-le-Street N York 64 K6
Wharton Ches W 55 Q13
Wharton Herefs 35 M9
Whashton N York 69 Q11
Whasset Cumb 61 U3
Whatcote Warwks 36 J12
Whateley Warwks 46 H14
Whatfield Suffk 40 H11
Whatley Somset 7 L3
Whatley Somset 17 T7
Whatley's End S Glos 28 C11
Whatlington E Susx 12 E12
Whatsole Street Kent 13 M7
Whatstandwell Derbys 46 K3
Whatton-in-the-Vale Notts 47 T6
Whauphill D & G 73 L10
Whaw N York 69 L12
Wheal Peevor Cnwll 2 J8
Wheal Rose Cnwll 2 J8
Wheatacre Norfk 41 S2
Wheatfield Oxon 30 E13
Wheathampstead Herts 31 Q10
Wheathill Shrops 35 P4
Wheathill Somset 17 Q10
Wheatley Hants 10 B2
Wheatley Oxon 30 C11
Wheatley Hill Dur 70 E5
Wheatley Hills Donc 57 S6
Wheatley Lane Lancs 62 G12
Wheaton Aston Staffs 45 U11
Wheddon Cross Somset 16 B9
Wheelbarrow Town Kent 13 M6
Wheeler End Bucks 20 D4
Wheeler's Green Wokham 20 C8
Wheelerstreet Surrey 10 E2
Wheelock Ches E 45 S2
Wheelock Heath Ches E 45 R2
Wheelton Lancs 55 P2
Wheldale Wakefd 57 Q1
Wheldrake C York 64 F11
Whelford Gloucs 29 N8
Whelpley Hill Bucks 31 L12
Whelpo Cumb 67 M5
Whelston Flints 54 F11
Whempstead Herts 31 T8
Whenby N York 64 E6
Whepstead Suffk 40 D9
Wherstead Suffk 41 L12
Wherwell Hants 19 N12
Wheston Derbys 56 H11
Whetsted Kent 12 C6
Whetstone Gt Lon 21 N4
Whetstone Leics 37 Q1
Wheyrigg Cumb 66 J3
Whicham Cumb 61 L3
Whichford Warwks 36 K14
Whickham Gatesd 77 Q13
Whiddon Devon 15 L13
Whiddon Down Devon 5 R2
Whigstreet Angus 91 Q3
Whilton Nhants 37 R8
Whimble Devon 14 J12
Whimple Devon 6 D5
Whimpwell Green Norfk 51 Q8
Whinburgh Norfk 50 H12
Whin Lane End Lancs 61 R11
Whinnieliggate D & G 73 S9
Whinnow Cumb 67 M2
Whinnyfold Abers 105 T9
Whinny Hill S on T 70 E9
Whippingham IoW 9 Q10
Whipsnade C Beds 31 M9
Whipsnade Zoo ZSL C Beds 31 M9
Whipton Devon 6 B6
Whirlow Sheff 57 M10
Whisby Lincs 58 F13
Whissendine Rutlnd 48 B11
Whissonsett Norfk 50 F9
Whistlefield Ag & B 88 F7
Whistlefield Inn Ag & B 88 D7
Whistley Green Wokham 20 C8
Whiston Knows 55 L8
Whiston Nhants 38 C8
Whiston Rothm 57 P9
Whiston Staffs 45 U11
Whiston Staffs 46 D4
Whiston Cross Shrops 45 S13
Whiston Eaves Staffs 46 D4
Whitacre Fields Warwks 36 J2
Whitbeck Cumb 61 L3
Whitbourne Herefs 35 R9
Whitburn S Tyne 77 U13
Whitburn W Loth 82 H6
Whitby Ches W 54 J11
Whitby N York 71 Q10
Whitbyheath Ches W 54 J12
Whitchester Border 84 J7
Whitchurch BaNES 17 R3
Whitchurch Bucks 30 H8
Whitchurch Cardif 27 M12
Whitchurch Devon 5 M6
Whitchurch Hants 19 Q11
Whitchurch Herefs 27 V4
Whitchurch Oxon 19 T5
Whitchurch Pembks 24 D5
Whitchurch Shrops 45 M5
Whitchurch Canonicorum Dorset 7 L5
Whitchurch Hill Oxon 19 T5
Whitcombe Dorset 7 T7
Whitcot Shrops 34 J2
Whitcott Keysett Shrops 34 G4
Whiteacre Kent 13 M6
Whiteacre Heath Warwks 36 H2
Whiteash Green Essex 22 J1
White Ball Somset 16 F13
Whitebridge Highld 102 E12
Whitebrook Mons 27 U6
Whitebushes Surrey 21 N13
Whitecairns Abers 105 Q12
Whitechapel Gt Lon 21 P6
White Chapel Lancs 62 B11
Whitechurch Pembks 25 L3
Whitecliff Gloucs 27 V6
White Colne Essex 23 L2
White Coppice Lancs 55 P3
Whitecraig E Loth 83 R4
Whitecroft Gloucs 28 B6
Whitecrook D & G 72 F8
Whitecross Cnwll 2 E10
White Cross Cnwll 2 H12
Whitecross Cnwll 3 P2
Whitecross Falk 82 J3
White End Worcs 35 S14
Whiteface Highld 109 N7
Whitefarland N Ayrs 79 R7
Whitefaulds S Ayrs 80 K11
Whitefield Bury 55 T5
Whitefield Devon 15 R5
Whitefield Somset 16 E11
Whitefield Lane End Knows 55 L9
Whiteford Abers 105 L10
Whitegate Ches W 55 P13
Whitehall Hants 20 B12
Whitehall Ork 106 v17
Whitehall W Susx 10 J6
Whitehaven Cumb 66 E9
Whitehill Hants 10 B4
Whitehill Kent 12 K4
Whitehill Leics 47 M11
Whitehills Abers 104 K2
Whitehouse Abers 104 K13
Whitehouse Ag & B 79 Q3
Whitehouse Common Birm 36 F1
Whitekirk E Loth 84 F2
White Kirkley Dur 69 M5
White Lackington Dorset 7 T5
Whitelackington Somset 17 L13
White Ladies Aston Worcs 36 B10
Whiteleaf Bucks 30 H12
White-le-Head Dur 69 Q2
Whiteley Hants 9 Q7
Whiteley Bank IoW 9 R12
Whiteley Green Ches E 56 D11
Whiteley Village Surrey 20 J10
Whitemans Green W Susx 11 N5
White Mill Carmth 25 S6
Whitemire Moray 103 Q5
Whitemoor C Nott 47 P5
Whitemoor Cnwll 3 P5
Whitemoor Derbys 47 L4
Whitemoor Staffs 45 U1
Whiteness Shet 106 t9
White Notley Essex 22 J4
Whiteoak Green Oxon 29 R5
White Ox Mead BaNES 17 T5
Whiteparish Wilts 8 J4
White Pit Lincs 59 Q11
Whiterashes Abers 105 P11
White Roding Essex 22 E5
Whiterow Highld 112 J7
Whiterow Moray 103 R4
Whiteshill Gloucs 28 F6
Whitesmith E Susx 11 S8
White Stake Lancs 55 M1
Whitestaunton Somset 6 J2
Whitestone Devon 5 V2
White Stone Herefs 35 N12
Whitestone Warwks 37 L3
Whitestone Cross Devon 6 A6
Whitestreet Green Suffk 40 G13
Whitewall Corner N York 64 H6
White Waltham W & M 20 D7
Whiteway BaNES 17 T4
Whiteway Gloucs 28 H5
Whitewell Lancs 62 D10
Whiteworks Devon 5 Q6
Whitfield C Dund 91 P5
Whitfield Kent 13 R6
Whitfield Nhants 30 D5
Whitfield Nthumb 76 F14
Whitfield S Glos 28 C9
Whitfield Hall Nthumb 68 G1
Whitford Devon 6 J5
Whitford Flints 54 D11
Whitgift E R Yk 58 D2
Whitgreave Staffs 46 B8
Whithorn D & G 73 L11
Whiting Bay N Ayrs 80 E7
Whitkirk Leeds 63 T13
Whitland Carmth 25 L7
Whitlaw Border 75 V3
Whitletts S Ayrs 81 M8
Whitley N York 57 S2
Whitley Readg 20 B8
Whitley Sheff 57 M8
Whitley Wilts 18 C7
Whitley Bay N Tyne 77 T11
Whitley Chapel Nthumb 76 J14
Whitley Heath Staffs 45 T8
Whitley Lower Kirk 56 K3
Whitley Row Kent 21 S12
Whitlock's End Solhll 36 F5
Whitminster Gloucs 28 E6
Whitmore Dorset 8 F7
Whitmore Staffs 45 T5
Whitnage Devon 16 D13
Whitnash Warwks 36 K8
Whitney-on-Wye Herefs 34 G11
Whitrigg Cumb 66 K5
Whitrigg Cumb 75 P14
Whitrigglees Cumb 66 K1
Whitsbury Hants 8 G5
Whitsome Border 85 M8
Whitson Newpt 27 R11
Whitstable Kent 13 M2
Whitstone Cnwll 14 G13
Whittingham Nthumb 77 M3
Whittingslow Shrops 34 K3
Whittington Derbys 57 N11
Whittington Gloucs 28 K3
Whittington Lancs 62 C4
Whittington Norfk 50 B14
Whittington Shrops 44 H7
Whittington Staffs 35 U4
Whittington Staffs 46 G12
Whittington Warwks 46 J14
Whittington Worcs 35 U10
Whittington Moor Derbys 57 N12
Whittlebury Nhants 30 E4
Whittle-le-Woods Lancs 55 N2
Whittlesey Cambs 39 L1
Whittlesford Cambs 39 Q11
Whittlestone Head Bl w D 55 R3
Whitton N Linc 58 F2
Whitton Nthumb 77 M5
Whitton Powys 34 G7
Whitton S on T 70 E8
Whitton Shrops 35 N6
Whitton Suffk 40 K11
Whittonditch Wilts 19 L6
Whittonstall Nthumb 69 N1
Whitway Hants 19 Q9
Whitwell Derbys 57 R11
Whitwell Herts 31 Q8
Whitwell IoW 9 Q13
Whitwell N York 69 S13
Whitwell Rutlnd 48 D12
Whitwell-on-the-Hill N York 64 G6
Whitwell Street Norfk 50 K9
Whitwick Leics 47 M10
Whitwood Wakefd 57 P2
Whitworth Lancs 56 C3
Whixall Shrops 45 M7
Whixley N York 63 U8
Whorlton Dur 69 P10
Whorlton N York 70 G12
Whyle Herefs 35 N8
Whyteleafe Surrey 21 P11
Wibdon Gloucs 27 V8
Wibsey C Brad 63 N13
Wibtoft Warwks 37 N3
Wichelstowe Swindn 29 M11
Wichenford Worcs 35 S8
Wichling Kent 12 H4
Wick BCP 8 H10
Wick Devon 6 G4
Wick Highld 112 J6
Wick S Glos 28 D13
Wick Somset 16 H8
Wick Somset 17 M11
Wick V Glam 16 B2
Wick W Susx 10 G10
Wick Wilts 8 H4
Wick Worcs 36 C11
Wicken Cambs 39 S6
Wicken Nhants 30 F5
Wicken Bonhunt Essex 39 Q14
Wickenby Lincs 58 J10
Wick End Bed 38 E10
Wicken Green Village Norfk 50 D7
Wickersley Rothm 57 Q8
Wicker Street Green Suffk 40 G12
Wickford Essex 22 H9
Wickham Hants 9 R6
Wickham W Berk 19 N6
Wickham Bishops Essex 22 K5
Wickhambreaux Kent 13 P4
Wickhambrook Suffk 40 C10
Wickhamford Worcs 36 E12
Wickham Green Suffk 40 J7
Wickham Green W Berk 19 P6
Wickham Heath W Berk 19 P7
Wickham Market Suffk 41 P9
Wickhampton Norfk 51 R12
Wickham St Paul Essex 40 D13
Wickham Skeith Suffk 40 J7
Wickham Street Suffk 40 C10
Wickham Street Suffk 40 J7
Wickhurst Green W Susx 10 J4
Wick John o' Groats Airport Highld 112 J6
Wicklewood Norfk 50 J13
Wickmere Norfk 51 L7
Wick St Lawrence N Som 17 L3
Wicksteed Park Nhants 38 C5
Wickstreet E Susx 11 S9
Wickwar S Glos 28 D10
Widdington Essex 22 D1
Widdop Calder 62 J13
Widdrington Nthumb 77 R6
Widdrington Station Nthumb 77 Q7
Widecombe in the Moor Devon 5 S5
Widegates Cnwll 4 H9
Widemouth Bay Cnwll 14 F12
Wide Open N Tyne 77 Q11
Widford Essex 22 G7
Widford Herts 22 B4
Widham Wilts 29 L10
Widley Hants 9 T7
Widmer End Bucks 20 E3
Widmerpool Notts 47 R8
Widmore Gt Lon 21 R9
Widnes Halton 55 M9
Widworthy Devon 6 H5
Wigan Wigan 55 N5
Wigborough Somset 17 M13
Wiggaton Devon 6 F6
Wiggenhall St Germans Norfk 49 S11
Wiggenhall St Mary Magdalen Norfk 49 S11
Wiggenhall St Mary the Virgin Norfk 49 S11
Wiggenhall St Peter Norfk 49 T11
Wiggens Green Essex 39 U12
Wiggenstall Staffs 46 E1
Wiggington Shrops 44 H6
Wigginton C York 64 E8
Wigginton Herts 30 K10
Wigginton Oxon 37 L14
Wigginton Staffs 46 H12
Wigginton Bottom Herts 30 K11
Wigglesworth N York 62 G8
Wiggonby Cumb 67 L2
Wiggonholt W Susx 10 H7
Wighill N York 64 B10
Wighton Norfk 50 F6
Wightwick Wolves 45 U14
Wigley Derbys 57 M12
Wigley Hants 9 L5
Wigmore Herefs 34 K7
Wigmore Medway 12 E3
Wigsley Notts 58 E12
Wigsthorpe Nhants 38 F4
Wigston Leics 47 R14
Wigston Fields Leics 47 R13
Wigston Parva Leics 37 N3
Wigthorpe Notts 57 S10
Wigtoft Lincs 49 L6
Wigton Cumb 67 L3
Wigtown D & G 73 L9
Wigtwizzle Sheff 56 K7
Wike Leeds 63 S11
Wilbarston Nhants 38 B3
Wilberfoss E R Yk 64 G9
Wilburton Cambs 39 Q5
Wilby Nhants 38 C7
Wilby Norfk 40 H3
Wilby Suffk 41 M6
Wilcot Wilts 18 H8
Wilcott Shrops 44 J10
Wilcove Cnwll 5 L9
Wilcrick Newpt 27 S10
Wilday Green Derbys 57 M12
Wildboarclough Ches E 56 E13
Wilden Bed 38 G9
Wilden Worcs 35 T6
Wilde Street Suffk 40 B5
Wildhern Hants 19 N10
Wildhill Herts 31 S11
Wildmanbridge S Lans 82 F8
Wildmill Brdgnd 26 G11
Wildmoor Hants 19 U9
Wildmoor Worcs 36 C5
Wildsworth Lincs 58 D7
Wilford C Nott 47 Q6
Wilkesley Ches E 45 P5
Wilkhaven Highld 109 S7
Wilkieston W Loth 83 M5
Wilkin's Green Herts 31 Q11
Wilksby Lincs 59 N14
Willand Devon 6 D2
Willards Hill E Susx 12 D11
Willaston Ches E 45 Q3
Willaston Ches W 54 H11
Willen M Keyn 30 J4
Willenhall Covtry 37 L5
Willenhall Wsall 46 C14
Willerby E R Yk 65 N13
Willerby N York 65 N4
Willersey Gloucs 36 F13
Willersley Herefs 34 H11
Willesborough Kent 12 K7
Willesborough Lees Kent 12 K7
Willesden Gt Lon 21 M6
Willesleigh Devon 15 P6
Willesley Wilts 28 G10
Willett Somset 16 F10
Willey Shrops 45 Q14
Willey Warwks 37 N4
Willey Green Surrey 20 F12
Williamscot Oxon 37 N11
Williamstown Rhondd 26 J9
William Herts 31 R6
Willicote Warwks 36 G11
Willingale Essex 22 E6
Willingdon E Susx 11 T10
Willingham Cambs 39 P6
Willingham by Stow Lincs 58 E10
Willingham Green Cambs 39 T10
Willingham St Mary Suffk 41 R4
Willington Bed 38 H11
Willington Derbys 46 J8
Willington Dur 69 Q5
Willington Kent 12 E5
Willington N Tyne 77 S12
Willington Warwks 36 J13
Willington Corner Ches W 55 M13
Willitoft E R Yk 64 G13
Williton Somset 16 E8
Willoughby Lincs 59 S12
Willoughby Warwks 37 P7
Willoughby Hills Lincs 49 N4
Willoughby-on-the-Wolds Notts 47 R8
Willoughby Waterleys Leics 37 Q2
Willoughton Lincs 58 F8
Willow Green Ches W 55 P11
Willows Green Essex 22 H4
Willsbridge S Glos 17 S2
Willsworthy Devon 5 N4
Willtown Somset 17 L11
Wilmcote Warwks 36 G9
Wilmington BaNES 17 S4
Wilmington Devon 6 H5
Wilmington E Susx 11 S10
Wilmington Kent 22 D13
Wilmslow Ches E 55 T10
Wilnecote Staffs 46 H13
Wilpshire Lancs 62 D13
Wilsden C Brad 63 M12
Wilsford Lincs 48 F5
Wilsford Wilts 18 H9
Wilsford Wilts 18 H13
Wilsham Devon 15 S3
Wilshaw Kirk 56 H5
Wilsill N York 63 P7
Wilsley Green Kent 12 E8
Wilsley Pound Kent 12 E8
Wilson Herefs 27 V3
Wilson Leics 47 M9
Wilsontown S Lans 82 H7
Wilstead Bed 31 N4
Wilsthorpe Lincs 48 G11
Wilstone Herts 30 K10
Wilstone Green Herts 30 K10
Wilton Cumb 66 F10
Wilton Herefs 28 A3
Wilton N York 64 K3
Wilton R & Cl 70 J9
Wilton Wilts 8 F2
Wilton Wilts 19 L8
Wilton Dean Border 75 U3
Wimbish Essex 39 S13
Wimbish Green Essex 39 T13
Wimbledon Gt Lon 21 M8
Wimblington Cambs 39 P2
Wimboldsley Ches W 55 Q14
Wimborne Minster Dorset 8 E9
Wimborne St Giles Dorset 8 E6
Wimbotsham Norfk 49 T12
Wimpole Cambs 39 N11
Wimpstone Warwks 36 H11
Wincanton Somset 17 T11
Winceby Lincs 59 P13
Wincham Ches W 55 Q11
Winchburgh W Loth 83 L4
Winchcombe Gloucs 28 K2
Winchelsea E Susx 12 H12
Winchelsea Beach E Susx 12 H12
Winchester Hants 9 P3
Winchester Services Hants 19 R13
Winchet Hill Kent 12 D7
Winchfield Hants 20 C12
Winchmore Hill Bucks 20 F3
Winchmore Hill Gt Lon 21 P4
Wincle Ches E 56 E13
Wincobank Sheff 57 N8
Winder Cumb 66 F9
Windermere Cumb 67 P13
Windermere Jetty Cumb 67 P13
Winderton Warwks 36 K12
Windhill Highld 102 F6
Windlehurst Stockp 56 E9
Windlesham Surrey 20 F10
Windmill Cnwll 3 M2
Windmill Derbys 56 J11
Windmill Hill E Susx 11 U8
Windmill Hill Somset 16 K13
Windrush Gloucs 29 N5
Windsole Abers 104 H3
Windsor W & M 20 G7
Windsor Castle W & M 20 G7
Windsoredge Gloucs 28 F7
Windsor Green Suffk 40 E10
Windygates Fife 91 N11
Windyharbour Ches E 55 T12
Windy Hill Wrexhm 44 H3
Wineham W Susx 11 L6
Winestead E R Yk 59 N2
Winewall Lancs 62 J11
Winfarthing Norfk 40 K3
Winford IoW 9 R12
Winford N Som 17 P3
Winforton Herefs 34 G11
Winfrith Newburgh Dorset 7 V8
Wing Bucks 30 J8
Wing Rutlnd 48 C13
Wingate Dur 70 F5
Wingates Bolton 55 Q5
Wingates Nthumb 77 M6
Wingerworth Derbys 57 N13
Wingfield C Beds 31 M7
Wingfield Suffk 41 M5
Wingfield Wilts 18 B9
Wingfield Green Suffk 41 M5
Wingham Kent 13 P4
Wingland Lincs 49 Q9
Wingmore Kent 13 N6
Wingrave Bucks 30 J9
Winkburn Notts 47 T2
Winkfield Br For 20 E8
Winkfield Row Br For 20 E8
Winkhill Staffs 46 E3
Winkhurst Green Kent 21 S13
Winkleigh Devon 15 P11
Winksley N York 63 R5
Winkton BCP 8 H9
Winlaton Gatesd 77 P13
Winlaton Mill Gatesd 77 P13
Winless Highld 112 H6
Winllan Powys 44 F9
Winmarleigh Lancs 61 T10
Winnall Hants 9 P3
Winnersh Wokham 20 C8
Winnington Ches W 55 P12
Winscales Cumb 66 F7
Winscombe N Som 17 M5
Winsford Ches W 55 Q13
Winsford Somset 16 B10
Winsham Devon 15 M5
Winsham Somset 7 L3
Winshill Staffs 46 J9
Winshwen Swans 26 B8
Winskill Cumb 67 S6
Winslade Hants 19 U11
Winsley Wilts 18 B8
Winslow Bucks 30 G7
Winson Gloucs 29 L6
Winsor Hants 9 L6
Winstanley Wigan 55 N6
Winster Cumb 67 P14
Winster Derbys 46 H1
Winston Dur 69 P9
Winston Suffk 41 L8
Winstone Gloucs 28 J6
Winston Green Suffk 41 L8
Winswell Devon 15 L10
Winterborne Came Dorset 7 T7
Winterborne Clenston Dorset 8 A8
Winterborne Herringston Dorset 7 S7
Winterborne Houghton Dorset 7 V4
Winterborne Kingston Dorset 8 B9
Winterborne Monkton Dorset 7 S7
Winterborne Stickland Dorset 8 A8
Winterborne Tomson Dorset 8 B9
Winterborne Whitechurch Dorset 8 A8
Winterborne Zelston Dorset 8 B9
Winterbourne S Glos 28 B11
Winterbourne W Berk 19 Q6
Winterbourne Abbas Dorset 7 R6
Winterbourne Bassett Wilts 18 G6
Winterbourne Dauntsey Wilts 8 H2
Winterbourne Earls Wilts 8 H2
Winterbourne Gunner Wilts 18 J13
Winterbourne Monkton Wilts 18 G6
Winterbourne Steepleton Dorset 7 R7
Winterbourne Stoke Wilts 18 G12
Winterbrook Oxon 19 T3
Winterburn N York 62 J8
Winteringham N Linc 58 F2
Winterley Ches E 45 R2
Wintersett Wakefd 57 N3
Winterslow Wilts 8 J2
Winterton N Linc 58 F3
Winterton-on-Sea Norfk 51 S10
Winthorpe Lincs 59 U13
Winthorpe Notts 48 B2
Winton BCP 8 F10
Winton Cumb 68 G10
Winton E Susx 11 S10
Winton N York 70 F13
Wintringham Cambs 38 K9
Wintringham N York 64 K5
Winwick Cambs 38 H4
Winwick Nhants 37 R6
Winwick Warrtn 55 P8
Wirksworth Derbys 46 J3
Wirral 54 G9
Wirswall Ches E 45 M5
Wisbech Cambs 49 Q12
Wisbech St Mary Cambs 49 P12
Wisborough Green W Susx 10 H5
Wiseman's Bridge Pembks 24 K9
Wiseton Notts 58 B9
Wishanger Gloucs 28 H6
Wishaw N Lans 82 E7
Wishaw Warwks 36 G2
Wisley Surrey 20 J11
Wisley Garden RHS Surrey 20 J11
Wispington Lincs 59 M12
Wissenden Kent 12 H7
Wissett Suffk 41 Q5
Wissington Norfk 49 U14
Wissington Suffk 40 G14
Wistanstow Shrops 34 K3
Wistanswick Shrops 45 Q8
Wistaston Ches E 45 Q3
Wistaston Green Ches E 45 Q3
Wisterfield Ches E 55 T12
Wiston Pembks 24 H7
Wiston S Lans 82 J12
Wiston W Susx 10 J8
Wistow Cambs 39 L4
Wistow Leics 37 R1
Wistow N York 64 D12
Wiswell Lancs 62 E12
Witcham Cambs 39 Q4
Witchampton Dorset 8 D7
Witchford Cambs 39 R5
Witcombe Somset 17 N12
Witham Essex 22 K5
Witham Friary Somset 17 U8
Witham on the Hill Lincs 48 G10
Witham St Hughs Lincs 58 E14
Withcall Lincs 59 N10
Withdean Br & H 11 N9
Witherenden Hill E Susx 12 B10
Witheridge Devon 15 T10
Witherley Leics 46 K14
Withern Lincs 59 R10
Withernsea E R Yk 59 Q1
Withernwick E R Yk 65 R11
Withersdale Street Suffk 41 N4
Withersfield Suffk 39 U11
Witherslack Cumb 61 S3
Withiel Cnwll 3 P3
Withiel Florey Somset 16 C10
Withielgoose Cnwll 3 Q3
Withington Gloucs 28 K4
Withington Herefs 35 N12
Withington Manch 55 T8
Withington Shrops 45 N11
Withington Staffs 46 D6
Withington Green Ches E 55 T12
Withington Marsh Herefs 35 N12
Withleigh Devon 6 B2
Withnell Lancs 55 P2
Withnell Fold Lancs 55 P2
Withybed Green Worcs 36 D6
Withybrook Warwks 37 M4
Withycombe Somset 16 D8
Withyham E Susx 11 R3
Withy Mills BaNES 17 S5
Withypool Somset 15 T6
Withywood Bristl 17 Q3
Witley Surrey 10 E3
Witnesham Suffk 41 L10
Witney Oxon 29 S5
Wittering C Pete 48 G13
Wittersham Kent 12 H10
Witton Birm 36 E2
Witton Norfk 51 P12
Witton Norfk 51 P7
Witton Gilbert Dur 69 R3
Witton Green Norfk 51 R13
Witton le Wear Dur 69 P6
Witton Park Dur 69 Q6
Wiveliscombe Somset 16 E11
Wivelrod Hants 19 U13
Wivelsfield E Susx 11 N6
Wivelsfield Green E Susx 11 P7
Wivelsfield Station W Susx 11 N7
Wivenhoe Essex 23 P3
Wivenhoe Cross Essex 23 P3
Wiveton Norfk 50 H5
Wix Essex 23 S2
Wixams Bed 31 N4
Wixford Warwks 36 E10
Wix Green Essex 23 S2
Wixhill Shrops 45 N8
Wixoe Suffk 40 B12
Woburn C Beds 30 K6
Woburn Safari Park C Beds 31 L6
Woburn Sands M Keyn 30 K5
Wokefield Park W Berk 19 U7
Woking Surrey 20 H11
Wokingham Wokham 20 D9
Wolborough Devon 5 V6
Woldingham Surrey 21 Q11
Wold Newton E R Yk 65 N5
Wold Newton NE Lin 59 M7
Wolfclyde S Lans 82 K11
Wolferlow Herefs 35 Q8
Wolferton Norfk 49 U8
Wolfhampcote Warwks 37 P7
Wolfhill P & K 90 J5
Wolf Hills Nthumb 76 E14
Wolf's Castle Pembks 24 G5
Wolfsdale Pembks 24 F6
Wollaston Dudley 35 U4
Wollaston Nhants 38 D8
Wollaston Shrops 44 H11
Wollaton C Nott 47 P6
Wollaton Hall & Park C Nott 47 P6
Wolleigh Devon 5 U4
Wollerton Shrops 45 P7
Wollescote Dudley 36 B4
Wolseley Bridge Staffs 46 D9
Wolsingham Dur 69 N5
Wolstanton Staffs 45 U4
Wolstenholme Rochdl 55 T4
Wolston Warwks 37 M5
Wolsty Cumb 66 H2
Wolvercote Oxon 29 U6
Wolverhampton Wolves 46 B14
Wolverhampton Halfpenny Green Airport Staffs 35 T2
Wolverley Shrops 45 L7
Wolverley Worcs 35 T5
Wolverton Hants 19 S9
Wolverton Kent 13 Q7
Wolverton M Keyn 30 H4
Wolverton Warwks 36 H8
Wolverton Wilts 17 U10
Wolverton Common Hants 19 S9
Wolvesnewton Mons 27 T8
Wolvey Warwks 37 M3
Wolvey Heath Warwks 37 M3
Wolviston S on T 70 G7
Wombleton N York 64 F3
Wombourne Staffs 35 U2
Wombwell Barns 57 P6
Womenswold Kent 13 P5
Womersley N York 57 R3
Wonastow Mons 27 T5
Wonersh Surrey 20 H13
Wonford Devon 6 B6
Wonson Devon 5 R3
Wonston Dorset 7 T3
Wonston Hants 19 Q13
Wooburn Bucks 20 F5
Wooburn Green Bucks 20 F5
Wooburn Moor Bucks 20 F5
Woodacott Devon 14 J11
Woodale N York 63 L4
Woodall Rothm 57 Q10
Woodall Services Rothm 57 Q10
Woodbank Ches W 54 J12
Woodbastwick Norfk 51 P10
Woodbeck Notts 58 C11
Wood Bevington Warwks 36 E10
Woodborough Notts 47 R4
Woodborough Wilts 18 H9
Woodbridge Devon 6 G5
Woodbridge Dorset 8 B5
Woodbridge Suffk 41 N11
Wood Burcote Nhants 37 S11
Woodbury Devon 6 D7
Woodbury Salterton Devon 6 D7
Woodchester Gloucs 28 F7
Woodchurch Kent 12 H9
Woodchurch Wirral 54 G9
Woodcombe Somset 16 C7
Woodcote Gt Lon 21 N10
Woodcote Oxon 19 T4
Woodcote Wrekin 45 S10
Woodcote Green Worcs 36 B6
Woodcott Hants 19 P10
Woodcroft Gloucs 27 U8
Woodcutts Dorset 8 D5
Wood Dalling Norfk 50 J8
Woodditton Cambs 39 U9
Woodeaton Oxon 30 B10
Wood Eaton Staffs 45 T10
Wooden Pembks 24 K9
Wood End Bed 38 F11
Wood End C Beds 31 L4
Wood End Cambs 39 N5
Wood End Gt Lon 20 K6
Wood End Herts 31 T7
Woodend Highld 93 T6
Woodend Nhants 37 R11
Woodend Staffs 46 G8
Woodend W Loth 82 J4
Woodend W Susx 10 C9
Wood End Warwks 36 F6
Wood End Warwks 36 H2
Wood End Warwks 36 J2
Wood End Wolves 46 B13
Wood Enderby Lincs 59 M14
Woodend Green Essex 22 E2
Woodfalls Wilts 8 H4
Woodford Cnwll 14 F10
Woodford Devon 5 T10
Woodford Gloucs 28 C8
Woodford Gt Lon 21 R4
Woodford Nhants 38 E5
Woodford Stockp 56 C10
Woodford Bridge Gt Lon 21 R4
Woodford Green Gt Lon 21 R4
Woodford Halse Nhants 37 P10
Woodford Wells Gt Lon 21 R4
Woodgate Birm 36 C4
Woodgate Devon 16 F13
Woodgate Norfk 50 E10
Woodgate Norfk 50 H10
Woodgate W Susx 10 E10
Woodgate Worcs 36 C7
Wood Green Gt Lon 21 P4
Woodgreen Hants 8 H5
Woodgreen Oxon 29 S5
Woodhall N York 62 K1
Woodhall Hill Leeds 63 Q12
Woodhall Spa Lincs 59 L14
Woodham Bucks 30 E9
Woodham Surrey 20 H10
Woodham Ferrers Essex 22 J8
Woodham Mortimer Essex 22 K7
Woodham Walter Essex 22 K6
Wood Hayes Wolves 46 B13
Woodhead Abers 105 M8
Woodhill Shrops 35 R4
Woodhill Somset 17 L11
Woodhorn Nthumb 77 R8
Woodhorn Demesne Nthumb 77 S8
Woodhouse Leeds 63 R13
Woodhouse Leics 47 P11
Woodhouse Sheff 57 P10
Woodhouse Wakefd 57 N2
Woodhouse Eaves Leics 47 P11
Woodhouse Green Staffs 56 C14
Woodhouselee Mdloth 83 P6
Woodhouselees D & G 75 S11
Woodhouse Mill Sheff 57 P9
Woodhouses Cumb 67 M2
Woodhouses Oldham 56 D6
Woodhouses Staffs 46 E12
Woodhouses Staffs 46 G10
Woodhuish Devon 6 B14
Woodhurst Cambs 39 M5
Woodingdean Br & H 11 P9
Woodkirk Leeds 57 L1
Woodland Abers 105 P11
Woodland Devon 5 Q9
Woodland Devon 5 T8
Woodland Dur 69 N7
Woodland Kent 13 M7
Woodland S Ayrs 80 H13
Woodland Head Devon 15 S13
Woodlands Donc 57 R5
Woodlands Dorset 8 F7
Woodlands Hants 9 L6
Woodlands Kent 21 U10
Woodlands N York 63 S9
Woodlands Somset 16 G8
Woodlands of Durris Abers 99 P4
Woodlands Park W & M 20 E7
Woodlands St Mary W Berk 19 M5
Woodland Street Somset 17 P9
Woodland View Sheff 57 M9
Wood Lane Shrops 44 K7
Wood Lane Staffs 45 T3
Woodleigh Devon 5 S11
Woodlesford Leeds 63 T14
Woodley Stockp 56 D8
Woodley Wokham 20 C8
Woodmancote Gloucs 28 E8
Woodmancote Gloucs 28 J2
Woodmancote Gloucs 28 K6
Woodmancote W Susx 10 B9
Woodmancote W Susx 11 L8
Woodmancote Worcs 36 B12
Woodmancott Hants 19 S12
Woodmansey E R Yk 65 P12
Woodmansgreen W Susx 10 D5
Woodmansterne Surrey 21 N11
Woodmanton Devon 6 D7
Woodmarsh Wilts 18 C9
Woodmill Staffs 46 F9
Woodminton Wilts 8 E4
Woodnesborough Kent 13 R4
Woodnewton Nhants 38 F2
Woodnook Notts 47 N3
Wood Norton Norfk 50 H8
Woodplumpton Lancs 61 U13
Woodrising Norfk 50 G13
Wood Row Leeds 57 N1
Woodrow Worcs 35 U5
Wood's Corner E Susx 11 V7
Woods Eaves Herefs 34 G11
Woodseaves Shrops 45 Q7
Woodseaves Staffs 45 S8
Woodsend Wilts 18 K5
Woodsetts Rothm 57 R10
Woodsford Dorset 7 U6
Wood's Green E Susx 12 B9
Woodside Br For 20 F8
Woodside Cumb 66 F6
Woodside Essex 22 C7
Woodside Fife 91 P10
Woodside Gt Lon 21 P9
Woodside Hants 9 L10
Woodside Herts 31 R11
Woodside P & K 90 K4
Woodside Green Kent 12 H5
Woodstock Oxon 29 T4
Woodstock Pembks 24 H5
Woodston C Pete 38 J1
Wood Street Norfk 51 Q9
Wood Street Village Surrey 20 G12
Woodthorpe Derbys 57 Q12
Woodthorpe Leics 47 P10
Woodthorpe Lincs 59 R10
Woodton Norfk 41 N1
Woodtown Devon 14 K8
Woodvale Sefton 54 H4
Woodville Derbys 46 K10
Woodwall Green Staffs 45 S7
Wood Walton Cambs 38 K4
Woodyates Dorset 8 E5
Woody Bay Devon 15 Q3
Woofferton Shrops 35 M7
Wookey Somset 17 P7
Wookey Hole Somset 17 P7
Wool Dorset 8 A11
Woolacombe Devon 15 L4
Woolage Green Kent 13 P6
Woolage Village Kent 13 P5
Woolaston Gloucs 28 A8
Woolaston Common Gloucs 28 A7
Woolavington Somset 16 K8
Woolbeding W Susx 10 D6
Woolbrook Devon 6 F7
Woolcotts Somset 16 C10
Wooldale Kirk 56 J5
Wooler Nthumb 85 P13
Woolfardisworthy Devon 14 H8
Woolfardisworthy Devon 15 T11
Woolfold Bury 55 S4
Woolfords S Lans 82 K7
Woolhampton W Berk 19 S7
Woolhope Herefs 35 P13
Woolland Dorset 7 U3
Woollard BaNES 17 R4
Woollensbrook Herts 31 U11
Woolley BaNES 17 T3
Woolley Cambs 38 J6
Woolley Cnwll 14 G9
Woolley Derbys 47 L1
Woolley Wakefd 57 M4
Woolley Bridge Derbys 56 F7
Woolley Edge Services Wakefd 57 M4
Woolley Green W & M 20 D6
Woolmere Green Worcs 36 C8
Woolmer Green Herts 31 S9
Woolmerston Somset 16 J10
Woolminstone Somset 7 M3
Woolpack Kent 12 G8
Woolpit Suffk 40 G8
Woolpit Green Suffk 40 G8
Woolscott Warwks 37 N7
Woolsgrove Devon 15 S12
Woolsington N u Ty 77 P11
Woolstaston Shrops 45 L14
Woolsthorpe by Belvoir Lincs 48 B7
Woolsthorpe-by-Colsterworth Lincs 48 D9
Woolston C Sotn 9 N7
Woolston Devon 5 S11
Woolston Devon 5 T10
Woolston Shrops 34 K3
Woolston Shrops 44 H9
Woolston Somset 16 E9
Woolston Somset 17 S11
Woolston Warrtn 55 P9
Woolstone Gloucs 28 J1
Woolstone M Keyn 30 J5
Woolstone Oxon 29 Q10
Woolston Green Devon 5 T7
Woolton Lpool 54 K9
Woolton Hill Hants 19 P8
Woolverstone Suffk 41 L13
Woolverton Somset 17 U6
Woolwich Gt Lon 21 R7
Woonton Herefs 34 H10
Woonton Herefs 35 N8
Wooperton Nthumb 77 L1
Woore Shrops 45 R5
Wootten Green Suffk 41 M6
Wootton Bed 31 M4
Wootton Hants 8 J9
Wootton Herefs 34 H10
Wootton IoW 9 Q10
Wootton Kent 13 P6
Wootton N Linc 58 J3
Wootton Nhants 37 U9
Wootton Oxon 29 T4
Wootton Oxon 29 U7
Wootton Shrops 44 H8
Wootton Staffs 45 T8
Wootton Staffs 46 F5
Wootton Bassett Wilts 29 L11
Wootton Bridge IoW 9 Q10
Wootton Broadmead Bed 31 M4
Wootton Common IoW 9 Q10
Wootton Courtenay Somset 16 B8
Wootton Fitzpaine Dorset 7 L5
Wootton Rivers Wilts 18 J8
Wootton St Lawrence Hants 19 S10
Wootton Wawen Warwks 36 G8
Worcester Worcs 35 U10
Worcester Park Gt Lon 21 M9
Wordsley Dudley 35 U3
Worfield Shrops 35 S1
Worgret Dorset 8 C11
Workhouse End Bed 38 H10
Workhouse Green Suffk 40 F13
Workington Cumb 66 F7
Worksop Notts 57 S11
Worlaby Lincs 59 P11
Worlaby N Linc 58 H4
Worlds End Bucks 30 J11
Worlds End Hants 9 S6
World's End W Berk 19 Q5
Worlds End W Susx 11 N7
Worle N Som 17 L4
Worleston Ches E 45 Q2
Worlingham Suffk 41 S3
Worlington Devon 15 S10
Worlington Suffk 39 U6
Worlingworth Suffk 41 M7
Wormald Green N York 63 S7
Wormbridge Herefs 27 S1
Wormegay Norfk 49 U11
Wormelow Tump Herefs 27 T1
Wormhill Derbys 56 H12
Wormhill Herefs 34 K13
Wormingford Essex 23 M1
Worminghall Bucks 30 D11
Wormington Gloucs 36 D13
Worminster Somset 17 Q8
Wormit Fife 91 N6
Wormleighton Warwks 37 N10
Wormley Herts 31 U11
Wormley Surrey 10 E3
Wormleybury Herts 31 U11
Wormley Hill Donc 57 U3
Wormshill Kent 12 G4
Wormsley Herefs 34 K11
Worplesdon Surrey 20 G12
Worrall Sheff 57 M8
Worrall Hill Gloucs 28 B5
Worsbrough Barns 57 N6
Worsbrough Bridge Barns 57 N6
Worsbrough Dale Barns 57 N6
Worsley Salfd 55 S6
Worstead Norfk 51 P8
Worsthorne Lancs 62 H13
Worston Devon 5 P10
Worston Lancs 62 F11
Worth Kent 13 R4
Worth Somset 17 P7
Worth W Susx 11 N3
Wortham Suffk 40 J5
Worthen Shrops 44 H13
Worthenbury Wrexhm 44 K4
Worthing Norfk 50 G10
Worthing W Susx 10 J10
Worthington Leics 47 M9
Worth Matravers Dorset 8 D13
Worthybrook Mons 27 T5
Worting Hants 19 S10
Wortley Barns 57 M7
Wortley Gloucs 28 E9
Wortley Leeds 63 R13
Worton N York 62 K2
Worton Wilts 18 E9
Wortwell Norfk 41 N4
Wotherton Shrops 44 G13
Wothorpe C Pete 48 F12
Wotter Devon 5 P8
Wotton Surrey 20 K13
Wotton-under-Edge Gloucs 28 E9
Wotton Underwood Bucks 30 E9
Woughton on the Green M Keyn 30 J5
Wouldham Kent 12 D3
Woundale Shrops 35 S2
Wrabness Essex 23 S1
Wrafton Devon 15 L5
Wragby Lincs 58 K11
Wragby Wakefd 57 P3
Wramplingham Norfk 50 K12
Wrangaton Devon 5 R9
Wrangbrook Wakefd 57 Q4
Wrangle Lincs 49 P3
Wrangle Common Lincs 49 P3
Wrangle Lowgate Lincs 49 P3
Wrangway Somset 16 F13
Wrantage Somset 16 K12
Wrawby N Linc 58 H5
Wraxall N Som 17 N2
Wraxall Somset 17 R9
Wray Lancs 62 C6
Wraysbury W & M 20 H8
Wrayton Lancs 62 C5
Wrea Green Lancs 61 R13
Wreaks End Cumb 61 N2
Wreay Cumb 67 P3
Wreay Cumb 67 Q8
Wrecclesham Surrey 10 C2
Wrekenton Gatesd 77 R14
Welton N York 64 H2
Wrenbury Ches E 45 N4
Wrench Green N York 65 M2
Wreningham Norfk 51 L14
Wrentham Suffk 41 S4
Wrenthorpe Wakefd 57 M2
Wrentnall Shrops 44 K13
Wressle E R Yk 64 G13
Wressle N Linc 58 G5
Wrestlingworth C Beds 39 L11
Wretton Norfk 49 U14
Wrexham Wrexhm 44 H3
Wrexham Industrial Estate Wrexhm 44 J3
Wribbenhall Worcs 35 S5
Wrickton Shrops 35 P4
Wrightington Bar Lancs 55 M4
Wright's Green Essex 22 D4
Wrinehill Staffs 45 S4
Wrington N Som 17 N4
Writhlington BaNES 17 S6
Writtle Essex 22 G6
Wrockwardine Wrekin 45 P11
Wroot N Linc 58 B6
Wrose C Brad 63 P12
Wrotham Kent 12 B4
Wrotham Heath Kent 12 B4
Wrottesley Staffs 45 T13
Wroughton Swindn 18 H4
Wroxall IoW 9 R12
Wroxall Warwks 36 H6
Wroxeter Shrops 45 N12
Wroxham Norfk 51 P10
Wroxton Oxon 37 M12
Wyaston Derbys 46 G5
Wyatt's Green Essex 22 E8
Wyberton East Lincs 49 M5
Wyboston Bed 38 J9
Wybunbury Ches E 45 Q4
Wychbold Worcs 36 B7
Wych Cross E Susx 11 Q4
Wychnor Staffs 46 G10
Wyck Hants 10 B3
Wyck Rissington Gloucs 29 N3
Wycliffe Dur 69 P10
Wycoller Lancs 62 J12
Wycomb Leics 47 U9
Wycombe Marsh Bucks 20 E4
Wyddial Herts 31 U6
Wye Kent 13 L6
Wyesham Mons 27 U5
Wyfordby Leics 47 U10
Wyke C Brad 56 J1
Wyke Devon 6 J5
Wyke Devon 15 U13
Wyke Dorset 17 U11
Wyke Shrops 45 P13
Wyke Surrey 20 F12
Wyke Champflower Somset 17 S10
Wykeham N York 65 L3
Wyken Covtry 37 L4
Wyken Shrops 35 S1
Wyke Regis Dorset 7 S9
Wykey Shrops 44 J9
Wykin Leics 37 M1
Wylam Nthumb 77 N13
Wylde Green Birm 36 F2
Wylye Wilts 18 F13
Wymeswold Leics 47 R9
Wymington Bed 38 E8
Wymondham Leics 48 B10
Wymondham Norfk 50 K13
Wyndham Brdgnd 26 G9
Wynford Eagle Dorset 7 Q5
Wynyard Park S on T 70 F7
Wynyard Village S on T 70 F7
Wyre Piddle Worcs 36 C11
Wysall Notts 47 R8
Wyson Herefs 35 M7
Wythall Worcs 36 E5
Wythall Green Worcs 36 E6
Wytham Oxon 29 U6
Wythburn Cumb 67 M10
Wythenshawe Manch 55 T9
Wythop Mill Cumb 66 J7
Wyton Cambs 39 L6
Wyton E R Yk 65 R13
Wyton on the Hill Cambs 39 L6
Wyverstone Suffk 40 H7
Wyverstone Street Suffk 40 H7
Wyville Lincs 48 C8

Y

Yaddlethorpe N Linc 58 E5
Yafford IoW 9 N12
Yafforth N York 70 D14
Yalberton Torbay 6 A13
Yalding Kent 12 C5
Yanwath Cumb 67 R7
Yanworth Gloucs 29 L5
Yapham E R Yk 64 H9
Yapton W Susx 10 F10
Yarborough N Som 17 L5
Yarbridge IoW 9 S11
Yarburgh Lincs 59 Q8
Yarcombe Devon 6 H3
Yard Devon 15 S8
Yardley Birm 36 F3
Yardley Gobion Nhants 30 G4
Yardley Hastings Nhants 38 C9
Yardley Wood Birm 36 F4
Yardro Powys 34 F9
Yarford Somset 16 H11
Yarkhill Herefs 35 P12
Yarley Somset 17 P8
Yarlington Somset 17 S11
Yarm S on T 70 F10
Yarmouth IoW 9 M11
Yarnacott Devon 15 P6
Yarnbrook Wilts 18 C10
Yarner Devon 5 T5
Yarnfield Staffs 45 U7
Yarnscombe Devon 15 N8
Yarnton Oxon 29 U5
Yarpole Herefs 35 L8
Yarrow Border 83 S13
Yarrow Somset 17 L7
Yarrow Feus Border 83 R13
Yarrowford Border 83 T12
Yarsop Herefs 34 K11
Yarwell Nhants 48 G14
Yate S Glos 28 D11
Yateley Hants 20 D10
Yatesbury Wilts 18 G6
Yattendon W Berk 19 S6
Yatton Herefs 34 K7
Yatton N Som 17 M3
Yatton Keynell Wilts 18 C5
Yaverland IoW 9 S11
Yawl Devon 6 K6
Yawthorpe Lincs 58 E8
Yaxham Norfk 50 H11
Yaxley Cambs 38 J2
Yaxley Suffk 40 K6
Yazor Herefs 34 K11
Yeading Gt Lon 20 K6
Yeadon Leeds 63 Q11
Yealand Conyers Lancs 61 U5
Yealand Redmayne Lancs 61 U4
Yealand Storrs Lancs 61 T4
Yealmbridge Devon 5 P10
Yealmpton Devon 5 P10
Yearby R & Cl 70 J8
Yearngill Cumb 66 H4
Yearsley N York 64 D5
Yeaton Shrops 44 K10
Yeaveley Derbys 46 G5
Yeavering Nthumb 85 N12
Yedingham N York 64 K4
Yelford Oxon 29 S7
Yell Shet 106 u5
Yelland Devon 15 L6
Yelling Cambs 39 L8
Yelvertoft Nhants 37 Q5
Yelverton Devon 5 N7
Yelverton Norfk 51 N13
Yenston Somset 17 T12
Yeoford Devon 15 S13
Yeolmbridge Cnwll 4 J3
Yeo Mill Devon 15 U8
Yeo Vale Devon 14 K8
Yeovil Somset 17 Q13
Yeovil Marsh Somset 17 P13
Yeovilton Somset 17 P12
Yerbeston Pembks 24 J9
Yesnaby Ork 106 r18
Yetlington Nthumb 77 L4
Yetminster Dorset 7 Q2
Yetson Devon 5 U9
Yettington Devon 6 E7
Yetts o'Muckhart Clacks 90 F11
Yews Green C Brad 63 M13
Yew Tree Sandw 36 D1
Y Felinheli Gwynd 52 H9
Y Ferwig Cerdgn 32 C11
Y Ffôr Gwynd 42 G6
Yielden Bed 38 F7
Yieldingtree Worcs 35 U5
Yieldshields S Lans 82 G8
Yiewsley Gt Lon 20 J6
Y Nant Wrexhm 44 G3
Ynys Gwynd 43 L7
Ynysboeth Rhondd 26 K8
Ynysddu Caerph 27 M9
Ynysforgan Swans 26 B8
Ynyshir Rhondd 26 J9
Ynyslas Cerdgn 33 M2
Ynysmaerdy Rhondd 26 J11
Ynysmeudwy Neath 26 C6
Ynystawe Swans 26 B7
Ynyswen Powys 26 E5
Ynyswen Rhondd 26 H8
Ynysybwl Rhondd 26 K9
Ynysymaengwyn Gwynd 43 L13
Yockenthwaite N York 62 J4
Yockleton Shrops 44 J11
Yokefleet E R Yk 58 D2
Yoker C Glas 89 M12
York C York 64 E9
York Lancs 62 E13
Yorkletts Kent 13 L3
Yorkley Gloucs 28 B6
Yorkshire Dales National Park 62 H4
York Town Surrey 20 E10
Yorton Heath Shrops 45 M9
Youlgreave Derbys 56 K14
Youlthorpe E R Yk 64 H8
Youlton N York 64 B7
Youngsbury Herts 31 U9
Young's End Essex 22 H4
Yoxall Staffs 46 F10
Yoxford Suffk 41 Q7
Y Rhiw Gwynd 42 D8
Ysbyty Cynfyn Cerdgn 33 Q5
Ysbyty Ifan Conwy 43 R4
Ysbyty Ystwyth Cerdgn 33 Q6
Ysceifiog Flints 54 E12
Ysgubor-y-Coed Cerdgn 33 N1
Ystalyfera Neath 26 D6
Ystrad Rhondd 26 H9
Ystrad Aeron Cerdgn 32 K9
Ystradfellte Powys 26 G5
Ystrad Ffin Carmth 33 Q11
Ystradgynlais Powys 26 D5
Ystrad Meurig Cerdgn 33 P7
Ystrad Mynach Caerph 27 L9
Ystradowen Carmth 26 D5
Ystradowen V Glam 26 J12
Ystumtuen Cerdgn 33 P5
Ythanbank Abers 105 Q9
Ythanwells Abers 104 J8
Ythsie Abers 105 P9

Z

Zeal Monachorum Devon 15 R12
Zeals Wilts 17 U10
Zelah Cnwll 3 L6
Zennor Cnwll 2 D9
Zoar Cnwll 2 K13
Zouch Notts 47 P9
ZSL London Zoo Gt Lon 21 N6
ZSL Whipsnade Zoo C Beds 31 M9